1993-94

Accredited Institutions of Postsecondary Education

1993-94 Accredited Institutions of Postsecondary Education
Programs
Candidates

A directory of accredited institutions, professionally accredited programs, and candidates for accreditation

Edited by William A. Wade
Published for the Commission on Recognition of Postsecondary Accreditation

American Council on Education
Washington, DC

American Council on Education
One Dupont Circle, NW
Washington, DC 20036

Printed in the United States of America

printing number
1 2 3 4 5 6 7 8 9 10

This publication was prepared on an Apple Macintosh IIsi computer, using QuarkXPress desktop publishing software, and was printed on an Apple LaserWriter IINT laser printer.

Library of Congress Cataloging in Publication Data

The Library of Congress has cataloged this serial as follows:

Accredited institutions of postsecondary education, programs,
     candidates / published by the American Council on Education,
     Washington, DC.

     v.; 24 cm.

     Annual
     Began with issue for 1976-77.
     A directory of accredited institutions, professionally accredited programs, and candidates for accreditation.
     Description based on: 1980-81.
     Spine title: Accredited Institutions of Postsecondary Education

     ISSN 0270-1715 = Accredited institutions of postsecondary education, programs, candidates.

I. Education, Higher—United States—Directories   I. American Council on Education.
II. Title: Accredited Institutions of Postsecondary Education.
     [DNLM: L901 A172]

L901.A48   378.73   81-641495
                                                                    AACR2   MARC-S

Table of Contents

About This Directory

Accredited Institutions of Postsecondary Education is published by the American Council on Education (ACE) for the Commission on Recognition of Postsecondary Accreditation (CORPA). Previous editions of the directory have been the joint effort of ACE and the Council on Postsecondary Accreditation (COPA). However, on December 31, 1993, COPA was dissolved and a new organization, CORPA, was created as a successor structure for the non-governmental recognition of accrediting bodies. There has been an orderly transition from COPA to CORPA, and those accrediting bodies previously recognized by COPA who wished to continue recognition were approved to do so by CORPA.

Neither CORPA nor ACE is an accrediting body; the listings in the directory are supplied by the national, regional, and specialized accrediting groups that have been evaluated by CORPA and recognized as meeting acceptable levels of quality and performance.

The institutions and programs listed, in turn, have been evaluated by the recognized accreditors and determined by their peers to meet acceptable levels of educational quality.

Those institutions designated as "candidates for accreditation" have achieved initial recognition from the appropriate accrediting commission or association. The designation "candidate" means that an institution is progressing toward accreditation, but is not assured accredited status.

Most of the data contained in each entry have been provided by the individual accrediting bodies. They, in turn, have had an opportunity to verify the listings as late in the publication process as possible.

Users of previous editions of the directory will notice that the current edition has been split into two primary sections: Accredited Degree Granting Institutions, and Accredited Non-Degree Granting Institutions. The reason for this is to provide the user with the opportunity to more easily identify those accredited institutions that grant degrees, and those that do not.

Users of the directory should note that the entries show only accredited institutions and indicate professional programs within those institutions that have sought and attained specialized accreditation. *The listings do not include all curricula offered by an institution.* For example, curricula in anthropology, English, physics, and many other disciplines are not listed because no recognized specialized accreditation exists in those fields. The absence of a particular discipline or course of study in these listings does not necessarily mean that it is not offered at that institution, nor that it is not a quality program if offered.

Also, the user is reminded that the process of accreditation is an ongoing one and that institutions and programs are accredited (or dropped from accredited status) throughout the year. Information about the accreditation status of a specific institution or program beyond what is given should be sought directly from the appropriate accrediting body. (Addresses, names, and telephone numbers of persons to contact begin on page 670.)

Please take time to review the section on how to use this directory and interpret the listings (page ix). For further clarification regarding entries in the directory, please contact the Commission on Recognition of Postsecondary Accreditation, One Dupont Circle, NW, Suite 305, Washington, DC 20036, (202) 452-1433.

To order this directory, contact Oryx Press, 4041 North Central Avenue, Phoenix, AZ 85012-3397, (800) 279-6799 or (602) 265-2651.

How to Use This Directory

Initial entry into the directory should be through the index, which lists over 5,500 accredited institutions alphabetically by institutional name, as well as numerous cross references.

The main body of the directory lists institutions alphabetically by state in two sections: Accredited Degree Granting Institutions and Accredited Non-Degree Granting Institutions.

Information for the individual listings is arranged as follows (not all categories are listed for each institution):

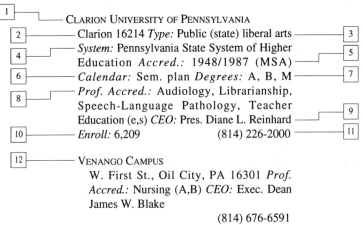

1. Name of the institution.

2. Address.

3. Brief description of (a) control (e.g., Public); (b) type of institution; and (c) type of student body (no indication means coeducational).

4. Indication of membership in a public system of higher education.

5. Dates of first accreditation (or of admission as candidate) and of latest renewal or reaffirmation of this status, followed by accrediting body. (Consult accrediting body for dates of interruption in or limitations on accreditation status.)

6. Type of academic calendar.

7. Level of degrees offered.

8. Specialized accreditation by 43 professional accrediting agencies, including one umbrella organization representing 20 joint review committees.

9. Name and title of chief executive officer.

10. Latest enrollment figure. Figures are included to provide indication of relative size of student body and indicate either total number enrolled or full time equivalent (FTE) calculated figures.

11. Telephone number.

12. Branch campus(es).

Abbreviations

A—associate degree or equivalent
ABA—American Bar Association
AMA—American Medical Association
B—bachelor's degree or equivalent
D—doctoral degree
e—elementary education curriculum (in Teacher Education)
4-1-4—academic year of two 4-month terms with a 1-month intersession
4-4-x—academic year of two 4-month terms with one term of flexible length
FTE—full time equivalent (enrollment calculation)
M—master's degree or equivalent
P—first professional degree (i.e., those degrees such as J.D., M.D., or M.Div.
     requiring six or more years of post-high school education)
p—personnel school service curriculum (in Teacher Education)
prelim.—preliminary
Qtr.—quarter (calendar year of four academic terms)
s—secondary school curriculum (in Teacher Education)
Sem.—semester (calendar year of two academic terms)
3-3—academic year of three terms
Tri.—trimester (calendar year of three 15-week terms, with students
     generally attending two of the three terms)

Key to Institutional Accrediting Bodies

AABC ....American Association of Bible Colleges
AARTS ....Association of Advanced Rabbinical and Talmudic Schools
ABHES ....Accrediting Bureau of Health Education Schools
ATS ....The Association of Theological Schools in the United States and Canada
ACCS/CT...................Accrediting Commission for Career Schools/Colleges of Technology
ACICS.......................Accrediting Council for Independent Colleges and Schools
MSA...........................Middle States Association of Colleges and Schools
NASC.........................The Northwest Association of Schools and Colleges
NCA ....North Central Association of Colleges and Schools.
NEASC-CIHE............New England Association of Schools and Colleges, Inc./Commission on
                       Institutions of Higher Education
NEASC-CTCI............New England Association of Schools and Colleges, Inc./Commission on
                       Technical and Career Institutions
NHSC.........................National Home Study Council
SACS-CC...................Southern Association of Colleges and Schools/Commission on Colleges
SACS-COEI...............Southern Association of Colleges and Schools/Commission on Occupational
                       Education Institutions
WASC-Jr....................Western Association of Schools and Colleges/Accrediting Commission for
                       Community and Junior Colleges
WASC-Sr. ....Western Association of Schools and Colleges/Accrediting Commission for
                       Senior Colleges and Universities

Key to Specialized Accrediting Bodies

Accounting..American Assembly of Collegiate Schools of Business

Acupuncture...National Accreditation Commission for Schools and Colleges of Acupuncture and Oriental Medicine

Administration Health Care Management......................................National Association of Schools of Public Affairs and Administration

Anesthesiologist Assisting....................American Medical Association

Art..National Association of Schools of Art and Design

Audiology ....American Speech-Language-Hearing Association

Blood Bank Technology ....American Medical Association

Business ....American Assembly of Collegiate Schools of Business

Cardiovascular Technology ....American Medical Association

Chiropractic Education ....The Council on Chiropractic Education

Clinical Psychology ....American Psychological Association

Combined Maxillofacial Prosthodontics..................................American Dental Association

Combined Professional-Scientific Psychology...American Psychological Association

Combined Prosthodontics ....American Dental Association

Community Health................................The Council on Education for Public Health

Community Health/Preventive Medicine ....The Council on Education for Public Health

Computer Science ....Computing Sciences Accreditation Board, Inc.

Construction Education..........................American Council for Construction Education

Counseling ....American Counseling Association

Counseling Psychology.........................American Psychological Association

Cytotechnology ....American Medical Association

Dance ....National Association of Schools of Dance

Dental Assisting...................................American Dental Association

Dental Hygiene ....American Dental Association

Dental Laboratory Technology ....American Dental Association

Dental Public Health ....American Dental Association

Dentistry...American Dental Association

Diagnostic Medical Sonography...........American Medical Association

Dietetics ....The American Dietetic Association

Electroneurodiagnostic Technology ......American Medical Association

EMT-Paramedic...................................American Medical Association

Endodontics..American Dental Association

Engineering ....Accreditation Board for Engineering and Technology, Inc.

Engineering Technology........................Accreditation Board for Engineering and Technology, Inc.

Forestry ....Society of American Foresters

Funeral Service Education ....American Board of Funeral Service Education, Inc.

General Dentistry..................................American Dental Association

General Practice Residency ....American Dental Association

Health Services Administration ....Accrediting Commission on Education for Health Services Administration

Histologic Technology..........................American Medical Association

Home Economics..................................American Home Economics Association

Interior Design ....Foundation for Interior Design Education Research

Journalism..Accrediting Council on Education in Journalism and Mass Communications

Key to Specialized Accrediting Bodies (continued)

Landscape Architecture ....American Society of Landscape Architects
Law ....American Bar Association/Association of American Law
          Schools
Librarianship ....American Library Association
Management ....National Association of Schools of Public Affairs and
          Administration
Marriage and Family Therapy ....American Association for Marriage and Family Therapy
Maxillofacial Prosthodontics ....American Dental Association
Medical Assisting ....Accrediting Bureau of Health Education
          Schools/American Medical Association
Medical Illustration ....American Medical Association
Medical Laboratory Technology ....Accrediting Bureau of Health Education
          Schools/American Medical Association
Medical Record Administration ....American Medical Association
Medical Record Technology ....American Medical Association
Medical Technology ....American Medical Association
Medicine ....American Medical Association
Mortuary Science ....American Board of Funeral Service Education, Inc.
Music ....National Association of Schools of Music
Nuclear Medicine Technology ....American Medical Association
Nurse Anesthesia Education ....Council on Accreditation of Nurse Anesthesia Educational
          Programs
Nursing ....National League for Nursing
Occupational Therapy ....American Medical Association
Occupational Therapy Assisting ....American Medical Association
Ophthalmic Medical Technology ....American Medical Association
Optometric Residency ....American Optometric Association
Optometry ....American Optometric Association
Oral and Maxillofacial Surgery ....American Dental Association
Oral Pathology ....American Dental Association
Orthodontics ....American Dental Association
Osteopathy ....American Osteopathic Association
Pediatric Dentistry ....American Dental Association
Perfusion ....American Medical Association
Periodontics ....American Dental Association
Physical Therapy ....American Physical Therapy Association
Physical Therapy Assisting ....American Physical Therapy Association
Physician Assisting ....American Medical Association
Planning ....Planning Accreditation Board
Podiatry ....American Podiatric Medical Association, Inc.
Policy Science ....National Association of Schools of Public Affairs and
          Administration
Practical Nursing ....National League for Nursing
Psychology Internship ....American Psychological Association
Public Administration ....National Association of Schools of Public Affairs and
          Administration
Public Affairs ....National Association of Schools of Public Affairs and
          Administration
Public Affairs and Administration ....National Association of Schools of Public Affairs and
          Administration
Public Health ....The Council on Education for Public Health

Key to Specialized Accrediting Bodies (continued)

Public Management ....National Association of Schools of Public Affairs and Administration

Public Management and Policy ....National Association of Schools of Public Affairs and Administration

Public Policy ....National Association of Schools of Public Affairs and Administration

Public Policy Administration.................National Association of Schools of Public Affairs and Administration

Public Policy and Administration ....National Association of Schools of Public Affairs and Administration

Radiation Therapy Technology..............American Medical Association

Radiography..American Medical Association

Recreation and Leisure Services............National Recreation and Park Association

Rehabilitation Counseling......................Council on Rehabilitation Education

Respiratory Therapy..............................American Medical Association

Respiratory Therapy Technology ....American Medical Association

School Psychology.................................American Psychological Association

Social Work ....Council on Social Work Education

Speech-Language Pathology..................American Speech-Language-Hearing Association

Surgeon Assisting ....American Medical Association

Surgical Technology ....American Medical Association

Teacher Education ....National Council for Accreditation of Teacher Education

Theatre ....National Association of Schools of Theatre

Urban Affairs and Policy Analysis ....National Association of Schools of Public Affairs and Administration

Urban Studies and Public
  Administration ....National Association of Schools of Public Affairs and Administration

Veterinary Medicine ....American Veterinary Medical Association

Veterinary Technology ....American Veterinary Medical Association

Accredited Degree Granting Institutions

ALABAMA

ALABAMA AGRICULTURAL AND MECHANICAL
UNIVERSITY
P.O. Box 1357, Normal 35762 *Type:* Public
(state) liberal arts *System:* Alabama Commission on Higher Education *Accred.:*
1963/1984 (SACS-CC) *Calendar:* Sem. plan
Degrees: A, B, M *Prof. Accred.:* Engineering Technology (civil/construction, electrical, mechanical, mechanical drafting/de-
sign), Home Economics, Planning (B,M),
Social Work (B), Teacher Education (e,s,p)
CEO: Pres. David B. Henson
FTE Enroll: 5,593   (205) 851-5000

ALABAMA AVIATION AND TECHNICAL COLLEGE
P.O. Box 1209, Ozark 36361-1209 *Type:*
Public (state) *Accred.:* 1991 (SACS-CC)
Calendar: Qtr. plan *Degrees:* A *CEO:* Pres.
Shirley H. Woodie
FTE Enroll: 326   (205) 774-5113

ALABAMA SOUTHERN COMMUNITY COLLEGE
P.O. Box 2000, Monroeville 36461 *Type:*
Public (state) *System:* State of Alabama De-
partment of Postsecondary Education *Ac-
cred.:* 1992 (SACS-CC) *Calendar:* Qtr. plan
Degrees: A *CEO:* Pres. John A. Johnson
FTE Enroll: 1,670   (205) 575-3156

THOMASVILLE CAMPUS
Hwy. 43, S., Thomasville 36784 *CEO:*
Pres. Hoyt Jones
          (205) 636-9642

ALABAMA STATE UNIVERSITY
915 S. Jackson St., Montgomery 36101-0271
Type: Public (state) liberal arts *System:* Alabama Commission on Higher Education *Accred.:* 1966/1990 (SACS-CC) *Calendar:*
Sem. plan *Degrees:* A, B, M *Prof. Accred.:*
Music, Social Work (B), Teacher Education
(e,s,p) *CEO:* Interim Pres. C.C. Baker
FTE Enroll: 5,221   (205) 293-4100

ATHENS STATE COLLEGE
300 N. Beaty St., Athens 35611 *Type:* Public
(state) liberal arts *System:* Alabama Commission on Higher Education *Accred.:* 1955/
1991 (SACS-CC) *Calendar:* Qtr. plan *Degrees:* B *CEO:* Pres. Jerry Bartlett
FTE Enroll: 2,387   (205) 233-8100

AUBURN UNIVERSITY
Auburn University 36849 *Type:* Public
(state) *System:* Auburn University System
Accred.: 1922/1993 (SACS-CC) *Calendar:*
Qtr. plan *Degrees:* B, M, D *Prof. Accred.:*
Art, Audiology, Business (B,M), Clinical
Psychology, Computer Science, Construc-
tion Education (B), Counseling, Counseling
Psychology, Engineering Technology (tex-
tile), Engineering (aerospace, agricultural,
chemical, civil, computer, electrical, indus-
trial, materials, mechanical), Forestry, Home
Economics, Interior Design, Landscape Ar-
chitecture (B), Marriage and Family Therapy
(M), Music, Nursing (B), Public Administra-
tion, Rehabilitation Counseling, Social Work
(B), Speech-Language Pathology, Teacher
Education (e,s,p), Theatre (associate), Veterinary Medicine *CEO:* Pres. William V.
Muse
FTE Enroll: 19,790   (205) 844-4000

AUBURN UNIVERSITY AT MONTGOMERY
7300 University Dr., Montgomery 36117-
3596 *Type:* Public (state) *System:* Auburn
University System *Accred.:* 1968/1988
(SACS-CC) *Calendar:* Qtr. plan *Degrees:* B,
M *Prof. Accred.:* Business (B,M), Medical
Technology, Nursing (B), Public Administra-
tion, Teacher Education (e,s,p) *CEO:* In-
terim Chanc. Guin A. Nance
FTE Enroll: 5,545   (205) 244-3000

BESSEMER STATE TECHNICAL COLLEGE
1100 Ninth Ave., S.W., Bessemer 35021
Type: Public (state) *Accred.:* 1972/1992
(SACS-COEI) *Calendar:* Qtr. plan *Degrees:*
A *Prof. Accred.:* Dental Assisting *CEO:*
Pres. W. Michael Bailey
FTE Enroll: 1,041   (205) 428-6391

BEVILL STATE COMMUNITY COLLEGE
P.O. Box 800, Sumiton 35148 *Type:* Public
(state) *Accred.:* 1992 (SACS-CC warning)
Calendar: Qtr. plan *Degrees:* A *CEO:* Pres.
Harold Wade
FTE Enroll: 2,859   (205) 648-3271

BREWER CAMPUS
2631 Temple Ave. N., Fayette 35555
CEO: Pres. Wayland K. DeWitt
          (205) 932-3221

BIRMINGHAM-SOUTHERN COLLEGE
900 Arkadelphia Rd., Birmingham 35254
Type: Private (United Methodist) liberal arts
Accred.: 1922/1984 (SACS-CC) *Calendar:*
4-1-4 plan *Degrees:* B, M *Prof. Accred.:*
Music, Teacher Education (e,s) *CEO:* Pres.
Neal R. Berte
FTE Enroll: 1,673   (205) 226-4600

BISHOP STATE COMMUNITY COLLEGE
351 N. Broad St., Mobile 36603-5898 *Type:*
Public (state) *System:* State of Alabama Department of Postsecondary Education *Accred.:* 1992 (SACS-CC) *Calendar:* Qtr. plan
Degrees: A *Prof. Accred.:* Mortuary Science, Nursing (A), Physical Therapy Assisting *CEO:* Pres. Yvonne Kennedy
FTE Enroll: 4,640   (205) 690-6416

BRANCH CAMPUS
414 Stanton St., Mobile 36617 *CEO:* Pres.
Earl Roberson, Sr.
     (205) 473-8692

SOUTHWEST CAMPUS
925 Dauphin Island Pkwy., Mobile 36605-
3299 *CEO:* Provost Earl Roberson, Sr.
     (205) 479-7476

CENTRAL ALABAMA COMMUNITY COLLEGE
908 Cherokee Rd., P.O. Box 699, Alexander
City 35010 *Type:* Public (state) *System:*
State of Alabama Department of Postsec-
ondary Education *Accred.:* 1969/1984
(SACS-CC) *Calendar:* Qtr. plan *Degrees:* A
CEO: Pres. James H. Cornell
FTE Enroll: 1,764   (205) 234-6346

CHATTAHOOCHEE VALLEY STATE COMMUNITY
COLLEGE
2602 College Dr., Phenix City 36869 *Type:*
Public (state) *System:* State of Alabama De-
partment of Postsecondary Education *Ac-
cred.:* 1976/1992 (SACS-CC) *Calendar:*
Qtr. plan *Degrees:* A *Prof. Accred.:* Nursing
(A) *CEO:* Pres. Richard J. Frederinko
FTE Enroll: 3,042   (205) 291-4900

COMMUNITY COLLEGE OF THE AIR FORCE
Simler Hall, Ste. 104, 130 W. Maxwell
Blvd., Maxwell Air Force Base 36112-6613
Type: Public (federal) technical *Accred.:*
1980/1986 (SACS-CC) *Calendar:* Courses
of varying lengths *Degrees:* A *CEO:* Pres.
Paul A. Reid
FTE Enroll: 167,931   (205) 953-7847

SCHOOL OF HEALTH SCIENCES
3790th MSTG, Sheppard Air Force Base,
TX 76311 *Prof. Accred.:* Medical Laboratory Technology (AMA), Physical Therapy Assisting, Physician Assisting, Radiography, Surgical Technology *CEO:* Commanding Ofcr. James R. Burchfield
     (817) 676-2700

CONCORDIA COLLEGE
1804 Green St., P.O. Box 1329, Selma
36701 *Type:* Private (Lutheran) *Accred.:*
1983/1989 (SACS-CC) *Calendar:* Sem. plan
Degrees: A, B (candidate) *CEO:* Pres. Julius
Jenkins
FTE Enroll: 348   (205) 874-5700

DOUGLAS MACARTHUR STATE TECHNICAL
COLLEGE
1708 N. Main St., Opp 36467 *Type:* Public
(state) *Accred.:* 1972/1992 (SACS-COEI)
Calendar: Qtr. plan *Degrees:* A *CEO:* Pres.
Raymond V. Chisum
FTE Enroll: 434   (205) 493-3573

DRAUGHONS JUNIOR COLLEGE
122 Commerce St., Montgomery 36104
Type: Private business *Accred.:* 1954/1991
(ACISC) *Calendar:* Qtr. plan *Degrees:* A
Prof. Accred.: Medical Assisting (AMA)
CEO: Dean Conley D. Siler
     (205) 263-1013

ENTERPRISE STATE JUNIOR COLLEGE
600 Plaza Dr., P.O. Box 1300, Enterprise
36331 *Type:* Public (state) *System:* State of
Alabama Department of Postsecondary Education *Accred.:* 1969/1984 (SACS-CC) *Calendar:* Qtr. plan *Degrees:* A *CEO:* Pres.
Joseph D. Talmadge
FTE Enroll: 2,225   (205) 347-2623

FAULKNER UNIVERSITY
5345 Atlanta Hwy., Montgomery 36109-
3378 *Type:* Private (Church of Christ) liberal
arts *Accred.:* 1971/1990 (SACS-CC) *Calendar:* Sem. plan *Degrees:* A, B, D *CEO:* Pres.
Billy D. Hilyer
FTE Enroll: 2,434   (205) 272-5820

FREDD STATE TECHNICAL COLLEGE
3401 Martin L. King, Jr. Blvd., Tuscaloosa
35401 *Type:* Public (state) *Accred.:* 1973/

1988 (SACS-COEI) *Calendar:* Qtr. plan *Degrees:* A *CEO:* Dir. Norman C. Cephus
FTE Enroll: 860 (205) 758-3361

GADSDEN STATE COMMUNITY COLLEGE
P.O. Box 227, Gadsden 35902-0227 *Type:* Public (state) *System:* State of Alabama Department of Postsecondary Education *Accred.:* 1968/1992 (SACS-CC) *Calendar:* Qtr. plan *Degrees:* A *Prof. Accred.:* EMT-Paramedic, Medical Laboratory Technology (AMA), Nursing (A), Radiography *CEO:* Pres. Victor B. Ficker
FTE Enroll: 5,084 (205) 549-8200

GEORGE C. WALLACE STATE COMMUNITY COLLEGE
Dothan 36303 *Type:* Public (state) *System:* State of Alabama Department of Postsecondary Education *Accred.:* 1969/1984 (SACS-CC) *Calendar:* Qtr. plan *Degrees:* A *Prof. Accred.:* EMT-Paramedic, Medical Assisting (AMA), Medical Laboratory Technology (AMA), Nursing (A), Radiography, Respiratory Therapy *CEO:* Pres. Larry Beaty
FTE Enroll: 3,884 (205) 983-3521

GEORGE CORLEY WALLACE STATE COMMUNITY COLLEGE
P.O. Drawer 1049, 3000 Range Line Rd., Selma 36702-1049 *Type:* Public (state) *System:* State of Alabama Department of Postsecondary Education *Accred.:* 1974/1989 (SACS-CC) *Calendar:* Qtr. plan *Degrees:* A *Prof. Accred.:* Nursing (A), Practical Nursing *CEO:* Pres. Julius R. Brown
FTE Enroll: 1,798 (205) 875-2634

HARRY M. AYERS STATE TECHNICAL COLLEGE
1801 Coleman Rd., Anniston 36202-1647 *Type:* Public (state) *Accred.:* 1972/1993 (SACS-COEI) *Calendar:* Qtr. plan *Degrees:* A *CEO:* Pres. Pierce C. Cain
FTE Enroll: 352 (205) 831-4540

HUNTINGDON COLLEGE
1500 E. Fairview Ave., Montgomery 36106-2148 *Type:* Private (United Methodist) liberal arts *Accred.:* 1928/1990 (SACS-CC) *Calendar:* Sem. plan *Degrees:* A, B *Prof. Accred.:* Music *CEO:* Pres. Wanda D. Bigham
FTE Enroll: 595 (205) 265-0511

INTERNATIONAL BIBLE COLLEGE
3625 Helton Dr., P.O. Box IBC, Florence 35630 *Type:* Private (Churches of Christ) *Accred.:* 1988 (AABC) *Calendar:* Sem. plan *Degrees:* A, B *CEO:* Pres. Dennis Jones
FTE Enroll: 65 (205) 766-6610

JACKSONVILLE STATE UNIVERSITY
700 N. Pelham Rd., Jacksonville 36265-9982 *Type:* Public (state) *System:* Alabama Commission on Higher Education *Accred.:* 1935/1983 (SACS-CC) *Calendar:* Sem. plan *Degrees:* B, M *Prof. Accred.:* Art (associate), Music (associate), Nursing (B), Social Work (B), Teacher Education (e,s,p) *CEO:* Pres. Harold J. McGee
FTE Enroll: 7,564 (205) 782-5781

JAMES H. FAULKNER STATE COMMUNITY COLLEGE
1900 Hwy. 31 S., Bay Minette 36507 *Type:* Public (state) *System:* State of Alabama Department of Postsecondary Education *Accred.:* 1970/1985 (SACS-CC) *Calendar:* Qtr. plan *Degrees:* A *Prof. Accred.:* Dental Assisting *CEO:* Pres. Gary L. Branch
FTE Enroll: 3,132 (205) 580-2100

JEFFERSON DAVIS STATE JUNIOR COLLEGE
P.O. Box 1119, Atmore 36504 *Type:* Public (state) *System:* State of Alabama Department of Postsecondary Education *Accred.:* 1968/1985 (SACS-CC) *Calendar:* Qtr. plan *Degrees:* A *Prof. Accred.:* Nursing (A) *CEO:* Pres. Sandra K. McLeod
FTE Enroll: 1,705 (205) 368-8118

JEFFERSON STATE COMMUNITY COLLEGE
2601 Carson Rd., Birmingham 35215-3098 *Type:* Public (state) *System:* State of Alabama Department of Postsecondary Education *Accred.:* 1968/1993 (SACS-CC) *Calendar:* Qtr. plan *Degrees:* A *Prof. Accred.:* Engineering Technology (electrical), Funeral Service Education, Medical Laboratory Technology (AMA), Nursing (A), Radiography *CEO:* Pres. Judy M. Merritt
FTE Enroll: 5,225 (205) 853-1200

J.F. DRAKE STATE TECHNICAL COLLEGE
3421 Meridian St., Huntsville 35811 *Type:* Public (state) *Accred.:* 1971/1991 (SACS-

COEI) *Calendar:* Qtr. plan *Degrees:* A
CEO: Pres. Johnny L. Harris, Ph.D.
FTE Enroll: 506   (205) 539-8161

J.F. INGRAM STATE TECHNICAL COLLEGE
5375 Ingram Rd., Deatsville 36022 *Type:*
Public (state) *Accred.:* 1977/1992 (SACS-
COEI) *Calendar:* Qtr. plan *Degrees:* A
CEO: Pres. Murry C. Gregg
FTE Enroll: 1,162   (205) 285-5177

JOHN C. CALHOUN STATE COMMUNITY COLLEGE
P.O. Box 2216, Decatur 35609-2216 *Type:*
Public (state) *System:* State of Alabama De-
partment of Postsecondary Education *Ac-
cred.:* 1968/1992 (SACS-CC) *Calendar:*
Qtr. plan *Degrees:* A *Prof. Accred.:* Dental
Assisting, Nursing (A), Practical Nursing
CEO: Pres. Richard G. Carpenter
FTE Enroll: 6,134   (205) 306-2500

JOHN M. PATTERSON STATE TECHNICAL
COLLEGE
3920 Troy Hwy., Montgomery 36116 *Type:*
Public (state) *Accred.:* 1972/1993 (SACS-
COEI) *Calendar:* Qtr. plan *Degrees:* A
CEO: Pres. J. Larry Taunton
FTE Enroll: 519   (205) 288-1080

JUDSON COLLEGE
P.O. Box 120, Marion 36756 *Type:* Private
(Southern Baptist) liberal arts for women *Ac-
cred.:* 1925/1984 (SACS-CC) *Calendar:*
Sem. plan *Degrees:* B *Prof. Accred.:* Music
CEO: Pres. David E. Potts
FTE Enroll: 338   (205) 683-5100

LAWSON STATE COMMUNITY COLLEGE
3060 Wilson Rd., S.W., Birmingham 35221
Type: Public (state) *System:* State of Alaba-
ma Department of Postsecondary Education
Accred.: 1968/1992 (SACS-CC) *Calendar:*
Qtr. plan *Degrees:* A *Prof. Accred.:* Nursing
(A) *CEO:* Pres. Perry W. Ward
FTE Enroll: 2,172   (205) 925-2515

LIVINGSTON UNIVERSITY
205 N. Washington St., Livingston 35470
Type: Public (state) liberal arts *System:* Al-
abama Commission on Higher Education *Ac-
cred.:* 1938/1992 (SACS-CC) *Calendar:*
Qtr. plan *Degrees:* A, B, M *Prof. Accred.:*
Nursing (A) *CEO:* Pres. Donald C. Hines
FTE Enroll: 1,977   (205) 652-9661

LURLEEN B. WALLACE STATE JUNIOR COLLEGE
P.O. Box 1418, Andalusia 36420 *Type:* Public (state) *System:* State of Alabama Department of Postsecondary Education *Accred.:*
1972/1987 (SACS-CC) *Calendar:* Qtr. plan
Degrees: A *CEO:* Pres. Seth Hammett
FTE Enroll: 998   (205) 222-6591

MARION MILITARY INSTITUTE
Washington St., Marion 36756 *Type:* Private
junior for men *Accred.:* 1926/1984 (SACS-
CC) *Calendar:* Sem. plan *Degrees:* A *CEO:*
Pres. Joseph Lewis Fant, III
FTE Enroll: 157   (205) 683-2301

MILES COLLEGE
P.O. Box 3800, Birmingham 35208 *Type:*
Private (Christian Methodist Episcopal) lib-
eral arts *Accred.:* 1969/1993 (SACS-CC)
Calendar: Sem. plan *Degrees:* A, B *CEO:*
Pres. Albert J.H. Sloan, II
FTE Enroll: 868   (205) 923-2771

NORTHEAST ALABAMA STATE COMMUNITY
COLLEGE
P.O. Box 159, Hwy. 35, Rainsville 35986
Type: Public (state) *System:* State of Alaba-
ma Department of Postsecondary Education
Accred.: 1969/1984 (SACS-CC) *Calendar:*
Qtr. plan *Degrees:* A *Prof. Accred.:* Nursing
(A) *CEO:* Pres. Charles M. Pendley
FTE Enroll: 1,547   (205) 228-6001

NORTHWEST ALABAMA COMMUNITY COLLEGE
Rte. 3, Box 77, Phil Campbell 35581 *Type:*
Public (state) *System:* State of Alabama De-
partment of Postsecondary Education *Ac-
cred.:* 1967/1992 (SACS-CC) *Calendar:*
Qtr. plan *Degrees:* A *Prof. Accred.:* Nursing
(A), Practical Nursing *CEO:* Pres. Larry
McCoy
FTE Enroll: 1,693   (205) 993-5331

OAKWOOD COLLEGE
Oakwood Rd., N.W., Huntsville 35896
Type: Private (Seventh-Day Adventist) liberal arts *Accred.:* 1958/1991 (SACS-CC) *Calendar:* Qtr. plan *Degrees:* A, B *Prof. Accred.:* Social Work (B), Teacher Education
(e,s) *CEO:* Pres. Benjamin F. Reaves
FTE Enroll: 1,392   (205) 726-7000

OPELIKA STATE TECHNICAL COLLEGE
1701 LaFayette Pkwy., Opelika 36803-2268
Type: Public (state) *Accred.:* 1971/1992

(SACS-COEI) *Calendar:* Qtr. plan *Degrees:* A *CEO:* Pres. Roy W. Johnson
FTE Enroll: 458   (205) 745-6437

PHILLIPS JUNIOR COLLEGE
3446 Demetropolis Rd., Mobile 36693 *Type:* Private junior *Accred.:* 1985 (ACISC) *Calendar:* Qtr. plan *Degrees:* A *CEO:* Dir. Lawrence Hasbrouck
                                        (205) 666-9696

PHILLIPS JUNIOR COLLEGE AT BIRMINGHAM
115 Office Park Dr., Mountain Brook 35223 *Type:* Private junior *Accred.:* 1969/1990 (ACISC) *Calendar:* Qtr. plan *Degrees:* A *CEO:* Dir. Diane S. Clower
FTE Enroll: 461   (205) 879-5100

PHILLIPS JUNIOR COLLEGE
4900 Corporate Dr., N.W., Ste. E, Huntsville 35805 *Accred.:* 1976/1989 (ACISC) *CEO:* Dir. Amanda Blanton
                                        (205) 430-3377

REID STATE TECHNICAL COLLEGE
I-65 at Hwy. 83, Evergreen 36401 *Type:* Public (state) *Accred.:* 1972/1988 (SACS-COEI) *Calendar:* Qtr. plan *Degrees:* A *CEO:* Pres. Ullysses McBride
FTE Enroll: 398   (205) 578-1313

SAMFORD UNIVERSITY
800 Lakeshore Dr., Birmingham 35229 *Type:* Private (Southern Baptist) *Accred.:* 1920/1986 (SACS-CC) *Calendar:* Sem. plan *Degrees:* A, B, M, D *Prof. Accred.:* Law, Music, Nursing (A,B), Teacher Education (e,s,p) *CEO:* Pres. Thomas E. Corts
FTE Enroll: 5,996   (205) 870-2011

SELMA UNIVERSITY
1501 Lapsley St., Selma 36701 *Type:* Private (Baptist) liberal arts and teachers *Accred.:* 1991 (SACS-CC) *Calendar:* Sem. plan *Degrees:* A, B *CEO:* Pres. W.L. Muse
FTE Enroll: 335   (205) 872-2533

SHELTON STATE COMMUNITY COLLEGE
202 Skyland Blvd., Tuscaloosa 35405 *Type:* Public (state) *System:* State of Alabama Department of Postsecondary Education *Accred.:* 1979/1984 (SACS-CC) *Calendar:* Sem. plan *Degrees:* A *Prof. Accred.:* Nursing (A) *CEO:* Pres. Thomas E. Umphrey
FTE Enroll: 2,468   (205) 759-1541

SHOALS COMMUNITY COLLEGE
P.O. Box 2545, George Wallace Blvd., Muscle Shoals 35662 *Type:* Public (state) *System:* State of Alabama Department of Postsecondary Education *Accred.:* 1991 (SACS-CC) *Calendar:* Qtr. plan *Degrees:* A *CEO:* Pres. Larry McCoy
FTE Enroll: 2,688   (205) 381-2813

SNEAD STATE COMMUNITY COLLEGE
P.O. Drawer D, 200 N. Walnut St., Boaz 35957 *Type:* Public (state) *System:* State of Alabama Department of Postsecondary Education *Accred.:* 1941/1993 (SACS-CC) *Calendar:* Qtr. plan *Degrees:* A *Prof. Accred.:* Veterinary Technology *CEO:* Pres. William H. Osborn
FTE Enroll: 1,451   (205) 593-5120

SOUTHEASTERN BIBLE COLLEGE
3001 Hwy. 280 E., Birmingham 35243 *Type:* Independent (nondenominational) *Accred.:* 1962/1983 (AABC) *Calendar:* Sem. plan *Degrees:* A, B *CEO:* Pres. John Talley, Jr.
FTE Enroll: 125   (205) 969-0880

SOUTHERN CHRISTIAN UNIVERSITY
P.O. Box 240240, Montgomery 36124-0240 *Type:* Private professional *Accred.:* 1989 (SACS-CC) *Calendar:* Qtr. plan *Degrees:* B, M, D (candidate) *CEO:* Pres. Rex A. Turner, Jr.
FTE Enroll: 84   (205) 277-2277

SOUTHERN UNION STATE COMMUNITY COLLEGE
P.O. Box 1000, Wadley 36276 *Type:* Public (state) *System:* State of Alabama Department of Postsecondary Education *Accred.:* 1970/1986 (SACS-CC) *Calendar:* Qtr. plan *Degrees:* A *Prof. Accred.:* Nursing (A) *CEO:* Pres. Roy W. Johnson
FTE Enroll: 2,600   (205) 395-2211

SPARKS STATE TECHNICAL COLLEGE
Hwy. 431, S., Eufaula 36072-0580 *Type:* Public (state) *Accred.:* 1973/1993 (SACS-COEI) *Calendar:* Qtr. plan *Degrees:* A *CEO:* Pres. Linda C. Young
FTE Enroll: 513   (205) 687-5288

SPRING HILL COLLEGE
4000 Dauphin St., Mobile 36608 *Type:* Private (Roman Catholic) liberal arts *Accred.:* 1922/1985 (SACS-CC) *Calendar:* Sem. plan

Degrees: B, M *CEO:* Pres. William J. Rewak, S.J.
FTE Enroll: 1,292   (205) 460-2121

STILLMAN COLLEGE
P.O. Drawer 1430, Tuscaloosa 35403 *Type:* Private (Presbyterian) liberal arts *Accred.:* 1953/1990 (SACS-CC) *Calendar:* Sem. plan *Degrees:* B *CEO:* Pres. Cordell Wynn
FTE Enroll: 945   (205) 349-4240

TALLADEGA COLLEGE
627 W. Battle St., Talladega 35160 *Type:* Private liberal arts *Accred.:* 1931/1989 (SACS-CC) *Calendar:* Sem. plan *Degrees:* B *Prof. Accred.:* Social Work (B) *CEO:* Pres. Joseph B. Johnson
FTE Enroll: 1,027   (205) 362-0206

TRENHOLM STATE TECHNICAL COLLEGE
1225 Air Base Blvd., Montgomery 36108 *Type:* Public (state) *Accred.:* 1972/1987 (SACS-COEI) *Calendar:* Qtr. plan *Degrees:* A *Prof. Accred.:* Dental Assisting, Dental Laboratory Technology, EMT-Paramedic, Medical Assisting (AMA), Practical Nursing *CEO:* Pres. Thad McClammy
FTE Enroll: 627   (205) 832-9000

TROY STATE UNIVERSITY
University Ave., Troy 36082 *Type:* Public (state) liberal arts and teachers *System:* Troy State University System *Accred.:* 1934/1983 (SACS-CC) *Calendar:* Qtr. plan *Degrees:* A, B, M *Prof. Accred.:* Nursing (A,B,M), Social Work (B), Teacher Education (e,s,p) *CEO:* Chanc. Jack Hawkins, Jr.
FTE Enroll: 11,882   (205) 670-3000

TROY STATE UNIVERSITY AT DOTHAN
P.O. Box 8368, 3601 U.S. Hwy. 231 N., Dothan 36304-0368 *Type:* Public (state) liberal arts and teachers *System:* Troy State University System *Accred.:* 1985/1990 (SACS-CC) *Calendar:* Qtr. plan *Degrees:* A, B, M *CEO:* Pres. Thomas E. Harrison
FTE Enroll: 2,500   (205) 983-6556

TROY STATE UNIVERSITY IN MONTGOMERY
231 Montgomery St., P.O. Drawer 4419, Montgomery 36103-4419 *Type:* Public (state) liberal arts and teachers *System:* Troy State University System *Accred.:* 1983/1989

(SACS-CC) *Calendar:* Qtr. plan *Degrees:* A, B, M *CEO:* Pres. Glenda S. McGaha
FTE Enroll: 2,383   (205) 834-1400

TUSKEGEE UNIVERSITY
Tuskegee 36088 *Type:* Private *Accred.:* 1933/1988 (SACS-CC) *Calendar:* Sem. plan *Degrees:* B, M, D *Prof. Accred.:* Engineering (aerospace, chemical, electrical, mechanical), Medical Technology, Nursing (B), Occupational Therapy, Social Work (B), Veterinary Medicine *CEO:* Pres. Benjamin F. Payton
FTE Enroll: 3,371   (205) 727-8011

UNITED STATES SPORTS ACADEMY
One Academy Dr., Daphne 36526 *Type:* Private professional *Accred.:* 1983/1988 (SACS-CC) *Calendar:* Qtr. plan *Degrees:* M, D (candidate) *CEO:* Pres. Thomas P. Rosandich
FTE Enroll: 189   (205) 626-3303

THE UNIVERSITY OF ALABAMA
P.O. Box 870166, Tuscaloosa 35487-0166 *Type:* Public (state) *System:* University of Alabama System *Accred.:* 1897/1984 (SACS-CC) *Calendar:* Sem. plan *Degrees:* B, M, D *Prof. Accred.:* Accounting (Type A,C), Art, Audiology, Business (B,M), Clinical Psychology, Computer Science, Counseling, Dietetics (coordinated), EMT-Paramedic, Engineering Technology (civil/construction, electrical), Engineering (aerospace, chemical, civil, electrical, industrial, mechanical, metallurgical, mineral), Home Economics, Interior Design, Journalism (B,M), Law, Librarianship, Music, Nursing (B), Rehabilitation Counseling, Social Work (B,M), Speech-Language Pathology, Teacher Education (e,s,p), Theatre *CEO:* Pres. E. Roger Sayers
FTE Enroll: 17,510   (205) 348-6010

. THE UNIVERSITY OF ALABAMA AT BIRMINGHAM
UAB Sta., Birmingham 35294 *Type:* Public (state) *System:* University of Alabama System *Accred.:* 1970/1984 (SACS-CC) *Calendar:* Qtr. plan *Degrees:* B, M, D *Prof. Accred.:* Accounting (Type A,C), Art (associate), Business (B,M), Clinical Psychology, Combined Prosthodontics (conditional), Cytotechnology, Dental Assisting, Dental Hygiene, Dental Public Health, Dentistry, Di-

etetics (internship), EMT-Paramedic, Endodontics, Engineering Technology (industrial hygiene), Engineering (civil, electrical, materials, mechanical), General Dentistry, General Practice Residency, Health Services Administration, Histologic Technology, Maxillofacial Prosthodontics (conditional), Medical Assisting (AMA), Medical Laboratory Technology (AMA), Medical Record Administration, Medical Record Technology, Medical Technology, Medicine, Music (associate), Nuclear Medicine Technology, Nurse Anesthesia Education, Nursing (B,M), Occupational Therapy, Occupational Therapy Assisting, Optometry, Oral Pathology, Oral and Maxillofacial Surgery, Orthodontics, Pediatric Dentistry, Periodontics, Physical Therapy, Psychology Internship, Public Administration, Public Health, Radiation Therapy Technology, Radiography, Rehabilitation Counseling, Respiratory Therapy, Social Work (B), Surgeon Assisting, Teacher Education (e,s,p) *CEO:* Pres. J. Claude Bennett
FTE Enroll: 15,331　　　　(205) 934-4011

THE UNIVERSITY OF ALABAMA IN HUNTSVILLE
Huntsville 35899 *Type:* Public (state) *System:* University of Alabama System *Accred.:* 1970/1985 (SACS-CC) *Calendar:* Qtr. plan *Degrees:* B, M, D *Prof. Accred.:* Computer Science, EMT-Paramedic, Engineering (chemical, civil, computer, electrical, industrial, mechanical), Music (associate), Nursing (B,M) *CEO:* Pres. Frank A. Franz
FTE Enroll: 5,337　　　　(205) 895-6120

UNIVERSITY OF MOBILE
P.O. Box 13220, Mobile 36663-0220 *Type:* Private (Southern Baptist) liberal arts *Accred.:* 1968/1993 (SACS-CC) *Calendar:* Sem. plan *Degrees:* A, B, M *Prof. Accred.:* Music (associate), Nursing (A,B) *CEO:* Pres. Michael A. Magnoli, Jr.
FTE Enroll: 1,656　　　　(205) 675-5990

UNIVERSITY OF MONTEVALLO
Sta. 6001, Montevallo 35115-6001 *Type:* Public (state) liberal arts and professional *System:* Alabama Commission on Higher Education *Accred.:* 1925/1990 (SACS-CC) *Calendar:* Sem. plan *Degrees:* B, M *Prof.*

Accred.: Art (associate), Audiology, Business (B), Home Economics, Music, Social Work (B), Speech-Language Pathology, Teacher Education (e,s) *CEO:* Pres. Robert M. McChesney
FTE Enroll: 2,904　　　　(205) 665-6000

UNIVERSITY OF NORTH ALABAMA
Box 5121, Florence 35632-0001 *Type:* Public (state) liberal arts and teachers *System:* Alabama Commission on Higher Education *Accred.:* 1934/1992 (SACS-CC) *Calendar:* Sem. plan *Degrees:* B, M *Prof. Accred.:* Art, Music, Nursing (B), Social Work (B), Teacher Education (e,s) *CEO:* Pres. Robert L. Potts
FTE Enroll: 5,425　　　　(205) 760-4100

UNIVERSITY OF SOUTH ALABAMA
307 University Blvd., Mobile 36688 *Type:* Public (state) liberal arts *System:* Alabama Commission on Higher Education *Accred.:* 1968/1993 (SACS-CC) *Calendar:* Qtr. plan *Degrees:* B, M, D *Prof. Accred.:* Audiology, Business (B,M), Computer Science, EMT-Paramedic, Engineering (chemical, civil, electrical, mechanical), Medical Technology, Medicine, Music, Nursing (B,M), Physical Therapy, Radiography, Respiratory Therapy, Speech-Language Pathology, Teacher Education (e,s,p) *CEO:* Pres. Frederick P. Whiddon
FTE Enroll: 12,382　　　　(205) 460-6101

WALKER COLLEGE
1411 Indiana Ave., Jasper 35501 *Type:* Private junior *Accred.:* 1959/1990 (SACS-CC) *Calendar:* Sem. plan *Degrees:* A *Prof. Accred.:* Nursing (A) *CEO:* Pres. Jack L. Mott
FTE Enroll: 750　　　　(205) 387-0511

WALLACE STATE COMMUNITY COLLEGE
801 Main St., Hanceville 35077 *Type:* Public (state) *System:* State of Alabama Department of Postsecondary Education *Accred.:* 1978/1984 (SACS-CC) *Calendar:* Qtr. plan *Degrees:* A *Prof. Accred.:* Dental Assisting, EMT-Paramedic, Medical Laboratory Technology (AMA), Medical Record Technology, Nursing (A), Physical Therapy Assisting, Radiography, Respiratory Therapy *CEO:* Pres. James C. Bailey
FTE Enroll: 4,456　　　　(205) 352-6403

ALASKA

ALASKA BIBLE COLLEGE
College Rd., Box 289, Glennallen 99588
Type: Independent *Accred.:* 1982/1992
(AABC) *Calendar:* Sem. plan *Degrees:* A,
B, certificates *CEO:* Pres. Gary J. Ridley, Sr.
FTE Enroll: 42   (907) 822-3201

ALASKA JUNIOR COLLEGE
Ste. 3-250, 800 E. Diamond Blvd., Anchorage 99515 *Type:* Private junior *Accred.:*
1970/1988 (ACISC) *Calendar:* Qtr. plan *Degrees:* A *CEO:* Dir. Linda Low
(907) 349-1905

ALASKA PACIFIC UNIVERSITY
4101 University Dr., Anchorage 99508 *Type:*
Private (United Methodist) *Accred.:* 1981/
1991 (NASC) *Calendar:* Tri. plan *Degrees:*
A, B, M *CEO:* Pres. F. Thomas Trotter
Enroll: 1,867   (907) 564-8248

PRINCE WILLIAM SOUND COMMUNITY COLLEGE
P.O. Box 97, Valdez 99686 *Type:* Public ju-
nior *System:* University of Alaska System
Accred.: 1989 (NASC) *Calendar:* Sem. plan
Degrees: A *CEO:* Pres. Jo Ann C. McDowell
Enroll: 1,237   (907) 835-2421

SHELDON JACKSON COLLEGE
801 Lincoln, Sitka 99835 *Type:* Private
(United Presbyterian) liberal arts *Accred.:*
1966/1988 (NASC) *Calendar:* 4-1-4 plan
Degrees: A, B *CEO:* Interim Pres. Kenneth
Cameron
Enroll: 299   (907) 747-5222

UNIVERSITY OF ALASKA ANCHORAGE
3211 Providence Dr., Anchorage 99508
Type: Public (state) *System:* University of
Alaska System *Accred.:* 1974/1990 (NASC)
Calendar: Sem. plan *Degrees:* A, B, M *Prof.
Accred.:* Art, Dental Assisting, Dental Hy-
giene, Engineering (civil), Journalism (B),
Medical Assisting (AMA), Medical Labora-
tory Technology (AMA), Nursing (A,B,M),
Social Work (B) *CEO:* Chanc. Donald
Behrend
Enroll: 19,268   (907) 786-1800

KENAI PENINSULA COLLEGE
34820 College Dr., Soldotna 99669 *CEO:*
Dir. Ginger Steffy
(907) 262-5801

KODIAK COLLEGE
Kodiak 99615 *CEO:* Dir. Carol Hagel
(907) 486-4161

MATANUSKA-SUSITNA COLLEGE
Box 2889, Palmer 99645 *CEO:* Dir. Glenn
Massay, Ph.D.
(907) 745-9774

UNIVERSITY OF ALASKA FAIRBANKS
320 Signers' Hall, Fairbanks 99775 *Type:*
Public (state) *System:* University of Alaska
System *Accred.:* 1934/1993 (NASC) *Calen-
dar:* Sem. plan *Degrees:* A, B, M, D *Prof.
Accred.:* Accounting (Type A), Business
(B,M), Computer Science, Engineering
(civil, electrical, geological/geophysical, me-
chanical, mining), Journalism (B), Music,
Social Work (B), Teacher Education (e,s,p)
CEO: Chanc. Joan K. Wadlow
Enroll: 8,123   (907) 474-7112

CHUKCHI CAMPUS
P.O. Box 297, Kotzebue 99752 *CEO:* Dir.
Lynn Johnson
(907) 442-3400

KUSKOKWIM CAMPUS
Bethel 99559 *CEO:* Pres. Linwood Laughy
(907) 543-4502

NORTHWEST CAMPUS
Pouch 400, Nome 99762 *CEO:* Dir.
Nancy Mendenhall
(907) 443-2201

UNIVERSITY OF ALASKA SOUTHEAST
11120 Glacier Hwy., Juneau 99801 *Type:*
Public (state) *System:* University of Alaska
System *Accred.:* 1983/1992 (NASC) *Calen-
dar:* Sem. plan *Degrees:* A, B, M *CEO:*
Chanc. Marshall L. Lind
Enroll: 4,783   (907) 789-4509

KETCHIKAN CAMPUS
Ketchikan 99901 *CEO:* Dir. Francis Fein-
erman
(907) 225-6177

SITKA CAMPUS
1332 Seward Ave., Sitka 99835 *CEO:* Dir.
Richard Griffin
(907) 747-6653

AMERICAN SAMOA

AMERICAN SAMOA COMMUNITY COLLEGE
P.O. Box 2609, Pago Pago 96799 *Type:* Public (territorial) junior *Accred.:* 1976/1991 (WASC-Jr.) *Calendar:* Sem. plan *Degrees:* A *CEO:* Pres. Saeu L. Scanlan
Enroll: 1,235   (684) 699-9155

ARIZONA

ACADEMY OF BUSINESS COLLEGE
Ste. 155, 3320 W. Cheryl Dr., Phoenix
85051 *Type:* Private business *Accred.:* 1985/
1990 (ACISC); 1993 (NCA candidate) *Calendar:* Courses of varying lengths *Degrees:*
A, certificates, diplomas *CEO:* Pres. Toby
D. Jalowsky
Enroll: 172   (602) 942-4141

AMERICAN GRADUATE SCHOOL OF
INTERNATIONAL MANAGEMENT
Thunderbird Campus, Glendale 85306 *Type:*
Private professional; graduate only *Accred.:*
1969/1985 (NCA) *Calendar:* Sem. plan *Degrees:* M *CEO:* Pres. Roy A. Herberger, Jr.
Enroll: 1,695   (602) 978-7200

AMERICAN INDIAN BIBLE COLLEGE
10020 N. 15th Ave., Phoenix 85021 *Type:*
Private (Assemblies of God) *Accred.:* 1988/
1993 (NCA) *Calendar:* Sem. plan *Degrees:*
A, B *CEO:* Pres. David J. Moore
Enroll: 126   (602) 944-3335

AMERICAN INSTITUTE
3443 N. Central Ave., Phoenix 85012 *Type:*
Private business *Accred.:* 1981/1987
(ACISC) *Calendar:* Sem. plan *Degrees:* A,
certificates, diplomas *CEO:* Exec. Dir. Mary
Park
                                 (602) 252-4986

ARIZONA COLLEGE OF THE BIBLE
2045 W. Northern Ave., Phoenix 85021
Type: Independent (nondenominational) *Accred.:* 1981/1991 (AABC) *Calendar:* Sem.
plan *Degrees:* A, B, certificates, diplomas
CEO: Pres. Robert W. Benton
FTE Enroll: 84   (602) 995-2670

ARIZONA INSTITUTE OF BUSINESS AND
TECHNOLOGY
Ste. 211, 4136 N. 75th Ave., Phoenix 85033
Type: Private business *Accred.:* 1982/1988
(ACISC) *Calendar:* Courses of varying
lengths *Degrees:* A, certificates, diplomas
CEO: Dir. Jeff Olson
                                 (602) 849-8208

BRANCH CAMPUS
Ste. 201, 925 S. Gilbert Rd., Mesa 85204
Accred.: 1991 (ACISC) *CEO:* Dir. Sue
Boyer
                                 (602) 545-8755

BRANCH CAMPUS
Ste. 104, 4136 N. 75th Ave., Phoenix
85033-3172 *Accred.:* 1988 (ACISC)
CEO: Dir. Jill Humphrey
                                 (602) 849-8208

ARIZONA STATE UNIVERSITY
Tempe 85287 *Type:* Public (state) *System:*
Arizona Board of Regents *Accred.:* 1931/
1993 (NCA) *Calendar:* Sem. plan *Degrees:*
B, P, M, D *Prof. Accred.:* Accounting (Type
A,C), Audiology, Business (B,M), Clinical
Psychology, Computer Science, Construction Education (B), Counseling Psychology,
Dance, Engineering Technology (aerospace,
electrical, manufacturing), Engineering
(aerospace, bioengineering, chemical, civil,
computer, electrical, general, industrial, mechanical), Health Services Administration,
Interior Design, Journalism (B,M), Law,
Medical Technology, Music, Nursing (B,M),
Planning (M), Psychology Internship, Public
Administration, School Psychology, Social
Work (B,M), Speech-Language Pathology,
Theatre *CEO:* Pres. Lattie F. Coor
Enroll: 40,444   (602) 965-9011

ARIZONA STATE UNIVERSITY WEST
4701 W. Thunderbird Rd., P.O. Box 37100,
Phoenix 85069-7100 *Type:* Public (state)
System: Arizona Board of Regents *Accred.:*
1992 (NCA) *Calendar:* Sem. plan *Degrees:*
B, M, certificates *Prof. Accred.:* Social
Work (B) *CEO:* Provost Ben R. Forsyth
Enroll: 4,946   (602) 543-5500

ARIZONA WESTERN COLLEGE
P.O. Box 929, Yuma 85366 *Type:* Public
(district) junior *System:* Arizona Community
College Board *Accred.:* 1968/1989 (NCA)
Calendar: Sem. plan *Degrees:* A, certificates
Prof. Accred.: Nursing (A) *CEO:* Pres.
James Carruthers
Enroll: 5,395   (602) 726-1000

CENTRAL ARIZONA COLLEGE
8470 N. Overfield Rd., Coolidge 85228 *Type:* Public (district) junior *System:* Arizona Community College Board *Accred.:* 1973/1993 (NCA) *Calendar:* Sem. plan *Degrees:* A, certificates *Prof. Accred.:* Nursing (A) *CEO:* Pres. John J. Klein
Enroll: 5,251   (602) 426-4444

CHANDLER-GILBERT COMMUNITY COLLEGE
2626 E. Pecos Rd., Chandler 85225-2479 *Type:* Public (district) junior *System:* Maricopa County Community College District *Accred.:* 1992 (NCA) *Calendar:* Sem. plan *Degrees:* A, certificates, diplomas *CEO:* Chanc. Arnette S. Ward
Enroll: 3,490   (602) 732-7000

CHAPARRAL CAREER COLLEGE
Ste. 204, 4585 E. Speedway Blvd., Tucson 85712 *Type:* Private business *Accred.:* 1969/ 1987 (ACISC) *Calendar:* Qtr. plan *Degrees:* A *CEO:* Pres. A. Lauren Rhude
                                   (602) 327-6866

COCHISE COLLEGE
Rte. 1, Box 100, Douglas 85607 *Type:* Public (district) junior *System:* Arizona Community College Board *Accred.:* 1969/1989 (NCA) *Calendar:* Sem. plan *Degrees:* A, certificates *Prof. Accred.:* Nursing (A) *CEO:* Pres. Dan Rehurek
Enroll: 4,938   (602) 364-7943

DEVRY INSTITUTE OF TECHNOLOGY, PHOENIX
2149 W. Dunlap Ave., Phoenix 85021 *Type:* Private *Accred.:* 1981/1992 (NCA)* *Calendar:* Sem. plan *Degrees:* A, B, certificates, diplomas *Prof. Accred.:* Engineering Technology (electrical) *CEO:* Pres. James A. Dugan
                                   (602) 870-9222

* Indirect accreditation through DeVry Institutes.

EASTERN ARIZONA COLLEGE
600 Church St., Thatcher 85552 *Type:* Public (district) junior *System:* Arizona Community College Board *Accred.:* 1966/1986 (NCA) *Calendar:* Sem. plan *Degrees:* A, certificates *CEO:* Pres. Gherald L. Hoopes, Jr.
Enroll: 4,943   (602) 428-8233

FRANK LLOYD WRIGHT SCHOOL OF ARCHITECTURE
Taliesin West, Scottsdale 85261 *Type:* Private professional *Accred.:* 1987/1992 (NCA) *Calendar:* Yearly plan *Degrees:* B, M *CEO:* Managing Trustee Richard Carney
Enroll: 33   (602) 860-2700

GATEWAY COMMUNITY COLLEGE
108 N. 40th St., Phoenix 85034 *Type:* Public (district) junior *System:* Maricopa County Community College District *Accred.:* 1971/ 1990 (NCA) *Calendar:* Sem. plan *Degrees:* A, certificates *Prof. Accred.:* Diagnostic Medical Sonography, Nuclear Medicine Technology, Nursing (A), Radiography, Respiratory Therapy, Respiratory Therapy Technology *CEO:* Pres. Phil D. Randolph
Enroll: 7,343   (602) 392-5000

GLENDALE COMMUNITY COLLEGE
6000 W. Olive Ave., Glendale 85302 *Type:* Public (district) junior *System:* Maricopa County Community College District *Accred.:* 1967/1992 (NCA) *Calendar:* Sem. plan *Degrees:* A, certificates *Prof. Accred.:* Engineering Technology (electrical), Nursing (A) *CEO:* Pres. John R. Waltrip
Enroll: 17,936   (602) 435-3000

GRAND CANYON UNIVERSITY
3300 W. Camelback Rd., P.O. Box 11097, Phoenix 85061 *Type:* Private (Southern Baptist) liberal arts and teachers *Accred.:* 1968/ 1987 (NCA) *Calendar:* 4-1-4 plan *Degrees:* B, M *Prof. Accred.:* Nursing (B) *CEO:* Pres. Bill Williams
Enroll: 1,747   (602) 249-3300

ITT TECHNICAL INSTITUTE
4837 E. McDowell Rd., Phoenix 85008-4292 *Type:* Private *Accred.:* 1977/1988 (ACCSCT) *Calendar:* Courses of varying lengths *Degrees:* A, certificates *CEO:* Dir. Michael M. Henry
                                   (602) 231-0871

ITT TECHNICAL INSTITUTE
1840 E. Benson Hwy., Tucson 85714-1770 *Type:* Private *Accred.:* 1986 (ACCSCT) *Calendar:* Courses of varying lengths *Degrees:* A *CEO:* Dir. William Fennelly
                                   (602) 294-2944

BRANCH CAMPUS
5100 Masthead St., N.E., Albuquerque, NM 87109-4366 *Accred.:* 1991 (ACC-SCT) *CEO:* Dir. Marianne Rittner
(505) 828-1114

LAMSON BUSINESS COLLEGE
Ste. 100, 6367 E. Tanque Verde Rd., Tucson 85715 *Type:* Private business *Accred.:* 1977/1989 (ACISC) *Calendar:* Qtr. plan *Degrees:* A, certificates, diplomas *CEO:* Dir. Robert A. Knapp
(602) 327-6851

LAMSON JUNIOR COLLEGE
1980 W. Main St., Mesa 85201 *Type:* Private junior *Accred.:* 1981/1988 (ACISC) *Calendar:* Qtr. plan *Degrees:* A, certificates, diplomas *CEO:* Interim Dir. George Tesner
(602) 898-7000

LAMSON JUNIOR COLLEGE
2701 W. Bethany Home Rd., Phoenix 85017 *Type:* Private junior *Accred.:* 1966/1988 (ACISC) *Calendar:* Qtr. plan *Degrees:* A *CEO:* Dir. Ralph H. Vieau
(602) 433-2000

MESA COMMUNITY COLLEGE
1833 W. Southern Ave., Mesa 85202 *Type:* Public (district) junior *System:* Maricopa County Community College District *Accred.:* 1967/1985 (NCA) *Calendar:* Sem. plan *Degrees:* A, certificates, diplomas *Prof. Accred.:* Nursing (A) *CEO:* Pres. Larry K. Christiansen
Enroll: 20,076   (602) 461-7000

MOHAVE COMMUNITY COLLEGE
1971 Jagerson Ave., Kingman 86401 *Type:* Public (district) junior *System:* Arizona Community College Board *Accred.:* 1981/1993 (NCA) *Calendar:* Sem. plan *Degrees:* A, certificates *CEO:* Pres. Charles W. Hall
Enroll: 5,744   (602) 757-4331

NAVAJO COMMUNITY COLLEGE
Tsaile 86556 *Type:* Public (local) junior *Accred.:* 1976/1990 (NCA) *Calendar:* Sem. plan *Degrees:* A, certificates, diplomas *CEO:* Pres. Tommy Lewis
Enroll: 1,804   (602) 724-3311

NORTHERN ARIZONA UNIVERSITY
Box 4092, Flagstaff 86011-4092 *Type:* Public (state) *System:* Arizona Board of Regents *Accred.:* 1930/1988 (NCA) *Calendar:* Sem. plan *Degrees:* B, M, D *Prof. Accred.:* Business (B,M), Dental Hygiene, Engineering Technology (civil/construction, electrical, mechanical), Engineering (civil, computer, electrical, mechanical), Forestry, Music, Nursing (B), Physical Therapy, Social Work (B), Speech-Language Pathology (probational) *CEO:* Pres. Clara Lovett
Enroll: 18,491   (602) 523-9011

NORTHLAND PIONEER COLLEGE
103 First Ave. at Hopi Dr., P.O. Box 610, Holbrook 86025 *Type:* Public (district) junior *System:* Arizona Community College Board *Accred.:* 1980/1990 (NCA) *Calendar:* Sem. plan *Degrees:* A, certificates, diplomas *CEO:* Pres. John H. Anderson
Enroll: 4,350   (602) 524-1993

PARADISE VALLEY COMMUNITY COLLEGE
18401 N. 32nd St., Phoenix 85032 *Type:* Public (district) junior *System:* Maricopa County Community College District *Accred.:* 1990 (NCA) *Calendar:* Sem. plan *Degrees:* A, certificates *CEO:* Pres. Raul Cardenas
Enroll: 5,315   (602) 493-2600

PARALEGAL INSTITUTE, INC.
3602 W. Thomas Rd., Ste. 9, P.O. Drawer 11408, Phoenix 85061-1408 *Type:* Private home study *Accred.:* 1979/1993 (NHSC) *Calendar:* Courses of varying lengths *Degrees:* A, certificates *CEO:* Pres. John W. Morrison
(602) 272-1855

PHOENIX COLLEGE
1202 W. Thomas Rd., Phoenix 85013 *Type:* Public (district) junior *System:* Maricopa County Community College District *Accred.:* 1928/1986 (NCA) *Calendar:* Sem. plan *Degrees:* A, certificates *Prof. Accred.:* Dental Assisting, Dental Hygiene, Medical Assisting (AMA), Medical Laboratory Technology (AMA), Medical Record Technology, Nursing (A) *CEO:* Pres. Marie Pepicello
Enroll: 13,385   (602) 264-2462

PIMA COUNTY COMMUNITY COLLEGE DISTRICT
4907 E. Broadway Blvd., Tucson 85709-1010 *Type:* Public (district) junior *System:* Arizona Community College Board *Accred.:* 1975/1991 (NCA) *Calendar:* Sem. plan *Degrees:* A, certificates *Prof. Accred.:* Dental Assisting, Dental Hygiene, Dental Laboratory Technology, Nursing (A), Radiography, Respiratory Therapy *CEO:* Chanc. Johnas F. Hockaday
Enroll: 30,175   (602) 748-4999

PIMA MEDICAL INSTITUTE
3350 E. Grant Rd., Tucson 85716 *Type:* Private *Accred.:* 1982/1988 (ABHES) *Calendar:* Courses of varying lengths *Degrees:* A *Prof. Accred.:* Radiography, Respiratory Therapy, Respiratory Therapy Technology *CEO:* Pres. Richard L. Luebke, Sr.
(602) 326-1600

BRANCH CAMPUS
2300 E. Broadway Rd., Tempe 85282 *Accred.:* 1986/1992 (ABHES) *Prof. Accred.:* Radiography *CEO:* Pres. Richard L. Luebke, Sr.
(602) 345-7777

BRANCH CAMPUS
1701 W. 72nd Ave., No. 130, Denver, CO 80221 *Accred.:* 1988 (ABHES) *Prof. Accred.:* Radiography *CEO:* Pres. Richard L. Luebke, Sr.
(303) 426-1800

BRANCH CAMPUS
2201 San Pedro Dr., N.E., Bldg. 3, Ste. 100, Albuquerque, NM 87110 *Accred.:* 1985/1991 (ABHES) *Prof. Accred.:* Radiography *CEO:* Pres. Richard L. Luebke, Sr.
(505) 881-1234

BRANCH CAMPUS
1627 Eastlake Ave. E., Seattle, WA 98102 *Accred.:* 1990 (ABHES) *CEO:* Dir. Walter Greenly
(206) 322-6100

PRESCOTT COLLEGE
220 Grove Ave., Prescott 86301 *Type:* Private liberal arts *Accred.:* 1984/1990 (NCA) *Calendar:* 4-1-4 plan *Degrees:* B, M *CEO:* Pres. Douglas M. North
Enroll: 782   (602) 776-5224

RIO SALADO COMMUNITY COLLEGE
640 N. First Ave., Phoenix 85003 *Type:* Public (district) junior *System:* Maricopa County Community College District *Accred.:* 1981/1992 (NCA) *Calendar:* Sem. plan *Degrees:* A, certificates *CEO:* Pres. Linda M. Thor
Enroll: 8,931   (602) 223-4000

SCOTTSDALE COMMUNITY COLLEGE
9000 E. Chaparral Rd., Scottsdale 85250 *Type:* Public (district) junior *System:* Maricopa County Community College District *Accred.:* 1975/1987 (NCA) *Calendar:* Sem. plan *Degrees:* A, certificates *Prof. Accred.:* Nursing (A) *CEO:* Pres. Arthur W. DeCabooter
Enroll: 10,102   (602) 423-6000

SOUTH MOUNTAIN COMMUNITY COLLEGE
7050 S. 24th St., Phoenix 85040 *Type:* Public (district) junior *System:* Maricopa County Community College District *Accred.:* 1984/1989 (NCA) *Calendar:* Sem. plan *Degrees:* A, certificates *CEO:* Pres. John A. Cordova
Enroll: 3,061   (602) 243-8000

SOUTHWESTERN COLLEGE
2625 E. Cactus Rd., Phoenix 85032 *Type:* Private (Conservative Baptist) *Accred.:* 1977/1987 (AABC); 1992 (NCA) *Calendar:* Sem. plan *Degrees:* A, B, certificates *CEO:* Pres. Wesley A. Olsen
Enroll: 160   (602) 992-6101

UNIVERSITY OF ARIZONA
Tucson 85721 *Type:* Public (state) *System:* Arizona Board of Regents *Accred.:* 1917/1990 (NCA) *Calendar:* Sem. plan *Degrees:* B, P, M, D *Prof. Accred.:* Audiology, Business (B,M), Clinical Psychology, Dance, Dietetics (internship), Engineering (aerospace, agricultural, chemical, civil, computer, electrical, geological/geophysical, industrial, materials, mechanical, mining, nuclear, systems), Journalism (B,M), Landscape Architecture (B), Law, Librarianship, Medical Technology, Medicine, Music, Nursing (B,M), Perfusion, Psychology Internship, Public Administration, Rehabilitation Counseling, School Psychology, Speech-Language Pathology, Theatre *CEO:* Pres. Manuel T. Pacheco
Enroll: 32,129   (602) 621-2211

UNIVERSITY OF PHOENIX
4615 E. Elwood St., 4th Fl., Phoenix 85040
Type: Private professional *Accred.:* 1978/
1992 (NCA) *Calendar:* Sem. plan *Degrees:*
A, B, M *Prof. Accred.:* Nursing (B) *CEO:*
Pres. William H. Gibbs
Enroll: 16,348   (602) 966-9577

ALBUQUERQUE MAIN CAMPUS
7471 Pan American Fwy., N.E., Albuquerque, NM 87109 *CEO:* Dir. Adrian
Mueller
                                 (505) 821-4800

CENTER FOR DISTANCE EDUCATION
4615 E. Elmwood St., P.O. Box 52069,
Phoenix 85071-2069 *CEO:* Dir. John
Sears
                                 (602) 921-8014

DENVER MAIN CAMPUS
7800 E. Dorado Pl., Englewood, CO
80111 *CEO:* Dir. Debra Kelin
                                 (303) 755-9090

FOUNTAIN VALLEY MAIN CAMPUS
10540 Talbert Ave., Fountain Valley, CA
92708 *CEO:* Dir. Tony Digiovanni
                                 (714) 968-2299

HAWAII MAIN CAMPUS
1585 Kapiolani Blvd., No. 722, Honolulu,
HI 96814 *CEO:* Dir. Grace Blodgett
                                 (808) 949-0573

ONLINE CAMPUS
101 California St., Ste. 505, San Francisco, CA 94111 *CEO:* Dir. Terri Hedegaard
                                 (415) 956-2121

PHOENIX MAIN CAMPUS
4605 E. Elmwood St., P.O. Box 52076,
Phoenix 85072-2076 *CEO:* Dir. Larry
Gudis
                                 (602) 966-7400

PUERTO RICO CAMPUS
P.O. Box 3870, R.D. 177 KM2, Guayn-
abo, PR 00657-3870 *CEO:* Dir. Candida
Acosta
                                 (809) 731-5400

SALT LAKE CITY MAIN CAMPUS
5251 Green St., Salt Lake City, UT 84123
CEO: Dir. Craig Swenson
                                 (801) 263-1444

SAN DIEGO CAMPUS
3870 Murphy Canyon Rd., Ste. 200, San
Diego, CA 92123 *CEO:* Dir. Terry
Klinger
                                 (619) 576-7469

SAN JOSE MAIN CAMPUS
2290 N. First St., Ste. 101, San Jose, CA
95131 *CEO:* Acting Dir. Robert Barker
                                 (408) 435-8500

TUCSON MAIN CAMPUS
3915 E. Broadway, Tucson 85711 *CEO:*
Dir. Kathy Alexander
                                 (602) 881-6512

WESTERN INTERNATIONAL UNIVERSITY
9215 N. Black Canyon Rd., Phoenix 85021
Type: Private *Accred.:* 1984/1992 (NCA)
Calendar: Tri. plan *Degrees:* A, B, M, cer-
tificates *CEO:* Pres. Robert S. Webber
Enroll: 1,201   (602) 943-2311

YAVAPAI COLLEGE
1100 E. Sheldon St., Prescott 86301 *Type:*
Public (district) junior *System:* Arizona
Community College Board *Accred.:* 1975/
1987 (NCA) *Calendar:* Sem. plan *Degrees:*
A, certificates *Prof. Accred.:* Nursing (A)
CEO: Pres. Doreen B. Dailey
Enroll: 5,739   (602) 445-7300

ARKANSAS

ARKANSAS BAPTIST COLLEGE
Dr. Martin Luther King, Jr., Dr., Little Rock 72202 *Type:* Private (Baptist) liberal arts *Accred.:* 1987/1990 (NCA) *Calendar:* Sem. plan *Degrees:* A, B, certificates *CEO:* Pres. W. Thomas Keaton
Enroll: 311   (501) 374-7856

ARKANSAS COLLEGE
P.O. Box 2317, Batesville 72503 *Type:* Private (Presbyterian) *Accred.:* 1959/1992 (NCA) *Calendar:* 4-1-4 plan *Degrees:* B *Prof. Accred.:* Social Work (B), Teacher Education (e,s,p) *CEO:* Pres. John V. Griffith
Enroll: 697   (501) 793-9813

ARKANSAS STATE UNIVERSITY
P.O. Box 10, State University 72467 *Type:* Public (state) *System:* Arkansas State University System Office *Accred.:* 1928/1993 (NCA) *Calendar:* Sem. plan *Degrees:* A, B, P, M, certificates *Prof. Accred.:* Art (associate), Business (B,M), Engineering (agricultural, general), Journalism (B,M), Medical Laboratory Technology (AMA), Medical Technology, Music, Nursing (A,B), Radiography, Rehabilitation Counseling, Social Work (B), Speech-Language Pathology, Teacher Education (e,s,p) *CEO:* Pres. John N. Mangieri
Enroll: 11,516   (501) 972-2100

ARKANSAS STATE UNIVERSITY—BEEBE BRANCH
Drawer H, Beebe 72012 *Type:* Public (state) junior *System:* Arkansas State University System Office *Accred.:* 1971/1992 (NCA) *Calendar:* Sem. plan *Degrees:* A, certificates *Prof. Accred.:* Medical Laboratory Technology (AMA) *CEO:* Chanc. William H. Owen, Jr.
Enroll: 2,605   (501) 882-8254

ARKANSAS TECH UNIVERSITY
Russellville 72801 *Type:* Public (state) liberal arts *System:* Arkansas Department of Higher Education *Accred.:* 1930/1991 (NCA) *Calendar:* Sem. plan *Degrees:* A, B, M *Prof. Accred.:* Engineering (general), Medical Assisting (AMA), Medical Record Administration, Music, Nursing (B), Teacher

Education (e,s,p) *CEO:* Pres. Robert C. Brown
Enroll: 4,756   (501) 968-0389

BLACK RIVER TECHNICAL COLLEGE
Hwy. 304 E., P.O. Box 468, Pocahontas 72455 *Type:* Public technical *Accred.:* 1993 (NCA candidate) *Calendar:* Sem. plan *Degrees:* A, certificates, diplomas *Prof. Accred.:* Respiratory Therapy Technology *CEO:* Dir. Richard Gaines
Enroll: 632   (501) 892-4565

CAPITAL CITY JUNIOR COLLEGE
P.O. Box 4818, 7723 Asher Ave., Little Rock 72214 *Type:* Private junior *Accred.:* 1987/1993 (NCA probational) *Calendar:* Qtr. plan *Degrees:* A, certificates *Prof. Accred.:* Medical Assisting (AMA) *CEO:* Pres. Carolyn Butler
Enroll: 364   (501) 562-0700

CENTRAL BAPTIST COLLEGE
1501 College Ave., Conway 72032 *Type:* Private (Missionary Baptist Association) *Accred.:* 1977/1987 (AABC); 1993 (NCA) *Calendar:* Sem. plan *Degrees:* A, B, certificates *CEO:* Pres. Charles E. Attebery
Enroll: 257   (501) 329-6872

EAST ARKANSAS COMMUNITY COLLEGE
Forrest City 72335-9598 *Type:* Public (district) junior *Accred.:* 1979/1989 (NCA) *Calendar:* Sem. plan *Degrees:* A, certificates *CEO:* Pres. Tom Spencer
Enroll: 1,797   (501) 633-4480

GARLAND COUNTY COMMUNITY COLLEGE
No. 100 College Dr., Mid-America Park, Hot Springs 71913 *Type:* Public (district) junior *Accred.:* 1981/1992 (NCA) *Calendar:* Sem. plan *Degrees:* A, certificates *Prof. Accred.:* Medical Laboratory Technology (AMA), Medical Record Technology, Nursing (A), Radiography *CEO:* Pres. Gerald H. Fisher
Enroll: 2,332   (501) 767-9371

HARDING UNIVERSITY
Box 2256, 900 E. Center Ave., Searcy 72149-0001 *Type:* Private (Churches of Christ) liberal arts *Accred.:* 1954/1985

(NCA) *Calendar:* Sem. plan *Degrees:* A, B, M *Prof. Accred.:* Music, Nursing (B), Social Work (B), Teacher Education (e,s) *CEO:* Pres. David B. Burks, Jr.
Enroll: 3,433　　　　　　(501) 279-4274

HENDERSON STATE UNIVERSITY
1100 Henderson St., Arkadelphia 71999-0001 *Type:* Public (state) liberal arts and teachers *System:* Arkansas Department of Higher Education *Accred.:* 1934/1992 (NCA) *Calendar:* Sem. plan *Degrees:* A, B, M *Prof. Accred.:* Music, Nursing (B), Teacher Education (e,s,p) *CEO:* Pres. Charles D. Dunn
Enroll: 4,466　　　　　　(501) 246-5511

HENDRIX COLLEGE
1601 Harkrider St., Conway 72032-3080 *Type:* Private (United Methodist) liberal arts *Accred.:* 1924/1989 (NCA) *Calendar:* Sem. plan *Degrees:* B *Prof. Accred.:* Music, Teacher Education (e,s) *CEO:* Pres. Ann H. Die
Enroll: 995　　　　　　(501) 329-6811

JOHN BROWN UNIVERSITY
Siloam Springs 72761 *Type:* Private liberal arts *Accred.:* 1962/1992 (NCA) *Calendar:* Sem. plan *Degrees:* A, B *Prof. Accred.:* Teacher Education (e,s) *CEO:* Pres. George R. Ford
Enroll: 1,018　　　　　　(501) 524-3131

MISSISSIPPI COUNTY COMMUNITY COLLEGE
P.O Drawer 1109, Blytheville 72316 *Type:* Public (district) junior *Accred.:* 1980/1992 (NCA) *Calendar:* Sem. plan *Degrees:* A, certificates *Prof. Accred.:* Nursing (A) *CEO:* Pres. John P. Sullins
Enroll: 1,745　　　　　　(501) 762-1020

NORTH ARKANSAS COMMUNITY/TECHNICAL COLLEGE
Pioneer Ridge, Harrison 72601 *Type:* Public (district) junior *Accred.:* 1979/1991 (NCA) *Calendar:* Sem. plan *Degrees:* A, certificates *Prof. Accred.:* Nursing (A) *CEO:* Pres. William Bert Baker
Enroll: 1,748　　　　　　(501) 743-3000

NORTHWEST ARKANSAS COMMUNITY COLLEGE
P.O. Box 1408, Bentonville 72712 *Type:* Public (district) junior *Accred.:* 1991/1993 (NCA candidate) *Calendar:* Sem. plan *De-*

grees: A, certificates *Prof. Accred.:* Physical Therapy Assisting, Radiation Therapy Technology *CEO:* Pres. Bob C. Burns
Enroll: 1,779　　　　　　(501) 636-7202

OUACHITA BAPTIST UNIVERSITY
410 Ouachita, OBU Box 3753, Arkadelphia 71998 *Type:* Private (Southern Baptist) *Accred.:* 1927/1990 (NCA) *Calendar:* Sem. plan *Degrees:* B, M *Prof. Accred.:* Music, Teacher Education (e,s,p) *CEO:* Pres. Ben Elrod
Enroll: 1,298　　　　　　(501) 245-5000

PHILANDER SMITH COLLEGE
812 W. 13th St., Little Rock 72202 *Type:* Private (United Methodist) liberal arts *Accred.:* 1949/1990 (NCA) *Calendar:* Sem. plan *Degrees:* B *Prof. Accred.:* Teacher Education (e,s) *CEO:* Pres. Myer L. Titus
Enroll: 940　　　　　　(501) 374-8343

PHILLIPS COUNTY COMMUNITY COLLEGE
Box 785, Helena 72342 *Type:* Public (district) junior *Accred.:* 1972/1985 (NCA) *Calendar:* Sem. plan *Degrees:* A, certificates *Prof. Accred.:* Medical Laboratory Technology (AMA), Nursing (A) *CEO:* Pres. Steven W. Jones
Enroll: 1,681　　　　　　(501) 338-6474

PULASKI TECHNICAL COLLEGE
3000 W. Scenic Rd., North Little Rock 72118-3399 *Type:* Public technical *Accred.:* 1993 (NCA candidate) *Calendar:* Sem. plan *Degrees:* A, certificates, diplomas *Prof. Accred.:* Dental Assisting, Respiratory Therapy Technology *CEO:* Pres. Benjamin Wyatt
Enroll: 972　　　　　　(501) 771-1000

RICH MOUNTAIN COMMUNITY COLLEGE
601 Bush St., Mena 71953 *Type:* Public (district) junior *Accred.:* 1990 (NCA) *Calendar:* Sem. plan *Degrees:* A, certificates *CEO:* Pres. Bill Abernathy
Enroll: 806　　　　　　(501) 394-5012

SHORTER COLLEGE
604 Locust St., North Little Rock 72114 *Type:* Private (African Methodist Episcopal) junior *Accred.:* 1981/1992 (NCA) *Calendar:* Sem. plan *Degrees:* A, certificates *CEO:* Pres. Katherine P. Mitchell
Enroll: 162　　　　　　(501) 374-6305

SOUTH ARKANSAS COMMUNITY COLLEGE
P.O. Box 7010, El Dorado 71731-7010
Type: Public (district) junior *Accred.:* 1983/
1988 (NCA) *Calendar:* Sem. plan *Degrees:*
A, certificates *Prof. Accred.:* Medical Labo-
ratory Technology (AMA), Radiography
CEO: Pres. Ben T. Whitfield
Enroll: 1,200   (501) 862-8131

SOUTHERN ARKANSAS UNIVERSITY
SAU Box 1402, Magnolia 71753 *Type:* Public (state) liberal arts and teachers *System:*
Arkansas Department of Higher Education
Accred.: 1929/1993 (NCA) *Calendar:* Sem.
plan *Degrees:* A, B, M, certificates *Prof. Accred.:* Music, Nursing (A), Teacher Education (e,s,p) *CEO:* Pres. Steven G. Gamble
Enroll: 2,742   (501) 235-4001

SOUTHERN ARKANSAS UNIVERSITY TECH
SAU Tech Sta., Camden 71701 *Type:* Public
(state) 2-year *Accred.:* 1980/1990 (NCA)
Calendar: Sem. plan *Degrees:* A, certificates
CEO: Chanc. George J. Brown
Enroll: 1,197   (501) 574-4500

UNIVERSITY OF ARKANSAS AT FAYETTEVILLE
Fayetteville 72701 *Type:* Public (state) *Sys-
tem:* University of Arkansas System Admin-
istration *Accred.:* 1924/1987 (NCA) *Calen-
dar:* Sem. plan *Degrees:* A, B, P, M, D *Prof.
Accred.:* Accounting (Type A,C), Business
(B,M), Engineering (agricultural, chemical,
civil, computer, electrical, industrial, me-
chanical), Home Economics, Interior Design,
Journalism (B,M), Landscape Architecture
(B), Law, Music, Nursing (A), Rehabilitation
Counseling, Social Work (B), Speech-Lan-
guage Pathology, Teacher Education (e,s,p)
CEO: Chanc. Daniel E. Ferritor
Enroll: 14,582   (501) 575-2000

UNIVERSITY OF ARKANSAS AT LITTLE ROCK
2801 S. University Ave., Little Rock 72204
Type: Public (state) *System:* University of
Arkansas System Administration *Accred.:*
1929/1990 (NCA) *Calendar:* Sem. plan *Degrees:* A, B, P, M, D *Prof. Accred.:* Art (associate), Audiology, Business (B,M), Computer Science, Dental Hygiene, Engineering
Technology (civil/construction, computer,
electrical, manufacturing, mechanical),
Health Services Administration, Journalism
(B,M), Law, Music, Nursing (A), Public Ad-

ministration, Social Work (M), Speech-Lan-
guage Pathology, Surgical Technology,
Teacher Education (e,s), Theatre *CEO:*
Chanc. Charles E. Hathaway
Enroll: 12,419   (501) 569-3362

UNIVERSITY OF ARKANSAS AT MONTICELLO
Monticello 71655 *Type:* Public (state) *System:* University of Arkansas System Administration *Accred.:* 1928/1985 (NCA) *Calendar:* Sem. plan *Degrees:* A, B, M, certificates *Prof. Accred.:* Forestry, Music (associate), Nursing (A), Teacher Education (e,s)
CEO: Chanc. Fred J. Taylor
Enroll: 2,520   (501) 460-1020

UNIVERSITY OF ARKANSAS AT PINE BLUFF
Pine Bluff 71601 *Type:* Public (state) *System:* University of Arkansas System Administration *Accred.:* 1950/1987 (NCA) *Calendar:* Sem. plan *Degrees:* A, B, M *Prof. Accred.:* Home Economics, Music, Nursing
(B), Social Work (B), Teacher Education
(e,s) *CEO:* Chanc. Lawrence A. Davis, Jr.
Enroll: 3,709   (501) 543-8000

UNIVERSITY OF ARKANSAS FOR MEDICAL
SCIENCES
4301 W. Markham St., Little Rock 72205
Type: Public (state) *System:* University of
Arkansas System Administration *Accred.:*
1987 (NCA) *Calendar:* Sem. plan *Degrees:*
A, B, M, D, certificates *Prof. Accred.:* Clini-
cal Psychology, Cytotechnology, Dietetics
(internship), Medical Technology, Medicine,
Nuclear Medicine Technology, Nursing
(B,M), Psychology Internship, Radiography,
Respiratory Therapy, Respiratory Therapy
Technology *CEO:* Chanc. Harry P. Ward
Enroll: 1,734   (501) 686-5000

UNIVERSITY OF CENTRAL ARKANSAS
Conway 73034 *Type:* Public (state) liberal
arts and teachers *System:* Arkansas Department of Higher Education *Accred.:* 1931/
1990 (NCA) *Calendar:* Sem. plan *Degrees:*
A, B, P, M *Prof. Accred.:* Business (B,M),
Music, Nursing (B,M), Occupational Therapy, Physical Therapy, Physical Therapy Assisting, Speech-Language Pathology, Teacher Education (e,s,p) *CEO:* Pres. Winfred L.
Thompson
Enroll: 9,473   (501) 450-3170

UNIVERSITY OF THE OZARKS
415 College Ave., Clarksville 72830 *Type:* Private (United Presbyterian) liberal arts *Accred.:* 1931/1993 (NCA) *Calendar:* 4-1-4 plan *Degrees:* A, B, M *Prof. Accred.:* Teacher Education (e,s) *CEO:* Pres. Gene Stephenson
Enroll: 579   (501) 754-3839

WESTARK COMMUNITY COLLEGE
P.O. Box 3649, Fort Smith 72913 *Type:* Public (district) junior *Accred.:* 1973/1985 (NCA) *Calendar:* Sem. plan *Degrees:* A, certificates *Prof. Accred.:* Medical Laboratory Technology (AMA), Nursing (A), Surgical Technology *CEO:* Pres. Joel Stubblefield
Enroll: 5,451   (501) 788-7000

WILLIAMS BAPTIST COLLEGE
Box 3667, Walnut Ridge 72476 *Type:* Private (Southern Baptist) *Accred.:* 1963/1987 (NCA) *Calendar:* Sem. plan *Degrees:* A, B, certificates *CEO:* Pres. Gary C. Huckabay
Enroll: 691   (501) 886-6741

CALIFORNIA

ACADEMY OF ART COLLEGE
540 Powell St., San Francisco 94108-3893
Type: Private *Accred.:* 1973/1990 (ACC-SCT) *Calendar:* Qtr. plan *Degrees:* B, M, certificates *Prof. Accred.:* Art (associate), Interior Design *CEO:* Vice Pres. Jan Schroeder
(510) 765-4200

ACADEMY OF CHINESE CULTURE AND HEALTH SCIENCES
1601 Clay St., Oakland 94612 *Type:* Private professional *Calendar:* Tri. plan *Degrees:* M *Prof. Accred.:* Acupuncture *CEO:* Pres. Wei Tsuei
FTE Enroll: 42   (510) 763-7787

ALLAN HANCOCK COLLEGE
800 S. College Dr., Santa Maria 93454 *Type:* Public (district) junior *System:* Allan Hancock Joint Community College District *Accred.:* 1952/1992 (WASC-Jr.) *Calendar:* Sem. plan *Degrees:* A *CEO:* Pres. Ann Foxworthy Stephenson
Enroll: 16,706   (805) 922-6966

AMERICAN ACADEMY OF DRAMATIC ARTS WEST
2550 Paloma St., Pasadena 91107 *Type:* Private professional *Accred.:* 1981/1991 (WASC-Jr.) *Calendar:* Sem. plan *Degrees:* A *Prof. Accred.:* Theatre *CEO:* Pres. George C. Cuttingham
Enroll: 300   (818) 798-0777

AMERICAN BAPTIST SEMINARY OF THE WEST
2606 Dwight Way, Berkeley 94704-3029 *Type:* Private (Baptist) graduate only *Accred.:* 1938/1989 (ATS) *Calendar:* Sem. plan *Degrees:* M, D *CEO:* Pres. Theodore Keaton
FTE Enroll: 40   (510) 841-1905

AMERICAN COLLEGE OF TRADITIONAL CHINESE MEDICINE
455 Arkansas St., San Francisco 94107 *Type:* Private professional *Calendar:* Qtr. plan *Degrees:* M *Prof. Accred.:* Acupuncture *CEO:* Acting Pres. Allan Brant
FTE Enroll: 56   (415) 282-7600

AMERICAN CONSERVATORY THEATER
30 Grant Ave., San Francisco 94108 *Type:* Independent professional *Accred.:* 1984/

1992 (WASC-Sr.) *Calendar:* Sem. plan *Degrees:* M *CEO:* Artistic Dir. Carey Perloff
FTE Enroll: 157   (415) 834-3350

THE AMERICAN FILM INSTITUTE CENTER FOR ADVANCED FILM AND TELEVISION STUDIES
2021 N. Western Ave., Los Angeles 90027 *Type:* Private professional; graduate only *Calendar:* 2-year program *Degrees:* M *Prof. Accred.:* Art *CEO:* Dir. Jean Firstenberg
Enroll: 160   (213) 856-7628

AMERICAN RIVER COLLEGE
4700 College Oak Dr., Sacramento 95841 *Type:* Public (district) junior *System:* Los Rios Community College District *Accred.:* 1959/1989 (WASC-Jr.) *Calendar:* Sem. plan *Degrees:* A *Prof. Accred.:* Respiratory Therapy *CEO:* Interim Pres. Max McDonald
Enroll: 20,824   (916) 484-8011

ANTELOPE VALLEY COLLEGE
3041 W. Ave. K, Lancaster 93536 *Type:* Public (district) junior *System:* Antelope Valley Community College District *Accred.:* 1952/1993 (WASC-Jr.) *Calendar:* Sem. plan *Degrees:* A *CEO:* Pres. Allan W. Kurki
Enroll: 10,409   (805) 943-3241

ARMSTRONG UNIVERSITY
2222 Harold Way, Berkeley 94704 *Type:* Private *Accred.:* 1979/1987 (ACISC) *Calendar:* Sem. plan *Degrees:* A, B, M *CEO:* Pres. Ron Hook
(510) 848-2500

ART CENTER COLLEGE OF DESIGN
1700 Lida St., P.O. Box 7197, Pasadena 91109 *Type:* Independent professional *Accred.:* 1955/1988 (WASC-Sr.) *Calendar:* Tri. plan *Degrees:* B, M *Prof. Accred.:* Art *CEO:* Pres. David R. Brown
FTE Enroll: 1,278   (818) 396-2200

BRANCH CAMPUS
Chateau de Sully, Rte. de Chailly 144, La Tour-de-Peliz CH-1814, Switzerland *Prof. Accred.:* Art *CEO:* Dir. Uwe Bahnsen
[41] (21) 944-6464

ART INSTITUTE OF SOUTHERN CALIFORNIA
2222 Laguna Canyon Rd., Laguna Beach
92651 *Type:* Independent *Accred.:* 1990
(WASC-Sr. candidate) *Calendar:* Sem. plan
Degrees: B *Prof. Accred.:* Art (associate)
CEO: Pres. John W. Lottes
FTE Enroll: 129   (714) 497-3309

AZUSA PACIFIC UNIVERSITY
901 E. Alosta, Azusa 91702-7000 *Type:* Independent liberal arts *Accred.:* 1992 (ATS);
1964/1992 (WASC-Sr.) *Calendar:* 4-4-1
plan *Degrees:* A, B, M *Prof. Accred.:* Nursing (B,M), Social Work (B) *CEO:* Pres.
Richard E. Felix
FTE Enroll: 3,132   (818) 969-3434

BAKERSFIELD COLLEGE
1801 Panorama Dr., Bakersfield 93305
Type: Public (district) junior *System:* Kern
Community College District *Accred.:* 1952/
1988 (WASC-Jr.) *Calendar:* Sem. plan *De-
grees:* A *Prof. Accred.:* Radiography *CEO:*
Pres. Richard L. Wright
Enroll: 12,242   (805) 395-4011

BARSTOW COLLEGE
2700 Barstow Rd., Barstow 92311 *Type:*
Public (district) junior *System:* Barstow
Community College District *Accred.:* 1962/
1989 (WASC-Jr.) *Calendar:* Sem. plan *Degrees:* A *CEO:* Pres. Judith A. Strattan
Enroll: 2,568   (619) 252-2411

BETHANY COLLEGE OF THE ASSEMBLIES OF GOD
800 Bethany Dr., Scotts Valley 95066 *Type:*
Independent (Assemblies of God) *Accred.:*
1966/1985 (WASC-Sr.) *Calendar:* 4-1-4 plan
Degrees: A, B *CEO:* Pres. Tom L. Duncan
FTE Enroll: 550   (408) 438-3800

BIOLA UNIVERSITY
13800 Biola Ave., La Mirada 90639 *Type:*
Independent liberal arts and professional *Ac-
cred.:* 1977/1988 (ATS); 1961/1988
(WASC-Sr.) *Calendar:* 4-1-4 plan *Degrees:*
B, P, M, D *Prof. Accred.:* Clinical Psycholo-
gy, Music, Nursing (B) *CEO:* Pres. Clyde
Cook
FTE Enroll: 2,757   (310) 903-4761

BROOKS COLLEGE
4825 E. Pacific Coast Hwy., Long Beach
90804 *Type:* Private 2-year *Accred.:* 1977/

1992 (WASC-Jr.) *Calendar:* Qtr. plan *Degrees:* A *CEO:* Exec. Dir. Steven B. Sotraidis
Enroll: 583   (310) 597-6611

BROOKS INSTITUTE OF PHOTOGRAPHY
801 Alston Rd., Santa Barbara 93108 *Type:*
Private *Accred.:* 1984/1990 (ACISC) *Calendar:* Tri. plan *Degrees:* B, M, certificates,
diplomas *CEO:* Vice Pres. Eugene C.
Streeter
       (805) 966-3888

BUTTE COLLEGE
3536 Butte Campus Dr., Oroville 95965
Type: Public (district) junior *System:* Butte
Community College District *Accred.:* 1972/
1991 (WASC-Jr.) *Calendar:* Sem. plan *De-
grees:* A *Prof. Accred.:* Respiratory Therapy
CEO: Pres. Betty M. Dean
Enroll: 12,400   (916) 895-2511

CABRILLO COLLEGE
6500 Soquel Dr., Aptos 95003 *Type:* Public
(district) junior *System:* Cabrillo Community
College District *Accred.:* 1961/1989
(WASC-Jr.) *Calendar:* Sem. plan *Degrees:*
A *Prof. Accred.:* Dental Hygiene, Radiogra-
phy *CEO:* Pres. John D. Hurd
Enroll: 13,529   (408) 479-6100

CALIFORNIA BAPTIST COLLEGE
8432 Magnolia Ave., Riverside 92504 *Type:*
Independent (Southern Baptist) liberal arts
Accred.: 1961/1987 (WASC-Sr.) *Calendar:*
Early sem. and Jan. term *Degrees:* B, M
Prof. Accred.: Music *CEO:* Pres. Russell R.
Tuck
FTE Enroll: 806   (909) 689-5771

CALIFORNIA COLLEGE FOR HEALTH SCIENCES
222 W. 24th St., National City 91950-9998
Type: Private professional and home study
Accred.: 1980/1987 (ACCSCT); 1981/1992
(NHSC) *Calendar:* Courses of varying
lengths *Degrees:* A, B, M, certificates *Prof.
Accred.:* Respiratory Therapy, Respiratory
Therapy Technology *CEO:* Pres. Ken B.
Scheiderman
       (619) 477-4800

CALIFORNIA COLLEGE OF ARTS AND CRAFTS
5212 Broadway, Oakland 94618 *Type:* Independent professional *Accred.:* 1954/1984
(WASC-Sr.) *Calendar:* Tri. plan *Degrees:*

B, M *Prof. Accred.:* Art, Interior Design
CEO: (Vacant)
FTE Enroll: 1,035   (510) 653-8118

CALIFORNIA COLLEGE OF PODIATRIC MEDICINE
1210 Scott St., San Francisco 94115 *Type:*
Independent professional *Accred.:* 1961/
1983 (WASC-Sr.) *Calendar:* Sem. plan *Degrees:* B, P, M, D *Prof. Accred.:* Podiatry
CEO: Interim Pres. Lawrence M. Oloff
FTE Enroll: 382   (415) 292-0439

CALIFORNIA FAMILY STUDY CENTER
5433 Laurel Canyon Blvd., North Hollywood 91607-2193 *Type:* Independent *Accred.:* 1983/1988 (WASC-Sr.) *Calendar:*
Sem. plan *Degrees:* M *CEO:* Pres. Edwin S.
Cox, Ph.D.
FTE Enroll: 290   (818) 509-5959

CALIFORNIA INSTITUTE OF INTEGRAL STUDIES
765 Ashbury St., San Francisco 94117 *Type:*
Independent graduate only *Accred.:* 1981/
1984 (WASC-Sr.) *Calendar:* Qtr. plan *Degrees:* M, D *CEO:* Pres. Robert McDermott
FTE Enroll: 698   (415) 753-6100

CALIFORNIA INSTITUTE OF TECHNOLOGY
1201 E. California Blvd., Pasadena 91125
Type: Independent *Accred.:* 1949/1990
(WASC-Sr.) *Calendar:* Qtr. plan *Degrees:*
B, M, D *Prof. Accred.:* Engineering (chemical, engineering physics/science) *CEO:* Pres.
Thomas E. Everhart
FTE Enroll: 1,992   (818) 395-6301

CALIFORNIA INSTITUTE OF THE ARTS
24700 McBean Pkwy., Valencia 91355
Type: Independent *Accred.:* 1955/1992
(WASC-Sr.) *Calendar:* Sem. plan *Degrees:*
B, M *Prof. Accred.:* Art, Dance, Music
CEO: Pres. Steven D. Lavine
FTE Enroll: 1,041   (805) 255-1050

CALIFORNIA LUTHERAN UNIVERSITY
60 Olsen Rd., Thousand Oaks 91360 *Type:*
Independent (Evangelical Lutheran Church)
liberal arts *Accred.:* 1962/1989 (WASC-Sr.)
Calendar: 4-1-4 plan *Degrees:* B, M *CEO:*
Pres. Luther S. Luedtke
FTE Enroll: 2,210   (805) 493-3100

CALIFORNIA MARITIME ACADEMY
200 Maritime Academy Dr., P.O. Box 1392,
Vallejo 94590-0644 *Type:* Public (state) *Accred.:* 1977/1992 (WASC-Sr.) *Calendar:*
Tri. plan *Degrees:* B *Prof. Accred.:* Engineering Technology (naval architecture/marine) *CEO:* Pres. Mary E. Lyons
FTE Enroll: 590   (707) 648-4200

CALIFORNIA POLYTECHNIC STATE UNIVERSITY,
SAN LUIS OBISPO
San Luis Obispo 93407 *Type:* Public (state)
System: California State University System
Accred.: 1951/1990 (WASC-Sr.) *Calendar:*
Qtr. plan *Degrees:* B, M *Prof. Accred.:* Business (B,M), Computer Science, Construction
Education (B), Engineering Technology (air
conditioning, electrical, manufacturing, mechanical, welding), Engineering (aerospace,
agricultural, architectural, civil, electrical,
environmental/sanitary, industrial, mechanical, metallurgical), Forestry (candidate), Interior Design, Landscape Architecture (B),
Planning (B,M), Recreation and Leisure Services *CEO:* Pres. Warren J. Baker
FTE Enroll: 14,073   (805) 756-1111

CALIFORNIA SCHOOL OF PROFESSIONAL
PSYCHOLOGY, BERKELEY/ALAMEDA
1005 Atlantic Ave., Alameda 94501 *Type:*
Independent professional *Accred.:* 1977/
1989 (WASC-Sr.) *Calendar:* Sem. plan *Degrees:* M, D *Prof. Accred.:* Clinical Psychology *CEO:* Chanc. Katsuyuki Sakamoto
FTE Enroll: 490   (510) 523-2300

CALIFORNIA SCHOOL OF PROFESSIONAL
PSYCHOLOGY, FRESNO
1350 M St., Fresno 93721 *Type:* Independent professional *Accred.:* 1977/1989
(WASC-Sr.) *Calendar:* Sem. plan *Degrees:*
M, D *Prof. Accred.:* Clinical Psychology
CEO: Chanc. Mary Beth Kenkel
FTE Enroll: 336   (209) 486-8420

CALIFORNIA SCHOOL OF PROFESSIONAL
PSYCHOLOGY, LOS ANGELES
1000 S. Fremont Ave., Alhambra 91803-
1360 *Type:* Independent professional *Accred.:* 1977/1989 (WASC-Sr.) *Calendar:*
Sem. plan *Degrees:* M, D *Prof. Accred.:*
Clinical Psychology *CEO:* Chanc. Lisa M.
Porche-Burke
FTE Enroll: 502   (818) 284-2777

CALIFORNIA SCHOOL OF PROFESSIONAL
PSYCHOLOGY, SAN DIEGO
6212 Ferris Sq., San Diego 92121-3250
Type: Independent professional *Accred.:*
1977/1989 (WASC-Sr.) *Calendar:* Sem.
plan *Degrees:* M, D *Prof. Accred.:* Clinical
Psychology (probational) *CEO:* Chanc. Raymond J. Trybus, Ph.D.
FTE Enroll: 465   (619) 452-1664

CALIFORNIA STATE POLYTECHNIC UNIVERSITY,
POMONA
3801 W. Temple Ave., Pomona 91768 *Type:*
Public (state) *System:* California State University System *Accred.:* 1970/1990 (WASC-
Sr.) *Calendar:* Qtr. plan *Degrees:* B, M *Prof.
Accred.:* Engineering Technology (general),
Engineering (aerospace, agricultural, chemical, civil, electrical, industrial, manufacturing, mechanical), Landscape Architecture
(B,M), Planning (B,M), Recreation and
Leisure Services, Social Work (B) *CEO:*
Pres. Bob H. Suzuki
FTE Enroll: 13,336   (909) 869-7659

CALIFORNIA STATE UNIVERSITY, BAKERSFIELD
9001 Stockdale Hwy., Bakersfield 93311-
1099 *Type:* Public (state) *System:* California
State University System *Accred.:* 1970/1990
(WASC-Sr.) *Calendar:* Qtr. plan *Degrees:*
B, M *Prof. Accred.:* Administration Health
Care Management, Business (B,M), Medical
Technology, Nursing (B,M), Public Administration, Teacher Education (e,s,p) *CEO:*
Pres. Tomás A. Arciniega
FTE Enroll: 4,151   (805) 664-2201

CALIFORNIA STATE UNIVERSITY, CHICO
First and Normal Sts., Chico 95929-0110
Type: Public (state) *System:* California State
University System *Accred.:* 1949/1989
(WASC-Sr.) *Calendar:* Sem. plan *Degrees:*
B, M *Prof. Accred.:* Art, Business (B,M),
Computer Science, Construction Education
(B), Engineering (civil, computer, electrical,
mechanical), Music, Nursing (B), Recreation
and Leisure Services, Social Work (B),
Speech-Language Pathology *CEO:* Pres.
Manuel A. Esteban
FTE Enroll: 13,007   (916) 898-6101

CALIFORNIA STATE UNIVERSITY, DOMINGUEZ
HILLS
1000 E. Victoria St., Carson 90747 *Type:*
Public (state) *System:* California State Uni-

versity System *Accred.:* 1965/1990 (WASC-
Sr.) *Calendar:* Qtr. plan *Degrees:* B, M *Prof.
Accred.:* Art, Medical Technology, Music,
Nuclear Medicine Technology, Nursing
(B,M), Public Administration, Teacher Education (e,s), Theatre (associate) *CEO:* Pres.
Robert C. Detweiler
FTE Enroll: 7,697   (310) 516-3300

CALIFORNIA STATE UNIVERSITY, FRESNO
5241 N. Maple Ave., Fresno 93740-0054
Type: Public (state) *System:* California State
University System *Accred.:* 1949/1989
(WASC-Sr.) *Calendar:* Sem. plan *Degrees:*
B, M *Prof. Accred.:* Audiology, Business
(B,M), Construction Education (B), Engineering (civil, electrical, industrial, mechanical, surveying), Interior Design, Journalism
(B,M), Music, Nursing (B,M), Physical
Therapy, Public Administration, Recreation
and Leisure Services, Rehabilitation Counseling, Social Work (B,M), Speech-Language Pathology, Teacher Education (e,s,p),
Theatre (associate) *CEO:* Pres. John D.
Welty
FTE Enroll: 14,839   (209) 278-4240

CALIFORNIA STATE UNIVERSITY, FULLERTON
P.O. Box 34080, Fullerton 92634 *Type:* Public (state) *System:* California State University
System *Accred.:* 1961/1991 (WASC-Sr.)
Calendar: Sem. plan *Degrees:* B, M *Prof.
Accred.:* Art, Business (B,M), Computer Science, Dance, Engineering (civil, electrical,
mechanical), Journalism (B,M), Music,
Nursing (B), Public Administration, Speech-
Language Pathology, Teacher Education
(e,s,p), Theatre *CEO:* Pres. Milton A.
Gordon
FTE Enroll: 15,741   (714) 773-2011

CALIFORNIA STATE UNIVERSITY, HAYWARD
25800 Carlos Bee Blvd., Hayward 94542
Type: Public (state) *System:* California State
University System *Accred.:* 1961/1989
(WASC-Sr.) *Calendar:* Qtr. plan *Degrees:*
B, M *Prof. Accred.:* Art, Business (B,M),
Music, Nursing (B), Public Administration,
Speech-Language Pathology, Teacher Education (e,s,p) *CEO:* Pres. Norma S. Rees
FTE Enroll: 10,384   (510) 881-3000

CALIFORNIA STATE UNIVERSITY, LONG BEACH
1250 Bellflower Blvd., Long Beach 90840
Type: Public (state) *System:* California State

University System *Accred.:* 1957/1992 (WASC-Sr.) *Calendar:* Sem. plan *Degrees:* B, M *Prof. Accred.:* Art, Audiology, Business (B,M), Community Health, Construction Education (B), Dance, Engineering (chemical, civil, computer, electrical, mechanical), Home Economics, Interior Design, Journalism (B), Music, Nurse Anesthesia Education, Nursing (B,M), Physical Therapy, Public Administration, Radiation Therapy Technology, Recreation and Leisure Services, Social Work (B,M), Speech-Language Pathology, Theatre *CEO:* Interim Pres. Karl W.E. Anatol
FTE Enroll: 19,761   (310) 985-4111

CALIFORNIA STATE UNIVERSITY, LOS ANGELES
5151 State University Dr., Los Angeles 90032 *Type:* Public (state) *System:* California State University System *Accred.:* 1954/1990 (WASC-Sr.) *Calendar:* Qtr. plan *Degrees:* B, M *Prof. Accred.:* Art, Audiology, Business (B,M), Counseling, Dietetics (coordinated), Engineering (civil, electrical, mechanical), Music, Nursing (B,M), Public Administration, Rehabilitation Counseling, Social Work (B), Speech-Language Pathology, Teacher Education (e,s,p) *CEO:* Pres. James M. Rosser
FTE Enroll: 12,089   (213) 343-3030

CALIFORNIA STATE UNIVERSITY, NORTHRIDGE
18111 Nordhoff St., Northridge 91330 *Type:* Public (state) *System:* California State University System *Accred.:* 1958/1991 (WASC-Sr.) *Calendar:* Sem. plan *Degrees:* B, M *Prof. Accred.:* Audiology, Business (B,M), Community Health, Computer Science, Counseling, Engineering (general), Home Economics, Journalism (B,M), Music, Physical Therapy, Radiography, Recreation and Leisure Services, Speech-Language Pathology, Teacher Education (e,s,p), Theatre (associate) *CEO:* Pres. Blenda J. Wilson
FTE Enroll: 20,325   (818) 885-2121

CALIFORNIA STATE UNIVERSITY, SACRAMENTO
6000 J St., Sacramento 95819-2694 *Type:* Public (state) *System:* California State University System *Accred.:* 1951/1990 (WASC-Sr.) *Calendar:* Sem. plan *Degrees:* B, M *Prof. Accred.:* Art, Audiology, Business (B,M), Computer Science, Construction Education (B), Counseling, Engineering Tech-

nology (civil/construction, mechanical), Engineering (civil, computer, electrical, mechanical), Interior Design, Music, Nursing (B,M), Recreation and Leisure Services, Rehabilitation Counseling, Social Work (B,M-conditional), Speech-Language Pathology, Theatre *CEO:* Pres. Donald R. Gerth
FTE Enroll: 18,103   (916) 278-6011

CALIFORNIA STATE UNIVERSITY, SAN BERNARDINO
5500 State University Pkwy., San Bernardino 92407-2397 *Type:* Public (state) *System:* California State University System *Accred.:* 1965/1989 (WASC-Sr.) *Calendar:* Qtr. plan *Degrees:* B, M *Prof. Accred.:* Art, Computer Science, Nursing (B), Public Administration, Rehabilitation Counseling, Social Work (M) *CEO:* Pres. Anthony H. Evans
FTE Enroll: 9,342   (909) 880-5000

CALIFORNIA STATE UNIVERSITY, SAN MARCOS
San Marcos 92069 *Type:* Public (state) *System:* California State University System *Accred.:* 1993 (WASC-Sr.) *Calendar:* Sem. plan *Degrees:* B, M *CEO:* Pres. Bill W. Stacy
FTE Enroll: 1,301   (619) 471-4100

CALIFORNIA STATE UNIVERSITY, STANISLAUS
801 W. Monte Vista Ave., Turlock 95382 *Type:* Public (state) *System:* California State University System *Accred.:* 1963/1991 (WASC-Sr.) *Calendar:* 4-1-4 plan *Degrees:* B, M *Prof. Accred.:* Art, Computer Science, Music, Nursing (B), Public Administration, Teacher Education (e,s,p), Theatre *CEO:* Pres. Lee R. Kerschner
FTE Enroll: 4,127   (209) 667-3082

CALIFORNIA WESTERN SCHOOL OF LAW
350 Cedar St., San Diego 92101 *Type:* Private professional *Calendar:* Sem. plan *Degrees:* P *Prof. Accred.:* Law *CEO:* Dean Michael H. Dessent
Enroll: 730   (619) 239-0391

CAÑADA COLLEGE
4200 Farm Hill Blvd., Redwood City 94061 *Type:* Public (district) junior *System:* San Mateo County Community College District *Accred.:* 1970/1992 (WASC-Jr.) *Calendar:*

Sem. plan *Degrees:* A *Prof. Accred.:* Radiography *CEO:* Pres. Miles Douglas Kechter
Enroll: 7,600   (415) 364-1212

CERRITOS COLLEGE
11110 Alondra Blvd., Norwalk 90650 *Type:* Public (district) junior *System:* Cerritos Community College District *Accred.:* 1959/1990 (WASC-Jr.) *Calendar:* Sem. plan *Degrees:* A *Prof. Accred.:* Dental Assisting, Dental Hygiene, Nursing (A), Physical Therapy Assisting *CEO:* Pres. Fred Gaskin
Enroll: 19,030   (310) 860-2451

CERRO COSO COMMUNITY COLLEGE
3000 College Heights Blvd., Ridgecrest 93555 *Type:* Public (district) junior *System:* Kern Community College District *Accred.:* 1975/1990 (WASC-Jr.) *Calendar:* Sem. plan *Degrees:* A *CEO:* Pres. Raymond A. McCue
Enroll: 4,085   (619) 375-5001

CHABOT COLLEGE
25555 Hesperian Blvd., Hayward 94545 *Type:* Public (district) junior *System:* Chabot-Las Positas Community College District *Accred.:* 1963/1991 (WASC-Jr.) *Calendar:* Qtr. plan *Degrees:* A *Prof. Accred.:* Dental Assisting, Dental Hygiene, Medical Assisting (AMA), Medical Record Technology *CEO:* Pres. Raul Cardoza
Enroll: 14,706   (510) 786-6600

CHAFFEY COLLEGE
5885 Haven Ave., Rancho Cucamonga 91701 *Type:* Public (district) junior *System:* Chaffey Community College District *Accred.:* 1952/1992 (WASC-Jr.) *Calendar:* Qtr. plan *Degrees:* A *Prof. Accred.:* Dental Assisting, Nursing (A), Radiography *CEO:* Pres. Jerry W. Young
Enroll: 15,497   (909) 941-2100

CHAPMAN UNIVERSITY
333 N. Glassell St., Orange 92666 *Type:* Independent (Disciples of Christ) liberal arts *Accred.:* 1956/1988 (WASC-Sr.) *Calendar:* 4-1-4 plan *Degrees:* A, B, M *Prof. Accred.:* Physical Therapy *CEO:* Pres. James Doti
FTE Enroll: 5,274   (714) 997-6826

CHARLES R. DREW UNIVERSITY OF MEDICINE AND SCIENCE
1621 E. 120th St., Los Angeles 90059 *Type:* Independent *Accred.:* 1988 (WASC-Sr. candidate) *Calendar:* Sem. plan *Degrees:* A, B, M, D *Prof. Accred.:* Dietetics (coordinated), Medical Record Technology, Medical Technology, Nuclear Medicine Technology, Physician Assisting, Radiography *CEO:* Pres. Reed V. Tuckson
FTE Enroll: 625   (213) 563-4800

CHRISTIAN HERITAGE COLLEGE
2100 Greenfield Dr., El Cajon 92019 *Type:* Independent (Scott Memorial Baptist Church) liberal arts *Accred.:* 1984 (WASC-Sr.) *Calendar:* Sem. plan *Degrees:* B *CEO:* Pres. David P. Jeremiah
FTE Enroll: 338   (619) 441-2200

CHURCH DIVINITY SCHOOL OF THE PACIFIC
2451 Ridge Rd., Berkeley 94709-1211 *Type:* Independent (Episcopal) professional; graduate only *Accred.:* 1954/1984 (ATS); 1978/1989 (WASC-Sr.) *Calendar:* Qtr. plan *Degrees:* P, M, D *CEO:* Pres. Charles A. Perry
FTE Enroll: 71   (510) 204-0700

CITRUS COLLEGE
1000 W. Foothill Blvd., Glendora 91741-1899 *Type:* Public (district) junior *System:* Citrus Community College District *Accred.:* 1952/1992 (WASC-Jr.) *Calendar:* Sem. plan *Degrees:* A *Prof. Accred.:* Dental Assisting *CEO:* Pres. Louis E. Zellers
Enroll: 12,374   (818) 963-0323

CITY COLLEGE OF SAN FRANCISCO
50 Phelan Ave., San Francisco 94112 *Type:* Public (district) junior *System:* San Francisco Community College District *Accred.:* 1952/1988 (WASC-Jr.) *Calendar:* Sem. plan *Degrees:* A *Prof. Accred.:* Dental Assisting, Dental Laboratory Technology, Engineering Technology (electrical, electromechanical, mechanical), Medical Assisting (AMA), Radiation Therapy Technology, Radiography *CEO:* Chanc. Evan S. Dobelle
Enroll: 64,085   (415) 239-3000

THE CLAREMONT GRADUATE SCHOOL
160 E. 10th St., Claremont 91711 *Type:* Independent graduate only *Accred.:* 1949/1993 (WASC-Sr.) *Calendar:* Sem. plan *Degrees:* M, D *Prof. Accred.:* Business (M) *CEO:* Pres. John D. Maguire
FTE Enroll: 1,000   (909) 621-8068

CLAREMONT MCKENNA COLLEGE
850 Columbia Ave., Claremont 91711 *Type:* Independent liberal arts *Accred.:* 1949/1991 (WASC-Sr.) *Calendar:* Sem. plan *Degrees:* B *CEO:* Pres. Jack L. Stark
FTE Enroll: 906   (909) 621-8111

CLEVELAND CHIROPRACTIC COLLEGE
590 N. Vermont Ave., Los Angeles 90004 *Type:* Independent professional *Accred.:* 1988 (WASC-Sr. candidate) *Calendar:* Tri. plan *Degrees:* B, P *Prof. Accred.:* Chiropractic Education *CEO:* Pres. Carl S. Cleveland, III, D.C.
FTE Enroll: 460   (213) 660-6166

COASTLINE COMMUNITY COLLEGE
11460 Warner Ave., Fountain Valley 92708 *Type:* Public (district) junior *System:* Coast Community College District *Accred.:* 1978/ 1988 (WASC-Jr.) *Calendar:* Sem. plan *Degrees:* A *CEO:* Acting Pres. Judith Valles
Enroll: 16,000   (714) 546-7600

COGSWELL POLYTECHNICAL COLLEGE
1174 Bordeaux Dr., Sunnyvale 94089-1299 *Type:* Independent technical *Accred.:* 1977/1982 (WASC-Sr. probational) *Calendar:* Tri. plan *Degrees:* A, B *Prof. Accred.:* Engineering Technology (electrical, mechanical) *CEO:* Pres. Ted Kastelic, Ph.D.
FTE Enroll: 321   (408) 541-0100

COLEMAN COLLEGE
7380 Parkway Dr., La Mesa 91942-1532 *Type:* Private *Accred.:* 1967/1988 (ACISC) *Calendar:* Qtr. plan *Degrees:* A, B, M, certificates, diplomas *CEO:* Pres. Michael J. Flood, C.D.P.
          (619) 465-3990

COLLEGE OF ALAMEDA
555 Atlantic Ave., Alameda 94501 *Type:* Public (district) junior *System:* Peralta Community College District *Accred.:* 1973/1993 (WASC-Jr.) *Calendar:* Qtr. plan *Degrees:* A *Prof. Accred.:* Dental Assisting *CEO:* Pres. Marie B. Smith
Enroll: 5,962   (510) 522-7221

COLLEGE OF MARIN
835 College Ave., Kentfield 94904 *Type:* Public (district) junior *System:* Marin Community College District *Accred.:* 1952/1993 (WASC-Jr.) *Calendar:* Sem. plan *Degrees:* A *Prof. Accred.:* Dental Assisting, Nursing (A) *CEO:* Pres. James E. Middleton
Enroll: 10,742   (415) 457-8811

COLLEGE OF NOTRE DAME
1500 Ralston Ave., Belmont 94002-9974 *Type:* Independent (Roman Catholic) liberal arts *Accred.:* 1955/1991 (WASC-Sr.) *Calendar:* Sem. plan *Degrees:* B, M *Prof. Accred.:* Music *CEO:* Pres. Veronica Skillin
FTE Enroll: 1,206   (415) 593-1601

COLLEGE OF OCEANEERING
Los Angeles Harbor, 272 S. Fries Ave., Wilmington 90744 *Type:* Private *Accred.:* 1982/1992 (WASC-Jr.) *Calendar:* Yearly plan *Degrees:* A *CEO:* Executive Dir. Ron Friedrich
Enroll: 261   (310) 834-2501

COLLEGE OF OSTEOPATHIC MEDICINE OF THE PACIFIC
309 E. Second St., Pomona 91766-1889 *Type:* Independent *Accred.:* 1990 (WASC-Sr. candidate) *Calendar:* Sem. plan *Degrees:* B, M *Prof. Accred.:* Osteopathy, Physician Assisting *CEO:* Pres. Philip Pumeranta
FTE Enroll: 832   (909) 623-6116

COLLEGE OF SAN MATEO
1700 W. Hillsdale Blvd., San Mateo 94402 *Type:* Public (district) junior *System:* San Mateo County Community College District *Accred.:* 1952/1989 (WASC-Jr.) *Calendar:* Sem. plan *Degrees:* A *Prof. Accred.:* Dental Assisting *CEO:* Pres. Peter J. Landsberger
Enroll: 14,485   (415) 574-6161

COLLEGE OF THE CANYONS
26455 N. Rockwell Canyon Rd., Santa Clarita 91355 *Type:* Public (district) junior *System:* Santa Clarita Community College District *Accred.:* 1972/1990 (WASC-Jr.) *Calendar:* Sem. plan *Degrees:* A *CEO:* Pres. Dianne G. Van Hook
Enroll: 6,300   (805) 259-7800

COLLEGE OF THE DESERT
43-500 Monterey Ave., Palm Desert 92260 *Type:* Public (district) junior *System:* Desert Community College District *Accred.:* 1963/ 1993 (WASC-Jr.) *Calendar:* Sem. plan *Degrees:* A *Prof. Accred.:* Nursing (A), Respiratory Therapy *CEO:* Pres. David A. George
Enroll: 11,029   (619) 346-8041

COLLEGE OF THE REDWOODS
7351 Tompkins Hill Rd., Eureka 95501
Type: Public (district) junior *System:* Redwoods Community College District *Accred.:* 1967/1989 (WASC-Jr.) *Calendar:* Sem. plan *Degrees:* A *Prof. Accred.:* Dental Assisting *CEO:* Pres. Cedric A. Sampson
Enroll: 7,369　　　　　　　(707) 445-6700

COLLEGE OF THE SEQUOIAS
915 S. Mooney Blvd., Visalia 93277 *Type:* Public (district) junior *System:* Sequoias Community College District *Accred.:* 1952/1989 (WASC-Jr.) *Calendar:* Sem. plan *Degrees:* A *CEO:* Interim Pres. David Erickson
Enroll: 9,086　　　　　　　(209) 730-3700

COLLEGE OF THE SISKIYOUS
800 College Ave., Weed 96094 *Type:* Public (district) junior *System:* Siskiyou Joint Community College District *Accred.:* 1961/1992 (WASC-Jr.) *Calendar:* Sem. plan *Degrees:* A *CEO:* Pres. Martha G. Romero
Enroll: 2,774　　　　　　　(916) 938-4461

COLUMBIA COLLEGE
P.O. Box 1849, Columbia 95310 *Type:* Public (district) junior *System:* Yosemite Community College District *Accred.:* 1972/1989 (WASC-Jr.) *Calendar:* Sem. plan *Degrees:* A *CEO:* Pres. Kenneth B. White
Enroll: 3,000　　　　　　　(209) 533-5100

COLUMBIA COLLEGE HOLLYWOOD
925 N. La Brea Ave., Los Angeles 90038-2392 *Type:* Private *Accred.:* 1979/1986 (ACCSCT) *Calendar:* Qtr. plan *Degrees:* A, B, diplomas *CEO:* Pres. Allan Rossman
　　　　　　　　　　　　(213) 851-0550

COMPTON COMMUNITY COLLEGE
1111 E. Artesia Blvd., Compton 90221 *Type:* Public (district) junior *System:* Compton Community College District *Accred.:* 1952/1993 (WASC-Jr.) *Calendar:* Sem. plan *Degrees:* A *CEO:* Pres. Byron Skinner
Enroll: 5,800　　　　　　　(310) 637-2660

CONCORDIA UNIVERSITY
1530 Concordia W., Irvine 92715-3299 *Type:* Independent (Lutheran-Missouri Synod) liberal arts *Accred.:* 1981/1985 (WASC-Sr.) *Calendar:* Qtr. plan *Degrees:* A, B, M *CEO:* Pres. D. Ray Halm
FTE Enroll: 762　　　　　　(714) 854-8002

CONTRA COSTA COLLEGE
2600 Mission Bell Dr., San Pablo 94806 *Type:* Public (district) junior *System:* Contra Costa Community College District *Accred.:* 1952/1989 (WASC-Jr.) *Calendar:* Sem. plan *Degrees:* A *Prof. Accred.:* Dental Assisting *CEO:* Pres. D. Candy Rose
Enroll: 9,700　　　　　　　(510) 235-7800

COSUMNES RIVER COLLEGE
8401 Center Pkwy., Sacramento 95823 *Type:* Public (district) junior *System:* Los Rios Community College District *Accred.:* 1972/1991 (WASC-Jr.) *Calendar:* Sem. plan *Degrees:* A *Prof. Accred.:* Medical Assisting (AMA), Medical Record Technology, Veterinary Technology *CEO:* Pres. Marc E. Hall
Enroll: 10,962　　　　　　(916) 688-7300

CRAFTON HILLS COLLEGE
11711 Sand Canyon Rd., Yucaipa 92399 *Type:* Public (district) junior *System:* San Bernardino Community College District *Accred.:* 1975/1990 (WASC-Jr.) *Calendar:* Sem. plan *Degrees:* A *Prof. Accred.:* EMT-Paramedic, Respiratory Therapy, Respiratory Therapy Technology *CEO:* Pres. Luis S. Gomez
Enroll: 5,111　　　　　　　(714) 794-2161

CUESTA COLLEGE
P.O. Box 8106, San Luis Obispo 93403 *Type:* Public (district) junior *System:* San Luis Obispo Community College District *Accred.:* 1968/1991 (WASC-Jr.) *Calendar:* Sem. plan *Degrees:* A *CEO:* Pres. Grace N. Mitchell
Enroll: 7,508　　　　　　　(805) 546-3100

CUYAMACA COLLEGE
2950 Jamacha Rd., El Cajon 92019 *Type:* Public (district) junior *System:* Grossmont-Cuyamaca Community College District *Accred.:* 1980/1990 (WASC-Jr.) *Calendar:* Sem. plan *Degrees:* A *CEO:* Pres. Sherrill L. Amador
Enroll: 5,003　　　　　　　(619) 670-1980

CYPRESS COLLEGE
9200 Valley View St., Cypress 90630 *Type:* Public (district) junior *System:* North Orange County Community College District *Accred.:* 1968/1986 (WASC-Jr.) *Calendar:* Sem. plan *Degrees:* A *Prof. Accred.:* Dental

Assisting, Dental Hygiene, Medical Record Technology, Mortuary Science, Radiography *CEO:* Pres. Tom K. Harris, Jr.
Enroll: 15,274   (714) 826-2220

DE ANZA COLLEGE
21250 Stevens Creek Blvd., Cupertino 95014 *Type:* Public (district) junior *System:* Foothill-DeAnza Community College District *Accred.:* 1969/1987 (WASC-Jr.) *Calendar:* Qtr. plan *Degrees:* A *Prof. Accred.:* Medical Assisting (AMA), Physical Therapy Assisting *CEO:* Pres. Martha J. Kanter
Enroll: 28,758   (408) 864-5678

DEEP SPRINGS COLLEGE
via Dyer, Nevada, Deep Springs 89010 *Type:* Private junior for men *Accred.:* 1952/1993 (WASC-Jr.) *Calendar:* Sem. plan *Degrees:* A *CEO:* Pres. Sherwin Howard
Enroll: 25   (619) 872-2000

DESIGN INSTITUTE OF SAN DIEGO
8555 Commerce Ave., San Diego 92121 *Type:* Private professional *Calendar:* Courses of varying lengths *Degrees:* B, P *Prof. Accred.:* Interior Design *CEO:* Dir. MaryJo Kalamon
                                    (619) 566-1200

DEVRY INSTITUTE OF TECHNOLOGY, CITY OF INDUSTRY
12801 Crossroads Pkwy. S., City of Industry 91746 *Type:* Private *Accred.:* 1981/1992 (NCA)* *Calendar:* Sem. plan *Degrees:* A, B, certificates, diplomas *Prof. Accred.:* Engineering Technology (electrical) *CEO:* Pres. David G. Moore
                                    (310) 699-9927

* Indirect accreditation through DeVry Institutes.

DIABLO VALLEY COLLEGE
321 Golf Club Rd., Pleasant Hill 94523 *Type:* Public (district) junior *System:* Contra Costa Community College District *Accred.:* 1952/1991 (WASC-Jr.) *Calendar:* Sem. plan *Degrees:* A *Prof. Accred.:* Dental Assisting, Dental Hygiene *CEO:* Pres. Phyllis L. Peterson
Enroll: 23,000   (510) 685-1230

DOMINICAN COLLEGE OF SAN RAFAEL
50 Acacia St., San Rafael 94901 *Type:* Independent (Roman Catholic) liberal arts *Accred.:* 1949/1987 (WASC-Sr.) *Calendar:*

Sem. plan *Degrees:* B, M *Prof. Accred.:* Nursing (B) *CEO:* Pres. Joseph R. Fink
FTE Enroll: 1,041   (415) 457-4440

DOMINICAN SCHOOL OF PHILOSOPHY AND THEOLOGY
2401 Ridge Rd., Berkeley 94709 *Type:* Independent (Roman Catholic) professional *Accred.:* 1978/1993 (ATS); 1964/1993 (WASC-Sr.) *Calendar:* Sem. plan *Degrees:* B, P, M *CEO:* Pres. Allen Duston, O.P.
FTE Enroll: 68   (510) 849-2030

DON BOSCO TECHNICAL INSTITUTE
1151 San Gabriel Blvd., Rosemead 91770 *Type:* Private (Roman Catholic) 2-year *Accred.:* 1972/1989 (WASC-Jr.) *Calendar:* Sem. plan *Degrees:* A *CEO:* Pres. Nicholas Reina, S.D.B.
Enroll: 205   (818) 307-6500

D-Q UNIVERSITY
P.O. Box 409, Davis 95617 *Type:* Public junior *Accred.:* 1977/1992 (WASC-Jr.) *Calendar:* Sem. plan *Degrees:* A *CEO:* Pres. Carlos Cordero
Enroll: 478   (916) 758-0470

EAST LOS ANGELES COLLEGE
1301 Brooklyn Ave., Monterey Park 91754 *Type:* Public (district) junior *System:* Los Angeles Community College District *Accred.:* 1952/1992 (WASC-Jr.) *Calendar:* Sem. plan *Degrees:* A *Prof. Accred.:* Medical Record Technology, Respiratory Therapy *CEO:* Acting Pres. Ernest Moreno
Enroll: 12,973   (213) 265-8650

EL CAMINO COLLEGE
16007 Crenshaw Blvd., Torrance 90506 *Type:* Public (district) junior *System:* El Camino Community College District *Accred.:* 1952/1990 (WASC-Jr.) *Calendar:* Sem. plan *Degrees:* A *Prof. Accred.:* Nursing (A), Radiography, Respiratory Therapy *CEO:* Pres. Sam Schauerman
Enroll: 27,330   (310) 715-3111

EMPEROR'S COLLEGE OF TRADITIONAL ORIENTAL MEDICINE
1807-B Wilshire Blvd., Santa Monica 90403 *Type:* Private professional *Calendar:* Qtr. plan *Degrees:* M *Prof. Accred.:* Acupuncture *CEO:* Pres. Bong Dal Kim
FTE Enroll: 182   (310) 453-8800

BRANCH CAMPUS
3625 W. 6th St., Ste. 220, Los Angeles 90020 *CEO:* Pres. Bong Dal Kim
(213) 738-8833

EMPIRE COLLEGE
Ste. 102, 3033 Cleveland Ave., Santa Rosa 95403 *Type:* Private business *Accred.:* 1969/ 1987 (ACISC) *Calendar:* Sem. plan *Degrees:* A, certificates, diplomas *CEO:* Pres. Roy O. Hurd
(707) 546-4000

EVERGREEN VALLEY COLLEGE
3095 Yerba Buena Rd., San Jose 95135 *Type:* Public (district) junior *System:* San Jose-Evergreen Community College District *Accred.:* 1977/1992 (WASC-Jr.) *Calendar:* Sem. plan *Degrees:* A *Prof. Accred.:* Nursing (A) *CEO:* Pres. Noelia Vela
Enroll: 11,255   (408) 274-7900

THE FASHION INSTITUTE OF DESIGN AND MERCHANDISING
919 S. Grand Ave., Los Angeles 90015 *Type:* Private 2-year *Accred.:* 1978/1993 (WASC-Jr.) *Calendar:* Qtr. plan *Degrees:* A *Prof. Accred.:* Interior Design *CEO:* Pres. Tonian Hohberg
Enroll: 2,484   (213) 624-1200

BRANCH CAMPUS
3420 S. Bristol St., Costa Mesa 92626 *CEO:* Dir. Dorothy Metcalfe
(714) 546-0930

BRANCH CAMPUS
1010 Second Ave., Ste. 200, San Diego 92101 *CEO:* Dir. Ann Poloko
(619) 235-4515

BRANCH CAMPUS
55 Stockton St., San Francisco 94108 *CEO:* Dir. Kathryn Caulfield
(415) 433-6691

FEATHER RIVER COLLEGE
P.O. Box 11110, Quincy 95971 *Type:* Public (district) junior *System:* Feather River Community College District *Accred.:* 1973/1988 (WASC-Jr.) *Calendar:* Sem. plan *Degrees:* A *CEO:* Pres. Donald J. Donato
Enroll: 1,435   (916) 283-0202

FIELDING INSTITUTE
2112 Santa Barbara St., Santa Barbara 93105 *Type:* Independent professional *Accred.:* 1982 (WASC-Sr.) *Calendar:* Tri. plan *Degrees:* M, D *CEO:* Pres. Donald J. MacIntyre
FTE Enroll: 792   (805) 687-1099

FOOTHILL COLLEGE
12345 El Monte Rd., Los Altos Hills 94022 *Type:* Public (district) junior *System:* Foothill-DeAnza Community College District *Accred.:* 1959/1988 (WASC-Jr.) *Calendar:* Qtr. plan *Degrees:* A *Prof. Accred.:* Dental Assisting, Dental Hygiene, Radiation Therapy Technology, Radiography, Respiratory Therapy, Veterinary Technology *CEO:* Pres. Thomas H. Clements
Enroll: 16,681   (415) 949-7200

FRANCISCAN SCHOOL OF THEOLOGY
1712 Euclid Ave., Berkeley 94709 *Type:* Independent (Roman Catholic) graduate only *Accred.:* 1975/1988 (ATS); 1975/1988 (WASC-Sr.) *Calendar:* Qtr. plan *Degrees:* M *CEO:* Pres. William M. Cieslak, O.F.M.
FTE Enroll: 63   (510) 848-5232

FRESNO CITY COLLEGE
1101 E. University Ave., Fresno 93741 *Type:* Public (district) junior *System:* State Center Community College District *Accred.:* 1952/1988 (WASC-Jr.) *Calendar:* Sem. plan *Degrees:* A *Prof. Accred.:* Dental Hygiene (conditional), Radiography, Respiratory Therapy *CEO:* Pres. Brice W. Harris
Enroll: 19,180   (209) 442-4600

FRESNO PACIFIC COLLEGE
1717 S. Chestnut Ave., Fresno 93702 *Type:* Independent (Mennonite Brethren) liberal arts *Accred.:* 1961/1986 (WASC-Sr.) *Calendar:* Sem. plan *Degrees:* A, B, M *CEO:* Pres. Richard Kriegbaum
FTE Enroll: 1,068   (209) 453-2000

FULLER THEOLOGICAL SEMINARY
135 N. Oakland Ave., Pasadena 91182 *Type:* Independent (interdenominational) professional; graduate only *Accred.:* 1957/1990 (ATS); 1969/1990 (WASC-Sr.) *Calendar:* Qtr. plan *Degrees:* P, M, D *Prof. Accred.:* Clinical Psychology, Marriage and Family

Therapy (M), Psychology Internship (provisional) *CEO:* Pres. Richard J. Mouw
FTE Enroll: 1,272   (818) 584-5200

FULLERTON COLLEGE
321 E. Chapman Ave., Fullerton 92634
Type: Public (district) junior *System:* North
Orange County Community College District
Accred.: 1952/1993 (WASC-Jr.) *Calendar:*
Sem. plan *Degrees:* A *CEO:* Pres. Philip W.
Borst
Enroll: 19,236   (714) 992-7000

GAVILAN COLLEGE
5055 Santa Teresa Blvd., Gilroy 95020
Type: Public (district) junior *System:* Gavilan Joint Community College District *Accred.:* 1952/1989 (WASC-Jr.) *Calendar:*
Sem. plan *Degrees:* A *CEO:* Pres. Glenn E.
Mayle
Enroll: 4,244   (408) 848-4712

GLENDALE COMMUNITY COLLEGE
1500 N. Verdugo Rd., Glendale 91208 *Type:*
Public (district) junior *System:* Glendale
Community College District *Accred.:* 1952/
1992 (WASC-Jr.) *Calendar:* Sem. plan *Degrees:* A *CEO:* Pres. John A. Davitt
Enroll: 14,516   (818) 240-1000

GOLDEN GATE BAPTIST THEOLOGICAL
SEMINARY
Strawberry Pt., Mill Valley 94941-3197
Type: Independent (Southern Baptist) professional; graduate only *Accred.:* 1962/1990
(ATS); 1971/1990 (WASC-Sr.) *Calendar:*
Sem. plan *Degrees:* P, M, D *Prof. Accred.:*
Music *CEO:* Pres. William O. Crews, Jr.
FTE Enroll: 545   (415) 388-8080

GOLDEN GATE UNIVERSITY
536 Mission St., San Francisco 94105-2968
Type: Independent business *Accred.:* 1959/
1986 (WASC-Sr.) *Calendar:* Tri. plan *Degrees:* A, B, P, M, D *Prof. Accred.:* Law
CEO: Pres. Thomas M. Stauffer
FTE Enroll: 4,413   (415) 442-7000

GOLDEN WEST COLLEGE
15744 Golden West St., Huntington Beach
92647 *Type:* Public (district) junior *System:*
Coast Community College District *Accred.:*
1969/1992 (WASC-Jr.) *Calendar:* Sem. plan

Degrees: A *Prof. Accred.:* Nursing (A)
CEO: Pres. Philip Westin
Enroll: 15,295   (714) 892-7711

GRADUATE THEOLOGICAL UNION
2400 Ridge Rd., Berkeley 94709 *Type:* Independent (interdenominational) graduate only
Accred.: 1969/1988 (ATS); 1966/1988
(WASC-Sr.) *Calendar:* Sem. plan *Degrees:*
M, D *CEO:* Pres. Glenn R. Bucher
FTE Enroll: 426   (510) 649-2400

GROSSMONT COLLEGE
8800 Grossmont College Dr., El Cajon
92020 *Type:* Public (district) junior *System:*
Grossmont-Cuyamaca Community College
District *Accred.:* 1963/1990 (WASC-Jr.)
Calendar: Sem. plan *Degrees:* A *Prof. Accred.:* Cardiovascular Technology, Nursing
(A), Perfusion, Respiratory Therapy *CEO:*
Pres. Richard Sanchez
Enroll: 17,441   (619) 465-1700

HARTNELL COLLEGE
156 Homestead Ave., Salinas 93901 *Type:*
Public (district) junior *System:* Hartnell
Community College District *Accred.:* 1952/
1989 (WASC-Jr.) *Calendar:* Sem. plan *Degrees:* A *Prof. Accred.:* Veterinary Technology *CEO:* Pres. James R. Hardt
Enroll: 7,554   (408) 755-6700

HARVEY MUDD COLLEGE
301 E. 12th St., Claremont 91711 *Type:* Independent professional *Accred.:* 1959/1987
(WASC-Sr.) *Calendar:* Sem. plan *Degrees:*
B, M *Prof. Accred.:* Engineering (general)
CEO: Pres. Henry E. Riggs
FTE Enroll: 667   (909) 621-8122

HEALD BUSINESS COLLEGE—CONCORD
2150 John Glenn Dr., Concord 94520 *Type:*
Private business *Accred.:* 1983/1989
(WASC-Jr.)* *Calendar:* Qtr. plan *Degrees:*
A *CEO:* Dir. Steven M. Kinzer
          (510) 827-1300

HEALD BUSINESS COLLEGE—FRESNO
255 W. Bullard Ave., Fresno 93704 *Type:*
Private business *Accred.:* 1983/1989
(WASC-Jr.)* *Calendar:* Qtr. plan *Degrees:*
A *CEO:* Dir. John Swiger
          (209) 438-4222

* Indirect accreditation through Heald Colleges.

HEALD BUSINESS COLLEGE—HAYWARD
777 Southland Dr., Hayward 94545 *Type:*
Private business *Accred.:* 1983/1989
(WASC-Jr.)* *Calendar:* Qtr. plan *Degrees:*
A *CEO:* Dir. Barbara Gordon
(510) 784-7000

HEALD BUSINESS COLLEGE—OAKLAND
1000 Broadway, Oakland 94607 *Type:* Private business *Accred.:* 1983/1989 (WASC-
Jr.)* *Calendar:* Qtr. plan *Degrees:* A *CEO:*
Dir. Jim Hermann
(510) 444-0201

HEALD BUSINESS COLLEGE—SACRAMENTO
2910 Prospect Park Dr., Rancho Cordova
95670 *Type:* Private business *Accred.:* 1983/
1989 (WASC-Jr.)* *Calendar:* Qtr. plan *Degrees:* A *CEO:* Dir. Phyllis Smith
(916) 638-1616

HEALD BUSINESS COLLEGE—SALINAS
1333 Schilling Pl., P.O. Box 3167, Salinas
93901 *Type:* Private business *Accred.:* 1983/
1989 (WASC-Jr.)* *Calendar:* Qtr. plan *Degrees:* A *CEO:* Dir. Chris Tilley
(408) 757-1700

HEALD BUSINESS COLLEGE—SAN FRANCISCO
1453 Mission St., San Francisco 94103
Type: Private business *Accred.:* 1983/1989
(WASC-Jr.)* *Calendar:* Qtr. plan *Degrees:*
A *CEO:* Dir. Linda Sempliner
(415) 673-5500

HEALD BUSINESS COLLEGE—SAN JOSE
2665 N. First St., Ste. 110, San Jose 95134
Type: Private business *Accred.:* 1983/1989
(WASC-Jr.)* *Calendar:* Qtr. plan *Degrees:*
A *CEO:* Dir. Peter Lee
(408) 955-9555

HEALD BUSINESS COLLEGE—SANTA ROSA
2425 Mendocino Ave., Santa Rosa 95403
Type: Private business *Accred.:* 1983/1989
(WASC-Jr.)* *Calendar:* Qtr. plan *Degrees:*
A *CEO:* Dir. Janet A. Engelbert
(707) 525-1300

HEALD BUSINESS COLLEGE—STOCKTON
1776 W. March La., 3rd Fl., Stockton 95207
Type: Private business *Accred.:* 1983/1989
(WASC-Jr.)* *Calendar:* Qtr. plan *Degrees:*
A *CEO:* Dir. Peter R. Tenney
(209) 477-1114

HEALD INSTITUTE OF TECHNOLOGY—HAYWARD
24301 Southland Dr., Ste. 500, Hayward
94545 *Type:* Private technical *Accred.:*
1983/1989 (WASC-Jr.)* *Calendar:* Qtr. plan
Degrees: A *CEO:* Dir. Dennis J. Morris
(510) 783-2100

HEALD INSTITUTE OF TECHNOLOGY—MARTINEZ
2860 Howe Rd., Martinez 94553 *Type:* Private technical *Accred.:* 1983/1989 (WASC-
Jr.)* *Calendar:* Qtr. plan *Degrees:* A *CEO:*
Dir. Douglas Cole
(510) 228-9000

HEALD INSTITUTE OF TECHNOLOGY—
SACRAMENTO
2920 Prospect Park Dr., Rancho Cordova
95670 *Type:* Private technical *Accred.:*
1983/1989 (WASC-Jr.)* *Calendar:* Qtr. plan
Degrees: A *CEO:* Dir. Bill Johnson
(916) 638-0999

HEALD INSTITUTE OF TECHNOLOGY—SAN
FRANCISCO
250 Executive Park Blvd., Ste. 1000, San
Francisco 94134 *Type:* Private technical *Ac-
cred.:* 1983/1989 (WASC-Jr.)* *Calendar:*
Qtr. plan *Degrees:* A *CEO:* Dir. James
Magri
(415) 822-2900

HEALD INSTITUTE OF TECHNOLOGY—SAN JOSE
684 El Paseo de Saratoga, Ste. A, San Jose
95130 *Type:* Private technical *Accred.:*
1983/1989 (WASC-Jr.)* *Calendar:* Qtr. plan
Degrees: A *CEO:* Dir. Kenneth Heinemann
(408) 295-8000

* Indirect accreditation through Heald Colleges.

HEBREW UNION COLLEGE—JEWISH INSTITUTE
OF RELIGION
3077 University Ave., Los Angeles 90007
Type: Independent (Reform Judaism) *Ac-
cred.:* 1960/1985 (WASC-Sr.) *Calendar:*
Sem. plan *Degrees:* B, M, D *CEO:* Exec.
Vice Pres. Uri D. Herscher
FTE Enroll: 76   (213) 749-3424

HOLY NAMES COLLEGE
3500 Mountain Blvd., Oakland 94619-9989
Type: Independent (Roman Catholic) liberal

arts *Accred.:* 1949/1986 (WASC-Sr.) *Calendar:* Sem., Tri., and weekend plans *Degrees:* B, M *Prof. Accred.:* Music, Nursing (B) *CEO:* Pres. Mary Alice Muellerleile
FTE Enroll: 825   (510) 436-1000

HUMBOLDT STATE UNIVERSITY
Arcata 95521 *Type:* Public (state) *System:* California State University System *Accred.:* 1949/1990 (WASC-Sr.) *Calendar:* Sem. plan *Degrees:* B, M *Prof. Accred.:* Art, Engineering (environmental/sanitary), Forestry, Journalism (B), Music, Nursing (B), Social Work (B-candidate), Theatre *CEO:* Pres. Alistair W. McCrone
FTE Enroll: 6,605   (707) 826-3011

HUMPHREYS COLLEGE
6650 Inglewood St., Stockton 95207 *Type:* Independent *Accred.:* 1992 (WASC-Sr.) *Calendar:* Qtr. plan *Degrees:* A, B, P, certificates *CEO:* Pres. Robert G. Humphreys
FTE Enroll: 666   (209) 478-0800

IMPERIAL VALLEY COLLEGE
P.O. Box 158, Imperial 92251 *Type:* Public (district) junior *System:* Imperial Community College District *Accred.:* 1952/1989 (WASC-Jr.) *Calendar:* Sem. plan *Degrees:* A *CEO:* Pres. John A. DePaoli, Jr.
Enroll: 5,151   (619) 352-8320

INTERIOR DESIGNERS INSTITUTE
1061 Camelback Rd., Newport Beach 92660 *Type:* Private *Accred.:* 1987 (ACCSCT) *Calendar:* Courses of varying lengths *Degrees:* A, B, certificates *Prof. Accred.:* Interior Design *CEO:* Exec. Dir. Judy Deaton
Enroll: 248   (714) 675-4451

IRVINE VALLEY COLLEGE
5500 Irvine Center Dr., Irvine 92720 *Type:* Public (district) junior *System:* Saddleback Community College District *Accred.:* 1988/1993 (WASC-Jr.) *Calendar:* Sem. plan *Degrees:* A *CEO:* Pres. Anna L. McFarlin
Enroll: 10,007   (714) 559-9300

ITT TECHNICAL INSTITUTE
7100 Knott Ave. Plaza, Buena Park 90620-1374 *Type:* Private *Accred.:* 1983/1988 (ACCSCT) *Calendar:* Courses of varying lengths *Degrees:* A, B *CEO:* Dir. Sanjay Advani
(714) 523-9080

ITT TECHNICAL INSTITUTE
2035 E. 223rd St., Carson 90810-1698 *Type:* Private *Accred.:* 1992 (ACCSCT) *Calendar:* Courses of varying lengths *Degrees:* A *CEO:* Dir. David Scarbro
(213) 835-5595

ITT TECHNICAL INSTITUTE
9700 Goethe Rd., Sacramento 95827-5281 *Type:* Private *Accred.:* 1991 (ACCSCT) *Calendar:* Courses of varying lengths *Degrees:* A *CEO:* Dir. Jeffrey Ortega
(916) 366-3900

ITT TECHNICAL INSTITUTE
630 E. Brier Dr., Ste. 150, San Bernardino 92408-2800 *Type:* Private *Accred.:* 1991 (ACCSCT) *Calendar:* Courses of varying lengths *Degrees:* A *CEO:* Dir. Michael C. Ackerman
(714) 889-3800

ITT TECHNICAL INSTITUTE
9680 Granite Ridge Dr., San Diego 92123-2662 *Type:* Private *Accred.:* 1983/1988 (ACCSCT) *Calendar:* Courses of varying lengths *Degrees:* A, B *CEO:* Dir. Robert Hammond
(619) 571-8500

ITT TECHNICAL INSTITUTE
6723 Van Nuys Blvd., Van Nuys 91405-4620 *Type:* Private *Accred.:* 1984/1989 (ACCSCT) *Calendar:* Courses of varying lengths *Degrees:* A *CEO:* Dir. Nader Mojtabai
(818) 989-1177

ITT TECHNICAL INSTITUTE
1530 W. Cameron Ave., West Covina 91790-2767 *Type:* Private *Accred.:* 1983/1989 (ACCSCT) *Calendar:* Courses of varying lengths *Degrees:* A, B *CEO:* Dir. Michele Huggard
(213) 960-8681

JESUIT SCHOOL OF THEOLOGY AT BERKELEY
1735 LeRoy Ave., Berkeley 94709-1193 *Type:* Independent (Roman Catholic) professional; graduate only *Accred.:* 1971/1989 (ATS); 1971/1989 (WASC-Sr.) *Calendar:* Sem. plan *Degrees:* P, M *CEO:* Pres. Thomas F. Gleeson, S.J.
FTE Enroll: 209   (510) 841-8804

JOHN F. KENNEDY UNIVERSITY
12 Altarinda Rd., Orinda 94563 *Type:* Independent liberal arts and professional *Accred.:* 1977/1985 (WASC-Sr.) *Calendar:* Qtr. plan *Degrees:* B, P, M *CEO:* Pres. Charles E. Glasser
FTE Enroll: 1,300   (510) 254-0200

KELSEY-JENNEY COLLEGE
7084 Miramar Rd., San Diego 92121 *Type:* Private *Accred.:* 1983/1989 (WASC-Jr.) *Calendar:* Qtr. plan *Degrees:* A *CEO:* Pres. J. Robert Evans
Enroll: 950   (619) 233-7418

KINGS RIVER COMMUNITY COLLEGE
995 N. Reed Ave., Reedley 93654 *Type:* Public (district) junior *System:* State Center Community College District *Accred.:* 1952/1988 (WASC-Jr.) *Calendar:* Sem. plan *Degrees:* A *Prof. Accred.:* Dental Assisting *CEO:* Pres. Richard J. Giese
Enroll: 6,189   (209) 638-3641

LA SIERRA UNIVERSITY
4700 Pierce St., Riverside 92515 *Type:* Independent (Seventh-Day Adventist) liberal arts and professional *Accred.:* 1960/1992 (WASC-Sr.) *Calendar:* Qtr. plan *Degrees:* A, B, P, M, D *Prof. Accred.:* Social Work (B) *CEO:* Pres. Lawrence T. Geraty
FTE Enroll: 1,477   (909) 785-2000

LAKE TAHOE COMMUNITY COLLEGE
One College Dr., South Lake Tahoe 96150 *Type:* Public (district) junior *System:* Lake Tahoe Community College District *Accred.:* 1979/1989 (WASC-Jr.) *Calendar:* Qtr. plan *Degrees:* A *CEO:* Pres. Guy F. Lease
Enroll: 3,086   (916) 541-4660

LANEY COLLEGE
900 Fallon St., Oakland 94607 *Type:* Public (district) junior *System:* Peralta Community College District *Accred.:* 1956/1991 (WASC-Jr.) *Calendar:* Sem. plan *Degrees:* A *CEO:* Pres. Odell Johnson
Enroll: 11,553   (510) 834-5740

LAS POSITAS COLLEGE
3033 Collier Canyon Rd., Livermore 94550 *Type:* Public (district) junior *System:* Chabot-Las Positas Community College District *Accred.:* 1991 (WASC-Jr.) *Calendar:*

Qtr. plan *Degrees:* A *CEO:* Pres. Susan A. Cota
Enroll: 5,723   (510) 373-5800

LASSEN COLLEGE
P.O. Box 3000, Susanville 96130 *Type:* Public (district) junior *System:* Lassen Community College District *Accred.:* 1952/1990 (WASC-Jr.) *Calendar:* Sem. plan *Degrees:* A *CEO:* Pres. Larry J. Blake
Enroll: 3,334   (916) 257-6181

L.I.F.E. BIBLE COLLEGE
1100 Covina Blvd., San Dimas 91773 *Type:* Private (International Church of Foursquare Gospel) *Accred.:* 1980/1990 (AABC) *Calendar:* Sem. plan *Degrees:* A, B, diplomas *CEO:* Interim Pres. Ron Mehl
FTE Enroll: 300   (714) 599-5433

LIFE CHIROPRACTIC COLLEGE-WEST
2005 Via Barrett, P.O. Box 367, San Lorenzo 94580 *Type:* Private professional *Calendar:* Sem. plan *Degrees:* P *Prof. Accred.:* Chiropractic Education *CEO:* Pres. Gerard W. Clum, D.C.
         (510) 276-9013

LINCOLN UNIVERSITY
281 Masonic Ave., San Francisco 94118 *Type:* Independent professional *Accred.:* 1990 (ACISC) *Calendar:* Sem. plan *Degrees:* B, M *CEO:* Pres. Luke T. Chang
         (415) 221-1212

LOMA LINDA UNIVERSITY
Loma Linda 92350 *Type:* Independent (Seventh-Day Adventist) liberal arts and professional *Accred.:* 1960/1992 (WASC-Sr.) *Calendar:* Qtr. plan *Degrees:* A, B, P, M, D *Prof. Accred.:* Cytotechnology, Dental Hygiene, Dentistry, Diagnostic Medical Sonography, Dietetics (coordinated), Endodontics, Marriage and Family Therapy (M), Medical Record Administration, Medical Technology, Medicine, Nuclear Medicine Technology, Nursing (B,M), Occupational Therapy, Occupational Therapy Assisting, Oral and Maxillofacial Surgery, Orthodontics, Periodontics, Physical Therapy, Physical Therapy Assisting, Public Health, Radiation Therapy Technology, Radiography, Respiratory

Therapy, Speech-Language Pathology *CEO:* Pres. B. Lyn Behrens, M.B.B.S.
FTE Enroll: 2,671   (909) 824-4300

LONG BEACH CITY COLLEGE
4901 E. Carson St., Long Beach 90808 *Type:* Public (district) junior *System:* Long Beach Community College District *Accred.:* 1952/1990 (WASC-Jr.) *Calendar:* Sem. plan *Degrees:* A *Prof. Accred.:* Nursing (A-warning), Radiography *CEO:* Pres. Barbara A. Adams
Enroll: 24,780   (310) 420-4111

LOS ANGELES CITY COLLEGE
855 N. Vermont Ave., Los Angeles 90029 *Type:* Public (district) junior *System:* Los Angeles Community College District *Accred.:* 1952/1992 (WASC-Jr.) *Calendar:* Sem. plan *Degrees:* A *Prof. Accred.:* Dental Laboratory Technology, Radiography *CEO:* Pres. Jose Robledo
Enroll: 17,087   (213) 953-4000

LOS ANGELES COLLEGE OF CHIROPRACTIC
16200 E. Amber Valley Dr., Whittier 90604 *Type:* Independent professional *Accred.:* 1993 (WASC-Sr.) *Calendar:* Sem. plan *Degrees:* B, P *Prof. Accred.:* Chiropractic Education *CEO:* Pres. Reed B. Phillips, D.C.
FTE Enroll: 781   (310) 947-8755

LOS ANGELES HARBOR COLLEGE
1111 Figueroa Pl., Wilmington 90744 *Type:* Public (district) junior *System:* Los Angeles Community College District *Accred.:* 1952/1990 (WASC-Jr.) *Calendar:* Sem. plan *Degrees:* A *CEO:* Pres. James Heinselman
Enroll: 9,613   (310) 522-8200

LOS ANGELES MISSION COLLEGE
13356 Eldridge Ave., Sylmar 91342-3244 *Type:* Public (district) junior *System:* Los Angeles Community College District *Accred.:* 1978/1991 (WASC-Jr.) *Calendar:* Sem. plan *Degrees:* A *CEO:* Pres. Jack Fujimoto
Enroll: 7,500   (818) 364-7600

LOS ANGELES PIERCE COLLEGE
6201 Winnetka Ave., Woodland Hills 91371 *Type:* Public (district) junior *System:* Los Angeles Community College District *Accred.:* 1952/1989 (WASC-Jr.) *Calendar:* Sem. plan *Degrees:* A *Prof. Accred.:* Nurs-

ing (A), Veterinary Technology (provisional) *CEO:* Pres. Lowell J. Erickson
Enroll: 18,584   (818) 347-0551

LOS ANGELES SOUTHWEST COLLEGE
1600 W. Imperial Hwy., Los Angeles 90047 *Type:* Public (district) junior *System:* Los Angeles Community College District *Accred.:* 1980/1989 (WASC-Jr.) *Calendar:* Sem. plan *Degrees:* A *CEO:* Pres. Carolyn G. Williams
Enroll: 6,935   (213) 241-5273

LOS ANGELES TRADE-TECHNICAL COLLEGE
400 W. Washington Blvd., Los Angeles 90015 *Type:* Public (district) junior *System:* Los Angeles Community College District *Accred.:* 1952/1992 (WASC-Jr.) *Calendar:* Sem. plan *Degrees:* A *Prof. Accred.:* Nursing (A) *CEO:* Pres. Thomas L. Stevens, Jr.
Enroll: 13,925   (213) 744-9500

LOS ANGELES VALLEY COLLEGE
5800 Fulton Ave., Van Nuys 91401 *Type:* Public (district) junior *System:* Los Angeles Community College District *Accred.:* 1952/1989 (WASC-Jr.) *Calendar:* Sem. plan *Degrees:* A *Prof. Accred.:* Nursing (A), Respiratory Therapy *CEO:* Pres. Mary E. Lee
Enroll: 18,803   (818) 781-1200

LOS MEDANOS COLLEGE
2700 E. Leland Rd., Pittsburg 94565 *Type:* Public (district) junior *System:* Contra Costa Community College District *Accred.:* 1977/1987 (WASC-Jr.) *Calendar:* Sem. plan *Degrees:* A *CEO:* Pres. Stanley H. Chin
Enroll: 7,493   (510) 798-3500

LOUISE SALINGER ACADEMY OF FASHION
101 Jessie St., San Francisco 94105-3593 *Type:* Private *Accred.:* 1971/1989 (ACC-SCT) *Calendar:* Qtr. plan *Degrees:* A, B, diplomas *CEO:* Pres. Esther Herschelle
                                       (415) 974-6666

LOYOLA MARYMOUNT UNIVERSITY
Loyola Blvd. at W. 80th St., Los Angeles 90045 *Type:* Independent (Roman Catholic) liberal arts and professional *Accred.:* 1949/1993 (WASC-Sr.) *Calendar:* Sem. plan *Degrees:* B, P, M *Prof. Accred.:* Art, Business (B,M), Dance, Engineering (civil, electrical,

mechanical), Law, Music (associate), Theatre *CEO:* Pres. Thomas P. O'Malley, S.J.
FTE Enroll: 6,178   (310) 338-2700

MARYMOUNT COLLEGE
30800 Palos Verdes Dr. E., Rancho Palos Verdes 90274-6299 *Type:* Private (Roman Catholic) junior *Accred.:* 1971/1989 (WASC-Jr.) *Calendar:* Sem. plan *Degrees:* A *CEO:* Pres. Thomas M. McFadden
Enroll: 1,074   (310) 377-5501

THE MASTER'S COLLEGE
21726 W. Placerita Canyon Rd., P.O. Box 221450, Newhall 91322-1450 *Type:* Independent (Baptist) liberal arts *Accred.:* 1975/ 1985 (WASC-Sr.) *Calendar:* Sem. plan *Degrees:* B *CEO:* Pres. John MacArthur, Jr.
FTE Enroll: 973   (805) 259-3540

MENDOCINO COLLEGE
P.O. Box 3000, Ukiah 95482 *Type:* Public (district) junior *System:* Mendocino-Lake Community College District *Accred.:* 1980/ 1990 (WASC-Jr.) *Calendar:* Sem. plan *Degrees:* A *CEO:* Pres. Carl J. Ehmann
Enroll: 4,000   (707) 468-3100

MENLO COLLEGE
1000 El Camino Real, Atherton 94027-4185 *Type:* Independent *Accred.:* 1952/1987 (WASC-Sr.) *Calendar:* 4-1-4 plan *Degrees:* A, B *CEO:* Pres. John R. Berthold
FTE Enroll: 440   (415) 323-6141

MENNONITE BRETHREN BIBLICAL SEMINARY
4824 E. Butler Ave., Fresno 93727-5097 *Type:* Independent (Mennonite) graduate only *Accred.:* 1977/1981 (ATS); 1972/1992 (WASC-Sr.) *Calendar:* 4-1-4 plan *Degrees:* M *CEO:* Pres. Henry J. Schmidt
FTE Enroll: 91   (209) 251-8628

MERCED COLLEGE
3600 M St., Merced 95340 *Type:* Public (district) junior *System:* Merced Community College District *Accred.:* 1965/1993 (WASC-Jr.) *Calendar:* Sem. plan *Degrees:* A *Prof. Accred.:* Dental Assisting, Dental Laboratory Technology, Radiography *CEO:* Pres. E. Jan Moser
Enroll: 7,803   (209) 384-6000

MERRITT COLLEGE
12500 Campus Dr., Oakland 94619 *Type:* Public (district) junior *System:* Peralta Community College District *Accred.:* 1956/1991 (WASC-Jr.) *Calendar:* Sem. plan *Degrees:* A *Prof. Accred.:* Radiography *CEO:* Pres. Stan R. Arterberry
Enroll: 6,023   (510) 531-4911

MILLS COLLEGE
Oakland 94613 *Type:* Independent liberal arts for women *Accred.:* 1949/1992 (WASC-Sr.) *Calendar:* Sem. plan *Degrees:* B, M *CEO:* Pres. Janet Holmgren McKay
FTE Enroll: 1,095   (510) 430-2255

MIRA COSTA COLLEGE
One Barnard Dr., Oceanside 92056 *Type:* Public (district) junior *System:* MiraCosta Community College District *Accred.:* 1952/ 1992 (WASC-Jr.) *Calendar:* Sem. plan *Degrees:* A *CEO:* Pres. H. Deon Holt
Enroll: 9,400   (619) 757-2121

MISSION COLLEGE
3000 Mission College Blvd., Santa Clara 95054 *Type:* Public (district) junior *System:* West Valley-Mission College District *Accred.:* 1979/1989 (WASC-Jr.) *Calendar:* Sem. plan *Degrees:* A *CEO:* Pres. Floyd M. Hogue
Enroll: 11,576   (408) 988-2200

MODESTO JUNIOR COLLEGE
435 College Ave., Modesto 95350 *Type:* Public (district) junior *System:* Yosemite Community College District *Accred.:* 1952/ 1989 (WASC-Jr.) *Calendar:* Sem. plan *Degrees:* A *Prof. Accred.:* Dental Assisting, Medical Assisting (AMA), Respiratory Therapy, Respiratory Therapy Technology *CEO:* Pres. Stanley L. Hodges
Enroll: 15,817   (209) 575-6067

MONTEREY INSTITUTE OF INTERNATIONAL STUDIES
425 Van Buren, Monterey 93940 *Type:* Independent liberal arts *Accred.:* 1961/1985 (WASC-Sr.) *Calendar:* Sem. plan *Degrees:* B, M *CEO:* Pres. Robert G. Gard, Jr.
FTE Enroll: 725   (408) 647-4100

MONTEREY PENINSULA COLLEGE
980 Fremont St., Monterey 93940 *Type:* Public (district) junior *System:* Monterey

Peninsula Community College District *Accred.:* 1952/1992 (WASC-Jr.) *Calendar:* Sem. plan *Degrees:* A *Prof. Accred.:* Dental Assisting, Nursing (A) *CEO:* Pres. David W. Hopkins, Jr.
Enroll: 10,500   (408) 646-4000

MOORPARK COLLEGE
7075 Campus Rd., Moorpark 93021 *Type:* Public (district) junior *System:* Ventura County Community College District *Accred.:* 1969/1992 (WASC-Jr.) *Calendar:* Sem. plan *Degrees:* A *Prof. Accred.:* Nursing (A), Radiography *CEO:* Pres. James W. Walker
Enroll: 10,562   (805) 378-1400

MOUNT ST. MARY'S COLLEGE
12001 Chalon Rd., Los Angeles 90049 *Type:* Independent (Roman Catholic) liberal arts primarily for women *Accred.:* 1949/1992 (WASC-Sr.) *Calendar:* 4-1-4 plan *Degrees:* A, B, M *Prof. Accred.:* Music, Nursing (B), Occupational Therapy Assisting, Physical Therapy, Physical Therapy Assisting *CEO:* Pres. Karen Kennelly, C.S.J.
FTE Enroll: 1,498   (310) 476-2237

DOHENY CAMPUS
10 Chester Pl., Los Angeles 90007 *CEO:* Dean Kathleen Kelly, C.S.J.
          (310) 746-0450

MOUNT SAN ANTONIO COLLEGE
1100 N. Grand Ave., Walnut 91789 *Type:* Public (district) junior *System:* Mount San Antonio Community College District *Accred.:* 1952/1993 (WASC-Jr.) *Calendar:* Sem. plan *Degrees:* A *Prof. Accred.:* Radiography, Respiratory Therapy, Veterinary Technology *CEO:* Pres. William H. Feddersen
Enroll: 23,615   (909) 594-5611

MOUNT SAN JACINTO COLLEGE
1499 N. State St., San Jacinto 92583 *Type:* Public (district) junior *System:* Mount San Jacinto Community College District *Accred.:* 1965/1988 (WASC-Jr.) *Calendar:* Sem. plan *Degrees:* A *CEO:* Pres. Roy B. Mason, II
Enroll: 7,022   (909) 654-8011

NAPA VALLEY COLLEGE
2277 Napa-Vallejo Hwy., Napa 94558 *Type:* Public (district) junior *System:* Napa Valley Community College District *Accred.:* 1952/

1992 (WASC-Jr.) *Calendar:* Sem. plan *Degrees:* A *Prof. Accred.:* Respiratory Therapy *CEO:* Pres. Diane E. Carey
Enroll: 7,102   (707) 253-3000

NATIONAL EDUCATION CENTER SAWYER CAMPUS
5500 S. Eastern Ave., Commerce 90040 *Type:* Private business *Accred.:* 1972/1990 (ACISC) *Calendar:* Courses of varying lengths *Degrees:* A *CEO:* Dir. Al Nederhood
          (213) 724-1800

NATIONAL EDUCATION CENTER SKADRON CAMPUS
825 E. Hospitality La., San Bernardino 92408 *Type:* Private business *Accred.:* 1962/1992 (ACISC) *Calendar:* Qtr. plan *Degrees:* A, certificates, diplomas *CEO:* Exec. Dir. David Corson
          (714) 885-3896

NATIONAL UNIVERSITY
4025 Camino del Rio S., Ste. 200, San Diego 92108 *Type:* Independent business *Accred.:* 1977/1992 (WASC-Sr.) *Calendar:* 12-term plan *Degrees:* A, B, P, M *CEO:* Pres. Jerry C. Lee
FTE Enroll: 7,653   (619) 563-7100

NAVAL POSTGRADUATE SCHOOL
One University Cir., Rm. 11, Monterey 93943-5000 *Type:* Public (federal) science and technology *Accred.:* 1955/1990 (WASC-Sr.) *Calendar:* Qtr. plan *Degrees:* B, M, D *Prof. Accred.:* Engineering (aerospace, electrical, mechanical), Public Management *CEO:* Supt. Ralph W. West, Jr.
FTE Enroll: 1,815   (408) 646-2411

NEW COLLEGE OF CALIFORNIA
50 Fell St., San Francisco 94102 *Type:* Independent liberal arts *Accred.:* 1976/1985 (WASC-Sr.) *Calendar:* Sem. plan *Degrees:* B, P, M *CEO:* Pres. Peter Gabel
FTE Enroll: 640   (415) 241-1300

OCCIDENTAL COLLEGE
1600 Campus Rd., Los Angeles 90041-3314 *Type:* Independent liberal arts *Accred.:* 1949/1990 (WASC-Sr.) *Calendar:* 3-term plan *Degrees:* B, M *CEO:* Pres. John B. Slaughter
FTE Enroll: 1,657   (213) 259-2500

OHLONE COLLEGE
43600 Mission Blvd., Fremont 94539 *Type:* Public (district) junior *System:* Fremont-Newark Community College District *Accred.:* 1970/1990 (WASC-Jr.) *Calendar:* Sem. plan *Degrees:* A *Prof. Accred.:* Nursing (A), Respiratory Therapy *CEO:* Pres. Peter Blomerley
Enroll: 9,827   (510) 659-6000

ORANGE COAST COLLEGE
2701 Fairview Rd., P.O. Box 5005, Costa Mesa 92628 *Type:* Public (district) junior *System:* Coast Community College District *Accred.:* 1952/1990 (WASC-Jr.) *Calendar:* Sem. plan *Degrees:* A *Prof. Accred.:* Dental Assisting, Diagnostic Medical Sonography, Electroneurodiagnostic Technology, Medical Assisting (AMA), Radiography, Respiratory Therapy *CEO:* Pres. David A. Grant
Enroll: 25,465   (714) 432-0202

OTIS COLLEGE OF ART AND DESIGN
2401 Wilshire Blvd., Los Angeles 90057 *Type:* Independent professional *Accred.:* 1956/1990 (WASC-Sr. probational) *Calendar:* Sem. plan *Degrees:* B, M *Prof. Accred.:* Art *CEO:* Pres. Neil J. Hoffman
FTE Enroll: 684   (213) 251-0500

OXNARD COLLEGE
4000 S. Rose Ave., Oxnard 93033 *Type:* Public (district) junior *System:* Ventura County Community College District *Accred.:* 1978/1993 (WASC-Jr.) *Calendar:* Sem. plan *Degrees:* A *CEO:* Pres. Elise D. Schneider
Enroll: 6,342   (805) 986-5800

PACIFIC CHRISTIAN COLLEGE
2500 E. Nutwood Ave., Fullerton 92631 *Type:* Independent (Christian Churches/Churches of Christ) liberal arts *Accred.:* 1969/1988 (WASC-Sr.) *Calendar:* 4-1-4 plan *Degrees:* A, B, M *CEO:* Pres. E. Leroy Lawson
FTE Enroll: 592   (714) 879-3901

PACIFIC COLLEGE OF ORIENTAL MEDICINE
7445 Mission Valley Rd., Ste. 103-106, San Diego 92108-4408 *Type:* Private professional *Calendar:* Tri. plan *Degrees:* M *Prof. Accred.:* Acupuncture *CEO:* Dean Jack Miller
FTE Enroll: 87   (619) 574-6909

BRANCH CAMPUS
915 Broadway, 3rd Fl., New York, NY 10010 *CEO:* Dean Jack Miller
       (212) 982-3456

PACIFIC GRADUATE SCHOOL OF PSYCHOLOGY
935 E. Meadow Dr., Palo Alto 94306 *Type:* Independent professional *Accred.:* 1986 (WASC-Sr.) *Calendar:* Qtr. plan *Degrees:* D *Prof. Accred.:* Clinical Psychology (provisional) *CEO:* Pres. Allen Calvin
FTE Enroll: 229   (415) 494-7477

PACIFIC LUTHERAN THEOLOGICAL SEMINARY
2770 Marin Ave., Berkeley 94708-5264 *Type:* Private (Evangelical Lutheran Church) graduate only *Accred.:* 1964/1991 (ATS) *Calendar:* Sem. plan *Degrees:* M *CEO:* Pres. Jerry L. Schmalenberger
FTE Enroll: 131   (510) 524-5264

PACIFIC OAKS COLLEGE
5 Westmoreland Pl., Pasadena 91103 *Type:* Independent professional *Accred.:* 1959/1985 (WASC-Sr.) *Calendar:* Sem. plan *Degrees:* B, M *CEO:* Pres. Katherine Gabel
FTE Enroll: 358   (818) 397-1321

PACIFIC SCHOOL OF RELIGION
1798 Scenic Ave., Berkeley 94709 *Type:* Independent (interdenominational) professional; graduate only *Accred.:* 1938/1988 (ATS); 1971/1988 (WASC-Sr.) *Calendar:* Sem. plan *Degrees:* P, M, D *CEO:* Pres. Eleanor Scott Meyers
FTE Enroll: 170   (510) 848-0528

PACIFIC UNION COLLEGE
One Angwin Ave., Angwin 94508-9707 *Type:* Independent (Seventh-Day Adventist) liberal arts *Accred.:* 1951/1991 (WASC-Sr.) *Calendar:* Qtr. plan *Degrees:* A, B, M *Prof. Accred.:* Music, Nursing (A,B), Social Work (B) *CEO:* Pres. D. Malcolm Maxwell
FTE Enroll: 1,406   (707) 965-6243

PALMER COLLEGE OF CHIROPRACTIC-WEST
90 E. Tasman Dr., San Jose 95134 *Type:* Private professional *Calendar:* Qtr. plan *Degrees:* P *Prof. Accred.:* Chiropractic Education *CEO:* Pres. Peter A. Martin, D.C.
Enroll: 591   (408) 944-6000

PALO VERDE COLLEGE
811 W. Chanslorway, Blythe 92225 *Type:* Public (district) junior *System:* Palo Verde Community College District *Accred.:* 1951/ 1990 (WASC-Jr.) *Calendar:* Sem. plan *Degrees:* A *CEO:* Pres. Wilford J. Beumel
Enroll: 1,386   (619) 922-6168

PALOMAR COLLEGE
1140 W. Mission Rd., San Marcos 92069 *Type:* Public (district) junior *System:* Palomar Community College District *Accred.:* 1951/1991 (WASC-Jr.) *Calendar:* Sem. plan *Degrees:* A *Prof. Accred.:* Dental Assisting, Nursing (A) *CEO:* Pres. George R. Boggs
Enroll: 21,264   (619) 744-1150

PASADENA CITY COLLEGE
1570 E. Colorado Blvd., Pasadena 91106 *Type:* Public (district) junior *System:* Pasadena Area Community College District *Accred.:* 1952/1991 (WASC-Jr.) *Calendar:* Sem. plan *Degrees:* A *Prof. Accred.:* Dental Assisting, Dental Hygiene, Dental Laboratory Technology, Medical Assisting (AMA), Nursing (A), Radiography *CEO:* Pres. Jack A. Scott
Enroll: 28,000   (818) 585-7123

PATTEN COLLEGE
2433 Coolidge Ave., Oakland 94601 *Type:* Independent (Christian Evangelical Church) liberal arts *Accred.:* 1980/1993 (WASC-Sr.) *Calendar:* Sem. plan *Degrees:* A, B *CEO:* Pres. Priscilla C. Benham
FTE Enroll: 695   (510) 533-8306

PEPPERDINE UNIVERSITY
24255 Pacific Coast Hwy., Malibu 90263 *Type:* Independent (Churches of Christ) liberal arts and professional *Accred.:* 1949/ 1993 (WASC-Sr.) *Calendar:* Tri. plan *Degrees:* B, P, M, D *Prof. Accred.:* Clinical Psychology, Law, Music *CEO:* Pres. David Davenport
FTE Enroll: 6,206   (310) 456-4000

PHILLIPS COLLEGE INLAND EMPIRE CAMPUS
4300 Central Ave., Riverside 92506 *Type:* Private business *Accred.:* 1982/1988 (ACISC) *Calendar:* Courses of varying lengths *Degrees:* A, certificates, diplomas *CEO:* Dir. Beverly Yourstone
            (714) 787-9300

PHILLIPS JUNIOR COLLEGE
8520 Balboa Blvd., Northridge 91325-3561 *Type:* Private *Accred.:* 1991 (ACCSCT) *Calendar:* Courses of varying lengths *Degrees:* A, diplomas *CEO:* Dir. Tom Azim-Zadeh
            (818) 895-2220

BRANCH CAMPUS
One Civic Plaza, Ste. 110, Carson 90745-2264 *Accred.:* 1991 (ACCSCT) *CEO:* Dir. Barbara Nyegaard
            (310) 518-2600

PHILLIPS JUNIOR COLLEGE CONDIE CAMPUS
One W. Campbell Ave., Campbell 95008 *Type:* Private junior *Accred.:* 1974/1990 (ACISC); 1991 (WASC-Jr.) *Calendar:* Qtr. plan *Degrees:* A *CEO:* Dir. Sylvia Karp
Enroll: 950   (408) 866-6666

PHILLIPS JUNIOR COLLEGE FRESNO CAMPUS
2048 N. Fine Ave., Fresno 93727 *Accred.:* 1989/1991 (ACISC) *CEO:* Dir. Diane Donally
            (209) 453-1000

PITZER COLLEGE
1050 N. Mills Ave., Claremont 91711-6110 *Type:* Independent liberal arts *Accred.:* 1965/1990 (WASC-Sr.) *Calendar:* Sem. plan *Degrees:* B *CEO:* Pres. Marilyn Chapin Massey
FTE Enroll: 844   (909) 621-8000

POINT LOMA NAZARENE COLLEGE
3900 Lomaland Dr., San Diego 92106 *Type:* Independent (Nazarene) liberal arts *Accred.:* 1949/1990 (WASC-Sr.) *Calendar:* Qtr. plan *Degrees:* A, B, M *Prof. Accred.:* Nursing (B) *CEO:* Pres. Jim L. Bond
FTE Enroll: 1,945   (619) 221-2200

POMONA COLLEGE
550 N. College Ave., Claremont 91711 *Type:* Independent liberal arts *Accred.:* 1949/1992 (WASC-Sr.) *Calendar:* Early sem. plan *Degrees:* B *CEO:* Pres. Peter W. Stanley
FTE Enroll: 1,499   (909) 621-8131

PORTERVILLE COLLEGE
100 E. College Ave., Porterville 93257 *Type:* Public (district) junior *System:* Kern Community College District *Accred.:* 1952/1989

(WASC-Jr.) *Calendar:* Sem. plan *Degrees:* A *CEO:* Interim Pres. John T. McCuen
Enroll: 2,780   (209) 781-3130

QUEEN OF THE HOLY ROSARY COLLEGE
43326 Mission Blvd., Mission San Jose 94539 *Type:* Private (Roman Catholic) junior *Accred.:* 1979/1989 (WASC-Jr.) *Calendar:* Sem. plan *Degrees:* A *CEO:* Pres. Renilde Cade, O.P.
Enroll: 280   (510) 657-2468

RANCHO SANTIAGO COMMUNITY COLLEGE
17th and Bristol Sts., Santa Ana 92706 *Type:* Public (district) junior *System:* Rancho Santiago Community College District *Accred.:* 1952/1990 (WASC-Jr.) *Calendar:* Sem. plan *Degrees:* A *CEO:* Pres. Vivian B. Blevins
Enroll: 26,379   (714) 564-6053

RAND GRADUATE SCHOOL OF POLICY STUDIES
1700 Main St., P.O. Box 2138, Santa Monica 90407-2138 *Type:* Independent graduate only *Accred.:* 1975/1990 (WASC-Sr.) *Calendar:* Qtr. plan *Degrees:* D *CEO:* Dean Charles Wolf, Jr.
FTE Enroll: 61   (310) 393-0411

RIO HONDO COLLEGE
3600 Workman Mill Rd., Whittier 90608 *Type:* Public (district) junior *System:* Rio Hondo Community College District *Accred.:* 1967/1990 (WASC-Jr.) *Calendar:* Sem. plan *Degrees:* A *Prof. Accred.:* Respiratory Therapy *CEO:* Pres. Alex A. Sanchez
Enroll: 18,400   (310) 692-0921

RIVERSIDE COMMUNITY COLLEGE
4800 Magnolia Ave., Riverside 92506-1299 *Type:* Public (district) junior *System:* Riverside Community College District *Accred.:* 1952/1989 (WASC-Jr.) *Calendar:* Sem. plan *Degrees:* A *Prof. Accred.:* Nursing (A) *CEO:* Pres. Salvatore G. Rotella
Enroll: 21,684   (909) 684-3240

SACRAMENTO CITY COLLEGE
3835 Freeport Blvd., Sacramento 95822 *Type:* Public (district) junior *System:* Los Rios Community College District *Accred.:* 1952/1992 (WASC-Jr.) *Calendar:* Sem. plan *Degrees:* A *Prof. Accred.:* Dental Assisting, Dental Hygiene *CEO:* Pres. Robert M. Harris
Enroll: 17,737   (916) 558-2100

SADDLEBACK COLLEGE
28000 Marguerite Pkwy., Mission Viejo 92692 *Type:* Public (district) junior *System:* Saddleback Community College District *Accred.:* 1971/1993 (WASC-Jr.) *Calendar:* Sem. plan *Degrees:* A *Prof. Accred.:* Nursing (A) *CEO:* Pres. Ned Doffoney
Enroll: 23,316   (714) 582-4500

ST. JOHN'S SEMINARY
5012 Seminary Rd., Camarillo 93012-2598 *Type:* Independent (Roman Catholic) professional; graduate only *Accred.:* 1976/1991 (ATS); 1951/1992 (WASC-Sr.) *Calendar:* Sem. plan *Degrees:* P, M *CEO:* Dean Jeremiah J. McCarthy
FTE Enroll: 131   (805) 482-2755

ST. JOHN'S SEMINARY COLLEGE
5118 E. Seminary Rd., Camarillo 93012-2599 *Type:* Independent (Roman Catholic) liberal arts *Accred.:* 1951/1981 (WASC-Sr.) *Calendar:* Sem. plan *Degrees:* B *CEO:* Pres./Rector Rafael Luevano
FTE Enroll: 100   (805) 482-2755

ST. MARY'S COLLEGE OF CALIFORNIA
1928 St. Marys Rd., Moraga 94575 *Type:* Independent (Roman Catholic) liberal arts *Accred.:* 1949/1993 (WASC-Sr.) *Calendar:* 4-1-4 plan *Degrees:* A, B, M *Prof. Accred.:* Nursing (B) *CEO:* Pres. Mel Anderson, F.S.C.
FTE Enroll: 3,682   (510) 631-4000

ST. PATRICK'S SEMINARY
320 Middlefield Rd., Menlo Park 94025 *Type:* Independent (Roman Catholic) professional; graduate only *Accred.:* 1971/1984 (ATS); 1971/1989 (WASC-Sr.) *Calendar:* Sem. plan *Degrees:* P, M *CEO:* Pres./Rector Gerald D. Coleman, S.S.
FTE Enroll: 63   (415) 325-5621

SALVATION ARMY SCHOOL FOR OFFICERS' TRAINING
30840 Hawthorne Blvd., Rancho Palos Verdes 90274 *Type:* Private *Accred.:* 1990 (WASC-Jr.) *Calendar:* Qtr. plan *Degrees:* A *CEO:* Training Principal Bill Luttrell
Enroll: 91   (310) 377-0481

SAMRA UNIVERSITY OF ORIENTAL MEDICINE
600 St. Paul Ave., Los Angeles 90017 *Type:* Private professional *Calendar:* Qtr. plan *De-*

grees: M *Prof. Accred.:* Acupuncture *CEO:* Pres. Norman Bleicher
FTE Enroll: 165   (213) 482-8448

SAMUEL MERRITT COLLEGE
370 Hawthorne Ave., Oakland 94609 *Type:* Private professional *Accred.:* 1984/1990 (WASC-Sr.) *Calendar:* 4-1-4 plan *Degrees:* A, B, M *Prof. Accred.:* Nursing (B), Physical Therapy *CEO:* Pres. Sharon L. Diaz
FTE Enroll: 433   (510) 420-6011

SAN BERNARDINO VALLEY COLLEGE
701 S. Mt. Vernon Ave., San Bernardino 92410 *Type:* Public (district) junior *System:* San Bernardino Community College District *Accred.:* 1952/1991 (WASC-Jr.) *Calendar:* Sem. plan *Degrees:* A *Prof. Accred.:* Nursing (A) *CEO:* Pres. Donald L. Singer
Enroll: 12,651   (714) 888-6511

SAN DIEGO CITY COLLEGE
1313 Twelfth Ave., San Diego 92101 *Type:* Public (district) junior *System:* San Diego Community College District *Accred.:* 1952/1992 (WASC-Jr.) *Calendar:* Sem. plan *Degrees:* A *CEO:* Pres. Jerome Hunter
Enroll: 13,000   (619) 230-2400

SAN DIEGO MESA COLLEGE
7250 Mesa College Dr., San Diego 92111 *Type:* Public (district) junior *System:* San Diego Community College District *Accred.:* 1966/1992 (WASC-Jr.) *Calendar:* Sem. plan *Degrees:* A *Prof. Accred.:* Medical Assisting (AMA), Medical Record Technology, Physical Therapy Assisting, Radiography, Veterinary Technology *CEO:* Pres. Constance M. Carroll
Enroll: 24,401   (619) 627-2600

SAN DIEGO MIRAMAR COLLEGE
10440 Black Mountain Rd., San Diego 92126 *Type:* Public (district) junior *System:* San Diego Community College District *Accred.:* 1982/1992 (WASC-Jr.) *Calendar:* Sem. plan *Degrees:* A *CEO:* Pres. Louis C. Murillo
Enroll: 7,342   (619) 536-7800

SAN DIEGO STATE UNIVERSITY
5300 Campanile Dr., San Diego 92182-0763 *Type:* Public (state) *System:* California State University System *Accred.:* 1949/1989 (WASC-Sr.) *Calendar:* Sem. plan *Degrees:* B, M *Prof. Accred.:* Accounting (Type A,B,C), Art, Audiology, Business (B,M), Clinical Psychology, Engineering (aerospace, civil, electrical, mechanical), Health Services Administration, Interior Design, Journalism (B,M), Music, Nursing (B,M), Public Administration, Public Health, Recreation and Leisure Services, Rehabilitation Counseling, Social Work (B,M), Speech-Language Pathology, Teacher Education (e,s,p), Theatre *CEO:* Pres. Thomas B. Day
FTE Enroll: 21,409   (619) 594-5200

SAN FRANCISCO ART INSTITUTE
800 Chestnut St., San Francisco 94133 *Type:* Public professional *System:* University of California Office of the President (Affiliate) *Accred.:* 1954/1984 (WASC-Sr.) *Calendar:* Sem. plan *Degrees:* B, M *Prof. Accred.:* Art *CEO:* Pres. William O. Barrett
FTE Enroll: 608   (415) 771-7020

SAN FRANCISCO COLLEGE OF MORTUARY SCIENCE
1598 Dolores St., San Francisco 94110 *Type:* Private professional *Accred.:* 1962/1992 (WASC-Jr. probational) *Calendar:* Sem. plan *Degrees:* A *Prof. Accred.:* Mortuary Science *CEO:* Pres. Jacquelyn S. Taylor
Enroll: 65   (415) 567-0674

SAN FRANCISCO CONSERVATORY OF MUSIC
1201 Ortega St., San Francisco 94122 *Type:* Independent professional *Accred.:* 1960/1988 (WASC-Sr.) *Calendar:* Sem. plan *Degrees:* B, M *Prof. Accred.:* Music *CEO:* Pres. Colin Murdoch
FTE Enroll: 250   (415) 564-8086

SAN FRANCISCO STATE UNIVERSITY
1600 Holloway Ave., San Francisco 94132 *Type:* Public (state) *System:* California State University System *Accred.:* 1949/1992 (WASC-Sr.) *Calendar:* Sem. plan *Degrees:* B, M *Prof. Accred.:* Art, Audiology, Business (B,M), Computer Science, Counseling, Engineering (civil, electrical, mechanical), Home Economics (provisional), Journalism (B,M), Medical Technology, Music, Nursing (B,M), Physical Therapy, Recreation and Leisure Services, Rehabilitation Counseling, Social Work (B,M), Speech-Language

Pathology, Teacher Education (e,s,p), Theatre *CEO:* Pres. Robert A. Corrigan
FTE Enroll: 18,544   (415) 338-1111

SAN FRANCISCO THEOLOGICAL SEMINARY
2 Kensington Rd., San Anselmo 94960
Type: Independent (Presbyterian) professional; graduate only *Accred.:* 1938/1988 (ATS); 1973/1988 (WASC-Sr.) *Calendar:* Sem. plan
Degrees: P, M, D *CEO:* Pres. J. Randolph Taylor
FTE Enroll: 388   (415) 258-6500

SAN JOAQUIN COLLEGE OF LAW
3385 E. Shields Ave., Fresno 93726 *Type:* Independent professional *Accred.:* 1993 (WASC-Sr.) *Calendar:* Sem. plan *Degrees:* P, M, certificates *CEO:* Dean Janice Pearson
FTE Enroll: 253   (209) 225-4953

SAN JOAQUIN DELTA COLLEGE
5151 Pacific Ave., Stockton 95207 *Type:* Public (district) junior *System:* San Joaquin Delta Community College District *Accred.:* 1952/1990 (WASC-Jr.) *Calendar:* Sem. plan *Degrees:* A *Prof. Accred.:* Nursing (A) *CEO:* Pres. L.H. Horton, Jr.
Enroll: 16,425   (209) 474-5051

SAN JOSE CHRISTIAN COLLEGE
P.O. Box 1090, 790 S. 12th St., San Jose 95112 *Type:* Independent (nondenominational) *Accred.:* 1969/1989 (AABC) *Calendar:* Qtr. plan *Degrees:* A, B, certificates *CEO:* Pres. Bryce L. Jessup
FTE Enroll: 217   (408) 293-9058

SAN JOSE CITY COLLEGE
2100 Moorpark Ave., San Jose 95128 *Type:* Public (district) junior *System:* San Jose-Evergreen Community College District *Accred.:* 1953/1992 (WASC-Jr.) *Calendar:* Sem. plan *Degrees:* A *Prof. Accred.:* Dental Assisting *CEO:* Pres. Del M. Anderson
Enroll: 12,507   (408) 298-2181

SAN JOSE STATE UNIVERSITY
One Washington Sq., San Jose 95192 *Type:* Public (state) *System:* California State University System *Accred.:* 1949/1989 (WASC-Sr.) *Calendar:* Sem. plan *Degrees:* B, M *Prof. Accred.:* Art, Audiology, Business (B,M), Community Health, Dance (associate), Engineering (aerospace, chemical, civil, computer, electrical, industrial, materials,

mechanical), Journalism (B,M), Librarianship, Music, Nursing (B,M), Occupational Therapy, Planning (M), Public Administration, Recreation and Leisure Services, Social Work (B,M), Speech-Language Pathology, Teacher Education (e,s,p), Theatre *CEO:* Pres. J. Handel Evans
FTE Enroll: 18,843   (408) 924-1000

SANTA BARBARA CITY COLLEGE
721 Cliff Dr., Santa Barbara 93109 *Type:* Public (district) junior *System:* Santa Barbara Community College District *Accred.:* 1952/1991 (WASC-Jr.) *Calendar:* Sem. plan *Degrees:* A *Prof. Accred.:* Dental Assisting, Nursing (A), Radiography *CEO:* Pres. Peter R. MacDougall
Enroll: 11,665   (805) 965-0581

SANTA CLARA UNIVERSITY
Santa Clara 95053 *Type:* Independent (Roman Catholic) liberal arts and professional *Accred.:* 1949/1988 (WASC-Sr.) *Calendar:* Qtr. plan *Degrees:* B, P, M, D *Prof. Accred.:* Business (B,M), Engineering (civil, computer, electrical, mechanical), Law, Music, Theatre *CEO:* Pres. Paul L. Locatelli, S.J.
FTE Enroll: 6,640   (408) 554-4764

SANTA MONICA COLLEGE
1900 Pico Blvd., Santa Monica 90405 *Type:* Public (district) junior *System:* Santa Monica Community College District *Accred.:* 1952/1992 (WASC-Jr.) *Calendar:* Sem. plan *Degrees:* A *Prof. Accred.:* Nursing (A), Respiratory Therapy *CEO:* Pres. Richard L. Moore
Enroll: 22,091   (310) 450-5150

SANTA ROSA JUNIOR COLLEGE
1501 Mendocino Ave., Santa Rosa 95401 *Type:* Public (district) junior *System:* Sonoma County Junior College District *Accred.:* 1952/1991 (WASC-Jr.) *Calendar:* Sem. plan *Degrees:* A *Prof. Accred.:* Dental Assisting, Radiography *CEO:* Pres. Robert F. Agrella
Enroll: 24,036   (707) 527-4431

SAYBROOK INSTITUTE
450 Pacific Ave., No. 300, San Francisco 94133 *Type:* Independent professional; graduate only *Accred.:* 1984/1988 (WASC-Sr.)

Calendar: Sem. plan *Degrees:* M, D *CEO:*
Pres. J. Bruce Frances
FTE Enroll: 304   (415) 441-5034

SCHOOL OF THEOLOGY AT CLAREMONT
1325 N. College Ave., Claremont 91711-
3199 *Type:* Independent (Disciples of Christ/
United Methodist) graduate only *Accred.:*
1944/1989 (ATS); 1971/1984 (WASC-Sr.)
Calendar: Sem. plan *Degrees:* P, M, D
CEO: Pres. Robert W. Edgar
FTE Enroll: 244   (909) 626-3521

SCRIPPS COLLEGE
1030 N. Columbia Ave., Claremont 91711
Type: Independent liberal arts for women
Accred.: 1949/1993 (WASC-Sr.) *Calendar:*
Sem. plan *Degrees:* B *CEO:* Pres. Nancy Y.
Bekavac
FTE Enroll: 572   (909) 621-8224

THE SCRIPPS RESEARCH INSTITUTE
10666 N. Torrey Pines Rd., La Jolla 92037
Type: Independent graduate only *Accred.:*
1993 (WASC-Sr.) *Calendar:* 9-month plan
Degrees: D *CEO:* Pres. Richard A. Lerner
FTE Enroll: 70   (619) 554-8265

SHASTA COLLEGE
P.O. Box 496006, Redding 96049 *Type:*
Public (district) junior *System:* Shasta-
Tehama-Trinity Joint Community College
District *Accred.:* 1952/1989 (WASC-Jr.)
Calendar: Sem. plan *Degrees:* A *CEO:* Pres.
Douglas M. Treadway
Enroll: 9,913   (916) 225-4600

SIERRA COLLEGE
5000 Rocklin Rd., Rocklin 95677 *Type:*
Public (district) junior *System:* Sierra Joint
Community College District *Accred.:* 1952/
1990 (WASC-Jr.) *Calendar:* Sem. plan *Degrees:* A *CEO:* Pres. Kevin M. Ramirez
Enroll: 11,194   (916) 624-3333

SIMPSON COLLEGE
2211 College View Dr., Redding 96003
Type: Independent (Christian and Mission-
ary Alliance) liberal arts *Accred.:* 1969/1981
(WASC-Sr.) *Calendar:* 4-1-4 plan *Degrees:*
B, M *CEO:* Pres. James M. Grant
FTE Enroll: 634   (916) 224-5600

SKYLINE COLLEGE
3300 College Dr., San Bruno 94066 *Type:*
Public (district) junior *System:* San Mateo
County Community College District *Ac-
cred.:* 1971/1989 (WASC-Jr.) *Calendar:*
Sem. plan *Degrees:* A *Prof. Accred.:* Respi-
ratory Therapy *CEO:* Pres. Linda Graef
Salter
Enroll: 9,371   (415) 355-7000

SOLANO COMMUNITY COLLEGE
4000 Suisun Valley Rd., Suisun 94585 *Type:*
Public (district) junior *System:* Solano County Community College District *Accred.:*
1952/1989 (WASC-Jr.) *Calendar:* Sem. plan
Degrees: A *CEO:* Pres. Virginia L. Holten
Enroll: 11,370   (707) 864-7000

SONOMA STATE UNIVERSITY
1801 E. Cotati Ave., Rohnert Park 94928
Type: Public (state) *System:* California State
University System *Accred.:* 1963/1989
(WASC-Sr.) *Calendar:* Sem. plan *Degrees:*
B, M *Prof. Accred.:* Art, Counseling, Music,
Nursing (B,M) *CEO:* Pres. Ruben Armiñana
FTE Enroll: 5,294   (707) 664-2880

SOUTH BAYLO UNIVERSITY
12012 S. Magnolia Ave., Garden Grove
92641 *Type:* Private professional *Calendar:*
Qtr. plan *Degrees:* M *Prof. Accred.:*
Acupuncture *CEO:* Pres. David Park
FTE Enroll: 235   (714) 530-9650

BRANCH CAMPUS
1543 W. Olympic Blvd., Los Angeles
90015 *CEO:* Pres. David Park
                                   (213) 738-1974

SOUTHERN CALIFORNIA COLLEGE
55 Fair Dr., Costa Mesa 92626 *Type:* Independent (Assemblies of God) liberal arts *Accred.:* 1964/1991 (WASC-Sr.) *Calendar:* 4-
1-4 plan *Degrees:* B, M *CEO:* Pres. Wayne
E. Kraiss
FTE Enroll: 818   (714) 556-3610

SOUTHERN CALIFORNIA COLLEGE OF
OPTOMETRY
2575 Yorba Linda Blvd., Fullerton 92631-
1699 *Type:* Independent professional *Ac-
cred.:* 1961/1991 (WASC-Sr.) *Calendar:*
Qtr. plan *Degrees:* A, B, P *Prof. Accred.:*
Optometry *CEO:* Pres. Richard L. Hopping
FTE Enroll: 376   (714) 449-7450

SOUTHWESTERN COLLEGE
900 Otay Lakes Rd., Chula Vista 91910
Type: Public (district) junior *System:* Southwestern Community College District *Accred.:* 1964/1991 (WASC-Jr.) *Calendar:* Sem. plan *Degrees:* A *CEO:* Pres. Joseph M. Conte
Enroll: 19,129   (619) 421-6700

SOUTHWESTERN UNIVERSITY SCHOOL OF LAW
675 S. Westmoreland Ave., Los Angeles 90005 *Type:* Private professional *Calendar:* Sem. plan *Degrees:* P *Prof. Accred.:* Law *CEO:* Dean Leigh H. Taylor
Enroll: 1,201   (213) 738-6710

STANFORD UNIVERSITY
Stanford 94305 *Type:* Independent liberal arts and professional *Accred.:* 1949/1991 (WASC-Sr.) *Calendar:* Qtr. plan *Degrees:* B, P, M, D *Prof. Accred.:* Business (M), Counseling Psychology, Engineering (aerospace, chemical, civil, electrical, industrial, mechanical, petroleum), Law, Medicine, Physician Assisting *CEO:* Pres. Gerhard Casper
FTE Enroll: 13,065   (415) 723-2300

STARR KING SCHOOL FOR THE MINISTRY
2441 LeConte Ave., Berkeley 94709 *Type:* Private (Unitarian Universalist) graduate only *Accred.:* 1978/1988 (ATS) *Calendar:* Sem. plan *Degrees:* M *CEO:* Pres. Rebecca Parker
FTE Enroll: 51   (510) 845-6232

TAFT COLLEGE
29 Emmons Park Dr., Taft 93268 *Type:* Public (district) junior *System:* West Kern Community College District *Accred.:* 1952/1991 (WASC-Jr.) *Calendar:* Sem. plan *Degrees:* A *CEO:* Pres. David Cothrun
Enroll: 1,200   (805) 763-4282

THOMAS AQUINAS COLLEGE
10000 N. Ojai Rd., Santa Paula 93060 *Type:* Independent liberal arts *Accred.:* 1980/1988 (WASC-Sr.) *Calendar:* Sem. plan *Degrees:* B *CEO:* Pres. Thomas E. Dillon
FTE Enroll: 205   (805) 525-4417

UNITED STATES INTERNATIONAL UNIVERSITY
10455 Pomerado Rd., San Diego 92131 *Type:* Independent liberal arts and professional *Accred.:* 1956/1992 (WASC-Sr. pro-

bational) *Calendar:* Qtr. plan *Degrees:* A, B, P, M, D *Prof. Accred.:* Engineering (civil) *CEO:* Pres. Garry D. Hays
FTE Enroll: 2,276   (619) 271-4300

UNIVERSITY OF CALIFORNIA, BERKELEY
Berkeley 94720 *Type:* Public (state) *System:* University of California Office of the President *Accred.:* 1949/1990 (WASC-Sr.) *Calendar:* Sem. plan *Degrees:* B, P, M, D *Prof. Accred.:* Business (B,M), Clinical Psychology, Dietetics (internship), Engineering (chemical, civil, computer, electrical, industrial, mechanical, mineral, naval architecture/ marine, nuclear), Forestry, Health Services Administration, Journalism (M), Landscape Architecture (M), Law, Librarianship, Optometry, Planning (M), Psychology Internship, Public Health, School Psychology, Social Work (M) *CEO:* Chanc. Chang-Lin Tien
FTE Enroll: 29,086   (510) 642-6000

UNIVERSITY OF CALIFORNIA, DAVIS
Davis 95616 *Type:* Public (state) *System:* University of California Office of the President *Accred.:* 1954/1992 (WASC-Sr.) *Calendar:* Qtr. plan *Degrees:* B, P, M, D *Prof. Accred.:* Business (M), Engineering (aerospace, agricultural, chemical, civil, computer, electrical, materials, mechanical), Landscape Architecture (B), Law, Medical Technology, Medicine, Physician Assisting, Psychology Internship, Veterinary Medicine *CEO:* Acting Chanc. Larry Vanderhoef
FTE Enroll: 21,251   (916) 752-1011

UNIVERSITY OF CALIFORNIA, HASTINGS COLLEGE OF THE LAW
200 McAllister St., San Francisco 94102 *Type:* Public (state) professional *System:* University of California Office of the President (Affiliate) *Calendar:* Sem. plan *Degrees:* P *Prof. Accred.:* Law *CEO:* Dean Frank T. Read
Enroll: 1,253   (415) 565-4600

UNIVERSITY OF CALIFORNIA, IRVINE
Irvine 92717 *Type:* Public (state) *System:* University of California Office of the President *Accred.:* 1965/1991 (WASC-Sr.) *Calendar:* Qtr. plan *Degrees:* B, P, M, D *Prof. Accred.:* Business (M), Engineering (civil, electrical, mechanical), Medical Technology,

Medicine, Psychology Internship, Theatre *CEO:* Chanc. Laurel L. Wilkening 924
FTE Enroll: 15,130 (714) 856-5011

UNIVERSITY OF CALIFORNIA, LOS ANGELES
405 Hilgard Ave., Los Angeles 90024 *Type:* Public (state) *System:* University of California Office of the President *Accred.:* 1949/1989 (WASC-Sr.) *Calendar:* Qtr. plan *Degrees:* B, P, M, D *Prof. Accred.:* Business (M), Clinical Psychology, Combined Prosthodontics, Dance, Dentistry, Endodontics, Engineering (aerospace, chemical, civil, computer, electrical, materials, mechanical), General Dentistry, General Practice Residency, Health Services Administration, Interior Design, Law, Librarianship, Maxillofacial Prosthodontics, Medical Technology, Medicine, Nurse Anesthesia Education, Nursing (B,M), Oral and Maxillofacial Surgery, Orthodontics, Pediatric Dentistry, Periodontics, Planning (M), Psychology Internship, Public Health, Radiography, Social Work (M) *CEO:* Chanc. Charles E. Young
FTE Enroll: 30,993 (310) 825-4321

UNIVERSITY OF CALIFORNIA, RIVERSIDE
Riverside 92521 *Type:* Public (state) *System:* University of California Office of the President *Accred.:* 1956/1988 (WASC-Sr.) *Calendar:* Qtr. plan *Degrees:* B, M, D *CEO:* Chanc. Raymond L. Orbach
FTE Enroll: 8,519 (909) 787-1012

UNIVERSITY OF CALIFORNIA, SAN DIEGO
La Jolla 92092 *Type:* Public (state) *System:* University of California Office of the President *Accred.:* 1964/1986 (WASC-Sr.) *Calendar:* Qtr. plan *Degrees:* B, P, M, D *Prof. Accred.:* Engineering (bioengineering, chemical, civil, electrical, mechanical, systems), Medicine, Psychology Internship *CEO:* Chanc. Richard C. Atkinson
FTE Enroll: 16,011 (619) 534-2230

UNIVERSITY OF CALIFORNIA, SAN FRANCISCO
513 Parnassus Ave., San Francisco 94143 *Type:* Public (state) *System:* University of California Office of the President *Accred.:* 1976/1986 (WASC-Sr.) *Calendar:* Qtr. plan *Degrees:* B, P, M, D *Prof. Accred.:* Combined Prosthodontics, Dental Hygiene, Dental Public Health, Dentistry, Dietetics (internship), General Dentistry, Medicine, Nu-

clear Medicine Technology, Nursing (B,M), Oral and Maxillofacial Surgery, Orthodontics, Pediatric Dentistry, Periodontics, Physical Therapy, Psychology Internship *CEO:* Chanc. Joseph B. Martin
FTE Enroll: 3,731 (415) 476-9000

UNIVERSITY OF CALIFORNIA, SANTA BARBARA
Santa Barbara 93106 *Type:* Public (state) *System:* University of California Office of the President *Accred.:* 1949/1991 (WASC-Sr.) *Calendar:* Qtr. plan *Degrees:* B, M, D *Prof. Accred.:* Combined Professional-Scientific Psychology (provisional), Computer Science, Counseling Psychology, Dance, Engineering (chemical, electrical, mechanical, nuclear), Psychology Internship *CEO:* Chanc. Barbara S. Uehling
FTE Enroll: 18,851 (805) 893-8000

UNIVERSITY OF CALIFORNIA, SANTA CRUZ
1156 High St., Santa Cruz 95064 *Type:* Public (state) *System:* University of California Office of the President *Accred.:* 1965/1986 (WASC-Sr.) *Calendar:* Qtr. plan *Degrees:* B, M, D *Prof. Accred.:* Engineering (computer), Psychology Internship (provisional) *CEO:* Chanc. Karl S. Pister
FTE Enroll: 10,100 (408) 459-2058

UNIVERSITY OF JUDAISM
15600 Mulholland Dr., Los Angeles 90077 *Type:* Independent *Accred.:* 1961/1988 (WASC-Sr.) *Calendar:* Sem. plan *Degrees:* B, M *CEO:* Pres. Robert Wexler
FTE Enroll: 196 (310) 476-9777

UNIVERSITY OF LA VERNE
1950 Third St., La Verne 91750 *Type:* Independent liberal arts and professional *Accred.:* 1955/1991 (WASC-Sr.) *Calendar:* 4-1-4 plan *Degrees:* B, P, M, D *CEO:* Pres. Stephen C. Morgan
FTE Enroll: 5,357 (909) 593-3511

UNIVERSITY OF REDLANDS
1200 E. Colton Ave., Redlands 92373-0999 *Type:* Independent liberal arts and professional *Accred.:* 1949/1992 (WASC-Sr.) *Calendar:* 4-1-4 plan *Degrees:* B, M *Prof. Accred.:* Music, Speech-Language Pathology *CEO:* Pres. James R. Appleton
FTE Enroll: 3,802 (909) 793-2121

UNIVERSITY OF SAN DIEGO
5998 Alcala Park, San Diego 92110-2492
Type: Independent (Roman Catholic) liberal arts and professional *Accred.:* 1956/1993 (WASC-Sr.) *Calendar:* 4-1-4 plan *Degrees:* B, P, M, D *Prof. Accred.:* Business (B,M), Diagnostic Medical Sonography, Engineering (electrical), Law, Marriage and Family Therapy (M), Nuclear Medicine Technology, Nursing (B,M), Radiation Therapy Technology *CEO:* Pres. Author Thomas
FTE Enroll: 5,324   (619) 260-4600

UNIVERSITY OF SAN FRANCISCO
2130 Fulton St., San Francisco 94117-1080
Type: Independent (Roman Catholic) liberal arts and professional *Accred.:* 1949/1981 (WASC-Sr.) *Calendar:* Sem. plan *Degrees:* B, P, M, D *Prof. Accred.:* Business (B,M), Law, Nursing (B) *CEO:* Pres. John P. Schlegel, S.J.
FTE Enroll: 6,974   (415) 666-6292

UNIVERSITY OF SOUTHERN CALIFORNIA
University Park, Los Angeles 90089-0012
Type: Independent liberal arts and professional *Accred.:* 1949/1987 (WASC-Sr.) *Calendar:* Sem. plan *Degrees:* B, P, M, D *Prof. Accred.:* Business (B,M), Clinical Psychology, Combined Prosthodontics, Computer Science, Counseling Psychology (provisional), Dental Hygiene, Dentistry, Dietetics (internship), Endodontics, Engineering (aerospace, chemical, civil, electrical, industrial, mechanical), Health Services Administration, Journalism (B,M), Law, Marriage and Family Therapy (D), Medicine, Music, Nursing (B), Occupational Therapy, Oral and Maxillofacial Surgery, Orthodontics, Pediatric Dentistry, Periodontics, Physical Therapy, Physician Assisting, Planning (M), Psychology Internship, Public Administration, Social Work (M) *CEO:* Pres. Steven B. Sample
FTE Enroll: 23,921   (213) 740-2311

UNIVERSITY OF THE PACIFIC
3601 Pacific Ave., Stockton 95211 *Type:* Independent liberal arts and professional *Accred.:* 1949/1987 (WASC-Sr.) *Calendar:* Sem. plan *Degrees:* B, P, M, D *Prof. Accred.:* Art, Business (B), Computer Science, Dentistry, Engineering (civil, computer, electrical, engineering physics/science, mechanical), General Dentistry, Law, Music,

Orthodontics, Physical Therapy, Speech-Language Pathology, Teacher Education (e,s,p) *CEO:* Pres. William L. Atchley
FTE Enroll: 5,527   (209) 946-2011

UNIVERSITY OF WEST LOS ANGELES
1155 W. Arbor Vitae St., Inglewood 90301-2902 *Type:* Independent professional *Accred.:* 1983/1988 (WASC-Sr.) *Calendar:* Tri. plan *Degrees:* B, P *CEO:* Pres. Bernard S. Jefferson
FTE Enroll: 595   (310) 215-3339

VENTURA COLLEGE
4667 Telegraph Rd., Ventura 93003 *Type:* Public (district) junior *System:* Ventura County Community College District *Accred.:* 1952/1990 (WASC-Jr.) *Calendar:* Sem. plan *Degrees:* A *CEO:* Pres. Jesus Carreon
Enroll: 12,350   (805) 642-3211

VICTOR VALLEY COLLEGE
18422 Bear Valley Rd., Victorville 92392
Type: Public (district) junior *System:* Victor Valley Community College District *Accred.:* 1963/1993 (WASC-Jr.) *Calendar:* Sem. plan *Degrees:* A *Prof. Accred.:* Nursing (A), Respiratory Therapy *CEO:* Pres. Edward O. Gould
Enroll: 7,744   (619) 245-4271

VISTA COLLEGE
2020 Milvia St., Berkeley 94704 *Type:* Public (district) junior *System:* Peralta Community College District *Accred.:* 1981/1991 (WASC-Jr.) *Calendar:* Sem. plan *Degrees:* A *CEO:* Pres. Barbara A. Beno
Enroll: 4,680   (510) 841-8431

WEST COAST UNIVERSITY
440 S. Shatto Pl., Los Angeles 90020 *Type:* Independent *Accred.:* 1963/1982 (WASC-Sr. probational) *Calendar:* Tri. plan *Degrees:* B, M *CEO:* Pres. Robert M.L. Baker, Jr.
FTE Enroll: 1,261   (213) 487-4433

WEST HILLS COMMUNITY COLLEGE
300 Cherry La., Coalinga 93210 *Type:* Public (district) junior *System:* West Hills Community College District *Accred.:* 1952/1993 (WASC-Jr.) *Calendar:* Sem. plan *Degrees:* A *CEO:* Pres. Francis P. Gornick
Enroll: 1,283   (209) 935-0801

WEST LOS ANGELES COLLEGE
4800 Freshman Dr., Culver City 90230 *Type:* Public (district) junior *System:* Los Angeles Community College District *Accred.:* 1971/1989 (WASC-Jr.) *Calendar:* Sem. plan *Degrees:* A *Prof. Accred.:* Dental Hygiene *CEO:* Pres. Evelyn C. Wong
Enroll: 8,852 (310) 287-4200

WEST VALLEY COLLEGE
14000 Fruitvale Ave., Saratoga 95070 *Type:* Public (district) junior *System:* West Valley-Mission College District *Accred.:* 1966/1990 (WASC-Jr.) *Calendar:* Sem. plan *Degrees:* A *Prof. Accred.:* Interior Design, Medical Assisting (AMA) *CEO:* Pres. Leo E. Chavez
Enroll: 13,084 (408) 867-2200

WESTERN STATE UNIVERSITY COLLEGE OF LAW OF ORANGE COUNTY
1111 N. State College Blvd., Fullerton 92631 *Type:* Private professional *Accred.:* 1976/1990 (WASC-Sr.) *Calendar:* Sem. plan *Degrees:* B, P *CEO:* Pres. John C. Monks
FTE Enroll: 1,470 (714) 738-1000

WESTERN STATE UNIVERSITY COLLEGE OF LAW OF SAN DIEGO
2121 San Diego Ave., San Diego 92110 *Type:* Private professional *Accred.:* 1976/1990 (WASC-Sr.) *Calendar:* Sem. plan *Degrees:* B, P *CEO:* Pres. John C. Monks
FTE Enroll: 554 (619) 297-9700

WESTMINSTER THEOLOGICAL SEMINARY IN CALIFORNIA
1725 Bear Valley Pkwy., Escondido 92027 *Type:* Independent (Presbyterian) professional *Accred.:* 1984 (WASC-Sr. probational) *Calendar:* 1-4-1-4 plan *Degrees:* P, M *CEO:* Pres. W. Robert Godfrey
FTE Enroll: 89 (619) 480-8474

WESTMONT COLLEGE
955 La Paz Rd., Santa Barbara 93108 *Type:* Independent liberal arts *Accred.:* 1957/1989 (WASC-Sr.) *Calendar:* Sem. plan *Degrees:* B *CEO:* Pres. David K. Winter
FTE Enroll: 1,281 (805) 565-6000

WHITTIER COLLEGE
P.O. Box 634, Whittier 90608 *Type:* Independent liberal arts *Accred.:* 1949/1990 (WASC-Sr.) *Calendar:* 4-1-4 modular curriculum *Degrees:* B, P, M *Prof. Accred.:* Law, Social Work (B) *CEO:* Pres. James L. Ash, Jr.
FTE Enroll: 1,356 (310) 907-4200

WOODBURY UNIVERSITY
7500 Glen Oaks Boulevard, Burbank 91510-7846 *Type:* Independent professional *Accred.:* 1961/1991 (WASC-Sr.) *Calendar:* Qtr. plan *Degrees:* B, M *Prof. Accred.:* Interior Design *CEO:* Pres. Paul E. Sago
FTE Enroll: 944 (818) 767-0888

WRIGHT INSTITUTE
2728 Durant Ave., Berkeley 94704 *Type:* Independent professional *Accred.:* 1977/1987 (WASC-Sr.) *Calendar:* Qtr. plan *Degrees:* D *Prof. Accred.:* Clinical Psychology *CEO:* Pres. Peter Dybwad
FTE Enroll: 230 (510) 841-9230

YESHIVA OHR ELCHONON-CHABAD/WEST COAST TALMUDIC SEMINARY
7215 Waring Ave., Los Angeles 90046 *Type:* Private professional *Accred.:* 1983/1989 (AARTS) *Calendar:* Sem. plan *Degrees:* B *CEO:* Pres. D. Weiss
Enroll: 37 (213) 937-3763

YO SAN UNIVERSITY OF TRADITIONAL CHINESE MEDICINE
1314 Second St., Santa Monica 90401 *Type:* Private professional *Calendar:* Tri. plan *Degrees:* M *Prof. Accred.:* Acupuncture *CEO:* Pres. Daoshing Ni
FTE Enroll: 26 (310) 917-2202

YUBA COLLEGE
2088 N. Beale Rd., Marysville 95901 *Type:* Public (district) junior *System:* Yuba Community College District *Accred.:* 1952/1989 (WASC-Jr.) *Calendar:* Sem. plan *Degrees:* A *Prof. Accred.:* Veterinary Technology *CEO:* Pres. Patricia L. Wirth
Enroll: 12,701 (916) 741-6700

COLORADO

ADAMS STATE COLLEGE
Alamosa 81102 *Type:* Public (state) liberal arts and teachers *System:* State Colleges in Colorado *Accred.:* 1950/1987 (NCA) *Calendar:* Sem. plan *Degrees:* A, B, M *Prof. Accred.:* Music, Teacher Education (e,s,p) *CEO:* Pres. William Fulkerson, Jr.
Enroll: 2,175   (719) 589-7341

AIMS COMMUNITY COLLEGE
5401 W. 20th St., P.O. Box 69, Greeley 80632 *Type:* Public (district) junior *Accred.:* 1977/1989 (NCA) *Calendar:* Qtr. plan *Degrees:* A, certificates *Prof. Accred.:* Radiography *CEO:* Pres. George R. Conger
Enroll: 9,459   (303) 330-8008

ARAPAHOE COMMUNITY COLLEGE
2500 W. College Dr., P.O. Box 9002, Littleton 80160-9002 *Type:* Public (state) junior *System:* Colorado Community College and Occupational Education System *Accred.:* 1970/1987 (NCA) *Calendar:* Sem. plan *Degrees:* A, certificates *Prof. Accred.:* Medical Laboratory Technology (AMA), Medical Record Technology, Physical Therapy Assisting *CEO:* Pres. James F. Weber
Enroll: 7,518   (303) 794-1550

BEL-REA INSTITUTE OF ANIMAL TECHNOLOGY
1681 S. Dayton St., Denver 80231-3048 *Type:* Private *Accred.:* 1975/1993 (ACC-SCT) *Calendar:* Qtr. plan *Degrees:* A *Prof. Accred.:* Veterinary Technology *CEO:* Dir. Marc Schapiro
                                   (800) 950-8001

BETH-EL COLLEGE OF NURSING
2790 N. Academy Blvd., Ste. 200, Colorado Springs 80917-5338 *Type:* Private professional *Accred.:* 1988/1993 (NCA) *Calendar:* Sem. plan *Degrees:* B, M, certificates *Prof. Accred.:* Nursing (B) *CEO:* Pres. and Dean Carole Schoffstall, Ph.D.
Enroll: 375   (719) 475-5170

BLAIR JUNIOR COLLEGE
828 Wooten Rd., Colorado Springs 80915 *Type:* Private junior *Accred.:* 1953/1988 (ACISC) *Calendar:* Qtr. plan *Degrees:* A *Prof. Accred.:* Medical Assisting (AMA) *CEO:* Dir. Darryl Armstrong
Enroll: 1,704   (719) 574-1082

COLORADO CHRISTIAN UNIVERSITY
180 S. Garrison St., Lakewood 80226 *Type:* Independent (interdenominational) *Accred.:* 1974/1984 (AABC); 1981/1989 (NCA) *Calendar:* Sem. plan *Degrees:* A, B, M, certificates, diplomas *CEO:* Pres. L. David Beckman
Enroll: 1,267   (303) 238-5386

COLORADO COLLEGE
14 E. Cache la Pourde St., Colorado Springs 80903 *Type:* Private liberal arts *Accred.:* 1915/1988 (NCA) *Calendar:* Sem. plan *Degrees:* B, M *CEO:* Pres. Kathryn Mohrman
Enroll: 1,945   (719) 389-6000

COLORADO INSTITUTE OF ART
200 E. Ninth Ave., Denver 80203-9947 *Type:* Private *Accred.:* 1977/1988 (ACC-SCT) *Calendar:* Qtr. plan *Degrees:* A, diplomas *CEO:* Pres. William C. Bottons
                                   (800) 275-2420

COLORADO MOUNTAIN COLLEGE
Box 10001, 215 Ninth St., Glenwood Springs 81602 *Type:* Public (district) junior *Accred.:* 1974/1992 (NCA) *Calendar:* Qtr. plan *Degrees:* A, certificates *Prof. Accred.:* Veterinary Technology *CEO:* Pres. Cynthia M. Heelan
Enroll: 8,081   (303) 945-8691

ALPINE CAMPUS
1370 Bob Adams Dr., Steamboat Springs 80477 *CEO:* Dean John Vickery
                                   (303) 879-3288

ROARING FORK CAMPUS
3000 County Rd. 114, Glenwood Springs 81601 *CEO:* Dean David Beyer
                                   (303) 945-7841

TIMBERLINE CAMPUS
901 S. Hwy. 24, Leadville 80461 *CEO:* Dean Joe Forrester
                                   (719) 486-2015

COLORADO NORTHWESTERN COMMUNITY COLLEGE
500 Kennedy Dr., Rangely 81648 *Type:* Public (district) junior *Accred.:* 1976/1993 (NCA) *Calendar:* Sem. plan *Degrees:* A,

certificates *Prof. Accred.:* Dental Hygiene *CEO:* Pres. Aubrey Holderness
Enroll: 1,525 (303) 562-1105

COLORADO SCHOOL OF MINES
1500 Illinois St., Golden 80401 *Type:* Public (state) technological *System:* Colorado Commission on Higher Education *Accred.:* 1929/1993 (NCA) *Calendar:* Sem. plan *Degrees:* B, M, D *Prof. Accred.:* Engineering (chemical, engineering physics/science, general, geological/geophysical, metallurgical, mining, petroleum) *CEO:* Pres. George S. Ansell
Enroll: 2,864 (303) 273-3000

COLORADO STATE UNIVERSITY
Fort Collins 80523 *Type:* Public (state) *System:* Colorado Commission on Higher Education *Accred.:* 1925/1984 (NCA) *Calendar:* Sem. plan *Degrees:* B, M, D *Prof. Accred.:* Audiology, Business (B,M), Construction Education (B), Counseling Psychology, Engineering (agricultural, chemical, civil, electrical, engineering physics/science, mechanical), Forestry, Interior Design, Journalism (B,M), Landscape Architecture (B-provisional), Marriage and Family Therapy (M), Medical Illustration, Music, Occupational Therapy, Psychology Internship, Recreation and Leisure Services, Social Work (B,M), Speech-Language Pathology, Teacher Education (s,p), Veterinary Medicine *CEO:* Pres. Albert C. Yates
Enroll: 21,210 (303) 491-1101

COLORADO TECHNICAL COLLEGE
4435 N. Chestnut St., Colorado Springs 80907 *Type:* Private *Accred.:* 1980/1991 (NCA) *Calendar:* Qtr. plan *Degrees:* A, B, M, certificates *Prof. Accred.:* Engineering Technology (bioengineering, electrical) *CEO:* Pres. David O'Donnell
Enroll: 1,496 (719) 598-0200

COMMUNITY COLLEGE OF AURORA
16000 E. Centretech Pkwy., Aurora 80011 *Type:* Public (state) junior *System:* Colorado Community College and Occupational Education System *Accred.:* 1988/1993 (NCA) *Calendar:* Sem. plan *Degrees:* A, certificates *CEO:* Pres. Larry D. Carter
Enroll: 5,067 (303) 360-4700

COMMUNITY COLLEGE OF DENVER
P.O. Box 173363, Denver 80217-3363 *Type:* Public (state) junior *System:* Colorado Community College and Occupational Education System *Accred.:* 1975/1988 (NCA) *Calendar:* Qtr. plan *Degrees:* A, certificates *Prof. Accred.:* Nuclear Medicine Technology, Radiation Therapy Technology, Radiography, Surgical Technology *CEO:* Pres. Byron N. McClenney
Enroll: 7,244 (303) 556-2600

DENVER BUSINESS COLLEGE
7350 N. Broadway, Denver 80221 *Type:* Private business *Accred.:* 1986 (ACISC) *Calendar:* Qtr. plan *Degrees:* A, certificates, diplomas *CEO:* Pres. Michael Schledorn
(303) 426-1000

BRANCH CAMPUS
1550 S. Alma School Rd., No. 101, Mesa, AZ 85210 *Accred.:* 1988 (ACISC) *CEO:* Dir. Tracy Lee
(602) 834-1000

BRANCH CAMPUS
1916 Young St., No. 101, Honolulu, HI 96816 *Accred.:* 1989 (ACISC) *CEO:* Dir. Jim Anderson
(808) 942-1000

DENVER CONSERVATIVE BAPTIST SEMINARY
P.O. Box 10000, Denver 80250-0100 *Type:* Private (Conservative Baptist) graduate only *Accred.:* 1970/1991 (ATS); 1972/1992 (NCA) *Calendar:* Qtr. plan *Degrees:* M, D *CEO:* Pres. Edward L. Hayes
Enroll: 671 (303) 761-2482

DENVER INSTITUTE OF TECHNOLOGY
7350 N. Broadway, Denver 80221-3653 *Type:* Private *Accred.:* 1968/1990 (ACCSCT) *Calendar:* Qtr. plan *Degrees:* A *CEO:* Dir. James Z. Turner
(303) 650-5050

HEALTH CAREERS DIVISION
7350 N. Broadway, Annex HCD, Denver 80221-3653 *Accred.:* 1992 (ACCSCT) *CEO:* Dir. Loretta E. Tyler
(303) 650-5050

DENVER TECHNICAL COLLEGE
925 S. Niagara St., Denver 80224-1658 *Type:* Private *Accred.:* 1979/1988 (ACC-

SCT) *Calendar:* Courses of varying lengths *Degrees:* A, certificates *Prof. Accred.:* Medical Assisting, Physical Therapy Assisting *CEO:* Pres. Raul Valdes-Pages

(303) 329-3000

DENVER TECHNICAL COLLEGE AT COLORADO SPRINGS
225 S. Union Blvd., Colorado Springs 80910-3138 *Accred.:* 1990 (ACCSCT) *Prof. Accred.:* Medical Assisting *CEO:* Dean of Educ. Don C. Jenkins

(719) 632-3000

FORT LEWIS COLLEGE
Durango 81301 *Type:* Public (state) liberal arts *System:* Colorado Commission on Higher Education *Accred.:* 1958/1986 (NCA) *Calendar:* Tri. plan *Degrees:* A, B *Prof. Accred.:* Business (B), Music *CEO:* Pres. Joel M. Jones
Enroll: 4,096   (303) 247-7100

FRONT RANGE COMMUNITY COLLEGE
3645 W. 112th Ave., Westminster 80030 *Type:* Public (state) junior *System:* Colorado Community College and Occupational Education System *Accred.:* 1975/1987 (NCA) *Calendar:* Sem. plan *Degrees:* A, certificates *Prof. Accred.:* Dental Assisting, Respiratory Therapy *CEO:* Pres. Thomas Gonzales
Enroll: 12,362   (303) 466-8811

ILIFF SCHOOL OF THEOLOGY
2201 S. University Blvd., Denver 80210 *Type:* Private (United Methodist) graduate only *Accred.:* 1938/1987 (ATS); 1973/1988 (NCA) *Calendar:* Qtr. plan *Degrees:* M, D *CEO:* Pres. Donald E. Messer
Enroll: 230   (303) 744-1287

INTERIOR DESIGN INSTITUTE OF DENVER
1401 Blake St., Denver 80202 *Type:* Private professional *Calendar:* Sem. plan *Degrees:* B *Prof. Accred.:* Interior Design *CEO:* Pres. Edward A. Jensen

(303) 893-3002

ITT TECHNICAL INSTITUTE
2121 S. Blackhawk St., Aurora 80014-1416 *Type:* Private *Accred.:* 1985 (ACCSCT) *Calendar:* Courses of varying lengths *Degrees:* A, B *CEO:* Dir. Coy D. Ritchie

(303) 695-1913

LAMAR COMMUNITY COLLEGE
2401 S. Main St., Lamar 81052 *Type:* Public (state) junior *System:* Colorado Community College and Occupational Education System *Accred.:* 1976/1992 (NCA) *Calendar:* Qtr. plan *Degrees:* A, certificates, diplomas *CEO:* Pres. Marvin E. Lane
Enroll: 1,469   (719) 336-2248

MESA STATE COLLEGE
P.O. Box 2647, Grand Junction 81502 *Type:* Public (state) *System:* State Colleges in Colorado *Accred.:* 1957/1989 (NCA) *Calendar:* Sem. plan *Degrees:* A, B, certificates *Prof. Accred.:* Nursing (A,B), Radiography *CEO:* Pres. Raymond N. Kieft
Enroll: 4,295   (303) 248-1020

METROPOLITAN STATE COLLEGE OF DENVER
P.O. Box 173362, Denver 80217-3362 *Type:* Public (state) liberal arts *System:* State Colleges in Colorado *Accred.:* 1971/1987 (NCA) *Calendar:* Sem. plan *Degrees:* B, certificates *Prof. Accred.:* Engineering Technology (civil/construction, electrical, mechanical), Music, Nursing (B), Recreation and Leisure Services, Teacher Education (e,s) *CEO:* Pres. Sheila Kaplan
Enroll: 16,998   (303) 556-3018

MILE HI COLLEGE, INC.
6464 W. 14th Ave., Lakewood 80214 *Type:* Private business *Accred.:* 1977/1986 (ACISC) *Calendar:* Qtr. plan *Degrees:* A, certificates, diplomas *CEO:* Dir. Roger Oviatt

(303) 233-7973

MORGAN COMMUNITY COLLEGE
17800 Rd. 20, Fort Morgan 80701 *Type:* Public (state) junior *System:* Colorado Community College and Occupational Education System *Accred.:* 1980/1989 (NCA) *Calendar:* Qtr. plan *Degrees:* A, certificates *Prof. Accred.:* Physical Therapy Assisting *CEO:* Pres. Richard Bond
Enroll: 934   (303) 867-3081

THE NAROPA INSTITUTE
2130 Arapahoe Ave., Boulder 80302 *Type:* Private *Accred.:* 1986/1990 (NCA) *Calendar:* Sem. plan *Degrees:* B, M, certificates *CEO:* Pres. John Whitehouse Cobb
Enroll: 441   (303) 444-0202

NATIONAL TECHNOLOGICAL UNIVERSITY
700 Centre Ave., Fort Collins 80526 *Type:* Private *Accred.:* 1986/1992 (NCA) *Calendar:* Sem. plan *Degrees:* M, certificates *CEO:* Pres. Lionel Baldwin
Enroll: 2,080   (303) 495-6411

NATIONAL THEATRE CONSERVATORY
1050 13th St., Denver 80204 *Type:* Private *Accred.:* 1992 (NCA) *Calendar:* Sem. plan *Degrees:* M *CEO:* Exec. Dir. Kevin Maifield
Enroll: 50   (303) 893-4000

NAZARENE BIBLE COLLEGE
P.O. Box 15749, 1111 Chapman Dr., Colorado Springs 80916 *Type:* Private (Church of the Nazarene) *Accred.:* 1976/1986 (AABC) *Calendar:* Qtr. plan *Degrees:* A, B, certificates, diplomas *CEO:* Pres. Jerry D. Lambert
FTE Enroll: 439   (719) 596-5110

EMMANUEL BIBLE COLLEGE
1605 E. Elizabeth St., Pasadena, CA 91104 *CEO:* Dir. Yeghia Babikian
FTE Enroll: 15   (818) 791-2575

INSTITUTO TEOLOGICO NAZARENO
1539 E. Howard St., Pasadena, CA 91104 *CEO:* Dir. Jose Rodríguez
FTE Enroll: 25   (818) 398-2389

NAZARENE INDIAN BIBLE COLLEGE
2315 Markham Rd., S.W., Albuquerque, NM 87105 *CEO:* Admin. Thomas McKinney
FTE Enroll: 44   (505) 877-0240

NORTHEASTERN JUNIOR COLLEGE
Sterling 80751 *Type:* Public (district) junior *Accred.:* 1964/1989 (NCA) *Calendar:* Qtr. plan *Degrees:* A, certificates, diplomas *CEO:* Pres. Henry M. Milander
Enroll: 3,251   (303) 522-6600

OTERO JUNIOR COLLEGE
1802 Colorado Ave., La Junta 81050 *Type:* Public (state) junior *System:* Colorado Community College and Occupational Education System *Accred.:* 1967/1987 (NCA) *Calendar:* Qtr. plan *Degrees:* A, certificates *Prof. Accred.:* Nursing (A) *CEO:* Pres. Joe M. Treece
Enroll: 950   (719) 384-8721

PARKS JUNIOR COLLEGE
9065 Grant St., Denver 80229 *Type:* Private junior *Accred.:* 1962/1990 (ACISC) *Calendar:* Qtr. plan *Degrees:* A, certificates, diplomas *Prof. Accred.:* Medical Assisting (AMA) *CEO:* Dir. Tara B. Pavlakovich
Enroll: 2,165   (303) 457-2757

BRANCH CAMPUS
6 Abilene St., Aurora 80011 *Accred.:* 1990 (ACISC) *CEO:* Dir. Patricia Draper-Hardy
                                   (303) 367-2757

PIKES PEAK COMMUNITY COLLEGE
5675 S. Academy Blvd., Colorado Springs 80906 *Type:* Public (state) junior *System:* Colorado Community College and Occupational Education System *Accred.:* 1975/1987 (NCA) *Calendar:* Sem. plan *Degrees:* A, certificates *Prof. Accred.:* Dental Assisting *CEO:* Pres. Marijane A. Paulsen
Enroll: 7,171   (719) 540-7551

PUEBLO COLLEGE OF BUSINESS AND TECHNOLOGY
330 Lake Ave., Pueblo 81004 *Type:* Private business *Accred.:* 1969/1987 (ACISC) *Calendar:* Qtr. plan *Degrees:* A, certificates, diplomas *CEO:* Dir. Karen Thompson
                                   (719) 545-3100

PUEBLO COMMUNITY COLLEGE
900 W. Orman Ave., Pueblo 81004 *Type:* Public (state) junior *System:* Colorado Community College and Occupational Education System *Accred.:* 1979/1991 (NCA) *Calendar:* Sem. plan *Degrees:* A, certificates *Prof. Accred.:* Dental Hygiene, Nursing (A), Occupational Therapy Assisting, Physical Therapy Assisting, Radiography, Respiratory Therapy *CEO:* Pres. Joe D. May
Enroll: 3,466   (719) 549-3400

RED ROCKS COMMUNITY COLLEGE
13300 W. Sixth Ave., Lakewood 80401 *Type:* Public (state) junior *System:* Colorado Community College and Occupational Education System *Accred.:* 1975/1988 (NCA) *Calendar:* Sem. plan *Degrees:* A, certificates *CEO:* Pres. Dorothy Horrell
Enroll: 6,427   (303) 988-6160

REGIS UNIVERSITY
3333 Regis Blvd., Denver 80221-1099 *Type:* Private (Roman Catholic) liberal arts *Accred.:* 1922/1988 (NCA) *Calendar:* Sem. plan *Degrees:* A, B, M, certificates *Prof. Accred.:* Medical Record Administration, Nursing (B) *CEO:* Pres. Michael J. Sheeran, S.J.
Enroll: 6,140   (303) 458-4100

ROCKY MOUNTAIN COLLEGE OF ART AND DESIGN
6875 E. Evans Ave., Denver 80224-2359 *Type:* Private *Accred.:* 1977/1989 (ACC-SCT) *Calendar:* Qtr. plan *Degrees:* A *CEO:* Pres. Steven M. Steele
       (303) 753-6046

ST. THOMAS THEOLOGICAL SEMINARY
1300 S. Steele St., Denver 80210-2599 *Type:* Private (Roman Catholic) for men; graduate only *Accred.:* 1970/1984 (ATS); 1961/1984 (NCA) *Calendar:* Qtr. plan *Degrees:* M *CEO:* Pres./Rector J. Dennis Martin
Enroll: 171   (303) 722-4687

TRINIDAD STATE JUNIOR COLLEGE
600 Prospect St., Trinidad 81082 *Type:* Public (state) junior *System:* Colorado Community College and Occupational Education System *Accred.:* 1962/1988 (NCA) *Calendar:* Qtr. plan *Degrees:* A, certificates *Prof. Accred.:* Nursing (A) *CEO:* Pres. Harold Deselms
Enroll: 1,630   (719) 621-8752

UNITED STATES AIR FORCE ACADEMY
USAF Academy 80840 *Type:* Public (federal) military and technological *Accred.:* 1959/1989 (NCA) *Calendar:* Sem. plan *Degrees:* B *Prof. Accred.:* Computer Science, Engineering (aerospace, civil, electrical, engineering mechanics, engineering physics/science, mechanical) *CEO:* Supt. Bradley C. Hosmer
Enroll: 4,287   (719) 472-2229

UNIVERSITY OF COLORADO AT BOULDER
Boulder 80309 *Type:* Public (state) *System:* University of Colorado Central Administration *Accred.:* 1913/1990 (NCA) *Calendar:* Sem. plan *Degrees:* B, P, M, D *Prof. Accred.:* Audiology, Business (B,M), Engineering (aerospace, architectural, chemical, civil, computer, electrical, mechanical), Journal-

ism (B,M), Law, Music, Speech-Language Pathology, Teacher Education (e,s,p) *CEO:* Chanc. James N. Corbridge, Jr.
Enroll: 25,089   (303) 492-1411

UNIVERSITY OF COLORADO AT COLORADO SPRINGS
P.O. Box 7150, Colorado Springs 80933-7150 *Type:* Public (state) *System:* University of Colorado Central Administration *Accred.:* 1970/1987 (NCA) *Calendar:* Sem. plan *Degrees:* B, M, D *Prof. Accred.:* Business (B,M), Computer Science, Engineering (electrical), Public Administration, Teacher Education (e,s) *CEO:* Chanc. Linda Bunnell Jones
Enroll: 5,772   (719) 593-3000

UNIVERSITY OF COLORADO AT DENVER
P.O. Box 173364, Denver 80217-3364 *Type:* Public (state) *System:* University of Colorado Central Administration *Accred.:* 1970/1991 (NCA) *Calendar:* Sem. plan *Degrees:* B, M, D *Prof. Accred.:* Business (B,M), Community Health/Preventive Medicine, Counseling, Engineering (civil, electrical, mechanical), Health Services Administration, Landscape Architecture (M), Music, Nursing (B,M), Planning (M), Public Administration, Teacher Education (e,s,p) *CEO:* Chanc. John C. Buechner
Enroll: 11,188   (303) 556-2400

UNIVERSITY OF COLORADO HEALTH SCIENCES CENTER
Denver 80262 *Type:* Public (state) *System:* University of Colorado Central Administration *Accred.:* 1913/1988 (NCA) *Calendar:* Sem. plan *Degrees:* B, M, D *Prof. Accred.:* Clinical Psychology, Dental Hygiene, Dentistry, General Practice Residency, Medical Technology, Medicine, Physical Therapy, Physician Assisting, Psychology Internship *CEO:* Chanc. Vincent A. Fulginiti
Enroll: 2,167   (303) 399-1211

UNIVERSITY OF DENVER
2199 S. University Blvd., Denver 80208 *Type:* Private (United Methodist) *Accred.:* 1914/1991 (NCA) *Calendar:* Qtr. plan *Degrees:* B, M, D, certificates *Prof. Accred.:* Accounting (Type A,B,C), Business (B,M), Clinical Psychology, Counseling Psychology, Engineering (electrical, mechanical),

Law, Music, Psychology Internship, Social Work (M) *CEO:* Chanc. Daniel L. Ritchie
Enroll: 8,108   (303) 871-2111

UNIVERSITY OF NORTHERN COLORADO
Greeley 80639 *Type:* Public (state) *System:* Colorado Commission on Higher Education *Accred.:* 1916/1985 (NCA) *Calendar:* Sem. plan *Degrees:* B, P, M, D *Prof. Accred.:* Accounting (Type A), Audiology, Business (B), Community Health, Counseling, Music, Nursing (B,M), Recreation and Leisure Services, Rehabilitation Counseling, School Psychology, Speech-Language Pathology, Teacher Education (e,s,p) *CEO:* Pres. Herman D. Lujan
Enroll: 12,679   (303) 351-1890

UNIVERSITY OF SOUTHERN COLORADO
2200 Bonforte Blvd., Pueblo 81001 *Type:* Public (state) liberal arts and technological *System:* Colorado Commission on Higher Education *Accred.:* 1951/1987 (NCA) *Cal-endar:* Sem. plan *Degrees:* B, M *Prof. Ac-cred.:* Engineering Technology (civil/con-struction, electrical, mechanical), Engineering (industrial), Music, Nursing (B), Social Work (B) *CEO:* Pres. Robert C. Shirley
Enroll: 4,869   (719) 549-2100

WESTERN STATE COLLEGE OF COLORADO
Gunnison 81231 *Type:* Public (state) liberal arts *System:* State Colleges in Colorado *Ac-cred.:* 1915/1993 (NCA) *Calendar:* Sem. plan *Degrees:* B *Prof. Accred.:* Music, Teacher Education (e,s,p) *CEO:* Pres. Kaye Howe
Enroll: 2,661   (303) 943-2114

YESHIVA TORAS CHAIM TALMUDIC SEMINARY
1400 Quitman St., P.O. Box 4067, Denver 80204 *Type:* Private professional *Accred.:* 1979/1990 (AARTS) *Calendar:* Sem. plan *Degrees:* B, M *CEO:* Pres. S. Beren
Enroll: 35   (303) 629-8200

CONNECTICUT

ALBERTUS MAGNUS COLLEGE
New Haven 06511-1189 *Type:* Private (Roman Catholic) liberal arts *Accred.:* 1932/1991 (NEASC-CIHE) *Calendar:* Sem. plan *Degrees:* A, B *CEO:* Pres. Julia M. McNamara
Enroll: 488   (203) 773-8550

ASNUNTUCK COMMUNITY-TECHNICAL COLLEGE
170 Elm St., Enfield 06082 *Type:* Public (state) junior *System:* State of Connecticut Board of Trustees of Community-Technical Colleges *Accred.:* 1976/1986 (NEASC-CIHE) *Calendar:* Sem. plan *Degrees:* A *CEO:* Pres. Harvey S. Irlen
Enroll: 814   (203) 253-3000

BERKELEY DIVINITY SCHOOL
363 St. Ronan St., New Haven 06511 *Type:* Private (Episcopal) graduate only *Accred.:* 1954/1991 (ATS) *Calendar:* Sem. plan *Degrees:* M *CEO:* Dean Philip Turner
            (203) 432-6105

BETH BENJAMIN ACADEMY OF CONNECTICUT
132 Prospect St., Stamford 06901 *Type:* Private professional *Accred.:* 1978/1990 (AARTS) *Calendar:* Tri. plan *Degrees:* Rabbinic (1st), Talmudic (1st) *CEO:* Pres. S. Schustal
Enroll: 29   (203) 325-4351

BRIARWOOD COLLEGE
2279 Mt. Vernon Rd., Southington 06489 *Type:* Private business *Accred.:* 1982/1992 (NEASC-CTCI) *Calendar:* Sem. plan *Degrees:* A, diplomas *Prof. Accred.:* Dental Assisting, Medical Record Technology, Mortuary Science (candidate) *CEO:* Pres. John J. LeConche
FTE Enroll: 301   (203) 628-4751

BRIDGEPORT ENGINEERING INSTITUTE
Fairfield 06430 *Type:* Private professional *Accred.:* 1977/1990 (NEASC-CIHE) *Calendar:* Tri. plan *Degrees:* A, B *CEO:* Pres. William M. Krummel
Enroll: 250   (203) 259-5717

CAPITAL COMMUNITY-TECHNICAL COLLEGE
61 Woodland St., Hartford 06105 *Type:* Public (state) 2-year *System:* State of Connecticut Board of Trustees of Community-

Technical Colleges *Accred.:* 1975/1986 (NEASC-CIHE) *Calendar:* Sem. plan *Degrees:* A *Prof. Accred.:* Engineering Technology (civil/construction, electrical, manufacturing, mechanical), Nursing (A) *CEO:* Pres. Conrad L. Mallett
Enroll: 1,322   (203) 520-7800

FLATBUSH CAMPUS
401 Flatbush Ave., Hartford 06106 *Prof. Accred.:* Engineering Technology (civil/construction, electrical, manufacturing, mechanical) *CEO:* Pres. Conrad L. Mallett
            (203) 527-4111

CENTRAL CONNECTICUT STATE UNIVERSITY
New Britain 06050 *Type:* Public liberal arts and teachers *System:* Connecticut State University Central Office *Accred.:* 1947/1988 (NEASC-CIHE) *Calendar:* Sem. plan *Degrees:* A, B, M *Prof. Accred.:* Computer Science, Engineering Technology (civil/construction, manufacturing), Nursing (B), Social Work (B-candidate) *CEO:* Pres. John W. Shumaker
Enroll: 8,739   (203) 827-7000

CHARTER OAK STATE COLLEGE
270 Farmington Ave., Ste. 171, Farmington 06032-1934 *Type:* Public (state) liberal arts *System:* State of Connecticut Department of Higher Education *Accred.:* 1981/1987 (NEASC-CIHE) *Calendar:* Sem. plan *Degrees:* A, B *CEO:* Pres. Merle W. Harris
Enroll: 1,145   (203) 566-7230

CONNECTICUT COLLEGE
New London 06320 *Type:* Private liberal arts *Accred.:* 1932/1987 (NEASC-CIHE) *Calendar:* Sem. plan *Degrees:* B, M *CEO:* Pres. Claire L. Gaudiani
Enroll: 1,673   (203) 447-1911

EASTERN CONNECTICUT STATE UNIVERSITY
Willimantic 06226-2295 *Type:* Public liberal arts and teachers *System:* Connecticut State University Central Office *Accred.:* 1958/1990 (NEASC-CIHE) *Calendar:* Sem. plan *Degrees:* A, B, M *CEO:* Pres. David G. Carter
Enroll: 3,139   (203) 456-2231

FAIRFIELD UNIVERSITY
Fairfield 06430-7524 *Type:* Private (Roman Catholic) liberal arts *Accred.:* 1953/1988 (NEASC-CIHE) *Calendar:* Sem. plan *Degrees:* B, M *Prof. Accred.:* Counseling, Nursing (B) *CEO:* Pres. Aloysius P. Kelley, S.J.
Enroll: 3,804   (203) 254-4000

GATEWAY COMMUNITY-TECHNICAL COLLEGE
60 Sargent Dr., New Haven 06511 *Type:* Public (state) 2-year *System:* State of Connecticut Board of Trustees of Community-Technical Colleges *Accred.:* 1981/1986 (NEASC-CIHE) *Calendar:* Sem. plan *Degrees:* A *Prof. Accred.:* Engineering Technology (mechanical), Nuclear Medicine Technology, Radiation Therapy Technology, Radiography *CEO:* Pres. Antonio Perez
Enroll: 2,587   (203) 789-7071

NORTH HAVEN CAMPUS
88 Bassett Rd., North Haven 06473 *Prof. Accred.:* Engineering Technology (mechanical) *CEO:* Pres. Antonio Perez
     (203) 234-3300

HARTFORD GRADUATE CENTER
275 Windsor St., Hartford 06120 *Type:* Private graduate only *Accred.:* 1966/1993 (NEASC-CIHE) *Calendar:* Sem. plan *Degrees:* M *CEO:* Pres. Ann Stuart
Enroll: 1,010   (203) 548-2400

HARTFORD SEMINARY
77 Sherman St., Hartford 06105 *Type:* Private (interdenominational) graduate only *Accred.:* 1938/1983 (ATS); 1983/1988 (NEASC-CIHE) *Calendar:* Sem. plan *Degrees:* M, D *CEO:* Pres. Barbara Brown Zikmund
FTE Enroll: 58   (203) 232-4451

HOLY APOSTLES COLLEGE AND SEMINARY
Cromwell 06416 *Type:* Private (Roman Catholic) liberal arts for men *Accred.:* 1979/1986 (NEASC-CIHE) *Calendar:* Sem. plan *Degrees:* A, B, M *CEO:* Pres./Rector Ronald D. Lawlor, O.F.M.
Enroll: 142   (203) 635-5311

HOUSATONIC COMMUNITY-TECHNICAL COLLEGE
510 Barnum Ave., Bridgeport 06608 *Type:* Public (state) junior *System:* State of Connecticut Board of Trustees of Community-Technical Colleges *Accred.:* 1972/1992

(NEASC-CIHE) *Calendar:* Sem. plan *Degrees:* A *Prof. Accred.:* Medical Laboratory Technology (AMA), Physical Therapy Assisting *CEO:* Pres. Vincent S. Darnowski
Enroll: 1,225   (203) 579-6400

KATHARINE GIBBS SCHOOL
142 East Ave., Norwalk 06851 *Type:* Private business *Accred.:* 1975/1991 (ACISC) *Calendar:* Sem. plan *Degrees:* A, certificates, diplomas *CEO:* Dir. Frank Bonilla
     (203) 838-4173

MANCHESTER COMMUNITY-TECHNICAL COLLEGE
60 Bidwell St., Manchester 06040 *Type:* Public (state) junior *System:* State of Connecticut Board of Trustees of Community-Technical Colleges *Accred.:* 1971/1992 (NEASC-CIHE) *Calendar:* Sem. plan *Degrees:* A *Prof. Accred.:* Medical Laboratory Technology (AMA), Occupational Therapy Assisting, Respiratory Therapy, Surgical Technology *CEO:* Pres. Jonathan M. Daube
Enroll: 3,523   (203) 647-6000

MIDDLESEX COMMUNITY-TECHNICAL COLLEGE
100 Training Hill Rd., Middletown 06457 *Type:* Public (state) junior *System:* State of Connecticut Board of Trustees of Community-Technical Colleges *Accred.:* 1973/1992 (NEASC-CIHE) *Calendar:* Sem. plan *Degrees:* A *Prof. Accred.:* Nuclear Medicine Technology, Radiography *CEO:* Pres. Leila G. Sullivan
Enroll: 1,361   (203) 344-3011

MITCHELL COLLEGE
New London 06320 *Type:* Private junior *Accred.:* 1956/1993 (NEASC-CIHE) *Calendar:* Sem. plan *Degrees:* A *CEO:* Pres. David A. Sandell
Enroll: 912   (203) 443-2811

NAUGATUCK VALLEY COMMUNITY-TECHNICAL COLLEGE
750 Chase Pkwy., Waterbury 06708 *Type:* Public (state) 2-year *System:* State of Connecticut Board of Trustees of Community-Technical Colleges *Accred.:* 1973/1992 (NEASC-CIHE) *Calendar:* Sem. plan *Degrees:* A *Prof. Accred.:* Engineering Technology (chemical, electrical, manufacturing, mechanical, mechanical drafting/design), Nursing (A), Radiography, Respiratory

Therapy Technology *CEO:* Pres. Richard L. Sanders
Enroll: 3,156   (203) 575-8082

NORTHWESTERN CONNECTICUT COMMUNITY-TECHNICAL COLLEGE
Park Pl. E., Winsted 06098 *Type:* Public (state) junior *System:* State of Connecticut Board of Trustees of Community-Technical Colleges *Accred.:* 1971/1993 (NEASC-CIHE) *Calendar:* Sem. plan *Degrees:* A *Prof. Accred.:* Medical Assisting (AMA) *CEO:* Pres. R. Eileen Baccus
Enroll: 941   (203) 738-6300

NORWALK COMMUNITY-TECHNICAL COLLEGE
188 Richards Ave., Norwalk 06854 *Type:* Public (state) 2-year *System:* State of Connecticut Board of Trustees of Community-Technical Colleges *Accred.:* 1973/1982 (NEASC-CIHE) *Calendar:* Sem. plan *Degrees:* A *Prof. Accred.:* Engineering Technology (architectural, civil/construction, computer, electrical, electromechanical, mechanical), Nursing (A) *CEO:* Pres. William H. Schwab
Enroll: 2,360   (203) 857-7000

PAIER COLLEGE OF ART
6 Prospect Ct., Hamden 06517-4025 *Type:* Private *Accred.:* 1991 (ACCSCT) *Calendar:* Courses of varying lengths *Degrees:* B, certificates, diplomas *CEO:* Pres. Edward T. Paier
                                   (203) 287-3030

QUINEBAUG VALLEY COMMUNITY-TECHNICAL COLLEGE
724 Upper Maple St., Danielson 06239 *Type:* Public (state) junior *System:* State of Connecticut Board of Trustees of Community-Technical Colleges *Accred.:* 1978/1991 (NEASC-CIHE) *Calendar:* Sem. plan *Degrees:* A *CEO:* Pres. Dianne E. Williams
Enroll: 571   (203) 774-1130

QUINNIPIAC COLLEGE
Hamden 06518-0569 *Type:* Private liberal arts and professional *Accred.:* 1958/1989 (NEASC-CIHE) *Calendar:* Sem. plan *Degrees:* A, B, M *Prof. Accred.:* Law (provisional), Medical Technology, Nursing (A), Occupational Therapy, Perfusion, Physical Therapy, Radiography, Respiratory Therapy,

Respiratory Therapy Technology, Veterinary Technology *CEO:* Pres. John L. Lahey
Enroll: 3,886   (203) 288-5251

SACRED HEART UNIVERSITY
5151 Park Ave., Fairfield 06432-1023 *Type:* Private (Roman Catholic) liberal arts *Accred.:* 1969/1993 (NEASC-CIHE) *Calendar:* Sem. plan *Degrees:* A, B, M *Prof. Accred.:* Nursing (B,M), Respiratory Therapy, Social Work (B) *CEO:* Pres. Anthony J. Cernera
Enroll: 3,132   (203) 371-7999

ST. JOSEPH COLLEGE
1678 Asylum Ave., West Hartford 06117 *Type:* Private (Roman Catholic) liberal arts *Accred.:* 1938/1986 (NEASC-CIHE) *Calendar:* Sem. plan *Degrees:* B, M *Prof. Accred.:* Dietetics (coordinated), Marriage and Family Therapy (M-candidate), Nursing (B,M), Social Work (B) *CEO:* Pres. Winifred E. Coleman
Enroll: 1,085   (203) 232-4571

SOUTHERN CONNECTICUT STATE UNIVERSITY
New Haven 06515-0901 *Type:* Public liberal arts and teachers *System:* Connecticut State University Central Office *Accred.:* 1952/1991 (NEASC-CIHE) *Calendar:* Sem. plan *Degrees:* A, B, M *Prof. Accred.:* Computer Science, Librarianship, Marriage and Family Therapy (M), Nurse Anesthesia Education, Nursing (B,M), Social Work (B,M), Speech-Language Pathology *CEO:* Pres. Michael J. Adanti
Enroll: 8,358   (203) 397-4000

TEIKYO POST UNIVERSITY
Waterbury 06708 *Type:* Private liberal arts *Accred.:* 1972/1985 (NEASC-CIHE) *Calendar:* Sem. plan *Degrees:* A, B *CEO:* Pres. Phyllis C. DeLeo
Enroll: 1,002   (203) 596-4500

THREE RIVERS COMMUNITY-TECHNICAL COLLEGE
P.O. Box 629, Mahan Dr., Norwich 06360 *Type:* Public (state) 2-year *System:* State of Connecticut Board of Trustees of Community-Technical Colleges *Accred.:* 1973/1992 (NEASC-CIHE) *Calendar:* Sem. plan *Degrees:* A *Prof. Accred.:* Engineering Technology (chemical, electrical, manufacturing, mechanical, mechanical drafting/design),

Nursing (A) *CEO:* Pres. Booker T. De-
Vaughn
Enroll: 2,149   (203) 886-1931

THAMES CAMPUS
574 New London Tpke., Norwich 06360
Prof. Accred.: Engineering Technology
(chemical, electrical, manufacturing, mechanical, nuclear) *CEO:* Pres. Booker T.
DeVaughn
                                   (203) 886-0177

TRINITY COLLEGE
Hartford 06106 *Type:* Private liberal arts *Ac-
cred.:* 1929/1986 (NEASC-CIHE) *Calendar:*
Sem. plan *Degrees:* B, M *CEO:* Interim
Pres. Borden W. Painter, Jr.
Enroll: 1,963   (203) 297-2000

TUNXIS COMMUNITY-TECHNICAL COLLEGE
Rtes. 6 and 177, Farmington 06032 *Type:*
Public (state) junior *System:* State of Con-
necticut Board of Trustees of Community-
Technical Colleges *Accred.:* 1975/1991
(NEASC-CIHE) *Calendar:* Sem. plan *De-
grees:* A *Prof. Accred.:* Dental Assisting,
Dental Hygiene *CEO:* Pres. Cathryn L.
Addy
Enroll: 1,672   (203) 677-7701

UNITED STATES COAST GUARD ACADEMY
15 Mohegan Ave., New London 06320-4195
Type: Public (federal) professional *Accred.:*
1952/1990 (NEASC-CIHE) *Calendar:* Sem.
plan *Degrees:* B *Prof. Accred.:* Engineering
(civil, electrical, naval architecture/marine)
CEO: Supt. Paul E. Versaw
Enroll: 946   (203) 444-8444

UNIVERSITY OF BRIDGEPORT
Bridgeport 06602 *Type:* Private *Accred.:*
1951/1989 (NEASC-CIHE) *Calendar:* Sem.
plan *Degrees:* A, B, M, D *Prof. Accred.:*
Art, Dental Hygiene, Engineering (computer,
electrical, mechanical) *CEO:* Pres. Edwin G.
Eigel, Jr.
Enroll: 937   (203) 576-4000

THE UNIVERSITY OF CONNECTICUT
Storrs 06269 *Type:* Public (state) *System:*
State of Connecticut Department of Higher
Education *Accred.:* 1931/1987 (NEASC-
CIHE) *Calendar:* Sem. plan *Degrees:* B, M,
D *Prof. Accred.:* Accounting (Type A,B),
Art, Audiology, Business (B,M), Clinical

Psychology, Community Health/Preventive
Medicine, Computer Science, Dietetics (coordinated), Engineering (chemical, civil,
computer, electrical, mechanical), Law, Marriage and Family Therapy (M,D), Music,
Nursing (B,M), Physical Therapy, Public Affairs, Recreation and Leisure Services, Social Work (M), Speech-Language Pathology,
Teacher Education (e,s,p), Theatre *CEO:*
Pres. Harry J. Hartley
Enroll: 18,393   (203) 486-2000

THE UNIVERSITY OF CONNECTICUT HEALTH
CENTER
263 Farmington Ave., Farmington 06030-
3800 *Type:* Public *System:* State of Con-
necticut Department of Higher Education
Accred.: 1931/1987 (NEASC-CIHE) *Calen-
dar:* 4-1-4 plan *Degrees:* B, P *Prof. Accred.:*
Cytotechnology, Dentistry, Endodontics,
General Dentistry, Medicine, Oral and Max-
illofacial Surgery, Orthodontics, Pediatric
Dentistry, Periodontics *CEO:* Vice Pres.
Leslie S. Cutler
Enroll: 507   (203) 679-2000

UNIVERSITY OF HARTFORD
200 Bloomfield Ave., West Hartford 06117
Type: Private *Accred.:* 1961/1991 (NEASC-
CIHE) *Calendar:* Sem. plan *Degrees:* A, B,
M, D *Prof. Accred.:* Art, Clinical Psychology (provisional), Engineering Technology
(electrical), Engineering (civil, electrical,
mechanical), Medical Technology, Music,
Nursing (B), Public Administration, Radiography, Respiratory Therapy, Teacher Education (e,s,p) *CEO:* Pres. Humphrey Tonkin
Enroll: 5,711   (203) 243-4100

UNIVERSITY OF NEW HAVEN
West Haven 06516 *Type:* Private *Accred.:*
1966/1990 (NEASC-CIHE) *Calendar:* Sem.
plan *Degrees:* A, B, M, D *Prof. Accred.:* Engineering (civil, electrical, industrial, mechanical) *CEO:* Pres. Lawrence J. DeNardis
Enroll: 3,198   (203) 932-7000

WESLEYAN UNIVERSITY
Middletown 06457 *Type:* Private liberal arts
Accred.: 1929/1992 (NEASC-CIHE) *Calen-
dar:* Sem. plan *Degrees:* B, M, D *CEO:*
Pres. William M. Chace
Enroll: 3,010   (203) 347-9411

WESTERN CONNECTICUT STATE UNIVERSITY
Danbury 06810 *Type:* Public liberal arts and teachers *System:* Connecticut State University Central Office *Accred.:* 1954/1984 (NEASC-CIHE) *Calendar:* Sem. plan *Degrees:* A, B, M *Prof. Accred.:* Nursing (B,M), Social Work (B) *CEO:* Pres. James R. Roach
Enroll: 3,704   (203) 797-4347

WILCOX COLLEGE OF NURSING
28 Crescent St., Middletown 06547 *Type:* Private *Accred.:* 1993 (NEASC-CTCI) *Calendar:* Sem. plan *Degrees:* A *CEO:* Pres. Susan E. Abbe
FTE Enroll: 126   (203) 344-6400

YALE UNIVERSITY
New Haven 06520 *Type:* Private *Accred.:* 1991 (ATS); 1929/1989 (NEASC-CIHE) *Calendar:* Sem. plan *Degrees:* B, M, D *Prof. Accred.:* Business (M), Clinical Psychology, Engineering (chemical, electrical, mechanical), Forestry, Health Services Administration, Law, Medicine, Music, Nursing (M), Physician Assisting, Psychology Internship, Public Health *CEO:* Pres. Richard C. Levin
Enroll: 10,731   (203) 432-4771

DELAWARE

DELAWARE STATE UNIVERSITY
1200 N. Dupont Hwy., Dover 19901 *Type:*
Public (state) *System:* Delaware Higher Education Commission *Accred.:* 1945/1992
(MSA) *Calendar:* Tri. plan *Degrees:* B, M
Prof. Accred.: Nursing (B), Social Work
(B,M) *CEO:* Pres. William B. DeLauder
Enroll: 2,882   (302) 739-4901

DELAWARE TECHNICAL & COMMUNITY COLLEGE
SOUTHERN CAMPUS
P.O. Box 610, Georgetown 19947 *Type:*
Public (state) 2-year technological *System:*
Delaware Technical & Community College
Office of the President *Accred.:* 1972/1988
(MSA) *Calendar:* Qtr. plan *Degrees:* A, certificates *Prof. Accred.:* Medical Laboratory
Technology (AMA), Occupational Therapy
Assisting, Radiography *CEO:* Vice Pres./
Campus Dir. Jack F. Owens
Enroll: 3,444   (302) 856-5400

DELAWARE TECHNICAL & COMMUNITY COLLEGE
STANTON/WILMINGTON CAMPUS
400 Stanton Christiana Rd., Newark 19713
Type: Public (state) 2-year technological
System: Delaware Technical & Community
College Office of the President *Accred.:*
1972/1988 (MSA) *Calendar:* Qtr. plan *Degrees:* A, certificates *Prof. Accred.:* Dental
Hygiene, Nuclear Medicine Technology,
Nursing (A), Physical Therapy Assisting,
Respiratory Therapy *CEO:* Vice Pres./
Campus Dir. Orlando J. George, Jr.
Enroll: 6,164   (302) 454-3917

DELAWARE TECHNICAL & COMMUNITY COLLEGE
TERRY CAMPUS
1832 N. Dupont Pkwy., Dover 19901 *Type:*
Public (state) 2-year technological *System:*
Delaware Technical & Community College
Office of the President *Accred.:* 1972/1988
(MSA) *Calendar:* Qtr. plan *Degrees:* A, cer-

tificates *Prof. Accred.:* Diagnostic Medical
Sonography, Histologic Technology, Radiography *CEO:* Acting Vice Pres./Campus Dir.
Wayne N. Dabson
Enroll: 1,969   (302) 739-5321

GOLDEY-BEACOM COLLEGE
4701 Limestone Rd., Wilmington 19808
Type: Private *Accred.:* 1976/1992 (MSA)
Calendar: Sem. plan *Degrees:* A, B, certificates *CEO:* Pres. William R. Baldt
Enroll: 1,852   (302) 998-8814

UNIVERSITY OF DELAWARE
Newark 19716 *Type:* Public (state-related)
System: Delaware Higher Education Commission *Accred.:* 1921/1992 (MSA) *Calendar:* 4-1-4 plan *Degrees:* A, B, M, D *Prof.
Accred.:* Accounting (Type A,C), Business
(B,M), Clinical Psychology, Dietetics (coordinated), Engineering Technology (agricultural, general), Engineering (chemical, civil,
electrical, mechanical), Medical Technology,
Music, Nursing (B,M), Physical Therapy,
Psychology Internship, Public Administration *CEO:* Pres. David P. Roselle
Enroll: 20,868   (302) 831-2000

WESLEY COLLEGE
120 N. State St., Dover 19901 *Type:* Private
(United Methodist) liberal arts *Accred.:*
1950/1988 (MSA) *Calendar:* Sem. plan *Degrees:* A, B, certificates *Prof. Accred.:* Nursing (A) *CEO:* Pres. Reed M. Stewart
Enroll: 1,294   (302) 736-2300

WILMINGTON COLLEGE
320 Dupont Hwy., New Castle 19720 *Type:*
Private *Accred.:* 1975/1991 (MSA) *Calendar:* Tri. plan *Degrees:* A, B, M, D *Prof. Accred.:* Nursing (B) *CEO:* Pres. Audrey K.
Doberstein
Enroll: 2,099   (302) 328-9401

DISTRICT OF COLUMBIA

THE AMERICAN UNIVERSITY
4400 Massachusetts Ave., N.W., Washington 20016 *Type:* Private (United Methodist) *Accred.:* 1928/1989 (MSA) *Calendar:* Sem. plan *Degrees:* A, B, P, M, D *Prof. Accred.:* Business (B,M), Clinical Psychology, Journalism (B,M), Law, Music, Public Administration, Teacher Education (e,s) *CEO:* Pres. Elliott S. Milstein
Enroll: 11,007 (202) 885-1000

THE CATHOLIC UNIVERSITY OF AMERICA
620 Michigan Ave., N.E., Washington 20064 *Type:* Private (Roman Catholic) *Accred.:* 1980/1985 (ATS); 1921/1990 (MSA) *Calendar:* Sem. plan *Degrees:* B, P, M, D *Prof. Accred.:* Clinical Psychology, Engineering (bioengineering, civil, electrical, mechanical), Law, Librarianship, Music, Nursing (B,M), Social Work (B,M), Teacher Education (e,s,p) *CEO:* Pres. F. Patrick Ellis, F.S.C.
Enroll: 6,632 (202) 319-5000

CORCORAN SCHOOL OF ART
500 17th St., N.W., Washington 20006-4899 *Type:* Private professional *Accred.:* 1985/1991 (MSA) *Calendar:* Sem. plan *Degrees:* B, certificates *Prof. Accred.:* Art *CEO:* Pres./Dir. David C. Levy
Enroll: 277 (202) 628-9484

DE SALES SCHOOL OF THEOLOGY
721 Lawrence St., N.E., Washington 20017 *Type:* Private (Roman Catholic) graduate only *Accred.:* 1991 (ATS); 1976/1992 (MSA) *Calendar:* Sem. plan *Degrees:* P, M *CEO:* Pres. John W. Crossin, O.S.F.S.
Enroll: 38 (202) 269-9412

DEFENSE INTELLIGENCE COLLEGE
Defense Intelligence Analysis Ctr., Washington 20340-5485 *Type:* Public (federal) graduate only *Accred.:* 1983/1988 (MSA) *Calendar:* Qtr. plan *Degrees:* M, certificates *CEO:* Commandant Charles J. Cunningham, Jr.
Enroll: 610 (202) 373-3344

DISTRICT OF COLUMBIA SCHOOL OF LAW
719 13th St., N.W., Washington 20005 *Type:* Public professional *Calendar:* Sem. plan *Degrees:* P *Prof. Accred.:* Law (ABA only) (provisional) *CEO:* Dean William L. Robinson
Enroll: 243 (202) 727-5225

DOMINICAN HOUSE OF STUDIES
487 Michigan Ave., N.E., Washington 20017 *Type:* Private (Roman Catholic) graduate for men *Accred.:* 1976/1986 (ATS); 1976/1992 (MSA) *Calendar:* Sem. plan *Degrees:* M *CEO:* Pres. Philip A. Smith, O.P.
Enroll: 40 (202) 529-5300

GALLAUDET UNIVERSITY
800 Florida Ave., N.E., Washington 20002 *Type:* Private liberal arts *Accred.:* 1957/1991 (MSA) *Calendar:* Sem. plan *Degrees:* A, B, M, D, certificates *Prof. Accred.:* Audiology, Counseling, Recreation and Leisure Services, Rehabilitation Counseling, Social Work (B,M-candidate), Speech-Language Pathology, Teacher Education (e,s,p) *CEO:* Pres. Irving King Jordan
Enroll: 2,175 (202) 651-5000

GEORGE WASHINGTON UNIVERSITY
Washington 20052 *Type:* Private *Accred.:* 1922/1988 (MSA) *Calendar:* Sem. plan *Degrees:* A, B, P, M, D, certificates *Prof. Accred.:* Audiology, Business (B,M), Clinical Psychology, Community Health/Preventive Medicine, Computer Science, Counseling, Engineering (civil, computer, electrical, mechanical, systems), Health Services Administration, Law, Medical Record Administration, Medical Technology, Medicine, Music, Nuclear Medicine Technology, Nurse Anesthesia Education, Physician Assisting, Psychology Internship, Public Administration, Radiation Therapy Technology, Rehabilitation Counseling, Speech-Language Pathology, Teacher Education (e,s,p) *CEO:* Pres. Stephen Joel Trachtenberg
Enroll: 19,210 (202) 994-1000

GEORGETOWN UNIVERSITY
37th and O Sts., N.W., Washington 20057 *Type:* Private (Roman Catholic) *Accred.:* 1921/1987 (MSA) *Calendar:* Sem. plan *Degrees:* B, P, M, D, certificates *Prof. Accred.:* Business (B,M), Law, Medicine, Nursing (B,M), Ophthalmic Medical Technology,

Psychology Internship *CEO:* Pres. Leo J. O'Donovan, S.J.
Enroll: 11,861   (202) 687-0100

HOWARD UNIVERSITY
2400 Sixth St., N.W., Washington 20059
Type: Private *Accred.:* 1940/1992 (ATS); 1921/1989 (MSA) *Calendar:* Sem. plan *Degrees:* B, P, M, D, certificates *Prof. Accred.:* Accounting (Type A), Art, Audiology, Business (B,M), Clinical Psychology, Computer Science, Dental Hygiene, Dentistry, Dietetics (coordinated), Engineering (chemical, civil, electrical, mechanical), General Dentistry, General Practice Residency, Health Services Administration, Journalism (B), Law, Medical Technology, Medicine, Music, Nursing (B,M), Occupational Therapy, Oral and Maxillofacial Surgery (conditional), Orthodontics, Pediatric Dentistry, Physical Therapy, Physician Assisting, Psychology Internship, Radiation Therapy Technology, Radiography, School Psychology (probational), Social Work (B,M), Speech-Language Pathology, Theatre (associate) *CEO:* Pres. Franklyn G. Jenifer
Enroll: 10,724   (202) 806-2500

MOUNT VERNON COLLEGE
2100 Foxhall Rd., N.W., Washington 20007
Type: Private liberal arts for women *Accred.:* 1958/1987 (MSA) *Calendar:* Modular plan *Degrees:* A, B *Prof. Accred.:* Interior Design *CEO:* Pres. LucyAnn Geiselman
Enroll: 412   (202) 625-0400

OBLATE COLLEGE
391 Michigan Ave., N.E., Washington 20017-1587 *Type:* Private (Roman Catholic) *Accred.:* 1976/1986 (ATS); 1966/1992 (MSA) *Calendar:* Sem. plan *Degrees:* B, P, M, certificates *CEO:* Pres. George F. Kirwin, O.M.I.
Enroll: 70   (202) 529-6544

SOUTHEASTERN UNIVERSITY
501 Eye St., S.W., Washington 20024 *Type:* Private *Accred.:* 1977 (MSA) *Calendar:* Qtr. plan *Degrees:* A, B, M *CEO:* Pres. W. Robert Higgins
Enroll: 538   (202) 488-8162

STRAYER COLLEGE
1025 15th St., N.W., Washington 20005
Type: Private business *Accred.:* 1981/1991 (MSA) *Calendar:* Qtr. plan *Degrees:* A, B, M, certificates *CEO:* Pres. Ron K. Bailey
Enroll: 3,957   (202) 408-2400

TRINITY COLLEGE
125 Michigan Ave., N.E., Washington 20017 *Type:* Private (Roman Catholic) liberal arts for women *Accred.:* 1921/1991 (MSA) *Calendar:* Sem. plan *Degrees:* B, M *CEO:* Pres. Patricia A. McGuire, J.D.
Enroll: 1,112   (202) 939-5000

UNIVERSITY OF THE DISTRICT OF COLUMBIA
4200 Connecticut Ave., N.W., Washington 20008 *Type:* Public (local) *Accred.:* 1971/1985 (MSA) *Calendar:* Sem. plan *Degrees:* A, B, M, certificates *Prof. Accred.:* Engineering Technology (aerospace, architectural, civil/construction, computer, electrical, electromechanical, mechanical), Engineering (civil, electrical, mechanical), Mortuary Science, Nursing (A,B), Planning (B,M-probational), Radiography, Respiratory Therapy, Social Work (B), Speech-Language Pathology *CEO:* Pres. Tilden J. LeMelle
Enroll: 11,422   (202) 282-7300

GEORGIA/HARVARD STREET CAMPUS
11th and Harvard Sts., N.W., Washington 20009 (federal) teacher education *Calendar:* Sem. plan *CEO:* Pres. Tilden J. LeMelle
      (202) 673-7021

MOUNT VERNON SQUARE CAMPUS
900 F St., N.W., Washington 20004 (federal) liberal arts *Calendar:* Sem. plan *CEO:* Pres. Tilden J. LeMelle
      (202) 282-7300

WESLEY THEOLOGICAL SEMINARY
4500 Massachusetts Ave., N.W., Washington 20016 *Type:* Private (United Methodist) graduate only *Accred.:* 1940/1990 (ATS); 1975/1991 (MSA) *Calendar:* Sem. plan *Degrees:* P, M, D, certificates *CEO:* Pres. G. Douglass Lewis
Enroll: 506   (202) 885-8600

FLORIDA

ART INSTITUTE OF FORT LAUDERDALE
1799 S.E. 17th St., Fort Lauderdale 33316-3000 *Type:* Private *Accred.:* 1971/1988 (ACCSCT) *Calendar:* Qtr. plan *Degrees:* A, B *CEO:* Pres. George Pry
(305) 463-3000

BARRY UNIVERSITY
11300 N.E. Second Ave., Miami Shores 33161-6695 *Type:* Private (Roman Catholic) *Accred.:* 1947/1993 (SACS-CC) *Calendar:* Sem. plan *Degrees:* B, M, D *Prof. Accred.:* Nurse Anesthesia Education, Nursing (B,M), Podiatry, Social Work (M) *CEO:* Pres. Jeanne O'Laughlin, O.P.
FTE Enroll: 4,491   (305) 899-3000

BAY AREA LEGAL ACADEMY
3924 Coconut Palm Dr., Tampa 33619 *Type:* Private business *Accred.:* 1979/1988 (ACISC) *Calendar:* Courses of varying lengths *Degrees:* A *CEO:* Dir. Isabelle Gibson
(813) 621-8074

BETHUNE-COOKMAN COLLEGE
640 Dr. Mary McLeod Bethune Blvd., Daytona Beach 32114-3099 *Type:* Private liberal arts *Accred.:* 1947/1990 (SACS-CC) *Calendar:* Sem. plan *Degrees:* B *Prof. Accred.:* Medical Technology, Teacher Education (e,s) *CEO:* Pres. Oswald P. Bronson, Sr.
FTE Enroll: 2,182   (904) 255-1401

BREVARD COMMUNITY COLLEGE
1519 Clearlake Rd., Cocoa 32922 *Type:* Public (district) junior *System:* Florida State Board of Community Colleges *Accred.:* 1963/1993 (SACS-CC) *Calendar:* Sem. plan *Degrees:* A *Prof. Accred.:* Dental Assisting, Dental Hygiene, EMT-Paramedic, Medical Laboratory Technology (AMA), Radiography, Respiratory Therapy *CEO:* Pres. Maxwell C. King
FTE Enroll: 12,913   (407) 632-1111

BRIARCLIFF COLLEGE
11401 S.W. 40th St., Miami 33165 *Type:* Private junior *Accred.:* 1987 (ACISC) *Calendar:* Courses of varying lengths *Degrees:* A *CEO:* Dir. Robert Hayward
(305) 551-9700

BROWARD COMMUNITY COLLEGE
225 E. Las Olas Blvd., Fort Lauderdale 33301 *Type:* Public (district) junior *System:* Florida State Board of Community Colleges *Accred.:* 1963/1993 (SACS-CC) *Calendar:* Sem. plan *Degrees:* A *Prof. Accred.:* Dental Assisting, Diagnostic Medical Sonography, EMT-Paramedic, Engineering Technology (electrical), Medical Assisting (AMA), Medical Laboratory Technology (AMA), Medical Record Technology, Nursing (A), Physical Therapy Assisting, Radiation Therapy Technology, Radiography, Respiratory Therapy, Respiratory Therapy Technology *CEO:* Pres. Willis N. Holcombe
FTE Enroll: 28,605   (305) 761-7409

CAREER CITY COLLEGE
1317 N.E. Fourth Ave., Fort Lauderdale 33304 *Type:* Private junior *Accred.:* 1986 (ACISC) *Calendar:* Courses of varying lengths *Degrees:* A, certificates, diplomas *CEO:* Pres. C.M. Fike, II
(305) 764-4660

BRANCH CAMPUS
2400 S.W. 13th St., Gainesville 32608 *Accred.:* 1989 (ACISC) *CEO:* Exec. Dir. Rhonda Olins
(904) 335-4000

CENTRAL FLORIDA COMMUNITY COLLEGE
P.O. Box 1388, Ocala 34478 *Type:* Public (district) junior *System:* Florida State Board of Community Colleges *Accred.:* 1964/1985 (SACS-CC) *Calendar:* Sem. plan *Degrees:* A *Prof. Accred.:* EMT-Paramedic, Nursing (A), Practical Nursing, Surgical Technology *CEO:* Pres. William J. Campion
FTE Enroll: 4,423   (904) 237-2111

CHIPOLA JUNIOR COLLEGE
3094 Indian Cir., Marianna 32446-2053 *Type:* Public (district) junior *System:* Florida State Board of Community Colleges *Accred.:* 1957/1988 (SACS-CC) *Calendar:* Sem. plan *Degrees:* A *CEO:* Pres. Jerry W. Kandzer
FTE Enroll: 1,804   (904) 526-2761

CLEARWATER CHRISTIAN COLLEGE
3400 Gulf-to-Bay Blvd., Clearwater 34619
Type: Private *Accred.:* 1984/1989 (SACS-CC) *Calendar:* 4-1-4 plan *Degrees:* A, B
CEO: Pres. George D. Youstra
FTE Enroll: 441 (813) 726-1153

COOPER ACADEMY OF COURT REPORTING
Ste. 110, 2247 Palm Beach Lakes Blvd., West Palm Beach 33401 *Type:* Private business *Accred.:* 1990 (ACISC) *Calendar:* Courses of varying lengths *Degrees:* A
CEO: Pres. Brenda J. Cooper
(407) 640-6999

DAYTONA BEACH COMMUNITY COLLEGE
P.O. Box 2811, Daytona Beach 32120-2811
Type: Public (district) junior *System:* Florida State Board of Community Colleges *Accred.:* 1963/1993 (SACS-CC) *Calendar:* Sem. plan *Degrees:* A *Prof. Accred.:* Dental Assisting, EMT-Paramedic, Medical Record Technology, Nursing (A), Respiratory Therapy, Respiratory Therapy Technology, Surgical Technology *CEO:* Pres. Philip R. Day, Jr.
FTE Enroll: 15,396 (904) 255-8131

ECKERD COLLEGE
4200 54th Ave. S., St. Petersburg 33711
Type: Private (Presbyterian) liberal arts
Accred.: 1963/1991 (SACS-CC) *Calendar:* 4-1-4 plan *Degrees:* B *CEO:* Pres. Peter H. Armacost
FTE Enroll: 2,261 (813) 867-1166

EDISON COMMUNITY COLLEGE
8099 College Pkwy., S.W., P.O. Box 06210, Fort Myers 33906-6210 *Type:* Public (district) junior *System:* Florida State Board of Community Colleges *Accred.:* 1964/1991 (SACS-CC) *Calendar:* Sem. plan *Degrees:* A *Prof. Accred.:* EMT-Paramedic, Respiratory Therapy *CEO:* Pres. Kenneth P. Walker
FTE Enroll: 6,783 (813) 489-9300

EDWARD WATERS COLLEGE
1658 Kings Rd., Jacksonville 32209 *Type:* Private (African Methodist Episcopal) liberal arts and teachers *Accred.:* 1979/1984 (SACS-CC warning) *Calendar:* Sem. plan *Degrees:* B *CEO:* Pres. Jesse Burns
FTE Enroll: 743 (904) 355-3030

EMBRY-RIDDLE AERONAUTICAL UNIVERSITY
600 S. Clyde Morris Blvd., Daytona Beach 32114-3900 *Type:* Private technological *Accred.:* 1968/1992 (SACS-CC) *Calendar:* Sem. plan *Degrees:* A, B, M *Prof. Accred.:* Engineering Technology (aerospace), Engineering (aerospace) *CEO:* Pres. Steven M. Sliwa
FTE Enroll: 11,385 (904) 226-6000

BRANCH CAMPUS
3200 N. Willow Creek Rd., Prescott, AZ 86301 *Prof. Accred.:* Engineering (aerospace) *CEO:* Dean Paul S. Daly
(602) 776-3728

FLAGLER CAREER INSTITUTE
3225 University Blvd. S., Jacksonville 32216-2736 *Type:* Private *Accred.:* 1982/1992 (ACCSCT) *Calendar:* Qtr. plan *Degrees:* A *Prof. Accred.:* Respiratory Therapy, Respiratory Therapy Technology *CEO:* Exec. Dir. Debra Schlofman
(904) 721-1622

FLAGLER COLLEGE
P.O. Box 1027, 74 King St., St. Augustine 32085-1027 *Type:* Private liberal arts *Accred.:* 1973/1988 (SACS-CC) *Calendar:* Sem. plan *Degrees:* B *CEO:* Pres. William L. Proctor
FTE Enroll: 1,389 (904) 829-6481

FLORIDA AGRICULTURAL AND MECHANICAL UNIVERSITY
400 Lee Hall, Tallahassee 32307 *Type:* Public (state) *System:* State University System of Florida *Accred.:* 1935/ 1988 (SACS-CC) *Calendar:* Sem. plan *Degrees:* B, M, D *Prof. Accred.:* Engineering Technology (civil/construction, electrical), Engineering (chemical, civil, electrical, industrial, mechanical), Journalism (B), Medical Record Administration, Nursing (B), Occupational Therapy, Physical Therapy, Respiratory Therapy, Social Work (B), Teacher Education (e,s,p)
CEO: Pres. Frederick S. Humphries
FTE Enroll: 9,910 (904) 599-3000

FLORIDA ATLANTIC UNIVERSITY
500 N.W. 20th St., Boca Raton 33431-0991
Type: Public (state) *System:* State University System of Florida *Accred.:* 1965/1992 (SACS-CC) *Calendar:* Sem. plan *Degrees:*

B, M, D *Prof. Accred.:* Business (B,M), Computer Science, Engineering (electrical, mechanical, ocean), Medical Technology, Music, Nursing (B,M), Public Administration, Social Work (B), Teacher Education (e,s,p) *CEO:* Pres. Anthony J. Catanese
FTE Enroll: 11,495   (407) 367-3000

FLORIDA BAPTIST THEOLOGICAL COLLEGE
P.O. Box 1306, Graceville 32440 *Type:* Private (Southern Baptist) *Accred.:* 1981/1987 (SACS-CC) *Calendar:* Sem. plan *Degrees:* B *CEO:* Pres. Thomas A. Kinchen
FTE Enroll: 456   (904) 263-3261

FLORIDA BIBLE COLLEGE
1701 N. Poinciana Blvd., Kissimmee 34758 *Type:* Private (Independent Fundamentalist Churches of America) *Accred.:* 1989 (AABC) *Calendar:* Sem. plan *Degrees:* A, B *CEO:* Acting Pres. Paul Goodnight
FTE Enroll: 102   (407) 933-4500

FLORIDA CAREER INSTITUTE
Ste. 200, 1685 Medical La., Fort Myers 33907 *Type:* Private business *Accred.:* 1984/1990 (ACISC) *Calendar:* Qtr. plan *Degrees:* A *CEO:* Exec. Dir. Sandra Duttko
      (813) 939-4766

FLORIDA CHRISTIAN COLLEGE
1011 Bill Beck Blvd., Kissimmee 34744 *Type:* Private (Christian Churches/Churches of Christ) *Accred.:* 1985/1990 (AABC); 1993 (SACS-CC candidate) *Calendar:* Qtr. plan *Degrees:* A, B *CEO:* Pres. A. Wayne Lowen
FTE Enroll: 145   (407) 847-8966

FLORIDA COLLEGE
119 Glen Arven Ave., Temple Terrace 33617 *Type:* Private junior *Accred.:* 1954/1988 (SACS-CC) *Calendar:* Sem. plan *Degrees:* A *CEO:* Pres. Charles G. Caldwell
FTE Enroll: 400   (813) 988-5131

FLORIDA COMMUNITY COLLEGE AT JACKSONVILLE
501 W. State St., Jacksonville 32202 *Type:* Public (district) junior *System:* Florida State Board of Community Colleges *Accred.:* 1969/1984 (SACS-CC) *Calendar:* Sem. plan *Degrees:* A *Prof. Accred.:* Dental Hygiene, EMT-Paramedic, Medical Laboratory Tech-

nology (AMA), Nursing (A), Respiratory Therapy *CEO:* Pres. Charles C. Spence
FTE Enroll: 30,619   (904) 632-3000

FLORIDA COMPUTER & BUSINESS SCHOOL
Ste. 200, 8300 Flagler St., Miami 33144 *Type:* Private business *Accred.:* 1985/1991 (ACISC) *Calendar:* Courses of varying lengths *Degrees:* A *CEO:* Pres. Carlos E. Rossie
      (305) 553-6065

FLORIDA INSTITUTE OF TECHNOLOGY
150 W. University Blvd., Melbourne 32901-6988 *Type:* Private technological *Accred.:* 1964/1985 (SACS-CC) *Calendar:* Sem. plan *Degrees:* A, B, M, D *Prof. Accred.:* Clinical Psychology, Engineering (aerospace, chemical, civil, computer, electrical, mechanical, ocean) *CEO:* Pres. Lynn E. Weaver
FTE Enroll: 4,982   (407) 768-8000

FLORIDA INTERNATIONAL UNIVERSITY
University Park, Miami 33199 *Type:* Public (state) liberal arts *System:* State University System of Florida *Accred.:* 1974/1990 (SACS-CC) *Calendar:* Sem. plan *Degrees:* A, B, M, D *Prof. Accred.:* Accounting (Type A,C), Business (B,M), Community Health/Preventive Medicine, Computer Science, Construction Education (B), Dietetics (coordinated), Engineering (civil, electrical, industrial, mechanical), Health Services Administration, Journalism (B,M), Landscape Architecture (M-initial), Medical Record Administration, Medical Technology, Nursing (B), Occupational Therapy, Physical Therapy, Public Administration, Social Work (B,M) *CEO:* Pres. Modesto A. Maidique
FTE Enroll: 17,945   (305) 348-2000

FLORIDA KEYS COMMUNITY COLLEGE
5901 W. Junior College Rd., Key West 33040 *Type:* Public (district) junior *System:* Florida State Board of Community Colleges *Accred.:* 1968/1992 (SACS-CC) *Calendar:* Sem. plan *Degrees:* A *CEO:* Pres. William A. Seeker
FTE Enroll: 1,012   (305) 296-9081

FLORIDA MEMORIAL COLLEGE
15800 N.W. 42nd Ave., Miami 33054 *Type:* Private (Baptist) liberal arts *Accred.:* 1951/

1992 (SACS-CC) *Calendar:* Sem. plan *Degrees:* B *CEO:* Pres. Albert E. Smith
FTE Enroll: 1,463   (305) 626-3600

FLORIDA SOUTHERN COLLEGE
111 Lake Hollingsworth Dr., Lakeland 33801 *Type:* Private (United Methodist) liberal arts *Accred.:* 1935/1988 (SACS-CC) *Calendar:* Sem. plan *Degrees:* B, M *CEO:* Pres. Thomas L. Reuschling
FTE Enroll: 2,496   (813) 680-4111

FLORIDA STATE UNIVERSITY
Tallahassee 32306 *Type:* Public (state) *System:* State University System of Florida *Accred.:* 1915/1984 (SACS-CC) *Calendar:* Sem. plan *Degrees:* A, B, M, D *Prof. Accred.:* Accounting (Type A,C), Art, Audiology, Business (B,M), Clinical Psychology, Computer Science, Dance, Engineering (chemical, civil, electrical, industrial, mechanical), Home Economics, Interior Design, Law, Librarianship, Music, Nursing (B,M), Planning (M), Public Administration, Recreation and Leisure Services, Rehabilitation Counseling, Social Work (B,M), Speech-Language Pathology, Teacher Education (e,s,p), Theatre *CEO:* Pres. Talbot D'Alemberte
FTE Enroll: 26,546   (904) 644-2525

FLORIDA TECHNICAL COLLEGE
8711 Lone Star Rd., Jacksonville 32211 *Type:* Private business *Accred.:* 1984/1988 (ACISC) *Calendar:* Courses of varying lengths *Degrees:* A, certificates, diplomas *CEO:* Dean Rufus J. Elliott
                              (904) 724-2229

FORT LAUDERDALE COLLEGE
1040 Bayview Dr., Fort Lauderdale 33304 *Type:* Private *Accred.:* 1968/1987 (ACISC) *Calendar:* Qtr. plan *Degrees:* A, B, M *CEO:* Dir. William P. Bedard
                              (305) 568-1600

GULF COAST COMMUNITY COLLEGE
5230 W. U.S. Hwy. 98, Panama City 32401-1041 *Type:* Public (district) junior *System:* Florida State Board of Community Colleges *Accred.:* 1962/1990 (SACS-CC) *Calendar:* Sem. plan *Degrees:* A *Prof. Accred.:* Dental Assisting, EMT-Paramedic, Nursing (A),

Radiography, Respiratory Therapy Technology *CEO:* Pres. Robert L. McSpadden
FTE Enroll: 3,933   (904) 769-1551

HILLSBOROUGH COMMUNITY COLLEGE
P.O. Box 31127, 39 Columbia Dr., Tampa 33631-3127 *Type:* Public (district) junior *System:* Florida State Board of Community Colleges *Accred.:* 1971/1986 (SACS-CC) *Calendar:* Sem. plan *Degrees:* A *Prof. Accred.:* Diagnostic Medical Sonography, EMT-Paramedic, Nuclear Medicine Technology, Radiation Therapy Technology, Radiography *CEO:* Pres. Andreas A. Paloumpis
FTE Enroll: 17,540   (813) 253-7000

HOBE SOUND BIBLE COLLEGE
P.O. Box 1065, 11305 S.E. Gomez Ave., Hobe Sound 33455 *Type:* Independent (Wesleyan) *Accred.:* 1986/1991 (AABC) *Calendar:* Sem. plan *Degrees:* A, B, certificates *CEO:* Pres. Robert Whitaker
FTE Enroll: 157   (407) 546-5534

INDIAN RIVER COMMUNITY COLLEGE
3209 Virginia Ave., Fort Pierce 34981-5599 *Type:* Public (district) junior *System:* Florida State Board of Community Colleges *Accred.:* 1963/1993 (SACS-CC) *Calendar:* Sem. plan *Degrees:* A *Prof. Accred.:* Dental Assisting, Dental Hygiene, Dental Laboratory Technology, EMT-Paramedic, Medical Laboratory Technology (AMA), Nursing (A), Radiography *CEO:* Pres. Edwin R. Massey
FTE Enroll: 9,530   (407) 462-4700

INTERNATIONAL ACADEMY OF MERCHANDISING AND DESIGN
211 S. Hoover St., Tampa 33609-9785 *Type:* Private *Accred.:* 1985/1989 (ACISC) *Calendar:* Sem. plan *Degrees:* A, B *Prof. Accred.:* Interior Design *CEO:* Pres. Michael Santoro
                              (813) 286-8585

INTERNATIONAL COLLEGE
2654 E. Tamiami Tr., Naples 33962-5790 *Type:* Private *Accred.:* 1990 (ACISC) *Calendar:* Sem. plan *Degrees:* A, B, M *CEO:* Pres. Terry McMahan
                              (813) 774-4700

BRANCH CAMPUS
Ste. 120, 8695 College Pkwy., Fort Myers 33919 *Accred.:* 1993 (ACISC) *CEO:* Pres. Terry McMahan
(813) 482-0019

INTERNATIONAL FINE ARTS COLLEGE
1737 N. Bayshore Dr., Miami 33132 *Type:* Private *Accred.:* 1979/1984 (SACS-CC) *Calendar:* Sem. plan *Degrees:* A *Prof. Accred.:* Interior Design *CEO:* Pres. Edward Porter
FTE Enroll: 667   (305) 373-4684

ITT TECHNICAL INSTITUTE
2600 Lake Lucien Dr., Maitland 32751-9754 *Type:* Private *Accred.:* 1990 (ACCSCT) *Calendar:* Courses of varying lengths *Degrees:* A, B *CEO:* Dir. Gary P. Cosgrove
(407) 660-2900

ITT TECHNICAL INSTITUTE
4809 Memorial Hwy., Tampa 33634-7350 *Type:* Private *Accred.:* 1983/1988 (ACCSCT) *Calendar:* Courses of varying lengths *Degrees:* A, B *CEO:* Dir. Dennis Alspaugh
(813) 885-2244

BRANCH CAMPUS
6600 Youngerman Cir., No. 10, Jacksonville 32244 *Accred.:* 1988 (ACCSCT) *CEO:* Dir. Carol Rouch
(904) 573-9100

JACKSONVILLE UNIVERSITY
2800 University Blvd. N., Jacksonville 32211 *Type:* Private *Accred.:* 1961/1993 (SACS-CC) *Calendar:* Sem. plan *Degrees:* B, M *Prof. Accred.:* Dance (associate), Music, Nursing (B) *CEO:* Pres. James J. Brady
FTE Enroll: 2,049   (904) 744-3950

JOHN B. STETSON UNIVERSITY
401 N. Woodland Blvd., DeLand 32720 *Type:* Private (Southern Baptist) *Accred.:* 1932/1991 (SACS-CC) *Calendar:* 4-1-4 plan *Degrees:* B, M, D *Prof. Accred.:* Law, Music *CEO:* Pres. H. Douglas Lee
FTE Enroll: 2,904   (904) 822-7000

JONES COLLEGE
5353 Arlington Expy., Jacksonville 32211-5588 *Type:* Private *Accred.:* 1957/1988 (ACISC) *Calendar:* Qtr. plan *Degrees:* A, B,

certificates, diplomas *CEO:* Pres. James M. Patch
(904) 743-1122

BRANCH CAMPUS
Ste. 100, 5975 Sunset Dr., South Miami 33143 *Accred.:* 1957/1988 (ACISC) *CEO:* Dir./Vice Pres. Juan Barreto
(305) 669-9606

KEISER COLLEGE
1500 N.W. 49th St., Fort Lauderdale 33309-3779 *Type:* Private *Accred.:* 1991 (SACS-CC) *Calendar:* Sem. plan *Degrees:* A, certificates *Prof. Accred.:* Medical Assisting, Medical Laboratory Technology *CEO:* Pres. Arthur Keiser
FTE Enroll: 953   (305) 776-4456

BRANCH CAMPUS
701 S. Babcock St., Melbourne 32901-1461 *Prof. Accred.:* Medical Assisting *CEO:* Exec. Dir. Carole A. Fuller
(407) 255-2255

BRANCH CAMPUS
1605 E. Plaza Dr., Tallahassee 32308 *Prof. Accred.:* Medical Assisting *CEO:* Exec. Dir. Maura Freeberg
(904) 942-9494

LAKE CITY COMMUNITY COLLEGE
Rte. 3, Box 7, Lake City 32055 *Type:* Public (district) junior *System:* Florida State Board of Community Colleges *Accred.:* 1964/1990 (SACS-CC) *Calendar:* Sem. plan *Degrees:* A *Prof. Accred.:* EMT-Paramedic, Medical Laboratory Technology (AMA) *CEO:* Pres. Muriel Kay Heimer
FTE Enroll: 3,574   (904) 752-1822

LAKE-SUMTER COMMUNITY COLLEGE
9501 U.S. Hwy. 441, Leesburg 34788-8751 *Type:* Public (district) junior *System:* Florida State Board of Community Colleges *Accred.:* 1965/1990 (SACS-CC) *Calendar:* Sem. plan *Degrees:* A *CEO:* Pres. Robert W. Westrick
FTE Enroll: 1,691   (904) 787-3747

LEGAL CAREER INSTITUTE
5225 W. Broward Blvd., Fort Lauderdale 33317 *Type:* Private business *Accred.:* 1985/1991 (ACISC) *Calendar:* Courses of varying

lengths *Degrees:* A, certificates, diplomas *CEO:* Vice Pres. Martha Metz
(305) 581-2223

BRANCH CAMPUS
Ste. 204, 7289 Garden Rd., Riviera Beach 33404 *Accred.:* 1989 (ACISC) *CEO:* Acad. Dir. Cynthia Dell Cioppia
(305) 848-2223

LYNN UNIVERSITY
3601 N. Military Tr., Boca Raton 33431 *Type:* Private *Accred.:* 1964/1991 (SACS-CC) *Calendar:* Sem. plan *Degrees:* A, B, M *Prof. Accred.:* Funeral Service Education *CEO:* Pres. Donald E. Ross
FTE Enroll: 1,173   (407) 994-0770

MANATEE COMMUNITY COLLEGE
5840 26th St. W., Bradenton 34207 *Type:* Public (district) junior *System:* Florida State Board of Community Colleges *Accred.:* 1963/1984 (SACS-CC) *Calendar:* Sem. plan *Degrees:* A *Prof. Accred.:* Nursing (A), Radiography, Respiratory Therapy *CEO:* Pres. Stephen J. Korcheck
FTE Enroll: 5,696   (813) 755-1511

MIAMI CHRISTIAN COLLEGE
500 N.E. First Ave., P.O. Box 019674, Miami 33101-9674 *Type:* Private (Evangelical Free Church) *Accred.:* 1975/1985 (AABC) *Calendar:* Sem. plan *Degrees:* A, B *CEO:* Pres. Kenneth M. Meyer
FTE Enroll: 238   (305) 577-4600

MIAMI-DADE COMMUNITY COLLEGE
300 N.E. Second Ave., Miami 33132 *Type:* Public (district) junior *System:* Florida State Board of Community Colleges *Accred.:* 1964/1985 (SACS-CC) *Calendar:* Sem. plan *Degrees:* A *Prof. Accred.:* Dental Hygiene, EMT-Paramedic, Electroneurodiagnostic Technology, Funeral Service Education, Medical Laboratory Technology (AMA), Medical Record Technology, Nursing (A), Physical Therapy Assisting, Radiation Therapy Technology, Radiography, Respiratory Therapy, Respiratory Therapy Technology *CEO:* Pres. Robert H. McCabe
FTE Enroll: 38,793   (305) 237-3221

NORTH FLORIDA JUNIOR COLLEGE
1000 Turner Davis Dr., Madison 32340 *Type:* Public (district) junior *System:* Florida

State Board of Community Colleges *Accred.:* 1963/1984 (SACS-CC) *Calendar:* Sem. plan *Degrees:* A *CEO:* Pres. William H. McCoy
FTE Enroll: 1,144   (904) 973-2288

NOVA SOUTHEASTERN UNIVERSITY
3301 College Ave., Fort Lauderdale 33314 *Type:* Private liberal arts and professional *Accred.:* 1971/1985 (SACS-CC) *Calendar:* Tri. plan *Degrees:* B, M, D *Prof. Accred.:* Clinical Psychology, Law, Marriage and Family Therapy (M-candidate), Psychology Internship, Speech-Language Pathology *CEO:* Pres. Stephen Feldman
FTE Enroll: 7,634   (305) 475-7300

OKALOOSA-WALTON COMMUNITY COLLEGE
100 College Blvd., Niceville 32578 *Type:* Public (district) junior *System:* Florida State Board of Community Colleges *Accred.:* 1965/1991 (SACS-CC) *Calendar:* Sem. plan *Degrees:* A *CEO:* Pres. James R. Richburg
FTE Enroll: 9,712   (904) 678-5111

ORLANDO COLLEGE
5500-5800 Diplomat Cir., Orlando 32810 *Type:* Private *Accred.:* 1957/1987 (ACISC) *Calendar:* Qtr. plan *Degrees:* A, B, M *CEO:* Dir. Ouida B. Kirby
Enroll: 1,902   (407) 628-5870

BRANCH CAMPUS
2411 Sand Lake Rd., Orlando 32809 *Accred.:* 1987 (ACISC) *CEO:* Pres. Barbara Huybers
(407) 851-2525

PALM BEACH ATLANTIC COLLEGE
1101 S. Flagler Dr., P.O. Box 24708, West Palm Beach 33416-4708 *Type:* Private liberal arts *Accred.:* 1972/1988 (SACS-CC) *Calendar:* Sem. plan *Degrees:* B, M *CEO:* Pres. Paul R. Corts
FTE Enroll: 1,867   (407) 650-7700

PALM BEACH COMMUNITY COLLEGE
4200 Congress Ave., Lake Worth 33461-4796 *Type:* Public (district) junior *System:* Florida State Board of Community Colleges *Accred.:* 1942/1991 (SACS-CC) *Calendar:* Sem. plan *Degrees:* A *Prof. Accred.:* Dental Assisting (prelim. provisional), Dental Hygiene, EMT-Paramedic, Occupational Therapy Assisting, Radiography, Respiratory

Therapy, Respiratory Therapy Technology
CEO: Pres. Edward M. Eissey
FTE Enroll: 12,622   (407) 439-8000

PASCO-HERNANDO COMMUNITY COLLEGE
36727 Blanton Rd., Dade City 33525-7599
Type: Public (district) junior *System:* Florida
State Board of Community Colleges *Ac-
cred.:* 1974/1989 (SACS-CC) *Calendar:*
Sem. plan *Degrees:* A *Prof. Accred.:* Dental
Hygiene, EMT-Paramedic *CEO:* Pres. Milton
O. Jones
FTE Enroll: 3,960   (904) 567-6701

PENSACOLA JUNIOR COLLEGE
1000 College Blvd., Pensacola 32504 *Type:*
Public (district) junior *System:* Florida State
Board of Community Colleges *Accred.:*
1956/1987 (SACS-CC) *Calendar:* Sem. plan
Degrees: A *Prof. Accred.:* Dental Assisting,
Dental Hygiene, Dental Laboratory Technology, EMT-Paramedic, Medical Assisting
(AMA), Medical Record Technology, Physical Therapy Assisting, Radiography, Respiratory Therapy, Respiratory Therapy Technology *CEO:* Pres. Horace E. Hartsell
FTE Enroll: 22,646   (904) 484-1000

PHILLIPS JUNIOR COLLEGE
2401 N. Harbor City Blvd., Melbourne
32935 *Type:* Private junior *Accred.:* 1966/
1987 (ACISC) *Calendar:* Qtr. plan *Degrees:*
A, certificates, diplomas *CEO:* Pres. Sharlee
Brittingham
                                 (407) 254-6459

BRANCH CAMPUS
1491 S. Nova Rd., Daytona Beach 32114
Accred.: 1989 (ACISC) *CEO:* Dir. Phillip
Rizzo
                                 (904) 255-1707

POLK COMMUNITY COLLEGE
999 Ave. H, N.E., Winter Haven 33881-
4299 *Type:* Public (district) junior *System:*
Florida State Board of Community Colleges
Accred.: 1965/1990 (SACS-CC) *Calendar:*
Sem. plan *Degrees:* A *Prof. Accred.:* EMT-
Paramedic, Nursing (A), Radiography *CEO:*
Pres. Maryly VanLeer Peck
FTE Enroll: 4,626   (813) 297-1000

PROSPECT HALL SCHOOL OF BUSINESS
2620 Hollywood Blvd., Hollywood 33020
Type: Private business *Accred.:* 1971/1986

(ACISC) *Calendar:* Qtr. plan *Degrees:* A
CEO: Dir. F. Moorghem
                                 (305) 923-8100

REGIONAL SEMINARY OF ST. VINCENT DE PAUL
10701 S. Military Tr., Boynton Beach
33436-4899 *Type:* Private (Roman Catholic)
graduate only *Accred.:* 1991 (ATS); 1968/
1990 (SACS-CC) *Calendar:* Sem. plan *Degrees:* M *CEO:* Rector/Pres. Pablo A.
Navarro
FTE Enroll: 80   (407) 732-4424

RINGLING SCHOOL OF ART AND DESIGN
2700 N. Tamiami Tr., Sarasota 34234 *Type:*
Private professional *Accred.:* 1979/1985
(SACS-CC) *Calendar:* Sem. plan *Degrees:*
B *Prof. Accred.:* Art, Interior Design *CEO:*
Pres. Arland F. Christ-Janer
FTE Enroll: 792   (813) 351-4614

ROLLINS COLLEGE
1000 Holt Ave., Winter Park 32789-4499
Type: Private liberal arts *Accred.:* 1927/1984
(SACS-CC) *Calendar:* 4-1-4 plan *Degrees:*
A, B, M *Prof. Accred.:* Business (M), Music
CEO: Pres. Rita Bornstein
FTE Enroll: 2,624   (407) 646-2000

ST. JOHN VIANNEY COLLEGE SEMINARY
2900 S.W. 87th Ave., Miami 33165 *Type:*
Private (Roman Catholic) for men *Accred.:*
1970/1986 (SACS-CC) *Calendar:* Sem. plan
Degrees: B *CEO:* Pres. George Garcia
FTE Enroll: 57   (305) 223-4561

ST. JOHNS RIVER COMMUNITY COLLEGE
5001 St. Johns Ave., Palatka 32177-3897
Type: Public (district) junior *System:* Florida
State Board of Community Colleges *Ac-
cred.:* 1963/1993 (SACS-CC) *Calendar:* Tri.
plan *Degrees:* A *CEO:* Pres. Robert L.
McLendon, Jr.
FTE Enroll: 2,809   (904) 328-1571

ST. LEO COLLEGE
P.O. Box 2187, St. Leo 33574 *Type:* Private
(Roman Catholic) liberal arts and teachers
Accred.: 1967/1991 (SACS-CC) *Calendar:*
Sem. plan *Degrees:* A, B, M (candidate)
Prof. Accred.: Social Work (B) *CEO:* Pres.
Frank M. Mouch
FTE Enroll: 5,179   (904) 588-8200

ST. PETERSBURG JUNIOR COLLEGE
P.O. Box 13489, St. Petersburg 33733-3489
Type: Public (district) junior *System:* Florida
State Board of Community Colleges *Ac-cred.:* 1931/1990 (SACS-CC) *Calendar:*
Sem. plan *Degrees:* A *Prof. Accred.:* Dental
Hygiene, EMT-Paramedic, Engineering
Technology (electrical), Funeral Service Ed-ucation (candidate), Medical Laboratory
Technology (AMA), Medical Record Tech-nology, Nursing (A), Physical Therapy As-sisting, Radiography, Respiratory Therapy,
Veterinary Technology *CEO:* Pres. Carl M.
Kuttler, Jr.
FTE Enroll: 13,496   (813) 341-3600

ST. THOMAS UNIVERSITY
16400 N.W. 32nd Ave., Miami 33054 *Type:*
Private (Roman Catholic) liberal arts *Ac-cred.:* 1968/1993 (SACS-CC) *Calendar:*
Sem. plan *Degrees:* B, M, D *Prof. Accred.:*
Law (ABA only) (provisional) *CEO:* Interim
Pres. Edward J. McCarthy
FTE Enroll: 2,255   (305) 625-6000

SANTA FE COMMUNITY COLLEGE
3000 N.W. 83rd St., Gainesville 32606
Type: Public (district) junior *System:* Florida
State Board of Community Colleges *Ac-cred.:* 1968/1992 (SACS-CC) *Calendar:*
Sem. plan *Degrees:* A *Prof. Accred.:* Dental
Assisting, Dental Hygiene, EMT-Paramedic,
Engineering Technology (computer), Nu-clear Medicine Technology, Nursing (A),
Radiation Therapy Technology, Radiogra-phy, Respiratory Therapy *CEO:* Pres.
Lawrence W. Tyree
FTE Enroll: 10,188   (904) 395-5000

SEMINOLE COMMUNITY COLLEGE
100 Weldon Blvd., Sanford 32773-6199
Type: Public (district) junior *System:* Florida
State Board of Community Colleges *Ac-cred.:* 1969/1993 (SACS-CC) *Calendar:*
Sem. plan *Degrees:* A *Prof. Accred.:* EMT-Paramedic, Interior Design, Nursing (A),
Physical Therapy Assisting, Respiratory
Therapy, Respiratory Therapy Technology
CEO: Pres. Earl S. Weldon
FTE Enroll: 10,196   (407) 323-1450

SOUTH COLLEGE
1760 N. Congress Ave., West Palm Beach
33409 *Type:* Private junior *Accred.:* 1984/

1989 (ACISC); 1985/1990 (SACS-CC) *Cal-endar:* Qtr. plan *Degrees:* A *Prof. Accred.:*
Medical Assisting (AMA) *CEO:* Dir. Charles
W. Stewart
FTE Enroll: 308   (407) 697-9200

SOUTH FLORIDA COMMUNITY COLLEGE
600 W. College Dr., Avon Park 33825 *Type:*
Public (district) junior *System:* Florida State
Board of Community Colleges *Accred.:*
1968/1992 (SACS-CC) *Calendar:* Sem.
plan *Degrees:* A *CEO:* Pres. Catherine P.
Cornelius
FTE Enroll: 7,727   (813) 453-6661

SOUTHEASTERN ACADEMY, INC.
233 Academy Dr., P.O. Box 421768,
Kissimmee 32742-1768 *Type:* Private com-bination home study and resident *Accred.:*
1986 (ACCSCT); 1977/1992 (NHSC) *Cal-endar:* Courses of varying lengths *Degrees:*
A, B, diplomas *CEO:* Pres. David L. Peoples
          (407) 847-4444

PEOPLES COLLEGE OF INDEPENDENT STUDIES
233 Academy Dr., P.O. Box 421768,
Kissimmee 34742-1768 *CEO:* Pres. David
L. Peoples
          (407) 847-4444

SOUTHEASTERN COLLEGE OF THE ASSEMBLIES OF
GOD
1000 Longfellow Blvd., Lakeland 33801
Type: Private (Assemblies of God) *Accred.:*
1954/1992 (AABC); 1986/1991 (SACS-CC)
Calendar: Sem. plan *Degrees:* B, diplomas
CEO: Pres. James L. Hennesy
FTE Enroll: 1,119   (813) 665-4404

SOUTHEASTERN UNIVERSITY OF THE HEALTH
SCIENCES
1750 N.E. 168th St., North Miami Beach
33162-3097 *Type:* Private professional *Cal-endar:* Sem. plan *Degrees:* B, P, M, D *Prof.
Accred.:* Optometry, Osteopathy *CEO:* Pres.
Morton Terry, D.O.
          (305) 949-4000

SOUTHERN COLLEGE
5600 Lake Underhill Rd., Orlando 32807
Type: Private junior *Accred.:* 1970/1988
(ACISC) *Calendar:* Qtr. plan *Degrees:* A,
certificates, diplomas *Prof. Accred.:* Dental

Assisting, Dental Laboratory Technology, Interior Design *CEO:* Pres. Daniel F. Moore
(407) 273-1000

TALLAHASSEE COMMUNITY COLLEGE
444 Appleyard Dr., Tallahassee 32304-2895
Type: Public (district) junior *System:* Florida State Board of Community Colleges *Accred.:* 1969/1984 (SACS-CC) *Calendar:* Sem. plan *Degrees:* A *Prof. Accred.:* Dental Hygiene, EMT-Paramedic, Respiratory Therapy *CEO:* Pres. James H. Hinson, Jr.
FTE Enroll: 7,037   (904) 488-9200

TALMUDIC COLLEGE OF FLORIDA
4014 Chase Ave., Miami Beach 32304-2895
Type: Private professional *Accred.:* 1977/1989 (AARTS) *Calendar:* Sem. plan *Degrees:* B, P, M, D *CEO:* Pres. Y. Zweig
Enroll: 55   (305) 534-7050

TAMPA COLLEGE
15064 U.S. Hwy. 19 N., Clearwater 34624
Type: Private *Accred.:* 1971/1989 (ACISC) *Calendar:* Qtr. plan *Degrees:* A, B, M *CEO:* Pres. Mark Page
(813) 530-9495

BRANCH CAMPUS
1200 U.S. Hwy. 98 S., Lakeland 33801
Accred.: 1990 (ACISC) *CEO:* Dir. Frances Morris
(813) 686-1444

TAMPA COLLEGE
3319 W. Hillsborough Ave., Tampa 33614
Type: Private *Accred.:* 1966/1987 (ACISC) *Calendar:* Qtr. plan *Degrees:* A, B, M *CEO:* Pres. David C. Zorn
(813) 879-6000

BRANCH CAMPUS
Sabal Business Ctr., 3924 Coconut Palm Dr., Tampa 33619 *Accred.:* 1990 (ACISC) *CEO:* Dir. Stan Banks
(813) 621-0041

UNIVERSITY OF CENTRAL FLORIDA
4000 Central Florida Blvd., Orlando 32816
Type: Public (state) liberal arts and professional *System:* State University System of Florida *Accred.:* 1970/1985 (SACS-CC) *Calendar:* Sem. plan *Degrees:* A, B, M, D *Prof. Accred.:* Accounting (Type A,C), Business (B,M), Computer Science, Engineering

Technology (aerospace, civil/construction, computer, electrical, environmental/sanitary, industrial, mechanical), Engineering (aerospace, civil, computer, electrical, environmental/sanitary, industrial, mechanical), Medical Record Administration, Medical Technology, Music, Nursing (B), Radiography, Respiratory Therapy, Social Work (B,M-candidate), Speech-Language Pathology, Teacher Education (e,s,p) *CEO:* Pres. John C. Hitt
FTE Enroll: 24,831   (407) 823-2000

UNIVERSITY OF FLORIDA
226 Tigert Hall, Gainesville 32611 *Type:* Public (state) *System:* State University System of Florida *Accred.:* 1913/1993 (SACS-CC) *Calendar:* Sem. plan *Degrees:* A, B, M, D *Prof. Accred.:* Accounting (Type A,C), Art, Audiology, Business (B,M), Clinical Psychology, Construction Education (B), Counseling, Counseling Psychology, Dental Public Health, Dentistry, Engineering Technology (surveying), Engineering (aerospace, agricultural, chemical, civil, computer, electrical, engineering physics/science, environmental/ sanitary, industrial, materials, mechanical, nuclear, ocean), Forestry, General Dentistry, Health Services Administration, Interior Design, Journalism (B,M), Landscape Architecture (B,M-initial), Law, Medical Technology, Medicine, Music, Nursing (B,M), Occupational Therapy, Ophthalmic Medical Technology, Oral and Maxillofacial Surgery, Orthodontics, Pediatric Dentistry, Periodontics, Physical Therapy, Physician Assisting, Planning (M), Psychology Internship, Recreation and Leisure Services, Rehabilitation Counseling, Speech-Language Pathology, Teacher Education (e,s,p), Theatre, Veterinary Medicine (limited) *CEO:* Pres. John V. Lombardi
FTE Enroll: 32,651   (904) 392-3261

UNIVERSITY OF MIAMI
P.O. Box 248006, Coral Gables 33124 *Type:* Private *Accred.:* 1940/1987 (SACS-CC) *Calendar:* Sem. plan *Degrees:* B, M, D *Prof. Accred.:* Accounting (Type A,C), Business (B,M), Clinical Psychology, Community Health/Preventive Medicine, Counseling Psychology (provisional), Cytotechnology, Diagnostic Medical Sonography, Engineering (architectural, civil, computer, electrical,

industrial, mechanical), General Practice Residency, Health Services Administration, Histologic Technology, Journalism (B,M), Law, Medicine, Music, Nuclear Medicine Technology, Nursing (B,M), Oral and Maxillofacial Surgery, Physical Therapy, Psychology Internship, Radiography, Teacher Education (e,s,p), Theatre (associate) *CEO:* Pres. Edward T. Foote, II
FTE Enroll: 15,398   (305) 284-2211

UNIVERSITY OF NORTH FLORIDA
4567 St. Johns Bluff Rd., S., Jacksonville 32224-2645 *Type:* Public (state) *System:* State University System of Florida *Accred.:* 1974/1989 (SACS-CC) *Calendar:* Sem. plan *Degrees:* B, M, D (candidate) *Prof. Accred.:* Business (B,M), Computer Science, Nursing (B), Teacher Education (e,s,p) *CEO:* Pres. Adam W. Herbert, Jr.
FTE Enroll: 6,614   (904) 646-2666

THE UNIVERSITY OF SARASOTA
5250 17th St., Sarasota 34235 *Type:* Private professional; graduate only *Accred.:* 1990 (SACS-CC) *Calendar:* Sem. plan *Degrees:* M, D *CEO:* C.E.O. and Provost Ned Wilson
FTE Enroll: 154   (813) 379-0404

UNIVERSITY OF SOUTH FLORIDA
4202 Fowler Ave., Tampa 33620-6100 *Type:* Public (state) *System:* State University System of Florida *Accred.:* 1963/1984 (SACS-CC) *Calendar:* Sem. plan *Degrees:* A, B, M, D *Prof. Accred.:* Accounting (Type A,C), Audiology, Business (B,M), Clinical Psychology, Computer Science, Engineering (chemical, civil, computer, electrical, industrial, mechanical), Journalism (B,M), Librarianship, Medicine, Music, Nursing (B,M), Psychology Internship, Public Administration, Public Health, Rehabilitation Counseling, Social Work (B,M), Speech-Language Pathology, Teacher Education (e,s,p), Theatre *CEO:* Pres. Betty Castor
FTE Enroll: 31,715   (813) 974-2011

UNIVERSITY OF TAMPA
401 W. Kennedy Blvd., Tampa 33606-1490 *Type:* Private liberal arts *Accred.:* 1951/1986 (SACS-CC) *Calendar:* Sem. plan *Degrees:*

A, B, M *Prof. Accred.:* Music, Nursing (B)
CEO: Pres. David G. Ruffer
FTE Enroll: 1,922   (813) 253-3333

THE UNIVERSITY OF WEST FLORIDA
11000 University Pkwy., Pensacola 32514-5750 *Type:* Public (state) liberal arts and professional *System:* State University System of Florida *Accred.:* 1969/1985 (SACS-CC) *Calendar:* Sem. plan *Degrees:* A, B, M *Prof. Accred.:* Engineering (systems), Journalism (B,M), Medical Technology, Music, Nursing (B), Public Administration, Social Work (B), Teacher Education (e,s,p) *CEO:* Pres. Morris L. Marx
FTE Enroll: 6,374   (904) 474-2000

VALENCIA COMMUNITY COLLEGE
P.O. Box 3028, Orlando 32802-3028 *Type:* Public (district) junior *System:* Florida State Board of Community Colleges *Accred.:* 1969/1993 (SACS-CC) *Calendar:* Sem. plan *Degrees:* A *Prof. Accred.:* Dental Hygiene, Diagnostic Medical Sonography, EMT-Paramedic, Medical Laboratory Technology (AMA), Nuclear Medicine Technology, Nursing (A), Radiation Therapy Technology, Radiography, Respiratory Therapy *CEO:* Pres. Paul C. Gianini, Jr.
FTE Enroll: 14,863   (407) 299-5000

WARD STONE COLLEGE
9020 S.W. 137th Ave., Miami 33186 *Type:* Private business *Accred.:* 1989 (ACISC) *Calendar:* Courses of varying lengths *Degrees:* A *CEO:* Pres. Leo Orsino
                              (305) 386-9900

WARNER SOUTHERN COLLEGE
5301 U.S. Hwy. 27 S., Lake Wales 33853-8725 *Type:* Private liberal arts *Accred.:* 1977/1992 (SACS-CC) *Calendar:* Sem. plan *Degrees:* A, B *CEO:* Pres. Gregory V. Hall
FTE Enroll: 496   (813) 638-1426

WEBBER COLLEGE
P.O. Box 96, Babson Park 33827 *Type:* Private business *Accred.:* 1969/1988 (SACS-CC) *Calendar:* Sem. plan *Degrees:* A, B *CEO:* Pres. Rex R. Yentes
FTE Enroll: 396   (813) 638-1431

GEORGIA

ABRAHAM BALDWIN AGRICULTURAL COLLEGE
P.O. Box 1, ABAC Sta., Tifton 31794-2601
Type: Public (state) junior *System:* Board of
Regents of the University System of Georgia
Accred.: 1953/1986 (SACS-CC) *Calendar:*
Qtr. plan *Degrees:* A *Prof. Accred.:* Nursing
(A) *CEO:* Pres. Harold J. Loyd
FTE Enroll: 2,531   (912) 386-3236

AGNES SCOTT COLLEGE
141 E. College Ave., Decatur 30030 *Type:*
Private liberal arts for women *Accred.:* 1907/
1984 (SACS-CC) *Calendar:* Sem. plan *Degrees:* B, M *CEO:* Pres. Ruth A. Schmidt
FTE Enroll: 572   (404) 371-6000

ALBANY STATE COLLEGE
504 College Dr., Albany 31705-2794 *Type:*
Public (state) liberal arts and professional
System: Board of Regents of the University
System of Georgia *Accred.:* 1951/1988
(SACS-CC) *Calendar:* Qtr. plan *Degrees:* B,
M *Prof. Accred.:* Nursing (B,M), Teacher
Education (e,s) *CEO:* Pres. Billy C. Black
FTE Enroll: 3,257   (912) 430-4600

THE AMERICAN COLLEGE FOR THE APPLIED
ARTS
3330 Peachtree Rd., N.E., Atlanta 30326
Type: Private professional *Accred.:* 1987/
1993 (SACS-CC) *Calendar:* Qtr. plan *De-
grees:* A, B *Prof. Accred.:* Interior Design
CEO: Pres. Rafael A. Lago
FTE Enroll: 1,925   (404) 231-9000

BRANCH CAMPUS
1651 Westwood Blvd., Los Angeles, CA
90024 *CEO:* Pres. Vicki McCarrell
                    (310) 477-8640

BRANCH CAMPUS
110 Marylebone High St., London, England, United Kingdom W1M 3DB *CEO:*
Pres. Mark Barnette
                    [44] (071) 486-1772

ANDREW COLLEGE
413 College St., Cuthbert 31740-1395 *Type:*
Private (United Methodist) junior *Accred.:*
1927/1986 (SACS-CC) *Calendar:* Qtr. plan
Degrees: A *CEO:* Pres. Kirk Treible
FTE Enroll: 306   (912) 732-2171

ARMSTRONG STATE COLLEGE
11935 Abercorn Ext., Savannah 31419-1997
Type: Public (state) liberal arts *System:*
Board of Regents of the University System
of Georgia *Accred.:* 1940/1992 (SACS-CC)
Calendar: Qtr. plan *Degrees:* A, B *Prof. Ac-
cred.:* Computer Science, Dental Hygiene,
Medical Technology, Music, Nursing (A,B),
Radiography, Respiratory Therapy, Teacher
Education (e,s) *CEO:* Pres. Robert A. Burnett
FTE Enroll: 5,187   (912) 927-5211

THE ART INSTITUTE OF ATLANTA
3376 Peachtree Rd., N.E., Atlanta 30326
Type: Private *Accred.:* 1985/1993 (SACS-
CC) *Calendar:* Qtr. plan *Degrees:* A *CEO:*
Pres. Hal R. Griffith
FTE Enroll: 1,422   (404) 266-1341

ATHENS AREA TECHNICAL INSTITUTE
U.S. Hwy. 29 N., Athens 30610 *Type:* Public
(state) 2-year *Accred.:* 1988/1993 (SACS-
CC) *Calendar:* Qtr. plan *Degrees:* A *Prof.
Accred.:* Engineering Technology (electri-
cal), Radiography, Respiratory Therapy,
Respiratory Therapy Technology *CEO:* Pres.
Kenneth C. Easom
FTE Enroll: 1,781   (706) 542-8050

ATLANTA CHRISTIAN COLLEGE
2605 Ben Hill Rd., East Point 30344 *Type:*
Private (Christian Churches/Churches of
Christ) *Accred.:* 1965/1984 (AABC); 1990
(SACS-CC) *Calendar:* Sem. plan *Degrees:*
A, B *CEO:* Pres. Edwin Groover
FTE Enroll: 235   (404) 761-8861

THE ATLANTA COLLEGE OF ART
1280 Peachtree St., N.E., Atlanta 30309
Type: Private professional *Accred.:* 1969/
1992 (SACS-CC) *Calendar:* Sem. plan *Degrees:* B *Prof. Accred.:* Art *CEO:* Pres. Ellen
L. Meyer
FTE Enroll: 505   (404) 898-1164

ATLANTA METROPOLITAN COLLEGE
1630 Stewart Ave., S.W., Atlanta 30310
Type: Public (state) junior *System:* Board of
Regents of the University System of Georgia
Accred.: 1976/1991 (SACS-CC) *Calendar:*

Qtr. plan *Degrees:* A *CEO:* Pres. Edwin A. Thompson
FTE Enroll: 1,475   (404) 756-4441

AUGUSTA COLLEGE
2500 Walton Way, Augusta 30904-2200 *Type:* Public (state) liberal arts *System:* Board of Regents of the University System of Georgia *Accred.:* 1926/1991 (SACS-CC) *Calendar:* Qtr. plan *Degrees:* A, B, M *Prof. Accred.:* Music, Nursing (A), Teacher Education (e,s) *CEO:* Pres. William A. Bloodworth
FTE Enroll: 5,009   (706) 737-1400

AUGUSTA TECHNICAL INSTITUTE
3116 Deans Bridge Rd., Augusta 30906 *Type:* Public (state) 2-year *Accred.:* 1988/1993 (SACS-CC) *Calendar:* Qtr. plan *Degrees:* A *Prof. Accred.:* Dental Assisting, Dental Laboratory Technology, Engineering Technology (mechanical), Medical Assisting (AMA), Medical Laboratory Technology (AMA), Practical Nursing, Respiratory Therapy Technology *CEO:* Pres. Jack B. Patrick
FTE Enroll: 1,987   (706) 771-4000

BAINBRIDGE COLLEGE
Hwy. 84 E., Bainbridge 31717 *Type:* Public (state) junior *System:* Board of Regents of the University System of Georgia *Accred.:* 1975/1990 (SACS-CC) *Calendar:* Qtr. plan *Degrees:* A *CEO:* Pres. Edward D. Mobley
FTE Enroll: 920   (912) 248-2500

BAUDER COLLEGE
Phipps Plaza, 3500 Peachtree Rd., N.E., Atlanta 30326-9975 *Type:* Private *Accred.:* 1973/1985 (ACCSCT); 1985/1990 (SACS-CC) *Calendar:* Qtr. plan *Degrees:* A *CEO:* Exec. Dir. Robert W. Schulte
FTE Enroll: 410   (404) 237-7573

BERRY COLLEGE
39 Mount Berry Sta., Rome 30149-0039 *Type:* Private liberal arts *Accred.:* 1957/1988 (SACS-CC) *Calendar:* Sem. plan *Degrees:* B, M *Prof. Accred.:* Music, Teacher Education (e,s) *CEO:* Pres. Gloria M. Shatto
FTE Enroll: 1,693   (706) 232-5374

BRENAU UNIVERSITY
One Centennial Cir., Gainesville 30501 *Type:* Private liberal arts *Accred.:* 1947/1991 (SACS-CC) *Calendar:* Qtr. plan *Degrees:* B,

M *Prof. Accred.:* Interior Design, Nursing (B) *CEO:* Pres. John S. Burd
FTE Enroll: 2,120   (404) 534-6299

BREWTON-PARKER COLLEGE
P.O. Box 197, Mount Vernon 30445-0197 *Type:* Private (Southern Baptist) liberal arts *Accred.:* 1962/1991 (SACS-CC) *Calendar:* Qtr. plan *Degrees:* A, B *Prof. Accred.:* Music (associate) *CEO:* Pres. Y. Lynn Holmes
FTE Enroll: 1,934   (912) 583-2241

BRUNSWICK COLLEGE
Altama Ave. at Fourth St., Brunswick 31523 *Type:* Public (state) junior *System:* Board of Regents of the University System of Georgia *Accred.:* 1965/1991 (SACS-CC) *Calendar:* Qtr. plan *Degrees:* A *Prof. Accred.:* Medical Laboratory Technology (AMA), Nursing (A), Radiography *CEO:* Pres. Dorothy L. Lord
FTE Enroll: 1,613   (912) 264-7235

CHATTAHOCHEE TECHNICAL INSTITUTE
980 S. Cobb Dr., Marietta 30060 *Type:* Public (state) 2-year *Accred.:* 1988/1993 (SACS-CC) *Calendar:* Qtr. plan *Degrees:* A *Prof. Accred.:* Engineering Technology (electrical, electromechanical) *CEO:* Pres. Harlon D. Crimm
FTE Enroll: 1,641   (404) 528-4500

CLARK ATLANTA UNIVERSITY
James P. Brawley Dr. at Fair St., Atlanta 30314 *Type:* Private (United Methodist) *Accred.:* 1932/1990 (SACS-CC) *Calendar:* Sem. plan *Degrees:* B, M, D *Prof. Accred.:* Business (M), Librarianship, Medical Record Administration, Social Work (B,M) *CEO:* Pres. Thomas W. Cole, Jr.
FTE Enroll: 5,128   (404) 880-8000

CLAYTON STATE COLLEGE
P.O. Box 285, Morrow 30260 *Type:* Public (state) *System:* Board of Regents of the University System of Georgia *Accred.:* 1971/1986 (SACS-CC) *Calendar:* Qtr. plan *Degrees:* A, B *Prof. Accred.:* Dental Hygiene, Nursing (A,B) *CEO:* Pres. Richard Skinner
FTE Enroll: 5,675   (404) 961-3400

COLUMBIA THEOLOGICAL SEMINARY
P.O. Box 520, 701 Columbia Dr., Decatur 30031 *Type:* Private (Presbyterian) graduate

only *Accred.:* 1938/1993 (ATS); 1983/1993 (SACS-CC) *Calendar:* 4-1-4 plan *Degrees:* M, D *CEO:* Pres. Douglas W. Oldenburg
FTE Enroll: 310   (404) 378-8821

COLUMBUS COLLEGE
4225 University Ave., Columbus 31907-5645*Type:* Public (state) liberal arts *System:* Board of Regents of the University System of Georgia *Accred.:* 1963/1985 (SACS-CC) *Calendar:* Qtr. plan *Degrees:* A, B, M *Prof. Accred.:* Dental Hygiene, Medical Laboratory Technology (AMA), Medical Technology, Music, Nursing (A,B), Respiratory Therapy, Teacher Education (e,s,p) *CEO:* Pres. Frank D. Brown
FTE Enroll: 5,241   (706) 568-2001

COLUMBUS TECHNICAL INSTITUTE
928 45th St., Columbus 31904-6572 *Type:* Public (state) 2-year *Accred.:* 1990 (SACS-CC) *Calendar:* Qtr. plan *Degrees:* A *Prof. Accred.:* Medical Assisting (AMA) *CEO:* Pres. W.G. Hartline
FTE Enroll: 1,440   (706) 649-1874

COVENANT COLLEGE
Scenic Hwy., Lookout Mountain 30750 *Type:* Private (Reformed Presbyterian) liberal arts *Accred.:* 1971/1987 (SACS-CC) *Calendar:* Sem. plan *Degrees:* A, B, M *CEO:* Pres. Frank A. Brock
FTE Enroll: 840   (706) 820-1560

DALTON COLLEGE
213 N. College Dr., Dalton 30720 *Type:* Public (state) junior *System:* Board of Regents of the University System of Georgia *Accred.:* 1969/1984 (SACS-CC) *Calendar:* Qtr. plan *Degrees:* A *Prof. Accred.:* Medical Laboratory Technology (AMA), Nursing (A) *CEO:* Pres. Derrell C. Roberts
FTE Enroll: 2,403   (706) 272-4436

DARTON COLLEGE
2400 Gillionville Rd., Albany 31707-3098 *Type:* Public (state) junior *System:* Board of Regents of the University System of Georgia *Accred.:* 1968/1993 (SACS-CC) *Calendar:* Qtr. plan *Degrees:* A *Prof. Accred.:* Dental Hygiene, Medical Laboratory Technology (AMA), Nursing (A) *CEO:* Pres. Peter J. Sireno
FTE Enroll: 2,096   (912) 430-6000

DEKALB COLLEGE
3251 Panthersville Rd., Decatur 30034 *Type:* Public (state) junior *System:* Board of Regents of the University System of Georgia *Accred.:* 1965/1992 (SACS-CC) *Calendar:* Qtr. plan *Degrees:* A *Prof. Accred.:* Dental Hygiene, Nursing (A) *CEO:* Pres. Marvin M. Cole
FTE Enroll: 12,863   (404) 244-5090

DEKALB TECHNICAL INSTITUTE
495 N. Indian Creek Dr., Clarkston 30021 *Type:* Public (state) 2-year *Accred.:* 1965/1992 (SACS-CC) *Calendar:* Qtr. plan *Degrees:* A *Prof. Accred.:* Engineering Technology (electrical, electromechanical), Medical Laboratory Technology (AMA), Surgical Technology *CEO:* Pres. Paul M. Starnes
FTE Enroll: 4,048   (404) 297-9522

DEVRY INSTITUTE OF TECHNOLOGY, ATLANTA
250 N. Arcadia Ave., Decatur 30030 *Type:* Private *Accred.:* 1981/1992 (NCA)* *Calendar:* Sem. plan *Degrees:* A, B, certificates, diplomas *Prof. Accred.:* Engineering Technology (electrical) *CEO:* Pres. Ronald W. Bush
                                    (404) 292-7900

* Indirect accreditation through DeVry Institutes.

EAST GEORGIA COLLEGE
237 Thigpen Dr., Swainsboro 30401 *Type:* Public (state) junior *System:* Board of Regents of the University System of Georgia *Accred.:* 1975/1990 (SACS-CC) *Calendar:* Qtr. plan *Degrees:* A *CEO:* Pres. Jeremiah J. Ashcroft
FTE Enroll: 779   (912) 237-7831

EMMANUEL COLLEGE
212 Spring St., P.O. Box 129, Franklin Springs 30639 *Type:* Private (Pentacostal Holiness Church) *Accred.:* 1967/1991 (SACS-CC) *Calendar:* Qtr. plan *Degrees:* A, B *CEO:* Pres. David R. Hopkins
FTE Enroll: 559   (706) 245-7226

EMORY UNIVERSITY
1380 S. Oxford Rd., Atlanta 30322 *Type:* Private (United Methodist) *Accred.:* 1938/1993 (ATS); 1917/1993 (SACS-CC) *Calendar:* Sem. plan *Degrees:* A, B, M, D *Prof. Accred.:* Anesthesiologist Assisting, Business (B,M), Clinical Psychology, Dietetics

(internship), Law, Medical Technology, Medicine, Music, Nursing (B,M), Oral Pathology, Oral and Maxillofacial Surgery, Physical Therapy, Physician Assisting, Psychology Internship, Public Health, Radiography *CEO:* Interim Pres. Billy E. Frye
FTE Enroll: 9,503   (404) 727-6123

FLOYD COLLEGE
P.O. Box 1864, Rome 30162-1864 *Type:* Public (state) junior *System:* Board of Regents of the University System of Georgia *Accred.:* 1972/1987 (SACS-CC) *Calendar:* Qtr. plan *Degrees:* A *Prof. Accred.:* Nursing (A) *CEO:* Pres. H. Lynn Cundiff
FTE Enroll: 3,235   (706) 802-5000

FORT VALLEY STATE COLLEGE
1005 State College Dr., Fort Valley 31030-3298 *Type:* Public (state) liberal arts and teachers *System:* Board of Regents of the University System of Georgia *Accred.:* 1951/1990 (SACS-CC) *Calendar:* Qtr. plan *Degrees:* A, B, M *Prof. Accred.:* Engineering Technology (electrical), Home Economics, Rehabilitation Counseling, Teacher Education (e,s,p), Veterinary Technology (probational) *CEO:* Pres. Oscar L. Prater
FTE Enroll: 2,748   (912) 825-6315

GAINESVILLE COLLEGE
Mundy Mill Rd., P.O. Box 1358, Gainesville 30503-1358 *Type:* Public (state) junior *System:* Board of Regents of the University System of Georgia *Accred.:* 1968/1992 (SACS-CC) *Calendar:* Qtr. plan *Degrees:* A *Prof. Accred.:* Dental Assisting, Dental Hygiene *CEO:* Pres. J. Foster Watkins
FTE Enroll: 2,309   (404) 535-6239

GEORGIA COLLEGE
C.P.O. Box 020, Milledgeville 31061 *Type:* Public (state) liberal arts *System:* Board of Regents of the University System of Georgia *Accred.:* 1925/1984 (SACS-CC) *Calendar:* Qtr. plan *Degrees:* A, B, M *Prof. Accred.:* Music, Nursing (B,M), Teacher Education (e,s) *CEO:* Pres. Edwin G. Speir, Jr.
FTE Enroll: 4,992   (912) 453-5350

GEORGIA INSTITUTE OF TECHNOLOGY
225 North Ave., N.W., Atlanta 30332-0325 *Type:* Public (state) technological *System:* Board of Regents of the University System

of Georgia *Accred.:* 1923/1984 (SACS-CC) *Calendar:* Qtr. plan *Degrees:* B, M, D *Prof. Accred.:* Business (B,M), Computer Science, Engineering (aerospace, ceramic, chemical, civil, computer, electrical, engineering mechanics, environmental/sanitary, industrial, materials, mechanical, nuclear, textile), Planning (M) *CEO:* Pres. John Patrick Crecine
FTE Enroll: 12,946   (404) 894-2000

GEORGIA MILITARY COLLEGE
201 E. Greene St., Milledgeville 31061-3398 *Type:* Public junior *Accred.:* 1940/1987 (SACS-CC) *Calendar:* Qtr. plan *Degrees:* A *CEO:* Pres. Peter J. Boylan
FTE Enroll: 2,419   (912) 454-2700

GEORGIA SOUTHERN UNIVERSITY
Landrum Box 8033, Statesboro 30460-8033 *Type:* Public (state) liberal arts and teachers *System:* Board of Regents of the University System of Georgia *Accred.:* 1935/1984 (SACS-CC) *Calendar:* Qtr. plan *Degrees:* A, B, M, D (candidate) *Prof. Accred.:* Business (B,M), Computer Science, Engineering Technology (civil/construction, electrical, industrial, mechanical), Music, Nursing (B,M), Public Administration, Recreation and Leisure Services, Teacher Education (e,s,p) *CEO:* Pres. Nicholas L. Henry
FTE Enroll: 13,720   (912) 681-5611

GEORGIA SOUTHWESTERN COLLEGE
800 Wheatley St., Americus 31709-4693 *Type:* Public (state) liberal arts *System:* Board of Regents of the University System of Georgia *Accred.:* 1932/1993 (SACS-CC) *Calendar:* Qtr. plan *Degrees:* A, B, M *Prof. Accred.:* Nursing (A,B), Teacher Education (e,s) *CEO:* Pres. William H. Capitan
FTE Enroll: 3,493   (912) 928-1279

GEORGIA STATE UNIVERSITY
University Plaza, Atlanta 30303-3083 *Type:* Public (state) *System:* Board of Regents of the University System of Georgia *Accred.:* 1952/1988 (SACS-CC) *Calendar:* Qtr. plan *Degrees:* A, B, M, D *Prof. Accred.:* Accounting (Type A,B,C), Art, Business (B,M), Clinical Psychology, Counseling, Counseling Psychology, Dietetics (coordinated), Health Services Administration, Law (ABA only), Medical Technology, Music, Nursing (B,M), Physical Therapy, Psychology Intern-

ship, Public Administration, Rehabilitation Counseling, Respiratory Therapy, Respiratory Therapy Technology, School Psychology, Social Work (B), Teacher Education (e,s,p) *CEO:* Pres. Carl V. Patton
FTE Enroll: 19,201   (404) 651-2000

GORDON COLLEGE
419 College Dr., Barnesville 30204 *Type:* Public (state) junior *System:* Board of Regents of the University System of Georgia *Accred.:* 1941/1986 (SACS-CC) *Calendar:* Qtr. plan *Degrees:* A *Prof. Accred.:* Nursing (A) *CEO:* Pres. Jerry M. Williamson
FTE Enroll: 2,381   (404) 358-5016

GUPTON-JONES COLLEGE OF FUNERAL SERVICE
5141 Snapfinger Woods Dr., Decatur 30035-4022 *Type:* Private professional *Calendar:* Courses of varying lengths *Degrees:* A, diplomas *Prof. Accred.:* Funeral Service Education *CEO:* Pres. Daniel E. Buchanan
(404) 593-2257

GWINNETT TECHNICAL INSTITUTE
1250 Atkinson Rd., P.O. Box 1505, Lawrenceville 30246-1505 *Type:* Public (local) 2-year *Accred.:* 1991 (SACS-CC) *Calendar:* Sem. plan *Degrees:* A, certificates *Prof. Accred.:* Dental Assisting, Dental Laboratory Technology, Physical Therapy Assisting, Radiography, Respiratory Therapy Technology *CEO:* Pres. J. Alvin Wilbanks
FTE Enroll: 3,542   (404) 962-7580

INSTITUTE OF PAPER SCIENCE AND TECHNOLOGY
500 10th St., N.W., Atlanta 30318 *Type:* Private graduate only *Accred.:* 1989/1992 (SACS-CC) *Calendar:* Qtr. plan *Degrees:* M, D *CEO:* Pres. Richard A. Matula
FTE Enroll: 78   (404) 853-9500

INTERDENOMINATIONAL THEOLOGICAL CENTER
671 Beckwith St., S.W., Atlanta 30314 *Type:* Private (interdenominational) graduate only *Accred.:* 1960/1991 (ATS); 1984/1991 (SACS-CC) *Calendar:* Sem. plan *Degrees:* M, D *CEO:* Pres. James H. Costen
FTE Enroll: 351   (404) 527-7700

KENNESAW STATE COLLEGE
P.O. Box 444, Marietta 30061 *Type:* Public (state) liberal arts *System:* Board of Regents of the University System of Georgia *Accred.:* 1968/1986 (SACS-CC) *Calendar:*

Qtr. plan *Degrees:* A, B, M *Prof. Accred.:* Music, Nursing (A,B), Teacher Education (e,s) *CEO:* Pres. Betty L. Siegel
FTE Enroll: 10,022   (404) 423-6000

LAGRANGE COLLEGE
601 Broad St., LaGrange 30240-2999 *Type:* Private (United Methodist) liberal arts *Accred.:* 1946/1992 (SACS-CC) *Calendar:* Qtr. plan *Degrees:* A, B, M *Prof. Accred.:* Nursing (A) *CEO:* Pres. Walter Y. Murphy
FTE Enroll: 1,009   (706) 882-2911

LIFE COLLEGE
1269 Barclay Cir., Marietta 30060 *Type:* Private professional *Accred.:* 1986/1991 (SACS-CC) *Calendar:* Qtr. plan *Degrees:* B, M, D *Prof. Accred.:* Chiropractic Education *CEO:* Pres. Sid E. Williams, D.C.
FTE Enroll: 3,384   (404) 424-0554

MACON COLLEGE
100 College Station Dr., Macon 31297 *Type:* Public (state) junior *System:* Board of Regents of the University System of Georgia *Accred.:* 1970/1985 (SACS-CC) *Calendar:* Qtr. plan *Degrees:* A *Prof. Accred.:* Dental Hygiene, Nursing (A) *CEO:* Pres. S. Aaron Hyatt
FTE Enroll: 3,724   (912) 471-2700

MASSEY BUSINESS COLLEGE
120 Ralph McGill Blvd., N.E., Atlanta 30308 *Type:* Private business *Accred.:* 1977/1987 (ACISC) *Calendar:* Qtr. plan *Degrees:* A *CEO:* Dir. Garrett S. Hall
(404) 872-1900

MASSEY INSTITUTE
Ste. 320, 5299 Roswell Rd., Atlanta 30342 *Accred.:* 1985/1987 (ACISC) *CEO:* Dir. Barry Cermak
(404) 256-3533

MEADOWS COLLEGE OF BUSINESS
1170 Brown Ave., Columbus 31906 *Type:* Private junior *Accred.:* 1974/1986 (ACISC) *Calendar:* Qtr. plan *Degrees:* A *CEO:* Pres. William F. Meadows, Jr.
(404) 327-7668

MEDICAL COLLEGE OF GEORGIA
1120 15th St., Augusta 30912 *Type:* Public (state) professional *System:* Board of Regents of the University System of Georgia

Accred.: 1973/1990 (SACS-CC) *Calendar:* Qtr. plan *Degrees:* A, B, M, D *Prof. Accred.:* Combined Prosthodontics, Dental Hygiene, Dentistry, Diagnostic Medical Sonography, Endodontics, General Practice Residency, Medical Illustration, Medical Record Administration, Medical Record Technology, Medical Technology, Medicine, Nuclear Medicine Technology, Nursing (B,M), Occupational Therapy, Occupational Therapy Assisting, Oral and Maxillofacial Surgery, Orthodontics, Pediatric Dentistry, Periodontics, Physical Therapy, Physical Therapy Assisting, Physician Assisting, Psychology Internship, Radiation Therapy Technology, Radiography, Respiratory Therapy *CEO:* Pres. Francis J. Tedesco
FTE Enroll: 1,998   (706) 721-0211

MERCER UNIVERSITY
1400 Coleman Ave., Macon 31207 *Type:* Private (Southern Baptist) *Accred.:* 1911/1984 (SACS-CC) *Calendar:* Qtr. plan *Degrees:* B, M, D *Prof. Accred.:* Engineering (general), Law, Medicine, Music *CEO:* Pres. R. Kirby Godsey
FTE Enroll: 4,704   (912) 752-2500

MIDDLE GEORGIA COLLEGE
1100 Second St., S.E., Cochran 31014 *Type:* Public (state) junior *System:* Board of Regents of the University System of Georgia *Accred.:* 1933/1989 (SACS-CC) *Calendar:* Qtr. plan *Degrees:* A *Prof. Accred.:* Nursing (A) *CEO:* Pres. Joe Ben Welch
FTE Enroll: 2,019   (912) 934-6221

MOREHOUSE COLLEGE
830 Westview Dr., S.W., Atlanta 30314 *Type:* Private liberal arts for men *Accred.:* 1932/1988 (SACS-CC) *Calendar:* Sem. plan *Degrees:* B *CEO:* Pres. Leroy Keith, Jr.
FTE Enroll: 2,864   (404) 681-2800

MOREHOUSE SCHOOL OF MEDICINE
720 Westview Dr., S.W., Atlanta 30310-1495 *Type:* Private professional *Accred.:* 1986/1991 (SACS-CC) *Calendar:* Sem. plan *Degrees:* D *Prof. Accred.:* Medicine *CEO:* Pres. Louis Sullivan
FTE Enroll: 153   (404) 752-1500

MORRIS BROWN COLLEGE
643 Martin Luther King, Jr. Dr., N.W., Atlanta 30314 *Type:* Private (African Methodist Episcopal) liberal arts *Accred.:* 1941/1989 (SACS-CC probational) *Calendar:* Sem. plan *Degrees:* B *CEO:* Pres. Samuel D. Jolly, Jr.
FTE Enroll: 1,858   (404) 220-0270

NORTH GEORGIA COLLEGE
College Ave., Dahlonega 30597 *Type:* Public (state) liberal arts and teachers *System:* Board of Regents of the University System of Georgia *Accred.:* 1948/1987 (SACS-CC) *Calendar:* Qtr. plan *Degrees:* A, B, M *Prof. Accred.:* Nursing (A,B), Teacher Education (e,s) *CEO:* Pres. Delmas J. Allen
FTE Enroll: 2,898   (706) 864-1400

OGLETHORPE UNIVERSITY
4484 Peachtree Rd., N.E., Atlanta 30319-2797 *Type:* Private liberal arts *Accred.:* 1950/1986 (SACS-CC) *Calendar:* Sem. plan *Degrees:* B, M *CEO:* Pres. Donald S. Stanton
FTE Enroll: 1,099   (404) 261-1441

PAINE COLLEGE
1235 15th St., Augusta 30901-3182 *Type:* Private (United Methodist/Christian Methodist Episcopal) liberal arts *Accred.:* 1944/1991 (SACS-CC) *Calendar:* Sem. plan *Degrees:* B *CEO:* Pres. Julius S. Scott, Jr.
FTE Enroll: 723   (706) 821-8200

PIEDMONT COLLEGE
P.O. Box 10, Demorest 30535 *Type:* Private liberal arts *Accred.:* 1965/1987 (SACS-CC) *Calendar:* Sem. plan *Degrees:* B, M (candidate) *CEO:* Pres. John F. Elger
FTE Enroll: 666   (706) 778-3000

REINHARDT COLLEGE
P.O. Box 128, Waleska 30183 *Type:* Private (United Methodist) *Accred.:* 1953/1988 (SACS-CC) *Calendar:* Qtr. plan *Degrees:* A, B (candidate) *CEO:* Pres. Floyd A. Falany
FTE Enroll: 765   (404) 720-5600

THE SAVANNAH COLLEGE OF ART AND DESIGN
201 W. Charlton St., Savannah 31401 *Type:* Private professional *Accred.:* 1983/1989 (SACS-CC) *Calendar:* Qtr. plan *Degrees:* B, M *CEO:* Pres. Richard G. Rowan
FTE Enroll: 2,287   (912) 238-2487

SAVANNAH STATE COLLEGE
State College Branch, P.O. Box 20449, Savannah 31404 *Type:* Public (state) liberal arts and professional *System:* Board of Regents of the University System of Georgia *Accred.:* 1951/1991 (SACS-CC) *Calendar:* Qtr. plan *Degrees:* B *Prof. Accred.:* Engineering Technology (civil/construction, computer, electrical, mechanical), Social Work (B) *CEO:* Pres. John T. Wolfe, Jr.
FTE Enroll: 3,384   (912) 356-2187

SAVANNAH TECHNICAL INSTITUTE
5717 White Bluff Rd., Savannah 31499 *Type:* Public (local) 2-year *Accred.:* 1991 (SACS-CC) *Calendar:* Qtr. plan *Degrees:* A *Prof. Accred.:* Dental Assisting, Engineering Technology (electrical, electromechanical), Medical Assisting (AMA), Practical Nursing, Surgical Technology *CEO:* Interim Pres. Don Stewart
FTE Enroll: 1,665   (912) 351-6362

SHORTER COLLEGE
315 Shorter Ave., Rome 30165-4298 *Type:* Private (Southern Baptist) liberal arts *Accred.:* 1923/1992 (SACS-CC) *Calendar:* Sem. plan *Degrees:* B, M (candidate) *Prof. Accred.:* Music *CEO:* Pres. Larry L. McSwain
FTE Enroll: 1,151   (706) 291-2121

SOUTH COLLEGE
709 Mall Blvd., Savannah 31406 *Type:* Private junior *Accred.:* 1975/1992 (ACISC); 1985/1990 (SACS-CC) *Calendar:* Qtr. plan *Degrees:* A *Prof. Accred.:* Medical Assisting (AMA) *CEO:* Pres. John T. South, III
FTE Enroll: 730   (912) 651-8100

SOUTH GEORGIA COLLEGE
100 W. College Park Dr., Douglas 31533-5098 *Type:* Public (state) junior *System:* Board of Regents of the University System of Georgia *Accred.:* 1934/1987 (SACS-CC) *Calendar:* Qtr. plan *Degrees:* A *Prof. Accred.:* Nursing (A) *CEO:* Pres.   Edward D. Jackson, Jr.
FTE Enroll: 1,241   (912) 383-4220

SOUTHERN COLLEGE OF TECHNOLOGY
1100 S. Marietta Pkwy., Marietta 30060-2896 *Type:* Public (state) *System:* Board of Regents of the University System of Georgia

Accred.: 1964/1988 (SACS-CC) *Calendar:* Qtr. plan *Degrees:* A, B, M *Prof. Accred.:* Construction Education (B), Engineering Technology (apparel, architectural, civil/construction, computer, electrical, industrial, mechanical, textile) *CEO:* Pres. Stephen R. Cheshier
FTE Enroll: 3,319   (404) 528-7230

SPELMAN COLLEGE
350 Spelman La., S.W., Atlanta 30314-4399 *Type:* Private liberal arts for women *Accred.:* 1932/1990 (SACS-CC) *Calendar:* Sem. plan *Degrees:* B *Prof. Accred.:* Music, Teacher Education (e,s) *CEO:* Pres. Johnnetta B. Cole
FTE Enroll: 2,027   (404) 681-3643

THOMAS COLLEGE
1501 Millpond Rd., Thomasville 31792-7499 *Type:* Private *Accred.:* 1984/1989 (SACS-CC) *Calendar:* Qtr. plan *Degrees:* A, B *CEO:* Pres. Homer R. Pankey
FTE Enroll: 585   (912) 226-1621

TOCCOA FALLS COLLEGE
Toccoa Falls 30598 *Type:* Private (Christian and Missionary Alliance) *Accred.:* 1957/1987 (AABC); 1983/1989 (SACS-CC) *Calendar:* Sem. plan *Degrees:* A, B *Prof. Accred.:* Music (associate) *CEO:* Pres. Paul L. Alford
FTE Enroll: 817   (706) 886-6831

TRUETT MCCONNELL COLLEGE
Rte. 6, Box 6000, Cleveland 30528 *Type:* Private (Southern Baptist) junior *Accred.:* 1966/1990 (SACS-CC) *Calendar:* Qtr. plan *Degrees:* A *Prof. Accred.:* Music *CEO:* Pres. Thomas Clark Bryan
FTE Enroll: 1,530   (706) 865-2134

THE UNIVERSITY OF GEORGIA
Athens 30602-1661 *Type:* Public (state) *System:* Board of Regents of the University System of Georgia *Accred.:* 1909/1991 (SACS-CC) *Calendar:* Qtr. plan *Degrees:* A, B, M, D *Prof. Accred.:* Accounting (Type A,B,C), Art, Audiology, Business (B,M), Clinical Psychology, Counseling, Counseling Psychology, Engineering (agricultural), Forestry, Home Economics, Interior Design, Journalism (B,M), Landscape Architecture (B,M), Law, Marriage and Family Therapy

(D), Music, Psychology Internship, Public Administration, Recreation and Leisure Services, Rehabilitation Counseling, School Psychology, Social Work (B,M), Speech-Language Pathology, Teacher Education (e,s,p), Theatre, Veterinary Medicine *CEO:* Pres. Charles B. Knapp
FTE Enroll: 28,776   (706) 542-3000

VALDOSTA STATE UNIVERSITY
1500 N. Patterson St., Valdosta 31698 *Type:* Public (state) liberal arts and teachers *System:* Board of Regents of the University System of Georgia *Accred.:* 1929/1990 (SACS-CC) *Calendar:* Qtr. plan *Degrees:* A, B, M *Prof. Accred.:* Art (associate), Business (B), Music, Nursing (B,M), Speech-Language Pathology, Teacher Education (e,s,p) *CEO:* Pres. Hugh C. Bailey
FTE Enroll: 8,710   (912) 333-5952

WAYCROSS COLLEGE
2001 Francis St., Waycross 31503 *Type:* Public (state) junior *System:* Board of Regents of the University System of Georgia *Accred.:* 1978/1993 (SACS-CC) *Calendar:* Qtr. plan *Degrees:* A *CEO:* Pres. James M. Dye
FTE Enroll: 658   (912) 285-6130

WESLEYAN COLLEGE
4760 Forsyth Rd., Macon 31297-4299 *Type:* Private (United Methodist) liberal arts for women *Accred.:* 1919/1984 (SACS-CC) *Calendar:* Sem. plan *Degrees:* B *Prof. Accred.:* Music *CEO:* Pres. Robert K. Ackerman
FTE Enroll: 451   (912) 477-1110

WEST GEORGIA COLLEGE
Carrollton 30118-0001 *Type:* Public (state) liberal arts and professional *System:* Board of Regents of the University System of Georgia *Accred.:* 1963/1993 (SACS-CC) *Calendar:* Qtr. plan *Degrees:* A, B, M *Prof. Accred.:* Business (B,M), Music, Nursing (A,B), Teacher Education (e,s,p) *CEO:* Acting Pres. Bruce W. Lyon
FTE Enroll: 7,947   (404) 836-6500

YOUNG HARRIS COLLEGE
P.O. Box 98, Young Harris 30582 *Type:* Private (United Methodist) junior *Accred.:* 1938/1991 (SACS-CC) *Calendar:* Qtr. plan *Degrees:* A *CEO:* Pres. Thomas S. Yow, III
FTE Enroll: 524   (706) 379-3111

GUAM

GUAM COMMUNITY COLLEGE
P.O. Box 23069, Guam Main Facility, Main Island 96921 *Type:* Public (territorial) junior *Accred.:* 1979/1989 (WASC-Jr.) *Calendar:* Sem. plan *Degrees:* A *CEO:* Pres. John T. Cruz
Enroll: 2,178   (671) 734-4311

UNIVERSITY OF GUAM
UOG Sta., Mangilao 96923 *Type:* Public (territorial) liberal arts and professional *Accred.:* 1963/1988 (WASC-Sr.) *Calendar:* Sem. plan *Degrees:* A, B, M *CEO:* Pres. John C. Salas
FTE Enroll: 3,740   (671) 734-9340

HAWAII

BRIGHAM YOUNG UNIVERSITY—HAWAII CAMPUS
55-220 Kulanui St., Laie 96762 *Type:* Independent (Latter-Day Saints) liberal arts *Accred.:* 1959/1986 (WASC-Sr.) *Calendar:* 4-4-2-2 plan *Degrees:* A, B *Prof. Accred.:* Social Work (B) *CEO:* Pres. Alton L. Wade
FTE Enroll: 1,940　　　　　(808) 293-3700

CANNON'S INTERNATIONAL BUSINESS COLLEGE
1500 Kapiolani Blvd., Honolulu 96814 *Type:* Private junior *Accred.:* 1954/1987 (ACISC) *Calendar:* Qtr. plan *Degrees:* A *CEO:* Pres. Evelyn A. Schemmel
　　　　　　　　　　　　(808) 955-1500

CHAMINADE UNIVERSITY OF HONOLULU
3140 Waialae Ave., Honolulu 96816-1578 *Type:* Independent (Roman Catholic) liberal arts and professional *Accred.:* 1960/1983 (WASC-Sr.) *Calendar:* Sem. plan *Degrees:* A, B, M *CEO:* Pres. Kent M. Keith
FTE Enroll: 1,533　　　　　(808) 735-4711

HAWAII COMMUNITY COLLEGE
523 W. Lanikaula St., Hilo 96720-4091 *Type:* Public (state) junior *System:* University of Hawaii Office of the Chancellor for Community Colleges *Accred.:* 1973/1989 (WASC-Jr.) *Calendar:* Sem. plan *Degrees:* A *CEO:* Provost Sandra Sakaguchi
Enroll: 1,857　　　　　(808) 933-3611

HAWAII PACIFIC UNIVERSITY
1166 Fort St. Mall, Honolulu 96813 *Type:* Independent liberal arts and business *Accred.:* 1973/1993 (WASC-Sr.) *Calendar:* Sem. plan *Degrees:* A, B, M *CEO:* Pres. Chatt G. Wright
FTE Enroll: 6,074　　　　　(808) 544-0200

HAWAII LOA COLLEGE CAMPUS
45-045 Kamehameha Hwy., Kaneohe 96744 *Prof. Accred.:* Nursing (B) *CEO:* Pres. Dwight M. Smith
　　　　　　　　　　　　(808) 235-3641

HONOLULU COMMUNITY COLLEGE
874 Dillingham Blvd., Honolulu 96817 *Type:* Public (state) junior *System:* University of Hawaii Office of the Chancellor for Community Colleges *Accred.:* 1970/1989

(WASC-Jr.) *Calendar:* Sem. plan *Degrees:* A *CEO:* Provost Peter R. Kessinger
Enroll: 4,523　　　　　(808) 845-9225

KANSAI GAIDAI HAWAII COLLEGE
5257 Kalanianaole Hwy., Honolulu 96821 *Type:* Private 2-year *Accred.:* 1985/1990 (WASC-Jr.) *Calendar:* Qtr. plan *Degrees:* A *CEO:* Dean of Admin. Kenji Nishimura
Enroll: 112　　　　　(808) 377-5402

KAPIOLANI COMMUNITY COLLEGE
4303 Diamond Head Rd., Honolulu 96816 *Type:* Public (state) junior *System:* University of Hawaii Office of the Chancellor for Community Colleges *Accred.:* 1970/1989 (WASC-Jr.) *Calendar:* Sem. plan *Degrees:* A *Prof. Accred.:* Medical Assisting (AMA), Medical Laboratory Technology (AMA), Nursing (A), Occupational Therapy Assisting, Physical Therapy Assisting, Radiography, Respiratory Therapy, Respiratory Therapy Technology *CEO:* Provost John E. Morton
Enroll: 7,000　　　　　(808) 734-9111

KAUAI COMMUNITY COLLEGE
3-1901 Kaumualii Hwy., Lihue 96766 *Type:* Public (state) junior *System:* University of Hawaii Office of the Chancellor for Community Colleges *Accred.:* 1971/1989 (WASC-Jr.) *Calendar:* Sem. plan *Degrees:* A *Prof. Accred.:* Nursing (A) *CEO:* Provost David Iha
Enroll: 1,563　　　　　(808) 245-8311

LEEWARD COMMUNITY COLLEGE
96-045 Ala Ike, Pearl City 96782 *Type:* Public (state) junior *System:* University of Hawaii Office of the Chancellor for Community Colleges *Accred.:* 1971/1989 (WASC-Jr.) *Calendar:* Sem. plan *Degrees:* A *CEO:* Provost Barbara B. Polk
Enroll: 5,804　　　　　(808) 455-0011

MAUI COMMUNITY COLLEGE
310 Kaahumanu Ave., Kahului 96732 *Type:* Public (state) junior *System:* University of Hawaii Office of the Chancellor for Community Colleges *Accred.:* 1980/1989 (WASC-Jr.) *Calendar:* Sem. plan *Degrees:* A *Prof.*

Accred.: Nursing (A) *CEO:* Provost Clyde M. Sakamoto
Enroll: 1,915   (808) 244-9181

TAI HSUAN FOUNDATION COLLEGE OF ACUPUNCTURE AND HERBAL MEDICINE
2600 S. King St., No. 206, Honolulu 96826 *Type:* Private professional *Calendar:* Sem. plan *Degrees:* M *Prof. Accred.:* Acupuncture *CEO:* Pres. Gayle Todoki
FTE Enroll: 25   (808) 947-4788

UNIVERSITY OF HAWAII AT HILO
200 W. Kawili St., Hilo 96720-4091 *Type:* Public (state) liberal arts and professional *System:* University of Hawaii Office of the President *Accred.:* 1976/1989 (WASC-Sr.) *Calendar:* Sem. plan *Degrees:* A, B *CEO:* Chanc. Kenneth L. Perrin
FTE Enroll: 2,255   (808) 933-3311

UNIVERSITY OF HAWAII AT MANOA
2444 Dole St., Honolulu 96822 *Type:* Public (state) liberal arts and professional *System:* University of Hawaii Office of the President *Accred.:* 1952/1991 (WASC-Sr.) *Calendar:* Sem. plan *Degrees:* A, B, P, M, D *Prof. Accred.:* Audiology, Business (B,M), Clinical Psychology, Dental Hygiene, Engineering (civil, electrical, mechanical, ocean), Journalism (B), Law, Librarianship, Medical Technology, Medicine, Music, Nursing (A,B,M), Planning (M), Psychology Internship (provisional), Public Health, Rehabilitation Counseling, Social Work (B,M), Speech-Language Pathology *CEO:* Chanc. Kenneth P. Mortimer
FTE Enroll: 16,149   (808) 956-8111

UNIVERSITY OF HAWAII AT WEST OAHU
96-043 Ala Ike, Pearl City 96782 *Type:* Public (state) liberal arts *System:* University of Hawaii Office of the President *Accred.:* 1981 (WASC-Sr.) *Calendar:* Sem. plan *Degrees:* B *CEO:* Chanc. Kenneth L. Perrin
FTE Enroll: 393   (808) 456-4718

WINDWARD COMMUNITY COLLEGE
45-720 Keaahala Rd., Kaneohe 96744 *Type:* Public (state) junior *System:* University of Hawaii Office of the Chancellor for Community Colleges *Accred.:* 1977/1989 (WASC-Jr.) *Calendar:* Sem. plan *Degrees:* A *CEO:* Provost Peter T. Dyer
Enroll: 1,633   (808) 235-0077

IDAHO

ALBERTSON COLLEGE
2112 Cleveland Blvd., Caldwell 83605 *Type:* Private (United Presbyterian) liberal arts *Accred.:* 1922/1992 (NASC) *Calendar:* 4-1-4 plan *Degrees:* B, M *CEO:* Pres. Robert L. Hendren, Jr.
Enroll: 981   (208) 459-5011

BOISE BIBLE COLLEGE
8695 Marigold St., Boise 83714 *Type:* Private (Christian Churches/Churches of Christ) *Accred.:* 1988 (AABC) *Calendar:* Sem. plan *Degrees:* A, B, certificates *CEO:* Pres. Charles A. Crane
FTE Enroll: 95   (208) 376-7731

BOISE STATE UNIVERSITY
Boise 83725 *Type:* Public liberal arts and teachers *System:* State Board of Education and Board of Regents of the University of Idaho *Accred.:* 1941/1990 (NASC) *Calendar:* Sem. plan *Degrees:* A, B, M *Prof. Accred.:* Accounting (Type A), Business (B,M), Construction Education (B), Dental Assisting, Medical Record Technology, Music, Nursing (A,B), Radiography, Respiratory Therapy, Respiratory Therapy Technology, Social Work (B,M-candidate), Surgical Technology, Teacher Education (e,s), Theatre (associate) *CEO:* Pres. Charles Ruch
Enroll: 14,908   (208) 385-1491

COLLEGE OF SOUTHERN IDAHO
315 Falls Ave., P.O. Box 1238, Twin Falls 83303-1238 *Type:* Public (district) junior *System:* State Board of Education and Board of Regents of the University of Idaho *Accred.:* 1968/1989 (NASC) *Calendar:* Sem. plan *Degrees:* A *Prof. Accred.:* Medical Assisting (AMA), Nursing (A) *CEO:* Pres. Gerald R. Meyerhoeffer
Enroll: 7,984   (208) 733-9554

EASTERN IDAHO TECHNICAL COLLEGE
1600 S. 2500 E., Idaho Falls 83404 *Type:* Public (district) 2-year *Accred.:* 1982/1992 (NASC) *Calendar:* Modified qtr. plan *Degrees:* A, certificates *CEO:* Dir. Grace Guemple
Enroll: 339   (208) 524-3000

IDAHO STATE UNIVERSITY
Pocatello 83209-0009 *Type:* Public (state) *System:* State Board of Education and Board of Regents of the University of Idaho *Accred.:* 1923/1989 (NASC) *Calendar:* Sem. plan *Degrees:* A, B, M, D *Prof. Accred.:* Audiology, Business (B,M), Counseling, Dental Hygiene, Dental Laboratory Technology (conditional), Engineering (general), Music, Nursing (B,M), Physical Therapy, Radiography, Social Work (B), Speech-Language Pathology, Teacher Education (e,s,p) *CEO:* Pres. Richard L. Bowen
Enroll: 11,756   (208) 236-3340

ITT TECHNICAL INSTITUTE
950 Lusk St., Boise 83706-2831 *Type:* Private *Accred.:* 1985/1990 (ACCSCT) *Calendar:* Courses of varying lengths *Degrees:* A, diplomas *CEO:* Dir. N. Dale Reynolds
(208) 344-8376

LEWIS-CLARK STATE COLLEGE
Lewiston 83501 *Type:* Public (state) 4-year liberal arts and teachers *System:* State Board of Education and Board of Regents of the University of Idaho *Accred.:* 1964/1989 (NASC) *Calendar:* Sem. plan *Degrees:* A, B *Prof. Accred.:* Nursing (A,B), Social Work (B-candidate), Teacher Education (e,s) *CEO:* Pres. Lee A. Vickers
Enroll: 3,029   (208) 799-2216

NORTH IDAHO COLLEGE
Coeur d'Alene 83814 *Type:* Public (district) junior *System:* State Board of Education and Board of Regents of the University of Idaho *Accred.:* 1947/1993 (NASC) *Calendar:* Sem. plan *Degrees:* A *Prof. Accred.:* Nursing (A) *CEO:* Pres. C. Robert Bennett
Enroll: 3,061   (208) 769-3300

NORTHWEST NAZARENE COLLEGE
Nampa 83686 *Type:* Private (Nazarene) liberal arts *Accred.:* 1930/1992 (NASC) *Calendar:* Qtr. plan *Degrees:* A, B, M *Prof. Accred.:* Music, Social Work (B), Teacher Education (e,s,p) *CEO:* Pres. Richard Hagood
Enroll: 1,258   (208) 467-8011

RICKS COLLEGE
  Rexburg 83460 *Type:* Private (Latter-Day Saints) junior *Accred.:* 1936/1989 (NASC) *Calendar:* Sem. plan *Degrees:* A *Prof. Accred.:* Engineering Technology (electrical, manufacturing, mechanical drafting/design, welding), Interior Design, Music, Nursing (A) *CEO:* Pres. Steven D. Bennion
  Enroll: 7,943   (208) 356-2411

UNIVERSITY OF IDAHO
  Moscow 83843 *Type:* Public (state) *System:* State Board of Education and Board of Regents of the University of Idaho *Accred.:* 1918/1989 (NASC) *Calendar:* Sem. plan *Degrees:* B, P, M, D *Prof. Accred.:* Business (B), Computer Science, Counseling, Dietetics (coordinated), Engineering (agricultural, chemical, civil, electrical, geological/geophysical, mechanical, metallurgical, mining), Forestry, Landscape Architecture (B), Law, Music, Recreation and Leisure Services, Teach- er Education (e,s,p) *CEO:* Pres. Elisabeth A. Zinser
  Enroll: 11,448   (208) 885-6365

ILLINOIS

ADLER SCHOOL OF PROFESSIONAL PSYCHOLOGY
65 E. Wacker Pl., Chicago 60601 *Type:* Private professional; graduate only *Accred.:* 1978/1990 (NCA) *Calendar:* Tri. plan *Degrees:* M, D, certificates *CEO:* Pres. Randall L. Thompson
Enroll: 372   (312) 201-5900

AMERICAN ACADEMY OF ART
332 S. Michigan Ave., No. 300, Chicago 60604-4301 *Type:* Private *Accred.:* 1974/1989 (ACCSCT) *Calendar:* Sem. plan *Degrees:* A *CEO:* Dir. John J. Balester
(312) 461-0600

AMERICAN CONSERVATORY OF MUSIC
16 N. Wabash Ave., Ste. 1850, Chicago 60602-4792 *Type:* Private *Calendar:* Courses of varying lengths *Degrees:* A, B, M, D, certificates *Prof. Accred.:* Music *CEO:* Dean Carl L. Waldschmidt
(312) 263-4161

AMERICAN SCHOOLS OF PROFESSIONAL PSYCHOLOGY
220 S. State St., No. 509, Chicago 60604 *Type:* Private graduate only *Accred.:* 1981/1991 (NCA) *Calendar:* Sem. plan *Degrees:* M, D *CEO:* Pres. Harold J. O'Donnell
Enroll: 925   (312) 341-6500

GEORGIA SCHOOL OF PROFESSIONAL PSYCHOLOGY
990 Hammond Dr., N.E., Atlanta, GA 30328 *CEO:* Dean Joseph Bascuas
(404) 872-0707

ILLINOIS SCHOOL OF PROFESSIONAL PSYCHOLOGY
220 S. State St., No. 509, Chicago 60604 *Prof. Accred.:* Clinical Psychology *CEO:* Dean Marc I. Lubin
(312) 341-6500

MINNESOTA SCHOOL OF PROFESSIONAL PSYCHOLOGY
3103 E. 80th St., Ste. 290, Bloomington, MN 55420 *Prof. Accred.:* Clinical Psychology (provisional) *CEO:* Dean Paul Olson
(612) 858-8800

AUGUSTANA COLLEGE
Rock Island 61201 *Type:* Private (Lutheran) liberal arts *Accred.:* 1913/1986 (NCA) *Calendar:* Qtr. plan *Degrees:* B *Prof. Accred.:* Music, Social Work (B), Teacher Education (e,s) *CEO:* Pres. Thomas Tredway
Enroll: 2,046   (309) 794-7208

AURORA UNIVERSITY
347 S. Gladstone Ave., Aurora 60506 *Type:* Private (Advent Christian) liberal arts *Accred.:* 1938/1989 (NCA) *Calendar:* Sem. plan *Degrees:* B, M *Prof. Accred.:* Nursing (B), Recreation and Leisure Services, Social Work (B,M) *CEO:* Pres. Thomas H. Zarle
Enroll: 2,025   (708) 892-6431

BARAT COLLEGE
700 E. Westleigh Rd., Lake Forest 60045 *Type:* Private (Roman Catholic) liberal arts *Accred.:* 1943/1993 (NCA) *Calendar:* Sem. plan *Degrees:* B *Prof. Accred.:* Nursing (B) *CEO:* Pres. Lucy S. Morros
Enroll: 719   (708) 234-3000

BELLEVILLE AREA COLLEGE
2500 Carlyle Rd., Belleville 62221 *Type:* Public (district) junior *System:* Illinois Community College Board *Accred.:* 1961/1993 (NCA) *Calendar:* Sem. plan *Degrees:* A, certificates *Prof. Accred.:* Medical Assisting (AMA), Medical Laboratory Technology (AMA), Medical Record Technology, Nursing (A), Physical Therapy Assisting, Radiography, Respiratory Therapy Technology *CEO:* Pres. Joseph J. Cipfl
Enroll: 15,633   (618) 235-7000

BETHANY THEOLOGICAL SEMINARY
Butterfield and Meyers Rds., Oak Brook 60521 *Type:* Private (Brethren) graduate only *Accred.:* 1940/1991 (ATS); 1971/1992 (NCA) *Calendar:* Qtr. plan *Degrees:* M, D *CEO:* Pres. Eugene F. Roop
Enroll: 92   (708) 620-2200

BLACK HAWK COLLEGE
6600 34th Ave., Moline 61265 *Type:* Public (district) junior *System:* Illinois Community College Board *Accred.:* 1986/1993 (NCA) *Calendar:* Sem. plan *Degrees:* A, certificates *Prof. Accred.:* Nursing (A), Respiratory

Therapy, Respiratory Therapy Technology
CEO: Pres. Judith A. Redwine
Enroll: 8,599   (309) 796-1311

BLACKBURN COLLEGE
700 College Ave., Carlinville 62626 *Type:*
Private (United Presbyterian) liberal arts *Accred.:* 1918/1986 (NCA) *Calendar:* Sem.
plan *Degrees:* B, M *CEO:* Pres. Miriam R.
Pride
Enroll: 489   (217) 854-3231

BLESSING-RIEMAN COLLEGE OF NURSING
Broadway at 11th St., P.O. Box C-3, Quincy
62301 *Type:* Private professional *Accred.:*
1989 (NCA) *Calendar:* Sem. plan *Degrees:*
B *CEO:* Dean Carole Piles
Enroll: 184   (217) 223-5811

BRADLEY UNIVERSITY
1501 W. Bradley Ave., Peoria 61625 *Type:*
Private *Accred.:* 1913/1990 (NCA) *Calendar:* Sem. plan *Degrees:* B, M *Prof. Accred.:*
Accounting (Type A), Art, Business (B,M),
Construction Education (B), Counseling, Engineering Technology (electrical, manufacturing, mechanical), Engineering (civil, electrical, industrial, manufacturing, mechanical), Music, Nurse Anesthesia Education,
Nursing (B), Teacher Education (e,s,p)
CEO: Pres. John R. Brazil
Enroll: 6,191   (309) 676-7611

CARL SANDBURG COLLEGE
2232 S. Lake Storey Rd., Galesburg 61401
Type: Public (district) junior *System:* Illinois
Community College Board *Accred.:* 1974/
1991 (NCA) *Calendar:* Sem. plan *Degrees:*
A, certificates *Prof. Accred.:* Radiography
CEO: Pres. Donald G. Crist
Enroll: 3,107   (309) 344-2518

CATHOLIC THEOLOGICAL UNION
5401 S. Cornell Ave., Chicago 60615-5698
Type: Private (Roman Catholic) graduate
only *Accred.:* 1972/1991 (ATS); 1972/1992
(NCA) *Calendar:* Qtr. plan *Degrees:* M, D
CEO: Pres. Donald Senior, C.P.
Enroll: 335   (312) 324-8000

CHICAGO COLLEGE OF COMMERCE
11 E. Adams St., Chicago 60603 *Type:* Private business *Accred.:* 1968/1986 (ACISC)
Calendar: Qtr. plan *Degrees:* A, certificates,

diplomas *CEO:* Chrmn. of the Bd. Mae S.
Glassbrenner
                                    (312) 236-3312

THE CHICAGO SCHOOL OF PROFESSIONAL
PSYCHOLOGY
806 S. Plymouth Ct., Chicago 60605 *Type:*
Private professional; graduate only *Accred.:*
1984/1992 (NCA) *Calendar:* Sem. plan *Degrees:* D *Prof. Accred.:* Clinical Psychology
CEO: Pres. Jeffrey C. Grip
Enroll: 166   (312) 786-9443

CHICAGO STATE UNIVERSITY
9501 S. King Dr., Chicago 60628 *Type:* Public (state) liberal arts and teachers *System:*
Illinois Board of Governors Universities *Accred.:* 1941/1993 (NCA) *Calendar:* Tri. plan
Degrees: B, M *Prof. Accred.:* Medical
Record Administration, Nursing (B), Occupational Therapy, Radiation Therapy Technology, Teacher Education (e,s,p) *CEO:*
Pres. Dolores E. Cross
Enroll: 8,675   (312) 995-2000

CHICAGO THEOLOGICAL SEMINARY
5757 S. University Ave., Chicago 60637
Type: Private (United Church of Christ)
graduate only *Accred.:* 1938/1986 (ATS);
1982/1987 (NCA) *Calendar:* Qtr. plan *Degrees:* M, D *CEO:* Pres. Kenneth B. Smith
Enroll: 212   (312) 752-5757

COLLEGE OF DUPAGE
22nd St. and Lambert Rd., Glen Ellyn 60137
Type: Public (district) junior *System:* Illinois
Community College Board *Accred.:* 1932/
1984 (NCA) *Calendar:* Qtr. plan *Degrees:*
A, certificates *Prof. Accred.:* Medical
Record Technology, Nuclear Medicine
Technology, Nursing (A), Occupational
Therapy Assisting, Radiography, Respiratory
Therapy Technology *CEO:* Pres. Harold D.
McAninch
Enroll: 36,115   (708) 858-2800

COLLEGE OF LAKE COUNTY
19351 W. Washington St., Grayslake 60030
Type: Public (district) junior *System:* Illinois
Community College Board *Accred.:* 1974/
1986 (NCA) *Calendar:* Sem. plan *Degrees:*
A, certificates *Prof. Accred.:* Medical Laboratory Technology (AMA), Medical Record

Technology, Nursing (A), Radiography *CEO:* Pres. Daniel J. LaVista
Enroll: 15,644   (708) 223-6601

COLLEGE OF ST. FRANCIS
500 N. Wilcox St., Joliet 60435 *Type:* Private (Roman Catholic) liberal arts *Accred.:* 1938/1989 (NCA) *Calendar:* Sem. plan *Degrees:* B, M *Prof. Accred.:* Recreation and Leisure Services, Social Work (B) *CEO:* Chanc. John C. Orr
Enroll: 4,138   (815) 740-3360

COLUMBIA COLLEGE
600 S. Michigan Ave., Chicago 60605 *Type:* Private liberal arts *Accred.:* 1974/1989 (NCA) *Calendar:* Sem. plan *Degrees:* B, M *CEO:* Pres. John B. Duff
Enroll: 7,133   (312) 663-1600

CONCORDIA UNIVERSITY
7400 Augusta St., River Forest 60305 *Type:* Private (Lutheran-Missouri Synod) *Accred.:* 1950/1992 (NCA) *Calendar:* Qtr. plan *Degrees:* B, M, certificates, diplomas *Prof. Accred.:* Clinical Psychology, Nursing (B), Teacher Education (e,s,p) *CEO:* Pres. Eugene L. Krentz
Enroll: 1,726   (708) 771-8300

DANVILLE AREA COMMUNITY COLLEGE
2000 E. Main St., Danville 61832 *Type:* Public (district) junior *System:* Illinois Community College Board *Accred.:* 1967/1989 (NCA) *Calendar:* Sem. plan *Degrees:* A, certificates *CEO:* Pres. Harry J. Braun
Enroll: 3,429   (217) 443-1811

DEPAUL UNIVERSITY
25 E. Jackson Blvd., Chicago 60604 *Type:* Private (Roman Catholic) liberal arts and professional *Accred.:* 1925/1987 (NCA) *Calendar:* Qtr. plan *Degrees:* B, M, D, certificates *Prof. Accred.:* Accounting (Type A,B,C), Business (B,M), Clinical Psychology, Law, Music, Nurse Anesthesia Education, Nursing (B,M), Teacher Education (e,s,p) *CEO:* Pres. John P. Minogue
Enroll: 16,499   (312) 362-8300

DEVRY INSTITUTE OF TECHNOLOGY, CHICAGO
3300 N. Campbell Ave., Chicago 60618 *Type:* Private *Accred.:* 1981/1992 (NCA)* *Calendar:* Sem. plan *Degrees:* A, B, certificates, diplomas *Prof. Accred.:* Engineering

Technology (electrical) *CEO:* Pres. E. Arthur Stunard
                             (312) 929-8500

DEVRY INSTITUTE OF TECHNOLOGY, DUPAGE
1221 N. Swift Rd., Addison 60101-6106 *Type:* Private *Accred.:* 1981/1992 (NCA)* *Calendar:* Sem. plan *Degrees:* A, B, certificates, diplomas *Prof. Accred.:* Engineering Technology (electrical) *CEO:* Pres. Jerry R. Dill
                             (708) 953-1300

* Indirect accreditation through DeVry Institutes.

DEVRY INSTITUTES
One Tower La., Oak Brook Terrace 60181 *Type:* Private *Accred.:* 1981/1992 (NCA) *Calendar:* Sem. plan *Degrees:* A, B, certificates, diplomas *CEO:* Pres. Ronald Taylor
Enroll: 22,231   (708) 571-7700

DR. WILLIAM M. SCHOLL COLLEGE OF PODIATRIC MEDICINE
1001 N. Dearborn St., Chicago 60610 *Type:* Private professional *Accred.:* 1985/1990 (NCA) *Calendar:* Sem. plan *Degrees:* B, D *Prof. Accred.:* Podiatry *CEO:* Pres. Richard B. Patterson
Enroll: 384   (312) 280-2880

EAST-WEST UNIVERSITY
816 S. Michigan Ave., Chicago 60605 *Type:* Private technical *Accred.:* 1983/1991 (NCA) *Calendar:* Qtr. plan *Degrees:* A, B *CEO:* Chanc. M. Wasi Khan
Enroll: 268   (312) 939-0111

EASTERN ILLINOIS UNIVERSITY
600 Lincoln Ave., Charleston 61920 *Type:* Public (state) *System:* Illinois Board of Governors Universities *Accred.:* 1915/1985 (NCA) *Calendar:* Sem. plan *Degrees:* B, P, M *Prof. Accred.:* Art (associate), Business (B,M), Home Economics, Journalism (B), Music, Recreation and Leisure Services, Speech-Language Pathology, Teacher Education (e,s,p) *CEO:* Pres. David L. Jorns
Enroll: 11,411   (217) 581-5000

ELGIN COMMUNITY COLLEGE
1700 Spartan Dr., Elgin 60123 *Type:* Public (district) junior *System:* Illinois Community College Board *Accred.:* 1968/1986 (NCA) *Calendar:* Sem. plan *Degrees:* A, certificates

Prof. Accred.: Dental Assisting, Nursing (A)
CEO: Pres. Paul R. Heath
Enroll: 9,156   (708) 697-1000

ELMHURST COLLEGE
190 Prospect St., Elmhurst 60126 *Type:* Private (United Church of Christ) liberal arts *Accred.:* 1924/1989 (NCA) *Calendar:* 4-1-4 plan *Degrees:* B *Prof. Accred.:* Nursing (B), Teacher Education (e,s) *CEO:* Pres. Ivan E. Frick
Enroll: 2,725   (708) 617-3100

EUREKA COLLEGE
300 E. College Ave., Eureka 61530 *Type:* Private (Disciples of Christ) liberal arts *Accred.:* 1924/1990 (NCA) *Calendar:* Four 8-week terms *Degrees:* B *CEO:* Pres. George A. Hearne
Enroll: 514   (309) 467-3721

FRONTIER COMMUNITY COLLEGE
Frontier Dr., Fairfield 62837 *Type:* Public (district) junior *System:* Illinois Eastern Community Colleges System *Accred.:* 1984/1988 (NCA)* *Calendar:* Sem. plan *Degrees:* A, certificates *Prof. Accred.:* Nursing (A) *CEO:* Pres. Richard L. Mason
                                         (618) 842-3711

* Indirect accreditation through Illinois Eastern Community Colleges System.

GARRETT-EVANGELICAL THEOLOGICAL SEMINARY
2121 Sheridan Rd., Evanston 60201 *Type:* Private (United Methodist) graduate only *Accred.:* 1938/1988 (ATS); 1972/1988 (NCA) *Calendar:* Qtr. plan *Degrees:* M, D *CEO:* Pres. Neal F. Fisher
Enroll: 478   (708) 866-3900

GEM CITY COLLEGE
700 State St., Quincy 62301 *Type:* Private business *Accred.:* 1954/1986 (ACISC) *Calendar:* Courses of varying lengths *Degrees:* A, certificates, diplomas *Prof. Accred.:* Medical Assisting *CEO:* Dir. Russell H. Hagenah
                                         (217) 222-0391

GOVERNORS STATE UNIVERSITY
University Park 60466 *Type:* Public (state) liberal arts *System:* Illinois Board of Governors Universities *Accred.:* 1975/1990 (NCA) *Calendar:* Tri. plan *Degrees:* B, M *Prof. Ac-*

cred.: Counseling, Health Services Administration, Medical Technology, Nursing (B,M), Social Work (B-candidate), Speech-Language Pathology *CEO:* Pres. Paula Wolff
Enroll: 5,133   (708) 534-5000

GREENVILLE COLLEGE
Greenville 62246 *Type:* Private (Free Methodist) liberal arts *Accred.:* 1948/1986 (NCA) *Calendar:* 4-1-4 plan *Degrees:* B *Prof. Accred.:* Teacher Education (e,s) *CEO:* Pres. Robert E. Smith
Enroll: 864   (618) 664-1840

HAROLD WASHINGTON COLLEGE
30 E. Lake St., Chicago 60601 *Type:* Public (city) junior *System:* City Colleges of Chicago *Accred.:* 1967/1986 (NCA) *Calendar:* Sem. plan *Degrees:* A, certificates *CEO:* Pres. Bernice J. Miller
Enroll: 14,359   (312) 781-9430

HARRINGTON INSTITUTE OF INTERIOR DESIGN
410 S. Michigan Ave., Chicago 60605 *Type:* Private professional *Calendar:* Sem. plan *Degrees:* A, P *Prof. Accred.:* Interior Design *CEO:* Pres. and Dean Robert C. Marks
                                         (312) 939-4975

HARRY S TRUMAN COLLEGE
1145 W. Wilson Ave., Chicago 60640 *Type:* Public (city) junior *System:* City Colleges of Chicago *Accred.:* 1967/1990 (NCA) *Calendar:* Sem. plan *Degrees:* A, certificates, diplomas *Prof. Accred.:* Medical Record Technology *CEO:* Pres. Wallace B. Appelson
Enroll: 4,760   (312) 878-1700

HIGHLAND COMMUNITY COLLEGE
2998 Pearl City Rd., Freeport 61032 *Type:* Public (district) junior *System:* Illinois Community College Board *Accred.:* 1973/1986 (NCA) *Calendar:* Sem. plan *Degrees:* A, certificates *CEO:* Pres. Ruth Mercedes Smith
Enroll: 3,180   (815) 235-6121

ILLINOIS BENEDICTINE COLLEGE
5700 College Rd., Lisle 60532 *Type:* Private (Roman Catholic) liberal arts *Accred.:* 1958/1986 (NCA) *Calendar:* Sem. plan *Degrees:* B, M *Prof. Accred.:* Nursing (B) *CEO:* Pres. Richard C. Becker
Enroll: 2,645   (708) 960-1500

ILLINOIS CENTRAL COLLEGE
One College Dr., East Peoria 61635 *Type:* Public (district) junior *System:* Illinois Community College Board *Accred.:* 1972/1992 (NCA) *Calendar:* Sem. plan *Degrees:* A, certificates *Prof. Accred.:* Dental Assisting, Dental Hygiene, Medical Laboratory Technology (AMA), Music, Nursing (A), Occupational Therapy Assisting, Physical Therapy Assisting, Radiography, Respiratory Therapy, Respiratory Therapy Technology, Surgical Technology *CEO:* Pres. Thomas K. Thomas
Enroll: 13,632   (309) 694-5011

ILLINOIS COLLEGE
1101 W. College St., Jacksonville 62650 *Type:* Private (United Presbyterian/United Church of Christ) liberal arts *Accred.:* 1913/ 1985 (NCA) *Calendar:* Sem. plan *Degrees:* B *CEO:* Pres. Richard A. Pfau
Enroll: 926   (217) 245-3000

ILLINOIS COLLEGE OF OPTOMETRY
3241 S. Michigan Ave., Chicago 60616 *Type:* Private professional *Accred.:* 1969/ 1989 (NCA) *Calendar:* Qtr. plan *Degrees:* B, D *Prof. Accred.:* Optometry *CEO:* Pres. Boyd B. Banwell
Enroll: 590   (312) 225-1700

ILLINOIS INSTITUTE OF TECHNOLOGY
3300 S. Federal St., Chicago 60616 *Type:* Private *Accred.:* 1941/1987 (NCA) *Calendar:* Sem. plan *Degrees:* B, M, D *Prof. Accred.:* Clinical Psychology, Engineering (aerospace, chemical, civil, electrical, mechanical, metallurgical), Law, Rehabilitation Counseling *CEO:* Pres. Lewis Collens
Enroll: 6,693   (312) 567-5198

ILLINOIS STATE UNIVERSITY
Normal 61790-1000 *Type:* Public (state) *System:* Regency Universities System Board of Regents *Accred.:* 1913/1985 (NCA) *Calendar:* Sem. plan *Degrees:* B, P, M, D, certificates *Prof. Accred.:* Accounting (Type A,C), Art, Audiology, Counseling, Home Economics, Medical Record Administration, Music, Psychology Internship, Recreation and Leisure Services, Social Work (B), Speech-Language Pathology, Teacher Education (e, s,p), Theatre *CEO:* Pres. Thomas P. Wallace
Enroll: 21,880   (309) 438-2111

ILLINOIS VALLEY COMMUNITY COLLEGE
2578 E. 350th Rd., Oglesby 61348 *Type:* Public (district) junior *System:* Illinois Community College Board *Accred.:* 1929/1988 (NCA) *Calendar:* Sem. plan *Degrees:* A, certificates *Prof. Accred.:* Dental Assisting, Nursing (A) *CEO:* Pres. Alfred E. Wisgoski
Enroll: 4,497   (815) 224-2720

ILLINOIS WESLEYAN UNIVERSITY
P.O. Box 2900, Bloomington 61702 *Type:* Private (United Methodist) *Accred.:* 1916/ 1993 (NCA) *Calendar:* Sem. plan *Degrees:* B *Prof. Accred.:* Music, Nursing (B) *CEO:* Pres. Minor Myers, Jr.
Enroll: 1,822   (309) 556-1000

INTERNATIONAL ACADEMY OF MERCHANDISING AND DESIGN
One N. State St., No. 400, Chicago 60602 *Type:* Private *Accred.:* 1981/1990 (ACISC) *Calendar:* Qtr. plan *Degrees:* A, B, diplomas *Prof. Accred.:* Interior Design *CEO:* Exec. Dir. Cynthia Reynolds
                                 (312) 541-3910

JOHN A. LOGAN COLLEGE
Carterville 62918 *Type:* Public (district) junior *System:* Illinois Community College Board *Accred.:* 1972/1987 (NCA) *Calendar:* Sem. plan *Degrees:* A, certificates *Prof. Accred.:* Dental Assisting *CEO:* Pres. J. Ray Hancock
Enroll: 4,971   (618) 985-3741

THE JOHN MARSHALL LAW SCHOOL
315 S. Plymouth Ct., Chicago 60604 *Type:* Private professional *Calendar:* Sem. plan *Degrees:* P, M *Prof. Accred.:* Law *CEO:* Acting Dean Fred R. Herzog
Enroll: 1,198   (312) 427-2737

JOHN WOOD COMMUNITY COLLEGE
150 S. 48th St., Quincy 62301 *Type:* Public (district) junior *System:* Illinois Community College Board *Accred.:* 1980/1992 (NCA) *Calendar:* Sem. plan *Degrees:* A, certificates *CEO:* Pres. Robert C. Keys
Enroll: 2,861   (217) 224-6500

JOLIET JUNIOR COLLEGE
1216 Houbolt Ave., Joliet 60436 *Type:* Public (district) junior *System:* Illinois Community College Board *Accred.:* 1917/1992 (NCA) *Calendar:* Sem. plan *Degrees:* A,

certificates *Prof. Accred.:* Nursing (A) *CEO:*
Pres. Raymond A. Pietak
Enroll: 10,427   (815) 729-9020

JUDSON COLLEGE
1151 N. State St., Elgin 60123 *Type:* Private
Accred.: 1973/1988 (NCA) *Calendar:* Tri. plan
Degrees: B *CEO:* Pres. James W. Didier
Enroll: 605   (708) 695-2500

KANKAKEE COMMUNITY COLLEGE
P.O. Box 888, Kankakee 60901 *Type:* Public
(district) junior *System:* Illinois Community
College Board *Accred.:* 1974/1984 (NCA)
Calendar: 4-1-4 plan *Degrees:* A, certifi-
cates *Prof. Accred.:* Medical Laboratory
Technology (AMA), Radiography, Respira-
tory Therapy Technology *CEO:* Pres.
Lawrence D. Huffman
Enroll: 3,824   (815) 933-0345

KASKASKIA COLLEGE
27210 College Rd., Centralia 62801 *Type:*
Public (district) junior *System:* Illinois Community College Board *Accred.:* 1964/1989
(NCA) *Calendar:* Sem. plan *Degrees:* A,
certificates *Prof. Accred.:* Dental Assisting,
Nursing (A), Radiography *CEO:* Pres. Raymond D. Woods
Enroll: 3,322   (618) 532-1981

KELLER GRADUATE SCHOOL OF MANAGEMENT
One Tower Lane, Oakbrook Terrace 60181
Type: Private professional *Accred.:* 1977/
1992 (NCA) *Calendar:* Qtr. plan *Degrees:*
M *CEO:* Pres. and C.E.O. Ronald L. Taylor
Enroll: 2,094   (708) 571-7700

EAST VALLEY CENTER
1201 S. Alma School Rd., Ste. 5450,
Mesa, AZ 85210 *CEO:* Dean Deborah B.
Robin
                    (602) 827-1511

KANSAS CITY DOWNTOWN
City Center Sq., 1100 Main St., Kansas
City, MO 64105-2112 *CEO:* Dean Martha
Gershun
                    (816) 221-1300

KANSAS CITY SOUTH
11224 Holmes Rd., Kansas City, MO
64131 *CEO:* Dean Martha Gershun
                    (816) 941-2224

MILWAUKEE CENTER
330 E. Kilbourn Ave., Milwaukee, WI
53202-3141 *CEO:* Dean Lee McConaghy
                    (414) 278-7677

NORTH SUBURBAN CENTER
Tri-State Intl. Office Ctr., Bldg. 25, Ste.
130, Lincolnshire 60069-4460 *CEO:* Dean
O. John Shubiak
                    (708) 940-7768

NORTHWEST SUBURBAN CENTER
1051 Perimeter Dr., Schaumburg 60173-
5009 *CEO:* Dean O. John Shubiak
                    (708) 330-0040

PHOENIX/NORTHWEST CENTER
2149 W. Dunlap Ave., Phoenix, AZ
85021 *CEO:* Dean Deborah B. Robin
                    (602) 870-0117

SOUTH SUBURBAN CENTER
15255 S. 94th Ave., Orland Park 60462-
3823 *CEO:* Dean O. John Shubiak
                    (708) 460-9580

WAUKESHA CENTER
20935 Swenson Dr., Waukesha, WI 53186
CEO: Dean Lee McConaghy
                    (414) 798-9889

WEST SUBURBAN CENTER
1101 31st St., Downers Grove 60515-
5515 *CEO:* Dean O. John Shubiak
                    (708) 969-6624

KENDALL COLLEGE
2408 Orrington Ave., Evanston 60201 *Type:*
Private (United Methodist) liberal arts *Accred.:* 1962/1993 (NCA) *Calendar:* 4-1-4
plan *Degrees:* A, B, certificates *CEO:* Pres.
Thomas J. Kerr, IV
Enroll: 403   (708) 866-1300

KENNEDY-KING COLLEGE
6800 S. Wentworth Ave., Chicago 60621
Type: Public (city) junior *System:* City Coll-
eges of Chicago *Accred.:* 1967/1988 (NCA)
Calendar: Sem. plan *Degrees:* A, certificates
CEO: Pres. Harold Pates
Enroll: 2,680   (312) 962-3200

KISHWAUKEE COLLEGE
21193 Malta Rd., Malta 60150 *Type:* Public
(district) junior *System:* Illinois Community

College Board *Accred.:* 1974/1989 (NCA) *Calendar:* Sem. plan *Degrees:* A, certificates *Prof. Accred.:* Radiography *CEO:* Pres. Norman L. Jenkins
Enroll: 3,388   (815) 825-2086

KNOWLEDGE SYSTEMS INSTITUTE
3420 Main St., Skokie 60076 *Type:* Private *Accred.:* 1991 (NCA) *Calendar:* Qtr. plan *Degrees:* M *CEO:* Pres. Shi-Kuo Chang
Enroll: 49   (708) 679-3135

KNOX COLLEGE
Galesburg 61401 *Type:* Private liberal arts *Accred.:* 1913/1989 (NCA) *Calendar:* 3-3-3 plan *Degrees:* B *CEO:* Pres. Frederick C. Nahm
Enroll: 954   (309) 343-0112

LAKE FOREST COLLEGE
555 N. Sheridan Rd., Lake Forest 60045 *Type:* Private (United Presbyterian) liberal arts *Accred.:* 1913/1987 (NCA) *Calendar:* Qtr. plan *Degrees:* B, M *CEO:* Pres. David Spadafora
Enroll: 975   (708) 234-3100

LAKE FOREST GRADUATE SCHOOL OF MANAGEMENT
240 N. Sheridan Rd., Lake Forest 60045 *Type:* Private graduate only *Accred.:* 1978/ 1993 (NCA) *Calendar:* Qtr. plan *Degrees:* M *CEO:* Pres. Raymond E. Britt, Jr.
Enroll: 810   (708) 234-5005

LAKE LAND COLLEGE
5001 Lake Land Blvd., Mattoon 61938 *Type:* Public (district) junior *System:* Illinois Community College Board *Accred.:* 1973/ 1988 (NCA) *Calendar:* Qtr. plan *Degrees:* A, certificates *Prof. Accred.:* Dental Hygiene, Nursing (A), Practical Nursing *CEO:* Pres. Robert K. Luther
Enroll: 4,543   (217) 235-3131

LEWIS AND CLARK COMMUNITY COLLEGE
5800 Godfrey Rd., Godfrey 62035 *Type:* Public (district) junior *System:* Illinois Community College Board *Accred.:* 1971/1993 (NCA) *Calendar:* Sem. plan *Degrees:* A, certificates *Prof. Accred.:* Dental Assisting, Medical Laboratory Technology (AMA), Nursing (A) *CEO:* Pres. Dale T. Chapman
Enroll: 5,853   (618) 466-3411

LEWIS UNIVERSITY
Rte. 53, Romeoville 60441 *Type:* Private (Roman Catholic) liberal arts *Accred.:* 1963/ 1987 (NCA) *Calendar:* 4-1-4 plan *Degrees:* A, B, M, certificates *Prof. Accred.:* Nursing (B,M) *CEO:* Pres. James Gaffney, F.S.C.
Enroll: 4,102   (815) 838-0500

LEXINGTON INSTITUTE OF HOSPITALITY CAREERS
10840 S. Western Ave., Chicago 60643 *Type:* Private *Accred.:* 1993 (NCA) *Calendar:* Sem. plan *Degrees:* A *CEO:* Pres. Ana Maria Boza
Enroll: 41   (312) 779-3800

LINCOLN CHRISTIAN COLLEGE AND SEMINARY
100 Campus View Dr., Lincoln 62656 *Type:* Private (Christian Churches/Churches of Christ) *Accred.:* 1954/1985 (AABC); 1991 (ATS); 1991 (NCA) *Calendar:* Sem. plan *Degrees:* A, B, M, certificates *CEO:* Pres. Charles A. McNeely
Enroll: 461   (217) 732-3168

LINCOLN COLLEGE
300 Keokuk St., Lincoln 62656 *Type:* Private junior *Accred.:* 1929/1986 (NCA) *Calendar:* 4-1-4 plan *Degrees:* A, certificates *CEO:* Pres. Jack D. Nutt
Enroll: 1,252   (217) 732-3155

LINCOLN LAND COMMUNITY COLLEGE
Shepherd Rd., Springfield 62794 *Type:* Public (district) junior *System:* Illinois Community College Board *Accred.:* 1973/1993 (NCA) *Calendar:* Sem. plan *Degrees:* A, certificates *Prof. Accred.:* Nursing (A), Radiography, Respiratory Therapy *CEO:* Pres. Norman L. Stephens, Jr.
Enroll: 7,965   (217) 786-2200

LINCOLN TRAIL COLLEGE
Rte. 3, Robinson 62454 *Type:* Public (district) junior *System:* Illinois Eastern Community Colleges System *Accred.:* 1984/1988 (NCA)* *Calendar:* Sem. plan *Degrees:* A, certificates *Prof. Accred.:* Nursing (A) *CEO:* Pres. Donald E. Donnay
                    (618) 544-8657

* Indirect accreditation through Illinois Eastern Community Colleges System.

LOYOLA UNIVERSITY OF CHICAGO
820 N. Michigan Ave., Chicago 60611 *Type:* Private (Roman Catholic) *Accred.:* 1921/ 1985 (NCA) *Calendar:* Sem. plan *Degrees:* B, M, D *Prof. Accred.:* Business (B,M), Clinical Psychology, Counseling Psychology, General Practice Residency, Law, Medicine, Nursing (B,M), Oral and Maxillofacial Surgery, Pediatric Dentistry, Social Work (B,M), Theatre (associate) *CEO:* Pres. John J. Piderit, S.J.
Enroll: 15,298   (312) 915-6000

LUTHERAN SCHOOL OF THEOLOGY AT CHICAGO
1100 E. 55th St., Chicago 60615-5199 *Type:* Private (Evangelical Lutheran) graduate only *Accred.:* 1945/1987 (ATS); 1982/1987 (NCA) *Calendar:* Qtr. plan *Degrees:* M, D, certificates *CEO:* Pres. William E. Lesher
Enroll: 389   (312) 753-0700

MACCORMAC JUNIOR COLLEGE
506 S. Wabash Ave., Chicago 60605-1667 *Type:* Private junior *Accred.:* 1979/1989 (NCA) *Calendar:* Qtr. plan *Degrees:* A, certificates, diplomas *CEO:* Pres. John Henry Allen
Enroll: 406   (312) 922-1884

MACMURRAY COLLEGE
447 E. College Ave., Jacksonville 62650 *Type:* Private (United Methodist) liberal arts *Accred.:* 1921/1989 (NCA) *Calendar:* 4-1-4 plan *Degrees:* A, B *Prof. Accred.:* Nursing (B), Social Work (B-candidate) *CEO:* Pres. Edward J. Mitchell
Enroll: 1,511   (217) 479-7025

MALCOLM X COLLEGE
1900 W. Van Buren St., Chicago 60612 *Type:* Public (city) junior *System:* City Colleges of Chicago *Accred.:* 1967/1991 (NCA) *Calendar:* Sem. plan *Degrees:* A, certificates *Prof. Accred.:* Medical Laboratory Technology (AMA), Mortuary Science, Radiography, Respiratory Therapy, Respiratory Therapy Technology *CEO:* Pres. Zerrie D. Campbell
Enroll: 3,263   (312) 850-7041

MCCORMICK THEOLOGICAL SEMINARY
5555 S. Woodlawn Ave., Chicago 60637 *Type:* Private (Presbyterian) graduate only *Accred.:* 1938/1987 (ATS); 1982/1987

(NCA) *Calendar:* Qtr. plan *Degrees:* M, D *CEO:* Pres. David Ramage, Jr.
Enroll: 627   (312) 947-6300

MCHENRY COUNTY COLLEGE
8900 U.S. Hwy. 14, Crystal Lake 60012-2794 *Type:* Public (district) junior *System:* Illinois Community College Board *Accred.:* 1976/1992 (NCA) *Calendar:* Sem. plan *Degrees:* A, certificates *CEO:* Pres. Robert C. Bartlett
Enroll: 4,671   (815) 455-3700

MCKENDREE COLLEGE
701 College Rd., Lebanon 62254 *Type:* Private (United Methodist) liberal arts *Accred.:* 1970/1989 (NCA) *Calendar:* 4-1-4 plan *Degrees:* A, B *Prof. Accred.:* Nursing (B) *CEO:* Pres. Gerrit J. TenBrink
Enroll: 1,450   (618) 537-4481

MEADVILLE/LOMBARD THEOLOGICAL SCHOOL
5701 S. Woodlawn Ave., Chicago 60637 *Type:* Private (Unitarian Universalist) graduate only *Accred.:* 1940/1987 (ATS) *Calendar:* Qtr. plan *Degrees:* M, D *CEO:* Pres./ Dean Spencer Lavan
FTE Enroll: 36   (312) 753-3195

MENNONITE COLLEGE OF NURSING
804 N. East St., Bloomington 61701 *Type:* Private *Accred.:* 1985/1991 (NCA) *Calendar:* Qtr. plan *Degrees:* B *Prof. Accred.:* Nursing (B) *CEO:* Pres. Kathleen Hogan
Enroll: 151   (309) 829-0715

MIDSTATE COLLEGE
244 S.W. Jefferson St., Peoria 61602 *Type:* Private junior *Accred.:* 1982/1992 (NCA) *Calendar:* Qtr. plan *Degrees:* A, certificates, diplomas *Prof. Accred.:* Medical Assisting (AMA) *CEO:* Pres. R. Dale Bunch
Enroll: 512   (309) 673-6365

MIDWESTERN UNIVERSITY
555 31st St., Downers Grove 60515 *Type:* Private professional *Accred.:* 1993 (NCA) *Calendar:* Sem. plan *Degrees:* B, D *Prof. Accred.:* Osteopathy *CEO:* Pres. Jack B. Kinsinger, Ph.D.
Enroll: 663   (708) 515-6060

MILLIKIN UNIVERSITY
1184 W. Main St., Decatur 62522 *Type:* Private (United Presbyterian) liberal arts and

professional *Accred.:* 1914/1987 (NCA) *Calendar:* 4-1-4 plan *Degrees:* B *Prof. Accred.:* Music, Nursing (B) *CEO:* Pres. Curtis L. McCray
Enroll: 1,911 (217) 424-6211

MONMOUTH COLLEGE
700 E. Broadway, Monmouth 61462 *Type:* Private (United Presbyterian) liberal arts *Accred.:* 1913/1988 (NCA) *Calendar:* 3-3-3 plan *Degrees:* B *CEO:* Pres. Bruce Haywood
Enroll: 585 (309) 457-2311

MONTAY COLLEGE
3750 W. Peterson Ave., Chicago 60659 *Type:* Private (Roman Catholic) 2-year *Accred.:* 1977/1989 (NCA) *Calendar:* 4-1-4 plan *Degrees:* A, certificates *CEO:* Pres. Charlene Endecavage
Enroll: 251 (312) 539-1919

MOODY BIBLE INSTITUTE
820 N. La Salle Dr., Chicago 60610 *Type:* Independent (interdenominational) *Accred.:* 1951/1992 (AABC); 1989 (NCA) *Calendar:* Sem. plan *Degrees:* A, B, M, certificates, diplomas *Prof. Accred.:* Music *CEO:* Pres. Joseph Stowell, III
Enroll: 4,693 (312) 329-4000

MORAINE VALLEY COMMUNITY COLLEGE
10900 S. 88th Ave., Palos Hills 60465 *Type:* Public (district) junior *System:* Illinois Community College Board *Accred.:* 1975/1986 (NCA) *Calendar:* Sem. plan *Degrees:* A, certificates *Prof. Accred.:* Medical Laboratory Technology (AMA), Medical Record Technology, Nursing (A), Radiography, Respiratory Therapy *CEO:* Pres. Vernon O. Crawley
Enroll: 14,074 (708) 974-4300

MORRISON INSTITUTE OF TECHNOLOGY
P.O. Box 410, Morrison 61270-0410 *Type:* Private 2-year *Calendar:* Sem. plan *Degrees:* A *Prof. Accred.:* Engineering Technology (general) *CEO:* C.E.O. Don D. Vandercreek
Enroll: 250 (815) 772-7218

MORTON COLLEGE
3801 S. Central Ave., Cicero 60650 *Type:* Public (district) junior *System:* Illinois Community College Board *Accred.:* 1927/1984 (NCA) *Calendar:* Sem. plan *Degrees:* A,

certificates *Prof. Accred.:* Dental Assisting, Physical Therapy Assisting *CEO:* Pres. Charles P. Ferro
Enroll: 4,698 (708) 656-8000

NAES COLLEGE
2838 W. Peterson Ave., Chicago 60659 *Type:* Private *Accred.:* 1984/1989 (NCA) *Calendar:* Sem. plan *Degrees:* B *CEO:* Pres. Faith Smith
Enroll: 75 (312) 761-5000

NATIONAL COLLEGE OF CHIROPRACTIC
200 E. Roosevelt Rd., Lombard 60148 *Type:* Private professional *Accred.:* 1981/1986 (NCA) *Calendar:* Tri. plan *Degrees:* B, D *Prof. Accred.:* Chiropractic Education *CEO:* Pres. James F. Winterstein, D.C.
Enroll: 711 (708) 826-6285

NATIONAL-LOUIS UNIVERSITY
2840 Sheridan Rd., Evanston 60201 *Type:* Private liberal arts and business *Accred.:* 1946/1991 (NCA) *Calendar:* Qtr. plan *Degrees:* B, P, M, D, certificates, diplomas *Prof. Accred.:* Medical Technology, Radiation Therapy Technology, Respiratory Therapy *CEO:* Pres. Orley R. Herron
Enroll: 7,575 (708) 475-1100

NORTH CENTRAL COLLEGE
30 N. Brainerd St., P.O. Box 3063, Naperville 60566-7063 *Type:* Private (United Methodist) liberal arts *Accred.:* 1914/1990 (NCA) *Calendar:* 3-3 plan *Degrees:* B, M *CEO:* Pres. Harold R. Wilde
Enroll: 2,535 (708) 420-3400

NORTH PARK COLLEGE AND THEOLOGICAL SEMINARY
3225 W. Foster Ave., Chicago 60625-4895 *Type:* Private (Evangelical Covenant) liberal arts and theology *Accred.:* 1963/1986 (ATS); 1926/1991 (NCA) *Calendar:* 3-3 plan *Degrees:* B, M *Prof. Accred.:* Music, Nursing (B) *CEO:* Pres. David G. Horner
Enroll: 1,392 (312) 583-2700

NORTHEASTERN ILLINOIS UNIVERSITY
5500 N. St. Louis Ave., Chicago 60625 *Type:* Public (state) liberal arts and teachers *System:* Illinois Board of Governors Universities *Accred.:* 1961/1987 (NCA) *Calendar:* Tri. plan *Degrees:* B, M *Prof. Accred.:* So-

cial Work (B), Teacher Education (e,s,p)
CEO: Pres. Gordon H. Lamb
Enroll: 10,820   (312) 794-4050

NORTHERN BAPTIST THEOLOGICAL SEMINARY
660 E. Butterfield Rd., Lombard 60148
Type: Private (Baptist) graduate only *Accred.:* 1968/1991 (ATS); 1947/1993 (NCA)
Calendar: Qtr. plan *Degrees:* M, D *CEO:*
Pres. Ian M. Chapman
Enroll: 193   (708) 620-2100

NORTHERN ILLINOIS UNIVERSITY
De Kalb 60115 *Type:* Public (state) *System:*
Regency Universities System Board of Regents *Accred.:* 1915/1984 (NCA) *Calendar:*
Sem. plan *Degrees:* B, P, M, D, certificates
Prof. Accred.: Accounting (Type A,C), Art,
Audiology, Business (B,M), Clinical Psychology, Counseling, Engineering (electrical, industrial, mechanical), Journalism
(B,M), Law, Librarianship, Marriage and
Family Therapy (M), Medical Technology,
Music, Nursing (B,M), Physical Therapy,
Psychology Internship, Public Administration, Rehabilitation Counseling, Speech-Language Pathology, Teacher Education
(e,s,p), Theatre *CEO:* Pres. John E. LaTourette
Enroll: 24,052   (815) 753-9500

NORTHWESTERN BUSINESS COLLEGE
4829 N. Lipps Ave., Chicago 60630 *Type:*
Private business *Accred.:* 1974/1986 (AC-ISC); 1991/1993 (NCA candidate) *Calendar:* Qtr. plan *Degrees:* A, certificates,
diplomas *Prof. Accred.:* Medical Assisting
(AMA) *CEO:* Pres. Lawrence W. Schumacher
Enroll: 928   (312) 777-4220

SOUTHWESTERN CAMPUS
8020 W. 87th St., Hickery Hills 60457 *Accred.:* 1989 (ACISC) *CEO:* Dir. Tony
Sapata
                                   (708) 430-0990

NORTHWESTERN UNIVERSITY
633 Clark St., Evanston 60208 *Type:* Private
Accred.: 1913/1985 (NCA) *Calendar:* Sem.
plan *Degrees:* B, M, D *Prof. Accred.:* Audiology, Business (M), Clinical Psychology,
Combined Prosthodontics, Counseling Psychology, Dentistry, Endodontics, Engineering (bioengineering, chemical, civil, electrical, environmental/sanitary, industrial, mate-

rials, mechanical), General Dentistry, Health
Services Administration, Journalism (B,M),
Law, Medicine, Music, Oral and Maxillofacial Surgery, Orthodontics, Pediatric Dentistry, Periodontics, Physical Therapy, Psychology Internship, Speech-Language
Pathology, Theatre *CEO:* Pres. Arnold R.
Weber
Enroll: 17,285   (708) 491-3741

OAKTON COMMUNITY COLLEGE
1600 E. Golf Rd., Des Plaines 60016 *Type:*
Public (district) junior *System:* Illinois Community College Board *Accred.:* 1976/1988
(NCA) *Calendar:* Sem. plan *Degrees:* A,
certificates, diplomas *Prof. Accred.:* Medical
Laboratory Technology (AMA), Medical
Record Technology, Nursing (A), Physical
Therapy Assisting *CEO:* Pres. Thomas Ten-Hoeve
Enroll: 13,356   (708) 635-1600

OLIVE-HARVEY COLLEGE
10001 S. Woodlawn Ave., Chicago 60628
Type: Public (city) junior *System:* City Colleges of Chicago *Accred.:* 1967/1990 (NCA)
Calendar: Sem. plan *Degrees:* A, certificates
CEO: Pres. Homer D. Franklin
Enroll: 3,698   (312) 291-6100

OLIVET NAZARENE UNIVERSITY
Kankakee 60901 *Type:* Private (Nazarene)
liberal arts *Accred.:* 1956/1985 (NCA) *Calendar:* Sem. plan *Degrees:* A, B, M, certificates *Prof. Accred.:* Music, Nursing (B), Social Work (B-candidate) *CEO:* Pres. John
Carl Bowling
Enroll: 1,973   (815) 939-5011

OLNEY CENTRAL COLLEGE
305 N. West St., Olney 62450 *Type:* Public
(district) junior *System:* Illinois Eastern
Community Colleges System *Accred.:* 1984/
1988 (NCA)* *Calendar:* Sem. plan *Degrees:*
A, certificates *Prof. Accred.:* Nursing (A),
Radiography *CEO:* Pres. Judith Hansen
                                   (618) 395-4351

* Indirect accreditation through Illinois Eastern
  Community Colleges System.

PARKLAND COLLEGE
2400 W. Bradley Ave., Champaign 61821
Type: Public (district) junior *System:* Illinois
Community College Board *Accred.:* 1972/

1993 (NCA) *Calendar:* Sem. plan *Degrees:* A, certificates *Prof. Accred.:* Dental Assisting, Dental Hygiene, Engineering Technology (electrical), Nursing (A), Occupational Therapy Assisting, Practical Nursing (warning), Radiography, Respiratory Therapy, Surgical Technology, Veterinary Technology *CEO:* Pres. Zelema M. Harris
Enroll: 9,343   (217) 351-2200

PHILLIPS COLLEGE OF CHICAGO
205 W. Randolph St., 2nd Fl., Chicago 60606 *Type:* Private business *Accred.:* 1969/1987 (ACISC) *Calendar:* Sem. plan *Degrees:* A, certificates, diplomas *CEO:* Dir. Camden McKinley
Enroll: 488   (312) 419-1711

PRAIRIE STATE COLLEGE
202 S. Halsted St., Chicago Heights 60411 *Type:* Public (district) junior *System:* Illinois Community College Board *Accred.:* 1965/1989 (NCA) *Calendar:* Sem. plan *Degrees:* A, certificates *Prof. Accred.:* Dental Hygiene, Nursing (A) *CEO:* Pres. E. Timothy Lightfield
Enroll: 5,785   (708) 756-3110

PRINCIPIA COLLEGE
Elsah 62028 *Type:* Private (Christian Science) liberal arts *Accred.:* 1923/1985 (NCA) *Calendar:* Qtr. plan *Degrees:* B *CEO:* Pres. David E. Pfeifer
Enroll: 589   (618) 374-2131

QUINCY UNIVERSITY
1800 College Ave., Quincy 62301 *Type:* Private (Roman Catholic) liberal arts *Accred.:* 1954/1992 (NCA) *Calendar:* Sem. plan *Degrees:* A, B, M *Prof. Accred.:* Music *CEO:* Pres. James F. Toal, O.F.M.
Enroll: 1,163   (217) 222-8020

RAY COLLEGE OF DESIGN
401 N. Wabash St., Chicago 60611-3532 *Type:* Private *Accred.:* 1975/1988 (ACCSCT) *Calendar:* Sem. plan *Degrees:* A, B *CEO:* Pres. Wade F. Ray
                                         (312) 280-3500

BRANCH CAMPUS
1051 Perimeter Dr., Schaumburg 60173-5070 *Accred.:* 1988/1993 (ACCSCT) *CEO:* Dir. Jeanne Flanagan
                                         (708) 619-3450

REND LAKE COLLEGE
Rural Rte. 1, Ina 62846 *Type:* Public (district) junior *System:* Illinois Community College Board *Accred.:* 1969/1989 (NCA) *Calendar:* Sem. plan *Degrees:* A, certificates *CEO:* Pres. Mark S. Kern
Enroll: 2,957   (618) 437-5321

RICHARD J. DALEY COLLEGE
7500 S. Pulaski Rd., Chicago 60652 *Type:* Public (city) junior *System:* City Colleges of Chicago *Accred.:* 1967/1991 (NCA) *Calendar:* Sem. plan *Degrees:* A, certificates *CEO:* Interim Pres. Donald B. Smith
Enroll: 9,431   (312) 838-7500

RICHLAND COMMUNITY COLLEGE
One College Park, Decatur 62521 *Type:* Public (district) junior *System:* Illinois Community College Board *Accred.:* 1978/1993 (NCA) *Calendar:* Qtr. plan *Degrees:* A, certificates *CEO:* Pres. Charles R. Novak
Enroll: 4,110   (217) 875-7200

ROBERT MORRIS COLLEGE
180 N. La Salle St., Chicago 60601 *Type:* Private *Accred.:* 1986/1991 (NCA) *Calendar:* Qtr. plan *Degrees:* A, B, diplomas *Prof. Accred.:* Medical Assisting (AMA) *CEO:* Pres. Richard D. Pickett
Enroll: 2,353   (312) 836-4802

ROCK VALLEY COLLEGE
3301 N. Mulford Rd., Rockford 61114 *Type:* Public (district) junior *System:* Illinois Community College Board *Accred.:* 1971/1984 (NCA) *Calendar:* Sem. plan *Degrees:* A, certificates *Prof. Accred.:* Respiratory Therapy, Respiratory Therapy Technology *CEO:* Pres. Karl J. Jacobs
Enroll: 3,214   (815) 654-4250

ROCKFORD BUSINESS COLLEGE
730 N. Church St., Rockford 61103 *Type:* Private business *Accred.:* 1968/1987 (ACISC) *Calendar:* Qtr. plan *Degrees:* A, certificates, diplomas *CEO:* Pres./Chrmn. of the Bd. David G. Swank
                                         (815) 965-8616

ROCKFORD COLLEGE
5050 E. State St., Rockford 61108 *Type:* Private liberal arts *Accred.:* 1913/1984 (NCA) *Calendar:* 4-1-4 plan *Degrees:* A, B, M

Prof. Accred.: Nursing (B) *CEO:* Pres. William A. Shields
Enroll: 1,025   (815) 226-4000

ROOSEVELT UNIVERSITY
430 S. Michigan Ave., Chicago 60605 *Type:* Private *Accred.:* 1946/1986 (NCA) *Calendar:* Sem. plan *Degrees:* B, M, D, certificates *Prof. Accred.:* Music, Teacher Education (e,s,p) *CEO:* Pres. Theodore L. Gross
Enroll: 6,318   (312) 341-3500

ROSARY COLLEGE
7900 W. Division St., River Forest 60305 *Type:* Private (Roman Catholic) liberal arts *Accred.:* 1919/1985 (NCA) *Calendar:* Sem. plan *Degrees:* B, M, certificates *Prof. Accred.:* Librarianship *CEO:* Pres. Jean Murray, O.P.
Enroll: 1,766   (708) 366-2490

RUSH UNIVERSITY
1653 W. Congress Pkwy., Chicago 60612 *Type:* Private professional *Accred.:* 1974/1988 (NCA) *Calendar:* Qtr. plan *Degrees:* B, M, D *Prof. Accred.:* Health Services Administration, Medicine, Nurse Anesthesia Education, Nursing (B,M) *CEO:* Pres. Leo M. Henikoff
Enroll: 1,301   (312) 942-5474

ST. AUGUSTINE COLLEGE
1333 W. Argyle St., Chicago 60640 *Type:* Private (Episcopal) *Accred.:* 1987/1992 (NCA) *Calendar:* Sem. plan *Degrees:* A, certificates *Prof. Accred.:* Respiratory Therapy *CEO:* Pres. Carlos A. Plazas
Enroll: 1,341   (312) 878-8756

ST. FRANCIS MEDICAL CENTER COLLEGE OF NURSING
511 N.E. Greenleaf St., Peoria 61603 *Type:* Private professional *Accred.:* 1991 (NCA) *Calendar:* Qtr. plan *Degrees:* B *Prof. Accred.:* Nursing (B) *CEO:* Dean Mary Ludgera Pieperbeck
Enroll: 153   (309) 655-2086

ST. JOSEPH COLLEGE OF NURSING
290 N. Springfield Ave., Joliet 60435 *Type:* Private *Accred.:* 1992 (NCA) *Calendar:* Qtr. plan *Degrees:* B *CEO:* Pres. Lois K. Benich
Enroll: 148   (815) 741-7132

ST. XAVIER UNIVERSITY
3700 W. 103rd St., Chicago 60655 *Type:* Private (Roman Catholic) liberal arts *Accred.:* 1937/1988 (NCA) *Calendar:* 4-1-4 plan *Degrees:* B, M *Prof. Accred.:* Music (associate), Nursing (B,M) *CEO:* Pres. Ronald O. Champagne
Enroll: 3,850   (312) 298-3000

SANGAMON STATE UNIVERSITY
Springfield 62794-9243 *Type:* Public (state) liberal arts *System:* Regency Universities System Board of Regents *Accred.:* 1975/1987 (NCA) *Calendar:* Sem. plan *Degrees:* B, M *Prof. Accred.:* Counseling, Medical Technology, Nursing (B), Public Administration *CEO:* Pres. Naomi B. Lynn
Enroll: 4,536   (217) 786-6600

SAUK VALLEY COMMUNITY COLLEGE
173 Illinois Rte. 2, Dixon 61021 *Type:* Public (district) junior *System:* Illinois Community College Board *Accred.:* 1972/1992 (NCA) *Calendar:* Sem. plan *Degrees:* A, certificates *Prof. Accred.:* Medical Laboratory Technology (AMA), Radiography *CEO:* Pres. Richard L. Behrendt
Enroll: 3,038   (815) 288-5511

SCHOOL OF THE ART INSTITUTE OF CHICAGO
37 S. Wabash Ave., Chicago 60603 *Type:* Private professional *Accred.:* 1936/1992 (NCA) *Calendar:* Sem. plan *Degrees:* B, M, certificates *Prof. Accred.:* Art *CEO:* Pres. G. David Pollick
Enroll: 1,667   (312) 899-5136

SEABURY-WESTERN THEOLOGICAL SEMINARY
2122 Sheridan Rd., Evanston 60201 *Type:* Private (Episcopal) *Accred.:* 1938/1987 (ATS); 1981/1987 (NCA) *Calendar:* Sem. plan *Degrees:* M, D, certificates *CEO:* Pres./Dean Mark S. Sisk
Enroll: 103   (708) 328-9300

SHAWNEE COMMUNITY COLLEGE
Rural Rte. 1, Box 53, Ullin 62992-9725 *Type:* Public (district) junior *System:* Illinois Community College Board *Accred.:* 1974/1990 (NCA) *Calendar:* Sem. plan *Degrees:* A, certificates *CEO:* Pres. Jack D. Hill
Enroll: 1,273   (618) 634-2242

SHIMER COLLEGE
P.O. Box A500, 438 N. Sheridan Rd., Waukegan 60079 *Type:* Private liberal arts *Accred.:* 1991 (NCA) *Calendar:* Sem. plan *Degrees:* B, diplomas *CEO:* Pres. Don P. Moon
Enroll: 106   (708) 623-8400

SOUTH SUBURBAN COLLEGE OF COOK COUNTY
15800 S. State St., South Holland 60473 *Type:* Public (district) junior *System:* Illinois Community College Board *Accred.:* 1933/1989 (NCA) *Calendar:* Sem. plan *Degrees:* A, certificates, diplomas *Prof. Accred.:* Music, Nursing (A), Occupational Therapy Assisting, Practical Nursing, Radiography *CEO:* Pres. Richard W. Fonte
Enroll: 11,024   (708) 596-2000

SOUTHEASTERN ILLINOIS COLLEGE
3575 College Rd., Harrisburg 62946 *Type:* Public (district) junior *System:* Illinois Community College Board *Accred.:* 1976/1988 (NCA) *Calendar:* Sem. plan *Degrees:* A, certificates *CEO:* Pres. Harry W. Abell
Enroll: 3,410   (618) 252-6376

SOUTHERN ILLINOIS COLLEGIATE COMMON MARKET
Rte. 3, Box 112, Carterville 62918 *Type:* Private *Calendar:* Courses of varying lengths *Degrees:* A *Prof. Accred.:* Medical Record Technology *CEO:* C.E.O. Ronald K. House
Enroll: 24   (618) 942-7740

SOUTHERN ILLINOIS UNIVERSITY AT CARBONDALE
Carbondale 62901 *Type:* Public (state) *System:* Southern Illinois University System *Accred.:* 1913/1989 (NCA) *Calendar:* Sem. plan *Degrees:* A, B, P, M, D *Prof. Accred.:* Accounting (Type A,C), Art, Business (B,M), Clinical Psychology, Counseling, Counseling Psychology, Dental Hygiene (conditional), Dental Laboratory Technology, Engineering Technology (civil/construction, electrical, mechanical), Engineering (civil, electrical, mechanical, mining), Forestry, Interior Design, Journalism (B,M), Law, Medicine, Mortuary Science, Music, Physical Therapy Assisting, Psychology Internship, Public Affairs, Radiography, Recreation and Leisure Services, Rehabilitation Counseling, Respiratory Therapy, Social Work

(B,M), Speech-Language Pathology, Teacher Education (e,s,p) *CEO:* Pres. John C. Guyon
Enroll: 24,766   (618) 453-2121

SOUTHERN ILLINOIS UNIVERSITY AT EDWARDSVILLE
Edwardsville 62026 *Type:* Public (state) *System:* Southern Illinois University System *Accred.:* 1969/1993 (NCA) *Calendar:* Qtr. plan *Degrees:* B, P, M, D *Prof. Accred.:* Accounting (Type A), Business (B,M), Dentistry, Engineering (civil, electrical, mechanical), General Dentistry (prelim. provisional), General Practice Residency, Music, Nurse Anesthesia Education, Nursing (B,M), Social Work (B), Speech-Language Pathology, Teacher Education (e,s,p) *CEO:* Pres. Nancy Belck
Enroll: 11,670   (618) 692-2000

SPERTUS COLLEGE OF JUDAICA
618 S. Michigan Ave., Chicago 60605 *Type:* Private (Jewish) liberal arts and teachers *Accred.:* 1971/1992 (NCA) *Calendar:* Qtr. plan *Degrees:* B, M, D, certificates *CEO:* Pres. Howard A. Sulkin
Enroll: 223   (312) 922-9012

SPOON RIVER COLLEGE
Rural Rte. 1, Canton 61520 *Type:* Public (district) junior *System:* Illinois Community College Board *Accred.:* 1977/1992 (NCA) *Calendar:* Sem. plan *Degrees:* A, certificates *CEO:* Pres. Felix T. Haynes, Jr.
Enroll: 2,191   (309) 647-4645

SPRINGFIELD COLLEGE IN ILLINOIS
1500 N. Fifth St., Springfield 62702 *Type:* Private (Roman Catholic) junior *Accred.:* 1933/1986 (NCA) *Calendar:* 4-1-4 plan *Degrees:* A *CEO:* Pres. H. Brent De Land
Enroll: 410   (217) 525-1420

STATE COMMUNITY COLLEGE OF EAST ST. LOUIS
601 James R. Thompson Blvd., East St. Louis 62201 *Type:* Public (state) junior *System:* Illinois Community College Board *Accred.:* 1978/1991 (NCA) *Calendar:* Sem. plan *Degrees:* A, certificates *CEO:* Interim Pres. Robert Randolph
Enroll: 1,119   (618) 583-2500

TAYLOR BUSINESS INSTITUTE
8th Fl., 36 S. State St., Chicago 60603 *Type:*
Private business *Accred.:* 1973/1990
(ACISC) *Calendar:* Courses of varying
lengths *Degrees:* A, certificates, diplomas
CEO: Pres. Janice C. Parker
(312) 236-6400

TELSHE YESHIVA-CHICAGO
3535 W. Foster Ave., Chicago 60625 *Type:*
Private professional *Accred.:* 1976/1989
(AARTS) *Calendar:* Sem. plan *Degrees:*
Rabbinic (1st and 2nd) *CEO:* Pres. A. Levin
Enroll: 74   (312) 463-7738

TRINITY CHRISTIAN COLLEGE
6601 W. College Dr., Palos Heights 60463
Type: Private (Christian Reformed) liberal
arts *Accred.:* 1976/1991 (NCA) *Calendar:*
Sem. plan *Degrees:* B *Prof. Accred.:* Nursing (B) *CEO:* Pres. Kenneth B. Bootsma
Enroll: 571   (708) 597-3000

TRINITY COLLEGE
2077 Half Day Rd., Deerfield 60015 *Type:*
Private (Evangelical Free Church) liberal
arts and professional *Accred.:* 1969/1987
(NCA) *Calendar:* Sem. plan *Degrees:* B
CEO: Pres. Kenneth M. Meyer
Enroll: 894   (708) 948-8980

TRINITY EVANGELICAL DIVINITY SCHOOL
2065 Half Day Rd., Deerfield 60015 *Type:*
Private (Evangelical Free Church) graduate
only *Accred.:* 1973/1989 (ATS); 1969/1990
(NCA) *Calendar:* Qtr. plan *Degrees:* M, D,
certificates *CEO:* Pres. Kenneth M. Meyer
Enroll: 1,618   (708) 945-8800

TRITON COLLEGE
2000 Fifth Ave., River Grove 60171 *Type:*
Public (district) junior *System:* Illinois Com-
munity College Board *Accred.:* 1972/1991
(NCA probational) *Calendar:* Sem. plan *De-
grees:* A, certificates *Prof. Accred.:* Dental
Laboratory Technology, Diagnostic Medical
Sonography, Engineering Technology (elec-
trical), Medical Laboratory Technology
(AMA), Nuclear Medicine Technology,
Nursing (A), Ophthalmic Medical Technolo-
gy, Practical Nursing, Radiography, Respira-
tory Therapy, Surgical Technology *CEO:*
Pres. George T. Jorndt
Enroll: 19,503   (708) 456-0300

UNIVERSITY OF CHICAGO
5801 S. Ellis Ave., Chicago 60637 *Type:* Pri-
vate *Accred.:* 1938/1992 (ATS); 1913/1986
(NCA) *Calendar:* Qtr. plan *Degrees:* B, M,
D, certificates *Prof. Accred.:* Accounting
(Type B), Business (M), General Practice
Residency, Health Services Administration,
Histologic Technology, Law, Maxillofacial
Prosthodontics, Medicine, Oral and Maxillo-
facial Surgery, Psychology Internship, Radi-
ation Therapy Technology, Social Work (M)
CEO: Pres. Hugo Freund Sonnenschein
Enroll: 11,286   (312) 702-1234

UNIVERSITY OF HEALTH SCIENCES/THE CHICAGO
MEDICAL SCHOOL
3333 Green Bay Rd., North Chicago 60064
Type: Private professional *Accred.:* 1980/
1988 (NCA) *Calendar:* Qtr. plan *Degrees:*
B, M, D *Prof. Accred.:* Clinical Psychology,
Medical Technology, Medicine, Nursing (B),
Physical Therapy *CEO:* C.E.O. and Pres.
Herman Finch
Enroll: 1,070   (708) 578-3000

UNIVERSITY OF ILLINOIS AT CHICAGO
P.O. Box 4348, Chicago 60680 *Type:* Public
(state) *System:* University of Illinois Central
Office *Accred.:* 1970/1987 (NCA) *Calendar:*
Qtr. plan *Degrees:* B, M, D *Prof. Accred.:*
Art, Blood Bank Technology, Business
(B,M), Clinical Psychology, Dentistry, Dietetics (coordinated), Endodontics, Engineering (bioengineering, chemical, civil, computer, electrical, industrial, mechanical, metallurgical), General Practice Residency (prelim. provisional), Medical Illustration, Medical Record Administration, Medical Technology, Medicine, Nursing (B,M), Occupational Therapy, Oral and Maxillofacial
Surgery, Orthodontics, Pediatric Dentistry,
Periodontics, Physical Therapy, Planning
(M), Psychology Internship, Public Administration, Public Health, Social Work (B,M)
CEO: Chanc. James J. Stukel
Enroll: 24,985   (312) 996-7000

UNIVERSITY OF ILLINOIS AT URBANA-
CHAMPAIGN
601 E. John St., Champaign 61820 *Type:*
Public (state) *System:* University of Illinois
Central Office *Accred.:* 1913/1989 (NCA)
Calendar: Sem. plan *Degrees:* B, M, D *Prof.
Accred.:* Accounting (Type A,C), Art, Audi-

ology, Business (B,M), Clinical Psychology, Community Health, Counseling Psychology, Dance, Engineering (aerospace, agricultural, ceramic, chemical, civil, computer, electrical, engineering mechanics, general, industrial, mechanical, metallurgical, nuclear), Forestry, Journalism (B,M), Landscape Architecture (B,M), Law, Librarianship, Music, Planning (B,M), Psychology Internship, Recreation and Leisure Services, Rehabilitation Counseling, Social Work (B,M), Speech-Language Pathology, Theatre, Veterinary Medicine *CEO:* Chanc. Michael Aiken
Enroll: 35,815   (217) 333-6290

UNIVERSITY OF ST. MARY OF THE LAKE
MUNDELEIN SEMINARY
Rte. 176, Mundelein 60060 *Type:* Private (Roman Catholic) graduate only *Accred.:* 1972/1992 (ATS) *Calendar:* Sem. plan *Degrees:* M, D *CEO:* Pres. Gerald F. Kicanas
FTE Enroll: 289   (708) 566-6401

VANDERCOOK COLLEGE OF MUSIC
3209 S. Michigan Ave., Chicago 60616 *Type:* Private professional *Accred.:* 1972/ 1992 (NCA) *Calendar:* Sem. plan *Degrees:* B, M *Prof. Accred.:* Music *CEO:* Pres. Roseanne K. Rosenthal
Enroll: 1,101   (312) 225-6288

WABASH VALLEY COLLEGE
2200 College Dr., Mount Carmel 62863 *Type:* Public (district) junior *System:* Illinois Eastern Community Colleges System *Accred.:* 1984/1988 (NCA)* *Calendar:* Sem. plan *Degrees:* A, certificates *Prof. Accred.:* Nursing (A) *CEO:* Pres. Harry K. Benson
                                          (618) 262-8641

* Indirect accreditation through Illinois Eastern Community Colleges System.

WAUBONSEE COMMUNITY COLLEGE
Illinois Rte. 47 at Harter Rd., Sugar Grove 60554 *Type:* Public (district) junior *System:* Illinois Community College Board *Accred.:*

1972/1986 (NCA) *Calendar:* Sem. plan *Degrees:* A, certificates *CEO:* Pres. John J. Swalec
Enroll: 7,550   (708) 466-4811

WEST SUBURBAN COLLEGE OF NURSING
Erie St. at Austin Blvd., Oak Park 60302 *Type:* Private professional *Accred.:* 1986/ 1989 (NCA) *Calendar:* Qtr. plan *Degrees:* B *Prof. Accred.:* Nursing (B) *CEO:* Provost Sandra A. Greniewicki
Enroll: 221   (708) 383-6200

WESTERN ILLINOIS UNIVERSITY
900 W. Adams St., Macomb 61455 *Type:* Public (state) *System:* Illinois Board of Governors Universities *Accred.:* 1913/1991 (NCA) *Calendar:* Sem. plan *Degrees:* B, P, M *Prof. Accred.:* Audiology, Business (B,M), Counseling, Music, Recreation and Leisure Services, Social Work (B-candidate), Speech-Language Pathology, Teacher Education (e,s,p) *CEO:* Pres. Donald S. Spencer
Enroll: 13,377   (309) 295-1414

WHEATON COLLEGE
501 E. College Ave., Wheaton 60187 *Type:* Private (interdenominational) *Accred.:* 1913/ 1984 (NCA) *Calendar:* Sem. plan *Degrees:* B, M, D, certificates *Prof. Accred.:* Music, Teacher Education (e,s) *CEO:* Pres. A. Duane Litfin
Enroll: 2,606   (708) 752-5000

WILBUR WRIGHT COLLEGE
4300 N. Narragansett Ave., Chicago 60634 *Type:* Public (city) junior *System:* City Colleges of Chicago *Accred.:* 1967/1992 (NCA) *Calendar:* Sem. plan *Degrees:* A, certificates *Prof. Accred.:* Diagnostic Medical Sonography, Occupational Therapy Assisting, Radiography *CEO:* Pres. Raymond F. Le Fevour
Enroll: 5,688   (312) 481-8182

WILLIAM RAINEY HARPER COLLEGE
1200 W. Algonquin Rd., Palatine 60067-
7398 *Type:* Public (district) junior *System:*
Illinois Community College Board *Accred.:*
1971/1988 (NCA) *Calendar:* Sem. plan *De-*
grees: A, certificates *Prof. Accred.:* Dental
Hygiene, Medical Assisting (AMA), Music,
Nursing (A) *CEO:* Pres. Paul N. Thompson
Enroll: 15,316   (708) 397-3000

INDIANA

ANCILLA COLLEGE
Donaldson 46513 *Type:* Private (Roman Catholic) junior *Accred.:* 1973/1988 (NCA) *Calendar:* Sem. plan *Degrees:* A, certificates *CEO:* Interim Pres. Candace Scheidt, P.H.J.C.
Enroll: 682   (219) 936-8898

ANDERSON UNIVERSITY
1100 E. Fifth St., Anderson 46012-3462 *Type:* Private (Church of God) *Accred.:* 1965/1989 (ATS); 1946/1989 (NCA) *Calendar:* Sem. plan *Degrees:* A, B, M *Prof. Accred.:* Music, Nursing (B), Social Work (B), Teacher Education (e,s) *CEO:* Pres. James L. Edwards
Enroll: 2,249   (317) 649-9071

ASSOCIATED MENNONITE BIBLICAL SEMINARY
3003 Benham Ave., Elkhart 46517-1999 *Type:* Private (Mennonite) graduate only *Accred.:* 1958/1989 (ATS); 1974/1989 (NCA) *Calendar:* Sem. plan *Degrees:* M, certificates *CEO:* Pres. Marlin E. Miller
FTE Enroll: 99   (219) 295-3726

BALL STATE UNIVERSITY
2000 University Ave., Muncie 47306 *Type:* Public (state) *System:* Indiana Commission for Higher Education *Accred.:* 1925/1984 (NCA) *Calendar:* Sem. plan *Degrees:* A, B, P, M, D *Prof. Accred.:* Accounting (Type A), Audiology, Business (B,M), Computer Science, Counseling, Counseling Psychology, Journalism (B,M), Landscape Architecture (B,M), Music, Nuclear Medicine Technology, Nursing (B,M), Planning (M), Psychology Internship, Radiography, Respiratory Therapy, School Psychology, Social Work (B), Speech-Language Pathology, Teacher Education (e,s,p) *CEO:* Pres. John E. Worthen
Enroll: 21,271   (317) 289-1241

BETHEL COLLEGE
1001 W. McKinley Ave., Mishawaka 46545 *Type:* Private (United Missionary) liberal arts *Accred.:* 1971/1991 (NCA) *Calendar:* Sem. plan *Degrees:* A, B, M *Prof. Accred.:* Nursing (A,B) *CEO:* Pres. Norman Bridges
Enroll: 981   (219) 257-3313

BUTLER UNIVERSITY
4600 Sunset Ave., Indianapolis 46208 *Type:* Private *Accred.:* 1915/1993 (NCA) *Calendar:* Sem. plan *Degrees:* A, B, M, certificates *Prof. Accred.:* Dance, Marriage and Family Therapy (M), Music, Psychology Internship (provisional), Teacher Education (e,s,p) *CEO:* Pres. Geoffrey Bannister
Enroll: 4,285   (317) 283-9900

CALUMET COLLEGE OF ST. JOSEPH
2400 New York Ave., Whiting 46394 *Type:* Private (Roman Catholic) liberal arts *Accred.:* 1968/1989 (NCA) *Calendar:* Sem. plan *Degrees:* A, B, certificates *CEO:* Pres. Dennis C. Rittenmeyer
Enroll: 1,086   (219) 473-7770

CHRISTIAN THEOLOGICAL SEMINARY
1000 W. 42nd St., Indianapolis 46208-3301 *Type:* Private (Christian Churches/Disciples of Christ) graduate only *Accred.:* 1944/1988 (ATS); 1973/1988 (NCA) *Calendar:* Sem. plan *Degrees:* M, D *Prof. Accred.:* Marriage and Family Therapy (M-candidate) *CEO:* Pres. Richard D.N. Dickinson, Jr.
Enroll: 344   (317) 924-1331

COMMONWEALTH BUSINESS COLLEGE
4200 W. 81st Ave., Merrillville 46410 *Type:* Private business *Accred.:* 1978/1990 (ACISC) *Calendar:* Qtr. plan *Degrees:* A *Prof. Accred.:* Medical Assisting *CEO:* Dir. Christine M. Piotrowicz
                    (219) 769-3321

BRANCH CAMPUS
1527 47th Ave., Moline, IL 61265 *Accred.:* 1986/1990 (ACISC) *CEO:* Dir. Don Watson
                    (309) 762-2100

BRANCH CAMPUS
8995 N. State Rte. 39, LaPorte 46350 *Accred.:* 1986/1990 (ACISC) *CEO:* Dir. Robert E. Mika
                    (219) 362-3338

CONCORDIA THEOLOGICAL SEMINARY
6600 N. Clinton St., Fort Wayne 46825-4996 *Type:* Private (Lutheran/Missouri Synod) graduate only *Accred.:* 1968/1991 (ATS);

1981/1991 (NCA) *Calendar:* Qtr. plan *Degrees:* M, D *CEO:* Pres. Robert D. Preus
Enroll: 377   (219) 481-2100

DEPAUW UNIVERSITY
Greencastle 46135 *Type:* Private (United Methodist) *Accred.:* 1915/1988 (NCA) *Calendar:* 4-1-4 plan *Degrees:* B *Prof. Accred.:* Music, Teacher Education (e,s) *CEO:* Pres. Robert G. Bottoms
Enroll: 2,058   (317) 658-4800

EARLHAM COLLEGE
701 National Rd. W., Richmond 47374 *Type:* Private (Society of Friends) liberal arts *Accred.:* 1973/1986 (ATS); 1915/1984 (NCA) *Calendar:* 3-3 plan *Degrees:* B, M *CEO:* Pres. Richard J. Wood
Enroll: 1,057   (317) 983-1200

FORT WAYNE SCHOOL OF RADIOGRAPHY
2200 Randallia Dr., Fort Wayne 46805 *Type:* Private *Calendar:* 24-month plan *Degrees:* A, certificates *Prof. Accred.:* Radiography *CEO:* C.E.O. David Ridderheim
Enroll: 46   (219) 484-6636

FRANKLIN COLLEGE OF INDIANA
501 E. Monroe St., Franklin 46131 *Type:* Private (Baptist) liberal arts *Accred.:* 1915/1992 (NCA) *Calendar:* 4-1-4 plan *Degrees:* A, B *Prof. Accred.:* Teacher Education (e,s) *CEO:* Pres. William Bryan Martin
Enroll: 899   (317) 738-8000

GOSHEN COLLEGE
1700 S. Main St., Goshen 46526 *Type:* Private (Mennonite) liberal arts *Accred.:* 1941/1985 (NCA) *Calendar:* Tri. plan *Degrees:* B, certificates *Prof. Accred.:* Nursing (B), Social Work (B), Teacher Education (e,s) *CEO:* Pres. Victor E. Stoltzfus
Enroll: 1,057   (219) 535-7000

GRACE COLLEGE
200 Seminary Dr., Winona Lake 46590 *Type:* Private (National Fellowship of Brethren Churches) liberal arts *Accred.:* 1976/1984 (NCA) *Calendar:* Sem. plan *Degrees:* A, B *CEO:* Pres. John J. Davis
Enroll: 682   (219) 372-5100

GRACE THEOLOGICAL SEMINARY
200 Seminary Dr., Winona Lake 46590 *Type:* Private (National Fellowship of Brethren Churches) graduate only *Accred.:* 1982/1987 (NCA) *Calendar:* Sem. plan *Degrees:* M, D, certificates, diplomas *CEO:* Pres. John J. Davis
Enroll: 130   (219) 372-5100

HANOVER COLLEGE
P.O. Box 108, Hanover 47243-0108 *Type:* Private (United Presbyterian) liberal arts *Accred.:* 1915/1990 (NCA) *Calendar:* 4-4-1 plan *Degrees:* B *Prof. Accred.:* Teacher Education (e,s) *CEO:* Pres. Russell L. Nichols
Enroll: 1,061   (812) 866-7000

HOLY CROSS COLLEGE
Box 308, Notre Dame 46556 *Type:* Private *Accred.:* 1987/1990 (NCA) *Calendar:* Sem. plan *Degrees:* A *CEO:* Pres. Richard B. Gilman, C.S.C.
Enroll: 431   (219) 233-6813

HUNTINGTON COLLEGE
2303 College Ave., Huntington 46750 *Type:* Private (United Brethren in Christ) liberal arts *Accred.:* 1961/1984 (NCA) *Calendar:* 4-1-4 plan *Degrees:* A, B, M, diplomas *CEO:* Pres. G. Blair Dowden
Enroll: 614   (219) 356-6000

INDIANA BUSINESS COLLEGE
802 N. Meridian St., Indianapolis 46204 *Type:* Private business *Accred.:* 1980/1986 (ACISC) *Calendar:* Courses of varying lengths *Degrees:* A, certificates, diplomas *CEO:* Pres. William N. Griffin, III
                    (800) 999-9229

BRANCH CAMPUS
Applegate Business Park, 1320 E. 53rd St., Ste. 106, Anderson 46103 *Accred.:* 1980/1986 (ACISC) *CEO:* Dir. Carla L. Burke
                    (317) 644-7414

BRANCH CAMPUS
3550 Two Mile House Rd., P.O. Box 1906, Columbus 47201 *Accred.:* 1980/1986 (ACISC) *CEO:* Dir. Judy J. Jackson
                    (812) 342-1000

BRANCH CAMPUS
4601 Theater Dr., Evansville 47715 *Accred.:* 1993 (ACISC) *CEO:* Dir. Donna Templeton
                    (812) 476-6000

BRANCH CAMPUS
Ste. 100, 5460 Victory Dr., Indianapolis 46203 *Accred.:* 1993 (ACISC) *CEO:* Dir. Linda Foster
(317) 783-5100

BRANCH CAMPUS
1170 S. Creasy La., Lafayette 47905 *Accred.:* 1980/1986 (ACISC) *CEO:* Dir. Doris Patton
(317) 447-9550

BRANCH CAMPUS
830 N. Miller Ave., Marion 46952 *Accred.:* 1980/1986 (ACISC) *CEO:* Dir. Teresa B. Wanbaudh
(317) 662-7497

BRANCH CAMPUS
1809 N. Walnut St., Muncie 47303 *Accred.:* 1980/1988 (ACISC) *CEO:* Dir. John E. Burton
(317) 288-8681

BRANCH CAMPUS
3175 S. Third St., Terre Haute 47802 *Accred.:* 1980/1986 (ACISC) *CEO:* Dir. Patricia J. Mozley
(812) 232-4458

BRANCH CAMPUS
1431 Willow St., Vincennes 47591 *Accred.:* 1980/1986 (ACISC) *CEO:* Dir. Dave Watson
(812) 882-2550

INDIANA INSTITUTE OF TECHNOLOGY
1600 E. Washington Blvd., Fort Wayne 46803 *Type:* Private technological *Accred.:* 1962/1986 (NCA) *Calendar:* Sem. plan *Degrees:* A, B, certificates *CEO:* Pres. Donald J. Andorfer
Enroll: 1,175 (219) 422-5561

INDIANA STATE UNIVERSITY
Terre Haute 47809 *Type:* Public (state) *System:* Indiana Commission for Higher Education *Accred.:* 1915/1990 (NCA) *Calendar:* Sem. plan *Degrees:* A, B, P, M, D *Prof. Accred.:* Art, Business (B,M), Clinical Psychology, Construction Education (B), Counseling Psychology, Dietetics (coordinated), Home Economics, Marriage and Family Therapy (M), Medical Laboratory Technology (AMA), Medical Technology, Music, Nurs-

ing (A,B,M), Recreation and Leisure Services, School Psychology, Speech-Language Pathology, Teacher Education (e,s,p) *CEO:* Pres. John W. Moore
Enroll: 12,271 (812) 237-6311

INDIANA UNIVERSITY AT KOKOMO
P.O. Box 9003, Kokomo 46904-9003 *Type:* Public (state) *System:* Indiana University System *Accred.:* 1969/1989 (NCA) *Calendar:* Sem. plan *Degrees:* A, B, M, certificates *Prof. Accred.:* Engineering Technology (electrical), Nursing (A), Teacher Education (e) *CEO:* Chanc. Emita B. Hill
Enroll: 3,522 (317) 455-9200

INDIANA UNIVERSITY AT SOUTH BEND
1700 Mishawaka Ave., P.O. Box 7111, South Bend 46634 *Type:* Public (state) *System:* Indiana University System *Accred.:* 1969/1990 (NCA) *Calendar:* Sem. plan *Degrees:* A, B, M, certificates *Prof. Accred.:* Business (B,M), Dental Assisting, Dental Hygiene, Public Affairs, Teacher Education (e,s,p) *CEO:* Chanc. H. Daniel Cohen
Enroll: 7,801 (219) 237-4111

INDIANA UNIVERSITY BLOOMINGTON
Bloomington 47405 *Type:* Public (state) *System:* Indiana University System *Accred.:* 1913/1987 (NCA) *Calendar:* Sem. plan *Degrees:* A, B, P, M, D, certificates *Prof. Accred.:* Art, Audiology, Business (B,M), Clinical Psychology, Interior Design, Journalism (B,M), Law, Librarianship, Music, Optometry, Public Affairs, Recreation and Leisure Services, Speech-Language Pathology, Teacher Education (e,s,p), Theatre *CEO:* Chanc. Kenneth R. Gros Louis
Enroll: 33,488 (812) 332-0211

INDIANA UNIVERSITY EAST
2325 N. Chester Blvd., Richmond 47374 *Type:* Public (state) *System:* Indiana University System *Accred.:* 1971/1992 (NCA) *Calendar:* Sem. plan *Degrees:* A, B, certificates *CEO:* Chanc. Charlie Nelms
Enroll: 2,411 (317) 966-8200

INDIANA UNIVERSITY NORTHWEST
3400 Broadway, Gary 46408 *Type:* Public (state) *System:* Indiana University System *Accred.:* 1969/1993 (NCA) *Calendar:* Sem. plan *Degrees:* A, B, M, certificates, diplo-

mas *Prof. Accred.:* Business (B,M), Dental Assisting, Dental Hygiene, Medical Laboratory Technology (AMA), Medical Record Technology, Nursing (A), Public Affairs, Radiography, Respiratory Therapy, Teacher Education (e,s) *CEO:* Chanc. Hilda Richards
Enroll: 5,962   (219) 980-6500

INDIANA UNIVERSITY-PURDUE UNIVERSITY AT FORT WAYNE
2101 Coliseum Blvd. E., Fort Wayne 46805
Type: Public (state) *System:* Indiana University System *Accred.:* 1969/1990 (NCA) *Calendar:* Sem. plan *Degrees:* A, B, M, certificates *Prof. Accred.:* Business (B,M), Dental Assisting, Dental Hygiene, Dental Laboratory Technology, Engineering Technology (architectural, civil/construction, electrical, industrial, manufacturing, mechanical, mechanical drafting/design), Engineering (electrical, mechanical), Medical Record Technology, Music, Nursing (A,B), Public Affairs, Teacher Education (e,s,p) *CEO:* Chanc. Joanne B. Lantz
Enroll: 12,090   (219) 481-6100

INDIANA UNIVERSITY-PURDUE UNIVERSITY AT INDIANAPOLIS
355 N. Lansing St., Indianapolis 46202
Type: Public (state) *System:* Indiana University System *Accred.:* 1969/1993 (NCA) *Calendar:* Sem. plan *Degrees:* A, B, P, M, D, certificates *Prof. Accred.:* Art, Combined Maxillofacial Prosthodontics, Combined Prosthodontics, Counseling Psychology, Cytotechnology, Dental Assisting, Dental Hygiene, Dentistry, Dietetics (internship), Endodontics, Engineering Technology (civil/construction, electrical, mechanical, mechanical drafting/design), Engineering (electrical, mechanical), Health Services Administration, Law, Medical Record Administration, Medical Technology, Medicine, Nuclear Medicine Technology, Nursing (A,B,M), Occupational Therapy, Occupational Therapy Assisting, Oral Pathology, Oral and Maxillofacial Surgery, Orthodontics, Pediatric Dentistry, Periodontics, Physical Therapy, Psychology Internship, Public Affairs, Radiation Therapy Technology, Radiography, Respiratory Therapy, School Psychology, Social Work (B,M) *CEO:* Chanc. Gerald L. Bepko
Enroll: 28,345   (317) 274-5555

INDIANA UNIVERSITY SOUTHEAST
4201 Grant Line Rd., New Albany 47150
Type: Public (state) *System:* Indiana University System *Accred.:* 1969/1990 (NCA) *Calendar:* Sem. plan *Degrees:* A, B, M, certificates *Prof. Accred.:* Business (B), Engineering Technology (mechanical), Teacher Education (e,s,p) *CEO:* Chanc. Leon Rand
Enroll: 5,942   (812) 941-2000

INDIANA VOCATIONAL TECHNICAL COLLEGE—
CENTRAL INDIANA TECHNICAL INSTITUTE
One W. 26th St., P.O. Box 1763, Indianapolis 46206 *Type:* Public (state) 2-year *System:* Indiana Vocational Technical College Office of the President *Accred.:* 1977/1987 (NCA) *Calendar:* Qtr. plan *Degrees:* A, certificates *Prof. Accred.:* Medical Assisting (AMA), Nursing (A), Practical Nursing, Radiography, Respiratory Therapy, Respiratory Therapy Technology, Surgical Technology *CEO:* Vice Pres./Chanc. Meredith L. Carter
Enroll: 5,780   (317) 921-4882

INDIANA VOCATIONAL TECHNICAL COLLEGE—
COLUMBUS/BLOOMINGTON TECHNICAL INSTITUTE
4475 Central Ave., Columbus 47203 *Type:* Public (state) 2-year *System:* Indiana Vocational Technical College Office of the President *Accred.:* 1978/1987 (NCA) *Calendar:* Qtr. plan *Degrees:* A, certificates *Prof. Accred.:* Medical Assisting (AMA) *CEO:* Vice Pres./Chanc. Homer B. Smith
Enroll: 2,629   (812) 372-9925

INDIANA VOCATIONAL TECHNICAL COLLEGE—
EASTCENTRAL TECHNICAL INSTITUTE
4301 S. Cowan Rd., P.O. Box 3100, Muncie 47307 *Type:* Public (state) 2-year *System:* Indiana Vocational Technical College Office of the President *Accred.:* 1979/1984 (NCA) *Calendar:* Qtr. plan *Degrees:* A, certificates *Prof. Accred.:* Medical Assisting (AMA) *CEO:* Exec. Dean Thomas Henry
Enroll: 2,445   (317) 289-2291

INDIANA VOCATIONAL TECHNICAL COLLEGE—
KOKOMO TECHNICAL INSTITUTE
1815 E. Morgan St., Kokomo 46901 *Type:* Public (state) 2-year *System:* Indiana Vocational Technical College Office of the President *Accred.:* 1978/1987 (NCA) *Calendar:* Qtr. plan *Degrees:* A, certificates *Prof. Ac-*

cred.: Medical Assisting (AMA) *CEO:* Exec
Dean Shanon L. Christiansen
Enroll: 1,808   (317) 459-0561

INDIANA VOCATIONAL TECHNICAL COLLEGE—
LAFAYETTE TECHNICAL INSTITUTE
3208 Ross Rd., P.O. Box 6299, Lafayette
47903 *Type:* Public (state) 2-year *System:*
Indiana Vocational Technical College Office
of the President *Accred.:* 1980/1990 (NCA)
Calendar: Qtr. plan *Degrees:* A, certificates
Prof. Accred.: Dental Assisting, Medical Assisting (AMA), Nursing (A), Respiratory
Therapy Technology, Surgical Technology
CEO: Exec. Dean Elizabeth J. Doversberger
Enroll: 1,833   (317) 477-9100

INDIANA VOCATIONAL TECHNICAL COLLEGE—
NORTHCENTRAL TECHNICAL INSTITUTE
1534 W. Sample St., South Bend 46619
Type: Public (state) 2-year *System:* Indiana
Vocational Technical College Office of the
President *Accred.:* 1977/1990 (NCA) *Calendar:* Qtr. plan *Degrees:* A, certificates *Prof.
Accred.:* Medical Assisting (AMA), Medical
Laboratory Technology (AMA), Nursing (A)
CEO: Vice Pres./Chanc. Carl F. Lutz
Enroll: 2,772   (219) 289-7001

INDIANA VOCATIONAL TECHNICAL COLLEGE—
NORTHEAST TECHNICAL INSTITUTE
3800 N. Anthony Blvd., Fort Wayne 46805
Type: Public (state) 2-year *System:* Indiana
Vocational Technical College Office of the
President *Accred.:* 1977/1990 (NCA) *Calendar:* Qtr. plan *Degrees:* A, certificates *Prof.
Accred.:* Medical Assisting (AMA), Respiratory Therapy, Respiratory Therapy Technology *CEO:* Vice Pres./Chanc. Jon L. Rupright
Enroll: 4,202   (219) 482-9171

INDIANA VOCATIONAL TECHNICAL COLLEGE—
NORTHWEST TECHNICAL INSTITUTE
1440 E. 35th Ave., Gary 46409 *Type:* Public
(state) 2-year *System:* Indiana Vocational
Technical College Office of the President
Accred.: 1981/1986 (NCA) *Calendar:* Qtr.
plan *Degrees:* A, certificates *CEO:* Vice
Pres./Chanc. Darnell E. Cole
Enroll: 2,575   (219) 981-1111

BRANCH CAMPUS
2401 Valley Dr., Valparaiso 46383 *Prof.
Accred.:* Medical Assisting (AMA), Practical Nursing, Respiratory Therapy Tech-

nology, Surgical Technology *CEO:* Exec.
Dean J. Robert Jeffs
                                   (219) 464-8514

INDIANA VOCATIONAL TECHNICAL COLLEGE—
SOUTHCENTRAL TECHNICAL INSTITUTE
8204 Hwy. 311 W., Sellersburg 47172 *Type:*
Public (state) 2-year *System:* Indiana Vocational Technical College Office of the President *Accred.:* 1980/1985 (NCA) *Calendar:*
Qtr. plan *Degrees:* A, certificates *Prof. Accred.:* Medical Assisting (AMA) *CEO:* Exec.
Dean Jonathan W. Thomas
Enroll: 2,094   (812) 246-3301

INDIANA VOCATIONAL TECHNICAL COLLEGE—
SOUTHEAST TECHNICAL INSTITUTE
590 Ivy Tech Dr., Madison 47250 *Type:*
Public (state) 2-year *System:* Indiana Vocational Technical College Office of the President *Accred.:* 1981/1986 (NCA) *Calendar:*
Qtr. plan *Degrees:* A, certificates *Prof. Accred.:* Medical Assisting (AMA) *CEO:* Vice
Pres. Homer B. Smith
Enroll: 963   (812) 265-2580

INDIANA VOCATIONAL TECHNICAL COLLEGE—
SOUTHWEST TECHNICAL INSTITUTE
3501 First Ave., Evansville 47710 *Type:*
Public (state) 2-year *System:* Indiana Vocational Technical College Office of the President *Accred.:* 1977/1986 (NCA) *Calendar:*
Qtr. plan *Degrees:* A, certificates *Prof. Accred.:* Medical Assisting (AMA), Nursing
(A), Practical Nursing, Surgical Technology
CEO: Exec. Dean Daniel L. Schenk
Enroll: 2,656   (812) 426-2865

INDIANA VOCATIONAL TECHNICAL COLLEGE—
WABASH VALLEY TECHNICAL INSTITUTE
7999 U.S. Hwy. 41, Terre Haute 47802
Type: Public (state) 2-year *System:* Indiana
Vocational Technical College Office of the
President *Accred.:* 1977/1985 (NCA) *Calendar:* Qtr. plan *Degrees:* A, certificates *Prof.
Accred.:* Medical Assisting (AMA), Medical
Laboratory Technology (AMA), Radiography *CEO:* Vice Pres./Chanc. Sam E. Borden
Enroll: 2,260   (812) 299-1121

INDIANA VOCATIONAL TECHNICAL COLLEGE—
WHITEWATER TECHNICAL INSTITUTE
2325 Chester Blvd., Richmond 47374 *Type:*
Public (state) 2-year *System:* Indiana Vocational Technical College Office of the Presi-

dent *Accred.:* 1981/1986 (NCA) *Calendar:* Qtr. plan *Degrees:* A, certificates *Prof. Accred.:* Nursing (A) *CEO:* Exec. Dean Jim Steck
Enroll: 1,189   (317) 966-2656

INDIANA WESLEYAN UNIVERSITY
4201 S. Washington St., Marion 46953 *Type:* Private (Wesleyan Methodist) liberal arts *Accred.:* 1966/1990 (NCA) *Calendar:* Sem. plan *Degrees:* A, B, M, certificates *Prof. Accred.:* Medical Laboratory Technology (AMA), Nursing (B,M), Social Work (B), Teacher Education (e,s) *CEO:* Pres. James Barnes
Enroll: 3,385   (317) 677-2100

INTERNATIONAL BUSINESS COLLEGE
3811 Illinois Rd., Fort Wayne 46804 *Type:* Private business *Accred.:* 1953/1986 (ACISC) *Calendar:* Courses of varying lengths *Degrees:* A, certificates, diplomas *Prof. Accred.:* Medical Assisting (AMA) *CEO:* Pres. Jack Smith
                                   (219) 432-8702

INTERNATIONAL BUSINESS COLLEGE
7205 Shadeland Sta., Indianapolis 46256 *Type:* Private business *Accred.:* 1986/1989 (ACISC) *Calendar:* Courses of varying lengths *Degrees:* A, certificates, diplomas *Prof. Accred.:* Medical Assisting (AMA) *CEO:* Dir. Scharme Smith
                                   (317) 841-6400

ITT TECHNICAL INSTITUTE
5115 Oak Grove Rd., Evansville 47715-2340 *Type:* Private *Accred.:* 1967/1989 (ACCSCT) *Calendar:* Courses of varying lengths *Degrees:* A *CEO:* Dir. Thomas Kielty
                                   (812) 479-1441

BRANCH CAMPUS
10509 Timberwood Cir., Louisville, KY 40223 *Accred.:* 1993 (ACCSCT) *CEO:* Dir. Alan Crews
                                   (502) 327-7424

BRANCH CAMPUS
1671 Worcester Rd., Framingham, MA 01701-9456 *Accred.:* 1990 (ACCSCT) *CEO:* Dir. Bruce Hedstrom
                                   (508) 879-6266

BRANCH CAMPUS
863 Glenrock Rd., Norfolk, VA 23502 *Accred.:* 1991 (ACCSCT) *CEO:* Dir. Jeffrey Abrams
                                   (804) 466-1260

ITT TECHNICAL INSTITUTE
4919 Coldwater Rd., Fort Wayne 46825-5532 *Type:* Private *Accred.:* 1968/1990 (ACCSCT) *Calendar:* Courses of varying lenths *Degrees:* A, B, diplomas *CEO:* Dir. Jack Cozad
                                   (219) 484-4107

BRANCH CAMPUS
3401 S. University Dr., Fort Lauderdale, FL 33328 *Accred.:* 1992 (ACCSCT) *CEO:* Dir. Nanelle Lough
                                   (305) 476-9300

BRANCH CAMPUS
1225 E. Big Beaver Rd., Troy, MI 48083-1905 *Accred.:* 1991/1993 (ACCSCT) *CEO:* Dir. Robert Martin
                                   (313) 524-1800

ITT TECHNICAL INSTITUTE
9511 Angola Ct., Indianapolis 46268-1119 *Type:* Private *Accred.:* 1967/1989 (ACCSCT) *Calendar:* Courses of varying lengths *Degrees:* A, B, diplomas *CEO:* Dir. Larry Graphman
                                   (317) 875-8640

BRANCH CAMPUS
375 W. Higgins Rd., Hoffman Estates, IL 60195 *Accred.:* 1990 (ACCSCT) *CEO:* Dir. Kenneth E. Butler, II
                                   (708) 519-9300

BRANCH CAMPUS
1821 Rutherford La., Austin, TX 78754-5101 *Accred.:* 1986 (ACCSCT) *CEO:* Dir. Jon A. Hittman
                                   (512) 339-8200

BRANCH CAMPUS
15621 Blue Ash Dr., Ste. 160, Houston, TX 77090-5818 *Accred.:* 1988 (ACCSCT) *CEO:* Dir. David D. Champlin
                                   (713) 879-6486

LUTHERAN COLLEGE OF HEALTH PROFESSIONS
535 Home Ave., Fort Wayne 46807 *Type:* Private *Accred.:* 1990/1992 (NCA candidate)

Calendar: Qtr. plan *Degrees:* A, B, certificates *Prof. Accred.:* Radiography *CEO:* Dean Marilyn R. Wilson
Enroll: 580   (219) 458-2451

MANCHESTER COLLEGE
604 College Ave., North Manchester 46962 *Type:* Private (Church of Brethren) liberal arts *Accred.:* 1932/1993 (NCA) *Calendar:* 4-1-4 plan *Degrees:* A, B, M *Prof. Accred.:* Social Work (B), Teacher Education (e,s) *CEO:* Interim Pres. Edgar C. Butterbaugh
Enroll: 1,090   (219) 982-5000

MARIAN COLLEGE
3200 Cold Spring Rd., Indianapolis 46222 *Type:* Private (Roman Catholic) liberal arts *Accred.:* 1956/1986 (NCA) *Calendar:* Sem. plan *Degrees:* A, B, certificates *Prof. Accred.:* Nursing (A,B), Radiography, Respiratory Therapy, Teacher Education (e,s) *CEO:* Pres. Daniel A. Felicetti
Enroll: 1,288   (317) 929-0123

MARTIN UNIVERSITY
2171 Avondale Pl., P.O. Box 18567, Indianapolis 46218 *Type:* Private *Accred.:* 1987/1990 (NCA) *Calendar:* Sem. plan *Degrees:* B, M *CEO:* Pres. Boniface Hardin
Enroll: 692   (317) 543-3235

MICHIANA COLLEGE
1030 E. Jefferson Blvd., South Bend 46617 *Type:* Private business *Accred.:* 1961/1991 (ACISC) *Calendar:* Qtr. plan *Degrees:* A, certificates, diplomas *Prof. Accred.:* Medical Assisting (AMA) *CEO:* Pres. David M. Krueper
                                            (219) 237-0774

BRANCH CAMPUS
4807 Illinois Rd., Fort Wayne 46804 *Accred.:* 1993 (ACISC) *CEO:* Dir. Anthony W. Conti
                                            (219) 436-2738

MID-AMERICA COLLEGE OF FUNERAL SERVICE
3111 Hamburg Pike, Jeffersonville 47130 *Type:* Private professional *Calendar:* Courses of varying lengths *Degrees:* A, diplomas *Prof. Accred.:* Funeral Service Education *CEO:* Pres. Glenn A. Morton
                                            (812) 288-8878

OAKLAND CITY COLLEGE
143 N. Lucretia St., Oakland City 47660 *Type:* Private (Baptist) liberal arts *Accred.:* 1977/1988 (NCA) *Calendar:* Sem. plan *Degrees:* A, B, M, certificates *Prof. Accred.:* Teacher Education (e,s) *CEO:* Chanc./Pres. James W. Murray
Enroll: 803   (812) 749-1213

PURDUE UNIVERSITY
West Lafayette 47907 *Type:* Public (state) *System:* Purdue University System *Accred.:* 1913/1990 (NCA) *Calendar:* Sem. plan *Degrees:* A, B, M, D, certificates *Prof. Accred.:* Audiology, Business (B,M), Clinical Psychology, Construction Education (B), Counseling, Dietetics (coordinated), Engineering Technology (electrical, mechanical), Engineering (aerospace, agricultural, chemical, civil, computer, construction, electrical, food process, industrial, mechanical, metallurgical, nuclear, surveying), Forestry, Landscape Architecture (B-provisional), Marriage and Family Therapy (D), Nursing (B), Social Work (B), Speech-Language Pathology, Teacher Education (e,s,p), Theatre (associate), Veterinary Medicine, Veterinary Technology *CEO:* Pres. Steven C. Beering
Enroll: 33,961   (317) 494-4600

PURDUE UNIVERSITY CALUMET
Hammond 46323 *Type:* Public (state) *System:* Purdue University System *Accred.:* 1969/1993 (NCA) *Calendar:* Sem. plan *Degrees:* A, B, certificates *Prof. Accred.:* Engineering Technology (architectural, civil/construction, electrical, industrial, mechanical), Engineering (electrical, mechanical), Marriage and Family Therapy (M-candidate), Nursing (A,B,M), Teacher Education (e,s) *CEO:* Chanc. James W. Yackel
Enroll: 9,466   (219) 989-2993

PURDUE UNIVERSITY NORTH CENTRAL
1401 S. U.S. Hwy. 421, Westville 46391 *Type:* Public (state) *System:* Purdue University System *Accred.:* 1971/1986 (NCA) *Calendar:* Sem. plan *Degrees:* A, certificates *Prof. Accred.:* Engineering Technology (electrical, industrial, mechanical), Nursing (A), Radiography *CEO:* Chanc. Dale W. Alspaugh
Enroll: 3,587   (219) 785-5200

ROSE-HULMAN INSTITUTE OF TECHNOLOGY
5500 Wabash Ave., Terre Haute 47803
Type: Private professional for men *Accred.:*
1916/1992 (NCA) *Calendar:* Qtr. plan *Degrees:* B, M *Prof. Accred.:* Engineering
(chemical, civil, electrical, mechanical)
CEO: Pres. Samuel F. Hulbert
Enroll: 1,409   (812) 877-1511

ST. FRANCIS COLLEGE
2701 Spring St., Fort Wayne 46808 *Type:*
Private (Roman Catholic) liberal arts *Accred.:* 1957/1986 (NCA) *Calendar:* Sem.
plan *Degrees:* A, B, M *Prof. Accred.:* Nursing (B), Social Work (B), Teacher Education
(e,s) *CEO:* Pres. M. Elise Kriss
Enroll: 933   (219) 434-3100

ST. JOSEPH'S COLLEGE
Rensselaer 47978 *Type:* Private (Roman
Catholic) liberal arts *Accred.:* 1932/1992
(NCA) *Calendar:* Sem. plan *Degrees:* A, B,
M *Prof. Accred.:* Teacher Education (e,s)
CEO: Pres. Albert J. Shannon
Enroll: 1,030   (219) 866-6157

ST. MARY-OF-THE-WOODS COLLEGE
St. Mary-of-the-Woods 47876 *Type:* Private
(Roman Catholic) liberal arts for women *Accred.:* 1919/1989 (NCA) *Calendar:* Sem.
plan *Degrees:* A, B, M, certificates *Prof. Accred.:* Music *CEO:* Pres. Barbara Doherty
Enroll: 1,258   (812) 535-5151

ST. MARY'S COLLEGE
Notre Dame 46556 *Type:* Private (Roman
Catholic) liberal arts primarily for women
Accred.: 1922/1986 (NCA) *Calendar:* Sem.
plan *Degrees:* B *Prof. Accred.:* Art, Music,
Nursing (B), Social Work (B-candidate),
Teacher Education (e,s) *CEO:* Pres. William
A. Hickey
Enroll: 1,576   (219) 284-4000

ST. MEINRAD COLLEGE
St. Meinrad 47577 *Type:* Private (Roman
Catholic) liberal arts *Accred.:* 1961/1991
(NCA) *Calendar:* Sem. plan *Degrees:* B
CEO: Pres./Rector Eugene Hensell, O.S.B.
Enroll: 116   (812) 357-6522

ST. MEINRAD SCHOOL OF THEOLOGY
St. Meinrad 47577 *Type:* Private (Roman
Catholic) graduate only *Accred.:* 1968/1993
(ATS); 1979/1984 (NCA) *Calendar:* Sem.

plan *Degrees:* M *CEO:* Pres./Rector Eugene
Hensell, O.S.B.
Enroll: 133   (812) 357-6611

SAWYER COLLEGE, INC.
6040 Hohman Ave., Hammond 46320 *Type:*
Private business *Accred.:* 1982/1988
(ACISC) *Calendar:* Qtr. plan *Degrees:* A
Prof. Accred.: Medical Assisting *CEO:* Dir.
Mary Jo Dixon
                    (219) 931-0436

BRANCH CAMPUS
3803 E. Lincoln Hwy., Merrillville 46410
Accred.: 1985/1988 (ACISC) *Prof. Accred.:* Medical Assisting *CEO:* Dir. Mary
Ann Livovich
                    (219) 736-0436

TAYLOR UNIVERSITY
500 W. Reade Ave., Upland 46989 *Type:*
Private liberal arts *Accred.:* 1947/1987
(NCA) *Calendar:* Sem. plan *Degrees:* A, B,
certificates *Prof. Accred.:* Music, Social
Work (B), Teacher Education (e,s) *CEO:*
Pres. Jay L. Kesler
Enroll: 2,227   (317) 998-2751

FORT WAYNE CAMPUS
1025 W. Rudisill Blvd., Fort Wayne
46807 *Degrees:* A, B, certificates, diplomas *CEO:* Pres. Donald D. Gerig
                    (219) 456-2111

TRI-STATE UNIVERSITY
Angola 46703 *Type:* Private business *Accred.:* 1966/1990 (NCA) *Calendar:* Qtr. plan
Degrees: A, B, certificates *Prof. Accred.:*
Engineering Technology (mechanical drafting/design), Engineering (aerospace, chemical, civil, electrical, mechanical) *CEO:* Pres.
R. John Reynolds
Enroll: 1,051   (219) 665-4100

UNIVERSITY OF EVANSVILLE
1800 Lincoln Ave., Evansville 47722 *Type:*
Private (United Methodist) *Accred.:* 1931/
1986 (NCA) *Calendar:* Qtr. plan *Degrees:*
A, B, M, certificates *Prof. Accred.:* Engineering (electrical, mechanical), Music,
Nursing (B,M), Physical Therapy, Physical
Therapy Assisting, Teacher Education (e,s,p)
CEO: Pres. James S. Vinson
Enroll: 2,928   (812) 479-2000

THE UNIVERSITY OF INDIANAPOLIS
1400 E. Hanna Ave., Indianapolis 46227
Type: Private (United Methodist) liberal arts
Accred.: 1947/1988 (NCA) *Calendar:* Qtr.
plan *Degrees:* A, B, M *Prof. Accred.:* Music,
Nursing (A,B), Occupational Therapy, Phys-
ical Therapy, Teacher Education (e,s) *CEO:*
Pres. G. Benjamin Lantz, Jr.
Enroll: 3,729   (317) 788-3368

UNIVERSITY OF NOTRE DAME
Notre Dame 46556 *Type:* Private (Roman
Catholic) *Accred.:* 1977/1983 (ATS); 1913/
1984 (NCA) *Calendar:* Sem. plan *Degrees:*
B, M, D *Prof. Accred.:* Accounting (Type
A), Business (B,M), Counseling Psychology,
Engineering (aerospace, chemical, civil,
electrical, mechanical, metallurgical), Law,
Music, Psychology Internship *CEO:* Pres.
Edward A. Malloy, C.S.C.
Enroll: 10,129   (219) 631-5000

UNIVERSITY OF SOUTHERN INDIANA
8600 University Blvd., Evansville 47712
Type: Public (state) *System:* Indiana Com-
mission for Higher Education *Accred.:* 1974/
1987 (NCA) *Calendar:* Sem. plan *Degrees:*
A, B, M, certificates *Prof. Accred.:* Dental
Assisting, Dental Hygiene, Engineering
Technology (civil/construction, electrical,
mechanical), Radiography, Respiratory
Therapy, Social Work (B), Teacher Educa-
tion (e,s) *CEO:* Pres. David L. Rice
Enroll: 7,430   (812) 464-8600

VALPARAISO UNIVERSITY
Valparaiso 46383 *Type:* Private (Lutheran-
Missouri Synod) *Accred.:* 1929/1988 (NCA)
Calendar: Sem. plan *Degrees:* A, B, M, D
Prof. Accred.: Business (B), Engineering
(civil, computer, electrical, mechanical),
Law, Music, Nursing (B,M), Social Work
(B), Teacher Education (e,s) *CEO:* Pres.
Alan F. Harre
Enroll: 3,872   (219) 464-5000

VINCENNES UNIVERSITY
1002 N. First St., Vincennes 47591 *Type:*
Public (state) junior *System:* Indiana Com-
mission for Higher Education *Accred.:* 1958/
1986 (NCA) *Calendar:* Sem. plan *Degrees:*
A, certificates *Prof. Accred.:* Art (associate),
Funeral Service Education, Medical Labora-
tory Technology (AMA), Medical Record
Technology, Nursing (A), Physical Therapy
Assisting, Practical Nursing, Respiratory
Therapy, Theatre *CEO:* Pres. Phillip M.
Summers
Enroll: 9,906   (812) 882-4208

WABASH COLLEGE
301 W. Wabash Ave., Crawfordsville 47933
Type: Private liberal arts for men *Accred.:*
1913/1993 (NCA) *Calendar:* Sem. plan *Degrees:* B *CEO:* Pres. Andrew T. Ford
Enroll: 768   (317) 362-1400

IOWA

AMERICAN INSTITUTE OF BUSINESS
2500 Fleur Dr., Des Moines 50321 *Type:*
Private junior *Accred.:* 1986/1989 (NCA)
Calendar: Qtr. plan *Degrees:* A, diplomas
CEO: Pres. Keith Fenton
Enroll: 956   (515) 244-4221

AMERICAN INSTITUTE OF COMMERCE
1801 E. Kimberly Rd., Davenport 52807
Type: Private junior *Accred.:* 1957/1989
(ACISC); 1993 (NCA) *Calendar:* Qtr. plan
Degrees: A, diplomas *Prof. Accred.:* Med-
ical Assisting (AMA) *CEO:* Pres. John Huston
Enroll: 814   (319) 355-3500

    BRANCH CAMPUS
    2302 W. First St., Cedar Falls 50613 *Ac-
    cred.:* 1987/1989 (ACISC) *CEO:* Dir.
    Ronald L. Sandler
                   (319) 277-0220

BRIAR CLIFF COLLEGE
3303 Rebecca St., Sioux City 51104 *Type:*
Private (Roman Catholic) liberal arts *Ac-
cred.:* 1945/1985 (NCA) *Calendar:* 3-3 plan
Degrees: A, B *Prof. Accred.:* Nursing (B),
Social Work (B) *CEO:* Pres. Margaret Wick
Enroll: 1,144   (712) 279-5321

BUENA VISTA COLLEGE
610 W. Fourth St., Storm Lake 50588 *Type:*
Private (United Presbyterian) liberal arts *Ac-
cred.:* 1952/1991 (NCA) *Calendar:* Sem.
plan *Degrees:* B *Prof. Accred.:* Social Work
(B), Teacher Education (e,s) *CEO:* Pres.
Keith G. Briscoe
Enroll: 2,316   (712) 749-2103

CENTRAL UNIVERSITY OF IOWA
812 University, Pella 50219 *Type:* Private
(Reformed Church in America) liberal arts
Accred.: 1942/1984 (NCA) *Calendar:* 3-3
plan *Degrees:* B *Prof. Accred.:* Music *CEO:*
Pres. William M. Wiebenga
Enroll: 1,599   (515) 628-9000

CLARKE COLLEGE
1550 Clarke Dr., Dubuque 52001 *Type:* Private (Roman Catholic) liberal arts *Accred.:*
1918/1984 (NCA) *Calendar:* Sem. plan *Degrees:* A, B, M *Prof. Accred.:* Music, Social
Work (B) *CEO:* Pres. Catherine Dunn, BVM
Enroll: 927   (319) 588-6300

CLINTON COMMUNITY COLLEGE
1000 Lincoln Blvd., Clinton 52732 *Type:*
Public (district) junior *System:* Eastern Iowa
Community College District *Accred.:* 1983/
1993 (NCA)* *Calendar:* Qtr. plan *Degrees:*
A, certificates, diplomas *CEO:* Pres. Desna
L. Wallin
                 (319) 242-6841

* Indirect accreditation through Eastern Iowa
  Community College District.

COE COLLEGE
Cedar Rapids 52402 *Type:* Private (United
Presbyterian) liberal arts *Accred.:* 1913/1988
(NCA) *Calendar:* 4-1-4 plan *Degrees:* B, M
Prof. Accred.: Music, Nursing (B) *CEO:*
Pres. John E. Brown
Enroll: 1,285   (319) 399-8000

CORNELL COLLEGE
600 First St. W., Mount Vernon 52314 *Type:*
Private (United Methodist) liberal arts *Accred.:* 1913/1993 (NCA) *Calendar:* Sem.
plan *Degrees:* B *Prof. Accred.:* Music *CEO:*
Acting Pres. C. William Heywood
Enroll: 1,144   (319) 895-4324

DES MOINES AREA COMMUNITY COLLEGE
2006 S. Ankeny Blvd., Ankeny 50021 *Type:*
Public (district) junior *System:* Iowa Depart-
ment of Education Division of Community
Colleges *Accred.:* 1974/1986 (NCA) *Calen-
dar:* Sem. plan *Degrees:* A, certificates,
diplomas *Prof. Accred.:* Dental Assisting,
Dental Hygiene, Medical Assisting (AMA),
Medical Laboratory Technology (AMA),
Nursing (A), Practical Nursing, Respiratory
Therapy *CEO:* Pres. Joseph A. Borgen,
Ph.D.
Enroll: 11,214   (515) 964-6260

DIVINE WORD COLLEGE
102 Jacoby Dr., S.W., Epworth 52045 *Type:*
Private liberal arts *Accred.:* 1970/1986
(NCA) *Calendar:* Sem. plan *Degrees:* A, B
CEO: Pres. Michael Hutchins
Enroll: 54   (319) 876-3353

DORDT COLLEGE
Sioux Center 51250 *Type:* Private (Christian Reformed) liberal arts *Accred.:* 1969/1992 (NCA) *Calendar:* Sem. plan *Degrees:* A, B *Prof. Accred.:* Engineering (general), Social Work (B) *CEO:* Pres. John B. Hulst
Enroll: 1,077   (712) 722-6000

DRAKE UNIVERSITY
26th St. and University Ave., Des Moines 50311 *Type:* Private *Accred.:* 1913/1988 (NCA) *Calendar:* Sem. plan *Degrees:* B, P, M, D *Prof. Accred.:* Art, Business (B,M), Journalism (B,M), Law, Music, Rehabilitation Counseling *CEO:* Pres. Michael R. Ferrari
Enroll: 6,333   (515) 271-2191

ELLSWORTH COMMUNITY COLLEGE
1100 College Ave., Iowa Falls 50126 *Type:* Public (district) junior *System:* Iowa Valley Community College District *Accred.:* 1963/1992 (NCA) *Calendar:* Qtr. plan *Degrees:* A, certificates, diplomas *CEO:* Dean Duane R. Lloyd
Enroll: 827   (515) 648-4611

EMMAUS BIBLE COLLEGE
2570 Asbury Rd., Dubuque 52001 *Type:* Independent (nondenominational) *Accred.:* 1986/1991 (AABC) *Calendar:* Sem. plan *Degrees:* A, B, certificates *CEO:* Pres. Daniel Smith
FTE Enroll: 168   (319) 588-8000

FAITH BAPTIST BIBLE COLLEGE AND
THEOLOGICAL SEMINARY
1900 N.W. Fourth St., Ankeny 50021 *Type:* Private (General Association of Regular Baptist Churches) *Accred.:* 1969/1989 (AABC); 1989/1993 (NCA candidate) *Calendar:* Sem. plan *Degrees:* A, B, M, certificates *CEO:* Pres. Robert L. Domokos
Enroll: 225   (515) 964-0601

GRACELAND COLLEGE
Lamoni 50140 *Type:* Private (Latter-Day Saints) liberal arts *Accred.:* 1920/1987 (NCA) *Calendar:* 4-1-4 plan *Degrees:* B *Prof. Accred.:* Nursing (B), Teacher Education (e,s) *CEO:* Pres. William T. Higdon
Enroll: 2,760   (515) 784-5000

GRAND VIEW COLLEGE
1200 Grandview Ave., Des Moines 50316 *Type:* Private (Lutheran) liberal arts *Accred.:* 1959/1985 (NCA) *Calendar:* 4-1-4 plan *Degrees:* A, B *Prof. Accred.:* Nursing (B) *CEO:* Pres. Arthur E. Puotinen
Enroll: 1,478   (515) 263-2800

GRINNELL COLLEGE
P.O. Box 805, Grinnell 50112 *Type:* Private liberal arts *Accred.:* 1913/1989 (NCA) *Calendar:* Sem. plan *Degrees:* B *CEO:* Pres. Pamela A. Ferguson
Enroll: 1,363   (515) 269-4000

HAMILTON TECHNICAL COLLEGE
1011 E. 53rd St., Davenport 52807-2616 *Type:* Private *Accred.:* 1974/1990 (ACCSCT) *Calendar:* Sem. plan *Degrees:* A *CEO:* Pres. MaryAnne Hamilton
                                   (319) 386-3570

HAWKEYE COMMUNITY COLLEGE
1501 E. Orange Rd., Waterloo 50704 *Type:* Public (district) junior *System:* Iowa Department of Education Division of Community Colleges *Accred.:* 1975/1987 (NCA) *Calendar:* Qtr. plan *Degrees:* A, certificates, diplomas *Prof. Accred.:* Dental Assisting, Dental Hygiene, Medical Laboratory Technology (AMA), Respiratory Therapy Technology *CEO:* Pres. Phillip O. Barry
Enroll: 2,467   (319) 296-2320

INDIAN HILLS COMMUNITY COLLEGE
525 Grandview Ave., Ottumwa 52501 *Type:* Public (district) junior *System:* Iowa Department of Education Division of Community Colleges *Accred.:* 1977/1990 (NCA) *Calendar:* Qtr. plan *Degrees:* A, certificates, diplomas *Prof. Accred.:* Medical Record Technology, Physical Therapy Assisting, Radiography *CEO:* Pres. Lyle Adrian Hellyer
Enroll: 3,295   (515) 683-5111

CENTERVILLE CAMPUS
Centerville 52544 *CEO:* Dean Richard Sharp
                                   (515) 856-2143

IOWA CENTRAL COMMUNITY COLLEGE
330 Ave. M, Fort Dodge 50501 *Type:* Public (district) junior *System:* Iowa Department of Education Division of Community Colleges *Accred.:* 1974/1991 (NCA) *Calendar:* Sem.

plan *Degrees:* A, certificates, diplomas *Prof. Accred.:* Medical Assisting (AMA), Radiography *CEO:* Pres. Jack Bottenfield
Enroll: 2,035   (515) 576-7201

IOWA LAKES COMMUNITY COLLEGE
19 S. 7th St., Estherville 51334 *Type:* Public (district) junior *System:* Iowa Department of Education Division of Community Colleges *Accred.:* 1976/1988 (NCA) *Calendar:* Sem. plan *Degrees:* A, certificates, diplomas *CEO:* Pres. Richard H. Blacker
Enroll: 1,798   (712) 362-2601

IOWA STATE UNIVERSITY
Ames 50011 *Type:* Public (state) *System:* Iowa State Board of Regents *Accred.:* 1916/1986 (NCA) *Calendar:* Sem. plan *Degrees:* B, P, M, D, certificates *Prof. Accred.:* Business (B,M), Computer Science, Counseling Psychology, Dietetics (coordinated), Engineering (aerospace, agricultural, ceramic, chemical, civil, computer, construction, electrical, engineering physics/science, industrial, mechanical, metallurgical, nuclear), Forestry, Home Economics, Interior Design, Journalism (B,M), Landscape Architecture (B), Marriage and Family Therapy (D), Music, Planning (B,M), Psychology Internship, Social Work (B), Veterinary Medicine *CEO:* Pres. Martin Charles Jischke
Enroll: 23,033   (515) 294-2042

IOWA WESLEYAN COLLEGE
601 N. Main St., Mount Pleasant 52641 *Type:* Private (United Methodist) liberal arts *Accred.:* 1916/1993 (NCA) *Calendar:* 4-1-4 plan *Degrees:* A, B, certificates *Prof. Accred.:* Nursing (B) *CEO:* Pres. Robert J. Prins
Enroll: 967   (319) 385-8021

IOWA WESTERN COMMUNITY COLLEGE
2700 College Rd., Council Bluffs 51501 *Type:* Public (district) junior *System:* Iowa Department of Education Division of Community Colleges *Accred.:* 1975/1990 (NCA) *Calendar:* Sem. plan *Degrees:* A, certificates *Prof. Accred.:* Dental Assisting, Engineering Technology (civil/construction), Medical Assisting (AMA) *CEO:* Pres. Carl L. Heinrich
Enroll: 4,506   (712) 325-3200

KIRKWOOD COMMUNITY COLLEGE
6301 Kirkwood Blvd., S.W., P.O. Box 2068, Cedar Rapids 52406-2068 *Type:* Public (district) junior *System:* Iowa Department of Education Division of Community Colleges *Accred.:* 1970/1990 (NCA) *Calendar:* Sem. plan *Degrees:* A, certificates, diplomas *Prof. Accred.:* Dental Assisting, Dental Laboratory Technology, Electroneurodiagnostic Technology, Medical Assisting (AMA), Medical Record Technology, Occupational Therapy Assisting, Respiratory Therapy, Veterinary Technology (probational) *CEO:* Pres. Norman R. Nielsen
Enroll: 17,924   (319) 398-5501

LORAS COLLEGE
1450 Alta Vista, Dubuque 52001 *Type:* Private (Roman Catholic) liberal arts *Accred.:* 1917/1990 (NCA) *Calendar:* Sem. plan *Degrees:* A, B, M *Prof. Accred.:* Social Work (B) *CEO:* Pres. James Barta
Enroll: 1,857   (319) 588-7103

LUTHER COLLEGE
Decorah 52101 *Type:* Private (Lutheran) liberal arts *Accred.:* 1915/1989 (NCA) *Calendar:* 4-1-4 plan *Degrees:* B *Prof. Accred.:* Music, Nursing (B), Social Work (B), Teacher Education (e,s) *CEO:* Pres. H. George Anderson
Enroll: 2,327   (319) 387-1001

MAHARISHI INTERNATIONAL UNIVERSITY
1000 N. Fourth St., DB 1113, Fairfield 52557 *Type:* Private liberal arts *Accred.:* 1980/1990 (NCA) *Calendar:* Sem. plan *Degrees:* A, B, M, D, certificates, diplomas *CEO:* Pres. Bevan Morris
Enroll: 796   (515) 472-5031

MARSHALLTOWN COMMUNITY COLLEGE
3700 S. Center St., P.O. Box 430, Marshalltown 50158 *Type:* Public (district) junior *System:* Iowa Valley Community College District *Accred.:* 1966/1992 (NCA) *Calendar:* Qtr. plan *Degrees:* A, certificates *Prof. Accred.:* Dental Assisting, Medical Assisting (AMA), Surgical Technology *CEO:* Dean William M. Simpson
Enroll: 1,248   (515) 752-7106

MORNINGSIDE COLLEGE
1501 Morningside Ave., Sioux City 51106
Type: Private (United Methodist) liberal arts
Accred.: 1913/1984 (NCA) *Calendar:* Sem.
plan *Degrees:* A, B, M *Prof. Accred.:* Music,
Nursing (B), Teacher Education (e,s) *CEO:*
Pres. Jerry M. Israel
Enroll: 1,306   (712) 274-5000

MOUNT MERCY COLLEGE
1330 Elmhurst Dr., N.E., Cedar Rapids
52402 *Type:* Private (Roman Catholic) liberal arts *Accred.:* 1932/1993 (NCA) *Calendar:*
4-1-4 plan *Degrees:* B *Prof. Accred.:* Nursing (B), Social Work (B) *CEO:* Pres.
Thomas R. Feld
Enroll: 1,392   (319) 363-8213

MOUNT ST. CLARE COLLEGE
400 N. Bluff Blvd., Clinton 52732 *Type:* Private (Roman Catholic) liberal arts *Accred.:*
1950/1989 (NCA) *Calendar:* Sem. plan *Degrees:* A, B, certificates *CEO:* Pres. James J.
Ross
Enroll: 396   (319) 242-4023

MUSCATINE COMMUNITY COLLEGE
152 Colorado St., Muscatine 52761 *Type:*
Public (district) junior *System:* Eastern Iowa
Community College District *Accred.:* 1983/
1993 (NCA)* *Calendar:* Qtr. plan *Degrees:*
A, certificates, diplomas *CEO:* Pres. Victor
G. McAvoy
                                   (319) 263-8250

* Indirect accreditation through Eastern Iowa
  Community College District.

NORTH IOWA AREA COMMUNITY COLLEGE
500 College Dr., Mason City 50401 *Type:*
Public (district) junior *System:* Iowa Department of Education Division of Community
Colleges *Accred.:* 1919/1984 (NCA) *Calendar:* Sem. plan *Degrees:* A, certificates,
diplomas *Prof. Accred.:* Nursing (A) *CEO:*
Pres. David L. Buettner
Enroll: 3,074   (515) 423-1264

NORTHEAST IOWA COMMUNITY COLLEGE
Box 400, Hwy. 150, Calmar 52132 *Type:*
Public (district) junior *System:* Iowa Department of Education Division of Community
Colleges *Accred.:* 1977/1991 (NCA) *Calendar:* Qtr. plan *Degrees:* A, certificates,
diplomas *Prof. Accred.:* Dental Assisting,

Medical Record Technology, Radiography,
Respiratory Therapy Technology *CEO:* Pres.
Don Roby
Enroll: 2,283   (319) 562-3263

NORTHWEST IOWA COMMUNITY COLLEGE
603 W. Park St., Sheldon 51201 *Type:* Public (district) junior *System:* Iowa Department
of Education Division of Community Colleges *Accred.:* 1980/1985 (NCA) *Calendar:*
Qtr. plan *Degrees:* A, certificates, diplomas
CEO: Pres. Carl H. Rolf
Enroll: 603   (712) 324-5061

NORTHWESTERN COLLEGE
Orange City 51041 *Type:* Private (Reformed
Church in America) liberal arts and teachers
Accred.: 1953/1986 (NCA) *Calendar:* Sem.
plan *Degrees:* A, B, M *Prof. Accred.:* Social
Work (B), Teacher Education (e,s) *CEO:*
Pres. James E. Bultman
Enroll: 1,045   (712) 737-4821

PALMER COLLEGE OF CHIROPRACTIC
1000 Brady St., Davenport 52803 *Type:* Private professional *Accred.:* 1984/1989 (NCA)
Calendar: Tri. plan *Degrees:* A, B, M, D,
certificates *Prof. Accred.:* Chiropractic Education *CEO:* Pres. Donald P. Kern, D.C.
Enroll: 1,898   (319) 326-9600

ST. AMBROSE UNIVERSITY
518 W. Locust St., Davenport 52803 *Type:*
Private (Roman Catholic) liberal arts *Accred.:* 1927/1988 (NCA) *Calendar:* Sem.
plan *Degrees:* B, M, certificates *Prof. Accred.:* Occupational Therapy *CEO:* Pres. Edward J. Rogalski
Enroll: 2,417   (319) 383-8700

SCOTT COMMUNITY COLLEGE
500 Belmont Rd., Bettendorf 52722 *Type:*
Public (district) junior *System:* Eastern Iowa
Community College District *Accred.:* 1983/
1993 (NCA)* *Calendar:* Qtr. plan *Degrees:*
A, certificates, diplomas *Prof. Accred.:* Medical Laboratory Technology (AMA), Radiography *CEO:* Pres. Lenny E. Stone
                                   (319) 359-7531

* Indirect accreditation through Eastern Iowa
  Community College District.

SIMPSON COLLEGE
701 N. C St., Indianola 50125 *Type:* Private (United Methodist) liberal arts *Accred.:* 1913/1986 (NCA) *Calendar:* 4-1-4 plan *Degrees:* B *Prof. Accred.:* Music *CEO:* Pres. Stephen G. Jennings
Enroll: 1,690   (515) 961-6251

SOUTHEASTERN COMMUNITY COLLEGE
Drawer F, West Burlington 52655 *Type:* Public (district) junior *System:* Iowa Department of Education Division of Community Colleges *Accred.:* 1974/1989 (NCA) *Calendar:* Qtr. plan *Degrees:* A, certificates, diplomas *Prof. Accred.:* Medical Assisting (AMA) *CEO:* Pres. R. Gene Gardner
Enroll: 2,918   (319) 752-2731

SOUTHWESTERN COMMUNITY COLLEGE
1501 Townline St., Creston 50801 *Type:* Public (district) junior *System:* Iowa Department of Education Division of Community Colleges *Accred.:* 1974/1989 (NCA) *Calendar:* Sem. plan *Degrees:* A, certificates, diplomas *CEO:* Supt./Pres. Richard L. Byerly
Enroll: 1,381   (515) 782-7081

TEIKYO MARYCREST UNIVERSITY
1607 W. 12th St., Davenport 52804 *Type:* Private liberal arts *Accred.:* 1955/1986 (NCA) *Calendar:* Sem. plan *Degrees:* A, B, M, certificates *Prof. Accred.:* Nursing (B), Social Work (B) *CEO:* Pres. Joseph D. Olander
Enroll: 1,264   (319) 326-9221

TEIKYO WESTMAR UNIVERSITY
1002 Third Ave., S.E., Le Mars 51031 *Type:* Private (United Methodist) liberal arts *Accred.:* 1953/1991 (NCA) *Calendar:* 4-1-4 plan *Degrees:* B, diplomas *CEO:* Pres. Joseph D. Olander
Enroll: 761   (712) 546-7081

UNIVERSITY OF DUBUQUE
2000 University Ave., Dubuque 52001 *Type:* Private (Presbyterian) liberal arts *Accred.:* 1944/1989 (ATS); 1921/1989 (NCA) *Calendar:* Sem. plan *Degrees:* A, B, M, D *Prof. Accred.:* Nursing (B), Social Work (B) *CEO:* Pres. John J. Agria
Enroll: 1,264   (319) 589-3223

UNIVERSITY OF IOWA
101 Jessup Hall, Iowa City 52242-1316 *Type:* Public (state) *System:* Iowa State Board of Regents *Accred.:* 1913/1988 (NCA) *Calendar:* Sem. plan *Degrees:* B, P, M, D *Prof. Accred.:* Audiology, Business (B,M), Clinical Psychology, Combined Prosthodontics, Counseling, Counseling Psychology, Dental Hygiene, Dental Public Health, Dentistry, Diagnostic Medical Sonography, Dietetics (internship), Endodontics, Engineering (bioengineering, chemical, civil, electrical, industrial, mechanical), General Dentistry, General Practice Residency, Health Services Administration, Journalism (B,M), Law, Librarianship, Medical Technology, Medicine, Music, Nuclear Medicine Technology, Nursing (B,M), Oral Pathology, Oral and Maxillofacial Surgery, Orthodontics, Pediatric Dentistry, Periodontics, Physical Therapy, Physician Assisting, Planning (M), Psychology Internship, Radiation Therapy Technology, Radiography, Recreation and Leisure Services, Rehabilitation Counseling, School Psychology, Social Work (B,M), Speech-Language Pathology, Theatre *CEO:* Pres. Hunter R. Rawlings, III
Enroll: 27,463   (319) 335-3500

UNIVERSITY OF NORTHERN IOWA
Cedar Falls 50614 *Type:* Public (state) *System:* Iowa State Board of Regents *Accred.:* 1913/1991 (NCA) *Calendar:* Sem. plan *Degrees:* B, P, M, D *Prof. Accred.:* Art, Audiology, Business (B,M), Construction Education (B), Counseling, Home Economics, Music, Recreation and Leisure Services, Social Work (B), Speech-Language Pathology *CEO:* Pres. Constantine W. Curris
Enroll: 13,045   (319) 273-2566

UNIVERSITY OF OSTEOPATHIC MEDICINE AND HEALTH SCIENCES
3200 Grand Ave., Des Moines 50312 *Type:* Private professional *Accred.:* 1986/1991 (NCA) *Calendar:* Sem. plan *Degrees:* B, M, D, certificates *Prof. Accred.:* Osteopathy, Physical Therapy, Physician Assisting, Podiatry *CEO:* Pres. David G. Marker
Enroll: 1,301   (515) 271-1400

UPPER IOWA UNIVERSITY
Box 1857, College and Washington Sts., Fayette 52142 *Type:* Private liberal arts *Accred.:* 1913/1991 (NCA) *Calendar:* 4-1-4

plan *Degrees:* A, B *CEO:* Pres. James R. Rocheleau
Enroll: 2,641   (319) 425-5200

VENNARD COLLEGE
Eighth Ave. E., P.O. Box 29, University Park 52595 *Type:* Independent (Wesleyan) *Accred.:* 1948/1984 (AABC) *Calendar:* Sem. plan *Degrees:* A, B *CEO:* Pres. Blake J. Neff
FTE Enroll: 142   (515) 673-8391

WALDORF COLLEGE
Forest City 50436 *Type:* Private (Lutheran) junior *Accred.:* 1948/1990 (NCA) *Calendar:* Sem. plan *Degrees:* A, certificates *CEO:* Pres. William E. Hamm
Enroll: 499   (515) 582-2450

WARTBURG COLLEGE
Waverly 50677 *Type:* Private (Lutheran) liberal arts *Accred.:* 1948/1987 (NCA) *Calendar:* 4-4-1 plan *Degrees:* B, certificates *Prof. Accred.:* Music, Social Work (B), Teacher Education (e,s) *CEO:* Pres. Robert L. Vogel
Enroll: 1,445   (319) 352-8200

WARTBURG THEOLOGICAL SEMINARY
333 Wartburg Pl., Dubuque 52003-7797 *Type:* Private (Lutheran) graduate only *Accred.:* 1944/1986 (ATS); 1976/1987 (NCA) *Calendar:* 4-1-4 plan *Degrees:* M, D *CEO:* Pres. Roger W. Fjeld
Enroll: 235   (319) 589-0200

WESTERN IOWA TECH COMMUNITY COLLEGE
4647 Stone Ave., P.O. Box 265, Sioux City 51102 *Type:* Public (district) junior *System:* Iowa Department of Education Division of Community Colleges *Accred.:* 1977/1992 (NCA) *Calendar:* Qtr. plan *Degrees:* A, certificates, diplomas *Prof. Accred.:* Dental Assisting, Practical Nursing, Surgical Technology *CEO:* Pres. Robert E. Dunker
Enroll: 2,578   (712) 274-6400

WILLIAM PENN COLLEGE
201 Trueblood Ave., Oskaloosa 52577 *Type:* Private (Society of Friends) liberal arts *Accred.:* 1913/1987 (NCA) *Calendar:* Sem. plan *Degrees:* B *CEO:* Pres. John D. Wagoner
Enroll: 689   (515) 673-1076

KANSAS

ALLEN COUNTY COMMUNITY COLLEGE
1801 N. Cottonwood, Iola 66749 *Type:* Public (district) junior *System:* Kansas State Board of Education *Accred.:* 1974/1989 (NCA) *Calendar:* Sem. plan *Degrees:* A, certificates *CEO:* Pres. John A. Masterson
Enroll: 1,717   (316) 365-5116

BAKER UNIVERSITY
606 W. 8th St., P.O. Box 65, Baldwin City 66006-0065 *Type:* Private (United Methodist) liberal arts *Accred.:* 1913/1992 (NCA) *Calendar:* 4-1-4 plan *Degrees:* A, B, M *Prof. Accred.:* Nursing (A,B) *CEO:* Pres. Daniel M. Lambert
Enroll: 1,840   (913) 594-6451

BARCLAY COLLEGE
607 N. Kingman, P.O. Box 288, Haviland 67059 *Type:* Private (Evangelical Friends International) *Accred.:* 1975/1985 (AABC) *Calendar:* Sem. plan *Degrees:* B, certificates *CEO:* Pres. Robin W. Johnston
FTE Enroll: 82   (316) 862-5252

BARTON COUNTY COMMUNITY COLLEGE
Rural Rte. 3, Box 136Z, Great Bend 67530 *Type:* Public (district) junior *System:* Kansas State Board of Education *Accred.:* 1974/1993 (NCA) *Calendar:* Sem. plan *Degrees:* A, certificates *Prof. Accred.:* Medical Laboratory Technology (AMA) *CEO:* Pres. Jimmie L. Downing
Enroll: 3,938   (316) 792-2701

BENEDICTINE COLLEGE
1020 N. Second St., Atchison 66002 *Type:* Private (Roman Catholic) liberal arts *Accred.:* 1971/1993 (NCA) *Calendar:* 4-1-4 plan *Degrees:* A, B, M *Prof. Accred.:* Music, Teacher Education (e,s) *CEO:* Pres. Thomas O. James
Enroll: 1,225   (913) 367-5340

BETHANY COLLEGE
421 N. First St., Lindsborg 67456 *Type:* Private (Lutheran) liberal arts *Accred.:* 1932/1990 (NCA) *Calendar:* 4-1-4 plan *Degrees:* B *Prof. Accred.:* Music, Social Work (B), Teacher Education (e,s) *CEO:* Pres. Joel M. McKean
Enroll: 694   (913) 227-3311

BETHEL COLLEGE
300 E. 27th St., North Newton 67117 *Type:* Private (Mennonite) liberal arts *Accred.:* 1938/1989 (NCA) *Calendar:* 4-1-4 plan *Degrees:* B *Prof. Accred.:* Nursing (B), Social Work (B) *CEO:* Pres. John E. Zehr
Enroll: 626   (316) 283-2500

THE BROWN MACKIE COLLEGE
126 S. Santa Fe Ave., Salina 67401 *Type:* Private business *Accred.:* 1980/1990 (NCA) *Calendar:* Qtr. plan *Degrees:* A, certificates, diplomas *CEO:* Pres. M. Gary Talley
Enroll: 654   (913) 825-5422

BUTLER COUNTY COMMUNITY COLLEGE
901 S. Haverhill Rd., El Dorado 67042 *Type:* Public (district) junior *System:* Kansas State Board of Education *Accred.:* 1970/1990 (NCA) *Calendar:* Sem. plan *Degrees:* A, certificates, diplomas *Prof. Accred.:* Nursing (A) *CEO:* Pres. Rodney V. Cox
Enroll: 6,627   (316) 312-2222

CENTRAL BAPTIST THEOLOGICAL SEMINARY
741 N. 31st St., Kansas City 66102-3964 *Type:* Private (Baptist) graduate only *Accred.:* 1962/1984 (ATS); 1979/1990 (NCA) *Calendar:* Sem. plan *Degrees:* M *CEO:* Pres. Thomas E. Clifton
Enroll: 104   (913) 371-5313

CENTRAL COLLEGE
1200 S. Main St., McPherson 67460 *Type:* Private (Free Methodist) *Accred.:* 1975/1987 (NCA) *Calendar:* 4-1-4 plan *Degrees:* A, B, certificates *CEO:* Pres. John A. Martin
Enroll: 335   (316) 241-0723

CLOUD COUNTY COMMUNITY COLLEGE
2221 Campus Dr., P.O. Box 1002, Concordia 66901-1002 *Type:* Public (district) junior *System:* Kansas State Board of Education *Accred.:* 1977/1991 (NCA) *Calendar:* Sem. plan *Degrees:* A, certificates *Prof. Accred.:* Nursing (A), Practical Nursing *CEO:* Pres. James P. Ihrig
Enroll: 2,875   (913) 243-1435

COFFEYVILLE COMMUNITY COLLEGE
11th and Willow Sts., Coffeyville 67337 *Type:* Public (district) junior *System:* Kansas

State Board of Education *Accred.:* 1972/ 1988 (NCA) *Calendar:* Sem. plan *Degrees:* A, certificates, diplomas *CEO:* Pres. Dan D. Kinney
Enroll: 1,838 (316) 251-7700

COLBY COMMUNITY COLLEGE
1255 S. Range, Colby 67701 *Type:* Public (district) junior *System:* Kansas State Board of Education *Accred.:* 1972/1985 (NCA) *Calendar:* Sem. plan *Degrees:* A, certificates, diplomas *Prof. Accred.:* Nursing (A), Physical Therapy Assisting, Practical Nursing, Veterinary Technology *CEO:* Pres. Mikel V. Ary
Enroll: 2,045 (913) 462-3984

COWLEY COUNTY COMMUNITY COLLEGE
125 S. Second St., P.O. Box 1147, Arkansas City 67005 *Type:* Public (district) junior *System:* Kansas State Board of Education *Accred.:* 1975/1990 (NCA) *Calendar:* Sem. plan *Degrees:* A, certificates *CEO:* Pres. Patrick J. McAtee
Enroll: 3,059 (316) 442-0430

DODGE CITY COMMUNITY COLLEGE
2501 N. 14th St., Dodge City 67801 *Type:* Public (district) junior *System:* Kansas State Board of Education *Accred.:* 1966/1986 (NCA) *Calendar:* Sem. plan *Degrees:* A, certificates, diplomas *Prof. Accred.:* Medical Record Technology, Nursing (A), Practical Nursing *CEO:* Pres. Thomas E. Gamble
Enroll: 2,283 (316) 225-1321

DONNELLY COLLEGE
608 N. 18th St., Kansas City 66102 *Type:* Private (Roman Catholic) junior *Accred.:* 1958/1989 (NCA) *Calendar:* Sem. plan *Degrees:* A, certificates *CEO:* Pres. John P. Murry
Enroll: 500 (913) 621-6070

EMPORIA STATE UNIVERSITY
1200 Commercial St., Emporia 66801 *Type:* Public (state) liberal arts and teachers *System:* Kansas Board of Regents *Accred.:* 1915/1985 (NCA) *Calendar:* Sem. plan *Degrees:* A, B, P, M, D *Prof. Accred.:* Librarianship, Music, Rehabilitation Counseling, Teacher Education (e,s,p) *CEO:* Pres. Robert E. Glennen, Jr.
Enroll: 6,006 (316) 343-1200

FORT HAYS STATE UNIVERSITY
600 Park St., Hays 67601 *Type:* Public (state) liberal arts and teachers *System:* Kansas Board of Regents *Accred.:* 1915/ 1992 (NCA) *Calendar:* Sem. plan *Degrees:* A, B, P, M *Prof. Accred.:* Music, Nursing (B), Radiography, Speech-Language Pathology, Teacher Education (e,s,p) *CEO:* Pres. Edward H. Hammond
Enroll: 5,603 (913) 628-4000

FORT SCOTT COMMUNITY COLLEGE
2108 S. Horton St., Fort Scott 66701 *Type:* Public (district) junior *System:* Kansas State Board of Education *Accred.:* 1976/1993 (NCA) *Calendar:* Sem. plan *Degrees:* A, certificates *Prof. Accred.:* Nursing (A) *CEO:* Pres. Laura Meeks
Enroll: 1,815 (316) 223-2700

FRIENDS UNIVERSITY
2100 University Ave., Wichita 67213 *Type:* Private (Friends) liberal arts *Accred.:* 1915/ 1991 (NCA) *Calendar:* Sem. plan *Degrees:* A, B, M *Prof. Accred.:* Marriage and Family Therapy (M-candidate), Music, Teacher Education (e,s) *CEO:* Pres. Biff Green
Enroll: 1,684 (316) 261-5800

GARDEN CITY COMMUNITY COLLEGE
801 Campus Dr., Garden City 67846 *Type:* Public (district) junior *System:* Kansas State Board of Education *Accred.:* 1975/1985 (NCA) *Calendar:* Sem. plan *Degrees:* A, certificates *Prof. Accred.:* Nursing (A) *CEO:* Pres. James H. Tangeman
Enroll: 2,216 (316) 276-7611

HASKELL INDIAN JUNIOR COLLEGE
155 Indian Ave., No. 1305, Lawrence 66046-4800 *Type:* Public (federal) junior *Accred.:* 1979/1993 (NCA) *Calendar:* Sem. plan *Degrees:* A, B *CEO:* Pres. Robert G. Martin
Enroll: 906 (913) 749-8404

HESSTON COLLEGE
P.O. Box 3000, Hesston 67062 *Type:* Private (Mennonite) junior *Accred.:* 1964/1991 (NCA) *Calendar:* 4-1-4 plan *Degrees:* A *Prof. Accred.:* Nursing (A) *CEO:* Pres. Kirk Alliman
Enroll: 491 (316) 327-4221

HIGHLAND COMMUNITY COLLEGE
Box 68, Highland 66035 *Type:* Public (district) junior *System:* Kansas State Board of Education *Accred.:* 1977/1989 (NCA) *Calendar:* Sem. plan *Degrees:* A, certificates *CEO:* Pres. Eric M. Priest
Enroll: 2,150   (913) 442-3236

HUTCHINSON COMMUNITY COLLEGE
1300 N. Plum St., Hutchinson 67501 *Type:* Public (district) junior *System:* Kansas State Board of Education *Accred.:* 1960/1984 (NCA) *Calendar:* Sem. plan *Degrees:* A, certificates *Prof. Accred.:* Medical Record Technology, Nursing (A), Radiography *CEO:* Pres. Edward E. Berger
Enroll: 4,508   (316) 665-3500

INDEPENDENCE COMMUNITY COLLEGE
College Ave. and Brookside Dr., Independence 67301 *Type:* Public (district) junior *System:* Kansas State Board of Education *Accred.:* 1957/1988 (NCA) *Calendar:* Sem. plan *Degrees:* A, certificates *CEO:* Pres. Don Schoening
Enroll: 1,470   (316) 331-4100

JOHNSON COUNTY COMMUNITY COLLEGE
12345 College Blvd. at Quivira Rd., Overland Park 66210 *Type:* Public (district) junior *System:* Kansas State Board of Education *Accred.:* 1975/1987 (NCA) *Calendar:* Sem. plan *Degrees:* A, certificates *Prof. Accred.:* Dental Hygiene, EMT-Paramedic, Nursing (A), Respiratory Therapy *CEO:* Pres. Charles J. Carlsen
Enroll: 15,492   (913) 469-8500

KANSAS CITY KANSAS COMMUNITY COLLEGE
7250 State Ave., Kansas City 66112 *Type:* Public (district) junior *System:* Kansas State Board of Education *Accred.:* 1951/1986 (NCA) *Calendar:* Sem. plan *Degrees:* A, certificates *Prof. Accred.:* Mortuary Science, Nursing (A) *CEO:* Pres. Thomas R. Burke
Enroll: 6,258   (913) 334-1100

KANSAS NEWMAN COLLEGE
3100 McCormick Ave., Wichita 67213 *Type:* Private (Roman Catholic) liberal arts *Accred.:* 1967/1987 (NCA) *Calendar:* Sem. plan *Degrees:* A, B, M *Prof. Accred.:* Nursing (A,B) *CEO:* Pres. Tarcisia Roths, Sr.
Enroll: 1,618   (316) 942-4291

KANSAS STATE UNIVERSITY
Manhattan 66506-0113 *Type:* Public (state) *System:* Kansas Board of Regents *Accred.:* 1916/1992 (NCA) *Calendar:* Sem. plan *Degrees:* A, B, M, D, certificates *Prof. Accred.:* Accounting (Type A,C), Business (B,M), Computer Science, Construction Education (B), Dietetics (coordinated), Engineering Technology (electrical, mechanical), Engineering (agricultural, architectural, chemical, civil, computer, electrical, industrial, manufacturing, mechanical, nuclear), Home Economics, Interior Design, Journalism (B,M), Landscape Architecture (B,M), Marriage and Family Therapy (M,D), Music, Planning (M), Psychology Internship, Public Administration, Recreation and Leisure Services, Social Work (B), Speech-Language Pathology, Teacher Education (e,s,p), Theatre, Veterinary Medicine *CEO:* Pres. Jon Wefald
Enroll: 21,222   (913) 532-6011

SALINA COLLEGE OF TECHNOLOGY
2409 Scanlan Ave., Salina 67401-8196 *Prof. Accred.:* Engineering Technology (chemical, civil/construction, computer, electrical, mechanical) *CEO:* Dean Jerry Cole
                                    (913) 825-0275

KANSAS WESLEYAN UNIVERSITY
100 E. Clafin, Salina 67401 *Type:* Private (United Methodist) liberal arts *Accred.:* 1916/1990 (NCA) *Calendar:* 4-1-4 plan *Degrees:* A, B *Prof. Accred.:* Nursing (A,B) *CEO:* Pres. Marshall P. Stanton
Enroll: 754   (913) 827-5541

LABETTE COMMUNITY COLLEGE
200 S. 14th St., Parsons 67357 *Type:* Public (district) junior *System:* Kansas State Board of Education *Accred.:* 1976/1988 (NCA) *Calendar:* Sem. plan *Degrees:* A, certificates *Prof. Accred.:* Nursing (A), Radiography, Respiratory Therapy, Respiratory Therapy Technology *CEO:* Pres. Joe Birmingham
Enroll: 2,236   (316) 421-6700

MANHATTAN CHRISTIAN COLLEGE
1415 Anderson Ave., Manhattan 66502 *Type:* Private (Christian Churches/Churches of Christ) *Accred.:* 1948/1986 (AABC) *Cal-*

endar: Sem. plan *Degrees:* A, B, certificates
CEO: Pres. Kenneth D. Cable
FTE Enroll: 206   (913) 539-3571

MCPHERSON COLLEGE
1600 E. Euclid, P.O. Box 1402, McPherson
67460 *Type:* Private (Church of Brethren)
liberal arts *Accred.:* 1921/1990 (NCA) *Calendar:* 4-1-4 plan *Degrees:* A, B, certificates
CEO: Pres. Paul W. Hoffman
Enroll: 479   (316) 241-0731

MIDAMERICA NAZARENE COLLEGE
2030 E. College Way, Olathe 66062-1899
Type: Private (Nazarene) liberal arts *Accred.:* 1974/1989 (NCA) *Calendar:* Sem.
plan *Degrees:* A, B, M *Prof. Accred.:* Music
(associate), Nursing (B) *CEO:* Pres. Richard
L. Spindle
Enroll: 1,446   (913) 782-3750

NEOSHO COUNTY COMMUNITY COLLEGE
1000 S. Allen, Chanute 66720 *Type:* Public
(district) junior *System:* Kansas State Board
of Education *Accred.:* 1976/1986 (NCA)
Calendar: Sem. plan *Degrees:* A, certificates, diplomas *Prof. Accred.:* Nursing (A)
CEO: Pres. Theodore W. Wischropp
Enroll: 1,819   (316) 431-2820

OTTAWA UNIVERSITY
1001 S. Cedar, Ottawa 66067-3399 *Type:*
Private (Baptist) liberal arts *Accred.:* 1914/
1989 (NCA) *Calendar:* Sem. plan *Degrees:*
B, M *CEO:* Pres. Harold D. Germer
Enroll: 3,481   (913) 242-5200

PITTSBURG STATE UNIVERSITY
1701 S. Broadway, Pittsburg 66762 *Type:*
Public (state) liberal arts and professional
System: Kansas Board of Regents *Accred.:*
1915/1993 (NCA) *Calendar:* Sem. plan *Degrees:* A, B, P, M, certificates *Prof. Accred.:*
Counseling, Engineering Technology (civil/
construction, electrical, manufacturing, mechanical, plastics), Music, Nursing (B), Social Work (B), Teacher Education (e,s,p)
CEO: Pres. Donald W. Wilson
Enroll: 6,516   (316) 231-7000

PRATT COMMUNITY COLLEGE
Hwy. 61, Pratt 67124 *Type:* Public (district)
junior *System:* Kansas State Board of Education *Accred.:* 1976/1988 (NCA) *Calendar:*
Sem. plan *Degrees:* A, certificates *Prof. Ac-*

cred.: Nursing (A) *CEO:* Pres. William A.
Wojciechowski
Enroll: 1,417   (316) 672-5641

ST. MARY COLLEGE
4100 S. 4th St. Trafficway, Leavenworth
66048-5082 *Type:* Private (Roman Catholic)
liberal arts primarily for women *Accred.:*
1928/1987 (NCA) *Calendar:* Sem. plan *Degrees:* A, B, M *Prof. Accred.:* Nursing (B),
Teacher Education (e,s) *CEO:* Pres. Peter
Clifford, F.S.C.
Enroll: 1,027   (913) 682-5151

SEWARD COUNTY COMMUNITY COLLEGE
1801 N. Kansas St., Box 1137, Liberal
67901 *Type:* Public (district) junior *System:*
Kansas State Board of Education *Accred.:*
1975/1990 (NCA) *Calendar:* Sem. plan *Degrees:* A, certificates *Prof. Accred.:* Medical
Laboratory Technology (AMA), Nursing
(A), Practical Nursing, Respiratory Therapy,
Respiratory Therapy Technology *CEO:* Pres.
Donald E. Guild
Enroll: 1,537   (316) 624-1951

SOUTHWESTERN COLLEGE
100 College St., Winfield 67156 *Type:* Private (United Methodist) liberal arts *Accred.:*
1918/1992 (NCA) *Calendar:* 4-1-4 plan *Degrees:* B, M, certificates *Prof. Accred.:*
Music, Nursing (B), Social Work (B) *CEO:*
Pres. Carl E. Martin
Enroll: 737   (316) 221-4150

STERLING COLLEGE
Sterling 67579 *Type:* Private (United Presbyterian) liberal arts *Accred.:* 1928/1987
(NCA) *Calendar:* 4-1-4 plan *Degrees:* A, B
CEO: Pres. John S. Devens
Enroll: 768   (316) 278-2173

TABOR COLLEGE
400 S. Jefferson St., Hillsboro 67063 *Type:*
Private (Mennonite) liberal arts *Accred.:*
1965/1985 (NCA) *Calendar:* Sem. plan *Degrees:* A, B *Prof. Accred.:* Music *CEO:* Pres.
LeVon Balzer
Enroll: 448   (316) 947-3121

TOPEKA SCHOOL OF MEDICAL TECHNOLOGY
1915 S.W. Sixth St., Ste. 207, Topeka 66604
Type: Private *Calendar:* 12-month plan *De-*

grees: B, certificates *Prof. Accred.:* Medical Technology *CEO:* Pres. Stephen White
Enroll: 16   (913) 295-8933

UNITED STATES ARMY COMMAND AND GENERAL STAFF COLLEGE
Fort Leavenworth 66027 *Type:* Public (federal) *Accred.:* 1976/1985 (NCA) *Calendar:* Sem. plan *Degrees:* M, diplomas *CEO:* Commandant Leonard Wishart
Enroll: 1,280   (913) 684-5621

UNIVERSITY OF KANSAS
Lawrence 66045 *Type:* Public (state) *System:* Kansas Board of Regents *Accred.:* 1913/1985 (NCA) *Calendar:* Sem. plan *Degrees:* B, P, M, D, certificates *Prof. Accred.:* Art, Audiology, Business (B,M), Clinical Psychology, Counseling Psychology, Engineering (aerospace, architectural, chemical, civil, computer, electrical, engineering physics/science, mechanical, petroleum), Health Services Administration, Journalism (B,M), Law, Music, Planning (M), Public Administration, School Psychology, Social Work (B,M), Speech-Language Pathology, Teacher Education (e,s,p) *CEO:* Chanc. Gene A. Budig
Enroll: 29,161   (913) 864-2700

UNIVERSITY OF KANSAS MEDICAL CENTER
200 Murphy Admin. Bldg., 39th St. and Rainbow Blvd., Kansas City 66103 *Type:* Public *Calendar:* Courses of varying lengths *Degrees:* B, M, certificates, diplomas *Prof. Accred.:* Cytotechnology, Dietetics (intern-ship), Medical Record Administration, Medical Technology, Medicine, Nurse Anesthesia Education, Nursing (B,M), Occupational Therapy, Physical Therapy, Radiation Therapy Technology, Respiratory Therapy *CEO:* Exec. Vice Chanc. D. Kay Clawson, M.D.
                    (913) 588-1401

WASHBURN UNIVERSITY OF TOPEKA
17th and College Sts., Topeka 66621 *Type:* Public (local) *Accred.:* 1913/1988 (NCA) *Calendar:* Sem. plan *Degrees:* A, B, M, D, certificates *Prof. Accred.:* Law, Medical Record Technology, Music, Nursing (B), Physical Therapy Assisting, Radiation Therapy Technology, Radiography, Respiratory Therapy, Respiratory Therapy Technology, Social Work (B,M-candidate), Teacher Education (e,s,p) *CEO:* Pres. Hugh L. Thompson
Enroll: 6,630   (913) 231-1010

WICHITA STATE UNIVERSITY
1845 Fairmont St., Wichita 67260 *Type:* Public (state) *System:* Kansas Board of Regents *Accred.:* 1927/1987 (NCA) *Calendar:* Sem. plan *Degrees:* A, B, P, M, D *Prof. Accred.:* Audiology, Business (B,M), Dance (associate), Dental Hygiene, Engineering (aerospace, electrical, industrial, mechanical), Medical Technology, Music, Nursing (B,M), Physical Therapy, Physician Assisting, Respiratory Therapy, Social Work (B), Speech-Language Pathology, Teacher Education (e,s,p) *CEO:* Pres. Eugene M. Hughes
Enroll: 15,120   (316) 689-3001

KENTUCKY

ALICE LLOYD COLLEGE
Purpose Rd., Pippa Passes 41844 *Type:* Private liberal arts *Accred.:* 1952/1987 (SACS-CC) *Calendar:* Sem. plan *Degrees:* B *CEO:* Acting Pres. Robert M. Duncan
FTE Enroll: 604   (606) 368-2101

ASBURY COLLEGE
One Macklem Dr., Wilmore 40390-1198 *Type:* Private liberal arts and teachers *Accred.:* 1940/1989 (SACS-CC) *Calendar:* Sem. plan *Degrees:* B *Prof. Accred.:* Music *CEO:* Pres. David Gyerston
FTE Enroll: 1,141   (606) 858-3511

ASBURY THEOLOGICAL SEMINARY
204 N. Lexington Ave., Wilmore 40390-1199 *Type:* Private (interdenominational) graduate only *Accred.:* 1946/1984 (ATS); 1984 (SACS-CC) *Calendar:* 4-1-4 plan *Degrees:* M, D *CEO:* Pres. David L. McKenna
FTE Enroll: 714   (606) 858-3581

ASHLAND COMMUNITY COLLEGE
1400 College Dr., Ashland 41101-3683 *Type:* Public (state) junior *System:* University of Kentucky Community College System *Accred.:* 1957/1991 (SACS-CC) *Calendar:* Sem. plan *Degrees:* A *CEO:* Pres. Charles R. Dassance
FTE Enroll: 2,496   (606) 329-2999

BELLARMINE COLLEGE
2001 Newburg Rd., Louisville 40205 *Type:* Private (Roman Catholic) liberal arts *Accred.:* 1949/1988 (SACS-CC) *Calendar:* Sem. plan *Degrees:* A, B, M *Prof. Accred.:* Nursing (B) *CEO:* Pres. Joseph J. McGowan, Jr.
FTE Enroll: 2,408   (502) 452-8211

BEREA COLLEGE
Berea 40404 *Type:* Private liberal arts *Accred.:* 1926/1985 (SACS-CC) *Calendar:* 4-1-4 plan *Degrees:* B *Prof. Accred.:* Nursing (B), Teacher Education (e,s) *CEO:* Pres. John B. Stephenson
FTE Enroll: 1,634   (606) 986-9341

BRESCIA COLLEGE
717 Frederica St., Owensboro 42301-3023 *Type:* Private (Roman Catholic) liberal arts

Accred.: 1957/1989 (SACS-CC) *Calendar:* Sem. plan *Degrees:* A, B, M (candidate) *CEO:* Pres. Ruth Gehres
FTE Enroll: 579   (502) 685-3131

CAMPBELLSVILLE COLLEGE
200 W. College St., Campbellsville 42718-2799 *Type:* Private (Southern Baptist) liberal arts *Accred.:* 1963/1984 (SACS-CC) *Calendar:* Sem. plan *Degrees:* A, B *Prof. Accred.:* Music (associate) *CEO:* Pres. Kenneth W. Winters
FTE Enroll: 1,029   (502) 465-8158

CAREERCOM JUNIOR COLLEGE OF BUSINESS
1102 S. Virginia St., Hopkinsville 42240 *Type:* Private junior *Accred.:* 1988 (ACISC) *Calendar:* Qtr. plan *Degrees:* A, certificates, diplomas *CEO:* Dir. Kim Hall
                                     (502) 886-1302

CENTRE COLLEGE
600 W. Walnut St., Danville 40422 *Type:* Private liberal arts *Accred.:* 1904/1985 (SACS-CC) *Calendar:* 4-1-4 plan *Degrees:* B *CEO:* Pres. Michael F. Adams
FTE Enroll: 947   (606) 238-5200

CLEAR CREEK BAPTIST BIBLE COLLEGE
300 Clear Creek Rd., Pineville 40977 *Type:* Private (Southern Baptist Convention) *Accred.:* 1986/1991 (AABC) *Calendar:* Sem. plan *Degrees:* A, B, certificates, diplomas *CEO:* Pres. Bill Whittaker
FTE Enroll: 136   (606) 337-3196

CUMBERLAND COLLEGE
6191 College Sta., Williamsburg 40769 *Type:* Private (Southern Baptist) liberal arts and teachers *Accred.:* 1964/1985 (SACS-CC) *Calendar:* Sem. plan *Degrees:* A, B, M *Prof. Accred.:* Music *CEO:* Pres. James H. Taylor
FTE Enroll: 1,388   (606) 549-2200

EASTERN KENTUCKY UNIVERSITY
Richmond 40475-3101 *Type:* Public (state) *System:* Kentucky Council on Higher Education *Accred.:* 1928/1986 (SACS-CC) *Calendar:* Sem. plan *Degrees:* A, B, M *Prof. Accred.:* Computer Science, Construction Education (B), EMT-Paramedic, Medical Assist-

ing (AMA), Medical Laboratory Technology (AMA), Medical Record Administration, Medical Record Technology, Medical Technology, Music, Nursing (A,B), Occupational Therapy, Public Administration, Recreation and Leisure Services, Social Work (B), Speech-Language Pathology, Teacher Education (e,s,p) *CEO:* Pres. H. Hanly Funderburk, Jr.
FTE Enroll: 15,735   (606) 622-1000

ELIZABETHTOWN COMMUNITY COLLEGE
600 College Street Rd., Elizabethtown 42701 *Type:* Public (state) junior *System:* University of Kentucky Community College System *Accred.:* 1964/1991 (SACS-CC) *Calendar:* Sem. plan *Degrees:* A *Prof. Accred.:* Nursing (A) *CEO:* Pres. Charles E. Stebbins
FTE Enroll: 2,803   (502) 769-2371

FUGAZZI COLLEGE
406 Lafayette Ave., Lexington 40502 *Type:* Private junior *Accred.:* 1957/1986 (ACISC) *Calendar:* Qtr. plan *Degrees:* A, certificates, diplomas *Prof. Accred.:* Medical Assisting (AMA) *CEO:* Dir. Sarah Wilkins
(606) 266-0401

BRANCH CAMPUS
5042 Lindbar Dr., Nashville, TN 37211 *Accred.:* 1991 (ACISC) *CEO:* Dir. Jane Kleiser
(615) 333-3344

GEORGETOWN COLLEGE
400 E. College St., Georgetown 40324 *Type:* Private (Southern Baptist) liberal arts *Accred.:* 1919/1992 (SACS-CC) *Calendar:* Sem. plan *Degrees:* B, M *CEO:* Pres. William H. Crouch, Jr.
FTE Enroll: 1,328   (502) 863-8011

HAZARD COMMUNITY COLLEGE
One Community College Dr., Hazard 41701 *Type:* Public (state) junior *System:* University of Kentucky Community College System *Accred.:* 1968/1991 (SACS-CC) *Calendar:* Sem. plan *Degrees:* A *CEO:* Pres. G. Edward Hughes
FTE Enroll: 1,570   (606) 436-5721

HENDERSON COMMUNITY COLLEGE
2660 S. Green St., Henderson 42420 *Type:* Public (state) junior *System:* University of Kentucky Community College System *Accred.:* 1960/1991 (SACS-CC) *Calendar:*

Sem. plan *Degrees:* A *Prof. Accred.:* Medical Laboratory Technology (AMA), Nursing (A) *CEO:* Pres. Patrick R. Lake
FTE Enroll: 1,029   (502) 827-1867

HOPKINSVILLE COMMUNITY COLLEGE
P.O. Box 2100, Hopkinsville 42241-2100 *Type:* Public (state) junior *System:* University of Kentucky Community College System *Accred.:* 1965/1991 (SACS-CC) *Calendar:* Sem. plan *Degrees:* A *Prof. Accred.:* Dental Hygiene *CEO:* Pres. A. James Kerley
FTE Enroll: 1,792   (502) 886-3921

INSTITUTE OF ELECTRONIC TECHNOLOGY
509 S. 30th St., Paducah 42001-0161 *Type:* Private *Accred.:* 1968/1989 (ACCSCT) *Calendar:* Sem. plan *Degrees:* A *CEO:* Dir. of Educ. Don Johnson
(502) 444-9676

LEXINGTON ELECTRONICS INSTITUTE
Clays Mill Shopping Ctr., 3340 Holwyn Rd., Lexington 40503-9938 *Accred.:* 1991 (ACCSCT) *CEO:* Dir. Judith A. Steinfeld
(606) 223-9608

JEFFERSON COMMUNITY COLLEGE
109 E. Broadway, Louisville 40202 *Type:* Public (state) junior *System:* University of Kentucky Community College System *Accred.:* 1968/1991 (SACS-CC) *Calendar:* Sem. plan *Degrees:* A *Prof. Accred.:* Nursing (A), Physical Therapy Assisting, Respiratory Therapy *CEO:* Pres. Ronald J. Horvath
FTE Enroll: 7,127   (502) 584-0181

KENTUCKY CHRISTIAN COLLEGE
617 N. Carol Malone Blvd., Grayson 41143-1199 *Type:* Private (Christian Churches/ Churches of Christ) *Accred.:* 1962/1991 (AABC); 1984/1989 (SACS-CC) *Calendar:* Sem. plan *Degrees:* A, B *CEO:* Pres. Keith P. Keeran
FTE Enroll: 530   (606) 474-6613

KENTUCKY COLLEGE OF BUSINESS
628 E. Main St., Lexington 40508 *Type:* Private junior *Accred.:* 1970/1989 (ACISC) *Calendar:* Qtr. plan *Degrees:* A, certificates, diplomas *CEO:* Dir. Kim Thomasson
(606) 253-0621

BRANCH CAMPUS
115 E. Lexington Ave., Danville 40422 *Accred.:* 1977/1989 (ACISC) *CEO:* Dir. Brent Brenard
(606) 236-6991

BRANCH CAMPUS
7627 Tanners La., Florence 41042 *Accred.:* 1989 (ACISC) *CEO:* Dir. Charlotte Brinnenman
(606) 525-6510

BRANCH CAMPUS
3950 Dixie Hwy., Louisville 40216 *Accred.:* 1970/1989 (ACISC) *CEO:* Dir. Bud Darland
(502) 447-7665

BRANCH CAMPUS
198 S. Mayo Tr., Pikeville 41501 *Accred.:* 1977/1989 (ACISC) *CEO:* Dir. Kristine Lentz
(606) 432-5477

BRANCH CAMPUS
139 Killarney La., Richmond 40475 *Accred.:* 1970/1989 (ACISC) *CEO:* Dir. Keeley Gadd
(606) 623-8956

KENTUCKY STATE UNIVERSITY
E. Main St., Frankfort 40601 *Type:* Public (state) liberal arts and teachers *System:* Kentucky Council on Higher Education *Accred.:* 1939/1989 (SACS-CC) *Calendar:* Sem. plan *Degrees:* A, B, M *Prof. Accred.:* Music, Nursing (A), Social Work (B), Teacher Education (e,s) *CEO:* Pres. Mary L. Smith
FTE Enroll: 1,953   (502) 227-6000

KENTUCKY WESLEYAN COLLEGE
3000 Frederica St., P.O. Box 1039, Owensboro 42302-1039 *Type:* Private (United Methodist) liberal arts *Accred.:* 1948/1988 (SACS-CC) *Calendar:* Sem. plan *Degrees:* A, B *CEO:* Interim Pres. Ray C. Purdom
FTE Enroll: 723   (502) 926-3111

LEES COLLEGE
601 Jefferson Ave., Jackson 41339 *Type:* Private (Presbyterian) *Accred.:* 1951/1989 (SACS-CC warning) *Calendar:* Sem. plan *Degrees:* A *CEO:* Pres. Charles M. Derrickson
FTE Enroll: 624   (606) 666-7521

LEXINGTON COMMUNITY COLLEGE
Oswald Bldg., Cooper Dr., Lexington 40506-0235 *Type:* Public (state) junior *System:* University of Kentucky Community College System *Accred.:* 1965/1991 (SACS-CC) *Calendar:* Sem. plan *Degrees:* A *Prof. Accred.:* Dental Hygiene, Dental Laboratory Technology, Nuclear Medicine Technology, Nursing (A), Radiography, Respiratory Therapy *CEO:* Acting Pres. Anthony Newberry
FTE Enroll: 3,967   (606) 257-4872

LEXINGTON THEOLOGICAL SEMINARY
631 S. Limestone St., Lexington 40508 *Type:* Private (Disciples of Christ) graduate only *Accred.:* 1938/1983 (ATS); 1984 (SACS-CC) *Calendar:* Sem. plan *Degrees:* M, D *CEO:* Pres. Richard L. Harrison, Jr.
FTE Enroll: 122   (606) 252-0361

LINDSEY WILSON COLLEGE
210 Lindsey Wilson St., Columbia 42728 *Type:* Private (United Methodist) *Accred.:* 1951/1993 (SACS-CC) *Calendar:* Sem. plan *Degrees:* A, B *CEO:* Pres. John B. Begley
FTE Enroll: 1,083   (502) 384-2126

LOUISVILLE PRESBYTERIAN THEOLOGICAL SEMINARY
1044 Alta Vista Rd., Louisville 40205 *Type:* Private (Presbyterian) graduate only *Accred.:* 1938/1989 (ATS); 1973/1989 (SACS-CC) *Calendar:* 4-1-4 plan *Degrees:* M, D *Prof. Accred.:* Marriage and Family Therapy (M) *CEO:* Pres. John M. Mulder
FTE Enroll: 201   (502) 895-3411

LOUISVILLE TECHNICAL INSTITUTE
3901 Atkinson Dr., Louisville 40218-4528 *Type:* Private *Accred.:* 1974/1992 (ACCSCT) *Calendar:* Qtr. plan *Degrees:* A, certificates, diplomas *CEO:* Exec. Dir. David B. Keene
(502) 456-6509

MADISONVILLE COMMUNITY COLLEGE
2000 College Dr., Madisonville 42431 *Type:* Public (state) junior *System:* University of Kentucky Community College System *Accred.:* 1968/1991 (SACS-CC) *Calendar:* Sem. plan *Degrees:* A *Prof. Accred.:* Respiratory Therapy *CEO:* Pres. Arthur D. Stumpf
FTE Enroll: 1,804   (502) 821-2250

MAYSVILLE COMMUNITY COLLEGE
1755 U.S. 68, Maysville 41056 *Type:* Public (state) junior *System:* University of Kentucky Community College System *Accred.:* 1968/1991 (SACS-CC) *Calendar:* Sem. plan *Degrees:* A *Prof. Accred.:* Dental Hygiene *CEO:* Pres. James C. Shires
FTE Enroll: 1,171　　　　　(606) 759-7141

MID-CONTINENT BAPTIST BIBLE COLLEGE
P.O. Box 7010, Mayfield 42066 *Type:* Private (Baptist) professional *Accred.:* 1987/1992 (SACS-CC) *Calendar:* Sem. plan *Degrees:* B *CEO:* Pres. LaVerne Butler
FTE Enroll: 84　　　　　　　(502) 247-8521

MIDWAY COLLEGE
512 E. Stephens St., Midway 40347-1120 *Type:* Private junior for women *Accred.:* 1949/1984 (SACS-CC) *Calendar:* Sem. plan *Degrees:* A, B *Prof. Accred.:* Nursing (A,B) *CEO:* Pres. Robert R. Botkin
FTE Enroll: 943　　　　　　(606) 846-4421

MOREHEAD STATE UNIVERSITY
University Blvd., Morehead 40351 *Type:* Public (state) *System:* Kentucky Council on Higher Education *Accred.:* 1930/1990 (SACS-CC) *Calendar:* Sem. plan *Degrees:* A, B, M *Prof. Accred.:* Music, Nursing (A,B), Radiography, Social Work (B), Teacher Education (e,s,p), Veterinary Technology *CEO:* Pres. Ronald G. Eaglin
FTE Enroll: 7,620　　　　　(606) 783-2221

MURRAY STATE UNIVERSITY
One Murray St., Murray 42071-3305 *Type:* Public (state) *System:* Kentucky Council on Higher Education *Accred.:* 1928/1984 (SACS-CC) *Calendar:* Sem. plan *Degrees:* A, B, M *Prof. Accred.:* Art, Business (B,M), Counseling, Engineering Technology (civil/construction, electrical, manufacturing), Journalism (B,M), Music, Nursing (B), Social Work (B), Speech-Language Pathology, Teacher Education (e,s,p), Veterinary Technology *CEO:* Pres. Ronald J. Kurth
FTE Enroll: 7,138　　　　　(502) 762-3011

NORTHERN KENTUCKY UNIVERSITY
Nunn Dr., Highland Heights 41099 *Type:* Public (state) *System:* Kentucky Council on Higher Education *Accred.:* 1973/1988 (SACS-CC) *Calendar:* Sem. plan *Degrees:*

A, B, M, D *Prof. Accred.:* Dental Hygiene, Law, Music (associate), Nursing (A,B), Radiography, Social Work (B), Teacher Education (e,s) *CEO:* Pres. Leon E. Boothe
FTE Enroll: 11,601　　　　(606) 572-5100

OWENSBORO COMMUNITY COLLEGE
4800 New Hartford Rd., Owensboro 42303 *Type:* Public (state) junior *System:* University of Kentucky Community College System *Accred.:* 1990 (SACS-CC) *Calendar:* Sem. plan *Degrees:* A *Prof. Accred.:* Radiography *CEO:* Pres. John M. McGuire
FTE Enroll: 1,862　　　　　(502) 686-4400

OWENSBORO JUNIOR COLLEGE OF BUSINESS
1515 E. 18th St., Owensboro 42303 *Type:* Private junior *Accred.:* 1969/1990 (ACISC) *Calendar:* Tri. plan *Degrees:* A *CEO:* Dir. Lenda Anderson
　　　　　　　　　　　　　　　(502) 926-4040

PADUCAH COMMUNITY COLLEGE
P.O. Box 7380, Paducah 42002-7380 *Type:* Public (state) junior *System:* University of Kentucky Community College System *Accred.:* 1932/1991 (SACS-CC) *Calendar:* Sem. plan *Degrees:* A *Prof. Accred.:* Nursing (A), Physical Therapy Assisting *CEO:* Pres. Leonard F. O'Hara
FTE Enroll: 2,250　　　　　(502) 554-9200

PIKEVILLE COLLEGE
214 Sycamore St., Pikeville 41501 *Type:* Private (United Presbyterian) liberal arts *Accred.:* 1961/1992 (SACS-CC) *Calendar:* Sem. plan *Degrees:* A, B *CEO:* Pres. William H. Owens
FTE Enroll: 846　　　　　　(606) 432-9200

PRESTONSBURG COMMUNITY COLLEGE
One Bert T. Combs Dr., Prestonsburg 41653 *Type:* Public (state) junior *System:* University of Kentucky Community College System *Accred.:* 1964/1991 (SACS-CC) *Calendar:* Sem. plan *Degrees:* A *CEO:* Pres. Deborah Lee Floyd
FTE Enroll: 2,473　　　　　(606) 886-3863

ST. CATHARINE COLLEGE
2735 Bardstown Rd., St. Catharine 40061 *Type:* Private (Roman Catholic) junior *Accred.:* 1957/1988 (SACS-CC) *Calendar:*

Sem. plan *Degrees:* A *CEO:* Pres. Martha L. Collins
FTE Enroll: 386   (606) 336-5082

SOMERSET COMMUNITY COLLEGE
808 Monticello Rd., Somerset 42501 *Type:* Public (state) junior *System:* University of Kentucky Community College System *Accred.:* 1965/1991 (SACS-CC) *Calendar:* Sem. plan *Degrees:* A *Prof. Accred.:* Medical Laboratory Technology (AMA), Physical Therapy Assisting *CEO:* Pres. Rollin J. Watson
FTE Enroll: 3,357   (606) 679-8501

SOUTHEAST COMMUNITY COLLEGE
700 College Rd., Cumberland 40823-1099 *Type:* Public (state) junior *System:* University of Kentucky Community College System *Accred.:* 1960/1991 (SACS-CC) *Calendar:* Sem. plan *Degrees:* A *CEO:* Pres. W. Bruce Ayers
FTE Enroll: 2,240   (606) 589-2145

THE SOUTHERN BAPTIST THEOLOGICAL SEMINARY
2825 Lexington Rd., Louisville 40280 *Type:* Private (Southern Baptist) graduate only *Accred.:* 1938/1983 (ATS); 1968/1993 (SACS-CC) *Calendar:* Sem. plan *Degrees:* M, D *Prof. Accred.:* Music, Social Work (M) *CEO:* Pres. R. Albert Mohler, Jr.
FTE Enroll: 1,468   (502) 897-4011

SOUTHWESTERN COLLEGE OF BUSINESS
2929 S. Dixie Hwy., Crestview Hills 41017 *Type:* Private business *Accred.:* 1980/1991 (ACISC) *Calendar:* Qtr. plan *Degrees:* A, certificates, diplomas *Prof. Accred.:* Medical Assisting *CEO:* Dir. Bruce Budesheim
                                    (606) 341-6633

SPALDING UNIVERSITY
851 S. Fourth St., Louisville 40203-2115 *Type:* Private (Roman Catholic) liberal arts *Accred.:* 1938/1986 (SACS-CC) *Calendar:* Sem. plan *Degrees:* A, B, M, D *Prof. Accred.:* Clinical Psychology, Nursing (B,M), Social Work (B), Teacher Education (e,s,p) *CEO:* Pres. Eileen M. Egan
FTE Enroll: 925   (502) 585-9911

SUE BENNETT COLLEGE
151 College St., London 40741 *Type:* Private (United Methodist) *Accred.:* 1932/1992

(SACS-CC) *Calendar:* Sem. plan *Degrees:* A *CEO:* Pres. Paul G. Bunnell
FTE Enroll: 497   (606) 864-2238

SULLIVAN COLLEGE
3101 Bardstown Rd., Louisville 40205 *Type:* Private *Accred.:* 1965/1991 (ACISC); 1979/1984 (SACS-CC) *Calendar:* Qtr. plan *Degrees:* A, B *CEO:* Pres. Al R. Sullivan
FTE Enroll: 1,654   (502) 456-6504

BRANCH CAMPUS
2659 Regency Rd., Lexington 40503 *Accred.:* 1985/1991 (ACISC) *CEO:* Dir. Bill Noel
                                    (606) 276-4357

THOMAS MORE COLLEGE
333 Thomas More Pkwy., Crestview Hills 41017 *Type:* Private (Roman Catholic) liberal arts *Accred.:* 1959/1990 (SACS-CC) *Calendar:* Sem. plan *Degrees:* A, B *Prof. Accred.:* Nursing (B) *CEO:* Pres. William F. Cleves
FTE Enroll: 929   (606) 341-5800

TRANSYLVANIA UNIVERSITY
300 N. Broadway, Lexington 40508-1797 *Type:* Private liberal arts *Accred.:* 1915/1993 (SACS-CC) *Calendar:* 4-1-4 plan *Degrees:* B *CEO:* Pres. Charles L. Shearer
FTE Enroll: 886   (606) 233-8300

UNION COLLEGE
310 College St., Barbourville 40906 *Type:* Private (United Methodist) liberal arts *Accred.:* 1932/1984 (SACS-CC) *Calendar:* Sem. plan *Degrees:* A, B, M *CEO:* Pres. Jack C. Phillips
FTE Enroll: 826   (606) 546-4151

UNIVERSITY OF KENTUCKY
206 Administration Bldg., Lexington 40506-0032 *Type:* Public (state) *System:* Kentucky Council on Higher Education *Accred.:* 1915/1992 (SACS-CC) *Calendar:* Sem. plan *Degrees:* A, B, M, D *Prof. Accred.:* Accounting (Type A,C), Business (B,M), Clinical Psychology, Counseling Psychology, Dentistry, Dietetics (coordinated), Dietetics (internship), Engineering (agricultural, chemical, civil, electrical, mechanical, metallurgical, mining), Forestry, General Practice Residency, Home Economics, Interior Design, Journalism (B), Landscape Architec-

ture (B), Law, Librarianship, Marriage and Family Therapy (M), Medical Technology, Medicine, Music, Nursing (B,M), Oral and Maxillofacial Surgery, Orthodontics, Pediatric Dentistry, Periodontics, Physical Therapy, Physician Assisting, Public Administration, Radiation Therapy Technology, Rehabilitation Counseling, School Psychology, Social Work (B,M), Speech-Language Pathology, Teacher Education (e,s,p) *CEO:* Pres. Charles T. Wethington, Jr.
FTE Enroll: 19,429   (606) 257-9000

UNIVERSITY OF LOUISVILLE
2301 S. Third St., Louisville 40292-0001
Type: Public (state) *System:* Kentucky Council on Higher Education *Accred.:* 1915/1987 (SACS-CC) *Calendar:* Sem. plan *Degrees:* A, B, M, D *Prof. Accred.:* Accounting (Type A), Audiology, Business (B,M), Clinical Psychology, Combined Prosthodontics, Cytotechnology, Dental Hygiene, Dentistry, Endodontics, Engineering (chemical, civil, computer, electrical, industrial, mechanical), General Dentistry, General Practice Residency, Law, Marriage and Family Therapy (post-D), Medical Technology, Medicine, Music, Nuclear Medicine Technology, Nursing (B,M), Oral and Maxillofacial Surgery, Orthodontics, Physical Therapy, Psychology Internship, Radiography, Respiratory Therapy, Social Work (M), Speech-Language Pathology, Teacher Education (e,s,p) *CEO:* Pres. Donald C. Swain
FTE Enroll: 17,254   (502) 588-5555

WESTERN KENTUCKY UNIVERSITY
1526 Big Red Way, Bowling Green 42101
Type: Public (state) *System:* Kentucky Council on Higher Education *Accred.:* 1926/1984 (SACS-CC) *Calendar:* Sem. plan *Degrees:* A, B, M *Prof. Accred.:* Art, Business (B), Computer Science, Dental Hygiene, Engineering Technology (civil/construction, electrical, mechanical), Journalism (B), Medical Record Technology, Music, Nursing (A,B), Recreation and Leisure Services, Social Work (B), Speech-Language Pathology, Teacher Education (e,s,p) *CEO:* Pres. Thomas C. Meredith
FTE Enroll: 12,841   (502) 745-0111

LOUISIANA

BOSSIER PARISH COMMUNITY COLLEGE
2719 Airline Dr. at I-220, Bossier City 71111 *Type:* Public (local) junior *Accred.:* 1983/1989 (SACS-CC) *Calendar:* Sem. plan *Degrees:* A *Prof. Accred.:* Respiratory Therapy Technology *CEO:* Chanc. James M. Conerly
FTE Enroll: 3,527   (318) 746-9851

CENTENARY COLLEGE OF LOUISIANA
P.O. Box 41188, Shreveport 71134-1188 *Type:* Private (United Methodist) liberal arts *Accred.:* 1925/1987 (SACS-CC) *Calendar:* Sem. plan *Degrees:* B, M *Prof. Accred.:* Music *CEO:* Pres. Kenneth L. Schwab
FTE Enroll: 1,065   (318) 869-5011

DELGADO COMMUNITY COLLEGE
501 City Park Ave., New Orleans 70119-4399 *Type:* Public (state/local) junior *System:* State of Louisiana Board of Trustees for State Colleges and Universities *Accred.:* 1971/1986 (SACS-CC) *Calendar:* Sem. plan *Degrees:* A *Prof. Accred.:* Funeral Service Education, Nuclear Medicine Technology, Physical Therapy Assisting, Radiography, Respiratory Therapy, Respiratory Therapy Technology, Surgical Technology *CEO:* Pres. Ione H. Elioff
FTE Enroll: 11,278   (504) 483-4114

DELTA JUNIOR COLLEGE
7290 Exchange Pl., Baton Rouge 70806 *Type:* Private junior *Accred.:* 1973/1989 (ACISC) *Calendar:* Qtr. plan *Degrees:* A, certificates, diplomas *CEO:* Pres. Billy B. Clark
                              (504) 927-7780

BRANCH CAMPUS
Ste. 30, 100 Covington Ctr., Covington 70433-3302 *Accred.:* 1990 (ACISC) *CEO:* Dir. Linda DeoGracias
                              (504) 892-5332

DELTA COLLEGE
3827 W. Main St., Houma 70360 *Accred.:* 1989 (ACISC) *CEO:* Regional Dir. Randall Wagley
                              (504) 362-5445

DELTA SCHOOL OF BUSINESS AND TECHNOLOGY
517 Broad St., Lake Charles 70601 *Type:* Private business *Accred.:* 1976/1988 (ACISC) *Calendar:* Courses of varying lengths *Degrees:* A, certificates, diplomas *CEO:* Pres. Gary J. Holt
                              (318) 439-5765

DILLARD UNIVERSITY
2601 Gentilly Blvd., New Orleans 70122 *Type:* Private (United Church of Christ/United Methodist) liberal arts *Accred.:* 1937/1989 (SACS-CC) *Calendar:* Sem. plan *Degrees:* B *Prof. Accred.:* Nursing (B-warning) *CEO:* Pres. Samuel D. Cook
FTE Enroll: 1,577   (504) 283-8822

ELAINE P. NUNEZ COMMUNITY COLLEGE
3700 LaFontaine St., Chalmette 70043 *Type:* Public (state) *System:* State of Louisiana Board of Trustees for State Colleges and Universities *Accred.:* 1992 (SACS-CC) *Calendar:* Sem. plan *Degrees:* A *CEO:* Pres. Carol F. Hopson
FTE Enroll: 1,958   (504) 278-7440

BRANCH CAMPUS
901 Delery St., New Orleans 70117 *CEO:* Dir. John J. Kane
                              (504) 278-7440

BRANCH CAMPUS
P.O. Drawer 944, Port Sulphur 70083 *CEO:* Dir. Martha McDaniel
                              (504) 564-2701

GRAMBLING STATE UNIVERSITY
P.O. Drawer 607, Grambling 71245 *Type:* Public (state) liberal arts and professional *System:* State of Louisiana Board of Trustees for State Colleges and Universities *Accred.:* 1949/1990 (SACS-CC) *Calendar:* Sem. plan *Degrees:* A, B, M, D *Prof. Accred.:* Journalism (B), Music, Nursing (B), Recreation and Leisure Services, Social Work (B,M), Teacher Education (e,s,p), Theatre (associate) *CEO:* Pres. Harold W. Lundy
FTE Enroll: 7,833   (318) 274-2000

GRANTHAM COLLEGE OF ENGINEERING
34641 Grantham College Rd., P.O. Box 5700, Slidell 70469-5700 *Type:* Private

home study *Accred.:* 1961/1991 (NHSC) *Calendar:* Courses of varying lengths *Degrees:* A, B *CEO:* Pres. Donald J. Grantham
(504) 649-4191

LOUISIANA COLLEGE
1140 College Dr., Pineville 71359 *Type:* Private (Southern Baptist) liberal arts *Accred.:* 1923/1991 (SACS-CC) *Calendar:* Sem. plan *Degrees:* A, B *Prof. Accred.:* Music, Nursing (B), Social Work (B-candidate) *CEO:* Pres. Robert L. Lynn
FTE Enroll: 1,134   (318) 487-7011

LOUISIANA STATE UNIVERSITY AND AGRICULTURAL AND MECHANICAL COLLEGE
Baton Rouge 70803 *Type:* Public (state) *System:* Louisiana State University System *Accred.:* 1913/1984 (SACS-CC) *Calendar:* Sem. plan *Degrees:* B, M, D *Prof. Accred.:* Art, Audiology, Business (B,M), Clinical Psychology, Construction Education (B), Engineering (agricultural, chemical, civil, computer, electrical, industrial, mechanical, petroleum), Forestry, Home Economics, Interior Design, Journalism (B,M), Landscape Architecture (B,M), Law, Librarianship, Music, Social Work (M), Speech-Language Pathology, Teacher Education (e,s,p), Veterinary Medicine *CEO:* Chanc. William E. Davis
FTE Enroll: 26,609   (504) 388-3202

LOUISIANA STATE UNIVERSITY AT ALEXANDRIA
8100 Hwy. 71 S., Alexandria 71302-9121 *Type:* Public (state) junior *System:* Louisiana State University System *Accred.:* 1960/1984 (SACS-CC) *Calendar:* Sem. plan *Degrees:* A *Prof. Accred.:* Nursing (A) *CEO:* Acting Chanc. Fred Beckerdite
FTE Enroll: 1,990   (318) 445-3672

LOUISIANA STATE UNIVERSITY AT EUNICE
P.O. Box 1129, Eunice 70535 *Type:* Public (state) junior *System:* Louisiana State University System *Accred.:* 1967/1984 (SACS-CC) *Calendar:* Sem. plan *Degrees:* A *Prof. Accred.:* Respiratory Therapy Technology *CEO:* Chanc. Michael Smith
FTE Enroll: 2,105   (318) 457-7311

LOUISIANA STATE UNIVERSITY IN SHREVEPORT
One University Pl., Shreveport 71115-2399 *Type:* Public (state) *System:* Louisiana State

University System *Accred.:* 1975/1984 (SACS-CC) *Calendar:* Sem. plan *Degrees:* B, M *Prof. Accred.:* Business (B,M), Computer Science, Medicine, Radiography, Teacher Education (e,s,p) *CEO:* Chanc. John R. Darling
FTE Enroll: 3,498   (318) 797-5000

LOUISIANA STATE UNIVERSITY MEDICAL CENTER
433 Bolivar St., New Orleans 70112-2223 *Type:* Public (state) *System:* Louisiana State University System *Accred.:* 1931/1984 (SACS-CC) *Calendar:* Sem. plan *Degrees:* A, B, M, D *Prof. Accred.:* Audiology, Combined Prosthodontics, Dental Hygiene, Dental Laboratory Technology, Dentistry, Endodontics, General Dentistry, Medical Technology, Medicine, Nursing (A,B,M), Occupational Therapy, Oral and Maxillofacial Surgery, Orthodontics, Pediatric Dentistry, Periodontics, Physical Therapy, Rehabilitation Counseling, Respiratory Therapy, Speech-Language Pathology *CEO:* Chanc. Perry G. Rigby
FTE Enroll: 3,074   (504) 568-4808

LOUISIANA TECH UNIVERSITY
P.O. Box 3168, Tech Sta., Ruston 71272 *Type:* Public (state) *System:* State of Louisiana Board of Trustees for State Colleges and Universities *Accred.:* 1927/1984 (SACS-CC) *Calendar:* Qtr. plan *Degrees:* A, B, M, D *Prof. Accred.:* Accounting (Type A,B,C), Art, Audiology, Business (B,M), Computer Science, Engineering Technology (civil/construction, electrical), Engineering (bioengineering, chemical, civil, electrical, industrial, mechanical, petroleum), Forestry, Home Economics, Interior Design, Medical Record Administration, Medical Record Technology, Music, Nursing (A), Speech-Language Pathology, Teacher Education (e,s,p) *CEO:* Pres. Daniel D. Reneau
FTE Enroll: 10,053   (318) 257-0211

LOYOLA UNIVERSITY
6363 St. Charles Ave., New Orleans 70118 *Type:* Private (Roman Catholic) *Accred.:* 1929/1985 (SACS-CC) *Calendar:* Sem. plan *Degrees:* B, M, D *Prof. Accred.:* Business (B,M), Law, Music, Nursing (B) *CEO:* Pres. James C. Carter, S.J.
FTE Enroll: 5,043   (504) 865-2011

McNEESE STATE UNIVERSITY
4100 Ryan St., Lake Charles 70609 *Type:* Public (state) liberal arts *System:* State of Louisiana Board of Trustees for State Colleges and Universities *Accred.:* 1954/1986 (SACS-CC) *Calendar:* Sem. plan *Degrees:* A, B, M *Prof. Accred.:* Business (B,M), Engineering (general), Music, Nursing (B), Radiography, Teacher Education (e,s,p) *CEO:* Pres. Robert D. Hebert
FTE Enroll: 7,382   (318) 475-5000

NEW ORLEANS BAPTIST THEOLOGICAL
SEMINARY
3939 Gentilly Blvd., New Orleans 70126 *Type:* Private (Southern Baptist) graduate only *Accred.:* 1954/1986 (ATS); 1965/1986 (SACS-CC) *Calendar:* Sem. plan *Degrees:* A, M, D *Prof. Accred.:* Music *CEO:* Pres. Landrum P. Leavell, II
FTE Enroll: 1,142   (504) 282-4455

NICHOLLS STATE UNIVERSITY
Louisiana Hwy. 1, Thibodaux 70310 *Type:* Public (state) liberal arts and teachers *System:* State of Louisiana Board of Trustees for State Colleges and Universities *Accred.:* 1964/1985 (SACS-CC) *Calendar:* Sem. plan *Degrees:* A, B, M *Prof. Accred.:* Business (B,M), Home Economics, Music, Nursing (A,B), Respiratory Therapy Technology, Teacher Education (e,s,p) *CEO:* Pres. Donald J. Ayo
FTE Enroll: 6,026   (504) 446-8111

NORTHEAST LOUISIANA UNIVERSITY
700 University Ave., Monroe 71209 *Type:* Public (state) *System:* State of Louisiana Board of Trustees for State Colleges and Universities *Accred.:* 1955/1989 (SACS-CC) *Calendar:* Sem. plan *Degrees:* A, B, M, D *Prof. Accred.:* Business (B,M), Computer Science, Construction Education (B), Counseling, Dental Hygiene, Home Economics, Marriage and Family Therapy (M), Music, Nursing (B), Occupational Therapy, Occupational Therapy Assisting, Radiography, Social Work (B), Speech-Language Pathology, Teacher Education (e,s,p) *CEO:* Pres. Lawson L. Swearingen, Jr.
FTE Enroll: 11,022   (318) 342-1000

NORTHWESTERN STATE UNIVERSITY
College Ave., Natchitoches 71497 *Type:* Public (state) liberal arts and professional *System:* State of Louisiana Board of Trustees for State Colleges and Universities *Accred.:* 1941/1986 (SACS-CC) *Calendar:* Sem. plan *Degrees:* A, B, M, D *Prof. Accred.:* Music, Nursing (A,B,M), Radiography, Social Work (B), Teacher Education (e,s,p), Veterinary Technology *CEO:* Pres. Robert A. Alost
FTE Enroll: 7,417   (318) 357-6491

NOTRE DAME SEMINARY GRADUATE SCHOOL OF
THEOLOGY
2901 S. Carrollton Ave., New Orleans 70118-4391 *Type:* Private (Roman Catholic) graduate only *Accred.:* 1979/1986 (ATS); 1951/1986 (SACS-CC) *Calendar:* Sem. plan *Degrees:* M *CEO:* Rector/Pres. Gregory M. Aymond
FTE Enroll: 113   (504) 866-7426

OUR LADY OF HOLY CROSS COLLEGE
4123 Woodland Dr., New Orleans 70131-7399 *Type:* Private (Roman Catholic) liberal arts and teachers *Accred.:* 1972/1986 (SACS-CC) *Calendar:* Sem. plan *Degrees:* A, B, M *Prof. Accred.:* Nursing (B) *CEO:* Pres. Thomas E. Chambers, Ph.D.
FTE Enroll: 1,053   (504) 394-7744

PHILLIPS JUNIOR COLLEGE
5001 Westbank Expy., Marrero 70072 *Type:* Private junior *Accred.:* 1984/1986 (ACISC) *Calendar:* Courses of varying lengths *Degrees:* A, certificates, diplomas *Prof. Accred.:* Medical Assisting (AMA) *CEO:* Dir. Bob Allen
          (504) 348-1182

PHILLIPS JUNIOR COLLEGE
822 S. Clearview Pkwy., New Orleans 70123 *Type:* Private junior *Accred.:* 1974/1986 (ACISC) *Calendar:* Courses of varying lengths *Degrees:* A, certificates, diplomas *Prof. Accred.:* Medical Assisting (AMA) *CEO:* Dir. Douglas Brill
          (504) 734-0123

ST. JOSEPH SEMINARY COLLEGE
St. Benedict 70457-9990 *Type:* Private (Roman Catholic) liberal arts *Accred.:* 1956/

1993 (SACS-CC) *Calendar:* Sem. plan *Degrees:* B *CEO:* Pres./Rector Scott J. Underwood
FTE Enroll: 80   (504) 892-1800

SOUTHEASTERN LOUISIANA UNIVERSITY
P.O. Box 784, University Sta., Hammond 70402 *Type:* Public (state) liberal arts and professional *System:* State of Louisiana Board of Trustees for State Colleges and Universities *Accred.:* 1946/1984 (SACS-CC) *Calendar:* Sem. plan *Degrees:* A, B, M *Prof. Accred.:* Accounting (Type A), Music, Nursing (B), Respiratory Therapy Technology, Social Work (B), Teacher Education (e,s,p) *CEO:* Pres. G. Warren Smith
FTE Enroll: 12,176   (504) 549-2000

SOUTHERN TECHNICAL COLLEGE
303 Rue Louis XIV, Lafayette 70508 *Type:* Private business *Accred.:* 1988 (ACISC) *Calendar:* Qtr. plan *Degrees:* A *CEO:* Dir. William Hughes
                                     (318) 981-4010

SOUTHERN UNIVERSITY AND AGRICULTURAL AND MECHANICAL COLLEGE AT BATON ROUGE
Southern Branch Post Office, Baton Rouge 70813 *Type:* Public (state) *System:* Southern University and Agricultural and Mechanical College System *Accred.:* 1938/1991 (SACS-CC) *Calendar:* Sem. plan *Degrees:* A, B, M, D *Prof. Accred.:* Computer Science, Engineering (civil, electrical, mechanical), Home Economics, Law (ABA only), Music, Nursing (B), Rehabilitation Counseling, Social Work (B), Teacher Education (e,s) *CEO:* Chanc. Marvin L. Yates
FTE Enroll: 9,596   (504) 771-4500

SOUTHERN UNIVERSITY AT NEW ORLEANS
6400 Press Dr., New Orleans 70126 *Type:* Public (state) *System:* Southern University and Agricultural and Mechanical College System *Accred.:* 1958/1990 (SACS-CC) *Calendar:* Sem. plan *Degrees:* A, B, M *Prof. Accred.:* Social Work (B,M) *CEO:* Chanc. Robert B. Gex
FTE Enroll: 4,242   (504) 286-5000

SOUTHERN UNIVERSITY/SHREVEPORT BOSSIER
3050 Martin Luther King, Jr. Dr., Shreveport 71107 *Type:* Public (state) junior *System:* Southern University and Agricultural and Mechanical College System *Accred.:* 1964/1991 (SACS-CC) *Calendar:* Sem. plan *De-*

grees: A *Prof. Accred.:* Medical Laboratory Technology (AMA), Radiography, Respiratory Therapy *CEO:* Chanc. Jerome G. Greene, Jr.
FTE Enroll: 1,083   (318) 674-3300

TULANE UNIVERSITY
6823 St. Charles Ave., New Orleans 70118 *Type:* Private *Accred.:* 1903/1990 (SACS-CC) *Calendar:* Sem. plan *Degrees:* B, M, D *Prof. Accred.:* Business (B,M), Computer Science, Engineering (bioengineering, chemical, civil, electrical, mechanical), Health Services Administration, Law, Medicine, Psychology Internship, Public Health, School Psychology (provisional), Social Work (M) *CEO:* Pres. Eamon M. Kelly
FTE Enroll: 10,064   (504) 865-5000

UNIVERSITY OF NEW ORLEANS
Lakefront, New Orleans 70148 *Type:* Public (state) *System:* Louisiana State University System *Accred.:* 1958/1984 (SACS-CC) *Calendar:* Sem. plan *Degrees:* A, B, M, D *Prof. Accred.:* Accounting (Type A,C), Art, Business (B,M), Computer Science, Counseling, Engineering (civil, electrical, mechanical, naval architecture/marine), Music, Planning (M), Teacher Education (e,s,p) *CEO:* Chanc. Gregory M. St. L. O'Brien
FTE Enroll: 12,446   (504) 286-6000

UNIVERSITY OF SOUTHWESTERN LOUISIANA
E. University Ave., Lafayette 70503 *Type:* Public (state) *System:* State of Louisiana Board of Trustees for State Colleges and Universities *Accred.:* 1925/1990 (SACS-CC) *Calendar:* Sem. plan *Degrees:* A, B, M, D *Prof. Accred.:* Audiology, Computer Science, EMT-Paramedic, Engineering (chemical, civil, electrical, mechanical, petroleum), Home Economics, Interior Design, Medical Record Administration, Music, Nursing (B), Speech-Language Pathology, Teacher Education (e,s,p) *CEO:* Pres. Ray P. Authement
FTE Enroll: 14,314   (318) 231-6000

XAVIER UNIVERSITY OF LOUISIANA
7325 Palmetto St., New Orleans 70125 *Type:* Private (Roman Catholic) *Accred.:* 1937/1990 (SACS-CC) *Calendar:* Sem. plan *Degrees:* B, M, D *Prof. Accred.:* Music, Nurse Anesthesia Education *CEO:* Pres. Norman C. Francis
FTE Enroll: 3,166   (504) 486-7411

MAINE

ANDOVER COLLEGE
901 Washington Ave., Portland 04103 *Type:* Private junior *Accred.:* 1970/1986 (ACISC) *Calendar:* Qtr. plan *Degrees:* A, certificates, diplomas *CEO:* C.E.O. Lee C. Jenkins
Enroll: 787   (207) 774-6126

BANGOR THEOLOGICAL SEMINARY
300 Union St., Bangor 04401 *Type:* Private (United Church of Christ) graduate only *Accred.:* 1974/1986 (ATS); 1968/1986 (NEASC-CIHE) *Calendar:* Sem. plan *Degrees:* M, D *CEO:* Pres. Malcolm L. Warford
FTE Enroll: 112   (207) 942-6781

BATES COLLEGE
Lewiston 04240 *Type:* Private liberal arts *Accred.:* 1929/1990 (NEASC-CIHE) *Calendar:* Sem. plan *Degrees:* B *CEO:* Pres. Donald W. Harward
Enroll: 1,506   (207) 786-6255

BEAL COLLEGE
629 Main St., Bangor 04401 *Type:* Private junior *Accred.:* 1966/1989 (ACISC) *Calendar:* Courses of varying lengths *Degrees:* A *Prof. Accred.:* Medical Assisting (AMA) *CEO:* Pres. Allen T. Stehle
                    (207) 947-4591

BOWDOIN COLLEGE
Brunswick 04011 *Type:* Private liberal arts *Accred.:* 1929/1987 (NEASC-CIHE) *Calendar:* Sem. plan *Degrees:* B, M *CEO:* Pres. Robert H. Edwards
Enroll: 1,432   (207) 725-3000

CASCO BAY COLLEGE
477 Congress St., Portland 04101 *Type:* Private junior *Accred.:* 1968/1986 (ACISC) *Calendar:* Sem. plan *Degrees:* A, certificates, diplomas *CEO:* Pres. Gene F. Stearns
                    (207) 772-0196

CENTRAL MAINE MEDICAL CENTER SCHOOL OF NURSING
Lewiston 04240 *Type:* Private 2-year technical *Accred.:* 1978/1989 (NEASC-CTCI) *Calendar:* Sem. plan *Degrees:* A *Prof. Accred.:* Nursing (A) *CEO:* Pres. William W. Young
FTE Enroll: 79   (207) 795-2840

CENTRAL MAINE TECHNICAL COLLEGE
1250 Turner St., Auburn 04210 *Type:* Public (state) 2-year *Accred.:* 1976/1991 (NEASC-CTCI) *Calendar:* Sem. plan *Degrees:* A, certificates *Prof. Accred.:* Engineering Technology (civil/construction), Nursing (A) *CEO:* Pres. William J. Hierstein
FTE Enroll: 555   (207) 784-2385

COLBY COLLEGE
Waterville 04901 *Type:* Private liberal arts *Accred.:* 1929/1988 (NEASC-CIHE) *Calendar:* 4-1-4 plan *Degrees:* B *CEO:* Pres. William R. Cotter
Enroll: 1,747   (207) 872-3000

COLLEGE OF THE ATLANTIC
103 Eden St., Bar Harbor 04609 *Type:* Private liberal arts *Accred.:* 1976/1988 (NEASC-CIHE) *Calendar:* Tri. plan *Degrees:* B, M *CEO:* Pres. Steven Katona
Enroll: 226   (207) 288-5015

EASTERN MAINE TECHNICAL COLLEGE
354 Hogan Rd., Bangor 04401 *Type:* Public (state) 2-year *Accred.:* 1973/1989 (NEASC-CTCI) *Calendar:* Sem. plan *Degrees:* A *Prof. Accred.:* Medical Laboratory Technology (AMA), Nursing (A), Radiography *CEO:* Pres. Darrel W. Staat
FTE Enroll: 957   (207) 941-4691

HUSSON COLLEGE
Bangor 04401 *Type:* Private 4-year business and professional *Accred.:* 1974/1993 (NEASC-CIHE) *Calendar:* Sem. plan *Degrees:* A, B, M, certificates, diplomas *Prof. Accred.:* Nursing (B) *CEO:* Pres. William H. Beardsley
Enroll: 1,359   (207) 947-1121

KENNEBEC VALLEY TECHNICAL COLLEGE
Fairfield 04937 *Type:* Public (state) 2-year *Accred.:* 1979/1989 (NEASC-CTCI) *Calendar:* Sem. plan *Degrees:* A *Prof. Accred.:* Nursing (A), Physical Therapy Assisting, Respiratory Therapy Technology *CEO:* Pres. Barbara W. Woodlee
FTE Enroll: 990   (207) 453-9762

MAINE COLLEGE OF ART
Portland 04101 *Type:* Private 4-year professional *Accred.:* 1978/1985 (NEASC-CIHE) *Calendar:* Sem. plan *Degrees:* B *Prof. Accred.:* Art *CEO:* Pres. Roger Gilmore
Enroll: 273   (207) 775-3052

MAINE MARITIME ACADEMY
Castine 04420 *Type:* Public (state) professional *Accred.:* 1971/1986 (NEASC-CIHE) *Calendar:* Sem. plan *Degrees:* B, M *Prof. Accred.:* Engineering Technology (naval architecture/marine) *CEO:* Pres. Kenneth M. Curtis
Enroll: 685   (207) 326-4311

MID-STATE COLLEGE
88 Hardscrabble Rd., Auburn 04210 *Type:* Private business *Accred.:* 1970/1987 (ACISC) *Calendar:* Sem. plan *Degrees:* A, certificates, diplomas *CEO:* Dir. Mary E. Wells
            (207) 783-1478

BRANCH CAMPUS
218 Water St., Augusta 04330 *Accred.:* 1977/1987 (ACISC) *CEO:* Dir. Valmond Landry
            (207) 623-3962

NORTHERN MAINE TECHNICAL COLLEGE
33 Edgemont Dr., Presque Isle 04769 *Type:* Public (state) 2-year *Accred.:* 1975/1989 (NEASC-CTCI) *Calendar:* Sem. plan *Degrees:* A *Prof. Accred.:* Nursing (A) *CEO:* Pres. Durward R. Huffman
FTE Enroll: 807   (207) 769-2461

ST. JOSEPH'S COLLEGE
Windham 04062-1198 *Type:* Private (Roman Catholic) liberal arts *Accred.:* 1961/1991 (NEASC-CIHE) *Calendar:* Sem. plan *Degrees:* B, M *Prof. Accred.:* Nursing (B) *CEO:* Pres. Loring E. Hart
Enroll: 2,234   (207) 892-6766

SOUTHERN MAINE TECHNICAL COLLEGE
Fort Rd., South Portland 04106 *Type:* Public (state) 2-year *Accred.:* 1974/1990 (NEASC-CTCI) *Calendar:* Sem. plan *Degrees:* A *Prof. Accred.:* Nursing (A), Radiation Therapy Technology, Radiography, Respiratory Therapy *CEO:* Pres. Wayne H. Ross
FTE Enroll: 1,907   (207) 767-9500

THOMAS COLLEGE
Waterville 04901 *Type:* Private liberal arts and business *Accred.:* 1969/1986 (NEASC-CIHE) *Calendar:* Sem. plan *Degrees:* A, B, M *CEO:* Pres. George R. Spann
Enroll: 616   (207) 873-0771

UNITY COLLEGE
Unity 04988-9502 *Type:* Private liberal arts *Accred.:* 1974/1992 (NEASC-CIHE) *Calendar:* Modular plan *Degrees:* A, B *CEO:* Pres. Wilson G. Hess
Enroll: 449   (207) 948-3131

UNIVERSITY OF MAINE
Orono 04469-0102 *Type:* Public (state) *System:* University of Maine System *Accred.:* 1929/1988 (NEASC-CIHE) *Calendar:* Sem. plan *Degrees:* A, B, M, D *Prof. Accred.:* Art, Business (B,M), Clinical Psychology, Dental Assisting, Dental Hygiene, Engineering Technology (civil/construction, electrical, mechanical), Engineering (agricultural, chemical, civil, electrical, engineering physics/science, forest, mechanical, surveying), Forestry, Law, Music, Nursing (B), Psychology Internship, Public Administration, Social Work (B,M), Speech-Language Pathology, Teacher Education (e,s,p), Veterinary Technology *CEO:* Pres. Frederick E. Hutchinson
Enroll: 10,269   (207) 581-1512

UNIVERSITY OF MAINE AT AUGUSTA
Augusta 04330 *Type:* Public (state) *System:* University of Maine System *Accred.:* 1973/1985 (NEASC-CIHE) *Calendar:* Sem. plan *Degrees:* A, B *Prof. Accred.:* Medical Laboratory Technology (AMA), Nursing (A) *CEO:* Pres. George P. Connick
Enroll: 2,186   (207) 621-3403

UNIVERSITY OF MAINE AT FARMINGTON
86 Main St., Farmington 04938 *Type:* Public (state) liberal arts and teachers *System:* University of Maine System *Accred.:* 1958/1992 (NEASC-CIHE) *Calendar:* Sem. plan *Degrees:* A, B *Prof. Accred.:* Teacher Education (e,s) *CEO:* Acting Pres. Sue A. Huseman
Enroll: 1,999   (207) 778-7000

UNIVERSITY OF MAINE AT FORT KENT
Pleasant St., Fort Kent 04743 *Type:* Public (state) liberal arts and teachers *System:* Uni-

versity of Maine System *Accred.:* 1970/1986 (NEASC-CIHE) *Calendar:* Sem. plan *Degrees:* A, B *Prof. Accred.:* Nursing (B) *CEO:* Pres. Richard G. Dumont
Enroll: 511   (207) 834-3162

UNIVERSITY OF MAINE AT MACHIAS
Machias 04654 *Type:* Public (state) liberal arts and teachers *System:* University of Maine System *Accred.:* 1970/1984 (NEASC-CIHE) *Calendar:* Sem. plan *Degrees:* A, B *Prof. Accred.:* Recreation and Leisure Services *CEO:* Pres. Paul E. Nordstrom
Enroll: 720   (207) 255-3313

UNIVERSITY OF MAINE AT PRESQUE ISLE
181 Main St., Presque Isle 04769 *Type:* Public (state) liberal arts and teachers *System:* University of Maine System *Accred.:* 1968/1984 (NEASC-CIHE) *Calendar:* Sem. plan *Degrees:* A, B *Prof. Accred.:* Medical Laboratory Technology (AMA), Recreation and Leisure Services *CEO:* Pres. W. Michael Easton
Enroll: 1,141   (207) 764-0311

UNIVERSITY OF NEW ENGLAND
11 Hills Beach Rd., Biddeford 04005 *Type:* Private liberal arts and professional *Accred.:* 1966/1986 (NEASC-CIHE) *Calendar:* 4-1-4 plan *Degrees:* A, B, M, D *Prof. Accred.:* Nurse Anesthesia Education, Nursing (A),

Occupational Therapy, Osteopathy, Physical Therapy, Social Work (M) *CEO:* Pres. Thomas Hadley Reynolds
Enroll: 1,232   (207) 283-0171

UNIVERSITY OF SOUTHERN MAINE
96 Falmouth St., Portland 04103 *Type:* Public (state) liberal arts and professional *System:* University of Maine System *Accred.:* 1960/1991 (NEASC-CIHE) *Calendar:* Sem. plan *Degrees:* A, B, M, D *Prof. Accred.:* Art, Counseling, Engineering (electrical), Music, Nursing (B,M), Rehabilitation Counseling, Social Work (B), Teacher Education (e,s) *CEO:* Pres. Richard L. Pattenaude
Enroll: 6,425   (207) 780-4141

WASHINGTON COUNTY TECHNICAL COLLEGE
Calais 04619 *Type:* Public (state) 2-year *Accred.:* 1976/1989 (NEASC-CTCI) *Calendar:* Sem. plan *Degrees:* A *CEO:* Pres. Ronald P. Renaud
FTE Enroll: 349   (207) 454-2144

WESTBROOK COLLEGE
Stevens Ave., Portland 04103 *Type:* Private liberal arts *Accred.:* 1934/1984 (NEASC-CIHE) *Calendar:* 4-1-4 plan *Degrees:* A, B *Prof. Accred.:* Dental Hygiene, Nursing (B) *CEO:* Pres. William D. Andrews
Enroll: 311   (207) 797-7261

MARYLAND

ALLEGANY COMMUNITY COLLEGE
Willowbrook Rd., Cumberland 21502 *Type:*
Public (local/state) two-year *System:* Maryland Higher Education Commission *Accred.:*
1965/1990 (MSA) *Calendar:* Sem. plan *Degrees:* A, certificates *Prof. Accred.:* Dental
Assisting, Dental Hygiene, Medical Laboratory Technology (AMA), Radiography, Respiratory Therapy *CEO:* Pres. Donald L.
Alexander
Enroll: 2,882   (301) 724-7700

ANNE ARUNDEL COMMUNITY COLLEGE
101 College Pkwy., Arnold 21012 *Type:*
Public (local/state) two-year *System:* Maryland Higher Education Commission *Accred.:*
1968/1989 (MSA) *Calendar:* Sem. plan *Degrees:* A, certificates *Prof. Accred.:* Nursing
(A) *CEO:* Pres. Thomas E. Florestano
Enroll: 12,401   (410) 647-7100

BALTIMORE CITY COMMUNITY COLLEGE
2901 Liberty Heights Ave., Baltimore 21215
Type: Public (state) two-year *System:* Maryland Higher Education Commission *Accred.:*
1963/1980 (MSA) *Calendar:* Sem. plan *Degrees:* A, certificates *Prof. Accred.:* Dental
Hygiene, Medical Record Technology, Nursing (A), Physical Therapy Assisting, Respiratory Therapy *CEO:* Pres. James D.
Tschechtelin
Enroll: 5,224   (410) 333-5555

HARBOR CAMPUS
600 E. Lombard St., Baltimore 21202
CEO: Exec. Dir. Mary Lynn Devlin
                                   (410) 333-8348

BALTIMORE HEBREW UNIVERSITY
5800 Park Heights Ave., Baltimore 21209
Type: Private *Accred.:* 1974/1991 (MSA)
Calendar: Sem. plan *Degrees:* B, M, D
CEO: Pres. Norma Fields Furst
Enroll: 294   (410) 578-6900

BALTIMORE INTERNATIONAL CULINARY COLLEGE
19-21 S. Gay St., Baltimore 21202-1503
Type: Private 2-year *Accred.:* 1991 (ACC-
SCT); 1989 (MSA candidate) *Calendar:*
Sem. plan *Degrees:* A, certificates *CEO:*
Pres. Roger Chylinski
Enroll: 378   (410) 752-1446

BOWIE STATE UNIVERSITY
14000 Jericho Park Rd., Bowie 20715 *Type:*
Public (state) *System:* University of Mary-
land System *Accred.:* 1961/1992 (MSA)
Calendar: Sem. plan *Degrees:* B, M *Prof.
Accred.:* Nursing (B), Social Work (B),
Teacher Education (e,s,p) *CEO:* Pres.
Nathaniel Pollard, Jr.
Enroll: 3,672   (301) 464-3000

CAPITOL COLLEGE
11301 Springfield Rd., Laurel 20708 *Type:*
Private technological *Accred.:* 1976/1991
(MSA) *Calendar:* Sem. plan *Degrees:* A, B,
M, certificates *Prof. Accred.:* Engineering
Technology (computer, electrical) *CEO:*
Pres. G. William Troxler
Enroll: 768   (301) 953-0060

CATONSVILLE COMMUNITY COLLEGE
800 S. Rolling Rd., Catonsville 21228 *Type:*
Public (local) two-year *System:* Maryland
Higher Education Commission *Accred.:*
1966/1991 (MSA) *Calendar:* Sem. plan *Degrees:* A, certificates *Prof. Accred.:* Mortuary Science, Occupational Therapy Assisting
CEO: Pres. Frederick J. Walsh
Enroll: 13,295   (410) 455-6050

CECIL COMMUNITY COLLEGE
1000 North East Rd., North East 21901-1999
Type: Public (local) two-year *System:* Maryland Higher Education Commission *Accred.:*
1974/1990 (MSA) *Calendar:* Sem. plan *Degrees:* A, certificates *Prof. Accred.:* Nursing
(A) *CEO:* Pres. Robert L. Gell
Enroll: 1,542   (410) 287-6060

CHARLES COUNTY COMMUNITY COLLEGE
Mitchell Rd., P.O. Box 910, La Plata 20646
Type: Public (state) two-year *System:* Mary-
land Higher Education Commission *Accred.:*
1969/1989 (MSA) *Calendar:* Sem. plan *De-
grees:* A, certificates *Prof. Accred.:* Nursing
(A), Practical Nursing *CEO:* Pres. John M.
Sine
Enroll: 5,817   (301) 934-2251

CHESAPEAKE COLLEGE
P.O. Box 8, Wye Mills 21679-0008 *Type:*
Public (local/state) two-year *System:* Mary-
land Higher Education Commission *Accred.:*

1970/1990 (MSA) *Calendar:* Sem. plan *Degrees:* A, certificates *Prof. Accred.:* Radiography *CEO:* Pres. John R. Kotula
Enroll: 2,042   (410) 822-5400

COLLEGE OF NOTRE DAME OF MARYLAND
4701 N. Charles St., Baltimore 21210 *Type:* Private (Roman Catholic) liberal arts primarily for women *Accred.:* 1925/1992 (MSA) *Calendar:* Sem. plan *Degrees:* B, M *Prof. Accred.:* Nursing (B) *CEO:* Pres. Rosemarie T. Nassif
Enroll: 2,647   (410) 435-0100

COLUMBIA UNION COLLEGE
7600 Flower Ave., Takoma Park 20912 *Type:* Private (Seventh-Day Adventist) liberal arts *Accred.:* 1942/1992 (MSA) *Calendar:* Sem. plan *Degrees:* A, B *Prof. Accred.:* Medical Laboratory Technology (AMA), Medical Technology, Nursing (B) *CEO:* Pres. Charles Scriven
Enroll: 1,211   (301) 270-9200

COPPIN STATE COLLEGE
2500 W. North Ave., Baltimore 21216-3698 *Type:* Public (state) *System:* University of Maryland System *Accred.:* 1962/1988 (MSA) *Calendar:* Sem. plan *Degrees:* B, M *Prof. Accred.:* Nursing (B), Rehabilitation Counseling, Social Work (B-conditional), Teacher Education (e,s) *CEO:* Pres. Calvin W. Burnett
Enroll: 2,816   (410) 383-5585

DUNDALK COMMUNITY COLLEGE
7200 Sollers Point Rd., Dundalk 21222-4692 *Type:* Public (local) two-year *System:* Maryland Higher Education Commission *Accred.:* 1975/1989 (MSA) *Calendar:* Sem. plan *Degrees:* A, certificates *CEO:* Pres. Martha A. Smith
Enroll: 3,574   (410) 282-6700

ESSEX COMMUNITY COLLEGE
7201 Rossville Blvd., Baltimore 21237 *Type:* Public (local) two-year *System:* Maryland Higher Education Commission *Accred.:* 1966/1992 (MSA) *Calendar:* Sem. plan *Degrees:* A, certificates *Prof. Accred.:* Medical Laboratory Technology (AMA), Medical Record Technology, Music, Nuclear Medicine Technology, Nursing (A), Physician Assisting, Radiation Therapy Technology,

Radiography, Respiratory Therapy Technology, Theatre, Veterinary Technology *CEO:* Pres. Donald J. Slowinski
Enroll: 11,475   (410) 682-6000

FREDERICK COMMUNITY COLLEGE
7932 Oppossumtown Pike, Frederick 21702 *Type:* Public (local) two-year *System:* Maryland Higher Education Commission *Accred.:* 1971/1991 (MSA) *Calendar:* Sem. plan *Degrees:* A, certificates *CEO:* Pres. Lee John Betts
Enroll: 4,235   (301) 846-2400

FROSTBURG STATE UNIVERSITY
Frostburg 21532-1099 *Type:* Public (state) *System:* University of Maryland System *Accred.:* 1953/1991 (MSA) *Calendar:* Sem. plan *Degrees:* B, M, certificates *Prof. Accred.:* Social Work (B-candidate) *CEO:* Pres. Catherine R. Gira
Enroll: 5,229   (301) 689-4000

GARRETT COMMUNITY COLLEGE
P.O. Box 151, Mosser Rd., McHenry 21541 *Type:* Public (local) two-year *System:* Maryland Higher Education Commission *Accred.:* 1975/1988 (MSA) *Calendar:* Sem. plan *Degrees:* A, certificates *CEO:* Pres. Stephen J. Herman
Enroll: 662   (301) 387-6666

GOUCHER COLLEGE
1021 Dulaney Valley Rd., Baltimore 21204 *Type:* Private liberal arts primarily for women *Accred.:* 1921/1989 (MSA) *Calendar:* Sem. plan *Degrees:* B, M *CEO:* Pres. Rhoda M. Dorsey
Enroll: 241   (410) 337-6000

HAGERSTOWN BUSINESS COLLEGE
18618 Crestwood Dr., Hagerstown 21740 *Type:* Private junior *Accred.:* 1968/1990 (ACISC) *Calendar:* Qtr. plan *Degrees:* A *Prof. Accred.:* Medical Record Technology *CEO:* Dir. Cheryl M. Hyslop
                                             (301) 739-2670

HAGERSTOWN JUNIOR COLLEGE
11400 Robinwood Dr., Hagerstown 21742-6590 *Type:* Public (local/state) two-year *System:* Maryland Higher Education Commission *Accred.:* 1968/1989 (MSA) *Calendar:* Sem. plan *Degrees:* A, certificates *Prof. Ac-*

cred.: Radiography *CEO:* Pres. Norman P. Shea
Enroll: 3,361   (301) 790-2800

HARFORD COMMUNITY COLLEGE
401 Thomas Run Rd., Bel Air 21015 *Type:* Public (local/state) two-year *System:* Maryland Higher Education Commission *Accred.:* 1967/1992 (MSA) *Calendar:* Sem. plan *Degrees:* A, certificates *Prof. Accred.:* Histologic Technology, Nursing (A) *CEO:* Pres. Richard J. Pappas
Enroll: 5,348   (410) 836-4000

HOME STUDY INTERNATIONAL
12501 Old Columbia Pike, P.O. Box 4437, Silver Spring 20914-4437 *Type:* Private home study *Accred.:* 1967/1993 (NHSC) *Calendar:* Courses of varying lengths *Degrees:* A, B, certificates *CEO:* Pres. Joseph E. Gurubatham
                                   (301) 680-6570

GRIGGS UNIVERSITY
12501 Old Columbia Pike, P.O. Box 4437, Silver Spring 20914-4437 *CEO:* Pres. Joseph E. Gurubatham
                                   (301) 680-6570

HOOD COLLEGE
401 Rosemont Ave., Frederick 21701-8575 *Type:* Private liberal arts primarily for women *Accred.:* 1922/1992 (MSA) *Calendar:* Sem. plan *Degrees:* B, M *Prof. Accred.:* Home Economics, Social Work (B) *CEO:* Pres. Martha E. Church
Enroll: 1,985   (301) 663-3131

HOWARD COMMUNITY COLLEGE
10901 Little Patuxent Pkwy., Columbia 21044 *Type:* Public (local/state) two-year *System:* Maryland Higher Education Commission *Accred.:* 1975/1990 (MSA) *Calendar:* Sem. plan *Degrees:* A, certificates *Prof. Accred.:* Nursing (A) *CEO:* Pres. Dwight A. Burrill
Enroll: 4,883   (410) 992-4800

JOHNS HOPKINS UNIVERSITY
34th and N. Charles Sts., Baltimore 21218 *Type:* Private *Accred.:* 1921/1989 (MSA) *Calendar:* Sem. plan *Degrees:* A, B, P, M, D *Prof. Accred.:* Engineering Technology (industrial hygiene), Engineering (bioengineering, chemical, civil, electrical, engineering mechanics, materials, mechanical), General Practice Residency, Health Services Administration, Medical Illustration, Medicine, Nursing (B,M), Public Health *CEO:* Pres. William C. Richardson
Enroll: 14,210   (410) 516-8068

COLUMBIA CENTER
6740 Alexander Bell Dr., Columbia 21046 *CEO:* Dir. Elizabeth Mayotte
                                   (410) 290-1777

PEABODY INSTITUTE OF THE JOHNS HOPKINS UNIVERSITY
One E. Mount Vernon Pl., Baltimore 21202-2397 *Prof. Accred.:* Music *CEO:* Dir. Robert O. Pierce
                                   (410) 659-8150

SCHOOL OF ADVANCED INTERNATIONAL STUDIES
1740 Massachusetts Ave., N.W., Washington, DC 20036 *CEO:* Dir. George R. Packard
                                   (202) 663-5600

LOYOLA COLLEGE IN MARYLAND
4501 N. Charles St., Baltimore 21210 *Type:* Private (Roman Catholic) *Accred.:* 1931/1990 (MSA) *Calendar:* Sem. plan *Degrees:* B, M, D, certificates *Prof. Accred.:* Accounting (Type A), Business (B,M), Computer Science, Counseling, Engineering (engineering physics/science), Speech-Language Pathology *CEO:* Acting Pres. Thomas E. Scheye
Enroll: 6,249   (410) 617-2000

THE MARYLAND COLLEGE OF ART AND DESIGN
10500 Georgia Ave., Silver Spring 20902 *Type:* Private professional *Calendar:* Qtr. plan *Degrees:* A *Prof. Accred.:* Art *CEO:* Pres. Edward Glynn
Enroll: 85   (301) 649-4454

THE MARYLAND INSTITUTE COLLEGE OF ART
1300 W. Mt. Royal Ave., Baltimore 21217 *Type:* Private professional *Accred.:* 1967/1988 (MSA) *Calendar:* Sem. plan *Degrees:* B, M, certificates *Prof. Accred.:* Art *CEO:* Pres. Fred Lazarus, IV
Enroll: 1,395   (410) 669-9200

MONTGOMERY COLLEGE—GERMANTOWN CAMPUS
20200 Observation Dr., Germantown 20874 *Type:* Public (local) two-year *System:* Montgomery College Central Administration *Accred.:* 1980/1992 (MSA) *Calendar:* Sem. plan *Degrees:* A, certificates *CEO:* Provost Noreen A. Lyne
Enroll: 3,989   (301) 353-7700

MONTGOMERY COLLEGE—ROCKVILLE CAMPUS
51 Mannakee St., Rockville 20850 *Type:* Public (local) two-year *System:* Montgomery College Central Administration *Accred.:* 1968/1992 (MSA) *Calendar:* Sem. plan *Degrees:* A, certificates *Prof. Accred.:* Engineering Technology (electrical), Medical Laboratory Technology (AMA), Medical Record Technology, Music, Radiography *CEO:* Provost Antoinette P. Hastings
Enroll: 14,998   (301) 279-5000

MONTGOMERY COLLEGE—TAKOMA PARK CAMPUS
Takoma Ave. and Fenton St., Takoma Park 20912 *Type:* Public (local) two-year *System:* Montgomery College Central Administration *Accred.:* 1950/1992 (MSA) *Calendar:* Sem. plan *Degrees:* A, certificates *Prof. Accred.:* Nursing (A) *CEO:* Provost O. Robert Brown
Enroll: 4,944   (301) 650-1300

MORGAN STATE UNIVERSITY
Hillen Rd. and Cold Spring La., Baltimore 21239 *Type:* Public (state) liberal arts *System:* Maryland Higher Education Commission *Accred.:* 1925/1988 (MSA) *Calendar:* Sem. plan *Degrees:* B, M, D *Prof. Accred.:* Engineering (civil, electrical, industrial), Landscape Architecture (M-initial), Medical Technology, Music, Planning (M), Social Work (B-conditional), Teacher Education (e,s,p) *CEO:* Pres. Earl S. Richardson
Enroll: 5,034   (410) 319-3333

MOUNT ST. MARY'S COLLEGE AND SEMINARY
Emmitsburg 21727 *Type:* Private (Roman Catholic) *Accred.:* 1987 (ATS); 1922/1990 (MSA) *Calendar:* Sem. plan *Degrees:* B, M *CEO:* Pres. James Loughran, S.J.
Enroll: 1,758   (301) 447-6122

NER ISRAEL RABBINICAL COLLEGE
400 Mount Wilson La., Baltimore 21208 *Type:* Private professional *Accred.:* 1974/1992 (AARTS) *Calendar:* Sem. plan *Degrees:* B, M, D *CEO:* Pres. Herman N. Neuberger
Enroll: 429   (410) 484-7200

PRINCE GEORGE'S COMMUNITY COLLEGE
301 Largo Rd., Largo 20772-2199 *Type:* Public (local) two-year *System:* Maryland Higher Education Commission *Accred.:* 1969/1990 (MSA) *Calendar:* Sem. plan *Degrees:* A *Prof. Accred.:* Engineering Technology (electrical), Medical Record Technology, Nuclear Medicine Technology, Nursing (A), Radiography, Respiratory Therapy *CEO:* Pres. Robert I. Bickford
Enroll: 13,307   (301) 336-6000

BRANCH CAMPUS
Andrews Air Force Base Degree Ctr., Patrick Ave., Bldg. 3611, Andrews Air Force Base 20331 *CEO:* Supervisor Kathy Sexton
          (301) 322-0778

ST. JOHN'S COLLEGE
60 College Ave., P.O. Box 2800, Annapolis 21404 *Type:* Private liberal arts *Accred.:* 1923/1989 (MSA) *Calendar:* Sem. plan *Degrees:* B, M *CEO:* Pres. Christopher B. Nelson
Enroll: 481   (410) 263-2371

ST. MARY'S COLLEGE OF MARYLAND
St. Mary's City 20686 *Type:* Public (state) liberal arts *System:* Maryland Higher Education Commission *Accred.:* 1959/1990 (MSA) *Calendar:* Sem. plan *Degrees:* B *Prof. Accred.:* Music *CEO:* Pres. Edward T. Lewis
Enroll: 1,569   (301) 862-0200

ST. MARY'S SEMINARY AND UNIVERSITY
5400 Roland Ave., Baltimore 21210 *Type:* Private (Roman Catholic) *Accred.:* 1971/1991 (ATS); 1951/1991 (MSA) *Calendar:* Sem. plan *Degrees:* B, P, M *CEO:* Pres./Rector Robert F. Leavitt
Enroll: 135   (410) 323-3200

SALISBURY STATE UNIVERSITY
Salisbury 21801 *Type:* Public (state) *System:* University of Maryland System *Accred.:* 1956/1991 (MSA) *Calendar:* Sem. plan *De-*

grees: B, M *Prof. Accred.:* Medical Technology, Nursing (B,M), Respiratory Therapy, Social Work (B) *CEO:* Pres. Thomas E. Bellavance
Enroll: 5,884   (410) 543-6000

SOJOURNER-DOUGLASS COLLEGE
500 N. Caroline St., Baltimore 21205 *Type:* Private *Accred.:* 1980/1990 (MSA) *Calendar:* Tri. plan *Degrees:* B *CEO:* Pres. Charles W. Simmons
Enroll: 252   (410) 276-0306

TOWSON STATE UNIVERSITY
Towson 21204-7097 *Type:* Public (state) *System:* University of Maryland System *Accred.:* 1949/1989 (MSA) *Calendar:* Sem. plan *Degrees:* B, M, certificates *Prof. Accred.:* Audiology, Business (B), Dance, Music, Nursing (B), Occupational Therapy, Psychology Internship, Speech-Language Pathology *CEO:* Pres. Hoke L. Smith
Enroll: 15,403   (410) 830-2000

TRADITIONAL ACUPUNCTURE INSTITUTE
American City Bldg., Ste. 100, 10227 Wincopin Cir., Columbia 21044-3422 *Type:* Private professional *Calendar:* Sem. plan *Degrees:* M *Prof. Accred.:* Acupuncture *CEO:* Pres. Robert M. Duggan
FTE Enroll: 48   (410) 596-6006

UNIFORMED SERVICES UNIVERSITY OF THE HEALTH SCIENCES
4301 Jones Bridge Rd., Bethesda 20814 *Type:* Public (federal) graduate only *Accred.:* 1984 (MSA) *Calendar:* Courses of varying lengths *Degrees:* P, M, D *Prof. Accred.:* Community Health/Preventive Medicine, Medicine *CEO:* Pres. James A. Zimble
Enroll: 790   (301) 295-3030

UNITED STATES NAVAL ACADEMY
121 Blake Rd., Annapolis 21402-5000 *Type:* Public (federal) military *Accred.:* 1947/1991 (MSA) *Calendar:* Sem. plan *Degrees:* B *Prof. Accred.:* Computer Science, Engineering (aerospace, electrical, mechanical, naval architecture/marine, ocean, systems) *CEO:* Supt. Thomas C. Lynch, U.S.N.
Enroll: 4,260   (410) 267-6100

UNIVERSITY OF BALTIMORE
1420 N. Charles St., Baltimore 21201 *Type:* Public (state) *System:* University of Maryland System *Accred.:* 1971/1992 (MSA) *Calendar:* Sem. plan *Degrees:* B, P, M, certificates *Prof. Accred.:* Business (B,M), Law, Public Administration *CEO:* Pres. H. Mebane Turner
Enroll: 5,983   (410) 625-3000

UNIVERSITY OF MARYLAND AT BALTIMORE
520 W. Lombard St., Baltimore 21201 *Type:* Public (state) *System:* University of Maryland System *Accred.:* 1921/1991 (MSA) *Calendar:* 4-1-4 plan *Degrees:* B, P, M, D, certificates *Prof. Accred.:* Combined Prosthodontics, Dental Hygiene, Dentistry, Endodontics, Engineering (chemical, mechanical), General Dentistry, General Practice Residency, Law, Medical Technology, Medicine, Nursing (B,M), Oral Pathology, Oral and Maxillofacial Surgery, Orthodontics, Pediatric Dentistry, Periodontics, Physical Therapy, Social Work (M-conditional) *CEO:* Interim Pres. John W. Ryan
Enroll: 4,982   (410) 706-3100

UNIVERSITY OF MARYLAND BALTIMORE COUNTY
5401 Wilkens Ave., Baltimore 21228 *Type:* Public (state) *System:* University of Maryland System *Accred.:* 1966/1991 (MSA) *Calendar:* 4-1-4 plan *Degrees:* B, M, D *Prof. Accred.:* Clinical Psychology, Diagnostic Medical Sonography, Policy Science, Psychology Internship (provisional), Social Work (B-conditional) *CEO:* Pres. Freeman A. Hrabowski, III
Enroll: 10,368   (410) 455-1000

UNIVERSITY OF MARYLAND COLLEGE PARK
College Park 20742 *Type:* Public (state) *System:* University of Maryland System *Accred.:* 1921/1992 (MSA) *Calendar:* Sem. plan *Degrees:* B, M, D, certificates *Prof. Accred.:* Audiology, Business (B,M), Clinical Psychology, Counseling, Counseling Psychology, Engineering (aerospace, agricultural, chemical, civil, electrical, fire protection, general, mechanical, nuclear), Journalism (B,M), Librarianship, Marriage and Family Therapy (M), Music, Planning (M), Psychology Internship, Rehabilitation Counseling, School Psychology, Speech-Language Pathology, Teacher Education (e,s,p), Veterinary Medicine *CEO:* Pres. William E. Kirwan
Enroll: 34,623   (301) 405-1000

UNIVERSITY OF MARYLAND EASTERN SHORE
Princess Anne 21853 *Type:* Public (state) *System:* University of Maryland System *Accred.:* 1937/1991 (MSA) *Calendar:* Sem. plan *Degrees:* B, M, D *Prof. Accred.:* Construction Education (B), Physical Therapy *CEO:* Pres. William P. Hytche
Enroll: 2,397   (410) 651-6101

UNIVERSITY OF MARYLAND UNIVERSITY
COLLEGE
University Blvd. at Adelphi Rd., College Park 20742-1600 *Type:* Public (state) *System:* University of Maryland System *Accred.:* 1946/1991 (MSA) *Calendar:* Sem. plan *Degrees:* A, B, M, certificates *CEO:* Pres. T. Benjamin Massey
Enroll: 40,029   (301) 985-7000

VILLA JULIE COLLEGE
1525 Green Spring Valley Rd., Stevenson 21153 *Type:* Private liberal arts *Accred.:* 1962/1988 (MSA) *Calendar:* Sem. plan *Degrees:* A, B *Prof. Accred.:* Medical Laboratory Technology (AMA) *CEO:* Pres. Carolyn Manuszak
Enroll: 1,681   (410) 486-7000

WASHINGTON BIBLE COLLEGE
6511 Princess Garden Pkwy., Lanham 20706 *Type:* Independent (nondenominational) *Accred.:* 1962/1991 (AABC) *Calendar:* Sem. plan *Degrees:* A, B, certificates, diplomas *CEO:* Pres. John A. Sproule
FTE Enroll: 200   (301) 552-1400

WASHINGTON COLLEGE
300 Washington Ave., Chestertown 21620 *Type:* Private liberal arts *Accred.:* 1925/1988 (MSA) *Calendar:* Sem. plan *Degrees:* B, M, certificates *CEO:* Pres. Charles H. Trout
Enroll: 981   (410) 778-2800

WASHINGTON THEOLOGICAL UNION
9001 New Hampshire Ave., Silver Spring 20903-3699 *Type:* Private (Roman Catholic) graduate only *Accred.:* 1973/1987 (ATS); 1973/1988 (MSA) *Calendar:* Sem. plan *Degrees:* P, M, certificates *CEO:* Pres. Vincent D. Cushing, O.F.M.
Enroll: 218   (301) 439-0551

WESTERN MARYLAND COLLEGE
2 College Hill, Westminster 21157 *Type:* Private liberal arts *Accred.:* 1922/1988 (MSA) *Calendar:* Sem. plan *Degrees:* B, M *Prof. Accred.:* Social Work (B) *CEO:* Pres. Robert Hunter Chambers, III
Enroll: 2,236   (410) 848-7000

WOR-WIC COMMUNITY COLLEGE
1409 Wesley Dr., Salisbury 21801 *Type:* Public (local) two-year *System:* Maryland Higher Education Commission *Accred.:* 1980/1990 (MSA) *Calendar:* Sem. plan *Degrees:* A, certificates *Prof. Accred.:* Radiography *CEO:* Pres. Arnold H. Maner
Enroll: 1,692   (410) 749-8181

MASSACHUSETTS

AMERICAN INTERNATIONAL COLLEGE
1000 State St., Springfield 01109-3189 *Type:* Private liberal arts and professional *Accred.:* 1933/1989 (NEASC-CIHE) *Calendar:* Sem. plan *Degrees:* B, M, D *Prof. Accred.:* Nursing (B) *CEO:* Pres. Harry J. Courniotes
Enroll: 1,418   (413) 737-7000

AMHERST COLLEGE
Amherst 01002 *Type:* Private liberal arts *Accred.:* 1929/1988 (NEASC-CIHE) *Calendar:* Sem. plan *Degrees:* B *CEO:* Pres. Peter R. Pouncey
Enroll: 1,579   (413) 542-2000

ANDOVER NEWTON THEOLOGICAL SCHOOL
210 Herrick Rd., Newton Centre 02159 *Type:* Private (United Church of Christ/Baptist) graduate only *Accred.:* 1938/1988 (ATS); 1978/1988 (NEASC-CIHE) *Calendar:* Sem. plan *Degrees:* M, D *CEO:* Pres. David T. Shannon
Enroll: 250   (617) 964-1100

ANNA MARIA COLLEGE
Paxton 01612-1198 *Type:* Private (Roman Catholic) liberal arts *Accred.:* 1955/1988 (NEASC-CIHE) *Calendar:* Sem. plan *Degrees:* A, B, M *Prof. Accred.:* Medical Laboratory Technology (AMA), Music, Nursing (B), Social Work (B) *CEO:* Pres. Rita Larivee, S.S.A.
Enroll: 906   (508) 757-4586

AQUINAS COLLEGE AT MILTON
303 Adams St., Milton 02186 *Type:* Private *Accred.:* 1975/1991 (NEASC-CTCI) *Calendar:* Modular plan *Degrees:* A *Prof. Accred.:* Medical Assisting (AMA) *CEO:* Pres. Dorothy M. Oppenheim
FTE Enroll: 243   (617) 696-3100

AQUINAS COLLEGE AT NEWTON
15 Walnut Park, Newton 02158 *Type:* Private *Accred.:* 1975/1991 (NEASC-CTCI) *Calendar:* Sem. plan *Degrees:* A *CEO:* Pres. Marian Batho, C.S.J.
FTE Enroll: 235   (617) 969-4400

ART INSTITUTE OF BOSTON
700 Beacon St., Boston 02215 *Type:* Private professional *Calendar:* Sem. plan *Degrees:* B, diplomas *Prof. Accred.:* Art *CEO:* Pres. Stan Trecker
Enroll: 350   (617) 262-1223

ARTHUR D. LITTLE MANAGEMENT EDUCATION INSTITUTE, INC.
Cambridge 02140-2390 *Type:* Private specialized graduate *Accred.:* 1976/1986 (NEASC-CIHE) *Calendar:* 10-month program *Degrees:* M *CEO:* Pres. Harland A. Riker, Jr.
Enroll: 62   (617) 864-5770

ASSUMPTION COLLEGE
500 Salisbury St., Worcester 01615-0005 *Type:* Private (Roman Catholic) liberal arts *Accred.:* 1949/1991 (NEASC-CIHE) *Calendar:* Sem. plan *Degrees:* A, B, M *Prof. Accred.:* Nursing (B), Rehabilitation Counseling *CEO:* Pres. Joseph H. Hagan
Enroll: 2,154   (508) 752-5615

ATLANTIC UNION COLLEGE
P.O. Box 1000, South Lancaster 01561 *Type:* Private (Seventh-Day Adventist) liberal arts *Accred.:* 1945/1988 (NEASC-CIHE) *Calendar:* Sem. plan *Degrees:* A, B, M *Prof. Accred.:* Music, Nursing (A,B), Social Work (B) *CEO:* Pres. James J. Londis
Enroll: 951   (508) 368-2000

BABSON COLLEGE
Babson Park, Wellesley 02157 *Type:* Private professional *Accred.:* 1950/1991 (NEASC-CIHE) *Calendar:* Sem. plan *Degrees:* B, M *Prof. Accred.:* Business (B,M) *CEO:* Pres. William F. Glavin
Enroll: 2,414   (617) 235-1200

BAY PATH COLLEGE
Longmeadow 01106 *Type:* Private for women *Accred.:* 1965/1985 (NEASC-CIHE) *Calendar:* Sem. plan *Degrees:* A, B *CEO:* Pres. Jeanette T. Wright
Enroll: 566   (413) 567-0621

BAY STATE COLLEGE
122 Commonwealth Ave., Boston 02116 *Type:* Private *Accred.:* 1989 (NEASC-CTCI)

Calendar: Sem. plan *Degrees:* A, diplomas *Prof. Accred.:* Medical Assisting *CEO:* Pres. Frederick G. Pfannenstiehl
FTE Enroll: 649   (617) 236-8000

BECKER COLLEGE
61 Sever St., Worcester 01615 *Type:* Private *Accred.:* 1976/1992 (NEASC-CIHE) *Calendar:* Sem. plan *Degrees:* A *Prof. Accred.:* Nursing (A), Occupational Therapy Assisting, Physical Therapy Assisting *CEO:* Pres. Arnold C. Weller, Jr.
Enroll: 1,705   (508) 791-9241

BRANCH CAMPUS
3 Paxton St., Leicester 01524 *Prof. Accred.:* Veterinary Technology *CEO:* Pres. Arnold C. Weller, Jr.
(508) 791-9241

BENTLEY COLLEGE
175 Forest St., Waltham 02154-4705 *Type:* Private professional *Accred.:* 1966/1992 (NEASC-CIHE) *Calendar:* Sem. plan *Degrees:* A, B, M *Prof. Accred.:* Business (B,M) *CEO:* Pres. Joseph M. Cronin
Enroll: 5,345   (617) 891-2000

BERKLEE COLLEGE OF MUSIC
1140 Boylston St., Boston 02215 *Type:* Private professional *Accred.:* 1973/1993 (NEASC-CIHE) *Calendar:* Sem. plan *Degrees:* B *CEO:* Pres. Lee E. Berk
Enroll: 2,371   (617) 266-1400

BERKSHIRE COMMUNITY COLLEGE
West St., Pittsfield 01201 *Type:* Public (state) junior *System:* Commonwealth of Massachusetts Higher Education Coordinating Council *Accred.:* 1964/1989 (NEASC-CIHE) *Calendar:* Sem. plan *Degrees:* A *Prof. Accred.:* Nursing (A), Physical Therapy Assisting, Respiratory Therapy *CEO:* Pres. Barbara Viniar
Enroll: 1,449   (413) 499-4660

BOSTON COLLEGE
Chestnut Hill 02167-3934 *Type:* Private (Roman Catholic) *Accred.:* 1935/1986 (NEASC-CIHE) *Calendar:* Sem. plan *Degrees:* B, P, M, D *Prof. Accred.:* Business (B,M), Counseling Psychology, Law, Nursing (B,M), Social Work (M), Teacher Education (e,s,p) *CEO:* Pres. J. Donald Monan, S.J.
Enroll: 12,744   (617) 552-8000

BOSTON CONSERVATORY
8 The Fenway, Boston 02215 *Type:* Private *Accred.:* 1968/1988 (NEASC-CIHE) *Calendar:* Sem. plan *Degrees:* B, M *Prof. Accred.:* Music *CEO:* Pres. William A. Seymour
Enroll: 368   (617) 536-6340

BOSTON UNIVERSITY
147 Bay State Rd., Boston 02215 *Type:* Private *Accred.:* 1938/1991 (ATS); 1929/1989 (NEASC-CIHE) *Calendar:* Sem. plan *Degrees:* B, P, M, D *Prof. Accred.:* Business (B,M), Clinical Psychology, Combined Prosthodontics, Counseling Psychology, Dental Public Health, Dentistry, Endodontics, Engineering (aerospace, bioengineering, computer, electrical, manufacturing, mechanical, systems), General Dentistry, Health Services Administration, Law, Medicine, Music, Occupational Therapy, Ophthalmic Medical Technology, Oral and Maxillofacial Surgery, Orthodontics, Pediatric Dentistry, Periodontics, Physical Therapy, Psychology Internship, Public Health, Rehabilitation Counseling, Social Work (B,M), Speech-Language Pathology, Teacher Education (e,s,p) *CEO:* Pres. John R. Silber
Enroll: 22,897   (617) 353-2000

BRADFORD COLLEGE
Bradford 01830 *Type:* Private *Accred.:* 1931/1986 (NEASC-CIHE) *Calendar:* 4-1-4 plan *Degrees:* A, B *CEO:* Pres. Joseph Short
Enroll: 434   (508) 372-7161

BRANDEIS UNIVERSITY
Waltham 02254-9110 *Type:* Private *Accred.:* 1953/1987 (NEASC-CIHE) *Calendar:* Sem. plan *Degrees:* B, M, D *CEO:* Pres. Samuel O. Thier
Enroll: 3,751   (617) 736-2000

BRIDGEWATER STATE COLLEGE
Bridgewater 02325 *Type:* Public (state) liberal arts and teachers *System:* Commonwealth of Massachusetts Higher Education Coordinating Council *Accred.:* 1953/1992 (NEASC-CIHE) *Calendar:* Sem. plan *Degrees:* B, M *Prof. Accred.:* Social Work (B), Teacher Education (e,s) *CEO:* Pres. Adrian Tinsley
Enroll: 6,353   (508) 697-1200

BRISTOL COMMUNITY COLLEGE
777 Elsbree St., Fall River 02720-7395
Type: Public (state) junior *System:* Common-
wealth of Massachusetts Higher Education
Coordinating Council *Accred.:* 1970/1984
(NEASC-CIHE) *Calendar:* Sem. plan *De-
grees:* A *Prof. Accred.:* Dental Hygiene,
Medical Laboratory Technology (AMA),
Nursing (A) *CEO:* Pres. Eileen T. Farley
Enroll: 3,079   (508) 678-2811

BUNKER HILL COMMUNITY COLLEGE
Rutherford Ave., Boston 02129 *Type:* Public
(state) junior *System:* Commonwealth of
Massachusetts Higher Education Coordinat-
ing Council *Accred.:* 1976/1990 (NEASC-
CIHE) *Calendar:* Sem. plan *Degrees:* A
Prof. Accred.: Nuclear Medicine Technolo-
gy, Nursing (A), Radiography *CEO:* Pres. C.
Scully Stikes
Enroll: 4,353   (617) 241-8600 x400

CAMBRIDGE COLLEGE
15 Mifflin Pl., Cambridge 02138 *Type:* Pri-
vate *Accred.:* 1981/1987 (NEASC-CIHE)
Calendar: Sem. plan *Degrees:* M *CEO:*
Pres. Eileen M. Brown
Enroll: 1,111   (617) 492-5108

CAPE COD COMMUNITY COLLEGE
Rte. 132, West Barnstable 02668 *Type:* Pub-
lic (state) junior *System:* Commonwealth of
Massachusetts Higher Education Coordinat-
ing Council *Accred.:* 1967/1988 (NEASC-
CIHE) *Calendar:* Sem. plan *Degrees:* A
Prof. Accred.: Dental Hygiene (conditional),
Nursing (A) *CEO:* Pres. Richard A. Kraus
Enroll: 2,001   (508) 362-2131

CLARK UNIVERSITY
Worcester 01610-1477 *Type:* Private *Ac-
cred.:* 1929/1986 (NEASC-CIHE) *Calendar:*
Modular plan *Degrees:* B, M, D *Prof. Ac-
cred.:* Business (B,M), Clinical Psychology,
Health Services Administration *CEO:* Pres.
Richard P. Traina
Enroll: 2,810   (508) 793-7711

COLLEGE OF OUR LADY OF THE ELMS
Chicopee 01013-2839 *Type:* Private (Roman
Catholic) liberal arts for women *Accred.:*
1942/1992 (NEASC-CIHE) *Calendar:* Sem.
plan *Degrees:* B, M *Prof. Accred.:* Nursing

(B), Social Work (B) *CEO:* Pres. Mary A.
Dooley, S.S.J.
Enroll: 735   (413) 594-2761

COLLEGE OF THE HOLY CROSS
Worcester 01610-2395 *Type:* Private (Ro-
man Catholic) liberal arts *Accred.:* 1930/
1990 (NEASC-CIHE) *Calendar:* Sem. plan
Degrees: B, M *CEO:* Pres. John E. Brooks,
S.J.
Enroll: 2,742   (508) 793-2011

CONWAY SCHOOL OF LANDSCAPE DESIGN
Delabarre Ave., Conway 01341 *Type:* Pri-
vate *Accred.:* 1989 (NEASC-CIHE) *Calen-
dar:* Tri. plan *Degrees:* M *CEO:* Dir. Mollie
Babize
Enroll: 18   (413) 369-4044

CURRY COLLEGE
Milton 02186 *Type:* Private liberal arts and
teachers *Accred.:* 1970/1992 (NEASC-
CIHE) *Calendar:* Sem. plan *Degrees:* B, M
Prof. Accred.: Nursing (B) *CEO:* Pres.
Catherine W. Ingold
Enroll: 1,078   (617) 333-0500

DEAN COLLEGE
Franklin 02038 *Type:* Private *Accred.:* 1957/
1986 (NEASC-CIHE) *Calendar:* Sem. plan
Degrees: A *CEO:* Pres. John A. Dunn, Jr.
Enroll: 1,508   (508) 528-9100

EASTERN NAZARENE COLLEGE
23 E. Elm Ave., Quincy 02170-2999 *Type:*
Private (Nazarene) liberal arts *Accred.:*
1943/1990 (NEASC-CIHE) *Calendar:* 4-1-4
plan *Degrees:* A, B, M *Prof. Accred.:* Social
Work (B) *CEO:* Pres. Kent R. Hill
Enroll: 1,229   (617) 773-6350

EMERSON COLLEGE
100 Beacon St., Boston 02116-1596 *Type:*
Private liberal arts *Accred.:* 1950/1992
(NEASC-CIHE) *Calendar:* Sem. plan *De-
grees:* B, M *Prof. Accred.:* Speech-Lan-
guage Pathology *CEO:* Pres. Jacqueline
Liebergott
Enroll: 2,434   (617) 578-8500

EUROPEAN INSTITUTE FOR INTERNATIONAL
COMMUNICATION
Brusselsestraat 84, 6211 PH Maastricht,
Netherlands *CEO:* Pres. Jacqueline
Liebergott
                              [31] (043) 25 82 82

EMMANUEL COLLEGE
400 The Fenway, Boston 02115 *Type:* Private (Roman Catholic) liberal arts primarily for women *Accred.:* 1933/1992 (NEASC-CIHE) *Calendar:* Sem. plan *Degrees:* B, M *Prof. Accred.:* Nursing (B) *CEO:* Pres. Janet Eisner, S.N.D.
Enroll: 1,268   (617) 277-9430

ENDICOTT COLLEGE
Beverly 01915 *Type:* Private liberal arts *Accred.:* 1952/1987 (NEASC-CIHE) *Calendar:* Sem. plan *Degrees:* A, B *Prof. Accred.:* Interior Design, Nursing (A) *CEO:* Pres. Richard E. Wylie
Enroll: 1,043   (508) 927-0585

EPISCOPAL DIVINITY SCHOOL
99 Brattle St., Cambridge 02138 *Type:* Private (Episcopal) graduate only *Accred.:* 1938/1988 (ATS) *Calendar:* Sem. plan *Degrees:* M, D *CEO:* Pres./Dean William W. Rankin
FTE Enroll: 104   (617) 868-3450

ESSEX AGRICULTURAL AND TECHNICAL INSTITUTE
562 Maple St., Hathorne 01937 *Type:* Public (state) *Accred.:* 1979/1991 (NEASC-CTCI) *Calendar:* Sem. plan *Degrees:* A, certificates *CEO:* Dir. Gustave D. Olson, Jr.
FTE Enroll: 429   (508) 774-0050

FISHER COLLEGE
118 Beacon St., Boston 02116 *Type:* Private *Accred.:* 1970/1990 (NEASC-CIHE) *Calendar:* Sem. plan *Degrees:* A *CEO:* Pres. Christian Fisher
Enroll: 2,115   (617) 262-3240

FITCHBURG STATE COLLEGE
160 Pearl St., Fitchburg 01420 *Type:* Public *System:* Commonwealth of Massachusetts Higher Education Coordinating Council *Accred.:* 1953/1992 (NEASC-CIHE) *Calendar:* Sem. plan *Degrees:* B, M *Prof. Accred.:* Medical Technology, Nursing (B) *CEO:* Pres. Vincent J. Mara
Enroll: 3,772   (508) 345-2151

FRAMINGHAM STATE COLLEGE
100 State St., Framingham 01701-9101 *Type:* Public liberal arts and teachers *System:* Commonwealth of Massachusetts Higher Education Coordinating Council *Accred.:* 1950/1984 (NEASC-CIHE) *Calendar:* Sem. plan *Degrees:* B, M *Prof. Accred.:* Dietetics (coordinated), Nursing (B) *CEO:* Pres. Paul F. Weller
Enroll: 3,877   (508) 626-4575

FRANKLIN INSTITUTE OF BOSTON
Boston 02116 *Type:* Private 2-year technical *Accred.:* 1970/1990 (NEASC-CTCI) *Calendar:* Sem. plan *Degrees:* A *Prof. Accred.:* Engineering Technology (architectural, civil/construction, computer, electrical, mechanical) *CEO:* Pres. Richard P. D'Onofrio
Enroll: 318   (617) 423-4630

GORDON COLLEGE
Wenham 01984 *Type:* Private liberal arts *Accred.:* 1961/1992 (NEASC-CIHE) *Calendar:* Tri. plan *Degrees:* B *Prof. Accred.:* Music, Social Work (B) *CEO:* Pres. R. Judson Carleberg
Enroll: 1,191   (508) 927-2300

GORDON-CONWELL THEOLOGICAL SEMINARY
130 Essex St., South Hamilton 01982 *Type:* Private (interdenominational) graduate only *Accred.:* 1964/1985 (ATS); 1985 (NEASC-CIHE) *Calendar:* Sem. plan *Degrees:* M, D *CEO:* Pres. Robert E. Cooley
FTE Enroll: 493   (508) 468-7111

GREENFIELD COMMUNITY COLLEGE
One College Dr., Greenfield 01301 *Type:* Public (state) junior *System:* Commonwealth of Massachusetts Higher Education Coordinating Council *Accred.:* 1966/1990 (NEASC-CIHE) *Calendar:* Sem. plan *Degrees:* A *Prof. Accred.:* Nursing (A) *CEO:* Pres. Katherine H. Sloan
Enroll: 1,964   (413) 774-3131

HAMPSHIRE COLLEGE
Amherst 01002 *Type:* Private liberal arts *Accred.:* 1974/1988 (NEASC-CIHE) *Calendar:* 4-1-4 plan *Degrees:* B *CEO:* Pres. Gregory S. Prince, Jr.
Enroll: 1,182   (413) 549-4600

HARVARD UNIVERSITY
Cambridge 02138 *Type:* Private (interdenominational) *Accred.:* 1940/1991 (ATS); 1929/1987 (NEASC-CIHE) *Calendar:* Sem. plan *Degrees:* A, B, P, M, D *Prof. Accred.:* Business (M), Combined Prosthodontics, Dental Public Health, Dentistry, Engineering

Technology (industrial hygiene), Engineering (engineering physics/science), Landscape Architecture (M), Law, Medicine, Oral Pathology (conditional), Orthodontics, Periodontics, Psychology Internship, Public Health *CEO:* Pres. Neil Rudenstine
Enroll: 18,114   (617) 495-1000

HEBREW COLLEGE
43 Hawes St., Brookline 02146 *Type:* Private (Jewish) teachers *Accred.:* 1955/1988 (NEASC-CIHE) *Calendar:* Sem. plan *Degrees:* B, M *CEO:* Pres. David M. Gordis
Enroll: 60   (617) 232-8710

HELLENIC COLLEGE/HOLY CROSS GREEK ORTHODOX SCHOOL OF THEOLOGY
50 Goddard Ave., Brookline 02146 *Type:* Private (Greek Orthodox) liberal arts and professional *Accred.:* 1974/1991 (ATS); 1974/1991 (NEASC-CIHE) *Calendar:* Sem. plan *Degrees:* B, M *CEO:* Pres. Methodios Tournas
FTE Enroll: 101   (617) 731-3500

HOLYOKE COMMUNITY COLLEGE
303 Homestead Ave., Holyoke 01040 *Type:* Public (state) junior *System:* Commonwealth of Massachusetts Higher Education Coordinating Council *Accred.:* 1970/1990 (NEASC-CIHE) *Calendar:* Sem. plan *Degrees:* A *Prof. Accred.:* Medical Record Technology, Nursing (A), Radiography, Veterinary Technology (probational) *CEO:* Pres. David M. Bartley
Enroll: 3,280   (413) 538-7000

KATHARINE GIBBS SCHOOL
126 Newbury St., Boston 02116 *Type:* Private business *Accred.:* 1967/1988 (ACISC) *Calendar:* Sem. plan *Degrees:* A, certificates, diplomas *CEO:* Dir. Jim P. Otten
                                   (617) 578-7100

LABOURE COLLEGE
2120 Dorchester Ave., Boston 02124 *Type:* Private (Roman Catholic) 2-year *Accred.:* 1975/1991 (NEASC-CTCI) *Calendar:* Sem. plan *Degrees:* A *Prof. Accred.:* Electroneurodiagnostic Technology, Medical Record Technology, Nursing (A), Radiation Therapy Technology *CEO:* Pres. Clarisse Correia, D.C.
FTE Enroll: 430   (617) 296-8300

LASELL COLLEGE
Newton 02166 *Type:* Private liberal arts for women *Accred.:* 1932/1992 (NEASC-CIHE) *Calendar:* Sem. plan *Degrees:* A, B *Prof. Accred.:* Physical Therapy Assisting *CEO:* Pres. Thomas E.J. de Witt
Enroll: 512   (617) 243-2000

LESLEY COLLEGE
29 Everett St., Cambridge 02138-2790 *Type:* Private teachers for women *Accred.:* 1952/1984 (NEASC-CIHE) *Calendar:* Sem. plan *Degrees:* A, B, M, D *CEO:* Pres. Margaret A. McKenna
Enroll: 2,585   (617) 868-9600

MARIAN COURT JUNIOR COLLEGE
35 Little's Point Rd., Swampscott 01907 *Type:* Private (Roman Catholic) *Accred.:* 1982/1992 (NEASC-CTCI) *Calendar:* Sem. plan *Degrees:* A *CEO:* Pres. Joanne Bibeau, R.S.M.
FTE Enroll: 195   (617) 595-6768

MASSACHUSETTS BAY COMMUNITY COLLEGE
50 Oakland St., Wellesley Hills 02181-5399 *Type:* Public (state) junior *System:* Commonwealth of Massachusetts Higher Education Coordinating Council *Accred.:* 1967/1984 (NEASC-CIHE) *Calendar:* Sem. plan *Degrees:* A *Prof. Accred.:* Radiography *CEO:* Pres. Roger A. Van Winkle
Enroll: 3,473   (617) 237-1100

MASSACHUSETTS COLLEGE OF ART
621 Huntington Ave., Boston 02115 *Type:* Public (state) teachers and professional *System:* Commonwealth of Massachusetts Higher Education Coordinating Council *Accred.:* 1954/1987 (NEASC-CIHE) *Calendar:* Sem. plan *Degrees:* B, M *Prof. Accred.:* Art *CEO:* Pres. William F. O'Neil
Enroll: 1,337   (617) 232-1555

MASSACHUSETTS COLLEGE OF PHARMACY AND ALLIED HEALTH SCIENCES
179 Longwood Ave., Boston 02115 *Type:* Private professional *Accred.:* 1974/1987 (NEASC-CIHE) *Calendar:* Sem. plan *Degrees:* A, B, M, D *Prof. Accred.:* Nuclear Medicine Technology, Nursing (B), Radiation Therapy Technology *CEO:* Pres. Sumner M. Robinson
Enroll: 1,249   (617) 732-2800

MASSACHUSETTS INSTITUTE OF TECHNOLOGY
Cambridge 02139 *Type:* Private *Accred.:* 1929/1989 (NEASC-CIHE) *Calendar:* Sem. plan *Degrees:* B, M, D *Prof. Accred.:* Business (B,M), Engineering (aerospace, chemical, civil, computer, electrical, materials, mechanical, nuclear, ocean), Planning (M) *CEO:* Pres. Charles M. Vest
Enroll: 9,406   (617) 253-1000

MASSACHUSETTS MARITIME ACADEMY
Academy Dr., Buzzards Bay 02532 *Type:* Public (state) professional *System:* Commonwealth of Massachusetts Higher Education Coordinating Council *Accred.:* 1974/1990 (NEASC-CIHE) *Calendar:* Qtr. plan *Degrees:* B *CEO:* Interim Pres. Christine M. Griffin
Enroll: 886   (617) 759-5761

MASSACHUSETTS SCHOOL OF PROFESSIONAL PSYCHOLOGY
322 Sprague St., Dedham 02026 *Type:* Private professional; graduate only *Accred.:* 1984/1992 (NEASC-CIHE) *Calendar:* Sem. plan *Degrees:* D *Prof. Accred.:* Clinical Psychology *CEO:* Pres. Bruce J. Weiss
Enroll: 131   (617) 329-6777

MASSASOIT COMMUNITY COLLEGE
One Massasoit Blvd., Brockton 02402 *Type:* Public (state) junior *System:* Commonwealth of Massachusetts Higher Education Coordinating Council *Accred.:* 1971/1987 (NEASC-CIHE) *Calendar:* Sem. plan *Degrees:* A *Prof. Accred.:* Dental Assisting (conditional), Medical Laboratory Technology (AMA), Nursing (A), Radiography, Respiratory Therapy *CEO:* Pres. Gerard F. Burke
Enroll: 4,298   (508) 588-9100

MERRIMACK COLLEGE
North Andover 01845 *Type:* Private (Roman Catholic) liberal arts *Accred.:* 1953/1991 (NEASC-CIHE) *Calendar:* Sem. plan *Degrees:* A, B *Prof. Accred.:* Engineering (civil, computer) *CEO:* Pres. John E. Deegan, O.S.A.
Enroll: 2,318   (508) 837-5000

MGH INSTITUTE OF HEALTH PROFESSIONS
101 Merrimac St., Boston 02114-4719 *Type:* Private professional *Accred.:* 1985/1990 (NEASC-CIHE) *Calendar:* Sem. plan *De-grees:* M *Prof. Accred.:* Nursing (M) *CEO:* Pres. Patrick E. McCarthy
Enroll: 216   (617) 726-8002

MIDDLESEX COMMUNITY COLLEGE
Springs Rd., Bedford 01730 *Type:* Public (state) junior *System:* Commonwealth of Massachusetts Higher Education Coordinating Council *Accred.:* 1973/1987 (NEASC-CIHE) *Calendar:* Sem. plan *Degrees:* A *Prof. Accred.:* Dental Assisting, Dental Hygiene, Dental Laboratory Technology, Diagnostic Medical Sonography, Medical Assisting (AMA), Medical Laboratory Technology (AMA), Nursing (A), Radiography *CEO:* Pres. Carole A. Cowan
Enroll: 4,338   (617) 275-8910

LOWELL CAMPUS
Kearney Sq., Lowell 01852 *CEO:* Dean Molly Sheehy
                    (508) 656-3200

MONTSERRAT COLLEGE OF ART
Dunham Rd., Box 26, Beverly 01915 *Type:* Private 4-year professional *Accred.:* 1982 (NEASC-CTCI) *Calendar:* Sem. plan *De-grees:* B, diplomas *Prof. Accred.:* Art *CEO:* Pres. Paul G. Marks
FTE Enroll: 229   (508) 922-8222

MOUNT HOLYOKE COLLEGE
South Hadley 01075 *Type:* Private liberal arts for women *Accred.:* 1929/1988 (NEASC-CIHE) *Calendar:* Sem. plan *De-grees:* B, M *CEO:* Pres. Elizabeth T. Kennan
Enroll: 1,894   (413) 538-2000

MOUNT IDA COLLEGE
777 Dedham St., Newton Centre 02159 *Type:* Private primarily for women *Accred.:* 1970/1988 (NEASC-CIHE) *Calendar:* 12-6-12 plan *Degrees:* A, B *Prof. Accred.:* Dental Assisting, Funeral Service Education, Occupational Therapy Assisting, Veterinary Technology *CEO:* Pres. Bryan E. Carlson
Enroll: 1,722   (617) 969-7000

MOUNT WACHUSETT COMMUNITY COLLEGE
444 Green St., Gardner 01440 *Type:* Public (state) junior *System:* Commonwealth of Massachusetts Higher Education Coordinating Council *Accred.:* 1968/1992 (NEASC-CIHE) *Calendar:* Sem. plan *Degrees:* A *Prof. Accred.:* Medical Laboratory Technol-

ogy (AMA), Nursing (A) *CEO:* Pres. Daniel M. Asquino
Enroll: 2,260   (508) 632-6600

THE NEW ENGLAND BANKING INSTITUTE
One Lincoln Plaza, 89 South St., Boston 02111 *Type:* Private *Accred.:* 1985 (NEASC-CTCI) *Calendar:* Sem. plan *Degrees:* A *CEO:* Pres. Robert A. Regan
FTE Enroll: 323   (617) 951-2350

NEW ENGLAND COLLEGE OF OPTOMETRY
424 Beacon St., Boston 02115 *Type:* Private professional *Accred.:* 1976/1986 (NEASC-CIHE) *Calendar:* Sem. plan *Degrees:* B, P, D *Prof. Accred.:* Optometry *CEO:* Pres. Larry R. Clausen
Enroll: 400   (617) 266-2030

NEW ENGLAND CONSERVATORY OF MUSIC
290 Huntington Ave., Boston 02115 *Type:* Private professional *Accred.:* 1951/1988 (NEASC-CIHE) *Calendar:* Sem. plan *Degrees:* B, M, D *Prof. Accred.:* Music *CEO:* Pres. Laurence Lesser
Enroll: 694   (617) 262-1120

NEW ENGLAND SCHOOL OF LAW
154 Stuart St., Boston 02116 *Type:* Private professional *Calendar:* Sem. plan *Degrees:* P *Prof. Accred.:* Law (ABA only) *CEO:* Dean John F. O'Brien
Enroll: 1,121   (617) 451-0010

NEWBURY COLLEGE
129 Fisher Ave., Brookline 02146 *Type:* Private *Accred.:* 1977/1992 (NEASC-CTCI) *Calendar:* Sem. plan *Degrees:* A *Prof. Accred.:* Physical Therapy Assisting, Respiratory Therapy, Respiratory Therapy Technology *CEO:* Pres. Edward J. Tassinari
FTE Enroll: 3,185   (617) 730-7000

NICHOLS COLLEGE
Dudley 01571 *Type:* Private business *Accred.:* 1965/1984 (NEASC-CIHE) *Calendar:* Sem. plan *Degrees:* A, B, M *CEO:* Pres. Lowell C. Smith
Enroll: 1,046   (508) 943-1560

NORTH ADAMS STATE COLLEGE
North Adams 01247 *Type:* Public teachers *System:* Commonwealth of Massachusetts Higher Education Coordinating Council *Accred.:* 1953/1993 (NEASC-CIHE) *Calendar:*

4-1-4 plan *Degrees:* B, M *CEO:* Pres. Thomas D. Aceto
Enroll: 1,753   (413) 664-4511

NORTH SHORE COMMUNITY COLLEGE
One Ferncroft Rd., Danvers 01923-4093 *Type:* Public (state) junior *System:* Commonwealth of Massachusetts Higher Education Coordinating Council *Accred.:* 1969/1989 (NEASC-CIHE) *Calendar:* Sem. plan *Degrees:* A *Prof. Accred.:* Nursing (A), Occupational Therapy Assisting, Physical Therapy Assisting, Radiography, Respiratory Therapy *CEO:* Pres. George Traicoff
Enroll: 3,291   (508) 762-4000

NORTHEASTERN UNIVERSITY
360 Huntington Ave., Boston 02115-5095 *Type:* Private *Accred.:* 1940/1988 (NEASC-CIHE) *Calendar:* Qtr. plan *Degrees:* A, B, P, M, D *Prof. Accred.:* Audiology, Business (B,M), Computer Science, Engineering Technology (electrical, mechanical), Engineering (chemical, civil, electrical, industrial, mechanical), Law, Medical Laboratory Technology (AMA), Medical Record Administration, Medical Technology, Nurse Anesthesia Education, Nursing (B,M), Perfusion, Physical Therapy, Physician Assisting, Public Administration, Radiography, Recreation and Leisure Services, Rehabilitation Counseling, Respiratory Therapy, Speech-Language Pathology *CEO:* Pres. John A. Curry
Enroll: 20,277   (617) 373-2000

NORTHERN ESSEX COMMUNITY COLLEGE
100 Elliott Way, Haverhill 01830-2399 *Type:* Public (state) junior *System:* Commonwealth of Massachusetts Higher Education Coordinating Council *Accred.:* 1969/1990 (NEASC-CIHE) *Calendar:* Sem. plan *Degrees:* A *Prof. Accred.:* Dental Assisting, Medical Record Technology, Nursing (A), Practical Nursing, Radiography, Respiratory Therapy, Respiratory Therapy Technology *CEO:* Pres. John R. Dimitry
Enroll: 3,723   (508) 374-3900

PINE MANOR COLLEGE
400 Heath St., Chestnut Hill 02167 *Type:* Private liberal arts for women *Accred.:* 1939/

1993 (NEASC-CIHE) *Calendar:* Sem. plan *Degrees:* A, B *CEO:* Pres. Rosemary Ashby
Enroll: 415   (617) 731-7000

POPE JOHN XXIII NATIONAL SEMINARY
558 South Ave., Weston 02193-2699 *Type:* Private (Roman Catholic) graduate only *Accred.:* 1983/1988 (ATS) *Calendar:* Sem. plan *Degrees:* M *CEO:* Rector Cornelius M. McRae
FTE Enroll: 62   (617) 899-5500

QUINCY COLLEGE
34 Coddington St., Quincy 02169 *Type:* Public (city) junior *Accred.:* 1980/1987 (NEASC-CIHE) *Calendar:* Sem. plan *Degrees:* A *Prof. Accred.:* Nursing (A), Practical Nursing, Surgical Technology *CEO:* Interim Pres. Donald L. Young
Enroll: 2,591   (617) 984-1600

QUINSIGAMOND COMMUNITY COLLEGE
670 W. Boylston St., Worcester 01606 *Type:* Public (state) junior *System:* Commonwealth of Massachusetts Higher Education Coordinating Council *Accred.:* 1967/1984 (NEASC-CIHE) *Calendar:* Sem. plan *Degrees:* A *Prof. Accred.:* Dental Hygiene, Nursing (A), Occupational Therapy Assisting, Radiography, Respiratory Therapy *CEO:* Pres. Clifford S. Peterson
Enroll: 2,843   (508) 853-2300

RADCLIFFE COLLEGE
10 Garden St., Cambridge 02138 *Type:* Private primarily for women *Accred.:* 1929/1987 (NEASC-CIHE)* *Calendar:* Sem. plan *Degrees:* A, B *CEO:* Pres. Linda S. Wilson
Enroll: 2,692   (617) 495-8601

* Indirect accreditation through Harvard University.

REGIS COLLEGE
Weston 02193 *Type:* Private (Roman Catholic) liberal arts for women *Accred.:* 1933/1986 (NEASC-CIHE) *Calendar:* Sem. plan *Degrees:* B, M *Prof. Accred.:* Nursing (B), Social Work (B) *CEO:* Pres. Sheila E. Megley, R.S.M.
Enroll: 801   (617) 893-1820

ROXBURY COMMUNITY COLLEGE
1234 Columbus Ave., Roxbury Crossing 02120-3400 *Type:* Public (state) junior *System:* Commonwealth of Massachusetts High-

er Education Coordinating Council *Accred.:* 1981/1986 (NEASC-CIHE) *Calendar:* Sem. plan *Degrees:* A *CEO:* Pres. Grace Carolyn Brown
Enroll: 1,524   (617) 427-0060

ST. HYACINTH COLLEGE AND SEMINARY
Granby 01033 *Type:* Private (Roman Catholic Order of Friars Minor Conventual) for men *Accred.:* 1967/1988 (NEASC-CIHE) *Calendar:* Sem. plan *Degrees:* B *CEO:* Pres. Daniel Pietrzak, O.P.M
Enroll: 31   (413) 467-7191

ST. JOHN'S SEMINARY
127 Lake St., Brighton 02135 *Type:* Private (Roman Catholic) *Accred.:* 1970/1989 (ATS); 1969/1989 (NEASC-CIHE) *Calendar:* Sem. plan *Degrees:* B, P, M *CEO:* Rector Timothy J. Moran
FTE Enroll: 101   (617) 254-2610

SALEM STATE COLLEGE
352 Lafayette St., Salem 01970-4589 *Type:* Public liberal arts and professional *System:* Commonwealth of Massachusetts Higher Education Coordinating Council *Accred.:* 1953/1991 (NEASC-CIHE) *Calendar:* Sem. plan *Degrees:* B, M *Prof. Accred.:* Art, Nuclear Medicine Technology, Nursing (B,M), Social Work (B,M), Teacher Education (e,s,p) *CEO:* Pres. Nancy D. Harrington
Enroll: 6,942   (508) 741-6000

SCHOOL OF THE MUSEUM OF FINE ARTS, BOSTON
230 The Fenway, Boston 02115-9975 *Type:* Private professional *Calendar:* Sem. plan *Degrees:* B, M, diplomas *Prof. Accred.:* Art *CEO:* Pres. Bruce K. MacDonald
                    (617) 267-6100

SIMMONS COLLEGE
Boston 02115 *Type:* Private liberal arts and professional for women *Accred.:* 1929/1990 (NEASC-CIHE) *Calendar:* Sem. plan *Degrees:* B, M, D *Prof. Accred.:* Librarianship, Nursing (B,M), Physical Therapy, Social Work (M) *CEO:* Pres. Jean A. Dowdall
Enroll: 2,342   (617) 738-2000

SIMON'S ROCK COLLEGE OF BARD
Great Barrington 01230-9702 *Type:* Private liberal arts *Accred.:* 1974/1986 (NEASC-

CIHE) *Calendar:* Sem. plan *Degrees:* A, B *CEO:* Pres. Leon Botstein
Enroll: 328   (413) 528-0771

SMITH COLLEGE
Northampton 01063 *Type:* Private liberal arts for women *Accred.:* 1929/1988 (NEASC-CIHE) *Calendar:* Sem. plan *Degrees:* B, M, D *Prof. Accred.:* Social Work (M) *CEO:* Pres. Mary Maples Dunn
Enroll: 2,522   (413) 584-2700

SPRINGFIELD COLLEGE
Springfield 01109 *Type:* Private liberal arts and professional *Accred.:* 1930/1989 (NEASC-CIHE) *Calendar:* Qtr. plan *Degrees:* B, M, D *Prof. Accred.:* Occupational Therapy, Physical Therapy, Recreation and Leisure Services, Rehabilitation Counseling, Social Work (M) *CEO:* Pres. Randolph W. Bromery
Enroll: 3,420   (413) 748-3000

SPRINGFIELD TECHNICAL COMMUNITY COLLEGE
One Armory Sq., Springfield 01105 *Type:* Public (state) 2-year *System:* Commonwealth of Massachusetts Higher Education Coordinating Council *Accred.:* 1971/1991 (NEASC-CIHE) *Calendar:* Sem. plan *Degrees:* A *Prof. Accred.:* Dental Assisting, Dental Hygiene, Medical Assisting (AMA), Medical Laboratory Technology (AMA), Nuclear Medicine Technology, Nursing (A), Physical Therapy Assisting, Radiation Therapy Technology, Radiography, Respiratory Therapy, Surgical Technology *CEO:* Pres. Andrew M. Scibelli
Enroll: 3,857   (413) 781-7822

STONEHILL COLLEGE
North Easton 02357 *Type:* Private (Roman Catholic) liberal arts *Accred.:* 1959/1989 (NEASC-CIHE) *Calendar:* Sem. plan *Degrees:* B *Prof. Accred.:* Teacher Education (e) *CEO:* Pres. Bartley MacPhaidin, C.S.C.
Enroll: 2,266   (508) 238-1081

SUFFOLK UNIVERSITY
8 Ashburton Pl., Beacon Hill, Boston 02108 *Type:* Private *Accred.:* 1952/1992 (NEASC-CIHE) *Calendar:* Sem. plan *Degrees:* A, B, P, M, D *Prof. Accred.:* Business (B,M),

Law, Public Administration *CEO:* Pres. David J. Sargent
Enroll: 9,703   (617) 723-4700

TUFTS UNIVERSITY
Medford 02155 *Type:* Private liberal arts *Accred.:* 1929/1992 (NEASC-CIHE) *Calendar:* Sem. plan *Degrees:* B, P, M, D *Prof. Accred.:* Combined Prosthodontics, Community Health/Preventive Medicine, Dentistry, Dietetics (internship), Endodontics, Engineering (chemical, civil, computer, electrical, mechanical), General Practice Residency, Medicine, Occupational Therapy, Oral and Maxillofacial Surgery, Orthodontics, Pediatric Dentistry, Periodontics, Psychology Internship, Veterinary Medicine *CEO:* Pres. John A. DiBiaggio
Enroll: 7,535   (617) 628-5000

UNIVERSITY OF MASSACHUSETTS AT AMHERST
Amherst 01003 *Type:* Public (state) *System:* University of Massachusetts President's Office *Accred.:* 1932/1988 (NEASC-CIHE) *Calendar:* Sem. plan *Degrees:* A, B, P, M, D *Prof. Accred.:* Audiology, Business (B,M), Clinical Psychology, Combined Professional-Scientific Psychology, Counseling Psychology, Engineering (chemical, civil, computer, electrical, environmental/sanitary, industrial, manufacturing, mechanical), Forestry, Interior Design, Landscape Architecture (B-initial,M), Music, Nursing (B,M), Planning (M), Psychology Internship, Public Administration, Public Health, Speech-Language Pathology, Teacher Education (e,s,p), Theatre *CEO:* Chanc. David K. Scott
Enroll: 21,996   (413) 545-3171

UNIVERSITY OF MASSACHUSETTS BOSTON
100 Morrisey Blvd., Boston 02125-3393 *Type:* Public (state) *System:* University of Massachusetts President's Office *Accred.:* 1972/1985 (NEASC-CIHE) *Calendar:* Sem. plan *Degrees:* B, M, D *Prof. Accred.:* Nursing (B,M), Rehabilitation Counseling *CEO:* Chanc. Sherry H. Penney
Enroll: 8,898   (617) 287-6800

UNIVERSITY OF MASSACHUSETTS DARTMOUTH
North Dartmouth 02747 *Type:* Public (state) *System:* University of Massachusetts President's Office *Accred.:* 1964/1990 (NEASC-CIHE) *Calendar:* Sem. plan *Degrees:* B, M

Prof. Accred.: Art, Computer Science, Engineering Technology (electrical, mechanical), Engineering (civil, computer, electrical, mechanical), Medical Technology, Nursing (B,M) *CEO:* Chanc. Peter Cressy
Enroll: 5,118   (508) 999-8004

UNIVERSITY OF MASSACHUSETTS LOWELL
One University Ave., Lowell 01854 *Type:* Public (state) *System:* University of Massachusetts President's Office *Accred.:* 1975/ 1987 (NEASC-CIHE) *Calendar:* Sem. plan *Degrees:* A, B, M, D *Prof. Accred.:* Art, Business (B,M), Computer Science, Engineering Technology (civil/construction, electrical, mechanical), Engineering (chemical, civil, electrical, mechanical, nuclear, plastics), Medical Technology, Music, Nursing (B,M), Physical Therapy, Teacher Education (e,s,p) *CEO:* Chanc. William T. Hogan
Enroll: 9,953   (508) 934-4000

UNIVERSITY OF MASSACHUSETTS MEDICAL CENTER AT WORCESTER
55 Lake Ave., N., Worcester 01605 *Type:* Public (state) *System:* University of Massachusetts President's Office *Calendar:* Sem. plan *Degrees:* B, P, M *Prof. Accred.:* Health Services Administration, Medicine, Nuclear Medicine Technology, Nursing (M), Radiation Therapy Technology *CEO:* Chanc. Aaron Lazare
Enroll: 407   (508) 856-6630

WELLESLEY COLLEGE
Wellesley 02181 *Type:* Private liberal arts for women *Accred.:* 1929/1989 (NEASC-CIHE) *Calendar:* 4-1-4 plan *Degrees:* B *CEO:* Pres. Diana Chapman Walsh
Enroll: 2,289   (617) 235-0320

WENTWORTH INSTITUTE OF TECHNOLOGY
Boston 02115 *Type:* Private technological *Accred.:* 1967/1991 (NEASC-CIHE) *Calendar:* Sem. plan *Degrees:* A, B *Prof. Accred.:* Engineering Technology (aerospace, architectural, civil/construction, computer, electrical, manufacturing, mechanical, mechanical drafting/design), Interior Design *CEO:* Pres. John F. Van Domelen
Enroll: 2,786   (617) 442-9010

WESTERN NEW ENGLAND COLLEGE
Springfield 01119 *Type:* Private liberal arts and professional *Accred.:* 1965/1992 (NEASC-CIHE) *Calendar:* Sem. plan *Degrees:* B, P, M, D *Prof. Accred.:* Engineering (electrical, industrial, mechanical), Law, Social Work (B) *CEO:* Pres. Beverly W. Miller
Enroll: 3,313   (413) 782-3111

WESTFIELD STATE COLLEGE
Western Ave., Westfield 01086 *Type:* Public (state) liberal arts and teachers *System:* Commonwealth of Massachusetts Higher Education Coordinating Council *Accred.:* 1957/ 1991 (NEASC-CIHE) *Calendar:* Sem. plan *Degrees:* B, M *Prof. Accred.:* Teacher Education (e,s) *CEO:* Pres. Ronald L. Applbaum
Enroll: 4,082   (413) 568-3311

WESTON SCHOOL OF THEOLOGY
3 Phillips Pl., Cambridge 02138 *Type:* Private (Roman Catholic) graduate only *Accred.:* 1968/1988 (ATS) *Calendar:* Sem. plan *Degrees:* M *CEO:* Pres. Robert A. Wild, S.J.
FTE Enroll: 121   (617) 492-1960

WHEATON COLLEGE
Norton 02766 *Type:* Private liberal arts *Accred.:* 1929/1989 (NEASC-CIHE) *Calendar:* Sem. plan *Degrees:* B *CEO:* Pres. Dale Rogers Marshall
Enroll: 1,299   (508) 285-7722

WHEELOCK COLLEGE
200 The Riverway, Boston 02215-4176 *Type:* Private teachers for women *Accred.:* 1950/1985 (NEASC-CIHE) *Calendar:* Tri. plan *Degrees:* A, B, M *Prof. Accred.:* Social Work (B) *CEO:* Acting Pres. Marjorie Bakken
Enroll: 1,260   (617) 734-5200

WILLIAMS COLLEGE
Williamstown 01267 *Type:* Private liberal arts *Accred.:* 1929/1988 (NEASC-CIHE) *Calendar:* 4-1-4 plan *Degrees:* B, M *CEO:* Pres. Harry C. Payne
Enroll: 2,094   (413) 597-3131

WORCESTER POLYTECHNIC INSTITUTE
100 Institute Rd., Worcester 01609-2280 *Type:* Private technological *Accred.:* 1937/ 1991 (NEASC-CIHE) *Calendar:* Sem. plan

Degrees: B, M, D *Prof. Accred.:* Computer Science, Engineering (chemical, civil, electrical, manufacturing, mechanical) *CEO:* Pres. Jon C. Strauss
Enroll: 3,575   (508) 831-5000

WORCESTER STATE COLLEGE
486 Chandler St., Worcester 01602-2597
Type: Public (state) liberal arts and teachers *System:* Commonwealth of Massachusetts Higher Education Coordinating Council *Accred.:* 1957/1992 (NEASC-CIHE) *Calendar:* Sem. plan *Degrees:* B, M *Prof. Accred.:* Nuclear Medicine Technology, Nursing (B), Occupational Therapy, Radiation Therapy Technology, Speech-Language Pathology *CEO:* Pres. Kalyan K. Ghosh
Enroll: 3,886   (508) 793-8000

MICHIGAN

ADRIAN COLLEGE
110 S. Madison St., Adrian 49221 *Type:* Private (United Methodist) liberal arts *Accred.:* 1916/1989 (NCA) *Calendar:* Sem. plan *Degrees:* A, B *CEO:* Pres. Stanley P. Caine
Enroll: 1,144   (517) 265-5161

ALBION COLLEGE
611 E. Porter St., Albion 49224 *Type:* Private (United Methodist) liberal arts *Accred.:* 1915/1991 (NCA) *Calendar:* Sem. plan *Degrees:* B *Prof. Accred.:* Music *CEO:* Pres. Melvin L. Vulgamore
Enroll: 1,677   (517) 629-1000

ALMA COLLEGE
Alma 48801 *Type:* Private (United Presbyterian) liberal arts *Accred.:* 1916/1990 (NCA) *Calendar:* 4-4-x plan *Degrees:* B *Prof. Accred.:* Music *CEO:* Pres. Alan J. Stone
Enroll: 1,296   (517) 463-7111

ALPENA COMMUNITY COLLEGE
666 Johnson St., Alpena 49707 *Type:* Public (district) junior *System:* Michigan Department of Education *Accred.:* 1963/1988 (NCA) *Calendar:* Sem. plan *Degrees:* A, certificates *CEO:* Pres. Donald L. Newport
Enroll: 2,118   (517) 356-9021

ANDREWS UNIVERSITY
Berrien Springs 49104 *Type:* Private (Seventh-Day Adventist) liberal arts and professional *Accred.:* 1970/1989 (ATS); 1922/1989 (NCA) *Calendar:* Qtr. plan *Degrees:* A, B, M, D, certificates *Prof. Accred.:* Counseling, Medical Technology, Music, Nursing (B,M), Physical Therapy, Social Work (B), Teacher Education (e,s,p) *CEO:* Pres. W. Richard Lesher
Enroll: 2,979   (616) 471-7771

AQUINAS COLLEGE
1607 Robinson Rd., S.E., Grand Rapids 49506 *Type:* Private (Roman Catholic) liberal arts *Accred.:* 1946/1987 (NCA) *Calendar:* Sem. plan *Degrees:* A, B, M *CEO:* Pres. R. Paul Nelson
Enroll: 2,544   (616) 459-8281

BAKER COLLEGE OF FLINT
G-1050 W. Bristol Rd., Flint 48507 *Type:* Private *Accred.:* 1985/1990 (NCA) *Calendar:* Qtr. plan *Degrees:* A, B, certificates, diplomas *Prof. Accred.:* Medical Assisting (AMA), Medical Record Technology *CEO:* Pres. Edward J. Kurtz
Enroll: 9,966   (313) 767-7600

BAKER COLLEGE OF MUSKEGON
141 Hartford St., Muskegon 49442 *Prof. Accred.:* Medical Assisting (AMA), Medical Record Technology, Physical Therapy Assisting *CEO:* Pres. Robert D. Jewell
                               (616) 726-4904

BAKER COLLEGE OF OWOSSO
1020 S. Washington St., Owosso 48867 *Prof. Accred.:* Medical Assisting (AMA) *CEO:* Pres. Rick E. Amidon
                               (517) 723-5251

BAY DE NOC COMMUNITY COLLEGE
2001 N. Lincoln Rd., Escanaba 49829 *Type:* Public (district) junior *System:* Michigan Department of Education *Accred.:* 1976/1991 (NCA) *Calendar:* Sem. plan *Degrees:* A, certificates *CEO:* Pres. Dwight E. Link
Enroll: 2,244   (906) 786-5802

CALVIN COLLEGE
3201 Burton St., S.E., Grand Rapids 49546 *Type:* Private (Christian Reformed) liberal arts *Accred.:* 1930/1985 (NCA) *Calendar:* 4-1-4 plan *Degrees:* B, M *Prof. Accred.:* Engineering (general), Music (associate), Social Work (B), Teacher Education (e,s) *CEO:* Pres. Anthony J. Diekema
Enroll: 3,725   (616) 957-6000

CALVIN THEOLOGICAL SEMINARY
3233 Burton St., S.E., Grand Rapids 49546 *Type:* Private (Christian Reformed) graduate only *Accred.:* 1944/1988 (ATS) *Calendar:* Qtr. plan *Degrees:* M, D *CEO:* Pres. James A. De Jong
FTE Enroll: 188   (616) 957-6036

THE CENTER FOR CREATIVE STUDIES—COLLEGE OF ART AND DESIGN
245 E. Kirby St., Detroit 48202-4013 *Type:* Private professional *Accred.:* 1982/1993

(NCA) *Calendar:* Sem. plan *Degrees:* B *Prof. Accred.:* Art *CEO:* Interim Pres. Frank Couzens, Jr.
Enroll: 860   (313) 872-3118

CENTER FOR HUMANISTIC STUDIES
40 E. Ferry Ave., Detroit 48202 *Type:* Private professional; graduate only *Accred.:* 1984/1989 (NCA) *Calendar:* Qtr. plan *Degrees:* P, M *CEO:* Pres. Clark Moustakas
Enroll: 68   (313) 875-7440

CENTRAL MICHIGAN UNIVERSITY
Mount Pleasant 48859 *Type:* Public (state) *System:* Michigan Department of Education *Accred.:* 1915/1986 (NCA) *Calendar:* Sem. plan *Degrees:* B, P, M, D, certificates *Prof. Accred.:* Accounting (Type A), Audiology, Business (B,M), Clinical Psychology (provisional), Dietetics (internship), Music, Recreation and Leisure Services, Speech-Language Pathology, Teacher Education (e,s,p) *CEO:* Pres. Leonard E. Plachta
Enroll: 24,724   (517) 774-4000

CHARLES STEWART MOTT COMMUNITY COLLEGE
1401 E. Court St., Flint 48503 *Type:* Public (district) junior *System:* Michigan Department of Education *Accred.:* 1926/1990 (NCA) *Calendar:* Sem. plan *Degrees:* A, certificates *Prof. Accred.:* Dental Assisting, Dental Hygiene, Nursing (A), Respiratory Therapy *CEO:* Pres. Allen D. Arnold
Enroll: 11,222   (313) 762-0200

CLEARY COLLEGE
2170 Washtenaw Ave., Ypsilanti 48197 *Type:* Private *Accred.:* 1988/1991 (NCA) *Calendar:* Qtr. plan *Degrees:* A, B, certificates, diplomas *CEO:* Pres. Thomas P. Sullivan
Enroll: 956   (313) 483-4400

CONCORDIA COLLEGE
4090 Geddes Rd., Ann Arbor 48105 *Type:* Private (Lutheran-Missouri Synod) liberal arts *Accred.:* 1968/1991 (NCA) *Calendar:* Qtr. plan *Degrees:* A, B *CEO:* Pres. James M. Koerschen
Enroll: 554   (313) 995-7300

CRANBROOK ACADEMY OF ART
500 Lone Pine Rd., Box 801, Bloomfield Hills 48303-0801 *Type:* Private professional; graduate only *Accred.:* 1960/1989 (NCA)

Calendar: Sem. plan *Degrees:* M *Prof. Accred.:* Art *CEO:* Pres. Roy Slade
Enroll: 146   (313) 645-3300

DAVENPORT COLLEGE OF BUSINESS
415 E. Fulton St., Grand Rapids 49503 *Type:* Private *Accred.:* 1976/1988 (NCA) *Calendar:* Qtr. plan *Degrees:* A, B, certificates, diplomas *Prof. Accred.:* Medical Assisting (AMA) *CEO:* Pres. Donald W. Maine
Enroll: 9,431   (616) 451-3511

BRANCH CAMPUS
7121 Grape Rd., Granger, IN 46530 *Prof. Accred.:* Medical Assisting *CEO:* Dir. Joyce Bono
                                   (219) 277-8447

BRANCH CAMPUS
8200 Georgia St., Merrillville, IN 46410 *Prof. Accred.:* Medical Assisting *CEO:* Dir. Patrick Comstock
                                   (219) 769-5556

BRANCH CAMPUS
643 Waverly Rd., Holland 49423 *CEO:* Dean Tom Carey
                                   (616) 395-4600

BRANCH CAMPUS
4123 N. Main St., Kalamazoo 49006 *Prof. Accred.:* Medical Assisting *CEO:* Dean C. Dexter Rohm
                                   (616) 382-2835

BRANCH CAMPUS
220 E. Kalamazoo St., Lansing 48933 *CEO:* Sr. Vice Pres. Don Colizzi
                                   (517) 484-2600

DELTA COLLEGE
University Center 48710 *Type:* Public (district) junior *System:* Michigan Department of Education *Accred.:* 1968/1984 (NCA) *Calendar:* Sem. plan *Degrees:* A, certificates *Prof. Accred.:* Dental Assisting, Dental Hygiene, Engineering Technology (electrical, mechanical), Nursing (A), Physical Therapy Assisting, Radiography, Respiratory Therapy, Surgical Technology *CEO:* Pres. Peter D. Boyse
Enroll: 11,774   (517) 686-9000

DETROIT COLLEGE OF BUSINESS
4801 Oakman Blvd., Dearborn 48126 *Type:* Private business *Accred.:* 1986/1990 (NCA) *Calendar:* Qtr. plan *Degrees:* A, B, certificates *CEO:* Senior Vice Pres. James Mendola
Enroll: 5,173   (313) 581-4400

DETROIT COLLEGE OF LAW
130 E. Elizabeth St., Detroit 48201 *Type:* Private professional *Calendar:* Sem. plan *Degrees:* P *Prof. Accred.:* Law *CEO:* Dean Arthur J. Lombard
Enroll: 791   (313) 226-0100

EASTERN MICHIGAN UNIVERSITY
Ypsilanti 48197 *Type:* Public (state) *System:* Michigan Department of Education *Accred.:* 1915/1991 (NCA) *Calendar:* Sem. plan *Degrees:* B, P, M, D, certificates *Prof. Accred.:* Business (B,M), Construction Education (B), Counseling, Dietetics (coordinated), Interior Design, Medical Technology, Music, Nursing (B), Occupational Therapy, Public Administration, Social Work (B,M-candidate), Speech-Language Pathology, Teacher Education (e,s,p) *CEO:* Pres. William E. Shelton
Enroll: 25,836   (313) 487-1849

FERRIS STATE UNIVERSITY
Big Rapids 49307 *Type:* Public (state) professional and technical *System:* Michigan Department of Education *Accred.:* 1959/ 1987 (NCA) *Calendar:* Qtr. plan *Degrees:* A, B, M, D, certificates *Prof. Accred.:* Construction Education (B), Dental Hygiene, Dental Laboratory Technology, Engineering (surveying), Medical Laboratory Technology (AMA), Medical Record Administration, Medical Record Technology, Medical Technology, Nuclear Medicine Technology, Nursing (B), Optometry, Radiography, Respiratory Therapy, Social Work (B) *CEO:* Pres. Helen Popovich
Enroll: 12,134   (616) 592-2100

GLEN OAKS COMMUNITY COLLEGE
62249 Shimmel Rd., Centreville 49032 *Type:* Public (district) junior *System:* Michigan Department of Education *Accred.:* 1975/ 1993 (NCA) *Calendar:* Sem. plan *Degrees:* A, certificates *CEO:* Pres. Philip G. Ward
Enroll: 1,409   (616) 467-9945

GMI ENGINEERING AND MANAGEMENT INSTITUTE
1700 W. Third Ave., Flint 48504 *Type:* Private technological *Accred.:* 1962/1987 (NCA) *Calendar:* Sem. plan *Degrees:* B, M *Prof. Accred.:* Engineering (electrical, industrial, manufacturing, mechanical) *CEO:* Pres. James E.A. John
Enroll: 2,382   (313) 762-9864

GOGEBIC COMMUNITY COLLEGE
E-4946 Jackson Rd., Ironwood 49938 *Type:* Public (district) junior *System:* Michigan Department of Education *Accred.:* 1949/1992 (NCA) *Calendar:* Sem. plan *Degrees:* A, certificates *CEO:* Pres. James R. Grote
Enroll: 1,392   (906) 932-4231

GRACE BIBLE COLLEGE
1011 Aldon St., S.W., P.O. Box 910, Grand Rapids 49509-9990 *Type:* Private (Grace Gospel Fellowship) *Accred.:* 1964/1983 (AABC); 1990 (NCA) *Calendar:* Sem. plan *Degrees:* A, B, certificates *CEO:* Pres. E. Bruce Kemper
Enroll: 100   (616) 538-2330

GRAND RAPIDS BAPTIST COLLEGE AND SEMINARY
1001 E. Beltline Ave., N.E., Grand Rapids 49505 *Type:* Private (Baptist) liberal arts and professional *Accred.:* 1977/1992 (NCA) *Calendar:* Sem. plan *Degrees:* A, B, M, D, diplomas *CEO:* Pres. Rex M. Rogers
Enroll: 928   (616) 949-5300

GRAND RAPIDS COMMUNITY COLLEGE
143 Bostwick St., N.E., Grand Rapids 49503 *Type:* Public (district) junior *System:* Michigan Department of Education *Accred.:* 1917/ 1991 (NCA) *Calendar:* Sem. plan *Degrees:* A, certificates *Prof. Accred.:* Dental Assisting, Dental Hygiene, Music, Nursing (A), Occupational Therapy Assisting, Practical Nursing, Radiography *CEO:* Pres. Richard W. Calkins
Enroll: 14,242   (616) 771-4000

GRAND VALLEY STATE UNIVERSITY
One Campus Dr., Allendale 49401 *Type:* Public (state) liberal arts *System:* Michigan Department of Education *Accred.:* 1968/ 1989 (NCA) *Calendar:* Sem. plan *Degrees:* B, M *Prof. Accred.:* Art, Engineering (gener-

al), Music, Nursing (B,M), Physical Therapy, Psychology Internship (provisional), Social Work (B,M), Teacher Education (e,s,p) *CEO:* Pres. Arend D. Lubbers
Enroll: 12,867   (616) 895-6611

GREAT LAKES CHRISTIAN COLLEGE
6211 W. Willow Hwy., Lansing 48917 *Type:* Private (Christian Churches/Churches of Christ) *Accred.:* 1977/1987 (AABC) *Calendar:* Sem. plan *Degrees:* A, B, certificates *CEO:* Acting Pres. Kenneth Henes
FTE Enroll: 162   (517) 321-0242

GREAT LAKES JUNIOR COLLEGE
310 S. Washington Ave., Saginaw 48607 *Type:* Private junior *Accred.:* 1993 (NCA) *Calendar:* Qtr. plan *Degrees:* A, certificates *CEO:* Pres. Angelo Guerriero
Enroll: 2,153   (517) 755-3455

HENRY FORD COMMUNITY COLLEGE
5101 Evergreen Rd., Dearborn 48128 *Type:* Public (district) junior *System:* Michigan Department of Education *Accred.:* 1949/1985 (NCA) *Calendar:* Sem. plan *Degrees:* A, certificates *Prof. Accred.:* Medical Assisting (AMA), Medical Record Technology, Nursing (A), Physical Therapy Assisting, Respiratory Therapy *CEO:* Pres. Andrew A. Mazzara
Enroll: 15,144   (313) 271-2750

HIGHLAND PARK COMMUNITY COLLEGE
Glendale Ave. at Third St., Highland Park 48203 *Type:* Public (district) junior *System:* Michigan Department of Education *Accred.:* 1921/1987 (NCA) *Calendar:* Sem. plan *Degrees:* A, certificates *Prof. Accred.:* Medical Laboratory Technology (AMA), Surgical Technology *CEO:* Pres. Thomas Lloyd
Enroll: 1,918   (313) 252-0475

HILLSDALE COLLEGE
33 E. College Ave., Hillsdale 49242 *Type:* Private liberal arts *Accred.:* 1915/1988 (NCA) *Calendar:* Sem. plan *Degrees:* B, certificates *CEO:* Pres. George Charles Roche, III
Enroll: 1,070   (517) 437-7341

HOPE COLLEGE
141 E. 12th St., P.O. Box 9000, Holland 49422-9000 *Type:* Private (Reformed Church in America) liberal arts *Accred.:* 1915/1984 (NCA) *Calendar:* Sem. plan *Degrees:* B *Prof. Accred.:* Art, Dance, Music, Nursing (B), Teacher Education (e,s), Theatre (associate) *CEO:* Pres. John H. Jacobson
Enroll: 2,755   (616) 392-5111

JACKSON COMMUNITY COLLEGE
2111 Emmons Rd., Jackson 49201 *Type:* Public (district) junior *System:* Michigan Department of Education *Accred.:* 1933/1986 (NCA) *Calendar:* Sem. plan *Degrees:* A, certificates *Prof. Accred.:* Diagnostic Medical Sonography, Radiography *CEO:* Pres. E. Lee Howser
Enroll: 8,441   (517) 787-0800

KALAMAZOO COLLEGE
1200 Academy St., Kalamazoo 49007 *Type:* Private (Baptist) liberal arts *Accred.:* 1915/1993 (NCA) *Calendar:* Qtr. plan *Degrees:* B *CEO:* Pres. Lawrence D. Bryan
Enroll: 1,250   (616) 337-7000

KALAMAZOO VALLEY COMMUNITY COLLEGE
6767 W. O Ave., Kalamazoo 49009 *Type:* Public (district) junior *System:* Michigan Department of Education *Accred.:* 1972/1986 (NCA) *Calendar:* Sem. plan *Degrees:* A, certificates *Prof. Accred.:* Dental Hygiene, Medical Assisting (AMA), Respiratory Therapy *CEO:* Pres. Marilyn J. Schlack
Enroll: 10,834   (616) 372-5200

KELLOGG COMMUNITY COLLEGE
450 North Ave., Battle Creek 49017-3397 *Type:* Public (district) junior *System:* Michigan Department of Education *Accred.:* 1965/1992 (NCA) *Calendar:* Sem. plan *Degrees:* A, certificates *Prof. Accred.:* Dental Hygiene, Medical Laboratory Technology (AMA), Physical Therapy Assisting, Radiography *CEO:* Pres. Paul R. Ohm
Enroll: 6,024   (616) 965-3931

KENDALL COLLEGE OF ART AND DESIGN
111 Division Ave. N., Grand Rapids 49503 *Type:* Private *Accred.:* 1981/1993 (NCA) *Calendar:* Sem. plan *Degrees:* B *Prof. Accred.:* Art, Interior Design *CEO:* Pres. Charles L. Deihl
Enroll: 632   (616) 451-2787

KIRTLAND COMMUNITY COLLEGE
10775 N. St. Helen Rd., Roscommon 48653 *Type:* Public (district) junior *System:* Michigan Department of Education *Accred.:* 1976/

1989 (NCA) *Calendar:* Sem. plan *Degrees:* A, certificates, diplomas *CEO:* Pres. Dorothy N. Franke
Enroll: 1,309   (517) 275-5121

LAKE MICHIGAN COLLEGE
2755 E. Napier St., Benton Harbor 49022 *Type:* Public (district) junior *System:* Michigan Department of Education *Accred.:* 1962/ 1989 (NCA) *Calendar:* Sem. plan *Degrees:* A, certificates *Prof. Accred.:* Dental Assisting, Nursing (A), Radiography *CEO:* Interim Pres. Greg Korock
Enroll: 3,816   (616) 927-3571

LAKE SUPERIOR STATE UNIVERSITY
1000 College Dr., Sault Ste. Marie 49783 *Type:* Public (state) liberal arts *System:* Michigan Department of Education *Accred.:* 1968/1991 (NCA) *Calendar:* Qtr. plan *Degrees:* A, B, M, certificates *Prof. Accred.:* Engineering Technology (automated systems, computer, electrical, mechanical, mechanical drafting/design), Nursing (B) *CEO:* Pres. Robert D. Arbuckle
Enroll: 3,366   (906) 632-6841

LANSING COMMUNITY COLLEGE
521 N. Washington Sq., Box 40010, Lansing 48901-7210 *Type:* Public (district) junior *System:* Michigan Department of Education *Accred.:* 1964/1984 (NCA) *Calendar:* Qtr. plan *Degrees:* A, certificates *Prof. Accred.:* Dental Assisting, Dental Hygiene, EMT-Paramedic, Nursing (A), Radiation Therapy Technology, Radiography, Respiratory Therapy, Respiratory Therapy Technology *CEO:* Pres. Abel B. Sykes, Jr.
Enroll: 21,828   (517) 483-1851

LAWRENCE TECHNOLOGICAL UNIVERSITY
21000 W. Ten Mile Rd., Southfield 48075 *Type:* Private professional and technological *Accred.:* 1967/1991 (NCA) *Calendar:* Qtr. plan *Degrees:* A, B, M *Prof. Accred.:* Engineering Technology (civil/construction, electrical, industrial, mechanical), Engineering (construction, electrical, mechanical), Interior Design *CEO:* Pres. Charles M. Chambers
Enroll: 4,500   (313) 356-0200

LEWIS COLLEGE OF BUSINESS
17370 Meyers Rd., Detroit 48235 *Type:* Private business *Accred.:* 1978/1990 (NCA)

Calendar: Tri. plan *Degrees:* A, certificates *CEO:* Pres. Marjorie L. Harris
Enroll: 322   (313) 862-6300

MACOMB COMMUNITY COLLEGE
14500 E. Twelve Mile Rd., Warren 48093 *Type:* Public (district) junior *System:* Michigan Department of Education *Accred.:* 1970/ 1987 (NCA) *Calendar:* Sem. plan *Degrees:* A, certificates *Prof. Accred.:* Medical Assisting (AMA), Nursing (A), Physical Therapy Assisting, Respiratory Therapy, Veterinary Technology *CEO:* Pres. Albert L. Lorenzo
Enroll: 28,165   (313) 445-7000

MADONNA UNIVERSITY
36600 Schoolcraft Rd., Livonia 48150 *Type:* Private (Roman Catholic) liberal arts *Accred.:* 1959/1988 (NCA) *Calendar:* Sem. plan *Degrees:* A, B, M, certificates *Prof. Accred.:* Nursing (B,M), Social Work (B), Teacher Education (e,s) *CEO:* Pres. Mary Francilene, C.S.S.F.
Enroll: 4,419   (313) 591-5000

MARYGROVE COLLEGE
8425 W. McNichols Rd., Detroit 48221 *Type:* Private (Roman Catholic) liberal arts *Accred.:* 1926/1987 (NCA) *Calendar:* Sem. plan *Degrees:* A, B, M, diplomas *Prof. Accred.:* Radiography, Respiratory Therapy, Social Work (B), Teacher Education (e,s,p) *CEO:* Pres. John E. Shay, Jr.
Enroll: 1,112   (313) 862-8000

MICHIGAN CHRISTIAN COLLEGE
800 W. Avon Rd., Rochester Hills 48307 *Type:* Private (Church of Christ) *Accred.:* 1974/1989 (NCA) *Calendar:* Sem. plan *Degrees:* A, B, certificates *CEO:* Pres. Kenneth L. Johnson
Enroll: 319   (313) 651-5800

MICHIGAN STATE UNIVERSITY
East Lansing 48824 *Type:* Public (state) *System:* Michigan Department of Education *Accred.:* 1915/1986 (NCA) *Calendar:* Qtr. plan *Degrees:* B, P, M, D *Prof. Accred.:* Accounting (Type A,B), Audiology, Business (B,M), Clinical Psychology, Counseling Psychology, Engineering (agricultural, chemical, civil, electrical, materials, mechanical), Forestry (probational), Interior Design, Journalism (B,M), Landscape Architecture (B),

Medical Technology, Medicine, Music, Nursing (B,M), Osteopathy, Planning (B,M), Psychology Internship, Recreation and Leisure Services, Rehabilitation Counseling, School Psychology, Social Work (B,M), Speech-Language Pathology, Teacher Education (e,s,p), Theatre, Veterinary Medicine, Veterinary Technology *CEO:* Pres. M. Peter McPherson
Enroll: 40,047   (517) 355-1855

MICHIGAN TECHNOLOGICAL UNIVERSITY
1400 Townsend Dr., Houghton 49931 *Type:* Public (state) *System:* Michigan Department of Education *Accred.:* 1928/1988 (NCA) *Calendar:* Qtr. plan *Degrees:* A, B, M, D, certificates *Prof. Accred.:* Engineering Technology (civil/construction, electrical, electromechanical, mechanical drafting/design, surveying), Engineering (chemical, civil, electrical, environmental/sanitary, general, geological/geophysical, materials, mechanical, mineral, mining), Forestry *CEO:* Pres. Curtis J. Tompkins
Enroll: 6,961   (906) 487-1885

MID MICHIGAN COMMUNITY COLLEGE
1375 S. Clare Ave., Harrison 48625 *Type:* Public (district) junior *System:* Michigan Department of Education *Accred.:* 1974/1992 (NCA) *Calendar:* Sem. plan *Degrees:* A, certificates *Prof. Accred.:* Radiography *CEO:* Pres. Charles J. Corrigan, Ph.D.
Enroll: 2,315   (517) 386-6622

MONROE COUNTY COMMUNITY COLLEGE
1555 S. Raisinville Rd., Monroe 48161 *Type:* Public (district) junior *System:* Michigan Department of Education *Accred.:* 1972/1990 (NCA) *Calendar:* Sem. plan *Degrees:* A, certificates *Prof. Accred.:* Nursing (A), Respiratory Therapy, Respiratory Therapy Technology *CEO:* Pres. Gerald D. Welch
Enroll: 3,924   (313) 242-7300

MONTCALM COMMUNITY COLLEGE
2800 College Dr., S.W., Sidney 48885 *Type:* Public (district) junior *System:* Michigan Department of Education *Accred.:* 1974/1986 (NCA) *Calendar:* Sem. plan *Degrees:* A, certificates *CEO:* Pres. Donald C. Burns
Enroll: 2,018   (517) 328-2111

MUSKEGON COMMUNITY COLLEGE
221 S. Quarterline Rd., Muskegon 49442 *Type:* Public (district) junior *System:* Michigan Department of Education *Accred.:* 1929/1991 (NCA) *Calendar:* Sem. plan *Degrees:* A, certificates *Prof. Accred.:* Respiratory Therapy, Respiratory Therapy Technology *CEO:* Pres. James L. Stevenson
Enroll: 5,216   (616) 773-0643

NORTH CENTRAL MICHIGAN COLLEGE
1515 Howard St., Petoskey 49770 *Type:* Public (district) junior *System:* Michigan Department of Education *Accred.:* 1972/1985 (NCA) *Calendar:* Sem. plan *Degrees:* A, certificates *CEO:* Pres. Robert B. Graham
Enroll: 2,230   (616) 348-6600

NORTHERN MICHIGAN UNIVERSITY
Marquette 49855 *Type:* Public (state) *System:* Michigan Department of Education *Accred.:* 1916/1985 (NCA) *Calendar:* Sem. plan *Degrees:* A, B, P, M, certificates *Prof. Accred.:* Medical Laboratory Technology (AMA), Medical Technology, Music, Nursing (B,M), Social Work (B), Speech-Language Pathology, Teacher Education (e,s,p) *CEO:* Pres. William E. Vandament
Enroll: 8,741   (906) 227-2242

NORTHWESTERN MICHIGAN COLLEGE
1701 E. Front St., Traverse City 49684 *Type:* Public (district) junior *System:* Michigan Department of Education *Accred.:* 1961/1990 (NCA) *Calendar:* Qtr. plan *Degrees:* A, certificates *Prof. Accred.:* Dental Assisting *CEO:* Pres. Timothy G. Quinn
Enroll: 4,275   (616) 922-0650

NORTHWOOD UNIVERSITY
3225 Cook Rd., Midland 48640 *Type:* Private business *Accred.:* 1974/1986 (NCA) *Calendar:* Qtr. plan *Degrees:* A, B, M, certificates *CEO:* Pres. David E. Fry
Enroll: 7,668   (517) 837-4200

BRANCH CAMPUS
2600 N. Military Trail, West Palm Beach, FL 33409 *CEO:* Provost John H. Haynie
Enroll: 600   (407) 478-5510

BRANCH CAMPUS
1114 W. FM 1382, P.O. Box 58, Cedar Hill, TX 75104 *CEO:* Provost Donald B. Tallman
Enroll: 400   (214) 291-1541

OAKLAND COMMUNITY COLLEGE
2480 Opdyke Rd., Bloomfield Hills 48304-2266 *Type:* Public (district) junior *System:* Michigan Department of Education *Accred.:* 1971/1988 (NCA) *Calendar:* Tri. plan *Degrees:* A, certificates *Prof. Accred.:* Diagnostic Medical Sonography, Radiography, Respiratory Therapy *CEO:* Chanc. Patsy J. Fulton
Enroll: 29,363   (313) 540-1500

AUBURN HILLS CAMPUS
2900 Featherstone Rd., Auburn Hills 48326 *CEO:* Pres. Richard T. Saunders
                             (313) 360-3032

HIGHLAND LAKES CAMPUS
7350 Cooley Lake Rd., Waterford 48327-4187 *Prof. Accred.:* Dental Hygiene, Medical Assisting (AMA), Medical Laboratory Technology (AMA), Nursing (A) *CEO:* Pres. Preston Pulliam
                             (313) 540-1500

ORCHARD RIDGE CAMPUS
27055 Orchard Lake Rd., Farmington Hills 48334 *CEO:* Pres. George F. Keith
                             (313) 471-7500

SOUTHFIELD CAMPUS
22322 Rutland Dr., Southfield 48075 *CEO:* Dean Martha R. Smydra
                             (313) 552-2600

OAKLAND UNIVERSITY
Rochester 48309 *Type:* Public (state) liberal arts and professional *System:* Michigan Department of Education *Accred.:* 1966/1989 (NCA) *Calendar:* Tri. plan *Degrees:* B, P, M, D *Prof. Accred.:* Business (B,M), Computer Science, Engineering (computer, electrical, mechanical, systems), Nurse Anesthesia Education, Nursing (B,M), Physical Therapy, Public Administration, Teacher Education (e,s,p) *CEO:* Pres. Sandra Packard
Enroll: 13,068   (313) 370-2100

OLIVET COLLEGE
Olivet 49076 *Type:* Private (United Church of Christ) liberal arts *Accred.:* 1913/1987 (NCA) *Calendar:* Sem. plan *Degrees:* B *Prof. Accred.:* Music (associate) *CEO:* Pres. Michael S. Bassis
Enroll: 735   (616) 749-7641

REFORMED BIBLE COLLEGE
3333 E. Beltline Ave., N.E., Grand Rapids 49505 *Type:* Independent (Reformed) *Accred.:* 1964/1984 (AABC) *Calendar:* Sem. plan *Degrees:* A, B, certificates *CEO:* Pres. Edwin D. Roels
FTE Enroll: 162   (616) 363-2050

SACRED HEART MAJOR SEMINARY
2701 Chicago Blvd., Detroit 48206 *Type:* Private (Roman Catholic) *Accred.:* 1991 (ATS); 1960/1984 (NCA) *Calendar:* Tri. plan *Degrees:* A, B, M *CEO:* Rector/Pres. John C. Nienstedt
Enroll: 309   (313) 883-8500

SAGINAW VALLEY STATE UNIVERSITY
7400 Bay Rd., University Center 48710 *Type:* Public (state) liberal arts *System:* Michigan Department of Education *Accred.:* 1970/1987 (NCA) *Calendar:* Tri. plan *Degrees:* B, M *Prof. Accred.:* Engineering (electrical, mechanical), Nursing (B,M), Social Work (B), Teacher Education (e,s,p) *CEO:* Pres. Eric R. Gilbertson
Enroll: 6,869   (517) 790-4000

ST. CLAIR COUNTY COMMUNITY COLLEGE
323 Erie St., P.O. Box 5015, Port Huron 48061-5015 *Type:* Public (district) junior *System:* Michigan Department of Education *Accred.:* 1930/1987 (NCA) *Calendar:* Sem. plan *Degrees:* A, certificates *CEO:* Pres. R. Ernest Dear
Enroll: 4,959   (313) 984-3881

ST. MARY'S COLLEGE
3535 Indian Tr., Orchard Lake 48324 *Type:* Private (Roman Catholic) liberal arts *Accred.:* 1976/1993 (NCA) *Calendar:* Sem. plan *Degrees:* A, B, certificates *CEO:* Pres. Edward D. Meyer
Enroll: 407   (313) 683-0504

SCHOOLCRAFT COLLEGE
18600 Haggerty Rd., Livonia 48152 *Type:* Public (district) junior *System:* Michigan Department of Education *Accred.:* 1968/1991 (NCA) *Calendar:* Sem. plan *Degrees:* A, certificates *Prof. Accred.:* Medical Record Technology, Occupational Therapy Assisting *CEO:* Pres. Richard W. McDowell
Enroll: 10,057   (313) 462-4400

SIENA HEIGHTS COLLEGE
1247 E. Siena Heights Dr., Adrian 49221
Type: Private (Roman Catholic) liberal arts
Accred.: 1940/1992 (NCA) *Calendar:* Sem.
plan *Degrees:* A, B, M, certificates *Prof. Accred.:* Art *CEO:* Pres. Cathleen Real
Enroll: 1,745   (517) 263-0731

SOUTHWESTERN MICHIGAN COLLEGE
58900 Cherry Grove Rd., Dowagiac 49047-9793 *Type:* Public (state) junior *System:*
Michigan Department of Education *Accred.:*
1971/1991 (NCA) *Calendar:* 4-1-4 plan *Degrees:* A, certificates *CEO:* Pres. David C.
Briegel
Enroll: 2,873   (616) 782-5113

SPRING ARBOR COLLEGE
Spring Arbor 49283 *Type:* Private (Free
Methodist) liberal arts *Accred.:* 1960/1987
(NCA) *Calendar:* Sem. plan *Degrees:* A, B
Prof. Accred.: Social Work (B-candidate),
Teacher Education (e,s) *CEO:* Pres. Allen
Carden
Enroll: 1,971   (517) 750-1200

SUOMI COLLEGE
601 Quincy St., Hancock 49930 *Type:* Private (Lutheran) junior *Accred.:* 1969/1989
(NCA) *Calendar:* Sem. plan *Degrees:* A,
certificates *CEO:* Pres. Robert A. Ubbelohde
Enroll: 582   (906) 482-5300

THOMAS M. COOLEY LAW SCHOOL
217 S. Capitol Ave., P.O. Box 13038, Lansing 48901-3038 *Type:* Private professional
Calendar: Sem. plan *Degrees:* P *Prof. Accred.:* Law (ABA only) *CEO:* Pres. Thomas
E. Brennan
Enroll: 1,536   (517) 371-5140

UNIVERSITY OF DETROIT MERCY
4001 W. McNichols Rd., P.O. Box 19900,
Detroit 48219 *Type:* Private (Roman
Catholic) liberal arts *Accred.:* 1931/1993
(NCA) *Calendar:* Sem. plan *Degrees:* A, B,
P, M, D, certificates *Prof. Accred.:* Business
(B,M), Clinical Psychology, Dental Hygiene,
Dentistry, Endodontics, Engineering (chemical, civil, electrical, mechanical), General
Practice Residency, Law, Medical Record
Administration, Medical Record Technology, Nurse Anesthesia Education, Orthodon-
tics, Physician Assisting, Social Work (B)
CEO: Pres. Maureen A. Fay, O.P.
Enroll: 5,426   (313) 927-1455

UNIVERSITY OF MICHIGAN
Ann Arbor 48109 *Type:* Public (state) *System:* University of Michigan System *Accred.:* 1913/1990 (NCA) *Calendar:* Tri. plan
Degrees: B, P, M, D, certificates *Prof. Accred.:* Art, Business (B,M), Clinical Psychology, Combined Prosthodontics, Dental Hygiene, Dentistry, Dietetics (internship), Endodontics, Engineering Technology (industrial hygiene), Engineering (aerospace,
chemical, civil, computer, electrical, industrial, materials, mechanical, naval architecture/marine, nuclear), Forestry, General Dentistry (prelim. provisional), General Practice
Residency, Health Services Administration,
Landscape Architecture (M), Law, Librarianship, Medical Illustration, Medicine,
Music, Nursing (B,M), Oral and Maxillofacial Surgery, Orthodontics, Pediatric Dentistry, Periodontics, Planning (M), Psychology Internship, Public Health, Radiation Therapy Technology, Social Work (M) *CEO:*
Pres. James J. Duderstadt
Enroll: 36,626   (313) 764-1817

UNIVERSITY OF MICHIGAN—DEARBORN
4901 Evergreen Rd., Dearborn 48128 *Type:*
Public (state) *System:* University of Michigan System *Accred.:* 1970/1984 (NCA) *Calendar:* Tri. plan *Degrees:* B, M *Prof. Accred.:* Engineering (electrical, industrial, mechanical) *CEO:* Chanc. James C. Renick
Enroll: 8,194   (313) 593-5000

UNIVERSITY OF MICHIGAN—FLINT
Flint 48502 *Type:* Public (state) *System:*
University of Michigan System *Accred.:*
1970/1990 (NCA) *Calendar:* Sem. plan *Degrees:* B, M, certificates *Prof. Accred.:* Business (B,M), Music, Nurse Anesthesia Education, Nursing (B), Physical Therapy, Teacher
Education (e,s) *CEO:* Chanc. James Renick
Enroll: 6,652   (313) 762-3000

WALSH COLLEGE OF ACCOUNTANCY AND
BUSINESS ADMINISTRATION
3838 Livernois Rd., P.O. Box 7006, Troy
48007-7006 *Type:* Private professional *Accred.:* 1975/1992 (NCA) *Calendar:* Sem.

plan *Degrees:* B, M *CEO:* Pres. David A. Spencer
Enroll: 3,578   (313) 689-8282

WASHTENAW COMMUNITY COLLEGE
4800 E. Huron River Dr., P.O. Box D-1, Ann Arbor 48106 *Type:* Public (district) junior *System:* Michigan Department of Education *Accred.:* 1973/1990 (NCA) *Calendar:* Sem. plan *Degrees:* A, certificates *Prof. Accred.:* Dental Assisting, Radiography, Respiratory Therapy *CEO:* Pres. Gunder A. Myran
Enroll: 10,944   (313) 973-3300

WAYNE COUNTY COMMUNITY COLLEGE
801 W. Fort St., Detroit 48226-3010 *Type:* Public (district) junior *System:* Michigan Department of Education *Accred.:* 1976/1993 (NCA) *Calendar:* Sem. plan *Degrees:* A, certificates *Prof. Accred.:* Dental Assisting, Dental Hygiene, Occupational Therapy Assisting, Veterinary Technology *CEO:* Pres. Rafael L. Cortada
Enroll: 9,577   (313) 496-2510

WAYNE STATE UNIVERSITY
Detroit 48202 *Type:* Public (state) *System:* Michigan Department of Education *Accred.:* 1915/1987 (NCA) *Calendar:* Sem. plan *Degrees:* B, P, M, D, certificates *Prof. Accred.:* Audiology, Business (B,M), Clinical Psychology, Cytotechnology, Dietetics (coordinated), Engineering (chemical, civil, electrical, industrial, materials, mechanical), Law, Librarianship, Medical Technology, Medicine, Mortuary Science, Music, Nurse Anesthesia Education, Nursing (B,M), Occupational Therapy, Physical Therapy, Psychology Internship, Public Administration, Radiation Therapy Technology, Social Work (B,M), Speech-Language Pathology, Teacher Education (e,s,p), Theatre *CEO:* Pres. David W. Adamany
Enroll: 34,945   (313) 577-2424

WEST SHORE COMMUNITY COLLEGE
3000 N. Stiles Rd., P.O. Box 277, Scottville 49454 *Type:* Public (district) junior *System:* Michigan Department of Education *Accred.:* 1974/1986 (NCA) *Calendar:* Sem. plan *Degrees:* A, certificates *CEO:* Pres. William M. Anderson
Enroll: 1,430   (616) 845-6211

WESTERN MICHIGAN UNIVERSITY
Kalamazoo 49008 *Type:* Public (state) *System:* Michigan Department of Education *Accred.:* 1915/1991 (NCA) *Calendar:* Tri. plan *Degrees:* B, P, M, D *Prof. Accred.:* Art, Audiology, Business (B,M), Clinical Psychology (provisional), Computer Science, Counseling, Counseling Psychology, Dance, Engineering Technology (manufacturing), Engineering (computer, electrical, industrial, mechanical), Music, Occupational Therapy, Physician Assisting, Social Work (B,M), Speech-Language Pathology, Teacher Education (e,s,p), Theatre *CEO:* Pres. Diether H. Haenicke
Enroll: 27,399   (616) 387-1000

WESTERN THEOLOGICAL SEMINARY
85 E. 13th St., Holland 49423 *Type:* Private (Reformed Church) graduate only *Accred.:* 1940/1992 (ATS) *Calendar:* Sem. plan *Degrees:* M, D *CEO:* Pres. Marvin D. Hoff
FTE Enroll: 114   (616) 392-8555

WILLIAM TYNDALE COLLEGE
35700 W. Twelve Mile Rd., Farmington Hills 48331 *Type:* Private *Accred.:* 1988/1993 (NCA) *Calendar:* Sem. plan *Degrees:* A, B, certificates *CEO:* Pres. James Clark McHann, Jr.
Enroll: 471   (313) 553-7200

YESHIVA BETH YEHUDA-YESHIVA GEDOLAH OF GREATER DETROIT
24600 Greenfield St., Oak Park 48237 *Type:* Private professional *Accred.:* 1986/1991 (AARTS) *Calendar:* Sem. plan *Degrees:* B, P, M, D *CEO:* Pres. Saul Weingarden
Enroll: 39   (313) 968-3360

MINNESOTA

ALEXANDRIA TECHNICAL COLLEGE
1601 Jefferson St., Alexandria 56308 *Type:*
Public (state) 2-year *Accred.:* 1980/1984
(NCA) *Calendar:* Qtr. plan *Degrees:* A, cer-
tificates, diplomas *Prof. Accred.:* Interior
Design, Medical Laboratory Technology
(AMA) *CEO:* Pres. Frank Starke
Enroll: 1,749   (612) 762-0221

ALFRED ADLER INSTITUTE OF MINNESOTA
1001 Hwy. 7, Ste. 344, Hopkins 55343 *Type:*
Private professional; graduate only *Accred.:*
1991 (NCA) *Calendar:* Qtr. plan *Degrees:* M,
diplomas *CEO:* Pres. Laurentius A. Hedberg
Enroll: 128   (612) 933-9363

ANOKA-RAMSEY COMMUNITY COLLEGE
11200 Mississippi Blvd., Coon Rapids
55433 *Type:* Public (state) junior *System:*
Minnesota Community College System *Accred.:* 1975/1987 (NCA) *Calendar:* Qtr. plan
Degrees: A, certificates *Prof. Accred.:* Nursing (A) *CEO:* Pres. Patrick M. Johns
Enroll: 6,250   (612) 422-3435

ANOKA TECHNICAL COLLEGE
1355 W. Hwy. 10, Anoka 55303 *Type:* Pri-
vate *Calendar:* Courses of varying lengths
Degrees: A, certificates, diplomas *Prof. Ac-
cred.:* Electroneurodiagnostic Technology,
Medical Assisting (AMA), Medical Record
Technology, Occupational Therapy Assist-
ing, Physical Therapy Assisting, Practical
Nursing, Surgical Technology *CEO:* Pres. G.
David Sayre
                              (612) 427-1880

AUGSBURG COLLEGE
731 21st Ave. S., Minneapolis 55454 *Type:*
Private (Lutheran) liberal arts *Accred.:* 1954/
1987 (NCA) *Calendar:* 4-1-4 plan *Degrees:*
B, M *Prof. Accred.:* Music, Nursing (B), Social Work (B,M-candidate), Teacher Education (e,s) *CEO:* Pres. Charles S. Anderson
Enroll: 2,924   (612) 330-1000

AUSTIN COMMUNITY COLLEGE
1600 8th Ave., N.W., Austin 55912 *Type:*
Public (state) junior *System:* Minnesota
Community College System *Accred.:* 1971/
1985 (NCA) *Calendar:* Qtr. plan *Degrees:* A
Prof. Accred.: Nursing (A), Occupational

Therapy Assisting *CEO:* Pres. Vicky R.
Smith
Enroll: 1,364   (507) 433-0508

BEMIDJI STATE UNIVERSITY
1500 Birchmont Dr., N.E., Bemidji 56601-
2699 *Type:* Public (state) liberal arts and
teachers *System:* Minnesota State University
System *Accred.:* 1943/1990 (NCA) *Calendar:* Qtr. plan *Degrees:* A, B, M *Prof. Accred.:* Music (associate), Nursing (B), Social
Work (B), Teacher Education (e,s,p) *CEO:*
Interim Pres. Linda L. Baer
Enroll: 5,260   (218) 755-2000

BETHANY LUTHERAN COLLEGE
734 Marsh St., Mankato 56001 *Type:* Private
(Lutheran) junior *Accred.:* 1974/1989 (NCA)
Calendar: Sem. plan *Degrees:* A *CEO:* Pres.
Marvin G. Meyer
Enroll: 317   (507) 625-2977

BETHEL COLLEGE
3900 Bethel Dr., St. Paul 55112 *Type:* Pri-
vate (Baptist) liberal arts *Accred.:* 1959/1990
(NCA) *Calendar:* Sem. plan *Degrees:* A, B,
M *Prof. Accred.:* Nursing (B), Social Work
(B), Teacher Education (e,s) *CEO:* Pres.
George K. Brushaber
Enroll: 1,963   (612) 638-6400

BETHEL THEOLOGICAL SEMINARY
3949 Bethel Dr., St. Paul 55112 *Type:* Private (Baptist) graduate only *Accred.:* 1966/
1991 (ATS); 1976/1991 (NCA) *Calendar:*
Qtr. plan *Degrees:* M, D *CEO:* Exec. Vice
Pres. and Dean Fred W. Prinzing
Enroll: 478   (612) 638-6180

WEST CAMPUS
6116 Arosa St., San Diego, CA 92115
CEO: Assoc. Dean Clifford V. Anderson
                              (619) 582-8118

BRAINERD COMMUNITY COLLEGE
501 W. College Dr., Brainerd 56401 *Type:*
Public (state) junior *System:* Minnesota
Community College System *Accred.:* 1977/
1993 (NCA) *Calendar:* Qtr. plan *Degrees:* A
CEO: Pres. Sally Jane Ihne
Enroll: 1,806   (218) 828-2525

CARLETON COLLEGE
One N. College St., Northfield 55057 *Type:* Private liberal arts *Accred.:* 1913/1989 (NCA) *Calendar:* 3-3 plan *Degrees:* B *CEO:* Pres. Stephen R. Lewis, Jr.
Enroll: 1,829   (507) 663-4000

COLLEGE OF ASSOCIATED ARTS
344 Summit Ave., St. Paul 55102-2199 *Type:* Private *Accred.:* 1978/1988 (ACC-SCT) *Calendar:* Sem. plan *Degrees:* B, certificates *CEO:* Pres. Chris R. Kabella
                                   (612) 224-3416

COLLEGE OF ST. BENEDICT
37 S. College Ave., St. Joseph 56374 *Type:* Private (Roman Catholic) liberal arts for women *Accred.:* 1933/1989 (NCA) *Calendar:* 4-1-4 plan *Degrees:* B *Prof. Accred.:* Dietetics (coordinated), Music (associate), Nursing (B), Social Work (B), Teacher Education (e,s) *CEO:* Pres. Colman O'Connell
Enroll: 1,996   (612) 363-5011

COLLEGE OF ST. CATHERINE
2004 Randolph Ave., St. Paul 55105 *Type:* Private (Roman Catholic) liberal arts for women *Accred.:* 1916/1993 (NCA) *Calendar:* 4-1-4 plan *Degrees:* A, B, M, certificates *Prof. Accred.:* Medical Record Technology, Music, Nursing (B), Occupational Therapy, Respiratory Therapy, Social Work (B,M), Teacher Education (e,s) *CEO:* Pres. Anita M. Pampusch, Ph.D.
Enroll: 2,638   (612) 690-6000

ST. MARY'S CAMPUS
2500 S. Sixth St., Minneapolis 55454-1494 *Prof. Accred.:* Nursing (A), Occupational Therapy Assisting, Physical Therapy Assisting *CEO:* Pres. Anita M. Pampusch, Ph.D.
                                   (612) 690-7702

COLLEGE OF ST. SCHOLASTICA
1200 Kenwood Ave., Duluth 55811 *Type:* Private (Roman Catholic) liberal arts *Accred.:* 1931/1993 (NCA) *Calendar:* Qtr. plan *Degrees:* B, M, certificates *Prof. Accred.:* Medical Record Administration, Medical Technology, Nursing (B,M), Physical Therapy, Social Work (B) *CEO:* Pres. Daniel H. Pilon
Enroll: 1,988   (218) 723-6033

CONCORDIA COLLEGE
901 S. 8th St., Moorhead 56562 *Type:* Private (Lutheran) liberal arts *Accred.:* 1959/1984 (NCA) *Calendar:* Tri. plan *Degrees:* B *Prof. Accred.:* Music, Social Work (B), Teacher Education (e,s,p) *CEO:* Pres. Paul J. Dovre
Enroll: 2,942   (218) 299-4000

CONCORDIA COLLEGE
275 N. Syndicate St., St. Paul 55104 *Type:* Private (Lutheran-Missouri Synod) liberal arts and teachers *Accred.:* 1959/1988 (NCA) *Calendar:* Qtr. plan *Degrees:* A, B, M *Prof. Accred.:* Teacher Education (e,s) *CEO:* Pres. Robert A. Holst
Enroll: 1,272   (612) 641-8278

CROWN COLLEGE
6425 County Rd. 30, St. Bonifacius 55375 *Type:* Private (Christian and Missionary Alliance) *Accred.:* 1950/1991 (AABC); 1980/1992 (NCA) *Calendar:* Sem. plan *Degrees:* A,B, certificates *CEO:* Pres. Bill W. Lanpher
Enroll: 501   (612) 446-4100

DAKOTA COUNTY TECHNICAL COLLEGE
1300 145th St. E., Rosemount 55068 *Type:* Private professional *Calendar:* Courses of varying lengths *Degrees:* A, P *Prof. Accred.:* Interior Design, Practical Nursing *CEO:* Dir. Karen Doyle
                                   (612) 423-8414

DR. MARTIN LUTHER COLLEGE
1884 College Heights, New Ulm 56073 *Type:* Private (Evangelical Lutheran Synod) *Accred.:* 1980/1992 (NCA) *Calendar:* Sem. plan *Degrees:* B *CEO:* Pres. John C. Lawrenz
Enroll: 568   (507) 354-8221

DULUTH TECHNICAL COLLEGE
2101 Trinity Rd., Duluth 55811-3399 *Type:* Private *Calendar:* Courses of varying lengths *Degrees:* A *Prof. Accred.:* Medical Laboratory Technology (AMA), Occupational Therapy Assisting, Physical Therapy Assisting *CEO:* Pres. Harold Erickson, Ph.D.
                                   (218) 722-2801

EAST GRAND FORKS TECHNICAL COLLEGE
Hwy. 220 N., P.O. Box 111, East Grand Forks 56721 *Type:* Private *Calendar:* Courses of varying lengths *Degrees:* A, certificates, diplomas *Prof. Accred.:* Medical As-

sisting (AMA), Medical Laboratory Technology (AMA), Radiography, Respiratory Therapy, Respiratory Therapy Technology, Surgical Technology *CEO:* Pres. Gerald Folstrom

(218) 773-3441

HUTCHINSON-WILLMAR REGIONAL TECHNICAL COLLEGE
P.O. Box 1097, Willmar 56201 *Type:* Public (state) 2-year *Accred.:* 1976/1992 (NCA) *Calendar:* Tri. plan *Degrees:* A, certificates, diplomas *Prof. Accred.:* Medical Assisting (AMA), Practical Nursing *CEO:* Pres. Ronald A. Erpelding
Enroll: 2,660   (612) 235-5114

FERGUS FALLS COMMUNITY COLLEGE
1414 College Way, Fergus Falls 56537 *Type:* Public (state) junior *System:* Minnesota Community College System *Accred.:* 1972/1993 (NCA) *Calendar:* Qtr. plan *Degrees:* A, certificates *Prof. Accred.:* Histologic Technology, Medical Laboratory Technology (AMA) *CEO:* Pres. Daniel F. True
Enroll: 1,421   (218) 739-7500

INVER HILLS COMMUNITY COLLEGE
8445 College Tr., Inver Grove Heights 55076 *Type:* Public (state) junior *System:* Minnesota Community College System *Accred.:* 1976/1988 (NCA) *Calendar:* Qtr. plan *Degrees:* A, certificates *Prof. Accred.:* Nursing (A) *CEO:* Pres. Steven R. Wallace
Enroll: 5,352   (612) 450-8500

GLOBE COLLEGE OF BUSINESS
Ste. 201, Box 60, 175 Fifth St. E., St. Paul 55101-2901 *Type:* Private business *Accred.:* 1953/1990 (ACISC) *Calendar:* Qtr. plan *Degrees:* A *CEO:* Pres. Terry L. Myhre
(612) 224-4378

ITASCA COMMUNITY COLLEGE
1851 E. Hwy. 169, Grand Rapids 55744 *Type:* Public (state) junior *System:* Arrowhead Community College Region *Accred.:* 1982/1989 (NCA)* *Calendar:* Qtr. plan *Degrees:* A, certificates *CEO:* Pres. Lawrence Dukes

(218) 327-4461

GUSTAVUS ADOLPHUS COLLEGE
800 W. College Ave., St. Peter 56082 *Type:* Private (Lutheran) liberal arts *Accred.:* 1915/1993 (NCA) *Calendar:* 4-1-4 plan *Degrees:* B *Prof. Accred.:* Music, Nursing (B), Teacher Education (e,s) *CEO:* Pres. Axel D. Steuer
Enroll: 2,278   (507) 933-8000

* Indirect accreditation through Arrowhead Community College Region.

LAKEWOOD COMMUNITY COLLEGE
3401 Century Ave., White Bear Lake 55110 *Type:* Public (state) junior *System:* Minnesota Community College System *Accred.:* 1974/1986 (NCA) *Calendar:* Qtr. plan *Degrees:* A *Prof. Accred.:* Nursing (A), Radiography *CEO:* Pres. James Meznek
Enroll: 6,414   (612) 779-3200

HAMLINE UNIVERSITY
1536 Hewitt Ave., St. Paul 55104 *Type:* Private (United Methodist) liberal arts *Accred.:* 1914/1988 (NCA) *Calendar:* 4-1-4 plan *Degrees:* B, M, D *Prof. Accred.:* Law, Music, Teacher Education (e,s) *CEO:* Pres. Larry G. Osnes
Enroll: 2,465   (612) 641-2800

LOWTHIAN COLLEGE
825 2nd Ave., S., Minneapolis 55402 *Type:* Private business *Accred.:* 1971/1989 (ACISC) *Calendar:* Courses of varying lengths *Degrees:* A *CEO:* Pres. Petrena Lowthian

(612) 332-3361

HIBBING COMMUNITY COLLEGE
1515 E. 25th St., Hibbing 55746 *Type:* Public (state) junior *System:* Arrowhead Community College Region *Accred.:* 1982/1989 (NCA)* *Calendar:* Qtr. plan *Degrees:* A, certificates *Prof. Accred.:* Radiography *CEO:* Pres. Anthony J. Kuznik
(218) 262-6700

LUTHER NORTHWESTERN THEOLOGICAL SEMINARY
2481 Como Ave., St. Paul 55108 *Type:* Private (Evangelical Lutheran) graduate only *Accred.:* 1991 (ATS); 1979/1984 (NCA)

* Indirect accreditation through Arrowhead Community College Region.

Calendar: Sem. plan *Degrees:* M, D *CEO:* Pres. David L. Tiede
Enroll: 783   (612) 641-3456

MACALESTER COLLEGE
1600 Grand Ave., St. Paul 55105 *Type:* Private (United Presbyterian) liberal arts *Accred.:* 1913/1986 (NCA) *Calendar:* 4-1-4 plan *Degrees:* B *Prof. Accred.:* Teacher Education (e,s) *CEO:* Pres. Robert M. Gavin, Jr.
Enroll: 1,838   (612) 696-6000

MANKATO STATE UNIVERSITY
Mankato 56002-8400 *Type:* Public (state) liberal arts and professional *System:* Minnesota State University System *Accred.:* 1916/1986 (NCA) *Calendar:* Qtr. plan *Degrees:* A, B, P, M, certificates *Prof. Accred.:* Art, Counseling, Dental Hygiene, Engineering Technology (electrical, manufacturing), Engineering (electrical), Music, Nursing (B), Recreation and Leisure Services, Rehabilitation Counseling, Social Work (B), Speech-Language Pathology, Teacher Education (e,s,p) *CEO:* Pres. Richard R. Rush
Enroll: 15,223   (507) 389-1111

MAYO GRADUATE SCHOOL
200 First St., S.W., Rochester 55905 *Type:* Private professional *Accred.:* 1984/1989 (NCA) *Calendar:* Sem. plan *Degrees:* M, D, certificates *Prof. Accred.:* Combined Maxillofacial Prosthodontics, Cytotechnology, Diagnostic Medical Sonography, Medical Laboratory Technology (AMA), Medicine, Nuclear Medicine Technology, Nurse Anesthesia Education, Oral and Maxillofacial Surgery (conditional), Orthodontics, Periodontics, Physical Therapy, Radiation Therapy Technology, Radiography *CEO:* C.E.O. Robert R. Waller
Enroll: 1,728   (507) 284-2511

MESABI COMMUNITY COLLEGE
905 W. Chestnut St., Virginia 55792 *Type:* Public (state) junior *System:* Arrowhead Community College Region *Accred.:* 1982/1989 (NCA)* *Calendar:* Qtr. plan *Degrees:* A, certificates *CEO:* Pres. Richard N. Kohlhase
                    (800) 657-3860

* Indirect accreditation through Arrowhead Community College Region.

METROPOLITAN STATE UNIVERSITY
700 E. 7th St., St. Paul 55106-5000 *Type:* Public (state) liberal arts *System:* Minnesota State University System *Accred.:* 1975/1985 (NCA) *Calendar:* Qtr. plan *Degrees:* B, M *Prof. Accred.:* Nursing (B) *CEO:* Pres. Susan A. Cole
Enroll: 5,390   (612) 772-7777

MINNEAPOLIS COLLEGE OF ART AND DESIGN
2501 Stevens Ave. S., Minneapolis 55404 *Type:* Private professional *Accred.:* 1960/1987 (NCA) *Calendar:* Sem. plan *Degrees:* B, M *Prof. Accred.:* Art *CEO:* Pres. John S. Slorp
Enroll: 585   (612) 874-3700

MINNEAPOLIS COMMUNITY COLLEGE
1501 Hennepin Ave., Minneapolis 55403 *Type:* Public (state) junior *System:* Minnesota Community College System *Accred.:* 1977/1993 (NCA) *Calendar:* Qtr. plan *Degrees:* A, certificates *Prof. Accred.:* Nursing (A) *CEO:* Pres. Jacquelyn M. Belcher
Enroll: 4,310   (612) 341-7000

MINNESOTA BIBLE COLLEGE
920 Mayowood Rd, S.W., Rochester 55902 *Type:* Private (Christian Churches/Churches of Christ) *Accred.:* 1948/1983 (AABC) *Calendar:* Qtr. plan *Degrees:* A, B *CEO:* Pres. Donald R. Lloyd
FTE Enroll: 107   (507) 288-4563

MOORHEAD STATE UNIVERSITY
1104 7th Ave. S., Moorhead 56563 *Type:* Public (state) liberal arts and teachers *System:* Minnesota State University System *Accred.:* 1916/1987 (NCA) *Calendar:* Qtr. plan *Degrees:* A, B, P, M *Prof. Accred.:* Art, Music, Nursing (B), Social Work (B), Speech-Language Pathology, Teacher Education (e,s,p) *CEO:* Pres. Roland Dille
Enroll: 8,308   (218) 236-2011

NORMANDALE COMMUNITY COLLEGE
9700 France Ave. S., Bloomington 55431 *Type:* Public (state) junior *System:* Minnesota Community College System *Accred.:* 1973/1991 (NCA) *Calendar:* Qtr. plan *Degrees:* A, certificates *Prof. Accred.:* Dental Assisting, Dental Hygiene, Nursing (A) *CEO:* Pres. Thomas J. Horak
Enroll: 9,221   (612) 832-6000

NORTH CENTRAL BIBLE COLLEGE
910 Elliot Ave. S., Minneapolis 55404 *Type:*
Private (Assemblies of God) *Accred.:* 1986/
1991 (NCA) *Calendar:* Sem. plan *Degrees:*
A, B, certificates *CEO:* Pres. Don H. Argue
Enroll: 1,042   (612) 332-3491

NORTH HENNEPIN COMMUNITY COLLEGE
7411 85th Ave. N., Brooklyn Park 55445
Type: Public (state) junior *System:* Minnesota
Community College System *Accred.:* 1972/
1986 (NCA) *Calendar:* Qtr. plan *Degrees:*
A, certificates *Prof. Accred.:* Nursing (A)
CEO: Pres. Frederick W. Capshaw
Enroll: 6,178   (612) 424-0820

NORTHEAST METRO TECHNICAL COLLEGE
3300 Century Ave. N., White Bear Lake
55110 *Type:* Public (local) 2-year *Accred.:*
1993 (NCA candidate) *Calendar:* Qtr. plan
Degrees: A, certificates, diplomas *Prof. Ac-
cred.:* Dental Assisting, Dental Laboratory
Technology (conditional), EMT-Paramedic,
Medical Assisting (AMA) *CEO:* Pres. Bill
Warner
Enroll: 2,155   (612) 770-2351

NORTHLAND COMMUNITY COLLEGE
Hwy. 1 E., Thief River Falls 56701 *Type:*
Public (state) junior *System:* Minnesota
Community College System *Accred.:* 1976/
1986 (NCA) *Calendar:* Qtr. plan *Degrees:* A
CEO: Provost James Haviland
Enroll: 862   (218) 681-2181

NORTHWEST TECHNICAL COLLEGE—MOORHEAD
1900 28th Ave. S., Moorhead 56560 *Type:*
Private *Calendar:* Courses of varying
lengths *Degrees:* A, certificates, diplomas
Prof. Accred.: Dental Assisting, Medical
Record Technology *CEO:* Dir. Nate Johnson
(218) 236-6277

NORTHWEST TECHNICAL INSTITUTE
11995 Singletree La., Eden Prairie 55344-
5351 *Type:* Private *Accred.:* 1972/1988
(ACCSCT) *Calendar:* Sem. plan *Degrees:* A
CEO: Pres. Norris J. Nelson
(612) 944-0080

NORTHWESTERN COLLEGE
3003 N. Snelling Ave., St. Paul 55113 *Type:*
Private liberal arts *Accred.:* 1978/1989
(NCA) *Calendar:* Qtr. plan *Degrees:* A, B,

certificates *Prof. Accred.:* Music *CEO:* Pres.
Donald O. Ericksen
Enroll: 1,340   (612) 631-5100

NORTHWESTERN COLLEGE OF CHIROPRACTIC
2501 W. 84th St., Bloomington 55431-1599
Type: Private professional *Accred.:* 1988/
1993 (NCA) *Calendar:* Tri. plan *Degrees:*
B, D *Prof. Accred.:* Chiropractic Education
CEO: Pres. John F. Allenburg
Enroll: 538   (612) 888-4777

OAK HILLS BIBLE COLLEGE
1600 Oak Hills Rd., S.W., Bemidji 56601
Type: Independent (interdenominational) *Ac-
cred.:* 1990 (AABC) *Calendar:* Qtr. plan
Degrees: A, B, certificates *CEO:* Pres. Mark
Hovestol
FTE Enroll: 126   (218) 751-8670

RAINY RIVER COMMUNITY COLLEGE
Hwy. 11-71 and 15th St., International Falls
56649 *Type:* Public (state) junior *System:*
Arrowhead Community College Region *Accred.:* 1982/1989 (NCA)* *Calendar:* Qtr.
plan *Degrees:* A, certificates *CEO:* Pres.
Allen Rasmussen
(218) 285-7722

* Indirect accreditation through Arrowhead
  Community College Region.

RANGE TECHNICAL COLLEGE
2900 E. Beltline, Hibbing 55746 *Type:* Private *Calendar:* Courses of varying lengths
Degrees: A *Prof. Accred.:* Dental Assisting,
Medical Laboratory Technology (AMA)
CEO: Dir. Gerald Stuhr
(218) 262-6688

RASMUSSEN BUSINESS COLLEGE
3500 Federal Dr., Eagan 55122 *Type:* Private business *Accred.:* 1953/1990 (ACISC)
Calendar: Courses of varying lengths *Degrees:* A, certificates, diplomas *CEO:* Dir.
Kristi Waite
(612) 687-9000

RASMUSSEN BUSINESS COLLEGE
Good Counsel Dr., Mankato 56001 *Type:*
Private business *Accred.:* 1973/1986
(ACISC) *Calendar:* Courses of varying
lengths *Degrees:* A, certificates, diplomas
CEO: Dir. Douglas Gardner
(507) 625-6556

RASMUSSEN BUSINESS COLLEGE
Ste. 315, 12450 Wayzata Blvd., Minnetonka 55305-9845 *Type:* Private business *Accred.:* 1973/1990 (ACISC) *Calendar:* Courses of varying lengths *Degrees:* A, certificates, diplomas *CEO:* Dir. Anne Scharff
(612) 545-2000

ROCHESTER COMMUNITY COLLEGE
851 30th Ave., S.E., Rochester 55904-4999 *Type:* Public (state) junior *System:* Minnesota Community College System *Accred.:* 1923/1991 (NCA) *Calendar:* Qtr. plan *Degrees:* A, certificates *Prof. Accred.:* Dental Assisting, Dental Hygiene, Engineering Technology (civil/construction, electrical), Medical Assisting (AMA), Nursing (A), Respiratory Therapy *CEO:* Pres. Karen E. Nagle
Enroll: 4,001   (507) 285-7210

ST. CLOUD STATE UNIVERSITY
740 Fourth Ave. S., St. Cloud 56301-4498 *Type:* Public (state) liberal arts and professional *System:* Minnesota State University System *Accred.:* 1915/1987 (NCA) *Calendar:* Qtr. plan *Degrees:* A, B, P, M *Prof. Accred.:* Art, Business (B,M), Computer Science, Engineering Technology (manufacturing), Engineering (electrical), Journalism (B,M), Music, Rehabilitation Counseling, Social Work (B), Speech-Language Pathology, Teacher Education (e,s,p) *CEO:* Pres. Robert Bess
Enroll: 16,047   (612) 255-0121

ST. CLOUD TECHNICAL COLLEGE
1540 Northway Dr., St. Cloud 56303 *Type:* Public (state) 2-year *Accred.:* 1985/1990 (NCA) *Calendar:* Qtr. plan *Degrees:* A, certificates, diplomas *Prof. Accred.:* Dental Assisting, Practical Nursing, Surgical Technology *CEO:* Pres. Larry Barnhardt
Enroll: 3,116   (612) 252-0101

ST. JOHN'S UNIVERSITY
Collegeville 56321 *Type:* Private (Roman Catholic) liberal arts and seminary for men *Accred.:* 1969/1988 (ATS); 1950/1989 (NCA) *Calendar:* 4-1-4 plan *Degrees:* B, M *Prof. Accred.:* Nursing (B), Social Work (B) *CEO:* Pres. Dietrich Reinhart, O.S.B.
Enroll: 1,812   (612) 363-2100

ST. MARY'S COLLEGE OF MINNESOTA
700 Terrace Heights, Winona 55987-1399 *Type:* Private (Roman Catholic) liberal arts *Accred.:* 1934/1987 (NCA) *Calendar:* Sem. plan *Degrees:* B, M *Prof. Accred.:* Nuclear Medicine Technology, Nurse Anesthesia Education *CEO:* Pres. Louis De Thomasis
Enroll: 6,276   (507) 457-1503

ST. OLAF COLLEGE
1520 St. Olaf Ave., Northfield 55057 *Type:* Private (Lutheran) liberal arts *Accred.:* 1915/1993 (NCA) *Calendar:* 4-1-4 plan *Degrees:* B *Prof. Accred.:* Dance, Music, Nursing (B), Social Work (B), Teacher Education (s), Theatre *CEO:* Pres. Melvin D. George
Enroll: 3,015   (507) 646-2222

ST. PAUL TECHNICAL COLLEGE
235 Marshall Ave., St. Paul 55102 *Type:* Public (local) 2-year *Accred.:* 1983/1993 (NCA) *Calendar:* Qtr. plan *Degrees:* A, certificates, diplomas *Prof. Accred.:* Medical Laboratory Technology (AMA), Practical Nursing, Respiratory Therapy *CEO:* Pres. Donovan Schwichtenberg
Enroll: 3,780   (612) 221-1300

SOUTHWEST STATE UNIVERSITY
1501 State St., Marshall 56258 *Type:* Public (state) liberal arts *System:* Minnesota State University System *Accred.:* 1972/1993 (NCA) *Calendar:* Qtr. plan *Degrees:* A, B *Prof. Accred.:* Music, Social Work (B-candidate) *CEO:* Pres. Oliver J. Ford, III
Enroll: 2,742   (507) 537-6272

SOUTHWESTERN TECHNICAL COLLEGE
1593 11th Ave., Granite Falls 56241 *Type:* Public (local) 2-year *Accred.:* 1991 (NCA) *Calendar:* Qtr. plan *Degrees:* A, certificates, diplomas *Prof. Accred.:* Dental Assisting *CEO:* Pres. Ralph Knapp
Enroll: 2,046   (612) 564-4511

UNITED THEOLOGICAL SEMINARY OF THE TWIN CITIES
3000 Fifth St., N.W., New Brighton 55112 *Type:* Private (United Church of Christ) *Accred.:* 1966/1992 (ATS); 1977/1992 (NCA) *Calendar:* Qtr. plan *Degrees:* M, D, certificates *CEO:* Pres. Benjamin Griffin
Enroll: 236   (612) 633-4311

UNIVERSITY OF MINNESOTA—CROOKSTON
Hwys. 2 and 75 N., Crookston 56716 *Type:*
Public (state) *System:* University of Min-
nesota System *Accred.:* 1971/1984 (NCA)
Calendar: Qtr. plan *Degrees:* A, B *CEO:*
Chanc. Donald G. Sargeant
Enroll: 1,352   (218) 281-6510

UNIVERSITY OF MINNESOTA—DULUTH
Duluth 55812 *Type:* Public (state) *System:*
University of Minnesota System *Accred.:*
1968/1988 (NCA) *Calendar:* Qtr. plan *De-
grees:* B, M, certificates *Prof. Accred.:*
Computer Science, Engineering (chemical,
computer, industrial), Medicine, Music, So-
cial Work (M), Speech-Language Pathology,
Teacher Education (e,s,p) *CEO:* Chanc.
Lawrence A. Ianni
Enroll: 7,680   (218) 726-8000

UNIVERSITY OF MINNESOTA—MORRIS
600 E. Fourth St., Morris 56267 *Type:* Pub-
lic (state) *System:* University of Minnesota
System *Accred.:* 1970/1990 (NCA) *Calen-
dar:* Qtr. plan *Degrees:* B *Prof. Accred.:*
Teacher Education (e,s) *CEO:* Chanc. David
C. Johnson
Enroll: 1,923   (612) 589-2211

UNIVERSITY OF MINNESOTA—TWIN CITIES
100 Church St., S.E., Minneapolis 55455
Type: Public (state) *System:* University of
Minnesota System *Accred.:* 1913/1986
(NCA) *Calendar:* Qtr. plan *Degrees:* A, B,
P, M, D, certificates *Prof. Accred.:* Accounting (Type A), Audiology, Business (B,M),
Clinical Psychology, Combined Prosthodontics, Counseling Psychology, Dance (associate), Dental Hygiene, Dentistry, Dietetics
(coordinated), Dietetics (internship), Endodontics (conditional), Engineering (aerospace, agricultural, chemical, civil, electrical,
geological/geophysical, materials, mechanical, metallurgical), Forestry, General Dentistry, General Practice Residency, Health
Services Administration, Interior Design,
Journalism (B,M), Landscape Architecture
(B,M-initial), Law, Marriage and Family
Therapy (D), Medical Technology, Medicine, Mortuary Science, Music, Nursing
(B,M), Occupational Therapy, Oral Pathology, Oral and Maxillofacial Surgery, Orthodontics, Pediatric Dentistry, Perfusion, Periodontics, Physical Therapy, Planning (M),

Psychology Internship, Public Health, Radia-
tion Therapy Technology, Radiography,
Recreation and Leisure Services, School
Psychology, Social Work (M), Speech-Lan-
guage Pathology, Teacher Education (e,s,p),
Theatre, Veterinary Medicine *CEO:* Pres.
Nils Hasselmo
Enroll: 38,019   (612) 625-5000

UNIVERSITY OF ST. THOMAS
2115 Summit Ave., St. Paul 55105 *Type:*
Private (Roman Catholic) liberal arts *Ac-
cred.:* 1974/1984 (ATS); 1916/1984 (NCA)
Calendar: 4-1-4 plan *Degrees:* B, P, M, D
Prof. Accred.: Music, Social Work (B,M),
Teacher Education (e,s,p) *CEO:* Pres. Dennis
J. Dease
Enroll: 10,423   (612) 962-5000

VERMILION COMMUNITY COLLEGE
1900 E. Camp St., Ely 55731 *Type:* Public
(state) junior *System:* Arrowhead Community College Region *Accred.:* 1982/1989
(NCA)* *Calendar:* Qtr. plan *Degrees:* A,
certificates *CEO:* Pres. Jon Harris
       (218) 365-7200

* Indirect accreditation through Arrowhead
Community College Region.

WALDEN UNIVERSITY
155 S. Fifth Ave., Minneapolis 55401 *Type:*
Private graduate only *Accred.:* 1990 (NCA)
Calendar: Tri. plan *Degrees:* D *CEO:* Pres.
Glendon F. Drake
Enroll: 753   (612) 338-7224

WILLIAM MITCHELL COLLEGE OF LAW
875 Summit Ave., St. Paul 55105 *Type:* Private professional *Calendar:* Sem. plan *Degrees:* P *Prof. Accred.:* Law *CEO:* Pres./
Dean James Hogg
Enroll: 1,156   (612) 227-9171

WILLMAR COMMUNITY COLLEGE
P.O. Box 797, Willmar 56201 *Type:* Public
(state) junior *System:* Minnesota Community
College System *Accred.:* 1972/1985 (NCA)
Calendar: Qtr. plan *Degrees:* A *CEO:* Pres.
Harold G. Conradi
Enroll: 1,383   (612) 231-5102

WINONA STATE UNIVERSITY
Winona 55987 *Type:* Public (state) liberal
arts and teachers *System:* Minnesota State

University System *Accred.:* 1913/1991 (NCA) *Calendar:* Qtr. plan *Degrees:* A, B, P, M, certificates *Prof. Accred.:* Music, Nursing (B,M), Social Work (B), Teacher Education (e,s,p) *CEO:* Pres. Darrell W. Krueger
Enroll: 7,329   (507) 457-5003

WORTHINGTON COMMUNITY COLLEGE
1450 Collegeway, Worthington 56187 *Type:* Public (state) junior *System:* Minnesota Community College System *Accred.:* 1973/1990 (NCA) *Calendar:* Qtr. plan *Degrees:* A, certificates, diplomas *CEO:* Pres. Conrad W. Burchill
Enroll: 906   (507) 372-2107

MISSISSIPPI

ALCORN STATE UNIVERSITY
P.O. Box 359, Lorman 39096-9402 *Type:* Public (state) teachers *System:* Mississippi Board of Trustees of State Institutions of Higher Learning *Accred.:* 1948/1991 (SACS-CC) *Calendar:* Sem. plan *Degrees:* A, B, M *Prof. Accred.:* Music, Nursing (A,B), Teacher Education (e,s) *CEO:* Pres. Walter Washington
FTE Enroll: 2,712   (601) 877-6100

BELHAVEN COLLEGE
1500 Peachtree St., Jackson 39202 *Type:* Private (Presbyterian) liberal arts *Accred.:* 1946/1987 (SACS-CC) *Calendar:* Sem. plan *Degrees:* B *Prof. Accred.:* Art (associate), Music *CEO:* Pres. Newton Wilson
FTE Enroll: 1,083   (601) 968-5919

BLUE MOUNTAIN COLLEGE
P.O. Box 338, Blue Mountain 38610 *Type:* Private (Southern Baptist) liberal arts primarily for women *Accred.:* 1927/1984 (SACS-CC) *Calendar:* Sem. plan *Degrees:* B *CEO:* Pres. E. Harold Fisher
FTE Enroll: 321   (601) 685-4771

COAHOMA COMMUNITY COLLEGE
3240 Friars Point Rd., Clarksdale 38614 *Type:* Public (district) junior *System:* Mississippi State Board for Community and Junior Colleges *Accred.:* 1975/1990 (SACS-CC) *Calendar:* Sem. plan *Degrees:* A *CEO:* Pres. Vivian M. Presley
FTE Enroll: 915   (601) 627-2571

COPIAH-LINCOLN COMMUNITY COLLEGE
P.O. Box 457, Wesson 39191 *Type:* Public (district) junior *System:* Mississippi State Board for Community and Junior Colleges *Accred.:* 1936/1985 (SACS-CC) *Calendar:* Sem. plan *Degrees:* A *Prof. Accred.:* Medical Laboratory Technology (AMA), Radiography *CEO:* Pres. Billy B. Thames
FTE Enroll: 2,706   (601) 643-5101

DELTA STATE UNIVERSITY
Hwy. 8 W., Cleveland 38733 *Type:* Public (state) liberal arts and teachers *System:* Mississippi Board of Trustees of State Institutions of Higher Learning *Accred.:* 1930/1984 (SACS-CC) *Calendar:* Sem. plan *Degrees:*

A, B, M, D *Prof. Accred.:* Art (associate), Counseling, Home Economics, Music, Nursing (B), Social Work (B), Teacher Education (e,s,p) *CEO:* Pres. F. Kent Wyatt
FTE Enroll: 3,357   (601) 846-3000

EAST CENTRAL COMMUNITY COLLEGE
P.O. Box 129, Decatur 39327-0129 *Type:* Public (district) junior *System:* Mississippi State Board for Community and Junior Colleges *Accred.:* 1939/1991 (SACS-CC) *Calendar:* Sem. plan *Degrees:* A *CEO:* Pres. Eddie M. Smith
FTE Enroll: 1,184   (601) 635-2111

EAST MISSISSIPPI COMMUNITY COLLEGE
P.O. Box 158, Scooba 39358 *Type:* Public (district) junior *System:* Mississippi State Board for Community and Junior Colleges *Accred.:* 1949/1987 (SACS-CC) *Calendar:* Sem. plan *Degrees:* A *Prof. Accred.:* Funeral Service Education *CEO:* Pres. Thomas L. Davis
FTE Enroll: 1,447   (601) 476-8442

HINDS COMMUNITY COLLEGE
Raymond 39154 *Type:* Public (district) junior *System:* Mississippi State Board for Community and Junior Colleges *Accred.:* 1928/1986 (SACS-CC) *Calendar:* Sem. plan *Degrees:* A *Prof. Accred.:* Dental Assisting, Medical Laboratory Technology (AMA), Medical Record Technology, Nursing (A), Respiratory Therapy, Respiratory Therapy Technology, Surgical Technology, Veterinary Technology (probational) *CEO:* Pres. V. Clyde Muse
FTE Enroll: 8,466   (601) 857-5261

HOLMES COMMUNITY COLLEGE
P.O. Box 369, Goodman 39079 *Type:* Public (district) junior *System:* Mississippi State Board for Community and Junior Colleges *Accred.:* 1934/1985 (SACS-CC) *Calendar:* Sem. plan *Degrees:* A *Prof. Accred.:* Nursing (A) *CEO:* Pres. Starkey A. Morgan
FTE Enroll: 1,992   (601) 472-2312

ITAWAMBA COMMUNITY COLLEGE
602 W. Hill St., Fulton 38843-1099 *Type:* Public (district) junior *System:* Mississippi State Board for Community and Junior Coll-

eges *Accred.:* 1955/1988 (SACS-CC) *Calendar:* Sem. plan *Degrees:* A *Prof. Accred.:* Nursing (A), Physical Therapy Assisting, Radiography, Respiratory Therapy, Respiratory Therapy Technology *CEO:* Pres. David Cole
FTE Enroll: 5,763   (601) 862-3101

JACKSON STATE UNIVERSITY
1400 J.R. Lynch St., Jackson 39217 *Type:* Public (state) liberal arts and teachers *System:* Mississippi Board of Trustees of State Institutions of Higher Learning *Accred.:* 1948/1991 (SACS-CC) *Calendar:* Sem. plan *Degrees:* B, M, D *Prof. Accred.:* Art, Computer Science, Journalism (B), Music, Public Policy and Administration, Rehabilitation Counseling, Social Work (B), Teacher Education (e,s,p) *CEO:* Pres. James E. Lyons
FTE Enroll: 6,346   (601) 968-2121

JONES COUNTY JUNIOR COLLEGE
900 Court St., Ellisville 39437 *Type:* Public (district) junior *System:* Mississippi State Board for Community and Junior Colleges *Accred.:* 1940/1987 (SACS-CC) *Calendar:* Sem. plan *Degrees:* A *Prof. Accred.:* EMT-Paramedic, Nursing (A) *CEO:* Pres. T. Terrel Tisdale
FTE Enroll: 4,441   (601) 477-4000

MAGNOLIA BIBLE COLLEGE
P.O. Box 1109, Kosciusko 39090 *Type:* Private (Churches of Christ) *Accred.:* 1989 (AABC); 1990 (SACS-CC) *Calendar:* Sem. plan *Degrees:* B *CEO:* Pres. Cecil May
FTE Enroll: 30   (601) 289-2896

MARY HOLMES COLLEGE
P.O. Box 1257, Hwy. 50 W., West Point 39773 *Type:* Private (United Presbyterian) 2-year *Accred.:* 1973/1989 (SACS-CC) *Calendar:* Sem. plan *Degrees:* A *CEO:* Pres. Sammie Potts
FTE Enroll: 403   (601) 494-6820

MERIDIAN COMMUNITY COLLEGE
910 Hwy. 19 N., Meridian 39307 *Type:* Public (district) junior *System:* Mississippi State Board for Community and Junior Colleges *Accred.:* 1942/1991 (SACS-CC) *Calendar:* Sem. plan *Degrees:* A *Prof. Accred.:* Dental Hygiene, Medical Laboratory Technology (AMA), Medical Record Technology, Nurs-

ing (A), Practical Nursing, Radiography, Respiratory Therapy Technology *CEO:* Pres. William F. Scaggs
FTE Enroll: 3,122   (601) 483-8241

MILLSAPS COLLEGE
1701 N. State St., Jackson 39210 *Type:* Private (United Methodist) liberal arts *Accred.:* 1912/1992 (SACS-CC) *Calendar:* Sem. plan *Degrees:* B, M *Prof. Accred.:* Business (B,M), Teacher Education (e,s) *CEO:* Pres. George M. Harmon
FTE Enroll: 1,240   (601) 974-1000

MISSISSIPPI COLLEGE
P.O. Box 4186, Clinton 39058 *Type:* Private (Southern Baptist) liberal arts *Accred.:* 1922/1992 (SACS-CC) *Calendar:* Sem. plan *Degrees:* B, M, D *Prof. Accred.:* Law, Music, Nursing (B), Social Work (B-candidate), Teacher Education (e,s,p) *CEO:* Acting Pres. Rory Lee
FTE Enroll: 3,745   (601) 925-3000

MISSISSIPPI DELTA COMMUNITY COLLEGE
P.O. Box 668, Moorhead 38761 *Type:* Public (district) junior *System:* Mississippi State Board for Community and Junior Colleges *Accred.:* 1930/1987 (SACS-CC) *Calendar:* Sem. plan *Degrees:* A *Prof. Accred.:* Medical Laboratory Technology (AMA), Nursing (A), Radiography *CEO:* Pres. Bobby S. Garvin
FTE Enroll: 3,491   (601) 246-5631

MISSISSIPPI GULF COAST COMMUNITY COLLEGE
P.O. Box 67, Perkinston 39573 *Type:* Public (district) junior *System:* Mississippi State Board for Community and Junior Colleges *Accred.:* 1929/1989 (SACS-CC) *Calendar:* Sem. plan *Degrees:* A *Prof. Accred.:* EMT-Paramedic, Medical Laboratory Technology (AMA), Nursing (A), Radiography *CEO:* Pres. Barry L. Mellinger
FTE Enroll: 8,077   (601) 928-5211

MISSISSIPPI STATE UNIVERSITY
Mississippi State 39762 *Type:* Public (state) *System:* Mississippi Board of Trustees of State Institutions of Higher Learning *Accred.:* 1926/1993 (SACS-CC) *Calendar:* Sem. plan *Degrees:* B, M, D *Prof. Accred.:* Accounting (Type A,C), Art, Business (B,M), Computer Science, Counseling, Engi-

neering (aerospace, agricultural, bioengineering, chemical, civil, computer, electrical, industrial, mechanical, nuclear, petroleum), Forestry, Home Economics, Interior Design, Landscape Architecture (B), Music (associate), Public Policy and Administration, Rehabilitation Counseling, Social Work (B-candidate), Teacher Education (e,s,p), Veterinary Medicine *CEO:* Pres. Donald W. Zacharias
FTE Enroll: 13,872   (601) 325-3920

MISSISSIPPI UNIVERSITY FOR WOMEN
P.O. Box W-1600, Columbus 39701 *Type:* Public (state) liberal arts and teachers for women *System:* Mississippi Board of Trustees of State Institutions of Higher Learning *Accred.:* 1921/1993 (SACS-CC) *Calendar:* Sem. plan *Degrees:* A, B, M *Prof. Accred.:* Art (associate), Home Economics, Music, Nursing (A,B,M), Teacher Education (e,s,p) *CEO:* Pres. Clyda S. Rent
FTE Enroll: 2,033   (601) 329-4750

MISSISSIPPI VALLEY STATE UNIVERSITY
1400 Hwy. 82 W., Itta Bena 38941 *Type:* Public (state) teachers *System:* Mississippi Board of Trustees of State Institutions of Higher Learning *Accred.:* 1968/1992 (SACS-CC) *Calendar:* Sem. plan *Degrees:* B, M *Prof. Accred.:* Art, Music (associate), Social Work (B), Teacher Education (e) *CEO:* Pres. William W. Sutton
FTE Enroll: 2,329   (601) 254-9041

NORTHEAST MISSISSIPPI COMMUNITY COLLEGE
Cunningham Blvd., Booneville 38829 *Type:* Public (district) junior *System:* Mississippi State Board for Community and Junior Colleges *Accred.:* 1956/1991 (SACS-CC) *Calendar:* Sem. plan *Degrees:* A *Prof. Accred.:* Dental Hygiene, Medical Assisting (AMA), Medical Laboratory Technology (AMA), Nursing (A), Respiratory Therapy Technology *CEO:* Pres. Joe M. Childers
FTE Enroll: 2,902   (601) 728-7751

NORTHWEST MISSISSIPPI COMMUNITY COLLEGE
510 N. Panola, Senatobia 38668 *Type:* Public (district) junior *System:* Mississippi State Board for Community and Junior Colleges *Accred.:* 1953/1988 (SACS-CC) *Calendar:* Sem. plan *Degrees:* A *Prof. Accred.:* Funeral

Service Education, Nursing (A), Respiratory Therapy *CEO:* Pres. David M. Haraway
FTE Enroll: 4,813   (601) 562-3200

PEARL RIVER COMMUNITY COLLEGE
101 Hwy. 11 N., Poplarville 39470-2298 *Type:* Public (district) junior *System:* Mississippi State Board for Community and Junior Colleges *Accred.:* 1929/1985 (SACS-CC) *Calendar:* Sem. plan *Degrees:* A *Prof. Accred.:* Dental Assisting (prelim. provisional), Nursing (A), Respiratory Therapy Technology *CEO:* Pres. Ted J. Alexander
FTE Enroll: 2,914   (601) 795-6801

PHILLIPS JUNIOR COLLEGE
2680 Insurance Center Dr., Jackson 39216 *Type:* Private junior *Accred.:* 1975/1990 (ACISC); 1987 (SACS-CC probational) *Calendar:* Qtr. plan *Degrees:* A *Prof. Accred.:* Medical Assisting (AMA) *CEO:* Pres. Nan Thompson
FTE Enroll: 350   (601) 362-6341

REFORMED THEOLOGICAL SEMINARY
5422 Clinton Blvd., Jackson 39209 *Type:* Private (interdenominational) graduate only *Accred.:* 1977/1982 (ATS); 1977/1992 (SACS-CC) *Calendar:* Sem. plan *Degrees:* M, D *Prof. Accred.:* Marriage and Family Therapy (M) *CEO:* Pres. Luder G. Whitlock, Jr.
FTE Enroll: 1,577   (601) 922-4988

RUST COLLEGE
150 E. Rust Ave., Holly Springs 38635 *Type:* Private (United Methodist) liberal arts *Accred.:* 1970/1984 (SACS-CC) *Calendar:* Sem. plan *Degrees:* A, B *CEO:* Pres. David L. Beckley
FTE Enroll: 1,180   (601) 252-8000

SOUTHEASTERN BAPTIST COLLEGE
4229 Hwy. 15 N., Laurel 39440 *Type:* Private (Baptist Missionary Association) *Accred.:* 1988 (AABC) *Calendar:* Sem. plan *Degrees:* A, B, certificates, diplomas *CEO:* Pres. Gerald Kellar
FTE Enroll: 55   (601) 426-6346

SOUTHWEST MISSISSIPPI COMMUNITY COLLEGE
Summit 39666 *Type:* Public (district) junior *System:* Mississippi State Board for Community and Junior Colleges *Accred.:* 1958/1990

(SACS-CC) *Calendar:* Sem. plan *Degrees:* A *CEO:* Pres. Horace C. Holmes
FTE Enroll: 1,513   (601) 276-2000

TOUGALOO COLLEGE
500 W. County Line Rd., Tougaloo 39174 *Type:* Private liberal arts *Accred.:* 1953/1990 (SACS-CC) *Calendar:* Sem. plan *Degrees:* A, B *CEO:* Pres. Adib A. Shakir
FTE Enroll: 1,153   (601) 977-7700

UNIVERSITY OF MISSISSIPPI
University 38677 *Type:* Public (state) *System:* Mississippi Board of Trustees of State Institutions of Higher Learning *Accred.:* 1895/1989 (SACS-CC) *Calendar:* Sem. plan *Degrees:* B, M, D *Prof. Accred.:* Accounting (Type A,C), Art, Audiology, Business (B,M), Clinical Psychology, Computer Science, Engineering (chemical, civil, electrical, geological/geophysical, mechanical), Home Economics, Journalism (B,M), Law, Music, Nursing (B,M), Psychology Internship, Social Work (B), Speech-Language Pathology, Teacher Education (e,s,p) *CEO:* Chanc. R. Gerald Turner
FTE Enroll: 10,233   (601) 232-7211

UNIVERSITY OF MISSISSIPPI MEDICAL CENTER
2500 N. State St., Jackson 39216-4505 *Type:* Public (state) *System:* Mississippi Board of Trustees of State Institutions of Higher Learning *Accred.:* 1991 (SACS-CC) *Calendar:* Qtr. plan *Degrees:* B, M, D *Prof. Accred.:* Cytotechnology, Dental Hygiene, Dentistry, EMT-Paramedic, General Dentistry (prelim. provisional), General Practice Residency, Medical Record Administration, Medical Technology, Medicine, Nuclear Medicine Technology, Occupational Therapy, Physical Therapy, Radiation Therapy Technology, Radiography, Respiratory Therapy, Respiratory Therapy Technology *CEO:* Vice Chanc. Norman Crooks Nelson, M.D.
FTE Enroll: 2,067   (601) 984-1000

THE UNIVERSITY OF SOUTHERN MISSISSIPPI
Southern Sta., Box 5001, Hattiesburg 39406-5001 *Type:* Public (state) *System:* Mississippi Board of Trustees of State Institutions of Higher Learning *Accred.:* 1929/1985 (SACS-CC) *Calendar:* Sem. plan *Degrees:*

B, M, D *Prof. Accred.:* Art, Audiology, Business (B,M), Clinical Psychology, Community Health/Preventive Medicine, Computer Science, Counseling, Counseling Psychology, Dance, Dietetics (coordinated), Engineering Technology (architectural, civil/construction, computer, electrical, industrial, mechanical), Home Economics, Interior Design, Journalism (B), Librarianship, Marriage and Family Therapy (M), Medical Technology, Music, Nursing (B,M), Recreation and Leisure Services, School Psychology, Social Work (B-candidate,M), Speech-Language Pathology, Teacher Education (e,s,p), Theatre *CEO:* Pres. Aubrey K. Lucas
FTE Enroll: 10,465   (601) 266-4111

GULF PARK CAMPUS
E. Beach Blvd., Long Beach 39560 *Prof. Accred.:* Engineering Technology (electrical) *CEO:* Dean James O. Williams
(601) 865-4500

WESLEY BIBLICAL SEMINARY
5980 Floral Dr., Jackson 39206 *Type:* Private (interdenominational) graduate only *Accred.:* 1991 (ATS) *Calendar:* Sem. plan *Degrees:* M *CEO:* Pres. Harold Spann
FTE Enroll: 45   (601) 957-1314

WESLEY COLLEGE
111 Wesley Cir., P.O. Box 1070, Florence 39073 *Type:* Private (Congregational Methodist Church) *Accred.:* 1979/1989 (AABC) *Calendar:* Sem. plan *Degrees:* B, certificates *CEO:* Pres. Samuel Bruce
FTE Enroll: 69   (601) 845-2265

WILLIAM CAREY COLLEGE
498 Tuscan Ave., Hattiesburg 39401-5499 *Type:* Private (Southern Baptist) liberal arts *Accred.:* 1958/1990 (SACS-CC) *Calendar:* Tri. plan *Degrees:* B, M *Prof. Accred.:* Medical Technology, Music, Nursing (B) *CEO:* Pres. James W. Edwards
FTE Enroll: 2,198   (601) 582-5051

WOOD COLLEGE
Wood College Rd., Mathiston 39752 *Type:* Private (United Methodist) junior *Accred.:* 1956/1990 (SACS-CC) *Calendar:* Sem. plan *Degrees:* A *CEO:* Pres. Doyce W. Gunter
FTE Enroll: 476   (601) 263-8128

MISSOURI

AQUINAS INSTITUTE OF THEOLOGY
3642 Lindell Blvd., St. Louis 63108-3396
Type: Private (Roman Catholic) graduate
only *Accred.:* 1968/1986 (ATS); 1964/1986
(NCA) *Calendar:* 4-1-4 plan *Degrees:* M, D
CEO: Pres. Charles E. Bouchard, O.P.
Enroll: 46   (314) 658-3882

ASSEMBLIES OF GOD THEOLOGICAL SEMINARY
1445 Boonville Ave., Springfield 65802
Type: Private (Assemblies of God) graduate
only *Accred.:* 1992 (ATS); 1978/1992
(NCA) *Calendar:* 4-4-1-1 plan *Degrees:* M
CEO: Pres. Delbert H. Tarr, Jr.
Enroll: 314   (417) 862-3344

AVILA COLLEGE
11901 Wornall Rd., Kansas City 64145
Type: Private (Roman Catholic) liberal arts
Accred.: 1946/1988 (NCA) *Calendar:* Sem.
plan *Degrees:* A, B, M, certificates *Prof. Ac-
cred.:* Medical Technology, Nursing (B),
Radiography, Social Work (B) *CEO:* Pres.
Larry Kramer
Enroll: 1,409   (816) 942-8400

BAPTIST BIBLE COLLEGE
628 E. Kearney St., Springfield 65803 *Type:*
Private (Baptist Bible Fellowship) *Accred.:*
1978/1988 (AABC) *Calendar:* Sem. plan
Degrees: A, B, certificates *CEO:* Pres.
Leland R. Kennedy
FTE Enroll: 889   (417) 869-9811

BASIC INSTITUTE OF TECHNOLOGY
4455 Chippewa Ave., St. Louis 63116-9990
Type: Private *Accred.:* 1974/1989 (ACC-
SCT) *Calendar:* Qtr. plan *Degrees:* A, diplomas *CEO:* Dir. J.A. Zoeller
       (314) 771-1200

CALVARY BIBLE COLLEGE
15800 Calvary Rd., Kansas City 64147-1341
Type: Independent (nondenominational) *Accred.:* 1961/1989 (AABC) *Calendar:* 4-4-1-
1 plan *Degrees:* A, B, certificates *CEO:*
Pres. Donald Urey
FTE Enroll: 223   (816) 322-0110

CENTRAL BIBLE COLLEGE
3000 N. Grant Ave., Springfield 65803
Type: Private (Assemblies of God) *Accred.:*

1948/1985 (AABC) *Calendar:* Sem. plan
Degrees: A, B, certificates, diplomas *CEO:*
Pres. Maurice Lednicky
FTE Enroll: 912   (417) 833-2551

CENTRAL CHRISTIAN COLLEGE OF THE BIBLE
911 Urbandale Dr. E., Moberly 65270 *Type:*
Private (Christian Churches/Churches of
Christ) *Accred.:* 1982/1992 (AABC) *Calen-
dar:* Sem. plan *Degrees:* A, B, diplomas
CEO: Pres. Lloyd M. Pelfrey
FTE Enroll: 77   (816) 263-3900

CENTRAL METHODIST COLLEGE
Fayette 65248 *Type:* Private (United
Methodist) liberal arts *Accred.:* 1913/1991
(NCA) *Calendar:* 4-1-4 plan *Degrees:* A, B
Prof. Accred.: Music *CEO:* Pres. Joe A.
Howell
Enroll: 994   (816) 248-3391

CENTRAL MISSOURI STATE UNIVERSITY
Warrensburg 64093 *Type:* Public (state) liberal arts and teachers *System:* Missouri Coordinating Board for Higher Education *Accred.:* 1915/1984 (NCA) *Calendar:* Qtr. plan
Degrees: A, B, P, M, certificates *Prof. Accred.:* Art (associate), Audiology, Construction Education (B), Home Economics,
Music, Nursing (B), Social Work (B),
Speech-Language Pathology, Teacher Education (e,s,p) *CEO:* Pres. Ed M. Elliott
Enroll: 11,631   (816) 543-4111

CLEVELAND CHIROPRACTIC COLLEGE
6401 Rockhill Rd., Kansas City 64131 *Type:*
Independent professional *Accred.:* 1984/
1989 (NCA) *Calendar:* Tri. plan *Degrees:* D
Prof. Accred.: Chiropractic Education *CEO:*
Pres. Carl S. Cleveland, III, D.C.
Enroll: 426   (816) 333-8230

COLLEGE OF THE OZARKS
Point Lookout 65726 *Type:* Private (Presby-
terian) liberal arts *Accred.:* 1961/1991
(NCA) *Calendar:* Tri. plan *Degrees:* B *Prof.
Accred.:* Teacher Education (e,s) *CEO:* Pres.
Jerry C. Davis
Enroll: 1,516   (417) 334-6411

COLUMBIA COLLEGE
1001 Rogers St., Columbia 65216 *Type:* Private (Disciples of Christ) *Accred.:* 1918/1993 (NCA) *Calendar:* Sem. plan *Degrees:* A, B *Prof. Accred.:* Social Work (B) *CEO:* Pres. Donald B. Ruthenberg
Enroll: 5,563 (314) 875-7200

CONCEPTION SEMINARY COLLEGE
P.O. Box 502, Conception 64433 *Type:* Private (Roman Catholic) *Accred.:* 1960/1984 (NCA) *Calendar:* Sem. plan *Degrees:* B, certificates *CEO:* Pres./Rector Gregory J. Polan
Enroll: 84 (816) 944-2218

CONCORDIA SEMINARY
801 De Mun Ave., St. Louis 63105 *Type:* Private (Lutheran/Missouri Synod) graduate only *Accred.:* 1963/1983 (ATS); 1978/1984 (NCA) *Calendar:* Qtr. plan *Degrees:* M, D, certificates *CEO:* Pres. John Franklin Johnson
Enroll: 526 (314) 721-5934

COTTEY COLLEGE
1000 W. Austin St., Nevada 64772 *Type:* Private junior for women *Accred.:* 1918/1993 (NCA) *Calendar:* Sem. plan *Degrees:* A *Prof. Accred.:* Music *CEO:* Pres. Helen R. Washburn
Enroll: 417 (417) 667-8181

COVENANT THEOLOGICAL SEMINARY
12330 Conway Rd., St. Louis 63141 *Type:* Private (Presbyterian) graduate only *Accred.:* 1988 (ATS); 1973/1988 (NCA) *Calendar:* Sem. plan *Degrees:* M, D, certificates *CEO:* Pres. Paul D. Kooistra
Enroll: 436 (314) 434-4044

CROWDER COLLEGE
601 Laclede, Neosho 64850 *Type:* Public (district) junior *System:* Missouri Coordinating Board for Higher Education *Accred.:* 1977/1992 (NCA) *Calendar:* Sem. plan *Degrees:* A, certificates *CEO:* Pres. Kent Farnsworth
Enroll: 1,784 (417) 451-3223

CULVER-STOCKTON COLLEGE
Canton 63435 *Type:* Private (Disciples of Christ) liberal arts *Accred.:* 1924/1992 (NCA) *Calendar:* Sem. plan *Degrees:* B *CEO:* Pres. Edward B. Strong, Jr.
Enroll: 1,145 (314) 288-5221

DEACONESS COLLEGE OF NURSING
6150 Oakland Ave., St. Louis 63139 *Type:* Private professional *Accred.:* 1985/1990 (NCA) *Calendar:* Sem. plan *Degrees:* A, B *Prof. Accred.:* Nursing (B) *CEO:* Pres. Elizabeth Anne Krekorian
Enroll: 338 (314) 768-3044

DEVRY INSTITUTE OF TECHNOLOGY, KANSAS CITY
11224 Holmes Rd., Kansas City 64131 *Type:* Private *Accred.:* 1981/1992 (NCA)* *Calendar:* Sem. plan *Degrees:* A, B, certificates, diplomas *Prof. Accred.:* Engineering Technology (electrical) *CEO:* Pres. Charles Robert Levalley
(816) 941-0430

* Indirect accreditation through DeVry Institutes.

DRURY COLLEGE
900 N. Benton Ave., Springfield 65802 *Type:* Private (United Church of Christ) liberal arts *Accred.:* 1915/1991 (NCA) *Calendar:* Sem. plan *Degrees:* A, B, M *Prof. Accred.:* Teacher Education (e,s) *CEO:* Pres. John E. Moore, Jr.
Enroll: 3,542 (417) 865-8731

EAST CENTRAL COLLEGE
P.O. Box 529, Union 63084 *Type:* Public (district) junior *System:* Missouri Coordinating Board for Higher Education *Accred.:* 1976/1990 (NCA) *Calendar:* Sem. plan *Degrees:* A, certificates *Prof. Accred.:* Dental Assisting *CEO:* Pres. Dale L. Gibson
Enroll: 3,216 (314) 583-5193

EDEN THEOLOGICAL SEMINARY
475 E. Lockwood Ave., St. Louis 63119-3192 *Type:* Private (United Church of Christ) graduate only *Accred.:* 1938/1988 (ATS); 1973/1989 (NCA) *Calendar:* 4-1-4 plan *Degrees:* M, D, certificates *CEO:* Pres. Charles R. Kniker
Enroll: 244 (314) 961-3627

EVANGEL COLLEGE
1111 N. Glenstone Ave., Springfield 65802 *Type:* Private (Assemblies of God) liberal arts *Accred.:* 1965/1988 (NCA) *Calendar:* Sem. plan *Degrees:* A, B *Prof. Accred.:* Music, Teacher Education (e,s) *CEO:* Pres. Robert H. Spence
Enroll: 1,420 (417) 865-2811

FONTBONNE COLLEGE
6800 Wydown Blvd., St. Louis 63105 *Type:*
Private (Roman Catholic) liberal arts *Ac-
cred.:* 1926/1993 (NCA) *Calendar:* Sem.
plan *Degrees:* B, M *Prof. Accred.:* Home
Economics, Speech-Language Pathology
CEO: Pres. Meneve Dunham
Enroll: 1,989   (314) 862-3456

FOREST INSTITUTE OF PROFESSIONAL
PSYCHOLOGY
1322 S. Campbell Ave., Springfield 65807
Type: Private *Accred.:* 1983/1992 (NCA
probational) *Calendar:* Tri. plan *Degrees:*
M, D *CEO:* Pres. Richard H. Cox
Enroll: 413   (417) 831-7902

HANNIBAL-LAGRANGE COLLEGE
2800 Palmyra Rd., Hannibal 63401 *Type:*
Private (Southern Baptist) liberal arts *Accred.:* 1958/1993 (NCA) *Calendar:* Sem.
plan *Degrees:* A, B, certificates *Prof. Accred.:* Nursing (A) *CEO:* Pres. Paul Brown
Enroll: 953   (314) 221-3675

HARRIS-STOWE STATE COLLEGE
3026 Laclede Ave., St. Louis 63103 *Type:*
Public (state) teachers *System:* Missouri Coordinating Board for Higher Education *Accred.:* 1924/1991 (NCA) *Calendar:* Sem.
plan *Degrees:* B *Prof. Accred.:* Teacher Education (e) *CEO:* Pres. Henry Givens, Jr.
Enroll: 1,978   (314) 340-3366

HEART OF THE OZARKS TECHNICAL COMMUNITY
COLLEGE
1417 N. Jefferson Ave., Springfield 65802
Type: Public (district) 2-year *System:* Missouri Coordinating Board for Higher Education *Accred.:* 1992 (NCA candidate) *Calendar:* Sem. plan *Degrees:* A, certificates *Prof.
Accred.:* Dental Assisting, Respiratory Therapy, Respiratory Therapy Technology *CEO:*
Pres. Norman K. Myers
Enroll: 2,073   (417) 895-7000

HICKEY SCHOOL
940 W. Port Plaza, St. Louis 63146 *Type:*
Private business *Accred.:* 1971/1989
(ACISC) *Calendar:* Courses of varying
lengths *Degrees:* A, certificates, diplomas
Prof. Accred.: Medical Assisting (AMA)
CEO: Dir. Michelle Birk
                                   (314) 434-2212

ITT TECHNICAL INSTITUTE
13505 Lakefront Dr., Earth City 63045-1416
Type: Private *Accred.:* 1965/1988 (ACC-
SCT) *Calendar:* Courses of varying lengths
Degrees: A, B *CEO:* Dir. Karen Finkenkeller
                                   (314) 298-7800

BRANCH CAMPUS
9814 M St., Omaha, NE 68127-2056 *Accred.:* 1991 (ACCSCT) *CEO:* Dir. Roger
B. Orensteen
                                   (402) 331-2900

JEFFERSON COLLEGE
1000 Viking Dr., Hillsboro 63050 *Type:*
Public (district) junior *System:* Missouri Coordinating Board for Higher Education *Accred.:* 1969/1989 (NCA) *Calendar:* Sem.
plan *Degrees:* A, certificates *Prof. Accred.:*
Music (associate), Veterinary Technology
(probational) *CEO:* Interim Pres. Ronald J.
Fundis
Enroll: 4,210   (314) 789-3951

KANSAS CITY ART INSTITUTE
4415 Warwick Blvd., Kansas City 64111
Type: Private professional *Accred.:* 1964/
1990 (NCA) *Calendar:* Sem. plan *Degrees:*
B *Prof. Accred.:* Art *CEO:* Pres. Beatrice
Rivas Sanchez
Enroll: 579   (816) 561-4852

KEMPER MILITARY SCHOOL AND COLLEGE
701 Third St., Boonville 65233 *Type:* Private
junior for men *Accred.:* 1927/1990 (NCA)
Calendar: Sem. plan *Degrees:* A *CEO:* Pres.
Roger D. Harms
Enroll: 275   (816) 882-5623

KENRICK-GLENNON SEMINARY
5200 Glennon Dr., St. Louis 63119-4399
Type: Private (Roman Catholic) graduate
only *Accred.:* 1973/1989 (ATS); 1964/1989
(NCA) *Calendar:* Sem. plan *Degrees:* M
CEO: Pres./Rector Ronald W. Ramson,
C.M.
Enroll: 69   (314) 644-0266

KIRKSVILLE COLLEGE OF OSTEOPATHIC
MEDICINE
800 W. Jefferson Ave., Kirksville 63501
Type: Private professional *Calendar:* Qtr.
plan *Degrees:* P *Prof. Accred.:* Osteopathy
CEO: Pres. Fred C. Tinning, Ph.D.
Enroll: 531   (816) 626-2354

LINCOLN UNIVERSITY
820 Chestnut St., Jefferson City 65102-0029
Type: Public (state) liberal arts and professional *System:* Missouri Coordinating Board for Higher Education *Accred.:* 1969/1988 (NCA) *Calendar:* Sem. plan *Degrees:* A, B, M *Prof. Accred.:* Music, Nursing (A), Teacher Education (e,s,p) *CEO:* Pres. Wendell G. Rayburn, Sr.
Enroll: 4,031   (314) 681-5000

LINDENWOOD COLLEGE
209 S. Kingshighway Blvd., St. Charles 63301 *Type:* Private (United Presbyterian) liberal arts *Accred.:* 1918/1984 (NCA) *Calendar:* 4-1-4 plan *Degrees:* B, M *Prof. Accred.:* Teacher Education (e,s) *CEO:* Pres. Dennis C. Spellmann
Enroll: 2,825   (314) 949-2000

LOGAN COLLEGE OF CHIROPRACTIC
1851 Schoettler Rd., P.O. Box 1065, Chesterfield 63006-1065 *Type:* Private professional *Accred.:* 1987/1992 (NCA) *Calendar:* Sem. plan *Degrees:* B, D *Prof. Accred.:* Chiropractic Education *CEO:* Pres. George A. Goodman, D.C.
Enroll: 696   (314) 227-2100

LONGVIEW COMMUNITY COLLEGE
500 Longview Rd., Lee's Summit 64081 *Type:* Public (district) junior *System:* Metropolitan Community College District *Accred.:* 1986 (NCA)* *Calendar:* Sem. plan *Degrees:* A, certificates *CEO:* Pres. Aldo W. Leker
                                        (816) 672-2000

MAPLE WOODS COMMUNITY COLLEGE
2601 N.E. Barry Rd., Kansas City 64156 *Type:* Public (district) junior *System:* Metropolitan Community College District *Accred.:* 1986 (NCA)* *Calendar:* Sem. plan *Degrees:* A, certificates *Prof. Accred.:* Veterinary Technology *CEO:* Pres. Stephen R. Brainard
                                        (816) 437-3000

* Indirect accreditation through Metropolitan Community College District.

MARYVILLE UNIVERSITY OF ST. LOUIS
13550 Conway Rd., St. Louis 63141 *Type:* Private liberal arts *Accred.:* 1941/1985 (NCA) *Calendar:* 4-4-1 plan *Degrees:* B, M, certificates *Prof. Accred.:* Art (associate), Interior Design, Nursing (B), Physical Thera-

py, Teacher Education (e,s) *CEO:* Pres. Keith H. Lovin
Enroll: 3,722   (314) 576-9300

MIDWESTERN BAPTIST THEOLOGICAL SEMINARY
5001 N. Oak St. Trafficway, Kansas City 64118 *Type:* Private (Southern Baptist) *Accred.:* 1964/1991 (ATS); 1971/1992 (NCA) *Calendar:* Sem. plan *Degrees:* M, D *CEO:* Pres. Milton U. Ferguson
Enroll: 524   (816) 453-4600

MINERAL AREA COLLEGE
P.O. Box 1000, Hwy. 67 and 32, Park Hills 63601 *Type:* Public (district) junior *System:* Missouri Coordinating Board for Higher Education *Accred.:* 1971/1988 (NCA) *Calendar:* Sem. plan *Degrees:* A, certificates *Prof. Accred.:* Dental Assisting *CEO:* Pres. Dixie A. Kohn
Enroll: 3,064   (314) 431-4593

MISSOURI BAPTIST COLLEGE
12542 Conway Rd., St. Louis 63141 *Type:* Private (Southern Baptist) liberal arts *Accred.:* 1978/1990 (NCA) *Calendar:* Sem. plan *Degrees:* A, B, certificates *CEO:* Interim Pres. Thomas S. Field
Enroll: 1,398   (314) 434-1115

MISSOURI SOUTHERN STATE COLLEGE
3950 Newman Rd., Joplin 64801 *Type:* Public (state) liberal arts and teachers *System:* Missouri Coordinating Board for Higher Education *Accred.:* 1949/1988 (NCA) *Calendar:* Sem. plan *Degrees:* A, B *Prof. Accred.:* Dental Hygiene, Nursing (A,B), Radiography, Teacher Education (e,s) *CEO:* Pres. Julio S. Leon
Enroll: 5,889   (417) 625-9300

MISSOURI VALLEY COLLEGE
500 E. College Dr., Marshall 65340 *Type:* Private (Presbyterian) liberal arts *Accred.:* 1916/1992 (NCA) *Calendar:* Sem. plan *Degrees:* A, B *CEO:* Pres. Earl J. Reeves
Enroll: 1,153   (816) 886-6924

MISSOURI WESTERN STATE COLLEGE
4525 Downs Dr., St. Joseph 64507 *Type:* Public (state) *System:* Missouri Coordinating Board for Higher Education *Accred.:* 1919/1990 (NCA) *Calendar:* Sem. plan *Degrees:* A, B, certificates *Prof. Accred.:* Engineering Technology (civil/construction, electrical),

Music, Nursing (B), Social Work (B), Teacher Education (e,s) *CEO:* Pres. Janet G. Murphy
Enroll: 5,093   (816) 271-4200

MOBERLY AREA COMMUNITY COLLEGE
College and Rollins Sts., Moberly 65270 *Type:* Public (district) junior *System:* Missouri Coordinating Board for Higher Education *Accred.:* 1980/1992 (NCA) *Calendar:* Sem. plan *Degrees:* A, certificates *CEO:* Pres. Andrew Komar, Jr.
Enroll: 1,846   (816) 263-4110

NAZARENE THEOLOGICAL SEMINARY
1700 E. Meyer Blvd., Kansas City 64131 *Type:* Private (Nazarene) graduate only *Accred.:* 1970/1989 (ATS) *Calendar:* Sem. plan *Degrees:* M, D *CEO:* Pres. A. Gordon Wetmore
FTE Enroll: 264   (816) 333-6254

NORTH CENTRAL MISSOURI COLLEGE
1301 Main St., Trenton 64683 *Type:* Public (district) junior *System:* Missouri Coordinating Board for Higher Education *Accred.:* 1983/1992 (NCA) *Calendar:* Sem. plan *Degrees:* A, certificates *CEO:* Pres. James E. Selby
Enroll: 1,044   (816) 359-3948

NORTHEAST MISSOURI STATE UNIVERSITY
Kirksville 63501 *Type:* Public (state) liberal arts and teachers *System:* Missouri Coordinating Board for Higher Education *Accred.:* 1914/1985 (NCA) *Calendar:* Sem. plan *Degrees:* B, P, M *Prof. Accred.:* Counseling, Music, Nursing (B), Speech-Language Pathology, Teacher Education (e,s,p) *CEO:* Pres. Russell G. Warren
Enroll: 6,249   (816) 785-4000

NORTHWEST MISSOURI COMMUNITY COLLEGE
4315 Pickett Rd., St. Joseph 64503-1635 *Type:* Private junior *Accred.:* 1980/1993 (NCA probational) *Calendar:* Qtr. plan *Degrees:* A, certificates, diplomas *CEO:* Pres. Stanley L. Shaver
Enroll: 1,255   (816) 223-9563

NORTHWEST MISSOURI STATE UNIVERSITY
800 University Dr., Maryville 64468-6001 *Type:* Public (state) liberal arts and teachers *System:* Missouri Coordinating Board for Higher Education *Accred.:* 1921/1988

(NCA) *Calendar:* Sem. plan *Degrees:* A, B, P, M, certificates, diplomas *Prof. Accred.:* Home Economics, Music, Teacher Education (e,s,p) *CEO:* Pres. Dean L. Hubbard
Enroll: 5,863   (816) 562-1110

OZARK CHRISTIAN COLLEGE
1111 N. Main St., Joplin 64801 *Type:* Private (Christian Churches/Churches of Christ) *Accred.:* 1988 (AABC) *Calendar:* Sem. plan *Degrees:* A, B, certificates *CEO:* Pres. Kenneth Idleman
FTE Enroll: 498   (417) 624-2518

PARK COLLEGE
8700 River Park Dr., Parkville 64152 *Type:* Private (Latter-Day Saints) liberal arts *Accred.:* 1913/1990 (NCA) *Calendar:* 4-1-4 plan *Degrees:* A, B, M *CEO:* Pres. Donald J. Breckon
Enroll: 7,252   (816) 741-2000

PENN VALLEY COMMUNITY COLLEGE
3201 S.W. Trafficway, Kansas City 64111 *Type:* Public (district) junior *System:* Metropolitan Community College District *Accred.:* 1986 (NCA)* *Calendar:* Sem. plan *Degrees:* A, certificates *Prof. Accred.:* Medical Record Technology, Nursing (A), Occupational Therapy Assisting, Physical Therapy Assisting, Radiography *CEO:* Pres. E. Paul Williams
                                   (816) 759-4000

* Indirect accreditation through Metropolitan Community College District.

PHILLIPS JUNIOR COLLEGE
1010 W. Sunshine St., Springfield 65807 *Type:* Private junior *Accred.:* 1981/1987 (ACISC) *Calendar:* Qtr. plan *Degrees:* A *Prof. Accred.:* Medical Assisting (AMA) *CEO:* Pres. Barbara Loven
                                   (417) 864-7220

RANKEN TECHNICAL COLLEGE
4431 Finney Ave., St. Louis 63113 *Type:* Private technical *Accred.:* 1989 (NCA) *Calendar:* Tri. plan *Degrees:* A, certificates *CEO:* Pres. Ben H. Ernst
Enroll: 1,373   (314) 371-0236

RESEARCH COLLEGE OF NURSING
2316 E. Meyer Blvd., Kansas City 64132 *Type:* Private professional *Accred.:* 1987/

1992 (NCA) *Calendar:* Sem. plan *Degrees:* B *Prof. Accred.:* Nursing (B) *CEO:* Dean Barbara Clemence
Enroll: 251   (816) 276-4700

ROCKHURST COLLEGE
1100 Rockhurst Rd., Kansas City 64110 *Type:* Private (Roman Catholic) liberal arts *Accred.:* 1934/1993 (NCA) *Calendar:* Sem. plan *Degrees:* B, M *Prof. Accred.:* Nursing (B), Physical Therapy *CEO:* Pres. Thomas J. Savage, S.J.
Enroll: 2,611   (816) 926-4000

ST. CHARLES COUNTY COMMUNITY COLLEGE
4601 Mid Rivers Mall Dr., P.O. Box 76975, St. Peters 63376 *Type:* Public (district) junior *System:* Missouri Coordinating Board for Higher Education *Accred.:* 1991 (NCA) *Calendar:* Sem. plan *Degrees:* A, certificates *Prof. Accred.:* Medical Record Technology, Nursing (A) *CEO:* Pres. Donald D. Shook
Enroll: 4,631   (314) 922-8000

ST. LOUIS CHRISTIAN COLLEGE
1360 Grandview Dr., Florissant 63033 *Type:* Private (Christian Churches/Churches of Christ) *Accred.:* 1977/1987 (AABC) *Calendar:* Sem. plan *Degrees:* A, B, certificates *CEO:* Pres. Thomas W. McGee
FTE Enroll: 118   (314) 837-6777

ST. LOUIS COLLEGE OF PHARMACY
4588 Parkview Pl., St. Louis 63110 *Type:* Private professional *Accred.:* 1967/1987 (NCA) *Calendar:* Sem. plan *Degrees:* B, M, D *CEO:* Thomas Patton
Enroll: 791   (314) 367-8700

ST. LOUIS COMMUNITY COLLEGE AT FLORISSANT VALLEY
3400 Pershall Rd., St. Louis 63135 *Type:* Public (district) junior *System:* St. Louis Community College District *Accred.:* 1988 (NCA)* *Calendar:* Sem. plan *Degrees:* A, certificates *Prof. Accred.:* Art, Engineering Technology (civil/construction, electrical, mechanical), Nursing (A) *CEO:* Pres. Michael T. Murphy
                    (314) 595-4200

* Indirect accreditation through St. Louis Community College District.

ST. LOUIS COMMUNITY COLLEGE AT FOREST PARK
5600 Oakland Ave., St. Louis 63110 *Type:* Public (district) junior *System:* St. Louis Community College District *Accred.:* 1988 (NCA)* *Calendar:* Sem. plan *Degrees:* A, certificates *Prof. Accred.:* Dental Hygiene, Diagnostic Medical Sonography, Funeral Service Education, Medical Laboratory Technology (AMA), Nursing (A), Radiography, Respiratory Therapy, Surgical Technology *CEO:* Pres. Henry D. Shannon
                    (314) 644-9100

ST. LOUIS COMMUNITY COLLEGE AT MERAMEC
11333 Big Bend Blvd., Kirkwood 63122 *Type:* Public (district) junior *System:* St. Louis Community College District *Accred.:* 1988 (NCA)* *Calendar:* Sem. plan *Degrees:* A, certificates *Prof. Accred.:* Dental Laboratory Technology, Nursing (A), Occupational Therapy Assisting, Physical Therapy Assisting *CEO:* Pres. Richard A. Black
                    (314) 984-7500

* Indirect accreditation through St. Louis Community College District.

ST. LOUIS UNIVERSITY
221 N. Grand Blvd., St. Louis 63103 *Type:* Private (Roman Catholic) *Accred.:* 1916/1992 (NCA) *Calendar:* Sem. plan *Degrees:* A, B, P, M, D, certificates *Prof. Accred.:* Business (B,M), Clinical Psychology, Dietetics (internship), Health Services Administration, Law, Medical Record Administration, Medical Technology, Medicine, Nuclear Medicine Technology, Nursing (B,M), Orthodontics, Perfusion, Physical Therapy, Physician Assisting, Public Administration, Public Health, Social Work (B,M), Speech-Language Pathology, Teacher Education (e,s,p) *CEO:* Pres. Lawrence Biondi, S.J.
Enroll: 11,747   (314) 658-2222

PARKS COLLEGE
Falling Springs Rd., Cahokia, IL 62206 *Prof. Accred.:* Engineering (aerospace, electrical) *CEO:* Vice Pres. Peggy Baty
                    (618) 337-7500

ST. PAUL SCHOOL OF THEOLOGY
5123 Truman Rd., Kansas City 64127 *Type:* Private (United Methodist) graduate only *Accred.:* 1964/1991 (ATS); 1976/1992 (NCA)

Calendar: Sem. plan *Degrees:* M, D *CEO:* Pres. Lovett H. Weems, Jr.
Enroll: 294   (816) 483-9600

SANFORD-BROWN BUSINESS COLLEGE
12006 Manchester Rd., Des Peres 63131 *Type:* Private business *Accred.:* 1982/1987 (ACISC) *Calendar:* Qtr. plan *Degrees:* A, certificates, diplomas *CEO:* Dir. Joyce Caton
FTE Enroll: 267   (314) 822-7100

BRANCH CAMPUS
355 Brooks Dr., Hazelwood 63042 *Accred.:* 1982/1988 (ACISC) *CEO:* Dir. Brett Combs
                                     (314) 731-5200

BRANCH CAMPUS
3901 Blue Ridge Cut-off, Kansas City 64113 *Accred.:* 1993 (ACISC) *CEO:* Dir. Pat Dixon
                                     (816) 737-5858

BRANCH CAMPUS
3555 Franks Dr., St. Charles 63301 *Accred.:* 1989 (ACISC) *CEO:* Dir. Jim Horstmeier
                                     (314) 724-7100

SOUTHEAST MISSOURI STATE UNIVERSITY
One University Plaza, Cape Girardeau 63701 *Type:* Public (state) liberal arts and teachers *System:* Missouri Coordinating Board for Higher Education *Accred.:* 1915/1991 (NCA) *Calendar:* Sem. plan *Degrees:* A, B, P, M, certificates *Prof. Accred.:* Music, Nursing (A,B), Social Work (B), Speech-Language Pathology, Teacher Education (e,s,p) *CEO:* Pres. Kala M. Stroup
Enroll: 8,438   (314) 651-2000

SOUTHWEST BAPTIST UNIVERSITY
1601 S. Springfield St., Bolivar 65613 *Type:* Private (Southern Baptist) liberal arts *Accred.:* 1957/1990 (NCA) *Calendar:* Sem. plan *Degrees:* A, B, M, certificates, diplomas *Prof. Accred.:* Music *CEO:* Pres. Roy Blunt
Enroll: 3,087   (417) 326-5281

SOUTHWEST MISSOURI STATE UNIVERSITY
901 S. National Ave., Springfield 65804 *Type:* Public (state) liberal arts and teachers *System:* Missouri Coordinating Board for Higher Education *Accred.:* 1915/1986

(NCA) *Calendar:* Sem. plan *Degrees:* A, B, P, M, certificates *Prof. Accred.:* Accounting (Type A,C), Business (B,M), Computer Science, Home Economics, Music, Nurse Anesthesia Education, Nursing (A,B), Public Administration, Recreation and Leisure Services, Social Work (B), Speech-Language Pathology, Teacher Education (e,s,p) *CEO:* Pres. John H. Keiser
Enroll: 19,002   (417) 836-5000

STATE FAIR COMMUNITY COLLEGE
3201 W. 16th St., Sedalia 65301 *Type:* Public (district) junior *System:* Missouri Coordinating Board for Higher Education *Accred.:* 1977/1989 (NCA) *Calendar:* Sem. plan *Degrees:* A, certificates *Prof. Accred.:* Respiratory Therapy Technology *CEO:* Pres. Marvin R. Fielding
Enroll: 2,418   (816) 530-5800

STEPHENS COLLEGE
Columbia 65215 *Type:* Private liberal arts primarily for women *Accred.:* 1918/1988 (NCA) *Calendar:* Sem. plan *Degrees:* A, B, certificates, diplomas *Prof. Accred.:* Medical Record Administration *CEO:* Pres. Patsy H. Sampson
Enroll: 1,045   (314) 876-7210

THREE RIVERS COMMUNITY COLLEGE
2080 Three Rivers Blvd., Poplar Bluff 63901 *Type:* Public (district) junior *System:* Missouri Coordinating Board for Higher Education *Accred.:* 1974/1987 (NCA) *Calendar:* Sem. plan *Degrees:* A, certificates *Prof. Accred.:* Medical Laboratory Technology (AMA), Nursing (A) *CEO:* Pres. Stephen M. Poort
Enroll: 3,261   (314) 840-9600

THE UNIVERSITY OF HEALTH SCIENCES
2105 Independence Blvd., Kansas City 64124 *Type:* Private professional *Calendar:* Tri. plan *Degrees:* P *Prof. Accred.:* Osteopathy *CEO:* Pres. John P. Perrin
Enroll: 500   (816) 283-2000

UNIVERSITY OF MISSOURI—COLUMBIA
Columbia 65211 *Type:* Public (state) *System:* University of Missouri System *Accred.:* 1913/1985 (NCA) *Calendar:* Sem. plan *Degrees:* B, P, M, D *Prof. Accred.:* Accounting (Type A,C), Business (B,M), Clinical Psy-

chology, Counseling Psychology, Dietetics (coordinated), Engineering (agricultural, chemical, civil, computer, electrical, industrial, mechanical), Forestry, Health Services Administration, Home Economics, Interior Design, Journalism (B,M), Law, Librarianship, Medicine, Music, Nuclear Medicine Technology, Nursing (B,M), Occupational Therapy, Physical Therapy, Psychology Internship, Public Administration, Radiography, Recreation and Leisure Services, Rehabilitation Counseling, Respiratory Therapy, Social Work (B,M), Speech-Language Pathology, Teacher Education (e,s,p), Veterinary Medicine *CEO:* Chanc. Charles A. Kiesler
Enroll: 23,430   (314) 882-2121

UNIVERSITY OF MISSOURI—KANSAS CITY
5100 Rockhill Rd., Kansas City 64110 *Type:* Public (state) *System:* University of Missouri System *Accred.:* 1938/1989 (NCA) *Calendar:* Sem. plan *Degrees:* B, P, M, D, certificates *Prof. Accred.:* Business (B,M), Combined Prosthodontics, Counseling Psychology, Dental Hygiene, Dentistry, Engineering (civil, electrical, mechanical), General Dentistry, Law, Maxillofacial Prosthodontics, Medicine, Music, Nursing (B,M), Oral and Maxillofacial Surgery, Orthodontics, Pediatric Dentistry, Periodontics, Psychology Internship, Public Administration, Teacher Education (e,s,p), Theatre *CEO:* Chanc. Eleanor B. Schwartz
Enroll: 14,052   (816) 235-1000

UNIVERSITY OF MISSOURI—ROLLA
Rolla 65401 *Type:* Public (state) *System:* University of Missouri System *Accred.:* 1913/1989 (NCA) *Calendar:* Sem. plan *Degrees:* B, M, D *Prof. Accred.:* Computer Science, Engineering (aerospace, ceramic, chemical, civil, electrical, engineering management, geological/geophysical, mechanical, metallurgical, mining, nuclear, petroleum) *CEO:* Chanc. John T. Park
Enroll: 5,657   (314) 341-4114

UNIVERSITY OF MISSOURI—ST. LOUIS
8001 Natural Bridge Rd., St. Louis 63121 *Type:* Public (state) *System:* University of Missouri System *Accred.:* 1960/1989 (NCA) *Calendar:* Sem. plan *Degrees:* B, M, D *Prof. Accred.:* Business (B,M), Clinical Psycholo-

gy, Music (associate), Nursing (B), Optometry, Public Policy Administration, Social Work (B), Teacher Education (e,s,p) *CEO:* Chanc. Blanche M. Touhill
Enroll: 14,052   (314) 553-5000

WASHINGTON UNIVERSITY
One Brookings Dr., Box 1192, St. Louis 63130 *Type:* Private *Accred.:* 1913/1984 (NCA) *Calendar:* Sem. plan *Degrees:* B, P, M, D, certificates *Prof. Accred.:* Art, Audiology, Business (B,M), Clinical Psychology, Engineering (chemical, civil, computer, electrical, general, mechanical, systems), Health Services Administration, Law, Medicine, Nurse Anesthesia Education, Occupational Therapy, Physical Therapy, Social Work (M), Teacher Education (e,s) *CEO:* Chanc. William H. Danforth
Enroll: 11,572   (314) 935-5000

WEBSTER UNIVERSITY
470 E. Lockwood Ave., St. Louis 63119 *Type:* Private liberal arts *Accred.:* 1925/1988 (NCA) *Calendar:* Sem. plan *Degrees:* B, M, D, certificates *Prof. Accred.:* Music, Nursing (B) *CEO:* Acting Pres. William J. Duggan
Enroll: 10,335   (314) 968-6900

WENTWORTH MILITARY ACADEMY AND JUNIOR COLLEGE
Washington Ave., Lexington 64067 *Type:* Private junior primarily for men *Accred.:* 1930/1991 (NCA) *Calendar:* Sem. plan *Degrees:* A, certificates *CEO:* Supt. Gerald Childress
Enroll: 1,050   (816) 259-2221

WESTMINSTER COLLEGE
501 Westminster Ave., Fulton 65251-1299 *Type:* Private (Presbyterian) liberal arts *Accred.:* 1913/1985 (NCA) *Calendar:* Sem. plan *Degrees:* B *CEO:* Pres. James F. Traer
Enroll: 731   (314) 642-3361

WILLIAM JEWELL COLLEGE
Liberty 64068 *Type:* Private (Southern Baptist) liberal arts *Accred.:* 1915/1991 (NCA) *Calendar:* 4-1-4 plan *Degrees:* B *Prof. Accred.:* Music, Nursing (B) *CEO:* Interim Pres. Jim Fanner
Enroll: 1,880   (816) 781-7700

WILLIAM WOODS UNIVERSITY
Fulton 65251 *Type:* Private (Disciples of Christ) liberal arts for women *Accred.:* 1919/1987 (NCA) *Calendar:* Sem. plan *Degrees:* A, B, M *Prof. Accred.:* Social Work (B-conditional), Teacher Education (e,s) *CEO:* Pres. Jahnae H. Barnett
Enroll: 833   (314) 642-2251

MONTANA

BILLINGS VOCATIONAL-TECHNICAL CENTER
3803 Central Ave., Billings 59102 *Type:* Public (state) 2-year *System:* Montana University System *Accred.:* 1979/1991 (NASC) *Calendar:* Sem. plan *Degrees:* A, certificates *CEO:* Dir. George E. Bell
Enroll: 422   (406) 656-4445

BLACKFEET COMMUNITY COLLEGE
Browning 59417 *Type:* Private (tribal) junior *Accred.:* 1985/1992 (NASC) *Calendar:* Qtr. plan *Degrees:* A *CEO:* Pres. Carol Murray
Enroll: 437   (406) 338-5441

BUTTE VOCATIONAL-TECHNICAL CENTER
Basin Creek Rd., Butte 59701 *Type:* Public (state) 2-year *System:* Montana University System *Accred.:* 1984/1993 (NASC) *Calendar:* Sem. plan *Degrees:* A, certificates *CEO:* Dir. Jane G. Baker
Enroll: 322   (406) 494-2894

CARROLL COLLEGE
N. Benton Ave., Helena 59625 *Type:* Private (Roman Catholic) liberal arts *Accred.:* 1949/1992 (NASC) *Calendar:* Sem. plan *Degrees:* B *Prof. Accred.:* Medical Record Administration, Nursing (B), Social Work (B) *CEO:* Pres. Matthew J. Quinn
Enroll: 1,384   (406) 447-4300

COLLEGE OF GREAT FALLS
1301 20th St., S., Great Falls 59405 *Type:* Private (Roman Catholic) liberal arts *Accred.:* 1935/1991 (NASC) *Calendar:* Sem. plan *Degrees:* B, M *CEO:* Pres. Frederick Gilliard
Enroll: 1,342   (406) 761-8210

DAWSON COMMUNITY COLLEGE
Glendive 59330 *Type:* Public (district) junior *System:* Montana Community College System *Accred.:* 1969/1989 (NASC) *Calendar:* Sem. plan *Degrees:* A *CEO:* Pres. Donald H. Kettner
Enroll: 553   (406) 365-3396

EASTERN MONTANA COLLEGE
Billings 59101 *Type:* Public (state) liberal arts and teachers *System:* Montana University System *Accred.:* 1932/1993 (NASC) *Calendar:* Sem. plan *Degrees:* B, M *Prof. Ac-*

cred.: Art, Music, Rehabilitation Counseling, Teacher Education (e,s,p) *CEO:* Pres. Bruce H. Carpenter
Enroll: 3,967   (406) 657-2011

FLATHEAD VALLEY COMMUNITY COLLEGE
777 Grandview Dr., Kalispell 59901 *Type:* Public (district) junior *System:* Montana Community College System *Accred.:* 1970/1992 (NASC) *Calendar:* Qtr. plan *Degrees:* A *CEO:* Pres. Howard L. Fryett
Enroll: 1,719   (406) 756-3822

FORT BELKNAP COLLEGE
P.O. Box 159, Harlem 59526-0159 *Type:* Private (tribal) junior *Accred.:* 1993 (NASC) *Calendar:* Sem. plan *Degrees:* A *CEO:* Pres. Margaret C. Perez
Enroll: 232   (406) 353-2205

FORT PECK COMMUNITY COLLEGE
P.O. Box 1027, Poplar 59255 *Type:* Private (tribal) junior *Accred.:* 1991/1993 (NASC) *Calendar:* Sem. plan *Degrees:* A *CEO:* Pres. James E. Shanley
Enroll: 395   (406) 768-5551

GREAT FALLS VOCATIONAL-TECHNICAL CENTER
2100 16th Ave., S., Great Falls 59405 *Type:* Public (state) 2-year *System:* Montana University System *Accred.:* 1979/1991 (NASC) *Calendar:* Sem. plan *Degrees:* A, certificates *Prof. Accred.:* Dental Assisting, Occupational Therapy, Respiratory Therapy, Respiratory Therapy Technology *CEO:* Dir. Willard R. Weaver
Enroll: 839   (406) 771-1240

HELENA VOCATIONAL-TECHNICAL CENTER
115 N. Roberts St., Helena 59620 *Type:* Public (state) 2-year *System:* Montana University System *Accred.:* 1977/1992 (NASC) *Calendar:* Sem. plan *Degrees:* A, certificates *CEO:* Dir. Alex Capdeville
Enroll: 569   (406) 444-6800

LITTLE BIG HORN COLLEGE
P.O. Box 370, Crow Agency 59022 *Type:* Private (tribal) junior *Accred.:* 1990/1992 (NASC) *Calendar:* Sem. plan *Degrees:* A *CEO:* Pres. Janine Pease-Windy Boy
Enroll: 226   (406) 638-7211

MILES COMMUNITY COLLEGE
Miles City 59301 *Type:* Public (district) junior *System:* Montana Community College System *Accred.:* 1971/1993 (NASC) *Calendar:* Sem. plan *Degrees:* A *CEO:* Pres. Judson H. Flower
Enroll: 695   (406) 232-3031

MISSOULA VOCATIONAL-TECHNICAL CENTER
909 South Ave., W., Missoula 59801 *Type:* Public (state) 2-year *System:* Montana University System *Accred.:* 1974/1991 (NASC) *Calendar:* Sem. plan *Degrees:* A, certificates *Prof. Accred.:* Respiratory Therapy Technology, Surgical Technology *CEO:* Dir. Dennis N. Lerum
Enroll: 612   (406) 542-6811

MONTANA COLLEGE OF MINERAL SCIENCE AND TECHNOLOGY
Butte 59701 *Type:* Public (state) technological *System:* Montana University System *Accred.:* 1932/1990 (NASC) *Calendar:* Sem. plan *Degrees:* B, M *Prof. Accred.:* Engineering (engineering physics/science, environmental/sanitary, geological/geophysical, metallurgical, mining, petroleum) *CEO:* Pres. Lindsay D. Norman, Jr.
Enroll: 1,975   (406) 496-4101

MONTANA STATE UNIVERSITY
Bozeman 59717 *Type:* Public (state) *System:* Montana University System *Accred.:* 1932/1990 (NASC) *Calendar:* Sem. plan *Degrees:* B, M, D *Prof. Accred.:* Art, Business (B), Computer Science, Counseling, Engineering Technology (civil/construction, electrical, mechanical), Engineering (agricultural, chemical, civil, electrical, industrial, mechanical), Music, Nursing (B,M), Psychology Internship, Teacher Education (e,s,p) *CEO:* Pres. Michael Malone
Enroll: 10,540   (406) 994-0211

NORTHERN MONTANA COLLEGE
P.O. Box 7751, Havre 59501 *Type:* Public (state) teachers *System:* Montana University

System *Accred.:* 1932/1992 (NASC) *Calendar:* Qtr. plan *Degrees:* A, B, M *Prof. Accred.:* Nursing (A,B) *CEO:* Pres. William Daehling
Enroll: 1,742   (406) 265-3221

ROCKY MOUNTAIN COLLEGE
1511 Poly Dr., Billings 59102 *Type:* Private liberal arts *Accred.:* 1949/1990 (NASC) *Calendar:* Sem. plan *Degrees:* A, B *CEO:* Pres. Arthur H. DeRosier
Enroll: 748   (406) 657-1020

SALISH KOOTENAI COLLEGE
P.O. Box 117, Pablo 59855 *Type:* Private (tribal) junior *Accred.:* 1984/1993 (NASC) *Calendar:* Qtr. plan *Degrees:* A, B *Prof. Accred.:* Dental Assisting, Nursing (A) *CEO:* Pres. Joseph F. McDonald
Enroll: 715   (406) 675-4800

STONE CHILD COMMUNITY COLLEGE
RR 1, Box 1082, Box Elder 59521-9796 *Type:* Private (tribal) junior *Accred.:* 1993 (NASC) *Calendar:* Sem. plan *Degrees:* A *CEO:* Pres. Margaret Nagel
Enroll: 226   (406) 395-4313

THE UNIVERSITY OF MONTANA
Missoula 59812 *Type:* Public (state) *System:* Montana University System *Accred.:* 1932/1989 (NASC) *Calendar:* Qtr. plan *Degrees:* A, B, M, D *Prof. Accred.:* Art, Business (B,M), Clinical Psychology, Forestry, Journalism (B,M), Law, Music, Physical Therapy, Social Work (B), Teacher Education (e,s,p), Theatre *CEO:* Pres. George M. Dennison
Enroll: 10,614   (406) 243-0211

WESTERN MONTANA COLLEGE
710 S. Atlantic St., Dillon 59725-3511 *Type:* Public (state) teachers *System:* Montana University System *Accred.:* 1932/1989 (NASC) *Calendar:* Sem. plan *Degrees:* A, B *CEO:* Pres. Sheila Sterns
Enroll: 1,022   (406) 683-7151

NEBRASKA

BELLEVUE COLLEGE
Galvin Rd. at Harvell Dr., Bellevue 68005
Type: Private liberal arts *Accred.:* 1977/1992
(NCA) *Calendar:* Sem. plan *Degrees:* B, M
CEO: Pres. John B. Muller
Enroll: 2,157   (402) 291-8100

CENTRAL COMMUNITY COLLEGE
P.O. Box 4903, Grand Island 68802-4903
Type: Public (state) 2-year technical *System:*
Nebraska Coordinating Commission for
Postsecondary Education *Accred.:* 1980/
1988 (NCA) *Calendar:* Qtr. plan *Degrees:*
A, certificates, diplomas *Prof. Accred.:* Med-
ical Assisting (AMA), Nursing (A) *CEO:*
Pres. Joseph W. Preusser
Enroll: 8,097   (308) 384-5220

CENTRAL TECHNICAL COMMUNITY COLLEGE
P.O. Box 1024, Hastings 68902-1024 *Type:*
Public 2-year technical *Calendar:* Courses of
varying lengths *Degrees:* A, certificates,
diplomas *Prof. Accred.:* Dental Assisting,
Dental Hygiene, Dental Laboratory Technology *CEO:* Pres. Judy Dresser
                                             (402) 463-9811

CHADRON STATE COLLEGE
10th and Main Sts., Chadron 69337 *Type:*
Public (state) liberal arts and teachers *Sys-
tem:* Nebraska Coordinating Commission for
Postsecondary Education *Accred.:* 1915/
1987 (NCA) *Calendar:* Sem. plan *Degrees:*
A, B, P, M *Prof. Accred.:* Social Work (B-
candidate), Teacher Education (e,s,p) *CEO:*
Pres. Samuel H. Rankin, Jr.
Enroll: 3,693   (308) 432-4451

CLARKSON COLLEGE
101 S. 42nd St., Omaha 68131 *Type:* Private
professional *Accred.:* 1984/1989 (NCA) *Calendar:* Sem. plan *Degrees:* B, M, certificates, diplomas *Prof. Accred.:* Nursing (B)
CEO: Pres. Fay Bower
Enroll: 515   (402) 552-3394

COLLEGE OF ST. MARY
1901 S. 72nd St., Omaha 68124 *Type:* Private (Roman Catholic) liberal arts primarily
for women *Accred.:* 1958/1988 (NCA) *Calendar:* Sem. plan *Degrees:* A, B, certificates
Prof. Accred.: Medical Record Administra-

tion, Medical Record Technology, Nursing
(A,B) *CEO:* Pres. Kenneth R. Nielsen
Enroll: 1,322   (402) 399-2400

CONCORDIA COLLEGE
800 N. Columbia Ave., Seward 68434 *Type:*
Private (Lutheran) *Accred.:* 1953/1988
(NCA) *Calendar:* Sem. plan *Degrees:* B, M,
certificates *Prof. Accred.:* Teacher Education
(e,s,p) *CEO:* Pres. Orville C. Walz
Enroll: 799   (402) 643-3651

CREIGHTON UNIVERSITY
2500 California Plaza, Omaha 68178 *Type:*
Private (Roman Catholic) *Accred.:* 1916/
1987 (NCA) *Calendar:* Sem. plan *Degrees:*
A, B, M, D, certificates *Prof. Accred.:* Ac-
counting (Type A), Business (B,M), Den-
tistry, EMT-Paramedic, General Dentistry,
Law, Medicine, Nursing (B,M), Occupational
Therapy, Social Work (B), Teacher Educa-
tion (e,s,p) *CEO:* Pres. Michael G. Morrison,
S.J.
Enroll: 6,225   (402) 280-2770

DANA COLLEGE
2848 College Dr., Blair 68008 *Type:* Private
(Lutheran) liberal arts and professional *Ac-
cred.:* 1958/1992 (NCA) *Calendar:* 4-1-4
plan *Degrees:* B *Prof. Accred.:* Social Work
(B), Teacher Education (e,s) *CEO:* Pres.
Myrvin Christopherson
Enroll: 572   (402) 426-7200

DOANE COLLEGE
1014 Boswell Ave., Crete 68333 *Type:* Pri-
vate (United Church of Christ) liberal arts
Accred.: 1913/1992 (NCA) *Calendar:* Sem.
plan *Degrees:* B, M *Prof. Accred.:* Teacher
Education (e,s) *CEO:* Pres. Frederic D.
Brown
Enroll: 1,643   (402) 826-2161

GRACE COLLEGE OF THE BIBLE
1515 S. 10th St., Omaha 68108 *Type:* Independent *Accred.:* 1948/1984 (AABC); 1992
(NCA candidate) *Calendar:* Sem. plan *Degrees:* A, B, certificates *CEO:* Pres. Neal F.
McBride
Enroll: 293   (402) 449-2800

HASTINGS COLLEGE
720 N. Turner Ave., P.O. Box 269, Hastings 68902-0269 *Type:* Private (United Presbyterian) liberal arts *Accred.:* 1916/1985 (NCA) *Calendar:* 4-1-4 plan *Degrees:* B, M *Prof. Accred.:* Music, Teacher Education (e,s) *CEO:* Pres. Thomas J. Reeves
Enroll: 954   (402) 463-2402

LINCOLN SCHOOL OF COMMERCE
P.O. Box 82826, 1821 K St., Lincoln 68501-2826 *Type:* Private junior *Accred.:* 1966/1987 (ACISC) *Calendar:* Sem. plan *Degrees:* A *CEO:* Dir. Gary Carlson
      (402) 474-5315

MCCOOK COMMUNITY COLLEGE
1205 E. Third St., McCook 69001 *Type:* Public (state) 2-year *System:* Mid-Plains Community College Area *Accred.:* 1980/1992 (NCA)* *Calendar:* Sem. plan *Degrees:* A, certificates, diplomas *CEO:* Pres. Robert G. Smallfoot
      (800) 658-4348

* Indirect accreditation through Mid-Plains Community College Area.

METROPOLITAN COMMUNITY COLLEGE
P.O. Box 3777, Omaha 68103 *Type:* Public (local) junior *System:* Nebraska Coordinating Commission for Postsecondary Education *Accred.:* 1979/1993 (NCA) *Calendar:* Qtr. plan *Degrees:* A, certificates, diplomas *Prof. Accred.:* Dental Assisting, Nursing (A), Respiratory Therapy, Respiratory Therapy Technology, Surgical Technology *CEO:* Pres. J. Richard Gilliland
Enroll: 10,301   (402) 449-8400

MID-PLAINS COMMUNITY COLLEGE
Rte. 4, Box 1, North Platte 69101 *Type:* Public (local) 2-year technical *System:* Mid-Plains Community College Area *Accred.:* 1986/1992 (NCA)* *Calendar:* Sem. plan *Degrees:* A, certificates, diplomas *Prof. Accred.:* Dental Assisting, Medical Laboratory Technology (AMA) *CEO:* Pres. Kenneth L. Aten
      (308) 532-8740

* Indirect accreditation through Mid-Plains Community College Area.

MIDLAND LUTHERAN COLLEGE
900 Clarkson St., Fremont 68025 *Type:* Private (Lutheran) liberal arts *Accred.:* 1947/1989 (NCA) *Calendar:* 4-1-4 plan *Degrees:* A, B *Prof. Accred.:* Nursing (B) *CEO:* Pres. Carl L. Hansen
Enroll: 961   (402) 721-5480

NEBRASKA CHRISTIAN COLLEGE
1800 Syracuse St., Norfolk 68701 *Type:* Private (Christian Churches/Churches of Christ) *Accred.:* 1985/1990 (AABC) *Calendar:* Sem. plan *Degrees:* A, B *CEO:* Pres. Ray Stites
FTE Enroll: 123   (402) 371-5960

NEBRASKA COLLEGE OF BUSINESS
3636 California St., Omaha 68131 *Type:* Private junior *Accred.:* 1968/1987 (ACISC) *Calendar:* Qtr. plan *Degrees:* A, certificates, diplomas *CEO:* Dir. Thomas Loggins
      (402) 553-8500

NEBRASKA COLLEGE OF TECHNICAL AGRICULTURE
Curtis 69025 *Type:* Private *Calendar:* Sem. plan *Degrees:* A *Prof. Accred.:* Veterinary Technology *CEO:* Dir. Ricky Sue Barnes-Wach, D.V.M.
      (308) 367-4124

NEBRASKA INDIAN COMMUNITY COLLEGE
P.O.Box 752, Winnebago 68071 *Type:* Public (federal) 2-year *Accred.:* 1986/1992 (NCA) *Calendar:* Sem. plan *Degrees:* A, certificates, diplomas *CEO:* Pres. Thelma Thomas
Enroll: 301   (402) 878-2414

NEBRASKA METHODIST COLLEGE OF NURSING AND ALLIED HEALTH
8501 W. Dodge Rd., Omaha 68114 *Type:* Private professional *Accred.:* 1989/1993 (NCA) *Calendar:* Sem. plan *Degrees:* A, B, certificates *Prof. Accred.:* Nursing (B), Respiratory Therapy *CEO:* Pres. Roger Koehler
Enroll: 474   (402) 390-4879

NEBRASKA WESLEYAN UNIVERSITY
5000 St. Paul Ave., Lincoln 68504 *Type:* Private (United Methodist) liberal arts *Accred.:* 1914/1990 (NCA) *Calendar:* Sem. plan *Degrees:* A, B *Prof. Accred.:* Music,

Nursing (B), Social Work (B), Teacher Education (e,s) *CEO:* Pres. John W. White, Jr.
Enroll: 1,694 (402) 466-2371

NORTHEAST COMMUNITY COLLEGE
801 E. Benjamin Ave., P.O. Box 469, Norfolk 68702-0469 *Type:* Public (local) junior *System:* Nebraska Coordinating Commission for Postsecondary Education *Accred.:* 1979/1984 (NCA) *Calendar:* Sem. plan *Degrees:* A, certificates, diplomas *CEO:* Pres. Robert P. Cox
Enroll: 3,257 (402) 371-2020

PERU STATE COLLEGE
Peru 68421 *Type:* Public (state) liberal arts and teachers *System:* Nebraska Coordinating Commission for Postsecondary Education *Accred.:* 1915/1991 (NCA) *Calendar:* Sem. plan *Degrees:* A, B, M *Prof. Accred.:* Teacher Education (e,s) *CEO:* Pres. Robert L. Burns
Enroll: 1,564 (402) 872-2239

SOUTHEAST COMMUNITY COLLEGE
8800 O St., Lincoln 68520 *Type:* Public (state/local) 2-year *System:* Nebraska Coordinating Commission for Postsecondary Education *Accred.:* 1983/1993 (NCA) *Calendar:* Qtr. plan *Degrees:* A, certificates, diplomas *Prof. Accred.:* Dental Assisting, Medical Assisting (AMA), Medical Laboratory Technology (AMA), Practical Nursing, Radiography, Respiratory Therapy, Respiratory Therapy Technology, Surgical Technology *CEO:* Interim Chanc. Jack Huck
Enroll: 8,150 (402) 437-2500

SPENCER SCHOOL OF BUSINESS
P.O. Box 399, 410 W. Second St., Grand Island 68802 *Type:* Private business *Accred.:* 1972/1988 (ACISC) *Calendar:* Qtr. plan *Degrees:* A, certificates, diplomas *CEO:* Dir. Connie J. Collin
(308) 382-8044

UNION COLLEGE
3800 S. 48th St., Lincoln 68506 *Type:* Private (Seventh-Day Adventist) liberal arts *Accred.:* 1923/1990 (NCA) *Calendar:* Sem. plan *Degrees:* A, B *Prof. Accred.:* Nursing (B), Social Work (B), Teacher Education (e,s) *CEO:* Pres. John G. Kerbs
Enroll: 558 (402) 488-2331

UNIVERSITY OF NEBRASKA AT KEARNEY
905 W. 25th St., Kearney 68849 *Type:* Public (state) *System:* University of Nebraska *Accred.:* 1916/1984 (NCA) *Calendar:* Sem. plan *Degrees:* B, P, M *Prof. Accred.:* Music, Nursing (B), Social Work (B), Speech-Language Pathology, Teacher Education (e,s,p) *CEO:* Chanc. Gladys Styles Johnston, Ph.D.
Enroll: 8,374 (308) 236-8441

UNIVERSITY OF NEBRASKA AT OMAHA
60th and Dodge Sts., Omaha 68182 *Type:* Public (state) *System:* University of Nebraska *Accred.:* 1939/1987 (NCA) *Calendar:* Sem. plan *Degrees:* B, P, M, D, certificates *Prof. Accred.:* Business (B,M), Counseling, Engineering Technology (civil/construction, electrical, manufacturing, mechanical drafting/design), Engineering (civil), Music (associate), Public Administration, Social Work (B,M), Speech-Language Pathology, Teacher Education (e,s,p) *CEO:* Chanc. Delbert D. Weber
Enroll: 16,227 (402) 554-2800

UNIVERSITY OF NEBRASKA—LINCOLN
Lincoln 68583 *Type:* Public (state) *System:* University of Nebraska *Accred.:* 1913/1987 (NCA) *Calendar:* Sem. plan *Degrees:* A, B, P, M, D, certificates *Prof. Accred.:* Accounting (Type A,C), Art, Audiology, Business (B,M), Clinical Psychology, Combined Prosthodontics, Construction Education (B), Counseling Psychology, Dental Hygiene, Dentistry, Endodontics, Engineering (agricultural, chemical, civil, electrical, industrial, mechanical), General Dentistry, General Practice Residency, Home Economics, Interior Design, Journalism (B,M), Law, Marriage and Family Therapy (M-candidate), Music, Oral and Maxillofacial Surgery, Orthodontics, Pediatric Dentistry, Periodontics, Planning (M), School Psychology, Speech-Language Pathology, Teacher Education (e,s,p), Theatre *CEO:* Chanc. Graham B. Spanier
Enroll: 24,573 (402) 472-7211

UNIVERSITY OF NEBRASKA MEDICAL CENTER
600 S. 42nd St., Omaha 68198-6605 *Type:* Public (state) *System:* University of Nebraska *Accred.:* 1913/1987 (NCA) *Calendar:* Sem. plan *Degrees:* B, M, D, certificates *Prof. Accred.:* Diagnostic Medical Sonogra-

phy, Dietetics (internship), Medical Technology, Medicine, Nuclear Medicine Technology, Nursing (B,M), Perfusion, Physical Therapy, Physician Assisting, Radiation Therapy Technology, Radiography *CEO:* Chanc. Carol A. Aschenbrener
Enroll: 2,757   (402) 559-4000

WAYNE STATE COLLEGE
200 E. 10th St., Wayne 68787 *Type:* Public (state) liberal arts and teachers *System:* Nebraska Coordinating Commission for Postsecondary Education *Accred.:* 1917/1992 (NCA) *Calendar:* Sem. plan *Degrees:* B, P, M *Prof. Accred.:* Teacher Education (e,s,p) *CEO:* Pres. Donald J. Mash
                    (402) 375-7200

WESTERN NEBRASKA COMMUNITY COLLEGE
1601 E. 27th St., Scottsbluff 69361 *Type:* Public (local) junior *System:* Nebraska Coordinating Commission for Postsecondary Education *Accred.:* 1988/1990 (NCA) *Calendar:* Sem. plan *Degrees:* A, certificates, diplomas *Prof. Accred.:* Practical Nursing *CEO:* Pres. John N. Harms
Enroll: 1,868   (308) 635-3606

YORK COLLEGE
9th and Kiplinger, York 68467 *Type:* Private (Church of Christ) *Accred.:* 1970/1984 (NCA) *Calendar:* Sem. plan *Degrees:* A, B, certificates *CEO:* Pres. Larry Roberts
Enroll: 396   (402) 362-4441

NEVADA

COMMUNITY COLLEGE OF SOUTHERN NEVADA
3200 E. Cheyenne Ave., North Las Vegas 89030 *Type:* Public (district) junior *System:* University and Community College System of Nevada *Accred.:* 1975/1990 (NASC) *Calendar:* Sem. plan *Degrees:* A *Prof. Accred.:* Dental Hygiene, Medical Laboratory Technology (AMA), Medical Record Technology, Nursing (A), Physical Therapy Assisting, Practical Nursing *CEO:* Pres. Paul E. Meacham
Enroll: 20,803   (702) 643-6060

MORRISON COLLEGE—RENO
140 Washington St., Reno 89503 *Type:* Private *Accred.:* 1990 (ACISC) *Calendar:* Qtr. plan *Degrees:* A, B *CEO:* Admin. Mary Morrison
                         (702) 323-4145

NORTHERN NEVADA COMMUNITY COLLEGE
901 Elm St., Elko 89801 *Type:* Public (district) junior *System:* University and Community College System of Nevada *Accred.:* 1974/1989 (NASC) *Calendar:* Sem. plan *Degrees:* A *Prof. Accred.:* Nursing (A) *CEO:* Pres. Ronald Remington
Enroll: 2,709   (702) 738-8493

PHILLIPS JUNIOR COLLEGE OF LAS VEGAS
Ste. 30, 3320 E. Flamingo Rd., Las Vegas 89121-4306 *Type:* Private junior *Accred.:* 1983/1987 (ACISC) *Calendar:* Qtr. plan *Degrees:* A *CEO:* Pres. Vincent Zocco
                         (702) 434-0486

SIERRA NEVADA COLLEGE
Incline Village 89450-4269 *Type:* Private liberal arts *Accred.:* 1977/1992 (NASC) *Calendar:* Sem. plan *Degrees:* B *CEO:* Pres. Mark Hurtubise
Enroll: 600   (702) 831-1314

TRUCKEE MEADOWS COMMUNITY COLLEGE
7000 Dandini Blvd., Reno 89512 *Type:* Public (district) junior *System:* University and Community College System of Nevada *Ac-*
cred.: 1980/1990 (NASC) *Calendar:* Sem. plan *Degrees:* A *Prof. Accred.:* Dental Assisting, Radiography *CEO:* Pres. John W. Gwaltney
Enroll: 9,022   (702) 673-7000

UNIVERSITY OF NEVADA, LAS VEGAS
4505 Maryland Pkwy., Las Vegas 89154 *Type:* Public (state) *System:* University and Community College System of Nevada *Accred.:* 1964/1992 (NASC) *Calendar:* Sem. plan *Degrees:* A, B, M, D *Prof. Accred.:* Accounting (Type A,C), Art, Business (B,M), Computer Science, Counseling, Engineering (civil, electrical, mechanical), Medical Technology, Music, Nuclear Medicine Technology, Nursing (B,M), Public Administration, Radiography, Social Work (B,M), Teacher Education (e,s,p), Theatre *CEO:* Pres. Robert C. Maxson
Enroll: 19,209   (702) 739-3201

UNIVERSITY OF NEVADA, RENO
Reno 89557 *Type:* Public (state) *System:* University and Community College System of Nevada *Accred.:* 1938/1993 (NASC) *Calendar:* Sem. plan *Degrees:* A, B, M, D *Prof. Accred.:* Business (B,M), Clinical Psychology, Engineering (chemical, civil, electrical, geological/geophysical, mechanical, metallurgical, mining), Journalism (B,M), Medical Laboratory Technology (AMA), Medical Technology, Medicine, Music, Nursing (B,M), Social Work (B,M-candidate), Speech-Language Pathology, Teacher Education (e,s,p) *CEO:* Pres. Joseph N. Crowley
Enroll: 11,307   (702) 784-4805

WESTERN NEVADA COMMUNITY COLLEGE
2201 W. Nye La., Carson City 89703 *Type:* Public (district) junior *System:* University and Community College System of Nevada *Accred.:* 1975/1990 (NASC) *Calendar:* Sem. plan *Degrees:* A *Prof. Accred.:* Nursing (A) *CEO:* Pres. Anthony D. Calabro
Enroll: 4,772   (702) 887-3000

NEW HAMPSHIRE

CASTLE COLLEGE
Searles Rd., Windham 03087 *Type:* Private *Accred.:* 1985/1989 (NEASC-CTCI) *Calendar:* Qtr. plan *Degrees:* A *CEO:* Pres. Sheila L. Garvey, R.S.M.
FTE Enroll: 395   (603) 893-6111

COLBY-SAWYER COLLEGE
100 Main St., New London 03257 *Type:* Private *Accred.:* 1933/1987 (NEASC-CIHE) *Calendar:* Sem. plan *Degrees:* A, B *Prof. Accred.:* Nursing (B) *CEO:* Pres. Peggy A. Stock
Enroll: 650   (603) 526-2010

COLLEGE FOR LIFELONG LEARNING
Durham 03824-3547 *Type:* Public (state) *System:* University System of New Hampshire *Accred.:* 1980/1986 (NEASC-CIHE) *Calendar:* Sem. plan *Degrees:* A, B *CEO:* Dean Victor B. Montana
Enroll: 1,054   (603) 862-1692

DANIEL WEBSTER COLLEGE
Nashua 03063 *Type:* Private *Accred.:* 1972/1986 (NEASC-CIHE) *Calendar:* Tri. plan *Degrees:* A, B *CEO:* Pres. Hannah M. McCarthy
Enroll: 739   (603) 883-3556

DARTMOUTH COLLEGE
Hanover 03755 *Type:* Private liberal arts *Accred.:* 1929/1988 (NEASC-CIHE) *Calendar:* Qtr. plan *Degrees:* B, P, M, D *Prof. Accred.:* Business (M), Engineering (general), Medicine, Psychology Internship, Theatre *CEO:* Pres. James O. Freedman
Enroll: 5,477   (603) 646-1110

FRANKLIN PIERCE COLLEGE
College Rd., Rindge 03461 *Type:* Private liberal arts *Accred.:* 1968/1988 (NEASC-CIHE) *Calendar:* Sem. plan *Degrees:* B *CEO:* Pres. Walter R. Peterson
Enroll: 2,644   (603) 899-5111

FRANKLIN PIERCE LAW CENTER
2 White St., Concord 03301 *Type:* Private professional *Calendar:* Sem. plan *Degrees:* P *Prof. Accred.:* Law (ABA only) *CEO:* Pres. Robert M. Viles
Enroll: 418   (603) 228-1541

HESSER COLLEGE
3 Sundial Ave., Manchester 03103 *Type:* Private junior business *Accred.:* 1985/1989 (NEASC-CTCI) *Calendar:* Sem. plan *Degrees:* A *CEO:* Pres. Linwood W. Galeucia
FTE Enroll: 1,985   (603) 668-6660

KEENE STATE COLLEGE
229 Main St., Keene 03431 *Type:* Public (state) liberal arts and teachers *System:* University System of New Hampshire *Accred.:* 1949/1990 (NEASC-CIHE) *Calendar:* Sem. plan *Degrees:* A, B, M *Prof. Accred.:* Music (associate), Teacher Education (e,s) *CEO:* Interim Pres. Richard E. Cunningham
Enroll: 3,980   (603) 352-1909

MCINTOSH COLLEGE
23 Cataract Ave., Dover 03820 *Type:* Private junior business *Accred.:* 1988 (NEASC-CTCI) *Calendar:* Sem. plan *Degrees:* A, diplomas *CEO:* Pres. Robert J. DeColfmacker
FTE Enroll: 732   (603) 742-1234

NEW ENGLAND COLLEGE
Henniker 03242-0788 *Type:* Private liberal arts *Accred.:* 1967/1984 (NEASC-CIHE) *Calendar:* 4-1-4 plan *Degrees:* B, M *Prof. Accred.:* Engineering (civil) *CEO:* Pres. William R. O'Connell, Jr.
Enroll: 1,069   (603) 428-2211

NEW HAMPSHIRE COLLEGE
2500 N. River Rd., Manchester 03104-1394 *Type:* Private *Accred.:* 1973/1991 (NEASC-CIHE) *Calendar:* Sem. plan *Degrees:* A, B, M *CEO:* Pres. Richard A. Gustafson
Enroll: 4,057   (603) 668-2211

NEW HAMPSHIRE TECHNICAL COLLEGE AT BERLIN
2020 Riverside Dr., Berlin 03570 *Type:* Public (state) 2-year technical *Accred.:* 1974/1990 (NEASC-CTCI) *Calendar:* Sem. plan *Degrees:* A *CEO:* Pres. Alex Easton
FTE Enroll: 589   (603) 752-1113

NEW HAMPSHIRE TECHNICAL COLLEGE AT CLAREMONT
One College Dr., Claremont 03743-9707 *Type:* Public (state) 2-year technical *Accred.:* 1973/1989 (NEASC-CTCI) *Calendar:* Sem. plan *Degrees:* A *Prof. Accred.:* Medical Assisting (AMA), Medical Laboratory

Technology (AMA), Medical Record Technology, Nursing (A), Occupational Therapy Assisting, Physical Therapy Assisting, Respiratory Therapy *CEO:* Pres. Willis Reed
FTE Enroll: 482   (603) 542-7744

NEW HAMPSHIRE TECHNICAL COLLEGE AT
LACONIA
Prescott Hill, Rte. 106, Laconia 03246 *Type:* Public (state) 2-year technical *Accred.:* 1974/1985 (NEASC-CTCI) *Calendar:* Sem. plan *Degrees:* A *CEO:* Pres. Larry Keller
FTE Enroll: 673   (603) 524-3207

NEW HAMPSHIRE TECHNICAL COLLEGE AT
MANCHESTER
1066 Front St., Manchester 03102 *Type:* Public (state) 2-year technical *Accred.:* 1974/1985 (NEASC-CTCI) *Calendar:* Sem. plan *Degrees:* A *CEO:* Pres. Patrick A. Roche, Ph.D.
FTE Enroll: 1,351   (603) 668-6706

NEW HAMPSHIRE TECHNICAL COLLEGE AT
NASHUA
505 Amherst St., P.O. Box 2052, Nashua 03061-2052 *Type:* Public (state) 2-year technical *Accred.:* 1974/1989 (NEASC-CTCI) *Calendar:* Sem. plan *Degrees:* A *CEO:* Pres. Robert E. Bloomfield
FTE Enroll: 850   (603) 882-6923

NEW HAMPSHIRE TECHNICAL COLLEGE AT
STRATHAM
P.O. Box 365, Stratham 03885 *Type:* Public (state) 2-year technical *Accred.:* 1975/1990 (NEASC-CTCI) *Calendar:* Sem. plan *Degrees:* A *CEO:* Pres. Jane P. Kilcoyne
FTE Enroll: 665   (603) 772-1194

NEW HAMPSHIRE TECHNICAL INSTITUTE
11 Institute Dr., Concord 03301-7412 *Type:* Public (state) 2-year technical *Accred.:* 1969/1991 (NEASC-CTCI) *Calendar:* Sem. plan *Degrees:* A *Prof. Accred.:* Dental Assisting, Dental Hygiene, EMT-Paramedic, Engineering Technology (architectural, computer, electrical, manufacturing, mechanical), Nursing (A), Radiography *CEO:* Pres. David E. Larrabee, Sr.
FTE Enroll: 2,193   (603) 225-1800

NOTRE DAME COLLEGE
Manchester 03104-2299 *Type:* Private (Roman Catholic) liberal arts *Accred.:*
1970/1992 (NEASC-CIHE) *Calendar:* Sem. plan *Degrees:* A, B, M *CEO:* Pres. Carol Descoteaux, CSC
Enroll: 1,019   (603) 669-4298

PLYMOUTH STATE COLLEGE
Plymouth 03264 *Type:* Public (state) liberal arts and professional *System:* University System of New Hampshire *Accred.:* 1955/1984 (NEASC-CIHE) *Calendar:* Sem. plan *Degrees:* A, B, M *Prof. Accred.:* Social Work (B-candidate), Teacher Education (e,s,p) *CEO:* Pres. Donald P. Wharton
Enroll: 3,893   (603) 535-5000

RIVIER COLLEGE
420 S. Main St., Nashua 03060-5086 *Type:* Private (Roman Catholic) liberal arts primarily for women *Accred.:* 1948/1992 (NEASC-CIHE) *Calendar:* Sem. plan *Degrees:* A, B, M *Prof. Accred.:* Nursing (A,B) *CEO:* Pres. Jeanne Perreault
Enroll: 1,747   (603) 888-1311

ST. ANSELM COLLEGE
Manchester 03102-1310 *Type:* Private (Roman Catholic) liberal arts *Accred.:* 1941/ 1989 (NEASC-CIHE) *Calendar:* Sem. plan *Degrees:* A, B *Prof. Accred.:* Nursing (B) *CEO:* Pres. Jonathan P. DeFelice, O.S.B.
Enroll: 1,902   (603) 641-7000

UNIVERSITY OF NEW HAMPSHIRE
Durham 03824 *Type:* Public (state) *System:* University System of New Hampshire *Accred.:* 1929/1985 (NEASC-CIHE) *Calendar:* Sem. plan *Degrees:* A, B, M, D *Prof. Accred.:* Computer Science, Engineering Technology (electrical, mechanical), Engineering (chemical, civil, electrical, mechanical), Forestry, Marriage and Family Therapy (M-candidate), Medical Technology, Music, Nursing (B,M), Occupational Therapy, Psychology Internship, Recreation and Leisure Services, Social Work (B), Speech-Language Pathology, Teacher Education (e,s,p) *CEO:* Pres. Dale F. Nitzschke
Enroll: 12,515   (603) 862-1234

UNIVERSITY OF NEW HAMPSHIRE AT
MANCHESTER
R.F.D. 4, Hackett Hill Rd., Manchester 03102 *CEO:* Dean Lewis Roberts, Jr.
                    (603) 668-0700

WHITE PINES COLLEGE
Chester 03036 *Type:* Private junior *Accred.:*
1975/1985 (NEASC-CIHE) *Calendar:* Sem.
plan *Degrees:* A *CEO:* Pres. Mary Scerra
Enroll: 71   (603) 887-4401

NEW JERSEY

ASSUMPTION COLLEGE FOR SISTERS
350 Bernardsville Rd., Mallinckrodt Convent, Mendham 07945-0800 *Type:* Private (Roman Catholic) junior *Accred.:* 1965/1990 (MSA) *Calendar:* Sem. plan *Degrees:* A, certificates *CEO:* Pres. Mary Gerard Gebler, S.C.C.
Enroll: 41   (201) 543-6528

ATLANTIC COMMUNITY COLLEGE
5100 Black Horse Pike, Mays Landing 08330-2699 *Type:* Public (local/state) junior *System:* Office of Community Colleges *Accred.:* 1971/1991 (MSA) *Calendar:* Sem. plan *Degrees:* A, certificates *Prof. Accred.:* Engineering Technology (electrical), Medical Laboratory Technology (AMA), Nursing (A), Occupational Therapy Assisting, Physical Therapy Assisting *CEO:* Pres. John T. May
Enroll: 5,581   (609) 625-1111

BERGEN COMMUNITY COLLEGE
400 Paramus Rd., Paramus 07652 *Type:* Public (local) junior *System:* Office of Community Colleges *Accred.:* 1972/1991 (MSA) *Calendar:* Sem. plan *Degrees:* A, certificates *Prof. Accred.:* Dental Hygiene, Diagnostic Medical Sonography, Medical Assisting (AMA), Medical Laboratory Technology (AMA), Nursing (A), Radiography, Respiratory Therapy, Surgical Technology *CEO:* Pres. Jose Lopez-Isa
Enroll: 12,333   (201) 447-7100

BERKELEY COLLEGE OF BUSINESS
44 Rifle Camp Rd., West Paterson 07424 *Type:* Private junior *Accred.:* 1983/1990 (MSA) *Calendar:* Qtr. plan *Degrees:* A, certificates *CEO:* Pres. Kevin L. Luing
Enroll: 1,585   (201) 278-5400

WALDWICK CAMPUS
100 W. Prospect St., Waldwick 07463 *CEO:* Admin. Dir. Teri Ovda
                    (201) 652-0388

WOODBRIDGE CAMPUS
430 Rahway Ave., Woodbridge 07095 *CEO:* Admin. Dir. David Baumol
                    (201) 750-1800

BETH MEDRASH GOVOHA
617 Sixth St., Lakewood 08701 *Type:* Private professional *Accred.:* 1974/1991 (AARTS) *Calendar:* Sem. plan *Degrees:* B, M *CEO:* Pres. M. Kotler
Enroll: 1,625   (908) 367-1060

BLOOMFIELD COLLEGE
467 Franklin St., Bloomfield 07003 *Type:* Private (Presbyterian) liberal arts *Accred.:* 1960/1992 (MSA) *Calendar:* 4-1-4 plan *Degrees:* B, certificates *Prof. Accred.:* Nursing (B) *CEO:* Pres. John F. Noonan
Enroll: 1,858   (201) 748-9000

BROOKDALE COMMUNITY COLLEGE
Newman Springs Rd., Lincroft 07738 *Type:* Public (local) junior *System:* Office of Community Colleges *Accred.:* 1972/1989 (MSA) *Calendar:* Sem. plan *Degrees:* A, certificates *Prof. Accred.:* Medical Laboratory Technology (AMA), Nursing (A) *CEO:* Pres. Peter F. Burnham
Enroll: 11,979   (908) 842-1900

ASBURY PARK LEARNING CENTER
Cookman St. and Grand Ave., Asbury Park 07712 *CEO:* Dir. Darrell Willis
                    (908) 842-1900

BAYSHORE LEARNING CENTER
311 Laurel Ave., West Keansburg 07734 *CEO:* Dir. Judith Simon
                    (908) 842-1900

FORT MONMOUTH LEARNING CENTER
918 Murphy Dr., Fort Monmouth 07703 *CEO:* Dir. John Westbrook
                    (908) 842-1900

FREEHOLD LEARNING CENTER
47 Throckmorton St., Freehold 07728 *CEO:* Dir. Cheryl Lenon
                    (908) 842-1900

LONG BRANCH LEARNING CENTER
Third Ave. and Broadway, Long Branch 07740 *CEO:* Dir. John Westbrook
                    (908) 842-1900

BURLINGTON COUNTY COLLEGE
County Rte. 530, Pemberton 08068-1599
Type: Public (local/state) junior *System:* Office of Community Colleges *Accred.:* 1972/
1989 (MSA) *Calendar:* Sem. plan *Degrees:*
A, certificates *Prof. Accred.:* Engineering
Technology (electrical), Medical Laboratory
Technology (AMA), Medical Record Technology, Nursing (A) *CEO:* Pres. Robert C.
Messina, Jr.
Enroll: 7,116   (609) 894-9311

CALDWELL COLLEGE
9 Ryerson Ave., Caldwell 07006-6195 *Type:*
Private (Roman Catholic) liberal arts *Accred.:* 1952/1990 (MSA) *Calendar:* Sem.
plan *Degrees:* B, certificates *CEO:* Pres.
Vivien Jennings, O.P.
Enroll: 1,304   (201) 228-4424

CAMDEN COUNTY COLLEGE
P.O. Box 200, Blackwood 08012 *Type:* Public (local/state) junior *System:* Office of
Community Colleges *Accred.:* 1972/1992
(MSA) *Calendar:* Sem. plan *Degrees:* A,
certificates *Prof. Accred.:* Dental Assisting,
Dental Hygiene, Medical Laboratory Technology (AMA), Veterinary Technology
CEO: Pres. Phyllis Della Vecchia
Enroll: 14,352   (609) 227-7200

BRANCH CAMPUS
Seventh and Cooper Sts., Camden 08102
CEO: Dir. Dhamiri B. Abayomi
(609) 338-1817

CENTENARY COLLEGE
400 Jefferson St., Hackettstown 07840 *Type:*
Private liberal arts primarily for women *Accred.:* 1932/1990 (MSA) *Calendar:* Sem.
plan *Degrees:* A, B *CEO:* Pres. Stephanie
M. Bennett-Smith
Enroll: 899   (908) 852-1400

COLLEGE OF ST. ELIZABETH
2 Convent Rd., Morristown 07960-6989
Type: Private (Roman Catholic) liberal arts
for women *Accred.:* 1921/1988 (MSA) *Calendar:* Sem. plan *Degrees:* B, certificates
Prof. Accred.: Nursing (B) *CEO:* Pres.
Jacqueline Burns, S.C.
Enroll: 1,202   (201) 292-6300

COUNTY COLLEGE OF MORRIS
Rte. 10 and Center Grove Rd., Randolph
07869 *Type:* Public (local/state) junior *System:* Office of Community Colleges *Accred.:*
1972/1988 (MSA) *Calendar:* Sem. plan *Degrees:* A, certificates *Prof. Accred.:* Engineering Technology (electrical, mechanical),
Medical Laboratory Technology (AMA),
Nursing (A) *CEO:* Pres. Edward J. Yaw
Enroll: 10,560   (201) 328-5000

CUMBERLAND COUNTY COLLEGE
College Dr., P.O. Box 517, Vineland 08360
Type: Public (local/state) junior *System:* Office of Community Colleges *Accred.:* 1970/
1991 (MSA) *Calendar:* Sem. plan *Degrees:* A,
certificates *Prof. Accred.:* Nursing (A), Radiography *CEO:* Pres. Roland J. Chapdelaine
Enroll: 2,700   (609) 691-8600

DEVRY TECHNICAL INSTITUTE
479 Green St., Woodbridge 07095 *Type:* Private *Accred.:* 1981/1992 (NCA)* *Calendar:*
Sem. plan *Degrees:* A, certificates, diplomas
Prof. Accred.: Engineering Technology
(electrical) *CEO:* Pres. Robert Bocchino
(201) 634-3460

* Indirect accreditation through DeVry Institutes.

DREW UNIVERSITY
Madison Ave., Rte. 24, Madison 07940
Type: Private (United Methodist) liberal arts
Accred.: 1938/1991 (ATS); 1932/1991
(MSA) *Calendar:* Sem. plan *Degrees:* B, P,
M, D *CEO:* Pres. Thomas H. Kean
Enroll: 2,068   (201) 408-3000

ESSEX COUNTY COLLEGE
303 University Ave., Newark 07102 *Type:*
Public (local/state) junior *System:* Office of
Community Colleges *Accred.:* 1974/1992
(MSA) *Calendar:* Sem. plan *Degrees:* A,
certificates *Prof. Accred.:* Nursing (A),
Physical Therapy Assisting, Radiography
CEO: Pres. A. Zachary Yamba
Enroll: 7,760   (201) 877-3000

WEST ESSEX BRANCH CAMPUS
730 Bloomfield Ave., West Caldwell
07006 *CEO:* Dir. Elizabeth Porcelli
(201) 228-3970

FAIRLEIGH DICKINSON UNIVERSITY
1000 River Rd., Teaneck 07666 *Type:* Private *Accred.:* 1948/1992 (MSA) *Calendar:* Sem. plan *Degrees:* A, B, P, M, D *Prof. Accred.:* Computer Science, Engineering (electrical) *CEO:* Pres. Francis J. Mertz
Enroll: 11,644 (201) 692-2000

FLORHAM-MADISON CAMPUS
285 Madison Ave., Madison 07940 *Prof. Accred.:* Physical Therapy Assisting *CEO:* Pres. Francis J. Mertz
(201) 593-8500

RUTHERFORD CAMPUS
223 Montrose Ave., Rutherford 07070 *Prof. Accred.:* Nursing (B), Public Administration *CEO:* Pres. Francis J. Mertz
(201) 460-5000

TEANECK-HACKENSACK CAMPUS
University Plaza 3, Hackensack 07840 *Prof. Accred.:* Clinical Psychology, Respiratory Therapy *CEO:* Pres. Francis J. Mertz
(201) 692-9170

FELICIAN COLLEGE
262 S. Main St., Lodi 07644 *Type:* Private (Roman Catholic) liberal arts *Accred.:* 1974/1990 (MSA) *Calendar:* Sem. plan *Degrees:* A, B, certificates *Prof. Accred.:* Medical Laboratory Technology (AMA), Nursing (A,B) *CEO:* Pres. Theresa Mary Martin
Enroll: 1,309 (201) 778-1190

GEORGIAN COURT COLLEGE
900 Lakewood Ave., Lakewood 08701 *Type:* Private (Roman Catholic) primarily for women *Accred.:* 1922/1989 (MSA) *Calendar:* Sem. plan *Degrees:* B, M *Prof. Accred.:* Social Work (B-candidate) *CEO:* Pres. Barbara Williams, R.S.M.
Enroll: 2,490 (908) 364-2200

GLOUCESTER COUNTY COLLEGE
Tanyard Rd., Deptford Twp., R.R. 4, P.O. Box 203, Sewell 08080 *Type:* Public (local/state) junior *System:* Office of Community Colleges *Accred.:* 1973/1988 (MSA) *Calendar:* Sem. plan *Degrees:* A, certificates *Prof. Accred.:* Nuclear Medicine Technology, Nursing (A), Respiratory Therapy Technology *CEO:* Pres. Richard H. Jones
Enroll: 4,755 (609) 468-5000

HUDSON COUNTY COMMUNITY COLLEGE
901 Bergen Ave., Jersey City 07306 *Type:* Public (local/state) junior *System:* Office of Community Colleges *Accred.:* 1981/1986 (MSA) *Calendar:* Sem. plan *Degrees:* A, certificates *Prof. Accred.:* Engineering Technology (electrical), Medical Assisting (AMA), Medical Record Technology *CEO:* Pres. Glen Gabert
Enroll: 2,878 (201) 656-2020

IMMACULATE CONCEPTION SEMINARY
400 S. Orange Ave., South Orange 07079 *Type:* Private (Roman Catholic) graduate only *Accred.:* 1977/1992 (ATS) *Calendar:* Sem. plan *Degrees:* M *CEO:* Rector/Dean Robert E. Harahan
FTE Enroll: 155 (201) 761-9575

JERSEY CITY STATE COLLEGE
2039 Kennedy Blvd., Jersey City 07305 *Type:* Public (state) *System:* Office of Senior Institutions *Accred.:* 1959/1990 (MSA) *Calendar:* Sem. plan *Degrees:* B, M, certificates *Prof. Accred.:* Art, Music, Nursing (B), Teacher Education (e,s,p) *CEO:* Pres. Carlos Hernandez
Enroll: 8,350 (201) 200-2000

KATHARINE GIBBS SCHOOL
33 Plymouth St., Montclair 07042 *Type:* Private business *Accred.:* 1967/1988 (ACISC) *Calendar:* Sem. plan *Degrees:* A, certificates, diplomas *CEO:* Dir. Beverly Ficon
(201) 744-6967

BRANCH CAMPUS
80 Kingsbridge Rd., Piscataway 08854 *Accred.:* 1985/1988 (ACISC) *CEO:* Dir. Terry Nighan
(908) 885-1580

KEAN COLLEGE OF NEW JERSEY
1000 Morris Ave., Union 07083 *Type:* Public (state) *System:* Office of Senior Institutions *Accred.:* 1960/1991 (MSA) *Calendar:* Sem. plan *Degrees:* B, M *Prof. Accred.:* Construction Education (B), Medical Record Administration, Music, Nursing (B), Occupational Therapy, Physical Therapy, Public Administration, Social Work (B), Speech-Language Pathology, Teacher Education (e,p) *CEO:* Pres. Elsa Gomez
Enroll: 11,692 (908) 527-2000

MERCER COUNTY COMMUNITY COLLEGE
1200 Old Trenton Rd., Box B, Trenton 08690-0182 *Type:* Public (local/state) junior *System:* Office of Community Colleges *Accred.:* 1967/1990 (MSA) *Calendar:* Sem. plan *Degrees:* A, certificates *Prof. Accred.:* Engineering Technology (civil/construction, electrical, mechanical), Funeral Service Education, Medical Laboratory Technology (AMA), Nursing (A), Radiography *CEO:* Pres. Thomas D. Sepe
Enroll: 8,749   (609) 586-4800

JAMES KERNEY CAMPUS
N. Broad and Academy Sts., Trenton 08690 *CEO:* Provost Beverly A. Richardson
        (609) 586-4800

MIDDLESEX COUNTY COLLEGE
155 Mill Rd., P.O. Box 3050, Edison 08818 *Type:* Public (local/state) junior *System:* Office of Community Colleges *Accred.:* 1970/1991 (MSA) *Calendar:* Sem. plan *Degrees:* A, certificates *Prof. Accred.:* Dental Hygiene, Engineering Technology (civil/construction, electrical, mechanical), Medical Laboratory Technology (AMA), Nursing (A), Radiography *CEO:* Pres. Flora Mancuso-Edwards
Enroll: 11,979   (908) 548-6000

MONMOUTH COLLEGE
Norwood and Cedar Aves., West Long Branch 07764-1898 *Type:* Private *Accred.:* 1952/1991 (MSA) *Calendar:* Sem. plan *Degrees:* A, B, M *Prof. Accred.:* Engineering (electrical), Nursing (B), Social Work (B) *CEO:* Pres. Rebecca Stafford
Enroll: 4,197   (908) 571-3400

MONTCLAIR STATE COLLEGE
Valley Rd. and Normal Ave., Upper Montclair 07043-1624 *Type:* Public (state) *System:* Office of Senior Institutions *Accred.:* 1937/1992 (MSA) *Calendar:* Sem. plan *Degrees:* B, M *Prof. Accred.:* Art (associate), Computer Science, Dance, Home Economics, Music, Recreation and Leisure Services, Speech-Language Pathology, Teacher Education (s,p), Theatre *CEO:* Pres. Irvin D. Reid
Enroll: 13,753   (201) 893-4000

NEW BRUNSWICK THEOLOGICAL SEMINARY
17 Seminary Pl., New Brunswick 08901-1196 *Type:* Private (Reformed Church) graduate only *Accred.:* 1938/1986 (ATS) *Calendar:* Sem. plan *Degrees:* M *CEO:* Pres. Norman J. Kansfield
FTE Enroll: 84   (908) 247-5241

NEW JERSEY INSTITUTE OF TECHNOLOGY
University Heights, Newark 07102-9938 *Type:* Public (state) technological *System:* Office of Senior Institutions *Accred.:* 1934/1992 (MSA) *Calendar:* Sem. plan *Degrees:* B, M, D *Prof. Accred.:* Computer Science, Engineering Technology (civil/construction, electrical, manufacturing, mechanical), Engineering (chemical, civil, electrical, industrial, mechanical) *CEO:* Pres. Saul K. Fenster
Enroll: 7,397   (201) 596-3000

OCEAN COUNTY COLLEGE
College Dr., CN 2001, Toms River 08753-2001 *Type:* Public (local/state) junior *System:* Office of Community Colleges *Accred.:* 1969/1989 (MSA) *Calendar:* Sem. plan *Degrees:* A, certificates *Prof. Accred.:* Engineering Technology (electrical), Medical Laboratory Technology (AMA), Nursing (A) *CEO:* Pres. Milton Shaw
Enroll: 8,117   (908) 255-4000

PASSAIC COUNTY COMMUNITY COLLEGE
One College Blvd., Paterson 07505-1179 *Type:* Public (local/state) junior *System:* Office of Community Colleges *Accred.:* 1978/1984 (MSA) *Calendar:* Sem. plan *Degrees:* A, certificates *Prof. Accred.:* Nursing (A), Radiography, Respiratory Therapy Technology *CEO:* Pres. Elliott Collins
Enroll: 3,435   (201) 684-6800

PRINCETON THEOLOGICAL SEMINARY
64 Mercer St., CN 821, Princeton 08542-0803 *Type:* Private (Presbyterian) graduate only *Accred.:* 1938/1987 (ATS); 1968/1988 (MSA) *Calendar:* Sem. plan *Degrees:* P, M, D *CEO:* Pres. Thomas W. Gillespie
Enroll: 778   (609) 921-8300

PRINCETON UNIVERSITY
Princeton 08544-0015 *Type:* Private *Accred.:* 1921/1989 (MSA) *Calendar:* Sem. plan *Degrees:* B, M, D *Prof. Accred.:* Engineering (aerospace, chemical, civil, electri-

cal, engineering physics/science, geological/
geophysical, mechanical) *CEO:* Pres. Harold
T. Shapiro
Enroll: 6,412   (609) 258-3000

RABBINICAL COLLEGE OF AMERICA
226 Sussex Ave., Morristown 07960 *Type:*
Private professional *Accred.:* 1979/1990
(AARTS) *Calendar:* Sem. plan *Degrees:* B
CEO: Pres. M. Herson
Enroll: 143   (201) 267-9404

RAMAPO COLLEGE OF NEW JERSEY
505 Ramapo Valley Rd., Mahwah 07430-
1680 *Type:* Public (state) liberal arts *System:*
Office of Senior Institutions *Accred.:* 1975/
1990 (MSA) *Calendar:* Sem. plan *Degrees:*
B *Prof. Accred.:* Social Work (B) *CEO:*
Pres. Robert A. Scott
Enroll: 4,711   (201) 529-7500

RARITAN VALLEY COMMUNITY COLLEGE
P.O. Box 3300, Hwy. 28 and Lamington Rd.,
Somerville 08876 *Type:* Public (local/state)
junior *System:* Office of Community Coll-
eges *Accred.:* 1972/1992 (MSA) *Calendar:*
Sem. plan *Degrees:* A, certificates *Prof. Ac-
cred.:* Nursing (A) *CEO:* Pres. S. Charles
Irace
Enroll: 5,638   (908) 526-1200

RIDER COLLEGE
2083 Lawrenceville Rd., Lawrenceville
08648-3099 *Type:* Private *Accred.:* 1955/
1991 (MSA) *Calendar:* 4-1-4 plan *Degrees:*
A, B, M, certificates *Prof. Accred.:* Business
(B,M), Teacher Education (e,s,p) *CEO:* Pres.
J. Barton Luedeke
Enroll: 5,651   (609) 896-5000

WESTMINSTER CHOIR COLLEGE
101 Walnut La., Princeton 08540 *Prof.
Accred.:* Music *CEO:* Pres. J. Barton
Luedeke
                                   (609) 921-7100

ROWAN COLLEGE OF NEW JERSEY
201 Mullica Hill Rd., Glassboro 08028-1701
Type: Public (state) *System:* Office of Senior
Institutions *Accred.:* 1958/1989 (MSA) *Cal-
endar:* Sem. plan *Degrees:* B, M, certificates
Prof. Accred.: Music, Teacher Education
(e,s,p) *CEO:* Pres. Herman D. James
Enroll: 9,803   (609) 863-5000

CAMDEN CAMPUS
One Broadway, Camden 08102 *CEO:* Dir.
Eric Clark
                                   (609) 757-2857

RUTGERS, THE STATE UNIVERSITY OF NEW
JERSEY CAMDEN CAMPUS
311 N. Fifth St., Camden 08102 *Type:* Public
(state) *System:* Rutgers, The State University
of New Jersey Central Office *Accred.:* 1950/
1988 (MSA) *Calendar:* Sem. plan *Degrees:*
B, P, M *Prof. Accred.:* Law, Nursing (B),
Physical Therapy, Public Administration,
Social Work (B,M) *CEO:* Provost Walter K.
Gordon
Enroll: 5,491   (609) 757-1766

RUTGERS, THE STATE UNIVERSITY OF NEW
JERSEY NEW BRUNSWICK CAMPUS
Old Queens Bldg., New Brunswick 08903
Type: Public (state) *System:* Rutgers, The
State University of New Jersey Central Of-
fice *Accred.:* 1921/1988 (MSA) *Calendar:*
Sem. plan *Degrees:* B, P, M, D *Prof. Ac-
cred.:* Accounting (Type A), Business (B),
Clinical Psychology, Dance (associate), En-
gineering (agricultural, ceramic, chemical,
civil, electrical, industrial, mechanical),
Landscape Architecture (B), Librarianship,
Music, Planning (M), School Psychology,
Social Work (B,M), Theatre *CEO:* Provost
Joseph A. Potenza
Enroll: 33,279   (908) 932-1766

RUTGERS, THE STATE UNIVERSITY OF NEW
JERSEY NEWARK CAMPUS
15 Washington St., Newark 07102 *Type:*
Public (state) *System:* Rutgers, The State
University of New Jersey Central Office *Accred.:* 1946/1988 (MSA) *Calendar:* Sem.
plan *Degrees:* B, P, M *Prof. Accred.:* Business (B,M), Law, Nursing (B,M), Public Administration, Social Work (B,M) *CEO:*
Provost Norman Samuels
Enroll: 9,833   (201) 648-1766

ST. PETER'S COLLEGE
2641 Kennedy Blvd., Jersey City 07306
Type: Private (Roman Catholic) *Accred.:*
1935/1988 (MSA) *Calendar:* Sem. plan *De-
grees:* A, B, M, certificates *Prof. Accred.:*
Nursing (B) *CEO:* Pres. Daniel A. Degnan,
S.J.
Enroll: 3,463   (201) 915-9000

ENGLEWOOD CLIFFS CAMPUS
Hudson Terrace, Englewood Cliffs 07632
CEO: Dir. Katherine Restaino-Dick
(201) 568-7730

SALEM COMMUNITY COLLEGE
460 Hollywood Ave., Carneys Point 08069
Type: Public (local/state) junior *System:* Office of Community Colleges *Accred.:* 1979/1990 (MSA) *Calendar:* Sem. plan *Degrees:* A, certificates *CEO:* Pres. Linda C. Jolly
Enroll: 1,507   (609) 299-2100

SETON HALL UNIVERSITY
400 S. Orange Ave., South Orange 07079
Type: Private (Roman Catholic) *Accred.:* 1932/1989 (MSA) *Calendar:* Sem. plan *Degrees:* B, P, M, D, certificates *Prof. Accred.:* Business (B,M), Nursing (B,M), Public Administration, Social Work (B), Teacher Education (e,s,p) *CEO:* Chanc. Thomas R. Peterson
Enroll: 10,199   (201) 761-9000

SCHOOL OF LAW
One Newark Ctr., Newark 07102-5210
Prof. Accred.: Law *CEO:* Dean Ronald J. Riccio
Enroll: 1,326   (201) 642-8500

STEVENS INSTITUTE OF TECHNOLOGY
Castle Point on the Hudson, Hoboken 07030
Type: Private technical *Accred.:* 1927/1987 (MSA) *Calendar:* Sem. plan *Degrees:* B, M, D *Prof. Accred.:* Computer Science, Engineering (chemical, civil, computer, electrical, engineering physics/science, general, mechanical, metallurgical) *CEO:* Pres. Harold J. Raveche
Enroll: 3,354   (201) 216-5100

STOCKTON STATE COLLEGE
Jimmy Leeds Rd., Pomona 08240 *Type:* Public (state) *System:* Office of Senior Institutions *Accred.:* 1975/1991 (MSA) *Calendar:* Sem. plan *Degrees:* B *Prof. Accred.:* Nursing (B), Physical Therapy, Social Work (B) *CEO:* Pres. Vera King Farris
Enroll: 5,650   (609) 652-1776

SUSSEX COUNTY COMMUNITY COLLEGE
College Hill, Newton 07860 *Type:* Public (local/state) junior *System:* Office of Community Colleges *Accred.:* 1993 (MSA) *Cal-*endar:* Sem. plan *Degrees:* A, certificates *CEO:* Pres. William A. Connor
Enroll: 2,042   (201) 579-5400

TALMUDICAL ACADEMY OF NEW JERSEY
Rte. 524, Adelphia 07710 *Type:* Private professional *Accred.:* 1980/1986 (AARTS) *Calendar:* Sem. plan *Degrees:* B *CEO:* Pres. Charles Semah
Enroll: 28   (201) 431-1600

THOMAS A. EDISON STATE COLLEGE
101 W. State St., Trenton 08608-1176 *Type:* Public (state) *System:* Office of Senior Institutions *Accred.:* 1977/1992 (MSA) *Calendar:* Sem. plan *Degrees:* A, B, P, certificates *Prof. Accred.:* Nursing (B) *CEO:* Pres. George A. Pruitt
Enroll: 8,019   (609) 984-1100

TRENTON STATE COLLEGE
Hillwood Lakes, CN 4700, Trenton 08650-4700 *Type:* Public (state) *System:* Office of Senior Institutions *Accred.:* 1939/1990 (MSA) *Calendar:* Sem. plan *Degrees:* B, M, certificates *Prof. Accred.:* Audiology, Counseling, Engineering Technology (industrial, mechanical), Interior Design, Music, Nursing (B), Speech-Language Pathology, Teacher Education (e,s,p) *CEO:* Pres. Harold W. Eickhoff
Enroll: 6,969   (609) 771-1855

UNION COUNTY COLLEGE
1033 Springfield Ave., Cranford 07016 *Type:* Public (local/state) junior *System:* Office of Community Colleges *Accred.:* 1957/1992 (MSA) *Calendar:* Sem. plan *Degrees:* A, certificates *Prof. Accred.:* Dental Laboratory Technology, Medical Laboratory Technology (AMA), Occupational Therapy Assisting, Physical Therapy Assisting, Respiratory Therapy *CEO:* Pres. Thomas H. Brown, Ph.D.
Enroll: 10,227   (908) 709-7000

ELIZABETH CAMPUS
12 W. Jersey St., Elizabeth 07206 *CEO:* Provost Marion Bonaparte
(908) 965-6090

PLAINFIELD CAMPUS
232 E. Second St., Plainfield 07060 *Prof. Accred.:* Practical Nursing *CEO:* Pres. Thomas H. Brown, Ph.D.
(908) 889-8500

UNIVERSITY OF MEDICINE AND DENTISTRY OF
NEW JERSEY
30 Bergen St., Newark 07107-3000 *Type:*
Public (state) professional *System:* Office of
Senior Institutions *Accred.:* 1979/1990
(MSA) *Calendar:* Sem. plan *Degrees:* A, B,
P, M, D, certificates *Prof. Accred.:* Cy-
totechnology, Diagnostic Medical Sonogra-
phy, Medical Technology, Nuclear Medicine
Technology, Nursing (A), Physician Assist-
ing, Radiography, Respiratory Therapy, Res-
piratory Therapy Technology, Surgical
Technology *CEO:* Pres. Stanley S. Bergen,
Jr.
Enroll: 3,406   (201) 982-4300

GRADUATE SCHOOL OF BIOMEDICAL SCIENCES
185 S. Orange Ave., Newark 07103 *CEO:*
Dean Vincent Lanzoni
Enroll: 734   (201) 456-4511

NEW JERSEY DENTAL SCHOOL
110 Bergen St., Newark 07103 *Prof. Accred.:* Combined Prosthodontics, Dental
Assisting, Dental Hygiene, Dentistry, Endodontics, General Dentistry, General
Practice Residency, Oral and Maxillofacial Surgery, Orthodontics, Pediatric Dentistry, Periodontics *CEO:* Dean Richard N.
Buchanan
Enroll: 353   (201) 456-4633

NEW JERSEY MEDICAL SCHOOL
185 S. Orange Ave., Newark 07103 *Prof.
Accred.:* Medicine, Psychology Internship
CEO: Dean Ruy V. Lourenco
Enroll: 703   (201) 465-4539

NEW JERSEY SCHOOL OF OSTEOPATHIC
MEDICINE
Academic Ctr., One Medical Center Dr.,
Stratford 08084 *Prof. Accred.:* Osteopathy
CEO: Dean Frederick J. Humphrey, II
Enroll: 231   (609) 566-6995

ROBERT WOOD JOHNSON MEDICAL SCHOOL
671 Hoes La., Piscataway 08854 *Prof. Accred.:* Community Health/Preventive
Medicine, Medicine, Psychology Internship *CEO:* Dean Norman H. Edelman
Enroll: 599   (908) 463-4557

SCHOOL OF HEALTH-RELATED PROFESSIONS
65 Bergen St., Newark 07107 *Prof. Accred.:* Dietetics (internship), Physical
Therapy *CEO:* Dean David M. Gibson
Enroll: 637   (201) 456-5453

UPSALA COLLEGE
Prospect St., East Orange 07019 *Type:* Pri-
vate (Evangelical Lutheran) *Accred.:* 1936/
1984 (MSA) *Calendar:* Sem. plan *Degrees:*
B, M *Prof. Accred.:* Social Work (B) *CEO:*
Pres. Robert E. Karsten
Enroll: 1,115   (201) 266-7000

WIRTHS EXTENSION CENTER
R.D. 3, Box 138-A, Sussex 07461 *CEO:*
Dir. James H. Stam
                    (201) 875-7187

WARREN COUNTY COMMUNITY COLLEGE
Box 55A, Rte. 57 W., Washington 07882
Type: Public (local/state) junior *System:* Of-
fice of Community Colleges *Accred.:* 1993
(MSA) *Calendar:* Sem. plan *Degrees:* A,
certificates *CEO:* Pres. Vincent De Sanctis
Enroll: 1,543   (908) 689-1090

WILLIAM PATERSON COLLEGE OF NEW JERSEY
300 Pompton Rd., Wayne 07470 *Type:* Pub-
lic (state) *System:* Office of Senior Institu-
tions *Accred.:* 1958/1991 (MSA) *Calendar:*
Sem. plan *Degrees:* B, M *Prof. Accred.:*
Music, Nursing (B), Speech-Language
Pathology, Teacher Education (e,s,p) *CEO:*
Pres. Arnold S. Speert
Enroll: 9,606   (201) 595-2000

NEW MEXICO

ALBUQUERQUE TECHNICAL VOCATIONAL
INSTITUTE
  525 Buena Vista Dr., S.E., Albuquerque
  87106 *Type:* Public 2-year *System:* New
  Mexico Commission on Higher Education
  Accred.: 1978/1993 (NCA) *Calendar:* Tri.
  plan *Degrees:* A, certificates *Prof. Accred.:*
  Engineering Technology (electrical, general
  drafting/design), Medical Laboratory Technology (AMA), Nursing (A), Practical Nursing, Respiratory Therapy, Respiratory Therapy Technology *CEO:* Pres. Ted F. Martinez
  Enroll: 19,622   (505) 224-3000

CLOVIS COMMUNITY COLLEGE
  417 Schepps Blvd., Clovis 88101 *Type:* Public (state) junior *System:* New Mexico Commission on Higher Education *Accred.:* 1987/
  1992 (NCA) *Calendar:* Sem. plan *Degrees:*
  A, certificates *Prof. Accred.:* Nursing (A),
  Radiography *CEO:* Pres. Jay Gurley
  Enroll: 3,343   (505) 769-2811

THE COLLEGE OF SANTA FE
  1600 St. Michael's Dr., Santa Fe 87501
  Type: Private (Roman Catholic) liberal arts
  Accred.: 1965/1991 (NCA) *Calendar:* Sem.
  plan *Degrees:* A, B, M *CEO:* Pres. James A.
  Fries
  Enroll: 1,468   (505) 473-6234

COLLEGE OF THE SOUTHWEST
  6610 Lovington Hwy., Hobbs 88240 *Type:*
  Private liberal arts *Accred.:* 1980/1993
  (NCA) *Calendar:* Sem. plan *Degrees:* B
  CEO: Pres. Joan M. Tucker
  Enroll: 352   (505) 392-6561

DONA ANA BRANCH COMMUNITY COLLEGE
  Box 30001, Las Cruces 88003 *Type:* Public
  2-year *System:* New Mexico State University
  System *Calendar:* Courses of varying
  lengths *Degrees:* A, certificates, diplomas
  Prof. Accred.: Radiography *CEO:* Provost
  Donaciano Gonzalez
                                (505) 527-7510

EASTERN NEW MEXICO UNIVERSITY
  Portales 88130 *Type:* Public (state) *System:*
  New Mexico Commission on Higher Educa-
  tion *Accred.:* 1947/1987 (NCA) *Calendar:*
  Sem. plan *Degrees:* A, B, M *Prof. Accred.:*

Music, Teacher Education (e,s) *CEO:* Pres.
Everett L. Frost
Enroll: 3,905   (505) 562-2121

EASTERN NEW MEXICO UNIVERSITY—ROSWELL
  P.O. Box 6000, Roswell 88202 *Type:* Public
  (state) *Accred.:* 1971/1992 (NCA) *Calendar:*
  Sem. plan *Degrees:* A, certificates *Prof. Ac-
  cred.:* Nursing (A) *CEO:* Provost Loyd R.
  Hughes
  Enroll: 2,140   (505) 624-7000

INSTITUTE OF AMERICAN INDIAN AND ALASKAN
NATIVE CULTURE AND ARTS DEVELOPMENT
  St. Michael's Dr., Box 20007, Santa Fe
  87504 *Type:* Public (federal) *Accred.:* 1984/
  1990 (NCA) *Calendar:* Sem. plan *Degrees:*
  A *Prof. Accred.:* Art *CEO:* Pres. Kathryn
  Harris Tijerina
  Enroll: 239   (505) 988-6440

INTERNATIONAL INSTITUTE OF CHINESE
MEDICINE
  P.O. Box 4991, Santa Fe 87502 *Type:* Pri-
  vate professional *Calendar:* Sem. plan *De-
  grees:* M *Prof. Accred.:* Acupuncture *CEO:*
  Pres. Michael Zeng
  FTE Enroll: 85   (505) 473-5233

LUNA VOCATIONAL TECHNICAL INSTITUTE
  P.O. Drawer K, Las Vegas 87701 *Type:* Public 2-year *System:* New Mexico Commission
  on Higher Education *Accred.:* 1982/1987
  (NCA) *Calendar:* Tri. plan *Degrees:* A, certificates *CEO:* Pres. Samuel F. Vigil
  Enroll: 1,208   (505) 454-2500

NEW MEXICO HIGHLANDS UNIVERSITY
  National Ave., Las Vegas 87701 *Type:* Pub-
  lic (state) liberal arts and professional *Sys-
  tem:* New Mexico Commission on Higher
  Education *Accred.:* 1926/1991 (NCA) *Cal-
  endar:* Sem. plan *Degrees:* A, B, M *Prof.
  Accred.:* Engineering Technology (electri-
  cal), Social Work (B,M) *CEO:* Pres. Gilbert
  Sanchez
  Enroll: 2,643   (505) 454-3229

NEW MEXICO INSTITUTE OF MINING AND
TECHNOLOGY
  Socorro 87801 *Type:* Public (state) techno-
  logical *System:* New Mexico Commission on

Higher Education *Accred.:* 1914/1985 (NCA) *Calendar:* Sem. plan *Degrees:* A, B, M,D *Prof. Accred.:* Engineering (petroleum) *CEO:* Pres. Daniel H. Lopez
Enroll: 1,602   (505) 835-5011

NEW MEXICO JUNIOR COLLEGE
5317 Lovington Hwy., Hobbs 88240 *Type:* Public (district) junior *System:* New Mexico Commission on Higher Education *Accred.:* 1970/1986 (NCA) *Calendar:* Sem. plan *Degrees:* A, certificates *Prof. Accred.:* Medical Laboratory Technology (AMA), Nursing (A) *CEO:* Pres. Charles D. Hays, Jr.
Enroll: 2,811   (505) 392-4510

NEW MEXICO MILITARY INSTITUTE
100 W. College Blvd., Roswell 88201 *Type:* Public (state) junior *System:* New Mexico Commission on Higher Education *Accred.:* 1938/1991 (NCA) *Calendar:* Sem. plan *Degrees:* A *CEO:* Supt. Winfield W. Scott, Jr.
Enroll: 538   (505) 624-8000

NEW MEXICO STATE UNIVERSITY
Box 30001, Las Cruces 88003 *Type:* Public (state) *System:* New Mexico State University System *Accred.:* 1926/1988 (NCA) *Calendar:* Sem. plan *Degrees:* A, B, P, M, D, certificates *Prof. Accred.:* Accounting (Type A,C), Computer Science, Engineering Technology (civil/construction, electrical, mechanical), Engineering (agricultural, chemical, civil, electrical, geological/geophysical, industrial, mechanical), Music, Nursing (A,B), Public Administration, Social Work (B,M), Speech-Language Pathology, Teacher Education (e,s,p) *CEO:* Pres. James E. Halligan
Enroll: 12,225   (505) 885-8831

NEW MEXICO STATE UNIVERSITY AT GRANTS
1500 3rd St., Grants 87020 *CEO:* Provost William E. Sailer
                    (505) 287-7981

NEW MEXICO STATE UNIVERSITY AT ALAMOGORDO
P.O. Box 477, Alamogordo 88311-0477 *Type:* Public (state) *System:* New Mexico State University System *Accred.:* 1973/1993 (NCA) *Calendar:* Sem. plan *Degrees:* A, certificates *Prof. Accred.:* Medical Laborato-

ry Technology (AMA), Nursing (A) *CEO:* Provost Charles R. Reidlinger
Enroll: 2,007   (505) 439-3600

NEW MEXICO STATE UNIVERSITY AT CARLSBAD
1500 University Dr., Carlsbad 88220 *Type:* Public (state) *System:* New Mexico State University System *Accred.:* 1980/1992 (NCA) *Calendar:* Sem. plan *Degrees:* A, certificates *Prof. Accred.:* Nursing (A) *CEO:* Provost Douglas E. Burgham
Enroll: 1,373   (505) 885-8831

NORTHERN NEW MEXICO COMMUNITY COLLEGE
1002 N. Onate St., Espanola 87532 *Type:* Public (state) junior *System:* New Mexico Commission on Higher Education *Accred.:* 1982/1987 (NCA) *Calendar:* Sem. plan *Degrees:* A, certificates *Prof. Accred.:* Radiography *CEO:* Pres. Connie A. Valdez
Enroll: 1,832   (505) 747-2100

PARKS COLLEGE
1023 Tijeras Ave., N.W., Albuquerque 87102 *Type:* Private junior *Accred.:* 1981/1987 (ACISC) *Calendar:* Qtr. plan *Degrees:* A, certificates, diplomas *CEO:* Pres. Cynthia S. Welch
                    (505) 843-7500

BRANCH CAMPUS
6922 E. Broadway, Tucson, AZ 85710 *Accred.:* 1987 (ACISC) *CEO:* Dir. Frank W. Welch
                    (602) 886-7979

ST. JOHN'S COLLEGE
Santa Fe 87501-4599 *Type:* Private liberal arts *Accred.:* 1969/1989 (NCA) *Calendar:* Sem. plan *Degrees:* B, M *CEO:* Pres. John Agresto
Enroll: 454   (505) 982-3691

SAN JUAN COLLEGE
4601 College Blvd., Farmington 87402 *Type:* Public (state) junior *System:* New Mexico Commission on Higher Education *Accred.:* 1973/1984 (NCA) *Calendar:* Sem. plan *Degrees:* A, certificates *Prof. Accred.:* Engineering Technology (mechanical drafting/design), Nursing (A) *CEO:* Pres. James C. Henderson
Enroll: 3,963   (505) 326-3311

SANTA FE COMMUNITY COLLEGE
P.O. Box 4187, Santa Fe 87502-4187 *Type:* Public (state) junior *System:* New Mexico Commission on Higher Education *Accred.:* 1988/1993 (NCA) *Calendar:* Sem. plan *Degrees:* A, certificates *Prof. Accred.:* Nursing (A) *CEO:* Pres. Leonardo de La Garza
Enroll: 3,296   (505) 471-8200

SOUTHWEST ACUPUNCTURE COLLEGE
712 W. San Mateo Rd., Santa Fe 87501 *Type:* Private professional *Calendar:* Tri. plan *Degrees:* M *Prof. Accred.:* Acupuncture *CEO:* Pres. Anthony Abbate
FTE Enroll: 65   (505) 988-3538

BRANCH CAMPUS
4308 Carlisle Blvd., N.E., Ste. 205, Albuquerque 87107 *CEO:* Pres. Anthony Abbate
                                    (505) 888-8898

SOUTHWESTERN INDIAN POLYTECHNIC INSTITUTE
9169 Coors Rd., N.W., Box 10146, Albuquerque 87184 *Type:* Public (federal) 2-year *Accred.:* 1975/1993 (NCA) *Calendar:* Qtr. plan *Degrees:* A, certificates *CEO:* Pres. Carolyn Elgin
Enroll: 519   (505) 897-5347

THE UNIVERSITY OF NEW MEXICO
Albuquerque 87131 *Type:* Public (state) *System:* New Mexico Commission on Higher Education *Accred.:* 1922/1989 (NCA) *Calendar:* Sem. plan *Degrees:* A, B, P, M, D, certificates *Prof. Accred.:* Audiology, Business (B,M), Clinical Psychology, Computer Science, Counseling, Dance, Dental Hygiene, Diagnostic Medical Sonography, EMT-Paramedic, Engineering (chemical, civil, computer, construction, electrical, mechanical, nuclear), Journalism (B,M), Law, Medical Technology, Medicine, Music, Nuclear Medicine Technology, Nursing (B,M), Physical Therapy, Planning (M), Psychology Internship, Public Administration, Radiation Therapy Technology, Radiography, Recreation and Leisure Services, Speech-Language Pathology, Teacher Education (e,s,p), Theatre *CEO:* Pres. Richard E. Peck
Enroll: 25,135   (505) 277-0111

GALLUP BRANCH
200 College Rd., Gallup 87301 *Prof. Accred.:* Medical Laboratory Technology (AMA), Nursing (A) *CEO:* Dir. John M. Phillips
                                    (505) 722-7221

LOS ALAMOS BRANCH
4000 University Dr., Los Alamos 87544 *CEO:* Dir. Carlos B. Ramirez
                                    (505) 662-5919

VALENCIA BRANCH
280 La Entrada, Los Lunas 87031 *CEO:* Dir. Ralph Sigala
                                    (505) 865-9596

WESTERN NEW MEXICO UNIVERSITY
P.O. Box 680, 1000 W. College Ave., Silver City 88062 *Type:* Public (state) liberal arts and professional *System:* New Mexico Commission on Higher Education *Accred.:* 1926/1992 (NCA) *Calendar:* Sem. plan *Degrees:* A, B, M, certificates *Prof. Accred.:* Nursing (A) *CEO:* Pres. John E. Counts
Enroll: 2,254   (505) 538-6238

NEW YORK

ADELPHI UNIVERSITY
South Ave., Garden City 11530 *Type:* Private *Accred.:* 1921/1988 (MSA) *Calendar:* Sem. plan *Degrees:* A, B, M, D, certificates *Prof. Accred.:* Audiology, Clinical Psychology, Nursing (B,M), Social Work (B,M), Speech-Language Pathology *CEO:* Pres. Peter Diamandopoulos
Enroll: 8,535   (516) 877-3000

ADIRONDACK COMMUNITY COLLEGE
Queensbury 12804 *Type:* Public (local/state) junior *System:* State University of New York Office of Community Colleges *Accred.:* 1971/1988 (MSA) *Calendar:* Sem. plan *Degrees:* A *CEO:* Pres. Roger C. Andersen
Enroll: 3,554   (518) 793-4491

ALBANY COLLEGE OF PHARMACY OF UNION UNIVERSITY
106 New Scotland Ave., Albany 12208 *Type:* Private professional *Accred.:* 1921/1992 (MSA) *Calendar:* Sem. plan *Degrees:* B, P, D *CEO:* Interim Pres. Ronald W. McLean
Enroll: 660   (518) 445-7211

ALBANY LAW SCHOOL
80 New Scotland Ave., Albany 12208 *Type:* Private professional *Calendar:* Sem. plan *Degrees:* P, D *Prof. Accred.:* Law *CEO:* Acting Dean John C. Welsh
Enroll: 785   (518) 445-2321

ALBANY MEDICAL COLLEGE OF UNION UNIVERSITY
47 New Scotland Ave., Albany 12208 *Type:* Private *Accred.:* 1921/1989 (MSA) *Calendar:* Sem. plan *Degrees:* P, M, D *Prof. Accred.:* Medicine, Nurse Anesthesia Education, Psychology Internship *CEO:* Pres. David Cornell
Enroll: 631   (518) 445-4970

ALFRED UNIVERSITY
Main St., Alfred 14802 *Type:* Private *Accred.:* 1921/1989 (MSA) *Calendar:* Sem. plan *Degrees:* B, M, D *Prof. Accred.:* Business (B) *CEO:* Pres. Edward G. Coll, Jr.
Enroll: 2,258   (607) 871-2111

NEW YORK STATE COLLEGE OF CERAMICS AT ALFRED UNIVERSITY
Alfred 14802 *System:* State University of New York System Office *Prof. Accred.:* Art, Engineering (ceramic, electrical, industrial, mechanical) *CEO:* Dean James W. McCauley
                (607) 871-2411

AMERICAN ACADEMY MCALLISTER INSTITUTE OF FUNERAL SERVICE, INC.
450 W. 56th St., New York 10019 *Type:* Private professional *Calendar:* Courses of varying lengths *Degrees:* A, diplomas *Prof. Accred.:* Funeral Service Education *CEO:* Pres. Patrick J. O'Connor
                (212) 757-1190

AMERICAN ACADEMY OF DRAMATIC ARTS
120 Madison Ave., New York 10016 *Type:* Private 2-year professional *Accred.:* 1983/1988 (MSA) *Calendar:* Sem. plan *Degrees:* A *Prof. Accred.:* Theatre *CEO:* Pres. George Cuttingham
Enroll: 386   (212) 686-9244

AUDREY COHEN COLLEGE
345 Hudson St., New York 10014-4598 *Type:* Private professional *Accred.:* 1984/1989 (MSA) *Calendar:* Sem. plan *Degrees:* B, M *CEO:* Pres. Audrey C. Cohen
Enroll: 952   (212) 989-2002

BANK STREET COLLEGE OF EDUCATION
610 W. 112th St., New York 10025 *Type:* Private graduate only *Accred.:* 1960/1992 (MSA) *Calendar:* Sem. plan *Degrees:* P, M, certificates *CEO:* Pres. Joseph Shenker
Enroll: 869   (212) 875-4400

BARD COLLEGE
Annandale-on-Hudson 12504 *Type:* Private liberal arts *Accred.:* 1922/1992 (MSA) *Calendar:* Sem. plan *Degrees:* B, M *CEO:* Pres. Leon Botstein
Enroll: 1,130   (914) 758-6822

BARNARD COLLEGE
3009 Broadway, New York 10027-6598 *Type:* Private liberal arts for women *Accred.:* 1921/1991 (MSA) *Calendar:* Sem. plan *De-*

grees: B *CEO:* Acting Pres. Kathryn J. Rodgers
Enroll: 2,132   (212) 854-5262

BERKELEY COLLEGE
W. Red Oak La., White Plains 10604 *Type:* Private 2-year *Accred.:* 1988 (MSA) *Calendar:* Qtr. plan *Degrees:* A, certificates *CEO:* Pres. Rose Mary Healy, Ph.D.
Enroll: 648   (914) 694-1122

THE BERKELEY SCHOOL OF NEW YORK
3 E. 43rd St., New York 10017 *Type:* Private 2-year *Accred.:* 1993 (MSA) *Calendar:* Qtr. plan *Degrees:* A, certificates *CEO:* Pres. Glen Zeitzer
Enroll: 767   (212) 986-4343

BERNARD M. BARUCH COLLEGE
17 Lexington Ave., New York 10010 *Type:* Public (local/state) *System:* City University of New York Office of the Chancellor *Accred.:* 1968/1990 (MSA) *Calendar:* Sem. plan *Degrees:* B, M *Prof. Accred.:* Accounting (Type A,B), Business (B,M), Health Services Administration, Public Administration *CEO:* Pres. Matthew Goldstein
Enroll: 15,351   (212) 447-3000

BETH HAMEDRASH SHAAREI YOSHER
4102 16th Ave., Brooklyn 11204 *Type:* Private professional *Accred.:* 1982/1990 (AARTS) *Calendar:* Sem. plan *Degrees:* Talmudic (1st and 2nd) *CEO:* Pres. J. Mayer
Enroll: 120   (718) 854-2290

BETH HATALMUD RABBINICAL COLLEGE
2127 82nd St., Brooklyn 11214 *Type:* Private professional *Accred.:* 1978/1990 (AARTS) *Calendar:* Sem. plan *Degrees:* Talmudic (1st and 2nd) *CEO:* Pres. Y. Meyer
Enroll: 207   (718) 259-2525

BORICUA COLLEGE
3755 Broadway, New York 10032 *Type:* Private liberal arts *Accred.:* 1980/1987 (MSA) *Calendar:* Tri. plan *Degrees:* A, B *CEO:* Pres. Victor G. Alicea
Enroll: 1,142   (212) 694-1000

BOROUGH OF MANHATTAN COMMUNITY COLLEGE
199 Chambers St., New York 10007 *Type:* Public (local/state) *System:* City University

of New York Office of the Chancellor *Accred.:* 1964/1987 (MSA) *Calendar:* Sem. plan *Degrees:* A *Prof. Accred.:* Medical Record Technology, Nursing (A), Respiratory Therapy *CEO:* Acting Pres. Stephen Curtis
Enroll: 14,867   (212) 346-8000

THE BRIARCLIFFE SCHOOL, INC.
250 Crossways Park Dr., Woodbury 11797-2015 *Type:* Private junior *Accred.:* 1977/1991 (ACISC); 1989 (MSA candidate) *Calendar:* Sem. plan *Degrees:* A, certificates *CEO:* Pres. Richard Turan
Enroll: 767   (516) 364-2055

BRANCH CAMPUS
10 Peninsula Blvd., Lynbrook 11563 *Accred.:* 1989/1992 (ACISC) *CEO:* Dir. Felicia Bruno
(516) 596-1313

BRANCH CAMPUS
10 Lake St., Patchogue 11772 *Accred.:* 1989/1992 (ACISC) *CEO:* Dir. Jeff Cohen
(516) 654-5300

BRONX COMMUNITY COLLEGE
W. 181st St. and University Ave., Bronx 10453 *Type:* Public (local/state) *System:* City University of New York Office of the Chancellor *Accred.:* 1961/1988 (MSA) *Calendar:* Sem. plan *Degrees:* A, certificates *Prof. Accred.:* Engineering Technology (electrical), Nuclear Medicine Technology, Nursing (A), Radiography *CEO:* Acting President Leo A. Corbie
Enroll: 6,737   (718) 220-6920

BROOKLYN COLLEGE
2900 Bedford Ave., Brooklyn 11210-2889 *Type:* Public (local/state) *System:* City University of New York Office of the Chancellor *Accred.:* 1933/1987 (MSA) *Calendar:* Sem. plan *Degrees:* B, M, certificates *Prof. Accred.:* Audiology (probational), Speech-Language Pathology (probational) *CEO:* Pres. Vernon E. Lattin
Enroll: 15,629   (718) 951-5000

BROOKLYN LAW SCHOOL
250 Joralemon St., Brooklyn 11201 *Type:* Private professional *Calendar:* Sem. plan *Degrees:* P *Prof. Accred.:* Law *CEO:* Dean David G. Trager
Enroll: 1,457   (718) 625-2200

BROOME COMMUNITY COLLEGE
Upper Front St., P.O. Box 1017, Binghamton 13902 *Type:* Public (local/state) junior *System:* State University of New York Office of Community Colleges *Accred.:* 1960/1990 (MSA) *Calendar:* Sem. plan *Degrees:* A, certificates *Prof. Accred.:* Dental Hygiene, Engineering Technology (chemical, civil/ construction, electrical, mechanical), Medical Assisting (AMA), Medical Laboratory Technology (AMA), Medical Record Technology, Nursing (A), Physical Therapy Assisting, Radiography *CEO:* Pres. Donald A. Dellow
Enroll: 6,730   (607) 778-5000

BRYANT & STRATTON BUSINESS INSTITUTE
1259 Central Ave., Albany 12205 *Type:* Private business *Accred.:* 1953/1988 (ACISC) *Calendar:* Qtr. plan *Degrees:* A *CEO:* Dir. Beth A. Tarquino
(518) 437-1802

BRYANT & STRATTON BUSINESS INSTITUTE
1028 Main St., Buffalo 14202 *Type:* Private business *Accred.:* 1953/1990 (ACISC) *Calendar:* Qtr. plan *Degrees:* A, certificates, diplomas *Prof. Accred.:* Medical Assisting (AMA) *CEO:* Dir. William B. Schatt
(716) 884-9120

BRANCH CAMPUS
1214 Abbott Rd., Lackawanna 14218 *Accred.:* 1990 (ACISC) *CEO:* Dir. Bonnie L. MacGregor
(716) 821-9331

BRANCH CAMPUS
1225 Jefferson Rd., Rochester 14623 *Accred.:* 1993 (ACISC) *CEO:* Dir. Eric B. Donaldson
(716) 292-5627

BRANCH CAMPUS
200 Bryant and Stratton Way, Williamsville 14221 *Accred.:* 1981/1990 (ACISC) *CEO:* Dir. Cameron J. Morton
(716) 631-0260

BRYANT & STRATTON BUSINESS INSTITUTE
82 St. Paul St., Rochester 14604-1381 *Type:* Private business *Accred.:* 1975/1988 (ACISC) *Calendar:* Qtr. plan *Degrees:* A, certificates, diplomas *Prof. Accred.:* Medical Assisting (AMA) *CEO:* Dir. Robin R. Courtenay
(716) 325-6010

BRYANT & STRATTON BUSINESS INSTITUTE
953 James St., Syracuse 13203-2502 *Type:* Private business *Accred.:* 1968/1987 (ACISC) *Calendar:* Qtr. plan *Degrees:* A, certificates, diplomas *Prof. Accred.:* Medical Assisting (AMA) *CEO:* Dir. Edward J. Heinrich
(315) 472-6603

BRANCH CAMPUS
5775 S. Bay Rd., Cicero 13039 *Accred.:* 1984/1986 (ACISC) *CEO:* Dir. David Reid
(315) 452-1105

CANISIUS COLLEGE
2001 Main St., Buffalo 14208 *Type:* Private *Accred.:* 1921/1990 (MSA) *Calendar:* Sem. plan *Degrees:* A, B, M *Prof. Accred.:* Business (B,M), Teacher Education (s,p) *CEO:* Pres. Vincent M. Cooke
Enroll: 4,629   (716) 883-7000

CAYUGA COUNTY COMMUNITY COLLEGE
Franklin St., Auburn 13021 *Type:* Public (local/state) junior *System:* State University of New York Office of Community Colleges *Accred.:* 1965/1991 (MSA) *Calendar:* Sem. plan *Degrees:* A, certificates *Prof. Accred.:* Nursing (A) *CEO:* Pres. Lawrence H. Poole
Enroll: 2,715   (315) 255-1743

CAZENOVIA COLLEGE
Seminary St., Cazenovia 13035 *Type:* Private liberal arts *Accred.:* 1961/1992 (MSA) *Calendar:* Sem. plan *Degrees:* A, B *CEO:* Pres. Stephen M. Schneeweiss
Enroll: 1,078   (315) 655-8283

CENTRAL YESHIVA TOMCHEI TMIMIM-
LUBAVITCH
841-853 Ocean Pkwy., Brooklyn 11230 *Type:* Private professional *Accred.:* 1976/ 1988 (AARTS) *Calendar:* Sem. plan *Degrees:* Rabbinic (1st and 2nd), Talmudic (1st and 2nd) *CEO:* Pres. J. Korf
Enroll: 415   (718) 434-0784

CHRIST THE KING SEMINARY
711 Knox Rd., P.O. Box 607, East Aurora 14052-0607 *Type:* Private (Roman Catholic)

Accred.: 1977/1992 (ATS); 1974/1993 (MSA) *Calendar:* Sem. plan *Degrees:* P, M *CEO:* Pres./Rector Frederick D. Leising, Ph.D.
Enroll: 102   (716) 652-8900

CITY COLLEGE
Convent Ave. at 138th St., New York 10031 *Type:* Public (local/state) *System:* City University of New York Office of the Chancellor *Accred.:* 1921/1992 (MSA) *Calendar:* Sem. plan *Degrees:* B, M, certificates *Prof. Accred.:* Clinical Psychology, Computer Science, Engineering Technology (electromechanical), Engineering (chemical, civil, electrical, mechanical), Landscape Architecture (B), Nursing (B), Physician Assisting, Teacher Education (e,s,p) *CEO:* Pres. Yolanda T. Moses
Enroll: 14,692   (212) 650-7000

CLARKSON UNIVERSITY
Box 5500, Potsdam 13699-5500 *Type:* Private technological *Accred.:* 1927/1988 (MSA) *Calendar:* Sem. plan *Degrees:* B, M, D *Prof. Accred.:* Business (B,M), Engineering (chemical, civil, computer, electrical, mechanical) *CEO:* Pres. Richard H. Gallagher
Enroll: 3,240   (315) 268-6400

CLINTON COMMUNITY COLLEGE
Rural Rte. 3, Box 8A, Plattsburgh 12901-9573 *Type:* Public (local/state) junior *System:* State University of New York Office of Community Colleges *Accred.:* 1975/1992 (MSA) *Calendar:* Sem. plan *Degrees:* A, certificates *Prof. Accred.:* Medical Laboratory Technology (AMA), Nursing (A) *CEO:* Pres. Jay L. Fennell
Enroll: 2,092   (518) 562-4200

COLGATE ROCHESTER DIVINITY SCHOOL/BEXLEY HALL/CROZER THEOLOGICAL SEMINARY
1100 S. Goodman St., Rochester 14620 *Type:* Private (interdenominational) graduate only *Accred.:* 1938/1993 (ATS) *Calendar:* Sem. plan *Degrees:* M, D *CEO:* Pres. James H. Evans, Jr.
FTE Enroll: 116   (716) 271-1320

COLGATE UNIVERSITY
13 Oak Dr., Hamilton 13346 *Type:* Private liberal arts *Accred.:* 1921/1988 (MSA) *Cal-*

endar: Sem. plan *Degrees:* B, M *CEO:* Pres. Neil R. Grabois
Enroll: 2,727   (315) 824-1000

COLLEGE OF AERONAUTICS
La Guardia Airport, Flushing 11371 *Type:* Private technical *Accred.:* 1969/1992 (MSA) *Calendar:* Tri. plan *Degrees:* A, B *Prof. Accred.:* Engineering Technology (aerospace) *CEO:* Pres. Richard B. Goetze, Jr.
Enroll: 1,207   (718) 429-6600

COLLEGE OF INSURANCE
101 Murray St., New York 10007 *Type:* Private professional *Accred.:* 1967/1988 (MSA) *Calendar:* Sem. plan *Degrees:* A, B, M, certificates *CEO:* Pres. Ellen Thrower
Enroll: 672   (212) 962-4111

COLLEGE OF MOUNT ST. VINCENT
6301 Riverdale Ave., Riverdale 10471 *Type:* Private liberal arts *Accred.:* 1921/1992 (MSA) *Calendar:* Sem. plan *Degrees:* A, B, M *Prof. Accred.:* Nursing (B) *CEO:* Pres. Mary C. Stuart
Enroll: 1,081   (212) 405-3200

COLLEGE OF NEW ROCHELLE
29 Castle Pl., New Rochelle 10805 *Type:* Private *Accred.:* 1921/1992 (MSA) *Calendar:* Sem. plan *Degrees:* B, M, certificates *Prof. Accred.:* Nursing (B,M), Social Work (B) *CEO:* Pres. Dorothy Ann Kelly, O.S.U.
Enroll: 5,696   (914) 632-5300

BROOKLYN CAMPUS
1368 Fulton St., Brooklyn 11216 *CEO:* Dir. Mary Ellen Shepard
        (718) 638-2500

CO-OP CITY CAMPUS
950 Baychester Ave., Bronx 10475 *CEO:* Dir. Carolyn Wiggins
        (212) 320-0300

DC 37 CAMPUS
125 Barclay St., New York 10007 *CEO:* Dir. James Taaffle
        (212) 815-1710

NEW YORK THEOLOGICAL SEMINARY CAMPUS
5 W. 29th St., New York 10001 *CEO:* Dir. Louis DeSalle
        (212) 689-6208

ROSA PARKS CAMPUS
144 W. 125th St., New York 10024 *CEO:*
Dir. Patricia Spradley
(212) 662-7500

SOUTH BRONX CAMPUS
332 E. 149th St., Bronx 10451 *CEO:* Dir.
Celeste Ashe-Johnson
(212) 665-1310

THE COLLEGE OF ST. ROSE
432 Western Ave., Albany 12203 *Type:* Private *Accred.:* 1928/1989 (MSA) *Calendar:*
Sem. plan *Degrees:* B, M *Prof. Accred.:* Art,
Cytotechnology, Speech-Language Pathology *CEO:* Pres. Louis C. Vaccaro
Enroll: 3,618   (518) 454-5111

COLLEGE OF STATEN ISLAND
130 Stuyvesant Pl., Staten Island 10301
Type: Public (local/state) *System:* City University of New York Office of the Chancellor *Accred.:* 1963/1990 (MSA) *Calendar:*
Sem. plan *Degrees:* A, B, M, certificates
Prof. Accred.: Computer Science, Engineering Technology (civil/construction, electrical, electromechanical, industrial, mechanical), Engineering (engineering physics/sci-
ence), Medical Laboratory Technology
(AMA), Nursing (A,B) *CEO:* Interim Pres.
Felix Cardegna
Enroll: 12,255   (718) 982-2000

SUNNYSIDE CAMPUS
715 Ocean Terr., Staten Island 10301
CEO: Exec. Vice Pres. and Provost Felix
Cardegna
(718) 390-7664

COLUMBIA-GREENE COMMUNITY COLLEGE
P.O. Box 1000, Hudson 12534 *Type:* Public
(local/state) junior *System:* State University
of New York Office of Community Colleges
Accred.: 1975/1991 (MSA) *Calendar:* Sem.
plan *Degrees:* A *Prof. Accred.:* Nursing (A)
CEO: Pres. Terry A. Cline
Enroll: 1,663   (518) 828-4181

COLUMBIA UNIVERSITY
116th St. and Broadway, New York 10027
Type: Private *Accred.:* 1921/1991 (MSA)
Calendar: Sem. plan *Degrees:* B, P, M, D,
certificates *Prof. Accred.:* Business (M),
Combined Prosthodontics, Dance, Dentistry,
Endodontics, Engineering (chemical, civil,

electrical, industrial, mechanical, metallurgi-
cal, mining), Journalism (M), Law, Medi-
cine, Nurse Anesthesia Education, Nursing
(B,M), Occupational Therapy, Orthodontics,
Pediatric Dentistry, Periodontics, Physical
Therapy, Planning (M), Public Health, So-
cial Work (M) *CEO:* Pres. George Rupp
Enroll: 19,079   (212) 854-1754

CONCORDIA COLLEGE
171 White Plains Rd., Bronxville 10708-
1923 *Type:* Private (Lutheran-Missouri
Synod) liberal arts *Accred.:* 1941/1991
(MSA) *Calendar:* Sem. plan *Degrees:* A, B
Prof. Accred.: Social Work (B) *CEO:* Pres.
Ralph C. Schultz
Enroll: 471   (914) 337-9300

THE COOPER UNION FOR THE ADVANCEMENT OF
SCIENCE AND ART
41 Cooper Sq., New York 10003 *Type:* Pri-
vate *Accred.:* 1946/1988 (MSA) *Calendar:*
Sem. plan *Degrees:* B, M *Prof. Accred.:* Art,
Engineering (chemical, civil, electrical, me-
chanical) *CEO:* Pres. John J. Iselin
Enroll: 1,085   (212) 254-6300

CORNELL UNIVERSITY
Ithaca 14853 *Type:* Private *Accred.:* 1921/
1992 (MSA) *Calendar:* Sem. plan *Degrees:*
B, P, M, D *Prof. Accred.:* Business (M), Engineering (agricultural, chemical, civil, electrical, engineering physics/science, industrial, materials, mechanical), Health Services
Administration, Interior Design, Landscape
Architecture (B,M), Law, Medicine, Planning (M), Social Work (B), Surgeon Assisting, Veterinary Medicine *CEO:* Pres. Frank
H. Rhodes
Enroll: 18,627   (607) 255-2000

CORNING COMMUNITY COLLEGE
Spencer Hill, Corning 14830 *Type:* Public
(local/state) junior *System:* State University
of New York Office of Community Colleges
Accred.: 1964/1990 (MSA) *Calendar:* Sem.
plan *Degrees:* A, certificates *Prof. Accred.:*
Nursing (A) *CEO:* Pres. Donald H. Hangen
Enroll: 3,800   (607) 962-9011

DAEMEN COLLEGE
4380 Main St., Amherst 14226-3592 *Type:*
Private liberal arts *Accred.:* 1956/1991
(MSA) *Calendar:* Sem. plan *Degrees:* B

Prof. Accred.: Medical Record Administration, Medical Technology, Nursing (B), Physical Therapy, Social Work (B) *CEO:* Pres. Robert S. Marshall
Enroll: 1,900   (716) 839-3600

DARKEI NO'AM RABBINICAL COLLEGE
2822 Ave. J, Brooklyn 11210 *Type:* Private professional *Accred.:* 1983/1988 (AARTS) *Calendar:* Sem. plan *Degrees:* Rabbinic (1st and 2nd) *CEO:* Pres. Chaim Scharf
Enroll: 65   (718) 338-6464

DOMINICAN COLLEGE OF BLAUVELT
470 Western Hwy., Orangeburg 10962 *Type:* Private liberal arts *Accred.:* 1972/1992 (MSA) *Calendar:* Sem. plan *Degrees:* A, B, certificates *Prof. Accred.:* Nursing (B), Occupational Therapy, Social Work (B) *CEO:* Pres. Kathleen Sullivan, O.P.
Enroll: 1,537   (914) 359-7800

DOWLING COLLEGE
Idle Hour Blvd., Oakdale 11769-1999 *Type:* Private *Accred.:* 1971/1985 (MSA) *Calendar:* Sem. plan *Degrees:* B, M *CEO:* Pres. Victor P. Meskill
Enroll: 4,695   (516) 244-3000

DUTCHESS COMMUNITY COLLEGE
53 Pendell Rd., Poughkeepsie 12601-1595 *Type:* Public (local/state) junior *System:* State University of New York Office of Community Colleges *Accred.:* 1964/1990 (MSA) *Calendar:* Sem. plan *Degrees:* A, certificates *Prof. Accred.:* Medical Laboratory Technology (AMA), Nursing (A) *CEO:* Pres. D. David Conklin
Enroll: 7,509   (914) 471-4500

BRANCH CAMPUS
Southern Dutchess Ext. Site, Blodgett House, Fishkill 12524 *CEO:* Dir. Roger Fazzone
     (914) 896-5775

BRANCH CAMPUS
Martha Lawrence Ext. Site, Spackenhill Rd., Poughkeepsie 12603 *CEO:* Dir. Roger Fazzone
     (914) 462-0063

D'YOUVILLE COLLEGE
320 Porter Ave., Buffalo 14201 *Type:* Private liberal arts primarily for women *Ac-*

cred.: 1928/1990 (MSA) *Calendar:* Sem. plan *Degrees:* B, M *Prof. Accred.:* Dietetics (coordinated), Nursing (B,M), Occupational Therapy, Physical Therapy, Social Work (B-conditional) *CEO:* Pres. Denise A. Roche, G.N.S.H.
Enroll: 1,581   (716) 881-3200

ELMIRA COLLEGE
Park Pl., Elmira 14901 *Type:* Private liberal arts *Accred.:* 1921/1989 (MSA) *Calendar:* Sem. plan *Degrees:* A, B, M *Prof. Accred.:* Nursing (B) *CEO:* Pres. Thomas K. Meier
Enroll: 1,685   (607) 735-1800

ERIE COMMUNITY COLLEGE CITY CAMPUS
121 Ellicott St., Buffalo 14203 *Type:* Public (local/state) junior *System:* Erie Community College Central Office *Accred.:* 1981/1990 (MSA) *Calendar:* Sem. plan *Degrees:* A, certificates *Prof. Accred.:* Medical Assisting (AMA), Medical Laboratory Technology (AMA), Nursing (A), Occupational Therapy Assisting, Radiation Therapy Technology, Acting Vice Pres. Thomas Adkins
Enroll: 3,807   (716) 851-1001

ERIE COMMUNITY COLLEGE NORTH (AMHERST) CAMPUS
6205 Main St., Williamsville 14221-7095 *Type:* Public (local/state) junior *System:* Erie Community College Central Office *Accred.:* 1972/1990 (MSA) *Calendar:* Sem. plan *Degrees:* A, certificates *Prof. Accred.:* Dental Hygiene, Engineering Technology (civil/construction, electrical, mechanical), Nursing (A) *CEO:* Interim Vice Pres. Dennis DiGiacomo
Enroll: 7,024   (716) 634-0800

ERIE COMMUNITY COLLEGE SOUTH CAMPUS
S-4041 Southwestern Blvd., Orchard Park 14127-2199 *Type:* Public (local/state) junior *System:* Erie Community College Central Office *Accred.:* 1981/1990 (MSA) *Calendar:* Sem. plan *Degrees:* A, certificates *Prof. Accred.:* Dental Laboratory Technology *CEO:* Vice Pres. Kenneth Gubala
Enroll: 3,501   (716) 851-1003

FASHION INSTITUTE OF TECHNOLOGY
Seventh Ave. at 27th St., New York 10001-5992 *Type:* Public (local/state) professional *System:* State University of New York Of-

fice of Community Colleges *Accred.:* 1957/
1992 (MSA) *Calendar:* 4-1-4 plan *Degrees:*
A, B, M, certificates *Prof. Accred.:* Art, Interior Design *CEO:* Pres. Allan F. Hershfield
Enroll: 12,120   (212) 760-7660

FINGER LAKES COMMUNITY COLLEGE
4355 Lake Shore Dr., Canandaigua 14424
Type: Public (local/state) junior *System:*
State University of New York Office of
Community Colleges *Accred.:* 1977/1992
(MSA) *Calendar:* Sem. plan *Degrees:* A,
certificates *Prof. Accred.:* Nursing (A) *CEO:*
Pres. Daniel T. Hayes
Enroll: 3,820   (716) 394-3500

FIVE TOWNS COLLEGE
305 N. Service Rd., Dix Hills 11746-6055
Type: Private *Accred.:* 1988 (MSA) *Calendar:* Sem. plan *Degrees:* A, B *CEO:* Pres.
Stanley G. Cohen
Enroll: 571   (516) 424-7000

FORDHAM UNIVERSITY
E. Fordham Rd., Bronx 10458 *Type:* Private
Accred.: 1921/1990 (MSA) *Calendar:* Sem.
plan *Degrees:* B, P, M, D, certificates *Prof.
Accred.:* Business (B,M), Clinical Psychology, Counseling Psychology, Law, School
Psychology, Social Work (M), Teacher Education (e,s,p) *CEO:* Pres. Joseph A. O'Hare,
S.J.
Enroll: 13,329   (718) 579-2000

FULTON-MONTGOMERY COMMUNITY COLLEGE
Rte. 67, Johnstown 12095 *Type:* Public
(local/state) junior *System:* State University
of New York Office of Community Colleges
Accred.: 1969/1991 (MSA) *Calendar:* Sem.
plan *Degrees:* A *CEO:* Pres. Jacqueline D.
Taylor
Enroll: 1,921   (518) 762-4651

THE GENERAL THEOLOGICAL SEMINARY
175 Ninth Ave., New York 10011-4977
Type: Private (Episcopal) graduate only *Accred.:* 1938/1988 (ATS) *Calendar:* Sem.
plan *Degrees:* M, D *CEO:* Pres./Dean Craig
Anderson
FTE Enroll: 104   (212) 243-5150

GENESEE COMMUNITY COLLEGE
One College Rd., Batavia 14020 *Type:* Public (local/state) junior *System:* State University of New York Office of Community

Colleges *Accred.:* 1971/1992 (MSA) *Calendar:* Sem. plan *Degrees:* A, certificates *Prof.
Accred.:* Nursing (A), Physical Therapy Assisting *CEO:* Pres. Stuart Steiner
Enroll: 3,667   (716) 343-0055

GRADUATE SCHOOL AND UNIVERSITY CENTER
33 W. 42nd St., New York 10036 *Type:* Public (local/state) graduate only *System:* City
University of New York Office of the Chancellor *Accred.:* 1961/1988 (MSA) *Calendar:*
Sem. plan *Degrees:* M, D *CEO:* Pres.
Frances Degen Horowitz
Enroll: 4,130   (212) 642-1600

HAMILTON COLLEGE
Clinton 13323 *Type:* Private liberal arts *Accred.:* 1921/1991 (MSA) *Calendar:* Sem.
plan *Degrees:* B *CEO:* Pres. Eugene M.
Tobin
Enroll: 1,723   (315) 859-4011

HARTWICK COLLEGE
Oneonta 13820 *Type:* Private liberal arts *Accred.:* 1949/1989 (MSA) *Calendar:* 4-1-4
plan *Degrees:* B *Prof. Accred.:* Art (associate), Music, Nursing (B) *CEO:* Pres. Richard
A. Detweiler
Enroll: 1,464   (607) 431-4200

HEBREW UNION COLLEGE—JEWISH INSTITUTE
OF RELIGION
One W. Fourth St., New York 10012 *Type:*
Private (Jewish) graduate only *Accred.:*
1960/1988 (MSA) *Calendar:* Sem. plan *Degrees:* P, M, D, certificates *CEO:* Pres.
Alfred Gottschalk
Enroll: 119   (212) 674-5300

HELENE FULD SCHOOL OF NURSING
1879 Madison Ave., New York 10035 *Type:*
Private professional *Accred.:* 1988 (MSA) *Calendar:* Qtr. plan *Degrees:* A *Prof. Accred.:*
Nursing (A) *CEO:* Dir./Dean Margaret
Wines, R.N.
Enroll: 216   (212) 423-1000

HERBERT H. LEHMAN COLLEGE
Bedford Park Blvd. W., Bronx 10468 *Type:*
Public (local/state) *System:* City University
of New York Office of the Chancellor *Accred.:* 1968/1988 (MSA) *Calendar:* Sem.
plan *Degrees:* B, M *Prof. Accred.:* Nurse
Anesthesia Education, Nursing (B,M), Social

Work (B), Speech-Language Pathology (probational) *CEO:* Pres. Ricardo R. Fernandez
Enroll: 9,955   (718) 960-8000

HERKIMER COUNTY COMMUNITY COLLEGE
Reservoir Rd., Herkimer 13350 *Type:* Public (local/state) junior *System:* State University of New York Office of Community Colleges *Accred.:* 1972/1988 (MSA) *Calendar:* Sem. plan *Degrees:* A, certificates *Prof. Accred.:* Occupational Therapy Assisting, Physical Therapy Assisting *CEO:* Pres. Ronald F. Williams
Enroll: 2,320   (315) 866-0300

HILBERT COLLEGE
5200 S. Park Ave., Hamburg 14075-1597 *Type:* Private liberal arts *Accred.:* 1976/1991 (MSA) *Calendar:* Sem. plan *Degrees:* A, B, certificates *CEO:* Pres. Edmunette Paczesny, F.S.S.J.
Enroll: 631   (716) 649-7900

HOBART & WILLIAM SMITH COLLEGES
Geneva 14456 *Type:* Private liberal arts *Accred.:* 1921/1989 (MSA) *Calendar:* Tri. plan *Degrees:* B *CEO:* Pres. Richard H. Hersh
Enroll: 1,829   (315) 789-5500

HOFSTRA UNIVERSITY
Hempstead 11550 *Type:* Private *Accred.:* 1940/1989 (MSA) *Calendar:* Sem. plan *Degrees:* A, B, P, M, D, certificates *Prof. Accred.:* Audiology, Business (B,M), Combined Professional-Scientific Psychology, Engineering (electrical, engineering physics/science, mechanical), Law, Rehabilitation Counseling, Speech-Language Pathology, Teacher Education (e,s,p) *CEO:* Pres. James M. Shuart
Enroll: 12,009   (516) 463-6600

HOSTOS COMMUNITY COLLEGE
475 Grand Concourse, Bronx 10451 *Type:* Public (local/state) *System:* City University of New York Office of the Chancellor *Accred.:* 1974/1990 (MSA) *Calendar:* Sem. plan *Degrees:* A *Prof. Accred.:* Dental Hygiene, Radiography *CEO:* Pres. Isaura Santiago
Enroll: 4,517   (718) 518-4444

HOUGHTON COLLEGE
Houghton 14744 *Type:* Private (Wesleyan) liberal arts *Accred.:* 1935/1991 (MSA) *Calendar:* Sem. plan *Degrees:* A, B *Prof. Ac-*

cred.: Music *CEO:* Pres. Daniel R. Chamberlain
Enroll: 1,148   (716) 567-9200

BUFFALO SUBURBAN CAMPUS
910 Union Rd., West Seneca 14224 *CEO:* Pres. Daniel R. Chamberlain
                    (716) 674-6363

HUDSON VALLEY COMMUNITY COLLEGE
80 Vandenburgh Ave., Troy 12180 *Type:* Public (local/state) junior *System:* State University of New York Office of Community Colleges *Accred.:* 1969/1989 (MSA) *Calendar:* Sem. plan *Degrees:* A, certificates *Prof. Accred.:* Construction Education (A), Dental Hygiene, Engineering Technology (civil/construction, electrical, mechanical), Medical Laboratory Technology (AMA), Mortuary Science, Nursing (A), Radiography, Respiratory Therapy *CEO:* Pres. Joseph J. Bulmer
Enroll: 9,766   (518) 283-1100

HUNTER COLLEGE
695 Park Ave., New York 10021 *Type:* Public (local/state) *System:* City University of New York Office of the Chancellor *Accred.:* 1921/1992 (MSA) *Calendar:* Sem. plan *Degrees:* B, M, certificates *Prof. Accred.:* Audiology (probational), Community Health, Nursing (B,M), Physical Therapy, Planning (M), Rehabilitation Counseling, Social Work (M), Speech-Language Pathology (probational) *CEO:* Acting Pres. Blanche D. Blank
Enroll: 18,854   (212) 772-4000

INTERBORO INSTITUTE
450 W. 56th St., New York 10019 *Type:* Private business *Accred.:* 1968/1985 (ACISC) *Calendar:* Sem. plan *Degrees:* A *CEO:* Pres. Bruce R. Kalisch
Enroll: 983   (212) 399-0091

IONA COLLEGE
715 North Ave., New Rochelle 10801-1890 *Type:* Private *Accred.:* 1952/1992 (MSA) *Calendar:* Sem. plan *Degrees:* B, M, certificates *Prof. Accred.:* Nursing (A), Practical Nursing, Social Work (B) *CEO:* Pres. John G. Driscoll, C.F.C.
Enroll: 5,983   (914) 633-2000

MANHATTAN CAMPUS
425 W. 33rd St., New York 10001 *CEO:*
Dir. Michael Jordan
(212) 714-9444

ROCKLAND CAMPUS
One Dutch Hill Rd., Orangeburg 10962
CEO: Dir. Barbara Witchel
(914) 359-2252

YONKERS CAMPUS
1061 N. Broadway, Yonkers 10701 *CEO:*
Dir. Marian McGowan
(914) 378-8000

ITHACA COLLEGE
Danby Rd., Ithaca 14850 *Type:* Private *Accred.:* 1955/1992 (MSA) *Calendar:* Sem. plan *Degrees:* B, M *Prof. Accred.:* Audiology, Medical Record Administration, Music, Physical Therapy, Recreation and Leisure Services, Speech-Language Pathology, Theatre *CEO:* Pres. James J. Whalen
Enroll: 6,444   (607) 274-3013

JAMESTOWN BUSINESS COLLEGE
P.O. Box 429, 7 Fairmont Ave., Jamestown 14702-0429 *Type:* Private business *Accred.:* 1968/1987 (ACISC) *Calendar:* Sem. plan *Degrees:* A *CEO:* Pres. Tyler C. Swanson
(716) 664-5100

JAMESTOWN COMMUNITY COLLEGE
525 Falconer St., Jamestown 14701 *Type:* Public (local/state) junior *System:* State University of New York Office of Community Colleges *Accred.:* 1956/1991 (MSA) *Calendar:* Sem. plan *Degrees:* A, certificates *Prof. Accred.:* Nursing (A) *CEO:* Pres. Timothy G. Davies
Enroll: 4,529   (716) 665-5220

CATTARAUGUS COUNTY CAMPUS
244 N. Union St., Olean 14760 *CEO:*
Dean Carol Scott
(716) 372-1661

JEFFERSON COMMUNITY COLLEGE
Outer Coffeen St., Watertown 13601 *Type:* Public (local/state) junior *System:* State University of New York Office of Community Colleges *Accred.:* 1969/1990 (MSA) *Calendar:* Sem. plan *Degrees:* A, certificates *Prof.*

Accred.: Nursing (A) *CEO:* Pres. John W. Deans
Enroll: 2,746   (315) 786-2200

JEWISH THEOLOGICAL SEMINARY OF AMERICA
3080 Broadway, New York 10027 *Type:* Private (Jewish) *Accred.:* 1954/1991 (MSA) *Calendar:* Sem. plan *Degrees:* B, P, M, D *CEO:* Chanc. Ismar Schorsch
Enroll: 435   (212) 678-8000

JOHN JAY COLLEGE OF CRIMINAL JUSTICE
899 10th Ave., New York 10019 *Type:* Public (local/state) *System:* City University of New York Office of the Chancellor *Accred.:* 1965/1988 (MSA) *Calendar:* Sem. plan *Degrees:* A, B, M, certificates *Prof. Accred.:* Public Administration *CEO:* Pres. Gerald W. Lynch
Enroll: 8,522   (212) 237-8000

THE JUILLIARD SCHOOL
60 Lincoln Center Plaza, New York 10023-6590 *Type:* Private professional *Accred.:* 1956/1988 (MSA) *Calendar:* Sem. plan *Degrees:* B, M, D, certificates *CEO:* Pres. Joseph W. Polisi
Enroll: 825   (212) 799-5000

KATHARINE GIBBS SCHOOL
535 Broad Hollow Rd., Melville 11747 *Type:* Private business *Accred.:* 1973/1990 (ACISC) *Calendar:* Sem. plan *Degrees:* A, certificates, diplomas *CEO:* Dir. Pat Martin
(516) 293-2460

KATHARINE GIBBS SCHOOL
200 Park Ave., New York 10166 *Type:* Private business *Accred.:* 1967/1990 (ACISC) *Calendar:* Courses of varying lengths *Degrees:* A, certificates, diplomas *CEO:* Dir. Julia Slick
(212) 867-9307

KEHILATH YAKOV RABBINICAL SEMINARY
206 Wilson St., Brooklyn 11211 *Type:* Private professional *Accred.:* 1981/1991 (AARTS) *Calendar:* Sem. plan *Degrees:* Rabbinic (1st and 2nd) *CEO:* Pres. Sandor Schwartz
Enroll: 100   (718) 963-3940

KEUKA COLLEGE
Keuka Park 14478 *Type:* Private liberal arts primarily for women *Accred.:* 1927/1992

(MSA) *Calendar:* 4-1-4 plan *Degrees:* B *Prof. Accred.:* Nursing (B), Occupational Therapy, Social Work (B) *CEO:* Pres. Arthur F. Kirk, Jr.
Enroll: 708　　　　　　　(315) 536-4411

THE KING'S COLLEGE
Lodge Rd., Briarcliff Manor 10510 *Type:* Private liberal arts *Accred.:* 1968/1984 (MSA) *Calendar:* Sem. plan *Degrees:* A, B *CEO:* Pres. Friedhelm K. Radandt
Enroll: 459　　　　　　　(914) 941-7200

KINGSBOROUGH COMMUNITY COLLEGE
2001 Oriental Blvd., Manhattan Beach, Brooklyn 11235 *Type:* Public (local/state) *System:* City University of New York Office of the Chancellor *Accred.:* 1964/1991 (MSA) *Calendar:* Sem. plan *Degrees:* A *Prof. Accred.:* Nursing (A) *CEO:* Pres. Leon M. Goldstein
Enroll: 14,466　　　　　(718) 368-5000

LA GUARDIA COMMUNITY COLLEGE
31-10 Thomson Ave., Long Island City 11101 *Type:* Public (local/state) *System:* City University of New York Office of the Chancellor *Accred.:* 1974/1992 (MSA) *Calendar:* Qtr. plan *Degrees:* A, certificates *Prof. Accred.:* Nursing (A), Occupational Therapy Assisting, Physical Therapy Assisting, Veterinary Technology *CEO:* Pres. Raymond C. Bowen
Enroll: 9,394　　　　　　(718) 482-7000

LABORATORY INSTITUTE OF MERCHANDISING
12 E. 53rd St., New York 10022 *Type:* Private *Accred.:* 1977/1992 (MSA) *Calendar:* 4-1-4 plan *Degrees:* A, B *CEO:* Pres. Adrian G. Marcuse
Enroll: 197　　　　　　　(212) 752-1530

LE MOYNE COLLEGE
Le Moyne Heights, Syracuse 13214 *Type:* Private liberal arts *Accred.:* 1953/1992 (MSA) *Calendar:* Sem. plan *Degrees:* B, M *CEO:* Interim Pres. Robert A. Mithcell, S.J.
Enroll: 2,436　　　　　　(315) 445-4100

LONG ISLAND UNIVERSITY
Northern Blvd., Brookville 11548 *Type:* Private *Accred.:* 1955/1989 (MSA) *Calendar:* Sem. plan *Degrees:* A, B, M, D, certificates *Prof. Accred.:* Clinical Psychology, Librarianship, Medical Record Administration,

Medical Technology, Radiography, Respiratory Therapy *CEO:* Pres. David J. Steinberg
Enroll: 17,504　　　　　(516) 299-2501

BRENTWOOD CAMPUS
Second Ave., Brentwood 11717 *CEO:* Provost Dennis L. Payette
　　　　　　　　　　　　(516) 273-5112

BROOKLYN CAMPUS
University Plaza, Brooklyn 11201 *Prof. Accred.:* Nursing (A,B), Physical Therapy *CEO:* Provost Gale Stevens-Haynes
　　　　　　　　　　　　(718) 488-1000

C.W. POST CAMPUS
Greenvale 11548 *Prof. Accred.:* Counseling, Nursing (B), Public Administration, Speech-Language Pathology *CEO:* Provost Doris Guidi
　　　　　　　　　　　　(516) 299-0200

ROCKLAND CAMPUS
Rte. 340, Orangeburg 10962 *CEO:* Provost Joram Warmund
　　　　　　　　　　　　(914) 359-7200

SOUTHAMPTON CAMPUS
Southampton 11968 *CEO:* Chanc. Robert F.X. Sillerman
　　　　　　　　　　　　(516) 283-4000

WESTCHESTER CAMPUS
555 Broadway, Dobbs Ferry 10522 *CEO:* Provost Dennis L. Payette
　　　　　　　　　　　　(914) 674-4000

MANHATTAN COLLEGE
Manhattan College Pkwy., Riverdale 10471 *Type:* Private *Accred.:* 1921/1992 (MSA) *Calendar:* Sem. plan *Degrees:* A, B, M *Prof. Accred.:* Engineering (chemical, civil, electrical, environmental/sanitary, mechanical), Nuclear Medicine Technology *CEO:* Pres. Thomas J. Scanlan, Ph.D.
Enroll: 3,698　　　　　　(212) 920-0100

MANHATTAN SCHOOL OF MUSIC
120 Claremont Ave., New York 10027 *Type:* Private professional *Accred.:* 1956/1988 (MSA) *Calendar:* Sem. plan *Degrees:* B, M, D, certificates *CEO:* Pres. Marta Istomin
Enroll: 869　　　　　　　(212) 749-2802

MANHATTANVILLE COLLEGE
2900 Purchase St., Purchase 10577 *Type:* Private liberal arts *Accred.:* 1926/1990 (MSA) *Calendar:* Sem. plan *Degrees:* B, M *CEO:* Pres. Marcia A. Savage
Enroll: 1,499   (914) 694-2200

MARIA COLLEGE OF ALBANY
700 New Scotland Ave., Albany 12208-1798 *Type:* Private junior for women *Accred.:* 1973/1988 (MSA) *Calendar:* Sem. plan *Degrees:* A *Prof. Accred.:* Nursing (A), Occupational Therapy Assisting, Physical Therapy Assisting *CEO:* Pres. Laureen Fitzgerald, R.S.M.
Enroll: 860   (518) 438-7170

MARIST COLLEGE
290 North Rd., Poughkeepsie 12601 *Type:* Private *Accred.:* 1964/1993 (MSA) *Calendar:* Sem. plan *Degrees:* B, M, certificates *Prof. Accred.:* Medical Technology, Social Work (B) *CEO:* Pres. Dennis J. Murray
Enroll: 4,992   (914) 575-3000

MARYKNOLL SCHOOL OF THEOLOGY
P.O. Box 305, Pinesbridge Rd., Maryknoll 10545-0305 *Type:* Private (Roman Catholic) graduate only *Accred.:* 1968/1992 (ATS); 1962/1988 (MSA) *Calendar:* Sem. plan *Degrees:* P, M *CEO:* Pres. John K. Halbert, M.M.
Enroll: 123   (914) 941-7590

MARYMOUNT COLLEGE
100 Marymount Ave., Tarrytown 10591-3796 *Type:* Private liberal arts *Accred.:* 1927/1990 (MSA) *Calendar:* Sem. plan *Degrees:* B *Prof. Accred.:* Social Work (B) *CEO:* Pres. Brigid Driscoll, R.S.H.M.
Enroll: 1,144   (914) 631-3200

MARYMOUNT MANHATTAN COLLEGE
221 E. 71st St., New York 10021 *Type:* Private liberal arts *Accred.:* 1961/1982 (MSA) *Calendar:* 4-1-4 plan *Degrees:* B *CEO:* Pres. Regina S. Peruggi
Enroll: 1,387   (212) 517-0400

MATER DEI COLLEGE
Rural Rte. 2, Box 45, Ogdensburg 13669-1034 *Type:* Private junior *Accred.:* 1974/1990 (MSA) *Calendar:* Sem. plan *Degrees:*

A, certificates *CEO:* Pres. Ronald M. Mrozinski, O.F.M.
Enroll: 582   (315) 393-5930

MEDAILLE COLLEGE
18 Agassiz Cir., Buffalo 14214 *Type:* Private liberal arts *Accred.:* 1951/1993 (MSA) *Calendar:* Sem. plan *Degrees:* A, B, certificates *CEO:* Pres. Kevin I. Sullivan
Enroll: 1,135   (716) 884-3281

MEDGAR EVERS COLLEGE
1650 Bedford Ave., Brooklyn 11225 *Type:* Public (local/state) *System:* City University of New York Office of the Chancellor *Accred.:* 1976/1992 (MSA) *Calendar:* Sem. plan *Degrees:* A, B, certificates *Prof. Accred.:* Nursing (B) *CEO:* Pres. Edison O. Jackson
Enroll: 3,924   (718) 270-4900

MERCY COLLEGE
555 Broadway, Dobbs Ferry 10522 *Type:* Private *Accred.:* 1968/1989 (MSA) *Calendar:* Sem. plan *Degrees:* A, B, M, certificates *Prof. Accred.:* Nursing (B,M), Social Work (B), Veterinary Technology *CEO:* Pres. Jay Sexter
Enroll: 3,103   (914) 693-4500

BRONX CAMPUS
50 Antin Pl., Bronx 10462 *CEO:* Dean Marilyn Nielsen
                    (212) 798-8952

PEEKSKILL CAMPUS
Peekskill 10566 *CEO:* Dean Wiley A. Dickerson
                    (914) 739-8300

WHITE PLAINS CAMPUS
Martine Ave. and S. Broadway, White Plains 10601 *CEO:* Dean John McGrath
                    (914) 948-3666

YORKTOWN CAMPUS
2651 Stang Blvd., Yorktown Heights 10598 *CEO:* Dean Thomas Barry
                    (914) 245-6100

MESIVTA OF EASTERN PARKWAY RABBINICAL SEMINARY
510 Dahill Rd., Brooklyn 11218 *Type:* Private professional *Accred.:* 1980/1991 (AARTS) *Calendar:* Sem. plan *Degrees:*

Talmudic (1st and 2nd) *CEO:* Pres. Joseph D. Epstein
Enroll: 57   (718) 438-1002

MESIVTA TIFERETH JERUSALEM OF AMERICA
141 E. Broadway, New York 10002 *Type:* Private professional *Accred.:* 1979/1989 (AARTS) *Calendar:* Sem. plan *Degrees:* Talmudic (1st and 2nd) *CEO:* Pres. D. Feinstein
Enroll: 89   (212) 964-2830

MESIVTA TORAH VODAATH SEMINARY
425 E. 9th St., Brooklyn 11218 *Type:* Private professional *Accred.:* 1976/1990 (AARTS) *Calendar:* Sem. plan *Degrees:* Talmudic (1st and 2nd) *CEO:* Dean Chaim H. Lashkowitz
Enroll: 383   (718) 941-8000

MIRRER YESHIVA CENTRAL INSTITUTE
1795 Ocean Pkwy., Brooklyn 11223 *Type:* Private professional *Accred.:* 1975/1988 (AARTS) *Calendar:* Sem. plan *Degrees:* Talmudic (1st and 2nd) *CEO:* Pres. S.M. Kalmanowitz
Enroll: 193   (718) 645-0536

MOHAWK VALLEY COMMUNITY COLLEGE
1101 Sherman Dr., Utica 13501 *Type:* Public (local/state) junior *System:* State University of New York Office of Community Colleges *Accred.:* 1960/1988 (MSA) *Calendar:* Sem. plan *Degrees:* A, certificates *Prof. Accred.:* Engineering Technology (civil/construction, electrical, mechanical, surveying), Medical Record Technology, Nursing (A), Respiratory Therapy Technology *CEO:* Pres. Michael I. Schafer
Enroll: 6,398   (315) 792-5400

BRANCH CAMPUS
Floyd Ave., Rome 13440 *CEO:* Dean Michael B. Sewall
                               (315) 339-3470

MOLLOY COLLEGE
1000 Hempstead Ave., Rockville Centre 11570 *Type:* Private *Accred.:* 1967/1993 (MSA) *Calendar:* 4-1-4 plan *Degrees:* A, B, M *Prof. Accred.:* Nursing (B,M), Respiratory Therapy, Respiratory Therapy Technology, Social Work (B) *CEO:* Pres. Janet A. Fitzgerald, O.P.
Enroll: 2,570   (516) 678-5000

MONROE COLLEGE
29 E. Fordham Rd., Bronx 10468 *Type:* Private junior *Accred.:* 1990 (MSA) *Calendar:* Sem. plan *Degrees:* A *CEO:* Pres. Stephen J. Jerome
Enroll: 1,827   (718) 933-6700

NEW ROCHELLE CAMPUS
434 Main St., New Rochelle 10801 *CEO:* Dir. Peter Neigler
                               (914) 632-5400

MONROE COMMUNITY COLLEGE
1000 E. Henrietta Rd., Rochester 14623 *Type:* Public (local/state) junior *System:* State University of New York Office of Community Colleges *Accred.:* 1965/1991 (MSA) *Calendar:* Sem. plan *Degrees:* A, certificates *Prof. Accred.:* Dental Hygiene, Engineering Technology (electrical), Medical Record Technology, Nursing (A), Radiography *CEO:* Pres. Peter A. Spina
Enroll: 13,406   (716) 292-2000

MOUNT ST. MARY COLLEGE
330 Powell Ave., Newburgh 12550 *Type:* Private liberal arts *Accred.:* 1968/1992 (MSA) *Calendar:* Sem. plan *Degrees:* B, M *Prof. Accred.:* Nursing (B) *CEO:* Pres. Ann Sakac, O.P.
Enroll: 1,513   (914) 561-0800

MOUNT SINAI SCHOOL OF MEDICINE
One Gustave L. Levy Pl., New York 10029 *Type:* Private *System:* City University of New York Office of the Chancellor (Affiliate) *Calendar:* Sem. plan *Degrees:* B, P, M, D *Prof. Accred.:* Health Services Administration, Medicine *CEO:* Dean John W. Rowe
Enroll: 483   (212) 650-6500

NASSAU COMMUNITY COLLEGE
One Education Dr., Garden City 11530 *Type:* Public (local/state) junior *System:* State University of New York Office of Community Colleges *Accred.:* 1967/1990 (MSA) *Calendar:* Sem. plan *Degrees:* A *Prof. Accred.:* Engineering Technology (civil/construction), Mortuary Science, Music, Nursing (A), Physical Therapy Assisting, Radiation Therapy Technology, Radiography, Respiratory Therapy, Surgical Technology *CEO:* Pres. Sean A. Fanelli
Enroll: 21,552   (516) 222-7205

NAZARETH COLLEGE OF ROCHESTER
4245 East Ave., Rochester 14618-3790 *Type:* Private *Accred.:* 1930/1991 (MSA) *Calendar:* Sem. plan *Degrees:* B, M *Prof. Accred.:* Music, Nursing (B), Social Work (B), Speech-Language Pathology *CEO:* Pres. Rose Marie Beston
Enroll: 2,786   (716) 586-2525

NEW SCHOOL FOR SOCIAL RESEARCH
66 W. 12th St., New York 10011 *Type:* Private *Accred.:* 1960/1991 (MSA) *Calendar:* Sem. plan *Degrees:* A, B, M, D, certificates *Prof. Accred.:* Clinical Psychology (probational), Urban Affairs and Policy Analysis *CEO:* Pres. Jonathan F. Fanton
Enroll: 6,242   (212) 229-5600

PARSONS SCHOOL OF DESIGN
66 Fifth Ave., New York 10011 *Prof. Accred.:* Art *CEO:* Dean Charles S. Olton
(212) 229-8950

PARSONS SCHOOL OF DESIGN
14 Rue Letellier, 75015 Paris, France *Prof. Accred.:* Art *CEO:* Dir. Janice Y. Nagourney
[33] (14) 577-3966

NEW YORK CHIROPRACTIC COLLEGE
2360 State Rte. 89, Seneca Falls 13148-0800 *Type:* Private professional *Accred.:* 1985 (MSA) *Calendar:* Tri. plan *Degrees:* P *Prof. Accred.:* Chiropractic Education *CEO:* Pres. Kenneth W. Padgett, D.C.
Enroll: 630   (315) 568-3000

NEW YORK CITY TECHNICAL COLLEGE
300 Jay St., Brooklyn 11201 *Type:* Public (local/state) *System:* City University of New York Office of the Chancellor *Accred.:* 1957/1992 (MSA) *Calendar:* Sem. plan *Degrees:* A, B, certificates *Prof. Accred.:* Dental Hygiene, Dental Laboratory Technology, Engineering Technology (civil/construction, electrical, electromechanical, mechanical), Nursing (A), Radiography *CEO:* Pres. Charles W. Meredith
Enroll: 10,309   (718) 260-5000

NEW YORK COLLEGE OF PODIATRIC MEDICINE
53 E. 124th St., New York 10035 *Type:* Private professional *Calendar:* Sem. plan *Degrees:* P *Prof. Accred.:* Podiatry *CEO:* Acting Pres. Monroe Seifer
Enroll: 554   (212) 410-8000

NEW YORK INSTITUTE OF TECHNOLOGY
268 Wheatley Rd., Old Westbury 11568-1036 *Type:* Private professional *Accred.:* 1969/1988 (MSA) *Calendar:* Sem. plan *Degrees:* A, B, P, M, certificates *Prof. Accred.:* Engineering Technology (electrical), Engineering (electrical, mechanical), Interior Design, Medical Technology, Osteopathy *CEO:* Pres. Matthew Schure
Enroll: 5,706   (516) 686-7516

CENTRAL ISLIP CAMPUS
211 Carleton Ave., Central Islip 11722 *Prof. Accred.:* Engineering Technology (electrical) *CEO:* Dean William C. Puffer
(516) 348-3000

MANHATTAN CAMPUS
1855 Broadway, New York 10023 *Prof. Accred.:* Engineering Technology (electrical), Engineering (electrical) *CEO:* Dean Felisa Kaplan
(212) 399-8300

NEW YORK LAW SCHOOL
57 Worth St., New York 10013 *Type:* Private *Calendar:* Sem. plan *Degrees:* P *Prof. Accred.:* Law *CEO:* Dean Harry H. Wellington
Enroll: 1,383   (212) 431-2840

NEW YORK MEDICAL COLLEGE
Sunshine Cottage, Administration Bldg., Valhalla 10595 *Type:* Private (Roman Catholic) professional *Accred.:* 1991 (MSA candidate) *Calendar:* Sem. plan *Degrees:* P, M, D *Prof. Accred.:* Medicine *CEO:* Pres. and C.E.O. Harry C. Barrett
Enroll: 1,261   (914) 993-4000

NEW YORK SCHOOL OF INTERIOR DESIGN
155 E. 56th St., New York 10022 *Type:* Private professional *Calendar:* Courses of varying lengths *Degrees:* B, P, diplomas *Prof. Accred.:* Interior Design *CEO:* Dir. of Acad. Affairs Christopher Walsh
(212) 753-5365

NEW YORK THEOLOGICAL SEMINARY
5 W. 29th St., New York 10001-4599 *Type:* Private (interdenominational) graduate only *Accred.:* 1958/1989 (ATS) *Calendar:* 4-1-4

plan *Degrees:* M, D *CEO:* Pres. M. William Howard, Jr.
FTE Enroll: 212   (212) 532-4012

NEW YORK UNIVERSITY
70 Washington Sq. S., New York 10012 *Type:* Private *Accred.:* 1921/1990 (MSA) *Calendar:* Sem. plan *Degrees:* A, B, P, M, D, certificates *Prof. Accred.:* Accounting (Type A,B,C), Business (B,M), Clinical Psychology, Combined Prosthodontics, Community Health, Counseling Psychology, Cytotechnology, Dance, Dental Assisting, Dental Hygiene, Dentistry, Diagnostic Medical Sonography, Endodontics, General Dentistry, Health Services Administration, Journalism (B,M), Law, Medicine, Music, Nuclear Medicine Technology, Nursing (B,M), Occupational Therapy, Oral and Maxillofacial Surgery, Orthodontics, Pediatric Dentistry, Periodontics, Physical Therapy, Physical Therapy Assisting, Planning (M), Psychology Internship, Public Administration, Rehabilitation Counseling, Respiratory Therapy, School Psychology, Social Work (B,M), Speech-Language Pathology *CEO:* Pres. L. Jay Oliva
Enroll: 33,446   (212) 998-1212

NIAGARA COUNTY COMMUNITY COLLEGE
3111 Saunders Settlement Rd., Sanborn 14132 *Type:* Public (local/state) junior *System:* State University of New York Office of Community Colleges *Accred.:* 1970/1991 (MSA) *Calendar:* Sem. plan *Degrees:* A, certificates *Prof. Accred.:* Electroneurodiagnostic Technology, Engineering Technology (electrical, mechanical), Nursing (A), Physical Therapy Assisting, Surgical Technology *CEO:* Pres. Gerald L. Miller
Enroll: 5,480   (716) 731-3271

NIAGARA UNIVERSITY
Niagara University 14109 *Type:* Private *Accred.:* 1922/1992 (MSA) *Calendar:* Sem. plan *Degrees:* A, B, M, certificates *Prof. Accred.:* Nursing (B), Social Work (B-conditional), Teacher Education (s,p) *CEO:* Pres. Brian J. O'Connell
Enroll: 3,006   (716) 285-1212

NORTH COUNTRY COMMUNITY COLLEGE
20 Winona Ave., P.O. Box 89, Saranac Lake 12983 *Type:* Public (local/state) junior *System:* State University of New York Office of Community Colleges *Accred.:* 1975/1990 (MSA) *Calendar:* Sem. plan *Degrees:* A, certificates *Prof. Accred.:* Radiography *CEO:* Pres. Gail Rogers Rice
Enroll: 1,533   (518) 891-2915

BRANCH CAMPUS
College Ave., Malone 12953 *CEO:* Dir. Wiley N. Kulia
                                   (518) 483-4550

BRANCH CAMPUS
Montcalm St., Ticonderoga 12883 *CEO:* Dir. Donna Condon
                                   (518) 585-4454

NYACK COLLEGE
One South Blvd., Nyack 10960-3698 *Type:* Private (Christian and Missionary Alliance) liberal arts *Accred.:* 1990 (ATS); 1962/1991 (MSA) *Calendar:* Sem. plan *Degrees:* A, B, M *Prof. Accred.:* Music *CEO:* Acting Chanc. Robert E. Nanfelt
Enroll: 903   (914) 358-1710

OHR HAMEIR THEOLOGICAL SEMINARY
Furnace Woods Rd., P.O. Box 2130, Peekskill 10566 *Type:* Private professional *Accred.:* 1979/1989 (AARTS) *Calendar:* Sem. plan *Degrees:* Talmudic (1st and 2nd) *CEO:* Pres. E. Kanarek
Enroll: 46   (914) 736-1500

OHR SOMAYACH-TANENBAUM EDUCATIONAL CENTER
P.O. Box 334, Monsey 10952 *Type:* Private professional *Accred.:* 1984/1989 (AARTS) *Calendar:* Tri. plan *Degrees:* Talmudic (1st and 2nd) *CEO:* Pres. Emil Tauber
Enroll: 62   (914) 425-1370

OLEAN BUSINESS INSTITUTE
301 N. Union St., Olean 14760 *Type:* Private business *Accred.:* 1969/1987 (ACISC) *Calendar:* Sem. plan *Degrees:* A *CEO:* Dir. Patrick J. McCarthy
                                   (716) 372-7978

ONONDAGA COMMUNITY COLLEGE
Rte. 173, Syracuse 13215 *Type:* Public (local/state) junior *System:* State University of New York Office of Community Colleges *Accred.:* 1972/1989 (MSA) *Calendar:* Sem. plan *Degrees:* A *Prof. Accred.:* Dental Hy-

giene, Engineering Technology (computer, electrical), Medical Record Technology, Nursing (A), Physical Therapy Assisting, Respiratory Therapy, Respiratory Therapy Technology, Surgical Technology *CEO:* Pres. Bruce H. Leslie
Enroll: 8,406   (315) 469-7741

ORANGE COUNTY COMMUNITY COLLEGE
115 South St., Middletown 10940 *Type:* Public (local/state) junior *System:* State University of New York Office of Community Colleges *Accred.:* 1962/1988 (MSA) *Calendar:* Sem. plan *Degrees:* A, certificates *Prof. Accred.:* Dental Hygiene, Engineering Technology (electrical), Medical Laboratory Technology (AMA), Nursing (A), Occupational Therapy Assisting, Physical Therapy Assisting, Radiography *CEO:* Pres. William F. Messner
Enroll: 5,963   (914) 343-1121

PACE UNIVERSITY
One Pace Plaza, New York 10038 *Type:* Private *Accred.:* 1957/1988 (MSA) *Calendar:* Sem. plan *Degrees:* A, B, P, M, D, certificates *Prof. Accred.:* Computer Science, Psychology Internship, School Psychology *CEO:* Pres. Patricia O'Donnell Ewers
Enroll: 7,644   (212) 346-1200

PLEASANTVILLE/BRIARCLIFF CAMPUS
861 Bedford Rd., Pleasantville 10570 *Prof. Accred.:* Nursing (A,B,M) *CEO:* Vice Pres. Richard S. Podgorski
(914) 773-3200

WHITE PLAINS CAMPUS
78 N. Broadway, White Plains 10603 *Prof. Accred.:* Law *CEO:* Vice Pres. Margaret R. Gotti
(914) 422-4213

PAUL SMITH'S COLLEGE
Paul Smiths 12970 *Type:* Private junior *Accred.:* 1977/1988 (MSA) *Calendar:* Sem. plan *Degrees:* A *CEO:* Pres. H. David Chamberlain
Enroll: 809   (518) 327-6211

PHILLIPS BETH ISRAEL SCHOOL OF NURSING
310 E. 22nd St., New York 10010 *Type:* Private *Calendar:* Sem. plan *Degrees:* A *Prof.*

Accred.: Nursing (A) *CEO:* Dean Julianne M. Hart
(212) 614-6104

PLAZA BUSINESS INSTITUTE
74-09 37th Ave., Jackson Heights 11372 *Type:* Private junior *Accred.:* 1974/1987 (ACISC) *Calendar:* Tri. plan *Degrees:* A, certificates, diplomas *CEO:* Pres. Charles E. Callahan
Enroll: 1,154   (718) 779-1430

POLYTECHNIC UNIVERSITY
6 MetroTech Ctr., Brooklyn 11201 *Type:* Private *Accred.:* 1927/1987 (MSA) *Calendar:* Sem. plan *Degrees:* B, M, D *Prof. Accred.:* Computer Science, Engineering (aerospace, chemical, civil, computer, electrical, industrial, mechanical, metallurgical) *CEO:* Pres. George Bugliarello
Enroll: 2,230   (718) 260-3600

LONG ISLAND CENTER
Rte. 110, Farmingdale 11735 *CEO:* Provost Ernest Racz
(516) 755-4400

WESTCHESTER GRADUATE CENTER
36 Saw Mill River Rd., Hawthorne 10532 *CEO:* Dir. Kathleen Voute MacDonald
(914) 347-6940

PRATT INSTITUTE
200 Willoughby Ave., Brooklyn 11205 *Type:* Private *Accred.:* 1950/1992 (MSA) *Calendar:* 4-1-4 plan *Degrees:* A, B, M, certificates *Prof. Accred.:* Art, Engineering (chemical, civil, electrical, mechanical), Interior Design, Librarianship, Planning (M) *CEO:* Pres. Thomas F. Schutte
Enroll: 3,218   (718) 636-3600

QUEENS COLLEGE
65-30 Kissena Blvd., Flushing 11367 *Type:* Public (local/state) *System:* City University of New York Office of the Chancellor *Accred.:* 1941/1991 (MSA) *Calendar:* Sem. plan *Degrees:* B, P, M *Prof. Accred.:* Audiology, Home Economics, Law (ABA only), Librarianship, Speech-Language Pathology *CEO:* Pres. Shirley Strum Kenny
Enroll: 16,268   (718) 997-5000

QUEENSBOROUGH COMMUNITY COLLEGE
222-05 56th Ave., Bayside 11364-1497
Type: Public (local/state) *System:* City University of New York Office of the Chancellor *Accred.:* 1963/1988 (MSA) *Calendar:* Sem. plan *Degrees:* A, certificates *Prof. Accred.:* Engineering Technology (computer, electrical, mechanical), Nursing (A) *CEO:* Pres. Kurt R. Schmeller
Enroll: 12,421   (718) 631-6262

RABBINICAL ACADEMY MESIVTA RABBI CHAIM BERLIN
1593 Coney Island Ave., Brooklyn 11230
Type: Private professional *Accred.:* 1975/1993 (AARTS) *Calendar:* Sem. plan *Degrees:* Talmudic (1st and 2nd) *CEO:* Pres. A.M. Schechter
Enroll: 416   (718) 377-0777

RABBINICAL COLLEGE BETH SHRAGA
28 Saddle River Rd., Monsey 10952 *Type:* Private professional *Accred.:* 1978/1991 (AARTS) *Calendar:* Sem. plan *Degrees:* Talmudic (1st and 2nd) *CEO:* Pres. S. Schiff
Enroll: 25   (914) 356-1980

RABBINICAL COLLEGE BOBOVER YESHIVA B'NEI ZION
1577 48th St., Brooklyn 11219 *Type:* Private professional *Accred.:* 1979/1991 (AARTS) *Calendar:* Sem. plan *Degrees:* Rabbinic (1st), Talmudic (1st and 2nd) *CEO:* Pres. N. Halberstam
Enroll: 350   (718) 438-2018

RABBINICAL COLLEGE CH'SAN SOFER
1876 50th St., Brooklyn 11204 *Type:* Private professional *Accred.:* 1979/1990 (AARTS) *Calendar:* Sem. plan *Degrees:* Talmudic (1st and 2nd) *CEO:* Pres. Jacob Hershkowitz
Enroll: 65   (718) 236-1171

RABBINICAL COLLEGE OF LONG ISLAND
201 Magnolia Blvd., Long Beach 11561 *Type:* Private professional *Accred.:* 1979/1990 (AARTS) *Calendar:* Sem. plan *Degrees:* Talmudic (1st) *CEO:* Pres. Y. Feigelstock
Enroll: 85   (516) 431-7304

RABBINICAL SEMINARY ADAS YEREIM
185 Wilson St., Brooklyn 11211 *Type:* Private professional *Accred.:* 1979/1990

(AARTS) *Calendar:* Sem. plan *Degrees:* Talmudic (1st) *CEO:* Pres. A. Schonberger
Enroll: 85   (718) 388-1751

RABBINICAL SEMINARY M'KOR CHAIM
1571 55th St., Brooklyn 11219 *Type:* Private professional *Accred.:* 1979/1990 (AARTS) *Calendar:* Sem. plan *Degrees:* Talmudic (1st and 2nd) *CEO:* Pres. Benjamin Lederer
Enroll: 74   (718) 851-0183

RABBINICAL SEMINARY OF AMERICA
92-15 69th Ave., Forest Hills 11375 *Type:* Private professional *Accred.:* 1975/1992 (AARTS) *Calendar:* Sem. plan *Degrees:* Talmudic (1st and 2nd) *CEO:* Pres. A.H. Leibowitz
Enroll: 203   (718) 268-4700

REGENTS COLLEGE OF THE UNIVERSITY OF THE STATE OF NEW YORK
7 Columbia Cir., Albany 12203-5159 *Type:* Private *Accred.:* 1977/1992 (MSA) *Calendar:* Sem. plan *Degrees:* A, B *Prof. Accred.:* Nursing (A,B) *CEO:* Pres. Thomas Sobol
Enroll: 12,668   (518) 464-8500

RENSSELAER POLYTECHNIC INSTITUTE
110 Eighth St., Troy 12180-3590 *Type:* Private *Accred.:* 1927/1991 (MSA) *Calendar:* Sem. plan *Degrees:* B, M, D *Prof. Accred.:* Business (B,M), Engineering (aerospace, bioengineering, chemical, civil, computer, electrical, environmental/sanitary, industrial, materials, mechanical, nuclear) *CEO:* Pres. R. Byron Pipes
Enroll: 6,663   (518) 276-6000

ROBERTS WESLEYAN COLLEGE
2301 Westside Dr., Rochester 14624-1997 *Type:* Private liberal arts *Accred.:* 1963/1990 (MSA) *Calendar:* Sem. plan *Degrees:* A, B, M *Prof. Accred.:* Art, Music, Nursing (B), Social Work (B) *CEO:* Pres. William C. Crothers
Enroll: 962   (716) 594-6000

ROCHESTER BUSINESS INSTITUTE
1850 Ridge Rd. E., Rochester 14622 *Type:* Private business *Accred.:* 1966/1990 (ACISC) *Calendar:* Qtr. plan *Degrees:* A *CEO:* Pres. Tom Conte
       (716) 266-0430

ROCHESTER INSTITUTE OF TECHNOLOGY
P.O. Box 9887, One Lomb Memorial Dr., Rochester 14623 *Type:* Private *Accred.:* 1958/1992 (MSA) *Calendar:* Qtr. plan *Degrees:* A, B, M, D, certificates *Prof. Accred.:* Art, Business (B,M), Computer Science, Diagnostic Medical Sonography, Dietetics (coordinated), Engineering Technology (architectural, civil/construction, computer, electrical, electromechanical, energy, manufacturing, mechanical, mechanical drafting/design), Engineering (computer, electrical, industrial, mechanical), Medical Record Technology, Nuclear Medicine Technology, Social Work (B) *CEO:* Pres. Albert J. Simone
Enroll: 12,078   (716) 475-2400

ROCKLAND COMMUNITY COLLEGE
145 College Rd., Suffern 10901 *Type:* Public (local/state) junior *System:* State University of New York Office of Community Colleges *Accred.:* 1968/1991 (MSA) *Calendar:* Sem. plan *Degrees:* A, certificates *Prof. Accred.:* Medical Laboratory Technology (AMA), Medical Record Technology, Nursing (A), Occupational Therapy Assisting, Respiratory Therapy *CEO:* Pres. Neal A. Raisman
Enroll: 8,271   (914) 574-4000

HAVERSTRAW LEARNING CENTER
36-39 Main St., Haverstraw 10927 *CEO:* Dir. Julia Kolovchevich
                               (914) 942-0624

NYACK LEARNING CENTER
92-94 Main St., Nyack 10960 *CEO:* Dir. Laurel Koras
                               (914) 358-9392

SPRING VALLEY LEARNING CENTER
185 N. Main St., Spring Valley 10977 *CEO:* Dir. Herman Stovall
                               (914) 352-5535

THE SAGE COLLEGES
45 Ferry St., Troy 12180 *Type:* Private *Accred.:* 1928/1990 (MSA) *Calendar:* 4-1-4 plan *Degrees:* A, B, M *Prof. Accred.:* Nursing (B,M), Physical Therapy *CEO:* Pres. Sara S. Chapman
Enroll: 4,212   (518) 270-2000

SAGE JUNIOR COLLEGE OF ALBANY
140 New Scotland Ave., Albany 12208 *Prof. Accred.:* Art, Nursing (A) *CEO:* Dean Sally A. Lawrence
                               (518) 445-1711

ST. BERNARD'S INSTITUTE
1100 S. Goodman St., Rochester 14620 *Type:* Private (Roman Catholic) graduate only *Accred.:* 1970/1993 (ATS) *Calendar:* Sem. plan *Degrees:* M *CEO:* Pres. Patricia A. Schoelles
FTE Enroll: 45   (716) 271-1320

ST. BONAVENTURE UNIVERSITY
Rte. 417, St. Bonaventure 14778 *Type:* Private *Accred.:* 1924/1989 (MSA) *Calendar:* Sem. plan *Degrees:* B, M *CEO:* Pres. Robert J. Wickenheiser
Enroll: 2,780   (716) 375-2000

ST. FRANCIS COLLEGE
180 Remsen St., Brooklyn 11201 *Type:* Private liberal arts *Accred.:* 1959/1991 (MSA) *Calendar:* Sem. plan *Degrees:* A, B *CEO:* Pres. Donald Sullivan, O.S.F.
Enroll: 1,911   (718) 522-2300

ST. JOHN FISHER COLLEGE
3690 East Ave., Rochester 14618 *Type:* Private *Accred.:* 1957/1991 (MSA) *Calendar:* Sem. plan *Degrees:* B, M *CEO:* Pres. William L. Pickett
Enroll: 2,348   (716) 385-8000

ST. JOHN'S UNIVERSITY
Grand Central and Utopia Pkwys., Jamaica 11439 *Type:* Private (Roman Catholic) *Accred.:* 1921/1991 (MSA) *Calendar:* Sem. plan *Degrees:* A, B, P, M, D, certificates *Prof. Accred.:* Audiology, Business (B,M), Clinical Psychology, Law, Librarianship, Speech-Language Pathology *CEO:* Pres. Donald J. Harrington, C.M.
Enroll: 19,037   (718) 990-6161

BRANCH CAMPUS
300 Howard Ave., Staten Island 10301 *CEO:* Sr. Vice Pres. James F. Kiernan, C.M.
                               (718) 390-4545

ST. JOSEPH'S COLLEGE
245 Clinton Ave., Brooklyn 11205-3688 *Type:* Private liberal arts *Accred.:* 1928/1992

(MSA) *Calendar:* Sem. plan *Degrees:* B, certificates *Prof. Accred.:* Nursing (B) *CEO:* Pres. George Aquin O'Connor, C.S.J.
Enroll: 866   (718) 636-6800

SUFFOLK CAMPUS
   155 Roe Blvd., Patchogue 11772 *CEO:* Pres. George Aquin O'Connor, C.S.J.
                    (516) 447-3200

ST. JOSEPH'S SEMINARY
   201 Seminary Ave., Yonkers 10704 *Type:* Private (Roman Catholic) graduate only *Accred.:* 1973/1993 (ATS); 1961/1988 (MSA) *Calendar:* Sem. plan *Degrees:* P, M *CEO:* Rector/Pres. Raymond T. Powers
Enroll: 76   (914) 968-6200

ST. LAWRENCE UNIVERSITY
   Canton 13617 *Type:* Private liberal arts *Accred.:* 1921/1988 (MSA) *Calendar:* Sem. plan *Degrees:* B, M *CEO:* Pres. Patti McGill Peterson
Enroll: 2,121   (315) 379-5011

ST. THOMAS AQUINAS COLLEGE
   Rte. 340, Sparkill 10976 *Type:* Private *Accred.:* 1972/1992 (MSA) *Calendar:* Sem. plan *Degrees:* A, B, M *CEO:* Pres. Donald T. McNelis
Enroll: 2,208   (914) 359-9500

ST. VLADIMIR'S ORTHODOX THEOLOGICAL SEMINARY
   575 Scarsdale Rd., Crestwood 10707 *Type:* Private (Orthodox Church in America) graduate only *Accred.:* 1973/1988 (ATS) *Calendar:* Sem. plan *Degrees:* M, D *CEO:* Pres. Metropolitan Theodosius
FTE Enroll: 68   (914) 961-8313

SARAH LAWRENCE COLLEGE
   One Meadway, Bronxville 10708 *Type:* Private liberal arts *Accred.:* 1937/1992 (MSA) *Calendar:* Sem. plan *Degrees:* B, M *CEO:* Pres. Alice Stone Ilchman
Enroll: 1,186   (914) 337-0700

SCHENECTADY COUNTY COMMUNITY COLLEGE
   78 Washington Ave., Schenectady 12305 *Type:* Public (local/state) junior *System:* State University of New York Office of Community Colleges *Accred.:* 1974/1989 (MSA) *Calendar:* Sem. plan *Degrees:* A,

certificates *Prof. Accred.:* Music *CEO:* Pres. Gabriel J. Basil
Enroll: 3,403   (518) 346-6211

SCHOOL OF VISUAL ARTS
   209 E. 23rd St., New York 10010 *Type:* Private professional *Accred.:* 1978/1992 (MSA) *Calendar:* Sem. plan *Degrees:* B, M *Prof. Accred.:* Art *CEO:* Pres. David J. Rhodes
Enroll: 4,861   (212) 679-7350

SEMINARY OF THE IMMACULATE CONCEPTION
   440 W. Neck Rd., Huntington 11743 *Type:* Private (Roman Catholic) graduate only *Accred.:* 1976/1991 (ATS); 1976/1992 (MSA) *Calendar:* Sem. plan *Degrees:* P, M, D, certificates *CEO:* Rector/Pres. John J. Strynkowski
Enroll: 187   (516) 423-0483

SH'OR YOSHUV RABBINICAL COLLEGE
   1526 Central Ave., Far Rockaway 11691 *Type:* Private professional *Accred.:* 1979/1992 (AARTS) *Calendar:* Sem. plan *Degrees:* Talmudic (1st and 2nd) *CEO:* Pres. Maurice Friedman
Enroll: 90   (718) 327-2048

SIENA COLLEGE
   515 Loudon Rd., Loudonville 12211-1462 *Type:* Private *Accred.:* 1943/1989 (MSA) *Calendar:* Sem. plan *Degrees:* B *Prof. Accred.:* Social Work (B) *CEO:* Pres. William E. McConville, O.F.M.
Enroll: 3,394   (518) 783-2300

SIMMONS INSTITUTE OF FUNERAL SERVICE
   1828 South Ave., Syracuse 13207 *Type:* Private professional *Calendar:* 16-mo. program *Degrees:* A *Prof. Accred.:* Funeral Service Education *CEO:* Pres. Thomas R. Taggart
                    (315) 475-5142

SKIDMORE COLLEGE
   814 N. Broadway, Saratoga Springs 12866-1632 *Type:* Private liberal arts *Accred.:* 1925/1989 (MSA) *Calendar:* Sem. plan *Degrees:* B *Prof. Accred.:* Art, Social Work (B) *CEO:* Pres. David H. Porter
Enroll: 2,645   (518) 584-5000

STATE UNIVERSITY COLLEGE AT BROCKPORT
   Brockport 14420 *Type:* Public (state) *System:* State University of New York System Office *Accred.:* 1952/1992 (MSA) *Calen-*

dar: Sem. plan *Degrees:* B, M, certificates *Prof. Accred.:* Counseling, Dance, Nursing (B), Public Administration, Recreation and Leisure Services, Social Work (B) *CEO:* Pres. John E. Van de Wetering
Enroll: 9,543   (716) 395-2211

STATE UNIVERSITY COLLEGE AT BUFFALO
1300 Elmwood Ave., Buffalo 14222 *Type:* Public (state) *System:* State University of New York System Office *Accred.:* 1948/1992 (MSA) *Calendar:* Sem. plan *Degrees:* B, M, certificates *Prof. Accred.:* Dietetics (coordinated), Engineering Technology (electrical, mechanical), Medical Technology, Nuclear Medicine Technology, Occupational Therapy, Social Work (B), Speech-Language Pathology, Teacher Education (e,s) *CEO:* Pres. F.C. Richardson
Enroll: 12,471   (716) 878-4000

STATE UNIVERSITY COLLEGE AT CORTLAND
P.O. Box 2000, Cortland 13045 *Type:* Public (state) *System:* State University of New York System Office *Accred.:* 1948/1992 (MSA) *Calendar:* Sem. plan *Degrees:* B, M, certificates *Prof. Accred.:* Recreation and Leisure Services *CEO:* Pres. James M. Clark
Enroll: 7,216   (607) 753-2201

STATE UNIVERSITY COLLEGE AT FREDONIA
Fredonia 14063 *Type:* Public (state) *System:* State University of New York System Office *Accred.:* 1952/1990 (MSA) *Calendar:* Sem. plan *Degrees:* B, M, certificates *Prof. Accred.:* Audiology, Music, Speech-Language Pathology, Theatre (associate) *CEO:* Pres. Donald A. MacPhee
Enroll: 4,957   (716) 673-3111

STATE UNIVERSITY COLLEGE AT GENESEO
Geneseo 14454 *Type:* Public (state) *System:* State University of New York System Office *Accred.:* 1952/1992 (MSA) *Calendar:* Sem. plan *Degrees:* B, M *Prof. Accred.:* Audiology, Speech-Language Pathology *CEO:* Pres. Carol C. Harter
Enroll: 5,630   (716) 245-5211

STATE UNIVERSITY COLLEGE AT NEW PALTZ
New Paltz 12561 *Type:* Public (state) *System:* State University of New York System Office *Accred.:* 1950/1991 (MSA) *Calendar:* Sem. plan *Degrees:* B, M, certificates

Prof. Accred.: Audiology, Computer Science, Engineering (electrical), Music, Nursing (B), Speech-Language Pathology *CEO:* Pres. Alice Chandler
Enroll: 8,475   (914) 257-2121

STATE UNIVERSITY COLLEGE AT OLD WESTBURY
P.O. Box 210, Old Westbury 11568 *Type:* Public (state) *System:* State University of New York System Office *Accred.:* 1976/1991 (MSA) *Calendar:* Sem. plan *Degrees:* B, certificates *CEO:* Pres. L. Eudora Pettigrew
Enroll: 4,194   (516) 876-3000

STATE UNIVERSITY COLLEGE AT ONEONTA
Oneonta 13820-4015 *Type:* Public (state) *System:* State University of New York System Office *Accred.:* 1949/1988 (MSA) *Calendar:* Sem. plan *Degrees:* B, M, certificates *Prof. Accred.:* Home Economics *CEO:* Pres. Alan B. Donovan
Enroll: 6,018   (607) 436-3500

STATE UNIVERSITY COLLEGE AT OSWEGO
Oswego 13126 *Type:* Public (state) *System:* State University of New York System Office *Accred.:* 1950/1992 (MSA) *Calendar:* Sem. plan *Degrees:* B, M, certificates *Prof. Accred.:* Music *CEO:* Pres. Stephen L. Weber
Enroll: 8,310   (315) 341-2500

STATE UNIVERSITY COLLEGE AT PLATTSBURGH
Plattsburgh 12901 *Type:* Public (state) *System:* State University of New York System Office *Accred.:* 1952/1992 (MSA) *Calendar:* Sem. plan *Degrees:* B, M, certificates *Prof. Accred.:* Audiology, Counseling, Nursing (B), Speech-Language Pathology *CEO:* Interim Pres. Walter Vom Saal
Enroll: 6,344   (518) 564-2000

STATE UNIVERSITY COLLEGE AT POTSDAM
Pierrepont Ave., Potsdam 13676 *Type:* Public (state) *System:* State University of New York System Office *Accred.:* 1952/1992 (MSA) *Calendar:* Sem. plan *Degrees:* B, M *Prof. Accred.:* Music *CEO:* Pres. William C. Merwin
Enroll: 4,419   (315) 267-2000

STATE UNIVERSITY COLLEGE AT PURCHASE
735 Anderson Hill Rd., Purchase 10577-1400 *Type:* Public (state) *System:* State University of New York System Office *Accred.:*

1976/1988 (MSA) *Calendar:* Sem. plan *Degrees:* B, M, certificates *CEO:* Pres. Bill Lacy
Enroll: 4,262   (914) 251-6000

STATE UNIVERSITY OF NEW YORK AT ALBANY
1400 Washington Ave., Albany 12222 *Type:* Public (state) *System:* State University of New York System Office *Accred.:* 1938/1990 (MSA) *Calendar:* Sem. plan *Degrees:* B, M, D, certificates *Prof. Accred.:* Business (B,M), Clinical Psychology, Computer Science, Counseling Psychology, Librarianship, Public Administration, Public Health, Rehabilitation Counseling, School Psychology, Social Work (B,M) *CEO:* Pres. H. Patrick Swygert
Enroll: 16,976   (518) 442-3300

STATE UNIVERSITY OF NEW YORK AT BINGHAMTON
P.O. Box 6000, Binghamton 13902-6000 *Type:* Public (state) *System:* State University of New York System Office *Accred.:* 1952/1991 (MSA) *Calendar:* Sem. plan *Degrees:* B, M, D, certificates *Prof. Accred.:* Business (B,M), Clinical Psychology, Computer Science, Engineering Technology (electrical, electromechanical, mechanical), Engineering (electrical, mechanical), Nursing (B,M) *CEO:* Pres. Lois B. DeFleur
Enroll: 11,883   (607) 777-2000

STATE UNIVERSITY OF NEW YORK AT BUFFALO
Buffalo 14260 *Type:* Public (state) *System:* State University of New York System Office *Accred.:* 1921/1989 (MSA) *Calendar:* Sem. plan *Degrees:* B, P, M, D, certificates *Prof. Accred.:* Accounting (Type A,B), Art, Audiology, Business (B,M), Clinical Psychology, Combined Prosthodontics, Counseling Psychology, Dental Assisting, Dentistry, Endodontics, Engineering (aerospace, chemical, civil, electrical, industrial, mechanical), General Dentistry, General Practice Residency, Law, Librarianship, Medicine, Music, Nurse Anesthesia Education, Nursing (B,M), Oral and Maxillofacial Surgery, Orthodontics, Periodontics, Physical Therapy, Planning (M), Psychology Internship, Rehabilitation Counseling, Social Work (M), Speech-Language Pathology *CEO:* Pres. William R. Greiner
Enroll: 26,015   (716) 645-2000

STATE UNIVERSITY OF NEW YORK AT STONY BROOK
Nicolls Rd., Stony Brook 11794-0701 *Type:* Public (state) *System:* State University of New York System Office *Accred.:* 1957/1989 (MSA) *Calendar:* Sem. plan *Degrees:* B, P, M, D, certificates *Prof. Accred.:* Cardiovascular Technology, Clinical Psychology, Dentistry, Engineering (computer, electrical, engineering physics/science, mechanical), General Dentistry, General Practice Residency, Medical Technology, Medicine, Nursing (B,M), Orthodontics, Periodontics, Physical Therapy, Physician Assisting, Psychology Internship, Respiratory Therapy, Social Work (B,M) *CEO:* Pres. John H. Marburger, III
Enroll: 17,697   (516) 632-6000

STATE UNIVERSITY OF NEW YORK COLLEGE OF AGRICULTURE AND TECHNOLOGY AT COBLESKILL
Cobleskill 12043 *Type:* Public (state) *System:* State University of New York System Office *Accred.:* 1952/1991 (MSA) *Calendar:* Sem. plan *Degrees:* A, B *Prof. Accred.:* Histologic Technology *CEO:* Pres. Kenneth E. Wing
Enroll: 2,574   (518) 234-5011

STATE UNIVERSITY OF NEW YORK COLLEGE OF AGRICULTURE AND TECHNOLOGY AT MORRISVILLE
Morrisville 13408 *Type:* Public (state) *System:* State University of New York System Office *Accred.:* 1952/1992 (MSA) *Calendar:* Sem. plan *Degrees:* A, certificates *Prof. Accred.:* Engineering Technology (electrical, mechanical), Nursing (A) *CEO:* Pres. Frederick Woodward
Enroll: 3,024   (315) 684-6000

STATE UNIVERSITY OF NEW YORK COLLEGE OF ENVIRONMENTAL SCIENCE AND FORESTRY AT SYRACUSE
Syracuse 13210 *Type:* Public (state) *System:* State University of New York System Office *Accred.:* 1952/1992 (MSA) *Calendar:* Sem. plan *Degrees:* A, B, M, D *Prof. Accred.:* Engineering (forest), Forestry, Landscape Architecture (B,M) *CEO:* Pres. Ross S. Whaley
Enroll: 1,709   (315) 470-6500

STATE UNIVERSITY OF NEW YORK COLLEGE OF OPTOMETRY AT NEW YORK CITY
100 E. 24th St., New York 10010 *Type:* Public (state) *System:* State University of New York System Office *Accred.:* 1976/1992 (MSA) *Calendar:* Qtr. plan *Degrees:* P, M, D *Prof. Accred.:* Optometry *CEO:* Pres. Alden N. Haffner
Enroll: 279 (212) 420-4900

STATE UNIVERSITY OF NEW YORK COLLEGE OF TECHNOLOGY AT ALFRED
Huntington Bldg., Alfred 14802 *Type:* Public (state) *System:* State University of New York System Office *Accred.:* 1952/1991 (MSA) *Calendar:* Sem. plan *Degrees:* A, B, certificates *Prof. Accred.:* Engineering Technology (air conditioning, architectural, civil/construction, electrical, electromechanical, general drafting/design, mechanical, surveying), Medical Laboratory Technology (AMA), Medical Record Technology, Nursing (A) *CEO:* Pres. William D. Rezak
Enroll: 2,615 (607) 587-4111

BRANCH CAMPUS
Wellsville 14895 *CEO:* Dir. Albert Vanderline
(607) 587-3105

STATE UNIVERSITY OF NEW YORK COLLEGE OF TECHNOLOGY AT CANTON
Cornell Dr., Canton 13617 *Type:* Public (state) *System:* State University of New York System Office *Accred.:* 1952/1992 (MSA) *Calendar:* Sem. plan *Degrees:* A, certificates *Prof. Accred.:* Engineering Technology (air conditioning, civil/construction, electrical, mechanical), Medical Laboratory Technology (AMA), Mortuary Science, Nursing (A), Veterinary Technology *CEO:* Pres. Joseph L. Kennedy
Enroll: 2,298 (315) 386-7011

STATE UNIVERSITY OF NEW YORK COLLEGE OF TECHNOLOGY AT DELHI
Delhi 13753 *Type:* Public (state) *System:* State University of New York System Office *Accred.:* 1952/1992 (MSA) *Calendar:* Sem. plan *Degrees:* A, certificates *Prof. Accred.:* Veterinary Technology *CEO:* Pres. Mary Ellen Duncan
Enroll: 2,330 (607) 746-4111

STATE UNIVERSITY OF NEW YORK COLLEGE OF TECHNOLOGY AT FARMINGDALE
Melville Rd., Farmingdale 11735 *Type:* Public (state) *System:* State University of New York System Office *Accred.:* 1952/1991 (MSA) *Calendar:* Sem. plan *Degrees:* A, B *Prof. Accred.:* Dental Hygiene, Engineering Technology (air conditioning, automotive, bioengineering, civil/construction, electrical, manufacturing, mechanical), Medical Laboratory Technology (AMA), Nursing (A), Veterinary Technology *CEO:* Pres. Frank A. Cipriani
Enroll: 9,684 (516) 420-2000

STATE UNIVERSITY OF NEW YORK EMPIRE STATE COLLEGE
One Union Ave., Saratoga Springs 12866 *Type:* Public (state) *System:* State University of New York System Office *Accred.:* 1974/1990 (MSA) *Calendar:* Sem. plan *Degrees:* A, B, M *CEO:* Pres. James W. Hall
Enroll: 6,322 (518) 587-2100

COLLEGEWIDE PROGRAMS
28 Union Ave., Saratoga Springs 12866-4309 *CEO:* Dean Douglas B. Johnstone
(518) 587-2100

GENESSEE VALLEY REGIONAL CENTER
8 Prince St., Rochester 14607 *CEO:* Dean James H. Matthews
(716) 244-3641

HUDSON VALLEY REGIONAL CENTER
200 N. Central Ave., Hartsdale 10530 *CEO:* Dean James Case
(914) 948-6206

LONG ISLAND REGIONAL CENTER
Trainor House, P.O. Box 130, Old Westbury 11568 *CEO:* Dean Patricia Lefor
(516) 997-4700

METROPOLITAN REGIONAL CENTER
666 Broadway, New York 10012 *CEO:* Dean Nancy Bunch
(212) 598-0640

NIAGARA FRONTIER REGIONAL CENTER
564 Franklin St., Buffalo 14202 *CEO:* Dean Thomas M. Rocco
(716) 886-8020

NORTHEAST CENTER
845 Central Ave., Albany 12206 *CEO:*
Dean Dennis R. Delong
(518) 485-5964

STATE UNIVERSITY OF NEW YORK HEALTH
SCIENCE CENTER AT BROOKLYN
450 Clarkson Ave., Brooklyn 11203 *Type:*
Public (state) *System:* State University of
New York System Office *Accred.:* 1952/
1991 (MSA) *Calendar:* Sem. plan *Degrees:*
B, P, M, D, certificates *Prof. Accred.:* Diag-
nostic Medical Sonography, Medical Record
Administration, Medicine, Nuclear Medicine
Technology, Nursing (B,M), Occupational
Therapy, Perfusion, Physical Therapy,
Physician Assisting, Radiography *CEO:* In-
terim Pres. Richard H. Schwarz
Enroll: 1,591   (718) 270-1000

STATE UNIVERSITY OF NEW YORK HEALTH
SCIENCE CENTER AT SYRACUSE
750 E. Adams St., Syracuse 13210 *Type:*
Public (state) *System:* State University of
New York System Office *Accred.:* 1952/
1989 (MSA) *Calendar:* Sem. plan *Degrees:*
A, B, P, M, D *Prof. Accred.:* Blood Bank
Technology, Cytotechnology, General Prac-
tice Residency, Medical Technology, Medi-
cine, Nursing (B,M), Perfusion, Physical
Therapy, Psychology Internship, Radiation
Therapy Technology, Radiography, Respira-
tory Therapy *CEO:* Pres. Gregory L. Eastwood
Enroll: 1,074   (315) 464-5540

STATE UNIVERSITY OF NEW YORK INSTITUTE OF
TECHNOLOGY AT UTICA/ROME
P.O. Box 3050, Utica 13504-3050 *Type:*
Public (state) *System:* State University of
New York System Office *Accred.:* 1979/
1990 (MSA) *Calendar:* Sem. plan *Degrees:*
B, M *Prof. Accred.:* Engineering Technolo-
gy (computer, electrical, industrial, mechani-
cal), Medical Record Administration, Nurs-
ing (B,M) *CEO:* Pres. Peter J. Cayan
Enroll: 2,614   (315) 792-7100

STATE UNIVERSITY OF NEW YORK MARITIME
COLLEGE
Fort Schuyler, Throggs Neck 10465 *Type:*
Public (state) *System:* State University of
New York System Office *Accred.:* 1952/
1991 (MSA) *Calendar:* Sem. plan *Degrees:*
B, M *Prof. Accred.:* Engineering (electrical,

naval architecture/marine) *CEO:* Pres. Floyd
H. Miller, U.S.N. (Ret.)
Enroll: 850   (212) 409-7200

STENOTYPE ACADEMY
291 Broadway, New York 10007 *Type:* Private business *Accred.:* 1978/1990 (ACISC)
Calendar: Courses of varying lengths *Degrees:* A *CEO:* Pres. Ivan Londa
(212) 962-0002

SUFFOLK COUNTY COMMUNITY COLLEGE
AMMERMAN CAMPUS
533 College Rd., Selden 11784 *Type:* Public
(local/state) junior *System:* Suffolk County
Community College Central Administration
Accred.: 1966/1992 (MSA) *Calendar:* Sem.
plan *Degrees:* A *Prof. Accred.:* Nursing (A),
Physical Therapy Assisting *CEO:* Exec.
Dean William C. Hudson
Enroll: 12,370   (516) 451-4110

SUFFOLK COUNTY COMMUNITY COLLEGE
EASTERN CAMPUS
Speonk-Riverhead Rd., Riverhead 11901
Type: Public (local/state) junior *System:* Suf-
folk County Community College Central
Administration *Accred.:* 1982/1992 (MSA)
Calendar: Sem. plan *Degrees:* A *CEO:*
Exec. Dean Steven T. Kenny
Enroll: 2,389   (516) 548-2500

SUFFOLK COUNTY COMMUNITY COLLEGE
WESTERN CAMPUS
Crooked Hill Rd., Brentwood 11717 *Type:*
Public (local/state) junior *System:* Suffolk
County Community College Central Admin-
istration *Accred.:* 1981/1992 (MSA) *Calen-
dar:* Sem. plan *Degrees:* A *Prof. Accred.:*
Nursing (A) *CEO:* Provost Salvatore La
Lima
Enroll: 5,625   (516) 434-6750

SULLIVAN COUNTY COMMUNITY COLLEGE
College Rd., Loch Sheldrake 12759 *Type:*
Public (local/state) junior *System:* State Uni-
versity of New York Office of Community
Colleges *Accred.:* 1968/1992 (MSA) *Calen-
dar:* 4-1-4 plan *Degrees:* A, certificates *Prof.
Accred.:* Nursing (A) *CEO:* Pres. Jeffrey B.
Willens
Enroll: 2,146   (914) 434-5750

SYRACUSE UNIVERSITY
Syracuse 13244 *Type:* Private *Accred.:* 1921/1988 (MSA) *Calendar:* Sem. plan *Degrees:* A, B, P, M, D, certificates *Prof. Accred.:* Art, Audiology, Business (B,M), Clinical Psychology, Dietetics (coordinated), Engineering (aerospace, bioengineering, chemical, civil, computer, electrical, mechanical), Interior Design, Journalism (B,M), Law, Librarianship, Marriage and Family Therapy (M,D-candidate), Music, Nursing (B,M), Public Administration, Rehabilitation Counseling, School Psychology, Social Work (B,M), Speech-Language Pathology *CEO:* Pres./Chanc. Kenneth A. Shaw
Enroll: 20,906   (315) 443-1870

TALMUDICAL SEMINARY OHOLEI TORAH
667 Eastern Pkwy., Brooklyn 11213 *Type:* Private professional *Accred.:* 1979/1990 (AARTS) *Calendar:* Sem. plan *Degrees:* Talmudic (1st) *CEO:* Pres. Teitelbaum
Enroll: 190   (718) 778-3340

TAYLOR BUSINESS INSTITUTE
One Penn Plaza, Concourse Level, New York 10019-0118 *Type:* Private junior *Accred.:* 1962/1987 (ACISC) *Calendar:* Sem. plan *Degrees:* A *CEO:* Dir. David Schuchman
          (212) 279-0510

TEACHERS COLLEGE OF COLUMBIA UNIVERSITY
525 W. 120th St., New York 10027 *Type:* Private professional; graduate only *Accred.:* 1921/1991 (MSA) *Calendar:* Sem. plan *Degrees:* M, D *Prof. Accred.:* Clinical Psychology, Counseling Psychology, Nursing (M), School Psychology, Speech-Language Pathology *CEO:* Pres. Michael Timpane
Enroll: 3,389   (212) 678-3000

TECHNICAL CAREER INSTITUTE
320 W. 31st St., New York 10001 *Type:* Private *Calendar:* Sem. plan *Degrees:* A *Prof. Accred.:* Engineering Technology (electrical) *CEO:* Pres. Harry D. Moss
          (212) 594-4000

TOMPKINS CORTLAND COMMUNITY COLLEGE
P.O. Box 139, 170 North St., Dryden 13053 *Type:* Public (local/state) junior *System:* State University of New York Office of Community Colleges *Accred.:* 1973/1988 (MSA) *Calendar:* Sem. plan *Degrees:* A,

certificates *Prof. Accred.:* Nursing (A) *CEO:* Pres. Eduardo J. Marti
Enroll: 2,904   (607) 844-8211

TORAH TEMIMAH TALMUDICAL SEMINARY
555 Ocean Pkwy., Brooklyn 11218 *Type:* Private professional *Accred.:* 1981/1991 (AARTS) *Calendar:* Sem. plan *Degrees:* Talmudic (1st and 2nd) *CEO:* Pres./Dean L. Margulies
Enroll: 240   (718) 853-8500

TOURO COLLEGE
Empire State Bldg., Ste. 5122, 350 Fifth Ave., New York 10118 *Type:* Private *Accred.:* 1976/1992 (MSA) *Calendar:* Sem. plan *Degrees:* A, B, P, M, certificates *Prof. Accred.:* Medical Record Administration, Occupational Therapy, Physical Therapy, Physician Assisting *CEO:* Pres. Bernard Lander
Enroll: 5,611   (212) 643-0700

HUNTINGTON BRANCH CAMPUS
300 Nassau Rd., Huntington 11743 *Prof. Accred.:* Law (ABA only) *CEO:* Dean Howard Glickstein
Enroll: 896   (516) 421-2244

TAINO TOWERS CAMPUS
844 Ave. of the Americas, New York 10001 *CEO:* Vice Pres. Stephen H. Adolphus
          (212) 447-0700

TROCAIRE COLLEGE
110 Red Jacket Pkwy., Buffalo 14220 *Type:* Private junior *Accred.:* 1974/1989 (MSA) *Calendar:* Sem. plan *Degrees:* A, certificates *Prof. Accred.:* Medical Laboratory Technology (AMA), Nursing (A), Radiography, Surgical Technology *CEO:* Pres. Barbara Ciarico, R.S.M.
Enroll: 1,148   (716) 826-1200

ULSTER COUNTY COMMUNITY COLLEGE
Stone Ridge 12484 *Type:* Public (local/state) junior *System:* State University of New York Office of Community Colleges *Accred.:* 1971/1991 (MSA) *Calendar:* Sem. plan *Degrees:* A, certificates *CEO:* Pres. Robert T. Brown
Enroll: 2,888   (914) 687-5000

UNION COLLEGE
Schenectady 12308 *Type:* Private liberal arts
Accred.: 1921/1991 (MSA) *Calendar:* Sem.
plan *Degrees:* B, M, D *Prof. Accred.:* Engi-
neering (civil, electrical, mechanical), Health
Services Administration *CEO:* Pres. Roger
H. Hull
Enroll: 2,744   (518) 370-6000

POUGHKEEPSIE BRANCH CAMPUS
249 Hooker Ave., Poughkeepsie 12603
CEO: Dir. Armen Fisher
                                   (914) 454-4490

UNION THEOLOGICAL SEMINARY
3041 Broadway, New York 10027-0003
Type: Private (interdenominational) graduate
only *Accred.:* 1938/1988 (ATS); 1967/1989
(MSA) *Calendar:* Sem. plan *Degrees:* P, M,
D *CEO:* Pres. Holland L. Hendrix
Enroll: 308   (212) 662-7100

UNITED STATES MERCHANT MARINE ACADEMY
Steamboat Rd., Kings Point 11024 *Type:*
Public (federal) technological *Accred.:* 1949/
1990 (MSA) *Calendar:* Qtr. plan *Degrees:* B
Prof. Accred.: Engineering (naval architecture/
marine) *CEO:* Supt. Thomas T. Matteson
Enroll: 936   (516) 773-5000

UNITED STATES MILITARY ACADEMY
West Point 10996-5000 *Type:* Public (feder-
al) professional *Accred.:* 1949/1989 (MSA)
Calendar: Sem. plan *Degrees:* B *Prof. Ac-
cred.:* Engineering (civil, electrical, engi-
neering management, mechanical) *CEO:*
Supt. Howard D. Graves
Enroll: 4,421   (914) 938-4011

UNITED TALMUDICAL ACADEMY
82 Lee Ave., Brooklyn 11211 *Type:* Private
professional *Accred.:* 1979/1987 (AARTS)
Calendar: Sem. plan *Degrees:* Rabbinic (1st
and 2nd) *CEO:* Pres. L. Lefkowitz
Enroll: 1,358   (718) 963-9260

UNIVERSITY OF ROCHESTER
River Sta., Rochester 14627 *Type:* Private
Accred.: 1921/1992 (MSA) *Calendar:* Sem.
plan *Degrees:* B, P, M, D, certificates *Prof.
Accred.:* Business (M), Clinical Psychology,
Community Health/Preventive Medicine,
Engineering (chemical, electrical, mechani-
cal), General Practice Residency, Marriage
and Family Therapy (post-D), Medicine,

Music, Nursing (B,M), Oral and Maxillofacial Surgery (conditional), Psychology Internship, Radiation Therapy Technology *CEO:*
Pres. G. Dennis O'Brien
Enroll: 9,291   (716) 275-2121

UTICA COLLEGE OF SYRACUSE UNIVERSITY
1600 Burrstone Rd., Utica 13502-4892 *Type:*
Private liberal arts *Accred.:* 1946/1988
(MSA) *Calendar:* Sem. plan *Degrees:* B
Prof. Accred.: Medical Technology, Nursing
(B), Occupational Therapy *CEO:* Pres.
Michael K. Simpson
Enroll: 2,620   (315) 792-3111

UTICA SCHOOL OF COMMERCE
201 Bleecker St., Utica 13501 *Type:* Private
business *Accred.:* 1969/1987 (ACISC) *Calendar:* Sem. plan *Degrees:* A *CEO:* Pres.
Philip M. Williams
                                   (315) 733-2307

BRANCH CAMPUS
P.O. Box 462, Rte. 5, Canastota 13032 *Ac-
cred.:* 1993 (ACISC) *CEO:* Dir. Darlene
Ballard
                                   (315) 697-8200

BRANCH CAMPUS
17-19 Elm St., Oneonta 13820 *Accred.:*
1993 (ACISC) *CEO:* Dir. John Frisch
                                   (607) 432-7003

VASSAR COLLEGE
Raymond Ave., Box 1, Poughkeepsie 12601
Type: Private liberal arts *Accred.:* 1921/1989
(MSA) *Calendar:* Sem. plan *Degrees:* B, M
CEO: Pres. Frances D. Fergusson
Enroll: 2,345   (914) 437-7000

VILLA MARIA COLLEGE OF BUFFALO
240 Pine Ridge Rd., Buffalo 14225-3999
Type: Private junior *Accred.:* 1972/1988
(MSA) *Calendar:* Sem. plan *Degrees:* A,
certificates *Prof. Accred.:* Interior Design
CEO: Pres. Marcella Marie Garus, C.S.S.F.
Enroll: 448   (716) 896-0700

WADHAMS HALL SEMINARY/COLLEGE
R.D. 4, Box 80, Ogdensburg 13669 *Type:*
Private (Roman Catholic) *Accred.:* 1972/
1992 (MSA) *Calendar:* Sem. plan *Degrees:*
B *CEO:* Pres. Richard W. Siepka
Enroll: 64   (315) 393-4231

WAGNER COLLEGE
Howard Ave. and Campus Rd., Staten Island 10301 *Type:* Private liberal arts *Accred.:* 1931/1991 (MSA) *Calendar:* Sem. plan *Degrees:* B, M *Prof. Accred.:* Nursing (B-warning,M) *CEO:* Pres. Norman R. Smith
Enroll: 1,521   (718) 390-3100

WEBB INSTITUTE OF NAVAL ARCHITECTURE
Crescent Beach Rd., Glen Cove 11542 *Type:* Private technological *Accred.:* 1930/1990 (MSA) *Calendar:* Sem. plan *Degrees:* B *Prof. Accred.:* Engineering (naval architecture/marine) *CEO:* Pres. James J. Conti
Enroll: 82   (516) 671-2213

WELLS COLLEGE
Aurora 13026-0500 *Type:* Private liberal arts for women *Accred.:* 1921/1992 (MSA) *Calendar:* 4-1-4 plan *Degrees:* B *CEO:* Pres. Robert A. Plane
Enroll: 350   (315) 364-3265

WESTCHESTER BUSINESS INSTITUTE
P.O. Box 710, 325 Central Ave., White Plains 10602 *Type:* Private business *Accred.:* 1966/1990 (ACISC) *Calendar:* Qtr. plan *Degrees:* A, certificates, diplomas *CEO:* Exec. Vice Pres. Kenneth A. Gabbert
                                   (914) 948-4442

WESTCHESTER COMMUNITY COLLEGE
75 Grasslands Rd., Valhalla 10595 *Type:* Public (local/state) junior *System:* State University of New York Office of Community Colleges *Accred.:* 1970/1990 (MSA) *Calendar:* Sem. plan *Degrees:* A *Prof. Accred.:* Radiography, Respiratory Therapy *CEO:* Pres. Joseph N. Hankin
Enroll: 11,131   (914) 285-6600

WOOD SCHOOL
8 E. 40th St., New York 10016 *Type:* Private business *Accred.:* 1967/1987 (ACISC) *Calendar:* Sem. plan *Degrees:* A *CEO:* Dir. Rosemary Duggan
                                   (212) 686-9040

YESHIVA DERECH CHAIM
1573 39th St., Brooklyn 11218 *Type:* Private professional *Accred.:* 1984/1993 (AARTS) *Calendar:* Sem. plan *Degrees:* Talmudic (1st and 2nd) *CEO:* Pres. Mordechai Rennert
Enroll: 165   (718) 438-5476

YESHIVA KARLIN STOLIN BETH AARON V'ISRAEL RABBINICAL INSTITUTE
1818 54th St., Brooklyn 11204 *Type:* Private professional *Accred.:* 1975/1990 (AARTS) *Calendar:* Sem. plan *Degrees:* Talmudic (1st and 2nd) *CEO:* Pres. Israel Pilchick
Enroll: 49   (718) 232-7800

YESHIVA MIKDASH MELECH
1326 Ocean Pkwy., Brooklyn 11230-5655 *Type:* Private professional *Accred.:* 1979/1993 (AARTS) *Calendar:* Sem. plan *Degrees:* Rabbinic (1st and 2nd) *CEO:* Dean Haim Benoliel
Enroll: 34   (718) 339-1090

YESHIVA OF NITRA—RABBINICAL COLLEGE YESHIVA FARM SETTLEMENT
Pines Bridge Rd., Mount Kisco 10549 *Type:* Private professional *Accred.:* 1980/1991 (AARTS) *Calendar:* Sem. plan *Degrees:* Rabbinic (1st and 2nd), Talmudic (1st and 2nd) *CEO:* Pres. Alexander Fischer
Enroll: 161   (718) 387-0422

YESHIVA SHAAR HATORAH TALMUDIC RESEARCH INSTITUTE
83-96 117th St., Kew Gardens 11415 *Type:* Private professional *Accred.:* 1984/1991 (AARTS) *Calendar:* Sem. plan *Degrees:* Rabbinic (1st), Talmudic (1st and 2nd) *CEO:* Pres. Z. Epstein
Enroll: 110   (718) 846-1940

YESHIVA UNIVERSITY
500 W. 185th St., New York 10033-3299 *Type:* Private *Accred.:* 1948/1991 (MSA) *Calendar:* Sem. plan *Degrees:* A, B, P, M, D, certificates *Prof. Accred.:* Clinical Psychology, Law, Medicine, School Psychology, Social Work (M-conditional) *CEO:* Pres. Norman Lamm
Enroll: 4,804   (212) 960-5400

YESHIVAS NOVOMINSK
1569 47th St., Brooklyn 11219 *Type:* Private professional *Accred.:* 1992 (AARTS) *Calendar:* Sem. plan *Degrees:* Talmudic (1st) *CEO:* Pres. Abraham Frankel
Enroll: 113   (718) 438-2727

YESHIVATH VIZNITZ
P.O. Box 446, Monsey 10952 *Type:* Private professional *Accred.:* 1980/1991 (AARTS)

Calendar: Sem. plan *Degrees:* Rabbinic (1st and advanced) *CEO:* Pres. Gershon Neiman
Enroll: 330   (914) 356-1010

YESIVATH ZICHRON MOSHE
Laurel Park Rd., South Fallsburg 12779
Type: Private professional *Accred.:* 1979/1992 (AARTS) *Calendar:* Sem. plan *Degrees:* Talmudic (1st and 2nd) *CEO:* Pres. A. Gorelick
Enroll: 104   (914) 434-5240

YORK COLLEGE
94-20 Guy R. Brewer Blvd., Jamaica 11451
Type: Public (local/state) *System:* City University of New York Office of the Chancellor *Accred.:* 1967/1987 (MSA) *Calendar:* Sem. plan *Degrees:* B *Prof. Accred.:* Nursing (B), Occupational Therapy, Social Work (B) *CEO:* Pres. Josephine D. Davis
Enroll: 5,505   (718) 262-2000

NORTH CAROLINA

ALAMANCE COMMUNITY COLLEGE
P.O. Box 8000, Graham 27253-8000 *Type:* Public (district) junior *System:* North Carolina Department of Community Colleges *Accred.:* 1969/1993 (SACS-CC) *Calendar:* Qtr. plan *Degrees:* A *Prof. Accred.:* Dental Assisting, Medical Laboratory Technology (AMA) *CEO:* Pres. W. Ronald McCarter
FTE Enroll: 2,993   (919) 578-2002

ANSON COMMUNITY COLLEGE
P.O. Box 126, Polkton 28135 *Type:* Public (district) junior *System:* North Carolina Department of Community Colleges *Accred.:* 1977/1993 (SACS-CC) *Calendar:* Qtr. plan *Degrees:* A *CEO:* Pres. Donald P. Altieri
FTE Enroll: 1,114   (704) 272-7635

APPALACHIAN STATE UNIVERSITY
Boone 28608 *Type:* Public (state) *System:* University of North Carolina General Administration *Accred.:* 1942/1992 (SACS-CC) *Calendar:* Sem. plan *Degrees:* B, M, D (candidate) *Prof. Accred.:* Business (B,M), Computer Science, Counseling, Home Economics, Music, Social Work (B), Speech-Language Pathology, Teacher Education (e,s,p) *CEO:* Chanc. Francis T. Borkowski
FTE Enroll: 11,373   (704) 262-2000

ASHEVILLE-BUNCOMBE TECHNICAL COMMUNITY COLLEGE
340 Victoria Rd., Asheville 28801 *Type:* Public (district) junior *System:* North Carolina Department of Community Colleges *Accred.:* 1969/1984 (SACS-CC) *Calendar:* Qtr. plan *Degrees:* A *Prof. Accred.:* Dental Assisting, Dental Hygiene, Medical Laboratory Technology (AMA), Radiography *CEO:* Pres. K. Ray Bailey
FTE Enroll: 4,256   (704) 254-1921

BARBER-SCOTIA COLLEGE
145 Cabarrus Ave., W., Concord 28025 *Type:* Private (Presbyterian) liberal arts and teachers *Accred.:* 1949/1993 (SACS-CC) *Calendar:* Sem. plan *Degrees:* B *CEO:* Pres. Joel O. Nwagbaraocha
FTE Enroll: 731   (704) 786-5171

BARTON COLLEGE
College Sta., Wilson 27893 *Type:* Private (Disciples of Christ) liberal arts *Accred.:* 1955/1988 (SACS-CC) *Calendar:* Sem. plan *Degrees:* B *Prof. Accred.:* Nursing (B), Social Work (B-candidate), Teacher Education (e,s) *CEO:* Pres. James B. Hemby, Jr.
FTE Enroll: 1,338   (919) 399-6300

BEAUFORT COUNTY COMMUNITY COLLEGE
P.O. Box 1069, Washington 27889 *Type:* Public (district) junior *System:* North Carolina Department of Community Colleges *Accred.:* 1973/1988 (SACS-CC) *Calendar:* Qtr. plan *Degrees:* A *Prof. Accred.:* Medical Laboratory Technology (AMA) *CEO:* Pres. U. Ronald Champion
FTE Enroll: 1,878   (919) 946-6194

BELMONT ABBEY COLLEGE
100 Belmont-Mount Holly Rd., Belmont 28012-2795 *Type:* Private (Roman Catholic) liberal arts *Accred.:* 1957/1989 (SACS-CC) *Calendar:* Sem. plan *Degrees:* B, M (candidate) *Prof. Accred.:* Teacher Education (e,s) *CEO:* Pres. Joseph S. Brosnan
FTE Enroll: 815   (704) 825-6700

BENNETT COLLEGE
900 E. Washington St., Greensboro 27401-3239 *Type:* Private (United Methodist) liberal arts for women *Accred.:* 1935/1990 (SACS-CC) *Calendar:* Sem. plan *Degrees:* B *Prof. Accred.:* Social Work (B), Teacher Education (e,s) *CEO:* Pres. Gloria Randall Scott
FTE Enroll: 655   (919) 273-4431

BLADEN COMMUNITY COLLEGE
P.O. Box 266, Dublin 28332-0266 *Type:* Public (district) junior *System:* North Carolina Department of Community Colleges *Accred.:* 1976/1992 (SACS-CC) *Calendar:* Qtr. plan *Degrees:* A *CEO:* Pres. Lynn G. King
FTE Enroll: 826   (910) 862-2164

BLUE RIDGE COMMUNITY COLLEGE
College Dr., Flat Rock 28731-9624 *Type:* Public (district) junior *System:* North Carolina Department of Community Colleges *Accred.:* 1973/1988 (SACS-CC) *Calendar:*

Qtr. plan *Degrees:* A *CEO:* Pres. David W. Sink, Jr.
FTE Enroll: 1,126　　　　(704) 692-3572

BREVARD COLLEGE
400 N. Broad St., Brevard 28712-3306 *Type:* Private (United Methodist) junior *Accred.:* 1949/1986 (SACS-CC) *Calendar:* Sem. plan *Degrees:* A *Prof. Accred.:* Music *CEO:* Pres. J. Thomas Bertrand
FTE Enroll: 722　　　　(704) 883-8292

BRUNSWICK COMMUNITY COLLEGE
P.O. Box 30, Supply 28462-0030 *Type:* Public (district) junior *System:* North Carolina Department of Community Colleges *Accred.:* 1983/1988 (SACS-CC) *Calendar:* Qtr. plan *Degrees:* A *CEO:* Pres. W. Michael Reaves
FTE Enroll: 1,005　　　　(910) 754-6900

CALDWELL COMMUNITY COLLEGE AND TECHNICAL INSTITUTE
P.O. Box 600, Lenoir 28645 *Type:* Public (district) junior *System:* North Carolina Department of Community Colleges *Accred.:* 1969/1986 (SACS-CC) *Calendar:* Qtr. plan *Degrees:* A *Prof. Accred.:* Diagnostic Medical Sonography, Occupational Therapy Assisting, Physical Therapy Assisting, Radiography *CEO:* Pres. Eric B. McKeithan
FTE Enroll: 2,982　　　　(704) 726-2200

CAMPBELL UNIVERSITY
P.O. Box 127, Buies Creek 27506 *Type:* Private (Southern Baptist) liberal arts *Accred.:* 1941/1990 (SACS-CC) *Calendar:* Sem. plan *Degrees:* B, M, D *Prof. Accred.:* Law (ABA only), Social Work (B-candidate), Teacher Education (e,s,p) *CEO:* Pres. Norman A. Wiggins
FTE Enroll: 4,194　　　　(919) 893-4111

CAPE FEAR COMMUNITY COLLEGE
411 N. Front St., Wilmington 28401-3993 *Type:* Public (district) junior *System:* North Carolina Department of Community Colleges *Accred.:* 1971/1986 (SACS-CC) *Calendar:* Qtr. plan *Degrees:* A *Prof. Accred.:* Dental Assisting (prelim. provisional) *CEO:* Interim Pres. Raymond A. Stone
FTE Enroll: 3,949　　　　(910) 251-5100

CARTERET COMMUNITY COLLEGE
3505 Arendell St., Morehead City 28557 *Type:* Public (district) junior *System:* North

Carolina Department of Community Colleges *Accred.:* 1974/1989 (SACS-CC) *Calendar:* Qtr. plan *Degrees:* A *Prof. Accred.:* Medical Assisting (AMA), Radiography, Respiratory Therapy, Respiratory Therapy Technology *CEO:* Pres. Donald W. Bryant
FTE Enroll: 1,981　　　　(919) 247-6000

CATAWBA COLLEGE
1300 W. Innes St., Salisbury 28144 *Type:* Private (United Church of Christ) liberal arts *Accred.:* 1928/1984 (SACS-CC) *Calendar:* Sem. plan *Degrees:* B, M *Prof. Accred.:* Teacher Education (e,s,p) *CEO:* Pres. J. Fred Corriher, Jr.
FTE Enroll: 966　　　　(704) 637-4111

CATAWBA VALLEY COMMUNITY COLLEGE
2550 Hwy. 70 SE, Hickory 28602-9699 *Type:* Public (district) junior *System:* North Carolina Department of Community Colleges *Accred.:* 1969/1984 (SACS-CC) *Calendar:* Qtr. plan *Degrees:* A *Prof. Accred.:* EMT-Paramedic, Engineering Technology (architectural, electrical, industrial, mechanical), Nursing (A) *CEO:* Pres. Cuyler A. Dunbar
FTE Enroll: 3,714　　　　(704) 327-7000

CECILS JUNIOR COLLEGE OF BUSINESS
1567 Patton Ave., Asheville 28806 *Type:* Private junior *Accred.:* 1971/1988 (ACISC) *Calendar:* Sem. plan *Degrees:* A *CEO:* Pres. John T. South, Jr.
　　　　　　　　　　(704) 252-2486

CENTRAL CAROLINA COMMUNITY COLLEGE
1105 Kelly Dr., Sanford 27330 *Type:* Public (district) junior *System:* North Carolina Department of Community Colleges *Accred.:* 1972/1987 (SACS-CC) *Calendar:* Qtr. plan *Degrees:* A *Prof. Accred.:* Veterinary Technology *CEO:* Pres. Marvin R. Joyner
FTE Enroll: 4,007　　　　(919) 775-5401

CENTRAL PIEDMONT COMMUNITY COLLEGE
P.O. Box 35009, Charlotte 28235 *Type:* Public (district) junior *System:* North Carolina Department of Community Colleges *Accred.:* 1969/1993 (SACS-CC) *Calendar:* Qtr. plan *Degrees:* A *Prof. Accred.:* Dental Assisting, Dental Hygiene (conditional), Engineering Technology (architectural, civil/construction, computer, electrical, manufac-

turing, mechanical), Medical Assisting (AMA), Medical Record Technology, Physical Therapy Assisting, Respiratory Therapy *CEO:* Pres. Paul Anthony Zeiss
FTE Enroll: 17,096   (704) 342-6633

CHOWAN COLLEGE
P.O. Box 1848, Murfreesboro 27855 *Type:* Private (Southern Baptist) *Accred.:* 1956/ 1988 (SACS-CC) *Calendar:* Sem. plan *Degrees:* A, B (candidate) *CEO:* Pres. Jerry F. Jackson
FTE Enroll: 802   (919) 398-4101

CLEVELAND COMMUNITY COLLEGE
137 S. Post Rd., Shelby 28150 *Type:* Public (district) junior *System:* North Carolina Department of Community Colleges *Accred.:* 1975/1991 (SACS-CC) *Calendar:* Qtr. plan *Degrees:* A *Prof. Accred.:* Radiography *CEO:* Pres. L. Steve Thornburg
FTE Enroll: 2,358   (704) 484-4000

COASTAL CAROLINA COMMUNITY COLLEGE
444 Western Blvd., Jacksonville 28546-6877 *Type:* Public (district) junior *System:* North Carolina Department of Community Colleges *Accred.:* 1972/1987 (SACS-CC) *Calendar:* Qtr. plan *Degrees:* A *Prof. Accred.:* Dental Assisting, Dental Hygiene, Medical Laboratory Technology (AMA), Surgical Technology *CEO:* Pres. Ronald K. Lingle
FTE Enroll: 3,423   (910) 455-1221

COLLEGE OF THE ALBEMARLE
P.O. Box 2327, Elizabeth City 27906-2327 *Type:* Public (district) junior *System:* North Carolina Department of Community Colleges *Accred.:* 1968/1993 (SACS-CC) *Calendar:* Qtr. plan *Degrees:* A *CEO:* Pres. Larry R. Donnithorne
FTE Enroll: 2,182   (919) 335-0821

CRAVEN COMMUNITY COLLEGE
800 College Ct., New Bern 28562 *Type:* Public (district) junior *System:* North Carolina Department of Community Colleges *Accred.:* 1971/1986 (SACS-CC) *Calendar:* Qtr. plan *Degrees:* A *CEO:* Pres. Lewis S. Redd
FTE Enroll: 1,949   (919) 638-4131

DAVIDSON COLLEGE
P.O. Box 1719, Davidson 28036 *Type:* Private (Presbyterian) liberal arts *Accred.:*

1917/1986 (SACS-CC) *Calendar:* Sem. plan *Degrees:* B *Prof. Accred.:* Teacher Education (e,s) *CEO:* Pres. John W. Kuykendall
FTE Enroll: 1,607   (704) 892-2000

DAVIDSON COUNTY COMMUNITY COLLEGE
P.O. Box 1287, Lexington 27293-1287 *Type:* Public (district) junior *System:* North Carolina Department of Community Colleges *Accred.:* 1968/1992 (SACS-CC) *Calendar:* Qtr. plan *Degrees:* A *Prof. Accred.:* Engineering Technology (electrical), Medical Record Technology, Nursing (A) *CEO:* Pres. J. Bryan Brooks
FTE Enroll: 2,633   (704) 249-8186

DUKE UNIVERSITY
P.O. Box 90001, Durham 27708-0001 *Type:* Private liberal arts and professional *Accred.:* 1938/ 1984 (ATS); 1895/1988 (SACS-CC) *Calendar:* Sem. plan *Degrees:* A, B, M, D *Prof. Accred.:* Blood Bank Technology, Business (M), Clinical Psychology, Electroneurodiagnostic Technology, Engineering (bioengineering, civil, electrical, mechanical), Forestry, Health Services Administration, Law, Medical Technology, Medicine, Nursing (M), Ophthalmic Medical Technology, Physical Therapy, Physician Assisting, Psychology Internship, Teacher Education (e,s,p) *CEO:* Pres. Nannerl O. Keohane
FTE Enroll: 11,096   (919) 684-8111

DURHAM TECHNICAL COMMUNITY COLLEGE
1637 Lawson St., Durham 27703 *Type:* Public (district) junior *System:* North Carolina Department of Community Colleges *Accred.:* 1971/1986 (SACS-CC) *Calendar:* Qtr. plan *Degrees:* A *Prof. Accred.:* Dental Laboratory Technology, Respiratory Therapy, Respiratory Therapy Technology *CEO:* Pres. Phail Wynn, Jr.
FTE Enroll: 4,096   (919) 598-9222

EAST CAROLINA UNIVERSITY
Fifth St., Greenville 27858-4353 *Type:* Public (state) *System:* University of North Carolina General Administration *Accred.:* 1927/1992 (SACS-CC) *Calendar:* Sem. plan *Degrees:* B, M, D *Prof. Accred.:* Art, Audiology, Business (B,M), Cytotechnology, General Practice Residency, Marriage and Family Therapy (M), Medical Record Administration, Medical Technology, Medi-

cine, Music, Nursing (B,M), Occupational Therapy, Physical Therapy, Recreation and Leisure Services, Rehabilitation Counseling, Social Work (B,M), Speech-Language Pathology, Teacher Education (e,s,p) *CEO:* Chanc. Richard R. Eakin
FTE Enroll: 18,221   (919) 757-6131

EAST COAST BIBLE COLLEGE
6900 Wilkinson Blvd., Charlotte 28214 *Type:* Private (Church of God) *Accred.:* 1985/1990 (AABC); 1989 (SACS-CC) *Calendar:* Sem. plan *Degrees:* A, B *CEO:* Pres. Ronald D. Martin
FTE Enroll: 212   (704) 394-2307

EDGECOMBE COMMUNITY COLLEGE
2009 W. Wilson St., Tarboro 27886 *Type:* Public (district) junior *System:* North Carolina Department of Community Colleges *Accred.:* 1973/1988 (SACS-CC) *Calendar:* Qtr. plan *Degrees:* A *Prof. Accred.:* Radiography *CEO:* Interim Pres. Hartwell H. Fuller
FTE Enroll: 2,579   (919) 823-5166

ELIZABETH CITY STATE UNIVERSITY
ECSU Box 790, Elizabeth City 27909 *Type:* Public (state) liberal arts and teachers *System:* University of North Carolina General Administration *Accred.:* 1947/1991 (SACS-CC) *Calendar:* Sem. plan *Degrees:* B *Prof. Accred.:* Teacher Education (e,s) *CEO:* Chanc. Jimmy R. Jenkins
FTE Enroll: 2,019   (919) 335-3230

ELON COLLEGE
Campus Box 2185, Elon College 27244-2010 *Type:* Private (United Church of Christ) liberal arts *Accred.:* 1947/1992 (SACS-CC) *Calendar:* Sem. plan *Degrees:* B, M *Prof. Accred.:* Teacher Education (e,s) *CEO:* Pres. J. Fred Young
FTE Enroll: 3,279   (910) 584-9711

FAYETTEVILLE STATE UNIVERSITY
1200 Murchison Rd., Newbold Sta., Fayetteville 28301-4298 *Type:* Public (state) liberal arts and teachers *System:* University of North Carolina General Administration *Accred.:* 1947/1991 (SACS-CC) *Calendar:* Sem. plan *Degrees:* A, B, M *Prof. Accred.:* Teacher Education (e,s) *CEO:* Chanc. Lloyd V. Hackley
FTE Enroll: 3,476   (910) 486-1111

FAYETTEVILLE TECHNICAL COMMUNITY COLLEGE
P.O. Box 35236, 2201 Hull Rd., Fayetteville 28303-0236 *Type:* Public (district) junior *System:* North Carolina Department of Community Colleges *Accred.:* 1967/1991 (SACS-CC) *Calendar:* Qtr. plan *Degrees:* A *Prof. Accred.:* Dental Assisting, Dental Hygiene, Engineering Technology (civil/construction, electrical), Funeral Service Education, Nursing (A), Physical Therapy Assisting, Radiography, Respiratory Therapy, Surgical Technology *CEO:* Pres. Robert Craig Allen
FTE Enroll: 12,423   (910) 678-8400

FORSYTH TECHNICAL COMMUNITY COLLEGE
2100 Silas Creek Pkwy., Winston-Salem 27103-5197 *Type:* Public (district) junior *System:* North Carolina Department of Community Colleges *Accred.:* 1968/1992 (SACS-CC) *Calendar:* Qtr. plan *Degrees:* A *Prof. Accred.:* Engineering Technology (electrical, manufacturing, mechanical drafting/design), Nuclear Medicine Technology, Radiation Therapy Technology, Radiography, Respiratory Therapy *CEO:* Pres. Bob H. Greene
FTE Enroll: 6,540   (919) 723-0371

GARDNER-WEBB UNIVERSITY
P.O. Box 997, Boiling Springs 28017 *Type:* Private (Southern Baptist) liberal arts *Accred.:* 1948/1986 (SACS-CC) *Calendar:* Sem. plan *Degrees:* A, B, M *Prof. Accred.:* Music, Nursing (A,B) *CEO:* Pres. M. Christopher White
FTE Enroll: 1,971   (704) 434-2361

GASTON COLLEGE
201 Hwy. 321 S., Dallas 28034-1499 *Type:* Public (district) junior *System:* North Carolina Department of Community Colleges *Accred.:* 1967/1991 (SACS-CC) *Calendar:* Qtr. plan *Degrees:* A *Prof. Accred.:* Engineering Technology (civil/construction, electrical, industrial, mechanical), Medical Assisting (AMA) *CEO:* Interim Pres. Paul Berrier
FTE Enroll: 4,431   (704) 922-6200

GREENSBORO COLLEGE
815 W. Market St., P.O. Box 26050, Greensboro 27420-6050 *Type:* Private (United

Methodist) liberal arts *Accred.:* 1926/1986 (SACS-CC) *Calendar:* Sem. plan *Degrees:* B *Prof. Accred.:* Teacher Education (e,s) *CEO:* Pres. Craven E. Williams
FTE Enroll: 784   (910) 272-7102

GUILFORD COLLEGE
5800 W. Friendly Ave., Greensboro 27410-4171 *Type:* Private liberal arts *Accred.:* 1926/1986 (SACS-CC) *Calendar:* Sem. plan *Degrees:* A, B *Prof. Accred.:* Teacher Education (e,s) *CEO:* Pres. William R. Rogers
FTE Enroll: 1,558   (910) 316-2000

GUILFORD TECHNICAL COMMUNITY COLLEGE
P.O. Box 309, Jamestown 27282 *Type:* Public (district) junior *System:* North Carolina Department of Community Colleges *Accred.:* 1969/1984 (SACS-CC) *Calendar:* Qtr. plan *Degrees:* A *Prof. Accred.:* Dental Assisting, Dental Hygiene, Engineering Technology (civil/construction, electrical, mechanical drafting/design), Medical Assisting (AMA) *CEO:* Pres. Donald W. Cameron
FTE Enroll: 30,643   (910) 334-4822

HALIFAX COMMUNITY COLLEGE
P.O. Drawer 809, Weldon 27890 *Type:* Public (district) junior *System:* North Carolina Department of Community Colleges *Accred.:* 1975/1990 (SACS-CC) *Calendar:* Qtr. plan *Degrees:* A *Prof. Accred.:* Medical Laboratory Technology (AMA) *CEO:* Pres. Elton L. Newbern, Jr.
FTE Enroll: 1,834   (919) 536-2551

HAYWOOD COMMUNITY COLLEGE
Freedlander Dr., Clyde 28721 *Type:* Public (district) junior *System:* North Carolina Department of Community Colleges *Accred.:* 1973/1988 (SACS-CC) *Calendar:* Qtr. plan *Degrees:* A *Prof. Accred.:* Medical Assisting (AMA) *CEO:* Pres. Dan W. Moore
FTE Enroll: 2,389   (704) 627-2821

HIGH POINT UNIVERSITY
University Sta., Montlieu Ave., High Point 27262-3598 *Type:* Private (United Methodist) liberal arts *Accred.:* 1951/1985 (SACS-CC) *Calendar:* Sem. plan *Degrees:* B, M (candidate) *Prof. Accred.:* Teacher Education (e,s) *CEO:* Pres. Jacob C. Martinson, Jr.
FTE Enroll: 2,245   (910) 841-9000

ISOTHERMAL COMMUNITY COLLEGE
P.O. Box 804, Spindale 28160 *Type:* Public (district) junior *System:* North Carolina Department of Community Colleges *Accred.:* 1970/1986 (SACS-CC) *Calendar:* Qtr. plan *Degrees:* A *CEO:* Pres. Willard L. Lewis, III
FTE Enroll: 1,880   (704) 286-3636

JAMES SPRUNT COMMUNITY COLLEGE
P.O. Box 398, Kenansville 28349-0398 *Type:* Public (district) junior *System:* North Carolina Department of Community Colleges *Accred.:* 1973/1988 (SACS-CC) *Calendar:* Qtr. plan *Degrees:* A *CEO:* Pres. Donald L. Reichard
FTE Enroll: 1,289   (910) 296-2400

JOHN WESLEY COLLEGE
2314 N. Centennial St., High Point 27265 *Type:* Independent (Wesleyan) *Accred.:* 1982/1992 (AABC) *Calendar:* Sem. plan *Degrees:* A, B, certificates *CEO:* Pres. Brian C. Donley
FTE Enroll: 63   (919) 889-2262

JOHNSON C. SMITH UNIVERSITY
100 Beatties Ford Rd., Charlotte 28216 *Type:* Private (Presbyterian) liberal arts *Accred.:* 1933/1986 (SACS-CC) *Calendar:* Sem. plan *Degrees:* B *Prof. Accred.:* Teacher Education (e,s) *CEO:* Interim Pres. Dorothy C. Yancy
FTE Enroll: 1,391   (704) 378-1000

JOHNSTON COMMUNITY COLLEGE
P.O. Box 2350, Smithfield 27577 *Type:* Public (district) junior *System:* North Carolina Department of Community Colleges *Accred.:* 1977/1992 (SACS-CC) *Calendar:* Qtr. plan *Degrees:* A *Prof. Accred.:* Radiography *CEO:* Pres. John L. Tart
FTE Enroll: 4,987   (919) 934-3051

LEES-MCRAE COLLEGE
P.O. Box 128, Banner Elk 28604 *Type:* Private (Presbyterian) liberal arts *Accred.:* 1953/1985 (SACS-CC) *Calendar:* Sem. plan *Degrees:* A, B *Prof. Accred.:* Teacher Education (e,s) *CEO:* Pres. James A. Schobel
FTE Enroll: 662   (704) 898-5241

LENOIR COMMUNITY COLLEGE
P.O. Box 188, Kinston 28502-0188 *Type:* Public (district) junior *System:* North Carolina Department of Community Colleges *Ac-*

cred.: 1968/1993 (SACS-CC) *Calendar:* Qtr. plan *Degrees:* A *Prof. Accred.:* Surgical Technology *CEO:* Pres. Lonnie H. Blizzard
FTE Enroll: 3,346   (919) 527-6223

LENOIR-RHYNE COLLEGE
Seventh Ave. and Eighth St., N.E., Hickory 28603 *Type:* Private (Lutheran) liberal arts *Accred.:* 1928/1992 (SACS-CC warning) *Calendar:* Sem. plan *Degrees:* B,M *Prof. Accred.:* Nursing (B), Teacher Education (e,s,p) *CEO:* Pres. John E. Trainer, Jr.
FTE Enroll: 1,377   (704) 328-1741

LIVINGSTONE COLLEGE
701 W. Monroe St., Salisbury 28144 *Type:* Private (African Methodist Episcopal) liberal arts *Accred.:* 1944/1991 (SACS-CC) *Calendar:* Sem. plan *Degrees:* B, M *Prof. Accred.:* Social Work (B), Teacher Education (e,s) *CEO:* Pres. Bernard W. Franklin
FTE Enroll: 662   (704) 638-5500

LOUISBURG COLLEGE
501 N. Main St., Louisburg 27549 *Type:* Private (United Methodist) junior *Accred.:* 1952/1986 (SACS-CC) *Calendar:* Sem. plan *Degrees:* A *CEO:* Pres. Ronald L. May
FTE Enroll: 568   (919) 496-2521

MARS HILL COLLEGE
Marshall St., Mars Hill 28754 *Type:* Private (Southern Baptist) liberal arts *Accred.:* 1926/1991 (SACS-CC) *Calendar:* Sem. plan *Degrees:* B *Prof. Accred.:* Music, Social Work (B), Teacher Education (e,s), Theatre (associate) *CEO:* Pres. Fred B. Bentley
FTE Enroll: 1,184   (704) 689-1111

MARTIN COMMUNITY COLLEGE
Kehukee Park Rd., Williamston 27892-9988 *Type:* Public (district) junior *System:* North Carolina Department of Community Colleges *Accred.:* 1972/1988 (SACS-CC) *Calendar:* Qtr. plan *Degrees:* A *Prof. Accred.:* Physical Therapy Assisting *CEO:* Pres. Martin H. Nadelman
FTE Enroll: 1,231   (919) 792-1521

MAYLAND COMMUNITY COLLEGE
P.O. Box 547, Spruce Pine 28777 *Type:* Public (district) junior *System:* North Carolina Department of Community Colleges *Accred.:* 1978/1984 (SACS-CC) *Calendar:*

Qtr. plan *Degrees:* A *CEO:* Interim Pres. Kenneth A. Bohan
FTE Enroll: 1,408   (704) 765-7351

MCDOWELL TECHNICAL COMMUNITY COLLEGE
Rte. 1, Box 170, Marion 28752 *Type:* Public (district) junior *System:* North Carolina Department of Community Colleges *Accred.:* 1975/1990 (SACS-CC) *Calendar:* Qtr. plan *Degrees:* A *CEO:* Pres. Robert M. Boggs
FTE Enroll: 1,177   (704) 652-6021

MEREDITH COLLEGE
3800 Hillsborough St., Raleigh 27607-5298 *Type:* Private (Southern Baptist) liberal arts for women *Accred.:* 1921/1990 (SACS-CC) *Calendar:* Sem. plan *Degrees:* B, M *Prof. Accred.:* Music, Social Work (B), Teacher Education (e,s) *CEO:* Pres. John Edgar Weems
FTE Enroll: 2,100   (919) 829-8600

METHODIST COLLEGE
5400 Ramsey St., Fayetteville 28311-1420 *Type:* Private (United Methodist) liberal arts *Accred.:* 1964/1989 (SACS-CC) *Calendar:* Sem. plan *Degrees:* A, B *Prof. Accred.:* Social Work (B-candidate), Teacher Education (e,s) *CEO:* Pres. M. Elton Hendricks
FTE Enroll: 1,701   (910) 630-7000

MITCHELL COMMUNITY COLLEGE
500 W. Broad St., Statesville 28677 *Type:* Public (district) junior *System:* North Carolina Department of Community Colleges *Accred.:* 1955/1989 (SACS-CC) *Calendar:* Qtr. plan *Degrees:* A *CEO:* Pres. Douglas O. Eason
FTE Enroll: 1,817   (704) 878-3200

MONTGOMERY COMMUNITY COLLEGE
P.O. Box 787, Troy 27371 *Type:* Public (district) junior *System:* North Carolina Department of Community Colleges *Accred.:* 1978/1993 (SACS-CC) *Calendar:* Qtr. plan *Degrees:* A *CEO:* Pres. Theodore H. Gasper, Jr.
FTE Enroll: 675   (910) 572-3691

MONTREAT-ANDERSON COLLEGE
P.O. Box 1267, Montreat 28757 *Type:* Private (Presbyterian) liberal arts *Accred.:* 1960/1990 (SACS-CC) *Calendar:* Sem. plan *Degrees:* A, B *CEO:* Pres. William W. Hurt
FTE Enroll: 318   (704) 669-8011

MOUNT OLIVE COLLEGE
634 Henderson St., Mount Olive 28365
Type: Private (Free Will Baptist) liberal arts
Accred.: 1960/1991 (SACS-CC) *Calendar:*
Sem. plan *Degrees:* A, B *CEO:* Pres. W.
Burkette Raper
FTE Enroll: 738   (919) 658-2502

NASH COMMUNITY COLLEGE
P.O. Box 7488, Rocky Mount 27804-0488
Type: Public (district) junior *System:* North
Carolina Department of Community Coll-
eges *Accred.:* 1976/1991 (SACS-CC) *Calen-
dar:* Qtr. plan *Degrees:* A *Prof. Accred.:*
Physical Therapy Assisting *CEO:* Pres. J.
Reid Parrott, Jr.
FTE Enroll: 1,847   (919) 443-4011

NORTH CAROLINA AGRICULTURAL AND
TECHNICAL STATE UNIVERSITY
1601 E. Market St., Greensboro 27411 *Type:*
Public (state) *System:* University of North
Carolina General Administration *Accred.:*
1936/1990 (SACS-CC) *Calendar:* Sem. plan
Degrees: B, M, D (candidate) *Prof. Accred.:*
Accounting (Type A), Business (B), Engi-
neering (aerospace, architectural, chemical,
civil, electrical, industrial, mechanical),
Home Economics, Landscape Architecture
(B-initial), Music (associate), Nursing (B),
Social Work (B), Teacher Education (e,s,p),
Theatre *CEO:* Chanc. Edward B. Fort
FTE Enroll: 8,013   (910) 334-7500

NORTH CAROLINA CENTRAL UNIVERSITY
1801 Fayetteville St., Durham 27707 *Type:*
Public (state) liberal arts and professional
System: University of North Carolina Gener-
al Administration *Accred.:* 1937/1989
(SACS-CC) *Calendar:* Sem. plan *Degrees:*
B, M *Prof. Accred.:* Law (ABA only), Li-
brarianship, Nursing (B), Speech-Language
Pathology, Teacher Education (e,s,p) *CEO:*
Chanc. Julius L. Chambers
FTE Enroll: 4,893   (919) 560-6100

NORTH CAROLINA SCHOOL OF THE ARTS
200 Waughtown St., P.O. Box 12189, Winston-Salem 27117-2189 *Type:* Public (state)
professional *System:* University of North
Carolina General Administration *Accred.:*
1970/1985 (SACS-CC) *Calendar:* Tri. plan

Degrees: B, M *CEO:* Chanc. Alexander C.
Ewing
FTE Enroll: 589   (919) 770-3399

NORTH CAROLINA STATE UNIVERSITY
P.O. Box 7001, Raleigh 27695-7001 *Type:*
Public (state) *System:* University of North
Carolina General Administration *Accred.:*
1928/1984 (SACS-CC) *Calendar:* Sem. plan
Degrees: A, B, M, D *Prof. Accred.:* Com-
puter Science, Counseling, Engineering
(aerospace, agricultural, chemical, civil,
computer, construction, electrical, industrial,
materials, mechanical, nuclear, textile),
Forestry, Landscape Architecture (M), Pub-
lic Affairs, Recreation and Leisure Services,
School Psychology, Social Work (B),
Teacher Education (e,s,p), Veterinary Medicine *CEO:* Chanc. Larry K. Monteith
FTE Enroll: 22,656   (919) 515-2011

NORTH CAROLINA WESLEYAN COLLEGE
3400 N. Wesleyan Blvd., Rocky Mount
27804 *Type:* Private (United Methodist) liberal arts *Accred.:* 1963/1990 (SACS-CC)
Calendar: Sem. plan *Degrees:* B *Prof. Accred.:* Teacher Education (e,s) *CEO:* Pres.
Leslie H. Garner, Jr.
FTE Enroll: 1,170   (919) 985-5100

PAMLICO COMMUNITY COLLEGE
P.O. Box 185, Hwy. 306 S., Grantsboro
28529 *Type:* Public (district) junior *System:*
North Carolina Department of Community
Colleges *Accred.:* 1977/1992 (SACS-CC)
Calendar: Qtr. plan *Degrees:* A *CEO:* Pres.
E. Douglas Kearney, Jr.
FTE Enroll: 259   (919) 249-1851

PEACE COLLEGE
15 E. Peace St., Raleigh 27604 *Type:* Private
(Presbyterian) junior for women *Accred.:*
1947/1985 (SACS-CC) *Calendar:* Sem. plan
Degrees: A *CEO:* Pres. Garrett Briggs
FTE Enroll: 437   (919) 832-2881

PEMBROKE STATE UNIVERSITY
One University Dr., Pembroke 28372 *Type:*
Public (state) liberal arts and teachers *Sys-
tem:* University of North Carolina General
Administration *Accred.:* 1951/1990 (SACS-
CC) *Calendar:* Sem. plan *Degrees:* B, M
Prof. Accred.: Music, Social Work (B),

Teacher Education (e,s,p) *CEO:* Chanc. Joseph B. Oxendine
FTE Enroll: 2,573   (910) 521-6000

PFEIFFER COLLEGE
P.O. Box 960, Misenheimer 28109-0960 *Type:* Private (United Methodist) liberal arts *Accred.:* 1959/1992 (SACS-CC) *Calendar:* Sem. plan *Degrees:* B, M *Prof. Accred.:* Music *CEO:* Pres. Zane E. Eargle
FTE Enroll: 829   (704) 463-1360

PIEDMONT BIBLE COLLEGE
716 Franklin St., Winston-Salem 27101 *Type:* Independent (Baptist) *Accred.:* 1956/1984 (AABC) *Calendar:* Sem. plan *Degrees:* B, diplomas *CEO:* Pres. Howard L. Wilburn
FTE Enroll: 264   (919) 725-8344

PIEDMONT COMMUNITY COLLEGE
P.O. Box 1197, Roxboro 27573 *Type:* Public (district) junior *System:* North Carolina Department of Community Colleges *Accred.:* 1977/1992 (SACS-CC) *Calendar:* Qtr. plan *Degrees:* A *CEO:* Pres. H. James Owen
FTE Enroll: 1,531   (910) 599-1181

PITT COMMUNITY COLLEGE
P.O. Drawer 7007, Greenville 27835-7007 *Type:* Public (district) junior *System:* North Carolina Department of Community Colleges *Accred.:* 1969/1993 (SACS-CC) *Calendar:* Qtr. plan *Degrees:* A *Prof. Accred.:* Diagnostic Medical Sonography, Medical Assisting (AMA), Medical Record Technology, Occupational Therapy Assisting, Radiation Therapy Technology, Radiography, Respiratory Therapy *CEO:* Pres. Charles E. Russell
FTE Enroll: 6,371   (919) 355-4200

QUEENS COLLEGE
1900 Selwyn Ave., Charlotte 28274 *Type:* Private (Presbyterian) liberal arts for women *Accred.:* 1932/1991 (SACS-CC) *Calendar:* Sem. plan *Degrees:* B, M *Prof. Accred.:* Music, Nursing (B), Teacher Education (e,s,p) *CEO:* Pres. Billy O. Wireman
FTE Enroll: 1,095   (704) 337-2200

RANDOLPH COMMUNITY COLLEGE
P.O. Box 1009, Asheboro 27204-1009 *Type:* Public (district) junior *System:* North Carolina Department of Community Colleges *Accred.:* 1974/1989 (SACS-CC) *Calendar:*

Qtr. plan *Degrees:* A *Prof. Accred.:* Nursing (A) *CEO:* Pres. Larry K. Linker
FTE Enroll: 2,117   (910) 629-1471

RICHMOND COMMUNITY COLLEGE
P.O. Box 1189, Hamlet 28345 *Type:* Public (district) junior *System:* North Carolina Department of Community Colleges *Accred.:* 1969/1993 (SACS-CC) *Calendar:* Qtr. plan *Degrees:* A *CEO:* Pres. Joseph W. Grimsley
FTE Enroll: 2,222   (919) 582-7000

ROANOKE BIBLE COLLEGE
714 First St., Elizabeth City 27909 *Type:* Private (Christian Churches/Churches of Christ) *Accred.:* 1979/1989 (AABC) *Calendar:* Sem. plan *Degrees:* A, B *CEO:* Pres. William A. Griffin
FTE Enroll: 113   (919) 338-5191

ROANOKE-CHOWAN COMMUNITY COLLEGE
Rte. 2, Box 46-A, Ahoskie 27910 *Type:* Public (district) junior *System:* North Carolina Department of Community Colleges *Accred.:* 1976/1992 (SACS-CC) *Calendar:* Qtr. plan *Degrees:* A *CEO:* Pres. Harold E. Mitchell
FTE Enroll: 2,696   (910) 332-5921

ROBESON COMMUNITY COLLEGE
P.O. Box 1420, Lumberton 28359 *Type:* Public (district) junior *System:* North Carolina Department of Community Colleges *Accred.:* 1975/1990 (SACS-CC) *Calendar:* Qtr. plan *Degrees:* A *CEO:* Pres. Frederick G. Williams, Jr.
FTE Enroll: 1,719   (910) 738-7101

ROCKINGHAM COMMUNITY COLLEGE
P.O. Box 38, Wentworth 27375-0038 *Type:* Public (district) junior *System:* North Carolina Department of Community Colleges *Accred.:* 1968/1993 (SACS-CC) *Calendar:* Qtr. plan *Degrees:* A *CEO:* Pres. N. Jerry Owens, Jr.
FTE Enroll: 2,598   (910) 342-4261

ROWAN-CABARRUS COMMUNITY COLLEGE
P.O. Box 1595, Salisbury 28144-1595 *Type:* Public (district) junior *System:* North Carolina Department of Community Colleges *Accred.:* 1970/1985 (SACS-CC) *Calendar:* Qtr. plan *Degrees:* A *Prof. Accred.:* Dental

Assisting, Nursing (A), Radiography *CEO:* Pres. Richard L. Brownell
FTE Enroll: 3,669   (704) 637-0760

ST. ANDREWS PRESBYTERIAN COLLEGE
1700 Dogwood Mile, Laurinburg 28352 *Type:* Private (Presbyterian) liberal arts *Accred.:* 1961/1990 (SACS-CC warning) *Calendar:* 4-1-4 plan *Degrees:* B *Prof. Accred.:* Teacher Education (e,s) *CEO:* Pres. Warren L. Board
FTE Enroll: 773   (910) 277-5000

ST. AUGUSTINE'S COLLEGE
1315 Oakwood Ave., Raleigh 27610-2298 *Type:* Private (Episcopal) liberal arts *Accred.:* 1942/1991 (SACS-CC) *Calendar:* Sem. plan *Degrees:* B *CEO:* Pres. Prezell R. Robinson
FTE Enroll: 1,745   (919) 516-4000

ST. MARY'S COLLEGE
900 Hillsborough St., Raleigh 27603-1689 *Type:* Private (Episcopal) junior for women *Accred.:* 1927/1989 (SACS-CC) *Calendar:* Sem. plan *Degrees:* A *CEO:* Pres. Clauston L. Jenkins
FTE Enroll: 215   (919) 828-2521

SALEM COLLEGE
Salem Sta., P.O. Box 10548, Winston-Salem 27108 *Type:* Private liberal arts for women *Accred.:* 1922/1990 (SACS-CC) *Calendar:* 4-1-4 plan *Degrees:* B, M *Prof. Accred.:* Music, Teacher Education (e,s,p) *CEO:* Pres. Julianne Still Thrift
FTE Enroll: 692   (919) 721-2600

SAMPSON COMMUNITY COLLEGE
P.O. Drawer 318, Clinton 28328 *Type:* Public (district) junior *System:* North Carolina Department of Community Colleges *Accred.:* 1977/1993 (SACS-CC) *Calendar:* Qtr. plan *Degrees:* A *CEO:* Pres. Clifton W. Paderick
FTE Enroll: 1,747   (910) 592-8081

SANDHILLS COMMUNITY COLLEGE
2200 Airport Rd., Pinehurst 28374 *Type:* Public (district) junior *System:* North Carolina Department of Community Colleges *Accred.:* 1968/1993 (SACS-CC) *Calendar:* Qtr. plan *Degrees:* A *Prof. Accred.:* Medical Laboratory Technology (AMA), Nursing (A), Radiography, Respiratory Therapy, Sur-

gical Technology *CEO:* Pres. John R. Dempsey
FTE Enroll: 2,801   (919) 692-6185

SHAW UNIVERSITY
118 E. South St., Raleigh 27601 *Type:* Private liberal arts *Accred.:* 1943/1993 (SACS-CC) *Calendar:* Sem. plan *Degrees:* A, B *Prof. Accred.:* Teacher Education (e,c) *CEO:* Pres. Talbert O. Shaw
FTE Enroll: 2,437   (919) 546-8200

SOUTHEASTERN BAPTIST THEOLOGICAL SEMINARY
P.O. Box 1889, Wake Forest 27588-1889 *Type:* Private (Southern Baptist) *Accred.:* 1958/1991 (ATS); 1978/1993 (SACS-CC) *Calendar:* Sem. plan *Degrees:* A, M, D *CEO:* Pres. L. Paige Patterson
FTE Enroll: 613   (919) 556-3101

SOUTHEASTERN COMMUNITY COLLEGE
P.O. Box 151, Whiteville 28472 *Type:* Public (district) junior *System:* North Carolina Department of Community Colleges *Accred.:* 1967/1991 (SACS-CC) *Calendar:* Qtr. plan *Degrees:* A *CEO:* Pres. Stephen C. Scott
FTE Enroll: 2,793   (910) 642-7141

SOUTHWESTERN COMMUNITY COLLEGE
275 Webster Rd., Sylva 28779 *Type:* Public (district) junior *System:* North Carolina Department of Community Colleges *Accred.:* 1971/1986 (SACS-CC) *Calendar:* Qtr. plan *Degrees:* A *Prof. Accred.:* Medical Laboratory Technology (AMA), Physical Therapy Assisting, Radiography, Respiratory Therapy, Respiratory Therapy Technology *CEO:* Pres. Barry W. Russell
FTE Enroll: 1,487   (704) 586-4091

STANLY COMMUNITY COLLEGE
141 College Dr., Albemarle 28001 *Type:* Public (district) junior *System:* North Carolina Department of Community Colleges *Accred.:* 1979/1984 (SACS-CC) *Calendar:* Qtr. plan *Degrees:* A *Prof. Accred.:* Occupational Therapy Assisting, Physical Therapy Assisting, Respiratory Therapy, Respiratory Therapy Technology *CEO:* Pres. Jan J. Crawford
FTE Enroll: 2,294   (704) 982-0121

SURRY COMMUNITY COLLEGE
P.O. Box 304, Dobson 27017 *Type:* Public (district) junior *System:* North Carolina Department of Community Colleges *Accred.:* 1969/1984 (SACS-CC) *Calendar:* Qtr. plan *Degrees:* A *CEO:* Pres. Swanson Richards
FTE Enroll: 2,667   (919) 386-8121

TRI-COUNTY COMMUNITY COLLEGE
2300 Hwy. 64 E., Murphy 28906 *Type:* Public (district) junior *System:* North Carolina Department of Community Colleges *Accred.:* 1975/1990 (SACS-CC) *Calendar:* Qtr. plan *Degrees:* A *CEO:* Pres. W. Harry Jarrett
FTE Enroll: 902   (704) 837-6810

THE UNIVERSITY OF NORTH CAROLINA AT ASHEVILLE
One University Heights, Asheville 28804 *Type:* Public (state) *System:* University of North Carolina General Administration *Accred.:* 1958/1992 (SACS-CC) *Calendar:* Sem. plan *Degrees:* B, M *Prof. Accred.:* Teacher Education (e,s) *CEO:* Interim Chanc. Larry Wilson
FTE Enroll: 2,667   (704) 251-6600

THE UNIVERSITY OF NORTH CAROLINA AT CHAPEL HILL
CB #9100, 103 South Bldg., Chapel Hill 27599-9100 *Type:* Public (state) *System:* University of North Carolina General Administration *Accred.:* 1895/1985 (SACS-CC) *Calendar:* Sem. plan *Degrees:* B, M, D *Prof. Accred.:* Audiology, Business (B,M), Clinical Psychology, Combined Prosthodontics, Counseling, Counseling Psychology, Cytotechnology, Dental Assisting, Dental Hygiene, Dentistry, Dietetics (coordinated), Endodontics, Engineering Technology (industrial hygiene), Engineering (environmental/sanitary), General Dentistry, General Practice Residency, Health Services Administration, Journalism (B,M), Law, Librarianship, Medical Technology, Medicine, Nuclear Medicine Technology, Nursing (B,M), Occupational Therapy, Oral and Maxillofacial Surgery, Orthodontics, Pediatric Dentistry, Periodontics, Physical Therapy, Planning (M), Psychology Internship, Public Administration, Public Health, Radiation Therapy Technology, Radiography, Recreation

and Leisure Services, Rehabilitation Counseling, School Psychology, Social Work (M), Speech-Language Pathology, Teacher Education (e,s,p) *CEO:* Chanc. Paul Hardin
FTE Enroll: 21,540   (919) 962-2211

THE UNIVERSITY OF NORTH CAROLINA AT CHARLOTTE
University City Blvd., Charlotte 28223 *Type:* Public (state) *System:* University of North Carolina General Administration *Accred.:* 1957/1992 (SACS-CC) *Calendar:* Sem. plan *Degrees:* B, M, D (candidate) *Prof. Accred.:* Accounting (Type A), Business (B,M), Engineering Technology (civil/construction, electrical, mechanical), Engineering (civil, electrical, mechanical), Nurse Anesthesia Education, Nursing (B,M), Public Administration, Social Work (B-candidate), Teacher Education (e,s,p) *CEO:* Chanc. James H. Woodward, Jr.
FTE Enroll: 13,206   (704) 547-2000

THE UNIVERSITY OF NORTH CAROLINA AT GREENSBORO
1000 Spring Garden St., Greensboro 27412 *Type:* Public (state) *System:* University of North Carolina General Administration *Accred.:* 1921/1993 (SACS-CC) *Calendar:* Sem. plan *Degrees:* B, M, D *Prof. Accred.:* Audiology, Business (B,M), Clinical Psychology, Counseling, Interior Design, Librarianship, Music, Nurse Anesthesia Education, Nursing (B,M), Public Affairs, Recreation and Leisure Services, Social Work (B), Speech-Language Pathology, Teacher Education (e,s,p), Theatre (associate) *CEO:* Chanc. William E. Moran
FTE Enroll: 10,821   (910) 334-5000

THE UNIVERSITY OF NORTH CAROLINA AT WILMINGTON
601 S. College Rd., Wilmington 28403-3297 *Type:* Public (state) *System:* University of North Carolina General Administration *Accred.:* 1952/1992 (SACS-CC) *Calendar:* Sem. plan *Degrees:* B, M *Prof. Accred.:* Business (B,M), Music (associate), Nursing (B), Recreation and Leisure Services, Teacher Education (e,s,p) *CEO:* Chanc. James R. Leutze
FTE Enroll: 7,530   (910) 395-3000

VANCE-GRANVILLE COMMUNITY COLLEGE
P.O. Box 917, Poplar Creek Rd., Henderson 27536 *Type:* Public (district) junior *System:* North Carolina Department of Community Colleges *Accred.:* 1977/1993 (SACS-CC) *Calendar:* Qtr. plan *Degrees:* A *Prof. Accred.:* Radiography *CEO:* Pres. Benjamin F. Currin
FTE Enroll: 3,164   (919) 492-2061

WAKE FOREST UNIVERSITY
1834 Wake Forest Rd., Winston-Salem 27109 *Type:* Private *Accred.:* 1921/1987 (SACS-CC) *Calendar:* Sem. plan *Degrees:* B, M, D *Prof. Accred.:* Accounting (Type A), Business (B,M), General Practice Residency, Law, Medical Technology, Medicine, Physician Assisting, Teacher Education (e,s,p) *CEO:* Pres. Thomas K. Hearn, Jr.
FTE Enroll: 5,496   (910) 759-5000

WAKE TECHNICAL COMMUNITY COLLEGE
9101 Fayetteville Rd., Raleigh 27603-5696 *Type:* Public (district) junior *System:* North Carolina Department of Community Colleges *Accred.:* 1970/1985 (SACS-CC) *Calendar:* Qtr. plan *Degrees:* A *Prof. Accred.:* Dental Assisting, Engineering Technology (civil/construction, computer, electrical, mechanical), Medical Assisting (AMA), Medical Laboratory Technology (AMA), Radiography *CEO:* Pres. Bruce I. Howell
FTE Enroll: 6,526   (919) 662-3240

WARREN WILSON COLLEGE
P.O. Box 9000, Asheville 28815-9000 *Type:* Private (United Presbyterian) liberal arts *Accred.:* 1952/1984 (SACS-CC) *Calendar:* Sem. plan *Degrees:* B, M *Prof. Accred.:* Social Work (B), Teacher Education (e,s) *CEO:* Pres. Douglas M. Orr, Jr.
FTE Enroll: 553   (704) 298-3325

WAYNE COMMUNITY COLLEGE
Caller Box 8002, Goldsboro 27533-8002 *Type:* Public (district) junior *System:* North Carolina Department of Community Colleges *Accred.:* 1970/1986 (SACS-CC) *Calendar:* Qtr. plan *Degrees:* A *Prof. Accred.:* Dental Assisting, Dental Hygiene *CEO:* Pres. Edward H. Wilson
FTE Enroll: 3,341   (919) 735-5151

WESTERN CAROLINA UNIVERSITY
Cullowhee 28723 *Type:* Public (state) *System:* University of North Carolina General Administration *Accred.:* 1946/1986 (SACS-CC) *Calendar:* Sem. plan *Degrees:* B, M *Prof. Accred.:* Business (B,M), Counseling, EMT-Paramedic, Engineering Technology (manufacturing), Home Economics (provisional), Medical Record Administration, Medical Technology, Music, Nursing (B), Social Work (B), Speech-Language Pathology, Teacher Education (e,s,p) *CEO:* Chanc. Myron L. Coulter
FTE Enroll: 5,966   (704) 227-7211

WESTERN PIEDMONT COMMUNITY COLLEGE
1001 Burkemont Ave., Morganton 28655-9978 *Type:* Public (district) junior *System:* North Carolina Department of Community Colleges *Accred.:* 1968/1993 (SACS-CC) *Calendar:* Qtr. plan *Degrees:* A *Prof. Accred.:* Dental Assisting, Medical Assisting (AMA), Medical Laboratory Technology (AMA), Nursing (A) *CEO:* Pres. James A. Richardson
FTE Enroll: 2,476   (704) 438-6000

WILKES COMMUNITY COLLEGE
P.O. Box 120, Collegiate Dr., Wilkesboro 28697-0120 *Type:* Public (district) junior *System:* North Carolina Department of Community Colleges *Accred.:* 1970/1985 (SACS-CC) *Calendar:* Qtr. plan *Degrees:* A *Prof. Accred.:* Dental Assisting *CEO:* Pres. James R. Randolph
FTE Enroll: 2,447   (919) 651-8600

WILSON TECHNICAL COMMUNITY COLLEGE
902 Herring Ave., P.O. Box 4305, Wilson 27893 *Type:* Public (district) junior *System:* North Carolina Department of Community Colleges *Accred.:* 1969/1984 (SACS-CC) *Calendar:* Qtr. plan *Degrees:* A *CEO:* Pres. Frank L. Eagles
FTE Enroll: 1,648   (919) 291-1195

WINGATE COLLEGE
Wingate 28174-0157 *Type:* Private (Southern Baptist) liberal arts *Accred.:* 1951/1985 (SACS-CC) *Calendar:* Sem. plan *Degrees:* A, B, M *Prof. Accred.:* Medical Assisting (AMA), Music, Nursing (B), Teacher Education (e,s,p) *CEO:* Pres. Jerry E. McGee
FTE Enroll: 1,416   (704) 233-8000

WINSTON-SALEM STATE UNIVERSITY
601 Martin Luther King, Jr. Dr., Winston-Salem 27110 *Type:* Public (state) liberal arts and teachers *System:* University of North Carolina General Administration *Accred.:* 1947/1990 (SACS-CC) *Calendar:* Sem. plan *Degrees:* B *Prof. Accred.:* Medical Technology, Music, Nursing (B), Teacher Education (e,s) *CEO:* Chanc. Cleon F. Thompson, Jr. *FTE Enroll:* 2,472   (910) 750-2000

NORTH DAKOTA

BISMARCK STATE COLLEGE
1500 Edwards Ave., Bismarck 58501 *Type:* Public (state) *System:* North Dakota University System *Accred.:* 1966/1988 (NCA) *Calendar:* Sem. plan *Degrees:* A, certificates *Prof. Accred.:* Medical Laboratory Technology (AMA) *CEO:* Pres. Kermit Lidstrom
Enroll: 2,472   (701) 224-5400

DICKINSON STATE UNIVERSITY
291 Campus Dr., Dickinson 58601 *Type:* Public (state) liberal arts and teachers *System:* North Dakota University System *Accred.:* 1928/1985 (NCA) *Calendar:* Sem. plan *Degrees:* A, B, certificates *Prof. Accred.:* Nursing (B) *CEO:* Pres. Albert A. Watrel
Enroll: 1,605   (701) 227-2507

FORT BERTHOLD COMMUNITY COLLEGE
P.O. Box 490, New Town 58763 *Type:* Public (tribal) junior *Accred.:* 1988/1991 (NCA) *Calendar:* Sem. plan *Degrees:* A, certificates *CEO:* Pres. Lyn Dockter-Pinnick
Enroll: 223   (701) 627-3665

JAMESTOWN COLLEGE
Jamestown 58405 *Type:* Private (United Presbyterian) liberal arts *Accred.:* 1920/1991 (NCA) *Calendar:* 4-1-4 plan *Degrees:* B *Prof. Accred.:* Nursing (B) *CEO:* Pres. James S. Walker
Enroll: 1,083   (701) 252-3467

LITTLE HOOP COMMUNITY COLLEGE
P.O. Box 269, Fort Totten 58335 *Type:* Public (tribal) junior *Accred.:* 1990/1993 (NCA) *Calendar:* Sem. plan *Degrees:* A, certificates, diplomas *CEO:* Pres. Merrill Berg
Enroll: 139   (701) 766-4415

MAYVILLE STATE UNIVERSITY
330 Third St., N.E., Mayville 58257 *Type:* Public (state) liberal arts and teachers *System:* North Dakota University System *Accred.:* 1917/1986 (NCA) *Calendar:* Qtr. plan *Degrees:* A, B, certificates *Prof. Accred.:* Teacher Education (e,s) *CEO:* Pres. Ellen E. Chaffee, Ph.D.
Enroll: 749   (701) 786-2301

MEDCENTER ONE COLLEGE OF NURSING
512 N. Seventh St., Bismarck 58501 *Type:* Private professional *Accred.:* 1990 (NCA) *Calendar:* Sem. plan *Degrees:* B *Prof. Accred.:* Nursing (B) *CEO:* Provost/Dean Rita Zaborowska
Enroll: 94   (701) 224-6832

MINOT STATE UNIVERSITY
Minot 58701 *Type:* Public (state) liberal arts and teachers *System:* North Dakota University System *Accred.:* 1917/1988 (NCA) *Calendar:* Qtr. plan *Degrees:* A, B, M *Prof. Accred.:* Audiology, Music, Nursing (B), Social Work (B), Speech-Language Pathology, Teacher Education (e,s) *CEO:* Pres. H. Erik Shaar
Enroll: 3,797   (701) 857-3300

NORTH DAKOTA STATE COLLEGE OF SCIENCE
800 N. Sixth St., Wahpeton 58076 *Type:* Public (state) junior *System:* North Dakota University System *Accred.:* 1971/1991 (NCA) *Calendar:* Qtr. plan *Degrees:* A, certificates, diplomas *Prof. Accred.:* Dental Assisting, Dental Hygiene, Medical Record Technology, Occupational Therapy Assisting, Practical Nursing *CEO:* Pres. Jerry C. Olson
Enroll: 2,147   (701) 671-2221

NORTH DAKOTA STATE UNIVERSITY
Fargo 58105 *Type:* Public (state) *System:* North Dakota University System *Accred.:* 1915/1986 (NCA) *Calendar:* Qtr. plan *Degrees:* A, B, P, M, D *Prof. Accred.:* Computer Science, Construction Education (B), Dietetics (coordinated), Engineering (agricultural, civil, construction, electrical, industrial, mechanical), Home Economics, Interior Design, Landscape Architecture (B-initial), Music, Nursing (B), Respiratory Therapy, Teacher Education (s,p), Veterinary Technology *CEO:* Pres. Jim L. Ozbun
Enroll: 9,229   (701) 237-8011

NORTH DAKOTA STATE UNIVERSITY—
BOTTINEAU
First St. and Simrall Blvd., Bottineau 58318 *Type:* Public (state) junior *System:* North Dakota University System *Accred.:* 1971/ 1989 (NCA) *Calendar:* Qtr. plan *Degrees:*

A, certificates, diplomas *CEO:* Dean J.W. Smith
Enroll: 411   (701) 228-2277

STANDING ROCK COLLEGE
HC1, Box 4, Fort Yates 58538 *Type:* Public (tribal) *Accred.:* 1984/1991 (NCA) *Calendar:* Sem. plan *Degrees:* A, certificates *CEO:* Pres. Ronald McNeil
Enroll: 218   (701) 854-3861

TRI-COLLEGE UNIVERSITY
306 Ceres Hall, North Dakota State Univ., Fargo 58105 *Type:* Private graduate only *Accred.:* 1979/1984 (NCA) *Calendar:* Qtr. plan *Degrees:* P, M *Prof. Accred.:* Nursing (B), Teacher Education (p) *CEO:* Provost William C. Nelson
Enroll: 210   (701) 237-8170

TRINITY BIBLE COLLEGE
50 S. Sixth St., Ellendale 58436 *Type:* Private (Assemblies of God) *Accred.:* 1980/1990 (AABC); 1991 (NCA probational) *Calendar:* Sem. plan *Degrees:* A, B, certificates, diplomas *CEO:* Pres. Ray Trask
Enroll: 424   (701) 349-3621

TURTLE MOUNTAIN COMMUNITY COLLEGE
P.O. Box 340, Belcourt 58316-0340 *Type:* Private (tribal) junior *Accred.:* 1984/1989 (NCA) *Calendar:* Sem. plan *Degrees:* A, certificates *CEO:* Pres. Gerald E. Monette
Enroll: 482   (701) 477-5605

UNITED TRIBES TECHNICAL COLLEGE
3315 University Dr., Bismarck 58504 *Type:* Private (tribal) *Accred.:* 1982/1990 (NCA) *Calendar:* Qtr. plan *Degrees:* A, certificates *CEO:* Pres. David M. Gipp
Enroll: 285   (701) 255-3285

UNIVERSITY OF MARY
7500 University Dr., Bismarck 58504 *Type:* Private (Roman Catholic) liberal arts *Accred.:* 1969/1993 (NCA) *Calendar:* 4-1-4 plan *Degrees:* A, B, M *Prof. Accred.:* Nurse Anesthesia Education, Nursing (B,M), Social Work (B) *CEO:* Pres. Thomas Welder, O.S.B.
Enroll: 1,851   (701) 255-7500

UNIVERSITY OF NORTH DAKOTA
Box 8232, University Sta., Grand Forks 58202-8232 *Type:* Public (state) *System:* North Dakota University System *Accred.:* 1913/1984 (NCA) *Calendar:* Sem. plan *Degrees:* A, B, P, M, D *Prof. Accred.:* Art, Business (B,M), Clinical Psychology, Computer Science, Counseling Psychology (provisional), Cytotechnology, Dietetics (coordinated), Engineering (chemical, civil, electrical, geological/geophysical, mechanical), Histologic Technology, Home Economics, Law, Medical Technology, Medicine, Music, Nurse Anesthesia Education, Nursing (B,M), Occupational Therapy, Physical Therapy, Physician Assisting, Social Work (B,M), Speech-Language Pathology, Teacher Education (e,s,p), Theatre *CEO:* Pres. Kendall L. Baker
Enroll: 14,887   (701) 777-2011

UNIVERSITY OF NORTH DAKOTA—LAKE REGION
N. College Dr., Devils Lake 58301 *Type:* Public (state) *System:* North Dakota University System *Accred.:* 1974/1991 (NCA) *Calendar:* Sem. plan *Degrees:* A, certificates, diplomas *CEO:* Exec. Dean Sharon L. Etemad
Enroll: 1,074   (701) 662-1600

UNIVERSITY OF NORTH DAKOTA—WILLISTON
P.O. Box 1326, Williston 58801 *Type:* Public (state) *System:* North Dakota University System *Accred.:* 1972/1990 (NCA) *Calendar:* Sem. plan *Degrees:* A, certificates, diplomas *CEO:* Exec. Dean Garvin L. Stevens
Enroll: 878   (701) 774-4200

VALLEY CITY STATE UNIVERSITY
College St., Valley City 58072 *Type:* Public (state) liberal arts and teachers *System:* North Dakota University System *Accred.:* 1915/1992 (NCA) *Calendar:* Qtr. plan *Degrees:* A, B *Prof. Accred.:* Teacher Education (e,s) *CEO:* Pres. Ellen E. Chaffee
Enroll: 1,003   (701) 845-7100

OHIO

ACADEMY OF COURT REPORTING
614 Superior Ave., N.W., Cleveland 44113
Type: Private business *Accred.:* 1980/1986
(ACISC) *Calendar:* Courses of varying
lengths *Degrees:* A, certificates, diplomas
CEO: Dir. Lynn Fisher
(216) 861-3222

BRANCH CAMPUS
Ste. 101, 26111 Evergreen Rd., Southfield, MI 48076 *Accred.:* 1989 (ACISC)
CEO: Mgr. Kathryn Trauben
(313) 353-4880

BRANCH CAMPUS
2930 W. Market St., Akron 44313 *Accred.:* 1986 (ACISC) *CEO:* Dir. Michelle
Endres
(216) 867-4030

BRANCH CAMPUS
630 E. Broad St., Columbus 43215 *Accred.:* 1988 (ACISC) *CEO:* Dir. Joseph A.
Trocchio
(614) 221-7770

AIR FORCE INSTITUTE OF TECHNOLOGY
2950 P St., Wright-Patterson Air Force Base
45433 *Type:* Public (federal) technological;
graduate only *Accred.:* 1960/1991 (NCA)
Calendar: Qtr. plan *Degrees:* M, D *Prof. Accred.:* Engineering (aerospace, computer,
electrical, engineering physics/science, nuclear, systems) *CEO:* Commandant Stuart R.
Boyd
Enroll: 775   (513) 255-6231

ANTIOCH UNIVERSITY
795 Livermore St., Yellow Springs 45387
Type: Private liberal arts and professional
Accred.: 1927/1988 (NCA) *Calendar:* Sem.
plan *Degrees:* B, M, D *CEO:* Pres. Alan E.
Guskin
Enroll: 4,115   (513) 767-7331

ANTIOCH COLLEGE
745 Livermore St., Yellow Springs 45387
CEO: Pres. Alan E. Guskin
(513) 767-7331

ANTIOCH NEW ENGLAND GRADUATE SCHOOL
Roxbury St., Keene, NH 03431 *Prof. Ac-
cred.:* Clinical Psychology, Marriage and
Family Therapy (M) *CEO:* Provost James
H. Craiglow
(603) 357-3122

ANTIOCH SEATTLE
2607 Second Ave., Seattle, WA 98121
CEO: Provost Gary Zimmerman
(206) 441-5352

ANTIOCH SOUTHERN CALIFORNIA—LOS
ANGELES
13274 Fiji Way, Marina del Rey, CA
90292 *CEO:* Provost Dale A. Johnston
(310) 578-1080

ANTIOCH SOUTHERN CALIFORNIA—SANTA
BARBARA
801 Garden St., Santa Barbara, CA 93101
CEO: Provost Dale A. Johnston
(805) 962-8179

GEORGE MEANY CENTER FOR LABOR STUDIES
10000 New Hampshire Ave., Silver
Spring, MD 20903 *CEO:* Dir. Robert
Pleasure
(301) 431-6400

SCHOOL FOR ADULT AND EXPERIENTIAL
LEARNING
800 Livermore St., Yellow Springs 45387
CEO: Provost Robert Miller
(513) 767-6321

ANTONELLI INSTITUTE OF ART AND
PHOTOGRAPHY
124 E. Seventh St., Cincinnati 45202-2592
Type: Private *Accred.:* 1975/1990 (ACC-
SCT) *Calendar:* Qtr. plan *Degrees:* A *CEO:*
Pres. Robert M. Resnick
(513) 241-4338

ART ACADEMY OF CINCINNATI
1125 St. Gregory St., Cincinnati 45202
Type: Private professional *Accred.:* 1990
(NCA) *Calendar:* Sem. plan *Degrees:* A, B,
certificates *Prof. Accred.:* Art *CEO:* Dir.
Roger Williams
Enroll: 224   (513) 562-8750

ASHLAND UNIVERSITY
401 College Ave., Ashland 44805 *Type:* Private (Brethren) liberal arts *Accred.:* 1969/1988 (ATS); 1930/1988 (NCA) *Calendar:* Sem. plan *Degrees:* A, B, M, D *Prof. Accred.:* Music, Nursing (B), Social Work (B), Teacher Education (e,s) *CEO:* Pres. G. William Benz
Enroll: 5,707   (419) 289-4142

ATHENAEUM OF OHIO
6616 Beechmont Ave., Cincinnati 45230-2091 *Type:* Private (Roman Catholic) graduate only *Accred.:* 1972/1992 (ATS); 1959/1993 (NCA) *Calendar:* Qtr. plan *Degrees:* M, certificates *CEO:* Pres. Robert J. Mooney
Enroll: 241   (513) 231-2223

BALDWIN-WALLACE COLLEGE
275 Eastland Rd., Berea 44017 *Type:* Private (United Methodist) liberal arts *Accred.:* 1913/1988 (NCA) *Calendar:* Qtr. plan *Degrees:* B, M, certificates *Prof. Accred.:* Music, Teacher Education (e,s,p) *CEO:* Pres. Neal Malicky
Enroll: 4,712   (216) 826-2900

BELMONT TECHNICAL COLLEGE
120 Fox-Shannon Pl., St. Clairsville 43950 *Type:* Public (state) 2-year *System:* Ohio Board of Regents *Accred.:* 1978/1988 (NCA) *Calendar:* Qtr. plan *Degrees:* A, certificates, diplomas *CEO:* Pres. Wesley R. Channell
Enroll: 1,750   (614) 695-9500

BLUFFTON COLLEGE
280 W. College Ave., Bluffton 45817-1196 *Type:* Private (Mennonite) liberal arts *Accred.:* 1953/1989 (NCA) *Calendar:* 4-1-4 plan *Degrees:* B *Prof. Accred.:* Music, Social Work (B) *CEO:* Pres. Elmer Neufeld
Enroll: 728   (419) 358-3000

BOHECKER'S BUSINESS COLLEGE
326 E. Main St., Ravenna 44266 *Type:* Private business *Accred.:* 1985/1989 (ACISC) *Calendar:* Courses of varying lengths *Degrees:* A *CEO:* C.E.O./Owner John Fitzpatrick
           (216) 297-7319

BOWLING GREEN STATE UNIVERSITY
Bowling Green 43403 *Type:* Public (state) *System:* Ohio Board of Regents *Accred.:* 1916/1993 (NCA) *Calendar:* Sem. plan *De-

grees: A, B, P, M, D *Prof. Accred.:* Art, Audiology, Business (B,M), Clinical Psychology, Journalism (B,M), Medical Record Technology, Medical Technology, Music, Nursing (B,M), Physical Therapy, Rehabilitation Counseling, Respiratory Therapy, Social Work (B), Speech-Language Pathology, Teacher Education (e,s,p), Theatre *CEO:* Pres. Paul J. Olscamp
Enroll: 19,568   (419) 372-2531

FIRELANDS COLLEGE
901 Rye Beach Rd., Huron 44839 *CEO:* Dean Robert Debard
           (419) 433-5560

BRADFORD SCHOOL
6170 Busch Blvd., Columbus 43229 *Type:* Private business *Accred.:* 1960/1988 (ACISC) *Calendar:* Qtr. plan *Degrees:* A, certificates, diplomas *CEO:* Pres. Patrick L. Denton
           (614) 846-9410

BRYANT & STRATTON BUSINESS INSTITUTE
12955 Snow Rd., Parma 44130-1013 *Type:* Private business *Accred.:* 1984/1990 (ACISC) *Calendar:* Qtr. plan *Degrees:* A, certificates, diplomas *CEO:* Dir. Alan J. Hyers
           (216) 265-3151

BRANCH CAMPUS
Sears Bldg., 3rd Fl., 691 Richmond Rd., Richmond Heights 44143 *Accred.:* 1988/1990 (ACISC) *CEO:* Dir. Charles Catley
           (216) 461-3151

CAPITAL UNIVERSITY
2199 E. Main St., Columbus 43209 *Type:* Private (Lutheran) liberal arts and professional *Accred.:* 1921/1993 (NCA) *Calendar:* 4-1-4 plan *Degrees:* B, M, D, certificates, diplomas *Prof. Accred.:* Law, Music, Nursing (B), Social Work (B), Teacher Education (e,s) *CEO:* Pres. Josiah H. Blackmore
Enroll: 3,680   (614) 236-6908

CASE WESTERN RESERVE UNIVERSITY
10900 Euclid Ave., Cleveland 44106-7001 *Type:* Private *Accred.:* 1913/1985 (NCA) *Calendar:* Sem. plan *Degrees:* B, M, D *Prof. Accred.:* Accounting (Type A,C), Anesthesiologist Assisting, Business (B,M), Clinical Psychology, Dentistry, Endodontics, Engi-

neering (bioengineering, chemical, civil, computer, electrical, engineering physics/science, materials, mechanical, polymer, systems), General Dentistry, Law, Medicine, Music, Nurse Anesthesia Education, Nursing (B,M), Oral and Maxillofacial Surgery, Orthodontics, Pediatric Dentistry, Periodontics, Psychology Internship, Social Work (M), Speech-Language Pathology *CEO:* Pres. Agnar Pytte
Enroll: 9,156   (216) 368-4344

CEDARVILLE COLLEGE
N. Main St., Box 601, Cedarville 45314-0601 *Type:* Private (Baptist) liberal arts *Accred.:* 1975/1987 (NCA) *Calendar:* Qtr. plan *Degrees:* A, B, certificates *Prof. Accred.:* Nursing (B) *CEO:* Pres. Paul Dixon
Enroll: 2,172   (513) 766-2211

CENTRAL OHIO TECHNICAL COLLEGE
1179 University Dr., Newark 43055-1767 *Type:* Public (district) 2-year *System:* Ohio Board of Regents *Accred.:* 1975/1988 (NCA) *Calendar:* Qtr. plan *Degrees:* A, certificates *Prof. Accred.:* Diagnostic Medical Sonography, Nursing (A), Physical Therapy Assisting, Radiography *CEO:* Pres. Julius S. Greenstein
Enroll: 1,860   (614) 366-1351

CENTRAL STATE UNIVERSITY
1400 Brush Row Rd., Wilberforce 45384 *Type:* Public (state) *System:* Ohio Board of Regents *Accred.:* 1949/1989 (NCA) *Calendar:* Qtr. plan *Degrees:* A, B *Prof. Accred.:* Engineering (manufacturing), Music *CEO:* Pres. Arthur E. Thomas
FTE Enroll: 3,261   (513) 376-6011

CHATFIELD COLLEGE
20918 State Rte. 251, St. Martin 45118 *Type:* Private liberal arts *Accred.:* 1971/1986 (NCA) *Calendar:* Sem. plan *Degrees:* A *CEO:* Pres. Ellen Doyle
Enroll: 176   (513) 875-3344

CINCINNATI BIBLE COLLEGE AND SEMINARY
2700 Glenway Ave., Cincinnati 45204 *Type:* Private (Christian Churches/Churches of Christ) *Accred.:* 1966/1986 (AABC); 1989 (NCA) *Calendar:* Sem. plan *Degrees:* A, B, M *CEO:* Pres. C. Barry McCarty
Enroll: 910   (513) 244-8100

CINCINNATI COLLEGE OF MORTUARY SCIENCE
Cohen Ctr., 3860 Pacific Ave., Cincinnati 45207-1033 *Type:* Private professional *Accred.:* 1982/1991 (NCA) *Calendar:* Qtr. plan *Degrees:* A, B *Prof. Accred.:* Mortuary Science *CEO:* Pres. Dan L. Flory
Enroll: 138   (513) 745-3631

CINCINNATI TECHNICAL COLLEGE
3520 Central Pkwy., Cincinnati 45223 *Type:* Public (state) 2-year *System:* Ohio Board of Regents *Accred.:* 1976/1991 (NCA) *Calendar:* Qtr. plan *Degrees:* A, certificates *Prof. Accred.:* Engineering Technology (bioengineering, civil/construction, computer, electrical, electromechanical, mechanical), Medical Assisting (AMA), Medical Laboratory Technology (AMA), Medical Record Technology, Occupational Therapy Assisting, Respiratory Therapy, Surgical Technology *CEO:* Pres. James P. Long
Enroll: 5,562   (513) 569-1500

CIRCLEVILLE BIBLE COLLEGE
1476 Lancaster Pike, P.O. Box 458, Circleville 43113 *Type:* Private (Churches of Christ in Christian Union) *Accred.:* 1976/1986 (AABC) *Calendar:* Sem. plan *Degrees:* A, B *CEO:* Pres. David Van Hoose
FTE Enroll: 167   (614) 474-8896

CLARK STATE COMMUNITY COLLEGE
570 E. Leffels La., P.O. Box 570, Springfield 45505 *Type:* Public (state) 2-year *System:* Ohio Board of Regents *Accred.:* 1974/1989 (NCA) *Calendar:* Qtr. plan *Degrees:* A, certificates *Prof. Accred.:* Engineering Technology (general drafting/design), Medical Laboratory Technology (AMA), Nursing (A) *CEO:* Pres. Albert A. Salerno
Enroll: 3,113   (513) 325-0691

CLERMONT COLLEGE
4200 Clermont College Dr., Batavia 45103 *Type:* Public (state) *System:* Ohio Board of Regents *Accred.:* 1978/1989 (NCA) *Calendar:* Qtr. plan *Degrees:* A, certificates *CEO:* Dean Roger J. Barry
Enroll: 1,745   (513) 732-5200

CLEVELAND COLLEGE OF JEWISH STUDIES
26500 Shaker Blvd., Beachwood 44122 *Type:* Private (Jewish) *Accred.:* 1988/1993

(NCA) *Calendar:* Sem. plan *Degrees:* B, M
CEO: Pres. David S. Ariel
Enroll: 308   (216) 464-4050

CLEVELAND INSTITUTE OF ART
11141 East Blvd., Cleveland 44106 *Type:*
Private professional *Accred.:* 1970/1991
(NCA) *Calendar:* Sem. plan *Degrees:* B
Prof. Accred.: Art *CEO:* Pres. Robert A.
Mayer
Enroll: 469   (216) 421-7400

CLEVELAND INSTITUTE OF ELECTRONICS, INC.
1776 E. 17th St., Cleveland 44114 *Type:* Private home study *Accred.:* 1956/1992
(NHSC) *Calendar:* Courses of varying
lengths *Degrees:* A, certificates *CEO:* Pres.
John R. Drinko
                                 (216) 781-9400

CLEVELAND INSTITUTE OF MUSIC
11021 East Blvd., Cleveland 44106 *Type:*
Private professional *Accred.:* 1980/1986
(NCA) *Calendar:* Sem. plan *Degrees:* B, M,
D, diplomas *Prof. Accred.:* Music *CEO:*
Pres. David Cerone
Enroll: 420   (216) 791-5000

CLEVELAND STATE UNIVERSITY
Euclid Ave. at E. 24th St., Cleveland 44115
Type: Public (state) *System:* Ohio Board of
Regents *Accred.:* 1940/1990 (NCA) *Calen-
dar:* Qtr. plan *Degrees:* B, P, M, D *Prof. Ac-
cred.:* Accounting (Type A,C), Audiology,
Business (B,M), Engineering (chemical,
civil, electrical, industrial, mechanical),
Health Services Administration, Law, Music,
Nursing (B), Occupational Therapy, Physical
Therapy, Public Administration, Social
Work (B), Speech-Language Pathology,
Teacher Education (e,s,p) *CEO:* Pres. Claire
A. Van Ummersen
FTE Enroll: 13,220   (216) 687-2000

COLLEGE OF MOUNT ST. JOSEPH
5701 Delhi Rd., Cincinnati 45233 *Type:* Private (Roman Catholic) liberal arts primarily
for women *Accred.:* 1932/1989 (NCA) *Calendar:* Sem. plan *Degrees:* A, B, M, certificates *Prof. Accred.:* Music, Nursing (B), Social Work (B-candidate) *CEO:* Pres. Francis
Marie Thrailkill, O.S.U.
Enroll: 2,594   (513) 244-4232

COLLEGE OF WOOSTER
Wooster 44691 *Type:* Private (United Pres-
byterian) liberal arts *Accred.:* 1915/1993
(NCA) *Calendar:* Qtr. plan *Degrees:* B *Prof.
Accred.:* Music *CEO:* Pres. Henry J.
Copeland
Enroll: 1,754   (216) 263-2311

COLUMBUS COLLEGE OF ART AND DESIGN
107 N. Ninth St., Columbus 43215 *Type:*
Private professional *Accred.:* 1986/1991
(NCA) *Calendar:* Sem. plan *Degrees:* B
Prof. Accred.: Art *CEO:* Pres. Joseph V.
Canzani
Enroll: 1,433   (614) 224-9101

COLUMBUS PARA-PROFESSIONAL INSTITUTE
1077 Lexington Ave., Columbus 43201
Type: Private *Accred.:* 1980/1990 (ACC-
SCT) *Calendar:* Qtr. plan *Degrees:* A, diplomas *CEO:* Dir. Sandra Moomaw
                                 (614) 299-0200

COLUMBUS STATE COMMUNITY COLLEGE
550 E. Spring St., P.O. Box 1609, Columbus
43216-1609 *Type:* Public (state) 2-year *System:* Ohio Board of Regents *Accred.:* 1973/
1990 (NCA) *Calendar:* Qtr. plan *Degrees:*
A, certificates *Prof. Accred.:* Dental Laboratory Technology, EMT-Paramedic, Engineering Technology (electrical), Histologic
Technology, Medical Laboratory Technology (AMA), Nursing (A), Respiratory Therapy, Respiratory Therapy Technology, Veterinary Technology *CEO:* Pres. Harold M.
Nestor
Enroll: 16,510   (614) 227-2400

CUYAHOGA COMMUNITY COLLEGE
700 Carnegie Ave., Cleveland 44115 *Type:*
Public (county) 2-year *System:* Ohio Board
of Regents *Accred.:* 1979/1989 (NCA) *Cal-
endar:* Qtr. plan *Degrees:* A, certificates
Prof. Accred.: Medical Assisting (AMA),
Medical Laboratory Technology (AMA),
Medical Record Technology, Occupational
Therapy Assisting, Physician Assisting,
Radiography, Respiratory Therapy, Surgical
Technology *CEO:* Pres. Jerry Sue Owens
Enroll: 25,488   (216) 987-6000

EASTERN CAMPUS
4250 Richmond Rd., Highland Hills 44122 *Prof. Accred.:* Nursing (A) *CEO:* Provost Paul Shumaker
(216) 987-2000

METROPOLITAN CAMPUS
2900 Community College Ave., Cleveland 44115 *Prof. Accred.:* Dental Assisting, Dental Hygiene, Dental Laboratory Technology, Nursing (A), Physical Therapy Assisting *CEO:* Provost Alex B. Johnson
(216) 987-4000

WESTERN CAMPUS
11000 W. Pleasant Valley Rd., Parma 44130 *Prof. Accred.:* Nursing (A) *CEO:* Provost Ronald M. Sobel
(216) 987-5000

DAVIS COLLEGE
4747 Monroe St., Toledo 43623 *Type:* Private junior *Accred.:* 1953/1986 (ACISC); 1991 (NCA) *Calendar:* Qtr. plan *Degrees:* A, certificates, diplomas *Prof. Accred.:* Medical Assisting (AMA) *CEO:* Pres. John M. Lambert
Enroll: 359 (419) 473-2700

THE DEFIANCE COLLEGE
701 N. Clinton St., Defiance 43512 *Type:* Private (United Church of Christ) liberal arts *Accred.:* 1916/1993 (NCA) *Calendar:* 4-1-4 plan *Degrees:* A, B, M *Prof. Accred.:* Social Work (B) *CEO:* Pres. Marvin J. Ludwig
Enroll: 998 (419) 784-4010

DENISON UNIVERSITY
P.O. Box B, Granville 43023 *Type:* Private (Baptist) liberal arts *Accred.:* 1913/1990 (NCA) *Calendar:* Sem. plan *Degrees:* B *CEO:* Pres. Michelle Tolela Myers
Enroll: 1,885 (614) 587-6281

DEVRY INSTITUTE OF TECHNOLOGY, COLUMBUS
1350 Alum Creek Dr., Columbus 43209 *Type:* Private *Accred.:* 1981/1992 (NCA)* *Calendar:* Sem. plan *Degrees:* A, B, certificates, diplomas *Prof. Accred.:* Engineering Technology (electrical) *CEO:* Pres. Richard A. Czerniak
(614) 253-7291

* Indirect accreditation through DeVry Institutes.

DYKE COLLEGE
112 Prospect Ave., S.E., Cleveland 44115 *Type:* Private *Accred.:* 1978/1990 (NCA) *Calendar:* Tri. plan *Degrees:* A, B, certificates, diplomas *CEO:* Pres. John C. Corfias
Enroll: 1,426 (216) 696-9000

EDISON STATE COMMUNITY COLLEGE
1973 Edison Dr., Piqua 45356 *Type:* Public (state) 2-year *System:* Ohio Board of Regents *Accred.:* 1981/1987 (NCA) *Calendar:* Qtr. plan *Degrees:* A, certificates *Prof. Accred.:* Nursing (A) *CEO:* Pres. Kenneth A. Yowell
Enroll: 3,297 (513) 778-8600

ETI TECHNICAL COLLEGE
4300 Euclid Ave., Cleveland 44103-9932 *Type:* Private *Accred.:* 1969/1989 (ACCSCT) *Calendar:* Qtr. plan *Degrees:* A, diplomas *CEO:* Pres. Jack Baron
(216) 431-4300

ETI TECHNICAL COLLEGE OF NILES
2076-86 Youngstown-Warren Rd., Niles 44446-4398 *Accred.:* 1989 (ACCSCT) *CEO:* Dir. Renee Zuzulo
(216) 652-9919

THE ETI TECHNICAL COLLEGE
1320 W. Maple St., N.W., North Canton 44720-2854 *Type:* Private *Accred.:* 1986 (ACCSCT) *Calendar:* Qtr. plan *Degrees:* A, diplomas *CEO:* Dir. Al Jablonski
(216) 494-1214

FRANCISCAN UNIVERSITY OF STEUBENVILLE
100 Franciscan Way, Steubenville 43952 *Type:* Private (Roman Catholic) liberal arts *Accred.:* 1960/1985 (NCA) *Calendar:* Sem. plan *Degrees:* A, B, M *Prof. Accred.:* Nursing (B) *CEO:* Pres. Michael Scanlan
Enroll: 1,812 (614) 283-3771

FRANKLIN UNIVERSITY
201 S. Grant Ave., Columbus 43215 *Type:* Private liberal arts and technical *Accred.:* 1976/1988 (NCA) *Calendar:* Tri. plan *Degrees:* A, B, M *Prof. Accred.:* Engineering Technology (electrical, mechanical), Nursing (B) *CEO:* Pres. Paul J. Otte
Enroll: 3,852 (614) 341-6237

GOD'S BIBLE COLLEGE
1810 Young St., Cincinnati 45210 *Type:* Independent (Wesleyan) *Accred.:* 1986/1991 (AABC) *Calendar:* Sem. plan *Degrees:* B, diplomas *CEO:* Pres. Bence Miller
FTE Enroll: 176   (513) 721-7944

HEBREW UNION COLLEGE—JEWISH INSTITUTE OF RELIGION
3101 Clifton Ave., Cincinnati 45220 *Type:* Private (Union of Hebrew Congregations) primarily for men *Accred.:* 1960/1991 (NCA) *Calendar:* Qtr. plan *Degrees:* M, D *CEO:* Pres. Alfred Gottschalk
Enroll: 123   (513) 221-1875

HEIDELBERG COLLEGE
310 E. Market St., Tiffin 44883 *Type:* Private (United Church of Christ) liberal arts *Accred.:* 1913/1985 (NCA) *Calendar:* Sem. plan *Degrees:* B, M *Prof. Accred.:* Music *CEO:* Pres. William C. Cassell
Enroll: 1,371   (419) 448-2202

HIRAM COLLEGE
Hiram 44234 *Type:* Private (Disciples of Christ) liberal arts *Accred.:* 1914/1990 (NCA) *Calendar:* Qtr. plan *Degrees:* B *Prof. Accred.:* Music *CEO:* Pres. G. Benjamin Oliver
Enroll: 1,301   (216) 569-3211

HOCKING TECHNICAL COLLEGE
3301 Hocking Pkwy., Nelsonville 45764 *Type:* Public (state) 2-year *System:* Ohio Board of Regents *Accred.:* 1976/1991 (NCA) *Calendar:* Qtr. plan *Degrees:* A, certificates *Prof. Accred.:* Engineering Technology (ceramic), Medical Assisting (AMA), Medical Record Technology, Nursing (A), Practical Nursing *CEO:* Pres. John J. Light
Enroll: 5,948   (614) 753-3591

THE INTERNATIONAL COLLEGE OF BROADCASTING
6 S. Smithville Rd., Dayton 45431-1833 *Type:* Private *Accred.:* 1976/1986 (ACCSCT) *Calendar:* Courses of varying lengths *Degrees:* A, diplomas *CEO:* Pres. Michael LeMaster
                              (513) 258-8251

ITT TECHNICAL INSTITUTE
3325 Stop Eight Rd., Dayton 45414-9915 *Type:* Private *Accred.:* 1991 (ACCSCT) *Cal-*endar: Courses of varying lengths *Degrees:* A *CEO:* Dir. William R. Miles
                              (513) 454-2267

ITT TECHNICAL INSTITUTE
P.O. Box 779, 655 Wick Ave., Youngstown 44501 *Type:* Private business *Accred.:* 1971/1989 (ACISC) *Calendar:* Courses of varying lengths *Degrees:* A, diplomas *CEO:* Dir. Michael Thompson
                              (216) 747-5555

BRANCH CAMPUS
8 Parkway Ctr., Pittsburgh, PA 15220 *Accred.:* 1992 (ACISC) *CEO:* Dir. James P. Callahan
                              (412) 937-9150

JEFFERSON TECHNICAL COLLEGE
4000 Sunset Blvd., Steubenville 43952 *Type:* Public (state) 2-year *System:* Ohio Board of Regents *Accred.:* 1973/1989 (NCA) *Calendar:* Qtr. plan *Degrees:* A, certificates *Prof. Accred.:* Dental Assisting, Medical Assisting (AMA), Medical Laboratory Technology (AMA), Radiography, Respiratory Therapy *CEO:* Pres. Edward L. Florak
Enroll: 1,691   (614) 264-5591

JOHN CARROLL UNIVERSITY
20700 N. Park Blvd., University Heights 44118 *Type:* Private (Roman Catholic) liberal arts and business *Accred.:* 1922/1984 (NCA) *Calendar:* Sem. plan *Degrees:* B, M, certificates *Prof. Accred.:* Business (B,M), Teacher Education (e,s,p) *CEO:* Pres. Michael J. Lavelle, S.J.
Enroll: 4,488   (216) 397-1886

KENT STATE UNIVERSITY
P.O. Box 5190, Kent 44242 *Type:* Public (state) *System:* Ohio Board of Regents *Accred.:* 1915/1984 (NCA) *Calendar:* Sem. plan *Degrees:* A, B, P, M, D *Prof. Accred.:* Art, Audiology, Business (B,M), Clinical Psychology, Counseling, Counseling Psychology, Interior Design, Journalism (B,M), Librarianship, Music, Nursing (A,B,M), Occupational Therapy Assisting, Psychology Internship (provisional), Public Administration, Radiography, Recreation and Leisure Services, Rehabilitation Counseling, School Psychology, Speech-Language Pathology,

Teacher Education (e,s,p) *CEO:* Pres. Carol A. Cartwright
Enroll: 33,139   (216) 672-3000

ASHTABULA CAMPUS
3325 W. 13th St., Ashtabula 44004 *Prof. Accred.:* Nursing (A) *CEO:* Dean John K. Mahan
(216) 964-3322

EAST LIVERPOOL CAMPUS
400 E. Fourth St., East Liverpool 43920 *Prof. Accred.:* Nursing (A), Physical Therapy Assisting *CEO:* Dean Suzanne B. Fitzgerald
(216) 385-3805

GEUAGA CAMPUS
14111 Claridon-Troy Rd., Burton Township 44021 *CEO:* Dean Larry Jones
(216) 834-4187

SALEM CAMPUS
2491 State Rte. 45 S., Salem 44460 *CEO:* Dean James F. Cooney
(216) 332-0361

STARK CAMPUS
6000 Frank Ave., N.W., Canton 44720 *CEO:* Dean William G. Bittle
(216) 499-9600

TRUMBULL CAMPUS
4314 Mahoning Ave., N.W., Warren 44483 *CEO:* Dean David A. Allen, Jr.
(216) 678-4281

TUSCARAWAS CAMPUS
University Dr., N.E., New Philadelphia 44663 *Prof. Accred.:* Engineering Technology (electrical, electromechanical), Nursing (A) *CEO:* Dean Harold D. Shade
(216) 339-3391

KENYON COLLEGE
Gambier 43022-9623 *Type:* Private (Episcopal) liberal arts *Accred.:* 1913/1991 (NCA) *Calendar:* Sem. plan *Degrees:* B *CEO:* Pres. Philip Harding Jordan, Jr.
Enroll: 1,523   (614) 427-5000

KETTERING COLLEGE OF MEDICAL ARTS
3737 Southern Blvd., Kettering 45429 *Type:* Private (Seventh-Day Adventist) junior *Accred.:* 1974/1990 (NCA) *Calendar:* Sem.

plan *Degrees:* A, certificates *Prof. Accred.:* Diagnostic Medical Sonography, Nursing (A), Physician Assisting, Radiography, Respiratory Therapy *CEO:* Provost Peter D.H. Bath
Enroll: 724   (513) 296-7218

LAKE ERIE COLLEGE
391 W. Washington St., Painesville 44077 *Type:* Private liberal arts *Accred.:* 1913/1989 (NCA) *Calendar:* Sem. plan *Degrees:* B, M *CEO:* Pres. Harold F. Laydon
Enroll: 718   (216) 352-3361

LAKELAND COMMUNITY COLLEGE
7700 Clocktower Dr., Mentor 44060 *Type:* Public (district) 2-year *System:* Ohio Board of Regents *Accred.:* 1973/1990 (NCA) *Calendar:* 4-1-4 plan *Degrees:* A, certificates *Prof. Accred.:* Dental Hygiene, Medical Laboratory Technology (AMA), Nursing (A), Radiography, Respiratory Therapy *CEO:* Pres. Ralph R. Doty
Enroll: 9,174   (216) 953-7118

LIMA TECHNICAL COLLEGE
4240 Campus Dr., Lima 45804 *Type:* Public (state) 2-year *System:* Ohio Board of Regents *Accred.:* 1979/1992 (NCA) *Calendar:* Qtr. plan *Degrees:* A, certificates *Prof. Accred.:* Dental Hygiene, Engineering Technology (electrical), Nursing (A), Physical Therapy Assisting, Radiography, Respiratory Therapy, Respiratory Therapy Technology *CEO:* Pres. James J. Countryman
Enroll: 2,750   (419) 221-1112

LORAIN COUNTY COMMUNITY COLLEGE
1005 N. Abbe Rd., Elyria 44035 *Type:* Public (district) 2-year *System:* Ohio Board of Regents *Accred.:* 1971/1984 (NCA) *Calendar:* Qtr. plan *Degrees:* A, certificates *Prof. Accred.:* Medical Laboratory Technology (AMA), Nursing (A), Practical Nursing (warning), Radiography *CEO:* Pres. Roy A. Church
Enroll: 7,681   (216) 365-4191

LOURDES COLLEGE
6832 Convent Blvd., Sylvania 43560 *Type:* Private (Roman Catholic) liberal arts *Accred.:* 1964/1992 (NCA) *Calendar:* Sem. plan *Degrees:* A, B, certificates, diplomas *Prof. Accred.:* Nursing (B), Occupational

Therapy Assisting, Social Work (B) *CEO:* Pres. Ann Francis Klimkowski, O.S.F.
Enroll: 1,469   (419) 885-4917

MALONE COLLEGE
515 25th St., N.W., Canton 44709 *Type:* Private (Friends) liberal arts *Accred.:* 1964/1984 (NCA) *Calendar:* Sem. plan *Degrees:* A, B, M *Prof. Accred.:* Nursing (B), Social Work (B) *CEO:* Pres. E. Arthur Self
Enroll: 1,805   (216) 471-8100

MARIETTA COLLEGE
Marietta 45750 *Type:* Private liberal arts *Accred.:* 1913/1986 (NCA) *Calendar:* Sem. plan *Degrees:* A, B, M, certificates, diplomas *Prof. Accred.:* Engineering (petroleum) *CEO:* Pres. Patrick D. McDonough
Enroll: 1,379   (614) 376-4643

MARION TECHNICAL COLLEGE
1467 Mt. Vernon Ave., Marion 43302-5694 *Type:* Public (state) 2-year *System:* Ohio Board of Regents *Accred.:* 1977/1987 (NCA) *Calendar:* Qtr. plan *Degrees:* A, certificates *Prof. Accred.:* Medical Laboratory Technology (AMA), Nursing (A) *CEO:* Pres. John Richard Bryson
Enroll: 1,698   (614) 389-4636

MEDICAL COLLEGE OF OHIO
Caller Service No. 10008, Toledo 43699 *Type:* Public (state) professional *System:* Ohio Board of Regents *Accred.:* 1980/1991 (NCA) *Calendar:* Sem. plan *Degrees:* M, D *Prof. Accred.:* General Practice Residency, Medicine, Nursing (B,M), Physical Therapy, Psychology Internship *CEO:* Pres. Roger C. Bone
Enroll: 383   (419) 381-4267

METHODIST THEOLOGICAL SCHOOL IN OHIO
P.O. Box 1204, 3081 Columbus Pike, Delaware 43015-0931 *Type:* Private (United Methodist) graduate only *Accred.:* 1965/1987 (ATS); 1976/1988 (NCA) *Calendar:* Qtr. plan *Degrees:* M, D *CEO:* Pres. Norman E. Dewire
Enroll: 225   (614) 363-1146

MIAMI-JACOBS JUNIOR COLLEGE OF BUSINESS
P.O. Box 1433, 400 E. Second St., Dayton 45401 *Type:* Private junior *Accred.:* 1957/1986 (ACISC) *Calendar:* Qtr. plan *Degrees:*

A, certificates, diplomas *CEO:* Pres. Charles G. Campbell
                                       (513) 461-5174

MIAMI UNIVERSITY
Oxford 45056 *Type:* Public (state) *System:* Ohio Board of Regents *Accred.:* 1913/1985 (NCA) *Calendar:* Sem. plan *Degrees:* A, B, P, M, D *Prof. Accred.:* Accounting (Type A,C), Art, Business (B,M), Clinical Psychology, Engineering (manufacturing), Home Economics, Music, Nursing (B), Speech-Language Pathology, Teacher Education (e,s,p) *CEO:* Pres. Paul G. Risser
Enroll: 19,806   (513) 529-1809

HAMILTON CAMPUS
1601 Peck Blvd., Hamilton 45011 *Prof. Accred.:* Nursing (A) *CEO:* Exec. Dir. Harriet V. Taylor
                                       (513) 863-8833

MIDDLETOWN CAMPUS
4200 E. University Blvd., Middletown 45042 *Prof. Accred.:* Nursing (A) *CEO:* Exec. Dir. Michael P. Governanti
                                       (513) 424-4444

MOUNT UNION COLLEGE
1972 Clark Ave., Alliance 44601 *Type:* Private (United Methodist) liberal arts *Accred.:* 1913/1992 (NCA) *Calendar:* Sem. plan *Degrees:* B, diplomas *Prof. Accred.:* Music *CEO:* Pres. Harold M. Kolenbrander
Enroll: 1,410   (216) 821-5320

MOUNT VERNON NAZARENE COLLEGE
800 Martinsburg Rd., Mount Vernon 43050 *Type:* Private (Nazarene) liberal arts *Accred.:* 1972/1989 (NCA) *Calendar:* 4-1-4 plan *Degrees:* A, B, M *CEO:* Pres. E. LeBron Fairbanks
Enroll: 1,126   (614) 397-1244

MTI BUSINESS COLLEGE
Ste. 310, 1901 E. 13th St., Cleveland 44114 *Type:* Private business *Accred.:* 1980/1989 (ACISC) *Calendar:* Courses of varying lengths *Degrees:* A, certificates, diplomas *Prof. Accred.:* Medical Assisting (AMA) *CEO:* Pres. Charles M. Kramer
                                       (216) 621-8228

MUSKINGUM AREA TECHNICAL COLLEGE
1555 Newark Rd., Zanesville 43701 *Type:* Public (state) 2-year *System:* Ohio Board of Regents *Accred.:* 1975/1988 (NCA) *Calendar:* Qtr. plan *Degrees:* A, certificates *Prof. Accred.:* Engineering Technology (electrical), Medical Assisting (AMA), Occupational Therapy Assisting, Radiography *CEO:* Pres. Lynn H. Willett
Enroll: 2,701   (614) 454-2501

MUSKINGUM COLLEGE
New Concord 43762 *Type:* Private (United Presbyterian) liberal arts *Accred.:* 1919/1993 (NCA) *Calendar:* Sem. plan *Degrees:* B, M *Prof. Accred.:* Music *CEO:* Pres. Samuel W. Speck, Jr.
Enroll: 1,092   (614) 826-8211

NORTH CENTRAL TECHNICAL COLLEGE
P.O. Box 698, Mansfield 44901-0698 *Type:* Public (state) 2-year *System:* Ohio Board of Regents *Accred.:* 1976/1988 (NCA) *Calendar:* Qtr. plan *Degrees:* A, certificates *Prof. Accred.:* Nursing (A), Radiography, Respiratory Therapy *CEO:* Pres. Byron E. Kee
Enroll: 2,966   (419) 755-4800

NORTHEASTERN OHIO UNIVERSITIES COLLEGE OF MEDICINE
4209 State Rte. 44, P.O. Box 95, Rootstown 44272-0095 *Type:* Public (state) professional *System:* Ohio Board of Regents *Calendar:* Sem. plan *Degrees:* P *Prof. Accred.:* Medicine, Psychology Internship *CEO:* Pres. and Dean Robert S. Blacklow, M.D.
Enroll: 420   (216) 325-2511

NORTHWEST TECHNICAL COLLEGE
22-600 State Rte. 34, Archbold 43502 *Type:* Public (state) 2-year *System:* Ohio Board of Regents *Accred.:* 1977/1989 (NCA) *Calendar:* Qtr. plan *Degrees:* A, certificates *Prof. Accred.:* Engineering Technology (electrical) *CEO:* Pres. Larry G. McDougle
Enroll: 2,054   (419) 267-5511

NORTHWESTERN COLLEGE
1441 N. Cable Rd., Lima 45805 *Type:* Private *Accred.:* 1987/1991 (NCA) *Calendar:* Qtr. plan *Degrees:* A, diplomas *CEO:* Pres. Loren R. Jarvis
Enroll: 1,331   (419) 227-3141

NOTRE DAME COLLEGE
4545 College Rd., South Euclid 44121 *Type:* Private (Roman Catholic) liberal arts for women *Accred.:* 1931/1991 (NCA) *Calendar:* Sem. plan *Degrees:* A, B, M, certificates, diplomas *CEO:* Pres. Marla Loehr, S.N.D.
Enroll: 810   (216) 381-1680

OBERLIN COLLEGE
Oberlin 44074 *Type:* Private liberal arts *Accred.:* 1913/1988 (NCA) *Calendar:* 4-1-4 plan *Degrees:* B, M, diplomas *Prof. Accred.:* Music *CEO:* Pres. S. Frederick Starr
Enroll: 2,818   (216) 775-8400

OHIO COLLEGE OF PODIATRIC MEDICINE
10515 Carnegie Ave., Cleveland 44106 *Type:* Private professional *Accred.:* 1987/1992 (NCA) *Calendar:* Sem. plan *Degrees:* D *Prof. Accred.:* Podiatry *CEO:* Pres. Thomas V. Melillo
Enroll: 374   (216) 231-3300

OHIO DOMINICAN COLLEGE
1216 Sunbury Rd., Columbus 43219 *Type:* Private (Roman Catholic) liberal arts *Accred.:* 1934/1988 (NCA) *Calendar:* Sem. plan *Degrees:* A, B, certificates *CEO:* Pres. Mary Andrew Matesich, O.P.
Enroll: 1,510   (614) 251-4690

OHIO NORTHERN UNIVERSITY
S. Main St., Ada 45810 *Type:* Private (United Methodist) *Accred.:* 1958/1985 (NCA) *Calendar:* Qtr. plan *Degrees:* B, D *Prof. Accred.:* Engineering (civil, electrical, mechanical), Law, Music *CEO:* Pres. DeBow Freed
Enroll: 2,872   (419) 772-2030

THE OHIO STATE UNIVERSITY
190 N. Oval Dr., Columbus 43210 *Type:* Public (state) *System:* Ohio Board of Regents *Accred.:* 1913/1987 (NCA) *Calendar:* Qtr. plan *Degrees:* A, B, M, D *Prof. Accred.:* Accounting (Type A,B), Art, Audiology, Blood Bank Technology, Business (B,M), Clinical Psychology, Combined Prosthodontics, Community Health/Preventive Medicine, Counseling Psychology, Dance, Dental Hygiene, Dentistry, Dietetics (coordinated), Endodontics, Engineering Technology (surveying), Engineering (aerospace, agricultural, ceramic, chemical, civil, electri-

cal, industrial, mechanical, metallurgical, welding), General Dentistry, General Practice Residency, Health Services Administration, Interior Design, Journalism (B,M), Landscape Architecture (B,M), Law, Medical Record Administration, Medical Technology, Medicine, Music, Nuclear Medicine Technology, Nursing (B,M), Occupational Therapy, Optometry, Oral Pathology, Oral and Maxillofacial Surgery, Orthodontics, Pediatric Dentistry, Perfusion, Periodontics, Physical Therapy, Planning (M), Psychology Internship, Public Administration, Radiation Therapy Technology, Radiography, Rehabilitation Counseling, Respiratory Therapy, Social Work (B,M), Speech-Language Pathology, Teacher Education (e,s,p), Theatre, Veterinary Medicine (limited) *CEO:* Pres. E. Gordon Gee
Enroll: 52,183   (614) 292-6446

AGRICULTURAL TECHNICAL INSTITUTE
1328 Dover Rd., Wooster 44691 *Accred.:* 1978/1993 (NCA) *Degrees:* A *CEO:* Dir. Dan D. Garrison
Enroll: 729   (216) 264-3911

LIMA CAMPUS
4240 Campus Dr., Lima 45804 *CEO:* Dean/Dir. Violette I. Meek
       (419) 221-1641

MANSFIELD CAMPUS
1680 University Dr., Mansfield 44906 *CEO:* Dean/Dir. John O. Riedl
       (419) 755-4011

MARION CAMPUS
1465 Mount Vernon Ave., Marion 43302 *CEO:* Acting Dean and Dir. Lynn A. Corbin
       (614) 389-2361

NEWARK CAMPUS
University Dr., Newark 43055 *CEO:* Dean/Dir. Julius S. Greenstein
       (614) 366-3321

OHIO UNIVERSITY
Athens 45701 *Type:* Public (state) *System:* Ohio Board of Regents *Accred.:* 1913/1984 (NCA) *Calendar:* Qtr. plan *Degrees:* A, B, M, D, certificates *Prof. Accred.:* Audiology, Business (B,M), Clinical Psychology, Counseling, Dance, Engineering (chemical, civil,

electrical, industrial, mechanical), Home Economics, Journalism (B,M), Music, Nursing (B), Osteopathy, Physical Therapy, Rehabilitation Counseling, Social Work (B), Speech-Language Pathology, Teacher Education (e,s,p) *CEO:* Pres. Charles J. Ping
Enroll: 27,249   (614) 593-1000

CHILLICOTHE CAMPUS
Chillicothe 45601 *CEO:* Dean Delbert E. Meyer
       (614) 774-7200

EASTERN CAMPUS
St. Clairsville 43950 *CEO:* Dean James W. Newton
       (614) 695-1720

IRONTON CAMPUS
1701 S. Seventh St., Ironton 45638 *CEO:* Dean Bill W. Dingus
       (614) 533-4600

LANCASTER CAMPUS
1570 Granville Pike, Lancaster 43130 *CEO:* Dean Raymond S. Wilkes
       (614) 654-6711

ZANESVILLE CAMPUS
Zanesville 43701 *Prof. Accred.:* Nursing (A) *CEO:* Dean Craig D. Laubenthal
       (614) 453-0762

OHIO VALLEY BUSINESS COLLEGE
P.O. Box 7000, 500 Maryland Ave., East Liverpool 43920 *Type:* Private business *Accred.:* 1985/1989 (ACISC) *Calendar:* Courses of varying lengths *Degrees:* A *Prof. Accred.:* Medical Assisting (AMA) *CEO:* Pres. Debra Sanford
       (216) 385-1070

OHIO WESLEYAN UNIVERSITY
61 S. Sanusky St., Delaware 43015 *Type:* Private (United Methodist) liberal arts *Accred.:* 1913/1989 (NCA) *Calendar:* 4-1-4 plan *Degrees:* B *Prof. Accred.:* Music, Nursing (B) *CEO:* Acting Pres. William C. Louthan
Enroll: 1,932   (614) 368-2000

OTTERBEIN COLLEGE
Westerville 43081 *Type:* Private (United Methodist) liberal arts *Accred.:* 1913/1985 (NCA) *Calendar:* 3-3 plan *Degrees:* B, M

Prof. Accred.: Music, Nursing (A,B), Teacher Education (e,s) *CEO:* Pres. C. Brent DeVore
Enroll: 2,532   (614) 898-1656

OWENS TECHNICAL COLLEGE
P.O. Box 10000, 30335 Oregon Rd., Toledo 43699 *Type:* Public (state) 2-year *System:* Ohio Board of Regents *Accred.:* 1976/1991 (NCA) *Calendar:* Sem. plan *Degrees:* A, certificates *Prof. Accred.:* Dental Hygiene, Diagnostic Medical Sonography, Engineering Technology (architectural, bioengineering, computer, electrical, electromechanical, industrial, mechanical, mechanical drafting/design), Nursing (A), Physical Therapy Assisting, Radiation Therapy Technology, Radiography, Surgical Technology *CEO:* Pres. Daniel H. Brown
Enroll: 10,159   (419) 666-0580

BRANCH CAMPUS
300 Davis St., Findlay 45840 *Prof. Accred.:* Engineering Technology (mechanical drafting/design) *CEO:* Exec. Dir. Kathleen Brubaker
(419) 423-6827

PONTIFICAL COLLEGE JOSEPHINUM
7625 N. High St., Columbus 43235 *Type:* Private (Roman Catholic) liberal arts and professional *Accred.:* 1970/1991 (ATS); 1977/1991 (NCA) *Calendar:* Sem. plan *Degrees:* B, M *CEO:* Pres./Rector Blase J. Cupich
Enroll: 141   (614) 885-5585

RABBINICAL COLLEGE OF TELSHE
28400 Euclid Ave., Wickliffe 44092-2523 *Type:* Private professional *Accred.:* 1974/1989 (AARTS) *Calendar:* Sem. plan *Degrees:* M, D *CEO:* Pres. M. Gifter
Enroll: 165   (216) 943-5300

RAYMOND WALTERS COLLEGE
9555 Plainfield Rd., Cincinnati 45236 *Type:* Public (state) *System:* Ohio Board of Regents *Accred.:* 1969/1989 (NCA) *Calendar:* Qtr. plan *Degrees:* A, certificates *Prof. Accred.:* Dental Hygiene, Medicine, Nursing (A), Veterinary Technology *CEO:* Acting Dean Roger J. Barry
Enroll: 4,230   (513) 745-5600

ST. MARY SEMINARY
28700 Euclid Ave., Wickliffe 44092-2585 *Type:* Private (Roman Catholic) graduate only *Accred.:* 1970/1985 (ATS); 1981/1986 (NCA) *Calendar:* Qtr. plan *Degrees:* M *CEO:* Pres./Rector Allan R. Laubenthal
Enroll: 69   (216) 943-7600

SHAWNEE STATE UNIVERSITY
940 Second St., Portsmouth 45662 *Type:* Public (state) 2-year *System:* Ohio Board of Regents *Accred.:* 1975/1993 (NCA) *Calendar:* Qtr. plan *Degrees:* A, B, certificates *Prof. Accred.:* Dental Hygiene, Medical Laboratory Technology (AMA), Occupational Therapy Assisting, Physical Therapy Assisting, Radiography, Respiratory Therapy *CEO:* Pres. Clive C. Veri
Enroll: 3,636   (614) 355-3205

SINCLAIR COMMUNITY COLLEGE
444 W. Third St., Dayton 45402 *Type:* Public (district) 2-year *System:* Ohio Board of Regents *Accred.:* 1970/1988 (NCA) *Calendar:* Qtr. plan *Degrees:* A, certificates *Prof. Accred.:* Dental Hygiene, Engineering Technology (electrical, industrial, mechanical, packaging), Medical Record Technology, Nursing (A), Occupational Therapy Assisting, Physical Therapy Assisting, Radiography, Respiratory Therapy, Surgical Technology *CEO:* Pres. David H. Ponitz
Enroll: 20,800   (513) 226-2500

SOUTHEASTERN BUSINESS COLLEGE
1855 Western Ave., Chillicothe 45601 *Type:* Private business *Accred.:* 1976/1986 (ACISC) *Calendar:* Courses of varying lengths *Degrees:* A *CEO:* Exec. Dir. John T. Danicki
(614) 774-6300

BRANCH CAMPUS
420 E. Main St., Jackson 45640 *Accred.:* 1976/1986 (ACISC) *CEO:* Dir. Janet Travis
(614) 286-1554

BRANCH CAMPUS
1522 Sheridan Dr., Lancaster 43130 *Accred.:* 1985/1986 (ACISC) *CEO:* Dir. Alex Bosserman
(614) 687-6126

BRANCH CAMPUS
3879 Rhodes Ave., New Boston 45662 *Accred.:* 1981/1986 (ACISC) *CEO:* Dir. Anita Thompson

(614) 456-4124

SOUTHEASTERN BUSINESS COLLEGE
Ste. 312, 529 Jackson Pike, Gallipolis 45631 *Type:* Private business *Accred.:* 1983/ 1989 (ACISC) *Calendar:* Courses of varying lengths *Degrees:* A *CEO:* Dir. Brent Patterson

(614) 446-4367

SOUTHEASTERN BUSINESS COLLEGE
1907 N. Ridge Rd., Lorain 44055 *Type:* Private business *Accred.:* 1991 (ACISC) *Calendar:* Courses of varying lengths *Degrees:* A *CEO:* Dir. Mary B. Kelleher

(216) 277-0021

BRANCH CAMPUS
4020 Milan Rd., Sandusky 44870 *Accred.:* 1992 (ACISC) *CEO:* Dir. Judith Shahan

(419) 627-8345

SOUTHERN OHIO COLLEGE
1055 Laidlaw Ave., Cincinnati 45237 *Type:* Private junior *Accred.:* 1964/1990 (ACISC); 1983/1992 (NCA probational) *Calendar:* Qtr. plan *Degrees:* A, certificates *Prof. Accred.:* Medical Assisting (AMA) *CEO:* Pres. Stephen Coppock
Enroll: 1,501

(513) 242-3791

BRANCH CAMPUS
2791 Mogadore Rd., Akron 44312 *Accred.:* 1980/1990 (ACISC) *Prof. Accred.:* Medical Assisting (AMA) *CEO:* Dir. Richard M. Thome

(216) 733-8766

BRANCH CAMPUS
4641 Bach La., Fairfield 45014 *Accred.:* 1983/1990 (ACISC) *Prof. Accred.:* Medical Assisting (AMA) *CEO:* Dir. Ruth A. Wysong

(513) 829-7100

NORTHERN KENTUCKY CAMPUS
309 Buttermilk Pike, Fort Mitchell, KY 41017 *Accred.:* 1988/1990 (ACISC) *CEO:* Dir. Terry Queeno

(606) 341-5627

SOUTHERN STATE COMMUNITY COLLEGE
200 Hobart Dr., Hillsboro 45133 *Type:* Public (state) 2-year *System:* Ohio Board of Regents *Accred.:* 1981/1990 (NCA) *Calendar:* Qtr. plan *Degrees:* A, certificates *Prof. Accred.:* Nursing (A) *CEO:* Pres. George R. McCormick
Enroll: 1,654

(513) 393-3431

SOUTHWESTERN COLLEGE OF BUSINESS
9910 Princeton-Glendale Rd., Cincinnati 45246 *Type:* Private business *Accred.:* 1982/ 1991 (ACISC) *Calendar:* Qtr. plan *Degrees:* A *Prof. Accred.:* Medical Assisting *CEO:* Dir. Susan Hatfield

(513) 874-0432

SOUTHWESTERN COLLEGE OF BUSINESS
225 W. First St., Dayton 45402 *Type:* Private business *Accred.:* 1973/1987 (ACISC) *Calendar:* Qtr. plan *Degrees:* A, certificates, diplomas *Prof. Accred.:* Medical Assisting *CEO:* Dir. Sharon Winstead

(513) 224-0061

BRANCH CAMPUS
717 Race St., Cincinnati 45202 *Accred.:* 1982/1991 (ACISC) *Prof. Accred.:* Medical Assisting *CEO:* Dir. Paul Bittner

(513) 421-3212

BRANCH CAMPUS
631 S. Briel Blvd., Middletown 45044 *Accred.:* 1982/1991 (ACISC) *Prof. Accred.:* Medical Assisting *CEO:* Dir. Rene Osterberger

(513) 423-3346

STARK TECHNICAL COLLEGE
6200 Frank Ave., N.W., Canton 44720 *Type:* Public (state) 2-year *System:* Ohio Board of Regents *Accred.:* 1976/1991 (NCA) *Calendar:* Qtr. plan *Degrees:* A, certificates *Prof. Accred.:* Engineering Technology (civil/construction, electrical, mechanical, mechanical drafting/design), Medical Assisting (AMA), Medical Laboratory Technology (AMA), Medical Record Technology, Occupational Therapy Assisting, Physical Therapy Assisting, Respiratory Therapy, Respiratory Therapy Technology *CEO:* Pres. John J. McGrath, Jr.
Enroll: 4,537

(216) 494-6170

STAUTZENBERGER COLLEGE—CENTRAL
5405 Southwyck Blvd., Toledo 43614 *Type:* Private business *Accred.:* 1987 (ACISC) *Calendar:* Courses of varying lengths *Degrees:* A, certificates, diplomas *CEO:* Dir. Kevin Rhea
(419) 474-2220

STAUTZENBERGER COLLEGE—FINDLAY
Ste. 150, 1637 Tiffin Ave., Findlay 54840 *Type:* Private business *Accred.:* 1986/1989 (ACISC) *Calendar:* Courses of varying lengths *Degrees:* A, certificates, diplomas *CEO:* Dir. Craig Burnside
(419) 423-2211

STAUTZENBERGER COLLEGE—SOUTH
5405 Southwyck Blvd., Toledo 43614 *Type:* Private business *Accred.:* 1962/1986 (ACISC) *Calendar:* Courses of varying lengths *Degrees:* A, certificates, diplomas *CEO:* Pres./Owner Charles Hawes
(419) 866-0261

TERRA TECHNICAL COLLEGE
2830 Napoleon Rd., Fremont 43420 *Type:* Public (state) 2-year *System:* Ohio Board of Regents *Accred.:* 1975/1987 (NCA) *Calendar:* Qtr. plan *Degrees:* A, certificates *CEO:* Pres. Charlotte J. Lee
Enroll: 2,940   (419) 334-8400

TIFFIN UNIVERSITY
155 Miami St., Tiffin 44883 *Type:* Private *Accred.:* 1985/1990 (NCA) *Calendar:* Sem. plan *Degrees:* A, B, M, certificates *CEO:* Pres. George Kidd, Jr.
Enroll: 1,041   (419) 447-6442

TRINITY LUTHERAN SEMINARY
2199 E. Main St., Columbus 43209-2334 *Type:* Private (Evangelical Lutheran) graduate only *Accred.:* 1940/1992 (ATS); 1974/1992 (NCA) *Calendar:* Sem. plan *Degrees:* M, D *CEO:* Pres. Dennis A. Anderson
Enroll: 238   (614) 235-4136

TRUMBULL BUSINESS COLLEGE
3200 Ridge Rd., Warren 44484 *Type:* Private business *Accred.:* 1976/1988 (ACISC) *Calendar:* Courses of varying lengths *Degrees:* A, certificates, diplomas *CEO:* Pres. Dennis R. Griffith
(216) 369-3200

THE UNION INSTITUTE
440 E. McMillan St., Cincinnati 45206-1947 *Type:* Private *Accred.:* 1985/1990 (NCA) *Calendar:* Qtr. plan *Degrees:* B, D *CEO:* Pres. Robert T. Conley
Enroll: 1,444   (513) 861-6400

UNITED THEOLOGICAL SEMINARY
1810 Harvard Blvd., Dayton 45406 *Type:* Private (United Methodist) graduate only *Accred.:* 1938/1990 (ATS); 1975/1991 (NCA) *Calendar:* 4-1-4 plan *Degrees:* M, D *CEO:* Pres. Daryl Ward
Enroll: 582   (513) 278-5817

THE UNIVERSITY OF AKRON
Akron 44325 *Type:* Public (state) *System:* Ohio Board of Regents *Accred.:* 1914/1987 (NCA) *Calendar:* Sem. plan *Degrees:* A, B, M, D, certificates *Prof. Accred.:* Accounting (Type A,B), Art, Audiology, Business (B,M), Counseling, Counseling Psychology, Dance, Dietetics (coordinated), Engineering Technology (civil/construction, electrical, mechanical, surveying), Engineering (chemical, civil, electrical, mechanical), Home Economics, Law, Medical Assisting (AMA), Music, Nurse Anesthesia Education, Nursing (B,M), Psychology Internship, Public Administration, Respiratory Therapy, Social Work (B), Speech-Language Pathology, Surgical Technology, Teacher Education (e,s,p) *CEO:* Pres. Peggy Gordon Elliott
Enroll: 27,079   (216) 972-7111

UNIVERSITY OF CINCINNATI
2624 Clifton Ave., Cincinnati 45221 *Type:* Public (state) *System:* Ohio Board of Regents *Accred.:* 1913/1989 (NCA) *Calendar:* Qtr. plan *Degrees:* A, B, P, M, D, certificates, diplomas *Prof. Accred.:* Art, Audiology, Blood Bank Technology, Business (B,M), Clinical Psychology, Construction Education (B), Counseling, Dental Hygiene, Dietetics (internship), EMT-Paramedic, Engineering Technology (architectural, chemical, civil/construction, electrical, industrial hygiene, manufacturing, mechanical), Engineering (aerospace, chemical, civil, computer, electrical, engineering mechanics, environmental/sanitary, industrial, materials, mechanical, nuclear), Interior Design, Law, Medical Technology, Music, Nuclear Medicine Technology, Nurse Anesthesia Educa-

tion, Nursing (B,M), Oral and Maxillofacial Surgery, Physical Therapy Assisting, Planning (B,M), Psychology Internship, Radiation Therapy Technology, Radiography, School Psychology, Social Work (B,M), Speech-Language Pathology, Teacher Education (e,s,p), Theatre (associate) *CEO:* Pres. Joseph A. Steger
Enroll: 34,660   (513) 556-6000

UNIVERSITY OF DAYTON
300 College Park Ave., Dayton 45469 *Type:* Private (Roman Catholic) *Accred.:* 1928/ 1988 (NCA) *Calendar:* Tri. plan *Degrees:* A, B, M, D, certificates *Prof. Accred.:* Business (B,M), Computer Science, Engineering Technology (electrical, industrial, manufacturing, mechanical), Engineering (chemical, civil, electrical, mechanical), Law, Medical Technology, Music, Teacher Education (e,s,p) *CEO:* Pres. Raymond L. Fitz, S.M.
Enroll: 10,658   (513) 229-1000

UNIVERSITY OF FINDLAY
1000 N. Main St., Findlay 45840 *Type:* Private (Churches of God) liberal arts *Accred.:* 1933/1984 (NCA) *Calendar:* Sem. plan *Degrees:* A, B, M *Prof. Accred.:* Nuclear Medicine Technology, Teacher Education (e,s) *CEO:* Pres. Kenneth E. Zirkle
Enroll: 3,284   (419) 422-4510

UNIVERSITY OF RIO GRANDE
E. College Ave., Rio Grande 45674 *Type:* Private liberal arts *Accred.:* 1969/1988 (NCA) *Calendar:* Qtr. plan *Degrees:* A, B, M, certificates *Prof. Accred.:* Medical Laboratory Technology (AMA), Nursing (A), Social Work (B) *CEO:* Pres. Barry M. Dorsey
Enroll: 2,160   (614) 245-5353

UNIVERSITY OF TOLEDO
2801 W. Bancroft St., Toledo 43606 *Type:* Public (state) *System:* Ohio Board of Regents *Accred.:* 1922/1992 (NCA) *Calendar:* Qtr. plan *Degrees:* A, B, P, M, D, certificates *Prof. Accred.:* Business (B,M), Clinical Psychology, Computer Science, Counseling, Engineering Technology (civil/construction, electrical, industrial, mechanical, mechanical drafting/design), Engineering (chemical, civil, computer, electrical, engineering physics/science, industrial, mechanical), Law, Medical Assisting (AMA), Music,

Nursing (A,B,M), Physical Therapy, Public Administration, Recreation and Leisure Services, Respiratory Therapy, Respiratory Therapy Technology, Social Work (B), Speech-Language Pathology, Teacher Education (e,s,p) *CEO:* Pres. Frank E. Horton
Enroll: 24,541   (419) 537-2696

URBANA UNIVERSITY
One College Way, Urbana 43078 *Type:* Private (Swedenborgian) liberal arts *Accred.:* 1975/1991 (NCA) *Calendar:* Sem. plan *Degrees:* A, B *CEO:* Pres. Francis E. Hazard
Enroll: 952   (513) 652-1301

URSULINE COLLEGE
2550 Lander Rd., Pepper Pike 44124 *Type:* Private (Roman Catholic) liberal arts primarily for women *Accred.:* 1931/1992 (NCA) *Calendar:* Sem. plan *Degrees:* B, M, certificates *Prof. Accred.:* Nursing (B), Social Work (B-candidate) *CEO:* Pres. Anne Marie Diederich, O.S.U.
Enroll: 1,588   (216) 449-4200

WALSH UNIVERSITY
2020 Easton St., N.W., Canton 44720 *Type:* Private (Roman Catholic) liberal arts *Accred.:* 1970/1990 (NCA) *Calendar:* Sem. plan *Degrees:* A, B, M *Prof. Accred.:* Nursing (A,B) *CEO:* Pres. Richard J. Mucowski, O.F.M.
Enroll: 1,550   (216) 499-7090

WASHINGTON STATE COMMUNITY COLLEGE
710 Colegate Dr., Marietta 45750 *Type:* Public (state) 2-year *System:* Ohio Board of Regents *Accred.:* 1979/1987 (NCA) *Calendar:* Qtr. plan *Degrees:* A, certificates *Prof. Accred.:* Medical Laboratory Technology (AMA) *CEO:* Pres. Carson K. Miller
Enroll: 2,108   (614) 374-8716

WAYNE COLLEGE
1901 Smucker Rd., Orrville 44667 *Type:* Public (state) *System:* Ohio Board of Regents *Accred.:* 1972/1991 (NCA) *Calendar:* Qtr. plan *Degrees:* A, certificates *CEO:* Dean Tyrone M. Turning
Enroll: 1,438   (216) 683-2010

WILBERFORCE UNIVERSITY
Wilberforce 45384 *Type:* Private (African Methodist Episcopal) liberal arts *Accred.:* 1993 (ATS candidate); 1939/1992 (NCA)

Calendar: Tri. plan *Degrees:* B *CEO:* Pres. John L. Henderson
Enroll: 844 (513) 376-2911

WILMINGTON COLLEGE
P.O. Box 1185, Wilmington 45177 *Type:* Private (Friends) liberal arts *Accred.:* 1944/1988 (NCA) *Calendar:* Sem. plan *Degrees:* A, B *CEO:* Pres. Neil A. Thorburn
Enroll: 2,028 (513) 382-6661

WINEBRENNER THEOLOGICAL SEMINARY
701 E. Melrose Ave., P.O. Box 478, Findlay 45839 *Type:* Private (Churches of God) graduate only *Accred.:* 1991 (ATS); 1986/1991 (NCA) *Calendar:* Sem. plan *Degrees:* M, certificates, diplomas *CEO:* Pres. David E. Draper
Enroll: 72 (419) 422-4824

WITTENBERG UNIVERSITY
P.O. Box 720, Springfield 45501 *Type:* Private (Lutheran) *Accred.:* 1916/1987 (NCA) *Calendar:* 3-3 plan *Degrees:* B *Prof. Accred.:* Music *CEO:* Pres. William Andrew Kinnison
Enroll: 2,135 (513) 327-6231

WRIGHT STATE UNIVERSITY
3640 Colonel Glenn Hwy., Dayton 45435 *Type:* Public (state) *System:* Ohio Board of Regents *Accred.:* 1968/1986 (NCA) *Calendar:* Qtr. plan *Degrees:* A, B, P, M, D, certificates *Prof. Accred.:* Accounting (Type A), Business (B,M), Clinical Psychology, Computer Science, Counseling, Engineering (bioengineering, computer, electrical, engineering physics/science, materials, mechanical), Medical Technology, Medicine, Music, Nursing (B,M), Psychology Internship, Rehabilitation Counseling, Social Work (B), Teacher Education (e,s,p) *CEO:* Pres. Harley E. Flack
Enroll: 17,657 (513) 873-3333

LAKE CAMPUS
7600 State Rte. 703, Celina 45822 *CEO:* Dean Donald E. Krischak
(419) 586-2365

XAVIER UNIVERSITY
3800 Victory Pkwy., Cincinnati 45207 *Type:* Private (Roman Catholic) *Accred.:* 1925/1989 (NCA) *Calendar:* Sem. plan *Degrees:* A, B, M *Prof. Accred.:* Health Services Administration, Nursing (A,B), Radiography, Social Work (B) *CEO:* Pres. James E. Hoff, S.J.
Enroll: 6,373 (513) 745-3000

YOUNGSTOWN STATE UNIVERSITY
410 Wick Ave., Youngstown 44555 *Type:* Public (state) *System:* Ohio Board of Regents *Accred.:* 1945/1988 (NCA) *Calendar:* Qtr. plan *Degrees:* A, B, M, D, certificates *Prof. Accred.:* Counseling, Dental Hygiene, Dietetics (coordinated), EMT-Paramedic, Engineering Technology (civil/construction, electrical, mechanical), Engineering (chemical, civil, electrical, industrial, mechanical), Medical Laboratory Technology (AMA), Music, Nursing (B), Respiratory Therapy, Social Work (B), Teacher Education (e,s,p) *CEO:* Pres. Leslie H. Cochran
Enroll: 14,806 (216) 742-3000

OKLAHOMA

BACONE COLLEGE
2299 Old Bacone Rd., Muskogee 74403-1597 *Type:* Private (Baptist) junior *Accred.:* 1965/1989 (NCA) *Calendar:* Sem. plan *Degrees:* A, certificates *Prof. Accred.:* Nursing (A), Radiography *CEO:* Pres. Dennis Tanner
Enroll: 686   (918) 683-4581

BARTLESVILLE WESLEYAN COLLEGE
2201 Silver Lake Rd., Bartlesville 74006 *Type:* Private (Wesleyan) liberal arts *Accred.:* 1978/1991 (NCA) *Calendar:* Sem. plan *Degrees:* A, B, certificates *CEO:* Pres. Paul R. Mills
Enroll: 502   (918) 333-6151

CAMERON UNIVERSITY
2800 Gore Blvd., Lawton 73505 *Type:* Public (state) liberal arts and professional *System:* Oklahoma State Regents for Higher Education *Accred.:* 1973/1991 (NCA) *Calendar:* Sem. plan *Degrees:* A, B, M *Prof. Accred.:* Music, Nursing (A), Teacher Education (e,s,p) *CEO:* Pres. Don Davis
Enroll: 5,809   (405) 581-2200

CARL ALBERT STATE COLLEGE
1507 S. McKenna, Poteau 74953-5208 *Type:* Public (state) junior *System:* Oklahoma State Regents for Higher Education *Accred.:* 1978/1993 (NCA) *Calendar:* Sem. plan *Degrees:* A, certificates *Prof. Accred.:* Nursing (A) *CEO:* Pres. Joe E. White
Enroll: 2,086   (918) 647-8660

CONNORS STATE COLLEGE
Rte. 1, Box 1000, Warner 74469 *Type:* Public (state) junior *System:* Oklahoma State Regents for Higher Education *Accred.:* 1963/1990 (NCA) *Calendar:* Sem. plan *Degrees:* A, certificates *Prof. Accred.:* Nursing (A) *CEO:* Pres. Carl O. Westbrook
Enroll: 2,383   (918) 463-2931

EAST CENTRAL UNIVERSITY
Ada 74820 *Type:* Public (state) liberal arts and teachers *System:* Oklahoma State Regents for Higher Education *Accred.:* 1922/1992 (NCA) *Calendar:* Sem. plan *Degrees:* B, M *Prof. Accred.:* Medical Record Administration, Nursing (B), Rehabilitation Counseling, Social Work (B), Teacher Education (e,s) *CEO:* Pres. Bill S. Cole
Enroll: 4,473   (405) 332-8000

EASTERN OKLAHOMA STATE COLLEGE
1301 W. Main St., Wilburton 74578 *Type:* Public (state) junior *System:* Oklahoma State Regents for Higher Education *Accred.:* 1954/1986 (NCA) *Calendar:* Sem. plan *Degrees:* A, certificates *Prof. Accred.:* Nursing (A) *CEO:* Pres. Bill H. Hill
Enroll: 2,041   (918) 465-2361

LANGSTON UNIVERSITY
P.O. Box 907, Langston 73050-0907 *Type:* Public (state) liberal arts and professional *System:* Oklahoma State Regents for Higher Education *Accred.:* 1948/1987 (NCA) *Calendar:* Sem. plan *Degrees:* B, M *Prof. Accred.:* Nursing (B), Physical Therapy, Teacher Education (e,s) *CEO:* Pres. Ernest L. Holloway
Enroll: 3,710   (405) 466-3201

MID-AMERICA BIBLE COLLEGE
3500 S.W. 119th St., Oklahoma City 73170-9797 *Type:* Private (Church of God) *Accred.:* 1968/1988 (AABC); 1985/1992 (NCA) *Calendar:* Sem. plan *Degrees:* A, B *CEO:* Pres. Forrest Robinson
Enroll: 290   (405) 691-3800

MURRAY STATE COLLEGE
1100 S. Murray, Tishomingo 73460 *Type:* Public (state) junior *System:* Oklahoma State Regents for Higher Education *Accred.:* 1964/1984 (NCA) *Calendar:* Sem. plan *Degrees:* A, certificates *Prof. Accred.:* Nursing (A), Veterinary Technology *CEO:* Pres. Clyde R. Kindell
Enroll: 1,667   (405) 371-2371

NORTHEASTERN OKLAHOMA A&M COLLEGE
200 I St. N.E., Miami 74354 *Type:* Public (state) junior *System:* Oklahoma State Regents for Higher Education *Accred.:* 1925/1987 (NCA) *Calendar:* Sem. plan *Degrees:* A, certificates *Prof. Accred.:* Medical Laboratory Technology (AMA), Nursing (A), Surgical Technology *CEO:* Pres. Jerry D. Carroll
Enroll: 2,725   (918) 542-8441

NORTHEASTERN STATE UNIVERSITY
Tahlequah 74464 *Type:* Public (state) liberal arts and teachers *System:* Oklahoma State Regents for Higher Education *Accred.:* 1922/1992 (NCA) *Calendar:* Sem. plan *Degrees:* B, M, D, certificates *Prof. Accred.:* Nursing (B), Optometry, Social Work (B), Teacher Education (e,s,p) *CEO:* Pres. W. Roger Webb
Enroll: 9,527   (918) 456-5511

NORTHERN OKLAHOMA COLLEGE
P.O. Box 310, Tonkawa 74653-0310 *Type:* Public (state) junior *System:* Oklahoma State Regents for Higher Education *Accred.:* 1948/1988 (NCA) *Calendar:* Sem. plan *Degrees:* A, certificates *Prof. Accred.:* Nursing (A) *CEO:* Pres. Joe M. Kinzer, Jr.
Enroll: 2,212   (405) 628-6200

NORTHWESTERN OKLAHOMA STATE UNIVERSITY
709 Oklahoma Blvd., Alva 73717 *Type:* Public (state) liberal arts and teachers *System:* Oklahoma State Regents for Higher Education *Accred.:* 1922/1984 (NCA) *Calendar:* Sem. plan *Degrees:* B, M, certificates *Prof. Accred.:* Nursing (B), Teacher Education (e,s) *CEO:* Pres. Joe J. Struckle
Enroll: 2,136   (405) 327-1700

OKLAHOMA BAPTIST UNIVERSITY
500 W. University, Shawnee 74801 *Type:* Private (Southern Baptist) liberal arts and professional *Accred.:* 1952/1988 (NCA) *Calendar:* 4-1-4 plan *Degrees:* A, B, M, certificates, diplomas *Prof. Accred.:* Music, Nursing (B), Teacher Education (e,s) *CEO:* Pres. Bob R. Agee
Enroll: 2,260   (405) 275-2850

OKLAHOMA CHRISTIAN UNIVERSITY OF SCIENCE AND ARTS
Box 11000, Oklahoma City 73136 *Type:* Private (Church of Christ) liberal arts *Accred.:* 1966/1986 (NCA) *Calendar:* Tri. plan *Degrees:* B, M *Prof. Accred.:* Engineering (electrical, mechanical), Music (associate), Teacher Education (e,s) *CEO:* Pres. J. Terry Johnson
Enroll: 1,636   (405) 425-5000

OKLAHOMA CITY COMMUNITY COLLEGE
7777 S. May Ave., Oklahoma City 73159 *Type:* Public (district) junior *System:* Okla-

homa State Regents for Higher Education *Accred.:* 1977/1992 (NCA) *Calendar:* 4-1-4 plan *Degrees:* A, certificates *Prof. Accred.:* Nursing (A), Occupational Therapy Assisting, Physical Therapy Assisting *CEO:* Pres. Bob D. Gaines
Enroll: 10,048   (405) 682-1611

OKLAHOMA CITY UNIVERSITY
2501 N. Blackwelder Ave., Oklahoma City 73106 *Type:* Private (United Methodist) *Accred.:* 1951/1983 (NCA) *Calendar:* Sem. plan *Degrees:* A, B, M, D *Prof. Accred.:* Law (ABA only), Music, Nursing (B) *CEO:* Pres. Jerald C. Walker
FTE Enroll: 3,485   (405) 521-5032

OKLAHOMA JUNIOR COLLEGE
3232 N.W. 65th St., Oklahoma City 73116 *Type:* Private business *Accred.:* 1989 (ACISC); 1991 (NCA candidate) *Calendar:* Tri. plan *Degrees:* A, certificates, diplomas *CEO:* Dir. Cameron Faili
FTE Enroll: 621   (405) 848-3400

OKLAHOMA JUNIOR COLLEGE
6019 S. 66th E. Ave., #107, Tulsa 74145-9209 *Type:* Private junior *Calendar:* Sem. plan *Degrees:* A *Prof. Accred.:* Medical Assisting *CEO:* Pres. Joel D. Boyd
                                   (918) 459-0200

OKLAHOMA PANHANDLE STATE UNIVERSITY
Box 430, Goodwell 73939 *Type:* Public (state) liberal arts *System:* Oklahoma State Regents for Higher Education *Accred.:* 1926/1985 (NCA) *Calendar:* Sem. plan *Degrees:* B, certificates *CEO:* Pres. Ron Meek
Enroll: 1,247   (405) 349-2611

OKLAHOMA STATE UNIVERSITY
Stillwater 74078 *Type:* Public (state) *System:* Oklahoma State University Office of the President *Accred.:* 1916/1986 (NCA) *Calendar:* Sem. plan *Degrees:* A, B, P, M, D, certificates, diplomas *Prof. Accred.:* Accounting (Type A,C), Business (B,M), Clinical Psychology, Counseling Psychology (provisional), Engineering Technology (civil/construction, electrical, fire protection/safety, manufacturing, mechanical), Engineering (aerospace, agricultural, architectural, chemical, civil, electrical, general, industrial, mechanical), Forestry, Home Economics, Interi-

or Design, Journalism (B,M), Landscape Architecture (B), Marriage and Family Therapy (M), Music, Recreation and Leisure Services, Speech-Language Pathology, Veterinary Medicine *CEO:* Interim Pres. Ray M. Bowen
Enroll: 19,477   (405) 744-5000

OKLAHOMA STATE UNIVERSITY COLLEGE OF OSTEOPATHIC MEDICINE
1111 W. 17th St., Tulsa 74107 *Type:* Public (state) professional *System:* Oklahoma State University Office of the President *Calendar:* Sem. plan *Degrees:* P *Prof. Accred.:* Osteopathy *CEO:* Provost/Dean Thomas Wesley Allen
Enroll: 271   (918) 582-1972

OKLAHOMA STATE UNIVERSITY—OKLAHOMA CITY
900 N. Portland Ave., Oklahoma City 73107 *Type:* Public (state) junior *System:* Oklahoma State University Office of the President *Accred.:* 1975/1990 (NCA) *Calendar:* Sem. plan *Degrees:* A, certificates *Prof. Accred.:* Nursing (A) *CEO:* Provost James E. Hooper
Enroll: 4,367   (405) 947-4421

OKLAHOMA STATE UNIVERSITY—OKMULGEE
1801 E. Fourth St., Okmulgee 74447 *Type:* Public (state) junior *System:* Oklahoma State University Office of the President *Accred.:* 1975/1990 (NCA) *Calendar:* Tri. plan *Degrees:* A, certificates, diplomas *CEO:* Provost Robert Klabenes
Enroll: 2,300   (918) 756-6211

ORAL ROBERTS UNIVERSITY
7777 S. Lewis Ave., Tulsa 74171 *Type:* Private (interdenominational) liberal arts and professional *Accred.:* 1980/1987 (ATS); 1971/1992 (NCA) *Calendar:* Sem. plan *Degrees:* B, M, D, certificates, diplomas *Prof. Accred.:* Music, Nursing (B,M), Social Work (B) *CEO:* Chanc. Granville Oral Roberts
Enroll: 4,332   (918) 495-6161

PHILLIPS GRADUATE SEMINARY
102 University Dr., P.O. Box 2335, University Sta., Enid 73702 *Type:* Private (Disciples of Christ) *Accred.:* 1952/1990 (ATS);

1992 (NCA) *Calendar:* Sem. plan *Degrees:* M, D *CEO:* Pres. William Tabbernee
Enroll: 229   (405) 237-4433

PHILLIPS UNIVERSITY
100 S. University Ave., Enid 73701 *Type:* Private *Accred.:* 1919/1989 (NCA) *Calendar:* Sem. plan *Degrees:* A, B, M *Prof. Accred.:* Music *CEO:* Pres. Robert D. Peck
Enroll: 807   (405) 237-4433

REDLANDS COMMUNITY COLLEGE
P.O. Box 370, El Reno 73036-0370 *Type:* Public (state) junior *System:* Oklahoma State Regents for Higher Education *Accred.:* 1978/1991 (NCA) *Calendar:* Sem. plan *Degrees:* A, certificates *Prof. Accred.:* Nursing (A) *CEO:* Pres. Larry F. Devane
Enroll: 1,908   (405) 262-2552

ROGERS STATE COLLEGE
Will Rogers and College Hill, Claremore 74017 *Type:* Public (state) junior *System:* Oklahoma State Regents for Higher Education *Accred.:* 1950/1987 (NCA) *Calendar:* Sem. plan *Degrees:* A, certificates *Prof. Accred.:* Nursing (A) *CEO:* Pres. Richard H. Mosier
Enroll: 3,922   (918) 341-7510

ROSE STATE COLLEGE
6420 S.E. 15th St., Midwest City 73110 *Type:* Public (state) junior *System:* Oklahoma State Regents for Higher Education *Accred.:* 1975/1988 (NCA) *Calendar:* Sem. plan *Degrees:* A, certificates *Prof. Accred.:* Dental Assisting, Dental Hygiene, Medical Laboratory Technology (AMA), Medical Record Technology, Nursing (A), Radiography, Respiratory Therapy, Respiratory Therapy Technology *CEO:* Pres. Larry Nutter
Enroll: 9,939   (405) 733-7311

ST. GREGORY'S COLLEGE
1900 W. MacArthur, Shawnee 74801 *Type:* Private (Roman Catholic) junior *Accred.:* 1969/1989 (NCA) *Calendar:* Sem. plan *Degrees:* A *CEO:* Pres. Carmen A. Notaro
Enroll: 328   (405) 878-5100

SEMINOLE JUNIOR COLLEGE
P.O. Box 351, Seminole 74868-0351 *Type:* Public (state) junior *System:* Oklahoma State Regents for Higher Education *Accred.:* 1975/1990 (NCA) *Calendar:* Tri. plan *De-

grees: A, certificates *Prof. Accred.:* Medical
Laboratory Technology (AMA), Nursing (A)
CEO: Pres. James J. Cook
Enroll: 1,844   (405) 382-9950

SOUTHEASTERN OKLAHOMA STATE UNIVERSITY
Sta. A, Durant 74701 *Type:* Public (state)
liberal arts and teachers *System:* Oklahoma
State Regents for Higher Education *Accred.:*
1922/1984 (NCA) *Calendar:* Sem. plan *Degrees:* B, M, certificates *Prof. Accred.:*
Music, Teacher Education (e,s) *CEO:* Pres.
Larry Williams
Enroll: 4,109   (405) 924-0121

SOUTHERN NAZARENE UNIVERSITY
6729 N.W. 39th Expy., Bethany 73008
Type: Private (Nazarene) liberal arts *Accred.:* 1956/1990 (NCA) *Calendar:* Sem.
plan *Degrees:* A, B, M *Prof. Accred.:* Nursing (B), Teacher Education (e,s) *CEO:* Pres.
Loren P. Gresham, Ph.D.
Enroll: 1,591   (405) 789-6400

SOUTHWESTERN COLLEGE OF CHRISTIAN
MINISTRIES
7210 N.W. 39th Expy., P.O. Box 340,
Bethany 73008-0340 *Type:* Private (Pentecostal Holiness) liberal arts *Accred.:* 1973/
1991 (NCA) *Calendar:* Sem. plan *Degrees:*
A, B *CEO:* Pres. Ronald Q. Moore
Enroll: 155   (405) 789-7661

SOUTHWESTERN OKLAHOMA STATE UNIVERSITY
100 Campus Dr., Weatherford 73096 *Type:*
Public (state) liberal arts and professional
System: Oklahoma State Regents for Higher
Education *Accred.:* 1922/1991 (NCA) *Calendar:* Sem. plan *Degrees:* A, B, M, certificates *Prof. Accred.:* Medical Record Administration, Music, Nursing (B), Radiography,
Teacher Education (e,s,p) *CEO:* Pres. Joe
Anna Hibler
Enroll: 5,543   (405) 772-6611

SAYRE CAMPUS
409 E. Mississippi, Sayre 73662 *Prof. Accred.:* Medical Laboratory Technology
CEO: Dean Don Roberts
                                   (405) 928-5533

TULSA JUNIOR COLLEGE
6111 E. Skelly Dr., Tulsa 74135 *Type:* Public (state) junior *System:* Oklahoma State Regents for Higher Education *Accred.:* 1974/

1989 (NCA) *Calendar:* Sem. plan *Degrees:*
A, certificates *Prof. Accred.:* Dental Hygiene, Medical Assisting (AMA), Medical
Laboratory Technology (AMA), Nursing
(A), Occupational Therapy Assisting, Physical Therapy Assisting, Radiography, Respiratory Therapy, Respiratory Therapy Technology *CEO:* Pres. Dean P. Van Trease
Enroll: 22,056   (918) 631-7000

UNIVERSITY OF CENTRAL OKLAHOMA
100 N. University Dr., Edmond 73060 *Type:*
Public (state) liberal arts and teachers *System:* Oklahoma State Regents for Higher Education *Accred.:* 1921/1993 (NCA) *Calendar:* Sem. plan *Degrees:* B, M, certificates
Prof. Accred.: Funeral Service Education,
Nursing (B), Speech-Language Pathology,
Teacher Education (e,s,p) *CEO:* Pres.
George Nigh
Enroll: 15,839   (405) 341-2980

UNIVERSITY OF OKLAHOMA
660 Parrington Oval, Norman 73019 *Type:*
Public (state) *System:* University of Oklahoma President's Office *Accred.:* 1913/1992
(NCA) *Calendar:* Sem. plan *Degrees:* B, M,
D, certificates *Prof. Accred.:* Accounting
(Type A,C), Business (B,M), Construction
Education (B), Counseling Psychology, Engineering (aerospace, chemical, civil, electrical, engineering physics/science, general, industrial, mechanical, petroleum), Interior
Design, Journalism (B,M), Law, Librarianship, Music, Planning (M), Public Health,
Social Work (B,M), Teacher Education
(e,s,p) *CEO:* Pres. Richard L. Van Horn
Enroll: 24,824   (405) 325-0311

UNIVERSITY OF OKLAHOMA HEALTH SCIENCES
CENTER
P.O. Box 26901, Oklahoma City 73126-
0901 *Type:* Public (state) *System:* University
of Oklahoma President's Office *Calendar:*
Sem. plan *Degrees:* A, B, P, M, D *Prof. Accred.:* Audiology, Combined Prosthodontics,
Cytotechnology, Dental Hygiene, Dentistry,
Diagnostic Medical Sonography, Dietetics
(coordinated), General Dentistry, Medical
Technology, Medicine, Nuclear Medicine
Technology, Nursing (B,M), Occupational
Therapy, Oral and Maxillofacial Surgery,
Orthodontics, Periodontics, Physical Therapy, Physician Assisting, Psychology Intern-

ship, Radiation Therapy Technology, Radiography, Speech-Language Pathology *CEO:* Provost Jay H. Stein
Enroll: 2,313 (405) 271-4000

UNIVERSITY OF SCIENCE AND ARTS OF OKLAHOMA
P.O. Box 82345, Chickasha 73018 *Type:* Public (state) liberal arts and teachers *System:* Oklahoma State Regents for Higher Education *Accred.:* 1920/1989 (NCA) *Calendar:* Tri. plan *Degrees:* B *Prof. Accred.:* Music, Teacher Education (e,s) *CEO:* Pres. Roy Troutt
Enroll: 1,653 (405) 224-3140

UNIVERSITY OF TULSA
600 S. College Ave., Tulsa 74104 *Type:* Private (United Presbyterian) *Accred.:* 1929/ 1988 (NCA) *Calendar:* 4-1-4 plan *Degrees:* B, M, D *Prof. Accred.:* Business (B,M), Clinical Psychology (provisional), Computer Science, Engineering (chemical, electrical, engineering physics/science, mechanical, petroleum), Law, Music, Nursing (B), Speech-Language Pathology, Teacher Education (e,s,p) *CEO:* Pres. Robert E. Donaldson
Enroll: 4,922 (918) 631-2000

WESTERN OKLAHOMA STATE COLLEGE
2801 N. Main St., Altus 73521 *Type:* Public (state) junior *System:* Oklahoma State Regents for Higher Education *Accred.:* 1976/1988 (NCA) *Calendar:* Sem. plan *Degrees:* A, certificates *CEO:* Pres. Stephen R. Hensley
Enroll: 1,803 (405) 477-2000

OREGON

BASSIST COLLEGE
2000 S.W. Fifth Ave., Portland 97201 *Type:* Private technical *Accred.:* 1977/1991 (NASC) *Calendar:* Qtr. plan *Degrees:* A, B *CEO:* Pres. Donald H. Bassist
Enroll: 150   (503) 228-6528

BLUE MOUNTAIN COMMUNITY COLLEGE
P.O. Box 100, Pendleton 97801 *Type:* Public (district) junior *System:* Oregon Office of Community College Services *Accred.:* 1968/1989 (NASC) *Calendar:* Qtr. plan *Degrees:* A *Prof. Accred.:* Dental Assisting, Engineering Technology (electrical) *CEO:* Pres. Ronald L. Daniels
Enroll: 5,588   (503) 276-1260

CENTRAL OREGON COMMUNITY COLLEGE
Bend 97701-5998 *Type:* Public (district) junior *System:* Oregon Office of Community College Services *Accred.:* 1966/1992 (NASC) *Calendar:* Qtr. plan *Degrees:* A *Prof. Accred.:* Medical Record Technology *CEO:* Pres. Robert Barber
Enroll: 3,138   (503) 385-6112

CHEMEKETA COMMUNITY COLLEGE
P.O. Box 14007, Salem 97309 *Type:* Public (district) junior *System:* Oregon Office of Community College Services *Accred.:* 1972/1992 (NASC) *Calendar:* Qtr. plan *Degrees:* A *Prof. Accred.:* Dental Assisting, Medical Assisting (AMA), Nursing (A) *CEO:* Pres. Gerard J. Berger
Enroll: 20,209   (503) 399-5000

CLACKAMAS COMMUNITY COLLEGE
19600 S. Molalla Ave., Oregon City 97045 *Type:* Public (district) junior *System:* Oregon Office of Community College Services *Accred.:* 1971/1991 (NASC) *Calendar:* Qtr. plan *Degrees:* A *Prof. Accred.:* Nursing (A) *CEO:* Pres. John S. Keyser
Enroll: 12,491   (503) 657-6958

CLATSOP COMMUNITY COLLEGE
1653 Jerome Ave., Astoria 97103 *Type:* Public (district) junior *System:* Oregon Office of Community College Services *Accred.:* 1965/1993 (NASC) *Calendar:* Qtr.

plan *Degrees:* A *CEO:* Pres. John W. Wubben
Enroll: 5,573   (503) 325-0910

CONCORDIA COLLEGE
2811 N.E. Holman St., Portland 97211 *Type:* Private (Lutheran) liberal arts *Accred.:* 1962/1991 (NASC) *Calendar:* Qtr. plan *Degrees:* A, B *CEO:* Pres. Charles E. Schlimpert
Enroll: 1,056   (503) 288-9371

EASTERN OREGON STATE COLLEGE
La Grande 97850 *Type:* Public (state) liberal arts and teachers *System:* Oregon State System of Higher Education *Accred.:* 1931/1993 (NASC) *Calendar:* Qtr. plan *Degrees:* A, B, M *Prof. Accred.:* Teacher Education (e,s) *CEO:* Pres. David E. Gilbert
Enroll: 2,881   (503) 962-3512

EUGENE BIBLE COLLEGE
2155 Bailey Hill Rd., Eugene 97405 *Type:* Private (Open Bible Standard Churches) *Accred.:* 1983/1988 (AABC) *Calendar:* Qtr. plan *Degrees:* B, certificates *CEO:* Pres. Jeffrey Farmer
FTE Enroll: 180   (503) 485-1780

GEORGE FOX COLLEGE
Newberg 97132 *Type:* Private liberal arts *Accred.:* 1959/1992 (NASC) *Calendar:* Sem. plan *Degrees:* A, B, M, D *Prof. Accred.:* Music *CEO:* Pres. Edward F. Stevens
Enroll: 1,420   (503) 538-8383

ITT TECHNICAL INSTITUTE
6035 N.E. 78th Ct., Portland 97218-2854 *Type:* Private *Accred.:* 1973/1988 (ACCSCT) *Calendar:* Courses of varying lengths *Degrees:* A, B *CEO:* Dir. James Horner
                                 (503) 255-6500

LANE COMMUNITY COLLEGE
4000 E. 30th Ave., Eugene 97405 *Type:* Public (district) junior *System:* Oregon Office of Community College Services *Accred.:* 1968/1989 (NASC) *Calendar:* Qtr. plan *Degrees:* A *Prof. Accred.:* Dental Assisting, Dental Hygiene, Nursing (A), Respiratory Therapy *CEO:* Pres. Jerry Moskus
Enroll: 9,350   (503) 747-4501

LEWIS AND CLARK COLLEGE
615 S.W. Palatine Hill Rd., Portland 97219 *Type:* Private (United Presbyterian) liberal arts *Accred.:* 1943/1993 (NASC) *Calendar:* Qtr. plan *Degrees:* B, M *Prof. Accred.:* Law, Music *CEO:* Pres. Michael J. Mooney
Enroll: 3,202   (503) 293-2770

LINFIELD COLLEGE
McMinnville 97128 *Type:* Private (Baptist) liberal arts *Accred.:* 1928/1993 (NASC) *Calendar:* 4-1-4 plan *Degrees:* B, M *Prof. Accred.:* Music, Nursing (B) *CEO:* Pres. Vivian A. Bull
Enroll: 2,806   (503) 472-4121

LINN-BENTON COMMUNITY COLLEGE
Albany 97321 *Type:* Public (district) junior *System:* Oregon Office of Community College Services *Accred.:* 1972/1992 (NASC) *Calendar:* Qtr. plan *Degrees:* A *Prof. Accred.:* Dental Assisting, Nursing (A) *CEO:* Pres. Jon Carnahan
Enroll: 6,357   (503) 967-6100

MARYLHURST COLLEGE
P.O. Box 261, Marylhurst 97036 *Type:* Private (Roman Catholic) liberal arts *Accred.:* 1977/1991 (NASC) *Calendar:* Qtr. plan *Degrees:* B, M *Prof. Accred.:* Music *CEO:* Pres. Nancy A. Wilgenbusch
Enroll: 1,240   (503) 636-8141

MOUNT ANGEL SEMINARY
St. Benedict 97373 *Type:* Private (Roman Catholic) *Accred.:* 1978/1985 (ATS); 1929/1992 (NASC) *Calendar:* Sem. plan *Degrees:* B, P, M *CEO:* Pres. Patrick S. Brennan
Enroll: 165   (503) 845-3951

MOUNT HOOD COMMUNITY COLLEGE
26000 S.E. Stark St., Gresham 97030 *Type:* Public (district) junior *System:* Oregon Office of Community College Services *Accred.:* 1972/1992 (NASC) *Calendar:* Qtr. plan *Degrees:* A *Prof. Accred.:* Dental Hygiene, Funeral Service Education, Medical Assisting (AMA), Nursing (A), Occupational Therapy Assisting, Physical Therapy Assisting, Respiratory Therapy, Surgical Technology *CEO:* Pres. Paul E. Kreider
Enroll: 7,960   (503) 667-6422

MULTNOMAH BIBLE COLLEGE
8435 N.E. Glisan St., Portland 97220 *Type:* Independent (interdenominational) *Accred.:* 1953/1983 (AABC); 1993 (ATS candidate) *Calendar:* Sem. plan *Degrees:* A, B, certificates *CEO:* Pres. Joseph C. Aldrich
FTE Enroll: 487   (503) 255-0332

NORTHWEST CHRISTIAN COLLEGE
Eugene 97401 *Type:* Private (Disciples of Christ) liberal arts *Accred.:* 1962/1992 (NASC) *Calendar:* Qtr. plan *Degrees:* A, B, M *CEO:* Pres. James E. Womack
Enroll: 325   (503) 343-1641

OREGON COLLEGE OF ORIENTAL MEDICINE
10525 Cherry Blossom Dr., Portland 97216 *Type:* Private professional *Calendar:* Qtr. plan *Degrees:* M *Prof. Accred.:* Acupuncture *CEO:* Pres. Elizabeth Goldblatt
FTE Enroll: 110   (503) 253-3443

OREGON GRADUATE INSTITUTE OF SCIENCE AND TECHNOLOGY
P.O. Box 91000, 20000 N.W. Walker Rd., Portland 97291-1000 *Type:* Private graduate only *Accred.:* 1973/1993 (NASC) *Calendar:* Qtr. plan *Degrees:* M, D *CEO:* Pres. Dwight A. Sangrey
Enroll: 551   (503) 690-1020

OREGON HEALTH SCIENCES UNIVERSITY
3181 S.W. Sam Jackson Park Rd., Portland 97201 *Type:* Public (state) professional *System:* Oregon State System of Higher Education *Accred.:* 1980/1990 (NASC) *Calendar:* Qtr. plan *Degrees:* A, B, M, D *Prof. Accred.:* Dental Hygiene, Dentistry, Dietetics (internship), EMT-Paramedic, Endodontics, Medical Technology, Medicine, Nursing (B,M), Oral and Maxillofacial Surgery, Orthodontics, Pediatric Dentistry, Periodontics, Psychology Internship, Radiation Therapy Technology *CEO:* Pres. Peter O. Kohler, M.D.
Enroll: 1,568   (503) 494-8252

OREGON INSTITUTE OF TECHNOLOGY
Klamath Falls 97601-8801 *Type:* Public (state) technological *System:* Oregon State System of Higher Education *Accred.:* 1962/1992 (NASC) *Calendar:* Qtr. plan *Degrees:* A, B *Prof. Accred.:* Dental Hygiene, Engineering Technology (civil/construction,

computer, electrical, manufacturing, mechanical, surveying), Nursing (B), Radiography *CEO:* Pres. Lawrence J. Wolf
Enroll: 2,758   (503) 885-1103

OREGON POLYTECHNIC INSTITUTE
900 S.E. Sandy Blvd., Portland 97214 *Type:* Private *Accred.:* 1977/1986 (ACCSCT) *Calendar:* Qtr. plan *Degrees:* A *CEO:* Dir. Mardell Lanfranco
                                   (503) 234-9333

OREGON STATE UNIVERSITY
Corvallis 97331 *Type:* Public (state) *System:* Oregon State System of Higher Education *Accred.:* 1924/1990 (NASC) *Calendar:* Qtr. plan *Degrees:* B, M, D *Prof. Accred.:* Accounting (Type A), Business (B,M), Construction Education (B), Counseling, Engineering (chemical, civil, computer, electrical, industrial, mechanical, nuclear), Forestry, Home Economics, Music, Teacher Education (e,s,p), Veterinary Medicine (limited) *CEO:* Pres. John V. Byrne
Enroll: 14,336   (503) 737-2565

PACIFIC NORTHWEST COLLEGE OF ART
1219 S.W. Park Ave., Portland 97205 *Type:* Private professional *Accred.:* 1961/1993 (NASC) *Calendar:* Sem. plan *Degrees:* B *Prof. Accred.:* Art *CEO:* Dir./C.E.O. Sally C. Lawrence
Enroll: 223   (503) 226-4391

PACIFIC UNIVERSITY
2043 College Way, Forest Grove 97116 *Type:* Private (United Church of Christ) *Accred.:* 1929/1992 (NASC) *Calendar:* Sem. plan *Degrees:* B, M, D *Prof. Accred.:* Clinical Psychology, Music, Occupational Therapy, Optometry, Physical Therapy *CEO:* Pres. Robert F. Duvall
Enroll: 1,621   (503) 357-6151

PORTLAND COMMUNITY COLLEGE
P.O. Box 19000, Portland 97219-0990 *Type:* Public (district) junior *System:* Oregon Office of Community College Services *Accred.:* 1970/1992 (NASC) *Calendar:* Qtr. plan *Degrees:* A *Prof. Accred.:* Dental Assisting, Dental Hygiene, Dental Laboratory Technology, Engineering Technology (electrical), Medical Assisting (AMA), Medical Laboratory Technology (AMA), Medical

Record Technology, Nursing (A), Radiography, Veterinary Technology *CEO:* Pres. Daniel F. Moriarty
Enroll: 23,710   (503) 244-6111

PORTLAND STATE UNIVERSITY
P.O. Box 751, Portland 97207 *Type:* Public (state) *System:* Oregon State System of Higher Education *Accred.:* 1955/1993 (NASC) *Calendar:* Qtr. plan *Degrees:* B, M, D *Prof. Accred.:* Accounting (Type A), Audiology, Business (B,M), Counseling, Engineering (civil, electrical, mechanical), Music, Planning (M), Public Administration, Rehabilitation Counseling, Social Work (M), Speech-Language Pathology, Teacher Education (e,s,p) *CEO:* Pres. Judith A. Ramaley
Enroll: 17,468   (503) 725-4419

REED COLLEGE
3203 S.E. Woodstock Blvd., Portland 97202-8199 *Type:* Private liberal arts *Accred.:* 1920/1989 (NASC) *Calendar:* Sem. plan *Degrees:* B, M *CEO:* Pres. Steven S. Koblik
Enroll: 1,230   (503) 771-1112

ROGUE COMMUNITY COLLEGE
3345 Redwood Hwy., Grants Pass 97527 *Type:* Public (district) junior *System:* Oregon Office of Community College Services *Accred.:* 1976/1991 (NASC) *Calendar:* Qtr. plan *Degrees:* A *Prof. Accred.:* Respiratory Therapy, Respiratory Therapy Technology *CEO:* Pres. Harvey Bennett
Enroll: 5,224   (503) 479-5541

SOUTHERN OREGON STATE COLLEGE
Ashland 97520 *Type:* Public (state) liberal arts and teachers *System:* Oregon State System of Higher Education *Accred.:* 1928/1992 (NASC) *Calendar:* Qtr. plan *Degrees:* B, M *Prof. Accred.:* Music, Nursing (B), Teacher Education (e,s) *CEO:* Pres. Joseph W. Cox
Enroll: 4,768   (503) 552-6111

SOUTHWESTERN OREGON COMMUNITY COLLEGE
1988 Newmark, Coos Bay 97420 *Type:* Public (district) junior *System:* Oregon Office of Community College Services *Accred.:* 1966/1992 (NASC) *Calendar:* Qtr. plan *Degrees:* A *CEO:* Pres. Stephen Kridelbaugh
Enroll: 5,095   (503) 888-2525

TREASURE VALLEY COMMUNITY COLLEGE
Ontario 97914 *Type:* Public (district) junior *System:* Oregon Office of Community College Services *Accred.:* 1966/1992 (NASC) *Calendar:* Qtr. plan *Degrees:* A *CEO:* Pres. Berton Glandon
Enroll: 3,094   (503) 889-6493

UMPQUA COMMUNITY COLLEGE
Roseburg 97470 *Type:* Public (district) junior *System:* Oregon Office of Community College Services *Accred.:* 1970/1990 (NASC) *Calendar:* Qtr. plan *Degrees:* A *Prof. Accred.:* Nursing (A) *CEO:* Pres. James M. Kraby
Enroll: 7,240   (503) 440-4600

UNIVERSITY OF OREGON
Eugene 97403-1226 *Type:* Public (state) *System:* Oregon State System of Higher Education *Accred.:* 1918/1992 (NASC) *Calendar:* Qtr. plan *Degrees:* B, M, D *Prof. Accred.:* Accounting (Type A), Business (B,M), Clinical Psychology, Counseling, Counseling Psychology, Interior Design, Journalism (B,M), Landscape Architecture (B), Law, Music, Planning (M), Psychology Internship, Public Affairs, Recreation and Leisure Services, Speech-Language Pathology *CEO:* Pres. Myles Brand
Enroll: 16,100   (503) 346-3036

UNIVERSITY OF PORTLAND
5000 N. Willamette Blvd., Portland 97203 *Type:* Private (Roman Catholic) *Accred.:* 1931/1993 (NASC) *Calendar:* Sem. plan *Degrees:* B, M *Prof. Accred.:* Business (B,M), Engineering (civil, electrical, mechanical), Nursing (B,M) *CEO:* Pres. David T. Tyson
Enroll: 3,183   (503) 283-7205

WARNER PACIFIC COLLEGE
2219 S.E. 68th Ave., Portland 97215 *Type:* Private (Church of God) liberal arts *Accred.:* 1961/1990 (NASC) *Calendar:* Sem. plan *Degrees:* A, B, M *CEO:* Pres. Marshall K. Christensen
Enroll: 551   (503) 775-4366

WESTERN BAPTIST COLLEGE
5000 Deer Park Dr., S.E., Salem 97301-9891 *Type:* Private (General Association of Regular Baptist Churches) *Accred.:* 1959/1991 (AABC); 1971/1991 (NASC) *Calendar:* Sem. plan *Degrees:* A, B, certificates *CEO:* Pres. David F. Miller
Enroll: 478   (503) 581-8600

WESTERN CONSERVATIVE BAPTIST SEMINARY
5511 S.E. Hawthorne Blvd., Portland 97215 *Type:* Private (Conservative Baptist) graduate only *Accred.:* 1991 (ATS candidate); 1969/1993 (NASC) *Calendar:* Sem. plan *Degrees:* M, D *CEO:* Interim Pres. Lawrence W. Ayers
Enroll: 540   (503) 233-8561

WESTERN EVANGELICAL SEMINARY
P.O. Box 23939, Portland 97281-3939 *Type:* Private (interdenominational) graduate only *Accred.:* 1974/1991 (ATS); 1976/1991 (NASC) *Calendar:* Qtr. plan *Degrees:* M, D *CEO:* Pres. David C. Le Shana
Enroll: 157   (503) 639-0559

WESTERN OREGON STATE COLLEGE
Monmouth 97361 *Type:* Public (state) *System:* Oregon State System of Higher Education *Accred.:* 1924/1993 (NASC) *Calendar:* Qtr. plan *Degrees:* A, B, M *Prof. Accred.:* Music, Rehabilitation Counseling, Teacher Education (e,s) *CEO:* Pres. Richard S. Meyers
Enroll: 4,041   (503) 838-8215

WESTERN STATES CHIROPRACTIC COLLEGE
2900 N.E. 132nd Ave., Portland 97230 *Type:* Private professional *Accred.:* 1986/1990 (NASC) *Calendar:* Qtr. plan *Degrees:* B, P *Prof. Accred.:* Chiropractic Education *CEO:* Pres. William H. Dallas, D.C.
Enroll: 363   (503) 256-3180

WILLAMETTE UNIVERSITY
Salem 97301 *Type:* Private (United Methodist) *Accred.:* 1924/1991 (NASC) *Calendar:* Sem. plan *Degrees:* B, M *Prof. Accred.:* Law, Music *CEO:* Pres. Jerry E. Hudson
Enroll: 2,425   (503) 370-6300

PENNSYLVANIA

ACADEMY OF THE NEW CHURCH
P.O. Box 278, Bryn Athyn 19009 *Type:* Private (Church of New Jerusalem) *Accred.:* 1952/1993 (MSA) *Calendar:* Tri. plan *Degrees:* A, B, P *CEO:* Pres. Daniel W. Goodenough
Enroll: 116   (215) 947-4200

ALBRIGHT COLLEGE
P.O. Box 15234, Reading 19612-5234 *Type:* Private (United Methodist) liberal arts *Accred.:* 1926/1988 (MSA) *Calendar:* 4-1-4 plan *Degrees:* B *Prof. Accred.:* Social Work (B) *CEO:* Pres. Ellen S. Hurwitz
Enroll: 1,566   (215) 921-2381

ALLEGHENY COLLEGE
520 N. Main St., Meadville 16335 *Type:* Private liberal arts *Accred.:* 1921/1990 (MSA) *Calendar:* Tri. plan *Degrees:* B, M *CEO:* Pres. Daniel F. Sullivan
Enroll: 1,881   (814) 332-3100

ALLENTOWN COLLEGE OF ST. FRANCIS DE SALES
Station Ave., Center Valley 18034 *Type:* Private (Roman Catholic) liberal arts *Accred.:* 1970/1988 (MSA) *Calendar:* Sem. plan *Degrees:* B, M *Prof. Accred.:* Nursing (B,M) *CEO:* Pres. Daniel G. Gambet, O.S.F.S.
Enroll: 2,083   (215) 282-1100

ALTOONA SCHOOL OF COMMERCE
508 58th St., Altoona 16602 *Type:* Private business *Accred.:* 1971/1989 (ACISC) *Calendar:* Qtr. plan *Degrees:* A *CEO:* Dir. J. William Laughlin
                                  (814) 944-6134

ALVERNIA COLLEGE
400 St. Bernadine St., Reading 19607 *Type:* Private (Roman Catholic) liberal arts *Accred.:* 1967/1991 (MSA) *Calendar:* Sem. plan *Degrees:* A, B *Prof. Accred.:* Nursing (A), Physical Therapy Assisting *CEO:* Pres. Daniel N. DeLucca
Enroll: 1,243   (215) 796-8200

THE AMERICAN COLLEGE
270 Bryn Mawr Ave., Bryn Mawr 19010 *Type:* Private professional *Accred.:* 1978/ 1987 (MSA) *Calendar:* Sem. plan *Degrees:* M, certificates *CEO:* Pres. Samuel H. Weese
Enroll: 26,831   (215) 526-1000

AMERICAN INSTITUTE OF DESIGN
1616 Orthodox St., Philadelphia 19124-3706 *Type:* Private *Accred.:* 1972/1987 (ACCSCT) *Calendar:* Qtr. plan *Degrees:* A, certificates *CEO:* Pres. Peter Klein
                                  (215) 288-8200

ANTONELLI INSTITUTE
2910 Jolly Rd., Plymouth Meeting 19462-0570 *Type:* Private *Accred.:* 1975/1990 (ACCSCT) *Calendar:* Sem. plan *Degrees:* A *CEO:* Dir. Thomas Treacy
                                  (215) 275-3040

ART INSTITUTE OF PHILADELPHIA
1622 Chestnut St., Philadelphia 19103-5198 *Type:* Private *Accred.:* 1973/1988 (ACCSCT) *Calendar:* Qtr. plan *Degrees:* A *CEO:* Pres. Robert P. Gioella
                                  (215) 567-7080

ART INSTITUTE OF PITTSBURGH
526 Penn Ave., Pittsburgh 15222-3269 *Type:* Private *Accred.:* 1970/1990 (ACCSCT) *Calendar:* Qtr. plan *Degrees:* A *CEO:* Pres. Saundra Van Dyke
                                  (412) 263-6600

BAPTIST BIBLE COLLEGE AND SEMINARY
P.O. Box 800, 538 Venard Rd., Clarks Summit 18411 *Type:* Private (Baptist) *Accred.:* 1968/1984 (AABC); 1984/1990 (MSA) *Calendar:* Sem. plan *Degrees:* A, B, M, certificates *CEO:* Pres. Milo Thompson
Enroll: 726   (717) 587-1172

BEAVER COLLEGE
Easton and Church Rds., Glenside 19038 *Type:* Private (United Presbyterian) *Accred.:* 1946/1989 (MSA) *Calendar:* 4-1-4 plan *Degrees:* A, B, M, certificates *Prof. Accred.:* Art, Physical Therapy *CEO:* Pres. Bette E. Landman
Enroll: 2,204   (215) 572-2900

BEREAN INSTITUTE
1901 W. Girard Ave., Philadelphia 19130-1599 *Type:* Private *Accred.:* 1974/1987

(ACISC); 1990 (ACCSCT) *Calendar:* Sem. plan *Degrees:* A *CEO:* Pres. Norman K. Spencer

(215) 763-4833

BIBLICAL THEOLOGICAL SEMINARY
200 N. Main St., Hatfield 19440 *Type:* Private (interdenominational) professional *Accred.:* 1990 (MSA) *Calendar:* Sem. plan *Degrees:* P, M, certificates *CEO:* Pres. David G. Dunbar
Enroll: 236   (215) 368-5000

BLOOMSBURG UNIVERSITY OF PENNSYLVANIA
Bloomsburg 17815 *Type:* Public (state) *System:* Pennsylvania State System of Higher Education *Accred.:* 1950/1989 (MSA) *Calendar:* Sem. plan *Degrees:* A, B, M, certificates *Prof. Accred.:* Audiology, Nursing (B,M), Social Work (B), Speech-Language Pathology, Teacher Education (e,s) *CEO:* Interim Pres. Curtis R. English
Enroll: 7,720   (717) 389-4000

BRADFORD SCHOOL
355 Fifth Ave., Pittsburgh 15222 *Type:* Private business *Accred.:* 1970/1988 (ACISC) *Calendar:* Courses of varying lengths *Degrees:* A, certificates, diplomas *Prof. Accred.:* Medical Assisting (AMA) *CEO:* Dir. Vincent S. Graziano
(412) 391-6710

BRADLEY ACADEMY FOR THE VISUAL ARTS
625 E. Philadelphia St., York 17403-1625 *Type:* Private *Accred.:* 1983/1988 (ACCSCT) *Calendar:* Sem. plan *Degrees:* A *CEO:* Dir. Loren H. Kroh
(717) 848-1447

BRYN MAWR COLLEGE
Bryn Mawr 19010-2899 *Type:* Private liberal arts for women *Accred.:* 1921/1989 (MSA) *Calendar:* Sem. plan *Degrees:* B, M, D, certificates *Prof. Accred.:* Social Work (M) *CEO:* Pres. Mary Patterson McPherson
Enroll: 1,881   (215) 526-5000

BUCKNELL UNIVERSITY
Lewisburg 17837-2086 *Type:* Private liberal arts *Accred.:* 1921/1988 (MSA) *Calendar:* 4-1-4 plan *Degrees:* B, M *Prof. Accred.:* Computer Science, Engineering (chemical,

civil, electrical, mechanical), Music *CEO:* Pres. Gary A. Sojka
Enroll: 3,562   (717) 523-1271

BUCKS COUNTY COMMUNITY COLLEGE
Swamp Rd., Newtown 18940 *Type:* Public (local/state) junior *Accred.:* 1968/1992 (MSA) *Calendar:* Sem. plan *Degrees:* A, certificates *Prof. Accred.:* Art, Music (associate), Nursing (A) *CEO:* Pres. James J. Linksz
Enroll: 11,485   (215) 968-8000

BUTLER COUNTY COMMUNITY COLLEGE
College Dr., Oak Hills, P.O. Box 1203, Butler 16001-1203 *Type:* Public (local/state) junior *Accred.:* 1971/1992 (MSA) *Calendar:* Sem. plan *Degrees:* A, certificates *CEO:* Pres. Thaddeus H. Penar
Enroll: 3,071   (412) 287-8711

CABRINI COLLEGE
610 King of Prussia Rd., Radnor 19087-3699 *Type:* Private (Roman Catholic) liberal arts for women *Accred.:* 1965/1990 (MSA) *Calendar:* Sem. plan *Degrees:* B, M *CEO:* Pres. and C.E.O. Antoinette Iadarola
Enroll: 1,557   (215) 971-8100

CALIFORNIA UNIVERSITY OF PENNSYLVANIA
250 University Ave., California 15419-1934 *Type:* Public (state) *System:* Pennsylvania State System of Higher Education *Accred.:* 1951/1990 (MSA) *Calendar:* Sem. plan *Degrees:* A, B, M *Prof. Accred.:* Nurse Anesthesia Education, Nursing (B), Social Work (B), Teacher Education (e,s,p) *CEO:* Pres. Angelo Armenti, Jr.
Enroll: 6,711   (412) 938-4000

CAMBRIA-ROWE BUSINESS COLLEGE
221 Central Ave., Johnstown 15902 *Type:* Private business *Accred.:* 1959/1987 (ACISC) *Calendar:* Qtr. plan *Degrees:* A *CEO:* Pres. Bill Coward
(814) 536-5168

BRANCH CAMPUS
422 S. 13th St., Indiana 15701 *Accred.:* 1993 (ACISC) *CEO:* Dir. Julianne D. Crimarki
(412) 463-0222

CARLOW COLLEGE
3333 Fifth Ave., Pittsburgh 15213-3165
Type: Private (Roman Catholic) liberal arts
for women *Accred.:* 1935/1991 (MSA) *Calendar:* Sem. plan *Degrees:* B, M *Prof. Accred.:* Nursing (B) *CEO:* Pres. Grace Ann
Geibel, R.S.M.
Enroll: 1,363   (412) 578-6000

CARNEGIE MELLON UNIVERSITY
5000 Forbes Ave., Pittsburgh 15213 *Type:*
Private *Accred.:* 1921/1988 (MSA) *Calendar:* Sem. plan *Degrees:* B, M, D *Prof. Accred.:* Art, Business (B,M), Engineering
(chemical, civil, computer, electrical, general, mechanical, metallurgical), Music, Public
Management, Public Management and Policy *CEO:* Pres. Robert Mehrabian
Enroll: 7,148   (412) 268-2000

CEDAR CREST COLLEGE
100 College Dr., Allentown 18104 *Type:*
Private (United Church of Christ) liberal arts
for women *Accred.:* 1944/1990 (MSA) *Cal-
endar:* Sem. plan *Degrees:* B *Prof. Accred.:*
Nuclear Medicine Technology, Nursing (B),
Social Work (B) *CEO:* Pres. Dorothy
Gulbenkian Blaney
Enroll: 1,051   (215) 437-4471

CENTRAL PENNSYLVANIA BUSINESS SCHOOL
College Hill Rd., Summerdale 17093-0309
Type: Private *Accred.:* 1977/1993 (MSA)
Calendar: Tri. plan *Degrees:* A *Prof. Ac-
cred.:* Medical Assisting (AMA), Physical
Therapy Assisting *CEO:* Pres. Todd A.
Milano
Enroll: 576   (717) 732-0702

CHATHAM COLLEGE
Woodland Rd., Pittsburgh 15232 *Type:* Pri-
vate liberal arts for women *Accred.:* 1924/
1988 (MSA) *Calendar:* 4-1-4 plan *Degrees:*
B *CEO:* Pres. Esther L. Barazzone
Enroll: 639   (412) 365-1100

CHESTNUT HILL COLLEGE
Germantown and Northwestern Aves.,
Philadelphia 19118-2695 *Type:* Private
(Roman Catholic) liberal arts for women *Ac-
cred.:* 1930/1992 (MSA) *Calendar:* Sem.
plan *Degrees:* A, B, M, certificates *CEO:*
Pres. Carol Jean Vale, Ph.D.
Enroll: 1,196   (215) 248-7000

CHEYNEY UNIVERSITY OF PENNSYLVANIA
Cheyney and Creek Rds., Cheyney 19319
Type: Public (state) *System:* Pennsylvania
State System of Higher Education *Accred.:*
1951/1991 (MSA) *Calendar:* Sem. plan
Degrees: A, B, M *Prof. Accred.:* Teacher
Education (e,s,p) *CEO:* Pres. H. Douglas
Covington
Enroll: 1,477   (215) 399-2000

THE CHUBB INSTITUTE—KEYSTONE SCHOOL
965 Baltimore Pike, Springfield 19064 *Type:*
Private business *Accred.:* 1968/1986
(ACISC) *Calendar:* Sem. plan *Degrees:* A
CEO: Dir. Charles A. Hamilton
                    (215) 543-1747

CHURCHMAN BUSINESS SCHOOL
355 Spring Garden St., Easton 18042 *Type:*
Private business *Accred.:* 1954/1987
(ACISC) *Calendar:* Tri. plan *Degrees:* A
CEO: Pres. Charles W. Churchman, Jr.
                    (215) 258-5345

CLARION UNIVERSITY OF PENNSYLVANIA
Clarion 16214 *Type:* Public (state) *System:*
Pennsylvania State System of Higher Educa-
tion *Accred.:* 1948/1987 (MSA) *Calendar:*
Sem. plan *Degrees:* A, B, M *Prof. Accred.:*
Audiology, Librarianship, Speech-Language
Pathology, Teacher Education (e,s) *CEO:*
Pres. Diane L. Reinhard
Enroll: 6,209   (814) 226-2000

VENANGO CAMPUS
W. First St., Oil City 16301 *Prof. Accred.:*
Nursing (A,B) *CEO:* Exec. Dean James
W. Blake
                    (814) 676-6591

COLLEGE MISERICORDIA
301 Lake St., Dallas 18612-1098 *Type:* Private (Roman Catholic) liberal arts primarily
for women *Accred.:* 1935/1990 (MSA) *Calendar:* Sem. plan *Degrees:* A, B, M, certificates *Prof. Accred.:* Nursing (B,M), Occupational Therapy, Radiography, Social Work
(B) *CEO:* Pres. Carol A. Jobe
Enroll: 1,610   (717) 674-6400

COMMUNITY COLLEGE OF ALLEGHENY COUNTY
ALLEGHENY CAMPUS
808 Ridge Ave., Pittsburgh 15212 *Type:*
Public (local/state) junior *System:* Community College of Allegheny County College Of-

fice *Accred.:* 1970/1989 (MSA) *Calendar:* Sem. plan *Degrees:* A, certificates *Prof. Accred.:* Medical Assisting (AMA), Medical Laboratory Technology (AMA), Medical Record Technology, Nuclear Medicine Technology, Nursing (A), Radiation Therapy Technology, Respiratory Therapy, Respiratory Therapy Technology *CEO:* Exec. Dean/ Vice Pres. J. David Griffin
Enroll: 7,847   (412) 237-2525

COMMUNITY COLLEGE OF ALLEGHENY COUNTY
BOYCE CAMPUS
595 Beatty Rd., Monroeville 15146 *Type:* Public (local/state) junior *System:* Community College of Allegheny County College Office *Accred.:* 1970/1989 (MSA) *Calendar:* Sem. plan *Degrees:* A, certificates *Prof. Accred.:* Diagnostic Medical Sonography, Occupational Therapy Assisting, Physical Therapy Assisting, Radiography, Surgical Technology *CEO:* Exec. Dean/Vice Pres. Carl A. DiSibio
Enroll: 4,478   (412) 371-8651

COMMUNITY COLLEGE OF ALLEGHENY COUNTY
NORTH CAMPUS
8701 Perry Hwy., Pittsburgh 15237 *Type:* Public (local/state) junior *System:* Community College of Allegheny County College Office *Accred.:* 1979/1989 (MSA) *Calendar:* Sem. plan *Degrees:* A, certificates *CEO:* Exec. Dean/Vice Pres. Fred F. Bartok
Enroll: 3,922   (412) 366-7000

COMMUNITY COLLEGE OF ALLEGHENY COUNTY
SOUTH CAMPUS
1750 Clairton Rd., Rte. 885, West Mifflin 15122 *Type:* Public (local/state) junior *System:* Community College of Allegheny County College Office *Accred.:* 1973/1989 (MSA) *Calendar:* Sem. plan *Degrees:* A, certificates *Prof. Accred.:* Medical Laboratory Technology (AMA) *CEO:* Exec. Dean/ Vice Pres. Thomas A. Juravich
Enroll: 5,491   (412) 469-1100

COMMUNITY COLLEGE OF BEAVER COUNTY
One Campus Dr., Monaca 15061-2588 *Type:* Public (local/state) junior *Accred.:* 1972/ 1989 (MSA) *Calendar:* Sem. plan *Degrees:* A, certificates *Prof. Accred.:* Medical Labo-

ratory Technology (AMA), Nursing (A) *CEO:* Pres. Margaret J. Williams-Betlyn
Enroll: 2,977   (412) 775-8561

COMMUNITY COLLEGE OF PHILADELPHIA
1700 Spring Garden St., Philadelphia 19130-3991 *Type:* Public (local/state) junior *Accred.:* 1968/1988 (MSA) *Calendar:* Sem. plan *Degrees:* A, certificates *Prof. Accred.:* Dental Assisting, Dental Hygiene, Medical Assisting (AMA), Medical Laboratory Technology (AMA), Medical Record Technology, Nursing (A), Radiography, Respiratory Therapy *CEO:* Pres. Frederick W. Capshaw
Enroll: 17,547   (215) 751-8000

COMPUTER TECH
107 Sixth St., Pittsburgh 15222 *Type:* Private business *Accred.:* 1971/1989 (ACISC) *Calendar:* Courses of varying lengths *Degrees:* A, certificates, diplomas *CEO:* Pres. Edward J. Boyd
                               (412) 391-4197

BRANCH CAMPUS
Country Club Rd. Ext., Fairmont, WV 26554 *Accred.:* 1989 (ACISC) *CEO:* Dir. Lawrence Grotstein
                               (304) 363-5100

CONSOLIDATED SCHOOL OF BUSINESS
Stes. I and J, 1817 Olde Homestead La., Lancaster 17601 *Type:* Private business *Accred.:* 1987/1990 (ACISC) *Calendar:* Courses of varying lengths *Degrees:* A, certificates, diplomas *CEO:* Dir. Vincent P. Safran
                               (717) 394-6211

CONSOLIDATED SCHOOL OF BUSINESS
1605 Clugston Rd., York 17404 *Type:* Private business *Accred.:* 1984/1990 (ACISC) *Calendar:* Courses of varying lengths *Degrees:* A, certificates, diplomas *CEO:* Exec. Dir. Betty J. Johnson
                               (717) 764-9950

THE CURTIS INSTITUTE OF MUSIC
1726 Locust St., Philadelphia 19103 *Type:* Private professional *Accred.:* 1993 (MSA) *Calendar:* Sem. plan *Degrees:* B, M, diplomas *Prof. Accred.:* Music *CEO:* Dir. Gary Graffman
Enroll: 160   (215) 893-5252

DEAN INSTITUTE OF TECHNOLOGY
1501 W. Liberty Ave., Pittsburgh 15226-1197 *Type:* Private *Accred.:* 1969/1990 (ACCSCT) *Calendar:* Qtr. plan *Degrees:* A, certificates, diplomas *CEO:* Dir. James S. Dean
(412) 531-4433

DELAWARE COUNTY COMMUNITY COLLEGE
901 S. Media Line Rd., Media 19063 *Type:* Public (local/state) junior *Accred.:* 1970/1991 (MSA) *Calendar:* Sem. plan *Degrees:* A, certificates *Prof. Accred.:* Medical Assisting (AMA), Nursing (A), Surgical Technology *CEO:* Pres. Richard D. DeCosmo
Enroll: 9,527   (215) 359-5000

DELAWARE VALLEY COLLEGE OF SCIENCE AND AGRICULTURE
700 E. Butler Ave., Doylestown 18901-2697 *Type:* Private *Accred.:* 1962/1988 (MSA) *Calendar:* Sem. plan *Degrees:* A, B *CEO:* Pres. George F. West
Enroll: 1,808   (215) 345-1500

DICKINSON COLLEGE
Carlisle 17013 *Type:* Private liberal arts *Accred.:* 1921/1992 (MSA) *Calendar:* Sem. plan *Degrees:* B *CEO:* Pres. A. Lee Fritschler
Enroll: 2,029   (717) 243-5121

DICKINSON SCHOOL OF LAW
150 S. College St., Carlisle 17013 *Type:* Private *Calendar:* Sem. plan *Degrees:* P *Prof. Accred.:* Law *CEO:* Dean John Maher
Enroll: 521   (717) 243-4611

DOUGLAS SCHOOL OF BUSINESS
130 Seventh St., Monessen 15062 *Type:* Private business *Accred.:* 1977/1986 (ACISC) *Calendar:* Tri. plan *Degrees:* A, certificates, diplomas *CEO:* Pres. Jeffrey D. Imbrescia
(412) 684-7644

DREXEL UNIVERSITY
32nd and Chestnut Sts., Philadelphia 19104 *Type:* Private *Accred.:* 1927/1991 (MSA) *Calendar:* Qtr. plan *Degrees:* B, M, D *Prof. Accred.:* Business (B,M), Computer Science, Engineering (architectural, chemical, civil, electrical, materials, mechanical), Librarianship *CEO:* Pres. Richard D. Breslin
Enroll: 11,594   (215) 895-2000

DUBOIS BUSINESS COLLEGE
One Beaver Dr., DuBois 15801 *Type:* Private business *Accred.:* 1954/1988 (ACISC) *Calendar:* Tri. plan *Degrees:* A *CEO:* Dir. Jackie D. Syktich
(814) 371-6920

DUFF'S BUSINESS INSTITUTE
110 Ninth St., Pittsburgh 15222 *Type:* Private business *Accred.:* 1961/1990 (ACISC) *Calendar:* Qtr. plan *Degrees:* A, certificates, diplomas *Prof. Accred.:* Medical Assisting (AMA) *CEO:* Dir. Mark A. Scott
(412) 261-4520

DUQUESNE UNIVERSITY
600 Forbes Ave., Pittsburgh 15282 *Type:* Private (Roman Catholic) *Accred.:* 1935/1983 (MSA) *Calendar:* Sem. plan *Degrees:* A, B, P, M, D *Prof. Accred.:* Business (B,M), Counseling, Law, Music, Nursing (B,M), Perfusion, Physical Therapy *CEO:* Pres. John E. Murray, Jr.
Enroll: 8,015   (412) 434-6000

EAST STROUDSBURG UNIVERSITY OF PENNSYLVANIA
200 Prospect St., East Stroudsburg 18301 *Type:* Public (state) *System:* Pennsylvania State System of Higher Education *Accred.:* 1950/1992 (MSA) *Calendar:* Sem. plan *Degrees:* A, B, M *Prof. Accred.:* Community Health, Nursing (B), Recreation and Leisure Services *CEO:* Pres. James E. Gilbert
Enroll: 5,494   (717) 424-3545

THE EASTERN BAPTIST THEOLOGICAL SEMINARY
6 Lancaster Ave., Wynnewood 19096-3494 *Type:* Private (Baptist) graduate only *Accred.:* 1954/1989 (ATS); 1954/1993 (MSA) *Calendar:* 4-1-4 plan *Degrees:* M, P, D *CEO:* Pres. Manfred T. Brauch
Enroll: 316   (215) 896-5000

EASTERN COLLEGE
10 Fairview Dr., St. Davids 19087-3696 *Type:* Private (Baptist) liberal arts *Accred.:* 1954/1992 (MSA) *Calendar:* Sem. plan *Degrees:* A, B, M, certificates *Prof. Accred.:* Nursing (B), Social Work (B) *CEO:* Pres. Roberta Hestenes
Enroll: 1,505   (215) 341-5800

EDINBORO UNIVERSITY OF PENNSYLVANIA
Edinboro 16444 *Type:* Public (state) *System:* Pennsylvania State System of Higher Education *Accred.:* 1949/1988 (MSA) *Calendar:* Sem. plan *Degrees:* A, B, M, certificates *Prof. Accred.:* Dietetics (coordinated), Nursing (B), Rehabilitation Counseling, Social Work (B), Speech-Language Pathology (probational) *CEO:* Pres. Foster F. Diebold
Enroll: 8,165   (814) 732-2000

ELECTRONIC INSTITUTES
19 Jamesway Plaza, Middletown 17057-4851 *Type:* Private *Accred.:* 1967/1987 (ACCSCT) *Calendar:* Courses of varying lengths *Degrees:* A, certificates *CEO:* Dir. William F. Margut
      (717) 944-2731

ELECTRONIC INSTITUTES
4634 Browns Hill Rd., Pittsburgh 15217-2919 *Type:* Private *Accred.:* 1971/1986 (ACCSCT) *Calendar:* Courses of varying lengths *Degrees:* A, certificates *CEO:* Pres. Philip Chosky
      (412) 521-8686

ELIZABETHTOWN COLLEGE
One Alpha Dr., Elizabethtown 17022-2298 *Type:* Private (Church of Brethren) liberal arts *Accred.:* 1948/1989 (MSA) *Calendar:* Sem. plan *Degrees:* B *Prof. Accred.:* Music, Occupational Therapy, Social Work (B) *CEO:* Pres. Gerhard E. Spiegler
Enroll: 1,809   (717) 367-1000

ERIE BUSINESS CENTER
246 W. Ninth St., Erie 16501 *Type:* Private business *Accred.:* 1954/1988 (ACISC) *Calendar:* Courses of varying lengths *Degrees:* A *CEO:* Pres. Charles P. McGeary
      (814) 456-7504

ERIE BUSINESS CENTER SOUTH
700 Moravia St., New Castle 16101 *Accred.:* 1985/1990 (ACISC) *CEO:* Dir. Irene Marburger
      (412) 658-9066

EVANGELICAL SCHOOL OF THEOLOGY
121 S. College St., Myerstown 17067 *Type:* Private (Evangelical Congregational Church) graduate only *Accred.:* 1987 (ATS); 1984/

1991 (MSA) *Calendar:* Sem. plan *Degrees:* P, M *CEO:* Pres. Ray A. Seilhamer
Enroll: 79   (717) 866-5775

FRANKLIN & MARSHALL COLLEGE
P.O. Box 3003, Lancaster 17604-3003 *Type:* Private liberal arts *Accred.:* 1921/1989 (MSA) *Calendar:* Sem. plan *Degrees:* A, B *CEO:* Pres. A. Richard Kneedler
Enroll: 1,792   (717) 291-3911

GANNON UNIVERSITY
University Sq., Erie 16541 *Type:* Private (Roman Catholic) *Accred.:* 1951/1987 (MSA) *Calendar:* Sem. plan *Degrees:* A, B, M, certificates *Prof. Accred.:* Dietetics (coordinated), Engineering (electrical, mechanical), Medical Assisting (AMA), Nurse Anesthesia Education, Nursing (A,B,M), Physical Therapy, Physician Assisting, Radiography, Respiratory Therapy, Social Work (B) *CEO:* Pres. David A. Rubino, Ph.D.
Enroll: 4,523   (814) 871-7000

GENEVA COLLEGE
College Ave., Beaver Falls 15010 *Type:* Private (Reformed Presbyterian) liberal arts *Accred.:* 1922/1988 (MSA) *Calendar:* Sem. plan *Degrees:* A, B, M *CEO:* Pres. John H. White
Enroll: 1,518   (412) 846-5100

GETTYSBURG COLLEGE
300 N. Washington St., Gettysburg 17325-1486 *Type:* Private liberal arts *Accred.:* 1921/1988 (MSA) *Calendar:* Sem. plan *Degrees:* B *CEO:* Pres. Gordon A. Haaland
Enroll: 2,152   (717) 337-6000

GRATZ COLLEGE
Old York Rd. and Melrose Ave., Melrose Park 19126 *Type:* Private liberal arts *Accred.:* 1967/1992 (MSA) *Calendar:* Sem. plan *Degrees:* B, M, certificates *CEO:* Pres. Gary S. Schiff
Enroll: 332   (215) 635-7300

GROVE CITY COLLEGE
100 Campus Dr., Grove City 16127-2104 *Type:* Private liberal arts *Accred.:* 1922/1990 (MSA) *Calendar:* Sem. plan *Degrees:* B *Prof. Accred.:* Engineering (electrical, mechanical) *CEO:* Pres. Jerry H. Combee
Enroll: 2,173   (412) 458-2000

GWYNEDD-MERCY COLLEGE
Gwynedd Valley 19437 *Type:* Private liberal arts primarily for women *Accred.:* 1958/1991 (MSA) *Calendar:* Sem. plan *Degrees:* A, B, M, certificates *Prof. Accred.:* Medical Record Technology, Nursing (A,B), Radiation Therapy Technology, Respiratory Therapy, Respiratory Therapy Technology *CEO:* Pres. Linda M. Bevilacqua, O.P.
Enroll: 1,968   (215) 646-7300

HAHNEMANN UNIVERSITY
Broad and Vine Sts., Philadelphia 19102-1192 *Type:* Private *Accred.:* 1978/1992 (MSA) *Calendar:* Sem. plan *Degrees:* A, B, P, M, D *Prof. Accred.:* Clinical Psychology, Marriage and Family Therapy (M), Medical Laboratory Technology (AMA), Medical Technology, Medicine, Nursing (A,B), Oral and Maxillofacial Surgery, Perfusion, Physical Therapy, Physical Therapy Assisting, Physician Assisting, Psychology Internship (provisional), Radiography *CEO:* Chanc. Iqbal F. Paroo
Enroll: 2,263   (215) 762-7000

HARCUM COLLEGE
Morris and Montgomery Aves., Bryn Mawr 19010 *Type:* Private junior for women *Accred.:* 1970/1990 (MSA) *Calendar:* Sem. plan *Degrees:* A *Prof. Accred.:* Dental Assisting, Dental Hygiene, Medical Assisting (AMA), Medical Laboratory Technology (AMA), Occupational Therapy Assisting, Physical Therapy Assisting, Veterinary Technology *CEO:* Pres. Narcisa A. Polonio
Enroll: 809   (215) 525-4100

HARRISBURG AREA COMMUNITY COLLEGE
One HACC Dr., Harrisburg 17110-2999 *Type:* Public (local/state) junior *Accred.:* 1967/1992 (MSA) *Calendar:* Sem. plan *Degrees:* A *Prof. Accred.:* Dental Assisting, Dental Hygiene, EMT-Paramedic, Engineering Technology (electrical, mechanical), Medical Laboratory Technology (AMA), Nursing (A), Practical Nursing, Respiratory Therapy, Respiratory Therapy Technology *CEO:* Pres. Mary L. Fifield
Enroll: 9,111   (717) 780-2300

LANCASTER CAMPUS
1008 New Holland Ave., Lancaster 17604 *CEO:* Dean Michael B. Klunk
(717) 293-5000

LEBANON CAMPUS
731 Cumberland St., Lebanon 17042 *CEO:* Dean Philip G. Hubbard
(717) 270-4222

HAVERFORD COLLEGE
370 Lancaster Ave., Haverford 19041-1392 *Type:* Private liberal arts *Accred.:* 1921/1988 (MSA) *Calendar:* Sem. plan *Degrees:* B *CEO:* Pres. Tom G. Kessinger
Enroll: 1,113   (215) 896-1000

HOLY FAMILY COLLEGE
Grant and Frankford Aves., Philadelphia 19114-2094 *Type:* Private (Roman Catholic) liberal arts *Accred.:* 1961/1991 (MSA) *Calendar:* Sem. plan *Degrees:* A, B, M *Prof. Accred.:* Nursing (B), Radiography *CEO:* Pres. M. Francesca Onley, Ph.D.
Enroll: 2,216   (215) 637-7700

HUSSIAN SCHOOL OF ART
1118 Market St., Philadelphia 19107-3679 *Type:* Private *Accred.:* 1972/1989 (ACCSCT) *Calendar:* Sem. plan *Degrees:* A *CEO:* Dir. Ronald Dove
(215) 238-9000

ICM SCHOOL OF BUSINESS
10 Wood St., Pittsburgh 15222 *Type:* Private business *Accred.:* 1967/1990 (ACISC) *Calendar:* Courses of varying lengths *Degrees:* A, certificates, diplomas *Prof. Accred.:* Medical Assisting (AMA) *CEO:* Dir. James D. Tussing
(412) 261-2647

IMMACULATA COLLEGE
Immaculata 19345 *Type:* Private (Roman Catholic) liberal arts for women *Accred.:* 1928/1989 (MSA) *Calendar:* Sem. plan *Degrees:* A, B, M, D *Prof. Accred.:* Music, Nursing (B) *CEO:* Pres. Marie Roseanne Bonfini, I.H.M.
Enroll: 2,345   (215) 647-4400

INDIANA UNIVERSITY OF PENNSYLVANIA
Indiana 15705 *Type:* Public (state) *System:* Pennsylvania State System of Higher Education *Accred.:* 1941/1990 (MSA) *Calendar:* Sem. plan *Degrees:* A, B, M, D, certificates *Prof. Accred.:* Clinical Psychology, Music, Nursing (B,M), Respiratory Therapy,

Speech-Language Pathology, Teacher Education (e,s,p) *CEO:* Pres. Lawrence K. Pettit
Enroll: 14,620   (412) 357-2100

ARMSTRONG COUNTY CAMPUS
Kittanning 16201 *CEO:* Dir. Robert H. Doerr
                    (814) 543-1078

PUNXSUTAWNEY CAMPUS
Punxsutawney 15767 *CEO:* Dir. Norman T. Storm
                    (814) 938-6711

INTERNATIONAL CORRESPONDENCE SCHOOLS
925 Oak St., Scranton 18515 *Type:* Private home study *Accred.:* 1956/1989 (NHSC) *Calendar:* Courses of varying lengths *Degrees:* A, certificates *CEO:* Pres. Gary M. Keisling
                    (717) 342-7701

THE ENGLISH LANGUAGE INSTITUTE OF AMERICA, INC.
925 Oak St., Scranton 18515 *Accred.:* 1981/1990 (NHSC) *CEO:* Pres. Gary M. Keisling
                    (717) 941-3406

ICS CENTER FOR DEGREE STUDIES
925 Oak St., Scranton 18515 *CEO:* Dir. Gerald E. Burns
                    (717) 342-7701

NORTH AMERICAN CORRESPONDENCE SCHOOLS
925 Oak St., Scranton 18515 *Accred.:* 1965/1990 (NHSC) *CEO:* Pres. Gary M. Keisling
                    (717) 342-7701

JOHNSON TECHNICAL INSTITUTE
3427 N. Main Ave., Scranton 18508-1495 *Type:* Private *Accred.:* 1979/1989 (ACCSCT) *Calendar:* Sem. plan *Degrees:* A *CEO:* Pres. Thomas W. Krause
                    (717) 342-6404

BRANCH CAMPUS
200 Shady La., Philipsburg 16866 *Accred.:* 1991 (ACCSCT) *CEO:* Dir. William Knight
                    (814) 342-5680

JUNIATA COLLEGE
1700 Moore St., Huntingdon 16652 *Type:* Private liberal arts *Accred.:* 1922/1993 (MSA) *Calendar:* Sem. plan *Degrees:* B *Prof. Accred.:* Social Work (B) *CEO:* Pres. Robert W. Neff
Enroll: 1,119   (814) 643-4310

KEYSTONE JUNIOR COLLEGE
P.O. Box 50, La Plume 18440-0200 *Type:* Private junior *Accred.:* 1936/1988 (MSA) *Calendar:* Sem. plan *Degrees:* A, certificates *CEO:* Pres. Robert E. Mooney, Jr.
Enroll: 1,024   (717) 945-5141

KING'S COLLEGE
133 N. River St., Wilkes-Barre 18711 *Type:* Private (Roman Catholic) liberal arts *Accred.:* 1955/1989 (MSA) *Calendar:* Sem. plan *Degrees:* A, B, M, certificates *Prof. Accred.:* Physician Assisting *CEO:* Pres. James R. Lackenmier, C.S.C.
Enroll: 2,294   (717) 826-5900

KUTZTOWN UNIVERSITY OF PENNSYLVANIA
Kutztown 19530 *Type:* Public (state) *System:* Pennsylvania State System of Higher Education *Accred.:* 1944/1988 (MSA) *Calendar:* Sem. plan *Degrees:* B, M *Prof. Accred.:* Nursing (B), Teacher Education (e,s,p) *CEO:* Pres. David E. McFarland
Enroll: 8,164   (215) 683-4000

LA ROCHE COLLEGE
9000 Babcock Blvd., Pittsburgh 15237 *Type:* Private (Roman Catholic) *Accred.:* 1973/1988 (MSA) *Calendar:* Sem. plan *Degrees:* B, M *Prof. Accred.:* Art (associate), Interior Design, Nurse Anesthesia Education, Nursing (B,M) *CEO:* Pres. William A. Kerr
Enroll: 1,851   (412) 367-9300

LA SALLE UNIVERSITY
1900 W. Olney Ave., Philadelphia 19141 *Type:* Private (Roman Catholic) *Accred.:* 1930/1991 (MSA) *Calendar:* Sem. plan *Degrees:* A, B, M *Prof. Accred.:* Nursing (B,M), Social Work (B) *CEO:* Pres. Joseph F. Burke, F.S.C.
Enroll: 6,069   (215) 951-1000

LACKAWANNA JUNIOR COLLEGE
901 Prospect Ave., Scranton 18505 *Type:* Private junior *Accred.:* 1973/1978 (MSA)

Calendar: Sem. plan *Degrees:* A, certificates *CEO:* Pres. Joseph G. Morelli
Enroll: 804   (717) 961-7810

LAFAYETTE COLLEGE
High St., Easton 18042 *Type:* Private liberal arts *Accred.:* 1921/1988 (MSA) *Calendar:* Sem. plan *Degrees:* B *Prof. Accred.:* Engineering (chemical, civil, electrical, mechanical) *CEO:* Acting Pres. Arthur J. Rothkopf
Enroll: 2,224   (215) 250-5000

LAKE ERIE COLLEGE OF OSTEOPATHIC MEDICINE
1858 W. Grandview Blvd., Erie 16509 *Type:* Independent *Calendar:* Sem. plan *Degrees:* P *Prof. Accred.:* Osteopathy *CEO:* Pres. Joseph John Namey
                  (814) 866-6641

LANCASTER BIBLE COLLEGE
901 Eden Rd., Lancaster 17601 *Type:* Independent *Accred.:* 1964/1989 (AABC); 1982/1992 (MSA) *Calendar:* Sem. plan *Degrees:* A, B, certificates *CEO:* Pres. Gilbert A. Peterson
Enroll: 392   (717) 569-7071

LANCASTER THEOLOGICAL SEMINARY
555 W. James St., Lancaster 17603-2897 *Type:* Private (United Church of Christ) graduate only *Accred.:* 1938/1989 (ATS); 1978/1989 (MSA) *Calendar:* 3-1-3 plan *Degrees:* P, M, D *CEO:* Pres. Peter M. Schmiechen
Enroll: 243   (717) 393-0654

THE LANSDALE SCHOOL OF BUSINESS
201 Church Rd., North Wales 19454 *Type:* Private junior *Accred.:* 1967/1986 (ACISC) *Calendar:* Courses of varying lengths *Degrees:* A *CEO:* Pres. Marlon D. Keller
                  (215) 699-5700

THE LAUREL BUSINESS INSTITUTE
11-15 Penn St., Uniontown 15401 *Type:* Private business *Accred.:* 1987/1991 (ACISC) *Calendar:* Courses of varying lengths *Degrees:* A, certificates, diplomas *CEO:* Pres. Christopher D. Decker
                  (412) 439-4900

LEBANON VALLEY COLLEGE
101 N. College Ave., Annville 17003-0501 *Type:* Private (United Methodist) liberal arts *Accred.:* 1922/1993 (MSA) *Calendar:* Sem.

plan *Degrees:* A, B, M *Prof. Accred.:* Music *CEO:* Pres. John A. Synodinos
Enroll: 1,488   (717) 867-6100

LEHIGH COUNTY COMMUNITY COLLEGE
4525 Education Park Dr., Schnecksville 18078-2598 *Type:* Public (local/state) junior *Accred.:* 1972/1988 (MSA) *Calendar:* Sem. plan *Degrees:* A, certificates *Prof. Accred.:* Medical Assisting (AMA), Medical Record Technology, Nursing (A), Occupational Therapy Assisting, Physical Therapy Assisting, Respiratory Therapy, Respiratory Therapy Technology *CEO:* Pres. James R. Davis
Enroll: 4,649   (215) 799-2121

LEHIGH UNIVERSITY
27 Memorial Dr. W., Bethlehem 18015 *Type:* Private *Accred.:* 1921/1988 (MSA) *Calendar:* Sem. plan *Degrees:* B, M, D *Prof. Accred.:* Accounting (Type A), Business (B,M), Computer Science, Engineering (chemical, civil, computer, electrical, industrial, materials, mechanical), School Psychology, Theatre *CEO:* Pres. Peter Likins, Jr.
Enroll: 6,556   (215) 758-3000

LINCOLN UNIVERSITY
Lincoln University 19352-0999 *Type:* Private (state) liberal arts *Accred.:* 1922/1988 (MSA) *Calendar:* Sem. plan *Degrees:* A, B, M *Prof. Accred.:* Recreation and Leisure Services *CEO:* Pres. Niara Sudarkasa
Enroll: 1,458   (215) 932-8300

LOCK HAVEN UNIVERSITY OF PENNSYLVANIA
Lock Haven 17745 *Type:* Public (state) *System:* Pennsylvania State System of Higher Education *Accred.:* 1949/1990 (MSA) *Calendar:* Sem. plan *Degrees:* A, B, M, certificates *Prof. Accred.:* Nursing (A), Social Work (B), Teacher Education (e,s) *CEO:* Pres. Craig D. Willis
Enroll: 3,712   (717) 893-2011

LUTHERAN THEOLOGICAL SEMINARY AT GETTYSBURG
61 N.W. Confederate Ave., Gettysburg 17325-1795 *Type:* Private (Evangelical Lutheran Church) graduate only *Accred.:* 1938/1989 (ATS); 1971/1991 (MSA) *Calen-*

dar: Qtr. plan *Degrees:* P, M *CEO:* Pres.
Darold H. Beekmann
Enroll: 236   (717) 334-6286

LUTHERAN THEOLOGICAL SEMINARY AT
PHILADELPHIA
7301 Germantown Ave., Philadelphia 19119
Type: Private (Evangelical Lutheran Church)
graduate only *Accred.:* 1938/1991 (ATS);
1971/1992 (MSA) *Calendar:* Sem. plan *Degrees:* P, M, D *CEO:* Pres. Robert G. Hughes
Enroll: 261   (215) 248-4616

LUZERNE COUNTY COMMUNITY COLLEGE
133 S. Prospect St., Nanticoke 18634 *Type:*
Public (local/state) junior *Accred.:* 1975/
1991 (MSA) *Calendar:* Tri. plan *Degrees:* A
Prof. Accred.: Dental Hygiene, Nursing (A),
Respiratory Therapy Technology *CEO:* Pres.
Donald R. Bronsard
Enroll: 6,881   (717) 829-7300

LYCOMING COLLEGE
Academy St., Williamsport 17701 *Type:* Private (United Methodist) liberal arts *Accred.:*
1934/1991 (MSA) *Calendar:* Sem. plan *Degrees:* B *Prof. Accred.:* Nursing (B) *CEO:*
Pres. James E. Douthat
Enroll: 1,405   (717) 321-4000

MANOR JUNIOR COLLEGE
700 Fox Chase Rd., Jenkintown 19046 *Type:*
Private (Ukrainian Catholic) for women *Accred.:* 1967/1988 (MSA) *Calendar:* Sem.
plan *Degrees:* A, certificates *Prof. Accred.:*
Dental Assisting, Medical Laboratory
Technology (AMA), Veterinary Technology
(probational) *CEO:* Pres. Mary Cecilia
Jurasinski, O.S.B.M.
Enroll: 570   (215) 885-2360

MANSFIELD UNIVERSITY OF PENNSYLVANIA
Academy St., Mansfield 16933 *Type:* Public
(state) *System:* Pennsylvania State System of
Higher Education *Accred.:* 1942/1992
(MSA) *Calendar:* Sem. plan *Degrees:* A, B,
M *Prof. Accred.:* Music, Radiography, Respiratory Therapy, Social Work (B), Teacher
Education (e,s) *CEO:* Pres. Rodney C.
Kelchner
Enroll: 3,371   (717) 662-4000

MARYWOOD COLLEGE
2300 Adams Ave., Scranton 18509 *Type:*
Private (Roman Catholic) liberal arts primar-

ily for women *Accred.:* 1921/1991 (MSA)
Calendar: Sem. plan *Degrees:* B, M *Prof.
Accred.:* Art, Dietetics (coordinated), Music,
Nursing (B), Social Work (B,M), Teacher
Education (e,s) *CEO:* Pres. Mary Reap,
I.H.M.
Enroll: 2,929   (717) 348-6231

MCCANN SCHOOL OF BUSINESS
Main and Pine Sts., Mahanoy City 17948
Type: Private business *Accred.:* 1962/1990
(ACISC) *Calendar:* Tri. plan *Degrees:* A
CEO: Dir. John J. Slodysko
                    (717) 773-1820

BRANCH CAMPUS
2004 Wyoming Ave., Wyoming 18644
Accred.: 1987 (ACISC) *CEO:* Pres. James
F. Noone
                    (717) 287-4400

MCCARRIE SCHOOLS OF HEALTH SCIENCES AND
TECHNOLOGY INC.
512-520 S. Broad St., Philadelphia 19146-
1613 *Type:* Private technical *Accred.:* 1983/
1989 (ABHES); 1973/1989 (ACCSCT) *Calendar:* Courses of varying lengths *Degrees:*
A, diplomas *Prof. Accred.:* Medical Assisting, Medical Laboratory Technology *CEO:*
Exec. Vice Pres. Robert J. Walder
                    (215) 545-7772

MEDIAN SCHOOL OF ALLIED HEALTH CAREERS
125 Seventh St., Pittsburgh 15222-3400
Type: Private *Accred.:* 1970/1986 (ACC-
SCT) *Calendar:* Qtr. plan *Degrees:* A, certificates, diplomas *Prof. Accred.:* Dental Assisting, Medical Assisting (AMA) *CEO:*
Pres. William B. Mosle, Jr.
                    (412) 391-7021

MEDICAL COLLEGE OF PENNSYLVANIA
3300 Henry Ave., Philadelphia 19129 *Type:*
Private professional *Accred.:* 1984/1991
(MSA) *Calendar:* Sem. plan *Degrees:* P, M,
D *Prof. Accred.:* General Practice Residency, Medicine, Nurse Anesthesia Education,
Psychology Internship *CEO:* Pres. Leonard
L. Ross
Enroll: 582   (215) 842-6000

MERCYHURST COLLEGE
501 E. 38th St., Erie 16546 *Type:* Private
(Roman Catholic) liberal arts *Accred.:* 1931/
1992 (MSA) *Calendar:* 4-2-4 plan *Degrees:*

A, B, M *Prof. Accred.:* Dietetics (coordinated), Social Work (B) *CEO:* Pres. William P. Garvey
Enroll: 2,186   (814) 824-2000

MESSIAH COLLEGE
Grantham 17027 *Type:* Private (Brethren in Christ) *Accred.:* 1963/1988 (MSA) *Calendar:* Sem. plan *Degrees:* B *Prof. Accred.:* Music, Nursing (B), Social Work (B) *CEO:* Pres. D. Ray Hostetter
Enroll: 2,259   (717) 766-2511

CITY CAMPUS
2026 N. Broad St., Philadelphia 19121 *CEO:* Dir. Don Wingert
(215) 769-2526

MILLERSVILLE UNIVERSITY OF PENNSYLVANIA
P.O. Box 1002, Millersville 17551-1002 *Type:* Public (state) *System:* Pennsylvania State System of Higher Education *Accred.:* 1950/1990 (MSA) *Calendar:* Sem. plan *Degrees:* A, B, M *Prof. Accred.:* Music, Nursing (B), Respiratory Therapy, Social Work (B), Teacher Education (e,s,p) *CEO:* Pres. Joseph A. Caputo
Enroll: 7,805   (717) 872-3011

MONTGOMERY COUNTY COMMUNITY COLLEGE
340 DeKalb Pike, Blue Bell 19422 *Type:* Public (local/state) junior *Accred.:* 1970/1991 (MSA) *Calendar:* Sem. plan *Degrees:* A, certificates *Prof. Accred.:* Dental Hygiene, Medical Laboratory Technology (AMA), Nursing (A) *CEO:* Pres. Edward M. Sweitzer
Enroll: 8,981   (215) 641-6300

MOORE COLLEGE OF ART AND DESIGN
The Parkway at 20th St., Philadelphia 19103 *Type:* Private professional for women *Accred.:* 1958/1992 (MSA) *Calendar:* Sem. plan *Degrees:* B *Prof. Accred.:* Art, Interior Design *CEO:* President Barbara Price
Enroll: 510   (215) 568-4515

MORAVIAN COLLEGE
1200 Main St., Bethlehem 18018 *Type:* Private (Moravian Church) *Accred.:* 1954/1988 (AABC); 1922/1988 (MSA) *Calendar:* 4-1-4 plan *Degrees:* B, P, M *CEO:* Pres. Roger H. Martin
Enroll: 1,308   (215) 861-1300

MOUNT ALOYSIUS COLLEGE
One College Dr., Cresson 16630 *Type:* Private (Roman Catholic) liberal arts *Accred.:* 1943/1990 (MSA) *Calendar:* Sem. plan *Degrees:* A, B, certificates *Prof. Accred.:* Medical Laboratory Technology (AMA), Nursing (A), Occupational Therapy Assisting, Surgical Technology *CEO:* Pres. Edward F. Pierce
Enroll: 1,037   (814) 886-4131

MUHLENBERG COLLEGE
24th and Chew Sts., Allentown 18104 *Type:* Private (Lutheran) liberal arts *Accred.:* 1921/1991 (MSA) *Calendar:* Sem. plan *Degrees:* A, B *CEO:* Pres. Arthur R. Taylor
Enroll: 2,071   (215) 821-3100

NATIONAL EDUCATION CENTER THOMPSON CAMPUS
5650 Derry St., Harrisburg 17111-4112 *Type:* Private business *Accred.:* 1962/1990 (ACISC) *Calendar:* Qtr. plan *Degrees:* A, certificates, diplomas *CEO:* Exec. Dir. Mike Seifert
(717) 564-8710

BRANCH CAMPUS
University City Science Ctr., 3440 Market St., Philadelphia 19104 *Accred.:* 1983/1986 (ACISC) *CEO:* Exec. Dir. Dom Montalzo
(215) 387-1530

NEUMANN COLLEGE
Concord Rd., Aston 19014 *Type:* Private (Roman Catholic) liberal arts *Accred.:* 1972/1991 (MSA) *Calendar:* Sem. plan *Degrees:* A, B, M *Prof. Accred.:* Medical Technology, Nursing (B) *CEO:* Pres. Nan B. Hechenberger
Enroll: 1,248   (215) 459-0905

NEW KENSINGTON COMMERCIAL SCHOOL
945 Greensburg Rd., New Kensington 15068 *Type:* Private business *Accred.:* 1959/1987 (ACISC) *Calendar:* Qtr. plan *Degrees:* A *CEO:* Pres. J. Bryant Mullen
(412) 339-7542

NORTHAMPTON COUNTY AREA COMMUNITY COLLEGE
3835 Green Pond Rd., Bethlehem 18017 *Type:* Public (local/state) junior *Accred.:* 1970/1990 (MSA) *Calendar:* Sem. plan *De-*

grees: A *Prof. Accred.:* Dental Hygiene, Funeral Service Education, Medical Laboratory Technology (AMA), Nursing (A), Practical Nursing, Radiography *CEO:* Pres. Robert J. Kopecek
Enroll: 6,055   (215) 861-5300

NORTHEAST INSTITUTE OF EDUCATION
P.O. Box 470, 314 Adams Ave., Scranton 18501-0470 *Type:* Private business *Accred.:* 1979/1988 (ACISC) *Calendar:* Courses of varying lengths *Degrees:* A *CEO:* Pres. Gregory C. Walker
                                   (717) 346-6666

BRANCH CAMPUS
Fountain Ct., Rte. 611, Box 574, Bartonsville 18321 *Accred.:* 1982/1988 (ACISC) *CEO:* Dir. Charles Gahwiler
                                   (717) 629-5555

NORTHEASTERN CHRISTIAN JUNIOR COLLEGE
1860 Montgomery Ave., Villanova 19085 *Type:* Private (Church of Christ) junior *Accred.:* 1978/1986 (MSA) *Calendar:* Tri. plan *Degrees:* A *CEO:* Pres. Bill D. Bowen
Enroll: 148   (215) 525-6780

PACE INSTITUTE
606 Court St., Reading 19601 *Type:* Private business *Accred.:* 1984/1990 (ACISC) *Calendar:* Courses of varying lengths *Degrees:* A, certificates, diplomas *CEO:* Pres. Rhoda E. Dersh
                                   (215) 375-1212

PALMER BUSINESS INSTITUTE
1457 Manheim Pike, Lancaster 17601 *Type:* Private business *Accred.:* 1985/1990 (ACISC) *Calendar:* Courses of varying lengths *Degrees:* A, certificates, diplomas *CEO:* Dir. Dennis P. Sheaffer
                                   (717) 392-1700

PEIRCE JUNIOR COLLEGE
1420 Pine St., Philadelphia 19102 *Type:* Private junior *Accred.:* 1971/1987 (MSA) *Calendar:* Sem. plan *Degrees:* A, certificates *CEO:* Pres. Arthur J. Lendo, Jr.
Enroll: 1,016   (215) 545-6400

PENN TECHNICAL INSTITUTE
110 Ninth St., Pittsburgh 15222-3618 *Type:* Private *Accred.:* 1967/1988 (ACCSCT) *Cal-*

endar: Qtr. plan *Degrees:* A *CEO:* Dir. Louis A. Dimasi
                                   (412) 355-0455

PENNCO TECH
3815 Otter St., Bristol 19007-3696 *Type:* Private *Accred.:* 1969/1993 (ACCSCT) *Calendar:* Courses of varying lengths *Degrees:* A, certificates, diplomas *CEO:* Pres. John A. Hobyak
                                   (215) 824-3200

PENNSYLVANIA ACADEMY OF THE FINE ARTS
118 N. Broad St., Philadelphia 19102 *Type:* Private professional *Calendar:* Courses of varying lengths *Degrees:* certificates, M *Prof. Accred.:* Art *CEO:* Dir. Frederick S. Osborne, Jr.
                                   (215) 972-7623

PENNSYLVANIA BUSINESS INSTITUTE
81 Robinson St., Pottstown 19464 *Type:* Private business *Accred.:* 1983/1986 (ACISC) *Calendar:* Courses of varying lengths *Degrees:* A *CEO:* Dir. June Stanbaugh
                                   (215) 326-6150

BRANCH CAMPUS
One Angelini Ave., Nesquehoning 18240 *Accred.:* 1993 (ACISC) *CEO:* Dir. Richard W. Miller
                                   (717) 669-9894

PENNSYLVANIA COLLEGE OF OPTOMETRY
1200 W. Godfrey Ave., Philadelphia 19141 *Type:* Private professional *Accred.:* 1954/1993 (MSA) *Calendar:* Sem. plan *Degrees:* B, P, M, certificates *Prof. Accred.:* Optometry *CEO:* Pres. Thomas L. Lewis, O.D.
Enroll: 634   (215) 276-6200

PENNSYLVANIA COLLEGE OF PODIATRIC MEDICINE
8th and Race Sts., Philadelphia 19107 *Type:* Private professional *Accred.:* 1990 (MSA) *Calendar:* Sem. plan *Degrees:* P, D *Prof. Accred.:* Podiatry *CEO:* Pres. James E. Bates
Enroll: 392   (215) 629-0300

PENNSYLVANIA COLLEGE OF TECHNOLOGY
One College Ave., Williamsport 17701 *Type:* Public (state) junior *Accred.:* 1970/1992 (MSA) *Calendar:* Sem. plan *Degrees:* A, certificates *Prof. Accred.:* Dental Hygiene, Engineering Technology (civil/con-

struction), Nursing (A), Occupational Therapy Assisting, Radiography *CEO:* Pres. Robert L. Breuder
Enroll: 4,719   (717) 326-3761

NORTH CAMPUS
Mansfield Rd., Wellsboro 16901 *CEO:* Dean William J. Lex
       (717) 724-7703

PENNSYLVANIA INSTITUTE OF TECHNOLOGY
800 Manchester Ave., Media 19063 *Type:* Private 2-year *Accred.:* 1983/1991 (MSA) *Calendar:* Qtr. plan *Degrees:* A, certificates *CEO:* Pres. Edward R. D'Alessio
Enroll: 370   (215) 565-7900

THE PENNSYLVANIA STATE UNIVERSITY
201 Old Main, University Park 16802 *Type:* Public (state) *Accred.:* 1921/1987 (MSA) *Calendar:* Sem. plan *Degrees:* A, B, M, D, certificates *Prof. Accred.:* Accounting (Type A,B,C), Art, Audiology, Business (B,M), Clinical Psychology, Counseling Psychology, Engineering (aerospace, agricultural, architectural, ceramic, chemical, civil, computer, electrical, engineering physics/science, industrial, mechanical, metallurgical, mining, nuclear, petroleum), Forestry, Health Services Administration, Journalism (B,M), Landscape Architecture (B), Music, Nursing (B,M), Psychology Internship, Public Administration, Recreation and Leisure Services, Rehabilitation Counseling, School Psychology, Social Work (B), Speech-Language Pathology, Teacher Education (e,s,p), Theatre *CEO:* Pres. Joab Langston Thomas
Enroll: 38,989   (814) 865-4700

ALLENTOWN CAMPUS
6090 Mohr La., Fogelsville 18051 *CEO:* Campus Exec. Ofcr. John V. Cooney
       (215) 285-4811

ALTOONA CAMPUS
Ivyside Park, Altoona 16601-3760 *Prof. Accred.:* Engineering Technology (electrical, mechanical) *CEO:* Acting Campus Exec. Ofcr. Kjell Meling
       (814) 949-5000

BEAVER CAMPUS
Brodhead Rd., Monaca 15061 *Prof. Accred.:* Engineering Technology (electrical,

mechanical, nuclear) *CEO:* Campus Exec. Ofcr. David B. Otto
       (412) 773-3500

BERKS CAMPUS
Tulpehocken Rd., Reading 19610 *Prof. Accred.:* Engineering Technology (electrical, mechanical) *CEO:* Campus Exec. Ofcr. Frederick H. Gaige
       (215) 320-4800

DELAWARE COUNTY CAMPUS
25 Yearsley Mill Rd., Media 19063 *Prof. Accred.:* Engineering Technology (electrical) *CEO:* Campus Exec. Ofcr. Edward S.J. Tomezsko
       (215) 565-3300

DUBOIS CAMPUS
College Pl., DuBois 15801 *Prof. Accred.:* Engineering Technology (electrical, mechanical) *CEO:* Campus Exec. Ofcr. Donald T. Hartman
       (814) 375-4700

FAYETTE CAMPUS
P.O. Box 519, Rte. 119 N., Uniontown 15401 *Prof. Accred.:* Engineering Technology (air conditioning, architectural, electrical) *CEO:* Campus Exec. Ofcr. August H. Simonsen
       (412) 430-4100

GREAT VALLEY GRADUATE CENTER
30 E. Swedesford Rd., Malvern 19355 *CEO:* Campus Exec. Ofcr. Lawrence S. Cote
       (215) 889-1300

HAZLETON CAMPUS
Highacres, Hazleton 18201 *Prof. Accred.:* Engineering Technology (electrical, mechanical), Medical Laboratory Technology (AMA), Physical Therapy Assisting *CEO:* Campus Exec. Ofcr. James J. Staudenmeier
       (717) 450-3000

HERSHEY MEDICAL CENTER
500 University Dr., Hershey 17033 *Prof. Accred.:* Medicine, Perfusion, Radiography *CEO:* Sr. Vice Pres./Dean C. McCollister Evarts
       (717) 531-8521

MCKEESPORT CAMPUS
University Dr., McKeesport 15132 *Prof. Accred.:* Engineering Technology (electrical, mechanical) *CEO:* Campus Exec. Ofcr. Joanne E. Burley
(412) 675-9000

MONT ALTO CAMPUS
Campus Dr., Mont Alto 17237 *Prof. Accred.:* Physical Therapy Assisting *CEO:* Campus Exec. Ofcr. Corrinne A. Caldwell
(717) 749-3111

NEW KENSINGTON CAMPUS
3550 Seventh Street Rd., New Kensington 15068 *Prof. Accred.:* Engineering Technology (bioengineering, electrical, mechanical), Medical Laboratory Technology (AMA), Radiography *CEO:* Campus Exec. Ofcr. Roy Myers
(412) 339-5466

OGONTZ CAMPUS
1600 Woodland Rd., Abington 19001 *Prof. Accred.:* Engineering Technology (electrical, mechanical) *CEO:* Campus Exec. Ofcr. Anthony Fusaro
(215) 886-9400

PENNSYLVANIA STATE UNIVERSITY AT ERIE-
BEHREND COLLEGE
Station Rd., Erie 16563 *Prof. Accred.:* Engineering Technology (electrical, mechanical) *CEO:* Provost/Dean John M. Lilley
(814) 898-6000

PENNSYLVANIA STATE UNIVERSITY AT
HARRISBURG-CAPITAL COLLEGE
Rte. 230, Middletown 17057 *Prof. Accred.:* Engineering Technology (civil/construction, electrical, environmental/sanitary, mechanical), Public Administration *CEO:* Provost/Dean Ruth Leventhal
(717) 948-6100

SCHUYLKILL CAMPUS
200 University Dr., Schuylkill Haven 17972 *Prof. Accred.:* Engineering Technology (computer, electrical), Radiography *CEO:* Campus Exec. Ofcr. Wayne D. Lammie
(717) 385-6000

SHENANGO CAMPUS
147 Shenango Ave., Sharon 16146 *Prof. Accred.:* Engineering Technology (electrical, mechanical) *CEO:* Campus Exec. Ofcr. Albert N. Skomra
(412) 983-5800

WILKES-BARRE CAMPUS
P.O. Box PSU, Lehman 18627 *Prof. Accred.:* Engineering Technology (bioengineering, electrical, mechanical, surveying) *CEO:* Campus Exec. Ofcr. William A. Pearman
(717) 675-2171

WORTHINGTON-SCRANTON CAMPUS
120 Ridge View Dr., Dunmore 18512 *Prof. Accred.:* Engineering Technology (architectural, electrical, mechanical) *CEO:* Campus Exec. Ofcr. James D. Gallagher
(717) 963-4757

YORK CAMPUS
1031 Edgecomb Ave., York 17403 *Prof. Accred.:* Engineering Technology (electrical, mechanical) *CEO:* Campus Exec. Ofcr. John J. Romano
(717) 771-4000

PHILADELPHIA COLLEGE OF BIBLE
200 Manor Ave., Langhorne 19047-2990 *Type:* Independent (interdenominational) *Accred.:* 1950/1986 (AABC); 1967/1991 (MSA) *Calendar:* Sem. plan *Degrees:* A, B, M, certificates *Prof. Accred.:* Music, Social Work (B) *CEO:* Pres. W. Sherrill Babb
Enroll: 685   (215) 752-5800

PHILADELPHIA COLLEGE OF OSTEOPATHIC
MEDICINE
4150 City Ave., Philadelphia 19131 *Type:* Private professional *Calendar:* Sem. plan *Degrees:* P, M, D *Prof. Accred.:* Osteopathy *CEO:* Pres. Leonard H. Finkelstein
Enroll: 808   (215) 871-2800

PHILADELPHIA COLLEGE OF PHARMACY AND
SCIENCE
600 S. 43rd St., Philadelphia 19104-4495 *Type:* Private professional *Accred.:* 1962/1988 (MSA) *Calendar:* Sem. plan *Degrees:* B, P, M, D *Prof. Accred.:* Physical Therapy *CEO:* Pres. Allen Misher
Enroll: 1,712   (215) 596-8800

PHILADELPHIA COLLEGE OF TEXTILES AND SCIENCE
Schoolhouse La. and Henry Ave., Philadelphia 19144 *Type:* Private professional *Accred.:* 1955/1991 (MSA) *Calendar:* Sem. plan *Degrees:* A, B, M *CEO:* Pres. James P. Gallagher
Enroll: 3,321   (215) 951-2700

PITTSBURGH INSTITUTE OF AERONAUTICS
P.O. Box 10897, Pittsburgh 15236-0897 *Type:* Private *Accred.:* 1970/1993 (ACC-SCT) *Calendar:* Qtr. plan *Degrees:* A, diplomas *CEO:* C.E.O. John Graham
                    (412) 466-1022

PITTSBURGH INSTITUTE OF MORTUARY SCIENCE
5808 Baum Blvd., Pittsburgh 15206 *Type:* Private professional *Calendar:* Courses of varying lengths *Degrees:* A, diplomas *Prof. Accred.:* Mortuary Science *CEO:* Pres. Eugene C. Ogrodnik
                    (412) 362-8500

PITTSBURGH TECHNICAL INSTITUTE
635 Smithfield St., Pittsburgh 15222-2560 *Type:* Private *Accred.:* 1976/1991 (ACC-SCT) *Calendar:* Sem. plan *Degrees:* A *CEO:* Pres. J.R. McCartan
                    (412) 471-1011

PITTSBURGH THEOLOGICAL SEMINARY
616 N. Highland Ave., Pittsburgh 15206 *Type:* Private (Presbyterian) graduate only *Accred.:* 1938/1992 (ATS); 1970/1993 (MSA) *Calendar:* Qtr. plan *Degrees:* P, M, D *CEO:* Pres. Carnegie Samuel Calian
Enroll: 311   (412) 362-5610

POINT PARK COLLEGE
201 Wood St., Pittsburgh 15222 *Type:* Private *Accred.:* 1968/1989 (MSA) *Calendar:* Sem. plan *Degrees:* A, B, M, certificates *Prof. Accred.:* Engineering Technology (civil/construction, electrical, mechanical) *CEO:* Pres. J. Matthew Simon
Enroll: 2,932   (412) 391-4100

READING AREA COMMUNITY COLLEGE
P.O. Box 1706, 10 S. 2nd St., Reading 19603-1706 *Type:* Public (state) junior *Accred.:* 1979/1988 (MSA) *Calendar:* Tri. plan *Degrees:* A, certificates *Prof. Accred.:* Medical Laboratory Technology (AMA) *CEO:* Pres. Gust Zogas
Enroll: 2,910   (215) 372-4721

RECONSTRUCTIONIST RABBINICAL COLLEGE
Greenwood Ave. and Church Rd., Wyncote 19095 *Type:* Private (Jewish) professional *Accred.:* 1990 (MSA) *Calendar:* Sem. plan *Degrees:* P, M *CEO:* Pres. David A. Teutsch
Enroll: 57   (215) 576-0800

ROBERT MORRIS COLLEGE
Narrows Run Rd., Coraopolis 15108 *Type:* Private *Accred.:* 1968/1992 (MSA) *Calendar:* Tri. plan *Degrees:* A, B, M *Prof. Accred.:* Radiography *CEO:* Pres. Edward A. Nicholson
Enroll: 5,492   (412) 262-8200

PITTSBURGH CAMPUS
600 Fifth Ave., Pittsburgh 15219 *CEO:* Dir. Daniel Pavlic
                    (412) 227-6800

ROSEMONT COLLEGE
1400 Montgomery Ave., Rosemont 19010-1699 *Type:* Private (Roman Catholic) liberal arts for women *Accred.:* 1930/1990 (MSA) *Calendar:* Sem. plan *Degrees:* B, M, certificates *CEO:* Pres. Ofelia Garcia
Enroll: 682   (215) 527-0200

ST. CHARLES BORROMEO SEMINARY
1000 E. Wynnewood Rd., Overbrook 19096-3099 *Type:* Private (Roman Catholic) *Accred.:* 1970/1986 (ATS); 1971/1991 (MSA) *Calendar:* Sem. plan *Degrees:* B, P, M, certificates *CEO:* Pres./Rector Daniel A. Murray
Enroll: 460   (215) 667-3394

ST. FRANCIS COLLEGE
Loretto 15940 *Type:* Private (Roman Catholic) *Accred.:* 1939/1991 (MSA) *Calendar:* Sem. plan *Degrees:* A, B, M *Prof. Accred.:* Nursing (B), Physician Assisting, Social Work (B) *CEO:* Pres. Christian Oravec
Enroll: 1,853   (814) 472-3000

ST. JOSEPH'S UNIVERSITY
5600 City Line Ave., Philadelphia 19131 *Type:* Private (Roman Catholic) *Accred.:* 1922/1984 (MSA) *Calendar:* Sem. plan *De-

grees: A, B, M, certificates *CEO:* Pres. Nicholas S. Rashford, S.J.
Enroll: 6,643   (215) 660-1000

ST. VINCENT COLLEGE AND SEMINARY
Frazier Purchase Rd., Latrobe 15650 *Type:* Private (Roman Catholic) liberal arts *Accred.:* 1984/1988 (ATS); 1921/1988 (MSA) *Calendar:* Sem. plan *Degrees:* B, P, M, certificates *CEO:* Pres. John F. Murtha, O.S.B.
Enroll: 1,263   (412) 539-9761

THE SAWYER SCHOOL
717 Liberty Ave., Pittsburgh 15222 *Type:* Private business *Accred.:* 1973/1991 (ACISC) *Calendar:* Courses of varying lengths *Degrees:* A *Prof. Accred.:* Medical Assisting, Medical Assisting (AMA) *CEO:* Pres. Thomas B. Sapienza
                                   (412) 261-5700

SCHUYLKILL BUSINESS INSTITUTE
2400 W. End Ave., Pottsville 17901 *Type:* Private business *Accred.:* 1980/1986 (ACISC) *Calendar:* Courses of varying lengths *Degrees:* A *CEO:* Pres. James Tarity, Jr.
                                   (717) 622-4835

SETON HILL COLLEGE
Greensburg 15601 *Type:* Private (Roman Catholic) liberal arts for women *Accred.:* 1921/1992 (MSA) *Calendar:* Sem. plan *Degrees:* B, certificates *Prof. Accred.:* Dietetics (coordinated), Music *CEO:* Pres. JoAnne W. Boyle
Enroll: 1,043   (412) 834-2200

SHENANGO VALLEY SCHOOL OF BUSINESS
335 Boyd Dr., Sharon 16146 *Type:* Private business *Accred.:* 1977/1986 (ACISC) *Calendar:* Courses of varying lengths *Degrees:* A *CEO:* Dir. Patricia McMahon
                                   (412) 983-0700

BRANCH CAMPUS
500 S. Mill St., New Castle 16101 *Accred.:* 1985/1986 (ACISC) *CEO:* Dir. Richard P. McMahon
                                   (412) 654-1976

BRANCH CAMPUS
124 W. Spring St., Titusville 16354 *Accred.:* 1993 (ACISC) *CEO:* Dir. Loran Johnson
                                   (814) 827-9567

SHIPPENSBURG UNIVERSITY OF PENNSYLVANIA
Shippensburg 17257 *Type:* Public (state) *System:* Pennsylvania State System of Higher Education *Accred.:* 1939/1989 (MSA) *Calendar:* Sem. plan *Degrees:* B, M *Prof. Accred.:* Business (B), Counseling, Social Work (B), Teacher Education (e,s,p) *CEO:* Pres. Anthony F. Ceddia
Enroll: 6,696   (717) 532-9121

SLIPPERY ROCK UNIVERSITY OF PENNSYLVANIA
Slippery Rock 16057 *Type:* Public (state) *System:* Pennsylvania State System of Higher Education *Accred.:* 1943/1991 (MSA) *Calendar:* Sem. plan *Degrees:* B, M *Prof. Accred.:* Music, Nursing (B), Physical Therapy, Recreation and Leisure Services, Social Work (B), Teacher Education (e,s,p) *CEO:* Pres. Robert N. Aebersold
Enroll: 7,844   (412) 738-0512

SOUTH HILLS BUSINESS SCHOOL
480 Waupelani Dr., State College 16801-4516 *Type:* Private business *Accred.:* 1976/1991 (ACISC) *Calendar:* Tri. plan *Degrees:* A *Prof. Accred.:* Medical Record Technology *CEO:* Dir. Maralyn J. Mazza
                                   (814) 234-7755

SUSQUEHANNA UNIVERSITY
Selinsgrove 17870 *Type:* Private (Lutheran) *Accred.:* 1930/1988 (MSA) *Calendar:* Sem. plan *Degrees:* A, B *Prof. Accred.:* Business (B), Music *CEO:* Pres. Joel L. Cunningham
Enroll: 1,559   (717) 374-0101

SWARTHMORE COLLEGE
500 College Ave., Swarthmore 19081 *Type:* Private liberal arts *Accred.:* 1921/1989 (MSA) *Calendar:* Sem. plan *Degrees:* B, M *Prof. Accred.:* Engineering (general) *CEO:* Pres. Alfred H. Bloom
Enroll: 1,346   (215) 328-8000

TALMUDICAL YESHIVA OF PHILADELPHIA
6063 Drexel Rd., Philadelphia 19131 *Type:* Private professional *Accred.:* 1975/1987 (AARTS) *Calendar:* Sem. plan *Degrees:* Rabbinic (1st), Talmudic (1st and 2nd) *CEO:* Pres. E. Weinberg
Enroll: 113   (215) 473-1212

TEMPLE UNIVERSITY
Broad and Montgomery Sts., Philadelphia 19122 *Type:* Private (state-related) *Accred.:*

1921/1989 (MSA) *Calendar:* Sem. plan *Degrees:* A, B, P, M, D, certificates *Prof. Accred.:* Art, Audiology, Business (B,M), Clinical Psychology, Combined Prosthodontics, Community Health, Counseling Psychology, Dance, Dentistry, Endodontics, Engineering Technology (civil/construction, electrical, mechanical), Engineering (civil, electrical, mechanical), General Dentistry, Health Services Administration, Journalism (B,M), Landscape Architecture (B-initial), Law, Medical Record Administration, Medicine, Music, Nuclear Medicine Technology, Nursing (B), Occupational Therapy, Oral and Maxillofacial Surgery, Orthodontics, Periodontics, Physical Therapy, Psychology Internship, Radiography, Recreation and Leisure Services, School Psychology, Social Work (B,M), Speech-Language Pathology, Teacher Education (e,s,p), Theatre *CEO:* Pres. Peter J. Liacouras
Enroll: 30,750   (215) 204-7000

THADDEUS STEVENS STATE SCHOOL OF TECHNOLOGY
750 E. King St., Lancaster 17602 *Type:* Public (state) junior *Accred.:* 1991 (MSA) *Calendar:* Sem. plan *Degrees:* A, certificates *CEO:* Pres. Alan K. Cohen
Enroll: 510   (717) 299-7730

THIEL COLLEGE
75 College Ave., Greenville 16125 *Type:* Private (Lutheran) liberal arts *Accred.:* 1922/1992 (MSA) *Calendar:* Sem. plan *Degrees:* A, B, certificates *Prof. Accred.:* Nursing (B), Respiratory Therapy Technology *CEO:* Pres. C. Carlyle Haaland
Enroll: 897   (412) 589-2000

THOMAS JEFFERSON UNIVERSITY
11th and Walnut Sts., Philadelphia 19107 *Type:* Private professional *Accred.:* 1976/1987 (MSA) *Calendar:* Qtr. plan *Degrees:* A, B, P, M, D, certificates *Prof. Accred.:* Cytotechnology, Dental Hygiene, Diagnostic Medical Sonography, General Practice Residency, Medical Technology, Medicine, Nursing (B,M), Occupational Therapy, Oral and Maxillofacial Surgery, Physical Therapy, Radiography *CEO:* Pres. Paul C. Brucker
Enroll: 2,596   (215) 955-6000

TRI-STATE BUSINESS INSTITUTE
5757 W. 26th St., Erie 16506 *Type:* Private business *Accred.:* 1990 (ACISC) *Calendar:* Courses of varying lengths *Degrees:* A, certificates, diplomas *CEO:* Vice Pres. Guy M. Euliano
      (814) 838-7673

TRIANGLE TECH
P.O. Box 551, DuBois 15801-9990 *Type:* Private *Accred.:* 1981/1986 (ACCSCT) *Calendar:* Courses of varying lengths *Degrees:* A, certificates *CEO:* Dir. Branda McCullough
      (814) 371-2090

TRIANGLE TECH
2000 Liberty St., Erie 16502-9987 *Type:* Private *Accred.:* 1978/1988 (ACCSCT) *Calendar:* Courses of varying lengths *Degrees:* A, certificates *CEO:* Dir. Mary M. Gill
      (814) 453-6016

TRIANGLE TECH
900 Greengate N. Plaza, Greensburg 15601-9944 *Type:* Private *Accred.:* 1970/1990 (ACCSCT) *Calendar:* Courses of varying lengths *Degrees:* A, certificates *CEO:* Dir. Jayne Kalp
      (412) 832-1050

BUSINESS CAREERS INSTITUTE
33 W. Otterman St., Greensburg 15601-2394 *Accred.:* 1991 (ACCSCT) *CEO:* Dir. Christine D. Sirnic
      (412) 834-1258

TRIANGLE TECH
1940 Perrysville Ave., Pittsburgh 15214-3897 *Type:* Private *Accred.:* 1970/1990 (ACCSCT) *Calendar:* Courses of varying lengths *Degrees:* A, certificates *CEO:* Dir. Brian James
      (412) 359-1000

MONROEVILLE SCHOOL OF BUSINESS
105 Mall Blvd., Expo Mart, 3rd Fl., Monroeville 15146-2229 *Accred.:* 1990 (ACCSCT) *CEO:* Dir. Marilyn McCarthy
      (412) 856-8040

TRINITY EPISCOPAL SCHOOL FOR MINISTRY
311 Eleventh St., Ambridge 15003 *Type:* Private (Episcopal) graduate only *Accred.:*

1985/1990 (ATS) *Calendar:* Sem. plan *Degrees:* M *CEO:* Pres./Dean William C. Frey
FTE Enroll: 87   (412) 266-3838

UNIVERSITY OF PENNSYLVANIA
34th and Spruce Sts., Philadelphia 19104
Type: Private *Accred.:* 1921/1989 (MSA)
Calendar: Sem. plan *Degrees:* A, B, P, M,
D, certificates *Prof. Accred.:* Business
(B,M), Clinical Psychology, Combined Professional-Scientific Psychology, Dentistry,
Endodontics, Engineering (bioengineering,
chemical, civil, electrical, materials, mechanical, systems), General Dentistry, Health
Services Administration, Landscape Architecture (M), Law, Medicine, Nuclear Medicine Technology, Nursing (B,M), Oral and
Maxillofacial Surgery, Orthodontics, Periodontics, Planning (M), Practical Nursing,
Psychology Internship, Social Work (M),
Veterinary Medicine *CEO:* Interim Pres.
Claire M. Fagin
Enroll: 22,229   (215) 898-5000

UNIVERSITY OF PITTSBURGH
4200 Fifth Ave., Pittsburgh 15260 *Type:*
Public (state-related) *Accred.:* 1921/1991
(MSA) *Calendar:* Tri. plan *Degrees:* B, P,
M, D, certificates *Prof. Accred.:* Audiology,
Business (B,M), Clinical Psychology, Combined Prosthodontics, Counseling, Counseling Psychology (provisional), Dental Hygiene, Dentistry, Dietetics (coordinated), Endodontics, Engineering (chemical, civil,
electrical, industrial, materials, mechanical,
metallurgical), General Dentistry, Health
Services Administration, Law, Librarianship,
Maxillofacial Prosthodontics, Medical
Record Administration, Medical Technology, Medicine, Nurse Anesthesia Education,
Nursing (B,M), Occupational Therapy, Oral
and Maxillofacial Surgery, Orthodontics, Pediatric Dentistry, Periodontics, Physical
Therapy, Planning (M), Psychology Internship, Public Administration, Public Health,
Rehabilitation Counseling, Social Work
(B,M), Speech-Language Pathology, Theatre
CEO: Chanc. J. Dennis O'Connor
Enroll: 27,973   (412) 624-4141

BRADFORD CAMPUS
Bradford 16701 *Prof. Accred.:* Nursing
(A) *CEO:* Pres. Richard E. McDowell
                    (814) 362-7500

GREENSBURG CAMPUS
1150 Mount Pleasant Rd., Greensburg
15601 *CEO:* Pres. George F. Chambers
                    (412) 837-7040

JOHNSTOWN CAMPUS
Johnstown 15904 *Prof. Accred.:* Engineering Technology (civil/construction,
electrical, mechanical), Respiratory Therapy *CEO:* Pres. Frank H. Blackington, III
                    (814) 269-7000

TITUSVILLE CAMPUS
504 E. Main St., Titusville 16354 *CEO:*
Pres. Michael A. Worman
                    (814) 827-4400

UNIVERSITY OF SCRANTON
800 Linden St., Scranton 18510-4501 *Type:*
Private (Roman Catholic) *Accred.:* 1927/
1988 (MSA) *Calendar:* 4-1-4 plan *Degrees:*
A, B, M *Prof. Accred.:* Computer Science,
Counseling, Nursing (B), Physical Therapy,
Rehabilitation Counseling, Teacher Education (s,p) *CEO:* Pres. Joseph A. Panuska, S.J.
Enroll: 5,113   (717) 941-7500

UNIVERSITY OF THE ARTS
Broad and Pine Sts., Philadelphia 19102
Type: Independent professional *Accred.:*
1969/1988 (MSA) *Calendar:* Sem. plan *Degrees:* A, B, M, certificates *Prof. Accred.:*
Art, Music *CEO:* Pres. Peter Solmssen
Enroll: 1,359   (215) 875-4800

URSINUS COLLEGE
Box 1000, Collegeville 19426-1000 *Type:*
Private liberal arts *Accred.:* 1921/1989
(MSA) *Calendar:* Sem. plan *Degrees:* A, B
CEO: Pres. Richard P. Richter
Enroll: 2,440   (215) 489-4111

VALLEY FORGE CHRISTIAN COLLEGE
1401 Charlestown Rd., VFCC Box 51,
Phoenixville 19460 *Type:* Private (Assemblies of God) *Accred.:* 1967/1987 (AABC)
Calendar: Sem. plan *Degrees:* B, certificates, diplomas *CEO:* Pres. Wesley W.
Smith
FTE Enroll: 495   (215) 935-0450

VALLEY FORGE MILITARY COLLEGE
1001 Eagle Rd., Wayne 19087-3695 *Type:*
Private junior for men *Accred.:* 1954/1992
(MSA) *Calendar:* 4-1-4 plan *Degrees:* A

CEO: Supt. N. Ronald Thunman, U.S.N. (Ret.)
Enroll: 137   (215) 688-1800

VILLANOVA UNIVERSITY
Lancaster Pike, Villanova 19085 *Type:* Private (Roman Catholic) *Accred.:* 1921/1991 (MSA) *Calendar:* Sem. plan *Degrees:* A, B, P, M, D *Prof. Accred.:* Accounting (Type A), Business (B,M), Computer Science, Counseling, Engineering (chemical, civil, electrical, mechanical), Law, Nursing (B,M)
CEO: Pres. Edmund J. Dobbin, O.S.A.
Enroll: 11,858   (215) 645-4500

WASHINGTON AND JEFFERSON COLLEGE
45 S. Lincoln St., Washington 15301 *Type:* Private liberal arts *Accred.:* 1921/1989 (MSA) *Calendar:* 4-1-4 plan *Degrees:* A, B, M *CEO:* Pres. Howard J. Burnett
Enroll: 1,273   (412) 222-4400

WAYNESBURG COLLEGE
51 W. College St., Waynesburg 15370 *Type:* Private (United Presbyterian) liberal arts *Accred.:* 1950/1990 (MSA) *Calendar:* Sem. plan *Degrees:* A, B, M *Prof. Accred.:* Nursing (B) *CEO:* Pres. Timothy R. Thyreen
Enroll: 1,332   (412) 627-8191

WEST CHESTER UNIVERSITY OF PENNSYLVANIA
S. High St., West Chester 19383 *Type:* Public (state) *System:* Pennsylvania State System of Higher Education *Accred.:* 1946/1990 (MSA) *Calendar:* Sem. plan *Degrees:* A, B, M *Prof. Accred.:* Music, Nursing (B), Respiratory Therapy, Social Work (B), Teacher Education (e,s,p) *CEO:* Pres. Madeleine Wing Adler
Enroll: 11,959   (215) 436-1000

WESTMINSTER COLLEGE
S. Market St., New Wilmington 16172 *Type:* Private (Presbyterian) liberal arts *Accred.:* 1921/1991 (MSA) *Calendar:* 4-1-4 plan *Degrees:* B, M *Prof. Accred.:* Music *CEO:* Pres. Oscar E. Remick
Enroll: 1,554   (412) 946-8761

WESTMINSTER THEOLOGICAL SEMINARY
Church Rd. and Willow Grove Ave., Glenside 19038 *Type:* Private (interdenominational) graduate only *Accred.:* 1986/1991 (ATS); 1954/1992 (MSA) *Calendar:* 4-1-4

plan *Degrees:* P, M, D *CEO:* Pres. Samuel T. Logan, Jr.
Enroll: 531   (215) 887-5511

WESTMORELAND COUNTY COMMUNITY COLLEGE
Armbrust Rd., Youngwood 15697-1895 *Type:* Public (local/state) junior *Accred.:* 1978/1988 (MSA) *Calendar:* Sem. plan *Degrees:* A, certificates *CEO:* Pres. Daniel C. Krezenski
Enroll: 6,425   (412) 925-4000

WIDENER UNIVERSITY
One University Pl., Chester 19013-5792 *Type:* Private *Accred.:* 1954/1991 (MSA) *Calendar:* Sem. plan *Degrees:* A, B, M, D, certificates *Prof. Accred.:* Clinical Psychology, Engineering (chemical, civil, electrical, general, mechanical), Health Services Administration, Nursing (B,M), Psychology Internship, Social Work (B,M-candidate) *CEO:* Pres. Robert J. Bruce
Enroll: 4,263   (215) 499-4000

SCHOOL OF LAW
4601 Concord Pike, P.O. Box 7474, Wilmington, DE 19803-0474 *Prof. Accred.:* Law *CEO:* Dean Arthur N. Frakt
Enroll: 1,404   (302) 477-2100

WIDENER UNIVERSITY AT HARRISBURG
3800 Vartan Way, Harrisburg 17110-9450 *Prof. Accred.:* Law (ABA only) *CEO:* Pres. Robert J. Bruce
Enroll: 797   (717) 541-3900

WILKES UNIVERSITY
170 S. Franklin St., Wilkes-Barre 18766 *Type:* Private *Accred.:* 1937/1990 (MSA) *Calendar:* Sem. plan *Degrees:* B, M *Prof. Accred.:* Engineering (electrical, materials), Nursing (B) *CEO:* Pres. Christopher N. Breiseth
Enroll: 3,263   (717) 824-4651

WILLIAMSPORT SCHOOL OF COMMERCE
941 W. Third St., Williamsport 17701 *Type:* Private business *Accred.:* 1963/1986 (ACISC) *Calendar:* Qtr. plan *Degrees:* A *CEO:* Dir. Benjamin H. Comfort, III
                    (717) 326-2869

WILSON COLLEGE
1015 Philadelphia Ave., Chambersburg 17201-1285 *Type:* Private (Presbyterian) liberal arts for women *Accred.:* 1922/1988

(MSA) *Calendar:* 4-1-4 plan *Degrees:* A, B, certificates *Prof. Accred.:* Veterinary Technology *CEO:* Pres. Gwendolyn Evans Jensen
Enroll: 900   (717) 264-4141

YESHIVA BETH MOSHE
930 Hickory St., Scranton 18505 *Type:* Private professional *Accred.:* 1976/1989 (AARTS) *Calendar:* Sem. plan *Degrees:* Talmudic (1st and 2nd) *CEO:* Pres. David Fink
Enroll: 80   (717) 346-1747

YORK COLLEGE OF PENNSYLVANIA
Country Club Rd., York 17405-7199 *Type:* Private *Accred.:* 1959/1991 (MSA) *Calen-*
dar: Sem. plan *Degrees:* A, B, M *Prof. Accred.:* Medical Record Administration, Nursing (B), Recreation and Leisure Services, Respiratory Therapy, Respiratory Therapy Technology *CEO:* Pres. George W. Waldner
Enroll: 5,013   (717) 846-7788

YORKTOWNE BUSINESS INSTITUTE
W. Seventh Ave., York 17404 *Type:* Private business *Accred.:* 1979/1991 (ACISC) *Calendar:* Courses of varying lengths *Degrees:* A, certificates, diplomas *CEO:* Pres. James P. Murphy
                                      (717) 846-5111

PUERTO RICO

AGUADILLA REGIONAL COLLEGE
P.O. Box 160, Ramey 00604 *Type:* Public
(state) junior *System:* University of Puerto
Rico Regional Colleges Administration *Ac-
cred.:* 1976/1992 (MSA) *Calendar:* Sem.
plan *Degrees:* A *CEO:* Dean/Dir. Miguel A.
Gonzalez
Enroll: 1,310   (809) 890-2681

AMERICAN UNIVERSITY OF PUERTO RICO
P.O. Box 2037, Bayamon 00621 *Type:* Pri-
vate liberal arts *Accred.:* 1982/1987 (MSA)
Calendar: Sem. plan *Degrees:* A, B *CEO:*
Pres. Juan B. Nazario-Negron
Enroll: 2,664   (809) 798-2022

BRANCH CAMPUS
P.O. Box 929, Dorado 00646 *CEO:* Dir.
Juan Osorio
                                   (809) 796-2169

BRANCH CAMPUS
P.O. Box 1082, Manati 00701 *CEO:* Dir.
Diana Javier
                                   (809) 854-2835

ARECIBO TECHNOLOGICAL UNIVERSITY COLLEGE
Box 4010, Arecibo 00613 *Type:* Public
(state) *System:* University of Puerto Rico Regional Colleges Administration *Accred.:*
1967/1988 (MSA) *Calendar:* Sem. plan *Degrees:* A, B *Prof. Accred.:* Nursing (A)
CEO: Dir. de Cano Ireneo Martin Duque
Enroll: 3,307   (809) 878-2830

ATLANTIC COLLEGE
Box 1774, Guaynabo 00651-1774 *Type:* Private junior *Accred.:* 1987 (ACISC) *Calendar:* Sem. plan *Degrees:* A, certificates,
diplomas *CEO:* Pres. Teresa de Dios
                                   (809) 720-1022

BAYAMON CENTRAL UNIVERSITY
P.O. Box 1725, Bayamon 00960-1725 *Type:*
Private (Roman Catholic) *Accred.:* 1971/
1988 (MSA) *Calendar:* Sem. plan *Degrees:*
A, B, M *CEO:* Pres. Vincent A.M. Van
Rooij, O.P.
Enroll: 2,846   (809) 786-3030

BAYAMON TECHNOLOGICAL UNIVERSITY
COLLEGE
Bayamon 00959-1919 *Type:* Public (state)
System: University of Puerto Rico Regional

Colleges Administration *Accred.:* 1960/1992
(MSA) *Calendar:* Sem. plan *Degrees:* A, B
CEO: Dean/Dir. Aida Canals de Bird
Enroll: 3,891   (809) 786-2885

CARIBBEAN CENTER FOR ADVANCED STUDIES
Apartado 3711, Old San Juan Sta., San Juan
00904-3711 *Type:* Private professional *Accred.:* 1974/1989 (MSA) *Calendar:* Sem.
plan *Degrees:* P, M, D *CEO:* Pres. Salvador
Santiago-Negron
Enroll: 370   (809) 725-6500

MIAMI INSTITUTE OF PSYCHOLOGY
8180 N.W. 36th St., 2nd Fl., Miami, FL
33166-6653 professional *Accred.:* 1981/
1989 (MSA) *Calendar:* Sem. plan *Degrees:* B, M, D, certificates *Prof. Accred.:*
Clinical Psychology (provisional) *CEO:*
Chanc. Evelyn Diaz
Enroll: 295   (305) 593-1223

CARIBBEAN UNIVERSITY
Box 493, Rd. 167 km. 21.2, Forest Hills,
Bayamon 00960-0493 *Type:* Private liberal
arts *Accred.:* 1977/1991 (MSA) *Calendar:*
Qtr. plan *Degrees:* A, B, M *CEO:* Pres.
Angel E. Juan-Ortega
Enroll: 1,752   (809) 780-0070

CAROLINA REGIONAL COLLEGE
P.O. Box 4800, Carolina 00984-4800 *Type:*
Public (state) junior *System:* University of
Puerto Rico Regional Colleges Administra-
tion *Accred.:* 1978/1992 (MSA) *Calendar:*
Sem. plan *Degrees:* A *CEO:* Dean/Dir.
Marta Arroyo
Enroll: 1,751   (809) 257-0000

CAYEY UNIVERSITY COLLEGE
Antonio R. Barcelo Ave., Cayey 00633
Type: Public (state) liberal arts *System:* Uni-
versity of Puerto Rico Central Administra-
tion *Accred.:* 1967/1990 (MSA) *Calendar:*
Sem. plan *Degrees:* A, B *CEO:* Chanc.
Margarita Benitez
Enroll: 3,243   (809) 738-2161

CENTRO DE ESTUDIOS AVANZADOS DE PUERTO
RICO Y EL CARIBE
Del Cristo St. No. 52, Box S 4467, San Juan
00904 *Type:* Private graduate only *Accred.:*

1982/1992 (MSA) *Calendar:* Sem. plan *Degrees:* M *CEO:* Exec. Dir. Ricardo Alegria
Enroll: 137   (809) 723-4481

COLEGIO BIBLICO PENTECOSTAL
Carretera 848, Km 0.5, P.O. Box 901, St. Just 00978 *Type:* Private (Church of God) *Accred.:* 1990 (AABC) *Calendar:* Sem. plan *Degrees:* B, certificates *CEO:* Pres. Ismael López Borrero
FTE Enroll: 159   (809) 761-0640

COLEGIO UNIVERSITARIO DEL ESTE
P.O. Box 2010, Carolina 00983-2010 *Type:* Private liberal arts *System:* Sistema Universitario Ana G. Mendez Central Office *Accred.:* 1959/1988 (MSA) *Calendar:* Sem. plan *Degrees:* A, B *Prof. Accred.:* Medical Record Technology *CEO:* Chanc. Alberto Maldonado Ruiz
Enroll: 4,018   (809) 257-7373

COLUMBIA COLLEGE
P.O. Box 8517, Carretera 183, KM 1.7, Caguas 00762-8517 *Type:* Private *Accred.:* 1976/1989 (ACISC) *Calendar:* Tri. plan *Degrees:* A, B, certificates, diplomas *CEO:* Pres. Alex A. De Jorge
                                   (809) 743-4041

BRANCH CAMPUS
Public Sq., San Jose St., Rio Grande 00745 *Accred.:* 1976/1989 (ACISC) *CEO:* Dir. Jesus M. Rivera
                                   (809) 887-3352

BRANCH CAMPUS
Box 3062, Yauco 00698 *Accred.:* 1976/1989 (ACISC) *CEO:* Dir. Sharon Santiago
                                   (809) 856-0845

CONSERVATORY OF MUSIC OF PUERTO RICO
P.O. Box 41227, Minillas Sta., Santurce 00940 *Type:* Public (state) *Accred.:* 1975/1989 (MSA) *Calendar:* Sem. plan *Degrees:* B *CEO:* Rector Raymond Torres Santos
Enroll: 290   (809) 751-0160

ELECTRONIC DATA PROCESSING COLLEGE
P.O. Box 2303, Hato Rey 00919 *Type:* Private *Accred.:* 1976/1989 (ACISC) *Calendar:* Courses of varying lengths *Degrees:* A, B *CEO:* Pres. Anibal N. Nieves
                                   (809) 765-3560

BRANCH CAMPUS
48 Betances St., P.O. Box 1674, San Sebastian 00755 *Accred.:* 1979/1989 (ACISC) *CEO:* Dir. Jose R. Soto
                                   (809) 896-2137

EVANGELICAL SEMINARY OF PUERTO RICO
776 Ponce de Leon Ave., San Juan 00925 *Type:* Private (interdenominational) graduate only *Accred.:* 1982/1987 (ATS); 1989 (MSA candidate) *Calendar:* Sem. plan *Degrees:* P, M *CEO:* Pres. Luis Fidel Mercado
Enroll: 165   (809) 751-6483

HUERTAS JUNIOR COLLEGE
Box 8429, Caguas 00626 *Type:* Private junior *Accred.:* 1977/1989 (ACISC) *Calendar:* Qtr. plan *Degrees:* A, certificates, diplomas *CEO:* Dir. Felix Rodriguez Matos
Enroll: 2,306   (809) 743-2156

HUMACAO COMMUNITY COLLEGE
101-103 Cruz Ortiz Stella, Box 8948, Humacao 00661 *Type:* Private business *Accred.:* 1979/1988 (ACISC) *Calendar:* Courses of varying lengths *Degrees:* A, certificates, diplomas *CEO:* Pres. Rafael Ramirez
                                   (809) 852-1430

BRANCH CAMPUS
P.O. Box 1185, Gerrido Morales No. 52, Fajardo 00648 *Accred.:* 1987 (ACISC) *CEO:* Dir. Maria Caracaballo
                                   (809) 863-5210

HUMACAO UNIVERSITY COLLEGE
CUH Sta., Rd. 908, Bo. Tejas, Humacao 00661 *Type:* Public (state) liberal arts *System:* University of Puerto Rico Central Administration *Accred.:* 1962/1989 (MSA) *Calendar:* Sem. plan *Degrees:* A, B *Prof. Accred.:* Nursing (A,B), Occupational Therapy Assisting, Physical Therapy Assisting, Social Work (B) *CEO:* Chanc. Felix A. Castrodad Ortiz
Enroll: 3,982   (809) 850-0000

INSTITUTO COMERCIAL DE PUERTO RICO JUNIOR COLLEGE
558 Munoz Rivera Ave., Box 304, Hato Rey 00919 *Type:* Private junior *Accred.:* 1985/1992 (MSA) *Calendar:* Tri. plan *Degrees:* A, certificates *CEO:* C.E.O. Ramon A. Negron
Enroll: 402   (809) 763-1010

ARECIBO CAMPUS
Rd. 2, KM 80.4, San Daniel Box 1606, Arecibo 00612-1606 *CEO:* Acad. Dean Angel L. Curbelo
(809) 878-0524

MAYAGUEZ CAMPUS
Mendez Vigo No. 55, P.O. Box 1108, Mayaguez 00708-1108 *CEO:* Dir. Genovena Christian
(809) 832-2250

INTER AMERICAN UNIVERSITY OF PUERTO RICO
AGUADILLA CAMPUS
Call Box 20000, Aguadilla 00605 *Type:* Private liberal arts *System:* Inter American University of Puerto Rico Central Administration *Accred.:* 1957/1987 (MSA) *Calendar:* Sem. plan *Degrees:* A, B, certificates *CEO:* Chanc. Hilda M. Bacó
Enroll: 4,083   (809) 891-0925

INTER AMERICAN UNIVERSITY OF PUERTO RICO
ARECIBO CAMPUS
Call Box UI, Arecibo 00613 *Type:* Private liberal arts *System:* Inter American University of Puerto Rico Central Administration *Accred.:* 1957/1987 (MSA) *Calendar:* Sem. plan *Degrees:* A, B, certificates *CEO:* Chanc. Zaida Vega-Lugo
Enroll: 4,576   (809) 878-5475

INTER AMERICAN UNIVERSITY OF PUERTO RICO
BARRANQUITAS CAMPUS
P.O. Box 517, Barranquitas 00794 *Type:* Private liberal arts *System:* Inter American University of Puerto Rico Central Administration *Accred.:* 1957/1987 (MSA) *Calendar:* Sem. plan *Degrees:* A, B, certificates *CEO:* Chanc. Vidal Rivera-Garcia
Enroll: 1,480   (809) 857-4040

INTER AMERICAN UNIVERSITY OF PUERTO RICO
BAYAMON CAMPUS
RD 174, Minillas Industrial Park, Bayamon 00959 *Type:* Private liberal arts *System:* Inter American University of Puerto Rico Central Administration *Accred.:* 1960/1987 (MSA) *Calendar:* Sem. plan *Degrees:* A, B, certificates *CEO:* Chanc. Felix Torres-Leon
Enroll: 5,169   (809) 780-4040

INTER AMERICAN UNIVERSITY OF PUERTO RICO
FAJARDO CAMPUS
P.O. Box 1029, Fajardo 00738 *Type:* Private liberal arts *System:* Inter American Universi-

ty of Puerto Rico Central Administration *Accred.:* 1961/1987 (MSA) *Calendar:* Sem. plan *Degrees:* A, B, certificates *CEO:* Chanc. Yolanda Robles-Garcia
Enroll: 1,915   (809) 863-2390

INTER AMERICAN UNIVERSITY OF PUERTO RICO
GUAYAMA CAMPUS
Call Box 10004, Guayama 00785 *Type:* Private liberal arts *System:* Inter American University of Puerto Rico Central Administration *Accred.:* 1957/1987 (MSA) *Calendar:* Sem. plan *Degrees:* A, B, certificates *CEO:* Chanc. Samuel F. Febres-Santiago
Enroll: 1,566   (809) 864-2222

INTER AMERICAN UNIVERSITY OF PUERTO RICO
METROPOLITAN CAMPUS
P.O. Box 1293, Hato Rey 00919-1293 *Type:* Private *System:* Inter American University of Puerto Rico Central Administration *Accred.:* 1960/1987 (MSA) *Calendar:* Sem. plan *Degrees:* A, B, P, M, D *Prof. Accred.:* Medical Technology, Nursing (B), Optometry, Social Work (B) *CEO:* Chanc. Manuel J. Fernos
Enroll: 13,857   (809) 250-1912

INTER AMERICAN UNIVERSITY OF PUERTO RICO
PONCE CAMPUS
Mercedita 00715 *Type:* Private liberal arts *System:* Inter American University of Puerto Rico Central Administration *Accred.:* 1962/1987 (MSA) *Calendar:* Sem. plan *Degrees:* A, B *CEO:* Chanc. Marilina L. Wayland
Enroll: 3,789   (809) 840-9090

INTER AMERICAN UNIVERSITY OF PUERTO RICO
SAN GERMAN CAMPUS
Harris Dr., Call Box 5100, San German 00683 *Type:* Private *System:* Inter American University of Puerto Rico Central Administration *Accred.:* 1944/1987 (MSA) *Calendar:* Sem. plan *Degrees:* A, B, M *Prof. Accred.:* Medical Technology *CEO:* Chanc. Agnes Mojica
Enroll: 5,959   (809) 264-1912

INTER AMERICAN UNIVERSITY OF PUERTO RICO
SCHOOL OF LAW
P.O. Box 8897, Fernandez Juncos Sta., Santurce 00910 *Type:* Private professional *System:* Inter American University of Puerto Rico Central Administration *Accred.:* 1961/1987 (MSA) *Calendar:* Sem. plan *Degrees:*

P *Prof. Accred.:* Law (ABA only) *CEO:*
Dean Carlos E. Ramos-Gonzalez
Enroll: 658   (809) 727-1930

INTER AMERICAN UNIVERSITY OF PUERTO RICO
SCHOOL OF OPTOMETRY
118 Eleanor Roosevelt St., Hato Rey 00919
Type: Private professional *System:* Inter
American University of Puerto Rico Central
Administration *Accred.:* 1985/1987 (MSA)
Calendar: Sem. plan *Degrees:* P *CEO:* Dean
Arthur J. Afanador
Enroll: 104   (809) 754-6690

INTERNATIONAL COLLEGE OF BUSINESS &
TECHNOLOGY
P.O. Box 8245, San Juan 00910 *Type:* Private
junior *Accred.:* 1984/1988 (ACISC) *Calen-
dar:* Courses of varying lengths *Degrees:* A
CEO: Chanc. Luz Zenida Fuentes-Ortiz
                                 (809) 725-8718

BRANCH CAMPUS
2nd Fl., Plaza San Alfonso, Caguas 00627
Accred.: 1984/1988 (ACISC) *CEO:* Dir.
William Rodriguez
                                 (809) 746-3777

BRANCH CAMPUS
Humacao Shopping Ctr., Font Martelo St.,
Humacao 00971 *Accred.:* 1993 (ACISC)
CEO: Dir. Reinaldo Gonzalez
                                 (809) 850-0055

LA MONTAÑA REGIONAL COLLEGE
Call Box 2500, Utuado 00641 *Type:* Public
(state) junior *System:* University of Puerto
Rico Regional Colleges Administration *Ac-
cred.:* 1986/1990 (MSA) *Calendar:* Sem.
plan *Degrees:* A *CEO:* Dean/Dir. Ramon A.
Toro
Enroll: 623   (809) 894-2828

NATIONAL COLLEGE OF BUSINESS &
TECHNOLOGY
Ramos Bldg., Hwy. No. 2, P.O. Box 2036,
Bayamon 00621 *Type:* Private business *Ac-
cred.:* 1983/1987 (ACISC) *Calendar:* Qtr.
plan *Degrees:* A, certificates, diplomas
CEO: Dir. Jesus Siveri Orta
                                 (809) 780-5134

BRANCH CAMPUS
Ste. 109, Ave. Gonzalo Marin, Arecibo
00612 *Accred.:* 1983/1989 (ACISC) *CEO:*
Dir. Iride M. Dumatt
                                 (809) 879-5044

PONCE SCHOOL OF MEDICINE
Ponce 00732 *Type:* Private professional *Cal-
endar:* Sem. plan *Degrees:* P *Prof. Accred.:*
Medicine *CEO:* Dean Luis F. Sala, M.D.
Enroll: 177   (809) 843-8288

PONCE TECHNOLOGICAL UNIVERSITY COLLEGE
Box 7186, Ponce 00732 *Type:* Public (state)
System: University of Puerto Rico Regional
Colleges Administration *Accred.:* 1970/1990
(MSA) *Calendar:* Sem. plan *Degrees:* A, B
Prof. Accred.: Physical Therapy Assisting
CEO: Dean/Dir. Pedro E. Laboy-Zengotita
Enroll: 2,192   (809) 844-8181

THE PONTIFICAL CATHOLIC UNIVERSITY OF
PUERTO RICO
Las Americas Ave., Sta. 6, Ponce 00732
Type: Private (Roman Catholic) *Accred.:*
1953/1993 (MSA) *Calendar:* Sem. plan *De-
grees:* A, B, P, M, certificates *Prof. Accred.:*
Law (ABA only), Medical Technology,
Nursing (B,M), Social Work (B) *CEO:* Pres.
Tosello O. Giangiacomo, C.S.Sp.
Enroll: 7,885   (809) 841-2000

ARECIBO BRANCH CAMPUS
P.O. Box 495, Arecibo 00613 *CEO:* Dean
Epifania Bonilla
                                 (809) 881-1212

GUAYAMA BRANCH CAMPUS
P.O. Box 809, Guayama 00654 *CEO:*
Dean Felix Rosa-Crespo
                                 (809) 864-0550

MAYAGUEZ BRANCH CAMPUS
P.O. Box 1326, Mayaguez 00709 *CEO:*
Dean Jaime Ortiz-Vega
                                 (809) 834-5151

RAMIREZ COLLEGE OF BUSINESS AND
TECHNOLOGY
P.O. Box 8074, 103 Munoz Rivera Ave.,
Santurce 00910 *Type:* Private junior *Ac-
cred.:* 1975/1987 (ACISC) *Calendar:* Tri.
plan *Degrees:* A *CEO:* Acting Pres. Morris
Brown
                                 (809) 763-3120

TECHNOLOGICAL COLLEGE OF THE MUNICIPALITY
OF SAN JUAN
Jose Oliver St., Industrial Park, Hato Rey
00918 *Type:* Public (local) junior *Accred.:*
1978/1992 (MSA) *Calendar:* Sem. plan *De-
grees:* A *Prof. Accred.:* Nursing (A) *CEO:*
Chanc. Peter J. Lugo de Menkini
Enroll: 1,043   (809) 250-7111

UNIVERSIDAD ADVENTISTA DE LAS ANTILLAS
P.O. Box 118, Mayaguez 00681 *Type:* Pri-
vate (Seventh-Day Adventist) liberal arts *Ac-
cred.:* 1978/1987 (MSA) *Calendar:* Sem. plan
Degrees: A, B *CEO:* Pres. Miguel Munoz
Enroll: 803   (809) 834-9595

UNIVERSIDAD CENTRAL DEL CARIBE
Call Box 60-327, Cayey 00621-6032 *Type:*
Private professional *Calendar:* Courses of
varying lengths *Degrees:* A, P *Prof. Accred.:*
Medicine, Radiography *CEO:* Pres. Raul A.
Marcial-Rojas, M.D.
                    (809) 798-3001

UNIVERSIDAD DE TURAPO
P.O. Box 30303, Esta. Universidad, Gurabo
00778 *Type:* Private *System:* Sistema Universitario Ana G. Mendez Central Office *Accred.:* 1974/1988 (MSA) *Calendar:* Sem.
plan *Degrees:* A, B, M *CEO:* Rector Dennis
Aliceo
Enroll: 7,367   (809) 743-7979

UNIVERSIDAD METROPOLITANA
Box 21150, Rio Piedras 00928 *Type:* Private
System: Sistema Universitario Ana G.
Mendez Central Office *Accred.:* 1983/1992
(MSA) *Calendar:* Sem. plan *Degrees:* A, B,
M *Prof. Accred.:* Nursing (A,B), Respiratory
Therapy *CEO:* Chanc. Rene L. Labarca
Enroll: 5,517   (809) 766-1717

UNIVERSIDAD POLITECNICA DE PUERTO RICO
Box 2017, Hato Rey 00918 *Type:* Private
Accred.: 1985/1990 (MSA) *Calendar:* Qtr.
plan *Degrees:* B *CEO:* Pres. Ernesto
Vazquez-Barquet
Enroll: 4,322   (809) 754-8000

UNIVERSITY OF PUERTO RICO MAYAGUEZ
CAMPUS
P.O. Box 5000, Mayaguez 00681 *Type:* Pub-
lic (state) *System:* University of Puerto Rico

Central Administration *Accred.:* 1946/1989
(MSA) *Calendar:* Sem. plan *Degrees:* A, B,
M, D *Prof. Accred.:* Engineering (chemical,
civil, electrical, industrial, mechanical),
Nursing (A,B) *CEO:* Chanc. Alejandro Ruiz-
Acevedo
Enroll: 10,416   (809) 832-4040

UNIVERSITY OF PUERTO RICO MEDICAL
SCIENCES CAMPUS
Box 365067, San Juan 00936-5067 *Type:*
Public (state) *System:* University of Puerto
Rico Central Administration *Accred.:* 1949/
1992 (MSA) *Calendar:* Sem. plan *Degrees:*
A, B, P, M, D, certificates *Prof. Accred.:*
Combined Prosthodontics, Dental Assisting,
Dental Hygiene, Dentistry, Dietetics (intern-
ship), General Practice Residency, Health
Services Administration, Medical Record
Administration, Medical Technology, Medi-
cine, Nuclear Medicine Technology, Nurse
Anesthesia Education, Nursing (B,M), Occu-
pational Therapy, Ophthalmic Medical Tech-
nology, Oral and Maxillofacial Surgery, Pe-
diatric Dentistry, Physical Therapy, Public
Health, Radiography, Respiratory Therapy,
Speech-Language Pathology *CEO:* Interim
Rector Uveles Garcia
Enroll: 2,854   (809) 758-2525

UNIVERSITY OF PUERTO RICO RIO PIEDRAS
CAMPUS
P.O. Box 23300, San Juan 00931-3300 *Type:*
Public (state) *System:* University of Puerto
Rico Central Administration *Accred.:*
1946/1990 (MSA) *Calendar:* Sem. plan *De-
grees:* A, B, P, M, D, certificates *Prof. Ac-
cred.:* Law, Librarianship, Planning (M), Re-
habilitation Counseling, Social Work (B,M),
Teacher Education (e,s,p) *CEO:* Rector
Efrain Gonzales Tejera
Enroll: 20,265   (809) 764-0000

UNIVERSITY OF THE SACRED HEART
Box 12383, Loiza Sta., Santurce 00914
Type: Private (Roman Catholic) *Accred.:*
1950/1992 (MSA) *Calendar:* Sem. plan *De-
grees:* A, B, M, certificates *Prof. Accred.:*
Medical Technology, Nursing (A,B), Social
Work (B) *CEO:* Pres. Jose Jaime Rivera
Enroll: 5,681   (809) 728-1515

RHODE ISLAND

BROWN UNIVERSITY
Providence 02912 *Type:* Private *Accred.:* 1929/1988 (NEASC-CIHE) *Calendar:* Sem. plan *Degrees:* B, P, M, D *Prof. Accred.:* Engineering (bioengineering, chemical, civil, electrical, materials, mechanical), Medicine, Psychology Internship *CEO:* Pres. Vartan Gregorian
Enroll: 7,361   (401) 863-1000

BRYANT COLLEGE
1150 Douglas Pike, Smithfield 02917-1284 *Type:* Private *Accred.:* 1964/1990 (NEASC-CIHE) *Calendar:* Sem. plan *Degrees:* A, B, M *CEO:* Pres. William E. Trueheart
Enroll: 4,120   (401) 232-6000

COMMUNITY COLLEGE OF RHODE ISLAND
400 East Ave., Warwick 02886-1805 *Type:* Public (state) *System:* State of Rhode Island Office of Higher Education *Accred.:* 1969/1984 (NEASC-CIHE) *Calendar:* Sem. plan *Degrees:* A, certificates, diplomas *Prof. Accred.:* Dental Assisting, Dental Hygiene, Medical Laboratory Technology (AMA), Nursing (A), Physical Therapy Assisting, Practical Nursing, Radiography, Respiratory Therapy *CEO:* Pres. Edward J. Liston
Enroll: 9,799   (401) 825-1000

JOHNSON & WALES UNIVERSITY
8 Abbott Park Pl., Providence 02903 *Type:* Private *Accred.:* 1954/1987 (ACISC) *Calendar:* Tri. plan *Degrees:* A, B, M, certificates, diplomas *CEO:* Pres. John A. Yena
Enroll: 7,903   (401) 456-1100

BRANCH CAMPUS
616 W. Lionshead Cir., Vail, CO 81657 *Accred.:* 1993 (ACISC) *CEO:* Dir. William Edwards Wilroy, III
                                   (303) 476-2993

BRANCH CAMPUS
1701 N.E. 127th St., North Miami, FL 33261 *Accred.:* 1993 (ACISC) *CEO:* Exec. Dir. Donald G. McGregor
                                   (305) 895-7111

BRANCH CAMPUS
701 E. Bay St., BTC Box 1409, Charleston, SC 29403 *Accred.:* 1984/1987 (ACISC) *CEO:* Dir. Paul W. Conco
                                   (803) 723-4638

BRANCH CAMPUS
2428 Almeda Ave., Stes. 316-318, Norfolk, VA 23513 *Accred.:* 1987 (ACISC) *CEO:* Dir. Debra C. Gray
                                   (804) 853-3508

KATHARINE GIBBS SCHOOL
178 Butler Ave., Providence 02906 *Type:* Private business *Accred.:* 1967/1991 (ACISC) *Calendar:* Sem. plan *Degrees:* A, certificates, diplomas *CEO:* Dir. Elaine K. Carroll
                                   (401) 861-1420

NAVAL WAR COLLEGE
Newport 02841-5010 *Type:* Public (federal) *Accred.:* 1989 (NEASC-CIHE) *Calendar:* Sem. plan *Degrees:* M *CEO:* Pres. Joseph C. Strasser
Enroll: 457   (401) 841-3089

NEW ENGLAND INSTITUTE OF TECHNOLOGY
2500 Post Rd., Warwick 02886-2251 *Type:* Private *Accred.:* 1972/1989 (ACCSCT); 1982/1993 (NEASC-CTCI) *Calendar:* Qtr. plan *Degrees:* A, B *CEO:* Pres. Richard I. Gouse
FTE Enroll: 2,064   (401) 739-5000

PROVIDENCE COLLEGE
Providence 02918 *Type:* Private (Roman Catholic) liberal arts *Accred.:* 1933/1987 (NEASC-CIHE) *Calendar:* Sem. plan *Degrees:* B, M, D *Prof. Accred.:* Social Work (B) *CEO:* Pres. John F. Cunningham, O.P.
Enroll: 3,853   (401) 865-1000

RHODE ISLAND COLLEGE
Providence 02908 *Type:* Public (state) liberal arts and teachers *System:* State of Rhode Island Office of Higher Education *Accred.:* 1958/1990 (NEASC-CIHE) *Calendar:* Sem. plan *Degrees:* B, M *Prof. Accred.:* Art, Music, Nursing (B), Social Work (B,M),

Teacher Education (e,s,p) *CEO:* Pres. John Nazarian
Enroll: 7,024   (401) 456-8000

RHODE ISLAND SCHOOL OF DESIGN
2 College St., Providence 02903 *Type:* Private professional *Accred.:* 1949/1986 (NEASC-CIHE) *Calendar:* Sem. plan *Degrees:* B, M *Prof. Accred.:* Art, Interior Design, Landscape Architecture (B) *CEO:* Pres. Roger Mandle
Enroll: 2,195   (401) 454-6402

ROGER WILLIAMS UNIVERSITY
One Old Ferry Rd., Bristol 02809-2921 *Type:* Private liberal arts *Accred.:* 1972/1986 (NEASC-CIHE) *Calendar:* Sem. plan *Degrees:* A, B *Prof. Accred.:* Engineering Technology (electrical, mechanical) *CEO:* Dean Anthony J. Santoro
Enroll: 2,649   (401) 253-1040

SALVE REGINA UNIVERSITY
100 Ochre Point Ave., Newport 02840-4192 *Type:* Private (Roman Catholic) liberal arts *Accred.:* 1956/1991 (NEASC-CIHE) *Calendar:* Sem. plan *Degrees:* A, B, M *Prof. Accred.:* Art (associate), Nursing (B), Social Work (B) *CEO:* Pres. Lucille McKillop, R.S.M.
Enroll: 1,906   (401) 847-6650

UNIVERSITY OF RHODE ISLAND
Kingston 02881-0806 *Type:* Public (state) *System:* State of Rhode Island Office of Higher Education *Accred.:* 1930/1987 (NEASC-CIHE) *Calendar:* Sem. plan *Degrees:* A, B, M, D *Prof. Accred.:* Audiology, Business (B,M), Clinical Psychology, Dental Hygiene, Engineering (chemical, civil, computer, electrical, industrial, manufacturing, mechanical), Landscape Architecture (B-initial), Librarianship, Marriage and Family Therapy (M), Music, Nursing (B,M), Physical Therapy, Planning (M), School Psychology, Speech-Language Pathology, Teacher Education (p) *CEO:* Pres. Robert L. Carothers
Enroll: 12,172   (401) 792-1000

SOUTH CAROLINA

AIKEN TECHNICAL COLLEGE
P.O. Box 696, Aiken 29802-0696 *Type:* Public (state) 2-year *System:* South Carolina State Board for Technical and Comprehensive Education *Accred.:* 1975/1990 (SACS-CC) *Calendar:* Qtr. plan *Degrees:* A *Prof. Accred.:* Dental Assisting *CEO:* Interim Pres. Don B. Campbell
FTE Enroll: 1,886   (803) 593-9231

ALLEN UNIVERSITY
1530 Harden St., Columbia 29204 *Type:* Private (African Methodist Episcopal) liberal arts and teachers *Accred.:* 1992 (SACS-CC warning) *Calendar:* Sem. plan *Degrees:* B *CEO:* Pres. Collie Coleman
FTE Enroll: 306   (803) 254-4165

ANDERSON COLLEGE
316 Blvd., Anderson 29621 *Type:* Private (Southern Baptist) *Accred.:* 1959/1990 (SACS-CC) *Calendar:* Sem. plan *Degrees:* A, B *Prof. Accred.:* Music (associate) *CEO:* Pres. Mark L. Hopkins
FTE Enroll: 1,065   (803) 231-2000

BENEDICT COLLEGE
Harden and Blanding Sts., Columbia 29204 *Type:* Private liberal arts *Accred.:* 1946/1991 (SACS-CC) *Calendar:* Sem. plan *Degrees:* B *Prof. Accred.:* Social Work (B) *CEO:* Interim Pres. Ruby W. Watts
FTE Enroll: 1,230   (803) 253-4220

CENTRAL CAROLINA TECHNICAL COLLEGE
506 N. Guignard Dr., Sumter 29150-2499 *Type:* Public (state) 2-year *System:* South Carolina State Board for Technical and Comprehensive Education *Accred.:* 1970/1985 (SACS-CC) *Calendar:* Qtr. plan *Degrees:* A *Prof. Accred.:* Engineering Technology (civil/construction) *CEO:* Pres. Herbert C. Robbins
FTE Enroll: 2,129   (803) 778-1961

CENTRAL WESLEYAN COLLEGE
P.O. Box 1020, Central 29630-1020 *Type:* Private (Wesleyan Methodist) liberal arts and teachers *Accred.:* 1973/1989 (SACS-CC) *Calendar:* Sem. plan *Degrees:* A, B, M *CEO:* Pres. John M. Newby
FTE Enroll: 1,365   (803) 639-2453

CHARLESTON SOUTHERN UNIVERSITY
P.O. Box 1108087, Charleston 29411 *Type:* Private (Southern Baptist) liberal arts and teachers *Accred.:* 1970/1986 (SACS-CC) *Calendar:* 4-1-4 plan *Degrees:* A, B, M *Prof. Accred.:* Music *CEO:* Pres. Jairy C. Hunter, Jr.
FTE Enroll: 1,962   (803) 863-7000

CHESTERFIELD-MARLBORO TECHNICAL COLLEGE
1201 Chesterfield Hwy., No. 9 W., P.O. Drawer 1007, Cheraw 29520-1007 *Type:* Public (state) 2-year *System:* South Carolina State Board for Technical and Comprehensive Education *Accred.:* 1973/1988 (SACS-CC) *Calendar:* Qtr. plan *Degrees:* A *CEO:* Pres. Ronald W. Hampton
FTE Enroll: 833   (803) 537-5286

THE CITADEL
Citadel Sta., 171 Moultrie St., Charleston 29409 *Type:* Public (state) primarily for men *System:* South Carolina Commission on Higher Education *Accred.:* 1924/1984 (SACS-CC) *Calendar:* Sem. plan *Degrees:* B, M *Prof. Accred.:* Engineering (civil, electrical), Teacher Education (s,p) *CEO:* Pres. Claudius E. Watts, III
FTE Enroll: 3,012   (803) 953-5000

CLAFLIN COLLEGE
700 College Ave., N.E., Orangeburg 29115 *Type:* Private (United Methodist) liberal arts *Accred.:* 1947/1991 (SACS-CC) *Calendar:* Sem. plan *Degrees:* B *CEO:* Pres. Oscar A. Rogers, Jr.
FTE Enroll: 991   (803) 534-2710

CLEMSON UNIVERSITY
201 Sikes Hall, Clemson 29634 *Type:* Public (state) liberal arts *System:* South Carolina Commission on Higher Education *Accred.:* 1927/1991 (SACS-CC) *Calendar:* Sem. plan *Degrees:* B, M, D *Prof. Accred.:* Accounting (Type A,C), Business (B,M), Computer Science, Construction Education (B), Engineering (agricultural, ceramic, chemical, civil, computer, electrical, environmental/sanitary, industrial, mechanical), Forestry, Nursing (B,M), Planning (M), Recreation and Leisure

Services, Teacher Education (e,s,p) *CEO:*
Pres. A. Max Lennon
FTE Enroll: 15,669   (803) 656-3311

COASTAL CAROLINA UNIVERSITY
P.O. Box 1954, Myrtle Beach 29577 *Type:*
Public (state) *System:* South Carolina Com-
mission on Higher Education *Accred.:* 1976/
1991 (SACS-CC) *Calendar:* Sem. plan *De-
grees:* A, B, M (candidate) *CEO:* Pres.
Ronald R. Ingle
FTE Enroll: 4,479   (803) 347-3161

COKER COLLEGE
300 E. College Ave., Hartsville 29550 *Type:*
Private liberal arts *Accred.:* 1923/1985
(SACS-CC) *Calendar:* Sem. plan *Degrees:*
B *Prof. Accred.:* Music *CEO:* Pres. James D.
Daniels
FTE Enroll: 800   (803) 383-8000

COLLEGE OF CHARLESTON
66 George St., Charleston 29424 *Type:* Pub-
lic (state) liberal arts *System:* South Carolina
Commission on Higher Education *Accred.:*
1916/1986 (SACS-CC) *Calendar:* Sem. plan
Degrees: B, M *Prof. Accred.:* Business (B),
Computer Science, Public Administration
CEO: Pres. Alexander M. Sanders, Jr.
FTE Enroll: 8,476   (803) 953-5507

COLUMBIA COLLEGE
1301 Columbia College Dr., Columbia
29203 *Type:* Private (United Methodist) lib-
eral arts for women *Accred.:* 1938/1991
(SACS-CC) *Calendar:* Sem. plan *Degrees:*
B, M *Prof. Accred.:* Music, Social Work (B)
CEO: Pres. Peter T. Mitchell
FTE Enroll: 1,095   (803) 786-3012

COLUMBIA INTERNATIONAL UNIVERSITY
P.O. Box 3122, Columbia 29203-3122 *Type:*
Independent (interdenominational) *Accred.:*
1948/1982 (AABC); 1985/1990 (ATS);
1982/1988 (SACS-CC) *Calendar:* Qtr. plan
Degrees: A, B, M, D, certificates *CEO:* Pres.
Johnny V. Miller
FTE Enroll: 1,341   (803) 754-4100

COLUMBIA JUNIOR COLLEGE OF BUSINESS
P.O. Box 1196, 3810 Main St., Columbia
29202 *Type:* Private junior *Accred.:* 1964/
1987 (ACISC) *Calendar:* Qtr. plan *Degrees:*

A, certificates, diplomas *CEO:* Pres. Michael
Gorman
                              (803) 799-9082

CONVERSE COLLEGE
580 E. Main St., Spartanburg 29302-0006
Type: Private liberal arts primarily for
women *Accred.:* 1912/1986 (SACS-CC)
Calendar: Sem. plan *Degrees:* B, M *Prof.
Accred.:* Interior Design, Music *CEO:* Inter-
im Pres. Thomas R. McDaniel
FTE Enroll: 899   (803) 596-9000

DENMARK TECHNICAL COLLEGE
P.O. Box 327, Denmark 29042 *Type:* Public
(state) 2-year *System:* South Carolina State
Board for Technical and Comprehensive Ed-
ucation *Accred.:* 1979/1984 (SACS-CC)
Calendar: Sem. plan *Degrees:* A *CEO:* Pres.
Joann R.G. Boyd
FTE Enroll: 780   (803) 793-3301

ERSKINE COLLEGE
2 Washington St., Due West 29639 *Type:*
Private (Presbyterian) liberal arts *Accred.:*
1981/1985 (ATS); 1925/1992 (SACS-CC)
Calendar: 4-1-4 plan *Degrees:* A, B, M, D
CEO: Pres. James W. Strobel
FTE Enroll: 751   (803) 379-2131

FLORENCE-DARLINGTON TECHNICAL COLLEGE
P.O. Box 100548, Florence 29501-0548
Type: Public (state) 2-year *System:* South
Carolina State Board for Technical and
Comprehensive Education *Accred.:* 1970/
1985 (SACS-CC) *Calendar:* Sem. plan *De-
grees:* A *Prof. Accred.:* Dental Assisting,
Dental Hygiene, Engineering Technology
(civil/construction, electrical, mechanical
drafting/design), Medical Laboratory Tech-
nology (AMA), Medical Record Technolo-
gy, Nursing (A), Radiography, Respiratory
Therapy, Respiratory Therapy Technology,
Surgical Technology *CEO:* Pres. Charles W.
Gould
FTE Enroll: 3,053   (803) 661-8324

FORREST JUNIOR COLLEGE
601 E. River St., Anderson 29624 *Type:* Private junior *Accred.:* 1965/1990 (ACISC)
Calendar: Qtr. plan *Degrees:* A *CEO:* Exec.
Dir./Dean William H. Taylor
                              (803) 225-7653

FRANCIS MARION UNIVERSITY
P.O. Box 100547, Florence 29501-0547 *Type:* Public (state) liberal arts *System:* South Carolina Commission on Higher Education *Accred.:* 1972/1987 (SACS-CC) *Calendar:* Sem. plan *Degrees:* A, B, M *CEO:* Pres. Thomas C. Stanton
FTE Enroll: 3,630   (803) 661-1362

FURMAN UNIVERSITY
3300 Poinsett Hwy., Greenville 29613 *Type:* Private (Southern Baptist) liberal arts *Accred.:* 1924/1987 (SACS-CC) *Calendar:* 3-2-3 plan *Degrees:* B, M *Prof. Accred.:* Music *CEO:* Pres. John E. Johns
FTE Enroll: 2,887   (803) 294-2000

GREENVILLE TECHNICAL COLLEGE
P.O. Box 5616, Greenville 29606 *Type:* Public (state) 2-year *System:* South Carolina State Board for Technical and Comprehensive Education *Accred.:* 1968/1992 (SACS-CC) *Calendar:* Sem. plan *Degrees:* A *Prof. Accred.:* Dental Assisting, Dental Hygiene, EMT-Paramedic, Engineering Technology (architectural, electrical, mechanical), Medical Laboratory Technology (AMA), Nursing (A), Physical Therapy Assisting, Practical Nursing, Radiography, Respiratory Therapy, Respiratory Therapy Technology, Surgical Technology *CEO:* Pres. Thomas E. Barton, Jr.
FTE Enroll: 7,103   (803) 250-8000

HORRY-GEORGETOWN TECHNICAL COLLEGE
P.O. Box 1966, Conway 29526 *Type:* Public (state) 2-year *System:* South Carolina State Board for Technical and Comprehensive Education *Accred.:* 1972/1988 (SACS-CC) *Calendar:* Sem. plan *Degrees:* A *Prof. Accred.:* Engineering Technology (electrical), Radiography *CEO:* Pres. D. Kent Sharples
FTE Enroll: 2,640   (803) 347-3286

LANDER UNIVERSITY
320 Stanley Ave., Greenwood 29649-2099 *Type:* Public (state) liberal arts *System:* South Carolina Commission on Higher Education *Accred.:* 1952/1986 (SACS-CC) *Calendar:* Sem. plan *Degrees:* B, M *Prof. Accred.:* Nursing (B) *CEO:* Pres. William C. Moran
FTE Enroll: 2,579   (803) 229-8300

LIMESTONE COLLEGE
1115 College Dr., Gaffney 29340 *Type:* Private liberal arts *Accred.:* 1928/1990 (SACS-CC) *Calendar:* Sem. plan *Degrees:* B *Prof. Accred.:* Music *CEO:* Pres. Walt Griffin
FTE Enroll: 1,155   (803) 489-7151

LUTHERAN THEOLOGICAL SOUTHERN SEMINARY
4201 N. Main St., Columbia 29203 *Type:* Private (Evangelical Lutheran Church) professional; graduate only *Accred.:* 1944/1993 (ATS); 1983/1993 (SACS-CC) *Calendar:* Sem. plan *Degrees:* M, D *CEO:* Pres. H. Frederick Reisz, Jr.
FTE Enroll: 211   (803) 786-5150

MEDICAL UNIVERSITY OF SOUTH CAROLINA
171 Ashley Ave., Charleston 29425 *Type:* Public (state) professional *System:* South Carolina Commission on Higher Education *Accred.:* 1971/1986 (SACS-CC) *Calendar:* Sem. plan *Degrees:* B, M, D *Prof. Accred.:* Blood Bank Technology, Cytotechnology, Dentistry, General Dentistry (prelim. provisional), Histologic Technology, Medical Record Administration, Medical Technology, Medicine, Nurse Anesthesia Education, Nursing (B,M), Occupational Therapy, Ophthalmic Medical Technology, Oral and Maxillofacial Surgery, Pediatric Dentistry, Perfusion, Periodontics, Physical Therapy, Psychology Internship, Radiation Therapy Technology *CEO:* Pres. James B. Edwards
FTE Enroll: 2,032   (803) 792-2211

MIDLANDS TECHNICAL COLLEGE
P.O. Box 2408, Columbia 29202 *Type:* Public (state) 2-year *System:* South Carolina State Board for Technical and Comprehensive Education *Accred.:* 1974/1989 (SACS-CC) *Calendar:* Sem. plan *Degrees:* A *Prof. Accred.:* Dental Assisting, Dental Hygiene, Engineering Technology (architectural, civil/construction, electrical, mechanical), Medical Laboratory Technology (AMA), Medical Record Technology, Nuclear Medicine Technology, Nursing (A), Practical Nursing, Radiography, Respiratory Therapy, Respiratory Therapy Technology, Surgical Technology *CEO:* Pres. James L. Hudgins
FTE Enroll: 7,855   (803) 738-1400

MORRIS COLLEGE
100 W. College St., Sumter 29150-3599
Type: Private (Baptist) liberal arts *Accred.:*
1978/1993 (SACS-CC) *Calendar:* Sem. plan
Degrees: B *CEO:* Pres. Luns C. Richardson
FTE Enroll: 932   (803) 775-9371

NEWBERRY COLLEGE
2100 College St., Newberry 29108 *Type:*
Private (Lutheran) liberal arts *Accred.:* 1936/
1992 (SACS-CC) *Calendar:* Sem. plan *Degrees:* B *Prof. Accred.:* Music, Teacher Education (e,p) *CEO:* Pres. Raymond M. Bost
FTE Enroll: 637   (803) 276-5010

NORTH GREENVILLE COLLEGE
P.O. Box 1892, Tigerville 29688-1892 *Type:*
Private (Southern Baptist) *Accred.:* 1957/
1989 (SACS-CC) *Calendar:* Sem. plan *De-
grees:* A,B (candidate) *CEO:* Pres. James B.
Epting
FTE Enroll: 599   (803) 895-1410

ORANGEBURG-CALHOUN TECHNICAL COLLEGE
3250 St. Matthews Rd., Orangeburg 29115
Type: Public (state) 2-year *System:* South
Carolina State Board for Technical and
Comprehensive Education *Accred.:* 1970/
1985 (SACS-CC) *Calendar:* Sem. plan *De-
grees:* A *Prof. Accred.:* Medical Laboratory
Technology (AMA), Nursing (A), Practical
Nursing, Radiography, Respiratory Therapy
Technology *CEO:* Pres. M. Rudolph Groomes
FTE Enroll: 1,898   (803) 536-1500

PIEDMONT TECHNICAL COLLEGE
P.O. Drawer 1467, Greenwood 29648 *Type:*
Public (state) 2-year *System:* South Carolina
State Board for Technical and Comprehen-
sive Education *Accred.:* 1972/1987 (SACS-
CC) *Calendar:* Sem. plan *Degrees:* A *Prof.
Accred.:* Engineering Technology (electrical,
general drafting/design), Radiography, Res-
piratory Therapy Technology *CEO:* Pres.
Lex D. Walters
FTE Enroll: 3,645   (803) 941-8324

PRESBYTERIAN COLLEGE
S. Broad St., P.O. Box 975, Clinton 29325
Type: Private (Presbyterian) liberal arts *Ac-
cred.:* 1949/1986 (SACS-CC) *Calendar:*
Sem. plan *Degrees:* B *CEO:* Pres. Kenneth
B. Orr
FTE Enroll: 1,159   (803) 833-2820

SHERMAN COLLEGE OF STRAIGHT CHIROPRACTIC
2020 Springfield Rd., P.O. Box 1452, Spartanburg 29304 *Type:* Private professional
Accred.: 1984 (SACS-CC probational) *Calendar:* Tri. plan *Degrees:* D *CEO:* Pres.
Thomas A. Gelardi
FTE Enroll: 143   (803) 578-8770

SOUTH CAROLINA STATE UNIVERSITY
300 College Ave. N.E., Orangeburg 29117
Type: Public (state) liberal arts *System:*
South Carolina Commission on Higher Education *Accred.:* 1941/1990 (SACS-CC) *Calendar:* Sem. plan *Degrees:* B, M, D *Prof.
Accred.:* Engineering Technology (civil/con-
struction, electrical, industrial, mechanical),
Home Economics, Rehabilitation Counseling, Social Work (B), Teacher Education
(e,s,p) *CEO:* Pres. Barbara Hatton
FTE Enroll: 6,218   (803) 536-7000

SPARTANBURG METHODIST COLLEGE
1200 Textile Rd., Spartanburg 29301-0009
Type: Private (United Methodist) junior *Ac-
cred.:* 1957/1988 (SACS-CC) *Calendar:*
Sem. plan *Degrees:* A *CEO:* Pres. George D.
Fields
FTE Enroll: 808   (803) 587-4000

SPARTANBURG TECHNICAL COLLEGE
P.O. Drawer 4386, Spartanburg 29305-4386
Type: Public (state) 2-year *System:* South
Carolina State Board for Technical and
Comprehensive Education *Accred.:* 1970/
1985 (SACS-CC) *Calendar:* Sem. plan *De-
grees:* A *Prof. Accred.:* Dental Assisting,
Engineering Technology (civil/construction,
electrical, mechanical), Medical Laboratory
Technology (AMA), Radiography, Respira-
tory Therapy, Respiratory Therapy Technol-
ogy, Surgical Technology *CEO:* Pres. Jack
A. Powers
FTE Enroll: 2,504   (803) 591-3600

TECHNICAL COLLEGE OF THE LOWCOUNTRY
100 S. Ribaut Rd., P.O. Box 1288, Beaufort
29901 *Type:* Public (state) 2-year *System:*
South Carolina State Board for Technical
and Comprehensive Education *Accred.:*
1978/1984 (SACS-CC) *Calendar:* Sem. plan
Degrees: A *Prof. Accred.:* Nursing (A)
CEO: Pres. Anne S. McNutt
FTE Enroll: 1,447   (803) 525-8324

TRI-COUNTY TECHNICAL COLLEGE
Hwy. 76, P.O. Box 587, Pendleton 29670
Type: Public (state) 2-year *System:* South
Carolina State Board for Technical and
Comprehensive Education *Accred.:* 1971/
1986 (SACS-CC) *Calendar:* Sem. plan *De-
grees:* A *Prof. Accred.:* Dental Assisting,
Engineering Technology (electrical), Med-
ical Laboratory Technology (AMA), Surgi-
cal Technology, Veterinary Technology
CEO: Pres. Don C. Garrison
FTE Enroll: 3,106   (803) 646-8361

TRIDENT TECHNICAL COLLEGE
P.O. Box 10367, Charleston 29423-8067
Type: Public (state) 2-year *System:* South
Carolina State Board for Technical and
Comprehensive Education *Accred.:* 1974/
1990 (SACS-CC) *Calendar:* Sem. plan *De-
grees:* A *Prof. Accred.:* Dental Assisting,
Dental Hygiene, Engineering Technology
(chemical, civil/ construction, electrical, me-
chanical), Medical Assisting (AMA), Med-
ical Laboratory Technology (AMA), Nursing
(A-warning), Occupational Therapy Assist-
ing, Physical Therapy Assisting, Radiography, Respiratory Therapy *CEO:* Pres. Mary
Dellamura Thornley
FTE Enroll: 7,512   (803) 572-6111

UNIVERSITY OF SOUTH CAROLINA—AIKEN
171 University Pkwy., Aiken 29801 *Type:*
Public (state) *System:* University of South
Carolina Central Office *Accred.:* 1961/1991
(SACS-CC) *Calendar:* Sem. plan *Degrees:*
A, B *Prof. Accred.:* Nursing (A,B) *CEO:*
Chanc. Robert E. Alexander
FTE Enroll: 2,500   (803) 648-6851

UNIVERSITY OF SOUTH CAROLINA—BEAUFORT
801 Carteret St., Beaufort 29902 *Type:* Pub-
lic (state) 2-year *System:* University of South
Carolina Central Office *Accred.:* 1959/1991
(SACS-CC)* *Calendar:* Sem. plan *Degrees:*
A *CEO:* Dean Chris Plyler
Enroll: 1,070   (803) 521-4100

* Indirect accreditation through University of
  South Carolina—Columbia.

UNIVERSITY OF SOUTH CAROLINA—COLUMBIA
Columbia 29208 *Type:* Public (state) *System:*
University of South Carolina Central Office
Accred.: 1917/1991 (SACS-CC) *Calendar:*
Sem. plan *Degrees:* A, B, M, D *Prof. Ac-
cred.:* Accounting (Type A,C), Audiology,
Business (B,M), Clinical Psychology, Com-
puter Science, Counseling, Engineering
(chemical, civil, electrical, mechanical),
Health Services Administration, Journalism
(B,M), Law, Librarianship, Medicine,
Music, Nursing (B,M), Psychology Intern-
ship, Public Administration, Public Health,
Rehabilitation Counseling, School Psycholo-
gy, Social Work (M), Speech-Language
Pathology, Teacher Education (e,s,p), The-
atre *CEO:* Pres. John M. Palms
FTE Enroll: 24,322   (803) 777-7000

UNIVERSITY OF SOUTH CAROLINA—LANCASTER
P.O. Box 889, Lancaster 29721 *Type:* Public
(state) 2-year *System:* University of South
Carolina Central Office *Accred.:* 1959/1991
(SACS-CC)* *Calendar:* Sem. plan *Degrees:*
A *CEO:* Dean John R. Arnold
Enroll: 1,031   (803) 285-7471

UNIVERSITY OF SOUTH CAROLINA—
SALKEHATCHIE
P.O. Box 617, Allendale 29810 *Type:* Public
(state) 2-year *System:* University of South
Carolina Central Office *Accred.:* 1965/1991
(SACS-CC)* *Calendar:* Sem. plan *Degrees:*
A *CEO:* Dean Carl A. Clayton
Enroll: 1,006   (803) 584-3446

UNIVERSITY OF SOUTH CAROLINA—
SPARTANBURG
800 University Way, Spartanburg 29303
Type: Public (state) *System:* University of
South Carolina Central Office *Accred.:*
1976/1991 (SACS-CC) *Calendar:* Sem. plan
Degrees: A, B, M (candidate) *Prof. Accred.:*
Nursing (A,B) *CEO:* Interim Chanc. William
J. Whitener
FTE Enroll: 2,732   (803) 599-2000

UNIVERSITY OF SOUTH CAROLINA—SUMTER
200 Miller Rd., Sumter 29150 *Type:* Public
(state) 2-year *System:* University of South
Carolina Central Office *Accred.:* 1976/1991
(SACS-CC)* *Calendar:* Sem. plan *Degrees:*
A *CEO:* Dean C. Leslie Carpenter
Enroll: 1,620   (803) 775-6341

* Indirect accreditation through University of
  South Carolina—Columbia.

UNIVERSITY OF SOUTH CAROLINA—UNION
P.O. Drawer 729, Union 29379 *Type:* Public (state) 2-year *System:* University of South Carolina Central Office *Accred.:* 1965/1991 (SACS-CC)* *Calendar:* Sem. plan *Degrees:* A *CEO:* Dean James W. Edwards
Enroll: 432   (803) 429-8728

* Indirect accreditation through University of South Carolina—Columbia.

VOORHEES COLLEGE
1141 Voorhees Rd., Denmark 29042 *Type:* Private (Episcopal) liberal arts *Accred.:* 1946/1992 (SACS-CC) *Calendar:* Sem. plan *Degrees:* A, B *CEO:* Pres. Leonard E. Dawson
FTE Enroll: 712   (803) 793-3351

WILLIAMSBURG TECHNICAL COLLEGE
601 Lane Rd., Kingstree 29556-4197 *Type:* Public (state) 2-year *System:* South Carolina State Board for Technical and Comprehensive Education *Accred.:* 1977/1992 (SACS-CC) *Calendar:* Sem. plan *Degrees:* A *CEO:* Interim Pres. James M. Donnelly
FTE Enroll: 388   (803) 354-2021

WINTHROP UNIVERSITY
701 Oakland Ave., Rock Hill 29733 *Type:* Public (state) liberal arts *System:* South Carolina Commission on Higher Education *Accred.:* 1923/1991 (SACS-CC) *Calendar:* Sem. plan *Degrees:* B, M *Prof. Accred.:* Art, Business (B,M), Computer Science, Interior Design, Music, Social Work (B), Teacher Education (e,s,p) *CEO:* Pres. Anthony J. DiGiorgio
FTE Enroll: 5,599   (803) 323-2211

WOFFORD COLLEGE
429 N. Church St., Spartanburg 29303-3663 *Type:* Private (United Methodist) liberal arts for men *Accred.:* 1917/1986 (SACS-CC) *Calendar:* 4-1-4 plan *Degrees:* B *CEO:* Pres. Joab M. Lesesne, Jr.
FTE Enroll: 1,093   (803) 597-4000

YORK TECHNICAL COLLEGE
452 S. Anderson Rd., Rock Hill 29730 *Type:* Public (state) 2-year *System:* South Carolina State Board for Technical and Comprehensive Education *Accred.:* 1970/1985 (SACS-CC) *Calendar:* Sem. plan *Degrees:* A *Prof. Accred.:* Dental Assisting (conditional), Dental Hygiene (provisional), Engineering Technology (electrical, mechanical drafting/design), Medical Laboratory Technology (AMA), Radiography *CEO:* Pres. Dennis F. Merrell
FTE Enroll: 2,666   (803) 327-8000

SOUTH DAKOTA

AUGUSTANA COLLEGE
29th St. and Summit Ave., Sioux Falls
57197 *Type:* Private (Lutheran) liberal arts
Accred.: 1931/1992 (NCA) *Calendar:* 4-1-4
plan *Degrees:* A, B, M *Prof. Accred.:* Music,
Nursing (B), Social Work (B), Teacher Education (e,s) *CEO:* Pres. Ralph H. Wagoner
Enroll: 1,890   (605) 336-4111

BLACK HILLS STATE UNIVERSITY
1200 University Ave., Spearfish 57799-9500
Type: Public (state) liberal arts and teachers
System: South Dakota Board of Regents *Accred.:* 1928/1993 (NCA) *Calendar:* Sem.
plan *Degrees:* A, B, M, certificates, diplomas *Prof. Accred.:* Music, Teacher Education (e,s) *CEO:* Pres. Clifford M. Trump
Enroll: 2,781   (605) 642-6011

DAKOTA STATE UNIVERSITY
820 N. Washington St., Madison 57042
Type: Public (state) liberal arts and teachers
System: South Dakota Board of Regents *Ac-
cred.:* 1920/1991 (NCA) *Calendar:* Sem.
plan *Degrees:* A, B *Prof. Accred.:* Medical
Record Administration, Medical Record
Technology, Respiratory Therapy, Teacher
Education (e,s) *CEO:* Pres. Jerald A.
Tunheim
Enroll: 1,504   (605) 256-5111

DAKOTA WESLEYAN UNIVERSITY
Mitchell 57301 *Type:* Private (United
Methodist) liberal arts *Accred.:* 1916/1987
(NCA) *Calendar:* Sem. plan *Degrees:* A, B,
M *Prof. Accred.:* Nursing (A) *CEO:* Acting
Pres. Neal Eddy
Enroll: 766   (605) 995-2600

HURON UNIVERSITY
333 Ninth St., S.W., Huron 57350 *Type:* Private liberal arts *Accred.:* 1915/1990 (NCA)
Calendar: Sem. plan *Degrees:* A, B, M, certificates *Prof. Accred.:* Nursing (A) *CEO:*
Pres. Norman Stewart
Enroll: 1,076   (605) 352-8721

KILIAN COMMUNITY COLLEGE
1600 S. Menlo Ave., Sioux Falls 57105
Type: Private *Accred.:* 1986/1990 (NCA)

Calendar: Qtr. plan *Degrees:* A, certificates,
diplomas *CEO:* Pres. Ronald F. MacDonald
Enroll: 185   (605) 336-1711

LAKE AREA VOCATIONAL-TECHNICAL INSTITUTE
230 11th St., N.E., Watertown 57201 *Type:*
Public (district) junior *Accred.:* 1980/1990
(NCA) *Calendar:* Qtr. plan *Degrees:* A, cer-
tificates, diplomas *Prof. Accred.:* Dental As-
sisting, Medical Laboratory Technology
(AMA), Practical Nursing *CEO:* Dir. Gary
D. Williams
Enroll: 829   (605) 886-5872

MITCHELL TECHNICAL INSTITUTE
821 N. Capital St., Mitchell 57301 *Type:*
Public (district) junior *Accred.:* 1980/1990
(NCA) *Calendar:* Sem. plan *Degrees:* A,
certificates, diplomas *Prof. Accred.:* Medical
Laboratory Technology (AMA) *CEO:* Dir.
Chris A. Paustian
Enroll: 550   (605) 995-3024

MOUNT MARTY COLLEGE
1105 W. Eighth St., Yankton 57078 *Type:*
Private (Roman Catholic) liberal arts *Accred.:* 1961/1993 (NCA) *Calendar:* Sem.
plan *Degrees:* A, B, M, certificates *Prof. Accred.:* Nurse Anesthesia Education, Nursing
(B), Respiratory Therapy *CEO:* Pres.
Jacquelyn Ernster
Enroll: 1,104   (605) 668-1514

NATIONAL COLLEGE
321 Kansas City St., P.O. Box 1780, Rapid
City 57701 *Type:* Private *Accred.:* 1985/
1992 (NCA probational) *Calendar:* Qtr. plan
Degrees: A, B, certificates, diplomas *Prof.
Accred.:* Medical Assisting (AMA), Medical
Record Technology, Veterinary Technology
CEO: Pres. Jerry L. Gallentine
Enroll: 1,871   (605) 394-4800

NETTLETON JUNIOR COLLEGE
100 S. Spring Ave., Sioux Falls 57104 *Type:*
Private junior *Accred.:* 1953/1990 (ACISC)
Calendar: Courses of varying lengths *De-
grees:* A, certificates, diplomas *CEO:* Dir.
Roger Hunt
       (605) 336-1837

NORTH AMERICAN BAPTIST SEMINARY
1321 W. 22nd St., Sioux Falls 57105-1599 *Type:* Private (Baptist) graduate only *Accred.:* 1968/1984 (ATS); 1979/1984 (NCA) *Calendar:* Sem. plan *Degrees:* M, D, certificates *CEO:* Pres. Charles M. Hiatt
Enroll: 180   (605) 336-6588

NORTHERN STATE UNIVERSITY
1200 S. Jay St., Aberdeen 57401 *Type:* Public (state) liberal arts and teachers *System:* South Dakota Board of Regents *Accred.:* 1918/1987 (NCA) *Calendar:* Sem. plan *Degrees:* A, B, M, certificates *Prof. Accred.:* Music, Teacher Education (e,s,p) *CEO:* Pres. John Hutchinson
Enroll: 2,868   (605) 622-2521

OGLALA LAKOTA COLLEGE
P.O. Box 490, Kyle 57752 *Type:* Public (tribal) *Accred.:* 1983/1993 (NCA) *Calendar:* Sem. plan *Degrees:* A, B, M, certificates *CEO:* Pres. Elgin Bad Wound
Enroll: 1,021   (605) 455-2321

PRESENTATION COLLEGE
1500 N. Main St., Aberdeen 57401 *Type:* Private (Roman Catholic) *Accred.:* 1971/ 1987 (NCA) *Calendar:* Sem. plan *Degrees:* A, B, certificates *Prof. Accred.:* Medical Laboratory Technology (AMA), Nursing (A) *CEO:* Pres. Alexander J. Popovics
Enroll: 482   (605) 225-8404

SINTE GLESKA UNIVERSITY
P.O. Box 490, Rosebud 57570 *Type:* Public (tribal) *Accred.:* 1983/1993 (NCA) *Calendar:* Sem. plan *Degrees:* A, B, M *CEO:* Pres. Lionel R. Bordeaux
Enroll: 652   (605) 747-2263

SIOUX FALLS COLLEGE
1501 S. Prairie Ave., Sioux Falls 57105 *Type:* Private (Baptist) liberal arts *Accred.:* 1931/1992 (NCA) *Calendar:* 4-1-4 plan *Degrees:* A, B, M *Prof. Accred.:* Social Work (B), Teacher Education (e,s) *CEO:* Pres. Thomas F. Johnson
Enroll: 906   (605) 331-5000

SISSETON-WAHPETON COMMUNITY COLLEGE
P.O. Box 689, Old Agency, Agency Village 57262 *Type:* Public (tribal) junior *Accred.:*

1990 (NCA) *Calendar:* Qtr. plan *Degrees:* A *CEO:* Pres. Gwen Hill
Enroll: 202   (605) 698-3966

SOUTH DAKOTA SCHOOL OF MINES AND TECHNOLOGY
501 E. St. Joseph St., Rapid City 57701 *Type:* Public (state) technological *System:* South Dakota Board of Regents *Accred.:* 1925/1986 (NCA) *Calendar:* Sem. plan *Degrees:* B, M, D *Prof. Accred.:* Computer Science, Engineering (chemical, civil, electrical, geological/geophysical, mechanical, metallurgical, mining) *CEO:* Pres. Richard J. Gowen
Enroll: 2,444   (605) 394-2411

SOUTH DAKOTA STATE UNIVERSITY
Box 2201, University Sta., Brookings 57007 *Type:* Public (state) *System:* South Dakota Board of Regents *Accred.:* 1916/1990 (NCA) *Calendar:* Sem. plan *Degrees:* A, B, M, D *Prof. Accred.:* Engineering (agricultural, civil, electrical, mechanical), Home Economics, Journalism (B,M), Music, Nursing (B,M), Teacher Education (s,p) *CEO:* Pres. Robert T. Wagner
Enroll: 9,701   (605) 688-4121

SOUTHEAST VOCATIONAL-TECHNICAL INSTITUTE
2301 Career Pl., 1001 E. 14th St., Sioux Falls 57107 *Type:* Public (district) 2-year *Accred.:* 1981/1993 (NCA) *Calendar:* Qtr. plan *Degrees:* A, certificates, diplomas *Prof. Accred.:* Nuclear Medicine Technology *CEO:* Dir. Terrence Sullivan
Enroll: 1,030   (605) 331-7624

THE UNIVERSITY OF SOUTH DAKOTA
414 E. Clark St., Vermillion 57069-2390 *Type:* Public (state) *System:* South Dakota Board of Regents *Accred.:* 1913/1991 (NCA) *Calendar:* Sem. plan *Degrees:* A, B, P, M, D *Prof. Accred.:* Art, Business (B,M), Clinical Psychology, Counseling, Dental Hygiene, Law, Medicine, Music, Nurse Anesthesia Education, Nursing (A), Physical Therapy, Public Administration, Social Work (B), Speech-Language Pathology, Teacher Education (e,s,p), Theatre (associate) *CEO:* Pres. Betty Turner Asher
Enroll: 7,591   (605) 677-5011

WESTERN DAKOTA TECHNICAL INSTITUTE
1600 Sedivy La., Rapid City 57701-4178
Type: Public (district) junior *Accred.:*
1983/1993 (NCA) *Calendar:* Qtr. plan *De-grees:* A, certificates, diplomas *CEO:* Dir.
Ken Gifford
Enroll: 663   (605) 394-4034

TENNESSEE

AMERICAN BAPTIST COLLEGE
1800 Baptist World Ctr., Nashville 37207
Type: Private (National Baptist/Southern
Baptist Conventions) *Accred.:* 1971/1992
(AABC) *Calendar:* Sem. plan *Degrees:* B,
certificates *CEO:* Pres. Bernard Lafayette, Jr.
FTE Enroll: 190   (615) 228-7877

AMERICAN TECHNICAL INSTITUTE
P.O. Box 8, Brunswick 38014 *Type:* Private
Accred.: 1989 (SACS-CC) *Calendar:* Sem.
plan *Degrees:* B *Prof. Accred.:* Engineering
Technology (nuclear) *CEO:* Pres. D. Wayne
Jones
FTE Enroll: 150   (901) 382-5857

AQUINAS COLLEGE
4210 Harding Rd., Nashville 37205 *Type:*
Private (Roman Catholic) 2-year *Accred.:*
1971/1986 (SACS-CC) *Calendar:* Sem. plan
Degrees: A, B (candidate) *Prof. Accred.:*
Nursing (A) *CEO:* Pres. Sr. Mary Reginald,
O.P.
FTE Enroll: 358   (615) 297-7545

AUSTIN PEAY STATE UNIVERSITY
601 College St., Clarksville 37044 *Type:*
Public (state) *System:* Tennessee Board of
Regents *Accred.:* 1947/1984 (SACS-CC)
Calendar: Sem. plan *Degrees:* A, B, M *Prof.
Accred.:* Art (associate), Medical Technolo-
gy, Music, Nursing (B), Social Work (B),
Teacher Education (e,s,p) *CEO:* Pres. Oscar
C. Page
FTE Enroll: 6,367   (615) 648-7011

BELMONT UNIVERSITY
1900 Belmont Blvd., Nashville 37212-3757
Type: Private (Baptist) liberal arts *Accred.:*
1959/1990 (SACS-CC) *Calendar:* Sem. plan
Degrees: A, B, M *Prof. Accred.:* Music,
Nursing (A) *CEO:* Pres. William E. Troutt
FTE Enroll: 2,488   (615) 383-7001

BETHEL COLLEGE
Cherry St., McKenzie 38201 *Type:* Private
(Presbyterian) liberal arts *Accred.:* 1952/
1988 (SACS-CC) *Calendar:* Qtr. plan *De-
grees:* B, M *CEO:* Pres. Bill J. Elkins
FTE Enroll: 439   (901) 352-1000

BRISTOL UNIVERSITY
Ste. 300, 1241 Volunteer Pkwy., Bristol
37620 *Type:* Private *Accred.:* 1970/1989
(ACISC) *Calendar:* Qtr. plan *Degrees:* A, B,
M *CEO:* Pres./Owner Craven H. Sumerell
          (615) 968-1442

BRANCH CAMPUS
Ste. 102, 5920 Castleway Dr. W., Indi-
anapolis, IN 45250 *Accred.:* 1970/1988
(ACISC) *CEO:* Dir. Hal Graves
          (317) 845-0882

BRYAN COLLEGE
Box 7000, Dayton 37321 *Type:* Private liber-
al arts *Accred.:* 1969/1984 (SACS-CC) *Cal-
endar:* Sem. plan *Degrees:* A, B *CEO:* Pres.
William E. Brown
FTE Enroll: 417   (615) 775-2041

CARSON-NEWMAN COLLEGE
1646 Russell Ave., P.O. Box 557, Jefferson
City 37760 *Type:* Private (Southern Baptist)
liberal arts *Accred.:* 1927/1993 (SACS-CC)
Calendar: Sem. plan *Degrees:* B, M *Prof.
Accred.:* Art (associate), Home Economics,
Music, Nursing (B), Teacher Education (e,s)
CEO: Pres. J. Cordell Maddox
FTE Enroll: 2,358   (615) 475-4000

CHATTANOOGA STATE TECHNICAL COMMUNITY
COLLEGE
4501 Amnicola Hwy., Chattanooga 37406
Type: Public (state) 2-year *System:* Ten-
nessee Board of Regents *Accred.:* 1967/1991
(SACS-CC) *Calendar:* Sem. plan *Degrees:*
A *Prof. Accred.:* Dental Assisting, Dental
Hygiene, Engineering Technology (comput-
er, electrical, mechanical), Medical Record
Technology, Nursing (A), Physical Therapy
Assisting, Radiation Therapy Technology,
Radiography, Respiratory Therapy *CEO:*
Pres. James L. Catanzaro
FTE Enroll: 9,763   (615) 697-4000

CHRISTIAN BROTHERS UNIVERSITY
650 East Pkwy. S., Memphis 38104 *Type:*
Private (Roman Catholic) liberal arts *Ac-
cred.:* 1958/1990 (SACS-CC) *Calendar:*
Sem. plan *Degrees:* A, B, M *Prof. Accred.:*
Engineering (chemical, civil, electrical, me-

chanical), Respiratory Therapy *CEO:* Pres. Stanislaus Sobcyk, F.S.C.
FTE Enroll: 1,362   (901) 722-0200

THE CHURCH OF GOD SCHOOL OF THEOLOGY
P.O. Box 3330, 900 Walker St., N.E., Cleveland 37311 *Type:* Private (Church of God) graduate only *Accred.:* 1989 (ATS); 1984/1989 (SACS-CC) *Calendar:* 4-1-4 plan *Degrees:* M *CEO:* Pres. Cecil B. Knight
FTE Enroll: 251   (615) 478-1131

CLEVELAND STATE COMMUNITY COLLEGE
P.O. Box 3570, Cleveland 37320-3570 *Type:* Public (state) junior *System:* Tennessee Board of Regents *Accred.:* 1969/1984 (SACS-CC) *Calendar:* Sem. plan *Degrees:* A *Prof. Accred.:* Medical Laboratory Technology (AMA), Nursing (A) *CEO:* Pres. Owen F. Cargol
FTE Enroll: 3,502   (615) 472-7141

COLUMBIA STATE COMMUNITY COLLEGE
P.O. Box 1315, Hwy. 412 W., Columbia 38402-1315 *Type:* Public (state) junior *System:* Tennessee Board of Regents *Accred.:* 1968/1983 (SACS-CC) *Calendar:* Sem. plan *Degrees:* A *Prof. Accred.:* Medical Laboratory Technology (AMA), Nursing (A), Radiography, Respiratory Therapy, Veterinary Technology *CEO:* Pres. L. Paul Sands
FTE Enroll: 2,577   (615) 540-2722

CRICHTON COLLEGE
P.O. Box 757830, Memphis 38175-7830 *Type:* Private *Accred.:* 1986/1992 (SACS-CC warning) *Calendar:* Sem. plan *Degrees:* B *CEO:* Pres. Larry R. Brooks
FTE Enroll: 354   (901) 367-9800

CUMBERLAND UNIVERSITY
S. Greenwood St., Lebanon 37087-3554 *Type:* Private *Accred.:* 1962/1990 (SACS-CC) *Calendar:* Sem. plan *Degrees:* A, B, M *CEO:* Pres. Ray C. Phillips
FTE Enroll: 841   (615) 444-2562

DAVID LIPSCOMB UNIVERSITY
3901 Granny White Pike, Nashville 37204-3951 *Type:* Private (Churches of Christ) liberal arts *Accred.:* 1954/1986 (SACS-CC) *Calendar:* Sem. plan *Degrees:* B, M *Prof. Accred.:* Social Work (B-candidate),

Teacher Education (e,s) *CEO:* Pres. Harold Hazelip
FTE Enroll: 2,386   (615) 269-1000

DRAUGHONS JUNIOR COLLEGE
Plus Park at Pavilion Blvd., Nashville 37217 *Type:* Private junior *Accred.:* 1954/1990 (ACISC) *Calendar:* Qtr. plan *Degrees:* A *CEO:* Chrmn. Charles W. Davidson
        (615) 361-7555

BRANCH CAMPUS
2424 Airway Dr. and Lovers La., Bowling Green, KY 42101 *Accred.:* 1954/1990 (ACISC) *CEO:* Dir. Peggy White
        (502) 843-6750

BRANCH CAMPUS
1860 Wilma Rudolph Blvd., Clarksville 37040 *Accred.:* 1988/1990 (ACISC) *CEO:* Dir. Jennie Stribling
        (615) 552-7600

DYERSBURG STATE COMMUNITY COLLEGE
P.O. Box 648, Dyersburg 38025-0648 *Type:* Public (state) junior *System:* Tennessee Board of Regents *Accred.:* 1971/ 1986 (SACS-CC) *Calendar:* Sem. plan *Degrees:* A *Prof. Accred.:* Nursing (A) *CEO:* Pres. Karen A. Bowyer
FTE Enroll: 1,497   (901) 286-3200

EAST TENNESSEE STATE UNIVERSITY
P.O. Box 70734, Johnson City 37614-0734 *Type:* Public (state) *System:* Tennessee Board of Regents *Accred.:* 1927/1993 (SACS-CC) *Calendar:* Sem. plan *Degrees:* A, B, M, D *Prof. Accred.:* Accounting (Type A,C), Art, Audiology, Business (B,M), Dental Assisting, Dental Hygiene, Dental Laboratory Technology, Engineering Technology (civil/construction, electrical, general drafting/design, manufacturing, surveying), Journalism (B), Medical Assisting (AMA), Medical Laboratory Technology (AMA), Medicine, Music, Nursing (A,B,M), Radiography, Respiratory Therapy Technology, Social Work (B), Speech-Language Pathology, Surgical Technology *CEO:* Pres. Roy S. Nicks
FTE Enroll: 11,521   (615) 929-4112

EMMANUEL SCHOOL OF RELIGION
One Walker Dr., Johnson City 37601 *Type:* Private (Christian Churches/Churches of Christ) graduate only *Accred.:* 1981/1986

(ATS); 1986 (SACS-CC) *Calendar:* Sem. plan *Degrees:* M, D (candidate) *CEO:* Pres. Calvin L. Phillips
FTE Enroll: 132   (615) 926-1186

FISK UNIVERSITY
1000 17th Ave. N., Nashville 37208-3051 *Type:* Private liberal arts *Accred.:* 1930/1989 (SACS-CC) *Calendar:* Sem. plan *Degrees:* B, M *Prof. Accred.:* Music *CEO:* Pres. Henry P. Ponder
FTE Enroll: 850   (615) 329-8500

FREE WILL BAPTIST BIBLE COLLEGE
P.O. Box 50117, 3606 W. End Ave., Nashville 37205 *Type:* Private (National Association of Free Will Baptist Churches) *Accred.:* 1958/1988 (AABC) *Calendar:* Sem. plan *Degrees:* A, B *CEO:* Pres. Thomas Malone
FTE Enroll: 284   (615) 383-1340

FREED-HARDEMAN UNIVERSITY
158 E. Main St., Henderson 38340-2399 *Type:* Private (Church of Christ) liberal arts *Accred.:* 1956/1991 (SACS-CC) *Calendar:* Sem. plan *Degrees:* B, M *Prof. Accred.:* Social Work (B), Teacher Education (e,s) *CEO:* Pres. Milton R. Sewell
FTE Enroll: 1,301   (901) 989-6000

HARDING UNIVERSITY GRADUATE SCHOOL OF RELIGION
1000 Cherry Rd., Memphis 38117 *Type:* Private *Accred.:* 1972/1987 (SACS-CC) *Calendar:* Sem. plan *Degrees:* M, D *CEO:* Exec. Dean Bill Flatt
FTE Enroll: 101   (901) 761-1350

HIWASSEE COLLEGE
HC Box 646, 225 Hiwassee College Dr., Madisonville 37354 *Type:* Private (United Methodist) junior *Accred.:* 1958/ 1990 (SACS-CC) *Calendar:* Sem. plan *Degrees:* A *CEO:* Pres. Stephen E. Fritz
FTE Enroll: 538   (615) 442-2091

ITT TECHNICAL INSTITUTE
1637 Downtown West Blvd., Knoxville 37919-9875 *Type:* Private *Accred.:* 1990 (ACCSCT) *Calendar:* Courses of varying lengths *Degrees:* A *CEO:* Dir. David Reynolds
                                     (615) 691-8111

ITT TECHNICAL INSTITUTE
441 Donelson Pike, Nashville 37214-8029 *Type:* Private *Accred.:* 1985/1990 (ACC-SCT) *Calendar:* Courses of varying lengths *Degrees:* A *CEO:* Dir. Nathan Blaede
                                     (615) 889-8700

BRANCH CAMPUS
Patewood Business Ctr., One Marcus Dr., Greenville, SC 29615 *Accred.:* 1993 (ACCSCT) *CEO:* Dir. Frederick Payne
                                     (803) 288-0777

JACKSON STATE COMMUNITY COLLEGE
2046 North Pkwy., Jackson 38301-3797 *Type:* Public (state) junior *System:* Tennessee Board of Regents *Accred.:* 1969/1984 (SACS-CC) *Calendar:* Sem. plan *Degrees:* A *Prof. Accred.:* EMT-Paramedic, Medical Laboratory Technology (AMA), Physical Therapy Assisting, Radiography, Respiratory Therapy *CEO:* Pres. Walter L. Nelms
FTE Enroll: 2,443   (901) 424-3520

JOHN A. GUPTON COLLEGE
1616 Church Street, Nashville 37203 *Type:* Private 2-year *Accred.:* 1971/1986 (SACS-CC) *Calendar:* Sem. plan *Degrees:* A *Prof. Accred.:* Mortuary Science *CEO:* Pres. John A. Gupton, III
FTE Enroll: 56   (615) 327-3927

JOHNSON BIBLE COLLEGE
7900 Johnson Dr., Knoxville 37998 *Type:* Private (Christian Churches/Churches of Christ) *Accred.:* 1970/1990 (AABC); 1979/ 1985 (SACS-CC) *Calendar:* Sem. plan *Degrees:* A, B, M, certificates *CEO:* Pres. David L. Eubanks
FTE Enroll: 446   (615) 573-4517

KING COLLEGE
1350 King College Rd., Bristol 37620-2699 *Type:* Private (Presbyterian) liberal arts *Accred.:* 1947/1988 (SACS-CC) *Calendar:* 4-1-4 plan *Degrees:* B *CEO:* Pres. Richard Stanislaw
FTE Enroll: 548   (615) 968-1187

KNOXVILLE BUSINESS COLLEGE
720 N. Fifth Ave., Knoxville 37917 *Type:* Private junior *Accred.:* 1955/1989 (ACISC) *Calendar:* Qtr. plan *Degrees:* A *CEO:* Pres. Stephen A. South
                                     (615) 524-3043

KNOXVILLE COLLEGE
901 College St., Knoxville 37921 *Type:* Private (Presbyterian) liberal arts *Accred.:* 1948/1992 (SACS-CC) *Calendar:* Sem. plan *Degrees:* A, B *Prof. Accred.:* Medical Assisting (AMA) *CEO:* Interim Pres. Peyton S. Hutchinson
FTE Enroll: 914   (615) 524-6500

LAMBUTH UNIVERSITY
705 Lambuth Blvd., Jackson 38301 *Type:* Private (United Methodist) liberal arts *Accred.:* 1954/1989 (SACS-CC) *Calendar:* Sem. plan *Degrees:* B *CEO:* Pres. Thomas F. Boyd
FTE Enroll: 932   (901) 425-2500

LANE COLLEGE
545 Lane Ave., Jackson 38301-4598 *Type:* Private (Christian Methodist Episcopal) liberal arts *Accred.:* 1949/1992 (SACS-CC) *Calendar:* Sem. plan *Degrees:* B *CEO:* Pres. Wesley Cornelious McClure
FTE Enroll: 744   (901) 426-7500

LEE COLLEGE
P.O. Box 3450, Cleveland 37320-3450 *Type:* Private (Churches of God) liberal arts *Accred.:* 1960/1984 (SACS-CC) *Calendar:* Sem. plan *Degrees:* B *CEO:* Pres. Charles Paul Conn
FTE Enroll: 2,011   (615) 472-2111

LEMOYNE-OWEN COLLEGE
807 Walker Ave., Memphis 38126 *Type:* Private (United Church of Christ/Baptist) liberal arts *Accred.:* 1960/1993 (SACS-CC) *Calendar:* Sem. plan *Degrees:* B, M (candidate) *CEO:* Pres. Burnett Joiner
FTE Enroll: 1,321   (901) 774-9090

LINCOLN MEMORIAL UNIVERSITY
Cumberland Gap Pkwy., Harrogate 37752-0901 *Type:* Private liberal arts *Accred.:* 1936/1989 (SACS-CC) *Calendar:* Sem. plan *Degrees:* A, B, M *Prof. Accred.:* Medical Technology, Nursing (A), Veterinary Technology *CEO:* Pres. Scott D. Miller
FTE Enroll: 1,460   (615) 869-3611

MARTIN METHODIST COLLEGE
433 W. Madison St., Pulaski 38478 *Type:* Private (United Methodist) *Accred.:* 1952/1989 (SACS-CC) *Calendar:* Sem. plan *Degrees:* A, B (candidate) *CEO:* Pres. George P. Miller, III
FTE Enroll: 496   (615) 363-7456

MARYVILLE COLLEGE
502 E. Lamar Alexander Pkwy., Maryville 37801 *Type:* Private (United Presbyterian) liberal arts *Accred.:* 1922/1993 (SACS-CC) *Calendar:* Sem. plan *Degrees:* B *Prof. Accred.:* Music *CEO:* Pres. Gerald W. Gibson
FTE Enroll: 774   (615) 981-8000

MEHARRY MEDICAL COLLEGE
1005 D.B. Todd Blvd., Nashville 37208 *Type:* Private professional *Accred.:* 1972/1988 (SACS-CC) *Calendar:* Sem. plan *Degrees:* M, D *Prof. Accred.:* Dental Hygiene, Dentistry, General Practice Residency, Health Services Administration, Medicine *CEO:* Acting Pres. Henry Foster, Jr.
FTE Enroll: 697   (615) 327-6111

MEMPHIS COLLEGE OF ART
Overton Park, 1930 Poplar Ave., Memphis 38112-2764 *Type:* Private professional *Accred.:* 1963/1984 (SACS-CC) *Calendar:* Sem. plan *Degrees:* B, M *Prof. Accred.:* Art *CEO:* Pres. Jeffrey D. Nesin
FTE Enroll: 247   (901) 726-4085

MEMPHIS STATE UNIVERSITY
Memphis 38152 *Type:* Public (state) *System:* Tennessee Board of Regents *Accred.:* 1927/1984 (SACS-CC) *Calendar:* Sem. plan *Degrees:* B, M, D *Prof. Accred.:* Accounting (Type A,B,C), Art, Audiology, Business (B,M), Clinical Psychology, Counseling Psychology, Dietetics (internship), Engineering Technology (architectural, computer, electrical, manufacturing), Engineering (civil, electrical, mechanical), Home Economics, Journalism (B,M), Law (ABA only), Music, Nursing (B), Planning (M), Psychology Internship, Public Administration, Rehabilitation Counseling, Social Work (B), Speech-Language Pathology, Teacher Education (e,s,p), Theatre *CEO:* Pres. V. Lane Rawlins
FTE Enroll: 17,193   (901) 678-2000

MEMPHIS THEOLOGICAL SEMINARY
168 East Pkwy. S., Memphis 38104 *Type:* Private (Cumberland Presbyterian) graduate only *Accred.:* 1973/1988 (ATS); 1988

(SACS-CC) *Calendar:* Sem. plan *Degrees:* M, D (candidate) *CEO:* Pres. J. David Hester *FTE Enroll:* 177　　　　　(901) 458-8232

MID-AMERICA BAPTIST THEOLOGICAL SEMINARY
1255 Poplar Ave., Memphis 38104 *Type:* Private (Baptist) professional *Accred.:* 1981/ 1986 (SACS-CC) *Calendar:* Sem. plan *Degrees:* A, M, D *CEO:* Pres. B. Gray Allison *FTE Enroll:* 372　　　　　(901) 726-9171

MIDDLE TENNESSEE STATE UNIVERSITY
Murfreesboro 37132 *Type:* Public (state) *System:* Tennessee Board of Regents *Accred.:* 1928/1985 (SACS-CC) *Calendar:* Sem. plan *Degrees:* A, B, M, D *Prof. Accred.:* Business (B,M), Home Economics, Journalism (B), Music, Nursing (B), Social Work (B), Teacher Education (e,s,p) *CEO:* Pres. James E. Walker
FTE Enroll: 17,765　　　　(615) 898-2300

MILLIGAN COLLEGE
Milligan College 37682 *Type:* Private liberal arts *Accred.:* 1960/1992 (SACS-CC) *Calendar:* Sem. plan *Degrees:* A, B, M *Prof. Accred.:* Teacher Education (e,s) *CEO:* Pres. Marshall J. Leggett
FTE Enroll: 737　　　　　(615) 461-8700

MOTLOW STATE COMMUNITY COLLEGE
P.O. Box 88100, Tullahoma 37388-8100 *Type:* Public (state) junior *System:* Tennessee Board of Regents *Accred.:* 1971/1986 (SACS-CC) *Calendar:* Sem. plan *Degrees:* A *Prof. Accred.:* Nursing (A) *CEO:* Pres. A. Frank Glass
FTE Enroll: 3,579　　　　(615) 455-8511

NASHVILLE SCHOOL OF INTERIOR DESIGN AT WATKINS INSTITUTE
601 Church St., Nashville 37219 *Type:* Private *Calendar:* Courses of varying lengths *Degrees:* A, certificates, diplomas *Prof. Accred.:* Interior Design *CEO:* Dir. Wanda Palus
　　　　　　　　　　　　(615) 242-1851

NASHVILLE STATE TECHNICAL INSTITUTE
120 White Bridge Rd., Nashville 37209-4515 *Type:* Public (state) 2-year *System:* Tennessee Board of Regents *Accred.:* 1972/ 1987 (SACS-CC) *Calendar:* Sem. plan *Degrees:* A *Prof. Accred.:* Engineering Technology (architectural, civil/construction,

computer, electrical, industrial, mechanical), Occupational Therapy Assisting *CEO:* Pres. George H. Van Allen
FTE Enroll: 3,151　　　　(615) 353-3333

NORTHEAST STATE TECHNICAL COMMUNITY COLLEGE
P.O. Box 246, 2425 Hwy. 75, Blountville 37617-0246 *Type:* Public (state) 2-year *System:* Tennessee Board of Regents *Accred.:* 1984/1989 (SACS-CC) *Calendar:* Sem. plan *Degrees:* A *Prof. Accred.:* Engineering Technology (computer, electrical, instrumentation) *CEO:* Pres. R. Wade Powers
FTE Enroll: 2,608　　　　(615) 323-3191

O'MORE COLLEGE OF DESIGN
423 S. Margin St., P.O. Box 908, Franklin 37065 *Type:* Private professional *Calendar:* Sem. plan *Degrees:* B *Prof. Accred.:* Interior Design *CEO:* Chair Chris Wyatt
　　　　　　　　　　　　(615) 794-4254

PELLISSIPPI STATE TECHNICAL COMMUNITY COLLEGE
10915 Hardin Valley Rd., P.O. Box 22990, Knoxville 37933-0990 *Type:* Public (state) 2-year *System:* Tennessee Board of Regents *Accred.:* 1977/1992 (SACS-CC) *Calendar:* Sem. plan *Degrees:* A *Prof. Accred.:* Engineering Technology (chemical, civil/construction, electrical, manufacturing, mechanical, mechanical drafting/design) *CEO:* Pres. Allen G. Edwards
FTE Enroll: 5,680　　　　(615) 694-6400

RHODES COLLEGE
2000 North Pkwy., Memphis 38112 *Type:* Private (Presbyterian) liberal arts *Accred.:* 1911/1990 (SACS-CC) *Calendar:* Sem. plan *Degrees:* B, M (candidate) *CEO:* Pres. James H. Daughdrill
FTE Enroll: 1,382　　　　(901) 726-3000

ROANE STATE COMMUNITY COLLEGE
Rte. 8, Box 69, Patton La., Harriman 37748 *Type:* Public (state) 2-year *System:* Tennessee Board of Regents *Accred.:* 1974/1989 (SACS-CC) *Calendar:* Sem. plan *Degrees:* A *Prof. Accred.:* Dental Assisting, Dental Hygiene, EMT-Paramedic, Medical Laboratory Technology (AMA), Medical Record Technology, Nursing (A), Physical Therapy Assisting, Radiography, Respiratory Thera-

py, Respiratory Therapy Technology *CEO:*
Pres. Sherry L. Hoppe
FTE Enroll: 4,165   (615) 354-3000

SHELBY STATE COMMUNITY COLLEGE
P.O. Box 40568, Memphis 38174-0568
Type: Public (state) junior *System:* Tennessee Board of Regents *Accred.:* 1974/1989
(SACS-CC) *Calendar:* Sem. plan *Degrees:*
A *Prof. Accred.:* EMT-Paramedic, Medical
Laboratory Technology (AMA), Nursing
(A), Physical Therapy Assisting, Radiography *CEO:* Pres. Lawrence M. Cox
FTE Enroll: 5,654   (901) 544-5000

SOUTHERN COLLEGE OF OPTOMETRY
1245 Madison Ave., Memphis 38104 *Type:*
Private professional *Accred.:* 1967/1992
(SACS-CC) *Calendar:* Qtr. plan *Degrees:* D
Prof. Accred.: Optometry *CEO:* Pres.
William E. Cochran, O.D.
FTE Enroll: 407   (901) 722-3200

SOUTHERN COLLEGE OF SEVENTH-DAY
ADVENTISTS
P.O. Box 370, Collegedale 37315-0370
Type: Private (Seventh-Day Adventist) liberal arts *Accred.:* 1950/1992 (SACS-CC warning) *Calendar:* Sem. plan *Degrees:* A, B
Prof. Accred.: Music, Nursing (A,B) *CEO:*
Pres. Donald R. Sahly
FTE Enroll: 1,388   (615) 238-2111

STATE TECHNICAL INSTITUTE AT MEMPHIS
5983 Macon Cove, Memphis 38134-7693
Type: Public (state) 2-year *System:* Tennessee Board of Regents *Accred.:* 1969/1984
(SACS-CC) *Calendar:* Sem. plan *Degrees:*
A *Prof. Accred.:* Engineering Technology
(architectural, bioengineering, chemical,
civil/construction, computer, electrical, industrial, mechanical) *CEO:* Pres. Charles M.
Temple
FTE Enroll: 6,149   (901) 377-4100

TENNESSEE STATE UNIVERSITY
3500 John Merritt Blvd., Nashville 37209-1561 *Type:* Public (state) *System:* Tennessee
Board of Regents *Accred.:* 1946/1990
(SACS-CC) *Calendar:* Sem. plan *Degrees:*
A, B, M, D *Prof. Accred.:* Dental Hygiene,
Engineering (architectural, civil, electrical,
mechanical), Home Economics, Medical
Record Administration, Medical Technolo-

gy, Music, Nursing (A,B), Physical Therapy,
Public Administration, Respiratory Therapy,
Social Work (B), Speech-Language Pathology, Teacher Education (e,s,p) *CEO:* Pres.
James A. Hefner
FTE Enroll: 6,168   (615) 320-3131

TENNESSEE TECHNOLOGICAL UNIVERSITY
N. Dixie Ave., Cookeville 38505 *Type:* Public (state) *System:* Tennessee Board of Regents *Accred.:* 1939/1985 (SACS-CC) *Calendar:* Sem. plan *Degrees:* A, B, M, D *Prof.
Accred.:* Accounting (Type A), Business
(B,M), Engineering (chemical, civil, electrical, industrial, mechanical), Music, Nursing
(B), Teacher Education (e,s,p) *CEO:* Pres.
Angelo A. Volpe
FTE Enroll: 9,311   (615) 372-3101

TENNESSEE TEMPLE UNIVERSITY
1815 Union Ave., Chattanooga 37404 *Type:*
Independent (Baptist) *Accred.:* 1984/1989
(AABC) *Calendar:* Sem. plan *Degrees:* A,
B, diplomas *CEO:* Interim Pres. Roger Stiles
FTE Enroll: 769   (615) 493-4100

TENNESSEE WESLEYAN COLLEGE
P.O. Box 40, Athens 37371 *Type:* Private
(United Methodist) liberal arts *Accred.:*
1958/1990 (SACS-CC) *Calendar:* Sem. plan
Degrees: B *CEO:* Interim Pres. Harry W.
Sherman
FTE Enroll: 522   (615) 745-7504

TREVECCA NAZARENE COLLEGE
333 Murfreesboro Rd., Nashville 37210
Type: Private (Nazarene) liberal arts and
teachers *Accred.:* 1969/1993 (SACS-CC)
Calendar: Sem. plan *Degrees:* A, B, M *Prof.
Accred.:* Medical Assisting (AMA), Music,
Physician Assisting, Social Work (B-candidate) *CEO:* Pres. Millard Reed
FTE Enroll: 1,357   (615) 248-1200

TUSCULUM COLLEGE
P.O. Box 5093, Greeneville 37743 *Type:* Private (Presbyterian) liberal arts *Accred.:*
1926/1991 (SACS-CC) *Calendar:* Sem. plan
Degrees: B, M *CEO:* Pres. Robert E. Knott
FTE Enroll: 1,117   (615) 636-7300

UNION UNIVERSITY
2447 Hwy. 45 By-Pass, Jackson 38305
Type: Private (Southern Baptist) liberal arts
Accred.: 1948/1987 (SACS-CC) *Calendar:*

Sem. plan *Degrees:* A, B, M *Prof. Accred.:* Music, Nursing (A,B) *CEO:* Pres. Hyran E. Barefoot
FTE Enroll: 2,477   (901) 668-1818

THE UNIVERSITY OF TENNESSEE AT CHATTANOOGA
615 McCallie Ave., Chattanooga 37403-2598 *Type:* Public (state) *System:* University of Tennessee System *Accred.:* 1910/1991 (SACS-CC) *Calendar:* Sem. plan *Degrees:* B, M *Prof. Accred.:* Business (B,M), Engineering (general), Music, Nursing (B), Physical Therapy, Social Work (B), Teacher Education (e,s,p) *CEO:* Chanc. Frederick W. Obear
FTE Enroll: 7,122   (615) 744-4111

THE UNIVERSITY OF TENNESSEE AT MARTIN
University St., Martin 38238 *Type:* Public (state) *System:* University of Tennessee System *Accred.:* 1951/1992 (SACS-CC) *Calendar:* Qtr. plan *Degrees:* A, B, M *Prof. Accred.:* Engineering Technology (civil/construction, electrical, mechanical), Home Economics, Music, Nursing (B), Social Work (B), Teacher Education (e,s,p) *CEO:* Chanc. Margaret N. Perry
FTE Enroll: 6,674   (901) 587-7000

THE UNIVERSITY OF TENNESSEE, KNOXVILLE
527 Andy Holt Tower, Knoxville 37996-0150 *Type:* Public (state) *System:* University of Tennessee System *Accred.:* 1897/1992 (SACS-CC) *Calendar:* Sem. plan *Degrees:* B, M, D *Prof. Accred.:* Accounting (Type A,C), Art, Audiology, Business (B,M), Community Health/Preventive Medicine, Counseling, Cytotechnology, Engineering (aerospace, agricultural, chemical, civil, electrical, engineering physics/science, industrial, materials, mechanical, nuclear), Forestry, General Practice Residency, Home Economics, Interior Design, Journalism (B,M), Law, Librarianship, Medical Technology, Music, Nuclear Medicine Technology, Nurse Anesthesia Education, Nursing (B,M), Oral and Maxillofacial Surgery, Planning (M), Psychology Internship, Radiography, Recreation and Leisure Services, Rehabilitation Counseling, Social Work (B,M), Speech-Language Pathology, Teacher Education (e,s,p), Veterinary Medicine *CEO:* Pres. Joseph E. Johnson
FTE Enroll: 23,198   (615) 974-1000

THE UNIVERSITY OF TENNESSEE, MEMPHIS
800 Madison Ave., Memphis 38163 *Type:* Public (state) *System:* University of Tennessee System *Accred.:* 1897/1993 (SACS-CC) *Calendar:* Sem. plan *Degrees:* B, M, D *Prof. Accred.:* Clinical Psychology, Counseling Psychology, Cytotechnology, Dental Hygiene, Dentistry, General Dentistry, Medical Record Administration, Medical Technology, Medicine, Nursing (B,M), Occupational Therapy, Oral and Maxillofacial Surgery, Orthodontics, Pediatric Dentistry, Periodontics, Physical Therapy, Psychology Internship, School Psychology, Social Work (M) *CEO:* Chanc. William R. Rice
FTE Enroll: 1,985   (901) 448-5500

THE UNIVERSITY OF THE SOUTH
735 University Ave., Sewanee 37375-1000 *Type:* Private (Episcopal) liberal arts *Accred.:* 1958/1985 (ATS); 1895/1985 (SACS-CC) *Calendar:* Sem. plan *Degrees:* B, M, D *CEO:* Pres. Samuel R. Williamson, Jr.
FTE Enroll: 1,218   (615) 598-1000

VANDERBILT UNIVERSITY
W. End Ave., Nashville 37240 *Type:* Private (interdenominational) *Accred.:* 1938/1983 (ATS); 1895/1986 (SACS-CC) *Calendar:* Sem. plan *Degrees:* B, M, D *Prof. Accred.:* Audiology, Business (M), Clinical Psychology, Counseling, Dietetics (internship), Engineering (bioengineering, chemical, civil, electrical, mechanical), General Practice Residency (prelim. provisional), Law, Medical Technology, Medicine, Music, Nuclear Medicine Technology, Nursing (M), Oral and Maxillofacial Surgery, Perfusion, Psychology Internship, Radiation Therapy Technology, Speech-Language Pathology, Teacher Education (e,s,p) *CEO:* Chanc. Joe B. Wyatt
FTE Enroll: 9,536   (615) 322-7311

VOLUNTEER STATE COMMUNITY COLLEGE
1360 Nashville Pike, Gallatin 37066 *Type:* Public (state) 2-year *System:* Tennessee Board of Regents *Accred.:* 1973/1989 (SACS-CC) *Calendar:* Qtr. plan *Degrees:* A *Prof. Accred.:* Dental Assisting, EMT-Paramedic, Medical Record Technology, Physical Therapy Assisting, Radiography, Respiratory Therapy Technology *CEO:* Pres. Hal R. Ramer
FTE Enroll: 4,092   (615) 452-8600

WALTERS STATE COMMUNITY COLLEGE
500 S. Davy Crockett Pkwy., Morristown
37813-6899 *Type:* Public (state) junior *System:* Tennessee Board of Regents *Accred.:*
1972/1987 (SACS-CC) *Calendar:* Sem. plan
Degrees: A *Prof. Accred.:* Nursing (A),
Physical Therapy Assisting *CEO:* Pres. Jack
E. Campbell
FTE Enroll: 3,913   (615) 587-2600

TEXAS

ABILENE CHRISTIAN UNIVERSITY
ACU Sta., Box 7000, Abilene 79699 *Type:* Private (Church of Christ) liberal arts *Accred.:* 1951/1991 (SACS-CC) *Calendar:* Sem. plan *Degrees:* A, B, M, D *Prof. Accred.:* Marriage and Family Therapy (M), Music, Social Work (B) *CEO:* Pres. Royce Money
FTE Enroll: 3,405   (915) 674-2000

ABILENE INTERCOLLEGIATE SCHOOL OF NURSING
2149 Hickory, Abilene 79601 *Type:* Private professional *Calendar:* Sem. plan *Degrees:* B *Prof. Accred.:* Nursing (B) *CEO:* Dean Corine Bonnet
                             (915) 672-2441

ALVIN COMMUNITY COLLEGE
3110 Mustang Rd., Alvin 77511-4898 *Type:* Public (district) junior *System:* Texas Higher Education Coordinating Board *Accred.:* 1959/1990 (SACS-CC) *Calendar:* Sem. plan *Degrees:* A *Prof. Accred.:* Medical Laboratory Technology (AMA), Nursing (A), Respiratory Therapy, Respiratory Therapy Technology *CEO:* Pres. A. Rodney Allbright
FTE Enroll: 4,289   (713) 331-6111

AMARILLO COLLEGE
P.O. Box 447, Amarillo 79178 *Type:* Public (district) junior *System:* Texas Higher Education Coordinating Board *Accred.:* 1933/1992 (SACS-CC) *Calendar:* Sem. plan *Degrees:* A *Prof. Accred.:* Dental Hygiene, Engineering Technology (electrical), Medical Laboratory Technology (AMA), Music, Nursing (A), Physical Therapy Assisting, Radiation Therapy Technology, Radiography, Respiratory Therapy, Surgical Technology *CEO:* Pres. Luther Bud Joyner
FTE Enroll: 6,153   (806) 371-5000

AMBER UNIVERSITY
1700 Eastgate Dr., Garland 75041 *Type:* Private (Church of Christ) *Accred.:* 1981/1987 (SACS-CC) *Calendar:* Sem. plan *Degrees:* B, M *CEO:* Pres. Douglas W. Warner
FTE Enroll: 1,520   (214) 279-6511

ANGELINA COLLEGE
P.O. Box 1768, Lufkin 75902 *Type:* Public (district) junior *System:* Texas Higher Education Coordinating Board *Accred.:* 1970/1985 (SACS-CC) *Calendar:* Sem. plan *Degrees:* A *Prof. Accred.:* Radiography, Respiratory Therapy Technology *CEO:* Pres. Larry M. Phillips
FTE Enroll: 2,944   (409) 639-1301

ANGELO STATE UNIVERSITY
2601 West Ave. N., San Angelo 76909 *Type:* Public (state) liberal arts *System:* Texas State University System *Accred.:* 1936/1992 (SACS-CC) *Calendar:* Sem. plan *Degrees:* A, B, M *Prof. Accred.:* Music, Nursing (A,B) *CEO:* Pres. Lloyd D. Vincent
FTE Enroll: 5,301   (915) 942-2073

ARLINGTON BAPTIST COLLEGE
3001 W. Division St., Arlington 76012-3425 *Type:* Private (World Baptist Fellowship) *Accred.:* 1981/1991 (AABC) *Calendar:* Sem. plan *Degrees:* B *CEO:* Interim Pres. Wendell Hiers
FTE Enroll: 146   (817) 461-8741

AUSTIN COLLEGE
900 N. Grand Ave., P.O. Box 1177, Sherman 75091-4440 *Type:* Private (Presbyterian) liberal arts *Accred.:* 1947/1989 (SACS-CC) *Calendar:* 4-1-4 plan *Degrees:* B, M *CEO:* Pres. Harry E. Smith
FTE Enroll: 1,389   (214) 813-2000

AUSTIN COMMUNITY COLLEGE
5930 Middle Fiskville Rd., Austin 78752-4390 *Type:* Public (district) junior *System:* Texas Higher Education Coordinating Board *Accred.:* 1978/1993 (SACS-CC) *Calendar:* Sem. plan *Degrees:* A *Prof. Accred.:* Diagnostic Medical Sonography, EMT-Paramedic, Medical Laboratory Technology (AMA), Nursing (A), Occupational Therapy Assisting, Physical Therapy Assisting, Radiography, Surgical Technology *CEO:* Pres. William E. Segura
FTE Enroll: 15,865   (512) 483-7000

AUSTIN PRESBYTERIAN THEOLOGICAL SEMINARY
100 E. 27th St., Austin 78705-5797 *Type:* Private (Presbyterian) graduate only *Accred.:* 1940/1989 (ATS); 1973/1989 (SACS-CC)

Calendar: Sem. plan *Degrees:* M, D *CEO:* Pres. Jack L. Stotts
FTE Enroll: 243   (512) 472-6736

BAPTIST MISSIONARY ASSOCIATION
THEOLOGICAL SEMINARY
1530 E. Pine St., Jacksonville 75766 *Type:* Private (Baptist) professional *Accred.:* 1986/1991 (SACS-CC) *Calendar:* Sem. plan *Degrees:* A, B, M *CEO:* Pres. Philip R. Bryan
FTE Enroll: 59   (903) 586-2501

BAUDER FASHION COLLEGE—ARLINGTON
508 S. Center St., Arlington 76010 *Type:* Private *Accred.:* 1985/1990 (SACS-CC) *Calendar:* Qtr. plan *Degrees:* A *CEO:* Exec. Dir. Steve O. Black
FTE Enroll: 156   (817) 277-6666

BAYLOR COLLEGE OF DENTISTRY
3302 Gaston Ave., Dallas 75246 *Type:* Private professional; graduate only *Accred.:* 1976/1989 (SACS-CC) *Calendar:* Qtr. plan *Degrees:* M, D *Prof. Accred.:* Combined Prosthodontics, Dental Hygiene, Dentistry, Dietetics (internship), Endodontics, General Dentistry, General Practice Residency (prelim. provisional), Oral and Maxillofacial Surgery, Orthodontics, Pediatric Dentistry, Periodontics, Radiation Therapy Technology, Radiography *CEO:* Pres. Dominick P. DePaola
FTE Enroll: 466   (214) 828-8100

BAYLOR COLLEGE OF MEDICINE
One Baylor Plaza, Houston 77030-3498 *Type:* Private professional; graduate only *Accred.:* 1970/1985 (SACS-CC) *Calendar:* Qtr. plan *Degrees:* M, D *Prof. Accred.:* Medicine, Nuclear Medicine Technology, Nurse Anesthesia Education, Perfusion, Physician Assisting, Psychology Internship *CEO:* Pres. William T. Butler
FTE Enroll: 1,116   (713) 798-4951

BAYLOR UNIVERSITY
Waco 76798 *Type:* Private (Southern Baptist) *Accred.:* 1914/1986 (SACS-CC) *Calendar:* Sem. plan *Degrees:* B, M, D *Prof. Accred.:* Accounting (Type A), Business (B,M), Clinical Psychology, Computer Science, Engineering (general), Health Services Administration, Law, Music, Nursing (B), Physical Therapy, Social Work (B), Speech-

Language Pathology, Teacher Education (e,s,p) *CEO:* Pres. Herbert H. Reynolds
FTE Enroll: 11,681   (817) 755-1011

BEE COUNTY COLLEGE
3800 Charco Rd., Beeville 78102 *Type:* Public (district) junior *System:* Texas Higher Education Coordinating Board *Accred.:* 1969/1984 (SACS-CC) *Calendar:* Sem. plan *Degrees:* A *Prof. Accred.:* Dental Hygiene *CEO:* Pres. Norman E. Wallace
FTE Enroll: 2,262   (512) 358-3130

BLINN COLLEGE
902 College Ave., Brenham 77833 *Type:* Public (district) junior *System:* Texas Higher Education Coordinating Board *Accred.:* 1950/1984 (SACS-CC) *Calendar:* Sem. plan *Degrees:* A *Prof. Accred.:* Nursing (A), Radiography *CEO:* Pres. Walter C. Schwartz
FTE Enroll: 6,816   (409) 830-4000

BRAZOSPORT COLLEGE
500 College Dr., Lake Jackson 77566 *Type:* Public (district) junior *System:* Texas Higher Education Coordinating Board *Accred.:* 1970/1985 (SACS-CC) *Calendar:* Sem. plan *Degrees:* A *CEO:* Pres. John R. Grable
FTE Enroll: 2,351   (409) 266-3000

BROOKHAVEN COLLEGE
3939 Valley View La., Farmers Branch 75244-4997 *Type:* Public (district) junior *System:* Dallas County Community College District *Accred.:* 1979/1993 (SACS-CC) *Calendar:* Sem. plan *Degrees:* A *CEO:* Pres. Walter G. Bumphus
FTE Enroll: 10,942   (214) 620-4700

CEDAR VALLEY COLLEGE
3030 N. Dallas Ave., Lancaster 75134 *Type:* Public (district) junior *System:* Dallas County Community College District *Accred.:* 1979/1993 (SACS-CC) *Calendar:* Sem. plan *Degrees:* A *Prof. Accred.:* Veterinary Technology *CEO:* Pres. Carol J. Spencer
FTE Enroll: 2,187   (214) 372-8201

CENTRAL TEXAS COLLEGE
P.O. Box 1800, Killeen 76540-9990 *Type:* Public (district) junior *System:* Texas Higher Education Coordinating Board *Accred.:* 1969/1984 (SACS-CC) *Calendar:* Sem. plan *Degrees:* A *Prof. Accred.:* Medical Labora-

tory Technology (AMA), Nursing (A) *CEO:* Chanc. James R. Anderson
FTE Enroll: 8,811   (817) 526-7161

CISCO JUNIOR COLLEGE
Rte. 3, Box 3, Cisco 76437 *Type:* Public (district) junior *System:* Texas Higher Education Coordinating Board *Accred.:* 1958/1989 (SACS-CC) *Calendar:* Sem. plan *Degrees:* A *Prof. Accred.:* Practical Nursing *CEO:* Pres. Roger C. Schustereit
FTE Enroll: 3,171   (817) 442-2567

CLARENDON COLLEGE
P.O. Box 968, Clarendon 79226 *Type:* Public (district) junior *System:* Texas Higher Education Coordinating Board *Accred.:* 1970/1985 (SACS-CC) *Calendar:* Sem. plan *Degrees:* A *CEO:* Pres. Jerry D. Stockton
FTE Enroll: 668   (806) 874-3571

COLLEGE OF THE MAINLAND
1200 Amburn Rd., Texas City 77591 *Type:* Public (district) junior *System:* Texas Higher Education Coordinating Board *Accred.:* 1969/1993 (SACS-CC) *Calendar:* Sem. plan *Degrees:* A *Prof. Accred.:* Nursing (A) *CEO:* Pres. Larry L. Stanley
FTE Enroll: 6,189   (409) 938-1211

COLLIN COUNTY COMMUNITY COLLEGE
2200 W. University Dr., P.O. Box 8001, McKinney 75070 *Type:* Public (district) junior *System:* Texas Higher Education Coordinating Board *Accred.:* 1989 (SACS-CC) *Calendar:* Sem. plan *Degrees:* A *CEO:* Pres. John H. Anthony
FTE Enroll: 6,534   (214) 548-6790

COMMONWEALTH INSTITUTE OF FUNERAL SERVICE
415 Barren Springs Dr., Houston 77090 *Type:* Private professional *Calendar:* Qtr. plan *Degrees:* A, diplomas *Prof. Accred.:* Funeral Service Education *CEO:* Pres. Terry McEnany
          (713) 873-0262

CONCORDIA LUTHERAN COLLEGE
3400 I.H. 35 N., Austin 78705 *Type:* Private (Lutheran) liberal arts *Accred.:* 1968/1988 (SACS-CC) *Calendar:* Sem. plan *Degrees:* A, B *CEO:* Pres. Pro-Tem Les Bayer
FTE Enroll: 622   (512) 452-7661

COOKE COUNTY COLLEGE
1525 W. California St., Gainesville 76240-4699 *Type:* Public (district) junior *System:* Texas Higher Education Coordinating Board *Accred.:* 1961/1991 (SACS-CC) *Calendar:* Sem. plan *Degrees:* A *Prof. Accred.:* Nursing (A), Occupational Therapy Assisting *CEO:* Pres. Ronnie Glassock
FTE Enroll: 2,641   (817) 668-7731

THE CRISWELL COLLEGE
4010 Gaston Ave., Dallas 75246 *Type:* Private (Baptist) *Accred.:* 1985/1990 (SACS-CC) *Calendar:* Sem. plan *Degrees:* A, B, M *CEO:* Pres. Richard R. Melick, Jr.
FTE Enroll: 233   (214) 821-5433

DALLAS BAPTIST UNIVERSITY
3000 Mountain Creek Pkwy., Dallas 75211-9299 *Type:* Private (Southern Baptist) liberal arts *Accred.:* 1959/1988 (SACS-CC) *Calendar:* 4-1-4 plan *Degrees:* B, M *Prof. Accred.:* Nursing (B) *CEO:* Pres. Gary R. Cook
FTE Enroll: 2,803   (214) 331-8311

DALLAS CHRISTIAN COLLEGE
2700 Christian Pkwy., Dallas 75234 *Type:* Private (Christian Churches/Churches of Christ) *Accred.:* 1978/1988 (AABC) *Calendar:* Sem. plan *Degrees:* A, B *CEO:* Pres. Gene Shepherd
FTE Enroll: 71   (214) 241-3371

DALLAS THEOLOGICAL SEMINARY
3909 Swiss Ave., Dallas 75204 *Type:* Private (interdenominational) graduate only *Accred.:* 1990 (ATS candidate); 1969/1993 (SACS-CC) *Calendar:* Sem. plan *Degrees:* M, D *CEO:* Pres. Donald K. Campbell
FTE Enroll: 961   (214) 824-3094

DEL MAR COLLEGE
101 Baldwin Blvd., Corpus Christi 78404-3897 *Type:* Public (district) junior *System:* Texas Higher Education Coordinating Board *Accred.:* 1946/1990 (SACS-CC) *Calendar:* Sem. plan *Degrees:* A *Prof. Accred.:* Art, Dental Assisting, Dental Hygiene, Diagnostic Medical Sonography, Engineering Technology (electrical), Medical Laboratory Technology (AMA), Music, Nursing (A), Radiography, Respiratory Therapy, Respira-

tory Therapy Technology, Surgical Technology *CEO:* Pres. Buddy R. Venters
FTE Enroll: 9,624   (512) 886-1200

DEVRY INSTITUTE OF TECHNOLOGY, DALLAS
4250 N. Beltline Rd., Irving 75038 *Type:* Private *Accred.:* 1981/1992 (NCA)* *Calendar:* Sem. plan *Degrees:* A, B, certificates, diplomas *Prof. Accred.:* Engineering Technology (electrical) *CEO:* Pres. Francis V. Cannon
           (214) 258-6767

* Indirect accreditation through DeVry Institutes.

EAST TEXAS BAPTIST UNIVERSITY
1209 N. Grove Ave., Marshall 75670-1498 *Type:* Private (Southern Baptist) liberal arts *Accred.:* 1957/1989 (SACS-CC) *Calendar:* 4-1-4 plan *Degrees:* A, B, M (candidate) *Prof. Accred.:* Music *CEO:* Pres. Bob E. Riley
FTE Enroll: 1,258   (903) 935-7963

EAST TEXAS STATE UNIVERSITY
ETSU Sta., Commerce 75429-3011 *Type:* Public (state) *System:* Texas Higher Education Coordinating Board *Accred.:* 1925/1983 (SACS-CC) *Calendar:* Sem. plan *Degrees:* B, M, D *Prof. Accred.:* Business (B,M), Counseling, Music, Social Work (B-conditional), Teacher Education (e,s,p) *CEO:* Pres. Jerry D. Morris
FTE Enroll: 6,502   (903) 886-5012

EAST TEXAS STATE UNIVERSITY AT TEXARKANA
P.O. Box 5518, Texarkana 75505-0518 *Type:* Public (state) *System:* Texas Higher Education Coordinating Board *Accred.:* 1979/1985 (SACS-CC) *Calendar:* Sem. plan *Degrees:* B, M *CEO:* Pres. John F. Moss
FTE Enroll: 759   (903) 838-6514

EASTFIELD COLLEGE
3737 Motley Dr., Mesquite 75150-2099 *Type:* Public (district) junior *System:* Dallas County Community College District *Accred.:* 1972/1993 (SACS-CC) *Calendar:* Sem. plan *Degrees:* A *CEO:* Pres. Roberto Aguero
FTE Enroll: 3,978   (214) 324-7001

EL CENTRO COLLEGE
Main and Lamar Sts., Dallas 75202-3604 *Type:* Public (district) junior *System:* Dallas

County Community College District *Accred.:* 1968/1993 (SACS-CC) *Calendar:* Sem. plan *Degrees:* A *Prof. Accred.:* Diagnostic Medical Sonography, Interior Design, Medical Laboratory Technology (AMA), Nursing (A), Radiography, Respiratory Therapy, Respiratory Therapy Technology, Surgical Technology *CEO:* Pres. Wright L. Lassiter, Jr.
FTE Enroll: 8,168   (214) 746-2010

EL PASO COMMUNITY COLLEGE
P.O. Box 20500, El Paso 79998 *Type:* Public (district) junior *System:* Texas Higher Education Coordinating Board *Accred.:* 1978/1983 (SACS-CC warning) *Calendar:* Sem. plan *Degrees:* A *Prof. Accred.:* Dental Assisting, Dental Hygiene, Diagnostic Medical Sonography, Medical Assisting (AMA), Medical Laboratory Technology (AMA), Medical Record Technology, Nursing (A), Physical Therapy Assisting, Radiation Therapy Technology, Radiography, Respiratory Therapy, Surgical Technology *CEO:* Interim Pres. Adriana Barrera
FTE Enroll: 14,610   (915) 594-2000

THE EPISCOPAL THEOLOGICAL SEMINARY OF THE SOUTHWEST
P.O. Box 2247, Austin 78768-2247 *Type:* Private (Episcopal) graduate only *Accred.:* 1958/1993 (ATS); 1983/1993 (SACS-CC) *Calendar:* 4-1-4 plan *Degrees:* M *CEO:* Dean Durstan R. McDonald
FTE Enroll: 62   (512) 472-4133

FRANK PHILLIPS COLLEGE
P.O. Box 5118, Borger 79008-5118 *Type:* Public (district) junior *System:* Texas Higher Education Coordinating Board *Accred.:* 1958/1989 (SACS-CC) *Calendar:* Sem. plan *Degrees:* A *CEO:* Pres. Vance W. Gipson
FTE Enroll: 1,160   (806) 274-5311

GALVESTON COLLEGE
4015 Ave. Q, Galveston 77550 *Type:* Public (district) junior *System:* Texas Higher Education Coordinating Board *Accred.:* 1969/1984 (SACS-CC) *Calendar:* Sem. plan *Degrees:* A *Prof. Accred.:* Nuclear Medicine Technology, Nursing (A), Radiation Therapy Technology, Radiography, Respiratory Therapy *CEO:* Pres. Marc A. Nigliazzo
FTE Enroll: 1,853   (409) 763-6551

GRAYSON COUNTY COLLEGE
6101 Grayson Dr., Denison 75020 *Type:*
Public (district) junior *System:* Texas Higher
Education Coordinating Board *Accred.:*
1967/1991 (SACS-CC) *Calendar:* Sem.
plan *Degrees:* A *Prof. Accred.:* Dental As-
sisting, Medical Laboratory Technology
(AMA), Nursing (A) *CEO:* Pres. James M.
Williams, Jr.
FTE Enroll: 2,916 (903) 465-6030

HARDIN-SIMMONS UNIVERSITY
2200 Hickory St., Abilene 79698 *Type:* Pri-
vate (Southern Baptist) *Accred.:* 1927/1987
(SACS-CC) *Calendar:* Sem. plan *Degrees:*
A, B, M *Prof. Accred.:* Music, Social Work
(B) *CEO:* Pres. Edwin L. Hall
FTE Enroll: 1,702 (915) 670-1000

HILL COLLEGE
P.O. Box 619, 112 Lamar Dr., Hillsboro
76645 *Type:* Public (district) junior *System:*
Texas Higher Education Coordinating Board
Accred.: 1963/1990 (SACS-CC) *Calendar:*
Sem. plan *Degrees:* A *CEO:* Pres. William
R. Auvenshine
FTE Enroll: 1,591 (817) 582-2555

HOUSTON BAPTIST UNIVERSITY
7502 Fondren Rd., Houston 77074-3298
Type: Private (Southern Baptist) liberal arts
Accred.: 1968/1991 (SACS-CC) *Calendar:*
Qtr. plan *Degrees:* A, B, M *Prof. Accred.:*
Nursing (A,B) *CEO:* Pres. E. Douglas Hodo
FTE Enroll: 2,174 (713) 774-7661

HOUSTON COMMUNITY COLLEGE
P.O. Box 7819, Houston 77270-7849 *Type:*
Public (district) junior *System:* Texas Higher
Education Coordinating Board *Accred.:*
1977/1992 (SACS-CC) *Calendar:* Sem. plan
Degrees: A *Prof. Accred.:* Dental Assisting,
Engineering Technology (electrical), Med-
ical Laboratory Technology (AMA), Med-
ical Record Technology, Nuclear Medicine
Technology, Occupational Therapy Assist-
ing, Physical Therapy Assisting, Radiogra-
phy, Respiratory Therapy, Respiratory Ther-
apy Technology, Surgical Technology *CEO:*
Chanc. Charles A. Green
FTE Enroll: 29,459 (713) 869-5021

CENTRAL COLLEGE
1300 Holman Ave., Houston 77004 *CEO:*
Pres. James P. Engle
(713) 630-7205

COLLEGE WITHOUT WALLS
4310 Dunlavy St., Houston 77270 *CEO:*
Pres. Baltazar A. Acevedo, Ph.D.
(713) 868-0795

NORTHEAST COLLEGE
4638 Airline Dr., P.O. Box 7849, Houston
77270-7849 *CEO:* Pres. Elaine P. Adams,
Ph.D.
(713) 694-5384

NORTHWEST COLLEGE
16360 Park Ten Pl., Houston 77084 *CEO:*
Pres. Judith K. Winn, Ph.D.
(713) 578-3487

SOUTHEAST COLLEGE
6815 Rustic St., Houston 77012 *CEO:*
Pres. Sylvia Ramos
(713) 641-2725

SOUTHWEST COLLEGE
5407 Gulfton St., Houston 77081 *CEO:*
Pres. Sue A. Cox
(713) 661-4589

HOUSTON GRADUATE SCHOOL OF THEOLOGY
6910 Fannin St., Ste. 207, Houston 77030-
2805 *Type:* Private *Accred.:* 1986/1991
(SACS-CC) *Calendar:* Sem. plan *Degrees:*
M, D (candidate) *CEO:* Pres. Delbert P.
Vaughn
FTE Enroll: 133 (713) 791-9505

HOWARD COLLEGE
1001 Birdwell La., Big Spring 79720 *Type:*
Public (district) junior *System:* Howard
County Junior College District *Accred.:*
1955/1986 (SACS-CC) *Calendar:* Sem. plan
Degrees: A *Prof. Accred.:* Dental Hygiene,
Nursing (A) *CEO:* Pres. Cheryl T. Sparks
FTE Enroll: 2,351 (915) 264-5000

HOWARD PAYNE UNIVERSITY
1000 Fisk Ave., Brownwood 76801 *Type:*
Private (Southern Baptist) liberal arts *Accred.:* 1948/1984 (SACS-CC) *Calendar:*
Sem. plan *Degrees:* B *Prof. Accred.:* Music

(associate), Social Work (B-candidate) *CEO:* Pres. Don Newbury, Jr.
FTE Enroll: 1,469   (915) 646-2502

HUSTON-TILLOTSON COLLEGE
900 Chicon St., Austin 78702 *Type:* Private (United Methodist/United Church of Christ) liberal arts *Accred.:* 1943/1990 (SACS-CC) *Calendar:* Sem. plan *Degrees:* B *CEO:* Pres. Joseph T. McMillan, Jr.
FTE Enroll: 539   (512) 505-3000

ICI UNIVERSITY
6300 N. Belt Line Rd., Irving 75063 *Type:* Private home study *Accred.:* 1977/1993 (NHSC) *Calendar:* Courses of varying lengths *Degrees:* A, B, diplomas *CEO:* Pres. George M. Flattery
          (800) 444-0424

INCARNATE WORD COLLEGE
4301 Broadway, San Antonio 78209 *Type:* Private (Roman Catholic) liberal arts *Accred.:* 1925/1985 (SACS-CC) *Calendar:* Sem. plan *Degrees:* B, M *Prof. Accred.:* Nuclear Medicine Technology, Nursing (B,M) *CEO:* Pres. Louis J. Agnese, Jr.
FTE Enroll: 2,239   (210) 829-6000

INSTITUTE FOR CHRISTIAN STUDIES
1909 University Ave. at 20th St., Austin 78705 *Type:* Private *Accred.:* 1987/1992 (SACS-CC) *Calendar:* Sem. plan *Degrees:* B *CEO:* Pres. David Worley
FTE Enroll: 29   (512) 476-2772

ITT TECHNICAL INSTITUTE
2201 Arlington Downs Rd., Arlington 76011-6319 *Type:* Private *Accred.:* 1983/1988 (ACCSCT) *Calendar:* Courses of varying lengths *Degrees:* A *CEO:* Dir. Tom D. Marley
          (817) 640-7100

ITT TECHNICAL INSTITUTE
1640 Eastgate Dr., Garland 75041-5585 *Type:* Private *Accred.:* 1989 (ACCSCT) *Calendar:* Courses of varying lengths *Degrees:* A *CEO:* Dir. Maureen K. Clements
          (214) 279-0500

ITT TECHNICAL INSTITUTE
9421 W. Sam Houston Pkwy., Houston 77099-1849 *Type:* Private *Accred.:* 1983/1988 (ACCSCT) *Calendar:* Courses of vary-

ing lengths *Degrees:* A *CEO:* Dir. Louis Christensen, Ph.D.
          (713) 270-1634

ITT TECHNICAL INSTITUTE
4242 Piedras Dr. E., Ste. 100, San Antonio 78228-1414 *Type:* Private *Accred.:* 1988 (ACCSCT) *Calendar:* Courses of varying lengths *Degrees:* A *CEO:* Dir. Barry S. Simich
          (210) 737-1881

JACKSONVILLE COLLEGE
500 W. Pine St., Jacksonville 75766-4798 *Type:* Private (Baptist) junior *Accred.:* 1974/1989 (SACS-CC) *Calendar:* Sem. plan *Degrees:* A *CEO:* Pres. Edwin Crank
FTE Enroll: 324   (903) 586-2518

JARVIS CHRISTIAN COLLEGE
P.O. Drawer G, Hwy. 80E, Hawkins 75765-9989 *Type:* Private (Disciples of Christ) liberal arts *Accred.:* 1967/1993 (SACS-CC) *Calendar:* Sem. plan *Degrees:* A, B *CEO:* Pres. Sebetha Jenkins
FTE Enroll: 497   (903) 769-5700

KD STUDIO
2600 Stemmons Fwy., No. 117, Dallas 75207 *Type:* Private *Calendar:* Sem. plan *Degrees:* A *Prof. Accred.:* Theatre *CEO:* Pres. Kathy Tyner
          (214) 638-0484

KILGORE COLLEGE
1100 Broadway, Kilgore 75662-3299 *Type:* Public (district) junior *System:* Texas Higher Education Coordinating Board *Accred.:* 1939/1989 (SACS-CC) *Calendar:* Sem. plan *Degrees:* A *Prof. Accred.:* Medical Laboratory Technology (AMA), Nursing (A), Physical Therapy Assisting, Radiography, Surgical Technology *CEO:* Pres. J. Frank Thornton
FTE Enroll: 5,165   (903) 984-8531

LAMAR UNIVERSITY AT BEAUMONT
4400 Martin Luther King, Jr. Pkwy. Blvd., Beaumont 77705 *Type:* Public (state) *System:* Lamar University System *Accred.:* 1955/1988 (SACS-CC) *Calendar:* Sem. plan *Degrees:* A, B, M, D *Prof. Accred.:* Audiology, Business (B,M), Dental Hygiene, Engineering (chemical, civil, electrical, industrial, mechanical), Music, Nursing (A,B), Radiography, Respiratory Therapy, Respira-

tory Therapy Technology, Social Work (B), Speech-Language Pathology, Teacher Education (e,s,p) *CEO:* Pres. Rex L. Cottle
FTE Enroll: 8,242   (409) 880-7011

LAMAR UNIVERSITY AT ORANGE
410 W. Front St., Orange 77630 *Type:* Public (state) junior *System:* Lamar University System *Accred.:* 1989 (SACS-CC) *Calendar:* Sem. plan *Degrees:* A *CEO:* Pres. Steve Maradian
FTE Enroll: 1,740   (409) 883-7750

LAMAR UNIVERSITY AT PORT ARTHUR
P.O. Box 310, Port Arthur 77641-0310 *Type:* Public (state) junior *System:* Lamar University System *Accred.:* 1988/1993 (SACS-CC) *Calendar:* Sem. plan *Degrees:* A *CEO:* Pres. W. Sam Monroe
FTE Enroll: 1,682   (409) 983-4921

LAREDO COMMUNITY COLLEGE
W. End Washington St., Laredo 78040-4395 *Type:* Public (district) junior *System:* Texas Higher Education Coordinating Board *Accred.:* 1957/1989 (SACS-CC) *Calendar:* Sem. plan *Degrees:* A *Prof. Accred.:* Medical Laboratory Technology (AMA), Nursing (A), Physical Therapy Assisting, Radiography *CEO:* Pres. Roger L. Worsley
FTE Enroll: 5,917   (210) 722-0521

LEE COLLEGE
511 S. Whiting St., Baytown 77520-0818 *Type:* Public (district) junior *System:* Texas Higher Education Coordinating Board *Accred.:* 1948/1985 (SACS-CC) *Calendar:* Sem. plan *Degrees:* A *Prof. Accred.:* Medical Record Technology, Nursing (A) *CEO:* Pres. Jackson N. Sasser
FTE Enroll: 4,752   (713) 427-5611

LETOURNEAU UNIVERSITY
P.O. Box 7001, Longview 75607 *Type:* Private liberal arts and professional *Accred.:* 1970/1986 (SACS-CC) *Calendar:* Sem. plan *Degrees:* A, B, M (candidate) *Prof. Accred.:* Engineering (general) *CEO:* Pres. Alvin O. Austin
FTE Enroll: 1,677   (903) 753-0231

LON MORRIS COLLEGE
822 College Ave., Jacksonville 75766 *Type:* Private (United Methodist) junior *Accred.:*

1927/1984 (SACS-CC) *Calendar:* Sem. plan *Degrees:* A *CEO:* Pres. Chappell Temple
FTE Enroll: 254   (903) 589-4000

LUBBOCK CHRISTIAN UNIVERSITY
5601 19th St., Lubbock 79407-2099 *Type:* Private (Church of Christ) liberal arts *Accred.:* 1963/1988 (SACS-CC) *Calendar:* Sem. plan *Degrees:* A, B, M *Prof. Accred.:* Social Work (B) *CEO:* Pres. Ken Jones
FTE Enroll: 992   (806) 796-8800

MCLENNAN COMMUNITY COLLEGE
1400 College Dr., Waco 76708 *Type:* Public (district) junior *System:* Texas Higher Education Coordinating Board *Accred.:* 1968/1992 (SACS-CC) *Calendar:* Sem. plan *Degrees:* A *Prof. Accred.:* Medical Laboratory Technology (AMA), Nursing (A), Physical Therapy Assisting, Radiography, Respiratory Therapy Technology *CEO:* Pres. Dennis F. Michaelis
FTE Enroll: 5,926   (817) 756-6551

MCMURRY UNIVERSITY
S. 14th St. and Sayles Blvd., Abilene 79697 *Type:* Private (United Methodist) liberal arts *Accred.:* 1949/1989 (SACS-CC) *Calendar:* Sem. plan *Degrees:* A, B *CEO:* Pres. Robert E. Shimp
FTE Enroll: 1,095   (915) 691-6200

MIDLAND COLLEGE
3600 N. Garfield St., Midland 79705 *Type:* Public (district) junior *System:* Texas Higher Education Coordinating Board *Accred.:* 1975/1990 (SACS-CC) *Calendar:* Sem. plan *Degrees:* A *Prof. Accred.:* Nursing (A), Radiography, Respiratory Therapy, Respiratory Therapy Technology, Veterinary Technology (probational) *CEO:* Pres. David E. Daniel
FTE Enroll: 2,682   (915) 685-4500

MIDWESTERN STATE UNIVERSITY
3400 Taft Blvd., Wichita Falls 76308-2099 *Type:* Public (state) *System:* Texas Higher Education Coordinating Board *Accred.:* 1950/1992 (SACS-CC) *Calendar:* Sem. plan *Degrees:* A, B, M *Prof. Accred.:* Dental Hygiene (conditional), Engineering Technology (manufacturing), Music, Nursing (B), Radiography, Social Work (B-candidate),

Teacher Education (e,s,p) *CEO:* Pres. Louis J. Rodriguez
FTE Enroll: 5,794   (817) 689-4000

MISS WADE'S FASHION MERCHANDISING COLLEGE
P.O. Box 586343, Ste. M5120, Dallas Apparel Mart, Dallas 75258 *Type:* Private *Accred.:* 1985/1990 (SACS-CC) *Calendar:* Tri. plan *Degrees:* A *CEO:* Pres. Frank J. Tortoriello, Jr.
FTE Enroll: 279   (214) 637-3530

MOUNTAIN VIEW COLLEGE
4849 W. Illinois Ave., Dallas 75211-6599 *Type:* Public (district) junior *System:* Dallas County Community College District *Accred.:* 1972/1993 (SACS-CC) *Calendar:* Sem. plan *Degrees:* A *CEO:* Pres. Monique Amerman
FTE Enroll: 5,360   (214) 333-8700

NAVARRO COLLEGE
3200 W. Seventh Ave., Corsicana 75110 *Type:* Public (district) junior *System:* Texas Higher Education Coordinating Board *Accred.:* 1954/1985 (SACS-CC) *Calendar:* Sem. plan *Degrees:* A *Prof. Accred.:* Medical Laboratory Technology *CEO:* Pres. Gerald E. Burson
FTE Enroll: 2,713   (903) 874-6501

NORTH HARRIS MONTGOMERY COUNTY COLLEGE
250 N. Sam Houston Pkwy., E., Houston 77060 *Type:* Public (district) junior *System:* Texas Higher Education Coordinating Board *Accred.:* 1976/1991 (SACS-CC) *Calendar:* Sem. plan *Degrees:* A *Prof. Accred.:* Nursing (A) *CEO:* Pres. John E. Pickelman
FTE Enroll: 17,553   (713) 591-3500

KINGWOOD COLLEGE
20000 Kingwood Dr., Kingwood 77339 *Prof. Accred.:* Respiratory Therapy, Respiratory Therapy Technology *CEO:* Pres. Stephen Head
                                   (713) 359-1600

TOMBALL COLLEGE
30555 Tomball Pkwy., Tomball 77375-4036 *Prof. Accred.:* Veterinary Technology *CEO:* Pres. Roy L. Lazenby
                                   (713) 351-3300

NORTH LAKE COLLEGE
5001 N. MacArthur Blvd., Irving 75038-3899 *Type:* Public (district) junior *System:* Dallas County Community College District *Accred.:* 1979/1993 (SACS-CC) *Calendar:* Sem. plan *Degrees:* A *Prof. Accred.:* Construction Education (A) *CEO:* Pres. James F. Horton
FTE Enroll: 3,887   (214) 659-5230

NORTHEAST TEXAS COMMUNITY COLLEGE
P.O. Drawer 1307, Mount Pleasant 75456-1307 *Type:* Public (district) junior *System:* Texas Higher Education Coordinating Board *Accred.:* 1987/1992 (SACS-CC) *Calendar:* Sem. plan *Degrees:* A *CEO:* Pres. Michael C. Bruner
FTE Enroll: 1,693   (903) 572-1911

OBLATE SCHOOL OF THEOLOGY
285 Oblate Dr., San Antonio 78216-6693 *Type:* Private (Roman Catholic) graduate only *Accred.:* 1982/1989 (ATS); 1968/1989 (SACS-CC) *Calendar:* Sem. plan *Degrees:* M *CEO:* Pres. Patrick Guidon, O.M.I.
FTE Enroll: 151   (210) 341-1366

ODESSA COLLEGE
201 W. University Blvd., Odessa 79764 *Type:* Public (district) junior *System:* Texas Higher Education Coordinating Board *Accred.:* 1952/1992 (SACS-CC) *Calendar:* Sem. plan *Degrees:* A *Prof. Accred.:* Medical Laboratory Technology (AMA), Music, Nursing (A), Physical Therapy Assisting, Radiography, Respiratory Therapy, Respiratory Therapy Technology, Surgical Technology *CEO:* Pres. Philip T. Speegle
FTE Enroll: 5,186   (915) 335-6400

OUR LADY OF THE LAKE UNIVERSITY
411 S.W. 24th St., San Antonio 78207-4689 *Type:* Private (Roman Catholic) liberal arts *Accred.:* 1923/1992 (SACS-CC) *Calendar:* Sem. plan *Degrees:* B, M, D *Prof. Accred.:* Marriage and Family Therapy (M), Social Work (B,M), Speech-Language Pathology *CEO:* Pres. Elizabeth Anne Sueltenfuss
FTE Enroll: 2,300   (210) 434-6711

PALO ALTO COLLEGE
1400 W. Villaret Blvd., San Antonio 78224-2499 *Type:* Public (district) junior *System:* Alamo Community College District *Accred.:*

1987/1993 (SACS-CC) *Calendar:* Sem. plan
Degrees: A *CEO:* Pres. Joel E. Vela
FTE Enroll: 7,613   (512) 921-5000

PANOLA COLLEGE
1109 W. Panola St., Carthage 75633 *Type:*
Public (district) junior *System:* Texas Higher
Education Coordinating Board *Accred.:*
1960/1990 (SACS-CC) *Calendar:* Sem. plan
Degrees: A *CEO:* Pres. William Edmonson
FTE Enroll: 1,247   (903) 693-2000

PARIS JUNIOR COLLEGE
2400 Clarksville St., Paris 75460 *Type:* Public (district) junior *System:* Texas Higher Education Coordinating Board *Accred.:* 1934/
1992 (SACS-CC) *Calendar:* Sem. plan *Degrees:* A *Prof. Accred.:* Nursing (A) *CEO:*
Pres. Bobby R. Walters
FTE Enroll: 1,913   (903) 785-7661

PARKER COLLEGE OF CHIROPRACTIC
2500 Walnut Hill La., Dallas 75229-5668
Type: Private professional *Accred.:* 1987/
1992 (SACS-CC) *Calendar:* Tri. plan *Degrees:* B, D *Prof. Accred.:* Chiropractic Education *CEO:* Pres. James W. Parker, D.C.
FTE Enroll: 1,007   (214) 438-6932

PAUL QUINN COLLEGE
3837 Simpson Stuart Rd., Dallas 75241
Type: Private (African Methodist Episcopal)
liberal arts *Accred.:* 1972/1987 (SACS-CC)
Calendar: Sem. plan *Degrees:* B *Prof. Ac-
cred.:* Social Work (B) *CEO:* Pres. Lee E.
Monroe
FTE Enroll: 665   (214) 376-1000

PRAIRIE VIEW A&M UNIVERSITY
P.O. Box 519, Prairie View 77446 *Type:*
Public (state) *System:* Texas A&M Universi-
ty System *Accred.:* 1934/1990 (SACS-CC)
Calendar: Sem. plan *Degrees:* B, M *Prof.
Accred.:* Computer Science, Engineering
Technology (computer, electrical), Engineer-
ing (civil, electrical, mechanical), Home
Economics, Nursing (B), Social Work (B),
Teacher Education (e,s) *CEO:* Pres. Julius
W. Becton, Jr.
FTE Enroll: 5,450   (409) 857-3311

RANGER COLLEGE
College Cir., Ranger 76470-3298 *Type:* Public (district) junior *System:* Texas Higher Education Coordinating Board *Accred.:* 1968/

1992 (SACS-CC) *Calendar:* Sem. plan *Degrees:* A *CEO:* Pres. Joe Mills
FTE Enroll: 785   (817) 647-3234

RICHLAND COLLEGE
12800 Abrams Rd., Dallas 75243-2199
Type: Public (district) junior *System:* Dallas
County Community College District *Ac-
cred.:* 1974/1993 (SACS-CC) *Calendar:*
Sem. plan *Degrees:* A *CEO:* Pres. Stephen
K. Mittelstet
FTE Enroll: 9,612   (214) 238-6209

ST. EDWARD'S UNIVERSITY
3001 S. Congress Ave., Austin 78704 *Type:*
Private liberal arts and teachers *Accred.:*
1958/1987 (SACS-CC) *Calendar:* Sem. plan
Degrees: B, M *Prof. Accred.:* Social Work
(B) *CEO:* Pres. Patricia A. Hayes
FTE Enroll: 2,414   (512) 448-8400

ST. MARY'S UNIVERSITY
One Camino Santa Maria, San Antonio
78228-8572 *Type:* Private (Roman Catholic)
Accred.: 1949/1984 (SACS-CC) *Calendar:*
Sem. plan *Degrees:* B, M, D *Prof. Accred.:*
Engineering (electrical, industrial), Law,
Marriage and Family Therapy (M), Music
(associate) *CEO:* Pres. John H. Moder
FTE Enroll: 4,129   (210) 436-3011

ST. PHILIP'S COLLEGE
1801 Martin Luther King Dr., San Antonio
78203 *Type:* Public (district) junior *System:*
Alamo Community College District *Accred.:*
1951/1985 (SACS-CC) *Calendar:* Sem. plan
Degrees: A *Prof. Accred.:* Medical Labora-
tory Technology (AMA), Medical Record
Technology, Occupational Therapy Assist-
ing, Physical Therapy Assisting, Practical
Nursing, Radiography, Respiratory Therapy
Technology, Surgical Technology *CEO:*
Pres. Hamice R. James
FTE Enroll: 5,475   (210) 531-3200

SAM HOUSTON STATE UNIVERSITY
Huntsville 77341 *Type:* Public (state) liberal
arts and teachers *System:* Texas State Uni-
versity System *Accred.:* 1925/1989 (SACS-
CC) *Calendar:* Sem. plan *Degrees:* B, M, D
Prof. Accred.: Music, Teacher Education
(e,s,p) *CEO:* Pres. Martin J. Anisman
FTE Enroll: 11,316   (409) 294-1111

SAN ANTONIO COLLEGE
1300 San Pedro Ave., San Antonio 78212-
4299 *Type:* Public (district) junior *System:*
Alamo Community College District *Accred.:*
1952/1985 (SACS-CC) *Calendar:* Sem. plan
Degrees: A *Prof. Accred.:* Dental Assisting,
Medical Assisting (AMA), Mortuary Sci-
ence, Nursing (A) *CEO:* Pres. Ruth Burgos-
Sasscer
FTE Enroll: 16,888   (210) 733-2000

SAN JACINTO COLLEGE
4624 Fairmont Pkwy., Pasadena 77504
Type: Public (district) junior *System:* Texas
Higher Education Coordinating Board *Ac-
cred.:* 1963/1989 (SACS-CC) *Calendar:*
Sem. plan *Degrees:* A *Prof. Accred.:* Med-
ical Laboratory Technology (AMA), Nursing
(A), Radiography, Respiratory Therapy, Res-
piratory Therapy Technology, Surgical
Technology *CEO:* Chanc. Thomas S. Sewell
FTE Enroll: 13,637   (713) 998-6100

SCHREINER COLLEGE
2100 Memorial Blvd., Kerrville 78028 *Type:*
Private (Presbyterian) *Accred.:* 1934/1989
(SACS-CC) *Calendar:* Sem. plan *Degrees:*
A, B *CEO:* Pres. Sam M. Junkin
FTE Enroll: 571   (210) 896-5411

SOUTH PLAINS COLLEGE
1401 College Ave., Levelland 79336 *Type:*
Public (district) junior *System:* Texas Higher
Education Coordinating Board *Accred.:*
1963/1993 (SACS-CC) *Calendar:* Sem. plan
Degrees: A *Prof. Accred.:* Medical Record
Technology, Nursing (A), Radiography, Res-
piratory Therapy, Respiratory Therapy Tech-
nology, Surgical Technology *CEO:* Pres.
Gary McDaniel
FTE Enroll: 4,606   (806) 894-9611

SOUTH TEXAS COLLEGE OF LAW
1303 San Jacinto St., Houston 77002-7000
Type: Private professional *Calendar:* Sem.
plan *Degrees:* P *Prof. Accred.:* Law (ABA
only) *CEO:* Pres./Dean William L. Wilks
Enroll: 1,352   (713) 659-8040

SOUTHERN METHODIST UNIVERSITY
6425 Boaz St., Dallas 75275 *Type:* Private
(United Methodist) *Accred.:* 1938/1991
(ATS); 1921/1991 (SACS-CC) *Calendar:*
Sem. plan *Degrees:* B, M, D *Prof. Accred.:*

Business (B,M), Dance, Engineering (civil,
computer, electrical, mechanical), Law,
Music *CEO:* Pres. A. Kenneth Pye
FTE Enroll: 7,837   (214) 768-2000

SOUTHWEST TEXAS JUNIOR COLLEGE
2401 Garner Field Rd., Uvalde 78801-6297
Type: Public (district) junior *System:* Texas
Higher Education Coordinating Board *Ac-
cred.:* 1964/1985 (SACS-CC) *Calendar:*
Sem. plan *Degrees:* A *CEO:* Pres. Billy Word
FTE Enroll: 2,286   (210) 278-4401

SOUTHWEST TEXAS STATE UNIVERSITY
601 University Dr., San Marcos 78666-4616
Type: Public (state) liberal arts and teachers
System: Texas State University System *Ac-
cred.:* 1925/1989 (SACS-CC) *Calendar:*
Sem. plan *Degrees:* A, B, M *Prof. Accred.:*
Health Services Administration, Home Eco-
nomics, Interior Design, Medical Record
Administration, Medical Technology, Music,
Physical Therapy, Public Administration,
Respiratory Therapy, Respiratory Therapy
Technology, Social Work (B), Speech-Lan-
guage Pathology *CEO:* Pres. Jerome H.
Supple
FTE Enroll: 18,174   (512) 245-2111

SOUTHWESTERN ADVENTIST COLLEGE
P.O. Box 567, Keene 76059 *Type:* Private
(Seventh-Day Adventist) liberal arts and
teachers *Accred.:* 1958/1985 (SACS-CC)
Calendar: Sem. plan *Degrees:* A, B, M *Prof.
Accred.:* Nursing (A,B), Social Work (B-
candidate) *CEO:* Pres. Marvin E. Anderson
FTE Enroll: 913   (817) 645-3921

SOUTHWESTERN ASSEMBLIES OF GOD COLLEGE
1200 Sycamore St., Waxahachie 75165
Type: Private (Assemblies of God) *Accred.:*
1948/1985 (AABC); 1968/1992 (SACS-CC)
Calendar: Sem. plan *Degrees:* A, B, diplomas *CEO:* Pres. Delmer R. Guynes
FTE Enroll: 894   (214) 937-4010

SOUTHWESTERN BAPTIST THEOLOGICAL
SEMINARY
2001 W. Seminary Dr., Fort Worth 76115
Type: Private (Southern Baptist) *Accred.:*
1944/1991 (ATS); 1969/1991 (SACS-CC)
Calendar: Sem. plan *Degrees:* A, B, M, D

Prof. Accred.: Music *CEO:* Acting Pres. William B. Tolar
FTE Enroll: 3,262   (817) 923-1921

SOUTHWESTERN CHRISTIAN COLLEGE
P.O. Box 10, Terrell 75160 *Type:* Private (Church of Christ) liberal arts *Accred.:* 1973/1989 (SACS-CC) *Calendar:* Sem. plan *Degrees:* A, B *CEO:* Pres. Jack Evans, Sr.
FTE Enroll: 182   (214) 563-3341

SOUTHWESTERN UNIVERSITY
University Ave. at Maple St., Georgetown 78627 *Type:* Private liberal arts *Accred.:* 1915/1992 (SACS-CC) *Calendar:* Sem. plan *Degrees:* B *Prof. Accred.:* Music *CEO:* Pres. Roy B. Shilling, Jr.
FTE Enroll: 1,220   (512) 863-6511

STEPHEN F. AUSTIN STATE UNIVERSITY
P.O. Box 6078, SFA Sta., Nacogdoches 75962 *Type:* Public (state) liberal arts and teachers *System:* Texas Higher Education Coordinating Board *Accred.:* 1927/1990 (SACS-CC) *Calendar:* Sem. plan *Degrees:* B, M, D *Prof. Accred.:* Business (B,M), Counseling, Forestry, Home Economics, Interior Design, Music, Nursing (B), Rehabilitation Counseling, Social Work (B), Speech-Language Pathology, Teacher Education (e,s), Theatre *CEO:* Pres. Daniel D. Angel
FTE Enroll: 11,580   (409) 568-2011

SUL ROSS STATE UNIVERSITY
Hwy. 90, Alpine 79832 *Type:* Public (state) liberal arts and teachers *System:* Texas State University System *Accred.:* 1929/1989 (SACS-CC) *Calendar:* Sem. plan *Degrees:* A, B, M *Prof. Accred.:* Veterinary Technology *CEO:* Pres. R. Victor Morgan
FTE Enroll: 2,884   (915) 837-8011

BRANCH CAMPUS
Uvalde Ctr., Uvalde 78801 *CEO:* Dean Frank W. Abbott
                                  (512) 278-3339

TARLETON STATE UNIVERSITY
1297 W. Washington St., Tarleton Sta., Stephenville 76402 *Type:* Public (state) liberal arts and professional *System:* Texas A&M University System *Accred.:* 1926/1990 (SACS-CC) *Calendar:* Sem. plan *Degrees:* A, B, M *Prof. Accred.:* Medical Tech-

nology, Music (associate), Social Work (B) *CEO:* Pres. Dennis P. McCabe
FTE Enroll: 5,785   (817) 968-9100

TARRANT COUNTY JUNIOR COLLEGE
1500 Houston St., Fort Worth 76102-6599 *Type:* Public (district) junior *System:* Texas Higher Education Coordinating Board *Accred.:* 1969/1993 (SACS-CC) *Calendar:* Sem. plan *Degrees:* A *Prof. Accred.:* Dental Hygiene, Medical Laboratory Technology (AMA), Medical Record Technology, Nursing (A), Physical Therapy Assisting, Radiography, Respiratory Therapy, Surgical Technology *CEO:* Chanc. C.A. Roberson
FTE Enroll: 20,739   (817) 336-7851

NORTHEAST CAMPUS
828 Harwood Rd., Hurst 76054 *CEO:* Pres. Herman L. Crow
                                  (817) 281-7860

NORTHWEST CAMPUS
4801 Marine Creek Pkwy., Fort Worth 76179 *CEO:* Pres. Michael Saenz
                                  (817) 232-2900

SOUTH CAMPUS
5301 Campus Dr., Fort Worth 76119 *CEO:* Pres. Jim Worden
                                  (817) 531-4501

TEMPLE JUNIOR COLLEGE
2600 S. First St., Temple 76504-7435 *Type:* Public (district) junior *System:* Texas Higher Education Coordinating Board *Accred.:* 1959/1990 (SACS-CC) *Calendar:* Sem. plan *Degrees:* A *Prof. Accred.:* Medical Laboratory Technology (AMA), Respiratory Therapy, Surgical Technology *CEO:* Pres. Marvin R. Felder
FTE Enroll: 2,748   (817) 773-9961

TEXARKANA COLLEGE
2500 N. Robinson Rd., Texarkana 75599 *Type:* Public (district) junior *System:* Texas Higher Education Coordinating Board *Accred.:* 1931/1985 (SACS-CC) *Calendar:* Sem. plan *Degrees:* A *Prof. Accred.:* Nursing (A) *CEO:* Pres. Carl M. Nelson
FTE Enroll: 3,613   (903) 838-4541

TEXAS A&M INTERNATIONAL UNIVERSITY
One W. End Washington St., Laredo 78041 *Type:* Public (state) *System:* Texas A&M

University System *Accred.:* 1970/1984 (SACS-CC) *Calendar:* Sem. plan *Degrees:* B, M *CEO:* Pres. Leo Sayavedra
FTE Enroll: 1,712   (210) 722-8001

TEXAS A&M UNIVERSITY
College Station 77843 *Type:* Public (state) *System:* Texas A&M University System *Accred.:* 1924/1993 (SACS-CC) *Calendar:* Sem. plan *Degrees:* B, M, D *Prof. Accred.:* Accounting (Type A,C), Business (B,M), Clinical Psychology, Computer Science, Construction Education (B), Counseling Psychology, Dietetics (internship), Engineering Technology (electrical, manufacturing, mechanical), Engineering (aerospace, agricultural, bioengineering, chemical, civil, electrical, industrial, mechanical, nuclear, ocean, petroleum, radiological health), Forestry, Journalism (B), Landscape Architecture (B,M), Medicine, Planning (M), Psychology Internship, Public Administration, School Psychology, Teacher Education (e,s,p), Veterinary Medicine (limited) *CEO:* Interim Pres. E. Dean Gage
FTE Enroll: 39,405   (409) 845-3211

TEXAS A&M UNIVERSITY AT GALVESTON
P.O. Box 1675, Galveston 77553 *Type:* Public (state) *System:* Texas A&M University System *Accred.:* 1978/1983 (SACS-CC) *Calendar:* Sem. plan *Degrees:* B *Prof. Accred.:* Engineering (naval architecture/marine) *CEO:* Pres. David J. Schmidly
FTE Enroll: 1,234   (409) 740-4400

TEXAS A&M UNIVERSITY—CORPUS CHRISTI
6300 Ocean Dr., Corpus Christi 78412 *Type:* Public (state) liberal arts *System:* Texas A&M University System *Accred.:* 1975/1990 (SACS-CC) *Calendar:* Sem. plan *Degrees:* B, M, D *Prof. Accred.:* Medical Technology, Music, Nursing (B,M) *CEO:* Pres. Robert R. Furgason
FTE Enroll: 2,945   (512) 991-6810

TEXAS A&M UNIVERSITY—KINGSVILLE
Campus Box 101, Kingsville 78363 *Type:* Public (state) *System:* Texas A&M University System *Accred.:* 1933/1984 (SACS-CC) *Calendar:* Sem. plan *Degrees:* B, M, D *Prof. Accred.:* Engineering (chemical, civil, electrical, mechanical, petroleum), Music *CEO:* Pres. Manuel L. Ibanez
FTE Enroll: 5,775   (512) 595-2111

TEXAS CHIROPRACTIC COLLEGE
5912 Spencer Hwy., Pasadena 77505 *Type:* Private professional *Accred.:* 1984/1990 (SACS-CC) *Calendar:* Tri. plan *Degrees:* B, D *Prof. Accred.:* Chiropractic Education *CEO:* Pres. Shelby M. Elliott, D.C.
FTE Enroll: 442   (713) 998-6000

TEXAS CHRISTIAN UNIVERSITY
2800 S. University Dr., Fort Worth 76129 *Type:* Private (Christian Church/Disciples of Christ) *Accred.:* 1942/1989 (ATS); 1922/1993 (SACS-CC) *Calendar:* Sem. plan *Degrees:* B, M, D *Prof. Accred.:* Business (B,M), Computer Science, Dietetics (coordinated), Interior Design, Journalism (B,M), Music, Nursing (B), Social Work (B), Speech-Language Pathology *CEO:* Chanc. William E. Tucker
FTE Enroll: 6,732   (817) 921-7000

TEXAS COLLEGE
2404 N. Grand Ave., Tyler 75712 *Type:* Private liberal arts and teachers *Accred.:* 1970/1984 (SACS-CC warning) *Calendar:* Sem. plan *Degrees:* B *CEO:* Pres. A.C. Mitchell Patton
FTE Enroll: 435   (903) 593-8311

TEXAS LUTHERAN COLLEGE
1000 W. Court St., Seguin 78155 *Type:* Private (Lutheran) liberal arts *Accred.:* 1953/1988 (SACS-CC) *Calendar:* Sem. plan *Degrees:* A, B *Prof. Accred.:* Social Work (B-candidate) *CEO:* Pres. Charles H. Oestreich
FTE Enroll: 1,082   (210) 372-8000

TEXAS SOUTHERN UNIVERSITY
3100 Cleburne St., Houston 77004 *Type:* Public *System:* Texas Higher Education Coordinating Board *Accred.:* 1948/1990 (SACS-CC) *Calendar:* Sem. plan *Degrees:* B, M, D *Prof. Accred.:* Law (ABA only), Medical Record Administration, Medical Technology, Respiratory Therapy, Social Work (B) *CEO:* Pres. Joann A. Horton
FTE Enroll: 9,937   (713) 527-7011

TEXAS SOUTHMOST COLLEGE
80 Fort Brown St., Brownsville 78520 *Type:* Public (district) junior *System:* Texas Higher

Education Coordinating Board *Accred.:* 1930/1991 (SACS-CC) *Calendar:* Sem. plan *Degrees:* A *Prof. Accred.:* Medical Laboratory Technology (AMA), Nursing (A), Radiography, Respiratory Therapy, Respiratory Therapy Technology *CEO:* Exec. Dir. Michael Putegnat
FTE Enroll: 5,194   (210) 544-8200

Texas Southmost College has entered into a legal partnership with The University of Texas at Brownsville.

TEXAS STATE TECHNICAL COLLEGE—AMARILLO
P.O. Box 11197, Amarillo 79111 *Type:* Public (state) 2-year *System:* Texas State Technical College System *Accred.:* 1970/1985 (SACS-CC) *Calendar:* Qtr. plan *Degrees:* A *CEO:* Pres. Ronald L. DeSpain
FTE Enroll: 528   (806) 335-2316

TEXAS STATE TECHNICAL COLLEGE—
HARLINGEN
2424 Boxwood, Harlingen 78550-3697 *Type:* Public (state) 2-year *System:* Texas State Technical College System *Accred.:* 1968/1985 (SACS-CC) *Calendar:* Qtr. plan *Degrees:* A *Prof. Accred.:* Medical Record Technology *CEO:* Pres. J. Gilbert Leal
FTE Enroll: 2,298   (210) 425-0600

TEXAS STATE TECHNICAL COLLEGE—
SWEETWATER
300 College Dr., Sweetwater 79556 *Type:* Public (state) 2-year *System:* Texas State Technical College System *Accred.:* 1979/1984 (SACS-CC) *Calendar:* Qtr. plan *Degrees:* A *CEO:* Pres. Clay G. Johnson
FTE Enroll: 1,881   (915) 235-7300

TEXAS STATE TECHNICAL COLLEGE—WACO
3801 Campus Dr., Waco 76705 *Type:* Public (state) 2-year *System:* Texas State Technical College System *Accred.:* 1968/1983 (SACS-CC) *Calendar:* Qtr. plan *Degrees:* A *Prof. Accred.:* Dental Assisting *CEO:* Pres. Don E. Goodwin
FTE Enroll: 3,218   (817) 867-4800

TEXAS TECH UNIVERSITY
Lubbock 79409 *Type:* Public (state) *System:* Texas Higher Education Coordinating Board *Accred.:* 1928/1984 (SACS-CC) *Calendar:* Sem. plan *Degrees:* B, M, D *Prof. Accred.:* Accounting (Type A,B,C), Art, Audiology,

Business (B,M), Clinical Psychology, Counseling Psychology, Dietetics (internship), Engineering Technology (civil/construction, electrical, mechanical), Engineering (agricultural, chemical, civil, electrical, engineering physics/science, industrial, mechanical, petroleum), Home Economics, Interior Design, Journalism (B), Landscape Architecture (B), Law, Marriage and Family Therapy (D), Music, Psychology Internship (probational), Public Administration, Social Work (B), Speech-Language Pathology, Teacher Education (e,s,p) *CEO:* Pres. Robert W. Lawless
FTE Enroll: 21,948   (806) 742-2011

TEXAS TECH UNIVERSITY HEALTH SCIENCES
CENTER
3601 Fourth St., Lubbock 79430 *Type:* Public (state) *System:* Texas Higher Education Coordinating Board *Calendar:* Sem. plan *Degrees:* B, M, D *Prof. Accred.:* EMT-Paramedic, Medical Technology, Medicine, Nursing (B,M), Occupational Therapy, Physical Therapy *CEO:* Pres. Robert W. Lawless, Ph.D.
Enroll: 876   (806) 743-2975

TEXAS WESLEYAN UNIVERSITY
1201 Wesleyan St., Fort Worth 76105-1536 *Type:* Private (United Methodist) liberal arts *Accred.:* 1949/1993 (SACS-CC) *Calendar:* Sem. plan *Degrees:* B, M, D *Prof. Accred.:* Music, Nurse Anesthesia Education *CEO:* Pres. Jake B. Schrum
FTE Enroll: 1,884   (817) 531-4444

TEXAS WOMAN'S UNIVERSITY
P.O. Box 23925, Denton 76204 *Type:* Public (state) for women *System:* Texas Higher Education Coordinating Board *Accred.:* 1923/1993 (SACS-CC) *Calendar:* Sem. plan *Degrees:* B, M, D *Prof. Accred.:* Dental Hygiene, Dietetics (internship), Librarianship, Medical Record Administration, Music, Nursing (B,M), Occupational Therapy, Physical Therapy, Psychology Internship, Social Work (B), Speech-Language Pathology *CEO:* Interim Pres. Patricia A. Sullivan
FTE Enroll: 7,423   (817) 898-2000

TRINITY UNIVERSITY
715 Stadium Dr., San Antonio 78212 *Type:* Private *Accred.:* 1946/1987 (SACS-CC) *Calendar:* Sem. plan *Degrees:* B, M *Prof. Ac-

cred.: Engineering (engineering physics/science), Health Services Administration, Music, Teacher Education (e,s,p) *CEO:* Pres. Ronald K. Calgaard
FTE Enroll: 2,465   (210) 736-7011

TRINITY VALLEY COMMUNITY COLLEGE
500 S. Prairieville, Athens 75751 *Type:* Public (district) junior *System:* Texas Higher Education Coordinating Board *Accred.:* 1952/1986 (SACS-CC) *Calendar:* Sem. plan *Degrees:* A *Prof. Accred.:* Nursing (A), Surgical Technology *CEO:* Pres. Ronald C. Baugh
FTE Enroll: 3,200   (903) 675-6200

TYLER JUNIOR COLLEGE
P.O. Box 9020, Tyler 75711 *Type:* Public (district) junior *System:* Texas Higher Education Coordinating Board *Accred.:* 1931/1990 (SACS-CC) *Calendar:* Sem. plan *Degrees:* A *Prof. Accred.:* Dental Hygiene, Medical Laboratory Technology (AMA), Radiography, Respiratory Therapy, Respiratory Therapy Technology *CEO:* Pres. Raymond M. Hawkins
FTE Enroll: 6,496   (903) 510-2200

UNIVERSITY OF CENTRAL TEXAS
P.O. Box 1416, U.S. Hwy. 190 W., Killeen 76540-1416 *Type:* Private *Accred.:* 1976/1985 (SACS-CC) *Calendar:* Sem. plan *Degrees:* B, M *CEO:* Pres. Jack W. Fuller
FTE Enroll: 863   (817) 526-8262

THE UNIVERSITY OF DALLAS
1845 E. Northgate Dr., Irving 75062 *Type:* Private (Roman Catholic) *Accred.:* 1963/1984 (SACS-CC) *Calendar:* Sem. plan *Degrees:* B, M, D *CEO:* Pres. Robert F. Sasseen
FTE Enroll: 2,244   (214) 721-5000

UNIVERSITY OF HOUSTON—CLEAR LAKE
2700 Bay Area Blvd., Houston 77058 *Type:* Public (state) *System:* University of Houston System *Accred.:* 1976/1992 (SACS-CC) *Calendar:* Sem. plan *Degrees:* B, M *Prof. Accred.:* Accounting (Type A,C), Business (B,M), Health Services Administration, Marriage and Family Therapy (M), Public Management, Teacher Education (e,s,p) *CEO:* Pres. Glenn A. Goerke
FTE Enroll: 7,194   (713) 283-7600

UNIVERSITY OF HOUSTON—DOWNTOWN
One Main St., Houston 77002 *Type:* Public (state) *System:* University of Houston System *Accred.:* 1976/1985 (SACS-CC) *Calendar:* Sem. plan *Degrees:* B *Prof. Accred.:* Engineering Technology (process/piping design) *CEO:* Pres. Max Castillo
FTE Enroll: 5,829   (713) 221-8000

UNIVERSITY OF HOUSTON—UNIVERSITY PARK
4800 Calhoun Blvd., Houston 77204-2162 *Type:* Public (state) *System:* University of Houston System *Accred.:* 1954/1987 (SACS-CC) *Calendar:* Sem. plan *Degrees:* B, M, D *Prof. Accred.:* Accounting (Type A,B,C), Business (B,M), Clinical Psychology, Computer Science, Counseling Psychology, Engineering Technology (civil/construction, computer, electrical, mechanical), Engineering (chemical, civil, electrical, industrial, mechanical), Law, Music, Optometry, Psychology Internship, Social Work (M), Speech-Language Pathology, Teacher Education (e,s,p) *CEO:* Pres. James H. Pickering
FTE Enroll: 32,124   (713) 743-1000

UNIVERSITY OF HOUSTON—VICTORIA
2506 E. Red River, Victoria 77901-4450 *Type:* Public (state) *System:* University of Houston System *Accred.:* 1978/1993 (SACS-CC) *Calendar:* Sem. plan *Degrees:* B, M *CEO:* Pres. Lesta Van Der Wert Turchen
FTE Enroll: 746   (512) 576-3151

UNIVERSITY OF MARY HARDIN-BAYLOR
Box 8001, 900 College St., Belton 76513 *Type:* Private (Southern Baptist) liberal arts primarily for women *Accred.:* 1926/1983 (SACS-CC) *Calendar:* Sem. plan *Degrees:* B, M *Prof. Accred.:* Nursing (B), Social Work (B-candidate) *CEO:* Pres. Jerry G. Bawcom
FTE Enroll: 1,827   (817) 939-4500

UNIVERSITY OF NORTH TEXAS
P.O. Box 13737, Denton 76203 *Type:* Public (state) *System:* Texas Higher Education Coordinating Board *Accred.:* 1925/1985 (SACS-CC) *Calendar:* Sem. plan *Degrees:* B, M, D *Prof. Accred.:* Accounting (Type A,C), Audiology (probational), Business (B,M), Clinical Psychology, Computer Science, Counseling, Counseling Psychology,

Interior Design, Journalism (B,M), Librarianship, Music, Public Administration, Recreation and Leisure Services, Rehabilitation Counseling, Social Work (B), Speech-Language Pathology *CEO:* Chanc. Alfred F. Hurley
FTE Enroll: 25,759   (817) 565-2000

UNIVERSITY OF NORTH TEXAS HEALTH SCIENCE CENTER AT FORT WORTH
3500 Camp Bowie Blvd., Fort Worth 76107-2970 *Type:* Public (state) professional *System:* Texas Higher Education Coordinating Board *Calendar:* Sem. plan *Degrees:* P *Prof. Accred.:* Osteopathy *CEO:* Pres. David M. Richards, D.O.
Enroll: 372   (817) 735-2000

UNIVERSITY OF ST. THOMAS
3800 Montrose Blvd., Houston 77006 *Type:* Private (Roman Catholic) liberal arts *Accred.:* 1990 (ATS); 1954/1984 (SACS-CC) *Calendar:* Sem. plan *Degrees:* B, M, D *Prof. Accred.:* Engineering (manufacturing) *CEO:* Pres. Joseph M. McFadden
FTE Enroll: 1,751   (713) 522-7911

THE UNIVERSITY OF TEXAS AT ARLINGTON
UTA Box 19125, Arlington 76019 *Type:* Public (state) *System:* University of Texas System *Accred.:* 1964/1986 (SACS-CC) *Calendar:* Sem. plan *Degrees:* B, M, D *Prof. Accred.:* Accounting (Type A,B,C), Business (B,M), Engineering (aerospace, civil, computer, electrical, industrial, mechanical), Interior Design, Music, Nursing (B,M), Planning (M), Social Work (B,M) *CEO:* Pres. Ryan C. Amacher
FTE Enroll: 25,267   (817) 273-2011

THE UNIVERSITY OF TEXAS AT AUSTIN
P.O. Box T, Austin 78713-7389 *Type:* Public (state) *System:* University of Texas System *Accred.:* 1901/1988 (SACS-CC) *Calendar:* Sem. plan *Degrees:* B, M, D *Prof. Accred.:* Accounting (Type A,C), Audiology, Business (B,M), Clinical Psychology, Counseling Psychology, Dance (associate), Dietetics (coordinated), Engineering (aerospace, architectural, chemical, civil, computer, electrical, environmental/sanitary, mechanical, petroleum), Home Economics, Interior Design, Journalism (B,M), Law, Librarianship, Music, Nursing (B,M), Planning (M), Psychology Internship, Public Affairs, Rehabili-

tation Counseling, School Psychology, Social Work (B,M), Speech-Language Pathology, Theatre *CEO:* Pres. Robert M. Berdahl
FTE Enroll: 44,850   (512) 471-3434

THE UNIVERSITY OF TEXAS AT BROWNSVILLE
80 Fort Brown, Brownsville 78520 *Type:* Public (state) *System:* University of Texas System *Accred.:* 1988 (SACS-CC) *Calendar:* Sem. plan *Degrees:* B, M *CEO:* Pres. Juliet V. Garcia
FTE Enroll: 1,492   (210) 544-8200

The University of Texas at Brownsville has entered into a legal partnership with Texas Southmost College.

THE UNIVERSITY OF TEXAS AT DALLAS
P.O. Box 830688, Richardson 75083-0688 *Type:* Public (state) *System:* University of Texas System *Accred.:* 1972/1988 (SACS-CC) *Calendar:* Sem. plan *Degrees:* B, M, D *Prof. Accred.:* Audiology, Engineering (electrical), Speech-Language Pathology *CEO:* Pres. Robert H. Rutford
FTE Enroll: 5,960   (214) 690-2111

THE UNIVERSITY OF TEXAS AT EL PASO
500 W. University Ave., El Paso 79968 *Type:* Public (state) *System:* University of Texas System *Accred.:* 1936/1986 (SACS-CC) *Calendar:* Sem. plan *Degrees:* B, M, D *Prof. Accred.:* Accounting (Type A,C), Business (B,M), Computer Science, Engineering (civil, electrical, industrial, mechanical, metallurgical), Medical Technology, Music, Nursing (B,M), Social Work (B-candidate), Speech-Language Pathology *CEO:* Pres. Diana S. Natalicio
FTE Enroll: 14,397   (915) 747-5000

THE UNIVERSITY OF TEXAS AT SAN ANTONIO
6900 N. Loop 1604 W., San Antonio 78249-0617 *Type:* Public (state) *System:* University of Texas System *Accred.:* 1974/1990 (SACS-CC) *Calendar:* Sem. plan *Degrees:* B, M *Prof. Accred.:* Art, Business (B,M), Engineering (civil, electrical, mechanical), Music, Nursing (B,M) *CEO:* Pres. Samuel A. Kirkpatrick
FTE Enroll: 14,338   (210) 691-4100

THE UNIVERSITY OF TEXAS AT TYLER
3900 University Blvd., Tyler 75799 *Type:* Public (state) *System:* University of Texas System *Accred.:* 1974/1990 (SACS-CC)

Calendar: Sem. plan *Degrees:* B, M *Prof. Accred.:* Medical Technology, Nursing (B,M) *CEO:* Pres. George F. Hamm
FTE Enroll: 4,477   (903) 566-7000

THE UNIVERSITY OF TEXAS HEALTH SCIENCE CENTER AT HOUSTON
P.O. Box 20036, Houston 77225 *Type:* Public (state) *System:* University of Texas System *Accred.:* 1973/1990 (SACS-CC) *Calendar:* Sem. plan *Degrees:* B, M, D *Prof. Accred.:* Combined Prosthodontics, Dental Hygiene, Dentistry, Dietetics (coordinated), Endodontics, General Dentistry (prelim. provisional), General Practice Residency, Medical Technology, Medicine, Nurse Anesthesia Education, Nursing (B,M), Oral and Maxillofacial Surgery, Orthodontics, Pediatric Dentistry, Perfusion, Periodontics, Psychology Internship, Public Health, Radiography, Respiratory Therapy *CEO:* Pres. M. David Low
FTE Enroll: 2,817   (713) 792-4975

THE UNIVERSITY OF TEXAS HEALTH SCIENCE CENTER AT SAN ANTONIO
7703 Floyd Curl Dr., San Antonio 78284-7834 *Type:* Public (state) *System:* University of Texas System *Accred.:* 1973/1989 (SACS-CC) *Calendar:* Sem. plan *Degrees:* B, M, D *Prof. Accred.:* Combined Prosthodontics, Dental Hygiene, Dental Laboratory Technology, Dentistry, EMT-Paramedic, Endodontics, General Dentistry, General Practice Residency, Medical Technology, Medicine, Nurse Anesthesia Education, Occupational Therapy, Oral and Maxillofacial Surgery, Pediatric Dentistry, Periodontics, Physical Therapy, Psychology Internship *CEO:* Pres. John P. Howe, III
FTE Enroll: 2,465   (210) 567-7000

THE UNIVERSITY OF TEXAS MEDICAL BRANCH AT GALVESTON
300 University Blvd., Galveston 77550-0133 *Type:* Public (state) *System:* University of Texas System *Accred.:* 1973/1988 (SACS-CC) *Calendar:* Sem. plan *Degrees:* B, M, D *Prof. Accred.:* Blood Bank Technology, Medical Record Administration, Medical Technology, Medicine, Nursing (B,M), Occupational Therapy, Oral and Maxillofacial Surgery, Physical Therapy, Physician Assist-

ing, Psychology Internship *CEO:* Pres. Thomas N. James
FTE Enroll: 1,940   (409) 772-1687

THE UNIVERSITY OF TEXAS OF THE PERMIAN BASIN
4901 E. University Blvd., Odessa 79762 *Type:* Public (state) *System:* University of Texas System *Accred.:* 1975/1990 (SACS-CC) *Calendar:* Sem. plan *Degrees:* B, M *CEO:* Pres. Charles A. Sorber
FTE Enroll: 1,602   (915) 367-2011

THE UNIVERSITY OF TEXAS—PAN AMERICAN
1201 W. University Dr., Edinburg 78539-2999 *Type:* Public (state) liberal arts *System:* University of Texas System *Accred.:* 1956/1986 (SACS-CC) *Calendar:* Sem. plan *Degrees:* A, B, M *Prof. Accred.:* Business (B,M), Dietetics (coordinated), Medical Technology, Nursing (A,B), Social Work (B) *CEO:* Pres. Miguel A. Nevarez
FTE Enroll: 13,754   (210) 381-2011

THE UNIVERSITY OF TEXAS SOUTHWESTERN MEDICAL CENTER AT DALLAS
5323 Harry Hines Blvd., Dallas 75235-9002 *Type:* Public (state) *System:* University of Texas System *Accred.:* 1973/1989 (SACS-CC) *Calendar:* Sem. plan *Degrees:* B, M, D *Prof. Accred.:* Blood Bank Technology, Clinical Psychology, Dietetics (coordinated), EMT-Paramedic, Medical Illustration, Medical Technology, Medicine, Oral and Maxillofacial Surgery, Physical Therapy, Physician Assisting, Psychology Internship, Rehabilitation Counseling *CEO:* Pres. C. Kern Wildenthal
FTE Enroll: 1,658   (214) 688-3111

VERNON REGIONAL JUNIOR COLLEGE
4400 College Dr., Vernon 76384-4092 *Type:* Public (district) junior *System:* Texas Higher Education Coordinating Board *Accred.:* 1974/1989 (SACS-CC) *Calendar:* Sem. plan *Degrees:* A *CEO:* Pres. R. Wade Kirk
FTE Enroll: 2,896   (817) 552-6291

THE VICTORIA COLLEGE
2200 E. Red River St., Victoria 77901-4494 *Type:* Public (district) junior *System:* Texas Higher Education Coordinating Board *Accred.:* 1951/1993 (SACS-CC) *Calendar:* Sem. plan *Degrees:* A *Prof. Accred.:* Med-

ical Laboratory Technology (AMA), Nursing (A), Respiratory Therapy Technology *CEO:* Pres. Jimmy L. Goodson
FTE Enroll: 2,703   (512) 573-3291

WAYLAND BAPTIST UNIVERSITY
1900 W. Seventh St., Plainview 79072 *Type:* Private (Southern Baptist) liberal arts *Accred.:* 1956/1989 (SACS-CC) *Calendar:* Sem. plan *Degrees:* A, B, M *CEO:* Pres. Wallace E. Davis, Jr.
FTE Enroll: 3,048   (806) 296-5521

WEATHERFORD COLLEGE
308 E. Park Ave., Weatherford 76086 *Type:* Public (district) junior *System:* Texas Higher Education Coordinating Board *Accred.:* 1956/1991 (SACS-CC) *Calendar:* Sem. plan *Degrees:* A *CEO:* Pres. James Boyd
FTE Enroll: 1,996   (817) 594-5471

WEST TEXAS A&M UNIVERSITY
2501 Fourth Ave., P.O. Box 999, W.T. Sta., Canyon 79016 *Type:* Public (state) liberal arts and professional *System:* Texas A&M University System *Accred.:* 1925/1985 (SACS-CC) *Calendar:* Sem. plan *Degrees:* B, M *Prof. Accred.:* Music, Nursing (B,M), Social Work (B) *CEO:* Pres. Barry B. Thompson
FTE Enroll: 6,640   (806) 656-2000

WESTERN TEXAS COLLEGE
6200 S. College Ave., Snyder 79549 *Type:* Public (district) junior *System:* Texas Higher

Education Coordinating Board *Accred.:* 1973/1988 (SACS-CC) *Calendar:* Sem. plan *Degrees:* A *CEO:* Pres. Harry L. Krenek
FTE Enroll: 1,169   (915) 573-8511

WHARTON COUNTY JUNIOR COLLEGE
911 Boling Hwy., Wharton 77488 *Type:* Public (district) junior *System:* Texas Higher Education Coordinating Board *Accred.:* 1951/1988 (SACS-CC) *Calendar:* Sem. plan *Degrees:* A *Prof. Accred.:* Dental Hygiene, Medical Laboratory Technology (AMA), Medical Record Technology, Physical Therapy Assisting, Radiography *CEO:* Pres. Elbert C. Hutchins
FTE Enroll: 2,075   (409) 532-4560

WILEY COLLEGE
711 Wiley Ave., Marshall 75670 *Type:* Private (United Methodist) liberal arts and teachers *Accred.:* 1933/1993 (SACS-CC) *Calendar:* Sem. plan *Degrees:* A, B *CEO:* Pres. Lamore J. Carter
FTE Enroll: 564   (903) 927-3300

WILLIAM MARSH RICE UNIVERSITY
6100 S. Main St., P.O. Box 1892, Houston 77251 *Type:* Private *Accred.:* 1914/1985 (SACS-CC) *Calendar:* Sem. plan *Degrees:* B, M, D *Prof. Accred.:* Engineering (chemical, civil, electrical, materials, mechanical) *CEO:* Pres. S. Malcolm Gillis
FTE Enroll: 4,167   (713) 527-8101

UTAH

BRIGHAM YOUNG UNIVERSITY
Provo 84602 *Type:* Private (Latter-Day Saints) *Accred.:* 1923/1991 (NASC) *Calendar:* Sem. plan *Degrees:* A, B, M, D *Prof. Accred.:* Accounting (Type A,C), Art, Audiology, Clinical Psychology, Computer Science, Construction Education (B), Dance (associate), Dietetics (coordinated), Engineering Technology (electrical, manufacturing, mechanical drafting/design), Engineering (chemical, civil, electrical, mechanical), Journalism (B,M), Law, Librarianship, Marriage and Family Therapy (M,D), Medical Technology, Music, Nursing (B,M), Psychology Internship, Public Administration, Recreation and Leisure Services, Social Work (B,M), Speech-Language Pathology, Teacher Education (e,s,p), Theatre, Veterinary Technology *CEO:* Pres. Rex E. Lee
Enroll: 38,548   (801) 378-4668

COLLEGE OF EASTERN UTAH
Price 84501 *Type:* Public (state) junior *System:* Utah System of Higher Education *Accred.:* 1945/1992 (NASC) *Calendar:* Qtr. plan *Degrees:* A *CEO:* Pres. Michael A. Petersen
Enroll: 2,746   (801) 637-2120

DIXIE COLLEGE
St. George 84770 *Type:* Public (state) junior *System:* Utah System of Higher Education *Accred.:* 1945/1992 (NASC) *Calendar:* Qtr. plan *Degrees:* A *Prof. Accred.:* Nursing (A) *CEO:* Pres. Robert C. Huddleston
Enroll: 2,963   (801) 673-4811

ITT TECHNICAL INSTITUTE
920 W. LeVoy Dr., Murray 84123-2500 *Type:* Private *Accred.:* 1985/1990 (ACCSCT) *Calendar:* Courses of varying lengths *Degrees:* A *CEO:* Dir. Dean L. Dalby
(801) 263-3313

LDS BUSINESS COLLEGE
411 E. S. Temple St., Salt Lake City 84111 *Type:* Private (Latter-Day Saints) *Accred.:* 1977/1992 (NASC) *Calendar:* Qtr. plan *Degrees:* A *Prof. Accred.:* Medical Assisting (AMA) *CEO:* Pres. Stephen Woodhouse
Enroll: 837   (801) 363-2765

PHILLIPS JUNIOR COLLEGE
3098 Highland Dr., Salt Lake City 84106 *Type:* Private junior *Accred.:* 1985/1990 (ACISC) *Calendar:* Courses of varying lengths *Degrees:* A *CEO:* Pres. Wayne Wilson
(801) 485-0221

SALT LAKE COMMUNITY COLLEGE
P.O. Box 30808, Salt Lake City 84130 *Type:* Public (state) junior *System:* Utah System of Higher Education *Accred.:* 1969/1989 (NASC) *Calendar:* Qtr. plan *Degrees:* A *Prof. Accred.:* Medical Assisting (AMA), Nursing (A), Practical Nursing, Radiography, Surgical Technology *CEO:* Pres. Frank W. Budd
Enroll: 24,794   (801) 967-4111

SNOW COLLEGE
Ephraim 84627 *Type:* Public (state) junior *System:* Utah System of Higher Education *Accred.:* 1953/1992 (NASC) *Calendar:* Qtr. plan *Degrees:* A *CEO:* Pres. Gerald J. Day
Enroll: 2,819   (801) 283-4021

SOUTHERN UTAH UNIVERSITY
Cedar City 84720 *Type:* Public (state) liberal arts and teachers *System:* Utah System of Higher Education *Accred.:* 1933/1993 (NASC) *Calendar:* Qtr. plan *Degrees:* A, B, M *Prof. Accred.:* Music, Nursing (A) *CEO:* Pres. Gerald R. Sherratt
Enroll: 4,434   (801) 586-7710

THE STEVENS-HENAGER COLLEGE OF BUSINESS
2168 Washington Blvd., Ogden 84401-1467 *Type:* Private junior *Accred.:* 1962/1989 (ACISC) *Calendar:* Qtr. plan *Degrees:* A, certificates, diplomas *CEO:* Dir. Vicky Dewsnup
(801) 394-7791

BRANCH CAMPUS
25 E. 1700 S., Provo 84606-6157 *Accred.:* 1993 (ACISC) *CEO:* Dir. Darrell Rhoten
(801) 375-5455

UNIVERSITY OF UTAH
Salt Lake City 84112 *Type:* Public (state) *System:* Utah System of Higher Education *Accred.:* 1933/1991 (NASC) *Calendar:* Qtr. plan *Degrees:* A, B, M, D *Prof. Accred.:* Ac-

counting (Type A,C), Audiology, Business (B,M), Clinical Psychology, Community Health/Preventive Medicine, Counseling Psychology, Cytotechnology, Dietetics (coordinated), Engineering Technology (industrial hygiene), Engineering (chemical, civil, electrical, geological/geophysical, materials, mechanical, metallurgical, mining), General Dentistry, General Practice Residency, Journalism (B,M), Law, Medical Technology, Medicine, Music, Nuclear Medicine Technology, Nursing (B,M), Physical Therapy, Physician Assisting, Psychology Internship, Public Administration, Radiation Therapy Technology, Recreation and Leisure Services, School Psychology, Social Work (M), Speech-Language Pathology *CEO:* Pres. Arthur K. Smith
Enroll: 26,799   (801) 581-7200

UTAH STATE UNIVERSITY
Logan 84322-1400 *Type:* Public (state) *System:* Utah System of Higher Education *Accred.:* 1924/1993 (NASC) *Calendar:* Qtr. plan *Degrees:* A, B, M, D *Prof. Accred.:* Accounting (Type A,C), Audiology, Business (B,M), Combined Professional-Scientific Psychology, Dietetics (coordinated), Engineering (agricultural, civil, electrical, manufacturing, mechanical), Forestry, Home Economics, Interior Design, Landscape Architecture (B,M), Music, Nursing (A), Rehabilitation Counseling, Social Work (B), Speech-Language Pathology, Teacher Education (e,s,p) *CEO:* Pres. George H. Emert
Enroll: 16,514   (801) 750-1000

UTAH VALLEY STATE COLLEGE
800 W. 1200 S., Orem 84058 *Type:* Public (state) junior *System:* Utah System of Higher Education *Accred.:* 1969/1984 (NASC) *Calendar:* Sem. plan *Degrees:* A, B *Prof. Accred.:* Engineering Technology (electrical) *CEO:* Pres. Kerry D. Romesburg
Enroll: 9,623   (801) 226-5000

WEBER STATE UNIVERSITY
3750 Harrison Blvd., Ogden 84408-1004 *Type:* Public (state) liberal arts and teachers *System:* Utah System of Higher Education *Accred.:* 1932/1989 (NASC) *Calendar:* Qtr. plan *Degrees:* A, B, M *Prof. Accred.:* Business (B,M), Dental Hygiene, Diagnostic Medical Sonography, EMT-Paramedic, Engineering Technology (automotive, electrical, manufacturing, mechanical), Medical Laboratory Technology (AMA), Medical Record Technology, Medical Technology, Music, Nuclear Medicine Technology, Nursing (A,B), Practical Nursing, Radiation Therapy Technology, Radiography, Respiratory Therapy, Respiratory Therapy Technology, Social Work (B), Teacher Education (e,s,p) *CEO:* Pres. Paul H. Thompson
Enroll: 14,993   (801) 626-6140

WESTMINSTER COLLEGE OF SALT LAKE CITY
1840 S. 1300 E., Salt Lake City 84105 *Type:* Private liberal arts and professional *Accred.:* 1936/1993 (NASC) *Calendar:* 4-1-4 plan *Degrees:* B, M *Prof. Accred.:* Nursing (B) *CEO:* Pres. Charles H. Dick
Enroll: 2,112   (801) 488-4298

VERMONT

BENNINGTON COLLEGE
Bennington 05201 *Type:* Private liberal arts *Accred.:* 1935/1987 (NEASC-CIHE) *Calendar:* Courses of varying lengths *Degrees:* B, M *CEO:* Pres. Elizabeth Coleman
Enroll: 544   (802) 442-5401

BURLINGTON COLLEGE
95 N. Ave., Burlington 05401-8477 *Type:* Private *Accred.:* 1982/1987 (NEASC-CIHE) *Calendar:* Tri. plan *Degrees:* A, B *CEO:* Pres. Steward La Casce
Enroll: 138   (802) 862-9616

CASTLETON STATE COLLEGE
Castleton 05735 *Type:* Public (state) liberal arts and teachers *System:* Vermont State Colleges *Accred.:* 1960/1991 (NEASC-CIHE) *Calendar:* Sem. plan *Degrees:* A, B, M *Prof. Accred.:* Nursing (A), Social Work (B) *CEO:* Interim Pres. Joseph T. Mack
Enroll: 2,217   (802) 468-5611

CHAMPLAIN COLLEGE
P.O. Box 670, Burlington 05402-0670 *Type:* Private *Accred.:* 1972/1990 (NEASC-CIHE) *Calendar:* Sem. plan *Degrees:* A, B *Prof. Accred.:* Engineering Technology (electrical), Radiography *CEO:* Pres. Roger H. Perry
Enroll: 1,425   (802) 658-0800

COLLEGE OF ST. JOSEPH
Rutland 05701 *Type:* Private (Roman Catholic) teachers *Accred.:* 1972/1986 (NEASC-CIHE) *Calendar:* Sem. plan *Degrees:* A, B, M *CEO:* Pres. Frank G. Miglorie, Jr.
Enroll: 297   (802) 773-5900

COMMUNITY COLLEGE OF VERMONT
Waterbury 05676 *Type:* Public (state) junior *System:* Vermont State Colleges *Accred.:* 1975/1992 (NEASC-CIHE) *Calendar:* Tri. plan *Degrees:* A *CEO:* Pres. Michael Holland
Enroll: 2,090   (802) 241-3535

GODDARD COLLEGE
Plainfield 05667 *Type:* Private liberal arts *Accred.:* 1959/1992 (NEASC-CIHE) *Calendar:* Sem. plan *Degrees:* B, M *CEO:* Pres. Jackson Kytle
Enroll: 543   (802) 454-8311

GREEN MOUNTAIN COLLEGE
Poultney 05764 *Type:* Private (United Methodist) liberal arts *Accred.:* 1934/1987 (NEASC-CIHE) *Calendar:* 4-1-4 plan *Degrees:* A, B *Prof. Accred.:* Recreation and Leisure Services *CEO:* Pres. James M. Pollock
Enroll: 766   (802) 287-9313

JOHNSON STATE COLLEGE
Johnson 05656 *Type:* Public (state) liberal arts and teachers *System:* Vermont State Colleges *Accred.:* 1961/1986 (NEASC-CIHE) *Calendar:* Sem. plan *Degrees:* A, B, M *CEO:* Pres. Robert T. Hahn
Enroll: 1,523   (802) 635-2356

LANDMARK COLLEGE
Putney 05346 *Type:* Private junior *Accred.:* 1991 (NEASC-CIHE) *Calendar:* Sem. plan *Degrees:* A *CEO:* Pres. Gene S. Cesari
Enroll: 71   (802) 387-4767

LYNDON STATE COLLEGE
Vail Hill, Lyndonville 05851 *Type:* Public (state) liberal arts and teachers *System:* Vermont State Colleges *Accred.:* 1965/1989 (NEASC-CIHE) *Calendar:* Sem. plan *Degrees:* A, B, M *Prof. Accred.:* Recreation and Leisure Services *CEO:* Pres. Margaret R. Williams
Enroll: 1,093   (802) 626-9371

MARLBORO COLLEGE
Marlboro 05344-0300 *Type:* Private liberal arts *Accred.:* 1965/1987 (NEASC-CIHE) *Calendar:* Sem. plan *Degrees:* B, M *CEO:* Pres. Roderick M. Gander
Enroll: 263   (802) 257-4333

MIDDLEBURY COLLEGE
Middlebury 05753 *Type:* Private liberal arts *Accred.:* 1929/1990 (NEASC-CIHE) *Calendar:* Sem. plan *Degrees:* B, M, D *CEO:* Pres. John McCardell
Enroll: 1,960   (802) 388-3711

NORWICH UNIVERSITY
Northfield 05663 *Type:* Private liberal arts *Accred.:* 1933/1990 (NEASC-CIHE) *Calendar:* Sem. plan *Degrees:* A, B, M, D *Prof. Accred.:* Engineering Technology (environmental/sanitary), Engineering (civil, electri-

cal, mechanical) *CEO:* Pres. Richard W. Schneider
Enroll: 2,512   (802) 485-2000

VERMONT COLLEGE
College St., Montpelier 05602 *Prof. Accred.:* Nursing (A,B) *CEO:* Vice Pres. Richard S. Hansen
                                   (802) 485-2000

ST. MICHAEL'S COLLEGE
Winooski Park, Colchester 05439 *Type:* Private (Roman Catholic) *Accred.:* 1939/1990 (NEASC-CIHE) *Calendar:* Sem. plan *Degrees:* B, M *CEO:* Pres. Paul J. Reiss
Enroll: 2,161   (802) 655-2000

SCHOOL FOR INTERNATIONAL TRAINING
P.O. Box 676, Brattleboro 05301-0676 *Type:* Private liberal arts *Accred.:* 1974/1992 (NEASC-CIHE) *Calendar:* Sem. plan *Degrees:* B, M *CEO:* Pres. Neal Mangham
Enroll: 658   (802) 257-7751

SOUTHERN VERMONT COLLEGE
Bennington 05201 *Type:* Private *Accred.:* 1979/1989 (NEASC-CIHE) *Calendar:* Sem. plan *Degrees:* A, B, certificates, diplomas *Prof. Accred.:* Nursing (A) *CEO:* Pres. William A. Glasser
Enroll: 513   (802) 442-5427

STERLING COLLEGE
Craftsbury Common 05827 *Type:* Private 2-year *Accred.:* 1987/1991 (NEASC-CTCI) *Calendar:* Qtr. plan *Degrees:* A *CEO:* Interim Pres. Ray Leonard
FTE Enroll: 90   (802) 586-7711

TRINITY COLLEGE OF VERMONT
208 Colchester Ave., Burlington 05401 *Type:* Private (Roman Catholic) liberal arts for women *Accred.:* 1952/1991 (NEASC-CIHE) *Calendar:* Sem. plan *Degrees:* B, M

Prof. Accred.: Social Work (B) *CEO:* Pres. Janice E. Ryan, R.S.M.
Enroll: 680   (802) 658-0337

UNIVERSITY OF VERMONT
Burlington 05405-0160 *Type:* Public (state) *Accred.:* 1929/1988 (NEASC-CIHE) *Calendar:* Sem. plan *Degrees:* A, B, P, M, D *Prof. Accred.:* Business (B,M), Clinical Psychology, Counseling, Dental Hygiene, Engineering (civil, electrical, mechanical), Forestry, Medical Technology, Medicine, Music, Nuclear Medicine Technology, Nursing (A,B,M), Physical Therapy, Radiation Therapy Technology, Social Work (B,M), Speech-Language Pathology, Teacher Education (e,s,p) *CEO:* Pres. Thomas P. Salmon
Enroll: 8,445   (802) 656-3131

VERMONT LAW SCHOOL
Chelsea St., P.O. Box 96, South Royalton 05068 *Type:* Private professional *Accred.:* 1980/1985 (NEASC-CIHE) *Calendar:* Sem. plan *Degrees:* P, D *Prof. Accred.:* Law *CEO:* Dean Maximilian W. Kempner
Enroll: 538   (802) 763-8303

VERMONT TECHNICAL COLLEGE
Randolph Center 05061 *Type:* Public (state) 2-year *System:* Vermont State Colleges *Accred.:* 1970/1989 (NEASC-CTCI) *Calendar:* Sem. plan *Degrees:* A *Prof. Accred.:* Engineering Technology (architectural, civil/construction, computer, electrical, mechanical), Veterinary Technology (probational) *CEO:* Pres. Robert G. Clarke
FTE Enroll: 725   (802) 728-3391

WOODBURY COLLEGE
660 Elm St., Montpelier 05602 *Type:* Private *Accred.:* 1984 (NEASC-CTCI) *Calendar:* Sem. plan *Degrees:* A *CEO:* Pres. Lawrence H. Mandell
FTE Enroll: 115   (802) 229-0516

VIRGIN ISLANDS

UNIVERSITY OF THE VIRGIN ISLANDS
St. Thomas 00802 *Type:* Public (state) *Accred.:* 1971/1991 (MSA) *Calendar:* Sem. plan *Degrees:* A, B, M *Prof. Accred.:* Nursing (A,B) *CEO:* Pres. Orville E. Kean, Ph.D. *Enroll:* 1,797   (809) 776-9200

BRANCH CAMPUS
St. Croix 00850 *CEO:* Dir. Mary M. Savage
(809) 778-1620

VIRGINIA

AVERETT COLLEGE
420 W. Main St., Danville 24541 *Type:* Private (Southern Baptist) liberal arts *Accred.:* 1928/1987 (SACS-CC) *Calendar:* Sem. plan *Degrees:* B, M *CEO:* Pres. Frank R. Campbell
FTE Enroll: 1,640   (804) 791-5600

BLUE RIDGE COMMUNITY COLLEGE
P.O. Box 80, Weyers Cave 24486 *Type:* Public (state) junior *System:* Virginia Community College System *Accred.:* 1969/1984 (SACS-CC) *Calendar:* Sem. plan *Degrees:* A *Prof. Accred.:* Veterinary Technology *CEO:* Pres. James R. Perkins
FTE Enroll: 2,002   (703) 234-9261

BLUEFIELD COLLEGE
3000 College Dr., Bluefield 24605 *Type:* Private (Southern Baptist) liberal arts *Accred.:* 1949/1993 (SACS-CC) *Calendar:* Sem. plan *Degrees:* A, B *CEO:* Pres. Roy A. Dobyns
FTE Enroll: 707   (703) 326-3682

BRIDGEWATER COLLEGE
Bridgewater 22812 *Type:* Private (Church of Brethren) liberal arts *Accred.:* 1925/1991 (SACS-CC) *Calendar:* 3-3-1-3 plan *Degrees:* B *CEO:* Pres. Wayne F. Geisert
FTE Enroll: 892   (703) 828-2501

CENTRAL VIRGINIA COMMUNITY COLLEGE
3506 Wards Rd., Lynchburg 24502-2498 *Type:* Public (state) junior *System:* Virginia Community College System *Accred.:* 1969/1984 (SACS-CC) *Calendar:* Sem. plan *Degrees:* A *Prof. Accred.:* Medical Laboratory Technology (AMA), Medical Record Technology, Radiography, Respiratory Therapy Technology *CEO:* Pres. Belle S. Wheelan
FTE Enroll: 2,419   (804) 386-4500

CHRISTENDOM COLLEGE
2101 Shenandoah Shores Rd., Front Royal 22630 *Type:* Private (Roman Catholic) liberal arts *Accred.:* 1987/1992 (SACS-CC) *Calendar:* Sem. plan *Degrees:* A, B *CEO:* Pres. Timothy O'Donnell
FTE Enroll: 144   (703) 636-2900

CHRISTOPHER NEWPORT UNIVERSITY
50 Shoe La., Newport News 23606-2998 *Type:* Public (state) liberal arts *System:* Commonwealth of Virginia Council of Higher Education *Accred.:* 1971/1986 (SACS-CC) *Calendar:* Sem. plan *Degrees:* B *Prof. Accred.:* Nursing (B), Social Work (B) *CEO:* Pres. Anthony R. Santoro
FTE Enroll: 3,848   (804) 594-7000

CLINCH VALLEY COLLEGE OF THE UNIVERSITY OF VIRGINIA
College Ave., Wise 24293 *Type:* Public (state) liberal arts and teachers *System:* University of Virginia Central Office *Accred.:* 1970/1985 (SACS-CC) *Calendar:* Sem. plan *Degrees:* B *CEO:* Chanc. L. Jay Lemons
FTE Enroll: 1,346   (703) 328-0100

THE COLLEGE OF WILLIAM AND MARY
Williamsburg 23187-8795 *Type:* Public (state) liberal arts *System:* College of William and Mary Central Office *Accred.:* 1921/1985 (SACS-CC) *Calendar:* Sem. plan *Degrees:* A, B, M, D *Prof. Accred.:* Accounting (Type A), Business (B,M), Law, Teacher Education (e,s,p) *CEO:* Pres. Timothy J. Sullivan
FTE Enroll: 6,876   (804) 221-4000

COMMONWEALTH COLLEGE
4160 Virginia Beach Blvd., Norfolk 23452 *Type:* Private *Accred.:* 1970/1990 (ACISC); 1992 (SACS-CC candidate) *Calendar:* Sem. plan *Degrees:* A, certificates, diplomas *CEO:* Pres. Maritza Samoorian
FTE Enroll: 1,114   (804) 340-0222

BRANCH CAMPUS
1120 W. Mercury Blvd., Hampton 23666-3309 *Accred.:* 1984/1988 (ACISC) *CEO:* Vice Pres./Dir. Julia Heffernan
                              (804) 838-2122

BRANCH CAMPUS
300 Boush St., Norfolk 23510-1216 *Accred.:* 1964/1991 (ACISC) *CEO:* Dir. James K. Tolbert
                              (804) 625-5891

BRANCH CAMPUS
5579 Portsmouth Blvd., Portsmouth 23701 *Accred.:* 1990 (ACISC) *CEO:* Dir. Robyn Rickenbach
(804) 488-7799

BRANCH CAMPUS
8141 Hull Street Rd., Richmond 23235-6411 *Accred.:* 1983/1991 (ACISC) *CEO:* Dir. Edward B. Abrams
(804) 745-2444

COMMUNITY HOSPITAL OF ROANOKE VALLEY COLLEGE OF HEALTH SCIENCES
P.O. Box 13186, Roanoke 24016 *Type:* Private *Accred.:* 1986/1991 (SACS-CC) *Calendar:* Sem. plan *Degrees:* A *Prof. Accred.:* EMT-Paramedic, Nursing (A), Physical Therapy Assisting, Respiratory Therapy *CEO:* Pres. Harry C. Nickens
FTE Enroll: 375   (703) 985-8483

DABNEY S. LANCASTER COMMUNITY COLLEGE
P.O. Box 1000, Clifton Forge 24422-1000 *Type:* Public (state) junior *System:* Virginia Community College System *Accred.:* 1969/1984 (SACS-CC) *Calendar:* Sem. plan *Degrees:* A *Prof. Accred.:* Nursing (A) *CEO:* Pres. John F. Backels
FTE Enroll: 927   (703) 862-4246

DANVILLE COMMUNITY COLLEGE
1008 S. Main St., Danville 24541 *Type:* Public (state) junior *System:* Virginia Community College System *Accred.:* 1970/1985 (SACS-CC) *Calendar:* Sem. plan *Degrees:* A *CEO:* Pres. B. Carlyle Ramsey
FTE Enroll: 1,911   (804) 797-2222

EASTERN MENNONITE COLLEGE AND SEMINARY
1200 Park Rd., Harrisonburg 22801-2462 *Type:* Private (Mennonite) liberal arts *Accred.:* 1986/1990 (ATS); 1959/1990 (SACS-CC) *Calendar:* Sem. plan *Degrees:* A, B, M *Prof. Accred.:* Nursing (B), Social Work (B), Teacher Education (e,s) *CEO:* Pres. Joseph L. Lapp
FTE Enroll: 1,034   (703) 432-4260

EASTERN SHORE COMMUNITY COLLEGE
29300 Lankford Hwy., Melfa 23410 *Type:* Public (state) junior *System:* Virginia Community College System *Accred.:* 1973/1988

(SACS-CC) *Calendar:* Sem. plan *Degrees:* A *CEO:* Pres. John C. Fiege
FTE Enroll: 780   (804) 787-5900

EASTERN VIRGINIA MEDICAL SCHOOL
825 Fairfax Ave., Norfolk 23507 *Type:* Private professional *Accred.:* 1984/1990 (SACS-CC) *Calendar:* Sem. plan *Degrees:* M, D *Prof. Accred.:* Medicine, Psychology Internship *CEO:* Pres. Edward E. Brickell
FTE Enroll: 527   (804) 446-5600

EMORY AND HENRY COLLEGE
P.O. Box 947, Emory 24327 *Type:* Private (United Methodist) liberal arts *Accred.:* 1925/1987 (SACS-CC) *Calendar:* Sem. plan *Degrees:* B *CEO:* Pres. Thomas R. Morris, Jr.
FTE Enroll: 831   (703) 944-4121

FERRUM COLLEGE
Ferrum 24088 *Type:* Private (United Methodist) liberal arts *Accred.:* 1960/1991 (SACS-CC) *Calendar:* Sem. plan *Degrees:* A, B *Prof. Accred.:* Recreation and Leisure Services, Social Work (B) *CEO:* Pres. Jerry M. Boone
FTE Enroll: 1,072   (703) 365-2121

GEORGE MASON UNIVERSITY
4400 University Dr., Fairfax 22030-4444 *Type:* Public (state) *System:* Commonwealth of Virginia Council of Higher Education *Accred.:* 1957/1991 (SACS-CC) *Calendar:* Sem. plan *Degrees:* B, M, D *Prof. Accred.:* Accounting (Type A,C), Business (B,M), Clinical Psychology, Engineering (electrical), Law, Nursing (B,M), Public Administration, Social Work (B), Teacher Education (e,s,p) *CEO:* Pres. George W. Johnson
FTE Enroll: 16,152   (703) 993-1000

GERMANNA COMMUNITY COLLEGE
P.O. Box 339, Locust Grove 22508 *Type:* Public (state) junior *System:* Virginia Community College System *Accred.:* 1972/1987 (SACS-CC) *Calendar:* Sem. plan *Degrees:* A *Prof. Accred.:* Nursing (A) *CEO:* Pres. Francis S. Turnage
FTE Enroll: 1,714   (703) 423-1333

HAMPDEN-SYDNEY COLLEGE
P.O. Box 128, Hampden-Sydney 23943 *Type:* Private (Presbyterian) liberal arts for men *Accred.:* 1919/1986 (SACS-CC) *Calen-*

dar: Sem. plan *Degrees:* B *CEO:* Pres. Samuel V. Wilson
FTE Enroll: 944   (804) 223-6000

HAMPTON UNIVERSITY
East Queen St., Hampton 23668 *Type:* Private liberal arts *Accred.:* 1932/1988 (SACS-CC) *Calendar:* Sem. plan *Degrees:* B, M, D *Prof. Accred.:* Computer Science, Engineering (chemical, electrical), Music, Nursing (B,M), Social Work (B), Speech-Language Pathology, Teacher Education (e,s,p) *CEO:* Pres. William R. Harvey
FTE Enroll: 5,388   (804) 727-5000

HOLLINS COLLEGE
P.O. Box 9688, Roanoke 24020 *Type:* Private liberal arts primarily for women *Accred.:* 1932/1986 (SACS-CC) *Calendar:* 4-1-4 plan *Degrees:* B, M *CEO:* Pres. Jane M. O'Brien
FTE Enroll: 948   (703) 362-6000

INSTITUTE OF TEXTILE TECHNOLOGY
P.O. Box 391, Charlottesville 22902 *Type:* Private professional; graduate only *Accred.:* 1987/1992 (SACS-CC) *Calendar:* Qtr. plan *Degrees:* M *CEO:* Pres. Charles G. Tewksbury
FTE Enroll: 34   (804) 296-5511

J. SARGEANT REYNOLDS COMMUNITY COLLEGE
P.O. Box 85622, Richmond 23285-5622 *Type:* Public (state) junior *System:* Virginia Community College System *Accred.:* 1974/1989 (SACS-CC) *Calendar:* Sem. plan *Degrees:* A *Prof. Accred.:* Dental Assisting, Dental Laboratory Technology, Medical Laboratory Technology (AMA), Nursing (A), Respiratory Therapy, Respiratory Therapy Technology *CEO:* Pres. S.A. Burnette
FTE Enroll: 6,153   (804) 371-3200

JAMES MADISON UNIVERSITY
Harrisonburg 22807 *Type:* Public (state) liberal arts and teachers *System:* Commonwealth of Virginia Council of Higher Education *Accred.:* 1927/1992 (SACS-CC) *Calendar:* Sem. plan *Degrees:* B, M *Prof. Accred.:* Accounting (Type A,C), Art, Audiology, Business (B,M), Counseling, Music, Nursing (B), Social Work (B), Speech-Language

Pathology, Teacher Education (e,s,p), Theatre *CEO:* Pres. Ronald E. Carrier
FTE Enroll: 10,744   (703) 568-6211

JOHN TYLER COMMUNITY COLLEGE
13101 Jefferson Davis Hwy., Chester 23831-5399 *Type:* Public (state) junior *System:* Virginia Community College System *Accred.:* 1969/1993 (SACS-CC) *Calendar:* Sem. plan *Degrees:* A *Prof. Accred.:* Engineering Technology (architectural, electrical), Funeral Service Education, Nursing (A), Physical Therapy Assisting *CEO:* Pres. Marshall W. Smith
FTE Enroll: 3,002   (804) 796-4000

THE JUDGE ADVOCATE GENERAL'S SCHOOL
600 Massie Rd., Charlottesville 22903-1781 *Type:* Public (federal) professional *Calendar:* Sem. plan *Degrees:* P *Prof. Accred.:* Law (ABA only) *CEO:* Commandant John T. Edwards
Enroll: 76   (804) 972-6310

LIBERTY UNIVERSITY
P.O. Box 20000, Lynchburg 24506-8001 *Type:* Private (Baptist) liberal arts *Accred.:* 1980/1986 (SACS-CC) *Calendar:* Sem. plan *Degrees:* A, B, M, D *Prof. Accred.:* Nursing (A) *CEO:* Pres. A. Pierre Guillermin
FTE Enroll: 10,001   (804) 582-2000

LONGWOOD COLLEGE
201 High St., Farmville 23909 *Type:* Public (state) liberal arts and teachers for women *System:* Commonwealth of Virginia Council of Higher Education *Accred.:* 1927/1993 (SACS-CC) *Calendar:* Sem. plan *Degrees:* B, M *Prof. Accred.:* Music, Recreation and Leisure Services, Social Work (B), Teacher Education (e,s,p) *CEO:* Pres. William F. Dorrill
FTE Enroll: 3,114   (804) 395-2000

LORD FAIRFAX COMMUNITY COLLEGE
P.O. Box 47, Middletown 22645 *Type:* Public (state) junior *System:* Virginia Community College System *Accred.:* 1972/1987 (SACS-CC) *Calendar:* Sem. plan *Degrees:* A *CEO:* Pres. Marilyn C. Beck
FTE Enroll: 1,738   (703) 869-1120

LYNCHBURG COLLEGE
1501 Lakeside Dr., Lynchburg 24501-3199 *Type:* Private (Disciples of Christ) liberal arts *Accred.:* 1927/1993 (SACS-CC) *Calen-*

dar: Sem. plan *Degrees:* B, M *Prof. Accred.:* Counseling, Nursing (B) *CEO:* Pres. Charles O. Warren
FTE Enroll: 1,895   (804) 522-8100

MARY BALDWIN COLLEGE
Frederick and New St., Staunton 24401 *Type:* Private (Presbyterian) liberal arts for women *Accred.:* 1931/1988 (SACS-CC) *Calendar:* 4-1-4 plan *Degrees:* B, M *CEO:* Pres. Cynthia H. Tyson
FTE Enroll: 1,050   (703) 887-7000

MARY WASHINGTON COLLEGE
1301 College Ave., Fredericksburg 22401 *Type:* Public (state) liberal arts *System:* Commonwealth of Virginia Council of Higher Education *Accred.:* 1930/1993 (SACS-CC) *Calendar:* Sem. plan *Degrees:* B, M *Prof. Accred.:* Music *CEO:* Pres. William M. Anderson, Jr.
FTE Enroll: 3,355   (703) 899-4100

MARYMOUNT UNIVERSITY
2807 N. Glebe Rd., Arlington 22207 *Type:* Private for women *Accred.:* 1958/ 1988 (SACS-CC) *Calendar:* Sem. plan *Degrees:* A, B, M *Prof. Accred.:* Interior Design, Nursing (A,B,M), Teacher Education (e,s) *CEO:* Pres. Eymard Gallagher, R.S.H.M.
FTE Enroll: 2,711   (703) 522-5600

MOUNTAIN EMPIRE COMMUNITY COLLEGE
P.O. Drawer 700, Big Stone Gap 24219 *Type:* Public (state) junior *System:* Virginia Community College System *Accred.:* 1974/ 1989 (SACS-CC) *Calendar:* Sem. plan *Degrees:* A *Prof. Accred.:* Nursing (A), Respiratory Therapy Technology *CEO:* Pres. Robert H. Sandel
FTE Enroll: 1,864   (703) 523-2400

NATIONAL BUSINESS COLLEGE
1813 E. Main St., Salem 24153 *Type:* Private junior *Accred.:* 1954/1986 (ACISC) *Calendar:* Qtr. plan *Degrees:* A *Prof. Accred.:* Medical Assisting (AMA) *CEO:* Pres. Anna Marie Counts
      (703) 986-1800

BRANCH CAMPUS
100 Logan St., Bluefield 24605 *Accred.:* 1984/1986 (ACISC) *CEO:* Dir. Denver Riffe
      (703) 326-3621

BRANCH CAMPUS
300A Piedmont Ave., Bristol 24201 *Accred.:* 1993 (ACISC) *CEO:* Admin. Pat Boltinghouse
      (703) 669-5333

BRANCH CAMPUS
1819 Emmet St., Charlottesville 22903 *Accred.:* 1979/1986 (ACISC) *CEO:* Dir. Karen Sheets
      (804) 295-0136

BRANCH CAMPUS
734 Main St., Danville 24541 *Accred.:* 1984/1986 (ACISC) *CEO:* Admin. John Scott
      (804) 793-6822

BRANCH CAMPUS
51-B Burgess Rd., Harrisonburg 22801 *Accred.:* 1988 (ACISC) *CEO:* Dir. Jack Raines
      (703) 432-0943

BRANCH CAMPUS
104 Candlewood Ct., Lynchburg 24502 *Accred.:* 1987 (ACISC) *CEO:* Dir. Victor Gosnell
      (804) 239-3500

BRANCH CAMPUS
10 Church St., Martinsville 24114 *Accred.:* 1987 (ACISC) *CEO:* Admin. June Ford
      (703) 632-5621

NEW RIVER COMMUNITY COLLEGE
P.O. Drawer 1127, Dublin 24084 *Type:* Public (state) junior *System:* Virginia Community College System *Accred.:* 1972/1987 (SACS-CC) *Calendar:* Sem. plan *Degrees:* A *Prof. Accred.:* Nursing (A) *CEO:* Pres. Edwin L. Barnes
FTE Enroll: 2,650   (703) 674-3600

NORFOLK STATE UNIVERSITY
2401 Corprew Ave., Norfolk 23504 *Type:* Public (state) liberal arts and teachers *System:* Commonwealth of Virginia Council of Higher Education *Accred.:* 1967/1988 (SACS-CC) *Calendar:* Sem. plan *Degrees:* A, B, M *Prof. Accred.:* Business (B), Computer Science, Medical Record Administration, Medical Technology, Music, Nursing

(A,B), Social Work (B,M), Teacher Education (e,s) *CEO:* Pres. Harrison B. Wilson
FTE Enroll: 8,652 (804) 683-8600

NORTHERN VIRGINIA COMMUNITY COLLEGE
4001 Wakefield Chapel Rd., Annandale 22003-3723 *Type:* Public (state) junior *System:* Virginia Community College System *Accred.:* 1968/1992 (SACS-CC) *Calendar:* Sem. plan *Degrees:* A *Prof. Accred.:* Dental Hygiene, EMT-Paramedic, Medical Laboratory Technology (AMA), Medical Record Technology, Nursing (A), Physical Therapy Assisting, Radiography, Respiratory Therapy, Respiratory Therapy Technology *CEO:* Pres. Richard J. Ernst
FTE Enroll: 22,404 (703) 323-3000

ALEXANDRIA CAMPUS
3001 N. Beauregard St., Alexandria 22311 *CEO:* Provost Barbara A. Wyles
(703) 845-6200

ANNANDALE CAMPUS
8333 Little River Tpke., Annandale 22003 *CEO:* Provost Barbara J. Guthrie-Morse
(703) 323-3010

LOUDOUN CAMPUS
1000 Harry Flood Byrd Hwy., Sterling 22170 *Prof. Accred.:* Veterinary Technology *CEO:* Provost R. Neil Reynolds
(703) 450-2500

MANASSAS CAMPUS
6901 Sudley Rd., Manassas 22110 *CEO:* Provost Gail B. Kettlewell
(703) 257-6600

WOODBRIDGE CAMPUS
15200 Neabsco Mills Rd., Woodbridge 22191 *CEO:* Provost Lionel B. Sylvas
(703) 878-5700

OLD DOMINION UNIVERSITY
5215 Hampton Blvd., Norfolk 23529 *Type:* Public (state) liberal arts and professional *System:* Commonwealth of Virginia Council of Higher Education *Accred.:* 1961/1992 (SACS-CC) *Calendar:* Sem. plan *Degrees:* B, M, D *Prof. Accred.:* Accounting (Type A), Business (B,M), Computer Science, Cytotechnology, Dental Assisting, Dental Hygiene, Engineering Technology (civil/construction, electrical, mechanical), Engineer-

ing (civil, computer, electrical, mechanical), Medical Technology, Music, Nuclear Medicine Technology, Nursing (B,M), Ophthalmic Medical Technology, Physical Therapy, Public Administration, Recreation and Leisure Services, Speech-Language Pathology, Teacher Education (e,s,p), Theatre *CEO:* Pres. James V. Koch
FTE Enroll: 13,582 (804) 683-3000

PATRICK HENRY COMMUNITY COLLEGE
P.O. Drawer 5311, Martinsville 24115-5311 *Type:* Public (state) junior *System:* Virginia Community College System *Accred.:* 1972/1987 (SACS-CC) *Calendar:* Qtr. plan *Degrees:* A *Prof. Accred.:* Nursing (A) *CEO:* Pres. Max F. Wingett
FTE Enroll: 1,578 (703) 638-8777

PAUL D. CAMP COMMUNITY COLLEGE
100 N. College Rd., P.O. Box 737, Franklin 23851 *Type:* Public (state) junior *System:* Virginia Community College System *Accred.:* 1973/1988 (SACS-CC) *Calendar:* Sem. plan *Degrees:* A *CEO:* Pres. Jerome J. Friga
FTE Enroll: 838 (804) 562-2171

PIEDMONT VIRGINIA COMMUNITY COLLEGE
Rte. 6, Box 1, Charlottesville 22902 *Type:* Public (state) junior *System:* Virginia Community College System *Accred.:* 1974/1989 (SACS-CC) *Calendar:* Qtr. plan *Degrees:* A *Prof. Accred.:* Nursing (A) *CEO:* Pres. Deborah M. DiCroce
FTE Enroll: 2,355 (804) 977-3900

PRESBYTERIAN SCHOOL OF CHRISTIAN EDUCATION
1205 Palmyra Ave., Richmond 23227 *Type:* Private (Presbyterian) graduate only *Accred.:* 1964/1988 (ATS); 1951/1988 (SACS-CC) *Calendar:* 4-1-4 plan *Degrees:* M, D *CEO:* Pres. Wayne G. Boulton
FTE Enroll: 114 (804) 359-5031

PROTESTANT EPISCOPAL THEOLOGICAL SEMINARY IN VIRGINIA
3737 Seminary Rd., Alexandria 22304 *Type:* Private (Episcopal) graduate only *Accred.:* 1938/1993 (ATS) *Calendar:* Sem. plan *Degrees:* M, D *CEO:* Pres./Dean Richard Reid
FTE Enroll: 198 (703) 370-6600

RADFORD UNIVERSITY
Radford 24142 *Type:* Public (state) liberal arts and teachers *System:* Commonwealth of Virginia Council of Higher Education *Accred.:* 1928/1993 (SACS-CC) *Calendar:* Sem. plan *Degrees:* B, M *Prof. Accred.:* Audiology, Business (B,M), Computer Science, Music, Nursing (B,M), Recreation and Leisure Services, Social Work (B), Speech-Language Pathology, Teacher Education (e,s,p) *CEO:* Pres. Donald N. Dedmon
FTE Enroll: 8,950   (703) 831-5000

RANDOLPH-MACON COLLEGE
P.O. Box 5005, Ashland 23005-5505 *Type:* Private (United Methodist) liberal arts *Accred.:* 1904/1987 (SACS-CC) *Calendar:* 4-1-4 plan *Degrees:* B *CEO:* Pres. Ladell Payne
FTE Enroll: 1,120   (804) 798-8372

RANDOLPH-MACON WOMAN'S COLLEGE
2500 Rivermont Ave., Lynchburg 24503 *Type:* Private (United Methodist) liberal arts for women *Accred.:* 1902/1990 (SACS-CC) *Calendar:* Sem. plan *Degrees:* B *CEO:* Interim Pres. Lambuth M. Clarke
FTE Enroll: 700   (804) 947-8000

RAPPAHANNOCK COMMUNITY COLLEGE
P.O. Box 287, Glenns 23149 *Type:* Public (state) junior *System:* Virginia Community College System *Accred.:* 1973/1988 (SACS-CC) *Calendar:* Sem. plan *Degrees:* A *CEO:* Pres. John H. Upton
FTE Enroll: 1,048   (804) 758-6700

REGENT UNIVERSITY
1000 Centerville Tpke., Virginia Beach 23464 *Type:* Private (interdenominational) graduate only *Accred.:* 1992 (ATS); 1984/1989 (SACS-CC) *Calendar:* Qtr. plan *Degrees:* M, D *Prof. Accred.:* Law (ABA only) (provisional) *CEO:* Pres. Terrence Lindvall
FTE Enroll: 1,155   (804) 523-7400

RICHARD BLAND COLLEGE
11301 Johnson Rd., Petersburg 23805 *Type:* Public (state) junior *System:* College of William and Mary Central Office *Accred.:* 1961/1988 (SACS-CC) *Calendar:* Sem. plan *Degrees:* A *CEO:* Pres. Clarence Maze, Jr.
FTE Enroll: 1,225   (804) 862-6100

ROANOKE COLLEGE
221 College La., Salem 24153-3794 *Type:* Private (Lutheran) liberal arts *Accred.:* 1927/1991 (SACS-CC) *Calendar:* 4-1-4 plan *Degrees:* B *CEO:* Pres. David M. Gring
FTE Enroll: 1,576   (703) 375-2500

ST. PAUL'S COLLEGE
406 Winsor Ave., Lawrenceville 23868 *Type:* Private (Episcopal) liberal arts and teachers *Accred.:* 1950/1990 (SACS-CC) *Calendar:* Sem. plan *Degrees:* B *CEO:* Pres. Thomas M. Law
FTE Enroll: 675   (804) 848-3111

SHENANDOAH UNIVERSITY
1460 College Dr., Winchester 22601 *Type:* Private (United Methodist) *Accred.:* 1973/1989 (SACS-CC) *Calendar:* Sem. plan *Degrees:* A, B, M *Prof. Accred.:* Music, Nursing (A), Physical Therapy, Respiratory Therapy *CEO:* Pres. James A. Davis
FTE Enroll: 1,294   (703) 665-4500

SOUTHERN VIRGINIA COLLEGE FOR WOMEN
One College Hill Dr., Buena Vista 24416 *Type:* Private for women *Accred.:* 1962/1983 (SACS-CC probational) *Calendar:* Sem. plan *Degrees:* A *CEO:* Pres. John W. Ripley
FTE Enroll: 179   (703) 261-8400

SOUTHSIDE VIRGINIA COMMUNITY COLLEGE
Rte. 1, Box 60, Alberta 23821 *Type:* Public (state) junior *System:* Virginia Community College System *Accred.:* 1972/1987 (SACS-CC) *Calendar:* Qtr. plan *Degrees:* A *CEO:* Pres. John J. Cavan
FTE Enroll: 1,997   (804) 949-7111

SOUTHWEST VIRGINIA COMMUNITY COLLEGE
P.O. Box SVCC, Richlands 24641 *Type:* Public (state) junior *System:* Virginia Community College System *Accred.:* 1970/1985 (SACS-CC) *Calendar:* Qtr. plan *Degrees:* A *Prof. Accred.:* Nursing (A), Radiography, Respiratory Therapy Technology *CEO:* Pres. Charles R. King
FTE Enroll: 2,772   (703) 964-2555

SWEET BRIAR COLLEGE
Sweet Briar 24595 *Type:* Private liberal arts for women *Accred.:* 1920/1990 (SACS-CC) *Calendar:* Sem. plan *Degrees:* B *CEO:* Pres. Barbara A. Hill
FTE Enroll: 528   (804) 381-6100

THOMAS NELSON COMMUNITY COLLEGE
P.O. Box 9407, Hampton 23670 *Type:* Public (state) junior *System:* Virginia Community College System *Accred.:* 1970/1985 (SACS-CC) *Calendar:* Sem. plan *Degrees:* A *Prof. Accred.:* Medical Laboratory Technology (AMA) *CEO:* Pres. Robert G. Templin, Jr.
FTE Enroll: 6,620   (804) 825-2700

TIDEWATER COMMUNITY COLLEGE
7000 College Dr., Portsmouth 23703 *Type:* Public (state) junior *System:* Virginia Community College System *Accred.:* 1971/1986 (SACS-CC) *Calendar:* Qtr. plan *Degrees:* A *Prof. Accred.:* Diagnostic Medical Sonography, Medical Record Technology, Nursing (A), Physical Therapy Assisting, Radiography, Respiratory Therapy, Respiratory Therapy Technology *CEO:* Pres. Larry L. Whitworth
FTE Enroll: 17,586   (804) 484-2121

UNION THEOLOGICAL SEMINARY IN VIRGINIA
3401 Brook Rd., Richmond 23227 *Type:* Private (Presbyterian) graduate only *Accred.:* 1938/1986 (ATS); 1971/1986 (SACS-CC) *Calendar:* Sem. plan *Degrees:* M, D *CEO:* Pres. T. Hartley Hall, IV
FTE Enroll: 246   (804) 355-0671

UNIVERSITY OF RICHMOND
Richmond 23173 *Type:* Private (Southern Baptist) liberal arts *Accred.:* 1910/1988 (SACS-CC) *Calendar:* Sem. plan *Degrees:* A, B, M, D *Prof. Accred.:* Accounting (Type A), Business (B,M), Law, Music *CEO:* Pres. Richard L. Morrill
FTE Enroll: 3,685   (804) 289-8000

UNIVERSITY OF VIRGINIA
P.O. Box 9011, Charlottesville 22906 *Type:* Public (state) *System:* University of Virginia Central Office *Accred.:* 1904/1986 (SACS-CC) *Calendar:* Sem. plan *Degrees:* B, M, D *Prof. Accred.:* Accounting (Type A,C), Audiology, Business (B,M), Clinical Psychology, Counseling, Dietetics (internship), Engineering (aerospace, chemical, civil, electrical, mechanical, nuclear, systems), General Practice Residency, Landscape Architecture (M), Law, Medical Technology, Medicine, Nuclear Medicine Technology, Nursing (B,M), Planning (B,M), Psychology Internship, Radiation Therapy Technology, Radio-

graphy, Speech-Language Pathology, Teacher Education (e,s,p) *CEO:* Pres. John T. Casteen, III
FTE Enroll: 20,600   (804) 924-3337

VIRGINIA COLLEGE
2163 Apperson Dr., Salem 24153-7235 *Type:* Private junior *Accred.:* 1990 (ACISC) *Calendar:* Qtr. plan *Degrees:* A *CEO:* Dir. Mark Nelson
                                   (703) 265-2895

BRANCH CAMPUS
1900 28th Ave. S., Birmingham, AL 35209 *Accred.:* 1993 (ACISC) *CEO:* Pres. Kenneth C. Horne
                                   (205) 802-1200

VIRGINIA COLLEGE AT HUNTSVILLE
2800-A Bob Wallace Ave., Huntsville, AL 35805 *Accred.:* 1993 (ACISC) *CEO:* Dir. Bernard Fortunoff
                                   (205) 533-7387

VIRGINIA COMMONWEALTH UNIVERSITY
910 W. Franklin St., Richmond 23284-2512 *Type:* Public (state) *System:* Commonwealth of Virginia Council of Higher Education *Accred.:* 1953/1984 (SACS-CC) *Calendar:* Sem. plan *Degrees:* A, B, M, D *Prof. Accred.:* Accounting (Type A,C), Art, Business (B,M), Clinical Psychology, Combined Prosthodontics, Computer Science, Counseling Psychology, Dental Hygiene, Dentistry, Dietetics (internship), Endodontics, General Dentistry (prelim. provisional), Health Services Administration, Interior Design, Journalism (B,M), Medical Record Administration, Medical Technology, Medicine, Music, Nuclear Medicine Technology, Nurse Anesthesia Education, Nursing (B,M), Occupational Therapy, Oral and Maxillofacial Surgery, Orthodontics, Pediatric Dentistry, Periodontics, Physical Therapy, Planning (M), Psychology Internship, Public Administration, Radiation Therapy Technology, Radiography, Recreation and Leisure Services, Rehabilitation Counseling, Social Work (B,M), Teacher Education (e,s,p) *CEO:* Pres. Eugene P. Trani
FTE Enroll: 17,196   (804) 367-0100

VIRGINIA HIGHLANDS COMMUNITY COLLEGE
P.O. Box 828, State Rte. 372 off Rte. 140,
Abingdon 24210 *Type:* Public (state) junior
System: Virginia Community College System *Accred.:* 1972/1987 (SACS-CC) *Calendar:* Sem. plan *Degrees:* A *Prof. Accred.:*
Nursing (A) *CEO:* Pres. N. DeWitt Moore,
Jr.
FTE Enroll: 1,472   (703) 628-6094

VIRGINIA INTERMONT COLLEGE
1013 Moore St., Bristol 24201 *Type:* Private
(Southern Baptist) liberal arts *Accred.:* 1925/
1987 (SACS-CC) *Calendar:* Sem. plan *Degrees:* A, B *Prof. Accred.:* Social Work (B)
CEO: Pres. Gary M. Poulton
FTE Enroll: 600   (703) 669-6101

VIRGINIA MILITARY INSTITUTE
Lexington 24450 *Type:* Public (state) primarily for men *System:* Commonwealth of
Virginia Council of Higher Education *Accred.:* 1926/1986 (SACS-CC) *Calendar:*
Sem. plan *Degrees:* B *Prof. Accred.:* Engineering (civil, electrical, mechanical) *CEO:*
Supt. John W. Knapp
FTE Enroll: 1,191   (703) 464-7000

VIRGINIA POLYTECHNIC INSTITUTE AND STATE
UNIVERSITY
210 Burruss Hall, Blacksburg 24061-0131
Type: Public (state) *System:* Commonwealth
of Virginia Council of Higher Education *Accred.:* 1923/1988 (SACS-CC) *Calendar:*
Sem. plan *Degrees:* A, B, M, D *Prof. Accred.:* Accounting (Type A,C), Business
(B,M), Clinical Psychology, Construction
Education (B), Engineering (aerospace, agricultural, chemical, civil, computer, electrical,
engineering mechanics, environmental/sanitary, industrial, materials, mechanical, mining, ocean), Forestry, Home Economics, Interior Design, Landscape Architecture
(B,M), Marriage and Family Therapy (M,D),
Planning (M), Teacher Education (e,s,p),
Theatre, Veterinary Medicine *CEO:* Pres.
Paul E. Torgersen
FTE Enroll: 26,030   (703) 231-6000

VIRGINIA STATE UNIVERSITY
P.O. Box 9001, One Hayden Dr., Petersburg
23806 *Type:* Public (state) liberal arts and
professional *System:* Commonwealth of Virginia Council of Higher Education *Accred.:*

1933/1988 (SACS-CC) *Calendar:* Sem. plan
Degrees: B, M *Prof. Accred.:* Engineering
Technology (electrical, mechanical), Music,
Social Work (B), Teacher Education (e,s,p)
CEO: Pres. Eddie N. Moore, Jr.
FTE Enroll: 4,024   (804) 524-5000

VIRGINIA UNION UNIVERSITY
1500 N. Lombardy St., Richmond 23220-
1711 *Type:* Private (Baptist) liberal arts *Accred.:* 1971/1987 (ATS); 1935/1990 (SACS-
CC) *Calendar:* Sem. plan *Degrees:* B, M, D
Prof. Accred.: Social Work (B) *CEO:* Pres.
S. Dallas Simmons
FTE Enroll: 1,549   (804) 257-5600

VIRGINIA WESLEYAN COLLEGE
Wesleyan Dr., Norfolk 23502-5599 *Type:*
Private (United Methodist) liberal arts and
teachers *Accred.:* 1970/1985 (SACS-CC)
Calendar: Sem. plan *Degrees:* B *Prof. Accred.:* Recreation and Leisure Services *CEO:*
Pres. William T. Greer, Jr.
FTE Enroll: 1,299   (804) 455-3200

VIRGINIA WESTERN COMMUNITY COLLEGE
3095 Colonial Ave., S.W., P.O. Box 14045,
Roanoke 24038 *Type:* Public (state) junior
System: Virginia Community College System *Accred.:* 1969/1993 (SACS-CC) *Calendar:* Sem. plan *Degrees:* A *Prof. Accred.:*
Dental Hygiene, Engineering Technology
(electrical), Nursing (A), Radiography *CEO:*
Pres. Charles L. Downs
FTE Enroll: 3,596   (703) 857-7311

WASHINGTON AND LEE UNIVERSITY
Lexington 24450 *Type:* Private liberal arts
Accred.: 1895/1990 (SACS-CC) *Calendar:*
4-4-2 plan *Degrees:* B, D *Prof. Accred.:*
Business (B), Journalism (B), Law *CEO:*
Pres. John D. Wilson
FTE Enroll: 1,972   (703) 463-8400

WYTHEVILLE COMMUNITY COLLEGE
1000 E. Main St., Wytheville 24382 *Type:*
Public (state) junior *System:* Virginia Community College System *Accred.:* 1970/1985
(SACS-CC) *Calendar:* Qtr. plan *Degrees:* A
Prof. Accred.: Dental Assisting, Dental Hygiene, Medical Laboratory Technology
(AMA), Nursing (A), Physical Therapy Assisting *CEO:* Pres. William F. Snyder
FTE Enroll: 1,832   (703) 228-5541

WASHINGTON

THE ART INSTITUTE OF SEATTLE
2323 Elliott Ave., Seattle 98121-1633 *Type:* Private *Accred.:* 1983 (ACCSCT); 1993 (NASC candidate) *Calendar:* Qtr. plan *Degrees:* A, diplomas *CEO:* Pres. Leslie E. Pritchard
(206) 448-0900

BASTYR UNIVERSITY
144 N.E. 54th St., Seattle 98105 *Type:* Private professional *Accred.:* 1989/1992 (NASC) *Calendar:* Qtr. plan *Degrees:* B, M, D *Prof. Accred.:* Acupuncture (candidate) *CEO:* Pres. Joseph E. Pizzorno, Jr.
Enroll: 323   (206) 523-9585

BELLEVUE COMMUNITY COLLEGE
3000 Landerholm Cir., S.E., Bellevue 98007-6484 *Type:* Public (district) junior *System:* Washington State Board for Community and Technical Colleges *Accred.:* 1970/1990 (NASC) *Calendar:* Qtr. plan *Degrees:* A *Prof. Accred.:* Diagnostic Medical Sonography, Nuclear Medicine Technology, Nursing (A), Radiation Therapy Technology, Radiography *CEO:* Pres. B. Jean Floten
Enroll: 16,879   (206) 641-0111

BIG BEND COMMUNITY COLLEGE
7662 Chanute St., Moses Lake 98837-3299 *Type:* Public (district) junior *System:* Washington State Board for Community and Technical Colleges *Accred.:* 1965/1992 (NASC) *Calendar:* Qtr. plan *Degrees:* A *CEO:* Pres. Gregory G. Fitch
Enroll: 2,753   (509) 762-5351

CENTRAL WASHINGTON UNIVERSITY
208 Bouillon, Ellensburg 98926 *Type:* Public (state) liberal arts and teachers *System:* Washington Higher Education Coordinating Board *Accred.:* 1918/1989 (NASC) *Calendar:* Qtr. plan *Degrees:* B, M *Prof. Accred.:* Construction Education (B), EMT-Paramedic, Engineering Technology (electrical), Medical Technology, Music, Recreation and Leisure Services, Teacher Education (e,s,p) *CEO:* Pres. Ivory V. Nelson
Enroll: 7,697   (509) 963-1111

CENTRALIA COLLEGE
600 W. Locust St., Centralia 98531 *Type:* Public (district) junior *System:* Washington State Board for Community and Technical Colleges *Accred.:* 1948/1992 (NASC) *Calendar:* Qtr. plan *Degrees:* A *CEO:* Pres. Henry P. Kirk
Enroll: 3,292   (206) 736-9391

CITY UNIVERSITY
16661 Northup Way, Bellevue 98008 *Type:* Private *Accred.:* 1978/1993 (NASC) *Calendar:* Qtr. plan *Degrees:* A, B, M *CEO:* Pres. Michael A. Pastore
Enroll: 3,520   (206) 643-2000

CLARK COLLEGE
1800 E. McLoughlin Blvd., Vancouver 98663 *Type:* Public (district) junior *System:* Washington State Board for Community and Technical Colleges *Accred.:* 1948/1989 (NASC) *Calendar:* Qtr. plan *Degrees:* A *Prof. Accred.:* Dental Hygiene, Nursing (A) *CEO:* Pres. Earl P. Johnson
Enroll: 10,488   (206) 694-6521

COGSWELL COLLEGE NORTH
10626 N.E. 37th Cir., Kirkland 98033 *Type:* Independent technical *Accred.:* 1992 (NASC candidate) *Calendar:* Tri. plan *Degrees:* A, B *Prof. Accred.:* Engineering Technology (electrical, mechanical) *CEO:* Pres. Ron Hundley
Enroll: 214   (206) 822-3137

COLUMBIA BASIN COLLEGE
2600 N. 20th Ave., Pasco 99302 *Type:* Public (district) junior *System:* Washington State Board for Community and Technical Colleges *Accred.:* 1960/1990 (NASC) *Calendar:* Qtr. plan *Degrees:* A *CEO:* Pres. Marvin Weiss
Enroll: 6,781   (509) 547-0511

CORNISH COLLEGE OF THE ARTS
710 E. Roy St., Seattle 98102 *Type:* Private professional *Accred.:* 1977/1992 (NASC) *Calendar:* Sem. plan *Degrees:* B *CEO:* Pres. Robert N. Funk
Enroll: 556   (206) 323-1400

EASTERN WASHINGTON UNIVERSITY
Cheney 99004 *Type:* Public (state) liberal arts and teachers *System:* Washington Higher Education Coordinating Board *Accred.:* 1919/1993 (NASC) *Calendar:* Qtr. plan *Degrees:* B, M *Prof. Accred.:* Business (B,M), Computer Science, Counseling, Dental Hygiene, Engineering Technology (computer, mechanical), Music, Nursing (B,M), Physical Therapy, Planning (B,M), Recreation and Leisure Services, Social Work (B,M), Speech-Language Pathology, Teacher Education (e,s,p) *CEO:* Pres. Marshall E. Drummond
Enroll: 8,363   (509) 359-6200

EDMONDS COMMUNITY COLLEGE
20000 68th Ave. W., Lynnwood 98036 *Type:* Public (district) junior *System:* Washington State Board for Community and Technical Colleges *Accred.:* 1973/1993 (NASC) *Calendar:* Qtr. plan *Degrees:* A *Prof. Accred.:* Medical Assisting (AMA) *CEO:* Pres. Thomas C. Nielsen
Enroll: 8,164   (206) 771-1500

EVERETT COMMUNITY COLLEGE
801 Wetmore Ave., Everett 98201-1327 *Type:* Public (district) junior *System:* Washington State Board for Community and Technical Colleges *Accred.:* 1948/1993 (NASC) *Calendar:* Qtr. plan *Degrees:* A *Prof. Accred.:* Nursing (A), Practical Nursing *CEO:* Pres. Susan Carroll
Enroll: 8,088   (206) 259-7151

EVERGREEN STATE COLLEGE
Olympia 98505 *Type:* Public (state) liberal arts *System:* Washington Higher Education Coordinating Board *Accred.:* 1941/1989 (NASC) *Calendar:* Qtr. plan *Degrees:* B, M *CEO:* Pres. Jane L. Jervis
Enroll: 3,410   (206) 866-6000

GONZAGA UNIVERSITY
Spokane 99258 *Type:* Private (Roman Catholic) *Accred.:* 1927/1992 (NASC) *Calendar:* Sem. plan *Degrees:* B, M, D *Prof. Accred.:* Business (B,M), Engineering (civil, electrical, mechanical), Law, Nurse Anesthesia Education, Nursing (B), Teacher Education (e,s,p) *CEO:* Pres. Bernard J. Coughlin, S.J.
Enroll: 5,332   (509) 328-4220

GRAYS HARBOR COLLEGE
Aberdeen 98520 *Type:* Public (district) junior *System:* Washington State Board for Community and Technical Colleges *Accred.:* 1948/1991 (NASC) *Calendar:* Qtr. plan *Degrees:* A *CEO:* Pres. Jewell C. Manspeaker
Enroll: 3,201   (206) 532-9020

GREEN RIVER COMMUNITY COLLEGE
12401 S.E. 320th St., Auburn 98002 *Type:* Public (district) junior *System:* Washington State Board for Community and Technical Colleges *Accred.:* 1967/1993 (NASC) *Calendar:* Qtr. plan *Degrees:* A *Prof. Accred.:* Occupational Therapy Assisting, Physical Therapy Assisting *CEO:* Pres. Richard A. Rutkowski
Enroll: 6,818   (206) 833-9111

HERITAGE COLLEGE
3240 Fort Rd., Toppenish 98948 *Type:* Private (Roman Catholic) liberal arts *Accred.:* 1986/1993 (NASC) *Calendar:* Sem. plan *Degrees:* A, B, M *CEO:* Pres. Kathleen Ross, S.N.J.M.
Enroll: 942   (509) 865-2244

HIGHLINE COMMUNITY COLLEGE
P.O. Box 98000, Des Moines 98198-9800 *Type:* Public (district) junior *System:* Washington State Board for Community and Technical Colleges *Accred.:* 1965/1993 (NASC) *Calendar:* Qtr. plan *Degrees:* A *Prof. Accred.:* Dental Assisting, Medical Assisting (AMA), Nursing (A), Respiratory Therapy *CEO:* Pres. Edward M. Command
Enroll: 9,201   (206) 878-3710

ITT TECHNICAL INSTITUTE
12720 Gateway Dr., Ste. 100, Seattle 98168-3333 *Type:* Private *Accred.:* 1977/1988 (ACCSCT) *Calendar:* Courses of varying lengths *Degrees:* A, B *CEO:* Dir. Carol A. Menck
                                   (206) 244-3300

ITT TECHNICAL INSTITUTE
N. 1050 Argonne Rd., Spokane 99212-2610 *Type:* Private *Accred.:* 1983/1988 (ACCSCT) *Calendar:* Courses of varying lengths *Degrees:* A *CEO:* Dir. Ralph Oscarson
                                   (509) 926-2900

LAKE WASHINGTON TECHNICAL COLLEGE
11605 132nd Ave., N.E., Kirkland 98034
Type: Public (district) *System:* Washington
State Board for Community and Technical
Colleges *Accred.:* 1981/1991 (NASC) *Calendar:* Sem. plan *Degrees:* A, certificates
Prof. Accred.: Dental Assisting *CEO:* Pres.
Donald W. Fowler
Enroll: 4,437   (206) 828-5600

LOWER COLUMBIA COLLEGE
P.O. Box 3010, Longview 98632-0310 *Type:*
Public (district) junior *System:* Washington
State Board for Community and Technical
Colleges *Accred.:* 1948/1992 (NASC) *Calendar:* Qtr. plan *Degrees:* A *Prof. Accred.:*
Nursing (A), Practical Nursing *CEO:* Pres.
Vernon R. Pickett
Enroll: 4,372   (206) 577-2300

LUTHERAN BIBLE INSTITUTE OF SEATTLE
Providence Heights, Issaquah 98027 *Type:*
Private (Lutheran) professional *Accred.:*
1982/1993 (NASC) *Calendar:* Qtr. plan *Degrees:* A, B *CEO:* Pres. Trygve R. Skarsten
Enroll: 156   (206) 392-0400

NORTH SEATTLE COMMUNITY COLLEGE
9600 College Way N., Seattle 98103 *Type:*
Public (district) junior *System:* Seattle Community College District *Accred.:* 1973/1993
(NASC) *Calendar:* Qtr. plan *Degrees:* A
Prof. Accred.: Medical Assisting (AMA)
CEO: Pres. Peter Ku
Enroll: 9,249   (206) 527-3600

NORTHWEST COLLEGE OF THE ASSEMBLIES OF GOD
P.O. Box 579, 5520 108th Ave., N.E., Kirkland 98033 *Type:* Private (Assemblies of
God) *Accred.:* 1952/1992 (AABC); 1973/
1993 (NASC) *Calendar:* Sem. plan *Degrees:*
A, B, certificates, diplomas *CEO:* Pres. Dennis
A. Davis
Enroll: 687   (206) 822-8266

NORTHWEST INDIAN COLLEGE
2522 Kwina Rd., Bellingham 98226 *Type:*
Private (tribal) junior *Accred.:* 1993 (NASC)
Calendar: Sem. plan *Degrees:* A *CEO:* Pres.
Robert J. Lorence
Enroll: 2,821   (206) 676-2772

NORTHWEST INSTITUTE OF ACUPUNCTURE AND
ORIENTAL MEDICINE
1307 N. 45th St., Seattle 98103 *Type:* Private professional *Calendar:* Qtr. plan *Degrees:* M *Prof. Accred.:* Acupuncture *CEO:*
Pres. Frederick O. Lanphear
FTE Enroll: 60   (206) 633-2419

OLYMPIC COLLEGE
1600 Chester Ave., Bremerton 98310 *Type:*
Public (district) junior *System:* Washington
State Board for Community and Technical
Colleges *Accred.:* 1948/1991 (NASC) *Calendar:* Qtr. plan *Degrees:* A *CEO:* Pres.
Wallace A. Simpson
Enroll: 6,589   (206) 478-4544

PACIFIC LUTHERAN UNIVERSITY
Tacoma 98447-0003 *Type:* Private (Lutheran) *Accred.:* 1936/1989 (NASC) *Calendar:*
4-1-4 plan *Degrees:* B, M *Prof. Accred.:* Accounting (Type A), Business (B,M), Computer Science, Marriage and Family Therapy
(M), Music, Nursing (B), Social Work (B),
Teacher Education (e,s,p) *CEO:* Pres. Loren
J. Anderson
Enroll: 3,451   (206) 531-6900

PENINSULA COLLEGE
1502 E. Lauridsen Blvd., Port Angeles
98362 *Type:* Public (district) junior *System:*
Washington State Board for Community and
Technical Colleges *Accred.:* 1965/1992
(NASC) *Calendar:* Qtr. plan *Degrees:* A
CEO: Pres. Joyce Helens
Enroll: 3,084   (206) 452-9277

PIERCE COLLEGE
9401 Farwest Dr., S.W., Tacoma 98498
Type: Public (district) junior *System:* Washington State Board for Community and
Technical Colleges *Accred.:* 1972/1992
(NASC) *Calendar:* Qtr. plan *Degrees:* A
Prof. Accred.: Dental Hygiene, Veterinary
Technology *CEO:* Pres. George A. Delaney
Enroll: 10,260   (206) 964-6500

PUGET SOUND CHRISTIAN COLLEGE
410 Fourth Ave. N., Edmonds 98020 *Type:*
Private (Christian Churches/Churches of
Christ) *Accred.:* 1979/1989 (AABC) *Calendar:* Qtr. plan *Degrees:* A, B, certificates
CEO: Pres. Glen Basey
FTE Enroll: 65   (206) 775-8686

RENTON TECHNICAL COLLEGE
3000 Fourth St., N.E., Renton 98056 *Type:*
Public (district) *System:* Washington State
Board for Community and Technical Col-

leges *Accred.:* 1978/1993 (NASC) *Calendar:* Sem. plan *Degrees:* A, certificates *Prof. Accred.:* Dental Assisting, Surgical Technology *CEO:* Pres. Robert C. Roberts
Enroll: 20,626   (206) 235-2352

St. MARTIN'S COLLEGE
Lacey 98503 *Type:* Private (Roman Catholic) liberal arts *Accred.:* 1933/1992 (NASC) *Calendar:* Sem. plan *Degrees:* A, B, M *Prof. Accred.:* Engineering (civil), Nursing (B) *CEO:* Pres. David R. Spangler
Enroll: 1,417   (206) 491-4700

SEATTLE CENTRAL COMMUNITY COLLEGE
1701 Broadway, Seattle 98122 *Type:* Public (district) junior *System:* Seattle Community College District *Accred.:* 1970/1990 (NASC) *Calendar:* Qtr. plan *Degrees:* A *Prof. Accred.:* Nursing (A), Respiratory Therapy, Surgical Technology *CEO:* Pres. Charles H. Mitchell
Enroll: 7,898   (206) 587-3800

SEATTLE PACIFIC UNIVERSITY
3307 Third Ave. W., Seattle 98119 *Type:* Private (Methodist) liberal arts *Accred.:* 1933/1993 (NASC) *Calendar:* Qtr. plan *Degrees:* B, M *Prof. Accred.:* Engineering (electrical), Music, Nursing (B), Teacher Education (e,s,p) *CEO:* Pres. Curtis A. Martin
Enroll: 8,918   (206) 281-2000

SEATTLE UNIVERSITY
12th Ave. and E. Columbia St., Seattle 98122 *Type:* Private (Roman Catholic) *Accred.:* 1993 (ATS); 1935/1992 (NASC) *Calendar:* Qtr. plan *Degrees:* B, M, D *Prof. Accred.:* Business (B,M), Diagnostic Medical Sonography, Engineering (civil, electrical, mechanical), Nursing (B), Teacher Education (e,s,p) *CEO:* Pres. William J. Sullivan, S.J.
Enroll: 4,830   (206) 296-6000

SHORELINE COMMUNITY COLLEGE
16101 Greenwood Ave. N., Seattle 98133 *Type:* Public (district) junior *System:* Washington State Board for Community and Technical Colleges *Accred.:* 1966/1992 (NASC) *Calendar:* Qtr. plan *Degrees:* A *Prof. Accred.:* Dental Hygiene, Histologic Technology, Medical Laboratory Technolo-

gy (AMA), Medical Record Technology, Nursing (A) *CEO:* Pres. Ronald E. Bell
Enroll: 8,352   (206) 546-4101

SKAGIT VALLEY COLLEGE
2405 College Way, Mount Vernon 98273 *Type:* Public (district) junior *System:* Washington State Board for Community and Technical Colleges *Accred.:* 1948/1989 (NASC) *Calendar:* Qtr. plan *Degrees:* A *Prof. Accred.:* Nursing (A), Practical Nursing *CEO:* Pres. James M. Ford
Enroll: 6,558   (206) 428-1261

SOUTH PUGET SOUND COMMUNITY COLLEGE
2011 Mottman Rd., S.W., Olympia 98502 *Type:* Public (district) junior *System:* Washington State Board for Community and Technical Colleges *Accred.:* 1975/1992 (NASC) *Calendar:* Qtr. plan *Degrees:* A *Prof. Accred.:* Dental Assisting, Nursing (A) *CEO:* Pres. Kenneth J. Minnaert
Enroll: 5,072   (206) 754-7711

SOUTH SEATTLE COMMUNITY COLLEGE
6000 16th Ave., S.W., Seattle 98106 *Type:* Public (district) junior *System:* Seattle Community College District *Accred.:* 1975/1990 (NASC) *Calendar:* Qtr. plan *Degrees:* A *CEO:* Pres. Jerry M. Brockey
Enroll: 6,917   (206) 764-5300

SPOKANE COMMUNITY COLLEGE
N. 1810 Greene St., Spokane 99207 *Type:* Public (district) junior *System:* Community Colleges of Spokane *Accred.:* 1967/1993 (NASC) *Calendar:* Qtr. plan *Degrees:* A *Prof. Accred.:* Cardiovascular Technology, Dental Assisting, EMT-Paramedic, Medical Record Technology, Nursing (A), Respiratory Therapy, Surgical Technology *CEO:* Pres. Donald R. Kolb
Enroll: 5,833   (509) 533-7000

SPOKANE FALLS COMMUNITY COLLEGE
W. 3410 Fort George Wright Dr., Spokane 99204 *Type:* Public (district) junior *System:* Community Colleges of Spokane *Accred.:* 1967/1993 (NASC) *Calendar:* Qtr. plan *Degrees:* A *CEO:* Pres. Vern Jerome Loland
Enroll: 5,949   (509) 459-3500

TACOMA COMMUNITY COLLEGE
5900 S. 12th St., Tacoma 98465 *Type:* Public (district) junior *System:* Washington State

Board for Community and Technical Colleges *Accred.:* 1967/1989 (NASC) *Calendar:* Qtr. plan *Degrees:* A *Prof. Accred.:* EMT-Paramedic, Medical Record Technology, Nursing (A), Radiography, Respiratory Therapy, Respiratory Therapy Technology *CEO:* Pres. Raymond J. Needham
Enroll: 6,319   (206) 566-5000

UNIVERSITY OF PUGET SOUND
Tacoma 98416 *Type:* Private (United Methodist) *Accred.:* 1923/1989 (NASC) *Calendar:* 4-1-4 plan *Degrees:* B, M *Prof. Accred.:* Law, Music, Occupational Therapy, Physical Therapy, Teacher Education (e,s) *CEO:* Pres. Susan Resneck Pierce
Enroll: 4,052   (206) 756-3100

UNIVERSITY OF WASHINGTON
Seattle 98195 *Type:* Public (state) *System:* Washington Higher Education Coordinating Board *Accred.:* 1918/1993 (NASC) *Calendar:* Qtr. plan *Degrees:* B, P, M, D *Prof. Accred.:* Accounting (Type A,C), Audiology, Business (B,M), Clinical Psychology, Combined Prosthodontics, Construction Education (B), Cytotechnology, Dentistry, EMT-Paramedic, Endodontics, Engineering (aerospace, ceramic, chemical, civil, computer, electrical, industrial, mechanical, metallurgical), Forestry, General Practice Residency, Health Services Administration, Journalism (B,M), Landscape Architecture (B,M), Law, Librarianship, Medical Record Administration, Medical Technology, Medicine, Music, Nursing (B,M), Occupational Therapy, Oral and Maxillofacial Surgery, Orthodontics, Periodontics, Physical Therapy, Physician Assisting, Planning (M), Psychology Internship, Public Health, School Psychology, Social Work (B,M), Speech-Language Pathology, Teacher Education (e,s,p), Theatre *CEO:* Pres. William P. Gerberding
Enroll: 40,003   (206) 543-2100

WALLA WALLA COLLEGE
204 S. College Ave., College Place 99324 *Type:* Private (Seventh-Day Adventist) liberal arts *Accred.:* 1932/1992 (NASC) *Calendar:* Qtr. plan *Degrees:* A, B, M *Prof. Accred.:* Engineering (general), Music, Nursing (B), Social Work (B,M) *CEO:* Pres. Niels-Erik Andreasen
Enroll: 1,734   (509) 527-2615

WALLA WALLA COMMUNITY COLLEGE
500 Tausick Way, Walla Walla 99362 *Type:* Public (district) junior *System:* Washington State Board for Community and Technical Colleges *Accred.:* 1969/1990 (NASC) *Calendar:* Qtr. plan *Degrees:* A *Prof. Accred.:* Nursing (A), Respiratory Therapy *CEO:* Pres. Steven L. Van Ausdle
Enroll: 5,904   (509) 522-2500

WASHINGTON STATE UNIVERSITY
Pullman 99164-1046 *Type:* Public (state) *System:* Washington Higher Education Coordinating Board *Accred.:* 1918/1990 (NASC) *Calendar:* Sem. plan *Degrees:* B, P, M, D *Prof. Accred.:* Accounting (Type A,C), Audiology, Business (B,M), Clinical Psychology, Construction Education (B), Counseling Psychology, Dietetics (coordinated), Engineering (agricultural, chemical, civil, electrical, geological/geophysical, materials, mechanical), Forestry, Interior Design, Landscape Architecture (B), Music, Nursing (B,M), Psychology Internship, Recreation and Leisure Services, Speech-Language Pathology, Teacher Education (e,s,p), Veterinary Medicine (limited) *CEO:* Pres. Samuel H. Smith
Enroll: 17,838   (509) 335-3564

WENATCHEE VALLEY COLLEGE
1300 Fifth St., Wenatchee 98801 *Type:* Public (district) junior *System:* Washington State Board for Community and Technical Colleges *Accred.:* 1948/1990 (NASC) *Calendar:* Qtr. plan *Degrees:* A *Prof. Accred.:* Medical Laboratory Technology (AMA), Radiography *CEO:* Interim Pres. Woody Ahn
Enroll: 4,082   (509) 662-1651

WESTERN WASHINGTON UNIVERSITY
Bellingham 98225 *Type:* Public (state) liberal arts and teachers *System:* Washington Higher Education Coordinating Board *Accred.:* 1921/1993 (NASC) *Calendar:* Qtr. plan *Degrees:* B, M *Prof. Accred.:* Audiology, Business (B,M), Computer Science, Counseling, Engineering Technology (electrical, manufacturing), Music, Recreation and Leisure Services, Speech-Language Pathology, Teacher Education (e,s,p) *CEO:* Pres. Karen W. Morse
Enroll: 11,232   (206) 650-3000

WHATCOM COMMUNITY COLLEGE
237 W. Kellogg Rd., Bellingham 98226
Type: Public (district) junior *System:* Washington State Board for Community and Technical Colleges *Accred.:* 1976/1991 (NASC) *Calendar:* Qtr. plan *Degrees:* A *CEO:* Pres. Harold G. Heiner
Enroll: 4,379   (206) 676-2170

WHITMAN COLLEGE
Walla Walla 99362 *Type:* Private liberal arts *Accred.:* 1918/1993 (NASC) *Calendar:* Sem. plan *Degrees:* B *CEO:* Pres. Thomas E. Cronin
Enroll: 1,205˙   (509) 527-5111

WHITWORTH COLLEGE
Spokane 99251-0002 *Type:* Private (United Presbyterian) liberal arts *Accred.:* 1933/1993 (NASC) *Calendar:* 4-1-4 plan *Degrees:* B, M *Prof. Accred.:* Music, Nursing (B,M), Teacher Education (e,s) *CEO:* Pres. William P. Robinson
Enroll: 1,735   (509) 466-1000

YAKIMA VALLEY COMMUNITY COLLEGE
P.O. Box 1647, Yakima 98907 *Type:* Public (district) junior *System:* Washington State Board for Community and Technical Colleges *Accred.:* 1948/1991 (NASC) *Calendar:* Qtr. plan *Degrees:* A, certificates *Prof. Accred.:* Dental Hygiene, Nursing (A), Occupational Therapy Assisting, Radiography *CEO:* Pres. V. Phillip Tullar
Enroll: 6,165   (509) 575-2350

WEST VIRGINIA

ALDERSON-BROADDUS COLLEGE
Philippi 26416 *Type:* Private (Baptist) liberal arts *Accred.:* 1959/1993 (NCA) *Calendar:* Sem. plan *Degrees:* A, B, M *Prof. Accred.:* Nursing (B), Physician Assisting *CEO:* Pres. W. Christian Sizemore
Enroll: 809   (304) 457-1700

APPALACHIAN BIBLE COLLEGE
N. Sand Branch Rd. and Rte. 16, P.O. Box ABC, Bradley 25818 *Type:* Independent (Baptist) *Accred.:* 1967/1987 (AABC) *Calendar:* Sem. plan *Degrees:* A, B, certificates *CEO:* Pres. Daniel L. Anderson
FTE Enroll: 188   (304) 877-6428

BETHANY COLLEGE
Bethany 26032 *Type:* Private (Disciples of Christ) liberal arts *Accred.:* 1926/1989 (NCA) *Calendar:* Sem. plan *Degrees:* B *Prof. Accred.:* Social Work (B), Teacher Education (e,s) *CEO:* Pres. D. Duane Cummins
Enroll: 751   (304) 829-7000

BLUEFIELD STATE COLLEGE
219 Rock St., Bluefield 24701 *Type:* Public (state) liberal arts and teachers *System:* State College System of West Virginia *Accred.:* 1951/1992 (NCA) *Calendar:* Sem. plan *Degrees:* A, B, certificates *Prof. Accred.:* Engineering Technology (architectural, civil/construction, electrical, mechanical, mining), Nursing (A), Radiography *CEO:* Pres. Robert E. Moore
Enroll: 2,931   (304) 327-4030

THE COLLEGE OF WEST VIRGINIA
609 S. Kanawha St., Beckley 25801 *Type:* Private *Accred.:* 1981/1985 (NCA) *Calendar:* Sem. plan *Degrees:* A, B, certificates *Prof. Accred.:* Respiratory Therapy *CEO:* Pres. Charles H. Polk
Enroll: 1,847   (304) 253-7351

CONCORD COLLEGE
Athens 24712 *Type:* Public (state) liberal arts and teachers *System:* State College System of West Virginia *Accred.:* 1931/1988 (NCA) *Calendar:* Sem. plan *Degrees:* A, B *Prof. Accred.:* Social Work (B), Teacher Education (e,s) *CEO:* Pres. Jerry L. Beasley
Enroll: 2,960   (304) 384-3115

DAVIS & ELKINS COLLEGE
100 Campus Dr., Elkins 26241 *Type:* Private (Presbyterian) liberal arts *Accred.:* 1946/1990 (NCA) *Calendar:* 4-1-4 plan *Degrees:* A, B, certificates *Prof. Accred.:* Nursing (A) *CEO:* Pres. Dorothy I. MacConkey
Enroll: 922   (304) 636-1900

FAIRMONT STATE COLLEGE
Locust Ave., Fairmont 26554 *Type:* Public (state) liberal arts and professional *System:* State College System of West Virginia *Accred.:* 1928/1992 (NCA) *Calendar:* Sem. plan *Degrees:* A, B, certificates *Prof. Accred.:* Engineering Technology (civil/construction, electrical, mechanical, mechanical drafting/design, mining), Medical Laboratory Technology (AMA), Medical Record Technology, Nursing (A), Teacher Education (e,s), Veterinary Technology *CEO:* Pres. Robert J. Dillman
Enroll: 6,613   (304) 367-4151

GLENVILLE STATE COLLEGE
200 High St., Glenville 26351 *Type:* Public (state) liberal arts and teachers *System:* State College System of West Virginia *Accred.:* 1949/1992 (NCA) *Calendar:* Sem. plan *Degrees:* A, B *Prof. Accred.:* Teacher Education (e,s) *CEO:* Pres. William K. Simmons
Enroll: 2,358   (304) 462-7361

HUNTINGTON JUNIOR COLLEGE OF BUSINESS
900 Fifth Ave., Huntington 25701 *Type:* Private junior *Accred.:* 1969/1988 (ACISC); 1993 (NCA candidate) *Calendar:* Qtr. plan *Degrees:* A, certificates, diplomas *CEO:* Dir. Carolyn Smith
Enroll: 510   (304) 697-7550

MARSHALL UNIVERSITY
Huntington 25755 *Type:* Public (state) *System:* University System of West Virginia *Accred.:* 1928/1986 (NCA) *Calendar:* Sem. plan *Degrees:* A, B, P, M, D, certificates *Prof. Accred.:* Counseling, Journalism (B,M), Medical Laboratory Technology (AMA), Medical Record Technology, Medical Technology, Medicine, Music, Nursing (A,B), Recreation and Leisure Services, Social Work (B), Speech-Language Pathology,

Teacher Education (e,s,p) *CEO:* Pres. J. Wade Gilley
Enroll: 13,094   (304) 696-2300

MOUNTAIN STATE COLLEGE
Spring at 16th St., Parkersburg 26101 *Type:* Private business *Accred.:* 1977/1989 (AC-ISC) *Calendar:* Qtr. plan *Degrees:* A, certificates, diplomas *CEO:* Pres. Judith Sutton
(304) 485-5487

OHIO VALLEY COLLEGE
College Pwy., Parkersburg 26101 *Type:* Private (Churches of Christ) *Accred.:* 1978/1993 (NCA) *Calendar:* Sem. plan *Degrees:* A, B, certificates *CEO:* Pres. E. Keith Stotts
Enroll: 243   (304) 485-7384

POTOMAC STATE COLLEGE OF WEST VIRGINIA UNIVERSITY
Fort Ave., Keyser 26726 *Type:* Public (state) junior *System:* University System of West Virginia *Accred.:* 1926/1984 (NCA) *Calendar:* Sem. plan *Degrees:* A, certificates *CEO:* Pres. Joseph M. Gratto
Enroll: 1,205   (304) 788-3011

SALEM-TEIKYO UNIVERSITY
Salem 26426 *Type:* Private liberal arts *Accred.:* 1963/1990 (NCA) *Calendar:* Sem. plan *Degrees:* A, B, M *CEO:* Pres. Ronald E. Ohl
Enroll: 970   (304) 782-5234

SHEPHERD COLLEGE
Shepherdstown 25443 *Type:* Public (state) liberal arts and teachers *System:* State College System of West Virginia *Accred.:* 1950/1992 (NCA) *Calendar:* Sem. plan *Degrees:* A, B *Prof. Accred.:* Nursing (A,B), Social Work (B), Teacher Education (e,s) *CEO:* Pres. Michael P. Riccards
Enroll: 3,559   (304) 876-2511

SOUTHERN WEST VIRGINIA COMMUNITY COLLEGE
P.O. Box 2900, Dempsey Branch Rd., Logan 25601-2900 *Type:* Public (state) junior *System:* State College System of West Virginia *Accred.:* 1971/1990 (NCA) *Calendar:* Sem. plan *Degrees:* A, certificates *Prof. Accred.:* Nursing (A) *CEO:* Pres. Harry J. Boyer
Enroll: 3,115   (304) 792-4300

THE UNIVERSITY OF CHARLESTON
2300 MacCorkle Ave., Charleston 25304 *Type:* Private liberal arts *Accred.:* 1958/1988 (NCA) *Calendar:* Sem. plan *Degrees:* A, B, M *Prof. Accred.:* Nursing (A,B), Radiography, Respiratory Therapy, Teacher Education (e,s) *CEO:* Pres. Edwin H. Welch
Enroll: 1,479   (304) 357-4713

WEBSTER COLLEGE
412 Fairmont Ave., Fairmont 26554 *Type:* Private business *Accred.:* 1968/1987 (ACISC) *Calendar:* Qtr. plan *Degrees:* A, certificates, diplomas *CEO:* Dir. Todd A. Matthews, Sr.
(304) 363-8824

BRANCH CAMPUS
N. Bridge Plaza, 2192 N. U.S. Rte. 1, Fort Pierce, FL 34946 *Accred.:* 1988 (ACISC) *CEO:* Dir. Lawrence Del Vecchio
(407) 464-7474

BRANCH CAMPUS
2002 N.W. 13th St., Gainesville, FL 32601 *Accred.:* 1987 (ACISC) *CEO:* Dir. Kathryn Herold
(904) 375-8014

BRANCH CAMPUS
5623 U.S. Hwy. 19, Ste. 300, New Port Richey, FL 34652 *Accred.:* 1993 (ACISC) *CEO:* Dir. Clair Walker
(813) 849-4993

BRANCH CAMPUS
1530 S.W. Third Ave., Ocala, FL 32671 *Accred.:* 1985/1987 (ACISC) *CEO:* Dir. Jay Lambeth
(904) 629-1941

WEST LIBERTY STATE COLLEGE
West Liberty 26074 *Type:* Public (state) liberal arts and professional *System:* State College System of West Virginia *Accred.:* 1942/1988 (NCA) *Calendar:* Sem. plan *Degrees:* A, B *Prof. Accred.:* Dental Hygiene, Medical Technology, Music *CEO:* Pres. Clyde D. Campbell
Enroll: 2,377   (304) 336-5000

WEST VIRGINIA BUSINESS COLLEGE
215 W. Main St., Clarksburg 26301 *Type:* Private business *Accred.:* 1966/1990 (AC-

ISC) *Calendar:* Qtr. plan *Degrees:* A, certificates, diplomas *CEO:* Dir. Jacinda Moore
(304) 624-7695

BRANCH CAMPUS
1052 Main St., Wheeling 26003 *Accred.:* 1990 (ACISC) *CEO:* Admin. Dir. Michelle L. Cottrell
(304) 232-0631

WEST VIRGINIA CAREER COLLEGE
1000 Virginia St., E., Charleston 25301 *Type:* Private business *Accred.:* 1971/1989 (ACISC) *Calendar:* Qtr. plan *Degrees:* A, certificates, diplomas *CEO:* Exec. Vice Pres. Thomas A. Crouse
(304) 345-2820

BRANCH CAMPUS
Nova Village Market Plaza, 1104 Beville Rd., Ste. J, Daytona Beach, FL 32114 *Accred.:* 1989 (ACISC) *CEO:* Exec. Dir. Sharron K. Stephens
(904) 255-0175

WEST VIRGINIA CAREER COLLEGE
148 Willey St., Morgantown 26505 *Type:* Private business *Accred.:* 1953/1988 (ACISC) *Calendar:* Qtr. plan *Degrees:* A, certificates, diplomas *CEO:* Exec. Dir. Patricia A. Callen
(304) 296-8282

BRANCH CAMPUS
200 College Dr., Lemont Furnace, PA 15456 *Accred.:* 1987 (ACISC) *CEO:* Dir. Trisha Gursky
(412) 437-4600

WEST VIRGINIA GRADUATE COLLEGE
P.O. Box 1003, Institute 25112 *Type:* Public (state) graduate only *System:* University System of West Virginia *Accred.:* 1972/1991 (NCA) *Calendar:* Sem. plan *Degrees:* M, certificates *Prof. Accred.:* Teacher Education (e,s,p) *CEO:* Pres. Dennis P. Prisk
Enroll: 3,322   (304) 766-2000

WEST VIRGINIA INSTITUTE OF TECHNOLOGY
Montgomery 25136 *Type:* Public (state) *System:* State College System of West Virginia *Accred.:* 1956/1989 (NCA) *Calendar:* Sem. plan *Degrees:* A, B, M, certificates *Prof. Accred.:* Dental Hygiene, Engineering Technology (electrical, mechanical, mechanical drafting/design), Engineering (chemical, civil, electrical, mechanical), Teacher Education (s) *CEO:* Pres. John P. Carrier
Enroll: 3,051   (304) 442-3071

WEST VIRGINIA NORTHERN COMMUNITY COLLEGE
College Sq., Wheeling 26003 *Type:* Public (state) junior *System:* State College System of West Virginia *Accred.:* 1972/1993 (NCA) *Calendar:* Sem. plan *Degrees:* A, certificates *Prof. Accred.:* Medical Laboratory Technology (AMA), Nursing (A), Respiratory Therapy, Surgical Technology *CEO:* Pres. Ronald M. Hutkin
Enroll: 2,991   (304) 233-5900

WEST VIRGINIA SCHOOL OF OSTEOPATHIC MEDICINE
400 N. Lee St., Lewisburg 24901 *Type:* Public (state) professional *System:* University System of West Virginia *Calendar:* Sem. plan *Degrees:* P *Prof. Accred.:* Osteopathy *CEO:* Pres. Olen E. Jones, Jr., PhD
Enroll: 233   (304) 645-6270

WEST VIRGINIA STATE COLLEGE
Institute 25112 *Type:* Public (state) liberal arts and professional *System:* State College System of West Virginia *Accred.:* 1927/1988 (NCA) *Calendar:* Sem. plan *Degrees:* A, B *Prof. Accred.:* Engineering Technology (electrical), Nuclear Medicine Technology, Recreation and Leisure Services, Social Work (B), Teacher Education (e,s) *CEO:* Pres. Hazo W. Carter, Jr.
Enroll: 4,896   (304) 766-3000

WEST VIRGINIA UNIVERSITY
Box 6201, Morgantown 26506-6201 *Type:* Public (state) *System:* University System of West Virginia *Accred.:* 1926/1984 (NCA) *Calendar:* Sem. plan *Degrees:* B, P, M, D *Prof. Accred.:* Art, Audiology, Business (B,M), Clinical Psychology, Counseling, Counseling Psychology, Dental Hygiene, Dentistry, Diagnostic Medical Sonography, Dietetics (internship), Endodontics, Engineering (aerospace, chemical, civil, computer, electrical, industrial, mechanical, mining, petroleum), Forestry, General Dentistry, General Practice Residency, Journalism (B,M), Landscape Architecture (B), Law, Medical Technology, Medicine, Music, Nu-

clear Medicine Technology, Nursing (B,M), Oral and Maxillofacial Surgery, Orthodontics, Physical Therapy, Psychology Internship, Public Administration, Radiation Therapy Technology, Radiography, Recreation and Leisure Services, Rehabilitation Counseling, Social Work (B,M), Speech-Language Pathology, Teacher Education (e,s,p), Theatre *CEO:* Pres. Neil S. Bucklew
Enroll: 22,712   (304) 293-0111

WEST VIRGINIA UNIVERSITY AT PARKERSBURG
Rte. 5, Box 167-A, Parkersburg 26101 *Type:* Public (state) *System:* University System of West Virginia *Accred.:* 1971/1987 (NCA) *Calendar:* Sem. plan *Degrees:* A, B, certificates *Prof. Accred.:* Nursing (A) *CEO:* Pres. Eldon L. Miller
Enroll: 3,979   (304) 424-8000

WEST VIRGINIA WESLEYAN COLLEGE
College Ave., Buckhannon 26201 *Type:* Private (United Methodist) liberal arts *Accred.:* 1927/1990 (NCA) *Calendar:* 4-1-4 plan *Degrees:* A, B, M *Prof. Accred.:* Music, Nursing (B) *CEO:* Pres. Thomas B. Courtice
Enroll: 1,655   (304) 473-8000

WHEELING JESUIT COLLEGE
316 Washington Ave., Wheeling 26003 *Type:* Private (Roman Catholic) liberal arts *Accred.:* 1962/1989 (NCA) *Calendar:* Sem. plan *Degrees:* B, M *Prof. Accred.:* Nuclear Medicine Technology, Nursing (B), Respiratory Therapy *CEO:* Pres. Thomas S. Acker, S.J.
Enroll: 1,438   (304) 243-2233

WISCONSIN

ALVERNO COLLEGE
3401 S. 39th St., P.O. Box 343922, Milwaukee 53234-3922 *Type:* Private (Roman Catholic) liberal arts primarily for women *Accred.:* 1951/1987 (NCA) *Calendar:* 4-1-4 plan *Degrees:* A, B, certificates *Prof. Accred.:* Music, Nursing (B), Teacher Education (e,s) *CEO:* Pres. Joel Read, O.S.F.
Enroll: 2,514   (414) 382-6000

BELLIN COLLEGE OF NURSING
929 Cass St., P.O. Box 1700, Green Bay 54305 *Type:* Private professional *Accred.:* 1989 (NCA) *Calendar:* 4-1-4 plan *Degrees:* B, certificates *Prof. Accred.:* Nursing (B) *CEO:* Pres. Joyce A. McCollum
Enroll: 214   (414) 433-3560

BELOIT COLLEGE
700 College St., Beloit 53511 *Type:* Private liberal arts *Accred.:* 1913/1987 (NCA) *Calendar:* Sem. plan *Degrees:* B, M, diplomas *CEO:* Pres. Victor E. Ferrall, Jr.
Enroll: 1,187   (608) 363-2000

BLACKHAWK TECHNICAL COLLEGE
6004 Prairie Rd., P.O. Box 5009, Janesville 53547-5009 *Type:* Public (district) 2-year *Accred.:* 1978/1990 (NCA) *Calendar:* Sem. plan *Degrees:* A, certificates, diplomas *Prof. Accred.:* Dental Assisting, Medical Assisting (AMA), Nursing (A), Physical Therapy Assisting *CEO:* Pres./District Dir. James C. Catania
Enroll: 2,485   (608) 756-4121

CARDINAL STRITCH COLLEGE
6801 N. Yates Rd., Milwaukee 53217 *Type:* Private (Roman Catholic) liberal arts *Accred.:* 1953/1984 (NCA) *Calendar:* Sem. plan *Degrees:* A, B, M, certificates *Prof. Accred.:* Nursing (A,B), Teacher Education (e,s) *CEO:* Pres. Mary Lea Schneider, O.S.F.
Enroll: 5,150   (414) 352-5400

CARROLL COLLEGE
100 N. East Ave., Waukesha 53186 *Type:* Private (Presbyterian) liberal arts *Accred.:* 1913/1988 (NCA) *Calendar:* 4-1-4 plan *Degrees:* B, M *Prof. Accred.:* Nursing (B), Social Work (B) *CEO:* Pres. Frank Falcone
Enroll: 2,108   (414) 547-1211

CARTHAGE COLLEGE
2001 Alford Dr., Kenosha 53140 *Type:* Private (Lutheran) liberal arts *Accred.:* 1916/1985 (NCA) *Calendar:* 4-1-4 plan *Degrees:* B, M *Prof. Accred.:* Music, Social Work (B) *CEO:* Pres. F. Gregory Campbell
Enroll: 2,099   (414) 551-8500

CHIPPEWA VALLEY TECHNICAL COLLEGE
620 W. Clairemont Ave., Eau Claire 54701 *Type:* Public (district) 2-year *Accred.:* 1973/1993 (NCA) *Calendar:* Sem. plan *Degrees:* A, certificates, diplomas *Prof. Accred.:* Diagnostic Medical Sonography, Histologic Technology, Medical Laboratory Technology (AMA), Medical Record Technology, Nursing (A), Radiography *CEO:* Dir. Norbert Wurtzel
Enroll: 3,273   (715) 833-6200

COLUMBIA COLLEGE OF NURSING
2121 E. Newport Ave., Milwaukee 53211 *Type:* Private professional *Accred.:* 1988/1993 (NCA) *Calendar:* Sem. plan *Degrees:* B *CEO:* Dean/C.E.O. Marion H. Snyder
Enroll: 321   (414) 961-3530

CONCORDIA UNIVERSITY WISCONSIN
12800 N. Lake Shore Dr., Mequon 53092 *Type:* Private (Lutheran) *Accred.:* 1964/1991 (NCA) *Calendar:* 4-1-4 plan *Degrees:* A, B, M *Prof. Accred.:* Nursing (B) *CEO:* Pres. R. John Buuck
Enroll: 2,312   (414) 243-5700

EDGEWOOD COLLEGE
855 Woodrow St., Madison 53711 *Type:* Private (Roman Catholic) liberal arts *Accred.:* 1958/1988 (NCA) *Calendar:* Sem. plan *Degrees:* A, B, M *Prof. Accred.:* Nursing (B), Teacher Education (e,s) *CEO:* Pres. James A. Ebben
Enroll: 1,690   (608) 257-4861

FOX VALLEY TECHNICAL INSTITUTE
1825 N. Bluemound Dr., P.O. Box 2277, Appleton 54913-2277 *Type:* Public (district) 2-year *Accred.:* 1974/1986 (NCA) *Calendar:* Sem. plan *Degrees:* A, certificates, diplomas *Prof. Accred.:* Dental Assisting, Nursing (A) *CEO:* Pres./District Dir. H. Victor Baldi
Enroll: 4,414   (414) 735-5600

GATEWAY TECHNICAL COLLEGE
3520 30th Ave., Kenosha 53141 *Type:* Public (district) 2-year *Accred.:* 1970/1990 (NCA) *Calendar:* Sem. plan *Degrees:* A, diplomas *Prof. Accred.:* Dental Assisting, Medical Assisting (AMA), Nursing (A), Surgical Technology *CEO:* Interim Pres. William P. Nickolai
Enroll: 20,925   (414) 656-6900

ITT TECHNICAL INSTITUTE
6300 W. Layton Ave., Greenfield 53220-4612 *Type:* Private *Accred.:* 1991 (ACC-SCT) *Calendar:* Courses of varying lengths *Degrees:* A *CEO:* Dir. Elizabeth A. Franck
(414) 282-9494

LAC COURTE OREILLES OJIBWA COMMUNITY COLLEGE
Rte. 2, Box 2357, Hayward 54843 *Type:* Public (tribal) junior *Accred.:* 1993 (NCA) *Calendar:* Sem. plan *Degrees:* A, certificates *CEO:* Pres. Jasjit S. Minhas
Enroll: 417   (715) 634-4790

LAKELAND COLLEGE
P.O. Box 359, Sheboygan 53082-0359 *Type:* Private (United Church of Christ) liberal arts *Accred.:* 1961/1992 (NCA) *Calendar:* 4-1-4 plan *Degrees:* A, B, M *CEO:* Pres. David R. Black
Enroll: 2,773   (414) 565-2111

LAKESHORE TECHNICAL COLLEGE
1290 North Ave., Cleveland 53015 *Type:* Public (district) 2-year *Accred.:* 1977/1992 (NCA) *Calendar:* Sem. plan *Degrees:* A, certificates, diplomas *Prof. Accred.:* Dental Assisting, Medical Assisting (AMA), Nursing (A), Radiography *CEO:* Pres./District Dir. Dennis Ladwig
Enroll: 10,286   (414) 458-4183

LAWRENCE UNIVERSITY
P.O. Box 599, Appleton 54912 *Type:* Private liberal arts *Accred.:* 1913/1989 (NCA) *Calendar:* Qtr. plan *Degrees:* B *Prof. Accred.:* Music *CEO:* Pres. Richard Warch
Enroll: 1,202   (414) 832-7000

MADISON AREA TECHNICAL COLLEGE
3550 Anderson St., Madison 53704 *Type:* Public (district) 2-year *Accred.:* 1969/1993 (NCA) *Calendar:* Sem. plan *Degrees:* A, certificates, diplomas *Prof. Accred.:* Dental

Assisting, Dental Hygiene, Medical Assisting (AMA), Medical Laboratory Technology (AMA), Nursing (A), Occupational Therapy Assisting, Radiography, Respiratory Therapy, Surgical Technology, Veterinary Technology *CEO:* Pres. Beverly S. Simone
Enroll: 19,738   (608) 246-6676

MADISON JUNIOR COLLEGE OF BUSINESS
1110 Spring Harbor Dr., Madison 53705 *Type:* Private junior *Accred.:* 1953/1984 (ACISC); 1992 (NCA candidate) *Calendar:* Tri. plan *Degrees:* A, certificates, diplomas *CEO:* Pres. Jeffry S. Sears
Enroll: 227   (608) 238-4266

MARANTHA BAPTIST BIBLE COLLEGE
745 W. Main St., P.O. Box 438, Watertown 53094 *Type:* Private *Accred.:* 1993 (NCA) *Calendar:* Sem. plan *Degrees:* A, B, M, certificates *CEO:* Pres. Arno Q. Weniger
Enroll: 500   (414) 261-9300

MARIAN COLLEGE OF FOND DU LAC
45 S. National Ave., Fond du Lac 54935 *Type:* Private (Roman Catholic) liberal arts *Accred.:* 1960/1989 (NCA) *Calendar:* Sem. plan *Degrees:* B, M *Prof. Accred.:* Nursing (B), Social Work (B), Teacher Education (e,s) *CEO:* Pres. Matthew G. Flanigan
Enroll: 2,271   (414) 923-7600

MARQUETTE UNIVERSITY
615 N. 11th St., Milwaukee 53233 *Type:* Private (Roman Catholic) *Accred.:* 1922/1993 (NCA) *Calendar:* Sem. plan *Degrees:* A, B, P, M, D *Prof. Accred.:* Accounting (Type A), Business (B,M), Combined Prosthodontics, Dental Hygiene, Dentistry, Endodontics, Engineering (bioengineering, civil, electrical, industrial, mechanical), General Dentistry (prelim. provisional), Journalism (B,M), Law, Nursing (B,M), Orthodontics, Physical Therapy, Social Work (B), Speech-Language Pathology, Teacher Education (e,s) *CEO:* Pres. Albert J. DiUlio, S.J.
Enroll: 11,017   (414) 288-7223

MEDICAL COLLEGE OF WISCONSIN
8701 Watertown Plank Rd., Milwaukee 53226 *Type:* Private *Accred.:* 1922/1987 (NCA) *Calendar:* Sem. plan *Degrees:* B, M, D, certificates *Prof. Accred.:* Community Health/ Preventive Medicine, Medicine, Oral and

Maxillofacial Surgery, Radiation Therapy Technology *CEO:* Pres. T. Michael Bolger
Enroll: 912   (414) 257-8225

MID-STATE TECHNICAL COLLEGE
500 32nd St. N., Wisconsin Rapids 54494 *Type:* Public (district) 2-year *Accred.:* 1979/1984 (NCA) *Calendar:* Sem. plan *Degrees:* A, certificates, diplomas *Prof. Accred.:* Medical Assisting (AMA), Respiratory Therapy, Surgical Technology *CEO:* Pres./District Dir. Mel K. Schneeberg
Enroll: 4,413   (715) 423-5650

MILWAUKEE AREA TECHNICAL COLLEGE
700 W. State St., Milwaukee 53233 *Type:* Public (district) 2-year *Accred.:* 1959/1989 (NCA) *Calendar:* Sem. plan *Degrees:* A, certificates, diplomas *Prof. Accred.:* Dental Hygiene, Dental Laboratory Technology, Funeral Service Education, Medical Assisting (AMA), Medical Laboratory Technology (AMA), Nursing (A), Occupational Therapy Assisting, Physical Therapy Assisting, Practical Nursing, Radiography, Respiratory Therapy, Respiratory Therapy Technology, Surgical Technology *CEO:* Acting Pres. John R. Birkholz
Enroll: 33,144   (414) 278-6600

MILWAUKEE INSTITUTE OF ART AND DESIGN
273 E. Erie St., Milwaukee 53202 *Type:* Private professional *Accred.:* 1987/1993 (NCA) *Calendar:* Sem. plan *Degrees:* B, diplomas *Prof. Accred.:* Art *CEO:* Pres. Terrence J. Coffman
Enroll: 521   (414) 276-7889

MILWAUKEE SCHOOL OF ENGINEERING
1025 N. Broadway, Milwaukee 53202-3109 *Type:* Private professional *Accred.:* 1971/1984 (NCA) *Calendar:* Qtr. plan *Degrees:* A, B, M, certificates *Prof. Accred.:* Engineering Technology (electrical, mechanical), Engineering (architectural, bioengineering, computer, electrical, industrial, mechanical) *CEO:* Pres. Hermann Viets
Enroll: 3,166   (414) 277-7300

MORAINE PARK TECHNICAL COLLEGE
235 N. National Ave., P.O. Box 1940, Fond du Lac 54936-1940 *Type:* Public (district) 2-year *Accred.:* 1975/1985 (NCA) *Calendar:* Sem. plan *Degrees:* A, certificates, diplomas

Prof. Accred.: Medical Record Technology, Nursing (A), Practical Nursing *CEO:* Pres. John J. Shanahan
Enroll: 5,836   (414) 922-8611

MOUNT MARY COLLEGE
2900 N. Menomonee River Pkwy., Milwaukee 53222 *Type:* Private (Roman Catholic) liberal arts primarily for women *Accred.:* 1926/1993 (NCA) *Calendar:* Sem. plan *Degrees:* B, M *Prof. Accred.:* Dietetics (coordinated), Interior Design, Occupational Therapy, Social Work (B), Teacher Education (e,s) *CEO:* Pres. Ruth Hollenbach, S.S.N.D.
Enroll: 1,526   (414) 258-4810

MOUNT SENARIO COLLEGE
1500 W. College Ave., Ladysmith 54848 *Type:* Independent liberal arts *Accred.:* 1975/1992 (NCA) *Calendar:* Sem. plan *Degrees:* A, B *CEO:* Pres. John N. Cable
Enroll: 599   (715) 532-5511

NASHOTAH HOUSE
2777 Mission Rd., Nashotah 53058-9793 *Type:* Private (Episcopal) graduate only *Accred.:* 1954/1988 (ATS) *Calendar:* Sem. plan *Degrees:* M *CEO:* Pres./Dean Gary W. Kriss
FTE Enroll: 37   (414) 646-3371

NICOLET AREA TECHNICAL COLLEGE
Box 518, Rhinelander 54501 *Type:* Public (district) junior *Accred.:* 1975/1990 (NCA) *Calendar:* Sem. plan *Degrees:* A, certificates, diplomas *Prof. Accred.:* Nursing (A) *CEO:* Pres. Adrian Lorbetske
Enroll: 1,701   (715) 365-4410

NORTHCENTRAL TECHNICAL COLLEGE
1000 Campus Dr., Wausau 54401 *Type:* Public (district) 2-year *Accred.:* 1970/1988 (NCA) *Calendar:* Sem. plan *Degrees:* A, certificates, diplomas *Prof. Accred.:* Dental Hygiene, Nursing (A), Radiography, Surgical Technology *CEO:* Pres. Robert Ernst
Enroll: 6,526   (715) 675-3331

NORTHEAST WISCONSIN TECHNICAL COLLEGE
P.O. Box 19042, 2740 W. Mason St., Green Bay 54307 *Type:* Public (district) 2-year *Accred.:* 1976/1991 (NCA) *Calendar:* Sem. plan *Degrees:* A, certificates, diplomas *Prof. Accred.:* Dental Assisting, Dental Hygiene, Medical Assisting (AMA), Nursing (A),

Physical Therapy Assisting, Respiratory Therapy, Surgical Technology *CEO:* Pres. Gerald Prindiville
Enroll: 4,839 (414) 498-5400

NORTHLAND COLLEGE
1411 Ellis Ave., Ashland 54806 *Type:* Private (United Church of Christ) liberal arts *Accred.:* 1957/1991 (NCA) *Calendar:* 4-1-4 plan *Degrees:* B *CEO:* Pres. Robert R. Parsonage
Enroll: 787 (715) 682-1699

NORTHWESTERN COLLEGE
1300 Western Ave., Watertown 53094 *Type:* Private (Evangelical Lutheran) liberal arts *Accred.:* 1981/1984 (NCA) *Calendar:* Sem. plan *Degrees:* B *CEO:* Pres. Robert J. Voss
Enroll: 205 (414) 261-4352

RIPON COLLEGE
300 Seward St., P.O. Box 248, Ripon 54971 *Type:* Private liberal arts *Accred.:* 1913/1990 (NCA) *Calendar:* Sem. plan *Degrees:* B *CEO:* Pres. William R. Stott, Jr.
Enroll: 793 (414) 748-8115

SACRED HEART SCHOOL OF THEOLOGY
P.O. Box 429, 7335 S. Hwy. 100, Hales Corners 53130-0429 *Type:* Private (Roman Catholic) graduate only *Accred.:* 1981/1988 (ATS) *Calendar:* Sem. plan *Degrees:* M *CEO:* Pres. John A. Kasparek
FTE Enroll: 124 (414) 425-8300

ST. FRANCIS SEMINARY
3257 S. Lake Dr., St. Francis 53235 *Type:* Private (Roman Catholic) *Accred.:* 1976/1990 (ATS); 1963/1991 (NCA) *Calendar:* Sem. plan *Degrees:* M *CEO:* Rector David A. Lichter
Enroll: 95 (414) 747-6400

ST. NORBERT COLLEGE
100 Grant St., De Pere 54115-2099 *Type:* Private (Roman Catholic) liberal arts *Accred.:* 1934/1992 (NCA) *Calendar:* Sem. plan *Degrees:* B, M *CEO:* Pres. Thomas A. Manion
Enroll: 1,965 (414) 337-3949

SILVER LAKE COLLEGE
2406 S. Alverno Rd., Manitowoc 54220 *Type:* Private (Roman Catholic) liberal arts *Accred.:* 1959/1988 (NCA) *Calendar:* Sem.

plan *Degrees:* A, B, M *Prof. Accred.:* Music, Nursing (B), Teacher Education (e,s) *CEO:* Pres. Barbara Belinske, O.S.F.
Enroll: 925 (414) 684-6691

SOUTHWEST WISCONSIN TECHNICAL COLLEGE
1800 Bronson Blvd., Fennimore 53809 *Type:* Public (district) 2-year *Accred.:* 1976/1988 (NCA) *Calendar:* Sem. plan *Degrees:* A, certificates, diplomas *Prof. Accred.:* Nursing (A), Practical Nursing *CEO:* Pres./District Dir. Richard A. Rogers
Enroll: 2,392 (608) 822-3262

STRATTON COLLEGE
1300 N. Jackson St., Milwaukee 53202-2608 *Type:* Private junior *Accred.:* 1966/1987 (ACISC) *Calendar:* Qtr. plan *Degrees:* A, certificates, diplomas *Prof. Accred.:* Medical Assisting (AMA) *CEO:* Dir. Robert H. Ley
(414) 276-5200

UNIVERSITY OF WISCONSIN CENTERS
150 E. Gilman St., P.O. Box 8680, Madison 53708-8680 *Type:* Public (state) *System:* University of Wisconsin System *Accred.:* 1977/1993 (NCA) *Calendar:* Sem. plan *Degrees:* A *CEO:* Chanc. Lee E. Grugel
Enroll: 10,960 (608) 262-1783

UNIVERSITY OF WISCONSIN CENTER—BARABOO-SAUK COUNTY
1006 Connie Rd., Baraboo 53913 *CEO:* Dean Aural M. Umhoefer
(608) 356-8351

UNIVERSITY OF WISCONSIN CENTER—BARRON COUNTY
1800 College Dr., Rice Lake 54868 *CEO:* Dean Mary H. Somers
(715) 234-8176

UNIVERSITY OF WISCONSIN CENTER—FOND DU LAC
Campus Dr., Fond du Lac 54935 *CEO:* Dean Bradley M. Gottfried
(414) 929-3600

UNIVERSITY OF WISCONSIN CENTER—FOX VALLEY
1478 Midway Rd., P.O. Box 8002, Menasha 54952-8002 *CEO:* Interim Dean Janice S. Green
(414) 832-2600

UNIVERSITY OF WISCONSIN CENTER—
MANITOWOC COUNTY
705 Viebahn St., Manitowoc 54220-6699
CEO: Dean Roland A. Baldwin
(414) 683-4700

UNIVERSITY OF WISCONSIN CENTER—
MARATHON COUNTY
518 S. Seventh Ave., Wausau 54401
CEO: Dean G. Dennis Massey
(715) 845-9602

UNIVERSITY OF WISCONSIN CENTER—
MARINETTE COUNTY
750 W. Bay Shore St., Marinette 54143
CEO: Dean William A. Schmidtke
(715) 735-7477

UNIVERSITY OF WISCONSIN CENTER—
MARSHFIELD-WOOD COUNTY
P.O. Box 150, Marshfield 54449 *CEO:*
Dean Carol L. McCart
(715) 387-1147

UNIVERSITY OF WISCONSIN CENTER—
RICHLAND
Hwy. 14 W., Richland Center 53581
CEO: Dean Dion Q. Kempthorne
(608) 647-6186

UNIVERSITY OF WISCONSIN CENTER—ROCK
COUNTY
2909 Kellogg Ave., Janesville 53546
CEO: Dean Jane E. Crisler
(608) 758-6522

UNIVERSITY OF WISCONSIN CENTER—
SHEBOYGAN COUNTY
One University Dr., Sheboygan 53081
CEO: Dean G. Kathleen O'Connor
(414) 459-6600

UNIVERSITY OF WISCONSIN CENTER—
WASHINGTON COUNTY
400 University Dr., West Bend 53095
CEO: Dean Joel M. Rodney
(414) 335-5200

UNIVERSITY OF WISCONSIN CENTER—
WAUKESHA COUNTY
1500 University Dr., Waukesha 53188
CEO: Dean Mary S. Knudten
(414) 521-5200

UNIVERSITY OF WISCONSIN—EAU CLAIRE
P.O. Box 4004, Eau Claire 54702 *Type:* Public (state) liberal arts and teachers *System:* University of Wisconsin System *Accred.:* 1950/1990 (NCA) *Calendar:* Sem. plan *Degrees:* A, B, P, M *Prof. Accred.:* Business (B), Journalism (B), Music, Nursing (B,M), Social Work (B), Speech-Language Pathology *CEO:* Chanc. Larry G. Schnack
Enroll: 10,431   (715) 836-2637

UNIVERSITY OF WISCONSIN—GREEN BAY
2420 Nicolet Dr., Green Bay 54311 *Type:* Public (state) liberal arts and teachers *System:* University of Wisconsin System *Accred.:* 1972/1988 (NCA) *Calendar:* Sem. plan *Degrees:* A, B, M *Prof. Accred.:* Music, Nursing (B), Social Work (B) *CEO:* Chanc. Mark Perkins
Enroll: 4,933   (414) 465-2000

UNIVERSITY OF WISCONSIN—LA CROSSE
1725 State St., La Crosse 54601 *Type:* Public (state) liberal arts and teachers *System:* University of Wisconsin System *Accred.:* 1928/1986 (NCA) *Calendar:* Sem. plan *Degrees:* A, B, M *Prof. Accred.:* Business (B,M), Community Health, Music, Physical Therapy, Recreation and Leisure Services, Social Work (B), Teacher Education (e,s,p) *CEO:* Chanc. Judith L. Kuipers, Ph.D.
Enroll: 8,362   (608) 785-8000

UNIVERSITY OF WISCONSIN—MADISON
500 Lincoln Dr., Madison 53706 *Type:* Public (state) liberal arts and teachers *System:* University of Wisconsin System *Accred.:* 1913/1989 (NCA) *Calendar:* Sem. plan *Degrees:* B, P, M, D, certificates *Prof. Accred.:* Accounting (Type A,B,C), Art, Audiology, Business (B,M), Clinical Psychology, Construction Education (B), Counseling Psychology, Cytotechnology, Diagnostic Medical Sonography, Dietetics (coordinated), Dietetics (internship), Engineering (agricultural, chemical, civil, electrical, engineering mechanics, industrial, mechanical, metallurgical, nuclear, surveying), Forestry, Health Services Administration, Interior Design, Journalism (B,M), Landscape Architecture (B), Law, Librarianship, Medical Technology, Medicine, Music, Nursing (B,M), Occupational Therapy, Physical Therapy, Physician Assisting, Planning (M), Psychology In-

ternship, Public Affairs and Administration, Radiation Therapy Technology, Radiography, Rehabilitation Counseling, School Psychology, Social Work (B,M), Speech-Language Pathology, Theatre, Veterinary Medicine *CEO:* Chanc. David Ward
Enroll: 37,878   (608) 262-1234

UNIVERSITY OF WISCONSIN—MILWAUKEE
P.O. Box 413, Milwaukee 53201 *Type:* Public (state) liberal arts and teachers *System:* University of Wisconsin System *Accred.:* 1969/1985 (NCA) *Calendar:* Sem. plan *Degrees:* B, P, M, D *Prof. Accred.:* Business (B,M), Clinical Psychology, Engineering (civil, electrical, industrial, materials, mechanical), Librarianship, Medical Record Administration, Medical Technology, Music, Nursing (B,M), Occupational Therapy, Planning (M), Public Administration, Rehabilitation Counseling, Social Work (B,M), Speech-Language Pathology *CEO:* Chanc. John H. Schroeder
Enroll: 24,343   (414) 229-4331

UNIVERSITY OF WISCONSIN—OSHKOSH
800 Algoma Blvd., Oshkosh 54901 *Type:* Public (state) liberal arts and teachers *System:* University of Wisconsin System *Accred.:* 1915/1987 (NCA) *Calendar:* Sem. plan *Degrees:* A, B, M *Prof. Accred.:* Audiology, Business (B,M), Counseling, Journalism (B), Music, Nursing (B,M), Social Work (B), Speech-Language Pathology *CEO:* Chanc. John E. Kerrigan
Enroll: 10,970   (414) 424-1234

UNIVERSITY OF WISCONSIN—PARKSIDE
Box 2000, Kenosha 53141-2000 *Type:* Public (state) liberal arts and teachers *System:* University of Wisconsin System *Accred.:* 1972/1993 (NCA) *Calendar:* Sem. plan *Degrees:* B, M *CEO:* Interim Chanc. John C. Stockwell
Enroll: 4,993   (414) 595-2345

UNIVERSITY OF WISCONSIN—PLATTEVILLE
One University Plaza, Platteville 53818-3099 *Type:* Public (state) liberal arts and teachers *System:* University of Wisconsin System *Accred.:* 1918/1987 (NCA) *Calendar:* Sem. plan *Degrees:* A, B, M *Prof. Accred.:* Engineering (civil, electrical, industrial, mechanical), Music (associate), Teacher

Education (e,s,p) *CEO:* Chanc. Robert G. Culbertson
Enroll: 5,265   (608) 342-1234

UNIVERSITY OF WISCONSIN—RIVER FALLS
River Falls 54022 *Type:* Public (state) liberal arts and teachers *System:* University of Wisconsin System *Accred.:* 1935/1988 (NCA) *Calendar:* Qtr. plan *Degrees:* A, B, M *Prof. Accred.:* Journalism (B), Music (associate), Social Work (B), Speech-Language Pathology *CEO:* Chanc. Gary A. Thibodeau
Enroll: 5,395   (715) 425-3201

UNIVERSITY OF WISCONSIN—STEVENS POINT
2100 Main St., Stevens Point 54481 *Type:* Public (state) liberal arts and teachers *System:* University of Wisconsin System *Accred.:* 1916/1988 (NCA) *Calendar:* Sem. plan *Degrees:* A, B, M *Prof. Accred.:* Art (associate), Audiology, Dance, Forestry, Music, Speech-Language Pathology, Theatre (associate) *CEO:* Chanc. Keith R. Sanders
Enroll: 9,202   (715) 346-0123

UNIVERSITY OF WISCONSIN—STOUT
Menomonie 54751-0790 *Type:* Public (state) liberal arts and teachers *System:* University of Wisconsin System *Accred.:* 1928/1986 (NCA) *Calendar:* Sem. plan *Degrees:* B, P, M *Prof. Accred.:* Art, Marriage and Family Therapy (M), Teacher Education (e,s,p) *CEO:* Chanc. Charles W. Sorensen
Enroll: 7,343   (715) 232-2441

UNIVERSITY OF WISCONSIN—SUPERIOR
1800 Grand Ave., Superior 54880 *Type:* Public (state) liberal arts and teachers *System:* University of Wisconsin System *Accred.:* 1916/1993 (NCA) *Calendar:* Sem. plan *Degrees:* A, B, P, M *Prof. Accred.:* Music, Social Work (B) *CEO:* Chanc. Betty J. Youngblood
Enroll: 2,969   (715) 394-8101

UNIVERSITY OF WISCONSIN—WHITEWATER
800 W. Main St., Whitewater 53190 *Type:* Public (state) liberal arts and teachers *System:* University of Wisconsin System *Accred.:* 1915/1986 (NCA) *Calendar:* Sem. plan *Degrees:* A, B, M *Prof. Accred.:* Business (B,M), Music, Social Work (B), Speech-Language Pathology, Teacher Edu-

cation (e,s,p) *CEO:* Chanc. H. Gaylon Greenhill
Enroll: 10,512   (414) 472-1918

VITERBO COLLEGE
815 S. Ninth St., La Crosse 54601 *Type:* Private (Roman Catholic) liberal arts *Accred.:* 1954/1989 (NCA) *Calendar:* Sem. plan *Degrees:* B, M *Prof. Accred.:* Dietetics (coordinated), Music, Nursing (B), Teacher Education (e,s) *CEO:* Pres. William J. Medland
Enroll: 1,392   (608) 791-0401

WAUKESHA COUNTY TECHNICAL COLLEGE
800 Main St., Pewaukee 53072 *Type:* Public (district) 2-year *Accred.:* 1975/1990 (NCA) *Calendar:* Sem. plan *Degrees:* A, certificates, diplomas *Prof. Accred.:* Medical Assisting (AMA), Nursing (A), Surgical Technology *CEO:* Pres. Richard Todd Anderson
Enroll: 16,257   (414) 691-5566

WESTERN WISCONSIN TECHNICAL COLLEGE
304 N. Sixth St., Box 908, La Crosse 54602 *Type:* Public (district) 2-year *Accred.:* 1972/1992 (NCA) *Calendar:* Qtr. plan *Degrees:* A, certificates, diplomas *Prof. Accred.:* Dental Assisting, Electroneurodiagnostic Technology, Medical Assisting (AMA), Medical Laboratory Technology (AMA), Medical Record Technology, Nursing (A), Physical

Therapy Assisting, Radiography, Respiratory Therapy, Surgical Technology *CEO:* Pres./District Dir. James Lee Rasch
Enroll: 4,006   (608) 785-9101

WISCONSIN INDIANHEAD TECHNICAL COLLEGE
HCR 69, Box 10B, 505 Pine Ridge Rd., Shell Lake 54871 *Type:* Public (district) 2-year *Accred.:* 1979/1984 (NCA) *Calendar:* Sem. plan *Degrees:* A, certificates, diplomas *Prof. Accred.:* Medical Assisting (AMA), Nursing (A) *CEO:* Pres./District Dir. David R. Hildebrand
Enroll: 3,341   (715) 468-2815

WISCONSIN LUTHERAN COLLEGE
8830 W. Bluemond Rd., Milwaukee 53226 *Type:* Private (Lutheran) *Accred.:* 1987/1990 (NCA) *Calendar:* Sem. plan *Degrees:* B *CEO:* Pres. Gary J. Greenfield
Enroll: 323   (414) 774-8620

WISCONSIN SCHOOL OF PROFESSIONAL PSYCHOLOGY
9120 W. Hampton Ave., Ste. 212, Milwaukee 53225 *Type:* Private professional *Accred.:* 1987/1990 (NCA) *Calendar:* Sem. plan *Degrees:* D *CEO:* Pres. Samuel H. Friedman
Enroll: 124   (414) 464-9777

WYOMING

CASPER COLLEGE
125 College Dr., Casper 82601 *Type:* Public (district) junior *System:* Wyoming Community College Commission *Accred.:* 1960/1989 (NCA) *Calendar:* Sem. plan *Degrees:* A, certificates *Prof. Accred.:* Music, Nursing (A), Radiography *CEO:* Pres. Leroy Strausner
Enroll: 4,088   (307) 268-2110

CENTRAL WYOMING COLLEGE
2660 Peck Ave., Riverton 82501 *Type:* Public (district) junior *System:* Wyoming Community College Commission *Accred.:* 1976/1988 (NCA) *Calendar:* Sem. plan *Degrees:* A, certificates, diplomas *Prof. Accred.:* Nursing (A) *CEO:* Pres. Jo Anne McFarland
Enroll: 1,607   (307) 856-9291

EASTERN WYOMING COLLEGE
3200 W. C St., Torrington 82240 *Type:* Public (district) junior *System:* Wyoming Community College Commission *Accred.:* 1976/1991 (NCA) *Calendar:* Sem. plan *Degrees:* A, certificates *Prof. Accred.:* Veterinary Technology *CEO:* Pres. Roy B. Mason
Enroll: 1,982   (307) 532-7111

LARAMIE COUNTY COMMUNITY COLLEGE
1400 E. College Dr., Cheyenne 82007 *Type:* Public (district) junior *System:* Wyoming Community College Commission *Accred.:* 1975/1990 (NCA) *Calendar:* Sem. plan *Degrees:* A, certificates *Prof. Accred.:* Dental Hygiene, Nursing (A), Practical Nursing, Radiography *CEO:* Pres. Charles H. Bohlen
Enroll: 4,291   (307) 778-1102

NORTHWEST COLLEGE
231 W. Sixth St., Powell 82435 *Type:* Public (district) junior *System:* Wyoming Community College Commission *Accred.:* 1964/1991 (NCA) *Calendar:* Sem. plan *Degrees:* A, certificates *Prof. Accred.:* Nursing (A), Practical Nursing *CEO:* Pres. John P. Hanna
Enroll: 1,937   (307) 754-6111

SHERIDAN COLLEGE
P.O. Box 1500, Sheridan 82801 *Type:* Public (district) junior *System:* Wyoming Community College Commission *Accred.:* 1968/1988 (NCA) *Calendar:* Sem. plan *Degrees:* A, certificates *Prof. Accred.:* Dental Assisting, Dental Hygiene, Nursing (A), Practical Nursing *CEO:* Pres. Stephen J. Maier
Enroll: 1,948   (307) 674-6446

GILLETTE CAMPUS
720 W. 8th St., Gillette 82716 *Prof. Accred.:* Nursing (A) *CEO:* Provost Jerome L. Winter
                                   (307) 686-0254

UNIVERSITY OF WYOMING
P.O. Box 3434, University Sta., Laramie 82071 *Type:* Public (state) *Accred.:* 1976/1990 (NCA) *Calendar:* Sem. plan *Degrees:* B, P, M, D *Prof. Accred.:* Audiology, Business (B,M), Clinical Psychology, Counseling, Engineering (agricultural, architectural, chemical, civil, electrical, mechanical, petroleum), Law, Medical Technology, Music, Nursing (B,M), Psychology Internship, Social Work (B), Speech-Language Pathology, Teacher Education (e,s,p) *CEO:* Pres. Terry P. Roark
Enroll: 12,052   (307) 766-1121

WESTERN WYOMING COLLEGE
P.O. Box 428, Rock Springs 82901 *Type:* Public (district) junior *System:* Wyoming Community College Commission *Accred.:* 1976/1987 (NCA) *Calendar:* Sem. plan *Degrees:* A, certificates *Prof. Accred.:* Radiography, Respiratory Therapy, Respiratory Therapy Technology *CEO:* Pres. Tex Boggs
Enroll: 2,579   (307) 382-1600

OUTSIDE THE UNITED STATES

CANADA

ACADIA DIVINITY COLLEGE
Wolfville, Nova Scotia B0P 1X0 *Type:* Private (Baptist) graduate only *Accred.:* 1984/1990 (ATS) *Calendar:* Sem. plan *Degrees:* M, D *CEO:* Prin./Dean Andrew D. MacRae
FTE Enroll: 120   (902) 542-2285

ATLANTIC SCHOOL OF THEOLOGY
640 Francklyn St., Halifax, Nova Scotia B3H 3B5 *Type:* Private (interdenominational) graduate only *Accred.:* 1976/1983 (ATS) *Calendar:* Sem. plan *Degrees:* M *CEO:* Pres. Gordon E. MacDermid
FTE Enroll: 109   (902) 423-6939

BETHANY BIBLE COLLEGE
26 Western St., Sussex, New Brunswick E0E 1P0 *Type:* Private (Wesleyan) *Accred.:* 1987/1992 (AABC) *Calendar:* Sem. plan *Degrees:* B, certificates, diplomas *CEO:* Pres. David Medders
FTE Enroll: 130   (506) 432-4400

BRIERCREST BIBLE COLLEGE
510 College Dr., Caronport, Saskatchewan S0H 0S0 *Type:* Independent *Accred.:* 1976/1986 (AABC) *Calendar:* Sem. plan *Degrees:* A, B, certificates *CEO:* Pres. John Barkman
FTE Enroll: 668   (306) 756-3200

CANADIAN BIBLE COLLEGE AND THEOLOGICAL SEMINARY
4400 Fourth Ave., Regina, Saskatchewan S4T 0H8 *Type:* Private (Christian and Missionary Alliance) *Accred.:* 1961/1991 (AABC); 1989 (ATS) *Calendar:* Sem. plan *Degrees:* A, B, M *CEO:* Pres. Robert A. Rose
FTE Enroll: 339   (306) 545-1515

CATHERINE BOOTH BIBLE COLLEGE
447 Webb Pl., Winnipeg, Manitoba R3B 2P2 *Type:* Private (Salvation Army) *Accred.:* 1991 (AABC) *Calendar:* Sem. plan *Degrees:* A, B, certificates *CEO:* Pres. Lloyd Hetherington
FTE Enroll: 69   (204) 947-6701

COLUMBIA BIBLE COLLEGE
2940 Clearbrook Rd., Clearbrook, British Columbia V2T 2Z8 *Type:* Private (Mennonite Brethren/Conference of Mennonites) *Accred.:* 1991 (AABC) *Calendar:* Sem. plan *Degrees:* A, B, certificates *CEO:* Pres. Walter Unger
FTE Enroll: 269   (604) 853-3358

DALHOUSIE UNIVERSITY
Halifax, Nova Scotia B3H 3J5 *Type:* Private *Calendar:* Sem. plan *Degrees:* B, P, M, D *Prof. Accred.:* Dentistry, Health Services Administration, Librarianship, Medicine, Oral and Maxillofacial Surgery, Periodontics *CEO:* Pres./Vice Chanc. Howard C. Clark, Ph.D.
Enroll: 11,046   (902) 424-2211

EASTERN PENTECOSTAL BIBLE COLLEGE
780 Argyle St., Peterborough, Ontario K9H 5T2 *Type:* Private (Pentacostal Assemblies of Canada) *Accred.:* 1989 (AABC) *Calendar:* Sem. plan *Degrees:* B, certificates, diplomas *CEO:* Pres. Robert Taitinger
FTE Enroll: 474   (705) 748-9111

EMMANUEL BIBLE COLLEGE
100 Fergus Ave., Kitchener, Ontario N2A 2H2 *Type:* Private (Missionary Church) *Accred.:* 1982/1992 (AABC) *Calendar:* Sem. plan *Degrees:* B, diplomas *CEO:* Pres. Thomas Dow
FTE Enroll: 180   (519) 894-8900

EMMANUEL COLLEGE OF VICTORIA UNIVERSITY
75 Queen's Park Crescent, E., Toronto, Ontario M5S 1K7 *Type:* Private (United Church of Canada) graduate only *Accred.:* 1938/1991 (ATS) *Calendar:* Sem. plan *Degrees:* M, D *CEO:* Prin. John C. Hoffman
FTE Enroll: 154   (416) 585-4539

HURON COLLEGE FACULTY OF THEOLOGY
1349 Western Rd., London, Ontario N6G 1H3 *Type:* Private (Anglican) graduate only *Accred.:* 1981/1985 (ATS) *Calendar:* Sem. plan *Degrees:* M *CEO:* Prin. Charles J. Jago
FTE Enroll: 39   (519) 438-7224

JOINT BOARD OF THEOLOGICAL COLLEGES
3473 University St., Montreal, Quebec H3A
2A8 *Type:* Private (interdenominational)
graduate only *Accred.:* 1989 (ATS) *Calendar:* Sem. plan *Degrees:* M *CEO:* Admin.
Ofcr. John Simons
FTE Enroll: 13　　　　　　　(514) 849-8511

KNOX COLLEGE
59 St. George St., Toronto, Ontario M5S
2E6 *Type:* Private (Presbyterian Church in
Canada) graduate only *Accred.:* 1948/1990
(ATS) *Calendar:* Sem. plan *Degrees:* M, D
CEO: Prin. Arthur Van Seters
FTE Enroll: 96　　　　　　　(416) 978-4500

LUTHERAN THEOLOGICAL SEMINARY
114 Seminary Crescent, Saskatoon,
Saskatchewan S7N 0X3 *Type:* Private
(Evangelical Lutheran Church) graduate
only *Accred.:* 1976/1988 (ATS) *Calendar:*
Sem. plan *Degrees:* M *CEO:* Pres. Roger W.
Nostbakken
FTE Enroll: 66　　　　　　　(306) 975-7004

MCGILL UNIVERSITY
845 Sherbrooke St. W., Montreal, Quebec
H3A 2T5 *Type:* Private (interdenominational)
Accred.: 1952/1990 (ATS) *Calendar:* Sem.
plan *Degrees:* B, M, D *Prof. Accred.:* Clinical Psychology, Dentistry, Librarianship,
Medicine, Oral and Maxillofacial Surgery,
Physical Therapy, Psychology Internship
CEO: Prin./Vice Chanc. D.L. Johnston
Enroll: 30,314　　　　　　　(514) 398-4455

MCMASTER UNIVERSITY
Hamilton, Ontario L8S 4L8 *Type:* Private
Accred.: 1954/1987 (ATS) *Calendar:* Sem.
plan *Degrees:* P, M, D *Prof. Accred.:* Medicine *CEO:* Pres. William H. Brackney
Enroll: 16,628　　　　　　　(416) 525-9140

MEMORIAL UNIVERSITY OF NEWFOUNDLAND
St. John's, Newfoundland A1B 3V6 *Type:*
Public *Calendar:* Sem. plan *Degrees:* B, P,
M, D *Prof. Accred.:* Medicine *CEO:* Pres.
Arthur May
Enroll: 15,606　　　　　　　(709) 737-8000

NER ISRAEL YESHIVA COLLEGE OF TORONTO
8950 Bathurst St., P.O. Box 5002, Thornhill,
Ontario L3T 6K1 *Type:* Private professional

Accred.: 1980/1989 (AARTS) *Calendar:* Sem.
plan *Degrees:* B *CEO:* Pres. S. Hofstadter
Enroll: 41　　　　　　　　(416) 731-1224

NEWMAN THEOLOGICAL COLLEGE
15611 St. Albert Tr., Edmonton, Alberta
T5L 4H8 *Type:* Private (Roman Catholic)
graduate only *Accred.:* 1991 (ATS) *Calendar:* Sem. plan *Degrees:* M *CEO:* Pres.
Kevin Carr
FTE Enroll: 83　　　　　　　(403) 447-2993

NORTH AMERICAN BAPTIST COLLEGE
11525 23rd Ave., Edmonton, Alberta T6J
4T3 *Type:* Private (North American Baptist
Conference) *Accred.:* 1969/1989 (AABC)
Calendar: Sem. plan *Degrees:* A, B, certificates, diplomas *CEO:* Pres. Paul Siewert
FTE Enroll: 240　　　　　　　(403) 437-1960

NORTHWEST BAPTIST THEOLOGICAL COLLEGE
22606 76A Ave., P.O. Box 790, Langley,
British Columbia V3A 8B8 *Type:* Private
(Fellowship of Evangelical Baptist Churches) *Accred.:* 1989 (AABC) *Calendar:* Sem.
plan *Degrees:* A, B, certificates *CEO:* Pres.
Doug Harris
FTE Enroll: 199　　　　　　　(604) 888-3310

ONTARIO BIBLE COLLEGE AND THEOLOGICAL
SEMINARY
25 Ballyconnor Ct., North York, Ontario
M2M 4B3 *Type:* Independent (interdenominational) *Accred.:* 1966/1988 (AABC); 1989
(ATS) *Calendar:* Sem. plan *Degrees:* B, M,
certificates, diplomas *CEO:* Pres. Bruce
Gordon
FTE Enroll: 366　　　　　　　(416) 226-6380

PROVIDENCE COLLEGE AND SEMINARY
Otterburne, Manitoba R0A 1G0 *Type:* Independent (interdenominational) *Accred.:*
1973/1983 (AABC); 1991 (ATS) *Calendar:*
Sem. plan *Degrees:* B, M, certificates, diplomas *CEO:* Pres. Larry McKinney
FTE Enroll: 243　　　　　　　(204) 433-7488

QUEEN'S THEOLOGICAL COLLEGE
Kingston, Ontario K7L 3N6 *Type:* Private
(United Church of Canada) graduate only
Accred.: 1986/1991 (ATS) *Calendar:* Sem.
plan *Degrees:* M *CEO:* Prin. Hallett E.
Llewellyn
FTE Enroll: 59　　　　　　　(613) 545-2110

REGENT COLLEGE
5800 University Blvd., Vancouver, British Columbia V6T 2E4 *Type:* Private (interdenominational) graduate only *Accred.:* 1985/1990 (ATS) *Calendar:* Sem. plan *Degrees:* M *CEO:* Pres. Walter C. Wright, Jr.
FTE Enroll: 211   (604) 224-3245

REGIS COLLEGE
15 St. Mary St., Toronto, Ontario M4Y 2R5 *Type:* Private (Roman Catholic) graduate only *Accred.:* 1970/1990 (ATS) *Calendar:* Sem. plan *Degrees:* M, D *CEO:* Pres. John E. Costello
FTE Enroll: 113   (416) 922-5474

ROCKY MOUNTAIN COLLEGE
4039 Brentwood Rd., N.W., Calgary, Alberta T2L 1L1 *Type:* Private (Evangelical Church in Canada) *Accred.:* 1989 (AABC) *Calendar:* Sem. plan *Degrees:* B, certificates, diplomas *CEO:* Pres. Randy Steinwand
FTE Enroll: 121   (403) 284-5100

RYERSON POLYTECHNICAL INSTITUTE
350 Victoria St., Toronto, Ontario M5B 2K3 *Degrees:* B *Prof. Accred.:* Interior Design *CEO:* Chrmn. Lorna Kelly
      (416) 979-5188

ST. AUGUSTINE'S SEMINARY OF TORONTO
2661 Kingston Rd., Scarborough, Ontario M1M 1M3 *Type:* Private (Roman Catholic) graduate only *Accred.:* 1980/1991 (ATS) *Calendar:* Sem. plan *Degrees:* M *CEO:* Rector James Wingle
FTE Enroll: 90   (416) 261-7207

ST. PETER'S SEMINARY
1040 Waterloo St. N., London, Ontario N6A 3Y1 *Type:* Private (Roman Catholic) graduate only *Accred.:* 1986/1991 (ATS) *Calendar:* Sem. plan *Degrees:* M *CEO:* Rector Patrick W. Fuerth
FTE Enroll: 73   (519) 432-1824

SIMON FRASER UNIVERSITY
Burnaby, British Columbia V5A 1S6 *Type:* Private *Calendar:* Sem. plan *Degrees:* A, B, certificates, diplomas *Prof. Accred.:* Clinical Psychology *CEO:* Chanc. Barbara Rae
      (604) 291-3111

STEINBACH BIBLE COLLEGE
Hwy. 12 N., Box 1420, Steinbach, Manitoba R0A 2A0 *Type:* Private (Mennonite Churches) *Accred.:* 1991 (AABC) *Calendar:* Sem. plan *Degrees:* B, certificates, diplomas *CEO:* Chair Stan Plett
FTE Enroll: 60   (204) 326-6451

TORONTO SCHOOL OF THEOLOGY
47 Queen's Park Crescent, E., Toronto, Ontario M5S 2C3 *Type:* Independent (interdenominational) graduate only *Accred.:* 1980/1991 (ATS) *Calendar:* Sem. plan *Degrees:* M, D *CEO:* Dir. Jean-Marc Laporte
      (416) 978-4039

TRINITY COLLEGE
6 Hoskin Ave., Toronto, Ontario M5S 1H8 *Type:* Private (Anglican Church of Canada) graduate only *Accred.:* 1938/1991 (ATS) *Calendar:* Sem. plan *Degrees:* M, D *CEO:* Dean David R. Holeton
FTE Enroll: 81   (416) 978-2133

UNIVÉRSITÉ DE MONTRÉAL
Case Postal 6128, Succursale A, Montreal, Quebec H3C 3J7 *Type:* Private *Calendar:* Sem. plan *Degrees:* B, P, M, D *Prof. Accred.:* Dentistry, Health Services Administration, Librarianship, Medicine, Optometry, Orthodontics, Pediatric Dentistry, Planning (B,M), Veterinary Medicine *CEO:* Rector G.G. Cloutier
Enroll: 49,837   (514) 343-6111

UNIVÉRSITÉ DE SHERBROOKE
2500 Blvd. de l'Universite, Sherbrooke, Quebec J1K 2R1 *Type:* Private *Calendar:* Sem. plan *Degrees:* B, P, M, D *Prof. Accred.:* Medicine *CEO:* Rector A. Cabana, Ph.D.
Enroll: 17,411   (819) 821-7000

UNIVÉRSITÉ LAVAL
Cite Universitaire, Quebec City, Quebec G1K 7P4 *Type:* Private *Calendar:* Sem. plan *Degrees:* B, P, M, D *Prof. Accred.:* Dentistry, Medicine, Oral and Maxillofacial Surgery *CEO:* Rector Michel Gervais
Enroll: 35,373   (418) 656-2131

UNIVERSITY OF ALBERTA
Edmonton, Alberta T6G 2E1 *Type:* Public *Calendar:* Sem. plan *Degrees:* B, P, M, D *Prof. Accred.:* Business (B,M), Dentistry,

Health Services Administration, Librarianship, Medicine, Orthodontics *CEO:* Pres./Vice Chanc. P. Davenport, Ph.D.
Enroll: 29,536　　　　　(403) 492-3111

UNIVERSITY OF BRITISH COLUMBIA
2075 Westbrook Mall, Vancouver, British Columbia V6T 1W5 *Type:* Public *Calendar:* Sem. plan *Degrees:* B, P, M, D *Prof. Accred.:* Clinical Psychology, Counseling, Dentistry, Librarianship, Medicine, Periodontics, Planning (M), Psychology Internship *CEO:* Pres./Vice Chanc. D.W. Strangway, Ph.D.
Enroll: 28,461　　　　　(604) 228-2375

UNIVERSITY OF CALGARY
2500 University Dr., N.W., Calgary, Alberta T2N 1N4 *Type:* Public *Calendar:* Sem. plan *Degrees:* B, P, M, D *Prof. Accred.:* Business (B,M), Medicine *CEO:* Prin. Toni Prediger
Enroll: 20,541　　　　　(403) 220-5110

UNIVERSITY OF GUELPH
Guelph, Ontario N1G 2W1 *Type:* Public *Calendar:* Sem. plan *Degrees:* B, M *Prof. Accred.:* Landscape Architecture (B,M), Marriage and Family Therapy (M), Veterinary Medicine *CEO:* Pres./Vice Chanc. B. Segal
Enroll: 12,723　　　　　(519) 824-4120

UNIVERSITY OF MANITOBA
Winnipeg, Manitoba R3T 2N2 *Type:* Public *Calendar:* Sem. plan *Degrees:* B, P, M, D *Prof. Accred.:* Clinical Psychology, Dentistry, Interior Design, Medicine, Oral and Maxillofacial Surgery, Orthodontics, Periodontics, Psychology Internship *CEO:* Pres./Vice Chanc. Arnold Naimark
Enroll: 23,462　　　　　(204) 474-8880

UNIVERSITY OF OTTAWA
Ottawa, Ontario K1N 6N5 *Type:* Public *Calendar:* Sem. plan *Degrees:* B, P, M, D *Prof. Accred.:* Clinical Psychology, Health Services Administration, Medicine, Psychology Internship *CEO:* Rector/Vice Chanc. M. Hamelin
Enroll: 23,694　　　　　(613) 564-3311

UNIVERSITY OF PRINCE EDWARD ISLAND
550 University Ave., Charlottetown, Prince Edward Island C1A 4P3 *Type:* Private *Calendar:* Sem. plan *Degrees:* A, B, certificates,

diplomas *Prof. Accred.:* Veterinary Medicine *CEO:* Chanc. G.L. Bennett
　　　　　(902) 566-0439

UNIVERSITY OF ST. MICHAEL'S COLLEGE
81 St. Mary St., Toronto, Ontario M5S 1J4 *Type:* Private (Roman Catholic) graduate only *Accred.:* 1972/1991 (ATS) *Calendar:* Sem. plan *Degrees:* M, D *CEO:* Dean Michael A. Fahey
FTE Enroll: 198　　　　　(416) 926-7140

UNIVERSITY OF SASKATCHEWAN
Saskatoon, Saskatchewan S7N 0W0 *Type:* Public *Calendar:* Sem. plan *Degrees:* B, P, M, D *Prof. Accred.:* Clinical Psychology, Dentistry, Medicine, Veterinary Medicine *CEO:* Pres./Vice Chanc. J.W.G. Ivany
Enroll: 15,546　　　　　(306) 244-4343

UNIVERSITY OF TORONTO
Toronto, Ontario M5S 1A1 *Type:* Public *Calendar:* Sem. plan *Degrees:* B, P, M, D *Prof. Accred.:* Combined Maxillofacial Prosthodontics, Dental Public Health, Dentistry, Health Services Administration, Landscape Architecture (B), Librarianship, Medicine, Oral Pathology, Oral and Maxillofacial Surgery, Orthodontics, Pediatric Dentistry, Periodontics *CEO:* Pres. J.R.S Prichard
Enroll: 53,313　　　　　(416) 978-2011

UNIVERSITY OF WATERLOO
University Ave., Waterloo, Ontario N2L 3G1 *Type:* Private *Calendar:* Sem. plan *Degrees:* B, P, M *Prof. Accred.:* Clinical Psychology, Optometry *CEO:* Pres./Vice Chanc. D.T. Wright
Enroll: 25,337　　　　　(519) 885-1211

UNIVERSITY OF WESTERN ONTARIO
London, Ontario N6A 3K7 *Type:* Private *Calendar:* Sem. plan *Degrees:* B, P, M, D *Prof. Accred.:* Clinical Psychology, Dentistry, Librarianship, Medicine, Oral Pathology, Orthodontics *CEO:* Pres./Vice Chanc. K.G. Pedersen
Enroll: 22,450　　　　　(519) 679-2111

UNIVERSITY OF WINDSOR
Windsor, Ontario N9B 3P4 *Type:* Public *Calendar:* Sem. plan *Degrees:* B, P, M, D *Prof. Accred.:* Clinical Psychology *CEO:* Pres./Vice Chanc. R.W. Ianni
Enroll: 14,079　　　　　(519) 253-4232

VANCOUVER SCHOOL OF THEOLOGY
6000 Iona Dr., Vancouver, British Columbia
V6T 1L4 *Type:* Private (interdenominational) graduate only *Accred.:* 1976/1990 (ATS)
Calendar: Sem. plan *Degrees:* M *CEO:*
Prin. William J. Phillips
FTE Enroll: 102   (604) 228-9031

WATERLOO LUTHERAN SEMINARY
75 University Ave., W., Waterloo, Ontario
N2L 3C5 *Type:* Private (Evangelical Luthern
Church) graduate only *Accred.:* 1982/1987
(ATS) *Calendar:* Sem. plan *Degrees:* M
CEO: Prin./Dean Richard C. Crossman
FTE Enroll: 95   (519) 884-1970

WESTERN PENTECOSTAL BIBLE COLLEGE
35235 Straiton Rd., Clayburn, British Columbia V0X 1E0 *Type:* Private (Pentecostal
Assemblies of Canada) *Accred.:* 1980/1990
(AABC) *Calendar:* Sem. plan *Degrees:* B,
certificates, diplomas *CEO:* Pres. James
Richards
FTE Enroll: 183   (604) 853-7491

WYCLIFFE COLLEGE
5 Hoskin Ave., Toronto, Ontario M5S 1H7
Type: Private (Anglican) graduate only *Accred.:* 1978/1991 (ATS) *Calendar:* Sem.
plan *Degrees:* M, D *CEO:* Acting Prin.
Harry St. Clair Hilchey
FTE Enroll: 91   (416) 979-2870

CAYMAN ISLANDS

INTERNATIONAL COLLEGE
P.O. Box Savannah, Newlands, Grand Cayman *Type:* Private *Accred.:* 1979/1987
(ACISC) *Calendar:* Qtr. plan *Degrees:* A, B,
M, certificates, diplomas *CEO:* Pres. Elsa M.
Cummings
                    (809) 947-1100

EGYPT

AMERICAN UNIVERSITY IN CAIRO
113 Sharia Dasr El Aini, Cairo *Type:* Private
Accred.: 1982/1988 (MSA) *Calendar:* Sem.
plan *Degrees:* B, M *CEO:* Pres. Donald McDonald
Enroll: 3,800   [20] 354-1830

FRANCE

THE AMERICAN UNIVERSITY OF PARIS
31 Ave. Bosquet, 75007 Paris *Type:* Private
liberal arts *Accred.:* 1973/1988 (MSA) *Calendar:* Sem. plan *Degrees:* B *CEO:* Pres.
Glenn W. Ferguson
Enroll: 992   [33] (1) 45 55 91 73

GERMANY

SCHILLER INTERNATIONAL UNIVERSITY
Friedrich-Ebert-Anlage 4, 69117 Heidelberg
Type: Private *Accred.:* 1983/1987 (ACISC)
Calendar: Sem. plan *Degrees:* A, B, M
CEO: Dir. Lisa Evans
                    [49] (62) 211-2046

THE AMERICAN COLLEGE OF SWITZERLAND
Leysin CH-1854, Switzerland *Accred.:*
1983/1992 (ACISC) *Calendar:* Sem. plan
CEO: Acting Provost Nancy Carroll
                    [41] (25) 342-223

BRANCH CAMPUS
453 Edgewater Dr., Dunedin, FL 34698-4964 *Accred.:* 1991 (ACISC) *CEO:* Dir.
Jeanette Brock
                    (813) 736-5082

BRANCH CAMPUS
32 Blvd. de Vaugirard, 75015 Paris,
France *Accred.:* 1983/1987 (ACISC)
CEO: Dir. Christiane Barody-Weiss
                    [33] (14) 538-5601

BRANCH CAMPUS
Chateau Pourtales, 161 rue Melanie, 6700
Strasbourg, France *Accred.:* 1986
(ACISC) *CEO:* Dir. Allen D. Olson
                    [33] (8) 831-0107

BRANCH CAMPUS
Calle de Rodriguez San Pedro, No. 10,
28015 Madrid, Spain *Accred.:* 1983/1987
(ACISC) *CEO:* Dir. Lynn Bergunde
                    [34] (1) 446-2349

BRANCH CAMPUS
Dorfstrasse 40, 6390 Engelberg, Switzerland *Accred.:* 1993 (ACISC) *CEO:* Dir.
Max Friedli
                    [41] (9) 44-343

BRANCH CAMPUS
Wickham Ct., W. Wickham, Kent, England, United Kingdom BR4 9HW *Accred.:* 1983/1987 (ACISC) *CEO:* Dir. Louise Cody

[44] (81) 777-8069

BRANCH CAMPUS
Royal Waterloo House, 51-55 Waterloo Rd., London, England, United Kingdom SE1 8TX *Accred.:* 1983/1987 (ACISC) *CEO:* Dir. Richard Taylor

[44] (71) 928-1372

GREECE

DEREE COLLEGE
P.O. Box 60018 GR-153, 10 Agnia, Paraskevi Attikis *Type:* Private liberal arts *Accred.:* 1981/1986 (NEASC-CIHE) *Calendar:* 4-1-4 plan *Degrees:* A, B *CEO:* Pres. John S. Bailey
Enroll: 4,139   [30] (1) 639-3250

MARSHALL ISLANDS

COLLEGE OF MICRONESIA
P.O. Box 159, Kolonia Pohnpei, FSM 96941 *Type:* Public junior *System:* College of Micronesia *Accred.:* 1978/1992 (WASC-Jr.) *Calendar:* Sem. plan *Degrees:* A *CEO:* Pres. Paul Gallen
Enroll: 502   (691) 320-2480

COLLEGE OF THE MARSHALL ISLANDS
P.O. Box 1258, Majuro, RMI 96960 *Type:* Public junior *System:* College of Micronesia *Accred.:* 1991 (WASC-Jr.) *Calendar:* Sem. plan *Degrees:* A *CEO:* Pres. Dorothy Nook
Enroll: 543   (692) 625-3394

MEXICO

FUNDACION UNIVERSIDAD DE LAS AMERICAS
Apartado Postal 100, Sta. Catarina Martir, Puebla 72820 *Type:* Private *Accred.:* 1959/1984 (SACS-CC) *Calendar:* Sem. plan *Degrees:* B, M *CEO:* Rector Enrique Cardenas
FTE Enroll: 6,138   [52] (22) 29-20-04

INSTITUTO TECNOLOGICO Y DE ESTUDIOS SUPERIORES DE MONTERREY
Ave. Eugenio Garza Sada, 2501 Sur, Monterrey, N.L. 64849 *Type:* Private *Accred.:*

1950/1989 (SACS-CC) *Calendar:* Sem. plan *Degrees:* B, M, D *CEO:* Pres. Rafael Rangel-Sostmann
FTE Enroll: 41,147   [52] (83) 58-25-32

UNIVERSIDAD DE LAS AMERICAS, A.C.
Calle de Puebla No. 223, Col. Roma, Mexico D.F. 06700 *Type:* Private *Accred.:* 1983/1988 (SACS-CC) *Calendar:* Sem. plan *Degrees:* B, M *CEO:* Pres. Margarita Gomez-Palacio
FTE Enroll: 1,614   [52] (5) 208-02-47

NIGERIA

THE NIGERIAN BAPTIST THEOLOGICAL SEMINARY
P.O. Box 30, Ogbomoso *Type:* Private (Southern Baptist) professional *Accred.:* 1983/1988 (SACS-CC) *Calendar:* Sem. plan *Degrees:* B *CEO:* Pres. Yusufu Ameh Obaje
FTE Enroll: 225   [234] (38) 710011

NORTHERN MARIANAS ISLANDS

NORTHERN MARIANAS COLLEGE
Box 1250, Saipan 96950 *Type:* Public junior *Accred.:* 1985/1990 (WASC-Jr.) *Calendar:* Sem. plan *Degrees:* A *CEO:* Pres. Agnes M. McPhetres
Enroll: 942   (670) 234-6932

PALAU

PALAU COMMUNITY COLLEGE
P.O. Box 9, Koror, RP 96940 *Type:* Public vocational *System:* College of Micronesia *Accred.:* 1977/1992 (WASC-Jr.) *Calendar:* Sem. plan *Degrees:* A *CEO:* Pres. Francis M. Matsutaro
Enroll: 391   (680) 488-2471

PANAMA

PANAMA CANAL COLLEGE
DoDDS, Panama Region, Unit No. 9025, APO Miami, FL 34002 *Type:* Public (federal) junior *Accred.:* 1941/1990 (MSA) *Calendar:* Sem. plan *Degrees:* A *CEO:* C.E.O. and Dean Ronald G. Woodbury
Enroll: 1,538   [507] 523-304

SWITZERLAND

FRANKLIN COLLEGE SWITZERLAND
Via Ponte Tresa 29, 6924 Sorengo (Lugano)
Type: Private liberal arts *Accred.:* 1975/1990
(MSA) *Calendar:* Sem. plan *Degrees:* A, B
CEO: Pres. Theo. E. Brenner
Enroll: 244   [41] (9) 155-0101

UNITED KINGDOM

IMC-INTERNATIONAL MANAGEMENT CENTRES
Castle St., Buckingham, England MK18 1BP
Type: Private home study *Accred.:* 1989
(NHSC) *Calendar:* Courses of varying
lengths *Degrees:* M, certificates *CEO:* Prin.
Gordon Wills
                [44] (280) 81-7222

RICHMOND COLLEGE, THE AMERICAN
INTERNATIONAL UNIVERSITY IN LONDON
Queens Rd., Richmond, Surrey, England
TW10 6JP *Type:* Private liberal arts *Accred.:*
1981/1991 (MSA) *Calendar:* Sem. plan *Degrees:* A, B, M *CEO:* Pres. Walter McCann
Enroll: 955   [44] (81) 332-8200

Accredited Non-Degree Granting Institutions

ALABAMA

ALABAMA REFERENCE LABORATORIES, INC.
543 S. Hull St., P.O. Box 4600, Montgomery 36103-4600 *Type:* Private *Calendar:* Courses of varying lengths *Degrees:* certificates *Prof. Accred.:* Medical Technology *CEO:* Pres. Robert B. Adams, M.D.
(205) 263-5745

ALABAMA STATE COLLEGE OF BARBER STYLING
9480 Pkwy. E., Birmingham 35215-8308 *Type:* Private *Accred.:* 1991 (ACCSCT) *Calendar:* Courses of varying lengths *Degrees:* certificates *CEO:* Owner/Dir. Donald S. Mathews
(205) 836-2404

ARMY ORDNANCE MISSILE AND MUNITIONS CENTER AND SCHOOL
Redstone Arsenal, Huntsville 35897-6000 *Type:* Public (federal) technical *Accred.:* 1976/1990 (SACS-COEI) *Calendar:* Courses of varying lengths *Degrees:* certificates *CEO:* Commandant James Boddie, U.S.A.
FTE Enroll: 1,471   (205) 876-3349

CAPPS COLLEGE
3100 Cottage Hill Rd., Bldg. 5, Mobile 36606 *Type:* Private *Accred.:* 1986/1992 (ABHES) *Calendar:* Courses of varying lengths *Degrees:* diplomas *Prof. Accred.:* Medical Assisting *CEO:* Dir./Pres. Morgan Landry
(205) 473-1393

CAREER DEVELOPMENT INSTITUTE
2233 Fourth Ave., N., Birmingham 35203 *Type:* Private *Accred.:* 1988/1993 (SACS-COEI) *Calendar:* Qtr. plan *Degrees:* diplomas *CEO:* Dir. Darlene Mosley
FTE Enroll: 100   (205) 252-6396

BRANCH CAMPUS
2314 Ninth Ave., N., Bessemer 35020 *CEO:* Dir. Darrell Glaze
(205) 425-6757

CAREER DEVELOPMENT INSTITUTE
1060 Springhill Ave., Mobile 36604 *Type:* Private *Accred.:* 1988/1993 (SACS-COEI) *Calendar:* Qtr. plan *Degrees:* diplomas *CEO:* Dir. Bertha George
FTE Enroll: 44   (205) 433-5042

CAREER DEVELOPMENT INSTITUTE
505 and 507 Montgomery St., Montgomery 36101-0766 *Type:* Private *Accred.:* 1988 (SACS-COEI) *Calendar:* Qtr. plan *Degrees:* diplomas *CEO:* Dir. Amie Garrett
FTE Enroll: 64   (205) 262-3131

CAREER DEVELOPMENT INSTITUTE
Parkview Ctr., 516 14th St., Tuscaloosa 35401 *Type:* Private *Accred.:* 1989/1991 (SACS-COEI) *Calendar:* Qtr. plan *Degrees:* diplomas *CEO:* Dir. Ralph Cheatham
FTE Enroll: 62   (205) 752-6025

CHOCTAW TRAINING INSTITUTE
218 W. Church St., Butler 36904 *Type:* Private *Accred.:* 1988/1991 (SACS-COEI) *Calendar:* Courses of varying lengths *Degrees:* certificates *CEO:* Dir. Ruth Corley
FTE Enroll: 15   (205) 459-4331

COASTAL TRAINING INSTITUTE
5950 S. Monticello Dr., Montgomery 36117-1964 *Type:* Private technical *Accred.:* 1985/1990 (SACS-COEI) *Calendar:* Courses of varying lengths *Degrees:* diplomas *CEO:* Dir. Larry McKay
FTE Enroll: 599   (205) 279-6241

BRANCH CAMPUS
Calle Comercial, No. 19-21, Aguadilla, PR 00603 *CEO:* Dir. Dave Barton, Sr.
(809) 792-5915

EXTENSION COURSE INSTITUTE OF THE UNITED STATES AIR FORCE
50 S. Turner Blvd., Gunter Annex, Maxwell Air Force Base 36118-5643 *Type:* Public (federal) home study *Accred.:* 1981/1991 (NHSC) *Calendar:* Courses of varying lengths *Degrees:* certificates, diplomas *CEO:* Commandant Jerry Sailors
(205) 416-4252

GADSDEN BUSINESS COLLEGE
750 Forrest Ave., P.O. Box 1544, Gadsden 35901 *Type:* Private business *Accred.:* 1962/1991 (ACISC) *Calendar:* Qtr. plan *Degrees:* certificates, diplomas *CEO:* Pres. Michael Beecham
(205) 546-2863

BRANCH CAMPUS
P.O. Box 1575, 630 S. Wilmer Ave., Anniston 36202-1575 *Accred.:* 1962/1991 (ACISC) *CEO:* Dir. Deborah Hawkins
(205) 237-7517

HERZING INSTITUTE
1218 S. 20th St., Birmingham 35205-3852 *Type:* Private *Accred.:* 1971/1993 (ACCSCT) *Calendar:* Courses of varying lengths *Degrees:* certificates, diplomas *CEO:* Dir. Donald Lewis
(205) 933-8536

HUNTSVILLE BUSINESS INSTITUTE SCHOOL OF COURT REPORTING
3315 S. Memorial Pkwy., No. 5, Huntsville 35801 *Type:* Private *Accred.:* 1990 (SACS-COEI) *Calendar:* Courses of varying lengths *Degrees:* certificates, diplomas *CEO:* Dir. Bonnie Gray
FTE Enroll: 12   (205) 880-7530

JOHN POPE EDEN AREA VOCATIONAL EDUCATION CENTER
Rte. 2, Box 1855, Ashville 35953 *Type:* Public (state) *Accred.:* 1984/1989 (SACS-COEI) *Calendar:* Courses of varying lengths *Degrees:* certificates *CEO:* Dir. John Hazelwood
FTE Enroll: 163   (205) 594-7055

J.R. PITTARD AREA VOCATIONAL SCHOOL
22401 Alabama Hwy. 21, Alpine 35160 *Type:* Public (state) *Accred.:* 1990 (SACS-COEI) *Calendar:* Courses of varying lengths *Degrees:* certificates *CEO:* Dir. L.C. McMurphy
FTE Enroll: 137   (205) 539-8161

NATIONAL CAREER COLLEGE
1351 McFarland Blvd., E., Tuscaloosa 35405 *Type:* Private business *Accred.:* 1984/1990 (ACISC) *Calendar:* Qtr. plan *Degrees:* certificates, diplomas *CEO:* Dir. Penny Mitchell
(205) 758-9091

NEW WORLD COLLEGE OF BUSINESS
1031 Noble St., Anniston 36201 *Type:* Private business *Accred.:* 1979/1991 (ACISC) *Calendar:* Qtr. plan *Degrees:* certificates, diplomas *CEO:* Pres. Barbara Turner
(205) 236-7578

PRINCE INSTITUTE OF PROFESSIONAL STUDIES
7735 Atlanta Hwy., Montgomery 36117 *Type:* Private business *Accred.:* 1984/1990

(ACISC) *Calendar:* Courses of varying lengths *Degrees:* certificates, diplomas *CEO:* Pres. Sara Prince
(205) 271-1670

RICE COLLEGE
2116 Bessemer Rd., Birmingham 35208 *Type:* Private *Accred.:* 1983/1988 (SACS-COEI) *Calendar:* Courses of varying lengths *Degrees:* certificates, diplomas *CEO:* Dir. William Bailey
FTE Enroll: 124   (205) 781-8600

RILEY COLLEGE
4129 Ross Clark Cir., N.W., Dothan 36303 *Type:* Private business *Accred.:* 1983/1988 (SACS-COEI) *Calendar:* Qtr. plan *Degrees:* certificates, diplomas *CEO:* Pres. Jeannine Benefield
FTE Enroll: 273   (205) 794-4296

BRANCH CAMPUS
901-A Jeff Davis St., Selma 36701 *CEO:* Dir. Michael Rawls
(205) 872-2904

BRANCH CAMPUS
610 W. Oglethorpe Blvd., Albany, GA 31701 *CEO:* Dir. Carlton Vurrell
(912) 883-8048

SOUTHEAST COLLEGE OF TECHNOLOGY
828 Downtowner Loop W., Mobile 36609-5404 *Type:* Private *Accred.:* 1986 (ACCSCT) *Calendar:* Courses of varying lengths *Degrees:* certificates *CEO:* Pres. Mike Lanouette
(205) 343-8200

SOUTHERN VOCATIONAL COLLEGE
205 S. Main St., Tuskegee 36083 *Type:* Private *Accred.:* 1983/1993 (SACS-COEI) *Calendar:* Courses of varying lengths *Degrees:* certificates, diplomas *Prof. Accred.:* Practical Nursing *CEO:* Pres. Lawrence F. Haygood, Jr.
FTE Enroll: 85   (205) 727-5220

TALLAPOOSA-ALEXANDER CITY AREA VOCATIONAL CENTER
100 E. Junior College Dr., Alexander City 35010 *Type:* Public (state) *Accred.:* 1984/1989 (SACS-COEI) *Calendar:* Courses of varying lengths *Degrees:* certificates *CEO:* Dir. Joe Martin
FTE Enroll: 139   (205) 329-8448

WINSTON COUNTY TECHNICAL CENTER
Holly Grove Rd., Double Springs 35553
Type: Public (state) *Accred.:* 1985/1990
(SACS-COEI) *Calendar:* Courses of varying
lengths *Degrees:* certificates *CEO:* Dir.
Betty Porter
FTE Enroll: 92   (205) 489-2121

ALASKA

CHARTER COLLEGE
Ste. 120, 2221 E. Northern Lights Blvd., Anchorage 99508 *Type:* Private business *Accred.:* 1988 (ACISC) *Calendar:* Courses of varying lengths *Degrees:* certificates, diplomas *CEO:* Pres. Milton Byrd
(907) 227-1000

THE TRAVEL ACADEMY
1415 E. Tudor Rd., Anchorage 99507-1033 *Type:* Private *Accred.:* 1987 (ACCSCT) *Calendar:* Courses of varying lengths *Degrees:* certificates *CEO:* Pres. Jennifer A. Deitz
(907) 563-7575

ARIZONA

ABC TECHNICAL & TRADE SCHOOLS
3761 E. Technical Dr., Tucson 85713 *Type:*
Private *Accred.:* 1977/1988 (ACCSCT) *Calendar:* Courses of varying lengths *Degrees:*
certificates, diplomas *CEO:* Vice Pres. Ron
B. Kessler
(602) 748-1762

AL COLLINS GRAPHIC DESIGN SCHOOL
1140 S. Priest Dr., Tempe 85281-5206 *Type:*
Private *Accred.:* 1981/1987 (ACCSCT) *Calendar:* Qtr. plan *Degrees:* certificates *CEO:*
Pres./C.E.O. Chuck Collins
(602) 966-3000

AMERICAN INSTITUTE OF TECHNOLOGY
440 S. 54th Ave., Phoenix 85043 *Type:* Private *Accred.:* 1985/1990 (ACCSCT) *Calendar:* Courses of varying lengths *Degrees:*
certificates *CEO:* Dir. R. Wade Murphree
(602) 233-2222

AMERICAN TELLER SCHOOLS
635 W. Indian School Rd., Ste. 201, Phoenix
85013-3118 *Type:* Private *Accred.:* 1988
(ACCSCT) *Calendar:* Courses of varying
lengths *Degrees:* certificates *CEO:* Pres.
Randy Utley
(602) 248-0885

BRANCH CAMPUS
1819 S. Dobson Rd., No. 215, Mesa
85202-5656 *Accred.:* 1988 (ACCSCT)
CEO: Dir. Shelli Navarro
(602) 730-8191

BRANCH CAMPUS
4023 E. Grant Rd., Ste. A, Tucson 85712-
2508 *Accred.:* 1988 (ACCSCT) *CEO:* Dir.
Bettie Moseman
(602) 881-1541

APOLLO COLLEGE—PHOENIX, INC.
8503 N. 27th Ave., Phoenix 85051 *Type:*
Private *Accred.:* 1978/1992 (ABHES); 1979/
1986 (ACCSCT) *Calendar:* Courses of varying lengths *Degrees:* certificates *Prof. Accred.:* Medical Assisting, Respiratory Therapy, Respiratory Therapy Technology *CEO:*
Dir. Cindy J. Carlson
(602) 864-1571

APOLLO COLLEGE—TRI-CITY, INC.
630 W. Southern Ave., Mesa 85210-5004
Type: Private *Accred.:* 1980/1992 (ABHES);
1986 (ACCSCT) *Calendar:* Courses of varying lengths *Degrees:* certificates *Prof. Accred.:* Medical Assisting *CEO:* Dir. Fredrick
D. Lockhart
(602) 831-6585

APOLLO COLLEGE—TUCSON, INC.
3870 N. Oracle Rd., Tucson 85705-3227
Type: Private *Accred.:* 1987/1992 (ABHES);
1986 (ACCSCT) *Calendar:* Courses of varying lengths *Degrees:* certificates *Prof. Accred.:* Medical Assisting *CEO:* Dir. Marvin
D. Ingram
(602) 888-5885

APOLLO COLLEGE—WESTRIDGE, INC.
7502 W. Thomas Rd., Phoenix 85033 *Type:*
Private *Accred.:* 1991 (ABHES); 1986 (ACC-
SCT) *Calendar:* Courses of varying lengths
Degrees: certificates *Prof. Accred.:* Medical
Assisting *CEO:* Dir. Dennis Delvalle
(602) 849-9000

THE ART CENTER
2525 N. Country Club Rd., Tucson 85716
Type: Private *Accred.:* 1993 (ACCSCT) *Calendar:* Courses of varying lengths *Degrees:*
certificates, diplomas *CEO:* Pres. Sharmon
R. Woods
(602) 325-0123

BRANCH CAMPUS
2268 Wyoming Blvd., N.E., Albuquerque,
NM 87112 *Accred.:* 1993 (ACCSCT)
CEO: Pres. Sharon R. Woods
(505) 298-1828

AZTECH COLLEGE
941 S. Dobson Rd., Ste. 120, Mesa 85202
Type: Private *Accred.:* 1991 (ACCSCT) *Calendar:* Courses of varying lengths *Degrees:*
diplomas *CEO:* Dir. David Brown
(602) 967-7813

BRANCH CAMPUS
2201 San Pedro Dr., N.E., Bldg. 3, Albuquerque, NM 87110-9877 *Accred.:* 1993
(ACCSCT) *CEO:* Dir. Judie Kautz
(505) 888-5800

THE BRYMAN SCHOOL
4343 N. 16th St., Phoenix 85016-5338 *Type:*
Private *Accred.:* 1990 (ACCSCT) *Calendar:*
Courses of varying lengths *Degrees:* certificates *Prof. Accred.:* Medical Assisting, Medical Assisting (AMA) *CEO:* Dir. Carole
Miller
(602) 274-4300

THE CAD INSTITUTE
Ste. 150, 4100 E. Broadway Rd., Phoenix
85040 *Type:* Private professional *Accred.:*
1993 (ACISC) *Calendar:* Courses of varying
lengths *Degrees:* certificates, diplomas
CEO: Pres. Dominic Pistillo
(602) 437-0405

CLINTON TECHNICAL INSTITUTE
2844 W. Deer Valley Rd., Phoenix 85027-
9951 *Type:* Private *Accred.:* 1979/1986
(ACCSCT) *Calendar:* Courses of varying
lengths *Degrees:* certificates *CEO:* Dir. Gary
Green
(602) 869-9644

MOTORCYCLE/MARINE MECHANICS INSTITUTE
9751 Delegates Dr., Orlando, FL 32837-
9835 *Accred.:* 1991 (ACCSCT) *CEO:* Dir.
Dennis Hendrix
(407) 240-2422

CONSERVATORY OF RECORDING ARTS &
SCIENCES
1110 E. Missouri Ave., No. 400, Phoenix
85014-2704 *Type:* Private *Accred.:* 1991
(ACCSCT) *Calendar:* Courses of varying
lengths *Degrees:* diplomas *CEO:* Admin.
Dir. Kirt R. Hamm
(602) 265-5566

DESERT INSTITUTE OF THE HEALING ARTS
639 N. Sixth Ave., Tucson 85705-8330
Type: Private *Accred.:* 1987 (ACCSCT) *Calendar:* Courses of varying lengths *Degrees:*
certificates *CEO:* Admin. Dir. Janice Hollender
(602) 882-0879

HIGH-TECH INSTITUTE
1515 E. Indian School Rd., Phoenix 85014-
4901 *Type:* Private *Accred.:* 1984/1989
(ACCSCT) *Calendar:* Courses of varying
lengths *Degrees:* certificates *CEO:* Dir.
Marilyn Pobiak
(602) 279-9700

BRANCH CAMPUS
1111 Howe Ave., Sacramento, CA 95825
Accred.: 1993 (ACCSCT) *CEO:* Dir. Glen
Laliberte
(916) 988-0986

INSTITUTE OF BUSINESS AND MEDICAL
TECHNOLOGY
20 E. Main St., No. 600, Mesa 85201-6502
Type: Private *Accred.:* 1992 (ACCSCT) *Calendar:* Courses of varying lengths *Degrees:*
certificates *CEO:* Pres. Craig W. Deonik
(602) 833-1028

LAURAL SCHOOL
2538 N. Eighth St., P.O. Box 5338, Phoenix
85010-5338 *Type:* Private home study *Accred.:* 1980/1991 (NHSC) *Calendar:* Courses of varying lengths *Degrees:* certificates,
diplomas *CEO:* Admin. Laura Orman
Fabricant
(602) 994-3460

LONG MEDICAL INSTITUTE
4126 N. Black Canyon Hwy., Phoenix
85017-4394 *Type:* Private *Accred.:* 1981/
1987 (ACCSCT) *Calendar:* Courses of varying lengths *Degrees:* diplomas *Prof. Accred.:* Respiratory Therapy Technology
CEO: Dir. Carol Martin
(602) 279-9333

METROPOLITAN COLLEGE OF COURT REPORTING
4640 E. Elwood St., Phoenix 85040 *Type:*
Private *Accred.:* 1992 (ACCSCT) *Calendar:*
Courses of varying lengths *Degrees:* certificates *CEO:* Pres./Owner David L. Stephenson
(602) 955-5900

MODERN SCHOOLS OF AMERICA, INC.
2538 N. 8th St., P.O. Box 5338, Phoenix
85010-5338 *Type:* Private home study *Accred.:* 1980/1991 (NHSC) *Calendar:* Courses of varying lengths *Degrees:* certificates
CEO: Admin. Laura Fabricant
(602) 990-8346

MUNDUS INSTITUTE
4745 N. Seventh St., Ste. 100, Phoenix
85014-3669 *Type:* Private *Accred.:* 1990
(ACCSCT) *Calendar:* Courses of varying
lengths *Degrees:* certificates *CEO:* Dir.
James Cox
(602) 248-8548

NATIONAL EDUCATION CENTER—ARIZONA
AUTOMOTIVE INSTITUTE
6829 N. 46th Ave., Glendale 85301-3597
Type: Private *Accred.:* 1972/1988 (ACC-
SCT) *Calendar:* Qtr. plan *Degrees:* diplomas *CEO:* Dir. John Frasure
(800) 528-0717

NORTHERN ARIZONA COLLEGE OF HEALTH
CAREERS
2575 E. Seventh Ave., Flagstaff 86004 *Type:*
Private *Accred.:* 1982/1989 (ABHES) *Calendar:* Courses of varying lengths *Degrees:*
certificates *Prof. Accred.:* Medical Assisting
CEO: Pres./Dir. Betty McCarty
(602) 526-0763

NORTHERN ARIZONA INSTITUTE OF TECHNOLOGY
1120 Kaibab La., Flagstaff 86001 *Type:* Private business *Accred.:* 1989 (ACISC) *Calendar:* Qtr. plan *Degrees:* certificates, diplomas *CEO:* Dir. Paul Deshler
(602) 779-4532

BRANCH CAMPUS
11300 Lomas Blvd., N.E., Albuquerque,
NM 87112 *Accred.:* 1993 (ACISC) *CEO:*
Dir. Daniel T. Chilenski
(505) 231-4097

PEDIGREE CAREER INSTITUTE
3037 W. Clarendon Ave., Phoenix 85017-
4612 *Type:* Private *Accred.:* 1987 (ACC-
SCT) *Calendar:* Courses of varying lengths
Degrees: certificates *CEO:* Dir. Connie
Long
(602) 264-3647

PEDIGREE CAREER INSTITUTE
3781 E. Technical Dr., No. 1, Tucson 85713-
5343 *Type:* Private *Accred.:* 1986 (ACC-
SCT) *Calendar:* Courses of varying lengths
Degrees: certificates *CEO:* Dir. Ron B.
Kessler
(602) 745-3647

THE REFRIGERATION SCHOOL
4210 E. Washington St., Phoenix 85034-
1894 *Type:* Private *Accred.:* 1973/1990
(ACCSCT) *Calendar:* Courses of varying
lengths *Degrees:* diplomas *CEO:* Dir. Ola
Lee Loney
(602) 275-7133

ROBERTO-VENN SCHOOL OF LUTHIERY
4011 S. 16th St., Phoenix 85040-1314 *Type:*
Private *Accred.:* 1979/1989 (ACCSCT) *Calendar:* Courses of varying lengths *Degrees:*
certificates *CEO:* Dir. John H. Roberts
(602) 243-1179

SCOTTSDALE CULINARY INSTITUTE
8100 E. Camelback Rd., Scottsdale 85251-
3940 *Type:* Private *Accred.:* 1989 (ACC-
SCT) *Calendar:* Courses of varying lengths
Degrees: certificates *CEO:* Pres. Elizabeth
S. Leite
(602) 990-3773

SOUTHWEST ACADEMY OF TECHNOLOGY
1660 S. Alma School Rd., No. 227, Mesa
85210-3073 *Type:* Private *Calendar:* Courses of varying lengths *Degrees:* certificates
Prof. Accred.: Respiratory Therapy, Respiratory Therapy Technology *CEO:* Dir. D.
Clark Fox
(602) 820-3003

SOUTHWESTERN ACADEMY
1660 S. Alma School Rd., No. 223, Mesa
85210 *Type:* Private home study *Accred.:*
1992 (NHSC) *Calendar:* Courses of varying
lengths *Degrees:* certificates *CEO:* Pres. D.
Clark Fox
(602) 820-3956

STERLING SCHOOL
801 E. Indian School Rd., Phoenix 85014
Type: Private business *Accred.:* 1981/1990
(ACISC) *Calendar:* Courses of varying
lengths *Degrees:* certificates, diplomas
CEO: Dir. Ruby Sterling
(602) 277-5276

TUCSON COLLEGE
7302-10 E. 22nd St., Tucson 85710 *Type:*
Private business *Accred.:* 1966/1990
(ACISC) *Calendar:* Courses of varying
lengths *Degrees:* certificates, diplomas *Prof.
Accred.:* Medical Assisting *CEO:* Pres. M.A.
Mikhail
(602) 296-3261

UNITED STATES ARMY INTELLIGENCE CENTER
AND FORT HUACHUCA
Attn.:ATSI-TDI-S, Fort Huachuca 85613
Type: Public (federal) *Accred.:* 1959/1990
(NCA) *Calendar:* Courses of varying lengths
Degrees: certificates, diplomas *CEO:* Com-
mandant Glen Kjos
Enroll: 4,153   (602) 533-5648

UNIVERSAL TECHNICAL INSTITUTE
3121 W. Weldon Ave., Phoenix 85017-4599
Type: Private *Accred.:* 1968/1993 (ACC-
SCT) *Calendar:* Courses of varying lengths
Degrees: certificates *CEO:* Dir. Randall R.
Smith

(602) 264-4164

BRANCH CAMPUS
601 Regency Dr., Glendale Heights, IL
60139-2208 *Accred.:* 1990 (ACCSCT)
CEO: Dir. Gerald A. Murphy

(708) 529-2662

ARKANSAS

ARKANSAS COLLEGE OF BARBERING AND HAIR DESIGN
200 Washington Ave., North Little Rock 72114-5615 *Type:* Private *Accred.:* 1991 (ACCSCT) *Calendar:* Courses of varying lengths *Degrees:* certificates *CEO:* Pres. Larry M. Little
(501) 376-9696

ARKANSAS VALLEY TECHNICAL INSTITUTE
1311 S. I St., Fort Smith 72901 *Type:* Private *Calendar:* Courses of varying lengths *Degrees:* diplomas *Prof. Accred.:* Respiratory Therapy Technology *CEO:* Pres. Carl Jones *Enroll:* 45   (501) 441-5256

CARTI SCHOOL OF RADIATION THERAPY TECHNOLOGY
P.O. Box 5210, Little Rock 72215 *Type:* Private *Calendar:* Courses of varying lengths *Degrees:* certificates *Prof. Accred.:* Radiation Therapy Technology *CEO:* Pres. Edward Rensch, Jr.
Enroll: 15   (501) 664-8573

COTTON BOLL TECHNICAL INSTITUTE
Box 36, Burdette 72321 *Type:* Private *Calendar:* Courses of varying lengths *Prof. Accred.:* Dental Assisting *CEO:* Pres. William Nelson
(501) 763-1486

EASTERN COLLEGE OF HEALTH VOCATIONS
6423 Forbing Rd., Little Rock 72209 *Type:* Private *Accred.:* 1984/1990 (ABHES) *Calendar:* Courses of varying lengths *Degrees:* diplomas *CEO:* Pres. Susan M. Dalto
(501) 568-0211

NATIONAL EDUCATION CENTER—ARKANSAS COLLEGE OF TECHNOLOGY
9720 Rodney Parham Rd., Little Rock 72207-6288 *Type:* Private *Accred.:* 1972/1988 (ACCSCT) *Calendar:* Qtr. plan *Degrees:* diplomas *CEO:* Exec. Dir. Byron Thompson
(501) 224-8200

NEW TYLER BARBER COLLEGE INC.
1221 E. Seventh St., North Little Rock 72114-4973 *Type:* Private *Accred.:* 1984/1989 (ACCSCT) *Calendar:* Courses of varying lengths *Degrees:* certificates *CEO:* Pres. Daniel Bryant
(501) 375-0377

RED RIVER TECHNICAL COLLEGE
Hwy. 29 S., P.O. Box 140, Hope 71801 *Type:* Private *Calendar:* Courses of varying lengths *Degrees:* certificates *Prof. Accred.:* Respiratory Therapy Technology *CEO:* Dir. Johnny Rapert
Enroll: 25   (501) 777-5722

SOUTH CENTRAL CAREER COLLEGE
4500 W. Commercial Dr., North Little Rock 72116 *Type:* Private business *Accred.:* 1979/1988 (ACISC) *Calendar:* Qtr. plan *Degrees:* certificates, diplomas *CEO:* Pres. Fred A. Ellis
(501) 758-6800

BRANCH CAMPUS
Ste. G, 2311 E. Nettleton, Jonesboro 72401 *Accred.:* 1987/1988 (ACISC) *CEO:* Dir. Landon Owens
(501) 972-6999

SOUTH CENTRAL CAREER COLLEGE
1614 Brentwood Dr., Pine Bluff 71601 *Type:* Private business *Accred.:* 1986 (ACISC) *Calendar:* Qtr. plan *Degrees:* certificates, diplomas *CEO:* Dir. Gene Owens
(501) 535-6800

SOUTHERN TECHNICAL COLLEGE
7601 Scott Hamilton Dr., Little Rock 72209 *Type:* Private business *Accred.:* 1988 (ACISC) *Calendar:* Qtr. plan *Degrees:* certificates, diplomas *CEO:* Dir. Karen Rosa
(501) 565-7000

BRANCH CAMPUS
3348 N. College St., Fayetteville 72703 *Accred.:* 1988 (ACISC) *CEO:* Dir. William Rodgers
(501) 442-2364

CALIFORNIA

ABS TRAINING CENTER
7132 Garden Grove Blvd., Westminster 92683
Type: Private *Accred.:* 1986 (ACCSCT) *Calendar:* Courses of varying lengths *Degrees:* certificates *CEO:* Dir. Linda Bonnette
(714) 895-9818

ACADEMY PACIFIC BUSINESS AND TRAVEL
COLLEGE
1777 N. Vine St., Hollywood 90028-5218
Type: Private *Accred.:* 1973/1990 (ACCSCT) *Calendar:* Courses of varying lengths *Degrees:* diplomas *CEO:* Pres. Marsha Toy
(213) 462-3211

THE ADVERTISING ARTS COLLEGE
10025 Mesa Rim Rd., San Diego 92121-2913 *Type:* Private *Accred.:* 1986 (ACCSCT) *Calendar:* Courses of varying lengths *Degrees:* certificates, diplomas *CEO:* Pres. Gary R. Cantor
(619) 546-0602

AMERICAN ACADEMY OF NUTRITION
3408 Sausalito, Corona del Mar 92625 *Type:* Private home study *Accred.:* 1989 (NHSC) *Calendar:* Courses of varying lengths *Degrees:* diplomas *CEO:* Admin. Peter Berwick
(714) 760-5081

AMERICAN COLLEGE OF OPTECHS
4021 Rosewood Ave., Los Angeles 90004-2932 *Type:* Private *Accred.:* 1983/1989 (ABHES); 1989 (ACCSCT) *Calendar:* Courses of varying lengths *Degrees:* certificates *CEO:* Pres./Dir. David A. Pyle
(213) 383-2862

AMERICAN NANNY COLLEGE
4650 Arrow Hwy., Ste. A10, Montclair 91763-1213 *Type:* Private *Accred.:* 1992 (ACCSCT) *Calendar:* Courses of varying lengths *Degrees:* certificates *CEO:* Pres. Beverly Benjamin
(909) 624-7711

AMERICAN TECHNICAL COLLEGE FOR CAREER
TRAINING
191 S. E St., San Bernardino 92401-1912
Type: Private *Accred.:* 1989 (ACCSCT) *Calendar:* Courses of varying lengths *Degrees:* certificates, diplomas *CEO:* Dir. Steve S. Hu
(714) 885-3857

AMERITECH COLLEGES
6843 Lennox Ave., Van Nuys 91405-4059
Type: Private *Accred.:* 1991 (ACCSCT) *Calendar:* Courses of varying lengths *Degrees:* certificates *CEO:* Dir. Tauni Murphy
(818) 901-7311

AMERITECH COLLEGES OF BAKERSFIELD
4300 Stine Rd., Ste. 700, Bakersfield 93313-2041 *Type:* Private *Accred.:* 1991 (ACCSCT) *Calendar:* Courses of varying lengths *Degrees:* certificates *CEO:* Dir. Jari Simpson
(805) 835-9225

ANDON COLLEGE AT MODESTO
1314 H St., Modesto 95354 *Type:* Private *Accred.:* 1983/1988 (ABHES) *Calendar:* Courses of varying lengths *Degrees:* certificates *CEO:* Pres. Gary D. Kerber
(209) 571-8777

ANDON COLLEGE AT STOCKTON
1201 N. El Dorado St., Stockton 95202
Type: Private *Accred.:* 1988 (ABHES) *Calendar:* Courses of varying lengths *Degrees:* certificates *CEO:* Pres. Gary D. Kerber
(209) 462-8777

ASSOCIATED TECHNICAL COLLEGE
1177 N. Magnolia Ave., Anaheim 92801-2606 *Type:* Private *Accred.:* 1987 (ACCSCT) *Calendar:* Courses of varying lengths *Degrees:* certificates *CEO:* Dir. Ali Khalaj
(714) 229-8785

ASSOCIATED TECHNICAL COLLEGE
1670 Wilshire Blvd., Los Angeles 90017-1690 *Type:* Private *Accred.:* 1969/1987 (ACCSCT) *Calendar:* Courses of varying lengths *Degrees:* certificates *CEO:* Dir. Antonio Sanges
(213) 484-2444

ASSOCIATED TECHNICAL COLLEGE
395 N. E St., San Bernardino 92401-1488
Type: Private *Accred.:* 1991 (ACCSCT) *Cal-*

endar: Courses of varying lengths *Degrees:* certificates *CEO:* Dir. F. Tony Galiardi
(714) 885-1888

ASSOCIATED TECHNICAL COLLEGE
1475 Sixth Ave., San Diego 92101-3245 *Type:* Private *Accred.:* 1984/1989 (ACCSCT) *Calendar:* Courses of varying lengths *Degrees:* certificates *CEO:* Dir. Ali Pourhosseini
(619) 234-2181

BRYAN COLLEGE OF COURT REPORTING
2511 Beverly Blvd., Los Angeles 90057 *Type:* Private business *Accred.:* 1971/1989 (ACISC) *Calendar:* Courses of varying lengths *Degrees:* certificates, diplomas *CEO:* Pres. James T. Patterson
(213) 484-8850

CABOT COLLEGE
41 E. 12th St., National City 92050-3397 *Type:* Private business *Accred.:* 1992 (ACISC) *Calendar:* Courses of varying lengths *Degrees:* certificates, diplomas *CEO:* Pres. Wayne Cox
(619) 474-8017

CALIFORNIA ACADEMY OF MERCHANDISING, ART & DESIGN
Ste. 150, 1333 Howe Ave., Sacramento 95825 *Type:* Private business *Accred.:* 1986/1990 (ACISC) *Calendar:* Courses of varying lengths *Degrees:* certificates, diplomas *CEO:* Admin. Linda Weldon
(916) 648-8168

CALIFORNIA CAREER SCHOOLS
392 W. Cerritos Ave., Anaheim 92805-6550 *Type:* Private *Accred.:* 1987 (ACCSCT) *Calendar:* Courses of varying lengths *Degrees:* certificates *CEO:* Owner Sidney Smith
(714) 635-6585

CALIFORNIA CULINARY ACADEMY
625 Polk St., San Francisco 94102-3368 *Type:* Private *Accred.:* 1982/1988 (ACCSCT) *Calendar:* Courses of varying lengths *Degrees:* certificates *CEO:* Pres. Thomas A. Bloom, Ph.D.
(415) 771-3536

CALIFORNIA INSTITUTE OF LOCKSMITHING
14721 Oxnard St., Van Nuys 91411 *Type:* Private *Accred.:* 1992 (ACCSCT) *Calendar:*

Courses of varying lengths *Degrees:* certificates *CEO:* Dir. Charles H. Merchant, Sr.
(818) 994-7426

CALIFORNIA NANNIE COLLEGE
910 Howe Ave., Sacramento 95825-3979 *Type:* Private *Accred.:* 1988 (ACCSCT) *Calendar:* Courses of varying lengths *Degrees:* certificates *CEO:* Owner Larry Lionetli
(916) 921-2400

CALIFORNIA PARAMEDICAL & TECHNICAL COLLEGE
3745 Long Beach Blvd., Long Beach 90807-3377 *Type:* Private *Accred.:* 1980/1987 (ACCSCT) *Calendar:* Courses of varying lengths *Degrees:* diplomas *Prof. Accred.:* Medical Assisting, Respiratory Therapy Technology, Surgical Technology *CEO:* Dir. Julia Morally
(310) 595-6638

CALIFORNIA PARAMEDICAL & TECHNICAL COLLEGE
4550 LaSierra Ave., Riverside 92505-2907 *Type:* Private *Accred.:* 1982/1987 (ACCSCT) *Calendar:* Courses of varying lengths *Degrees:* diplomas *Prof. Accred.:* Medical Assisting, Respiratory Therapy Technology *CEO:* Dir. Julia Morally
(714) 687-9006

CALIFORNIA SCHOOL OF COURT REPORTING
3510 Adams St., Riverside 92504 *Type:* Private business *Accred.:* 1986/1989 (ACISC) *Calendar:* Courses of varying lengths *Degrees:* certificates, diplomas *CEO:* Pres. Virginia Wilcke
(714) 359-0293

CALIFORNIA SCHOOL OF COURT REPORTING
1201 N. Main St., Santa Ana 92701 *Type:* Private business *Accred.:* 1979/1989 (ACISC) *Calendar:* Courses of varying lengths *Degrees:* certificates, diplomas *CEO:* Dir. Joan Arntson
(714) 541-6892

CAREER MANAGEMENT INSTITUTE
1855 W. Katella Ave., Ste. 150, Orange 92667 *Type:* Private *Accred.:* 1993 (ACCSCT) *Calendar:* Courses of varying lengths *Degrees:* certificates, diplomas *CEO:* Owner/C.E.O. Nino Duccini
(714) 771-5077

CAREER WEST ACADEMY
2505B Zanella Way, Chico 95928 *Type:* Private *Accred.:* 1992 (ACCSCT) *Calendar:* Courses of varying lengths *Degrees:* certificates *CEO:* Admin. Christine Howell Payton
(916) 893-1388

CATHERINE COLLEGE
Ste. 200, 8155 Van Nuys Blvd., Panorama City 91402 *Type:* Private business *Accred.:* 1983/1990 (ACISC) *Calendar:* Courses of varying lengths *Degrees:* certificates, diplomas *CEO:* Dir. Barbara Thomas
(818) 989-9000

CENTRAL CALIFORNIA SCHOOL OF CONTINUING EDUCATION
3195 McMillan St., Ste. F, San Luis Obispo 93401 *Type:* Private *Accred.:* 1993 (ACCSCT) *Calendar:* Courses of varying lengths *Degrees:* certificates *CEO:* Admin. Gene R. Appleby
(805) 543-9123

CENTURY BUSINESS COLLEGE
2665 Fifth Ave., San Diego 92103-6613 *Type:* Private *Accred.:* 1985/1990 (ACCSCT) *Calendar:* Courses of varying lengths *Degrees:* certificates *CEO:* Vice Pres. Wayne G. Miletta
(619) 233-0184

BRANCH CAMPUS
3325 Wilshire Blvd., Los Angeles 90010-1703 *Accred.:* 1985/1990 (ACCSCT) *CEO:* Vice Pres. Wayne G. Miletta
(213) 383-1585

CENTURY SCHOOLS
3075 E. Flamingo Rd., Ste. 114, Las Vegas, NV 89121 *Accred.:* 1990 (ACCSCT) *CEO:* Dir. Richard Gallion
(702) 451-6666

CHAMPION INSTITUTE OF COSMETOLOGY
72261 Hwy. 111, Palm Desert 92260 *Type:* Private *Accred.:* 1993 (ACCSCT) *Calendar:* Courses of varying lengths *Degrees:* certificates, diplomas *CEO:* Pres. Virginia Slough
(619) 322-2227

CHAMPION INSTITUTE OF COSMETOLOGY
559 S. Palm Canyon Dr., Palm Springs 92264 *Type:* Private *Accred.:* 1993 (ACCSCT) *Calendar:* Courses of varying lengths

Degrees: certificates, diplomas *CEO:* Pres. Virginia Slough
(619) 322-2227

COLLEGE FOR RECORDING ARTS
665 Harrison St., San Francisco 94107-1312 *Type:* Private *Accred.:* 1977/1990 (ACCSCT) *Calendar:* Sem. plan *Degrees:* diplomas *CEO:* Pres. Leo de Gar Kulka
(415) 781-6306

COLLEGEAMERICA—SAN FRANCISCO
814 Mission St., Ste. 300, San Francisco 94103-9748 *Type:* Private *Accred.:* 1993 (ACCSCT) *Calendar:* Courses of varying lengths *Degrees:* certificates *CEO:* Dir. Tami Freedman
(415) 882-4545

COMBAT SYSTEMS TECHNICAL SCHOOLS COMMAND
Mare Island, Vallejo 94592 *Type:* Public (federal) technical *Accred.:* 1986/1990 (SACS-COEI) *Calendar:* Courses of varying lengths *Degrees:* certificates *CEO:* Commanding Ofcr. Shannon R. Butler, U.S.N. *FTE Enroll:* 481　　　　(707) 554-8550

COMPUTER LEARNING CENTER
222 S. Harbor Blvd., Anaheim 92805 *Type:* Private business *Accred.:* 1990 (ACISC) *Calendar:* Courses of varying lengths *Degrees:* certificates, diplomas *CEO:* Dir. Mary Langdon
(714) 956-8060

BRANCH CAMPUS
4371 Latham St., Riverside 92507 *Accred.:* 1993 (ACISC) *CEO:* Dir. Mary Langdon
(800) 464-4252

COMPUTER LEARNING CENTER
3130 Wilshire Blvd., Los Angeles 90010 *Type:* Private business *Accred.:* 1990 (ACISC) *Calendar:* Courses of varying lengths *Degrees:* certificates, diplomas *CEO:* Dir. Stephen J. Woody
(213) 386-6311

COMPUTER LEARNING CENTER
661 Howard St., San Francisco 94105 *Type:* Private business *Accred.:* 1980/1992 (ACISC) *Calendar:* Courses of varying

lengths *Degrees:* certificates, diplomas *CEO:* Dir. Elaine Cue
(415) 498-0800

COMPUTER LEARNING CENTER
111 N. Market St., San Jose 95113 *Type:* Private business *Accred.:* 1990 (ACISC) *Calendar:* Courses of varying lengths *Degrees:* certificates, diplomas *CEO:* Dir. Donald L. McMullen, Jr.
(408) 983-5950

CONCORDE CAREER INSTITUTE
1717 S. Brookhurst St., Anaheim 92804-6461 *Type:* Private *Accred.:* 1991 (ACCSCT) *Calendar:* Courses of varying lengths *Degrees:* certificates *Prof. Accred.:* Medical Assisting (AMA) *CEO:* Dir. William G. Carver
(714) 635-3450

CONCORDE CAREER INSTITUTE
4150 Lankershim Blvd., North Hollywood 91602-2896 *Type:* Private *Accred.:* 1991 (ACCSCT) *Calendar:* Courses of varying lengths *Degrees:* certificates *Prof. Accred.:* Respiratory Therapy Technology, Surgical Technology *CEO:* Dir. Jeri Weinstein
(818) 766-8151

CONCORDE CAREER INSTITUTE
600 N. Sierra Way, San Bernardino 92410-4414 *Type:* Private *Accred.:* 1991 (ACCSCT) *Calendar:* Courses of varying lengths *Degrees:* certificates *Prof. Accred.:* Practical Nursing *CEO:* Dir. Mary Ellen Kontra
(714) 884-8891

CONCORDE CAREER INSTITUTE
123 Camino de la Reina, San Diego 92108 *Type:* Private *Accred.:* 1991 (ACCSCT) *Calendar:* Courses of varying lengths *Degrees:* certificates *CEO:* Dir. Nelson Melchior
(619) 280-5005

CONCORDE CAREER INSTITUTE
1290 N. First St., San Jose 95112-4709 *Type:* Private *Accred.:* 1989 (ACCSCT) *Calendar:* Courses of varying lengths *Degrees:* certificates *CEO:* Dir. Rosalie Lampone
(408) 441-6411

CONCORDE CAREER INSTITUTE
6850 Van Nuys Blvd., Van Nuys 91405 *Type:* Private *Accred.:* 1982/1988 (ABHES)

Calendar: Courses of varying lengths *Degrees:* certificates *Prof. Accred.:* Medical Assisting *CEO:* Dir. Celiene T. Ramsey
(818) 780-5252

CONSOLIDATED WELDING SCHOOLS
4343 E. Imperial Hwy., Lynwood 90262-2396 *Type:* Private *Accred.:* 1985/1990 (ACCSCT) *Calendar:* Courses of varying lengths *Degrees:* certificates *CEO:* Pres. Robert Swanson
(310) 638-0418

DEFENSE LANGUAGE INSTITUTE
Presidio of Monterey 93944 *Type:* Public (federal) technical *Accred.:* 1979/1989 (WASC-Jr.) *Calendar:* Courses of varying lengths *Degrees:* certificates *CEO:* Commandant Vladimir Sobichevsky
Enroll: 2,985
(408) 647-5118

DELL'ARTE SCHOOL OF PHYSICAL THEATRE
P.O. Box 816, Blue Lake 95525 *Type:* Private *Calendar:* Courses of varying lengths *Degrees:* certificates *Prof. Accred.:* Theatre (associate) *CEO:* Dir. Peter Buckley
(707) 668-5663

DENTAL TECHNOLOGY INSTITUTE
1937 W. Chapman Ave., No. 100, Orange 92668-2630 *Type:* Private *Accred.:* 1976/1989 (ACCSCT) *Calendar:* Courses of varying lengths *Degrees:* diplomas *CEO:* Dir. Paul Nichols
(714) 937-3989

DICKINSON-WARREN BUSINESS COLLEGE
1001 S. 57th St., Richmond 94804 *Type:* Private business *Accred.:* 1979/1988 (ACISC) *Calendar:* Courses of varying lengths *Degrees:* certificates, diplomas *CEO:* Pres. Ramon Flores
(510) 231-7555

EAST LOS ANGELES OCCUPATIONAL CENTER
2100 Marengo St., Los Angeles 90033 *Type:* Private professional *Calendar:* Courses of varying lengths *Degrees:* certificates *Prof. Accred.:* Dental Assisting *CEO:* Prin. Joe Tijerina
(213) 223-1283

EDUCORP CAREER COLLEGE
230 E. Third St., Long Beach 90802-3140 *Type:* Private *Accred.:* 1975/1987 (ACC-

SCT) *Calendar:* Courses of varying lengths *Degrees:* certificates, diplomas *CEO:* Dir. Kenneth Boyle

(213) 437-0501

EDUTEK PROFESSIONAL COLLEGES
1541 Broadway, San Diego 92101-5788 *Type:* Private *Accred.:* 1991 (ACCSCT) *Calendar:* Courses of varying lengths *Degrees:* certificates *CEO:* Exec. Dir. Carol Ruiz

(619) 239-4138

BRANCH CAMPUS
4560 Alvarado Canyon Rd., San Diego 92120-4309 *Accred.:* 1991 (ACCSCT) *CEO:* Dir. Carol Ruiz

(619) 582-1319

BRANCH CAMPUS
5952 El Cajon Blvd., San Diego 92115-3828 *Accred.:* 1991 (ACCSCT) *CEO:* Dir. Carol Ruiz

(619) 582-1319

ELDORADO COLLEGE
Ste. 104, 2204 El Camino Real, Oceanside 92054 *Type:* Private business *Accred.:* 1980/ 1986 (ACISC) *Calendar:* Qtr. plan *Degrees:* certificates, diplomas *CEO:* Dir. Martha B. Cockell

(619) 433-3660

BRANCH CAMPUS
385 N. Escondido Blvd., Escondido 92025 *Accred.:* 1989 (ACISC) *CEO:* Dir. Martha B. Cockell

(619) 743-2100

BRANCH CAMPUS
Ste. 200, 2255 Camino Del Rio, San Diego 92108-3605 *Accred.:* 1992 (ACISC) *CEO:* (Vacant)

(619) 294-9256

ELDORADO COLLEGE
1901 Pacific Ave., West Covina 91790 *Type:* Private business *Accred.:* 1985 (ACISC) *Calendar:* Qtr. plan *Degrees:* certificates, diplomas *CEO:* Dir. Delores Moran Coe

(818) 960-5173

ELEGANCE INTERNATIONAL
4929 Wilshire Blvd., Los Angeles 90010-1734 *Type:* Private *Accred.:* 1978/1989

(ACCSCT) *Calendar:* Sem. plan *Degrees:* diplomas *CEO:* Pres. Wynna Miller

(213) 937-4838

ELITE PROGRESSIVE SCHOOL OF COSMETOLOGY
5522 Garfield Ave., Sacramento 95841 *Type:* Private *Accred.:* 1993 (ACCSCT) *Calendar:* Courses of varying lengths *Degrees:* certificates *CEO:* Owner Manhal Mansour

(916) 338-1885

ESTELLE HARMAN ACTORS WORKSHOP
522 N. La Brea Ave., Los Angeles 90036-2095 *Type:* Private *Accred.:* 1976/1988 (ACCSCT) *Calendar:* Qtr. plan *Degrees:* certificates *CEO:* Dir. Estelle Harman

(213) 931-8137

FASHION CAREERS OF CALIFORNIA
1923 Morena Blvd., San Diego 92110 *Type:* Private business *Accred.:* 1983/1989 (ACISC) *Calendar:* Courses of varying lengths *Degrees:* certificates, diplomas *CEO:* Dir. Patricia G. O'Connor

(619) 275-4700

FRESNO INSTITUTE OF TECHNOLOGY
1545 N. Fulton St., Fresno 93720 *Type:* Private *Accred.:* 1991 (ACCSCT) *Calendar:* Courses of varying lengths *Degrees:* certificates *CEO:* Dir. Fred Freedman

(209) 442-3574

GALEN COLLEGE OF MEDICAL AND DENTAL ASSISTANTS
1325 N. Wishon Ave., Fresno 93728-2381 *Type:* Private *Accred.:* 1974/1988 (ACCSCT) *Calendar:* Courses of varying lengths *Degrees:* diplomas *CEO:* Pres. Stella Mesple

(209) 264-9726

BRANCH CAMPUS
1604 Ford Ave., Ste. 10, Modesto 95350-4665 *Accred.:* 1988 (ACCSCT) *CEO:* Pres. Stella Mesple

(209) 527-5084

BRANCH CAMPUS
3746 W. Mineral King Ave., Ste. C, Visalia 93291-5510 *Accred.:* 1988 (ACCSCT) *CEO:* Pres. Stella Mesple

(209) 264-9726

GEMOLOGICAL INSTITUTE OF AMERICA
P.O. Box 2110, 1660 Stewart St., Santa
Monica 90404-4088 *Type:* Private technical
and home study *Accred.:* 1973/1986 (ACC-
SCT); 1965/1987 (NHSC) *Calendar:* Courses of varying lengths *Degrees:* certificates,
diplomas *CEO:* Accreditation Offcr. Raymond
Page
(310) 829-2991

BRANCH CAMPUS
580 Fifth Ave., New York, NY 10036-
4794 *Accred.:* 1986 (ACCSCT) *CEO:*
Mgr. Patrick B. Ball
(212) 944-5900

GLENDALE CAREER COLLEGE
1021 Grandview Ave., Glendale 91201
Type: Private *Calendar:* Courses of varying
lengths *Degrees:* diplomas *Prof. Accred.:*
Medical Assisting *CEO:* Exec. Dir. Gloria
Green
(818) 243-1131

GOLF ACADEMY OF SAN DIEGO
P.O. Box 3050, Rancho Santa Fe 92067
Type: Private business *Accred.:* 1982/1988
(ACISC) *Calendar:* Courses of varying
lengths *Degrees:* certificates, diplomas
CEO: Pres. Frederick L. Schwartz
(619) 756-2486

GOLF ACADEMY OF THE SOUTH
P.O. Box 3609, Winter Springs, FL 32708
Accred.: 1990 (ACISC) *CEO:* Dir.
Richard B. Rogers
(407) 699-1990

HEMPHILL SCHOOLS
510 S. Alvarado St., Los Angeles 90057-
2998 *Type:* Private home study *Accred.:*
1966/1992 (NHSC) *Calendar:* Courses of
varying lengths *Degrees:* diplomas *CEO:*
Pres. Arturo Delgado
(213) 413-6323

HUNTINGTON COLLEGE OF DENTAL TECHNOLOGY
7466 Edinger Ave., Huntington Beach
92647-3510 *Type:* Private *Accred.:* 1987
(ACCSCT) *Calendar:* Courses of varying
lengths *Degrees:* certificates *CEO:* Pres.
Edward M. Beram
(714) 841-9500

HYPNOSIS MOTIVATION INSTITUTE
18607 Ventura Blvd., Ste. 310, Tarzana
91356 *Type:* Private home study *Accred.:*
1989 (NHSC) *Calendar:* Courses of varying
lengths *Degrees:* certificates *CEO:* Pres.
John J. Kappas
(818) 344-4464

INSTITUTE FOR BUSINESS & TECHNOLOGY
2550 Scott Blvd., Santa Clara 95050-9998
Type: Private *Accred.:* 1979/1986 (ACC-
SCT) *Calendar:* Courses of varying lengths
Degrees: certificates *Prof. Accred.:* Medical
Assisting *CEO:* Pres. M.A. Mikhail
(408) 727-1060

NATIONAL CAREER EDUCATION
6060 Sunrise Vista Dr., Ste. 3000, Citrus
Heights 95610-7053 *Accred.:* 1986 (ACC-
SCT) *Prof. Accred.:* Medical Assisting
CEO: Dir. Lynn M. Kretzinger
(916) 969-4900

INSTITUTE OF BUSINESS AND MEDICAL
TECHNOLOGY
75-110 St. Charles Pl., Palm Desert 92260
Type: Private *Accred.:* 1992 (ACCSCT) *Calendar:* Courses of varying lengths *Degrees:*
certificates *CEO:* Pres. Craig W. Deonik
(619) 776-5873

INSTITUTE OF COMPUTER TECHNOLOGY
3200 Wilshire Blvd., No. 400, Los Angeles
90010-1308 *Type:* Private *Accred.:* 1985/
1990 (ACCSCT) *Calendar:* Courses of varying lengths *Degrees:* diplomas *CEO:* Pres.
K.C. You
(213) 381-3333

INTERNATIONAL DEALERS SCHOOL
6329 E. Washington Blvd., Commerce
90040 *Type:* Private *Accred.:* 1985/1990
(ACCSCT) *Calendar:* Courses of varying
lengths *Degrees:* certificates, diplomas
CEO: Admin. Candetta Simone
(213) 890-0030

IRVINE COLLEGE OF BUSINESS
16591 Noyes Ave., Irvine 92714 *Type:* Private business *Accred.:* 1977/1989 (ACISC)
Calendar: Courses of varying lengths *Degrees:* certificates, diplomas *CEO:* Pres.
William D. Polick, Sr.
(714) 863-1145

JOHN TRACY CLINIC
806 W. Adams Blvd., Los Angeles 90007
Type: Private home study *Accred.:* 1965/
1992 (NHSC) *Calendar:* Courses of varying
lengths *Degrees:* certificates *CEO:* Dir.
Sandra Meyer
(213) 748-5481

LEARNING TREE UNIVERSITY
20916 Knapp St., Chatsworth 91311 *Type:*
Independent *Calendar:* Qtr. plan *Degrees:*
certificates *Prof. Accred.:* Art (associate)
CEO: Dir. Christy Wilson
(818) 882-5685

LEDERWOLFF CULINARY ACADEMY
3300 Stockton Blvd., Sacramento 95820-
1450 *Type:* Private *Accred.:* 1991 (ACC-
SCT) *Calendar:* Courses of varying lengths
Degrees: certificates *CEO:* Owner Kristine
Wolff
(916) 456-7002

LEICESTER SCHOOL
1106 W. Olympic Blvd., Los Angeles 90015
Type: Private *Accred.:* 1992 (ACCSCT) *Calendar:* Courses of varying lengths *Degrees:*
certificates *CEO:* Dir./Owner Victor Weintraub
(213) 746-7666

LOS ANGELES ORT TECHNICAL INSTITUTE
635 S. Harvard Blvd., Los Angeles 90005-
2586 *Type:* Private *Accred.:* 1988 (ACC-
SCT) *Calendar:* Courses of varying lengths
Degrees: certificates *CEO:* Dir. Joseph
Neman
(213) 387-4244

VALLEY BRANCH
15130 Ventura Blvd., No. 250, Sherman
Oaks 91403-3301 *Accred.:* 1988 (ACC-
SCT) *CEO:* Coord. Chris Mahdesian
(818) 788-7222

MANAGEMENT COLLEGE OF SAN FRANCISCO
1255 Post St., No. 450, San Francisco 94109
Type: Private *Accred.:* 1993 (ACCSCT) *Calendar:* Courses of varying lengths *Degrees:*
certificates *CEO:* Owner Marilyn Mayer
(405) 776-7244

MARIC COLLEGE OF MEDICAL CAREERS
7202 Princess View Dr., San Diego 92120-
1390 *Type:* Private *Accred.:* 1982/1987
(ABHES); 1982/1988 (ACCSCT) *Calendar:*

Courses of varying lengths *Degrees:* certificates *Prof. Accred.:* Medical Assisting *CEO:*
Dir. Ken Humphrey
(619) 583-8232

MARIC COLLEGE OF MEDICAL CAREERS
1300 Rancheros Dr., San Marcos 92069-
3033 *Type:* Private *Accred.:* 1985/1987
(ABHES); 1984/1990 (ACCSCT) *Calendar:*
Courses of varying lengths *Degrees:* certificates *Prof. Accred.:* Medical Assisting *CEO:*
Dir. Kay Sherburne
(619) 747-1555

VISTA CAMPUS BRANCH
1593-C E. Vista Way, Vista 92084-3577
Accred.: 1990 (ABHES); 1990 (ACC-
SCT) *CEO:* Dir. Susan Race
(619) 758-8640

MARIN BALLET SCHOOL
100 Elm St., San Rafael 94901 *Type:* Private
Calendar: Courses of varying lengths *Degrees:* certificates *Prof. Accred.:* Dance
CEO: Artistic Dir. Margaret Swarthout
(415) 453-6705

MASTERS INSTITUTE
50 Airport Pkwy., Ste. 8, San Jose 95110-
1011 *Type:* Private *Accred.:* 1984/1989
(ACCSCT) *Calendar:* Courses of varying
lengths *Degrees:* certificates *CEO:* Pres.
David T. Ruggieri
(408) 441-1800

MED-HELP TRAINING SCHOOL
2702 Clayton Rd., Ste. 201, Concord 94519-
2726 *Type:* Private *Accred.:* 1981/1987
(ACCSCT) *Calendar:* Courses of varying
lengths *Degrees:* certificates *CEO:* Dir.
Ronald Hare
(510) 682-2030

MERIT COLLEGE
7101 Sepulveda Blvd., Van Nuys 91405
Type: Private business *Accred.:* 1972/1986
(ACISC) *Calendar:* Courses of varying
lengths *Degrees:* certificates, diplomas
CEO: Chrmn. and C.E.O. J. Robert Evans
(818) 988-6640

MODERN TECHNOLOGY SCHOOL OF X-RAY
1232 E. Katella Ave., Anaheim 92805-6623
Type: Private *Accred.:* 1987 (ACCSCT) *Calendar:* Courses of varying lengths *Degrees:*

certificates *CEO:* Admin. Dir. Harvey S. Caplan
(714) 978-7702

MODERN TECHNOLOGY SCHOOL OF X-RAY
6180 Laurel Canyon Blvd., North Hollywood 91606 *Type:* Private *Accred.:* 1987/1993 (ACCSCT) *Calendar:* Courses of varying lengths *Degrees:* certificates *CEO:* Exec. Dir. Beverly Yourstone
(818) 763-2563

MOLER BARBER COLLEGE
3500 Broadway St., Oakland 94611-5729 *Type:* Private *Accred.:* 1980/1988 (ACCSCT) *Calendar:* Courses of varying lengths *Degrees:* certificates, diplomas *CEO:* Owner Willie C. McHenry
(510) 652-4177

MOLER BARBER COLLEGE
727 J St., Sacramento 95814-2501 *Type:* Private *Accred.:* 1980/1993 (ACCSCT) *Calendar:* Courses of varying lengths *Degrees:* diplomas *CEO:* Dir. James A. Murray, Jr.
(916) 441-0072

BRANCH CAMPUS
2645 El Camino Ave., Sacramento 95821-2901 *Accred.:* 1991/1993 (ACCSCT) *CEO:* Dir. James D. Knauss
(916) 482-0871

BRANCH CAMPUS
410 E. Weber Ave., Stockton 95202-3025 *Accred.:* 1991 (ACCSCT) *CEO:* Dir. James D. Knauss
(209) 465-3218

MOLER BARBER COLLEGE
50 Mason St., San Francisco 94102-2890 *Type:* Private *Accred.:* 1980/1987 (ACCSCT) *Calendar:* Courses of varying lengths *Degrees:* diplomas *CEO:* Dir. Donald A. Forfang, II
(415) 362-5885

MTI BUSINESS COLLEGE OF STOCKTON INC.
6006 N. El Dorado St., Stockton 95207-4349 *Type:* Private *Accred.:* 1987 (ACCSCT) *Calendar:* Courses of varying lengths *Degrees:* certificates *CEO:* Dir. Felix G. Brenner
(209) 957-3030

MTI COLLEGE
2011 W. Chapman Ave., Ste. 100, Orange 92668-2632 *Type:* Private *Accred.:* 1988 (ACCSCT) *Calendar:* Qtr. plan *Degrees:* certificates, diplomas *CEO:* Dir. Ton Bui
(714) 385-1132

BRANCH CAMPUS
760 Via Lata, No. 300, Colton 92324-3916 *Accred.:* 1988 (ACCSCT) *CEO:* Dir. Sheri Talmadge
(714) 424-0123

MTI-WESTERN BUSINESS COLLEGE
2731 Capitol Ave., Sacramento 95816 *Type:* Private business *Accred.:* 1975/1987 (ACISC) *Calendar:* Courses of varying lengths *Degrees:* certificates, diplomas *CEO:* Pres. John A. Zimmerman
(916) 442-8933

MUSICIANS INSTITUTE
1655 N. McCadden Pl., Hollywood 90028 *Type:* Private *Calendar:* Courses of varying lengths *Degrees:* certificates *Prof. Accred.:* Music *CEO:* Pres. Patrick Hicks
(213) 462-1384

NATIONAL EDUCATION CENTER—BRYMAN CAMPUS
1120 N. Brookhurst St., Anaheim 92801-1702 *Type:* Private *Accred.:* 1983/1990 (ACCSCT) *Calendar:* Courses of varying lengths *Degrees:* diplomas *CEO:* Dir. Cheryl K. Smith
(714) 778-6500

NATIONAL EDUCATION CENTER—BRYMAN CAMPUS
5350 Atlantic Ave., Long Beach 90805-6020 *Type:* Private *Accred.:* 1968/1989 (ACCSCT) *Calendar:* Courses of varying lengths *Degrees:* diplomas *Prof. Accred.:* Medical Assisting (AMA) *CEO:* Exec. Dir. Roger Gugelmeyer
(310) 422-6007

NATIONAL EDUCATION CENTER—BRYMAN CAMPUS
1017 Wilshire Blvd., Los Angeles 90017-2493 *Type:* Private *Accred.:* 1973/1990 (ACCSCT) *Calendar:* Courses of varying lengths *Degrees:* diplomas *CEO:* Dir. Dick Whitaker
(213) 481-1640

NATIONAL EDUCATION CENTER—BRYMAN CAMPUS
3505 N. Hart Ave., Rosemead 91770-2096 *Type:* Private *Accred.:* 1968/1990 (ACC-SCT) *Calendar:* Courses of varying lengths *Degrees:* diplomas *Prof. Accred.:* Medical Assisting (AMA) *CEO:* Dir. George Ballew
(818) 573-5470

BRANCH CAMPUS
1600 Broadway, 3rd Fl., Oakland 94612-2142 *Accred.:* 1990 (ACCSCT) *CEO:* Dir. Nancy Bailey
(510) 763-0800

NATIONAL EDUCATION CENTER—BRYMAN CAMPUS
731 Market St., San Francisco 94103-9946 *Type:* Private *Accred.:* 1972/1990 (ACC-SCT) *Calendar:* Courses of varying lengths *Degrees:* diplomas *Prof. Accred.:* Medical Assisting (AMA) *CEO:* Dir. Vicki L. Wallace
(415) 777-2500

NATIONAL EDUCATION CENTER—BRYMAN CAMPUS
2015 Naglee Ave., San Jose 95128-4801 *Type:* Private *Accred.:* 1973/1986 (ACC-SCT) *Calendar:* Courses of varying lengths *Degrees:* diplomas *Prof. Accred.:* Medical Assisting (AMA) *CEO:* Exec. Dir. Sandra Pella
(408) 275-8800

BRANCH CAMPUS
2322 Canal St., New Orleans, LA 70119-6504 *Accred.:* 1991 (ACCSCT) *CEO:* Dir. Deborah L. Roberts
(504) 822-4500

NATIONAL EDUCATION CENTER—BRYMAN CAMPUS
4212 W. Artesia Blvd., Torrance 90504-3198 *Type:* Private *Accred.:* 1973/1990 (ACCSCT) *Calendar:* Courses of varying lengths *Degrees:* diplomas *Prof. Accred.:* Medical Assisting (AMA) *CEO:* Dir. Judy Kavenaush
(310) 542-6951

NATIONAL EDUCATION CENTER—BRYMAN CAMPUS
20835 Sherman Way, Winnetka 91306-2795 *Type:* Private *Accred.:* 1974/1987 (ACC-SCT) *Calendar:* Courses of varying lengths

Degrees: diplomas *Prof. Accred.:* Medical Assisting *CEO:* Dir. Tapas Ghosh
(818) 887-7911

NATIONAL EDUCATION CENTER SAWYER CAMPUS
8475 Jackson Rd., Sacramento 95826 *Type:* Private business *Accred.:* 1973/1991 (ACISC) *Calendar:* Courses of varying lengths *Degrees:* certificates, diplomas *CEO:* Dir. Albert H. Plante
(916) 383-1909

THE NATIONAL HISPANIC UNIVERSITY
Ste. 201, 135 E. Gish Rd., San Jose 95112 *Type:* Private *Accred.:* 1993 (ACISC) *Calendar:* Courses of varying lengths *Degrees:* certificates, diplomas *CEO:* (Vacant)
(408) 441-2000

BRANCH CAMPUS
2nd Fl., 262 Grand Ave., Oakland 94601 *Accred.:* 1993 (ACISC) *CEO:* (Vacant)
(510) 451-0511

NAVAL AMPHIBIOUS SCHOOL
Bldg. 401, San Diego 92155 *Type:* Public (federal) technical *Accred.:* 1979/1989 (SACS-COEI) *Calendar:* Courses of varying lengths *Degrees:* certificates *CEO:* Commanding Ofcr. R.S. Cloward, U.S.N.
FTE Enroll: 246   (619) 437-2236

NAVAL CONSTRUCTION TRAINING CENTER
Port Hueneme 93043 *Type:* Public (federal) technical *Accred.:* 1979/1988 (SACS-COEI) *Calendar:* Courses of varying lengths *Degrees:* certificates *CEO:* Commanding Ofcr. W.L. Dillinger, U.S.N.
FTE Enroll: 296   (805) 982-5556

NAVAL SERVICE SCHOOL COMMAND
Naval Training Ctr., San Diego 92133 *Type:* Public (federal) technical *Accred.:* 1985/1989 (SACS-COEI) *Calendar:* Courses of varying lengths *Degrees:* certificates *CEO:* Commanding Ofcr. J.R. Beinbrink, U.S.N.
FTE Enroll: 2,172   (619) 524-4857

NAVAL TECHNICAL TRAINING CENTER
Treasure Island, 1070 M Ave., San Francisco 94130 *Type:* Public (federal) technical *Accred.:* 1987/1992 (SACS-COEI) *Calendar:* Courses of varying lengths *Degrees:* certifi-

cates *CEO:* Commanding Ofcr. Deane K. Gibson, U.S.N.
FTE Enroll: 263   (415) 395-3073

NAVAL TRANSPORTATION MANAGEMENT SCHOOL
Oakland Army Base, Bldg. 790, Oakland 94626 *Type:* Public (federal) technical *Accred.:* 1986/1991 (SACS-COEI) *Calendar:* Courses of varying lengths *Degrees:* certificates *CEO:* Commanding Ofcr. Richard Elgin, U.S.N.
FTE Enroll: 59   (510) 466-2155

NEWBRIDGE COLLEGE
700 El Camino Real, Tustin 92680 *Type:* Private *Accred.:* 1991 (ACCSCT) *Calendar:* Courses of varying lengths *Degrees:* certificates *CEO:* Owner J. Ramon Villanueva
(714) 573-8787

NEWSCHOOL OF ARCHITECTURE
1249 F St., San Diego 92101-6634 *Type:* Private *Accred.:* 1991 (ACCSCT) *Calendar:* Courses of varying lengths *Degrees:* certificates *CEO:* Pres. Gordon Bishop
(619) 235-4100

NORTH PARK COLLEGE
3956 30th St., San Diego 92104-3005 *Type:* Private *Accred.:* 1991 (ACCSCT) *Calendar:* Courses of varying lengths *Degrees:* certificates *CEO:* Pres. Ross Lipsker
(619) 297-3333

BRANCH CAMPUS
4718 Clairemont Mesa Blvd., San Diego 92117 *Accred.:* 1993 (ACCSCT) *CEO:* Dir. Gerald Faskas
(619) 297-3333

NORTH VALLEY OCCUPATIONAL CENTER
11450 Sharp Ave., Mission Hills 91345 *Type:* Private professional *Calendar:* Courses of varying lengths *Prof. Accred.:* Dental Assisting *CEO:* Prin. Gloria Martinez
(818) 365-9645

NORTHWEST COLLEGE OF MEDICAL & DENTAL ASSISTANTS
530 E. Union Ave., Pasadena 91101-1744 *Type:* Private *Accred.:* 1983/1988 (ACCSCT) *Calendar:* Courses of varying lengths

Degrees: diplomas *CEO:* Exec. Dir. Marla Mittskys
(818) 796-5815

NORTHWEST COLLEGE OF MEDICAL & DENTAL ASSISTANTS
134 W. Holt Ave., Pomona 91768-3199 *Type:* Private *Accred.:* 1976/1988 (ACCSCT) *Calendar:* Courses of varying lengths *Degrees:* diplomas *CEO:* Exec. Dir. Susan Hutchison
(714) 623-1552

NORTHWEST COLLEGE OF MEDICAL & DENTAL ASSISTANTS
2121 W. Garvey Ave., West Covina 91790-2097 *Type:* Private *Accred.:* 1973/1990 (ACCSCT) *Calendar:* Courses of varying lengths *Degrees:* diplomas *CEO:* Exec. Dir. Jacky Ford
(818) 960-5046

BRANCH CAMPUS
124 S. Glendale Ave., Glendale 91205-1109 *Accred.:* 1986 (ACCSCT) *CEO:* Dir. Marsha Fuerst
(818) 242-0205

NOVA INSTITUTE OF HEALTH TECHNOLOGY
3000 S. Robertson Blvd., Los Angeles 90034-9158 *Type:* Private *Accred.:* 1991 (ACCSCT) *Calendar:* Courses of varying lengths *Degrees:* certificates, diplomas *CEO:* Dir. Rashed B. Elyas
(310) 840-5777

NOVA INSTITUTE OF HEALTH TECHNOLOGY
520 N. Euclid Ave., Ontario 91762-3591 *Type:* Private *Accred.:* 1991 (ACCSCT) *Calendar:* Courses of varying lengths *Degrees:* certificates, diplomas *CEO:* Dir. Martha L. Escobar
(714) 984-5027

NOVA INSTITUTE OF HEALTH TECHNOLOGY
11416 Whittier Blvd., Whittier 90601-3198 *Type:* Private *Accred.:* 1991 (ACCSCT) *Calendar:* Courses of varying lengths *Degrees:* certificates, diplomas *CEO:* Dir. Nagui Elyas
(310) 695-0771

OAKLAND COLLEGE OF COURT REPORTING
449 15th St., Oakland 94612 *Type:* Private business *Accred.:* 1982/1988 (ACISC) *Calendar:* Courses of varying lengths *Degrees:*

certificates, diplomas *CEO:* Pres. Brandy McGill
(510) 287-5290

ORANGE COUNTY BUSINESS COLLEGE
2035 E. Ball Rd., Anaheim 92805 *Type:* Private business *Accred.:* 1973/1990 (ACISC) *Calendar:* Courses of varying lengths *Degrees:* certificates, diplomas *CEO:* Dir. Susan A. Fechtman
(714) 772-6941

PACIFIC COAST COLLEGE
1261 Third Ave., Ste. B, Chula Vista 91911-3237 *Type:* Private *Accred.:* 1989 (ACCSCT) *Calendar:* Courses of varying lengths *Degrees:* diplomas *CEO:* Exec. Dir. Marian M. Smith
(619) 691-0882

PACIFIC COAST COLLEGE
118 W. Fifth St., Santa Ana 92701-4634 *Type:* Private *Accred.:* 1972/1987 (ACCSCT) *Calendar:* Courses of varying lengths *Degrees:* diplomas *CEO:* Exec. Dir. James J. Vernetti
(714) 558-8700

PACIFIC GATEWAY COLLEGE
3018 Carmel St., Los Angeles 90065-1401 *Type:* Private *Accred.:* 1990 (ACCSCT) *Calendar:* Courses of varying lengths *Degrees:* certificates *CEO:* Pres. John R. Phalen
(818) 247-9544

PACIFIC TRAVEL SCHOOL
2515 N. Main St., Santa Ana 92701-1300 *Type:* Private *Accred.:* 1968/1990 (ACCSCT) *Calendar:* Courses of varying lengths *Degrees:* diplomas *CEO:* Dir. Celia Sifry
(714) 543-9495

PLATT COLLEGE
10900 E. 183rd St., Ste. 290, Cerritos 90701-5342 *Type:* Private *Accred.:* 1991 (ACCSCT) *Calendar:* Courses of varying lengths *Degrees:* certificates *CEO:* Dir. Margaret Potter Simons
(310) 809-5100

PLATT COLLEGE
2361 McGaw Ave., Irvine 92714-5831 *Type:* Private *Accred.:* 1991 (ACCSCT) *Calendar:*

Courses of varying lengths *Degrees:* certificates *CEO:* Pres. William W. Lockwood
(714) 833-2300

PLATT COLLEGE
7470 N. Figueroa St., Los Angeles 90041-1717 *Type:* Private *Accred.:* 1987/1993 (ACCSCT) *Calendar:* Courses of varying lengths *Degrees:* certificates *CEO:* Dir. William W. Lockwood
(213) 258-8050

PLATT COLLEGE
2920 Inland Empire Blvd., No. 102, Ontario 91764-4801 *Type:* Private *Accred.:* 1989 (ACCSCT) *Calendar:* Courses of varying lengths *Degrees:* certificates *CEO:* Pres. Jan E. Hartz
(909) 989-1187

PLATT COLLEGE
6250 El Cajon Blvd., San Diego 92115-3919 *Type:* Private *Accred.:* 1985/1990 (ACCSCT) *Calendar:* Courses of varying lengths *Degrees:* certificates *CEO:* Pres. Robert D. Leiker
(619) 265-0107

PLATT COLLEGE
301 Mission St., No. 450, San Francisco 94105-2243 *Type:* Private *Accred.:* 1991 (ACCSCT) *Calendar:* Courses of varying lengths *Degrees:* certificates *CEO:* Dir. Carel R. Thomas
(415) 495-4000

PRACTICAL SCHOOLS
900 E. Ball Rd., Anaheim 92805-5915 *Type:* Private *Accred.:* 1973/1990 (ACCSCT) *Calendar:* Courses of varying lengths *Degrees:* diplomas *CEO:* Pres. Marlyn B. Sheehan
(714) 535-6000

ROSSTON SCHOOL OF HAIR DESIGN
673 W. Fifth St., San Bernardino 92410-3201 *Type:* Private *Accred.:* 1976/1988 (ACCSCT) *Calendar:* Courses of varying lengths *Degrees:* certificates, diplomas *CEO:* Pres. John Olivas
(714) 884-2719

SAN FRANCISCO BALLET SCHOOL
455 Franklin St., San Francisco 94102 *Type:* Private *Calendar:* Courses of varying

lengths *Degrees:* certificates *Prof. Accred.:* Dance *CEO:* Dir. Nancy Johnson

(415) 861-5600

SAN FRANCISCO BARBER COLLEGE
64 Sixth St., San Francisco 94103-1608 *Type:* Private *Accred.:* 1984/1989 (ACC-SCT) *Calendar:* Courses of varying lengths *Degrees:* certificates *CEO:* Pres. Frank Yorkis

(415) 621-6802

SAN JOAQUIN VALLEY COLLEGE
201 New Stine Rd., Bakersfield 93309-2606 *Type:* Private *Accred.:* 1982/1988 (ACC-SCT) *Calendar:* Courses of varying lengths *Degrees:* diplomas *Prof. Accred.:* Medical Assisting *CEO:* Dir. Cherie Mendez

(805) 834-0126

SAN JOAQUIN VALLEY COLLEGE
3333 N. Bond St., Fresno 93726-9941 *Type:* Private *Accred.:* 1981/1987 (ACCSCT) *Calendar:* Courses of varying lengths *Degrees:* diplomas *Prof. Accred.:* Medical Assisting *CEO:* Dir. Janet Caldwell

(209) 229-7800

SAN JOAQUIN VALLEY COLLEGE OF AERONAUTICS
4985 E. Andersen Ave., Fresno 93726 *Accred.:* 1993 (ACCSCT) *CEO:* Dir. Janet Caldwell

(209) 229-7800

SAN JOAQUIN VALLEY COLLEGE
8400 W. Mineral King Ave., Visalia 93291-9283 *Type:* Private *Accred.:* 1981/1987 (ACCSCT) *Calendar:* Courses of varying lengths *Degrees:* diplomas *Prof. Accred.:* Medical Assisting, Respiratory Therapy Technology *CEO:* Pres. Robert F. Perry

(209) 651-2500

SANTA BARBARA BUSINESS COLLEGE
211 S. Real Rd., Bakersfield 93301 *Type:* Private business *Accred.:* 1983/1991 (ACISC) *Calendar:* Qtr. plan *Degrees:* certificates, diplomas *Prof. Accred.:* Medical Assisting *CEO:* Dir. DiAnne Davis

(805) 322-3006

SANTA BARBARA BUSINESS COLLEGE
4333 Hansen Ave., Fremont 94536 *Type:* Private business *Accred.:* 1976/1986

(ACISC) *Calendar:* Qtr. plan *Degrees:* certificates, diplomas *Prof. Accred.:* Medical Assisting *CEO:* Dir. Susan Rocha

(510) 793-4342

SANTA BARBARA BUSINESS COLLEGE
4025 Foothill Rd., Santa Barbara 93110 *Type:* Private business *Accred.:* 1976/1990 (ACISC) *Calendar:* Qtr. plan *Degrees:* certificates, diplomas *Prof. Accred.:* Medical Assisting *CEO:* Dir. Susan Corvino

(805) 967-9677

SANTA BARBARA BUSINESS COLLEGE
303 E. Plaza Dr., Santa Maria 93454 *Type:* Private business *Accred.:* 1983/1991 (ACISC) *Calendar:* Qtr. plan *Degrees:* certificates, diplomas *Prof. Accred.:* Medical Assisting *CEO:* Dir. Carol Gastiger

(805) 922-8256

SAWYER COLLEGE
441 W. Trimble Rd., San Jose 95131 *Type:* Private business *Accred.:* 1973/1990 (ACISC) *Calendar:* Courses of varying lengths *Degrees:* certificates, diplomas *CEO:* Dir. Laura James

(408) 954-8200

SAWYER COLLEGE AT POMONA
1021 E. Holt Ave., Pomona 91767 *Type:* Private business *Accred.:* 1967/1990 (ACISC) *Calendar:* Courses of varying lengths *Degrees:* certificates, diplomas *CEO:* Dir. Denise Berson

(714) 629-2534

SAWYER COLLEGE AT VENTURA
2101 E. Gonzales Rd., Oxnard 93030 *Type:* Private business *Accred.:* 1969/1987 (ACISC) *Calendar:* Courses of varying lengths *Degrees:* certificates, diplomas *CEO:* Pres. Doreen E. Adamache

(805) 485-6000

SCHOOL OF COMMUNICATION ELECTRONICS
184 Second St., San Francisco 94105-3809 *Type:* Private *Accred.:* 1986 (ACCSCT) *Calendar:* Courses of varying lengths *Degrees:* certificates *CEO:* Owner Robert W. Lew

(415) 896-0858

SEQUOIA INSTITUTE
420 Whitney Pl., Fremont 94539-7663 *Type:* Private *Accred.:* 1977/1989 (ACCSCT) *Cal-*

endar: Courses of varying lengths *Degrees:* certificates *CEO:* Pres. Timothy T. Schutz

(510) 490-6900

SIERRA ACADEMY OF AERONAUTICS
TECHNICIANS INSTITUTE
Oakland International Airport, Oakland 94614-0429 *Type:* Private *Accred.:* 1987 (ACCSCT) *Calendar:* Courses of varying lengths *Degrees:* certificates, diplomas *CEO:* Pres. Norris N. Everett

(510) 568-6100

SIERRA VALLEY BUSINESS COLLEGE
Bldg. D, 4747 N. First St., Fresno 93726 *Type:* Private business *Accred.:* 1981/1987 (ACISC) *Calendar:* Courses of varying lengths *Degrees:* certificates, diplomas *CEO:* Pres. Donald D. Goodpaster

(209) 222-0947

SILICON VALLEY COLLEGE
41350 Christy St., Fremont 94538 *Type:* Private *Accred.:* 1992 (ACCSCT) *Calendar:* Courses of varying lengths *Degrees:* certificates *CEO:* Chrmn./Dean Ellis C. Gedney

(510) 623-9966

SIMI VALLEY ADULT SCHOOL
3192 Los Angeles Ave., Simi Valley 93065 *Type:* Private *Calendar:* Courses of varying lengths *Degrees:* certificates, diplomas *Prof. Accred.:* Respiratory Therapy Technology, Surgical Technology *CEO:* Dir. Sondra Jones

(805) 527-4840

SOUTH COAST COLLEGE OF COURT REPORTING
1380 S. Sanderson Ave., Anaheim 92806 *Type:* Private business *Accred.:* 1984/1990 (ACISC) *Calendar:* Courses of varying lengths *Degrees:* certificates, diplomas *CEO:* Dir. Jean Gonzalez

(714) 897-6464

SOUTHERN CALIFORNIA COLLEGE OF BUSINESS AND LAW
595 W. Lambert Rd., Brea 92621 *Type:* Private business *Accred.:* 1993 (ACISC) *Calendar:* Courses of varying lengths *Degrees:* certificates, diplomas *CEO:* Pres. Cynthia L. Cramer

(714) 529-1055

SOUTHERN CALIFORNIA COLLEGE OF COURT REPORTING
1100 S. Claudina Pl., Anaheim 92805 *Type:* Private business *Accred.:* 1991 (ACISC) *Calendar:* Courses of varying lengths *Degrees:* certificates, diplomas *CEO:* Dir. Debra D. Lee

(714) 758-1500

SUTECH SCHOOL OF VOCATIONAL-TECHNICAL TRAINING
3427 E. Olympic Blvd., Los Angeles 90023-3076 *Type:* Private *Accred.:* 1992 (ACCSCT) *Calendar:* Courses of varying lengths *Degrees:* certificates *CEO:* Pres. Oswaldo Forero

(213) 262-3210

BRANCH CAMPUS
1815 S. Lewis St., Anaheim 90023-3076 *CEO:* Pres. Oswaldo Forero

(213) 262-3210

SYSTEMS PROGRAMMING DEVELOPMENT INSTITUTE
4900 Triggs St., City of Commerce 90022-4832 *Type:* Private *Accred.:* 1984/1989 (ACCSCT) *Calendar:* Courses of varying lengths *Degrees:* certificates *CEO:* Pres. Jose Luis Segura

(213) 261-8181

TECHNICAL HEALTH CAREERS SCHOOL
11603 S. Western Ave., Los Angeles 90047 *Type:* Private *Accred.:* 1982/1988 (ABHES) *Calendar:* Courses of varying lengths *Degrees:* certificates *Prof. Accred.:* Medical Assisting *CEO:* Pres. Sharon L. Hughes

(213) 757-0273

TRAVEL AND TRADE CAREER INSTITUTE
3635 Atlantic Ave., Long Beach 90807 *Type:* Private *Accred.:* 1972/1989 (ACCSCT) *Calendar:* Courses of varying lengths *Degrees:* diplomas *CEO:* Pres. Rodger Erickson

(310) 426-8841

BRANCH CAMPUS
12541 Brookhurst St., Ste. 100, Garden Grove 92640-9802 *Accred.:* 1972/1989 (ACCSCT) *CEO:* Exec. Vice Pres. Karen R. Erickson

(714) 636-2611

TRAVEL UNIVERSITY INTERNATIONAL
3655 Ruffin Rd. N., Ste. 225, San Diego 92123-1853 *Type:* Private *Accred.:* 1988 (ACCSCT) *Calendar:* Courses of varying lengths *Degrees:* certificates *CEO:* Pres. Nancy Chappie

(619) 292-9755

BRANCH CAMPUS
1441 Kapiolani Blvd., Ste. 1414, Honolulu, HI 96814-4401 *Accred.:* 1988 (ACCSCT) *CEO:* Dir. Susan James

(808) 946-3535

TRUCK DRIVING ACADEMY
5168 N. Blythe Ave., No. 102, Fresno 93722-6429 *Type:* Private *Accred.:* 1988 (ACCSCT) *Calendar:* Courses of varying lengths *Degrees:* certificates *CEO:* Dir. Shirley Ross

(209) 276-5708

TRUCK DRIVING ACADEMY
5711 Florin-Perkins Rd., Sacramento 95828-1002 *Type:* Private *Accred.:* 1988 (ACCSCT) *Calendar:* Courses of varying lengths *Degrees:* certificates *CEO:* Owner Charles J. Grant

(916) 381-2285

TRUCK MARKETING INSTITUTE
1090 Eugenia Pl., P.O. Box 5000, Carpinteria 93014-5000 *Type:* Private home study *Accred.:* 1968/1989 (NHSC) *Calendar:* Courses of varying lengths *Degrees:* diplomas *CEO:* Dir. Robert Godfrey

(805) 684-4558

UCC VOCATIONAL CENTER
1322 Coronado Ave., Long Beach 90804-3504 *Type:* Private *Accred.:* 1992 (ACCSCT) *Calendar:* Courses of varying lengths *Degrees:* certificates *CEO:* Dir. Smith Leng

(310) 597-3798

VALLEY COMMERCIAL COLLEGE
910 Twelfth St., Modesto 95354 *Type:* Private business *Accred.:* 1970/1989 (ACISC) *Calendar:* Courses of varying lengths *Degrees:* certificates, diplomas *CEO:* Pres./C.E.O. Gregory L. Martin

(209) 578-0616

WATTERSON COLLEGE
1165 E. Colorado Blvd., Pasadena 91106 *Type:* Private business *Accred.:* 1953/1990 (ACISC) *Calendar:* Qtr. plan *Degrees:* certificates, diplomas *CEO:* Dir. Rita A. Totten

(818) 449-3990

WATTERSON COLLEGE
1422 S. Azusa Ave., West Covina 91791 *Type:* Private business *Accred.:* 1988 (ACISC) *Calendar:* Qtr. plan *Degrees:* certificates, diplomas *CEO:* Dir. Al Parsons

(818) 919-8701

WATTERSON COLLEGE PACIFIC
815 N. Oxnard Blvd., Oxnard 93030 *Type:* Private business *Accred.:* 1979/1990 (ACISC) *Calendar:* Courses of varying lengths *Degrees:* certificates, diplomas *CEO:* Dir. Julie Martin

(805) 656-5566

BRANCH CAMPUS
2030 University Dr., Vista 92083 *Accred.:* 1985/1990 (ACISC) *CEO:* Dir. P. Kevin Michie

(619) 724-1500

WESTECH COLLEGE
500 W. Mission Blvd., Pomona 91766-1532 *Type:* Private *Accred.:* 1991 (ACCSCT) *Calendar:* Courses of varying lengths *Degrees:* certificates *CEO:* Exec. Dir. Barry Maleki

(714) 622-6486

WESTERN CAREER COLLEGE
8909 Folsom Blvd., Sacramento 95826 *Type:* Private *Accred.:* 1970/1987 (ACCSCT) *Calendar:* Courses of varying lengths *Degrees:* diplomas *Prof. Accred.:* Medical Assisting *CEO:* Pres. Richard G. Nathanson

(916) 361-1660

WESTERN CAREER COLLEGE
170 Bayfair Mall, San Leandro 94578-3711 *Type:* Private *Accred.:* 1986 (ACCSCT) *Calendar:* Courses of varying lengths *Degrees:* diplomas *Prof. Accred.:* Medical Assisting *CEO:* Dir. Jay Harris

(510) 278-3888

WESTERN TRUCK SCHOOL
4565 N. Golden State Blvd., Fresno 93722-3829 *Type:* Private *Accred.:* 1988 (ACCSCT) *Calendar:* Courses of varying lengths

Degrees: certificates *CEO:* Dir. Gerald Payne

          (209) 276-1220

WESTERN TRUCK SCHOOL
4612 E. Nunes Rd., Turlock 95308-9518 *Type:* Private *Accred.:* 1987 (ACCSCT) *Calendar:* Courses of varying lengths *Degrees:* certificates *CEO:* Dir. Don Laughlin

          (209) 472-1500

WESTERN TRUCK SCHOOL
4521 W. Capitol Ave., West Sacramento 95691-2121 *Type:* Private *Accred.:* 1980/ 1993 (ACCSCT) *Calendar:* Courses of varying lengths *Degrees:* certificates *CEO:* Pres. Everett G. Nord

          (916) 372-6500

BRANCH CAMPUS
1835 S. Black Canyon Hwy., Phoenix, AZ 85040-1905 *Accred.:* 1987/1993 (ACC-SCT) *CEO:* Dir. Bill Williams

          (602) 437-5303

BRANCH CAMPUS
5800 State Rd., Bakersfield 93308 *Accred.:* 1992 (ACCSCT) *CEO:* Dir. Mitzy Bennett

          (805) 399-0701

BRANCH CAMPUS
4757 Old Cliffs Rd., San Diego 92120 *Accred.:* 1992 (ACCSCT) *CEO:* Dir. Dale Shubert

          (619) 229-8301

BRANCH CAMPUS
1053 N. Broadway, Stockton 95205-3924 *Accred.:* 1991 (ACCSCT) *CEO:* Dir. Douglas Millen

          (209) 946-0569

WESTLAKE INSTITUTE OF TECHNOLOGY
31826A Village Center Rd., Westlake Village 91361 *Type:* Private *Accred.:* 1992 (ACCSCT) *Calendar:* Courses of varying lengths *Degrees:* certificates *CEO:* Owner Bruce H. Dotson

          (818) 991-9992

COLORADO

ACADEMY OF FLORAL DESIGN
837 Acoma St., Denver 80204 *Type:* Private business *Accred.:* 1983/1987 (ACISC) *Calendar:* Courses of varying lengths *Degrees:* certificates, diplomas *CEO:* Pres./Dir. Noel S. Valnes
(303) 623-8855

AMERICAN DIESEL & AUTOMOTIVE COLLEGE
1002 S. Jason St., Denver 80223-2868 *Type:* Private *Accred.:* 1981/1987 (ACCSCT) *Calendar:* Courses of varying lengths *Degrees:* diplomas *CEO:* Dir. Mel Jones
(303) 778-5522

BARNES BUSINESS COLLEGE
150 N. Sheridan Blvd., Denver 80226 *Type:* Private business *Accred.:* 1953/1987 (ACISC) *Calendar:* Qtr. plan *Degrees:* certificates, diplomas *CEO:* Dir. Shirley C. Lowery
(303) 922-8454

BOULDER SCHOOL OF MASSAGE THERAPY
3285 30th St., Boulder 80301-1451 *Type:* Private *Accred.:* 1991 (ACCSCT) *Calendar:* Courses of varying lengths *Degrees:* certificates *CEO:* Dir. Lorraine M. Zinn
(303) 443-5131

BOULDER VALLEY AREA VOCATIONAL-
TECHNICAL CENTER
6600 E. Arapahoe Ave., Boulder 80303 *Type:* Private *Calendar:* Courses of varying lengths *Degrees:* certificates *Prof. Accred.:* Medical Assisting (AMA) *CEO:* Exec. Dir. Lonnie M. Hart, Ph.D.
Enroll: 36   (303) 447-5247

COLLEGEAMERICA—DENVER
720 S. Colorado Blvd., Ste. 260, Denver 80222-1912 *Type:* Private *Accred.:* 1993 (ACCSCT) *Calendar:* Courses of varying lengths *Degrees:* certificates *CEO:* Dir. Kathy A. Metcalf
(303) 691-9756

COLORADO AERO TECH
10851 W. 120th Ave., Broomfield 80021-3465 *Type:* Private *Accred.:* 1972/1987 (ACCSCT) *Calendar:* Courses of varying lengths *Degrees:* certificates *CEO:* Exec. Dir. Erik Brumme
(800) 888-3995

COLORADO ASSOCIATION OF PARAMEDICAL EDUCATION, INC.
9191 Grant St., Thornton 80229 *Type:* Private *Calendar:* Courses of varying lengths *Degrees:* certificates *Prof. Accred.:* EMT-Paramedic *CEO:* Dir. Donald Massey
(303) 451-7800

COLORADO CAREER ACADEMY
13790 E. Rice Pl., Aurora 80015-1092 *Type:* Private *Accred.:* 1992 (ACCSCT) *Calendar:* Courses of varying lengths *Degrees:* certificates *CEO:* Pres./Dir. Vaios N. Athanasiou
(303) 690-6900

COLORADO CAREER ACADEMY
95 S. Wadsworth Blvd., Lakewood 80226-1513 *Type:* Private *Accred.:* 1985/1990 (ACCSCT) *Calendar:* Courses of varying lengths *Degrees:* certificates *CEO:* Owner/Dir. Madeleine Athanasiou
(303) 234-0401

COLORADO SCHOOL OF TRADES
1575 Hoyt St., Lakewood 80215-2996 *Type:* Private *Accred.:* 1973/1990 (ACCSCT) *Calendar:* Courses of varying lengths *Degrees:* certificates *CEO:* Dir. Robert E. Martin
(303) 233-4697

COLORADO SCHOOL OF TRAVEL
608 Garrison St., Unit J, Lakewood 80215-5881 *Type:* Private *Accred.:* 1991 (ACCSCT) *Calendar:* Courses of varying lengths *Degrees:* certificates *CEO:* Pres. Paula E. Wagner
(303) 233-8654

COLUMBINE COLLEGE
5801 W. 44th Ave., Denver 80212-5528 *Type:* Private *Accred.:* 1991/1993 (ACCSCT) *Calendar:* Courses of varying lengths *Degrees:* certificates *CEO:* Pres. Roger Hartman
(303) 935-2266

BRANCH CAMPUS
3754 E. LaSalle St., Colorado Springs
80909 *Accred.:* 1991/1993 (ACCSCT)
CEO: Owner/Dir. Peter Schlosser
(719) 574-8777

CONCORDE CAREER INSTITUTE
770 Grant St., Denver 80203-3517 *Type:*
Private *Accred.:* 1991 (ACCSCT) *Calendar:*
Courses of varying lengths *Degrees:* certificates *Prof. Accred.:* Surgical Technology
CEO: Dir. Richard K. Shepard
(303) 861-1151

DENVER ACADEMY OF COURT REPORTING
2nd Fl., 7290 Samuel Dr., Denver 80221-
2792 *Type:* Private business *Accred.:* 1982/
1987 (ACISC) *Calendar:* Courses of varying
lengths *Degrees:* certificates, diplomas
CEO: Dir. Charles W. Jarstfer
(303) 629-1291

BRANCH CAMPUS
220 Ruskin Dr., Colorado Springs 80910
Accred.: 1992 (ACISC) *CEO:* Dir. Wayne
L. Frantz
(719) 574-5010

DENVER AUTOMOTIVE AND DIESEL COLLEGE
405 S. Platte River Dr., Denver 80223-9960
Type: Private *Accred.:* 1968/1988 (ACC-
SCT) *Calendar:* Courses of varying lengths
Degrees: diplomas *CEO:* Dir. Joseph R.
Chalupa
(303) 722-5724

DENVER PARALEGAL INSTITUTE
1401 19th St., Denver 80202-1213 *Type:*
Private *Accred.:* 1979/1990 (ACCSCT) *Calendar:* Courses of varying lengths *Degrees:*
certificates *CEO:* Dir. Betsy O'Neil
Covington
(800) 848-0550

BRANCH CAMPUS
105 E. Vermijo Ave., Ste. 415, Colorado
Springs 80903 *Accred.:* 1992 (ACCSCT)
CEO: Dir. Brenda A. Mientka
(719) 444-0190

DURANGO AIR SERVICE
1300 County Rd. 309, Durango 81301 *Type:*
Private *Accred.:* 1993 (ACCSCT) *Calendar:*
Courses of varying lengths *Degrees:* certificates, diplomas *CEO:* Pres. Donley E.
Watkins
(303) 247-5535

EMILY GRIFFITH OPPORTUNITY SCHOOL
1250 Welton St., Denver 80204 *Type:* Private *Calendar:* Courses of varying lengths
Degrees: certificates *Prof. Accred.:* Dental
Assisting, Medical Assisting (AMA) *CEO:*
Prin. Mary Ann Parthum, Ph.D.
(303) 572-8218

HERITAGE COLLEGE OF HEALTH CAREERS
12 Lakeside La., Denver 80212-7413 *Type:*
Private *Accred.:* 1991 (ACCSCT) *Calendar:*
Courses of varying lengths *Degrees:* certificates *CEO:* Pres. Richard Herold
(303) 477-7240

MEDICAL CAREERS TRAINING CENTER
4020 S. College Ave., Fort Collins 80524
Type: Private *Accred.:* 1990 (ABHES) *Calendar:* Courses of varying lengths *Degrees:*
certificates *CEO:* Pres. Richard B. Laub
(303) 223-2669

PLATT COLLEGE
3100 S. Parker Rd., Aurora 80014-3141
Type: Private *Accred.:* 1987 (ACCSCT) *Calendar:* Courses of varying lengths *Degrees:*
certificates, diplomas *CEO:* Dir. Jerald Sirbu
(303) 369-5151

PPI HEALTH CAREERS SCHOOL
2345 N. Academy Blvd., Colorado Springs
80909 *Type:* Private *Accred.:* 1983/1990
(ABHES) *Calendar:* Courses of varying
lengths *Degrees:* diplomas *Prof. Accred.:*
Medical Assisting, Medical Laboratory
Technology *CEO:* Pres. Thomas J.
Twardowski
(719) 596-7400

PRESBYTERIAN-ST. LUKE CENTER FOR HEALTH
SCIENCE EDUCATION
1719 E. 19th Ave., Denver 80218 *Type:* Private *Calendar:* Courses of varying lengths
Degrees: certificates, diplomas *Prof. Accred.:* Medical Technology, Radiography
CEO: Pres. Thomas Petty, M.D.
(303) 839-6740

TECHNICAL TRADES INSTITUTE
2315 E. Pikes Peak Ave., Colorado Springs
80909 *Type:* Private *Accred.:* 1983/1988

(ACCSCT) *Calendar:* Courses of varying lengths *Degrees:* certificates, diplomas *CEO:* Dir. Frederick W. Harring
(719) 632-7626

EMERY AVIATION COLLEGE
1245A Aviation Way, Colorado Springs 80916 *Accred.:* 1990 (ACCSCT) *CEO:* Dir. Charles R. Hannum
(719) 591-9488

TECHNICAL TRADES INSTITUTE
772 Horizon Dr., Grand Junction 81501-9977 *Type:* Private *Accred.:* 1987 (ACC-

SCT) *Calendar:* Courses of varying lengths *Degrees:* certificates *CEO:* Dir. Kim E. Rosenquist
(303) 245-8101

T.H. PICKENS TECHNICAL CENTER
500 Buckley Rd., Aurora 80011 *Type:* Private *Calendar:* Courses of varying lengths *Degrees:* certificates *Prof. Accred.:* Dental Assisting, Medical Assisting (AMA), Medical Laboratory Technology (AMA), Respiratory Therapy Technology *CEO:* Exec. Dir. Dale McCall, Ph.D.
(303) 344-4910

CONNECTICUT

ALBERT I. PRINCE REGIONAL VOCATIONAL-
TECHNICAL SCHOOL
500 Bookfield St., Hartford 06106 *Type:* Private *Calendar:* Courses of varying lengths *Degrees:* certificates *Prof. Accred.:* Dental Assisting *CEO:* Dir. Silas Shannon
(203) 246-8594

ALLSTATE TRACTOR TRAILER TRAINING SCHOOL
2064 Main St., Bridgeport 06004-2720 *Type:* Private *Accred.:* 1989 (ACCSCT) *Calendar:* Courses of varying lengths *Degrees:* certificates *CEO:* Pres. George Delibro
(800) 245-9422

BARAN INSTITUTE OF TECHNOLOGY
611 Day Hill Rd., Windsor 06095 *Type:* Private *Accred.:* 1993 (ACCSCT) *Calendar:* Courses of varying lengths *Degrees:* certificates *CEO:* Dir./Owner Bradley R. Baran
(203) 688-3353

BRANFORD HALL CAREER INSTITUTE
9 Business Park Dr., Branford 06405 *Type:* Private business *Accred.:* 1977/1987 (ACISC) *Calendar:* Courses of varying lengths *Degrees:* certificates, diplomas *CEO:* Pres. Nelson Bernabucci
(203) 488-2525

BUTLER BUSINESS SCHOOL
2710 North Ave., Bridgeport 06604 *Type:* Private business *Accred.:* 1979/1991 (ACISC) *Calendar:* Courses of varying lengths *Degrees:* certificates, diplomas *CEO:* Pres. Robert M. Butler
(203) 333-3601

CONNECTICUT BUSINESS INSTITUTE
605 Broad St., Stratford 06497 *Type:* Private business *Accred.:* 1972/1988 (ACISC) *Calendar:* Tri. plan *Degrees:* certificates, diplomas *CEO:* Pres. Robert Moir
(203) 377-1775

BRANCH CAMPUS
809 Main St., East Hartford 06108 *Accred.:* 1993 (ACISC) *CEO:* Dir. Edward J. Dupre
(203) 291-2880

BRANCH CAMPUS
984 Chapel St., New Haven 06510 *Accred.:* 1972/1988 (ACISC) *CEO:* Dir. Katherine Palmieri
(203) 562-8114

CONNECTICUT CENTER FOR MASSAGE THERAPY
75 Kitts La., Newington 06111-3954 *Type:* Private *Accred.:* 1985/1990 (ACCSCT) *Calendar:* Courses of varying lengths *Degrees:* certificates *CEO:* Dir. Stephen Kitts
(203) 667-1886

BRANCH CAMPUS
25 Sylvan Rd. S., Westport 06880 *Accred.:* 1993 (ACCSCT) *CEO:* Dir. John A. Varanelli
(203) 221-7325

CONNECTICUT INSTITUTE OF ART
581 W. Putnam Ave., Greenwich 06830-6005 *Type:* Private *Accred.:* 1980/1990 (ACCSCT) *Calendar:* Sem. plan *Degrees:* diplomas *CEO:* Chrmn./Pres. August J. Propersi
(203) 869-4430

CONNECTICUT INSTITUTE OF HAIR DESIGN
1681 Meriden Rd., Wolcott 06716-3322 *Type:* Private *Accred.:* 1980/1987 (ACCSCT) *Calendar:* Courses of varying lengths *Degrees:* diplomas *CEO:* Dir. John A. Varanelli
(203) 879-4247

CONNECTICUT SCHOOL OF ELECTRONICS
586 Ella T. Grasso Blvd., New Haven 06519-0308 *Type:* Private *Accred.:* 1968/1989 (ACCSCT) *Calendar:* Sem. plan *Degrees:* certificates, diplomas *CEO:* Dir./Vice Pres. Karen George
(203) 624-2121

DATA INSTITUTE
745 Burnside Ave., East Hartford 06108 *Type:* Private business *Accred.:* 1983/1987 (ACISC) *Calendar:* Courses of varying lengths *Degrees:* certificates, diplomas *CEO:* Pres. Mark Scheinberg
(203) 528-4111

BRANCH CAMPUS
101 Pierpont Rd., Waterbury 06705 *Accred.:* 1993 (ACISC) *CEO:* Dir. Irmagard Witenko
(203) 756-5500

ELI WHITNEY REGIONAL VOCATIONAL-
TECHNICAL SCHOOL
71 Jones Rd., Hamden 06514 *Type:* Private *Calendar:* Courses of varying lengths *Degrees:* certificates *Prof. Accred.:* Dental Assisting *CEO:* Dir. Cecil Robinson
(203) 397-4031

HARTFORD CAMERATA CONSERVATORY
834 Asylum Ave., Hartford 06105 *Type:* Private professional *Accred.:* 1979/1990 (NEASC-CTCI) *Calendar:* Sem. plan *Degrees:* diplomas *CEO:* Dir. Claudia Bell
FTE Enroll: 32   (203) 246-2588

HARTFORD SECRETARIAL SCHOOL
765 Asylum Ave., Hartford 06105 *Type:* Private business *Accred.:* 1979/1990 (ACISC) *Calendar:* Qtr. plan *Degrees:* certificates, diplomas *CEO:* Pres. Patrick J. Fox
(203) 522-2888

HUNTINGTON INSTITUTE
193 Broadway, Norwich 06360 *Type:* Private business *Accred.:* 1980/1986 (ACISC) *Calendar:* Courses of varying lengths *Degrees:* certificates, diplomas *CEO:* Dir. Thomas Haggerty
(203) 886-0507

INDUSTRIAL MANAGEMENT AND TRAINING, INC.
233 Mill St., Waterbury 06706 *Type:* Private *Accred.:* 1993 (ACCSCT) *Calendar:* Courses of varying lengths *Degrees:* certificates *CEO:* Owner/C.E.O. Marcel Veronneau
(203) 753-7910

LYME ACADEMY OF FINE ARTS
84 Lyme St., Old Lyme 06371 *Type:* Independent *Calendar:* Courses of varying lengths *Degrees:* certificates *Prof. Accred.:* Art (associate) *CEO:* Academic Dean Sharon Hunter
(203) 434-5232

MORSE SCHOOL OF BUSINESS
275 Asylum St., Hartford 06103 *Type:* Private business *Accred.:* 1953/1990 (ACISC) *Calendar:* Courses of varying lengths *De-*

grees: certificates, diplomas *Prof. Accred.:* Medical Assisting (AMA) *CEO:* Pres. Michael S. Taub
(203) 522-2261

NEW ENGLAND TECHNICAL INSTITUTE OF
CONNECTICUT
200 John Downey Dr., New Britain 06051-0651 *Type:* Private *Accred.:* 1983/1988 (ACCSCT) *Calendar:* Courses of varying lengths *Degrees:* diplomas *CEO:* Dir. Paul S. Taub
(203) 225-8641

NEW ENGLAND TRACTOR TRAILER TRAINING
SCHOOL OF CONNECTICUT
32 Field Rd., Somers 06071-0326 *Type:* Private *Accred.:* 1982/1988 (ACCSCT) *Calendar:* Courses of varying lengths *Degrees:* diplomas *CEO:* Dir. Arlan Greenberg
(203) 749-0711

PORTER AND CHESTER INSTITUTE
P.O. Box 364, Stratford 06497-0364 *Type:* Private *Accred.:* 1972/1990 (ACCSCT) *Calendar:* Qtr. plan *Degrees:* diplomas *CEO:* Dir. Raymond R. Clark
(203) 375-4463

BRANCH CAMPUS
138 Weymouth St., Enfield 06082-6028 *Accred.:* 1980/1990 (ACCSCT) *CEO:* Dir. Joseph M. Doering
(800) 870-6789

BRANCH CAMPUS
320 Sylvan Lake Rd., Watertown 06779-1400 *Accred.:* 1972/1987 (ACCSCT) *CEO:* Dir. Louis Giannelli
(203) 274-9294

BRANCH CAMPUS
125 Silas Deane Hwy., Wethersfield 06109-1238 *Accred.:* 1979/1990 (ACCSCT) *CEO:* Dir. John D. Mashia
(203) 529-2519

RIDLEY-LOWELL BUSINESS AND TECHNICAL
INSTITUTE
P.O. Box 652, New London 06320 *Type:* Private business *Accred.:* 1979/1989 (ACISC) *Calendar:* Courses of varying lengths *Degrees:* certificates, diplomas *CEO:* Dir. W.T. Weymouth, III
(203) 443-7441

ROFFLER ACADEMY FOR HAIRSTYLISTS
454 Park St., Hartford 06106-1525 *Type:* Private *Accred.:* 1974/1990 (ACCSCT) *Calendar:* Courses of varying lengths *Degrees:* diplomas *CEO:* Dir. Carlos J. Vigo
(203) 522-2359

BRANCH CAMPUS
709 Queen St., Southington 06489 *Accred.:* 1990 (ACCSCT) *CEO:* Dir. Gabriel A. Termine
(203) 620-9260

SCHOOL OF THE HARTFORD BALLET
Hartford Courant Arts Ctr., 224 Farmington Ave., Hartford 06105 *Type:* Private *Calendar:* Courses of varying lengths *Degrees:* certificates *Prof. Accred.:* Dance *CEO:* Dir. Enid Lynn
(203) 525-9396

STONE ACADEMY
1315 Dixwell Ave., Hamden 06514 *Type:* Private business *Accred.:* 1974/1990 (ACISC) *Calendar:* Courses of varying lengths *Degrees:* certificates, diplomas *Prof. Accred.:* Medical Assisting (AMA) *CEO:* Pres. Janet S. Arena
(203) 288-7474

TECHNICAL CAREERS INSTITUTE
11 Kimberly Ave., West Haven 06516-4499 *Type:* Private *Accred.:* 1974/1987 (ACCSCT) *Calendar:* Courses of varying lengths *Degrees:* certificates *CEO:* Dir. Ronald G. Anderson
(203) 932-2282

BRANCH CAMPUS
605 Day Hill Rd., Windsor 06095-0126 *Accred.:* 1986 (ACCSCT) *CEO:* Dir. Linda Perkins
(203) 688-8351

WESTLAWN SCHOOL OF MARINE TECHNOLOGY
733 Summer St., Stamford 06901 *Type:* Private home study *Accred.:* 1971/1992 (NHSC) *Calendar:* Courses of varying lengths *Degrees:* certificates *CEO:* Dir. Norman Nudelman
(203) 359-0500

WINDHAM REGIONAL VOCATIONAL-TECHNICAL SCHOOL
210 Birch St., Willimantic 06226 *Type:* Private *Calendar:* Courses of varying lengths *Degrees:* certificates *Prof. Accred.:* Dental Assisting *CEO:* Dir. Charles Wilt
(203) 456-3879

DELAWARE

DAWN TRAINING INSTITUTE
New Castle County Airport, 120 Old Churchmans Rd., New Castle 19720-3116 *Type:* Private *Accred.:* 1991 (ACCSCT) *Calendar:* Courses of varying lengths *Degrees:* certificates *CEO:* Pres. Hollis Anglin
(302) 328-9695

STAR TECHNICAL INSTITUTE
Graystone Plaza, 631 W. Newport Pike, Wilmington 19804 *Type:* Private *Accred.:* 1988/1993 (ACCSCT) *Calendar:* Courses of varying lengths *Degrees:* diplomas *CEO:* Dir. Edward Webber
(302) 999-7827

BRANCH CAMPUS
Sunburst Office Bldg., 1st Fl., 1541 Alta Dr., Whitehall, PA 18052-5632 *Accred.:* 1988 (ACCSCT) *CEO:* Dir. Fred Galletti
(215) 434-9963

DISTRICT OF COLUMBIA

AUTOMATION ACADEMY
666 11th St., N.W., Ste. 750, Washington 20001-4542 *Type:* Private *Accred.:* 1988 (ACCSCT) *Calendar:* Courses of varying lengths *Degrees:* certificates *CEO:* Pres. Gerald W. Newman
(202) 638-6677

HANNAH HARRISON CAREER SCHOOL
4470 MacArthur Blvd., N.W., Washington 20007 *Type:* Private *Calendar:* Courses of varying lengths *Degrees:* diplomas *Prof. Accred.:* Practical Nursing *CEO:* Dir. Jane Town
(202) 333-3500

LEVINE SCHOOL OF MUSIC
1690 36th St., N.W., Washington 20007 *Type:* Independent *Calendar:* Courses of varying lengths *Degrees:* certificates *Prof. Accred.:* Music *CEO:* Dir. Joanne Hoover
(202) 337-2227

MARGARET MURRAY WASHINGTON VOCATIONAL SCHOOL
27 O St., N.W., Washington 20001 *Type:* Public *Calendar:* Courses of varying lengths *Degrees:* certificates *Prof. Accred.:* Dental Assisting, Practical Nursing (warning) *CEO:* Prin. Alethia Spraggins
(202) 673-7224

MARINE CORPS INSTITUTE
Marine Barracks, 8th and Eye Sts., S.E., Washington 20390 *Type:* Public (federal) home study *Accred.:* 1977/1992 (NHSC) *Calendar:* Courses of varying lengths *Degrees:* certificates *CEO:* Dir. J.C. Flynn
(202) 433-2728

MCGRAW-HILL CONTINUING EDUCATION CENTER
4401 Connecticut Ave., N.W., Washington 20008 *Type:* Private home study *Accred.:* 1956/1992 (NHSC) *Calendar:* Courses of varying lengths *Degrees:* certificates *CEO:* Pres. Harold B. Reeb
(202) 244-1600

NRI SCHOOLS
4401 Connecticut Ave., N.W., Washington 20008 *CEO:* Pres. Harold B. Reeb
(202) 244-1600

NATIONAL CONSERVATORY OF DRAMATIC ARTS
1556 Wisconsin Ave., N.W., Washington 20007-2758 *Type:* Private *Accred.:* 1980/1987 (ACCSCT) *Calendar:* Courses of varying lengths *Degrees:* diplomas *CEO:* Pres. C. Wayne Rudisill
(202) 333-2202

NATIONAL EDUCATION CENTER CAPITOL HILL CAMPUS
810 First St., N.E., Washington 20002 *Type:* Private business *Accred.:* 1971/1989 (ACISC) *Calendar:* Qtr. plan *Degrees:* certificates, diplomas *Prof. Accred.:* Medical Assisting *CEO:* Dir. Beth Wilson
(202) 289-7700

PTC CAREER INSTITUTE
529 14th St., N.W., Ste. 350, Washington 20004 *Type:* Private *Accred.:* 1991 (ACCSCT) *Calendar:* Courses of varying lengths *Degrees:* certificates *CEO:* Dir. Bill Little
(202) 638-5300

WASHINGTON CONSERVATORY OF MUSIC, INC.
5144 Massachusetts Ave., N.W., P.O. Box 5758, Washington 20816 *Type:* Private professional *Calendar:* Courses of varying lengths *Degrees:* certificates *Prof. Accred.:* Music (associate) *CEO:* Admin. Joan T. Willoughby
(301) 320-2770

FLORIDA

ACADEMY OF CREATIVE HAIR DESIGN
2911 Jacksonville Rd., Ocala 32670 *Type:*
Private *Accred.:* 1993 (SACS-COEI) *Calendar:* Courses of varying lengths *Degrees:*
certificates *CEO:* Dir. Jim Smith
(904) 351-5900

ACADEMY OF HEALING ARTS, MASSAGE &
FACIAL SKIN CARE
3141 S. Military Tr., Lake Worth 33463-2113 *Type:* Private *Accred.:* 1992 (ACC-SCT) *Calendar:* Courses of varying lengths
Degrees: certificates *CEO:* C.E.O. M.J.
Artemik
(407) 965-5550

AMERICAN FLYERS COLLEGE
5400 N.W. 21st Terr., Fort Lauderdale
33309 *Type:* Private *Accred.:* 1993 (ACC-SCT) *Calendar:* Courses of varying lengths
Degrees: diplomas *CEO:* Exec. Dir. Edward
C. Hertberg
(305) 772-7500

ATI CAREER TRAINING CENTER
3501 N.W. 9th Ave., Oakland Park 33309-5900 *Type:* Private *Accred.:* 1984/1989
(ACCSCT) *Calendar:* Qtr. plan *Degrees:*
certificates *CEO:* Dir. Donald Neman
(305) 563-5899

BRANCH CAMPUS
One N.E. 19th St., Miami 33132 *Accred.:*
1991 (ACCSCT) *CEO:* Dir. Mark Gutmann
(305) 573-1600

ATI CAREER TRAINING CENTER ELECTRONIC
CAMPUS
2880 N.W. 62nd St., Fort Lauderdale 33309-9731 *Type:* Private *Accred.:* 1989 (ACC-SCT) *Calendar:* Qtr. plan *Degrees:* certificates *CEO:* Dir. David L. Withers
(305) 973-4760

ATI—HEALTH EDUCATION CENTER
1395 N.W. 167th St., Ste. 200, Miami
33169-5745 *Type:* Private *Accred.:* 1991
(ACCSCT) *Calendar:* Qtr. plan *Degrees:*
certificates *CEO:* Dir. Barbara Monk
(305) 628-1000

ATLANTIC VOCATIONAL-TECHNICAL CENTER
4700 Coconut Creek Pkwy., Coconut Creek
33063 *Type:* Public (state) technical *Accred.:*
1978/1989 (SACS-COEI) *Calendar:* Courses of varying lengths *Degrees:* certificates
Prof. Accred.: Practical Nursing *CEO:* Dir.
Robert Crawford
FTE Enroll: 3,087   (305) 977-2000

BRANCH CAMPUS
1400 N.E. 6th St., Pompano Beach 33060
CEO: Dir. Robert Crawford
(305) 786-7630

AUTOMOTIVE TRANSMISSION SCHOOL
453 E. Okeechobee Rd., Hialeah 33010-5350 *Type:* Private *Accred.:* 1985/1990
(ACCSCT) *Calendar:* Courses of varying
lengths *Degrees:* certificates *CEO:* Pres.
Manuel J. Safon, Jr.
(305) 888-4898

AVANTI HAIR TECH
905 E. Memorial Blvd., Lakeland 33801-1919 *Type:* Private *Accred.:* 1987 (ACC-SCT) *Calendar:* Courses of varying lengths
Degrees: diplomas *CEO:* Dir. Joan Ogden
(813) 686-2224

AVANTI HAIR TECH
8803 N. Florida Ave., Tampa 33604 *Type:*
Private *Accred.:* 1981/1988 (ACCSCT) *Calendar:* Courses of varying lengths *Degrees:*
diplomas *CEO:* Dir. Dwayne Adams
(813) 931-8500

BRANCH CAMPUS
5433 Lake Howell Rd., Winter Park
32792-1033 *Accred.:* 1991 (ACCSCT)
CEO: Dir. Glenda Dunson
(305) 657-0700

AVANTI HAIR TECH
8851 N. 56th St., Temple Terrace 33617
Type: Private *Accred.:* 1988 (ACCSCT) *Calendar:* Courses of varying lengths *Degrees:*
diplomas *CEO:* Pres. Stewart A. Smith
(813) 985-8785

BARNA INSTITUTE
1050 N.E. Fifth Terr., Fort Lauderdale
33304 *Type:* Private technical *Accred.:*

1984/1989 (SACS-COEI) *Calendar:* Courses of varying lengths *Degrees:* certificates *CEO:* Dir. Patricia A. Wetstein
FTE Enroll: 165 (305) 525-5069

BAY AREA VOCATIONAL-TECHNICAL SCHOOL
1976 Lewis Turner Blvd., Fort Walton Beach 32547 *Type:* Public (state) technical *Accred.:* 1979/1989 (SACS-COEI) *Calendar:* Courses of varying lengths *Degrees:* certificates *CEO:* Dir. Edward V. Baker
FTE Enroll: 498 (904) 833-3500

BEACON CAREER INSTITUTE
2900 N.W. 183rd St., Miami 33056 *Type:* Private technical *Accred.:* 1992 (SACS-COEI) *Calendar:* Courses of varying lengths *Degrees:* diplomas *CEO:* Dir. Eddie Pabon
FTE Enroll: 259 (305) 620-4637

BEAUTY SCHOOLS OF AMERICA
7942 W. Sample Rd., Margate 33063 *Type:* Private *Accred.:* 1989/1992 (SACS-COEI) *Calendar:* Courses of varying lengths *Degrees:* diplomas *CEO:* Dir. Lisbeth Ruiz
FTE Enroll: 763 (305) 755-2014

BRANCH CAMPUS
1176 S.W. 67th Ave., Miami 33144 *CEO:* Dir. Lisbeth Ruiz
(305) 267-6604

BRANELL INSTITUTE
Bldg. 2, Ste. 2, 1700 Halstead Blvd., Tallahassee 32308 *Type:* Private business *Accred.:* 1988/1991 (ACISC); 1992 (SACS-COEI) *Calendar:* Qtr. plan *Degrees:* certificates, diplomas *CEO:* Dir. Judy Marvin
FTE Enroll: 303 (904) 668-0200

BRANELL INSTITUTE
Ste. 115, 1408 N. Westshore Blvd., Tampa 33607 *Type:* Private business *Accred.:* 1986/1990 (ACISC); 1992 (SACS-COEI) *Calendar:* Courses of varying lengths *Degrees:* certificates, diplomas *CEO:* Dir. Susan J. Siemsglusz
FTE Enroll: 124 (813) 287-0400

BUSINESS & TECHNOLOGY INSTITUTE
42 N.W. 27th Ave., Ste. 323, Miami 33125 *Type:* Private *Accred.:* 1991 (SACS-COEI) *Calendar:* Courses of varying lengths *Degrees:* diplomas *CEO:* Dir. Fernando N. Llerena
FTE Enroll: 12 (305) 541-4463

BUSINESS TRAINING INSTITUTE
Ste. 200, 21649 U.S. 19 N., Clearwater 34625-2835 *Type:* Private business *Accred.:* 1987 (ACISC) *Calendar:* Courses of varying lengths *Degrees:* certificates, diplomas *CEO:* Dir. Edward Murphy
(813) 791-7833

BUSINESS TRAINING INSTITUTE
Ste. 131, 1900 Evans Rd., Melbourne 32901 *Type:* Private business *Accred.:* 1988/1990 (ACISC) *Calendar:* Courses of varying lengths *Degrees:* certificates, diplomas *CEO:* Dir. Darlene Wohl
(407) 724-0707

THE CAREER CENTER
1750 45th St., West Palm Beach 33407-2192 *Type:* Private *Accred.:* 1993 (ACCSCT) *Calendar:* Courses of varying lengths *Degrees:* certificates *CEO:* Pres. Donald W. Schaefer
(407) 881-0220

CAREER TRAINING INSTITUTE
101 W. Main St., Leesburg 34748-5173 *Type:* Private *Accred.:* 1992 (ACCSCT) *Calendar:* Courses of varying lengths *Degrees:* diplomas *CEO:* Dir. Nancy Bradley
(904) 326-5134

CAREER TRAINING INSTITUTE
2120 W. Colonial Dr., Orlando 32804-6948 *Type:* Private *Accred.:* 1992 (ACCSCT) *Calendar:* Courses of varying lengths *Degrees:* diplomas *CEO:* Dir. Roger Bradley
(407) 843-3984

CHARLOTTE VOCATIONAL-TECHNICAL CENTER
18300 Toledo Blade Blvd., Port Charlotte 33948-3399 *Type:* Public (state) technical *Accred.:* 1983/1988 (SACS-COEI) *Calendar:* Courses of varying lengths *Degrees:* certificates *Prof. Accred.:* Dental Assisting *CEO:* Dir. Roseann Keller Samson
FTE Enroll: 572 (813) 629-6819

CONCORDE CAREER INSTITUTE
7960 Arlington Expy., Jacksonville 32211-7429 *Type:* Private *Accred.:* 1991 (ACCSCT) *Calendar:* Courses of varying lengths

Degrees: certificates *CEO:* Dir. Sonnie Willingham

(904) 725-0525

CONCORDE CAREER INSTITUTE
4000 N. State Rd. 7, Lauderdale Lakes 33319 *Type:* Private *Accred.:* 1991 (ACC-SCT) *Calendar:* Courses of varying lengths *Degrees:* certificates *CEO:* Dir. Patricia Trax

(305) 731-8880

CONCORDE CAREER INSTITUTE
4202 W. Spruce St., Tampa 33607-4127 *Type:* Private *Accred.:* 1991 (ACCSCT) *Calendar:* Courses of varying lengths *Degrees:* certificates *CEO:* Dir. Thomas L. Buck

(813) 874-0094

BRANCH CAMPUS
285 N.W. 199th St., Miami 33169-2920 *Accred.:* 1992 (ACCSCT) *CEO:* Dir. Patricia Trax

(305) 652-0055

CROWN BUSINESS INSTITUTE
1223 S.W. Fourth St., Miami 33135 *Type:* Private business *Accred.:* 1981/1990 (ACISC) *Calendar:* Courses of varying lengths *Degrees:* certificates, diplomas *CEO:* Dir. Zuleica Perdomo-Martell

(305) 643-1600

DAVID G. ERWIN TECHNICAL CENTER
2010 E. Hillsborough Ave., Tampa 33610 *Type:* Public (state) technical *Accred.:* 1981/1991 (SACS-COEI) *Calendar:* Courses of varying lengths *Degrees:* certificates *Prof. Accred.:* Medical Assisting (AMA), Medical Laboratory Technology (AMA), Respiratory Therapy Technology, Surgical Technology *CEO:* Dir. Michael Donohue
FTE Enroll: 934   (813) 238-8631

DEFENSE EQUAL OPPORTUNITY MANAGEMENT INSTITUTE
EOMI Library, Bldg. 560, Patrick Air Force Base 32925 *Type:* Public (federal) *Accred.:* 1983/1988 (SACS-COEI) *Calendar:* Courses of varying lengths *Degrees:* certificates *CEO:* Dir. Ronald M. Joe, U.S.A.
FTE Enroll: 162   (305) 494-6976

DIANA RAMSAY'S SPECIALTY BEAUTY SCHOOL
2245 W. Hillsboro Blvd., Deerfield Beach 33442 *Type:* Private *Accred.:* 1990 (SACS-COEI) *Calendar:* Courses of varying lengths *Degrees:* certificates, diplomas *CEO:* Dir. Diana Ramsay
FTE Enroll: 12   (305) 429-8358

ELKINS INSTITUTE OF JACKSONVILLE
3947 Boulevard Center Dr., Ste. 6, Jacksonville 32207 *Type:* Private *Accred.:* 1989 (SACS-COEI) *Calendar:* Courses of varying lengths *Degrees:* certificates *CEO:* Dir. Alan Shinall
FTE Enroll: 74   (904) 398-6211

EURO HAIR DESIGN INSTITUTE
1964 W. Tennessee St., No. 14, Tallahassee 32304-3238 *Type:* Private *Accred.:* 1983/1988 (ACCSCT) *Calendar:* Courses of varying lengths *Degrees:* diplomas *CEO:* Pres. Stewart A. Smith

(904) 576-2174

EURO-SKILL THERAPEUTIC TRAINING CENTER
500 N.E. Spanish River Blvd., Stes. 25-26, Boca Raton 33431 *Type:* Private *Accred.:* 1992 (SACS-COEI) *Calendar:* Courses of varying lengths *Degrees:* certificates *CEO:* Dir. Edith Szasz
FTE Enroll: 18   (407) 395-3089

FAA CENTER FOR MANAGEMENT DEVELOPMENT
4500 Palm Coast Pkwy., S.E., Palm Coast 32137 *Type:* Private *Accred.:* 1989 (SACS-COEI) *Calendar:* Courses of varying lengths *Degrees:* certificates *CEO:* Dir. Raymond A. Salazar
FTE Enroll: 310   (904) 446-7136

FEDERAL CORRECTIONAL INSTITUTION
501 Capital Cir., N.E., Tallahassee 32301-3572 *Type:* Public (federal) *Accred.:* 1985/1990 (SACS-COEI) *Calendar:* Courses of varying lengths *Degrees:* certificates *CEO:* Dir. Lewis James
FTE Enroll: 350   (904) 878-2173

FLIGHTSAFETY INTERNATIONAL
Vero Beach Airport, P.O. Box 2708, Vero Beach 32961-2708 *Type:* Private *Accred.:* 1975/1988 (ACCSCT) *Calendar:* Courses of varying lengths *Degrees:* certificates *CEO:* Admin. Jeffrey Krell

(407) 567-5178

FLORIDA INSTITUTE OF MASSAGE THERAPY &
ESTHETICS
5453 N. University Dr., Lauderhill 33351
Type: Private *Accred.:* 1991 (ACCSCT) *Calendar:* Courses of varying lengths *Degrees:*
certificates *CEO:* Dir. Neal R. Heller
(305) 742-8399

FLORIDA INSTITUTE OF ULTRASOUND, INC.
P.O. Box 15135, 8800 University Pkwy.,
Bldg. A, Pensacola 32514 *Type:* Private
technical *Accred.:* 1985/1992 (ABHES) *Calendar:* Courses of varying lengths *Degrees:*
certificates *CEO:* Dir. J. Jay Crittenden,
M.D.
(904) 478-7300

FLORIDA SCHOOL OF BUSINESS
2990 N.W. 81st Terr., Miami 33147 *Type:*
Private business *Accred.:* 1986 (ACISC)
Calendar: Qtr. plan *Degrees:* certificates,
diplomas *CEO:* Dir. Michael D. Beauregard
(305) 696-6312

FLORIDA SCHOOL OF BUSINESS
405 E. Polk St., Tampa 33602 *Type:* Private
business *Accred.:* 1986 (ACISC) *Calendar:*
Qtr. plan *Degrees:* certificates, diplomas
CEO: Dir. James Howard
(813) 221-4200

FLORIDA TECHNICAL COLLEGE
1819 N. Semoran Blvd., Orlando 32807
Type: Private business *Accred.:* 1982/1987
(ACISC) *Calendar:* Courses of varying
lengths *Degrees:* certificates, diplomas
CEO: Dean Sunil Wadhwa
(407) 678-5600

FLORIDA TECHNICAL COLLEGE
4750 E. Adamo Dr., Tampa 33605 *Type:*
Private business *Accred.:* 1982/1987
(ACISC) *Calendar:* Courses of varying
lengths *Degrees:* certificates, diplomas
CEO: Dir. Kenneth B. Dowling
(813) 247-1700

FULL SAIL CENTER FOR THE RECORDING ARTS
3300 University Blvd., Winter Park 32792-
7429 *Type:* Private *Accred.:* 1986/1993
(ACCSCT) *Calendar:* Courses of varying
lengths *Degrees:* diplomas *CEO:* Pres.
Edward E. Haddock, Jr.
(407) 679-6333

GARCES COMMERCIAL COLLEGE
1301 S.W. First St., Miami 33135 *Type:* Private *Accred.:* 1990 (SACS-COEI) *Calendar:*
Courses of varying lengths *Degrees:* diplomas *CEO:* Dir. Elena Nespereira
FTE Enroll: 688   (305) 643-1044

BRANCH CAMPUS
5385 N.W. 36th St., Miami Springs 33166
CEO: Dir. Gabriel Torres
(305) 871-6535

GEORGE STONE VOCATIONAL-TECHNICAL
CENTER
2400 Longleaf Dr., Pensacola 32526 *Type:*
Public (state) *Accred.:* 1981/1991 (SACS-
COEI) *Calendar:* Courses of varying lengths
Degrees: certificates *CEO:* Dir. Robert
Lindner
FTE Enroll: 877   (904) 944-1424

GEORGE T. BAKER AVIATION SCHOOL
3275 N.W. 42nd Ave., Miami 33142 *Type:*
Private technical *Accred.:* 1978/1993
(SACS-COEI) *Calendar:* Courses of varying
lengths *Degrees:* certificates *CEO:* Dir.
Doris Southern
FTE Enroll: 622   (305) 871-3143

THE HAIR DESIGN SCHOOL
5110 University Blvd., Bldg. C, Jacksonville
32216-5940 *Type:* Private *Accred.:* 1979/
1986 (ACCSCT) *Calendar:* Courses of varying lengths *Degrees:* diplomas *CEO:* Exec.
Vice Pres. Stewart A. Smith
(904) 731-7500

HENRY W. BREWSTER TECHNICAL CENTER
2222 N. Tampa St., Tampa 33602 *Type:*
Public (state) *Accred.:* 1989/1990 (SACS-
COEI) *Calendar:* Courses of varying lengths
Degrees: certificates *CEO:* Dir. Joe Kolinsky
FTE Enroll: 254   (813) 273-9240

HI-TECH SCHOOL OF MIAMI
10350 W. Flagler St., Miami 33174 *Type:*
Private *Accred.:* 1993 (ACCSCT) *Calendar:*
Courses of varying lengths *Degrees:* certificates *CEO:* Pres. Eric Arencibia
(305) 221-3423

HIALEAH TECHNICAL CENTER
1780 E. 4th Ave., Hialeah 33012-3122 *Type:*
Private *Accred.:* 1991 (ACCSCT) *Calendar:*

Courses of varying lengths *Degrees:* certificates *CEO:* Dir. Roberto Luna

(305) 884-4387

HUMANITIES CENTER INSTITUTE OF ALLIED HEALTH/SCHOOL OF MASSAGE
4045 Park Blvd., Pinellas Park 34665-3634 *Type:* Private *Accred.:* 1984/1989 (ACC-SCT) *Calendar:* Courses of varying lengths *Degrees:* certificates *CEO:* Dir. Sherry L. Fears

(813) 541-5200

JAMES L. WALKER VOCATIONAL-TECHNICAL CENTER
3702 Estey Ave., Naples 33942-4498 *Type:* Public (state) *Accred.:* 1980/1990 (SACS-COEI) *Calendar:* Courses of varying lengths *Degrees:* certificates *Prof. Accred.:* Dental Assisting (prelim. provisional) *CEO:* Dir. Edmund Magero
FTE Enroll: 1,363   (813) 643-0919

LAKE COUNTY AREA VOCATIONAL-TECHNICAL CENTER
2001 Kurt St., Eustis 32726 *Type:* Public (state) *Accred.:* 1974/1989 (SACS-COEI) *Calendar:* Courses of varying lengths *Degrees:* certificates *Prof. Accred.:* EMT-Paramedic *CEO:* Dir. Maxine Felts
FTE Enroll: 1,032   (904) 357-8222

LEE COUNTY VOCATIONAL HIGH TECH CENTER
3800 Michigan Ave., Fort Myers 33916 *Type:* Public (state) *Accred.:* 1978/1993 (SACS-COEI) *Calendar:* Courses of varying lengths *Degrees:* certificates *CEO:* Dir. Ronald E. Pentiuk
FTE Enroll: 1,134   (813) 334-4544

LINDSEY HOPKINS TECHNICAL EDUCATION CENTER
750 N.W. 20th St., Miami 33127 *Type:* Public (state) *Accred.:* 1972/1992 (SACS-COEI) *Calendar:* Courses of varying lengths *Degrees:* certificates *Prof. Accred.:* Dental Assisting, Dental Laboratory Technology, Practical Nursing, Surgical Technology *CEO:* Dir. John Leyva
FTE Enroll: 3,431   (305) 324-6070

LIVELY AREA VOCATIONAL-TECHNICAL CENTER
500 N. Appleyard Dr., Tallahassee 32304-2895 *Type:* Public (state) *Accred.:* 1977/1992 (SACS-COEI) *Calendar:* Courses of

varying lengths *Degrees:* certificates *CEO:* Dir. Tom Dunn
FTE Enroll: 1,788   (904) 487-7401

MANATEE AREA VOCATIONAL-TECHNICAL CENTER
5603 34th St., W., Bradenton 34210 *Type:* Public (state) *Accred.:* 1980/1990 (SACS-COEI) *Calendar:* Courses of varying lengths *Degrees:* certificates *Prof. Accred.:* Dental Assisting, EMT-Paramedic *CEO:* Dir. Walter Bucklin
FTE Enroll: 586   (813) 755-2641

MARION COUNTY SCHOOL OF RADIOLOGIC TECHNOLOGY
438 S.W. Third St., Ocala 32674 *Type:* Private *Calendar:* 2-year program *Degrees:* certificates *Prof. Accred.:* Radiography *CEO:* Admin. Sam Lauff, Jr.
Enroll: 36   (904) 629-7545

MARTIN COLLEGE
1901 N.W. Seventh St., Miami 33125-3462 *Type:* Private *Accred.:* 1978/1986 (ACC-SCT) *Calendar:* Courses of varying lengths *Degrees:* certificates, diplomas *CEO:* Dir. Fernando A. Alvarez

(305) 541-8140

MASTER SCHOOLS
824 S.W. 24th St., Fort Lauderdale 33315-2644 *Type:* Private *Accred.:* 1991 (ACC-SCT) *Calendar:* Courses of varying lengths *Degrees:* certificates *CEO:* Owner Marta Alvarez

(305) 467-8829

MASTER SCHOOLS
4315 N.W. Seventh St., Ste. 36, Miami 33126 *Type:* Private *Accred.:* 1991 (ACC-SCT) *Calendar:* Courses of varying lengths *Degrees:* certificates *CEO:* Dir. Mindy Levine

(305) 373-3036

MEDICAL ARTS TRAINING CENTER, INC.
441 S. State Rd. 7, Margate 33068-1934 *Type:* Private technical *Accred.:* 1982/1986 (ABHES) *Calendar:* Courses of varying lengths *Degrees:* certificates *Prof. Accred.:* EMT-Paramedic, Medical Assisting *CEO:* Chrmn. Lauren Hemedinger

(305) 968-3500

MIAMI INSTITUTE OF TECHNOLOGY
1001 S.W. First St., Miami 33130-1008
Type: Private *Accred.:* 1980/1987 (ACC-
SCT) *Calendar:* Courses of varying lengths
Degrees: certificates *CEO:* Dir. Octavio
Gutierrez
(305) 324-6781

MIAMI JOB CORPS CENTER
660 S.W. Third St., Miami 33130 *Type:* Private *Accred.:* 1986/1991 (SACS-COEI) *Calendar:* Courses of varying lengths *Degrees:*
certificates *CEO:* Dir. Don E. DeJarnett
FTE Enroll: 222   (305) 325-1276

MIAMI LAKES TECHNICAL EDUCATION CENTER
5780 N.W. 158th St., Miami 33014 *Type:*
Public (state) *Accred.:* 1983/1993 (SACS-
COEI) *Calendar:* Courses of varying lengths
Degrees: certificates *Prof. Accred.:* Practical
Nursing *CEO:* Dir. Noward Dean
FTE Enroll: 1,242   (305) 557-1100

MIAMI TECHNICAL INSTITUTE
14701 N.W. 7th Ave., North Miami 33168-
3103 *Type:* Private *Accred.:* 1987 (ACC-
SCT) *Calendar:* Courses of varying lengths
Degrees: certificates
(305) 688-8811

BRANCH CAMPUS
7061 W. Flagler St., Miami 33144-2453
Accred.: 1991 (ACCSCT) *CEO:* Dir.
Orlando Tiferino
(305) 263-9832

MID-FLORIDA TECHNICAL INSTITUTE
2900 W. Oak Ridge Rd., Orlando 32809-
3799 *Type:* Public (state) *Accred.:* 1974/
1989 (SACS-COEI) *Calendar:* Courses of
varying lengths *Degrees:* certificates *CEO:*
Dir. Robert J. Clark
FTE Enroll: 3,901   (305) 855-5880

NATIONAL AVIATION ACADEMY
St. Pete/Clearwater Airport, No. 228, Clearwater 34622 *Type:* Private technical *Accred.:*
1991 (SACS-COEI) *Calendar:* Courses of
varying lengths *Degrees:* diplomas *CEO:*
Pres. Jon Lelekis
FTE Enroll: 139   (813) 531-2080

NATIONAL CAREER INSTITUTE
3910 U.S. Hwy. 301 N., Ste. 200, Tampa
33619-1259 *Type:* Private *Accred.:* 1985/

1990 (ACCSCT) *Calendar:* Courses of varying lengths *Degrees:* diplomas *CEO:* Pres.
Carroll L. Gossage
(813) 620-1446

NATIONAL EDUCATION CENTER—BAUDER
COLLEGE CAMPUS
4801 N. Dixie Hwy., Fort Lauderdale 33334-
3971 *Type:* Private *Accred.:* 1970/1988
(ACCSCT) *Calendar:* Qtr. plan *Degrees:*
diplomas *CEO:* Exec. Dir. Peter Crocitto
(305) 491-7171

BRANCH CAMPUS
7955 N.W. 12th St., Ste. 300, Miami
33126-1823 *Accred.:* 1988 (ACCSCT)
CEO: Dir. Allen Rice
(305) 477-0251

NATIONAL EDUCATION CENTER—TAMPA
TECHNICAL INSTITUTE
2410 E. Busch Blvd., Tampa 33612 *Type:*
Private *Accred.:* 1991 (ACCSCT) *Calendar:*
Courses of varying lengths *Degrees:* diplomas *CEO:* Pres. Mark W. Johnson
(813) 935-5700

NATIONAL EDUCATION CENTER—FORT
WORTH CAMPUS
300 E. Loop 820, Fort Worth, TX 76112-
1225 *Accred.:* 1991 (ACCSCT) *CEO:* Dir.
Tom Stose
(817) 451-0017

NATIONAL SCHOOL OF TECHNOLOGY
16150 N.E. 17th Ave., North Miami Beach
33162-4799 *Type:* Private *Accred.:* 1983/
1988 (ACCSCT) *Calendar:* Courses of varying lengths *Degrees:* diplomas *Prof. Accred.:* Medical Assisting *CEO:* Dir. Arthur
Ortiz
(305) 949-9500

BRANCH CAMPUS
4355 W. 16th Ave., Hialeah 33012-7628
Accred.: 1988 (ACCSCT) *Prof. Accred.:*
Medical Assisting *CEO:* Dir. Neil Berris
(305) 558-9500

NATIONAL TRAINING, INC.
188 College Dr., P.O. Box 1899, Orange
Park 32067-1899 *Type:* Private combination
home study and resident *Accred.:* 1982/1992
(NHSC) *Calendar:* Courses of varying

lengths *Degrees:* certificates *CEO:* Pres.
Frank Lark

(904) 272-4000

NAVAL DIVING AND SALVAGE TRAINING CENTER
Panama City 32407 *Type:* Public (federal)
Accred.: 1983/1988 (SACS-COEI) *Calendar:* Courses of varying lengths *Degrees:*
certificates *CEO:* Commandant D.P. McCampbell, U.S.N.
FTE Enroll: 231   (904) 235-5207

NAVAL SERVICE SCHOOL COMMAND
Naval Training Ctr., Orlando 32813 *Type:*
Public (federal) technical *Accred.:* 1976/
1991 (SACS-COEI) *Calendar:* Courses of
varying lengths *Degrees:* certificates *CEO:*
Commandant Harry L. Smith, U.S.N.
FTE Enroll: 1,186   (407) 646-4122

NAVAL TECHNICAL TRAINING CENTER
Corry Sta., 640 Roberts Ave., Rm. 112, Pensacola 32511 *Type:* Public (federal) technical
Accred.: 1975/1990 (SACS-COEI) *Calendar:* Courses of varying lengths *Degrees:*
certificates *CEO:* Commander Ivan Dunn,
U.S.N.
FTE Enroll: 1,925   (904) 452-6558

NEW ENGLAND INSTITUTE OF TECHNOLOGY AT
PALM BEACH
1126 53rd Ct., West Palm Beach 33407-2384 *Type:* Private *Accred.:* 1984 (ACCSCT); 1992 (SACS-COEI candidate) *Calendar:* Qtr. plan *Degrees:* certificates *CEO:*
Pres. John W. Anderson
FTE Enroll: 538   (407) 842-8324

NORTH TECHNICAL EDUCATION CENTER
7071 Garden Rd., Riviera Beach 33404
Type: Public (state) *Accred.:* 1976/1991
(SACS-COEI) *Calendar:* Courses of varying
lengths *Degrees:* certificates *CEO:* Dir.
Patricia I. Nugent
FTE Enroll: 990   (407) 881-4600

OMNI TECHNICAL SCHOOL
2242 W. Broward Blvd., Fort Lauderdale
33312-1460 *Type:* Private *Accred.:* 1992
(ACCSCT) *Calendar:* Courses of varying
lengths *Degrees:* diplomas *CEO:* Pres. Stewart
A. Smith

(305) 584-4730

OMNI TECHNICAL SCHOOL
1710 N.W. Seventh St., Miami 33125-3502
Type: Private *Accred.:* 1992 (ACCSCT) *Calendar:* Courses of varying lengths *Degrees:*
diplomas *CEO:* Dir. Hipolito Ramos

(305) 541-6200

ORLANDO VOCATIONAL-TECHNICAL CENTER
301 W. Amelia St., Orlando 32801 *Type:*
Public (state) *Accred.:* 1983/1988 (SACS-COEI) *Calendar:* Courses of varying lengths
Degrees: certificates *Prof. Accred.:* Dental
Assisting *CEO:* Dir. Joseph A. McCoy
FTE Enroll: 1,357   (305) 425-2756

PALM BEACH BEAUTY & BARBER SCHOOL
4645 Gun Club Rd., West Palm Beach
33415-2882 *Type:* Private *Accred.:* 1991
(ACCSCT) *Calendar:* Courses of varying
lengths *Degrees:* diplomas *CEO:* Dir. Rex
Anderson

(407) 683-1238

PARALEGAL CAREERS
Ste. 100, 1211 N. Westshore Blvd., Tampa
33607 *Type:* Private *Accred.:* 1988 (SACS-COEI) *Calendar:* Courses of varying lengths
Degrees: diplomas *CEO:* Dir. Charles Sweet
FTE Enroll: 35   (813) 289-6025

PHD HAIR ACADEMY
27380 U.S. Hwy. 19 N., Clearwater 34621-2953 *Type:* Private *Accred.:* 1988 (ACCSCT) *Calendar:* Courses of varying lengths
Degrees: diplomas *CEO:* Dir. Gayl E.
McCanless

(813) 791-7438

PINELLAS AREA VOCATIONAL-TECHNICAL
INSTITUTE
6100 154th Ave., N., Clearwater 34620
Type: Public (state) *Accred.:* 1970/1990
(SACS-COEI) *Calendar:* Courses of varying
lengths *Degrees:* certificates *CEO:* Dir.
Clide Cassity
FTE Enroll: 1,865   (813) 531-3531

BRANCH CAMPUS
14400 49th St., N., Clearwater 34620
CEO: Dir. Clide Cassity

(813) 531-3531

BRANCH CAMPUS
2375 Whitney Rd., Clearwater 34620
CEO: Dir. Clide Cassity

(813) 530-0617

PINELLAS TECHNICAL EDUCATION CENTER—ST.
PETERSBURG CAMPUS
910 34th St., St. Petersburg 33711-2298
Type: Public (state) *Accred.:* 1975/1990
(SACS-COEI) *Calendar:* Courses of varying
lengths *Degrees:* certificates *Prof. Accred.:*
Dental Assisting, Medical Assisting (AMA),
Respiratory Therapy Technology *CEO:* Dir.
Warren Laux
FTE Enroll: 1,869   (813) 327-3671

POLITECHNICAL INSTITUTE
11865 (H3) Coral Way, Miami 33165 *Type:*
Private *Accred.:* 1989 (SACS-COEI) *Calendar:* Courses of varying lengths *Degrees:*
certificates *CEO:* Dir. Ivan Curiel
FTE Enroll: 560   (305) 226-8099

POMPANO ACADEMY OF AERONAUTICS
1006 N.E. 10th St., Pompano Beach 33060-
5722 *Type:* Private *Accred.:* 1992 (ACC-
SCT) *Calendar:* Courses of varying lengths
Degrees: certificates *CEO:* Dir. Gardner H.
Craft
                                (800) 545-7262

THE POYNTER INSTITUTE FOR MEDIA STUDIES
801 Third St., S., St. Petersburg 33701 *Type:*
Private *Accred.:* 1983/1988 (SACS-COEI)
Calendar: Courses of varying lengths *Degrees:* certificates *CEO:* Pres. Robert J.
Haiman
FTE Enroll: 1,277   (813) 821-9494

QUALTEC INSTITUTE FOR COMPETITIVE
ADVANTAGE
11760 U.S. Hwy. 1, North Palm Beach
33408 *Type:* Private *Accred.:* 1990 (SACS-
COEI) *Calendar:* Courses of varying lengths
Degrees: certificates *CEO:* Dir. Elizabeth
Hirst
FTE Enroll: 205   (800) 247-9871

RADFORD M. LOCKLIN VOCATIONAL-TECHNICAL
CENTER
5330 Berryhill Rd., Milton 32570 *Type:*
Public (state) *Accred.:* 1988 (SACS-COEI)
Calendar: Courses of varying lengths *Degrees:* certificates *CEO:* Dir. Raymond
Rogers
FTE Enroll: 341   (904) 626-1918

RADIATION THERAPY REGIONAL CENTERS
7341 Gladiolus Dr., Fort Myers 33908 *Type:*
Private *Calendar:* Courses of varying

lengths *Degrees:* certificates *Prof. Accred.:*
Radiation Therapy Technology *CEO:* C.E.O.
Daniel E. Dosoretz, M.D.
                                (813) 489-0380

RECREATIONAL VEHICLE SERVICE ACADEMY
721 Cattleman Rd., Sarasota 34232-2852
Type: Private *Accred.:* 1991 (ACCSCT) *Calendar:* Courses of varying lengths *Degrees:*
certificates *CEO:* Dir. Thomas J. Santoro
                                (813) 379-9511

REESE INSTITUTE SCHOOL OF MASSAGE THERAPY
425 Geneva Dr., Oviedo 32765-9115 *Type:*
Private *Accred.:* 1991 (ACCSCT) *Calendar:*
Courses of varying lengths *Degrees:* certificates *CEO:* Assoc. Dir. Geri F. Parsons
                                (407) 365-9283

RIDGE VOCATIONAL-TECHNICAL CENTER
7700 State Rd. 544, Winter Haven 33881
Type: Public (state) *Accred.:* 1982/1992
(SACS-COEI) *Calendar:* Courses of varying
lengths *Degrees:* certificates *CEO:* Dir. Carl
Ray
FTE Enroll: 1,450   (813) 422-6402

ROBERT MORGAN VOCATIONAL-TECHNICAL
CENTER
18180 S.W. 122nd Ave., Miami 33177 *Type:*
Public (state) *Accred.:* 1983/1988 (SACS-
COEI) *Calendar:* Courses of varying lengths
Degrees: certificates *Prof. Accred.:* Dental
Assisting *CEO:* Dir. Frederick Reed
FTE Enroll: 1,109   (305) 253-9920

ROMAR HAIRSTYLING ACADEMY
1608 S. Federal Hwy., Boynton Beach
33435 *Type:* Private *Accred.:* 1990 (SACS-
COEI) *Calendar:* Courses of varying lengths
Degrees: certificates, diplomas *CEO:* Dir.
Peter Ross
FTE Enroll: 127   (407) 737-3430

RTI TECHNICAL INSTITUTE
Fairfield Plaza, 1412 W. Fairfield Dr., Pensacola 32501-1105 *Type:* Private *Accred.:*
1985/1990 (ACCSCT) *Calendar:* Courses of
varying lengths *Degrees:* certificates *CEO:*
Dir. Larry Bryant
                                (904) 433-6547

ST. AUGUSTINE TECHNICAL CENTER
2980 Collins Ave., St. Augustine 32095-
9970 *Type:* Public (state) *Accred.:* 1980/

1990 (SACS-COEI) *Calendar:* Courses of varying lengths *Degrees:* certificates *Prof. Accred.:* EMT-Paramedic *CEO:* Dir. Steve Hand
FTE Enroll: 1,883   (904) 824-4401

BRANCH CAMPUS
113 Putnam County Blvd., East Palatka 32131 *CEO:* Dir. Bernie Masters
(904) 557-2468

SARASOTA COUNTY TECHNICAL INSTITUTE
4748 Beneva Rd., Sarasota 34233 *Type:* Public (state) *Accred.:* 1971/1991 (SACS-COEI) *Calendar:* Courses of varying lengths *Degrees:* certificates *Prof. Accred.:* EMT-Paramedic, Medical Assisting (AMA), Practical Nursing *CEO:* Dir. Steve Harvey
FTE Enroll: 2,228   (813) 924-1365

SEGAL INSTITUTE OF COURT REPORTING
18850 U.S. Hwy. 19, N., No. 565, Clearwater 34618-6822 *Type:* Private *Accred.:* 1991 (SACS-COEI) *Calendar:* Courses of varying lengths *Degrees:* certificates *CEO:* Dir. Susan Segal
FTE Enroll: 64   (813) 535-0608

SER-IBM BUSINESS INSTITUTE
42 N.W. 27th Ave., No. 421, Miami 33125 *Type:* Private *Accred.:* 1985/1990 (SACS-COEI) *Calendar:* Courses of varying lengths *Degrees:* certificates *CEO:* Dir. Melvin Chaves
FTE Enroll: 195   (305) 649-7500

BRANCH CAMPUS
4238 W. 12th Ave., Unit B-19, Hialeah 33012 *CEO:* Dir. Lola Gonzalez
(305) 557-2468

BRANCH CAMPUS
7100 Pine Blvd., Pembroke Pines 33024 *CEO:* Dir. Lola Gonzalez
(305) 983-5700

SHERIDAN VOCATIONAL-TECHNICAL CENTER
5400 Sheridan St., Hollywood 33021 *Type:* Public (state) *Accred.:* 1974/1989 (SACS-COEI) *Calendar:* Courses of varying lengths *Degrees:* certificates *Prof. Accred.:* Medical Laboratory Technology (AMA), Practical Nursing *CEO:* Dir. Robert Boegli
FTE Enroll: 1,754   (305) 985-3233

SOUTH TECHNICAL EDUCATION CENTER
1300 S.W. 30th Ave., Boynton Beach 33426 *Type:* Public (state) *Accred.:* 1980/1990 (SACS-COEI) *Calendar:* Courses of varying lengths *Degrees:* certificates *CEO:* Dir. James L. Rasco
FTE Enroll: 2,212   (407) 369-7000

SOUTHERN TECHNICAL CENTER
19151 S. Dixie Hwy., Miami 33157 *Type:* Private *Accred.:* 1988 (ACCSCT) *Calendar:* Courses of varying lengths *Degrees:* certificates *CEO:* Dir. Joaquin Bassolles
(305) 254-0995

STENOTYPE INSTITUTE OF JACKSONVILLE
500 Ninth Ave., N., P.O. Box 50009, Jacksonville Beach 32250 *Type:* Private business and home study *Accred.:* 1968/1989 (ACISC); 1987/1992 (NHSC) *Calendar:* Courses of varying lengths *Degrees:* certificates, diplomas *CEO:* Pres. Thyra D. Ellis
(904) 246-7466

SUNCOAST CENTER FOR NATURAL HEALTH/SUNCOAST SCHOOL
4910 Cypress St., Tampa 33607-3802 *Type:* Private *Accred.:* 1986 (ACCSCT) *Calendar:* Courses of varying lengths *Degrees:* diplomas *CEO:* Dir. Daniel A. Ulrich
(813) 287-1099

SUNSTATE ACADEMY OF HAIR DESIGN
2418 Colonial Blvd., Fort Myers 33907-1491 *Type:* Private *Accred.:* 1990 (ACCSCT) *Calendar:* Courses of varying lengths *Degrees:* diplomas *CEO:* Dir. Kenneth F. Stone
(813) 278-1311

SUNSTATE ACADEMY OF HAIR DESIGN
1825 Tamiami Tr., No. E6, Port Charlotte 33948 *Type:* Private *Accred.:* 1983/1986 (ACCSCT) *Calendar:* Courses of varying lengths *Degrees:* diplomas *CEO:* Dir. Kenneth F. Stone
(813) 255-1366

SUNSTATE ACADEMY OF HAIR DESIGN
4424 Bee Ridge Rd., Sarasota 34233-2502 *Type:* Private *Accred.:* 1983/1989 (ACCSCT) *Calendar:* Courses of varying lengths *Degrees:* diplomas *CEO:* Dir. James A. Stone
(813) 377-4880

SUWANEE-HAMILTON AREA VOCATIONAL-
TECHNICAL AND ADULT EDUCATION CENTER
415 Pinewood Dr., S.W., Live Oak 32060
Type: Public (state) *Accred.:* 1973/1990
(SACS-COEI) *Calendar:* Courses of varying
lengths *Degrees:* certificates *CEO:* Dir. Bill
McMillian
FTE Enroll: 373   (904) 362-2751

TECHNICAL CAREER INSTITUTE
720 N.W. 27th Ave., Miami 33125 *Type:*
Private *Accred.:* 1993 (SACS-COEI) *Calendar:* Courses of varying lengths *Degrees:*
certificates, diplomas *CEO:* Dir. James Ladd
FTE Enroll: 17   (305) 442-4480

TOM P. HANEY VOCATIONAL-TECHNICAL
CENTER
3016 Hwy. 77, Panama City 32405 *Type:*
Public (state) *Accred.:* 1977/1992 (SACS-
COEI) *Calendar:* Courses of varying lengths
Degrees: certificates *CEO:* Dir. Marion
Riviere
FTE Enroll: 688   (904) 769-2191

BRANCH CAMPUS
Bay St. Joseph Care Ctr., Port St. Joe
32456 *CEO:* Dir. Marion Riviere

TRAVISS VOCATIONAL-TECHNICAL CENTER
3225 Winter Lake Rd., Eaton Park 33803
Type: Public (state) *Accred.:* 1978/1988
(SACS-COEI) *Calendar:* Courses of varying
lengths *Degrees:* certificates *CEO:* Dir. Carl
Ray
FTE Enroll: 1,045   (813) 665-1220

U.S. SCHOOLS
100 N. Plaza, Miami 33147 *Type:* Private
Accred.: 1989/1992 (SACS-COEI) *Calendar:* Courses of varying lengths *Degrees:*
certificates *CEO:* Dir. Hugh Alpeter
FTE Enroll: 207   (305) 836-7424

VAN DYCK INSTITUTE OF TOURISM
1301 66th St. N., St. Petersburg 33710 *Type:*
Private *Accred.:* 1992 (ACCSCT) *Calendar:*
Courses of varying lengths *Degrees:* certificates *CEO:* Pres. Claus Van Dyck
                                     (813) 347-0074

WASHINGTON-HOLMES AREA VOCATIONAL-
TECHNICAL CENTER
209 Hoyt St., Chipley 32428 *Type:* Public
(state) *Accred.:* 1976/1991 (SACS-COEI)

Calendar: Courses of varying lengths *Degrees:* certificates *CEO:* Dir. Gene Prough
FTE Enroll: 816   (904) 638-1180

WEST TECHNICAL EDUCATION CENTER
2625 State Rd. 715, Belle Glade 33430
Type: Public (state) *Accred.:* 1984/1989
(SACS-COEI) *Calendar:* Courses of varying
lengths *Degrees:* certificates *CEO:* Dir.
Shirley W. Maxson
FTE Enroll: 503   (407) 996-4930

WESTSIDE VOCATIONAL-TECHNICAL CENTER
731 E. Story Rd., Winter Garden 34787
Type: Public (state) *Accred.:* 1981/1991
(SACS-COEI) *Calendar:* Courses of varying
lengths *Degrees:* certificates *CEO:* Dir. Walt
Cobb
FTE Enroll: 1,189   (305) 656-2851

BRANCH CAMPUS
Technology Information Ctr., 6628 Old
Winter Garden Rd., Orlando 32811 *CEO:*
Asst. Dir. Tom Winters
                                     (407) 292-8696

WILLIAM T. MCFATTER VOCATIONAL-
TECHNICAL CENTER
6500 Nova Dr., Davie 33317 *Type:* Public
(state) *Accred.:* 1989 (SACS-COEI) *Calendar:* Courses of varying lengths *Degrees:*
certificates *Prof. Accred.:* Dental Laboratory
Technology, Practical Nursing *CEO:* Dir.
Horace McLeod
FTE Enroll: 1,250   (305) 370-8324

BRANCH CAMPUS
Broward Fire Acad., 2600 S.W. 71 Terr.,
Davie 33314 *CEO:* Asst. Prin. Patricia
Gaiefsky
                                     (305) 474-8219

BRANCH CAMPUS
Criminal Justice Inst., 3501 S.W. Davie
Rd., Davie 33314 *CEO:* Asst. Prin. Patricia
Gaiefsky
                                     (305) 474-8219

WINTER PARK ADULT VOCATIONAL CENTER
901 Webster Ave., Winter Park 32789 *Type:*
Public (state) *Accred.:* 1986/1988 (SACS-
COEI) *Calendar:* Courses of varying lengths
Degrees: certificates *Prof. Accred.:* Medical
Assisting (AMA) *CEO:* Dir. Kaye Chastain
FTE Enroll: 916   (407) 647-6366

WITHLACOOHEE TECHNICAL INSTITUTE
1201 W. Main St., Inverness 34450 *Type:*
Public (state) *Accred.:* 1984/1989 (SACS-
COEI) *Calendar:* Courses of varying lengths
Degrees: certificates *CEO:* Dir. Steven S.
Kinard
FTE Enroll: 690   (904) 726-2430

GEORGIA

ALBANY TECHNICAL INSTITUTE
1021 Lowe Rd., Albany 31708 *Type:* Public (state) *Accred.:* 1974/1989 (SACS-COEI) *Calendar:* Courses of varying lengths *Degrees:* certificates *Prof. Accred.:* Dental Assisting, Radiography *CEO:* Dir. Alvin Anderson
FTE Enroll: 971   (912) 888-1320

ALLIANCE TRACTOR TRAILER TRAINING CENTER
333 Industrial Blvd., P.O. Box 1008, McDonough 30253-1008 *Type:* Private *Accred.:* 1988/1993 (ACCSCT) *Calendar:* Courses of varying lengths *Degrees:* certificates *CEO:* Dir. Scott McElrath
(404) 957-6401

ALTAMAHA TECHNICAL INSTITUTE
1777 W. Cherry St., Jesup 31545 *Type:* Public (state) *Accred.:* 1992 (SACS-COEI) *Calendar:* Courses of varying lengths *Degrees:* diplomas *CEO:* Pres. C. Paul Scott
FTE Enroll: 244   (912) 427-5800

BRANCH CAMPUS
Cromatie St., Hazlehurst 31319 *CEO:* Dir. Molly Hinson
(912) 375-5480

ARMSTRONG UNIVERSITY OF BEAUTY
101 E. Fourth St., Rome 30161 *Type:* Private *Accred.:* 1989 (SACS-COEI) *Calendar:* Courses of varying lengths *Degrees:* diplomas *CEO:* Dir. Bobbie Wilson
FTE Enroll: 37   (404) 232-6565

ARMY SIGNAL CENTER AND SCHOOL
Fort Gordon 30905-5080 *Type:* Public (federal) technical *Accred.:* 1976/1991 (SACS-COEI) *Calendar:* Courses of varying lengths *Degrees:* certificates *CEO:* Commandant Robert E. Gray, U.S.A.
FTE Enroll: 8,022   (404) 791-4588

ARTISTIC BEAUTY COLLEGE
1820 Hwy. 20, Ste. 200, Conyers 30208 *Type:* Private *Accred.:* 1990 (SACS-COEI) *Calendar:* Courses of varying lengths *Degrees:* certificates, diplomas *CEO:* Dir. Connie Manning
FTE Enroll: 133   (404) 922-7653

ASHER SCHOOL OF BUSINESS
100 Pinnacle Way, Ste. 110, Norcross 30071 *Type:* Private *Accred.:* 1990 (SACS-COEI) *Calendar:* Courses of varying lengths *Degrees:* certificates *CEO:* Dir. Joe Voyles
FTE Enroll: 183   (404) 368-0800

ATLANTA AREA TECHNICAL SCHOOL
1560 Stewart Ave., S.W., Atlanta 30310 *Type:* Public (state) *Accred.:* 1971/1991 (SACS-COEI) *Calendar:* Courses of varying lengths *Degrees:* certificates *Prof. Accred.:* Dental Laboratory Technology (provisional), Medical Assisting (AMA), Medical Laboratory Technology (AMA) *CEO:* Dir. Gerald Allen
FTE Enroll: 9,800   (404) 758-9451

BRANCH CAMPUS
4191 Northside Dr., N.W., Atlanta 30342 *CEO:* Dir. Gerald Allen
(404) 842-3117

ATLANTA JOB CORPS CENTER
239 W. Lake Ave., N.W., Atlanta 30314 *Type:* Public (district) *Accred.:* 1985/1990 (SACS-COEI) *Calendar:* Courses of varying lengths *Degrees:* diplomas *CEO:* Dir. Lonnie Hall
FTE Enroll: 579   (404) 794-9512

ATLANTA SCHOOL OF MASSAGE
2300 Peachford Rd., Ste. 3200, Atlanta 30338-5820 *Type:* Private *Accred.:* 1988 (ACCSCT) *Calendar:* Courses of varying lengths *Degrees:* certificates *CEO:* Dir. Beth Geno
(404) 454-7167

BEN HILL-IRWIN TECHNICAL INSTITUTE
667 Perry House Rd., Fitzgerald 31750 *Type:* Public (state) *Accred.:* 1973/1989 (SACS-COEI) *Calendar:* Courses of varying lengths *Degrees:* certificates *CEO:* Dir. Edgar B. Greene
FTE Enroll: 451   (912) 468-7487

BRANCH CAMPUS
210 W. Jackson St., Douglas 31533 *CEO:* Dir. Jim Mills
(912) 384-7520

BRANELL INSTITUTE
1000 Circle 75 Pkwy., Ste. 100, Atlanta
30339 *Type:* Private business *Accred.:* 1987/
1991 (ACISC); 1992 (SACS-COEI) *Calendar:* Courses of varying lengths *Degrees:*
certificates, diplomas *CEO:* Dir. James F.
McCoy, Jr.
FTE Enroll: 353   (404) 951-0051

BRANELL INSTITUTE
Ste. A, 4876 Riverdale Rd., College Park
30337 *Type:* Private business *Accred.:* 1972/
1991 (ACISC); 1988 (SACS-COEI) *Calendar:* Courses of varying lengths *Degrees:*
certificates, diplomas *CEO:* Dir. Marilyn
Kniery
FTE Enroll: 363   (404) 997-1300

   BRANCH CAMPUS
   7505 Fannin Ctr., Ste. 400, Houston, TX
   77054 *CEO:* Dir. Jim Gifford
                          (713) 795-0031

BRANELL INSTITUTE
Ste. 120, 5255 Snapfinger Park Dr., Decatur
30035 *Type:* Private business *Accred.:* 1972/
1990 (ACISC); 1992 (SACS-COEI) *Calendar:* Courses of varying lengths *Degrees:*
certificates, diplomas *CEO:* Dir. Polly Neal
FTE Enroll: 223   (404) 593-1097

BROWN COLLEGE OF COURT REPORTING &
MEDICAL TRANSCRIPTION
1100 Spring St., N.W., No. 200, Atlanta
30309 *Type:* Private *Accred.:* 1984/1989
(SACS-COEI) *Calendar:* Courses of varying
lengths *Degrees:* certificates *CEO:* Dir.
Forrest Brown
FTE Enroll: 248   (404) 876-1227

   BRANCH CAMPUS
   501 Spur 63, Ste. B-3, Longview, TX
   75601 *CEO:* Dir. Phyllis Lorenzen
                          (903) 757-4338

CARROLL TECHNICAL INSTITUTE
997 S. Hwy. 16, Carrollton 30117 *Type:*
Public (state) *Accred.:* 1973/1992 (SACS-COEI) *Calendar:* Courses of varying lengths
Degrees: certificates *CEO:* Pres. Judy
Hulsey
FTE Enroll: 542   (404) 834-6800

CLASSIC NAIL CARE SCHOOL
2227 Godby Rd., Ste. 114, College Park
30349 *Type:* Private *Accred.:* 1993 (ACC-SCT) *Calendar:* Courses of varying lengths
Degrees: certificates, diplomas *CEO:* Pres.
Diane Kirk
                          (404) 762-6047

COOSA VALLEY TECHNICAL INSTITUTE
112 Hemlock St., Rome 30161 *Type:* Public
(state) *Accred.:* 1972/1992 (SACS-COEI)
Calendar: Courses of varying lengths *Degrees:* certificates *Prof. Accred.:* Respiratory
Therapy Technology *CEO:* Dir. J.D. Powell
FTE Enroll: 425   (404) 235-1142

DALTON VOCATIONAL SCHOOL OF HEALTH
OCCUPATIONS
1221 Elkwood Dr., Dalton 30720 *Type:* Public (state) technical *Accred.:* 1975/1990
(SACS-COEI) *Calendar:* Courses of varying
lengths *Degrees:* certificates *CEO:* Dir.
Rubye P. Sane
FTE Enroll: 95   (404) 278-8922

DEKALB BEAUTY COLLEGE
6254 Memorial Dr., No. M, Stone Mountain
30032 *Type:* Private *Accred.:* 1987/1992
(SACS-COEI) *Calendar:* Courses of varying
lengths *Degrees:* certificates *CEO:* Dir.
Betty Lyon
FTE Enroll: 184   (404) 879-6673

DERMA CLINIC ACADEMY
5600 Roswell Rd., No. 110, Atlanta 30342
Type: Private *Accred.:* 1987 (SACS-COEI)
Calendar: Courses of varying lengths *Degrees:* certificates *CEO:* Dir. Margaret A.
Ruffin
FTE Enroll: 35   (404) 250-9600

EXECUTIVE TRAVEL INSTITUTE
5775 Peachtree Dunwoody Rd., Ste. 300-E,
Atlanta 30342-1505 *Type:* Private *Accred.:*
1991 (ACCSCT) *Calendar:* Courses of varying lengths *Degrees:* certificates *CEO:* Dir.
Joseph M. Brown
                          (404) 303-2929

FLINT RIVER TECHNICAL INSTITUTE
1533 Hwy. 19, S., Thomaston 30286 *Type:*
Public (state) *Accred.:* 1973/1990 (SACS-COEI) *Calendar:* Courses of varying lengths

Degrees: certificates *CEO:* Dir. Carlos Schmitt
FTE Enroll: 183   (404) 647-0928

GEORGIA MEDICAL INSTITUTE
40 Marietta St., Fls. 5 and 13, Atlanta 30303 *Type:* Private *Accred.:* 1985/1987 (ABHES) *Calendar:* Courses of varying lengths *Degrees:* diplomas *CEO:* Pres./Dir. Dominic J. Dean
       (404) 525-3272

GRIFFIN TECHNICAL INSTITUTE
501 Varsity Rd., Griffin 30223 *Type:* Public (state) *Accred.:* 1971/1991 (SACS-COEI) *Calendar:* Courses of varying lengths *Degrees:* certificates *Prof. Accred.:* Radiography *CEO:* Dir. Coy L. Hodges
FTE Enroll: 827   (404) 228-7365

GWINNETT COLLEGE
4230 Hwy. 29, Ste. 11, Liburn 30247 *Type:* Private business *Accred.:* 1988 (ACISC) *Calendar:* Qtr. plan *Degrees:* certificates, diplomas *CEO:* Exec. Vice Pres. Billy L. Clark
       (404) 381-7200

HEART OF GEORGIA TECHNICAL INSTITUTE
Rte. 5, Box 136A-1, Dublin 31021 *Type:* Public (state) *Accred.:* 1986/1991 (SACS-COEI) *Calendar:* Courses of varying lengths *Degrees:* certificates *CEO:* Pres. Ron Henderson
FTE Enroll: 403   (912) 275-6589

BRANCH CAMPUS
1124 College St., Eastman 31023 *CEO:* Pres. Ron Henderson
       (912) 374-7122

HOUSTON AERONAUTICAL COLLEGE
Rte. 3, Box 250, Sandersville 31082 *Type:* Private *Accred.:* 1990/1992 (SACS-COEI) *Calendar:* Courses of varying lengths *Degrees:* certificates, diplomas *CEO:* Pres. Ray Houston
FTE Enroll: 436   (912) 552-6100

INTERACTIVE LEARNING SYSTEMS
480 N. Thomas St., Athens 30601 *Type:* Private business *Accred.:* 1984/1992 (ACISC); 1989 (SACS-COEI) *Calendar:* Courses of

varying lengths *Degrees:* certificates, diplomas *CEO:* Dir. Fannie Smith
FTE Enroll: 66   (404) 548-9800

INTERACTIVE LEARNING SYSTEMS
5600 Roswell Rd., N.E., Atlanta 30342 *Type:* Private *Accred.:* 1989 (SACS-COEI) *Calendar:* Courses of varying lengths *Degrees:* certificates *CEO:* Pres. Fonya Gail Hester
FTE Enroll: 459   (404) 250-9000

BRANCH CAMPUS
4812 Old National Hwy., College Park 30337 *CEO:* Dir. JoAnn Wilson
       (404) 765-9777

BRANCH CAMPUS
2759 Delk Rd., Ste. 101, Marietta 30067 *CEO:* Dir. Lynn Haltiwanger
       (404) 951-2367

BRANCH CAMPUS
2171 Northlake Pkwy., Ste. 100, Tucker 30084 *CEO:* Dir. Doug Cole
       (404) 939-6008

BRANCH CAMPUS
6612 Dixie Hwy., Ste. 2, Florence, KY 41042 *CEO:* Dir. Richard Ellison
       (606) 282-8989

BRANCH CAMPUS
103 S. Main St., Williamstown, KY 41097 *CEO:* Dir. Janelle McKinney
       (606) 824-3573

INTERNATIONAL SCHOOL OF SKIN & NAILCARE
5600 Roswell Rd., N.E., Atlanta 30342 *Type:* Private *Accred.:* 1987/1992 (SACS-COEI) *Calendar:* Courses of varying lengths *Degrees:* certificates *CEO:* Dir. Sissy McQuinn
FTE Enroll: 102   (404) 843-1005

KERR BUSINESS COLLEGE
P.O. Box 976, 3011 Hogansville Rd., La-Grange 30241 *Type:* Private business *Accred.:* 1976/1990 (ACISC) *Calendar:* Qtr. plan *Degrees:* certificates, diplomas *CEO:* Dir. Fred Randall Kerr
       (404) 884-1751

BRANCH CAMPUS
P.O. Box 1986, 2623 Washington Rd., Bldg. B, Augusta 30903 *Accred.:* 1984/1990 (ACISC) *CEO:* Dir. Darryl H. Kerr
(404) 738-5046

LANIER TECHNICAL INSTITUTE
2990 Landrum Education Dr., Oakwood 30566 *Type:* Public (state) *Accred.:* 1972/1986 (SACS-COEI) *Calendar:* Courses of varying lengths *Degrees:* certificates *Prof. Accred.:* Dental Assisting, Dental Hygiene, Medical Laboratory Technology (AMA) *CEO:* Pres. Joe E. Hill
FTE Enroll: 808   (404) 531-6300

MABLE BAILEY FASHION COLLEGE
1332 13th St., Columbus 31901 *Type:* Private *Accred.:* 1983/1988 (SACS-COEI) *Calendar:* Courses of varying lengths *Degrees:* certificates *CEO:* Dir. Mable Bailey
FTE Enroll: 20   (404) 324-4295

MACON BEAUTY SCHOOL
630-J North Ave., Macon 31211 *Type:* Private *Accred.:* 1990 (SACS-COEI) *Calendar:* Courses of varying lengths *Degrees:* certificates, diplomas *CEO:* Dir. Joyce Meadows
FTE Enroll: 121   (912) 746-3243

MACON TECHNICAL INSTITUTE
3300 Macon Tech Dr., Macon 31206 *Type:* Public (state) *Accred.:* 1973/1993 (SACS-COEI) *Calendar:* Courses of varying lengths *Degrees:* certificates *Prof. Accred.:* Medical Laboratory Technology (AMA) *CEO:* Pres. Melton Palmer
FTE Enroll: 927   (912) 781-0551

BRANCH CAMPUS
940 Forsyth St., Macon 31206 *CEO:* Pres. Melton Palmer
(912) 744-4812

MEADOWS COLLEGE OF BUSINESS
832 S. Slappey Blvd., Albany 31701 *Type:* Private business *Accred.:* 1976/1991 (ACISC) *Calendar:* Qtr. plan *Degrees:* certificates, diplomas *CEO:* Dir. Diane Phipps
(912) 883-1736

BRANCH CAMPUS
1118-C 280 By-Pass, Phenix City, AL 36867 *Accred.:* 1993 (ACISC) *CEO:* Dir. Deborah Beatty
(205) 291-0273

METROPOLITAN COLLEGE OF BUSINESS
4319 Covington Hwy., No. 303, Decatur 30035 *Type:* Private *Accred.:* 1990 (SACS-COEI) *Calendar:* Courses of varying lengths *Degrees:* certificates, diplomas *CEO:* Pres. Bernard Clay
FTE Enroll: 16   (404) 288-6241

METROPOLITAN SCHOOL OF HAIR DESIGN
5481 Memorial Dr., Ste. E, Stone Mountain 30083 *Type:* Private *Accred.:* 1989/1991 (SACS-COEI) *Calendar:* Courses of varying lengths *Degrees:* diplomas *CEO:* Dir. Jerry Vaughn
FTE Enroll: 40   (404) 294-5697

MIDDLE GEORGIA TECHNICAL INSTITUTE
1311 Corder Rd., Warner Robins 31088 *Type:* Public (state) *Accred.:* 1978/1988 (SACS-COEI) *Calendar:* Courses of varying lengths *Degrees:* certificates, diplomas *CEO:* Pres. Billy G. Edenfield
FTE Enroll: 316   (912) 929-6800

BRANCH CAMPUS
Robbins Air Force Museum, Robbins Air Force Base 31098 *CEO:* Pres. Billy G. Edenfield
(912) 929-6783

MOULTRIE AREA TECHNICAL INSTITUTE
315 Industrial Park Dr., Moultrie 31776 *Type:* Public (state) *Accred.:* 1974/1990 (SACS-COEI) *Calendar:* Courses of varying lengths *Degrees:* certificates *CEO:* Pres. Jack N. Gay
FTE Enroll: 506   (912) 985-2297

BRANCH CAMPUS
314 E. 14th St., Tifton 31794 *CEO:* Dir. Wanda Golden
(912) 382-2767

THE NATIONAL BUSINESS INSTITUTE
243 W. Ponce de Leon Ave., Decatur 30030 *Type:* Private *Accred.:* 1990 (SACS-COEI) *Calendar:* Courses of varying lengths *Degrees:* certificates *CEO:* Pres. Mark Lavinsky
FTE Enroll: 53   (404) 352-0800

NATIONAL EDUCATION CENTER—BRYMAN CAMPUS
40 Marietta St., 8th Fl., Atlanta 30303-2816 *Type:* Private *Accred.:* 1973/1986 (ACC-

SCT) *Calendar:* Courses of varying lengths *Degrees:* diplomas *Prof. Accred.:* Medical Assisting (AMA) *CEO:* Dir. John Mathias
(404) 524-8800

NAVY SUPPLY CORPS SCHOOL
Athens 30606 *Type:* Public (federal) technical *Accred.:* 1981/1991 (SACS-COEI) *Calendar:* Courses of varying lengths *Degrees:* certificates *CEO:* Commanding Ofcr. Justin D, McCarthy, U.S.N.
FTE Enroll: 374   (404) 354-7200

NORTH FULTON BEAUTY COLLEGE
10930 Crabapple Rd., Roswell 30075 *Type:* Private *Accred.:* 1992 (SACS-COEI) *Calendar:* Courses of varying lengths *Degrees:* certificates *CEO:* Dir. Jane Champion
FTE Enroll: 28   (404) 552-9570

NORTH GEORGIA TECHNICAL INSTITUTE
Hwy. 197, N., Clarkesville 30523 *Type:* Public (state) *Accred.:* 1972/1992 (SACS-COEI) *Calendar:* Courses of varying lengths *Degrees:* certificates *Prof. Accred.:* Medical Laboratory Technology (AMA) *CEO:* Dir. James H. Marlowe
FTE Enroll: 540   (404) 754-7702

NORTH METRO TECHNICAL INSTITUTE
5198 Ross Rd., Acworth 30101 *Type:* Public (state) *Accred.:* 1991 (SACS-COEI) *Calendar:* Courses of varying lengths *Degrees:* diplomas *CEO:* Pres. Kenneth Allen
FTE Enroll: 265   (404) 975-4010

OCCUPATIONAL EDUCATION CENTER—CENTRAL
3075 Alton Rd., Chamblee 30341 *Type:* Public (state) *Accred.:* 1988/1993 (SACS-COEI) *Calendar:* Courses of varying lengths *Degrees:* certificates *CEO:* Dir. Robert Burns
FTE Enroll: 122   (404) 457-3393

OCCUPATIONAL EDUCATION CENTER—NORTH
1995 Womack Rd., Dunwoody 30338 *Type:* Public (state) *Accred.:* 1988 (SACS-COEI) *Calendar:* Courses of varying lengths *Degrees:* certificates *CEO:* Dir. Frank Hall
FTE Enroll: 277   (404) 394-0321

OCCUPATIONAL EDUCATION CENTER—SOUTH
3303 Pantherville Rd., Decatur 30034 *Type:* Public (state) *Accred.:* 1988/1993 (SACS-

COEI) *Calendar:* Courses of varying lengths *Degrees:* certificates *CEO:* Dir. Larry Ladner
FTE Enroll: 215   (404) 241-9400

OGEECHEE TECHNICAL INSTITUTE
One Joe Kennedy Blvd., Statesboro 30458 *Type:* Public (state) *Accred.:* 1992 (SACS-COEI) *Calendar:* Courses of varying lengths *Degrees:* diplomas *CEO:* Pres. Robert C. Ernst
FTE Enroll: 248   (912) 764-8530

OKEFENOKEE TECHNICAL INSTITUTE
1701 Carswell Ave., Waycross 31503 *Type:* Public (state) *Accred.:* 1972/1992 (SACS-COEI) *Calendar:* Courses of varying lengths *Degrees:* certificates *Prof. Accred.:* Medical Laboratory Technology (AMA), Radiography, Surgical Technology *CEO:* Dir. Joseph Ray Miller
FTE Enroll: 327   (912) 283-2002

PICKENS TECHNICAL INSTITUTE
100 Pickens Tech Dr., Jasper 30143 *Type:* Public (state) *Accred.:* 1971/1991 (SACS-COEI) *Calendar:* Courses of varying lengths *Degrees:* certificates *CEO:* Dir. Tom Harrison
FTE Enroll: 425   (404) 692-3411

PORTFOLIO CENTER
125 Bennett St., N.W., Atlanta 30309 *Type:* Private professional *Accred.:* 1982/1992 (SACS-COEI) *Calendar:* Courses of varying lengths *Degrees:* certificates *CEO:* Dir. Gemma Gatt
FTE Enroll: 320   (404) 351-5055

PRO-WAY HAIR SCHOOL
8-B Franklin Rd., Newnan 30263 *Type:* Private *Accred.:* 1983/1990 (SACS-COEI) *Calendar:* Courses of varying lengths *Degrees:* certificates *CEO:* Dir. Francis Sullivan
FTE Enroll: 88   (404) 251-4592

BRANCH CAMPUS
3099 S. Perkins Rd., Memphis, TN 38118 *CEO:* Dir. Steve Sullivan
(901) 363-3553

QUALITY PLUS OFFICE SKILLS AND MOTIVATIONAL TRAINING CENTER
Ste. 450, 1655 Peachtree St., Atlanta 30309 *Type:* Private business *Accred.:* 1990 (ACISC) *Calendar:* Courses of varying

lengths *Degrees:* certificates, diplomas *CEO:* Pres. Kathleen Bacon
(404) 892-6669

ROFFLER MOLER HAIRSTYLING COLLEGE
P.O. Box 518, Forest Park 30050-0518 *Type:* Private *Accred.:* 1985/1990 (ACCSCT) *Calendar:* Courses of varying lengths *Degrees:* certificates *CEO:* Dir. Ruby Sheffield
(404) 366-2838

BRANCH CAMPUS
1311 Roswell Rd., Marietta 30062 *Accred.:* 1988 (ACCSCT) *CEO:* Dir. Ruby Sheffield
(404) 565-3285

SAMVERLY COLLEGE
210 Edgewood Ave., N.E., Atlanta 30303-2322 *Type:* Private *Accred.:* 1992 (ACCSCT) *Calendar:* Courses of varying lengths *Degrees:* certificates *CEO:* Dir. Beverly Purdie
(404) 522-4370

SOUTH GEORGIA TECHNICAL INSTITUTE
728 Southerfield Rd., Americus 31709-9691 *Type:* Public (state) *Accred.:* 1973/1993 (SACS-COEI) *Calendar:* Courses of varying lengths *Degrees:* certificates *CEO:* Dir. Dea Pounders
FTE Enroll: 438   (912) 928-0283

SOUTHEASTERN CENTER FOR THE ARTS
1935 Cliff Valley Way, Ste. 210, Atlanta 30329 *Type:* Private *Accred.:* 1983/1988 (SACS-COEI) *Calendar:* Courses of varying lengths *Degrees:* certificates *CEO:* Dir. Fred Rich
FTE Enroll: 43   (404) 633-1990

SOUTHEASTERN FLIGHT ACADEMY
Herbert Smart Airport, Macon 31201 *Type:* Private *Accred.:* 1992 (SACS-COEI) *Calendar:* Courses of varying lengths *Degrees:* certificates, diplomas *CEO:* Pres. Patrick Murphy
FTE Enroll: 61   (800) 423-7510

SOUTHEASTERN TECHNICAL INSTITUTE
3001 E. First St., Vidalia 30474 *Type:* Private *Accred.:* 1992 (SACS-COEI) *Calendar:* Courses of varying lengths *Degrees:* certificates *CEO:* Dir. Larry Siefferman
FTE Enroll: 670   (912) 537-0386

SWAINSBORO TECHNICAL INSTITUTE
201 Kite Rd., Swainsboro 30401 *Type:* Public (state) *Accred.:* 1973/1988 (SACS-COEI) *Calendar:* Courses of varying lengths *Degrees:* certificates *CEO:* Dir. Donald Speir
FTE Enroll: 627   (912) 237-6465

THOMAS TECHNICAL INSTITUTE
Hwy. 19 at Rte. 319, Thomasville 31799 *Type:* Public (state) *Accred.:* 1973/1988 (SACS-COEI) *Calendar:* Courses of varying lengths *Degrees:* certificates *Prof. Accred.:* Medical Assisting (AMA), Physical Therapy Assisting, Radiography, Respiratory Therapy Technology, Surgical Technology *CEO:* Dir. Charles R. DeMott
FTE Enroll: 1,015   (912) 225-4094

TRIDENT TRAINING FACILITY
1040 USS Georgia Ave., Kings Bay 31547 *Type:* Public (federal) *Accred.:* 1993 (SACS-COEI) *Calendar:* Courses of varying lengths *Degrees:* certificates *CEO:* Commandant K. Kevan, U.S.N.
FTE Enroll: 558   (912) 922-8304

TURNER JOB CORPS CENTER
2000 Schilling Ave., Albany 31708 *Type:* Public (district) *Accred.:* 1984/1989 (SACS-COEI) *Calendar:* Courses of varying lengths *Degrees:* certificates *CEO:* Dir. Hal Schmitz
FTE Enroll: 993   (912) 431-1820

VALDOSTA TECHNICAL INSTITUTE
Val-Tech Rd., Valdosta 31602 *Type:* Public (state) *Accred.:* 1974/1990 (SACS-COEI) *Calendar:* Courses of varying lengths *Degrees:* certificates *Prof. Accred.:* Medical Assisting (AMA), Radiography *CEO:* Dir. James Bridges
FTE Enroll: 611   (912) 333-2100

WALKER TECHNICAL INSTITUTE
Hwy. 27, N., Rock Spring 30739 *Type:* Public (state) *Accred.:* 1972/1992 (SACS-COEI) *Calendar:* Courses of varying lengths *Degrees:* certificates *CEO:* Dir. Ray Brooks
FTE Enroll: 430   (404) 764-1016

WEST GEORGIA TECHNICAL INSTITUTE
303 Fort Dr., LaGrange 30240 *Type:* Public (state) *Accred.:* 1973/1988 (SACS-COEI) *Calendar:* Courses of varying lengths *Degrees:* certificates *Prof. Accred.:* Radiography *CEO:* Dir. Roger Slater
FTE Enroll: 379   (404) 882-2518

GUAM

INTERNATIONAL BUSINESS COLLEGE OF GUAM
P.O. Box 3783, Agana 96910 *Type:* Private business *Accred.:* 1978/1990 (ACISC) *Calendar:* Qtr. plan *Degrees:* certificates, diplomas *CEO:* Dir. Gerald Schemmel
(671) 646-6901

HAWAII

ELECTRONIC INSTITUTE
1270 Queen Emma St., Rm. 107, Honolulu 96813 *Type:* Private *Accred.:* 1993 (ACC-SCT) *Calendar:* Courses of varying lengths *Degrees:* certificates *CEO:* Acting Prin. Herbert Yamada
(808) 521-5290

HAWAII BUSINESS COLLEGE
111 N. King Penthouse, Honolulu 96817 *Type:* Private business *Accred.:* 1976/1988 (ACISC) *Calendar:* Courses of varying lengths *Degrees:* certificates, diplomas *CEO:* Pres. Walter Omori
(808) 524-4014

HAWAII INSTITUTE OF HAIR DESIGN
71 S. Hotel St., Honolulu 96813-3112 *Type:* Private *Accred.:* 1978/1990 (ACCSCT) *Calendar:* Courses of varying lengths *Degrees:* certificates, diplomas *CEO:* Pres. Margaret Williams
(808) 533-6596

MED-ASSIST SCHOOL OF HAWAII
1149 Bethel St., Ste. 605, Honolulu 96813 *Type:* Private *Accred.:* 1984/1990 (ABHES) *Calendar:* Courses of varying lengths *Degrees:* certificates *Prof. Accred.:* Medical Assisting *CEO:* Pres. James Takemoto
(808) 524-3363

NEW YORK TECHNICAL INSTITUTE OF HAWAII
1375 Dillingham Blvd., Honolulu 96817-4415 *Type:* Private *Accred.:* 1991 (ACC-SCT) *Calendar:* Courses of varying lengths *Degrees:* certificates *CEO:* Owner Tracy Hamilton
(808) 841-5827

TRAVEL INSTITUTE OF THE PACIFIC
1314 S. King St., Ste. 1164, Honolulu 96814-2004 *Type:* Private *Accred.:* 1991 (ACCSCT) *Calendar:* Courses of varying lengths *Degrees:* certificates *CEO:* Dir. James Hughes
(808) 591-2708

IDAHO

AMERICAN INSTITUTE OF HEALTH TECHNOLOGY,
INC.
6600 Emerald St., Boise 83704 *Type:* Private
Accred.: 1982/1988 (ABHES) *Calendar:*
Courses of varying lengths *Degrees:* certificates *CEO:* Pres./Dir. Judy L. Groothuis
(208) 377-8080

ILLINOIS

AMERICAN CAREER TRAINING
237 S. State St., Chicago 60604 *Type:* Private *Accred.:* 1991 (ACCSCT) *Calendar:* Courses of varying lengths *Degrees:* certificates *CEO:* Exec. Dir. David C. Kujawa
(312) 461-0700

AMERICAN COLLEGE OF TECHNOLOGY
1300 W. Washington St., Bloomington 61701-4712 *Type:* Private *Accred.:* 1983/ 1988 (ACCSCT) *Calendar:* Courses of varying lengths *Degrees:* diplomas *CEO:* Vice Pres. Douglas E. Minter
(309) 828-5151

AMERICAN HEALTH INFORMATION MANAGEMENT ASSOCIATION
919 N. Michigan Ave., Ste. 1400, Chicago 60611 *Type:* Private home study *Accred.:* 1970/1990 (NHSC) *Calendar:* Courses of varying lengths *Degrees:* certificates *CEO:* Dir. Karen Patena, RRA
(312) 787-2672

AUTOMOTIVE TECHNICAL INSTITUTE
5567 N. Elston Ave., Chicago 60630 *Type:* Private *Accred.:* 1985/1990 (ACCSCT) *Calendar:* Courses of varying lengths *Degrees:* certificates, diplomas *CEO:* Exec. Dir. Robert H. Snow
(312) 792-8300

BELLEVILLE BARBER COLLEGE
329 N. Illinois St., Belleville 62220-1291 *Type:* Private *Accred.:* 1985/1990 (ACCSCT) *Calendar:* Courses of varying lengths *Degrees:* certificates *CEO:* Owner/Mgr. Betty Boeving
(618) 234-4424

BLOOMINGTON-NORMAL SCHOOL OF RADIOGRAPHY
900 Franklin Ave., Normal 61761 *Type:* Private *Calendar:* 24-month course *Degrees:* certificates *Prof. Accred.:* Radiography *CEO:* Sr. Vice Pres. Scott M. Harrison *Enroll:* 22   (309) 452-2834

BROWN'S BUSINESS COLLEGE
601 Bruns La., Springfield 62702 *Type:* Private business *Accred.:* 1987 (ACISC) *Calendar:* Courses of varying lengths *Degrees:*

certificates, diplomas *CEO:* Admin. Florence Lee Wellons
(217) 787-8797

CAIN'S BARBER COLLEGE
365 E. 51st St., Chicago 60615 *Type:* Private *Accred.:* 1993 (ACCSCT) *Calendar:* Courses of varying lengths *Degrees:* diplomas *CEO:* Dir. Leroy Cain
(312) 536-4623

CAPITAL AREA VOCATIONAL CENTER
12201 Toronto Rd., Springfield 62707 *Type:* Private *Calendar:* Courses of varying lengths *Degrees:* certificates, diplomas *Prof. Accred.:* Practical Nursing *CEO:* Dir. Shirley McConnaughay
(217) 529-5431

CATHERINE COLLEGE
Mezzanine Level, 2 N. La Salle St., Chicago 60602 *Type:* Private business *Accred.:* 1969/ 1988 (ACISC) *Calendar:* Courses of varying lengths *Degrees:* certificates, diplomas *CEO:* Pres. Richard H. Otto
(312) 263-7800

CAVE TECHNICAL INSTITUTE
2842 S. State St., Lockport 60441-4915 *Type:* Private *Accred.:* 1988 (ACCSCT) *Calendar:* Courses of varying lengths *Degrees:* certificates *CEO:* Dir. Harold C. Jones
(815) 727-1576

THE COLLEGE OF OFFICE TECHNOLOGY
2nd Fl., 1514-20 W. Division St., Chicago 60622 *Type:* Private business *Accred.:* 1985/ 1989 (ACISC) *Calendar:* Courses of varying lengths *Degrees:* certificates, diplomas *CEO:* Dir. Pedro A. Galva
(312) 278-0042

COMPUTER LEARNING CENTER
3rd Fl., 200 S. Michigan Ave., Chicago 60604-2404 *Type:* Private business *Accred.:* 1985/1991 (ACISC) *Calendar:* Courses of varying lengths *Degrees:* certificates, diplomas *CEO:* Dir. Marty Ehrenberg
(312) 427-2700

CONNECTICUT SCHOOL OF BROADCASTING
200 W. 22nd St., Ste. 202, Lombard 60148
Type: Private *Accred.:* 1993 (ACCSCT) *Calendar:* Courses of varying lengths *Degrees:* certificates *CEO:* Pres. Robert Mills
(708) 916-1700

COOKING AND HOSPITALITY INSTITUTE OF CHICAGO
361 W. Chestnut St., Chicago 60610-3050
Type: Private *Accred.:* 1988 (ACCSCT) *Calendar:* Courses of varying lengths *Degrees:* certificates *CEO:* Pres. Linda Calafiore
(312) 944-2725

COYNE AMERICAN INSTITUTE
1235 W. Fullerton Ave., Chicago 60614-2102 *Type:* Private *Accred.:* 1965/1993 (ACCSCT) *Calendar:* Qtr. plan *Degrees:* diplomas *CEO:* Pres. John J. Freeman
(312) 935-2520

ENVIRONMENTAL TECHNICAL INSTITUTE
1054 E. Irving Park, Bensenville 60106-2283 *Type:* Private *Accred.:* 1988 (ACCSCT) *Calendar:* Courses of varying lengths *Degrees:* certificates *CEO:* Dir. Lynn Tortorello
(708) 350-9100

BRANCH CAMPUS
13010 S. Division St., Blue Island 60406-2606 *Accred.:* 1988 (ACCSCT) *CEO:* Admin. Lynn Tortorello
(708) 385-0707

FOX SECRETARIAL COLLEGE
4201 W. 93rd St., Oak Lawn 60453 *Type:* Private business *Accred.:* 1987 (ACISC) *Calendar:* Qtr. plan *Degrees:* certificates, diplomas *CEO:* Pres. Edward L. Kapelinski
(708) 636-7700

THE HADLEY SCHOOL FOR THE BLIND
700 Elm St., Winnetka 60093 *Type:* Private home study *Accred.:* 1958/1989 (NHSC) *Calendar:* Courses of varying lengths *Degrees:* certificates *CEO:* Pres. Robert J. Winn
(708) 446-8111

HEARTLAND SCHOOL OF BUSINESS
Ste. 209, 211 W. State St., Jacksonville 62650 *Type:* Private business *Accred.:* 1993 (ACISC) *Calendar:* Courses of varying

lengths *Degrees:* certificates, diplomas *CEO:* Dir. Mark G. Woodworth
(217) 243-9001

LINCOLN TECHNICAL INSTITUTE
7320 W. Agatite Ave., Norridge 60656-9975 *Type:* Private *Accred.:* 1971/1985 (ACCSCT) *Calendar:* Courses of varying lengths *Degrees:* certificates, diplomas *CEO:* Exec. Dir. James O. Yeaman
(312) 625-1535

LINCOLN TECHNICAL INSTITUTE
8920 S. Cicero Ave., Oak Lawn 60453-1315 *Type:* Private *Accred.:* 1986 (ACCSCT) *Calendar:* Courses of varying lengths *Degrees:* certificates *CEO:* Dir. Kenneth R. Ruff
(708) 423-9000

M G INSTITUTE
40 E. Delaware Pl., Chicago 60611 *Type:* Private *Accred.:* 1993 (ACCSCT) *Calendar:* Courses of varying lengths *Degrees:* certificates *CEO:* Pres. Mary Ghorbanian
(312) 943-4190

MARYCREST COLLEGE
280 E. Merchant St., Kankakee 60901 *Type:* Private business *Accred.:* 1979/1987 (ACISC) *Calendar:* Qtr. plan *Degrees:* certificates, diplomas *CEO:* Dir. Steve Gibson
(815) 932-8724

MEDICAL CAREERS INSTITUTE
116 S. Michigan Ave., 2nd Fl., Chicago 60603 *Type:* Private *Accred.:* 1986 (ABHES) *Calendar:* Courses of varying lengths *Degrees:* diplomas *CEO:* Dir. William Zane
(312) 782-9804

MOLER HAIRSTYLING COLLEGE
5840 W. Madison St., Chicago 60644-3839 *Type:* Private *Accred.:* 1982/1988 (ACCSCT) *Calendar:* Courses of varying lengths *Degrees:* certificates *CEO:* Dir. Kenneth M. Edwards
(312) 287-2552

MUSIC CENTER OF THE NORTH SHORE
300 Green Bay Rd., Winnetka 60093 *Type:* Private *Calendar:* Courses of varying lengths *Degrees:* certificates *Prof. Accred.:* Music *CEO:* Exec. Dir. Frank Little
(708) 446-3822

NAPOLEON HILL FOUNDATION
1440 Paddock Dr., Northbrook 60062 *Type:*
Private home study *Accred.:* 1986/1991
(NHSC) *Calendar:* Courses of varying
lengths *Degrees:* certificates *CEO:* Exec.
Dir. Michael J. Ritt, Jr.
(708) 998-0408

NATIONAL BARBER COLLEGE
1035 W. Jefferson St., Springfield 62702-
4835 *Type:* Private *Accred.:* 1989/1993
(ACCSCT) *Calendar:* Courses of varying
lengths *Degrees:* certificates *CEO:* Owner/
Dir. Gerald R. Higgins
(217) 793-3222

NATIONAL EDUCATION CENTER—BRYMAN
CAMPUS
17 N. State St., Chicago 60602-7103 *Type:*
Private *Accred.:* 1991 (ACCSCT) *Calendar:*
Courses of varying lengths *Degrees:* diplomas *CEO:* Exec. Dir. Sally Mol
(312) 368-4911

NATIONAL EDUCATION CENTER—BRYMAN
CAMPUS
4101 W. 95th St., Oak Lawn 60453-1000
Type: Private *Accred.:* 1991 (ACCSCT) *Calendar:* Courses of varying lengths *Degrees:*
diplomas *CEO:* Dir. Doloris Reynolds
(708) 423-0911

OMAR RIVAS ACADEMY OF BARBER ARTS AND
SCIENCE
5912 W. Roosevelt Rd., Chicago 60650-
1139 *Type:* Private *Accred.:* 1986 (ACC-
SCT) *Calendar:* Courses of varying lengths
Degrees: diplomas *CEO:* Dir. Omar Rivas
(312) 287-3400

PATHFINDER
19 E. 21st St., Chicago 60616-1701 *Type:*
Private *Accred.:* 1992 (ACCSCT) *Calendar:*
Courses of varying lengths *Degrees:* certificates *CEO:* Pres. Melvyn R. May
(312) 842-7272

PBS TRAINING CENTER
529 S. Wabash Ave., 2nd Fl., Chicago 60605
Type: Private *Accred.:* 1991 (ACCSCT) *Calendar:* Courses of varying lengths *Degrees:*
certificates *CEO:* Pres. Anthony McElligott
(312) 427-9006

PTC CAREER INSTITUTE
11 E. Adams St., Ste. 400, Chicago 60603
Type: Private *Accred.:* 1991 (ACCSCT) *Calendar:* Courses of varying lengths *Degrees:*
certificates *CEO:* Dir. Greg Reger
(312) 922-2005

QUINCY TECHNICAL SCHOOLS
501 N. Third St., Quincy 62301-9990 *Type:*
Private *Accred.:* 1977/1988 (ACCSCT) *Calendar:* Qtr. plan *Degrees:* diplomas *CEO:*
Dir. William G. Dubuque, Jr.
(800) 438-5621

ROCKFORD SCHOOL OF PRACTICAL NURSING
978 Haskell Ave., Rockford 61103 *Type:*
Private *Calendar:* Courses of varying
lengths *Degrees:* certificates, diplomas *Prof.
Accred.:* Practical Nursing *CEO:* Dir.
Shirley Asher
(815) 966-3716

SANFORD-BROWN BUSINESS COLLEGE
3237 W. Chain of Rocks Rd., Granite City
62040 *Type:* Private business *Accred.:* 1988
(ACISC) *Calendar:* Courses of varying
lengths *Degrees:* certificates, diplomas
CEO: Dir. Chris Kern
(618) 931-0300

SPARKS COLLEGE
131 S. Morgan St., Shelbyville 62565 *Type:*
Private business *Accred.:* 1954/1990
(ACISC) *Calendar:* Courses of varying
lengths *Degrees:* certificates, diplomas
CEO: Dir. Paula W. Bitzer
(217) 774-5112

TYLER SCHOOL OF SECRETARIAL SCIENCES
8030 S. Kedzie Ave., Chicago 60652 *Type:*
Private business *Accred.:* 1984/1988
(ACISC) *Calendar:* Courses of varying
lengths *Degrees:* certificates, diplomas
CEO: Pres. Michael Franzak
(312) 436-5050

WORSHAM COLLEGE OF MORTUARY SCIENCE
495 Northgate Pkwy., Wheeling 60090
Type: Private professional *Calendar:* 1-year
program *Degrees:* diplomas *Prof. Accred.:*
Mortuary Science *CEO:* Chf. Admin.
Frederick C. Cappetta
(708) 808-8444

INDIANA

ACADEMY OF HAIR DESIGN
2150 Lafayette Rd., Indianapolis 46222-2394 *Type:* Private *Accred.:* 1982/1988 (ACCSCT) *Calendar:* Courses of varying lengths *Degrees:* diplomas *CEO:* Dir./Owner Jack Hale
(317) 637-7227

ARISTOTLE COLLEGE OF MEDICAL AND DENTAL TECHNOLOGY
5425 S. U.S. 31, Indianapolis 46227 *Type:* Private technical *Accred.:* 1982/1986 (ABHES) *Calendar:* Courses of varying lengths *Degrees:* certificates, diplomas *Prof. Accred.:* Medical Assisting *CEO:* Pres. Michael A. Walker
(317) 784-5400

BRANCH CAMPUS
5255 Hohman Ave., Hammond 46320 *Accred.:* 1987 (ABHES) *CEO:* Pres. Michael A. Walker
(219) 931-1917

COLLEGE OF COURT REPORTING
Ste. 111, 111 W. 10th St., Hobart 46342 *Type:* Private business *Accred.:* 1989 (ACISC) *Calendar:* Courses of varying lengths *Degrees:* certificates, diplomas *CEO:* Dir. Kay Moody
(219) 942-1459

DEFENSE INFORMATION SCHOOL
Bldg. 400, Fort Benjamin Harrison 46216-6200 *Type:* Public (federal) *Accred.:* 1979/1990 (NCA) *Calendar:* Courses of varying lengths *Degrees:* certificates *CEO:* Commandant Kristian L. Wells
Enroll: 1,745   (317) 542-4046

INDIANA BARBER/STYLIST COLLEGE
5536 E. Washington St., Indianapolis 46219-6426 *Type:* Private *Accred.:* 1973/1988 (ACCSCT) *Calendar:* Courses of varying lengths *Degrees:* diplomas *CEO:* Pres. Rachel Merritt
(317) 356-8222

INSTITUTE OF DATA PROCESSING INC.
9521 Indianapolis Blvd., Highland 46322-2617 *Type:* Private *Accred.:* 1988 (ACCSCT) *Calendar:* Courses of varying lengths *Degrees:* certificates *CEO:* Dir. Eileen Georegijewski
(219) 924-1553

LAKESHORE MEDICAL LABORATORY TRAINING PROGRAM
402 Franklin St., Michigan City 46953 *Type:* Private *Calendar:* Courses of varying lengths *Degrees:* certificates *Prof. Accred.:* Cytotechnology, Medical Laboratory Technology (AMA) *CEO:* Chrmn. Thomas H. Roberts, M.D.
(219) 872-7032

LINCOLN TECHNICAL INSTITUTE
1201 Stadium Dr., Indianapolis 46202-2194 *Type:* Private *Accred.:* 1968/1988 (ACCSCT) *Calendar:* Courses of varying lengths *Degrees:* certificates, diplomas *CEO:* Exec. Dir. Merlyn Cooper
(317) 632-5553

PROFESSIONAL CAREERS INSTITUTE
2611 Waterfront Pkwy., East Dr., Indianapolis 46214-2028 *Type:* Private *Accred.:* 1970/1990 (ACCSCT) *Calendar:* Courses of varying lengths *Degrees:* certificates *Prof. Accred.:* Dental Assisting, Medical Assisting (AMA) *CEO:* Dir. Richard H. Weiss
(317) 299-6001

UNITED STATES ARMY SOLDIER SUPPORT INSTITUTE
Fort Benjamin Harrison 46216-5505 *Type:* Public (federal) *Accred.:* 1980/1985 (NCA) *Calendar:* Courses of varying lengths *Degrees:* certificates *CEO:* Commandant Robert J. Bavis, III
(317) 542-4969

IOWA

CAPRI COSMETOLOGY COLLEGE
395 Main St., P.O. Box 873, Dubuque 52004-0873 *Type:* Private *Accred.:* 1991 (ACCSCT) *Calendar:* Courses of varying lengths *Degrees:* certificates *CEO:* Owner Chuck Fiegin

(319) 588-4545

CEDAR RAPIDS SCHOOL OF HAIRSTYLING
1531 First Ave., S.E., Cedar Rapids 52402-5123 *Type:* Private *Accred.:* 1991 (ACCSCT) *Calendar:* Courses of varying lengths *Degrees:* certificates *CEO:* Pres. T.L. Millis
(515) 362-1488

COLLEGE OF HAIR DESIGN
810 LaPorte Rd., Waterloo 50702-1834 *Type:* Private *Accred.:* 1991 (ACCSCT) *Calendar:* Courses of varying lengths *Degrees:* certificates *CEO:* Pres. Joe O. Squires
(319) 232-9995

HAMILTON BUSINESS COLLEGE
1924 D St., S.W., Cedar Rapids 52404 *Type:* Private business *Accred.:* 1957/1991 (ACISC); 1990/1992 (NCA candidate) *Calendar:* Courses of varying lengths *Degrees:* diplomas *CEO:* Pres. John Huston
Enroll: 826   (319) 363-0481

BRANCH CAMPUS
2300 Euclid Ave., Des Moines 50310 *Accred.:* 1989/1991 (ACISC) *CEO:* Dir. Nancy Baker

(515) 279-0253

BRANCH CAMPUS
100 First St., N.W., Mason City 50401 *Accred.:* 1957/1991 (ACISC) *CEO:* Pres. Dave Tracy

(515) 423-2530

IOWA SCHOOL OF BARBERING AND HAIRSTYLING
603 E. Sixth St., Des Moines 50309-5478 *Type:* Private *Accred.:* 1975/1986 (ACCSCT) *Calendar:* Courses of varying lengths *Degrees:* diplomas *CEO:* Pres. T.L. Millis
(515) 244-0971

NATIONAL EDUCATION CENTER—NATIONAL INSTITUTE OF TECHNOLOGY CAMPUS
1119 Fifth St., West Des Moines 50265-2698 *Type:* Private *Accred.:* 1968/1986 (ACCSCT) *Calendar:* Qtr. plan *Degrees:* diplomas *CEO:* Dir. Pat Bishop
(515) 223-1486

SPENCER SCHOOL OF BUSINESS
217 W. Fifth St., P.O. Box 5065, Spencer 51301 *Type:* Private professional *Accred.:* 1972/1990 (ACISC); 1989/1993 (NCA candidate) *Calendar:* Qtr. plan *Degrees:* diplomas *Prof. Accred.:* Medical Assisting (AMA) *CEO:* Pres. James R. Grove
Enroll: 157   (712) 262-7290

KANSAS

ADVANCED HAIR TECH
4323 State Ave., Kansas City 66101 *Type:*
Private *Accred.:* 1992 (ACCSCT) *Calendar:*
Courses of varying lengths *Degrees:* certificates *CEO:* Dir. Douglas Rushing
(913) 321-0214

AMTECH INSTITUTE
4011 E. 31st St. S., Wichita 67210-1588
Type: Private *Accred.:* 1986 (ACCSCT) *Calendar:* Courses of varying lengths *Degrees:*
certificates *CEO:* Dir. Rex Spaulding
(316) 682-6548

BRYAN INSTITUTE
1004 S. Oliver St., Wichita 67214 *Type:* Private *Accred.:* 1971/1988 (ACCSCT) *Calendar:* Courses of varying lengths *Degrees:*
diplomas *Prof. Accred.:* Medical Assisting
CEO: Dir. Jeffrey Baughman
(316) 685-2284

BRANCH CAMPUS
1719 W. Pioneer Pkwy., Arlington, TX
76013-4799 *Accred.:* 1982/1992 (ACCSCT) *Prof. Accred.:* Medical Assisting
CEO: Dir. Sandra Dickerson
(817) 265-5588

BRYAN TRAVEL COLLEGE
1527 Fairlawn Rd., Topeka 66604 *Type:* Private business *Accred.:* 1990 (ACISC) *Calendar:* Courses of varying lengths *Degrees:*
certificates, diplomas *CEO:* Admin. Rosie
Beltch
(913) 272-7511

CENTER FOR TRAINING IN BUSINESS AND
INDUSTRY
2211 Silicon Ave., Lawrence 66046 *Type:*
Private business *Accred.:* 1989 (ACISC)
Calendar: Courses of varying lengths *Degrees:* certificates, diplomas *CEO:* Pres.
Patricia M. Anderson
(913) 841-9640

CLIMATE CONTROL INSTITUTE
3030 N. Hillside St., Wichita 67219-3902
Type: Private *Accred.:* 1976/1985 (ACCSCT) *Calendar:* Courses of varying lengths
Degrees: certificates *CEO:* Dir. Susan
Hampton
(316) 686-7355

TRAVEL CAREERS DIVISION
568 Colonial Rd., Ste. 102, Memphis, TN
38117-9939 *Accred.:* 1992 (ACCSCT)
CEO: Dir. Tim Hampton
(901) 761-5730

FLINT HILLS TECHNICAL SCHOOL
3301 W. 18th Ave., Emporia 66801 *Type:*
Private *Calendar:* Courses of varying
lengths *Degrees:* certificates *Prof. Accred.:*
Dental Assisting (conditional) *CEO:* Dir.
Keith Stover
(316) 342-6404

KANSAS SCHOOL OF HAIRSTYLING
1207 E. Douglas Ave., Wichita 67211-1693
Type: Private *Accred.:* 1985/1990 (ACCSCT) *Calendar:* Courses of varying lengths
Degrees: certificates *CEO:* Owner/Dir. John
Jewell
(316) 264-4891

NORTH CENTRAL KANSAS AREA VOCATIONAL-
TECHNICAL SCHOOL
P.O. Box 507, Beloit 67420 *Type:* Public
professional *Accred.:* 1981/1992 (NCA) *Calendar:* Qtr. plan *Degrees:* certificates *Prof.
Accred.:* Practical Nursing *CEO:* Dir. D.
William Reeves
Enroll: 428   (913) 738-2276

SOUTHERN TECHNICAL COLLEGE
2105 S. Meridian St., Wichita 67213-1993
Type: Private *Accred.:* 1981/1986 (ACCSCT) *Calendar:* Courses of varying lengths
Degrees: certificates *CEO:* Dir. Todd Kraus
(316) 942-7733

TOPEKA TECHNICAL COLLEGE
1620 N.W. Gage Blvd., Topeka 66618-2830
Type: Private *Accred.:* 1971/1987 (ACCSCT) *Calendar:* Qtr. plan *Degrees:* diplomas *CEO:* Pres. Ann K. Colgan
(913) 232-5858

WICHITA AREA VOCATIONAL-TECHNICAL SCHOOL
324 N. Emporia St., Wichita 67202 *Type:*
Private *Calendar:* Courses of varying
lengths *Degrees:* certificates *Prof. Accred.:*
Medical Laboratory Technology (AMA),
Practical Nursing, Surgical Technology
CEO: Dir. Rosemary A. Kirby, Ph.D.
(316) 833-4664

WICHITA BUSINESS COLLEGE
Ste. 515, 501 E. Pawnee St., Wichita 67211
Type: Private business *Accred.:* 1963/1987
(ACISC) *Calendar:* Qtr. plan *Degrees:* certificates, diplomas *CEO:* Dir. Faith Kite
(316) 263-1261

WICHITA TECHNICAL INSTITUTE
942 S. West St., Wichita 67213-1681 *Type:*
Private *Accred.:* 1971/1988 (ACCSCT) *Calendar:* Courses of varying lengths *Degrees:*
certificates, diplomas *Prof. Accred.:* Dental
Assisting *CEO:* Pres. Paul D. Moore
(316) 943-2241

WRIGHT BUSINESS SCHOOL
9500 Marshall Dr., Lenexa 66215 *Type:* Private business *Accred.:* 1984/1988 (ACISC)
Calendar: Courses of varying lengths *Degrees:* certificates, diplomas *CEO:* Dir. Anna
Selleck
(913) 599-0220

BRANCH CAMPUS
5528 N.E. Antioch Rd., Kansas City, MO
64119 *Accred.:* 1989 (ACISC) *CEO:* Dir.
Ruth Frye
(816) 452-4411

KENTUCKY

BALLARD COUNTY AREA VOCATIONAL CENTER
Rte. 1, Box 214, Barlow 42024 *Type:* Public
(state) technical *Accred.:* 1975/1990 (SACS-
COEI) *Calendar:* Courses of varying lengths
Degrees: certificates *CEO:* Dir. Donald G.
Wells
FTE Enroll: 86   (502) 665-5112

BARRETT & COMPANY SCHOOL OF HAIR DESIGN
973 Kimberly Sq., Nicholasville 40356
Type: Private *Accred.:* 1987/1992 (SACS-
COEI) *Calendar:* Courses of varying lengths
Degrees: certificates *CEO:* Dir. James Barrett
FTE Enroll: 34   (606) 885-9136

CARL D. PERKINS JOB CORPS CENTER
Box G-11, Goble Roberts Rd., Prestonsburg
41653 *Type:* Private *Accred.:* 1985/1990
(SACS-COEI) *Calendar:* Courses of varying
lengths *Degrees:* certificates *CEO:* Dir.
Edna Higginbotham
FTE Enroll: 287   (606) 886-1037

COMPUTER EDUCATION SERVICES
981 S. Third St., Ste. 106, Louisville 40203
Type: Private *Accred.:* 1992 (SACS-COEI)
Calendar: Courses of varying lengths *De-
grees:* certificates *CEO:* Pres. Linda Crowe
FTE Enroll: 15   (502) 583-2860

THE COMPUTER SCHOOL
820 Lane Allen Rd., Lexington 40504-3615
Type: Private *Accred.:* 1992 (ACCSCT) *Calendar:* Courses of varying lengths *Degrees:*
certificates *CEO:* Pres./Owner John J.
Weikel
                              (606) 276-1929

EARLE C. CLEMENTS JOB CORPS CENTER
Hwy. 60, Morganfield 42437 *Type:* Private
Accred.: 1983/1988 (SACS-COEI) *Calen-
dar:* Courses of varying lengths *Degrees:*
certificates *CEO:* Dir. Jack Carson
FTE Enroll: 959   (502) 389-2419

HUMANA HEALTH INSTITUTE
612 S. Fourth St., No. 400, Louisville 40202
Type: Private *Accred.:* 1983/1991 (SACS-
COEI) *Calendar:* Courses of varying lengths
Degrees: certificates *Prof. Accred.:* Practical
Nursing *CEO:* Dir. Linda Blair
FTE Enroll: 545   (502) 580-3660

BRANCH CAMPUS
11500 Ninth St., N., Ste. 140, St. Petersburg, FL 33716 *CEO:* Dir. Sharon Roberts
                              (813) 577-1497

BRANCH CAMPUS
6800 Park Ten Blvd., Ste. 160, S., San
Antonio, TX 78213 *CEO:* Dir. Adrienne
Lyons
                              (512) 580-3660

KENTUCKY CAREER INSTITUTE
P.O. Box 143, 8095 Connector Dr., Florence
41022 *Type:* Private *Accred.:* 1993
(ACISC); 1991 (SACS-COEI) *Calendar:*
Courses of varying lengths *Degrees:* certifi-
cates, diplomas *CEO:* Pres. Harry Beck
FTE Enroll: 92   (606) 371-9393

BRANCH CAMPUS
113 S. Hubbard La., Louisville 40207
CEO: Dir. Pam Drury
                              (502) 895-7336

KENTUCKY COLLEGE OF BARBERING AND
HAIRSTYLING
1230 S. Third St., Louisville 40203-2906
Type: Private *Accred.:* 1983/1988 (ACC-
SCT) *Calendar:* Courses of varying lengths
Degrees: diplomas *CEO:* Dir. David Durbin
                              (502) 634-0521

KENTUCKY SCHOOL OF FINANCIAL EDUCATION
1930 Bishop La., Ste. 720, Louisville 40218
Type: Private *Accred.:* 1991 (SACS-COEI)
Calendar: Courses of varying lengths *De-
grees:* certificates *CEO:* Pres. J. Martin
Gossman
FTE Enroll: 33   (502) 451-7615

KENTUCKY TECH—ASHLAND STATE
VOCATIONAL-TECHNICAL SCHOOL
4818 Roberts Dr., Ashland 41102 *Type:*
Public (state) technical *System:* Kentucky
Tech Northeast Region *Accred.:* 1971/1989
(SACS-COEI) *Calendar:* Courses of varying
lengths *Degrees:* certificates *CEO:* Prin.
Marsha Burks
                              (606) 928-6427

KENTUCKY TECH—BARREN COUNTY AREA
VOCATIONAL EDUCATION CENTER
491 Trojan Tr., Glasgow 42141 *Type:* Public
(state) technical *System:* Kentucky Tech

Southern Region *Accred.:* 1972/1992 (SACS-COEI) *Calendar:* Courses of varying lengths *Degrees:* certificates *CEO:* Coord. Max Doty

(502) 651-2196

KENTUCKY TECH—BELFRY AREA VOCATIONAL EDUCATION CENTER
P.O. Box 280, Belfry 41514 *Type:* Public (state) technical *System:* Kentucky Tech Northeast Region *Accred.:* 1974/1989 (SACS-COEI) *Calendar:* Courses of varying lengths *Degrees:* certificates *CEO:* Prin. Brad W. May

(606) 353-4951

KENTUCKY TECH—BELL COUNTY AREA VOCATIONAL EDUCATION CENTER
Box 199-A, Rte. 7, Pineville 40977 *Type:* Public (state) technical *System:* Kentucky Tech Southeast Region *Accred.:* 1975/1990 (SACS-COEI) *Calendar:* Courses of varying lengths *Degrees:* certificates *CEO:* Coord. Ron Mason

(606) 337-3094

KENTUCKY TECH—BOONE COUNTY AREA VOCATIONAL EDUCATION CENTER
3320 Cougar Path, Hebron 41048 *Type:* Public (state) technical *System:* Kentucky Tech North Central Region *Accred.:* 1973/1993 (SACS-COEI) *Calendar:* Courses of varying lengths *Degrees:* certificates *CEO:* Coord. Stephanie Rottman

(606) 689-7855

KENTUCKY TECH—BOWLING GREEN STATE TRANSPORTATION CENTER
6198 Nashville Rd., Bowling Green 42101 *Type:* Public (state) technical *Accred.:* 1972/1992 (SACS-COEI) *Calendar:* Courses of varying lengths *Degrees:* certificates *CEO:* Coord. Robert Bierman

(502) 781-0711

KENTUCKY TECH—BOWLING GREEN STATE VOCATIONAL-TECHNICAL SCHOOL
1845 Loop Dr., Bowling Green 42102 *Type:* Public (state) technical *System:* Kentucky Tech Southern Region *Accred.:* 1972/1992 (SACS-COEI) *Calendar:* Courses of varying lengths *Degrees:* certificates *Prof. Accred.:* Dental Assisting, Radiography, Respiratory Therapy Technology, Surgical Technology *CEO:* Prin. Donald R. Williams

(502) 843-5461

KENTUCKY TECH—BREATHITT COUNTY AREA VOCATIONAL EDUCATION CENTER
P.O. Box 786, Jackson 41339 *Type:* Public (state) technical *System:* Kentucky Tech Southeast Region *Accred.:* 1973/1988 (SACS-COEI) *Calendar:* Courses of varying lengths *Degrees:* certificates *CEO:* Coord. Fred Deaton

(606) 666-5153

KENTUCKY TECH—BRECKINRIDGE COUNTY AREA VOCATIONAL EDUCATION CENTER
P.O. Box 68, Harnet 40144 *Type:* Public (state) technical *System:* Kentucky Tech Northwest Region *Accred.:* 1974/1992 (SACS-COEI) *Calendar:* Courses of varying lengths *Degrees:* certificates *CEO:* Coord. Wayne A. Spencer

(502) 756-2138

KENTUCKY TECH—BULLITT COUNTY AREA VOCATIONAL EDUCATION CENTER
395 High School Dr., Sheperdsville 40165 *Type:* Public (state) technical *System:* Kentucky Tech Northwest Region *Accred.:* 1973/1993 (SACS-COEI) *Calendar:* Courses of varying lengths *Degrees:* certificates *CEO:* Coord. Robert Hazelrigg

(502) 543-7018

KENTUCKY TECH—CALDWELL COUNTY AREA VOCATIONAL EDUCATION CENTER
P.O. Box 350, Princeton 42445 *Type:* Public (state) technical *System:* Kentucky Tech West Region *Accred.:* 1971/1991 (SACS-COEI) *Calendar:* Courses of varying lengths *Degrees:* certificates *CEO:* Coord. Arthur Dunn

(502) 365-5563

KENTUCKY TECH—CARROLL COUNTY AREA VOCATIONAL EDUCATION CENTER
1704 Highland Ave., Carrollton 41008 *Type:* Public (state) technical *System:* Kentucky Tech North Central Region *Accred.:* 1973/1993 (SACS-COEI) *Calendar:* Courses of varying lengths *Degrees:* certificates *CEO:* Coord. Donald W. Garner

(502) 732-4479

KENTUCKY TECH—CASEY COUNTY AREA
VOCATIONAL EDUCATION CENTER
Rte. 4, Box 49, Liberty 42539 *Type:* Public
(state) technical *System:* Kentucky Tech
Southern Region *Accred.:* 1974/1989
(SACS-COEI) *Calendar:* Courses of varying
lengths *Degrees:* certificates *CEO:* Coord.
J.D. Shugars
(606) 787-6241

KENTUCKY TECH—CENTRAL KENTUCKY STATE
VOCATIONAL-TECHNICAL SCHOOL
105 Vo-Tech Rd., Lexington 40510 *Type:*
Public (state) technical *System:* Kentucky
Tech North Central Region *Accred.:* 1972/
1992 (SACS-COEI) *Calendar:* Courses of
varying lengths *Degrees:* certificates *Prof.
Accred.:* Dental Assisting, Respiratory Therapy Technology, Surgical Technology *CEO:*
Prin. Ron Baugh
(606) 255-8500

KENTUCKY TECH—CHRISTIAN COUNTY AREA
VOCATIONAL EDUCATION CENTER
109 Hamond Plaza, Ste. 2, Fort Campbell
Blvd., Hopkinsville 42240 *Type:* Public
(state) technical *System:* Kentucky Tech
West Region *Accred.:* 1971/1991 (SACS-
COEI) *Calendar:* Courses of varying lengths
Degrees: certificates *CEO:* Coord. Ann
Claxton
(502) 887-2524

KENTUCKY TECH—CLARK COUNTY AREA
VOCATIONAL EDUCATION CENTER
650 Boone Ave., Winchester 40391 *Type:*
Public (state) technical *System:* Kentucky
Tech North Central Region *Accred.:* 1972/
1992 (SACS-COEI) *Calendar:* Courses of
varying lengths *Degrees:* certificates *CEO:*
Coord. William Lockhart
(606) 744-1250

KENTUCKY TECH—CLAY COUNTY AREA
VOCATIONAL EDUCATION CENTER
Rte. 2, Box 256, Manchester 40962 *Type:*
Public (state) technical *System:* Kentucky
Tech Southeast Region *Accred.:* 1975/1990
(SACS-COEI) *Calendar:* Courses of varying
lengths *Degrees:* certificates *CEO:* Coord.
Charles McWhorter
(606) 598-2194

KENTUCKY TECH—CLINTON COUNTY AREA
VOCATIONAL EDUCATION CENTER
Rte. 3, Box 8, Albany 42602 *Type:* Public
(state) technical *System:* Kentucky Tech
Southern Region *Accred.:* 1974/1989
(SACS-COEI) *Calendar:* Courses of varying
lengths *Degrees:* certificates *CEO:* Coord.
Preston Sparks
(606) 387-6448

KENTUCKY TECH—CORBIN AREA VOCATIONAL
EDUCATION CENTER
1909 S. Snyder Ave., Corbin 40701 *Type:*
Public (state) technical *System:* Kentucky
Tech Southeast Region *Accred.:* 1975/1990
(SACS-COEI) *Calendar:* Courses of varying
lengths *Degrees:* certificates *CEO:* Coord.
Ronnie Partin
(606) 528-5338

KENTUCKY TECH—CUMBERLAND VALLEY
HEALTH OCCUPATIONS CENTER
U.S. 25E S., P.O. Box 187, Pineville 40977
Type: Public (state) technical *System:* Ken-
tucky Tech Southeast Region *Accred.:*
1975/1990 (SACS-COEI) *Calendar:* Courses
of varying lengths *Degrees:* certificates *Prof.
Accred.:* Radiography, Respiratory Therapy
Technology, Surgical Technology *CEO:*
Coord. Mildred Winkler
(606) 337-3106

KENTUCKY TECH—DANVILLE SCHOOL OF
HEALTH OCCUPATIONS
448 S. Third St., Danville 40422 *Type:* Public (state) technical *System:* Kentucky Tech
North Central Region *Accred.:* 1972/1992
(SACS-COEI) *Calendar:* Courses of varying
lengths *Degrees:* certificates *CEO:* Coord.
Sandra Houston
(606) 236-2053

KENTUCKY TECH—DAVIESS COUNTY
VOCATIONAL-TECHNICAL SCHOOL
P.O. Box 1677, Owensboro 42303-1677
Type: Public (state) technical *System:* Ken-
tucky Tech West Region *Accred.:* 1973/1988
(SACS-COEI) *Calendar:* Courses of varying
lengths *Degrees:* certificates *CEO:* Prin. Ray
Gillaspie
(502) 686-3321

KENTUCKY TECH—ELIZABETHTOWN STATE
VOCATIONAL-TECHNICAL SCHOOL
505 University Dr., Elizabethtown 42701
Type: Public (state) technical *System:* Ken-

tucky Tech Northwest Region *Accred.:* 1974/1992 (SACS-COEI) *Calendar:* Courses of varying lengths *Degrees:* certificates *CEO:* Prin. Neil Ramer

(502) 765-2104

KENTUCKY TECH—FULTON COUNTY AREA VOCATIONAL EDUCATION CENTER
Rte. 4, Hickman 42050 *Type:* Public (state) technical *System:* Kentucky Tech West Region *Accred.:* 1975/1990 (SACS-COEI) *Calendar:* Courses of varying lengths *Degrees:* certificates *CEO:* Coord. Larry Lynch

(502) 236-2517

KENTUCKY TECH—GARRARD COUNTY AREA VOCATIONAL EDUCATION CENTER
306 W. Maple Ave., Lancaster 40444 *Type:* Public (state) technical *System:* Kentucky Tech North Central Region *Accred.:* 1972/1992 (SACS-COEI) *Calendar:* Courses of varying lengths *Degrees:* certificates *CEO:* Coord. James Spurlin

(606) 792-2144

KENTUCKY TECH—GARTH AREA VOCATIONAL EDUCATION CENTER
HC 79, Box 205, Martin 41649 *Type:* Public (state) technical *System:* Kentucky Tech Northeast Region *Accred.:* 1974/1989 (SACS-COEI) *Calendar:* Courses of varying lengths *Degrees:* certificates *CEO:* Prin. Ronald Turner

(606) 285-3088

KENTUCKY TECH—GLASGOW HEALTH OCCUPATIONS SCHOOL
1215 N. Race St., Glasgow 42141 *Type:* Public (state) technical *System:* Kentucky Tech Southern Region *Accred.:* 1972/1992 (SACS-COEI) *Calendar:* Courses of varying lengths *Degrees:* certificates *CEO:* Coord. Rebecca Forrest

(502) 651-5673

KENTUCKY TECH—GREEN COUNTY AREA VOCATIONAL EDUCATION CENTER
P.O. Box H, Greensburg 42743 *Type:* Public (state) technical *System:* Kentucky Tech Southern Region *Accred.:* 1974/1989 (SACS-COEI) *Calendar:* Courses of varying lengths *Degrees:* certificates *CEO:* Coord. Jerry O. Rogers

(502) 932-4263

KENTUCKY TECH—GREENUP COUNTY AREA VOCATIONAL EDUCATION CENTER
P.O. Box 7, South Shore 41175 *Type:* Public (state) technical *System:* Kentucky Tech Northeast Region *Accred.:* 1971/1989 (SACS-COEI) *Calendar:* Courses of varying lengths *Degrees:* certificates *CEO:* Coord. Helen Spears

(606) 932-3107

KENTUCKY TECH—HARLAN STATE VOCATIONAL-TECHNICAL SCHOOL
21 Ballpark Rd., Harlan 40831 *Type:* Public (state) technical *System:* Kentucky Tech Southeast Region *Accred.:* 1975/1990 (SACS-COEI) *Calendar:* Courses of varying lengths *Degrees:* certificates *CEO:* Prin. Harve J. Couch

(606) 573-1506

KENTUCKY TECH—HARRISON COUNTY AREA VOCATIONAL EDUCATION CENTER
551 Webster Ave., Cynthiana 41031 *Type:* Public (state) technical *System:* Kentucky Tech North Central Region *Accred.:* 1972/1992 (SACS-COEI) *Calendar:* Courses of varying lengths *Degrees:* certificates *CEO:* Coord. James Plummer

(606) 234-5286

KENTUCKY TECH—HARRODSBURG AREA VOCATIONAL EDUCATION CENTER
661 Tapt Rd., P.O. Box 628, Harrodsburg 40330 *Type:* Public (state) technical *System:* Kentucky Tech North Central Region *Accred.:* 1972/1992 (SACS-COEI) *Calendar:* Courses of varying lengths *Degrees:* certificates *CEO:* Coord. L. Hughes Jones

(606) 734-9329

KENTUCKY TECH—HAZARD STATE VOCATIONAL-TECHNICAL SCHOOL
101 Vo-Tech Dr., Hazard 41701 *Type:* Public (state) technical *System:* Kentucky Tech Southeast Region *Accred.:* 1973/1988 (SACS-COEI) *Calendar:* Courses of varying lengths *Degrees:* certificates *CEO:* Prin. Connie W. Johnson

(606) 436-3101

KENTUCKY TECH—HENDERSON COUNTY AREA VOCATIONAL EDUCATION CENTER
2440 Zion Rd., Henderson 42420 *Type:* Public (state) technical *System:* Kentucky Tech

West Region *Accred.:* 1973/1988 (SACS-COEI) *Calendar:* Courses of varying lengths *Degrees:* certificates *CEO:* Prin. Dennis Harrell

(502) 827-3810

KENTUCKY TECH—JEFFERSON STATE VOCATIONAL-TECHNICAL CENTER
727 W. Chestnut St., Louisville 40202 *Type:* Public (state) technical *System:* Kentucky Tech Northwest Region *Accred.:* 1973/1993 (SACS-COEI) *Calendar:* Courses of varying lengths *Degrees:* certificates *CEO:* Prin. Sandra Parks

(502) 588-4223

KENTUCKY TECH—KENTUCKY ADVANCED TECHNOLOGY CENTER
1845 Loop Dr., Bowling Green 42102 *Type:* Public (state) technical *System:* Kentucky Tech Southern Region *Accred.:* 1972/1992 (SACS-COEI) *Calendar:* Courses of varying lengths *Degrees:* certificates *CEO:* Coord. Jack Thomas

(502) 843-5807

KENTUCKY TECH—KNOTT COUNTY AREA VOCATIONAL EDUCATION CENTER
HCR 60, Box 1100, Hindman 41822 *Type:* Public (state) technical *System:* Kentucky Tech Southeast Region *Accred.:* 1973/1988 (SACS-COEI) *Calendar:* Courses of varying lengths *Degrees:* certificates *CEO:* Coord. Sonny Smith

(606) 785-5350

KENTUCKY TECH—KNOX COUNTY AREA VOCATIONAL EDUCATION CENTER
210 Wall St., Barbourville 40906 *Type:* Public (state) technical *System:* Kentucky Tech Southeast Region *Accred.:* 1975/1990 (SACS-COEI) *Calendar:* Courses of varying lengths *Degrees:* certificates *CEO:* Coord. Charles Frasier

(606) 546-5320

KENTUCKY TECH—LAUREL COUNTY STATE VOCATIONAL-TECHNICAL SCHOOL
1711 S. Main St., London 40741 *Type:* Public (state) technical *System:* Kentucky Tech Southeast Region *Accred.:* 1975/1990 (SACS-COEI) *Calendar:* Courses of varying

lengths *Degrees:* certificates *CEO:* Prin. Ronnie Partin

(606) 864-7311

KENTUCKY TECH—LEE COUNTY AREA VOCATIONAL EDUCATION CENTER
P.O. Box B, Beattyville 41311 *Type:* Public (state) technical *System:* Kentucky Tech Southeast Region *Accred.:* 1973/1988 (SACS-COEI) *Calendar:* Courses of varying lengths *Degrees:* certificates *CEO:* Coord. Fred Kincaid

(606) 464-2475

KENTUCKY TECH—LESLIE COUNTY AREA VOCATIONAL EDUCATION CENTER
P.O. Box 902, Hyden 41749 *Type:* Public (state) technical *System:* Kentucky Tech Southeast Region *Accred.:* 1973/1988 (SACS-COEI) *Calendar:* Courses of varying lengths *Degrees:* certificates *CEO:* Coord. Betty Huff

(606) 672-2859

KENTUCKY TECH—LETCHER COUNTY AREA VOCATIONAL EDUCATION CENTER
610 Circle Dr., Whitesburg 41858 *Type:* Public (state) technical *System:* Kentucky Tech Southeast Region *Accred.:* 1973/1988 (SACS-COEI) *Calendar:* Courses of varying lengths *Degrees:* certificates *CEO:* Coord. James G. Estep

(606) 633-5053

KENTUCKY TECH—MADISON COUNTY AREA VOCATIONAL EDUCATION CENTER
P.O. Box 809, 703 N. Second St., Richmond 40476-0809 *Type:* Public (state) technical *System:* Kentucky Tech North Central Region *Accred.:* 1972/1992 (SACS-COEI) *Calendar:* Courses of varying lengths *Degrees:* certificates *CEO:* Coord. Evelyn Watson

(606) 623-4061

KENTUCKY TECH—MADISONVILLE HEALTH OCCUPATIONS SCHOOL
701 N. Laffoon, Madisonville 42431 *Type:* Public (state) technical *System:* Kentucky Tech West Region *Accred.:* 1971/1991 (SACS-COEI) *Calendar:* Courses of varying lengths *Degrees:* certificates *CEO:* Coord. Mary Stanley

(502) 825-6552

KENTUCKY TECH—MADISONVILLE STATE
VOCATIONAL-TECHNICAL SCHOOL
150 School Ave., Madisonville 42431 *Type:*
Public (state) technical *System:* Kentucky
Tech West Region *Accred.:* 1971/1991
(SACS-COEI) *Calendar:* Courses of varying
lengths *Degrees:* certificates *CEO:* Prin.
James Pfeffer, Jr.

(502) 825-6544

KENTUCKY TECH—MARION COUNTY AREA
VOCATIONAL EDUCATION CENTER
Rte. 3, Box 100, Lebanon 40033 *Type:* Pub-
lic (state) technical *System:* Kentucky Tech
Northwest Region *Accred.:* 1974/1992
(SACS-COEI) *Calendar:* Courses of varying
lengths *Degrees:* certificates *CEO:* Coord.
John Coyle

(502) 692-3155

KENTUCKY TECH—MARTIN COUNTY AREA
VOCATIONAL EDUCATION CENTER
HC 68, Box 2177, Inez 41224 *Type:* Public
(state) technical *System:* Kentucky Tech
Northeast Region *Accred.:* 1974/1989
(SACS-COEI) *Calendar:* Courses of varying
lengths *Degrees:* certificates *CEO:* Coord.
Robert L. Allen

(606) 298-3879

KENTUCKY TECH—MASON COUNTY AREA
VOCATIONAL EDUCATION CENTER
646 Kent Station Rd., Maysville 41056
Type: Public (state) technical *System:* Kentucky Tech Northeast Region *Accred.:*
1975/1988 (SACS-COEI) *Calendar:* Courses
of varying lengths *Degrees:* certificates
CEO: Coord. Glenn Collins

(606) 759-7101

KENTUCKY TECH—MAYFIELD AREA
VOCATIONAL EDUCATION CENTER
710 Doughtit Rd., Mayfield 42066 *Type:*
Public (state) technical *System:* Kentucky
Tech West Region *Accred.:* 1975/1990
(SACS-COEI) *Calendar:* Courses of varying
lengths *Degrees:* certificates *CEO:* Coord.
Jim Lawson

(502) 247-4710

KENTUCKY TECH—MAYO STATE VOCATIONAL-
TECHNICAL SCHOOL
513 Third St., Paintsville 41240 *Type:* Public
(state) technical *System:* Kentucky Tech

Northeast Region *Accred.:* 1974/1989
(SACS-COEI) *Calendar:* Courses of varying
lengths *Degrees:* certificates *CEO:* Prin.
Gary Coleman

(606) 789-5321

KENTUCKY TECH—MCCORMICK AREA
VOCATIONAL EDUCATION CENTER
50 Orchard La., Alexandria 41001 *Type:*
Public (state) technical *System:* Kentucky
Tech North Central Region *Accred.:* 1973/
1993 (SACS-COEI) *Calendar:* Courses of
varying lengths *Degrees:* certificates *CEO:*
Coord. Kenneth McCormick

(606) 635-4101

KENTUCKY TECH—MEADE COUNTY AREA
VOCATIONAL EDUCATION CENTER
Old State Rd., Brandenburg 40108 *Type:*
Public (state) technical *System:* Kentucky
Tech Northwest Region *Accred.:* 1974/1992
(SACS-COEI) *Calendar:* Courses of varying
lengths *Degrees:* certificates *CEO:* Coord.
William Whalen

(502) 422-3955

KENTUCKY TECH—MILLARD AREA VOCATIONAL
EDUCATION CENTER
430 Millard Hwy., Pikeville 41501 *Type:*
Public (state) technical *System:* Kentucky
Tech Northeast Region *Accred.:* 1974/1989
(SACS-COEI) *Calendar:* Courses of varying
lengths *Degrees:* certificates *CEO:* Prin.
William Justice

(606) 437-6059

KENTUCKY TECH—MONROE COUNTY AREA
VOCATIONAL EDUCATION CENTER
4th and Emmerton Sts., Tompkinsville
42167 *Type:* Public (state) technical *System:*
Kentucky Tech Southern Region *Accred.:*
1972/1992 (SACS-COEI) *Calendar:* Courses of varying lengths *Degrees:* certificates
CEO: Coord. Bill Polland

(502) 487-8261

KENTUCKY TECH—MONTGOMERY COUNTY
AREA VOCATIONAL EDUCATION CENTER
682 Woodford Dr., Mount Sterling 40353
Type: Public (state) technical *System:* Kentucky Tech Northeast Region *Accred.:*
1975/1988 (SACS-COEI) *Calendar:* Courses

of varying lengths *Degrees:* certificates *CEO:* Coord. Norma Willoughby

(606) 498-1103

KENTUCKY TECH—MORGAN COUNTY AREA VOCATIONAL EDUCATION CENTER

P.O. Box 249, West Liberty 41472 *Type:* Public (state) technical *System:* Kentucky Tech Northeast Region *Accred.:* 1975/1988 (SACS-COEI) *Calendar:* Courses of varying lengths *Degrees:* certificates *CEO:* Coord. Willis Lyon

(606) 743-4321

KENTUCKY TECH—MUHLENBERG COUNTY AREA VOCATIONAL EDUCATION CENTER

R.R. Box 67, Greenville 42345 *Type:* Public (state) technical *System:* Kentucky Tech West Region *Accred.:* 1971/1991 (SACS-COEI) *Calendar:* Courses of varying lengths *Degrees:* certificates *CEO:* Coord. Andrew Swansey

(502) 338-1271

KENTUCKY TECH—MURRAY AREA VOCATIONAL EDUCATION CENTER

18th and Sycamore Sts., Murray 42071 *Type:* Public (state) technical *System:* Kentucky Tech West Region *Accred.:* 1975/1990 (SACS-COEI) *Calendar:* Courses of varying lengths *Degrees:* certificates *CEO:* Prin. Lynn Tackett

(502) 753-1870

KENTUCKY TECH—NELSON COUNTY AREA VOCATIONAL EDUCATION CENTER

1060 Bloomfield Rd., Bardstown 40004 *Type:* Public (state) technical *System:* Kentucky Tech Northwest Region *Accred.:* 1974/1992 (SACS-COEI) *Calendar:* Courses of varying lengths *Degrees:* certificates *CEO:* Coord. John T. Kromer

(502) 348-9096

KENTUCKY TECH—NORTHERN CAMPBELL COUNTY VOCATIONAL-TECHNICAL SCHOOL

Campbell Dr., Highland Heights 41076 *Type:* Public (state) technical *System:* Kentucky Tech North Central Region *Accred.:* 1973/1993 (SACS-COEI) *Calendar:* Courses of varying lengths *Degrees:* certificates *CEO:* Coord. Earl Wittenrock

(606) 441-2010

KENTUCKY TECH—NORTHERN KENTUCKY HEALTH OCCUPATIONS CENTER

790 Thomas More Pkwy., Edgewood 41017 *Type:* Public (state) technical *System:* Kentucky Tech North Central Region *Accred.:* 1973/1993 (SACS-COEI) *Calendar:* Courses of varying lengths *Degrees:* certificates *CEO:* Coord. Wade Halsey

(606) 341-5200

KENTUCKY TECH—NORTHERN KENTUCKY STATE VOCATIONAL-TECHNICAL SCHOOL

1025 Amsterdam Rd., Covington 41018 *Type:* Public (state) technical *System:* Kentucky Tech North Central Region *Accred.:* 1973/1993 (SACS-COEI) *Calendar:* Courses of varying lengths *Degrees:* certificates *CEO:* Prin. Edward Burton

(606) 431-2700

KENTUCKY TECH—OHIO COUNTY AREA VOCATIONAL EDUCATION CENTER

P.O. Box 1406, U.S. 231 S., Hartford 42347 *Type:* Public (state) technical *System:* Kentucky Tech West Region *Accred.:* 1973/1988 (SACS-COEI) *Calendar:* Courses of varying lengths *Degrees:* certificates *CEO:* Coord. Ray Price

(502) 274-9612

KENTUCKY TECH—OLDHAM COUNTY AREA VOCATIONAL EDUCATION CENTER

P.O. Box 127, Hwy. 393, Buckner 40065 *Type:* Public (state) technical *System:* Kentucky Tech Northwest Region *Accred.:* 1973/1993 (SACS-COEI) *Calendar:* Courses of varying lengths *Degrees:* certificates *CEO:* Prin. Jeanette Stratton

(502) 222-0131

KENTUCKY TECH—OWENSBORO VOCATIONAL-TECHNICAL SCHOOL

1501 Frederica St., Owensboro 42301 *Type:* Public (state) technical *System:* Kentucky Tech West Region *Accred.:* 1973/1988 (SACS-COEI) *Calendar:* Courses of varying lengths *Degrees:* certificates *CEO:* Prin. Beverly Bosley

(502) 686-3255

KENTUCKY TECH—PADUCAH AREA VOCATIONAL EDUCATION CENTER

2400 Adams St., Paducah 42001 *Type:* Public (state) technical *System:* Kentucky Tech

West Region *Accred.:* 1975/1990 (SACS-COEI) *Calendar:* Courses of varying lengths *Degrees:* certificates *CEO:* Prin. Robert Rouff

(502) 443-6592

KENTUCKY TECH—PATTON AREA VOCATIONAL EDUCATION CENTER
3234 Turkeyfoot Rd., Fort Mitchell 41017 *Type:* Public (state) technical *System:* Kentucky Tech North Central Region *Accred.:* 1973/1993 (SACS-COEI) *Calendar:* Courses of varying lengths *Degrees:* certificates *CEO:* Coord. Eugene Penn

(606) 341-2266

KENTUCKY TECH—PHELPS AREA VOCATIONAL EDUCATION CENTER
HC 67, No. 1002, Phelps 41553 *Type:* Public (state) technical *System:* Kentucky Tech Northeast Region *Accred.:* 1974/1989 (SACS-COEI) *Calendar:* Courses of varying lengths *Degrees:* certificates *CEO:* Prin. Curtis Akers

(606) 456-8136

KENTUCKY TECH—ROCKCASTLE COUNTY AREA VOCATIONAL EDUCATION CENTER
P.O. Box 275, Mount Vernon 40456 *Type:* Public (state) technical *System:* Kentucky Tech Southeast Region *Accred.:* 1975/1990 (SACS-COEI) *Calendar:* Courses of varying lengths *Degrees:* certificates *Prof. Accred.:* Respiratory Therapy Technology *CEO:* Coord. Donna Hopkins

(606) 256-4346

KENTUCKY TECH—ROWAN STATE VOCATIONAL-TECHNICAL SCHOOL
100 Vo-Tech Dr., 32 N., Morehead 40351 *Type:* Public (state) technical *System:* Kentucky Tech Northeast Region *Accred.:* 1975/1988 (SACS-COEI) *Calendar:* Courses of varying lengths *Degrees:* certificates *Prof. Accred.:* Respiratory Therapy Technology *CEO:* Prin. Jamie Brown

(606) 783-1538

KENTUCKY TECH—RUSSELL AREA VOCATIONAL EDUCATION CENTER
705 Red Devil La., Russell 41169 *Type:* Public (state) technical *System:* Kentucky Tech Northeast Region *Accred.:* 1971/1989 (SACS-COEI) *Calendar:* Courses of varying lengths *Degrees:* certificates *CEO:* Coord. Michael Chapman

(606) 836-1256

KENTUCKY TECH—RUSSELL COUNTY AREA VOCATIONAL EDUCATION CENTER
P.O. Box 599, Russell Springs 42642 *Type:* Public (state) technical *System:* Kentucky Tech Southern Region *Accred.:* 1974/1989 (SACS-COEI) *Calendar:* Courses of varying lengths *Degrees:* certificates *CEO:* Prin. Chester Taylor

(502) 866-6175

KENTUCKY TECH—RUSSELLVILLE AREA VOCATIONAL EDUCATION CENTER
1103 W. 9th St., Russellville 42276 *Type:* Public (state) technical *System:* Kentucky Tech Southern Region *Accred.:* 1972/1992 (SACS-COEI) *Calendar:* Courses of varying lengths *Degrees:* certificates *CEO:* Coord. Maurice Grayson

(502) 726-8433

KENTUCKY TECH—SHELBY COUNTY AREA VOCATIONAL EDUCATION CENTER
Rte. 7, Box 331, Shelbyville 40065 *Type:* Public (state) technical *System:* Kentucky Tech Northwest Region *Accred.:* 1973/1993 (SACS-COEI) *Calendar:* Courses of varying lengths *Degrees:* certificates *CEO:* Coord. Ruth Bunch

(502) 633-6554

KENTUCKY TECH—SOMERSET STATE VOCATIONAL-TECHNICAL SCHOOL
714 Airport Rd., Somerset 42501 *Type:* Public (state) technical *System:* Kentucky Tech Southern Region *Accred.:* 1974/1989 (SACS-COEI) *Calendar:* Courses of varying lengths *Degrees:* certificates *CEO:* Prin. Carol Ann Van Hook

(606) 679-4303

KENTUCKY TECH—WAYNE COUNTY AREA VOCATIONAL EDUCATION CENTER
Rte. 4, Box 1B, Monticello 42633 *Type:* Public (state) technical *System:* Kentucky Tech Southern Region *Accred.:* 1974/1989 (SACS-COEI) *Calendar:* Courses of varying lengths *Degrees:* certificates *CEO:* Coord. Sharon Tiller

(606) 348-8424

KENTUCKY TECH—WEBSTER COUNTY AREA
VOCATIONAL EDUCATION CENTER
P.O. Box 188, Dixon 42409 *Type:* Public
(state) technical *System:* Kentucky Tech
West Region *Accred.:* 1971/1991 (SACS-
COEI) *Calendar:* Courses of varying lengths
Degrees: certificates *CEO:* Coord. Claude
Hicks
(502) 639-5035

KENTUCKY TECH—WEST KENTUCKY STATE
VOCATIONAL-TECHNICAL SCHOOL
Hwy. 60, W., Paducah 42002 *Type:* Public
(state) technical *System:* Kentucky Tech
West Region *Accred.:* 1975/1990 (SACS-
COEI) *Calendar:* Courses of varying lengths
Degrees: certificates *Prof. Accred.:* Dental
Assisting, Diagnostic Medical Sonography,
Medical Assisting (AMA), Physical Therapy
Assisting, Radiography, Respiratory Therapy
Technology, Surgical Technology *CEO:*
Prin. Lee Hicklin
(502) 554-4991

PURCHASE TRAINING CENTER
Rte. 2, Lee Powell Rd., Mayfield 42006
CEO: Acting Dir. Bob Town
(502) 247-9633

MADISONVILLE HEALTH TECHNOLOGY CENTER
P.O. Box 608, Madisonville 42431 *Type:*
Private *Calendar:* Courses of varying
lengths *Degrees:* certificates *Prof. Accred.:*
Medical Laboratory Technology (AMA),
Radiography, Respiratory Therapy Technol-
ogy, Surgical Technology *CEO:* Dir. Bill M.
Hatley
(502) 825-6546

MARSHALL COUNTY AREA VOCATIONAL
EDUCATION CENTER
Rte. 7, Box 100-A, Benton 42025 *Type:*
Public (state) technical *Accred.:* 1975/1989
(SACS-COEI) *Calendar:* Courses of varying
lengths *Degrees:* certificates *CEO:* Dir.
James Cothran
FTE Enroll: 88   (502) 527-8648

NATIONAL EDUCATION CENTER—KENTUCKY
COLLEGE OF TECHNOLOGY
300 High Rise Dr., Louisville 40213-3200
Type: Private *Accred.:* 1968/1986 (ACC-
SCT) *Calendar:* Courses of varying lengths

Degrees: diplomas *CEO:* Exec. Dir. Greg
Cawthon
(502) 966-5555

NEW IMAGE CAREERS
109 E. Sixth St., Corbin 40701 *Type:* Private
Accred.: 1984/1989 (SACS-COEI) *Calendar:* Courses of varying lengths *Degrees:*
certificates *CEO:* Dir. Wanda Powers
FTE Enroll: 87   (606) 528-1490

NU-TEK ACADEMY OF BEAUTY
Ste. 6, Mount Sterling Plaza, Mount Sterling
40353 *Type:* Private *Accred.:* 1990/1993
(SACS-COEI) *Calendar:* Courses of varying
lengths *Degrees:* certificates, diplomas
CEO: Dir. Rebecca Taylor
FTE Enroll: 64   (606) 498-4460

PATHOLOGY AND CYTOLOGY LABORATORIES, INC.
290 Big Run Rd., Lexington 40503 *Type:*
Private *Calendar:* Courses of varying
lengths *Degrees:* certificates *Prof. Accred.:*
Cytotechnology *CEO:* Exec. Vice Pres.
James L. Bauer, M.D.
Enroll: 10   (606) 278-9513

PJ'S COLLEGE OF COSMETOLOGY
Russellville Rd., Bowling Green 42101
Type: Private *Accred.:* 1986/1991 (SACS-
COEI) *Calendar:* Courses of varying lengths
Degrees: certificates *CEO:* Dir. Elnora
Wade
FTE Enroll: 823   .   (502) 842-8149

BRANCH CAMPUS
113 N. Washington St., Crawfordsville,
IN 47933 *CEO:* Dir. Elnora Wade
(800) 627-2566

BRANCH CAMPUS
1400 W. Main St., Greenfield, IN 46140
CEO: Dir. Elnora Wade
(800) 627-2566

BRANCH CAMPUS
5539 S. Madison Ave., Indianapolis, IN
46227 *CEO:* Dir. Elnora Wade
(800) 627-2566

BRANCH CAMPUS
3023 S. Lafountain St., Kokomo, IN
46902 *CEO:* Dir. Elnora Wade
(800) 627-2566

BRANCH CAMPUS
2006 N. Walnut St., Muncie, IN 47303
CEO: Dir. Elnora Wade
(800) 627-2566

BRANCH CAMPUS
2026 Stafford Rd., Plainfield, IN 46168
CEO: Dir. Elnora Wade
(800) 627-2566

PJ'S COLLEGE OF COSMETOLOGY
124 W. Washington St., Glasgow 42141
Type: Private *Accred.:* 1987/1992 (SACS-COEI) *Calendar:* Courses of varying lengths *Degrees:* certificates *CEO:* Dir. Elnora Wade
FTE Enroll: 42   (502) 651-6553

RETS ELECTRONIC INSTITUTE
4146 Outer Loop, Louisville 40219-9977
Type: Private *Accred.:* 1978/1988 (ACC-SCT) *Calendar:* Sem. plan *Degrees:* certificates, diplomas *CEO:* Dir. Frank S. Jordan
(502) 968-7191

ROY'S OF LOUISVILLE BEAUTY ACADEMY
151 Chenoweth La., Louisville 40207 *Type:* Private *Accred.:* 1989 (SACS-COEI) *Calendar:* Courses of varying lengths *Degrees:* certificates *CEO:* Dir. Thomas Esrey
FTE Enroll: 189   (502) 897-9401

BRANCH CAMPUS
5200 Dixie Hwy., Louisville 40216 *CEO:* Dir. Thomas Esrey
(502) 448-1016

SPENCERIAN COLLEGE
4627 Dixie Hwy., P.O. Box 16418, Louisville 40216 *Type:* Private business *Accred.:* 1954/1990 (ACISC); 1977/1987 (SACS-COEI) *Calendar:* Qtr. plan *Degrees:* certificates, diplomas *Prof. Accred.:* Medical Assisting (AMA) *CEO:* Exec. Dir. David E. Gray
FTE Enroll: 292   (502) 447-1000

FASHION DIVISION
3901 Atkinson Dr., Louisville 40222 *Accred.:* 1987/1990 (ACISC) *CEO:* Dir. Glenn Sullivan
(502) 456-6653

TRI-STATE BEAUTY ACADEMY
219 W. Main St., Morehead 40351 *Type:* Private *Accred.:* 1983/1993 (SACS-COEI) *Calendar:* Courses of varying lengths *Degrees:* certificates *CEO:* Dir. Betty Stucky
FTE Enroll: 80   (606) 784-6725

LOUISIANA

ABBEVILLE BEAUTY ACADEMY
1828 Veterans Memorial Dr., Abbeville
70510 *Type:* Private *Accred.:* 1991 (SACS-
COEI) *Calendar:* Courses of varying lengths
Degrees: certificates *CEO:* Dir. Hazel
Doucet
FTE Enroll: 56   (318) 893-1228

ACADIAN TECHNICAL INSTITUTE
1933 W. Hutchinson Ave., Crowley 70527
Type: Public (state) *Accred.:* 1976/1991
(SACS-COEI) *Calendar:* Courses of varying
lengths *Degrees:* certificates *CEO:* Dir.
Richard A. Arnaud
FTE Enroll: 231   (318) 788-7521

ALEXANDRIA REGIONAL TECHNICAL INSTITUTE
4311 S. MacArthur Dr., Alexandria 71302
Type: Public (state) *Accred.:* 1976/1991
(SACS-COEI) *Calendar:* Courses of varying
lengths *Degrees:* certificates *CEO:* Dir.
Patricia F. Juneau
FTE Enroll: 372   (318) 487-5698

AMERICAN SCHOOL OF BUSINESS
701 Professional Dr. N., Shreveport 71105
Type: Private business *Accred.:* 1988
(ACISC) *Calendar:* Courses of varying
lengths *Degrees:* certificates, diplomas
CEO: Dir. Judith Killough
                                (318) 798-3333

ASCENSION COLLEGE
320 E. Ascension St., Gonzales 70737 *Type:*
Private technical *Accred.:* 1991 (SACS-
COEI) *Calendar:* Courses of varying lengths
Degrees: certificates, diplomas *CEO:* Dir.
Midge Jacobsen
FTE Enroll: 55   (504) 647-6609

ASCENSION TECHNICAL INSTITUTE
9697 Airline Hwy., Sorrento 70778 *Type:*
Public (state) *Accred.:* 1982/1992 (SACS-
COEI) *Calendar:* Courses of varying lengths
Degrees: certificates *CEO:* Dir. Charles A.
Tassin
FTE Enroll: 168   (504) 675-5397

AVOYELLES TECHNICAL INSTITUTE
Hwy. 107, Choupique St., Cottonport 71327
Type: Public (state) *Accred.:* 1979/1991
(SACS-COEI) *Calendar:* Courses of varying

lengths *Degrees:* certificates *CEO:* Dir.
Ward Nash
FTE Enroll: 445   (318) 876-2701

AYERS INSTITUTE
Ste. 318, 2924 Knight St., Shreveport 71105
Type: Private business *Accred.:* 1963/1986
(ACISC) *Calendar:* Courses of varying
lengths *Degrees:* certificates, diplomas
CEO: Dir. Ellie Higginbotham
                                (318) 868-3000

BASTROP TECHNICAL INSTITUTE
Kammell St., Bastrop 71221 *Type:* Public
(state) *Accred.:* 1981/1989 (SACS-COEI)
Calendar: Courses of varying lengths *De-
grees:* certificates *CEO:* Dir. Norene Smith
FTE Enroll: 132   (318) 283-0836

BATON ROUGE REGIONAL TECHNICAL INSTITUTE
3250 N. Acadian Thruway, Baton Rouge
70805 *Type:* Public (state) *Accred.:* 1973/
1992 (SACS-COEI) *Calendar:* Courses of
varying lengths *Degrees:* certificates *CEO:*
Dir. Robert R. Buck
FTE Enroll: 547   (504) 359-9201

J.M. FRAZIER VOCATIONAL-TECHNICAL
SCHOOL
555 Julia St., Baton Rouge 70802 *CEO:*
Dir. Robert R. Buck
                                (504) 359-9201

BATON ROUGE SCHOOL OF COMPUTERS
9255 Interline Ave., Baton Rouge 70809-
1971 *Type:* Private *Accred.:* 1982/1988
(ACCSCT) *Calendar:* Courses of varying
lengths *Degrees:* diplomas *CEO:* Pres. Betty
Truxillo
                                (504) 923-2525

BOLTON AVENUE BEAUTY SCHOOL
5623 Jackson St., Alexandria 71301 *Type:*
Private *Accred.:* 1988 (SACS-COEI) *Calendar:* Courses of varying lengths *Degrees:*
certificates *CEO:* Dir. Winn Johnson
FTE Enroll: 62   (318) 422-6143

CAMELOT CAREER COLLEGE
P.O. Box 53326, 2618 Wooddale Blvd.,
Baton Rouge 70805 *Type:* Private business
Accred.: 1990 (ACISC) *Calendar:* Courses

of varying lengths *Degrees:* certificates, diplomas *CEO:* Pres. Ronnie Williams
(504) 928-3005

CAMERON COLLEGE
2740 Canal St., New Orleans 70119 *Type:* Private technical *Accred.:* 1982/1993 (SACS-COEI) *Calendar:* Courses of varying lengths *Degrees:* certificates *CEO:* Dir. Eleanor Cameron
FTE Enroll: 153 (504) 821-5881

CAREER TRAINING SPECIALISTS
1611 Louisville Ave., Monroe 71201 *Type:* Private *Accred.:* 1989 (SACS-COEI) *Calendar:* Courses of varying lengths *Degrees:* certificates, diplomas *CEO:* Dir. Lloydelle Hopkins
FTE Enroll: 230 (318) 323-2889

CHARLES B. COREIL TECHNICAL INSTITUTE
One Vocational Dr., Ville Platte 70586 *Type:* Public (state) *Accred.:* 1981/1986 (SACS-COEI) *Calendar:* Courses of varying lengths *Degrees:* certificates *CEO:* Dir. Danny Lemoine
FTE Enroll: 349 (318) 363-2197

CLAIBORNE TECHNICAL INSTITUTE
3001 Minden Rd., Homer 71040 *Type:* Public (state) *Accred.:* 1989/1992 (SACS-COEI) *Calendar:* Courses of varying lengths *Degrees:* certificates *CEO:* Dir. Thomas Ragland
FTE Enroll: 139 (318) 927-2034

CLOYD'S BEAUTY SCHOOL NO. 2
1311 Winnsboro Rd., Monroe 71202 *Type:* Private *Accred.:* 1991 (SACS-COEI) *Calendar:* Courses of varying lengths *Degrees:* certificates, diplomas *CEO:* Dir. William R. Mathieu
FTE Enroll: 22 (318) 322-5314

CLOYD'S BEAUTY SCHOOL NO. 3
2514 Ferrand St., Monroe 71201 *Type:* Private *Accred.:* 1991 (SACS-COEI) *Calendar:* Courses of varying lengths *Degrees:* certificates, diplomas *CEO:* Dir. William R. Mathieu
FTE Enroll: 36 (318) 322-5314

COASTAL COLLEGE
1410 Canal St., New Orleans 70112 *Type:* Private *Accred.:* 1985/1990 (SACS-COEI)

Calendar: Courses of varying lengths *Degrees:* certificates *CEO:* Dir. Randi Reboul
FTE Enroll: 2,656 (504) 522-2400

BRANCH CAMPUS
5520 Industrial Dr. Ext., Bossier City 71112 *CEO:* Dir. L.C. Farrier
(318) 746-8800

BRANCH CAMPUS
119 Yokum Rd., Hammond 70403 *CEO:* Dir. Randi Reboul
(504) 345-3200

BRANCH CAMPUS
2318 W. Park Ave., Houma 70364 *CEO:* Dir. Mac Le Blanc
(504) 872-2800

BRANCH CAMPUS
320 Howze Beach Rd., Slidell 70461 *CEO:* Dir. Kay Cook
(504) 641-2121

COMMERCIAL COLLEGE OF BATON ROUGE
5677 Florida Blvd., Baton Rouge 70806 *Type:* Private business *Accred.:* 1972/1989 (ACISC) *Calendar:* Courses of varying lengths *Degrees:* certificates, diplomas *CEO:* Dir. Glenna McCollister
(504) 927-3470

COMMERCIAL COLLEGE OF SHREVEPORT
2640 Youree Dr., Shreveport 71104 *Type:* Private business *Accred.:* 1971/1989 (ACISC) *Calendar:* Courses of varying lengths *Degrees:* certificates, diplomas *CEO:* Dir. John Kelsall
(318) 865-6571

CONCORDIA TECHNICAL INSTITUTE
E.E. Wallace Blvd., Ferriday 71334 *Type:* Public (state) *Accred.:* 1980/1990 (SACS-COEI) *Calendar:* Courses of varying lengths *Degrees:* certificates *CEO:* Dir. Ray King
FTE Enroll: 130 (318) 757-6501

CULINARY ARTS INSTITUTE OF LOUISIANA
427 Lafayette St., Baton Rouge 70802 *Type:* Private *Accred.:* 1992 (ACCSCT) *Calendar:* Courses of varying lengths *Degrees:* certificates, diplomas *CEO:* Pres. Violet Harrington
(504) 343-6233

DELTA CAREER COLLEGE
3900 Lee St. Ext., Alexandria 71302 *Type:*
Private business *Accred.:* 1970/1988
(ACISC) *Calendar:* Qtr. plan *Degrees:* cer-
tificates, diplomas *CEO:* Pres. John F. Mc-
Cray
                                (318) 442-9586

    BRANCH CAMPUS
    4358 Hwy. 84 W., Vidalia 71373 *Accred.:*
    1988 (ACISC) *CEO:* Dir. Royal Hill
                                (318) 336-8896

DELTA CAREER COLLEGE
1900 Cameron St., Lafayette 70506 *Type:*
Private business *Accred.:* 1990 (SACS-
COEI) *Calendar:* Qtr. plan *Degrees:* certifi-
cates, diplomas *CEO:* Dir. Phil Mayeaux
FTE Enroll: 103   (318) 235-1147

DELTA CAREER COLLEGE
1702 Hudson La., Monroe 71201 *Type:* Private business *Accred.:* 1990 (SACS-COEI)
Calendar: Qtr. plan *Degrees:* certificates,
diplomas *CEO:* Dir. James Jenkins
FTE Enroll: 150   (318) 322-8870

DELTA-OUACHITA REGIONAL TECHNICAL
INSTITUTE
609 Vocational Pkwy., West Monroe 71292
Type: Public (state) *Accred.:* 1976/1991
(SACS-COEI) *Calendar:* Courses of varying
lengths *Degrees:* certificates *CEO:* Dir. Irving
D. Adkins
FTE Enroll: 346   (318) 396-7431

DELTA SCHOOLS
4549 Johnston St., Lafayette 70503 *Type:*
Private business *Accred.:* 1971/1989
(ACISC) *Calendar:* Courses of varying
lengths *Degrees:* certificates, diplomas
CEO: Vice Pres. Darlene Touchete
                                (318) 988-2211

    BRANCH CAMPUS
    413 W. Admiral Doyle St., New Iberia
    70560 *Accred.:* 1979/1989 (ACISC) *CEO:*
    Dir. Georgia Thompson
                                (318) 365-7348

DENHAM SPRINGS BEAUTY COLLEGE
923 Florida Ave., S.E., Denham Springs
70726 *Type:* Private *Accred.:* 1989 (SACS-
COEI) *Calendar:* Courses of varying lengths

Degrees: certificates *CEO:* Dir. Frances
Hand
FTE Enroll: 91   (504) 665-6188

DIESEL DRIVING ACADEMY
8136 Airline Hwy., Baton Rouge 70815
Type: Private *Accred.:* 1990/1992 (SACS-
COEI) *Calendar:* Courses of varying lengths
Degrees: certificates *CEO:* Dir. Willie Price
FTE Enroll: 55   (504) 929-9990

DIESEL DRIVING ACADEMY
4709 Greenwood Rd., Shreveport 71133
Type: Private *Accred.:* 1982/1988 (SACS-
COEI) *Calendar:* Courses of varying lengths
Degrees: certificates *CEO:* Dir. Bruce Busada
FTE Enroll: 144   (318) 636-6300

    BRANCH CAMPUS
    9725 Interstate 30, Little Rock, AR 72209
    CEO: Dir. Ron Nahlen
                                (501) 565-1166

DOMESTIC HEALTH CARE INSTITUTE
4826 Jamestown Ave., Baton Rouge 70808
Type: Private *Accred.:* 1990 (ABHES) *Calendar:* Courses of varying lengths *Degrees:*
certificates, diplomas *CEO:* Pres. Dan
Chavis
                                (504) 925-5312

EASTERN COLLEGE OF HEALTH VOCATIONS
3540 I-10 Service Rd., S., Metairie 70001
Type: Private *Accred.:* 1986/1992 (ABHES)
Calendar: Courses of varying lengths *Degrees:* diplomas *CEO:* Pres. Susan Dalto
                                (504) 834-8644

EVANGELINE TECHNICAL INSTITUTE
600 S. M.L.K., Jr. Dr., Martinville 70582
Type: Public (state) *Accred.:* 1974/1989
(SACS-COEI) *Calendar:* Courses of varying
lengths *Degrees:* certificates *CEO:* Dir.
Prosper Chretien
FTE Enroll: 209   (318) 394-6466

FINED, SCHOOL OF FINANCIAL EDUCATION
5745 Essen La., No. 207, Baton Rouge
70810 *Type:* Private *Accred.:* 1991 (SACS-
COEI) *Calendar:* Courses of varying lengths
Degrees: certificates, diplomas *CEO:* Dir.
Mark A. Reichel
FTE Enroll: 10   (504) 767-7983

FLORIDA PARISHES TECHNICAL INSTITUTE
100 College Dr., Greensburg 70441 *Type:* Public (state) *Accred.:* 1977/1991 (SACS-COEI) *Calendar:* Courses of varying lengths *Degrees:* certificates *CEO:* Dir. Jimmie Meadows
FTE Enroll: 144   (504) 222-4251

FOLKES TECHNICAL INSTITUTE
3337 Hwy. 10, E., Jackson 70748 *Type:* Public (state) *Accred.:* 1981/1987 (SACS-COEI) *Calendar:* Courses of varying lengths *Degrees:* certificates *CEO:* Dir. James V. Soileau
FTE Enroll: 191   (504) 634-2636

BRANCH CAMPUS
Dixon Correctional Inst., Hwy. 68, Jackson 70748 *CEO:* Dir. George Clark
(504) 634-2636

BRANCH CAMPUS
Wakefield Abattoir, Hwy. 61, Wakefield 70784 *CEO:* Dir. George Clark
(504) 634-2636

FRANKLIN COLLEGE OF COURT REPORTING
1200 S. Clearview Pkwy., New Orleans 70123 *Type:* Private *Accred.:* 1990 (SACS-COEI) *Calendar:* Courses of varying lengths *Degrees:* certificates *CEO:* Pres. Mary Franklin
FTE Enroll: 119   (504) 734-1000

GULF AREA TECHNICAL INSTITUTE
1115 Clover St., Abbeville 70510 *Type:* Public (state) *Accred.:* 1975/1990 (SACS-COEI) *Calendar:* Courses of varying lengths *Degrees:* certificates *CEO:* Dir. Ray Lavergne
FTE Enroll: 201   (318) 893-4984

HAMMOND AREA TECHNICAL INSTITUTE
Hwy. 190 and Pride Blvd., Hammond 70404 *Type:* Public (state) *Accred.:* 1975/1990 (SACS-COEI) *Calendar:* Courses of varying lengths *Degrees:* certificates *CEO:* Dir. Francis N. Bickham
FTE Enroll: 153   (504) 549-5063

HUEY P. LONG TECHNICAL INSTITUTE
303 S. Jones St., Winnfield 71483 *Type:* Public (state) *Accred.:* 1977/1993 (SACS-COEI) *Calendar:* Courses of varying lengths

Degrees: certificates *CEO:* Dir. Larry Williams
FTE Enroll: 425   (318) 628-4342

BRANCH CAMPUS
E. Bradford St., Jena 71342 *CEO:* Dir. Larry Williams
(318) 992-2910

ITI TECHNICAL COLLEGE
13944 Airline Hwy., Baton Rouge 70817-5998 *Type:* Private *Accred.:* 1981/1988 (ACCSCT) *Calendar:* Courses of varying lengths *Degrees:* certificates *CEO:* Pres. Earl J. Martin, Jr.
(504) 752-4233

JEFFERSON COLLEGE
12 Westbank Expy., Gretna 70053 *Type:* Private business *Accred.:* 1991 (ACISC) *Calendar:* Courses of varying lengths *Degrees:* certificates, diplomas *CEO:* Vice Pres. Michael A. Chatelain
(504) 362-5787

JEFFERSON DAVIS TECHNICAL INSTITUTE
1230 N. Main St., Jennings 70546 *Type:* Public (state) *Accred.:* 1976/1991 (SACS-COEI) *Calendar:* Courses of varying lengths *Degrees:* certificates *CEO:* Dir. Johnnie Smith
FTE Enroll: 85   (318) 824-4811

JEFFERSON TECHNICAL INSTITUTE
5200 Blair Dr., Metairie 70001 *Type:* Public (state) *Accred.:* 1975/1989 (SACS-COEI) *Calendar:* Courses of varying lengths *Degrees:* certificates *CEO:* Dir. Justin LeMaitre
FTE Enroll: 294   (504) 736-7076

JOCELYN DASPIT BEAUTY COLLEGE
3204 Independence St., Metairie 70006 *Type:* Private *Accred.:* 1987 (SACS-COEI) *Calendar:* Courses of varying lengths *Degrees:* certificates *CEO:* Dir. John A. Daspit
FTE Enroll: 136   (504) 888-8983

BRANCH CAMPUS
507 Cypress St., Hammond 70401 *CEO:* Dir. Jocelyn Fletcher
(504) 345-6307

BRANCH CAMPUS
1727 W. Airline Hwy., La Place 70068 *CEO:* Dir. Lisa Bailey
(504) 652-6807

JUMONVILLE MEMORIAL TECHNICAL INSTITUTE
Hwy. 3131, Hospital Rd., New Roads 70760
Type: Public (state) *Accred.:* 1976/1991
(SACS-COEI) *Calendar:* Courses of varying
lengths *Degrees:* certificates *CEO:* Dir.
George L. Grace
FTE Enroll: 679   (504) 638-8613

BRANCH CAMPUS
Loiusiana State Penitentiary, General De-
livery, Angola 70712 *CEO:* Dir. George
L. Grace
                         (504) 655-4411

BRANCH CAMPUS
3233 Rosedale Rd., Port Allen 70767
CEO: Dir. George L. Grace

BRANCH CAMPUS
Louisiana Correctional Inst. for Women,
P.O. Box 40, St. Gabriel 70776 *CEO:* Dir.
George L. Grace
                         (504) 642-5529

BRANCH CAMPUS
Hunt Correctional Ctr., St. Gabriel 70776
CEO: Dir. George L. Grace
                         (504) 642-3306

LAFAYETTE REGIONAL TECHNICAL INSTITUTE
1101 Bertrand Dr., Lafayette 70506 *Type:*
Public (state) technical *Accred.:* 1981/1991
(SACS-COEI) *Calendar:* Courses of varying
lengths *Degrees:* certificates *Prof. Accred.:*
Medical Laboratory Technology (AMA)
CEO: Dir. Ted Ardoin
FTE Enroll: 613   (318) 265-5962

LAMAR SALTER TECHNICAL INSTITUTE
Hwy. 171, S., Leesville 71446 *Type:* Public
(state) *Accred.:* 1983/1993 (SACS-COEI)
Calendar: Courses of varying lengths *De-
grees:* certificates *CEO:* Dir. Tommy Cordova
FTE Enroll: 235   (318) 537-3135

LOUISIANA ART INSTITUTE
7380 Exchange Pl., Baton Rouge 70806-
3851 *Type:* Private *Accred.:* 1988 (ACC-
SCT) *Calendar:* Courses of varying lengths
Degrees: certificates *CEO:* Dir./Owner
David W. Clark
                         (504) 928-7770

LOUISIANA HAIR DESIGN COLLEGE
7909 Airline Hwy., Metairie 70003-6438
Type: Private *Accred.:* 1991 (ACCSCT) *Calendar:* Courses of varying lengths *Degrees:*
certificates, diplomas *CEO:* Dir. Shirley
Whitaker
                         (504) 737-2376

LOUISIANA INSTITUTE OF TECHNOLOGY
3349 Masonic Dr., Alexandria 71301 *Type:*
Private *Accred.:* 1991 (SACS-COEI) *Calendar:* Courses of varying lengths *Degrees:*
certificates *CEO:* Pres. Jackie Davis
FTE Enroll: 139   (318) 442-1864

LOUISIANA INSTITUTE OF TECHNOLOGY
3412 Williams Blvd., Kenner 70065 *Type:*
Private *Accred.:* 1983/1988 (SACS-COEI)
Calendar: Courses of varying lengths *De-
grees:* certificates *CEO:* Pres. Ralph White
FTE Enroll: 123   (504) 443-3418

BRANCH CAMPUS
115 Henderson Rd., Lafayette 70508
CEO: Dir. Darrell Augurson
                         (318) 233-0776

LOUISIANA TRAINING CENTER
942-A Arizona St., Sulphur 70663 *Type:* Private *Accred.:* 1992 (SACS-COEI) *Calendar:*
Courses of varying lengths *Degrees:* certificates *CEO:* Pres. Pat Bedford
FTE Enroll: 17   (318) 625-9469

NATCHITOCHES TECHNICAL INSTITUTE
200 Hwy. 3110, S. Bypass, Natchitoches
71458 *Type:* Public (state) *Accred.:* 1982/
1992 (SACS-COEI) *Calendar:* Courses of
varying lengths *Degrees:* certificates *CEO:*
Dir. Dolores H. Tucker
FTE Enroll: 178   (318) 357-3162

NEW ORLEANS REGIONAL TECHNICAL INSTITUTE
980 Navarre Ave., New Orleans 70124
Type: Public (state) *Accred.:* 1988/1993
(SACS-COEI) *Calendar:* Courses of varying
lengths *Degrees:* certificates *CEO:* Dir.
Simone Charbonnet
FTE Enroll: 293   (504) 483-4666

NICK RANDAZZO VOCATIONAL TRAINING
INSTITUTE
125 Lafayette St., Gretna 70053-5835 *Type:*
Private *Accred.:* 1993 (ACCSCT) *Calendar:*

Courses of varying lengths *Degrees:* certificates *CEO:* Pres./C.E.O. Nick Randazzo
(504) 366-5409

NORTH CENTRAL TECHNICAL INSTITUTE
605 N. Boundary, Farmerville 71241 *Type:* Public (state) *Accred.:* 1979/1993 (SACS-COEI) *Calendar:* Courses of varying lengths *Degrees:* certificates *CEO:* Dir. Johnny Bridges
FTE Enroll: 86   (318) 368-3179

NORTHEAST LOUISIANA TECHNICAL INSTITUTE
1710 Warren St., Winnsboro 71295 *Type:* Public (state) *Accred.:* 1976/1992 (SACS-COEI) *Calendar:* Courses of varying lengths *Degrees:* certificates *CEO:* Dir. John Pinckard
FTE Enroll: 137   (318) 435-2163

NORTHWEST LOUISIANA TECHNICAL INSTITUTE
814 Constable St., Minden 71055 *Type:* Public (state) *Accred.:* 1975/1990 (SACS-COEI) *Calendar:* Courses of varying lengths *Degrees:* certificates *CEO:* Dir. Charles T. Strong
FTE Enroll: 283   (318) 371-3035

OAKDALE TECHNICAL INSTITUTE
Old Pelican Hwy., Oakdale 71463 *Type:* Public (state) *Accred.:* 1983/1991 (SACS-COEI) *Calendar:* Courses of varying lengths *Degrees:* certificates *CEO:* Dir. Darrell Rodriguez
FTE Enroll: 208   (318) 335-3944

OCHSNER SCHOOL OF ALLIED HEALTH SCIENCES
880 Commerce Rd., W., New Orleans 70123 *Type:* Private technical *Accred.:* 1978/1988 (SACS-COEI) *Calendar:* Courses of varying lengths *Degrees:* certificates *Prof. Accred.:* Blood Bank Technology, Diagnostic Medical Sonography, Medical Technology, Nuclear Medicine Technology, Perfusion, Radiation Therapy Technology, Radiography, Respiratory Therapy, Respiratory Therapy Technology, Surgical Technology *CEO:* Dir. George Porter
FTE Enroll: 120   (504) 838-3232

OUR LADY OF THE LAKE COLLEGE OF NURSING AND ALLIED HEALTH
5000 Hennessy Blvd., Baton Rouge 70809 *Type:* Private *Calendar:* Courses of varying

lengths *Prof. Accred.:* Surgical Technology *CEO:* Exec. Dir. Robert C. Davidge
(504) 765-8802

REFRIGERATION SCHOOL OF NEW ORLEANS
1201 Mazant St., New Orleans 70117-9909 *Type:* Private *Accred.:* 1992 (ACCSCT) *Calendar:* Courses of varying lengths *Degrees:* certificates *CEO:* Pres. Earl J. Martin, Jr.
(504) 949-2712

RETS TRAINING CENTER
3321 Hessmer Ave., Metairie 70002-4726 *Type:* Private *Accred.:* 1990/1993 (ACCSCT) *Calendar:* Courses of varying lengths *Degrees:* certificates, diplomas *CEO:* Pres. Harold M. Zlatnicky
(504) 888-6848

RIVER PARISHES TECHNICAL INSTITUTE
Airline Pkwy. at 10th St., Reserve 70084 *Type:* Public (state) *Accred.:* 1984/1989 (SACS-COEI) *Calendar:* Courses of varying lengths *Degrees:* certificates *CEO:* Dir. Jack Worrell
FTE Enroll: 315   (504) 536-4418

RUSTON TECHNICAL INSTITUTE
1010 James St., Ruston 71270 *Type:* Public (state) *Accred.:* 1982/1988 (SACS-COEI) *Calendar:* Courses of varying lengths *Degrees:* certificates *CEO:* Dir. Donald Walsworth
FTE Enroll: 137   (318) 251-4145

SABINE VALLEY TECHNICAL INSTITUTE
Hwy. 171, S., Many 71449 *Type:* Public (state) *Accred.:* 1977/1988 (SACS-COEI) *Calendar:* Courses of varying lengths *Degrees:* certificates *CEO:* Dir. David B. Crittenden
FTE Enroll: 122   (318) 256-5663

SHREVEPORT-BOSSIER REGIONAL TECHNICAL INSTITUTE
2010 N. Market St., Shreveport 71137 *Type:* Public (state) *Accred.:* 1976/1991 (SACS-COEI) *Calendar:* Courses of varying lengths *Degrees:* certificates *CEO:* Dir. Sam Merritt
FTE Enroll: 490   (318) 226-7811

SIDNEY N. COLLIER TECHNICAL INSTITUTE
3727 Louisa St., New Orleans 70126 *Type:* Public (state) *Accred.:* 1977/1988 (SACS-

COEI) *Calendar:* Courses of varying lengths *Degrees:* certificates *CEO:* Dir. Levi Lewis
FTE Enroll: 259   (504) 942-8333

SLIDELL TECHNICAL INSTITUTE
1000 Canulette Rd., Slidell 70459 *Type:* Public (state) *Accred.:* 1974/1989 (SACS-COEI) *Calendar:* Courses of varying lengths *Degrees:* certificates *CEO:* Dir. Gerald J. Ayo
FTE Enroll: 217   (504) 646-6430

SOUTH LOUISIANA BEAUTY COLLEGE
300 Howard Ave., Houma 70363 *Type:* Private *Accred.:* 1987/1992 (SACS-COEI) *Calendar:* Courses of varying lengths *Degrees:* certificates *CEO:* Dir. Catherine A. Nagy
FTE Enroll: 60   (504) 873-8978

SOUTH LOUISIANA REGIONAL TECHNICAL INSTITUTE
201 St. Charles St., Houma 70361 *Type:* Public (state) *Accred.:* 1975/1990 (SACS-COEI) *Calendar:* Courses of varying lengths *Degrees:* certificates *CEO:* Dir. Kenneth Callahan
FTE Enroll: 263   (504) 857-3655

BRANCH CAMPUS
Louisiana Marine & Petroleum Inst., Sta. 1, Box 10251, Houma 70361 *CEO:* Dir. Kenneth Callahan
          (504) 857-3698

SOWELA REGIONAL TECHNICAL INSTITUTE
3820 Legion St., Lake Charles 70616 *Type:* Public (state) *Accred.:* 1971/1992 (SACS-COEI) *Calendar:* Courses of varying lengths *Degrees:* certificates *CEO:* Dir. W. Stanley Leger
FTE Enroll: 840   (318) 491-2698

BRANCH CAMPUS
Louisiana Correctional & Industrial Inst., P.O. Box 1056, DeQuincy 70633 *CEO:* Asst. Dir. Colin Fake
          (318) 491-2688

SULLIVAN TECHNICAL INSTITUTE
1710 Sullivan Dr., Bogalusa 70427 *Type:* Public (state) *Accred.:* 1970/1988 (SACS-COEI) *Calendar:* Courses of varying lengths *Degrees:* certificates *CEO:* Dir. M.J. Murphy
FTE Enroll: 349   (504) 732-6640

BRANCH CAMPUS
Washington Correctional Inst., Rte. 2, Box 500, Angie 70426 *CEO:* Guidance Counselor Gary Ledet
          (504) 732-6640

TALLULAH TECHNICAL INSTITUTE
Old Hwy. 65 S., Tallulah 71284 *Type:* Public (state) *Accred.:* 1980/1990 (SACS-COEI) *Calendar:* Courses of varying lengths *Degrees:* certificates *CEO:* Dir. Patrick T. Murphy
FTE Enroll: 151   (318) 574-4820

BRANCH CAMPUS
Hwy. 883-1, Lake Providence 71254 *CEO:* Asst. Dir. Ralph Moore
          (318) 559-0864

TECHE AREA TECHNICAL INSTITUTE
Ave. C, Acadiana Airport, New Iberia 70560 *Type:* Public (state) *Accred.:* 1976/1991 (SACS-COEI) *Calendar:* Courses of varying lengths *Degrees:* certificates *CEO:* Dir. Paul Fair
FTE Enroll: 287   (318) 373-0011

T.H. HARRIS TECHNICAL INSTITUTE
337 E. South St., Opelousas 70570 *Type:* Public (state) *Accred.:* 1970/1990 (SACS-COEI) *Calendar:* Courses of varying lengths *Degrees:* certificates *CEO:* Dir. Raymond Lalonde
FTE Enroll: 434   (318) 948-0239

THIBODAUX AREA TECHNICAL INSTITUTE
1425 Tiger Dr., Thibodaux 70302 *Type:* Public (state) *Accred.:* 1988 (SACS-COEI) *Calendar:* Courses of varying lengths *Degrees:* certificates *CEO:* Dir. Joyce M. Viguerie
FTE Enroll: 140   (504) 447-0924

WEST JEFFERSON TECHNICAL INSTITUTE
475 Manhattan Blvd., Harvey 70058 *Type:* Public (state) *Accred.:* 1982/1993 (SACS-COEI) *Calendar:* Courses of varying lengths *Degrees:* certificates *Prof. Accred.:* Respiratory Therapy Technology *CEO:* Dir. Donna H. Wilson
FTE Enroll: 182   (504) 361-6464

WESTSIDE TECHNICAL INSTITUTE
1201 Bayou Rd., Plaquemine 70765 *Type:* Public (state) *Accred.:* 1974/1992 (SACS-COEI) *Calendar:* Courses of varying lengths *Degrees:* certificates *CEO:* Dir. Alfred S. Bell
FTE Enroll: 129   (504) 342-8228

YOUNG MEMORIAL TECHNICAL INSTITUTE
900 Youngs Rd., Morgan City 70380 *Type:* Public (state) *Accred.:* 1976/1991 (SACS-COEI) *Calendar:* Courses of varying lengths *Degrees:* certificates *CEO:* Dir. Greg Garrett
FTE Enroll: 318   (504) 380-2436

MAINE

AIR-TECH INC.
Rural Rte. 1, Box 170, Limerick 04048 *Type:* Private *Accred.:* 1993 (ACCSCT) *Calendar:* Courses of varying lengths *Degrees:* diplomas *CEO:* Treas. Patricia B. Smith
(207) 793-8020

THE LANDING SCHOOL OF BOAT BUILDING AND DESIGN
P.O. Box 1490, Kennebunkport 04046-1490 *Type:* Private *Accred.:* 1987 (ACCSCT) *Cal-* *endar:* Courses of varying lengths *Degrees:* certificates *CEO:* Dir. David Van Cleef
(207) 985-7976

NEW ENGLAND SCHOOL OF BROADCASTING
One College Cir., Bangor 04401-2999 *Type:* Private *Accred.:* 1986 (ACCSCT) *Calendar:* Courses of varying lengths *Degrees:* diplomas *CEO:* Pres. George E. Wildey
(207) 947-6083

MARYLAND

ABBIE BUSINESS INSTITUTE
5310 Spectrum Dr., Frederick 21701 *Type:*
Private business *Accred.:* 1981/1988
(ACISC) *Calendar:* Courses of varying
lengths *Degrees:* certificates, diplomas
CEO: Pres. Allan R. Short
(301) 694-0211

ARMY ORDNANCE CENTER AND SCHOOL
Bldg. 3071, Aberdeen Proving Ground
21005-5201 *Type:* Public (federal) technical
Accred.: 1978/1993 (SACS-COEI) *Calen-dar:* Courses of varying lengths *Degrees:*
certificates *CEO:* Commandant Russell
Childress, Jr.
FTE Enroll: 3,080   (410) 278-3373

ARUNDEL INSTITUTE OF TECHNOLOGY
1808 Edison Hwy., Baltimore 21213-1549
Type: Private *Accred.:* 1971/1988 (ACC-SCT) *Calendar:* Qtr. plan *Degrees:* diplo-mas *CEO:* Dir. R. Wayne Moore
(410) 327-6640

BROADCASTING INSTITUTE OF MARYLAND
7200 Harford Rd., Baltimore 21234-7765
Type: Private *Accred.:* 1980/1990 (ACC-SCT) *Calendar:* Sem. plan *Degrees:* diplo-mas *CEO:* Pres. John C. Jeppi, Sr.
(410) 254-2770

DIESEL INSTITUTE OF AMERICA
Rte. 40, P.O. Box 69, Grantsville 21536-0069 *Type:* Private *Accred.:* 1988 (ACC-SCT) *Calendar:* Courses of varying lengths
Degrees: diplomas *CEO:* Dir. F.C. Bud
Poland
(301) 895-5139

EMERGENCY MANAGEMENT INSTITUTE
16825 S. Seton Ave., Emmitsburg 21727
Type: Public (federal) home study *Accred.:*
1988/1992 (NHSC) *Calendar:* Courses of
varying lengths *Degrees:* certificates *CEO:*
Dir. Linda Straka
(301) 447-1076

FLEET BUSINESS SCHOOL
Ste. 201, 2530 Riva Rd., Annapolis 21401
Type: Private business *Accred.:* 1971/1989
(ACISC) *Calendar:* Qtr. plan *Degrees:* cer-

tificates, diplomas *CEO:* Dir. James H.
Graves
(410) 266-8500

JOHNSTON SCHOOL OF PRACTICAL NURSING
201 E. University Pkwy., Baltimore 21218
Type: Private professional *Calendar:* Courses
of varying lengths *Degrees:* certificates *Prof.
Accred.:* Practical Nursing *CEO:* Dir. Judith
Feustle
(410) 554-2327

LINCOLN TECHNICAL INSTITUTE
3200 Wilkens Ave., Baltimore 21229-4289
Type: Private *Accred.:* 1968/1989 (ACC-SCT) *Calendar:* Courses of varying lengths
Degrees: certificates, diplomas *CEO:* Dir.
Stephen Buchenot
(410) 646-5480

LINCOLN TECHNICAL INSTITUTE
7800 Central Ave., Landover 20785-4807
Type: Private *Accred.:* 1968/1988 (ACC-SCT) *Calendar:* Courses of varying lengths
Degrees: certificates, diplomas *CEO:* Dir.
Daniel J. Tokarski
(301) 336-7250

MARYLAND DRAFTING INSTITUTE
2045 University Blvd. E., Langley Park
20783-4137 *Type:* Private *Accred.:* 1974/
1989 (ACCSCT) *Calendar:* Courses of vary-ing lengths *Degrees:* certificates, diplomas
CEO: Dir. Carol B. Sawyer
(301) 439-7776

BRANCH CAMPUS
8001 Forbes Pl., North Springfield, VA
22151-2205 *Accred.:* 1985/1990 (ACC-SCT) *CEO:* Dir. Carol B. Sawyer
(703) 321-9777

THE MEDIX SCHOOL
1017 York Rd., Towson 21204-2511 *Type:*
Private *Accred.:* 1976/1988 (ACCSCT) *Cal-endar:* Courses of varying lengths *Degrees:*
certificates *Prof. Accred.:* Dental Assisting
(provisional), Medical Assisting (AMA)
CEO: Dir. Ben E. Wilke
(410) 337-5155

BRANCH CAMPUS
2480 Windy Hill Rd., Marietta, GA
30067-9744 *Accred.:* 1988 (ACCSCT)
Prof. Accred.: Dental Assisting (conditional), Medical Assisting (AMA) *CEO:*
Dir. Larry H. Ritchie
(404) 980-0002

NATIONAL CRYPTOLOGIC SCHOOL
9800 Savage Rd., Fort George G. Meade
20755 *Type:* Public (federal) *Accred.:* 1990
(SACS-COEI) *Calendar:* Courses of varying
lengths *Degrees:* certificates, diplomas
CEO: Commanding Ofcr. Whitney E. Reed
FTE Enroll: 2,020   (410) 859-6136

NATIONAL EDUCATION CENTER TEMPLE SCHOOL
CAMPUS
3601 O'Donnell St., Baltimore 21224 *Type:*
Private business *Accred.:* 1988 (ACISC)
Calendar: Qtr. plan *Degrees:* certificates,
diplomas *CEO:* Exec. Dir. Jane Parker
(410) 675-6000

NAVAL HEALTH SCIENCES EDUCATION AND
TRAINING COMMAND
National Naval Medical Ctr., Bethesda
20889 *Type:* Public (federal) technical *Ac-
cred.:* 1984/1990 (SACS-COEI) *Calendar:*
Courses of varying lengths *Degrees:* certifi-
cates *Prof. Accred.:* Psychology Internship,
Radiography *CEO:* Commanding Ofcr.
David G. Kemp, U.S.N.
FTE Enroll: 3,937   (301) 295-0203

FIELD MEDICAL SERVICE SCHOOL
Camp Pendleton, CA 92055 *CEO:* Commanding Ofcr. George J. Hansel, U.S.N.
(619) 725-7139

FIELD MEDICAL SERVICE SCHOOL
Camp Lejeune, NC 28542 *CEO:* Commandant A.E. Mataldi, U.S.N.
(919) 451-0929

NAVAL AEROSPACE MEDICAL INSTITUTE
Pensacola, FL 32508 *CEO:* Commandant
Charles Bercier, U.S.N.
(904) 452-4554

NAVAL DENTAL SCHOOL—MAXILLOFACIAL
National Naval Dental Ctr., Bethesda
20889 *Prof. Accred.:* Combined Prosthodontics, Endodontics, General Dentistry,
Maxillofacial Prosthodontics, Oral Pathol-

ogy, Periodontics *CEO:* Commandant
Francis J. Robertello, U.S.N.
(301) 295-0064

NAVAL HOSPITAL CORPS SCHOOL
Great Lakes, IL 60088 *CEO:* Commandant C.W. Cote, U.S.N.
(708) 688-5680

NAVAL SCHOOL OF DENTAL ASSISTING
Naval Sta., San Diego, CA 92136 *CEO:*
Ofcr. in Charge Robert Flinton, U.S.N.
(619) 556-8262

NAVAL SCHOOL OF HEALTH SCIENCE
Oakland, CA 94627 *Prof. Accred.:* Surgical Technology *CEO:* Ofcr. in Charge T.
Bratton, U.S.N.
(510) 633-6065

NAVAL SCHOOL OF HEALTH SCIENCE
San Diego, CA 92134 *Prof. Accred.:*
Medical Laboratory Technology (AMA),
Physician Assisting, Surgical Technology
CEO: Commanding Ofcr. M. Iczkowski,
U.S.N.
(619) 532-7700

NAVAL SCHOOL OF HEALTH SCIENCE
National Naval Medical Ctr., Bethesda
20889 *Prof. Accred.:* Cytotechnology,
Electroneurodiagnostic Technology, Medical Laboratory Technology (AMA), Nuclear Medicine Technology, Surgical
Technology *CEO:* Commanding Ofcr.
Kenneth D. Gibson, U.S.N.
(301) 295-1204

NAVAL SCHOOL OF HEALTH SCIENCE
Portsmouth, VA 23708 *Prof. Accred.:*
Surgical Technology *CEO:* Ofcr. in
Charge J.E. Shepherd, U.S.N.
(804) 398-5032

NAVAL UNDERSEA MEDICAL INSTITUTE
Groton, CT 06349 *CEO:* Ofcr. in Charge
D.M. Sack, U.S.N.
(203) 449-3365

NEW ENGLAND TRACTOR TRAILER TRAINING
SCHOOL
1410 Bush St., Baltimore 21230-9910 *Type:*
Private *Accred.:* 1991 (ACCSCT) *Calendar:*

Courses of varying lengths *Degrees:* diplomas *CEO:* Dir. Henry Holder, III
                                                                                (410) 783-0100

OSCAR B. HUNTER MEMORIAL LABORATORY
8218 Wisconsin Ave., Ste. 202, Bethesda 20814 *Type:* Private *Calendar:* Courses of varying lengths *Degrees:* certificates *Prof. Accred.:* Medical Technology *CEO:* Dir. Oscar B. Hunter, Jr.
Enroll: 8   (301) 656-9093

PSI INSTITUTE
1310 Apple Ave., Silver Spring 20910-3354 *Type:* Private *Accred.:* 1986 (ACCSCT) *Calendar:* Courses of varying lengths *Degrees:* certificates *CEO:* Dir. Burl Dicken
                                                                                (301) 589-0900

PTC CAREER INSTITUTE
201 E. Baltimore St., Baltimore 21202 *Type:* Private *Accred.:* 1986 (ACCSCT) *Calendar:* Courses of varying lengths *Degrees:* certificates *CEO:* Dir. Susan L. Sherwood
                                                                                (410) 837-3270

RETS TECHNICAL TRAINING CENTER
1520 S. Caton Ave., Baltimore 21227-1063 *Type:* Private *Accred.:* 1973/1988 (ACCSCT) *Calendar:* Courses of varying lengths

Degrees: certificates, diplomas *CEO:* Pres. H.V. Leslie
                                                                                (410) 644-6400

TESST ELECTRONICS AND COMPUTER INSTITUTE
5122 Baltimore Ave., Hyattsville 20781-2080 *Type:* Private *Accred.:* 1975/1993 (ACCSCT) *Calendar:* Courses of varying lengths *Degrees:* diplomas *CEO:* Vice Pres. Richard J. Armbruster
                                                                                (301) 864-5750

WOODBRIDGE BUSINESS INSTITUTE
309 E. Main St., Salisbury 21801 *Type:* Private business *Accred.:* 1982/1988 (ACISC) *Calendar:* Qtr. plan *Degrees:* certificates, diplomas *CEO:* Dir. Patricia L. Keeton
                                                                                (410) 742-6700

BRANCH CAMPUS
1310 Mercantile Dr., Highland, IL 62249 *Accred.:* 1982/1988 (ACISC) *CEO:* Dir. Kevin Cochrane
                                                                                (618) 654-2539

BRANCH CAMPUS
14573-H Jefferson Davis Hwy., Woodbridge, VA 22191 *Accred.:* 1988 (ACISC) *CEO:* Dir. C.L. Marshall
                                                                                (703) 491-3715

MASSACHUSETTS

ALLSTATE INSTITUTE OF TECHNOLOGY
165 Front St., Door D, 5th Fl., Chicopee
01013 *Type:* Private *Accred.:* 1993 (ACC-
SCT) *Calendar:* Courses of varying lengths
Degrees: certificates, diplomas *CEO:* Dir./
Owner Bart O'Connor, Jr.
(413) 594-8248

ASSOCIATED TECHNICAL INSTITUTE
345 W. Cummings Park, Woburn 01801
Type: Private *Accred.:* 1975/1989 (ACC-
SCT) *Calendar:* Courses of varying lengths
Degrees: certificates *CEO:* Pres. Brian
Matza
(617) 935-3838

BANCROFT SCHOOL OF MASSAGE THERAPY
50 Franklin St., Worcester 01608-1996
Type: Private *Accred.:* 1988 (ACCSCT) *Calendar:* Courses of varying lengths *Degrees:*
certificates *CEO:* Pres. Steven Tankanow
(508) 757-7923

BAY STATE SCHOOL OF APPLIANCES
225 Turnpike St., Rte. 138, Canton 02021
Type: Private *Accred.:* 1988 (ACCSCT) *Calendar:* Courses of varying lengths *Degrees:*
certificates *CEO:* Dir. Robert Mason
(617) 828-3434

BURDETT SCHOOL
745 Boylston St., Boston 02116 *Type:* Private business *Accred.:* 1954/1990 (ACISC)
Calendar: Courses of varying lengths *Degrees:* certificates, diplomas *CEO:* Pres.
Maralin Manning
(617) 859-1900

BRANCH CAMPUS
100 Front St., Worcester 01608 *Accred.:*
1993 (ACISC) *CEO:* Dir. Thomas E.
Langford
(508) 849-1900

BUTERA SCHOOL OF ART
111 Beacon St., Boston 02116-1597 *Type:*
Private *Accred.:* 1977/1989 (ACCSCT) *Calendar:* Sem. plan *Degrees:* diplomas *CEO:*
Pres. Joseph L. Butera
(617) 536-4623

THE CAMBRIDGE SCHOOL OF CULINARY ARTS
2020 Massachusetts Ave., Cambridge
02140-2124 *Type:* Private *Accred.:* 1992
(ACCSCT) *Calendar:* Courses of varying
lengths *Degrees:* certificates *CEO:* Dir.
Roberta Dowling
(617) 354-3836

CATHERINE E. HINDS INSTITUTE OF ESTHETICS
65 Riverside Pl., Woburn 02155-4604 *Type:*
Private *Accred.:* 1987 (ACCSCT) *Calendar:*
Courses of varying lengths *Degrees:* certificates *CEO:* Dir. Catherine E. Hinds
(617) 391-3733

CHARLES H. MCCANN TECHNICAL SCHOOL
Hodges Crossroad, North Adams 01247
Type: Private *Calendar:* Courses of varying
lengths *Degrees:* certificates *Prof. Accred.:*
Dental Assisting *CEO:* Supt. Howard
Brookner
(413) 663-5383

COMPUTER LEARNING CENTER
5 Middlesex Ave., Somerville 02145 *Type:*
Private business *Accred.:* 1982/1991
(ACISC) *Calendar:* Courses of varying
lengths *Degrees:* certificates, diplomas
CEO: Exec. Dir. Mark Dugan
(617) 776-3500

BRANCH CAMPUS
436 Broadway, Methuen 01844 *Accred.:*
1993 (ACISC) *CEO:* Dir. Doris Lannoy
Inslee
(508) 794-0233

COMPUTER PROCESSING INSTITUTE
615 Massachusetts Ave., Cambridge 02139
Type: Private business *Accred.:* 1982/1988
(ACISC) *Calendar:* Courses of varying
lengths *Degrees:* certificates, diplomas
CEO: Dir. Fred Aloi
(617) 354-6900

EAST COAST AERO TECHNICAL SCHOOL
696 Virginia Rd., Concord 01742 *Type:* Private *Accred.:* 1970/1986 (ACCSCT) *Calendar:* Courses of varying lengths *Degrees:*
certificates *CEO:* Dir. Robert McTique
(508) 371-9977

FORSYTH SCHOOL FOR DENTAL HYGIENISTS
140 The Fenway, Boston 02115 *Type:* Private *Calendar:* Courses of varying lengths *Degrees:* certificates *Prof. Accred.:* Dental Hygiene *CEO:* Dir. John W. Hein
(617) 262-5200

HALLMARK INSTITUTE OF PHOTOGRAPHY
P.O. Box 308, Turners Falls 01376-0308 *Type:* Private *Accred.:* 1982/1993 (ACC-SCT) *Calendar:* Courses of varying lengths *Degrees:* certificates *CEO:* Pres. George J. Rosa, III
(413) 863-2478

HICKOX SCHOOL
200 Tremont St., Boston 02116 *Type:* Private business *Accred.:* 1968/1986 (ACISC) *Calendar:* Courses of varying lengths *Degrees:* certificates, diplomas *CEO:* Pres. S. Arthur Verenis
(617) 482-7655

KINYON-CAMPBELL BUSINESS SCHOOL
59 Linden St., New Bedford 02740 *Type:* Private business *Accred.:* 1971/1988 (ACISC) *Calendar:* Qtr. plan *Degrees:* certificates, diplomas *CEO:* Dir. David B. Daganhardt
(508) 992-5448

LIFE LABORATORIES
299 Carew St., Springfield 01104 *Type:* Private *Calendar:* Courses of varying lengths *Degrees:* certificates *Prof. Accred.:* Medical Technology *CEO:* Pres. Kenneth Geromini *Enroll:* 8
(413) 747-0820

LONGY SCHOOL OF MUSIC, INC.
One Follen St., Cambridge 02138 *Type:* Private *Calendar:* Courses of varying lengths *Degrees:* diplomas *Prof. Accred.:* Music *CEO:* Dir. Victor Rosenbaum
(617) 876-0956

MASSACHUSETTS SCHOOL OF BARBERING & MEN'S HAIRSTYLING
152 Parkingway St., Quincy 02169-5058 *Type:* Private *Accred.:* 1978/1990 (ACC-SCT) *Calendar:* Sem. plan *Degrees:* certificates *CEO:* Gen. Mgr. Richard Conragan
(617) 770-4444

NATIONAL EDUCATION CENTER—BRYMAN CAMPUS
323 Boylston St., Brookline 02146-7685 *Type:* Private *Accred.:* 1973/1990 (ACC-SCT) *Calendar:* Courses of varying lengths *Degrees:* diplomas *CEO:* Exec. Dir. Dennis Hirsch
(617) 232-6035

BRANCH CAMPUS
4244 Oakman Blvd., Detroit, MI 48204-2024 *Accred.:* 1987 (ACCSCT) *CEO:* Dir. Myra Dembiec
(313) 834-1400

NEW ENGLAND HAIR ACADEMY
492-500 Main St., Malden 02148-5105 *Type:* Private *Accred.:* 1979/1989 (ACC-SCT) *Calendar:* Courses of varying lengths *Degrees:* certificates *CEO:* Dir. Anthony Clemente
(617) 324-6799

NEW ENGLAND SCHOOL OF ACCOUNTING
155 Ararat St., Worcester 01606 *Type:* Private business *Accred.:* 1969/1987 (ACISC) *Calendar:* Sem. plan *Degrees:* certificates, diplomas *CEO:* Dir. Kevin Albano
(508) 853-8972

NEW ENGLAND SCHOOL OF ACUPUNCTURE
30 Common St., Watertown 02172 *Type:* Private professional *Calendar:* Sem. plan *Degrees:* diplomas *Prof. Accred.:* Acupuncture *CEO:* Pres. Daniel Seitz
FTE Enroll: 120   (617) 926-1788

NEW ENGLAND SCHOOL OF ART AND DESIGN
28 Newbury St., Boston 02116-3276 *Type:* Private *Accred.:* 1968/1989 (ACCSCT) *Calendar:* Sem. plan *Degrees:* diplomas *Prof. Accred.:* Interior Design *CEO:* Pres. William M. Davis
(617) 536-0383

NEW ENGLAND SCHOOL OF PHOTOGRAPHY
537 Commonwealth Ave., Boston 02215-2005 *Type:* Private *Accred.:* 1981/1986 (ACCSCT) *Calendar:* Courses of varying lengths *Degrees:* diplomas *CEO:* Pres. William R. Carruthers
(617) 437-1868

NEW ENGLAND TRACTOR TRAILER TRAINING SCHOOL OF MASSACHUSETTS
1093 N. Montello St., Brockton 02401-1642 *Type:* Private *Accred.:* 1982/1992 (ACC-

SCT) *Calendar:* Courses of varying lengths *Degrees:* diplomas *CEO:* Dir. John Henry
(508) 587-1100

NORTH BENNET STREET SCHOOL
39 N. Bennet St., Boston 02113-1998 *Type:* Private *Accred.:* 1982/1987 (ACCSCT) *Calendar:* Courses of varying lengths *Degrees:* diplomas *CEO:* Exec. Dir. Cynthia Stone
(617) 227-0155

NORTHEAST BROADCASTING SCHOOL
142 Berkeley St., Boston 02116-5100 *Type:* Private *Accred.:* 1972/1987 (ACCSCT) *Calendar:* Sem. plan *Degrees:* certificates *CEO:* Pres. Howard E. Horton
(617) 267-7910

NORTHEAST INSTITUTE OF INDUSTRIAL TECHNOLOGY
41 Phillips St., Boston 02114-3699 *Type:* Private *Accred.:* 1971/1987 (ACCSCT) *Calendar:* Sem. plan *Degrees:* certificates, diplomas *CEO:* Assoc. Dir. Richard Riman
(617) 523-2869

PEDIGREE CAREER INSTITUTE
Harbor Mall, Rte. 1A, Lynnway, Lynn 01901-1797 *Type:* Private *Accred.:* 1982/1987 (ACCSCT) *Calendar:* Courses of varying lengths *Degrees:* certificates *CEO:* Dir. Russell L. Carriker
(617) 592-3647

RETS ELECTRONIC SCHOOLS
965 Commonwealth Ave., Boston 02215-1397 *Type:* Private *Accred.:* 1974/1989 (ACCSCT) *Calendar:* Courses of varying lengths *Degrees:* certificates, diplomas *CEO:* Dir. Don Harris
(617) 783-1197

ST. JOHN'S SCHOOL OF BUSINESS
P.O. Box 1190, West Springfield 01090-1190 *Type:* Private business *Accred.:* 1981/1988 (ACISC) *Calendar:* Qtr. plan *Degrees:* certificates, diplomas *CEO:* Dir. Kenneth C. Ballard
(413) 781-0390

THE SALTER SCHOOL
155 Ararat St., Worcester 01606 *Type:* Private business *Accred.:* 1953/1988 (ACISC)

Calendar: Sem. plan *Degrees:* certificates, diplomas *CEO:* Dir. John F. Albano
(508) 853-1074

BRANCH CAMPUS
One Grove St., New Britain, CT 06053 *Accred.:* 1953/1987 (ACISC) *CEO:* Dir. Janet Cyr
(203) 224-8838

BRANCH CAMPUS
458 Bridge St., Cambridge 01103 *Accred.:* 1993 (ACISC) *CEO:* Dir. Louis S. Gozzi
(413) 731-7353

SOUTHEASTERN TECHNICAL INSTITUTE
250 Foundry St., South Easton 02375 *Type:* Private *Calendar:* Courses of varying lengths *Degrees:* certificates *Prof. Accred.:* Dental Assisting, Medical Assisting (AMA), Medical Laboratory Technology (AMA) *CEO:* Supt. Paul K. O'Leary
(508) 238-4374

TAD TECHNICAL INSTITUTE
45 Spruce St., Chelsea 02150-2397 *Type:* Private *Accred.:* 1991 (ACCSCT) *Calendar:* Courses of varying lengths *Degrees:* certificates *CEO:* Pres. Rod Kruse
(617) 889-3600

TRAVEL EDUCATION CENTER
100 Cambridge Park Dr., Cambridge 02140 *Type:* Private *Accred.:* 1979/1990 (ACCSCT) *Calendar:* Courses of varying lengths *Degrees:* certificates *CEO:* Pres. Linda Paresky
(617) 547-7750

BRANCH CAMPUS
402 Amherst St., Nashua, NH 03063-1278 *Accred.:* 1985/1990 (ACCSCT) *CEO:* Pres. Linda Paresky
(603) 880-7200

TRAVEL SCHOOL OF AMERICA
1047 Commonwealth Ave., Boston 02215-1099 *Type:* Private *Accred.:* 1978/1988 (ACCSCT) *Calendar:* Courses of varying lengths *Degrees:* certificates *CEO:* Pres. Bernard Garber
(617) 787-1214

WENTWORTH TECHNICAL SCHOOL
191 Spring Ave., Lexington 02173-8045
Type: Private *Accred.:* 1973/1988 (ACC-SCT) *Calendar:* Courses of varying lengths
Degrees: diplomas *CEO:* Dir. Dorothy G. Pesek

(617) 674-1000

WORCESTER TECHNICAL INSTITUTE
251 Belmont St., Worcester 01605 *Type:*
Public (state) technical *Accred.:* 1982/1992
(NEASC-CTCI) *Calendar:* Sem. plan *Degrees:* certificates *Prof. Accred.:* Dental Assisting *CEO:* Dir. Janet M. Doe
FTE Enroll: 337   *(508) 799-1945*

MICHIGAN

ACADEMY OF HEALTH CAREERS
27301 Dequindre Rd., Ste. 200, Madison Heights 48071 *Type:* Private *Accred.:* 1991 (ACCSCT) *Calendar:* Courses of varying lengths *Degrees:* certificates *CEO:* Pres. Dale Saham
(313) 547-8400

AMERICAN EDUCATION CENTER
26075 Woodward Ave., Huntington Woods 48070 *Type:* Private *Accred.:* 1988 (ACCSCT) *Calendar:* Courses of varying lengths *Degrees:* certificates *CEO:* Dir. Susan Lefever
(313) 399-5522

BLACK FOREST HALL
2787 Quick Rd., P.O. Box 140, Harbor Springs 49740-0140 *Type:* Private *Accred.:* 1988/1993 (ACCSCT) *Calendar:* Courses of varying lengths *Degrees:* certificates *CEO:* Pres. Ceejay Heckenberg
(616) 526-7066

CARNEGIE INSTITUTE
550 Stephenson Hwy., Ste. 100, Troy 48083-1159 *Type:* Private *Accred.:* 1968/1993 (ACCSCT) *Calendar:* Qtr. plan *Degrees:* diplomas *Prof. Accred.:* Medical Assisting (AMA) *CEO:* Pres. Gloria J. McEachern
(313) 589-1078

CENTER FOR CREATIVE STUDIES—INSTITUTE OF MUSIC AND DANCE
201 E. Kirby St., Detroit 48202 *Type:* Private *Calendar:* Courses of varying lengths *Degrees:* certificates *Prof. Accred.:* Music *CEO:* Chrmn. Michael Stockdale
(313) 872-3118

DETROIT BUSINESS INSTITUTE
115 State St., Detroit 48226 *Type:* Private business *Accred.:* 1961/1987 (ACISC) *Calendar:* Qtr. plan *Degrees:* certificates, diplomas *CEO:* Dir. Leon D. Gust
(313) 962-6534

DETROIT BUSINESS INSTITUTE
Ste. 515, 21700 Northwestern Hwy., Southfield 48075 *Type:* Private business *Accred.:* 1986 (ACISC) *Calendar:* Qtr. plan *Degrees:* certificates, diplomas *CEO:* Dir. Thomas E. Kretschmer
(313) 557-5744

DETROIT BUSINESS INSTITUTE—DOWNRIVER
19100 Fort St., Riverview 48192 *Type:* Private business *Accred.:* 1983/1989 (ACISC) *Calendar:* Qtr. plan *Degrees:* certificates, diplomas *CEO:* Dir. Becky Fratangalo
(313) 479-0660

DETROIT INSTITUTE OF OPHTHALMOLOGY
15415 E. Jefferson Ave., Grosse Pointe Park 48230 *Type:* Private *Calendar:* Courses of varying lengths *Degrees:* certificates *Prof. Accred.:* Ophthalmic Medical Technology *CEO:* Pres. Philip C. Hessburg, M.D. *Enroll:* 16
(313) 824-4800

DORSEY BUSINESS SCHOOL
30821 Barrington Ave., Madison Heights 48071 *Type:* Private business *Accred.:* 1984/1990 (ACISC) *Calendar:* Courses of varying lengths *Degrees:* certificates, diplomas *CEO:* Dir. Paula Maake
(313) 585-9200

   BRANCH CAMPUS
   Ste. 202, 24901 Northwestern Hwy., Southfield 48075 *Accred.:* 1985/1990 (ACISC) *CEO:* Dir. Elayne Steinhart
   (313) 352-7830

DORSEY BUSINESS SCHOOL
31542 Gratiot Ave., Roseville 48066 *Type:* Private business *Accred.:* 1961/1990 (ACISC) *Calendar:* Qtr. plan *Degrees:* certificates, diplomas *CEO:* Dir. Cheryl Steinmetz
(313) 296-3225

DORSEY BUSINESS SCHOOL
15755 Northline Rd., Southgate 48195 *Type:* Private business *Accred.:* 1972/1990 (ACISC) *Calendar:* Qtr. plan *Degrees:* certificates, diplomas *CEO:* Exec. Dir. Jack Peeples
(313) 285-5400

DORSEY BUSINESS SCHOOL
34841 Veteran's Plaza, Wayne 48184 *Type:* Private business *Accred.:* 1984/1990 (ACISC) *Calendar:* Courses of varying

lengths *Degrees:* certificates, diplomas *CEO:* Dir. Edward Wolfe

(313) 595-1540

EDUCATIONAL INSTITUTE OF THE AMERICAN HOTEL AND MOTEL ASSOCIATION
1407 S. Harrison Rd., P.O. Box 1240, East Lansing 48826 *Type:* Private home study *Accred.:* 1963/1993 (NHSC) *Calendar:* Courses of varying lengths *Degrees:* certificates, diplomas *CEO:* Pres. E. Ray Swan

(517) 353-5500

ELLIOTT TRAVEL SCHOOL
30000 Orchard Lake, Farmington Hills 48334 *Type:* Private *Accred.:* 1993 (ACCSCT) *Calendar:* Courses of varying lengths *Degrees:* certificates *CEO:* Dir. Jared M. Schubiner

(313) 855-7730

BRANCH CAMPUS
5460 Arden Ave., Warren 48092 *Accred.:* 1993 (ACCSCT) *CEO:* Dir. Colette VanElsachker

(313) 497-9010

FLINT INSTITUTE OF BARBERING
3214 Flushing Rd., Flint 48504-4395 *Type:* Private *Accred.:* 1972/1988 (ACCSCT) *Calendar:* Courses of varying lengths *Degrees:* diplomas *CEO:* Pres. John L. Ayre

(313) 232-4711

GRAND RAPIDS EDUCATIONAL CENTER
1750 Woodworth St., N.E., Grand Rapids 49505 *Type:* Private *Accred.:* 1985/1991 (ABHES); 1978/1989 (ACCSCT) *Calendar:* Courses of varying lengths *Degrees:* certificates *CEO:* Pres. Robert J. Malone

(616) 364-8464

BRANCH CAMPUS
Golf Ridge Ctr., 5349 W. Main St., Kalamazoo 49009-1083 *Accred.:* 1990 (ABHES); 1989 (ACCSCT) *CEO:* Dir. Gloria J. Stender

(616) 381-9616

ITT TECHNICAL INSTITUTE
4020 Sparks Dr., S.E., Grand Rapids 49546 *Type:* Private *Accred.:* 1972/1989 (ACCSCT) *Calendar:* Courses of varying lengths

Degrees: diplomas *CEO:* Dir. Dennis Hormel

(616) 956-1060

BRANCH CAMPUS
600 Holiday Plaza Dr., Matteson, IL 60443 *Accred.:* 1993 (ACCSCT) *CEO:* Dir. Blair Hoy

JACKSON BUSINESS INSTITUTE
234 S. Mechanic St., Jackson 49201 *Type:* Private business *Accred.:* 1953/1987 (ACISC) *Calendar:* Qtr. plan *Degrees:* certificates, diplomas *CEO:* Pres. Jack D. Bunce

(517) 789-6123

LANSING COMPUTER INSTITUTE
501 N. Marshall St., Ste. 101, Lansing 48912-2300 *Type:* Private *Accred.:* 1985/1990 (ACCSCT) *Calendar:* Courses of varying lengths *Degrees:* certificates *CEO:* Dir. Virginia Hilbert

(517) 482-8896

LAWTON SCHOOL
21800 Greenfield, Oak Park 48237 *Type:* Private *Accred.:* 1991 (ACCSCT) *Calendar:* Courses of varying lengths *Degrees:* certificates *CEO:* Exec. Dir. Audrey Gaylor

(313) 968-2421

MICHIGAN BARBER SCHOOL INC.
8988-90 Grand River Ave., Detroit 48204-2244 *Type:* Private *Accred.:* 1988 (ACCSCT) *Calendar:* Courses of varying lengths *Degrees:* certificates *CEO:* Mgr./Dir. Forrest F. Green, Jr.

(313) 894-2300

MICHIGAN CAREER INSTITUTE
14520 Gratiot Ave., Detroit 48205-2395 *Type:* Private *Accred.:* 1969/1989 (ACCSCT) *Calendar:* Courses of varying lengths *Degrees:* diplomas *CEO:* Dir. Andrew G. Vignone

(313) 526-6600

MICHIGAN INSTITUTE OF AERONAUTICS
Willow Run Airport, 47884 D St., Belleville 48111-1278 *Type:* Private *Accred.:* 1991 (ACCSCT) *Calendar:* Courses of varying lengths *Degrees:* certificates *CEO:* Pres. Charles Hawes

(800) 447-1310

MOTECH EDUCATION CENTER
35155 Industrial Rd., Livonia 48150-1238
Type: Private *Accred.:* 1976/1990 (ACC-SCT) *Calendar:* Sem. plan *Degrees:* certificates *CEO:* Dir. Paul Alberts
(313) 522-9510

NATIONAL EDUCATION CENTER—NATIONAL
INSTITUTE OF TECHNOLOGY CAMPUS
15115 Deerfield Rd., East Pointe 48021-1599 *Type:* Private *Accred.:* 1980/1990 (ACCSCT) *Calendar:* Qtr. plan *Degrees:* diplomas *CEO:* Exec. Dir. Jerry Smith
(313) 779-5530

NATIONAL EDUCATION CENTER—NATIONAL
INSTITUTE OF TECHNOLOGY CAMPUS
18000 Newburgh Rd., Livonia 48152-2695
Type: Private *Accred.:* 1970/1990 (ACC-SCT) *Calendar:* Qtr. plan *Degrees:* diplomas *CEO:* Dir. Harry Strong
(313) 464-7387

NATIONAL EDUCATION CENTER—NATIONAL
INSTITUTE OF TECHNOLOGY CAMPUS
2620/2630 Remico St., S.W., Wyoming 49509-9990 *Type:* Private *Accred.:* 1980/1990 (ACCSCT) *Calendar:* Qtr. plan *Degrees:* diplomas *CEO:* Dir. Jenell L. McKinney
(616) 538-3170

NATIONAL EDUCATION CENTER
1302 N. Fourth St., San Jose, CA 95112
Accred.: 1991 (ACCSCT) *CEO:* Exec. Dir. Terry R. Johnson
(408) 452-8800

NORTHEASTERN SCHOOL OF COMMERCE
P.O. Box 819, 701 N. Madison Ave., Bay City 48707 *Type:* Private business *Accred.:* 1953/1988 (ACISC) *Calendar:* Qtr. plan *Degrees:* certificates, diplomas *CEO:* Dir. Louis H. Bork
(517) 893-4502

PAYNE-PULLIAM SCHOOL OF TRADE AND
COMMERCE
2345 Cass Ave., Detroit 48201 *Type:* Private business *Accred.:* 1978/1987 (ACISC) *Calendar:* Courses of varying lengths *Degrees:* certificates, diplomas *CEO:* Pres. Betty E. Pulliam
(313) 963-4710

PONTIAC BUSINESS INSTITUTE
755 W. Drahner Rd., P.O. Box 459, Oxford 48371 *Type:* Private business *Accred.:* 1979/1986 (ACISC) *Calendar:* Qtr. plan *Degrees:* certificates, diplomas *CEO:* Dir. Patricia Fischer
(313) 628-4847

ROSS BUSINESS INSTITUTE
22293 Eureka Rd., Taylor 48180 *Type:* Private business *Accred.:* 1983/1989 (ACISC) *Calendar:* Qtr. plan *Degrees:* certificates, diplomas *Prof. Accred.:* Medical Assisting *CEO:* Dir. Judith Sierota
(313) 374-2135

BRANCH CAMPUS
1285 N. Telegraph Rd., Monroe 48161
Accred.: 1987 (ACISC) *Prof. Accred.:* Medical Assisting *CEO:* Dir. JoAnn Haedicke
(313) 243-5456

BRANCH CAMPUS
37065 S. Gratiot Ave., Mount Clemens 48043-7002 *Accred.:* 1979/1989 (ACISC) *Prof. Accred.:* Medical Assisting *CEO:* Dir. Beth Stirzinger
(313) 954-3083

ROSS MEDICAL EDUCATION CENTER
1036 Gilbert Rd., Flint 48532-3527 *Type:* Private *Accred.:* 1978/1987 (ACCSCT) *Calendar:* Courses of varying lengths *Degrees:* certificates *Prof. Accred.:* Medical Assisting *CEO:* Dir. Margaret Scheneman
(313) 230-1100

BRANCH CAMPUS
1188 N. West Ave., Jackson 49202 *Accred.:* 1987 (ACCSCT) *Prof. Accred.:* Medical Assisting *CEO:* Dir. Susan C. Travers
(517) 782-7677

BRANCH CAMPUS
950 W. Norton Ave., Roosevelt Park 48441-4156 *Accred.:* 1987 (ACCSCT) *Prof. Accred.:* Medical Assisting *CEO:* Dir. Melanie Jackson
(616) 739-1531

BRANCH CAMPUS
4054 Bay Rd., Saginaw 48603-1201 *Accred.:* 1987 (ACCSCT) *Prof. Accred.:*

Medical Assisting *CEO:* Dir. Robin Thomas

(517) 793-9800

ROSS MEDICAL EDUCATION CENTER
913 W. Holmes Rd., Ste. 260, Lansing 48910-4490 *Type:* Private *Accred.:* 1982/ 1987 (ACCSCT) *Calendar:* Courses of varying lengths *Degrees:* certificates *Prof. Accred.:* Medical Assisting *CEO:* Exec. Dir. Sharon McCaughrim

(517) 887-0180

BRANCH CAMPUS
2035 28th St., S.E., Ste. 0, Grand Rapids 49508-1539 *Accred.:* 1987 (ACCSCT) *Prof. Accred.:* Medical Assisting *CEO:* Dir. Mary Clabeaux

(616) 243-3070

ROSS MEDICAL EDUCATION CENTER
26417 Hoover Rd., Warren 48089-1190 *Type:* Private *Accred.:* 1981/1986 (ACCSCT) *Calendar:* Courses of varying lengths *Degrees:* certificates *Prof. Accred.:* Medical Assisting *CEO:* Dir. Dolores Jurko

(313) 758-7200

BRANCH CAMPUS
15670 E. Eight Mile Rd., Detroit 48205-1496 *Accred.:* 1990 (ACCSCT) *CEO:* Dir. Sandra Maniaci

(313) 371-2131

BRANCH CAMPUS
253 Summit Dr., Waterford 48328-3364 *Accred.:* 1993 (ACCSCT) *Prof. Accred.:* Medical Assisting *CEO:* Dir. Susan Switzer

(313) 683-1166

ROSS TECHNICAL INSTITUTE
1490 S. Military Tr., Ste. 11, West Palm Beach, FL 33415-9141 *Accred.:* 1991 (ACCSCT) *Prof. Accred.:* Medical Assisting *CEO:* Dir. Teri Sullivan

(407) 433-1288

ROSS TECHNICAL INSTITUTE
5757 Whitmore Lake Rd., Ste. 800, Brighton 48116 *Type:* Private *Accred.:* 1992/1993 (ACCSCT) *Calendar:* Courses of varying lengths *Degrees:* certificates *Prof. Accred.:* Medical Assisting *CEO:* Dir. Cindy Barnett

(313) 227-0160

BRANCH CAMPUS
4703 Washtenaw Ave., Ann Arbor 48108-1411 *Accred.:* 1991 (ACCSCT) *Prof. Accred.:* Medical Assisting *CEO:* Dir. Elizabeth Elliot

(313) 434-7320

ROSS TECHNICAL INSTITUTE
1553 Woodward Ave., Ste. 650, Detroit 48226-1695 *Type:* Private *Accred.:* 1979/ 1989 (ACCSCT) *Calendar:* Courses of varying lengths *Degrees:* certificates *Prof. Accred.:* Medical Assisting *CEO:* Dir. Aimee B. Davis

(313) 965-7451

BRANCH CAMPUS
20820 Greenfield Rd., 1st Fl., Oak Park 48237-3011 *Accred.:* 1990 (ACCSCT) *Prof. Accred.:* Medical Assisting *CEO:* Dir. Julie Gadowski

(313) 967-3100

SAGINAW BEAUTY ACADEMY
P.O. Box 423, Saginaw 48601-0423 *Type:* Private *Accred.:* 1992 (ACCSCT) *Calendar:* Courses of varying lengths *Degrees:* certificates *CEO:* Dir. Carlean Gill

(517) 752-9261

SAWYER SCHOOL OF BUSINESS
26051 Hoover Rd., Warren 48089 *Type:* Private business *Accred.:* 1973/1990 (ACISC) *Calendar:* Courses of varying lengths *Degrees:* certificates, diplomas *CEO:* Pres./Dir. Joseph T. Belliotti

(313) 758-2300

SER BUSINESS AND TECHNICAL INSTITUTE
9301 Michigan Ave., Detroit 48210 *Type:* Private business *Accred.:* 1989 (ACISC) *Calendar:* Courses of varying lengths *Degrees:* certificates, diplomas *CEO:* Educ. Dir. Eva G. Dewaelsche

(313) 846-2240

SHARP'S ACADEMY OF HAIRSTYLING
115 Main St., Flushing 48433 *Type:* Private *Accred.:* 1993 (ACCSCT) *Calendar:* Courses of varying lengths *Degrees:* certificates *CEO:* Owner Patricia Sharp

(313) 659-3348

BRANCH CAMPUS
8166 Holly Rd., Grand Blanc 48499 *Ac-cred.:* 1993 (ACCSCT) *CEO:* Owner Patricia Sharp

(313) 695-6742

SPECS HOWARD SCHOOL OF BROADCAST ARTS INC.
16900 W. Eight Mile Rd., Ste. 115, Southfield 48075-5273 *Type:* Private *Accred.:* 1978/1990 (ACCSCT) *Calendar:* Courses of varying lengths *Degrees:* diplomas *CEO:* Exec. Dir. Specs Howard

(313) 569-0101

TRAVEL TRAINING CENTER
5003-05 Schaefer Rd., Dearborn 48126-3539 *Type:* Private *Accred.:* 1991 (ACCSCT) *Calendar:* Courses of varying lengths *Degrees:* certificates *CEO:* Dir. M.R. Younis

(313) 584-5000

MINNESOTA

ACADEMY EDUCATION CENTER
Ste. 200, 3050 Metro Dr., Minneapolis 55425 *Type:* Private business *Accred.:* 1993 (ACISC) *Calendar:* Courses of varying lengths *Degrees:* certificates *CEO:* Dir. Mary Erickson
(612) 851-0066

ART INSTRUCTION SCHOOLS
500 S. Fourth St., Minneapolis 55415 *Type:* Private home study *Accred.:* 1956/1991 (NHSC) *Calendar:* Courses of varying lengths *Degrees:* certificates *CEO:* Pres. Thomas R. Stuart
(612) 339-8721

AVANTE SCHOOL OF COSMETOLOGY
1650 White Bear Ave., St. Paul 55106-1610 *Type:* Private *Accred.:* 1987 (ACCSCT) *Calendar:* Courses of varying lengths *Degrees:* diplomas *CEO:* Dir. James Turner
(612) 772-1417

BEMIDJI TECHNICAL COLLEGE
905 Grant Ave., S.E, Bemidji 56601 *Type:* Private *Calendar:* Courses of varying lengths *Degrees:* certificates *Prof. Accred.:* Dental Assisting *CEO:* Pres. Melvin Salberge
(218) 759-3200

BRAINERD/STAPLES REGIONAL TECHNICAL COLLEGE
300 Quince St., Brainerd 56401 *Type:* Private *Calendar:* Courses of varying lengths *Degrees:* certificates *Prof. Accred.:* Dental Assisting *CEO:* Dir. Craig Oliver
(218) 828-5344

CONCORDE CAREER INSTITUTE
12 N. 12th St., Minneapolis 55403-1331 *Type:* Private *Accred.:* 1991 (ACCSCT) *Calendar:* Courses of varying lengths *Degrees:* certificates *Prof. Accred.:* Dental Assisting *CEO:* Dir. Susan Cooke
(612) 341-3850

DULUTH BUSINESS UNIVERSITY
412 W. Superior St., Duluth 55802 *Type:* Private business *Accred.:* 1970/1987 (ACISC) *Calendar:* Qtr. plan *Degrees:* cer-

tificates, diplomas *CEO:* Pres. James R. Gessner
(218) 722-3361

DUNWOODY INDUSTRIAL INSTITUTE
818 Dunwoody Blvd., Minneapolis 55403-1192 *Type:* Private *Accred.:* 1972/1988 (ACCSCT) *Calendar:* Courses of varying lengths *Degrees:* diplomas *CEO:* Pres. M. James Bensen
(612) 374-5800

HENNEPIN TECHNICAL COLLEGE
9000 Brooklyn Blvd., Brooklyn Park 55455 *Type:* Private *Calendar:* Courses of varying lengths *Degrees:* certificates *Prof. Accred.:* Dental Assisting, Practical Nursing *CEO:* Dir. Marty Patterson
(612) 425-3800

LAKELAND MEDICAL-DENTAL ACADEMY
1402 W. Lake St., Minneapolis 55408-2682 *Type:* Private *Accred.:* 1968/1989 (ACCSCT) *Calendar:* Qtr. plan *Degrees:* diplomas *Prof. Accred.:* Dental Assisting, Medical Assisting (AMA), Medical Laboratory Technology (AMA) *CEO:* Dir. Lorrie Laurin
(612) 827-5656

THE McCONNELL SCHOOL
831 Second Ave. S., Minneapolis 55402-2861 *Type:* Private *Accred.:* 1967/1989 (ACCSCT) *Calendar:* Courses of varying lengths *Degrees:* diplomas *CEO:* Dir. William McKay
(612) 332-4238

MEDICAL INSTITUTE OF MINNESOTA
5503 Green Valley Dr., Bloomington 55437 *Type:* Private *Accred.:* 1985/1989 (ABHES) *Calendar:* Courses of varying lengths *Degrees:* certificates *Prof. Accred.:* Veterinary Technology *CEO:* Pres. Phillip Miller
(612) 844-0064

MINNEAPOLIS BUSINESS COLLEGE
1711 W. County Rd. B, Roseville 55113 *Type:* Private business *Accred.:* 1962/1989 (ACISC) *Calendar:* Courses of varying lengths *Degrees:* certificates, diplomas *Prof.*

Accred.: Medical Assisting (AMA) *CEO:* Pres. Joseph Greco

(612) 636-7406

MINNEAPOLIS DRAFTING SCHOOL
5700 W. Broadway, Minneapolis 55428-3548 *Type:* Private *Accred.:* 1972/1988 (ACCSCT) *Calendar:* Qtr. plan *Degrees:* certificates, diplomas *CEO:* Pres. Robert X. Casserly

(612) 535-8843

MINNEAPOLIS TECHNICAL COLLEGE
1415 Hennepin Ave. S., Rm. 446, Minneapolis 55403 *Type:* Private *Calendar:* Courses of varying lengths *Degrees:* certificates *Prof. Accred.:* Dental Assisting, Practical Nursing *CEO:* Pres. Harvey Rucker

(612) 370-9400

MINNESOTA RIVERLAND TECHNICAL COLLEGE
1926 Collegeview Rd., S.E., Rochester 55904 *Type:* Private *Calendar:* Courses of varying lengths *Degrees:* diplomas *Prof. Accred.:* Dental Assisting, Practical Nursing, Surgical Technology *CEO:* Pres. Marlin Wacholz

(507) 285-8616

BRANCH CAMPUS
1900 N.W. Eighth Ave., Austin 55912 *Prof. Accred.:* Radiography *CEO:* Pres. John Gedker

(507) 433-0600

BRANCH CAMPUS
1225 S.W. Third St., Faribault 55021 *Prof. Accred.:* Medical Laboratory Technology (AMA) *CEO:* Vice Pres. Donald T. Olson

(507) 334-3965

MINNESOTA SCHOOL OF BARBERING
3615 E. Lake St., Minneapolis 55406 *Type:* Private *Accred.:* 1983/1988 (ACCSCT) *Calendar:* Courses of varying lengths *Degrees:* certificates *CEO:* Dir. Margaret Schmidt

(612) 722-1996

MINNESOTA SCHOOL OF BUSINESS
1401 W. 76th St., Minneapolis 55423 *Type:* Private business *Accred.:* 1953/1990 (ACISC) *Calendar:* Qtr. plan *Degrees:* certificates, diplomas *CEO:* Dir. Patricia Peick

(612) 861-2000

BRANCH CAMPUS
6120 Earle Brown Dr., Brooklyn Center 55430 *Accred.:* 1990 (ACISC) *CEO:* Dir. Mary Sackett

(612) 566-7777

MOLER BARBER SCHOOL OF HAIRSTYLING
1411 Nicollet Ave., Minneapolis 55403-2666 *Type:* Private *Accred.:* 1983/1988 (ACCSCT) *Calendar:* Courses of varying lengths *Degrees:* certificates *CEO:* Owner Delano Martinson

(612) 871-3754

MUSIC TECH
304 N. Washington Ave., Minneapolis 55401 *Type:* Private *Calendar:* Courses of varying lengths *Degrees:* diplomas *Prof. Accred.:* Music *CEO:* Educ. Dir. Douglas W. Smith

(612) 338-0175

NATIONAL EDUCATION CENTER—BROWN INSTITUTE CAMPUS
2225 E. Lake St., Minneapolis 55407-1900 *Type:* Private *Accred.:* 1967/1988 (ACCSCT) *Calendar:* Courses of varying lengths *Degrees:* diplomas *CEO:* Pres. Bonnie Hugeback

(612) 721-2481

NEI COLLEGE OF TECHNOLOGY
825 41st Ave., N.E., Columbia Heights 55421-2974 *Type:* Private *Accred.:* 1968/1988 (ACCSCT) *Calendar:* Qtr. plan *Degrees:* certificates, diplomas *CEO:* Pres. Charles R. Dettmann

(612) 781-4881

ST. CLOUD BUSINESS COLLEGE
245 N. 37th Ave., St. Cloud 56303 *Type:* Private business *Accred.:* 1969/1987 (ACISC) *Calendar:* Qtr. plan *Degrees:* certificates, diplomas *CEO:* Dir. Cathy Wogen

(612) 251-5600

SCHOOL OF COMMUNICATION ARTS
2526 27th Ave. S., Minneapolis 55406-1310 *Type:* Private *Accred.:* 1980/1990 (ACCSCT) *Calendar:* Sem. plan *Degrees:* certificates *CEO:* Pres. Roger Klietz

(612) 721-5357

SOUTH CENTRAL TECHNICAL COLLEGE
2200 Tech Dr., Albert Lea 56007-3499
Type: Private *Calendar:* Courses of varying
lengths *Degrees:* certificates *Prof. Accred.:*
Dental Assisting *CEO:* Pres. John Votca
(507) 373-0656

TWIN CITY SCHOOL OF PET GROOMING INC.
2556 Hwy. 10, Mounds View 55112-4032
Type: Private *Accred.:* 1991 (ACCSCT) *Calendar:* Courses of varying lengths *Degrees:*
certificates *CEO:* Dir. Mary Bourke
(612) 755-9463

MISSISSIPPI

AMHERST CAREER CENTER
201 W. Park Ave., Greenwood 38930 *Type:*
Private *Accred.:* 1991 (SACS-COEI) *Calendar:* Courses of varying lengths *Degrees:*
certificates *CEO:* Dir. Gladys Flaggs
FTE Enroll: 227   (601) 453-0480

BRANCH CAMPUS
330 N. Mart Plaza, Jackson 37206 *CEO:*
Dir. Melvin Brantley
                        (601) 336-0392

BATESVILLE JOB CORPS CENTER
Hwy. 51, S., Batesville 38606 *Type:* Public
(state) *Accred.:* 1989 (SACS-COEI) *Calendar:* Courses of varying lengths *Degrees:*
certificates *CEO:* Dir. Laura Bruton
FTE Enroll: 360   (601) 563-4656

BROCK'S HAIR DESIGN COLLEGE
116 Franklin St., Carthage 39051-3716
Type: Private *Accred.:* 1991 (ACCSCT) *Calendar:* Courses of varying lengths *Degrees:*
certificates *CEO:* Pres. Clinton E. Brock
                        (601) 267-3678

BROCK'S HAIR DESIGN COLLEGE
1508 S. Glouster St., Tupelo 38801-6510
Type: Private *Accred.:* 1991 (ACCSCT) *Calendar:* Courses of varying lengths *Degrees:*
certificates *CEO:* Dir. Laura Moore
                        (601) 680-4802

DELTA TECHNICAL INSTITUTE
323 Central Ave., Cleveland 38732-2647
Type: Private *Accred.:* 1988 (ACCSCT) *Calendar:* Courses of varying lengths *Degrees:*
certificates *CEO:* Pres. Van P. Carmicle
                        (601) 843-6063

GEIGER'S SCHOOL OF COSMETOLOGY
600 N. 26th Ave., Hattiesburg 39401 *Type:*
Private *Accred.:* 1991 (SACS-COEI) *Calendar:* Courses of varying lengths *Degrees:*
certificates *CEO:* Dir. Howard Steed
FTE Enroll: 51   (601) 583-2523

GULFPORT JOB CORPS CENTER
3300 20th St., Gulfport 39501 *Type:* Public
(state) *Accred.:* 1985/1992 (SACS-COEI)
Calendar: Courses of varying lengths *Degrees:* certificates *CEO:* Dir. Karen Kennedy
FTE Enroll: 350   (601) 864-9691

HATTIESBURG RADIOLOGY GROUP
5000 W. Fourth St., Hattiesburg 39402 *Type:*
Private *Calendar:* Courses of varying
lengths *Degrees:* certificates *Prof. Accred.:*
Radiography *CEO:* Admin. Jim Sumrall
Enroll: 28   (601) 288-4241

JACKSON ACADEMY OF BEAUTY
2525 Robinson Rd., Jackson 39209 *Type:*
Private *Accred.:* 1990 (SACS-COEI) *Calendar:* Courses of varying lengths *Degrees:*
certificates *CEO:* Dir. Jim Bailey
FTE Enroll: 124   (601) 352-3003

JACKSON HAIR DESIGN COLLEGE
2845 Suncrest Dr., Jackson 39212-2529
Type: Private *Accred.:* 1980/1990 (ACCSCT) *Calendar:* Courses of varying lengths
Degrees: diplomas *CEO:* Owner/Dir. Clovis
V. Martin, Jr.
                        (601) 372-7667

BRANCH CAMPUS
852 W. Capitol St., Jackson 39203 *Accred.:* 1990 (ACCSCT) *CEO:* Dir. Susan
M. Martin
                        (601) 353-8122

MISSISSIPPI JOB CORPS CENTER
501 Harmony Rd., Crystal Springs 39059
Type: Public (state) *Accred.:* 1984/1989
(SACS-COEI) *Calendar:* Courses of varying
lengths *Degrees:* certificates *CEO:* Dir.
Debbie Zeiger
FTE Enroll: 435   (601) 892-3348

MOORE CAREER COLLEGE
2460 Terry Rd., Jackson 39204 *Type:* Private *Accred.:* 1985/1990 (SACS-COEI) *Calendar:* Courses of varying lengths *Degrees:*
certificates, diplomas *CEO:* Dir. Acka
Dolloff
FTE Enroll: 659   (601) 371-2900

BRANCH CAMPUS
1500 N. 31st Ave., Hattiesburg 39401
CEO: Dir. Linda Foley
                        (601) 583-4100

BRANCH CAMPUS
1500 Hwy. 19, N., Meridian 39307 *CEO:* Dir. Mac LeBlanc
(601) 693-2900

BRANCH CAMPUS
880 Cliff Gookin Blvd., Tupelo 38801 *CEO:* Dir. Joanna Schaffner
(601) 842-7600

NAVAL CONSTRUCTION TRAINING CENTER
5510 CBC 8th St., Gulfport 39501 *Type:* Public (federal) technical *Accred.:* 1975/1990 (SACS-COEI) *Calendar:* Courses of varying lengths *Degrees:* certificates *CEO:* Commandant G.R. Henderson, U.S.N.
FTE Enroll: 425
(601) 865-2531

NAVAL TECHNICAL TRAINING CENTER
Naval Air Sta., Meridian 39309 *Type:* Public (federal) technical *Accred.:* 1976/1991 (SACS-COEI) *Calendar:* Courses of varying lengths *Degrees:* certificates *CEO:* Commandant Corey Whitehead, U.S.N.
FTE Enroll: 958
(601) 679-2724

SOUTHERN DRIVER'S ACADEMY
3906 I-55, S., Jackson 39212 *Type:* Private *Accred.:* 1990 (SACS-COEI) *Calendar:* Courses of varying lengths *Degrees:* certificates, diplomas *CEO:* Dir. Johnnie E. Twiner
FTE Enroll: 49
(601) 371-1371

MISSOURI

AERO MECHANICS SCHOOL
Riverside 64150 *Type:* Private *Accred.:* 1991
(ACCSCT) *Calendar:* Courses of varying
lengths *Degrees:* certificates *CEO:* Exec.
Dir. Robert J. Andrist, Jr.
(816) 741-7700

AL-MED ACADEMY
10963 St. Charles Rock Rd., St. Louis 63074
Type: Private *Accred.:* 1985/1991 (ABHES)
Calendar: Courses of varying lengths *Degrees:* diplomas *Prof. Accred.:* Medical Assisting *CEO:* Pres. C. Larkin Hicks
(314) 739-4450

BEREAN COLLEGE
1445 Boonville Ave., Springfield 65802
Type: Private home study *Accred.:* 1985/
1990 (NHSC) *Calendar:* Courses of varying
lengths *Degrees:* certificates *CEO:* Pres.
Zenas J. Bicket
(417) 862-2781

BRYAN INSTITUTE
12184 Natural Bridge Rd., Bridgeton 63044-
2078 *Type:* Private *Accred.:* 1979/1989
(ACCSCT) *Calendar:* Sem. plan *Degrees:*
diplomas *Prof. Accred.:* Medical Assisting
CEO: Dir. Robert D. Johnston
(314) 291-0241

BRYAN TRAVEL COLLEGE
Ste. B, 500 W. University St., Springfield
65807 *Type:* Private business *Accred.:* 1991
(ACISC) *Calendar:* Courses of varying
lengths *Degrees:* certificates, diplomas
CEO: Dir. Debra Lee
(417) 862-5700

CAPE GIRARDEAU AREA VOCATIONAL-
TECHNICAL SCHOOL
301 N. Clark St., Cape Girardeau 63701
Type: Private *Calendar:* Courses of varying
lengths *Degrees:* certificates *Prof. Accred.:*
Respiratory Therapy Technology *CEO:* Dir.
Harold C. Tilley
(314) 334-3358

CONCORDE CAREER INSTITUTE
3239 Broadway, Kansas City 64111-2407
Type: Private *Accred.:* 1990 (ACCSCT) *Calendar:* Qtr. plan *Degrees:* diplomas *Prof.*

Accred.: Medical Assisting (AMA) *CEO:*
Dir. Peggy Ammons
(816) 531-5223

DIAMOND COUNCIL OF AMERICA
9140 Ward Pkwy., Kansas City 64114 *Type:*
Private home study *Accred.:* 1984/1993
(NHSC) *Calendar:* Courses of varying
lengths *Degrees:* certificates *CEO:* Exec.
Dir. Jerry Fogel
(816) 444-3500

DICK HILL INTERNATIONAL FLIGHT SCHOOL
P.O. Box 10603, Springfield 65808-0603
Type: Private *Accred.:* 1988 (ACCSCT) *Calendar:* Courses of varying lengths *Degrees:*
certificates *CEO:* Dir. Marlene J. Hill
(417) 485-3474

EASTERN JACKSON COUNTY COLLEGE OF ALLIED
HEALTH
808 S. 15th St., Blue Springs 64015 *Type:*
Private *Accred.:* 1984/1991 (ABHES) *Calendar:* Courses of varying lengths *Degrees:*
certificates *CEO:* Pres./Dir. Kathryn L.
Harmon
(816) 229-4720

ELECTRONIC INSTITUTE
15329 Kensington Ave., Kansas City 64147-
1212 *Type:* Private *Accred.:* 1971/1987
(ACCSCT) *Calendar:* Qtr. plan *Degrees:*
certificates *CEO:* Pres./Owner Jeff Freeman
(816) 331-5700

FLORISSANT UPHOLSTERY SCHOOL
1420 N. Vandeventer St., St. Louis 63113-
3416 *Type:* Private *Accred.:* 1988/1993
(ACCSCT) *Calendar:* Courses of varying
lengths *Degrees:* certificates *CEO:* Dir.
Charles S. Davis
(314) 534-1886

HANNIBAL AREA VOCATIONAL-TECHNICAL
SCHOOL
4500 McMasters Ave., Hannibal 63401
Type: Private *Calendar:* Courses of varying
lengths *Degrees:* certificates *Prof. Accred.:*
Respiratory Therapy Technology *CEO:* Dir.
Harold D. Ward
(314) 221-4430

IHM HEALTH STUDIES CENTER
2500 Ecoff Ave., St. Louis 63143 *Type:* Private *Accred.:* 1992 (ABHES) *Calendar:* Courses of varying lengths *Degrees:* certificates *CEO:* Dir. D. Ann Bullock
(314) 768-1234

INTERNATIONAL HAIR INSTITUTE
415 S. Florissant Rd., Ferguson 63135-2715 *Type:* Private *Accred.:* 1984/1989 (ACC-SCT) *Calendar:* Courses of varying lengths *Degrees:* diplomas *CEO:* Dir. Lawrence H. Coleman
(314) 524-3460

LEONARD'S BARBER COLLEGE
4974 Natural Bridge Rd., St. Louis 63115 *Type:* Private *Accred.:* 1993 (ACCSCT) *Calendar:* Courses of varying lengths *Degrees:* certificates *CEO:* Dir. Leonard Hall
(314) 382-3000

METRO BUSINESS COLLEGE
1732 N. Kingshighway Blvd., Cape Girardeau 63701 *Type:* Private business *Accred.:* 1979/1987 (ACISC) *Calendar:* Courses of varying lengths *Degrees:* certificates, diplomas *Prof. Accred.:* Medical Assisting *CEO:* Dir. Mary Emmenderfer
(314) 334-9181

BRANCH CAMPUS
1407 Southwest Blvd., Jefferson City 65109 *Accred.:* 1986 (ACISC) *Prof. Accred.:* Medical Assisting *CEO:* Dir. Charles DeSha
(314) 635-6600

METRO BUSINESS COLLEGE
2305 N. Bishop Ave., Hwy. 63 N., Rolla 65401 *Type:* Private business *Accred.:* 1985/1990 (ACISC) *Calendar:* Courses of varying lengths *Degrees:* certificates, diplomas *Prof. Accred.:* Medical Assisting *CEO:* Pres. Raymond Buchli
(314) 364-8464

MID-AMERICA PARALEGAL INSTITUTE
Ste. 211, 8008 Carondelet, Clayton 63105 *Type:* Private business *Accred.:* 1993 (ACISC) *Calendar:* Courses of varying lengths *Degrees:* certificates, diplomas *CEO:* Dir. Robert C. Withington
(314) 863-3331

MIDWEST INSTITUTE FOR MEDICAL ASSISTANTS
112 W. Jefferson St., Ste. 120, Kirkwood 63122 *Type:* Private *Accred.:* 1978/1990 (ABHES) *Calendar:* Courses of varying lengths *Degrees:* diplomas *CEO:* Dir. Elizabeth Shreffler
(314) 965-8363

MISSOURI SCHOOL FOR DOCTORS' ASSISTANTS
10121 Manchester Rd., St. Louis 63122-1583 *Type:* Private *Accred.:* 1970/1988 (ACCSCT) *Calendar:* Courses of varying lengths *Degrees:* certificates, diplomas *Prof. Accred.:* Medical Assisting *CEO:* Assoc. Dir. Michael Vander Velde
(314) 821-7700

MISSOURI SCHOOL OF BARBERING AND HAIRSTYLING
1125 N. Hwy. 67, Florissant 63031 *Type:* Private *Accred.:* 1992 (ACCSCT) *Calendar:* Courses of varying lengths *Degrees:* diplomas *CEO:* Pres. T.L. Millis
(314) 839-0310

MISSOURI SCHOOL OF BARBERING AND HAIRSTYLING
3740 Noland Rd., Independence 64055-3343 *Type:* Private *Accred.:* 1987 (ACCSCT) *Calendar:* Courses of varying lengths *Degrees:* diplomas *CEO:* Dir. Lana Jones
(816) 836-4118

MISSOURI TECHNICAL SCHOOL
1167 Corporate Lake Dr., St. Louis 63132-2907 *Type:* Private *Accred.:* 1985/1990 (ACCSCT) *Calendar:* Courses of varying lengths *Degrees:* diplomas *CEO:* Dir. Paul C. Dodge
(314) 569-3600

NATIONAL CAREER INSTITUTE
17601-A E. 40 Hwy., Independence 64055 *Type:* Private business *Accred.:* 1985/1991 (ACISC) *Calendar:* Courses of varying lengths *Degrees:* certificates, diplomas *CEO:* Dir. Jim Mullen
(816) 373-6292

BRANCH CAMPUS
1209 N. Seventh St., Harlingen, TX 78550 *Accred.:* 1989 (ACISC) *CEO:* Dir. Alim Ansari
(512) 425-4183

NICHOLS CAREER CENTER
609 Union St., Jefferson City 65101 *Type:*
Private *Calendar:* Courses of varying
lengths *Degrees:* certificates *Prof. Accred.:*
Dental Assisting, Practical Nursing *CEO:*
Dir. Harold Lynch
(314) 659-3000

PATRICIA STEVENS COLLEGE
1000 St. Louis Union Sta., St. Louis 63103
Type: Private business *Accred.:* 1968/1986
(ACISC) *Calendar:* Qtr. plan *Degrees:* certificates, diplomas *CEO:* Exec. Dir. Richard
R. Harvey
(314) 421-0949

ROLLA AREA VOCATIONAL-TECHNICAL SCHOOL
1304 E. Tenth St., Rolla 65401-3699 *Type:*
Private *Calendar:* Courses of varying
lengths *Degrees:* certificates *Prof. Accred.:*
Radiography *CEO:* Dir. Bob Chapman
(314) 364-3726

ST. LOUIS COLLEGE OF HEALTH CAREERS
4484 W. Pine Blvd., St. Louis 63108 *Type:*
Private *Accred.:* 1986/1992 (ABHES) *Calendar:* Courses of varying lengths *Degrees:*
certificates *CEO:* Pres. Rush L. Robinson
(314) 652-0300

ST. LOUIS CONSERVATORY AND SCHOOLS FOR
THE ARTS
560 Trinity Ave. at Delmar Blvd., St. Louis
63130 *Type:* Private *Calendar:* Courses of
varying lengths *Degrees:* diplomas *Prof. Accred.:* Music *CEO:* Dean Shirley Bartzen
(314) 863-3033

ST. LOUIS TECH
4144 Cypress Rd., St. Ann 63074-1521
Type: Private *Accred.:* 1977/1988 (ACC-
SCT) *Calendar:* Courses of varying lengths
Degrees: certificates, diplomas *CEO:* Pres./
Owner Ted M. Petry
(314) 427-3600

STE. GENEVIEVE BEAUTY COLLEGE
755 Market St., Ste. Genevieve 63670-1525
Type: Private *Accred.:* 1991 (ACCSCT) *Calendar:* Courses of varying lengths *Degrees:*
certificates *CEO:* Mgr. Vicky Fithian
(314) 883-5550

SOUTHWEST SCHOOL OF BROADCASTING
1031 E. Battlefield Rd., Ste. 212B, Springfield 65807-5083 *Type:* Private *Accred.:*
1988 (ACCSCT) *Calendar:* Courses of varying lengths *Degrees:* certificates *CEO:* Vice
Pres. Johnie F. Jones
(417) 883-4060

SULLIVAN EDUCATIONAL CENTERS
1001 Harrison St., Kansas City 64106-3073
Type: Private *Accred.:* 1982/1993 (ACC-
SCT) *Calendar:* Courses of varying lengths
Degrees: diplomas *CEO:* Pres. Phillip C.
Sullivan
(816) 471-1811

TAD TECHNICAL INSTITUTE
7910 Troost Ave., Kansas City 64131-1920
Type: Private *Accred.:* 1989 (ACCSCT) *Calendar:* Qtr. plan *Degrees:* certificates, diplomas *CEO:* Pres. Waunda Thomas
(816) 361-5140

TRANS WORLD TRAVEL ACADEMY
Lindbergh Training Ctr., 11495 Natural
Bridge Rd., St. Louis 63044-9842 *Type:* Pri-
vate home study *Accred.:* 1981/1993
(NHSC) *Calendar:* Courses of varying
lengths *Degrees:* certificates *CEO:* Exec.
Dir. Frank A. Bugler
(314) 895-6754

THE VANDERSCHMIDT SCHOOL
4625 Lindell Blvd., St. Louis 63108 *Type:*
Private business *Accred.:* 1985/1991
(ACISC) *Calendar:* Courses of varying
lengths *Degrees:* certificates, diplomas
CEO: Exec. Dir. Nancy S. Rendleman
(314) 361-6000

VATTEROTT COLLEGE
3925 Industrial Dr., St. Ann 63074-1807
Type: Private *Accred.:* 1982/1987 (ACC-
SCT) *Calendar:* Courses of varying lengths
Degrees: certificates, diplomas *CEO:* Dir.
Turner Brooks
(314) 428-5900

BRANCH CAMPUS
210 S. Main St., Independence 64050 *Accred.:* 1987 (ACCSCT) *CEO:* Dir. Paula
Jerden
(816) 252-3997

BRANCH CAMPUS
N. Main St., Joplin 64801 *Accred.:* 1987
(ACCSCT) *CEO:* Dir. Linda Lynch
(417) 781-5633

BRANCH CAMPUS
1258 E. Trafficway, Springfield 65801
Accred.: 1987 (ACCSCT) *CEO:* Dir. J.
Barry Mannion
(417) 831-8116

VATTEROTT EDUCATIONAL CENTERS
3854 Washington Ave., St. Louis 63108-
3406 *Type:* Private *Accred.:* 1976/1986

(ACCSCT) *Calendar:* Courses of varying
lengths *Degrees:* certificates, diplomas
CEO: Pres. John C. Vatterott
(314) 534-2586

WATTERSON COLLEGE
3323 S. Kingshighway Blvd., St. Louis
63139 *Type:* Private business *Accred.:* 1988
(ACISC) *Calendar:* Courses of varying
lengths *Degrees:* certificates, diplomas
CEO: Dir. Thomas M. Barlow
(314) 351-8020

MONTANA

BIG SKY COLLEGE OF BARBER STYLING
750 Kensington Ave., Missoula 59801-5720
Type: Private *Accred.:* 1987 (ACCSCT) *Calendar:* Courses of varying lengths *Degrees:* diplomas *CEO:* Pres. Gary T. Lucht
(406) 721-5588

BILLINGS BUSINESS COLLEGE
2520 Fifth Ave., S., Billings 59101 *Type:* Private business *Accred.:* 1990 (ACISC) *Calendar:* Courses of varying lengths *Degrees:* certificates, diplomas *CEO:* Dir. Ray L. Mace
(406) 256-1000

BILLINGS SCHOOL OF BARBERING & HAIRSTYLING
922-1/2 Grand Ave., Billings 59101 *Type:* Private *Accred.:* 1985/1990 (ACCSCT) *Cal-endar:* Courses of varying lengths *Degrees:* diplomas *CEO:* Dir. Monte Krause
(406) 259-9369

MAY TECHNICAL COLLEGE
1306 Central Ave., Billings 59102-5531
Type: Private *Accred.:* 1983/1988 (ACCSCT) *Calendar:* Courses of varying lengths *Degrees:* diplomas *CEO:* Pres. Michael May
(406) 259-7000

BRANCH CAMPUS
1807 Third St., N.W., Great Falls 59404-1922 *Accred.:* 1988 (ACCSCT) *CEO:* Dir. Richard T. Norine
(406) 761-4000

NEBRASKA

COLLEGE OF HAIR DESIGN
304 S. 11th St., Lincoln 68508-2199 *Type:* Private *Accred.:* 1977/1987 (ACCSCT) *Calendar:* Qtr. plan *Degrees:* diplomas *CEO:* Pres. Alyce Howard
(402) 474-4244

DR. WELBES COLLEGE OF MASSAGE THERAPY
2602 J St., Omaha 68107-1643 *Type:* Private *Accred.:* 1991 (ACCSCT) *Calendar:* Courses of varying lengths *Degrees:* certificates *CEO:* Owner John Welbes
(402) 731-6768

GATEWAY ELECTRONICS INSTITUTE
4862 S. 96th St., Omaha 68127-2048 *Type:* Private *Accred.:* 1973/1988 (ACCSCT) *Calendar:* Qtr. plan *Degrees:* diplomas *CEO:* Dir. John E. Queen
(402) 593-9000

GATEWAY ELECTRONICS INSTITUTE OF LINCOLN
1033 O St., Ste. 130, Lincoln 68508-3126 *Accred.:* 1985/1990 (ACCSCT)
(402) 434-6060

INSTITUTE OF COMPUTER SCIENCE
808 S. 74th Plaza, Ste. 200, Omaha 68114-4666 *Type:* Private *Accred.:* 1984/1989 (ACCSCT) *Calendar:* Courses of varying lengths *Degrees:* certificates *CEO:* Owner David M. Weller
(402) 393-7064

NEBRASKA CUSTOM DIESEL DRIVER TRAINING
14243 C Cir., Omaha 68144-5600 *Type:* Private *Accred.:* 1986 (ACCSCT) *Calendar:* Courses of varying lengths *Degrees:* certificates *CEO:* Dir. Charles H. Reece
(402) 393-7773

OMAHA COLLEGE OF BUSINESS
1052 Park Ave., Omaha 68105 *Type:* Private business *Accred.:* 1984/1988 (ACISC) *Calendar:* Courses of varying lengths *Degrees:* certificates, diplomas *CEO:* Dir. Kimball Reeves
(402) 342-1818

OMAHA COLLEGE OF HEALTH CAREERS
10845 Harney St., Omaha 68154 *Type:* Private *Accred.:* 1986 (ACCSCT) *Calendar:* Courses of varying lengths *Degrees:* certificates, diplomas *Prof. Accred.:* Dental Assisting, Medical Assisting (AMA), Veterinary Technology (probational) *CEO:* Pres. William J. Stuckey
(402) 333-1400

OMAHA OPPORTUNITIES INDUSTRIALIZATION CENTER
2724 N. 24th St., Omaha 68110-2100 *Type:* Private *Accred.:* 1986 (ACCSCT) *Calendar:* Courses of varying lengths *Degrees:* diplomas *CEO:* Exec. Dir. Bernice Dodd
(402) 457-4222

UNIVERSAL TECHNICAL INSTITUTE
902 Capitol Ave., Omaha 68102-9954 *Type:* Private *Accred.:* 1967/1987 (ACCSCT) *Calendar:* Courses of varying lengths *Degrees:* certificates, diplomas *CEO:* Owner Ivan Abdouch
(402) 345-2422

NEVADA

ACADEMY OF MEDICAL CAREERS
5243 W. Charleston Blvd., No. 11, Las
Vegas 89102 *Type:* Private *Accred.:* 1993
(ACCSCT) *Calendar:* Courses of varying
lengths *Degrees:* certificates, diplomas
CEO: Pres. William M. Paul
(818) 896-2272

AMERICAN ACADEMY OF CAREER EDUCATION
3120 E. Desert Inn Rd., Las Vegas 89121-
3857 *Type:* Private *Accred.:* 1977/1987
(ACCSCT) *Calendar:* Courses of varying
lengths *Degrees:* certificates *CEO:* Dir.
Grant Gailey
(702) 732-7748

CAREER COLLEGE OF NORTHERN NEVADA
1195-A Corporate Blvd., Reno 89502-2331
Type: Private *Accred.:* 1991 (ACCSCT) *Calendar:* Courses of varying lengths *Degrees:*
certificates *CEO:* Pres. Larry F. Clark
(702) 856-2266

EDUCATION DYNAMICS INSTITUTE
2635 N. Decatur Blvd., Las Vegas 89108-
2913 *Type:* Private *Accred.:* 1973/1988
(ACCSCT) *Calendar:* Courses of varying
lengths *Degrees:* diplomas *CEO:* Exec. Dir.
Robert McCart
(702) 648-1522

EDUCATION DYNAMICS INSTITUTE
953 E. Sahara Ave., Bldg. 35-B, Ste. 102,
Las Vegas 89108-2906 *Type:* Private *Accred.:* 1993 (ACCSCT) *Calendar:* Courses
of varying lengths *Degrees:* diplomas *CEO:*
Dir. Erick Mendoza
(702) 731-6421

INTERIOR DESIGN INSTITUTE
4225 S. Eastern Ave., No. 4, Las Vegas
89119-5427 *Type:* Private *Accred.:* 1993
(ACCSCT) *Calendar:* Courses of varying
lengths *Degrees:* certificates *CEO:* Pres.
Nancy Wolff
(702) 369-9944

INTERNATIONAL DEALERS SCHOOL
503 E. Fremont St., Las Vegas 89101 *Type:*
Private *Accred.:* 1988 (ACCSCT) *Calendar:*
Courses of varying lengths *Degrees:* certificates *CEO:* Dir. Karen Reilly
(702) 385-7665

INTERNATIONAL DEALERS SCHOOL
1055 S. Virginia St., Reno 89502-2417
Type: Private *Accred.:* 1988 (ACCSCT) *Degrees:* certificates *CEO:* Dir. Jim Greene
(702) 322-8330

LAS VEGAS GAMING & TECHNICAL SCHOOL
3030 S. Highland Dr., Las Vegas 89109-
1047 *Type:* Private *Accred.:* 1991 (ACC-
SCT) *Calendar:* Courses of varying lengths
Degrees: certificates, diplomas *CEO:* Dir.
Carol A. Adams
(800) 847-5484

NATIONAL ACADEMY FOR CASINO DEALERS
557 S. Sahara Ave., Ste. 108, Las Vegas
89104 *Type:* Private *Accred.:* 1984/1989
(ACCSCT) *Calendar:* Courses of varying
lengths *Degrees:* certificates, diplomas
CEO: Pres. Al Rodrigues
(702) 735-4884

PCI DEALERS SCHOOL
920 S. Valley View Blvd., Las Vegas 89107-
4416 *Type:* Private *Accred.:* 1991 (ACC-
SCT) *Calendar:* Courses of varying lengths
Degrees: certificates *CEO:* Pres. Joel Lauer
(702) 877-4724

PROFESSIONAL CAREERS
P.O. Box 96895, Las Vegas 89193-6895
Type: Private *Accred.:* 1991 (ACCSCT) *Calendar:* Courses of varying lengths *Degrees:*
certificates *CEO:* Pres. Mathew Klabacka
(702) 368-2338

VEGAS CAREER SCHOOL
2101 S. Decatur Blvd., Las Vegas 89102
Type: Private *Accred.:* 1991 (ACCSCT) *Calendar:* Courses of varying lengths *Degrees:*
certificates *CEO:* Owner John Rosich
(702) 362-8488

NEW HAMPSHIRE

NORTHEAST CAREER SCHOOLS
749 E. Industrial Park Dr., Manchester 03109 *Type:* Private *Accred.:* 1988 (ACC-SCT) *Calendar:* Courses of varying lengths *Degrees:* certificates *CEO:* Pres. Chris Liponis

(603) 669-1151

NEW JERSEY

ACADEMY OF PROFESSIONAL DEVELOPMENT
98 Mayfield Ave., Edison 08837 *Type:* Private business *Accred.:* 1986 (ACISC) *Calendar:* Courses of varying lengths *Degrees:* certificates, diplomas *CEO:* Pres. A. Roy Kirkley, Jr.
(908) 417-9100

BRANCH CAMPUS
Mercer County Airport Terminal, West Trenton 08628 *Accred.:* 1991 (ACISC) *CEO:* Dir. Jean Battaglia
(609) 538-0400

AMERICAN BARTENDERS SCHOOL
398-412 Bloomfield Ave., Montclair 07042-2006 *Type:* Private *Accred.:* 1991 (ACCSCT) *Calendar:* Courses of varying lengths *Degrees:* certificates *CEO:* Dir. Michele Ungaro
(201) 783-7100

AMERICAN BUSINESS ACADEMY
66 Moore St., Hackensack 07601 *Type:* Private business *Accred.:* 1976/1988 (ACISC) *Calendar:* Qtr. plan *Degrees:* certificates, diplomas *CEO:* Pres. Theodore S. Takvorian
(201) 488-9400

AVIATION CAREER ACADEMY
Fostertown Rd., Medford 08055-9626 *Type:* Private *Accred.:* 1991 (ACCSCT) *Calendar:* Courses of varying lengths *Degrees:* certificates *CEO:* Owner/C.E.O. Fred Trepper
(609) 267-1200

BERDAN INSTITUTE
265 Rte. 46 W., Totowa 07512-1819 *Type:* Private *Accred.:* 1980/1990 (ACCSCT) *Calendar:* Courses of varying lengths *Degrees:* certificates, diplomas *Prof. Accred.:* Dental Assisting, Medical Assisting (AMA) *CEO:* Dir. E. Lynn Thacker
(201) 256-3444

BILINGUAL INSTITUTE
685 Broad St., Newark 07102 *Type:* Private business *Accred.:* 1982/1988 (ACISC) *Calendar:* Courses of varying lengths *Degrees:* certificates, diplomas *CEO:* Dir. Antonio Cordoba
(201) 624-3883

BRANCH CAMPUS
2 W. Broadway, Paterson 07505 *Accred.:* 1989 (ACISC) *CEO:* Dir. Eduardo L. Gonzalez
(201) 279-8988

BOARDWALK AND MARINA CASINO DEALERS SCHOOL
2709 Atlantic Ave., Atlantic City 08401-6401 *Type:* Private *Accred.:* 1991 (ACCSCT) *Calendar:* Courses of varying lengths *Degrees:* certificates *CEO:* Pres. Arnold Hasson
(609) 344-1986

BRICK COMPUTER SCIENCE INSTITUTE
515 Hwy. 70, Brick 08723-4043 *Type:* Private *Accred.:* 1974/1990 (ACCSCT) *Calendar:* Courses of varying lengths *Degrees:* diplomas *CEO:* Dir. Robert H. Forshee, Jr.
(908) 477-0975

BUSINESS TRAINING INSTITUTE
4 Forest Ave., Paramus 07652 *Type:* Private business *Accred.:* 1985/1990 (ACISC) *Calendar:* Courses of varying lengths *Degrees:* certificates, diplomas *CEO:* Pres. James P. Mellett, Jr.
(201) 845-9300

THE CHUBB INSTITUTE
8 Sylvan Way, Parsippany 07054-0342 *Type:* Private *Accred.:* 1972/1987 (ACCSCT) *Calendar:* Courses of varying lengths *Degrees:* diplomas *CEO:* Dir. Todd A. Brown
(201) 682-4900

BRANCH CAMPUS
40 Journal Sq., Jersey City 07306-4009 *Accred.:* 1987 (ACCSCT) *CEO:* Dir. George C. Kiesel
(201) 656-0330

CITTONE INSTITUTE
1697 Oak Tree Rd., Edison 08820 *Type:* Private business *Accred.:* 1975/1988 (ACISC) *Calendar:* Courses of varying lengths *Degrees:* certificates, diplomas *CEO:* Dir. Simon Cittone
(908) 548-8798

BRANCH CAMPUS
523 Fellowship Rd., Mount Laurel 08054-3414 *Accred.:* 1991 (ACISC) *CEO:* Dir. Walter Whalen
(609) 722-9333

BRANCH CAMPUS
100 Canal Pointe Blvd., Princeton 08540 *Accred.:* 1989 (ACISC) *CEO:* Dir. Rita Harris
(609) 520-8798

COMPUTER LEARNING CENTER
160 E. Rte. 4, Paramus 07652 *Type:* Private business *Accred.:* 1984/1991 (ACISC) *Calendar:* Courses of varying lengths *Degrees:* certificates, diplomas *CEO:* Pres./Dir. Graeme Dorras
(201) 845-6868

DIVERS ACADEMY OF THE EASTERN SEABOARD
2500 S. Broadway, Camden 08104-2431 *Type:* Private *Accred.:* 1981/1986 (ACCSCT) *Calendar:* Courses of varying lengths *Degrees:* certificates, diplomas *CEO:* Dir. Tamara M. Brown
(800) 238-3483

DOVER BUSINESS COLLEGE
15 E. Blackwell St., Dover 07801 *Type:* Private business *Accred.:* 1974/1986 (ACISC) *Calendar:* Qtr. plan *Degrees:* certificates, diplomas *CEO:* Dir. Susan Baumstein
(201) 366-6700

BRANCH CAMPUS
E. 81 Rte. 4 W., Paramus 07652 *Accred.:* 1974/1986 (ACISC) *CEO:* Dir. Christopher Coutts
(201) 843-8500

DRAKE COLLEGE OF BUSINESS
9 Caldwell Pl., Elizabeth 07201 *Type:* Private business *Accred.:* 1982/1988 (ACISC) *Calendar:* Sem. plan *Degrees:* certificates, diplomas *CEO:* Pres. Freida Kay
(201) 352-5509

BRANCH CAMPUS
60 Evergreen Pl., East Orange 07018 *Accred.:* 1993 (ACISC) *CEO:* Dir. Catherine Palmer
(201) 352-5509

DU CRET SCHOOL OF THE ARTS
1030 Central Ave., Plainfield 07060-2898 *Type:* Private *Accred.:* 1979/1989 (ACCSCT) *Calendar:* Sem. plan *Degrees:* certificates, diplomas *CEO:* Dir. Frank J. Falotico
(908) 757-7171

EMPIRE TECHNICAL SCHOOLS OF NEW JERSEY
576 Central Ave., East Orange 07018-1983 *Type:* Private *Accred.:* 1969/1990 (ACCSCT) *Calendar:* Courses of varying lengths *Degrees:* certificates *CEO:* Dir. Timothy M. Rodgers
(201) 675-0565

ENGINE CITY TECHNICAL INSTITUTE
Rte. 22 W., Box 3116, Union 07083-8517 *Type:* Private *Accred.:* 1984/1989 (ACCSCT) *Calendar:* Courses of varying lengths *Degrees:* certificates *CEO:* Dir. Larry L. Berlin
(201) 964-1450

GENERAL TECHNICAL INSTITUTE WELDING TRADE SCHOOL
1118 Baltimore Ave., Linden 07036-1899 *Type:* Private *Accred.:* 1967/1987 (ACCSCT) *Calendar:* Courses of varying lengths *Degrees:* certificates, diplomas *CEO:* Pres. Gregory G. Sytch
(201) 486-9353

HARRIS SCHOOL OF BUSINESS
654 Longwood Ave., Cherry Hill 08002 *Type:* Private business *Accred.:* 1978/1987 (ACISC) *Calendar:* Courses of varying lengths *Degrees:* certificates, diplomas *CEO:* Dir. Alan Harris
(609) 662-5300

HOHOKUS SCHOOL
27 S. Franklin Tpke., Ramsey 07446 *Type:* Private business *Accred.:* 1976/1991 (ACISC) *Calendar:* Courses of varying lengths *Degrees:* certificates, diplomas *CEO:* Pres. Thomas M. Eastwick
(201) 327-8877

HUDSON AREA SCHOOL OF RADIOLOGIC TECHNOLOGY
29 E. 29th St., Bayonne 07002 *Type:* Private *Calendar:* Courses of varying lengths *Degrees:* diplomas *Prof. Accred.:* Radiography *CEO:* Exec. Vice Pres. Michael R. D'Agnes
(201) 858-5202

JOE KUBERT SCHOOL OF CARTOON AND GRAPHIC ART
37 Myrtle Ave., Dover 07801-4054 *Type:* Private *Accred.:* 1980/1990 (ACCSCT) *Calendar:* Sem. plan *Degrees:* diplomas *CEO:* Owner Joseph Kubert
(201) 361-1327

KANE BUSINESS INSTITUTE
206 Haddonfield Rd., Cherry Hill 08002 *Type:* Private business *Accred.:* 1985/1989 (ACISC) *Calendar:* Courses of varying lengths *Degrees:* certificates, diplomas *CEO:* Dir. Kathleen Mahaney
(609) 488-1166

LINCOLN TECHNICAL INSTITUTE
Haddonfield Rd. at Rte. 130N, Pennsauken 08110-1208 *Type:* Private *Accred.:* 1988 (ACCSCT) *Calendar:* Courses of varying lengths *Degrees:* certificates *CEO:* Exec. Dir. Deborah M. Ramentol
(609) 665-3010

LINCOLN TECHNICAL INSTITUTE
2299 Vauxhall Rd., Union 07083-5032 *Type:* Private *Accred.:* 1967/1988 (ACCSCT) *Calendar:* Courses of varying lengths *Degrees:* certificates *CEO:* Exec. Dir. Robert P. Gioella
(908) 964-7800

METROPOLITAN TECHNICAL INSTITUTE
11 Daniel Rd., Fairfield 07004-2506 *Type:* Private *Accred.:* 1983/1988 (ACCSCT) *Calendar:* Courses of varying lengths *Degrees:* certificates *CEO:* Dir. Frank Gergelyi
(201) 227-8191

THE NASH ACADEMY OF ANIMAL ARTS
595 Anderson Ave., Cliffside Park 07010-1830 *Type:* Private *Accred.:* 1982/1987 (ACCSCT) *Calendar:* Courses of varying lengths *Degrees:* certificates, diplomas *CEO:* Pres. John Nash
(201) 945-2710

BRANCH CAMPUS
857 Lane Allen Plaza, Lexington, KY 40504-3605 *Accred.:* 1987 (ACCSCT) *CEO:* Dir. Vivian Henderson
(606) 276-5301

NATIONAL EDUCATION CENTER—RETS CAMPUS
103 Park Ave., Nutley 07110-3505 *Type:* Private *Accred.:* 1977/1988 (ACCSCT) *Calendar:* Qtr. plan *Degrees:* diplomas *CEO:* Dir. Martin Klangasky
(201) 661-0600

NAVAL AIR TECHNICAL TRAINING CENTER
Hangar 1, Lakehurst 08733 *Type:* Public (federal) *Accred.:* 1984/1989 (SACS-COEI) *Calendar:* Courses of varying lengths *Degrees:* certificates *CEO:* Commandant D.R. Murphy, U.S.N.
FTE Enroll: 151   (908) 323-2300

OMEGA INSTITUTE
Cinnaminson Mall, Rte. 130 S., Cinnaminson 08077 *Type:* Private business *Accred.:* 1982/1988 (ACISC) *Calendar:* Courses of varying lengths *Degrees:* certificates, diplomas *Prof. Accred.:* Medical Assisting *CEO:* Dir. Lee Cobleigh
(609) 786-2200

PENNCO TECH
P.O. Box 1427, Blackwood 08012-9961 *Type:* Private *Accred.:* 1980/1993 (ACCSCT) *Calendar:* Courses of varying lengths *Degrees:* diplomas *CEO:* Dir. Donald S. VanDemark, Jr.
(609) 232-0310

THE PLAZA SCHOOL
The Bergen Mall, Paramus 07652-9948 *Type:* Private *Accred.:* 1971/1988 (ACCSCT) *Calendar:* Courses of varying lengths *Degrees:* diplomas *CEO:* Pres. Leslie Balter
(201) 843-0344

PTC CAREER INSTITUTE UNIVERSITY HEIGHTS CAMPUS
200 Washington St., Newark 07102 *Type:* Private *Accred.:* 1991 (ACCSCT) *Calendar:* Courses of varying lengths *Degrees:* certificates *CEO:* Dir. Bill Wildish
(201) 623-1100

SAWYER SCHOOL
664 Newark Ave., Elizabeth 07208 *Type:* Private business *Accred.:* 1972/1987 (ACISC) *Calendar:* Courses of varying lengths *Degrees:* certificates, diplomas *CEO:* Pres. George Vomacka
(201) 351-5150

SCS BUSINESS AND TECHNICAL INSTITUTE
516 Main St., East Orange 07017 *Type:* Private business *Accred.:* 1988 (ACISC) *Calendar:* Courses of varying lengths *Degrees:* certificates, diplomas *CEO:* Dir. Ellen Scott
(201) 675-4300

SCS BUSINESS AND TECHNICAL INSTITUTE
756 Broad St., Newark 07102 *Type:* Private business *Accred.:* 1986/1989 (ACISC) *Calendar:* Courses of varying lengths *Degrees:* certificates, diplomas *CEO:* Dir. Peter Mameli
(201) 623-3939

BRANCH CAMPUS
714 Market St., Philadelphia, PA 19106 *Accred.:* 1989 (ACISC) *CEO:* Dir. Alexandra Abramsky
(215) 592-8600

SCS BUSINESS AND TECHNICAL INSTITUTE
2200 Bergenline Ave., Union City 07087 *Type:* Private business *Accred.:* 1987/1990 (ACISC) *Calendar:* Courses of varying lengths *Degrees:* certificates, diplomas *CEO:* Dir. Judy Gacita
(201) 867-3500

STAR TECHNICAL INSTITUTE
Deptwood Ctr., 251 N. Delsea Dr., Deptford 08096 *Type:* Private *Accred.:* 1991 (ACCSCT) *Calendar:* Courses of varying lengths *Degrees:* diplomas *CEO:* Dir. B.J. Torres
(609) 384-2888

STAR TECHNICAL INSTITUTE
2224 U.S. Hwy., 130 Park Pl., Edgewater Park 08010-3105 *Type:* Private *Accred.:* 1985/1992 (ACCSCT) *Calendar:* Courses of varying lengths *Degrees:* diplomas *CEO:* Dir. Barbara Torres
(609) 877-2727

BRANCH CAMPUS
212 Wyoming Ave., Kingston, PA 18704 *Accred.:* 1985/1992 (ACCSCT) *CEO:* Dir. Jane M. Acri
(717) 287-9777

BRANCH CAMPUS
Greenridge Plaza, 1600 Nay Aug Ave., Scranton, PA 18509 *Accred.:* 1985/1992 (ACCSCT) *CEO:* Dir. Maureen Ryneski
(717) 963-0144

STAR TECHNICAL INSTITUTE
Somerdale Sq., Ste. 2, Somerdale 08083-1345 *Type:* Private *Accred.:* 1985/1992 (ACCSCT) *Calendar:* Courses of varying lengths *Degrees:* diplomas *CEO:* Dir. Marcie Evans
(609) 435-7827

BRANCH CAMPUS
1255 Rte. 70, Ste. 12N, Lakewood 08701-5947 *Accred.:* 1985/1992 (ACCSCT) *CEO:* Dir. James C. Howey
(908) 901-0001

STAR TECHNICAL INSTITUTE
1386 S. Delsea Dr., Vineland 08360-6210 *Type:* Private *Accred.:* 1985/1992 (ACCSCT) *Calendar:* Courses of varying lengths *Degrees:* diplomas *CEO:* Dir. Niles Commisso
(609) 696-0500

BRANCH CAMPUS
2105 Hwy. 35, Ocean Township 07712-7201 *Accred.:* 1985/1992 (ACCSCT) *CEO:* Dir. James Mannion
(908) 493-1660

STUART SCHOOL OF BUSINESS ADMINISTRATION
2400 Belmar Blvd., Wall 07719 *Type:* Private business *Accred.:* 1967/1991 (ACISC) *Calendar:* Sem. plan *Degrees:* certificates, diplomas *CEO:* Dir. Letitia M. Cooper
(201) 681-7200

TECHNICAL INSTITUTE OF CAMDEN COUNTY
343 Berlin-Cross Keys Rd., Sicklerville 08081-9709 *Type:* Private *Calendar:* Courses of varying lengths *Degrees:* certificates *Prof. Accred.:* Dental Assisting, Medical Assisting (AMA) *CEO:* Supt. R. Sanders Haldeman
(609) 767-7000

TETERBORO SCHOOL OF AERONAUTICS
80 Moonachie Ave., Teterboro Airport, Teterboro 07608-1083 *Type:* Private *Accred.:* 1973/1993 (ACCSCT) *Calendar:* Courses of varying lengths *Degrees:* certificates, diplomas *CEO:* Dir. Edward Chudzik
(201) 288-6300

TITAN HELICOPTER ACADEMY
Bldg. 90, Easterwood St., Millville 08332-4810 *Type:* Private *Accred.:* 1992 (ACCSCT) *Calendar:* Courses of varying lengths *Degrees:* diplomas *CEO:* Pres. Peter Amico
(609) 327-5203

NEW MEXICO

ALBUQUERQUE BARBER COLLEGE
525 San Pedro Dr., N.E., Ste. 104, Albuquerque 87108-1847 *Type:* Private *Accred.:* 1988 (ACCSCT) *Calendar:* Courses of varying lengths *Degrees:* certificates *CEO:* Owner/Pres. Gene J. Varoz
(505) 266-4900

INTERNATIONAL BUSINESS COLLEGE
3200 N. White Sands Blvd., Alamogordo 88310 *Type:* Private business *Accred.:* 1982/ 1987 (ACISC) *Calendar:* Courses of varying lengths *Degrees:* certificates, diplomas *CEO:* Dir. Linda Wallace
(505) 437-1854

INTERNATIONAL BUSINESS COLLEGE
Ste. F, 650 E. Montana Ave., Las Cruces 88001 *Type:* Private business *Accred.:* 1981/ 1987 (ACISC) *Calendar:* Courses of varying lengths *Degrees:* certificates, diplomas *CEO:* Dir. Larry Madrid
(505) 526-5579

INTERNATIONAL SCHOOL
301 Victory La., Sunland 88063 *Type:* Private *Accred.:* 1992 (ACCSCT) *Calendar:* Courses of varying lengths *Degrees:* certificates *CEO:* Owner Bob C. Lewis
(505) 589-1414

LUJAC BUSINESS COLLEGE
5716 U.S. Hwy. 64, Farmington 87401-1414 *Type:* Private business *Accred.:* 1988/1991 (ACISC) *Calendar:* Courses of varying lengths *Degrees:* certificates, diplomas *CEO:* Dir. Lucy C. Jacquez
(505) 326-6153

METROPOLITAN COLLEGE OF COURT REPORTING
2201 San Pedro St., N.E., Bldg. 1, No. 1300, Albuquerque 87110 *Type:* Private *Accred.:* 1993 (ACCSCT) *Calendar:* Courses of varying lengths *Degrees:* certificates *CEO:* Dir. Bob Evans
(505) 888-3400

UNITED TRAINING INSTITUTE, INC.
2620 San Mateo Blvd., N.E., Ste. C, Albuquerque 87710 *Type:* Private home study *Accred.:* 1989 (NHSC) *Calendar:* Courses of varying lengths *Degrees:* certificates *CEO:* Pres. Lee Schwuchow
(505) 881-2840

NEW YORK

ACADEMY FOR CAREER EDUCATION
55-05 Myrtle Ave., Ridgewood 11385 *Type:* Private business *Accred.:* 1990 (ACISC) *Calendar:* Courses of varying lengths *Degrees:* certificates, diplomas *CEO:* Pres. Chana Schachner
(718) 497-4900

ADVANCED SOFTWARE ANALYSIS
2nd Fl., 151 Lawrence St., Brooklyn 11201 *Type:* Private business *Accred.:* 1991 (ACISC) *Calendar:* Courses of varying lengths *Degrees:* certificates, diplomas *CEO:* Dir. Alex Schegol
(718) 522-9073

ADVANCED SOFTWARE ANALYSIS
Ste. 700, 5 Beekman St., New York 10038 *Type:* Private business *Accred.:* 1987/1991 (ACISC) *Calendar:* Courses of varying lengths *Degrees:* certificates, diplomas *CEO:* Dir. Leon Rabinovich
(212) 349-9768

THE ALVIN AILEY AMERICAN DANCE CENTER
211 W. 61st St., 3rd Fl., New York 10023 *Type:* Private *Calendar:* Courses of varying lengths *Degrees:* certificates *Prof. Accred.:* Dance *CEO:* Dance Exec. Denise Jefferson
(212) 767-0940

AMERICAN BALLET CENTER/JOFFREY BALLEY SCHOOL
434 Ave. of the Americas, New York 10011 *Type:* Private *Calendar:* Courses of varying lengths *Degrees:* certificates *Prof. Accred.:* Dance *CEO:* Exec. Dir. Edith D'Addario
(212) 254-8520

AMERICAN BARTENDERS SCHOOL
105A Madison Ave., New York 10016-7418 *Type:* Private *Accred.:* 1988 (ACCSCT) *Calendar:* Courses of varying lengths *Degrees:* certificates *CEO:* Dir. Mark Salis
(212) 532-4200

AMERICAN BUSINESS INSTITUTE
1657 Broadway, New York 10019 *Type:* Private business *Accred.:* 1978/1989 (ACISC) *Calendar:* Sem. plan *Degrees:* certificates, diplomas *CEO:* Dir. Gary Cottone
(212) 582-9040

THE AMERICAN MUSICAL AND DRAMATIC ACADEMY
2109 Broadway, New York 10023 *Type:* Private *Calendar:* Courses of varying lengths *Degrees:* certificates *Prof. Accred.:* Theatre *CEO:* Exec. Dir. Jan Martin
(212) 787-5300

APEX TECHNICAL SCHOOL
635 Ave. of the Americas, New York 10011 *Type:* Private *Accred.:* 1968/1989 (ACCSCT) *Calendar:* Courses of varying lengths *Degrees:* certificates *CEO:* Pres. Bill Cann
(212) 645-3300

BERK TRADE AND BUSINESS SCHOOL
311 W. 35th St., New York 10001-1725 *Type:* Private *Accred.:* 1973/1988 (ACCSCT) *Calendar:* Courses of varying lengths *Degrees:* certificates *CEO:* Dir. Irving Berk
(212) 629-3736

BLAKE BUSINESS SCHOOL
P.O. Box 1052, 20 Cooper Sq., New York 10276 *Type:* Private business *Accred.:* 1974/1986 (ACISC) *Calendar:* Courses of varying lengths *Degrees:* certificates, diplomas *CEO:* Pres. Barbara Marion
(212) 254-1233

BUSINESS INFORMATICS CENTER
134 S. Central Ave., Valley Stream 11580-5431 *Type:* Private *Accred.:* 1991 (ACCSCT) *Calendar:* Courses of varying lengths *Degrees:* certificates *CEO:* Dir. Joseph Brown
(516) 561-0050

CAREER INSTITUTE
500 Eighth Ave., 2nd Fl., New York 10018 *Type:* Private *Accred.:* 1991/1993 (ACCSCT) *Calendar:* Courses of varying lengths *Degrees:* certificates *CEO:* Pres. Harry Lokos
(212) 564-0589

CASHIER TRAINING INSTITUTE
500 Eighth Ave., New York 10018-6504 *Type:* Private *Accred.:* 1985 (ACCSCT) *Calendar:* Courses of varying lengths *Degrees:* certificates *CEO:* Pres. Harry Lokos
(212) 564-0500

CHARLES STUART SCHOOL OF DIAMOND SETTING
1420 Kings Hwy., Brooklyn 11229 *Type:* Private *Accred.:* 1993 (ACCSCT) *Calendar:* Courses of varying lengths *Degrees:* certificates *CEO:* Dir. Charles Wechsler
(718) 339-2640

CHAUFFEURS TRAINING SCHOOL
12 Railroad Ave., Albany 12205-5727 *Type:* Private *Accred.:* 1980/1990 (ACCSCT) *Calendar:* Courses of varying lengths *Degrees:* certificates *CEO:* Dir. Albert V. Hanley
(518) 482-8601

CHERYL FELL'S SCHOOL OF BUSINESS
2541 Military Rd., Niagara Falls 14304 *Type:* Private business *Accred.:* 1981/1990 (ACISC) *Calendar:* Courses of varying lengths *Degrees:* certificates, diplomas *CEO:* Dir. Cheryl Anne Fell
(716) 297-2750

CIRCLE IN THE SQUARE THEATRE SCHOOL
1633 Broadway, New York 10019 *Type:* Private *Calendar:* Courses of varying lengths *Degrees:* certificates *Prof. Accred.:* Theatre *CEO:* Exec. Dir. E. Colin O'Leary
(212) 307-3732

COMMERCIAL DRIVER TRAINING
600 Patton Ave., West Babylon 11704-1421 *Type:* Private *Accred.:* 1984/1989 (ACCSCT) *Calendar:* Courses of varying lengths *Degrees:* certificates *CEO:* Pres. John B. Rayne
(516) 249-1330

COMPUTER CAREER CENTER
474 Fulton Ave., Hempstead 11550 *Type:* Private *Accred.:* 1993 (ACISC) *Calendar:* Courses of varying lengths *Degrees:* certificates, diplomas *CEO:* Pres. Kenneth G. Barrett
(516) 486-2526

CONTINENTAL DENTAL ASSISTANT SCHOOL
633 Jefferson Rd., Rochester 14623 *Type:* Private *Accred.:* 1983/1990 (ABHES) *Calendar:* Courses of varying lengths *Degrees:* certificates *CEO:* Pres. Arthur J. Resso
(716) 272-8060

COPE INSTITUTE
84 Williams St., New York 10038 *Type:* Private business *Accred.:* 1981/1987 (ACISC)

Calendar: Qtr. plan *Degrees:* certificates, diplomas *CEO:* Dir. Yerachmiel Barash
(718) 436-1700

DANCE THEATRE OF HARLEM, INC.
466 W. 152nd St., New York 10031 *Type:* Private *Calendar:* Courses of varying lengths *Degrees:* certificates *Prof. Accred.:* Dance *CEO:* Dir. Walter R. Raines
(212) 690-2800

DRAKE BUSINESS SCHOOL
2488 Grand Concourse, Bronx 10458 *Type:* Private business *Accred.:* 1974/1986 (ACISC) *Calendar:* Courses of varying lengths *Degrees:* certificates, diplomas *CEO:* Dir. Hugh Brooms
(212) 295-6200

DRAKE BUSINESS SCHOOL
6th Fl., 36-09 Main St., Flushing 11354 *Type:* Private business *Accred.:* 1974/1986 (ACISC) *Calendar:* Courses of varying lengths *Degrees:* certificates, diplomas *CEO:* Dir. Cheryl R. Caro
(718) 353-3535

DRAKE BUSINESS SCHOOL
225 Broadway, New York 10007 *Type:* Private business *Accred.:* 1974/1986 (ACISC) *Calendar:* Courses of varying lengths *Degrees:* certificates, diplomas *CEO:* Dir. Phyllis Haimson
(212) 349-7900

DRAKE BUSINESS SCHOOL
25 Victory Blvd., Staten Island 10301 *Type:* Private business *Accred.:* 1974/1986 (ACISC) *Calendar:* Courses of varying lengths *Degrees:* certificates, diplomas *CEO:* Dir. Richard De Crescenzo
(718) 447-1515

ELMIRA BUSINESS INSTITUTE
180 Clemens Center Pkwy., Elmira 14901 *Type:* Private business *Accred.:* 1969/1986 (ACISC) *Calendar:* Sem. plan *Degrees:* certificates, diplomas *CEO:* Pres. Brad C. Phillips
(607) 733-7177

FEGS TRADES AND BUSINESS SCHOOL
17 Battery Pl., Ste. 6 N., New York 10004 *Type:* Private *Accred.:* 1986 (ACCSCT) *Calendar:* Courses of varying lengths *Degrees:*

certificates *CEO:* Vice Pres. Virginia Cruickshank

(212) 440-8130

BRANCH CAMPUS
199 Jay St., Brooklyn 11201 *Accred.:* 1986 (ACCSCT) *CEO:* Dir. James Leggio

(718) 448-0120

FOLK ART INSTITUTE OF THE MUSEUM OF AMERICAN FOLK ART
61 W. 62nd St., New York 10023-7015 *Type:* Private *Calendar:* 2-year program *Degrees:* certificates *Prof. Accred.:* Art (associate) *CEO:* Dir. Barbara Kaufman-Cate

(212) 977-7170

FRENCH CULINARY INSTITUTE
462 Broadway, New York 10013 *Type:* Private *Accred.:* 1985/1990 (ACCSCT) *Calendar:* Courses of varying lengths *Degrees:* certificates *CEO:* Pres. Dorothy Cann Hamilton

(212) 219-8890

GLOBAL BUSINESS INSTITUTE
1931 Mott Ave., Far Rockaway 11691 *Type:* Private business *Accred.:* 1984/1988 (ACISC) *Calendar:* Courses of varying lengths *Degrees:* certificates, diplomas *CEO:* Dir. Sandy Basso

(718) 327-2220

BRANCH CAMPUS
33 Journal Sq., Jersey City, NJ 07306 *Accred.:* 1993 (ACISC) *CEO:* Dir. George P. Blount

(201) 420-7900

BRANCH CAMPUS
209 W. 125th St., New York 10027 *Accred.:* 1990 (ACISC) *CEO:* Dir. Ethel C. Jones

(212) 663-1500

HUNTER BUSINESS SCHOOL
3601 Hempstead Tpke., Levittown 11756 *Type:* Private business *Accred.:* 1982/1986 (ACISC) *Calendar:* Courses of varying lengths *Degrees:* certificates, diplomas *CEO:* Pres. Florence Kruman

(516) 935-7420

INSTITUTE OF ALLIED MEDICAL PROFESSIONS
No. 23D, 106 Central Park S., New York 10019 *Type:* Private *Calendar:* Courses of varying lengths *Degrees:* certificates *Prof. Accred.:* Nuclear Medicine Technology *CEO:* Pres. Eugene Vinciguerra

(212) 757-0520

INSTITUTE OF AUDIO RESEARCH
64 University Pl., New York 10003-4595 *Type:* Private *Accred.:* 1985/1990 (ACCSCT) *Calendar:* Courses of varying lengths *Degrees:* certificates *CEO:* Dir. Miriam Friedman

(212) 677-7580

ISABELLA G. HART SCHOOL OF PRACTICAL NURSING
1425 Portland Ave., Rochester 14621 *Type:* Private professional *Calendar:* Courses of varying lengths *Degrees:* certificates *Prof. Accred.:* Practical Nursing *CEO:* Dir. Judith Sawyer

(716) 338-4784

ISLAND DRAFTING & TECHNICAL INSTITUTE
128 Broadway, Amityville 11701-2789 *Type:* Private *Accred.:* 1967/1987 (ACCSCT) *Calendar:* Courses of varying lengths *Degrees:* diplomas *CEO:* Pres. Joseph P. DiLiberto

(516) 691-8733

KRISSLER BUSINESS INSTITUTE
166 Mansion Sq. Park, Poughkeepsie 12601 *Type:* Private business *Accred.:* 1975/1990 (ACISC) *Calendar:* Courses of varying lengths *Degrees:* certificates, diplomas *CEO:* Dir. Edgar H. Krissler

(914) 471-0330

LABAN/BARTENIEFF INSTITUTE OF MOVEMENT STUDIES, INC.
11 E. 4th St., New York 10003-6902 *Type:* Private *Calendar:* Courses of varying lengths *Degrees:* certificates *Prof. Accred.:* Dance *CEO:* Exec. Dir. Martha Eddy

(212) 477-4299

LEWIS A. WILSON TECHNICAL CENTER
17 Westminster Ave., Dix Hills 11746 *Type:* Private *Calendar:* Courses of varying lengths *Degrees:* certificates *Prof. Accred.:*

Practical Nursing *CEO:* Coord. Margaret A. Shields

(516) 667-6000

LONG ISLAND BUSINESS INSTITUTE
6500 Jericho Tpke., Commack 11725 *Type:* Private business *Accred.:* 1978/1990 (ACISC) *Calendar:* Qtr. plan *Degrees:* certificates, diplomas *CEO:* Dir. Genevieve Baron

(516) 499-7100

MANDL SCHOOL
254 W. 54th St., New York 10019-5516 *Type:* Private *Accred.:* 1987 (ABHES); 1987 (ACCSCT) *Calendar:* Courses of varying lengths *Degrees:* certificates, diplomas *CEO:* Pres. Melvyn P. Weiner

(212) 247-3434

MARION S. WHELAN SCHOOL OF PRACTICAL NURSING
196-198 North St., Geneva 14456 *Type:* Private professional *Calendar:* Courses of varying lengths *Degrees:* certificates *Prof. Accred.:* Practical Nursing *CEO:* Dir. Ann McGuane

(315) 789-4222

MARTHA GRAHAM SCHOOL OF CONTEMPORARY DANCE, INC.
316 E. 63rd St., New York 10021 *Type:* Private *Calendar:* Courses of varying lengths *Degrees:* certificates *Prof. Accred.:* Dance *CEO:* Dir. Diane Gray

(212) 838-5886

MERCE CUNNINGHAM STUDIO
55 Bethune St., New York 10014 *Type:* Private *Calendar:* Courses of varying lengths *Degrees:* certificates *Prof. Accred.:* Dance *CEO:* Artistic Dir. Merce Cunningham

(212) 255-3130

MILDRED ELLEY BUSINESS SCHOOL
2 Computer Dr. S., Albany 12205 *Type:* Private business *Accred.:* 1982/1988 (ACISC) *Calendar:* Sem. plan *Degrees:* certificates, diplomas *CEO:* Pres. Faith Ann Takes

(518) 446-0595

BRANCH CAMPUS
400 Columbus Ave., Pittsfield, MA 01201 *Accred.:* 1993 (ACISC) *CEO:* Dir. Joe Moltzen

(413) 499-8618

MODERN WELDING SCHOOL
1740 Broadway, Schenectady 12306-4998 *Type:* Private *Accred.:* 1984/1989 (ACCSCT) *Calendar:* Courses of varying lengths *Degrees:* certificates *CEO:* Dir. Dana J. Gillenwalters

(518) 374-1216

MUNSON-WILLIAMS-PROCTOR INSTITUTE
310 Genesee St., Utica 13502 *Type:* Private *Calendar:* 2-year program *Degrees:* diplomas *Prof. Accred.:* Art *CEO:* Dir. Clyde E. McCulley

(315) 797-8260

NATIONAL SHAKESPEARE CONSERVATORY
591 Broadway, New York 10012 *Type:* Private *Calendar:* Courses of varying lengths *Degrees:* certificates *Prof. Accred.:* Theatre *CEO:* Dir. Albert Schoemann

(212) 219-9874

NATIONAL TAX TRAINING SCHOOL
4 Melnick Dr., P.O. Box 382, Monsey 10952 *Type:* Private home study *Accred.:* 1965/1991 (NHSC) *Calendar:* Courses of varying lengths *Degrees:* certificates *CEO:* Dir. Ben D. Eisenberg

(914) 352-3634

NATIONAL TRACTOR TRAILER SCHOOL
P.O. Box 208, Liverpool 13088-0208 *Type:* Private *Accred.:* 1984/1989 (ACCSCT) *Calendar:* Courses of varying lengths *Degrees:* certificates *CEO:* Pres. Harry Kowalchyk, Jr.

(315) 451-2430

BRANCH CAMPUS
175 Katherine St., Buffalo 14210-2007 *Accred.:* 1991 (ACCSCT) *CEO:* Dir. Judith A. O'Brocta

(716) 849-6887

NEW SCHOOL OF CONTEMPORARY RADIO
50 Colvin Ave., Albany 12206-1106 *Type:* Private *Accred.:* 1981/1993 (ACCSCT) *Calendar:* Courses of varying lengths *Degrees:* certificates *CEO:* Dir. Thomas Brownlie, III

(518) 438-7682

NEW YORK FOOD & HOTEL MANAGEMENT SCHOOL
154 W. 14th St., New York 10011-7307 *Type:* Private *Accred.:* 1973/1989 (ACC-

SCT) *Calendar:* Sem. plan *Degrees:* certificates *CEO:* Dir. Joseph S. Monaco
(212) 675-6655

NEW YORK INSTITUTE OF BUSINESS AND TECHNOLOGY
2nd Fl., 401 Park Ave. S., New York 10016 *Type:* Private business *Accred.:* 1974/1991 (ACISC) *Calendar:* Courses of varying lengths *Degrees:* certificates, diplomas *CEO:* Dir. Leith E. Yetman
(212) 725-9400

NEW YORK SCHOOL FOR MEDICAL/DENTAL ASSISTANTS
116-16 Queens Blvd., Forest Hills 11375-2330 *Type:* Private *Accred.:* 1973/1988 (ACCSCT) *Calendar:* Courses of varying lengths *Degrees:* certificates, diplomas *CEO:* Pres. Clinton Arnaboldi
(718) 793-2330

NEW YORK SCHOOL OF DOG GROOMING
248 E. 34th St., New York 10016-4873 *Type:* Private *Accred.:* 1973/1989 (ACCSCT) *Calendar:* Courses of varying lengths *Degrees:* certificates *CEO:* Dir. Sam Kohl
(212) 685-3776

BRANCH CAMPUS
265-17 Union Tpke., New Hyde Park 11040-1425 *Accred.:* 1992 (ACCSCT) *CEO:* Dir. Cynthia Kohl
(718) 343-3130

NIKOLAIS AND LOUIS DANCE LAB
375 W. Broadway, 5th Fl., New York 10012 *Type:* Private *Calendar:* Courses of varying lengths *Degrees:* certificates *Prof. Accred.:* Dance *CEO:* Dir. Lynn Lesniak Needle
(212) 226-7000

NORTHEAST INSTITUTE
2643 Main St., Buffalo 14214-2015 *Type:* Private *Accred.:* 1991 (ACCSCT) *Calendar:* Courses of varying lengths *Degrees:* certificates *CEO:* Dir. James Sterphie
(716) 838-6984

PACE BUSINESS SCHOOL
210 E. 188th St., Bronx 10458 *Type:* Private business *Accred.:* 1988 (ACISC) *Calendar:* Courses of varying lengths *Degrees:* certificates, diplomas *CEO:* Dir. Neil Brenner
(718) 933-7400

PACE BUSINESS SCHOOL
164 Ashburton Ave., Yonkers 10701 *Type:* Private business *Accred.:* 1980/1989 (ACISC) *Calendar:* Courses of varying lengths *Degrees:* certificates, diplomas *CEO:* Pres./Dir. Richard J. Pfundstein
(914) 963-7945

PRACTICAL BIBLE TRAINING SCHOOL
400 Riverside Dr., Johnson City 13790 *Type:* Independent (Baptist) *Accred.:* 1985/1990 (AABC) *Calendar:* Sem. plan *Degrees:* certificates, diplomas *CEO:* Pres. Dale Linebaugh
FTE Enroll: 137   (607) 729-1581

PRINTING TRADES SCHOOL LTD.
233 Park Ave. S., New York 10003-1690 *Type:* Private *Accred.:* 1975/1993 (ACCSCT) *Calendar:* Courses of varying lengths *Degrees:* certificates *CEO:* Pres. Elizabeth G. Jenkins
(212) 677-0505

PROFESSIONAL BUSINESS INSTITUTE
125 Canal St., New York 10002 *Type:* Private business *Accred.:* 1985/1989 (ACISC) *Calendar:* Courses of varying lengths *Degrees:* certificates, diplomas *CEO:* Dir. Elayne S. Zinbarg
(212) 226-7300

RIDLEY-LOWELL BUSINESS AND TECHNICAL INSTITUTE
116 Front St., Binghamton 13905 *Type:* Private business *Accred.:* 1977/1987 (ACISC) *Calendar:* Courses of varying lengths *Degrees:* certificates, diplomas *CEO:* Dir. Carol Zindle
(607) 724-2941

ROYAL BARBER & BEAUTY SCHOOL
108-112 Broadway, Schenectady 12305-2592 *Type:* Private *Accred.:* 1987 (ACCSCT) *Calendar:* Courses of varying lengths *Degrees:* certificates *CEO:* Dir. Sondra Kaczmarek
(518) 346-2288

ST. FRANCIS SCHOOL OF PRACTICAL NURSING
2221 W. State St., Olean 14760 *Type:* Private professional *Calendar:* Courses of varying lengths *Degrees:* certificates *Prof. Accred.:*

Practical Nursing *CEO:* Dir. Redempta Grawunder

(716) 375-7316

SCS BUSINESS AND TECHNICAL INSTITUTE
2467 Jerome Ave., Bronx 10468 *Type:* Private business *Accred.:* 1986/1989 (ACISC) *Calendar:* Courses of varying lengths *Degrees:* certificates, diplomas *CEO:* Dir. Michael Tolarico

(212) 733-5200

SCS BUSINESS AND TECHNICAL INSTITUTE
884 Flatbush Ave., Brooklyn 11226 *Type:* Private business *Accred.:* 1987 (ACISC) *Calendar:* Courses of varying lengths *Degrees:* certificates, diplomas *CEO:* Dir. Marvin Smith

(718) 856-6100

SCS BUSINESS AND TECHNICAL INSTITUTE
394 Bridge St., Brooklyn 11201 *Type:* Private business *Accred.:* 1987/1989 (ACISC) *Calendar:* Courses of varying lengths *Degrees:* certificates, diplomas *CEO:* Dir. Lydia Gonzales

(718) 802-9500

SCS BUSINESS AND TECHNICAL INSTITUTE
163-02 Jamaica Ave., Jamaica 11432 *Type:* Private business *Accred.:* 1986/1989 (ACISC) *Calendar:* Courses of varying lengths *Degrees:* certificates, diplomas *CEO:* Dir. Sylvester Lewis

(718) 658-8855

SCS BUSINESS AND TECHNICAL INSTITUTE
25 W. 17th St., New York 10022 *Type:* Private business *Accred.:* 1984/1988 (ACISC) *Calendar:* Courses of varying lengths *Degrees:* certificates, diplomas *CEO:* Dir. Kenneth Herskovits

(212) 366-1666

SIMMONS SCHOOL
190 E. Post Rd., White Plains 10601 *Type:* Private business *Accred.:* 1983/1988 (ACISC) *Calendar:* Courses of varying lengths *Degrees:* certificates, diplomas *CEO:* Dir. Muriel Adler

(914) 761-2701

THE SONIA MOORE STUDIO OF THE THEATRE
485 Park Ave., No. 6A, New York 10022 *Type:* Private *Calendar:* Courses of varying lengths *Degrees:* certificates *Prof. Accred.:* Theatre (associate) *CEO:* Pres. Sonia Moore

(212) 755-5120

SOTHEBY'S EDUCATIONAL STUDIES
1334 York Ave., New York 10021 *Type:* Private *Calendar:* Courses of varying lengths *Degrees:* certificates *Prof. Accred.:* Art *CEO:* Vice Pres./Acting Dir. Elisabeth D. Garrett

(212) 606-7822

SPANISH-AMERICAN INSTITUTE
215 W. 43rd St., New York 10036 *Type:* Private business *Accred.:* 1986/1989 (ACISC) *Calendar:* Courses of varying lengths *Degrees:* certificates, diplomas *CEO:* Pres. Frank J. Ferraro

(212) 840-7111

SPENCER BUSINESS AND TECHNICAL INSTITUTE
200 State St., Schenectady 12305 *Type:* Private business *Accred.:* 1981/1987 (ACISC) *Calendar:* Courses of varying lengths *Degrees:* certificates, diplomas *CEO:* Dir. Stephen Rall

(518) 374-7619

STENOTOPIA, THE WORLD OF COURT REPORTING
45 S. Service Rd., Plainview 11803 *Type:* Private business *Accred.:* 1990 (ACISC) *Calendar:* Courses of varying lengths *Degrees:* certificates, diplomas *CEO:* Pres. Randy Scheff Gordon

(516) 777-1117

SUBURBAN TECHNICAL SCHOOL
175 Fulton Ave., Hempstead 11550-3771 *Type:* Private *Accred.:* 1972/1987 (ACCSCT) *Calendar:* Courses of varying lengths *Degrees:* diplomas *CEO:* Pres. Randy S. Proto

(516) 481-6660

BRANCH CAMPUS
2650 Sunrise Hwy., East Islip 11730-1017 *Accred.:* 1987 (ACCSCT) *Calendar:* Courses of varying lengths *Degrees:* diplomas *CEO:* Dir. Jay Fund

(516) 224-5001

SUPERIOR CAREER INSTITUTE
116 W. 14th St., New York 10011-7395 *Type:* Private *Accred.:* 1983/1988 (ACCSCT) *Calendar:* Courses of varying lengths

Degrees: certificates *CEO:* Dir. Carolyn Moffett

(212) 675-2140

THE SWEDISH INSTITUTE
226 W. 26th St., 5th Fl., New York 10001-6700 *Type:* Private *Accred.:* 1981/1986 (ACCSCT) *Calendar:* Sem. plan *Degrees:* diplomas *CEO:* Pres. Patricia J. Eckardt

(212) 924-5900

SYRIT COMPUTER SCHOOL SYSTEMS
1760 53rd St., Brooklyn 11204-9004 *Type:* Private *Accred.:* 1981/1986 (ACCSCT) *Calendar:* Courses of varying lengths *Degrees:* diplomas *CEO:* Dir. Elliot Amsel

(718) 853-1212

TECHNO-DENT TRAINING CENTER
101 W. 31st St., 4th Fl., New York 10001-3507 *Type:* Private *Accred.:* 1983/1988 (ACCSCT) *Calendar:* Tri. plan *Degrees:* certificates *CEO:* Pres. George A. Nossa

(212) 695-1818

TRAVEL INSTITUTE
15 Park Row, No. 617, New York 10038-2301 *Type:* Private *Accred.:* 1991 (ACCSCT) *Calendar:* Courses of varying lengths *Degrees:* certificates *CEO:* Owner/Dir. Robert Berger

(212) 349-3331

TRI-STATE INSTITUTE OF TRADITIONAL CHINESE ACUPUNCTURE
Box 890, Planetarium Sta., New York 10024-0890 *Type:* Private professional *Calendar:* Sem. plan *Degrees:* diplomas *Prof. Accred.:* Acupuncture *CEO:* Pres. Mark Seem
FTE Enroll: 95   (212) 496-7869

ULTRASOUND DIAGNOSTIC SCHOOL
121 W. 27th St., Ste. 504, New York 10001 *Type:* Private *Accred.:* 1984/1990 (ABHES) *Calendar:* Courses of varying lengths *Degrees:* certificates *CEO:* Exec. Dir. William Spier, Ph.D.

(212) 645-9116

BRANCH CAMPUS
1099 Southside Blvd., Ste. 106, Jacksonville, FL 32256 *Accred.:* 1993 (ABHES) *CEO:* Admin. Richard Vallone

(904) 363-6221

BRANCH CAMPUS
2760 E. Atlantic Blvd., Pompano Beach, FL 33062 *Accred.:* 1989 (ABHES) *CEO:* Admin. Irwin Kroll

(305) 942-6551

BRANCH CAMPUS
5804 E. Breckenridge Pkwy., Tampa, FL 33610 *Accred.:* 1989 (ABHES) *CEO:* Admin. M. Lorraine Gittings

(813) 621-0072

BRANCH CAMPUS
13 Corp. Sq. Office Park, Ste. 140, Atlanta, GA 30329 *Accred.:* 1990 (ABHES) *CEO:* Admin. Roger N. Phillips, III

(404) 248-9070

BRANCH CAMPUS
1320 Fenwick La., Silver Spring, MD 20910 *Accred.:* 1987 (ABHES) *CEO:* Admin. Marilyn Lavender

(301) 588-0786

BRANCH CAMPUS
33 Boston Post Rd. W., Ste. 140, Marlborough, MA 01752 *Accred.:* 1988 (ABHES) *CEO:* Admin. Jim Scheffler

(508) 485-1213

BRANCH CAMPUS
Plaza One at Gill La., Ste. 6B, 675 Rte. 1, Iselin, NJ 08830 *Accred.:* 1985/1987 (ABHES) *CEO:* Admin. Estelle Wilchins

(908) 634-1131

BRANCH CAMPUS
One Old Country Rd., Carle Place 11514 *Accred.:* 1985/1987 (ABHES) *CEO:* Admin. Ria Salice-Iannittei

(516) 248-6060

BRANCH CAMPUS
2269 Saw Mill River Rd., Elmsford 10523 *Accred.:* 1985/1987 (ABHES) *CEO:* Admin. Wayne Engel

(914) 347-6817

BRANCH CAMPUS
3511 Cottman Ave., Philadelphia, PA 19149 *Accred.:* 1986/1992 (ABHES) *CEO:* Admin. Maura Gilligan-Gardy

(215) 624-8245

BRANCH CAMPUS
5830 Ellsworth Ave., Ste. 201, Pittsburgh, PA 15232 *Accred.:* 1993 (ABHES) *CEO:* Admin. Jane Takielo

(412) 362-9404

BRANCH CAMPUS
6575 W. Loop S., Ste. 200, Bellaire, TX 77401 *Accred.:* 1992 (ABHES) *CEO:* Admin. Catherine Doughty
(713) 664-9632

BRANCH CAMPUS
102 Decker Ct., Ste. 205, Irving, TX 75062 *Accred.:* 1993 (ABHES) *CEO:* Admin. Pam Castleman
(214) 791-1120

UNIVERSAL BUSINESS AND MEDIA SCHOOL
220 E. 106th St., New York 10029 *Type:* Private business *Accred.:* 1991 (ACISC) *Calendar:* Courses of varying lengths *De-grees:* certificates, diplomas *CEO:* Pres. Georgina Falu
(212) 360-1210

UPSTATE CAREER INSTITUTE
913 Culver Rd., Rochester 14609-7141 *Type:* Private *Accred.:* 1992 (ACCSCT) *Calendar:* Courses of varying lengths *Degrees:* certificates *CEO:* Dir. John L. Gillard
(716) 482-1280

WESTCHESTER CONSERVATORY OF MUSIC
20 Soundview Ave., White Plains 10606 *Type:* Private *Calendar:* Courses of varying lengths *Degrees:* certificates *Prof. Accred.:* Music *CEO:* Exec. Dir. Laura Calzolari
(914) 761-3715

NORTH CAROLINA

ACADEMY OF ARTISTIC HAIR DESIGN
314 Tenth St., North Wilkesboro 28659
Type: Private *Accred.:* 1987/1992 (SACS-COEI) *Calendar:* Courses of varying lengths *Degrees:* certificates *CEO:* Dir. Hazel T. Mayes
FTE Enroll: 57   (919) 838-4571

ADVANCE INSTITUTE
1330-B Patton Ave., Asheville 28806 *Type:* Private *Accred.:* 1990/1991 (SACS-COEI) *Calendar:* Courses of varying lengths *Degrees:* certificates *CEO:* Dir. Linda Parker
FTE Enroll: 62   (704) 251-1713

BRANCH CAMPUS
1005 Buncombe Rd., Greenville, SC 29609 *CEO:* Dir. Jo Drucker
(803) 233-5647

ALLIANCE TRACTOR TRAILER TRAINING CENTER
P.O. Box 883, Arden 28704-0883 *Type:* Private *Accred.:* 1986 (ACCSCT) *Calendar:* Courses of varying lengths *Degrees:* certificates *CEO:* Vice Pres. Brenda Rice
(704) 684-4454

BRANCH CAMPUS
P.O. Box 950, Lebanon, TN 37088-0950 *Accred.:* 1986 (ACCSCT) *CEO:* Asst. Dir. Jeff Carlton
(615) 449-6363

AMERICAN BUSINESS AND FASHION INSTITUTE
Ste. 600, 1515 Mockingbird La., Charlotte 28209-3236 *Type:* Private business *Accred.:* 1978/1987 (ACISC) *Calendar:* Courses of varying lengths *Degrees:* certificates, diplomas *CEO:* Dir. Elizabeth M. Hummel
(704) 523-3738

ARNOLD'S BEAUTY COLLEGE
3117 Shannon Rd., Durham 27707 *Type:* Private *Accred.:* 1989/1991 (SACS-COEI) *Calendar:* Courses of varying lengths *Degrees:* diplomas *CEO:* Dir. Arnold Braun
FTE Enroll: 231   (919) 493-9557

BLACK WORLD COLLEGE OF HAIR DESIGN
P.O. Box 669403, Charlotte 28266-9403 *Type:* Private *Accred.:* 1986 (ACCSCT) *Cal-*endar: Courses of varying lengths *Degrees:* diplomas *CEO:* Vice Pres./Dir. Luther Gore
(704) 372-8172

BRADFORD SCHOOL
335 Lamar Ave., Charlotte 28204 *Type:* Private *Calendar:* Courses of varying lengths *Degrees:* certificates *Prof. Accred.:* Medical Assisting (AMA) *CEO:* Pres. Gary L. Pritchett
(704) 372-4304

BROOKSTONE COLLEGE OF BUSINESS
Ste. 240, 8307 University Executive Park Dr., Charlotte 28213 *Type:* Private business *Accred.:* 1984/1990 (ACISC); 1992 (SACS-COEI candidate) *Calendar:* Qtr. plan *Degrees:* certificates, diplomas *CEO:* Dir. Jack Henderson, III
FTE Enroll: 192   (704) 547-8600

BRANCH CAMPUS
Airport W., 7815 National Service Rd., Greensboro 27409 *Accred.:* 1988/1990 (ACISC) *CEO:* Dir. Michael Thompson
(919) 668-2627

BURKE ACADEMY OF COSMETIC ART
304 W. Union St., Morganton 28655 *Type:* Private *Accred.:* 1991 (SACS-COEI) *Calendar:* Courses of varying lengths *Degrees:* certificates, diplomas *CEO:* Dir. Emily Lowe
FTE Enroll: 37   (704) 437-1028

BRANCH CAMPUS
609 W. 29th St., Newton 28658 *CEO:* Dir. Emily Lowe
(704) 465-7281

CAROLINA BEAUTY COLLEGE
801 English Rd., High Point 27262 *Type:* Private *Accred.:* 1984/1989 (SACS-COEI) *Calendar:* Courses of varying lengths *Degrees:* certificates *CEO:* Dir. Marion Fields
FTE Enroll: 1,371   (919) 886-4712

BRANCH CAMPUS
240-246 E. Front St., Burlington 27215 *CEO:* Dir. Amaka Uchebo
(919) 227-7658

BRANCH CAMPUS
5430-0 N. Tryon St., Charlotte 28213
CEO: Dir. Billie Kelley
(704) 597-5641

BRANCH CAMPUS
5100 N. Roxboro Rd., Durham 22704
CEO: Dir. Sybil Caulder
(919) 477-4014

BRANCH CAMPUS
1483-B E. Franklin Blvd., Gastonia 28053
CEO: Dir. Margaret Freeman
(704) 864-8723

BRANCH CAMPUS
2001 E. Wendover Ave., Greensboro
27405 *CEO:* Dir. Celia Chambers
(919) 272-2966

BRANCH CAMPUS
930 Floyd St., Kannapolis 28081 *CEO:*
Dir. Viola Childers
(704) 932-5651

BRANCH CAMPUS
338 N. Main St., Kernersville 27284
CEO: Dir. Lorraine Stevens
(919) 993-6050

BRANCH CAMPUS
810 E. Winston Rd., Lexington 27292
CEO: Dir. Susan Lowe
(704) 249-1518

BRANCH CAMPUS
1201 Stafford St., Ste. 12, Monroe 28110
CEO: Dir. Nancy Reinders
(704) 283-2514

BRANCH CAMPUS
501 S. South St., Mount Airy 27030 *CEO:*
Dir. Blanche Murphy
(919) 786-2791

BRANCH CAMPUS
1902 S. Main St., Salisbury 28144 *CEO:*
Dir. Dale Bare
(704) 637-7045

BRANCH CAMPUS
231 N. Lafayette St., Shelby 28150 *CEO:*
Dir. Myrtice Myers
(704) 487-0557

BRANCH CAMPUS
123 Berry St., Statesville 28677 *CEO:*
Dir. Treva Lail
(704) 872-6662

BRANCH CAMPUS
1253-24 Corporation Pkwy., Winston-
Salem 27127 *CEO:* Dir. Libby Martin
(919) 723-9510

FAYETTEVILLE BEAUTY COLLEGE
2018 Ft. Bragg Rd., Fayetteville 28303
Type: Private *Accred.:* 1989/1993 (SACS-
COEI) *Calendar:* Courses of varying lengths
Degrees: diplomas *CEO:* Dir. Bonnie Henry
FTE Enroll: 124   (919) 484-7191

HAIRSTYLING INSTITUTE OF CHARLOTTE
209-B S. Kings Dr., Charlotte 28204-2621
Type: Private *Accred.:* 1983/1988 (ACC-
SCT) *Calendar:* Courses of varying lengths
Degrees: diplomas *CEO:* Owner/Pres.
Costas Melissaris
(704) 334-5511

KING'S COLLEGE
322 Lamar Ave., Charlotte 28204 *Type:* Private business *Accred.:* 1954/1986 (ACISC)
Calendar: Qtr. plan *Degrees:* certificates,
diplomas *Prof. Accred.:* Medical Assisting
(AMA) *CEO:* Pres. C. Edward Arrington, Jr.
(704) 372-0266

LYNDON B. JOHNSON CIVILIAN CONSERVATION
CENTER
466 Job Corps Dr., Franklin 29734 *Type:*
Public (state) *Accred.:* 1991 (SACS-COEI)
Calendar: Courses of varying lengths
Degrees: certificates *CEO:* Dir. Edward
Washington
FTE Enroll: 234   (704) 524-4446

MARIA PARHAM HOSPITAL, INC.
Ruin Creek Rd. at I-85, P.O. Drawer 59,
Henderson 27536 *Type:* Private *Calendar:*
Courses of varying lengths *Degrees:* certifi-
cates *Prof. Accred.:* Medical Laboratory
Technology *CEO:* Admin. Winn Clayton
(919) 438-4143

MR. DAVID'S SCHOOL OF HAIR DESIGN
4348 Market St., Wilmington 28403 *Type:*
Private *Accred.:* 1989/1992 (SACS-COEI)

Calendar: Courses of varying lengths *Degrees:* diplomas *CEO:* Dir. David Atkinson
FTE Enroll: 108   (919) 763-4418

NORTHERN HOSPITAL OF SURRY COUNTY
SCHOOL OF MEDICAL TECHNOLOGY
P.O. Box 1101, 830 Rockford St., Mount Airy 27030 *Type:* Private *Calendar:* Courses of varying lengths *Degrees:* certificates *Prof. Accred.:* Medical Laboratory Technology *CEO:* Technical Dir. David A. McCullough
(919) 789-9541

OCONALUFTEE JOB CORPS CIVILIAN
CONSERVATION CENTER
200 Park Cir., Cherokee 28719 *Type:* Public (federal) *Accred.:* 1984/1989 (SACS-COEI) *Calendar:* Courses of varying lengths *Degrees:* certificates *CEO:* Dir. Delmar P. Robinson
FTE Enroll: 280   (704) 497-5411

SALISBURY BUSINESS COLLEGE
1400 Jake Alexander Blvd. W., Salisbury 28144 *Type:* Private business *Accred.:* 1975/1987 (ACISC) *Calendar:* Qtr. plan *Degrees:* certificates, diplomas *CEO:* Pres. Bill Hensley
(704) 636-4071

SCHENCK CIVILIAN CONSERVATION CENTER
98 Schenck Dr., Pisgah Forest 28768 *Type:* Public (federal) *Accred.:* 1985/1990 (SACS-COEI) *Calendar:* Courses of varying lengths

Degrees: certificates, diplomas *CEO:* Dir. John Henry Young
FTE Enroll: 237   (704) 877-3291

SHERRILLS ACADEMY
3421 Murchison Rd., Ste. M, Fayetteville 28311-9954 *Type:* Private *Accred.:* 1991 (ACCSCT) *Calendar:* Courses of varying lengths *Degrees:* diplomas *CEO:* Dir. Van Michael Welch
(919) 630-1140

SKYLAND ACADEMY OF COSMETIC ARTS
415 Seventh Ave., S.W., Hickory 29601 *Type:* Private *Accred.:* 1990 (SACS-COEI) *Calendar:* Courses of varying lengths *Degrees:* certificates *CEO:* Dir. Luci Ratliff
FTE Enroll: 42   (704) 327-2887

SKYLAND ACADEMY OF COSMETIC ARTS
170 Rosscraggon Rd., Skyland 28776 *Type:* Private *Accred.:* 1988 (SACS-COEI) *Calendar:* Courses of varying lengths *Degrees:* certificates *CEO:* Dir. Luci Ratliff
FTE Enroll: 75   (704) 687-1643

WINSTON-SALEM BARBER SCHOOL
1531 Silas Creek Pkwy., Winston-Salem 27127-3757 *Type:* Private *Accred.:* 1991 (ACCSCT) *Calendar:* Courses of varying lengths *Degrees:* diplomas *CEO:* Pres. Joseph Long
(919) 724-1459

NORTH DAKOTA

AAKER'S BUSINESS COLLEGE
P.O. Box 876, 201 N. Third St., Grand Forks 58206-0876 *Type:* Private business *Accred.:* 1966/1991 (ACISC) *Calendar:* Courses of varying lengths *Degrees:* certificates, diplomas *CEO:* Admin. Robert C. Hadlich
(701) 772-6646

INTERSTATE BUSINESS COLLEGE
2720 32nd Ave., S.W., Fargo 58103 *Type:* Private business *Accred.:* 1953/1989 (ACISC) *Calendar:* Courses of varying lengths *Degrees:* certificates, diplomas *Prof. Accred.:* Dental Assisting (prelim. provisional) *CEO:* Dir. Tony Grindberg
(701) 232-2477

BRANCH CAMPUS
520 E. Main Ave., Bismarck 58501 *Accred.:* 1984/1989 (ACISC) *CEO:* Dir. Rodney Wentz
(701) 255-0779

MEYER VOCATIONAL TECHNICAL SCHOOL
P.O. Box 2126, Minot 58702-2126 *Type:* Private *Accred.:* 1991 (ACCSCT) *Calendar:* Courses of varying lengths *Degrees:* certificates *CEO:* Dir. Scott Meyer
(701) 852-0427

MINOT SCHOOL FOR ALLIED HEALTH
110 Burdick Expy. W., Minot 58701 *Type:* Private *Calendar:* Courses of varying lengths *Degrees:* certificates *Prof. Accred.:* Radiography *CEO:* Acting Pres. Terry Hoff
(701) 857-5620

MOLER BARBER COLLEGE OF HAIRSTYLING
16 S. Eighth St., Fargo 58103 *Type:* Private *Accred.:* 1989 (ACCSCT) *Calendar:* Courses of varying lengths *Degrees:* certificates *CEO:* Pres. Joel K. Cannon
(701) 232-6773

TRAVEL CAREER INSTITUTE
855 Basin Ave., Bismarck 58504-9967 *Type:* Private *Accred.:* 1991 (ACCSCT) *Calendar:* Courses of varying lengths *Degrees:* certificates *CEO:* Dir. Pam Wentz-Baccus
(701) 258-9419

TURTLE MOUNTAIN SCHOOL OF PARAMEDICAL TECHNIQUE
Box 203, 322 W. 4th St., Bottineau Medical Arts Clinic Bldg., Bottineau 58318 *Type:* Private *Calendar:* Courses of varying lengths *Degrees:* certificates *Prof. Accred.:* Medical Laboratory Technology *CEO:* Exec. Dir. Kenneth W. Kihle, M.D.
(701) 228-3390

OHIO

ACA COLLEGE OF DESIGN
2528 Kemper La., Cincinnati 45206-2014
Type: Private *Accred.:* 1979/1989 (ACC-SCT) *Calendar:* Qtr. plan *Degrees:* certificates *CEO:* Pres. Marion Allman
(513) 751-1206

ACADEMY OF HAIR DESIGN
1440 Whipple Ave., Canton 44708 *Type:* Private *Accred.:* 1991 (ACCSCT) *Calendar:* Courses of varying lengths *Degrees:* certificates *CEO:* Dir. Franklin D. Ferren
(216) 477-6695

AKRON BARBER COLLEGE
3200 S. Arlington Rd., Ste. 2, Akron 44312-5269 *Type:* Private *Accred.:* 1986 (ACC-SCT) *Calendar:* Courses of varying lengths *Degrees:* diplomas *CEO:* Dir./Owner Mary Jane Sabotin
(216) 644-9114

AKRON MACHINING INSTITUTE INC.
2959 Barber Rd., Barberton 44203-1005
Type: Private *Accred.:* 1986 (ACCSCT) *Calendar:* Courses of varying lengths *Degrees:* diplomas *CEO:* Dir. Joan Cook
(216) 745-1111

CLEVELAND MACHINING INSTITUTE
2500 Brookpark Rd., Cleveland 44134-1407 *Accred.:* 1989 (ACCSCT) *CEO:* Dir. Debra Schlofman
(216) 741-1100

AKRON MEDICAL-DENTAL INSTITUTE
733 W. Market St., Akron 44303-1078 *Type:* Private *Accred.:* 1977/1987 (ACCSCT) *Calendar:* Qtr. plan *Degrees:* diplomas *Prof. Accred.:* Medical Assisting (AMA) *CEO:* Dir. Elizabeth Husk
(216) 762-9788

AKRON SCHOOL OF PRACTICAL NURSING
619 Sumner St., Akron 44311 *Type:* Private professional *Calendar:* Courses of varying lengths *Degrees:* certificates *Prof. Accred.:* Practical Nursing *CEO:* Dir. Dottie Stiles
(216) 376-4129

ALLSTATE HAIRSTYLING AND BARBER COLLEGE
2546 Lorain Ave., Cleveland 44113-3413
Type: Private *Accred.:* 1985/1990 (ACC-SCT) *Calendar:* Courses of varying lengths *Degrees:* diplomas *CEO:* Dir. Phil D'Amico
(216) 241-6684

AMERICAN SCHOOL OF NAIL TECHNIQUES & COSMETOLOGY
924 E. Tallmadge Ave., Akron 44310 *Type:* Private *Accred.:* 1992 (ACCSCT) *Calendar:* Courses of varying lengths *Degrees:* certificates *CEO:* Dir. Nancy L. Kolson
(216) 633-9427

AMERICAN SCHOOL OF TECHNOLOGY
4599-4605 Morse Center Dr., Columbus 43229-6665 *Type:* Private *Accred.:* 1991 (ACCSCT) *Calendar:* Courses of varying lengths *Degrees:* diplomas *CEO:* Dir. Susan R. Stella
(614) 436-4820

ARISTOTLE INSTITUTE OF MEDICAL AND DENTAL TECHNOLOGY
5900 Westerville Rd., Westerville 43081
Type: Private *Accred.:* 1984/1991 (ABHES) *Calendar:* Courses of varying lengths *Degrees:* diplomas *CEO:* Pres. Michael A. Walker
(614) 891-1800

ART ADVERTISING ACADEMY
4343 Bridgetown Rd., Cincinnati 45211-4427 *Type:* Private *Accred.:* 1984/1989 (ACCSCT) *Calendar:* Courses of varying lengths *Degrees:* certificates *CEO:* Owner/Dir. Jerry E. Neff
(513) 574-1010

CENTRAL SCHOOL OF PRACTICAL NURSING
3300 Chester Ave., Cleveland 44114 *Type:* Private professional *Calendar:* Courses of varying lengths *Degrees:* certificates *Prof. Accred.:* Practical Nursing *CEO:* Dir. Pat Turk
(216) 391-8434

CHOFFIN CAREER CENTER
200 E. Wood St., Youngtown 44503 *Type:* Private *Calendar:* Courses of varying lengths *Degrees:* certificates *Prof. Accred.:*

Dental Assisting, Practical Nursing, Surgical Technology *CEO:* Prin. Raymond Brown
(216) 744-8700

CINCINNATI SCHOOL OF COURT REPORTING
600 Executive Bldg., 35 E. Seventh St., Cincinnati 45202 *Type:* Private business *Accred.:* 1982/1988 (ACISC) *Calendar:* Courses of varying lengths *Degrees:* certificates, diplomas *CEO:* Pres. Adeline M. Womack
(513) 241-1011

CLEVELAND INSTITUTE OF DENTAL AND MEDICAL ASSISTANTS, INC.
1836 Euclid Ave., Rm. 401, Cleveland 44115-2285 *Type:* Private *Accred.:* 1982/1989 (ABHES); 1989 (ACCSCT) *Calendar:* Courses of varying lengths *Degrees:* certificates, diplomas *Prof. Accred.:* Medical Assisting *CEO:* Pres. Beverly A. Davis
(216) 241-2930

BRANCH CAMPUS
5564 Mayfield Rd., Lyndhurst 44124-2928 *Accred.:* 1986/1992 (ABHES); 1989 (ACCSCT) *CEO:* Dir. Beverly A. Davis
(216) 473-6273

BRANCH CAMPUS
5733 Hopkins Rd., Mentor 44060-2035 *Accred.:* 1983/1989 (ABHES); 1989 (ACCSCT) *CEO:* Pres. Beverly A. Davis
(216) 257-5524

CONNECTICUT SCHOOL OF BROADCASTING
4790 Red Bank Expy., No. 102, Cincinnati 45227-1509 *Type:* Private *Accred.:* 1992 (ACCSCT) *Calendar:* Courses of varying lengths *Degrees:* certificates *CEO:* Pres. Robert Mills
(216) 271-6060

CONNECTICUT SCHOOL OF BROADCASTING
6701 Rockside Rd., Ste. 204, Independence 44131-2316 *Type:* Private *Accred.:* 1992 (ACCSCT) *Calendar:* Courses of varying lengths *Degrees:* certificates *CEO:* Pres. Robert Mills
(216) 447-9117

ESI CAREER CENTER
25301 Euclid Ave., Euclid 44117-2609 *Type:* Private *Accred.:* 1981/1991 (ACCSCT) *Calendar:* Courses of varying lengths

Degrees: certificates *CEO:* Pres. Thomas Strong
(216) 289-1299

BRANCH CAMPUS
1770 Fort St., Lincoln Park, MI 48146-1988 *Accred.:* 1991/1993 (ACCSCT) *CEO:* Dir. Raymond Kuhn
(313) 381-7800

BRANCH CAMPUS
1985 N. Ridge Rd., Lorain 44055-9990 *Accred.:* 1991 (ACCSCT) *CEO:* Pres. Thomas Strong
(216) 277-8832

HAMMEL COLLEGE
885 E. Buchtel Ave., Akron 44305 *Type:* Private business *Accred.:* 1953/1987 (ACISC) *Calendar:* Courses of varying lengths *Degrees:* certificates, diplomas *CEO:* Dir. Michael Kovalck
(216) 762-7491

HAMRICK TRUCK DRIVING SCHOOL
1156 Medina Rd., Medina 44256-9615 *Type:* Private *Accred.:* 1988/1993 (ACCSCT) *Calendar:* Courses of varying lengths *Degrees:* certificates *CEO:* Pres. Denver Hamrick
(216) 239-2229

HANNAH E. MULLINS SCHOOL OF PRACTICAL NURSING
2094 E. State St., Salem 44460 *Type:* Private professional *Calendar:* Courses of varying lengths *Degrees:* certificates *Prof. Accred.:* Practical Nursing *CEO:* Coord. Donna J. Lynn
(216) 332-8940

HOBART INSTITUTE OF WELDING TECHNOLOGY
Trade Sq. E., Troy 45373-9989 *Type:* Private *Accred.:* 1991 (ACCSCT) *Calendar:* Courses of varying lengths *Degrees:* certificates *CEO:* Registrar Ruth E. Ogletree
(513) 332-5214

HOSPITALITY TRAINING CENTER
220 N. Main St., Hudson 44236 *Type:* Private home study *Accred.:* 1986/1991 (NHSC) *Calendar:* Courses of varying lengths *Degrees:* diplomas *CEO:* Pres. Duane R. Hills
(216) 653-9151

INSTITUTE OF MEDICAL AND DENTAL
TECHNOLOGY
375 Glensprings Dr., Ste. 201, Cincinnati
45246 *Type:* Private *Accred.:* 1983/1989
(ABHES) *Calendar:* Courses of varying
lengths *Degrees:* diplomas *CEO:* Pres./Dir.
Vincent J. Sofia
(513) 851-8500

BRANCH CAMPUS
4452 Eastgate Blvd., Ste. 209, Cincinnati
45244 *Accred.:* 1992 (ABHES) *CEO:*
Pres. Vincent J. Sofia
(513) 753-5030

KNOX COUNTY CAREER CENTER
306 Martinsburg Rd., Mount Vernon 43050
Type: Private *Calendar:* Courses of varying
lengths *Degrees:* certificates *Prof. Accred.:*
Medical Assisting (AMA) *CEO:* Supt. Ray
Richardson
(614) 397-5820

MARYCREST COLLEGE
4404 Secor Rd., Toledo 43623 *Type:* Private
business *Accred.:* 1982/1988 (ACISC) *Calendar:* Courses of varying lengths *Degrees:*
certificates, diplomas *Prof. Accred.:* Medical
Assisting *CEO:* Dir. Renee Hampton
(419) 472-2115

MARYCREST COLLEGE
4615 Woodville Rd., P.O. Box 23245, Toledo 43623-0245 *Type:* Private business *Accred.:* 1984/1988 (ACISC) *Calendar:* Courses
of varying lengths *Degrees:* certificates,
diplomas *Prof. Accred.:* Medical Assisting
CEO: Dir. Connie Buhr
(419) 472-2115

MARYMOUNT SCHOOL OF PRACTICAL NURSING
12300 McCracken Rd., Garfield Heights
44125 *Type:* Private professional *Calendar:*
Courses of varying lengths *Degrees:* certificates *Prof. Accred.:* Practical Nursing *CEO:*
Dir. Louise Evans
(216) 587-8160

McKIM TECHNICAL INSTITUTE
1791 S. Jacoby Rd., Akron 44321-2299
Type: Private *Accred.:* 1991 (ACCSCT) *Calendar:* Courses of varying lengths *Degrees:*
certificates *CEO:* Pres. Carol L. Swaney
(216) 666-4014

MEDINA COUNTY CAREER CENTER
1101 W. Liberty St., Medina 44256-9969
Type: Private *Calendar:* Courses of varying
lengths *Degrees:* certificates *Prof. Accred.:*
Medical Assisting (AMA) *CEO:* Supt.
Thomas Horwedel
(216) 953-7118

NATIONAL EDUCATION CENTER—NATIONAL
INSTITUTE OF TECHNOLOGY CAMPUS
1225 Orlen Ave., Cuyahoga Falls 44221-
2955 *Type:* Private *Accred.:* 1969/1990
(ACCSCT) *Calendar:* Qtr. plan *Degrees:*
diplomas *CEO:* Dir. Donald Miller
(216) 923-9959

NHAW HOME STUDY INSTITUTE
1389 Dublin Rd., P.O. Box 16790, Columbus 43216 *Type:* Private home study *Accred.:* 1969/1991 (NHSC) *Calendar:* Courses
of varying lengths *Degrees:* diplomas *CEO:*
Dir. James H. Healy
(614) 488-1835

OHIO AUTO-DIESEL TECHNICAL INSTITUTE
1421 E. 49th St., Cleveland 44103-1269
Type: Private *Accred.:* 1973/1988 (ACC-
SCT) *Calendar:* Courses of varying lengths
Degrees: certificates *CEO:* Pres. Marc L.
Brenner
(216) 881-1700

OHIO INSTITUTE OF PHOTOGRAPHY AND
TECHNOLOGY
2029 Edgefield Rd., Dayton 45439-1984
Type: Private *Accred.:* 1976/1993 (ACC-
SCT) *Calendar:* Sem. plan *Degrees:* certificates, diplomas *CEO:* Pres. Terry Guthrie
(513) 294-6155

OHIO STATE COLLEGE OF BARBER STYLING
329 Superior St., Toledo 43604-1421 *Type:*
Private *Accred.:* 1983/1988 (ACCSCT) *Calendar:* Courses of varying lengths *Degrees:*
diplomas *CEO:* Pres. Roger Bradley
(419) 241-5618

BRANCH CAMPUS
4614 E. Broad St., Columbus 43223 *Accred.:* 1977/1987 (ACCSCT) *CEO:* Mgr.
Kathryn Mitchell
(614) 868-1015

BRANCH CAMPUS
4390 Karl Rd., Columbus 43224-1107 *Accred.:* 1989 (ACCSCT) *CEO:* Mgr. Jerome Voldness
(614) 267-4247

PENN-OHIO COLLEGE
3517 Market St., Youngstown 44507 *Type:* Private business *Accred.:* 1971/1990 (ACISC) *Calendar:* Sem. plan *Degrees:* certificates, diplomas *CEO:* Pres. Jim Sheppard
(216) 788-5084

PROFESSIONAL SKILLS INSTITUTE
1232 Flaire Dr., Toledo 43615 *Type:* Private *Accred.:* 1986/1992 (ABHES) *Calendar:* Courses of varying lengths *Degrees:* certificates, diplomas *Prof. Accred.:* Physical Therapy Assisting *CEO:* Dir. Patricia A. Finch
(419) 531-9610

RAEDEL COLLEGE AND INDUSTRIAL WELDING SCHOOL
137 Sixth St., N.E., Canton 44702 *Type:* Private professional *Accred.:* 1986 (ACISC) *Calendar:* Courses of varying lengths *Degrees:* certificates, diplomas *CEO:* Dir. Fred G. Holloway
(216) 454-9006

RETS TECH CENTER
P.O. Box 130, Centerville 45459-6120 *Type:* Private *Accred.:* 1974/1989 (ACCSCT) *Calendar:* Qtr. plan *Degrees:* certificates, diplomas *CEO:* Pres. Michael A. LeMaster
(513) 433-3410

SAWYER COLLEGE OF BUSINESS
13027 Lorain Ave., Cleveland 44111 *Type:* Private business *Accred.:* 1979/1988 (ACISC) *Calendar:* Qtr. plan *Degrees:* certificates, diplomas *CEO:* Dir. Betty Gray
(216) 941-7666

SAWYER COLLEGE OF BUSINESS
3150 Mayfield Rd., Cleveland Heights 44118 *Type:* Private business *Accred.:* 1973/1990 (ACISC) *Calendar:* Qtr. plan *Degrees:* certificates, diplomas *CEO:* Dir. Bruce T. Shields
(216) 932-0911

SCHOOL OF ADVERTISING ART
2900 Acosta St., Kettering 45420-3467 *Type:* Private *Accred.:* 1988 (ACCSCT) *Calendar:* Courses of varying lengths *Degrees:* certificates *CEO:* Business Mgr. Terry Wilson
(513) 294-0592

TDDS
1688 N. Princetown Rd., Diamond 44412-9608 *Type:* Private *Accred.:* 1991 (ACCSCT) *Calendar:* Courses of varying lengths *Degrees:* certificates *CEO:* Pres. Richard Rathburn
(216) 538-2216

TECHNOLOGY EDUCATION CENTER
288 S. Hamilton Rd., Columbus 43213-2087 *Type:* Private *Accred.:* 1980/1991 (ACCSCT) *Calendar:* Courses of varying lengths *Degrees:* certificates *CEO:* Dir. Thomas D. Greenhouse
(614) 759-7700

TOTAL TECHNICAL INSTITUTE
6500 Pearl Rd., Parma Heights 44130 *Type:* Private *Accred.:* 1985/1990 (ACCSCT) *Calendar:* Courses of varying lengths *Degrees:* certificates *CEO:* Dir. David Mondi
(216) 843-2323

VIRGINIA MARTI COLLEGE OF FASHION AND ART
P.O. Box 580, Lakewood 44107-3002 *Type:* Private *Accred.:* 1975/1990 (ACCSCT) *Calendar:* Courses of varying lengths *Degrees:* certificates, diplomas *CEO:* Dir. Virginia Marti
(216) 221-8584

WEST SIDE INSTITUTE OF TECHNOLOGY
9801 Walford Ave., Cleveland 44102-4758 *Type:* Private *Accred.:* 1969/1988 (ACCSCT) *Calendar:* Courses of varying lengths *Degrees:* certificates *CEO:* Dir. Richard R. Pountney
(216) 651-1656

WOOSTER BUSINESS COLLEGE
11610 Euclid Ave., Cleveland 44106 *Type:* Private *Calendar:* Courses of varying lengths *Degrees:* diplomas *Prof. Accred.:* Medical Assisting (AMA) *CEO:* Dir. Phillip Drummond
(216) 231-0000

OKLAHOMA

BRYAN INSTITUTE
2843 E. 51st St., Tulsa 74105-6247 *Type:*
Private *Accred.:* 1974/1989 (ACCSCT) *Calendar:* Courses of varying lengths *Degrees:*
diplomas *Prof. Accred.:* Medical Assisting
CEO: Dir. Carla Schaefer
(918) 749-6891

CENTRAL OKLAHOMA AREA VOCATIONAL-
TECHNICAL CENTER
3 CVT Cir., Drumright 74030 *Type:* Private
Calendar: Courses of varying lengths *Degrees:* certificates *Prof. Accred.:* Practical
Nursing *CEO:* Supt. John Hopper
(918) 352-2551

CLIMATE CONTROL INSTITUTE
708 S. Sheridan Rd., Tulsa 74112-3140
Type: Private *Accred.:* 1978/1988 (ACCSCT) *Calendar:* Qtr. plan *Degrees:* certificates *CEO:* Pres. Sue Kloehr
(918) 836-6656

FRANCIS TUTTLE VOCATIONAL-TECHNICAL
CENTER
12777 N. Rockwell Ave., Oklahoma City
73142 *Type:* Private *Calendar:* Courses of
varying lengths *Degrees:* certificates *Prof.
Accred.:* Practical Nursing, Respiratory
Therapy Technology *CEO:* Supt. Bruce
Gray
(405) 722-7799

GREAT PLAINS AREA VOCATIONAL-TECHNICAL
CENTER
4500 W. Lee Blvd., Lawton 73505 *Type:*
Private *Calendar:* Courses of varying
lengths *Degrees:* certificates *Prof. Accred.:*
Practical Nursing, Radiography, Surgical
Technology *CEO:* Supt. Kenneth Bridges
(405) 355-6371

HOLLYWOOD COSMETOLOGY CENTER
P.O. Box 890488, Oklahoma City 73189
Type: Private *Accred.:* 1992 (ACCSCT) *Calendar:* Courses of varying lengths *Degrees:*
diplomas *CEO:* Dir. Crystal Burgess
(405) 364-3375

INDIAN MERIDIAN VOCATIONAL-TECHNICAL
CENTER
1312 S. Sangre St., Stillwater 74074 *Type:*
Private *Calendar:* Courses of varying

lengths *Degrees:* certificates *Prof. Accred.:*
Radiography *CEO:* Supt. Fred A. Shultz
(405) 377-3333

METROPOLITAN COLLEGE OF COURT REPORTING
2525 Northwest Expy., No. 215, Oklahoma
City 73112 *Type:* Private *Accred.:* 1992
(ACCSCT) *Calendar:* Courses of varying
lengths *Degrees:* certificates *CEO:* Pres./
Owner David L. Stephenson
(405) 840-2181

METROPOLITAN COLLEGE OF LEGAL STUDIES
2865 E. Skelly Dr., Tulsa 74105 *Type:* Private *Accred.:* 1992 (ACCSCT) *Calendar:*
Courses of varying lengths *Degrees:* certificates *CEO:* Pres./Owner David L. Stephenson
(918) 745-9946

MID-DEL COLLEGE
3420 S. Sunny La., Del City 73115-3535
Type: Private *Accred.:* 1981/1986 (ACCSCT) *Calendar:* Courses of varying lengths
Degrees: certificates, diplomas *CEO:* Dir.
Sidney Carey
(405) 677-8311

MISS SHIRLEY'S BEAUTY COLLEGE
309 S.W. 59th St., Ste. 305, Oklahoma City
73109 *Type:* Private *Accred.:* 1991 (ACCSCT) *Calendar:* Courses of varying lengths
Degrees: certificates *CEO:* Owner Glynn
Mize
(405) 631-0055

NATIONAL EDUCATION CENTER—SPARTAN
SCHOOL OF AERONAUTICS
P.O. Box 582833, Tulsa 74158-2833 *Type:*
Private *Accred.:* 1969/1986 (ACCSCT) *Calendar:* Courses of varying lengths *Degrees:*
diplomas *CEO:* Pres. Ross L. Alloway
(918) 836-6886

OKLAHOMA FARRIER'S COLLEGE
Rte. 2, Box 88, Sperry 74073-9446 *Type:*
Private *Accred.:* 1980/1993 (ACCSCT) *Calendar:* Courses of varying lengths *Degrees:*
diplomas *CEO:* Pres. Bud Beaston
(918) 288-7221

OKLAHOMA HORSESHOEING SCHOOL
3000 N. Interstate 35, Oklahoma City 73111-9987 *Type:* Private *Accred.:* 1988/ 1993 (ACCSCT) *Calendar:* Courses of varying lengths *Degrees:* certificates *CEO:* Dir. Jack Roth
(405) 424-3842

OKLAHOMA STATE HORSESHOEING SCHOOL
Rte. 1, Box 28-B, Ardmore 73401-9707 *Type:* Private *Accred.:* 1992 (ACCSCT) *Calendar:* Courses of varying lengths *Degrees:* certificates *CEO:* Owner Reggie Kester
(405) 223-0064

O.T. AUTRY AREA VOCATIONAL-TECHNICAL CENTER
1201 W. Willow St., Enid 73703 *Type:* Private *Calendar:* Courses of varying lengths *Degrees:* certificates *Prof. Accred.:* Radiography *CEO:* Supt. James Strate
(405) 242-2750

PLATT COLLEGE
4821 S. 72nd E. Ave., Tulsa 74145-6502 *Type:* Private *Accred.:* 1985/1990 (ACCSCT) *Calendar:* Courses of varying lengths *Degrees:* certificates *CEO:* Pres. George Gillard
(918) 663-9000

BRANCH CAMPUS
3737 N. Portland Ave., Oklahoma City 73112 *Accred.:* 1985/1990 (ACCSCT) *CEO:* Dir. Michael Pugliese
(405) 942-8683

STATE BARBER & HAIR DESIGN COLLEGE INC.
2514 S. Agnew Ave., Oklahoma City 73108-6220 *Type:* Private *Accred.:* 1988 (ACCSCT) *Calendar:* Courses of varying lengths

Degrees: certificates *CEO:* Owner Bobby Lewis
(405) 631-8621

TULSA BARBER STYLING COLLEGE
1314 E. Third St., Tulsa 74120-2802 *Type:* Private *Accred.:* 1985/1990 (ACCSCT) *Calendar:* Courses of varying lengths *Degrees:* certificates *CEO:* Owner Manly E. Jones
(918) 599-0803

TULSA TECHNOLOGY CENTER
3420 S. Memorial Dr., Tulsa 74145-1390 *Type:* Private *Calendar:* Courses of varying lengths *Degrees:* certificates *Prof. Accred.:* Practical Nursing, Radiography, Surgical Technology *CEO:* Supt. Gene Callahan
(918) 627-7200

TULSA WELDING SCHOOL
3038 Southwest Blvd., Tulsa 74107-3818 *Type:* Private *Accred.:* 1970/1990 (ACCSCT) *Calendar:* Courses of varying lengths *Degrees:* diplomas *CEO:* Pres. Roger Hess
(918) 587-6789

UNITED STATES COAST GUARD INSTITUTE
P.O. Substation 18, Oklahoma City 73169-6999 *Type:* Public (federal) home study *Accred.:* 1981/1992 (NHSC) *Calendar:* Courses of varying lengths *Degrees:* certificates *CEO:* Commander Roland Isnor
(405) 680-4262

WRIGHT BUSINESS SCHOOL
Ste. 122, 2219 S.W. 74th St., Oklahoma City 73159 *Type:* Private business *Accred.:* 1986/1988 (ACISC) *Calendar:* Courses of varying lengths *Degrees:* certificates, diplomas *CEO:* Dir. Jim Coyte
(405) 681-2300

OREGON

AIRMAN PROFICIENCY CENTER
3565 N.E. Cornell Rd., Hillsboro 97124
Type: Private *Accred.:* 1992 (ACCSCT) *Calendar:* Courses of varying lengths *Degrees:* certificates *CEO:* Dir. Gail Young
(503) 648-2831

APOLLO COLLEGE OF MEDICAL-DENTAL
CAREERS
2600 S.E. 98th St., Portland 97266-1302
Type: Private *Accred.:* 1985/1990 (ABHES)
Calendar: Courses of varying lengths *Degrees:* certificates *CEO:* Pres. Margaret M. Carlson
(503) 761-6100

BROADCAST PROFESSIONALS COMPLETE SCHOOL
OF RADIO BROADCASTING
11507-D S.W. Pacific Hwy., Portland 97223-8628 *Type:* Private *Accred.:* 1991 (ACCSCT) *Calendar:* Courses of varying lengths *Degrees:* certificates *CEO:* Exec. Dir. Keith Allen Glutsch
(503) 244-5113

COLLEGE OF LEGAL ARTS
Ste. 308, 527 S.W. Hall St., Portland 97201
Type: Private business *Accred.:* 1978/1990 (ACISC) *Calendar:* Courses of varying lengths *Degrees:* certificates, diplomas *CEO:* Pres./Dir. Billy P. Ellis
(503) 223-5100

COLLEGEAMERICA
921 S.W. Washington St., Ste. 200, Portland 97205-2820 *Type:* Private *Accred.:* 1982/1987 (ACCSCT) *Calendar:* Courses of varying lengths *Degrees:* certificates *Prof. Accred.:* Dental Assisting, Medical Assisting (AMA) *CEO:* Dir. Floyd W. King
(503) 242-9000

COMMERCIAL TRAINING SERVICES
2416 N. Marine Dr., Portland 97217-7741
Type: Private *Accred.:* 1973/1990 (ACCSCT) *Calendar:* Courses of varying lengths *Degrees:* certificates *CEO:* Pres. Clifford Georgioff
(503) 285-7542

CONCORDE CAREER INSTITUTE
1827 N.E. 44th Ave., Portland 97213 *Type:* Private *Accred.:* 1991 (ACCSCT) *Calendar:* Courses of varying lengths *Degrees:* certificates *CEO:* Dir. Larry W. Cartmill
(503) 281-4181

DIESEL TRUCK DRIVER TRAINING SCHOOL
90801 Hwy. 99 N., Eugene 97402-9624
Type: Private *Accred.:* 1991 (ACCSCT) *Calendar:* Courses of varying lengths *Degrees:* certificates *CEO:* Dir. John Klabacka
(800) 888-7075

EAST-WEST COLLEGE OF THE HEALING ARTS
812 S.W. Tenth Ave., Portland 97205-2593
Type: Private *Accred.:* 1991 (ACCSCT) *Calendar:* Courses of varying lengths *Degrees:* certificates *CEO:* Pres. David Slawson
(503) 226-1137

LA GRANDE COLLEGE OF BUSINESS
703 Washington St., La Grande 97850 *Type:* Private business *Accred.:* 1979/1988 (ACISC) *Calendar:* Courses of varying lengths *Degrees:* certificates, diplomas *CEO:* Pres. Ronald L. Vincent
(503) 963-6485

MOLER BARBER COLLEGE
517 S.W. Fourth St., Portland 97204-2118
Type: Private *Accred.:* 1988 (ACCSCT) *Calendar:* Courses of varying lengths *Degrees:* certificates *CEO:* Pres. Gordon Scarbrough
(503) 223-9818

OREGON DENTURIST COLLEGE
19001 S.E. McLaughlin Blvd., Milwaukie 97268-0289 *Type:* Private *Accred.:* 1991 (ACCSCT) *Calendar:* Courses of varying lengths *Degrees:* certificates *CEO:* Dean Joanne D. Thibert
(503) 655-7561

OREGON SCHOOL OF ARTS AND CRAFTS
8245 S.W. Barnes Rd., Portland 97225 *Type:* Private professional *Calendar:* Courses of varying lengths *Degrees:* certificates, diplomas *Prof. Accred.:* Art (associate) *CEO:* Pres. Paul C. Magnusson
Enroll: 65
(503) 297-5544

PARAMEDIC TRAINING INSTITUTE
P.O. Box 1878, Beaverton 97075 *Type:* Private *Calendar:* Courses of varying lengths *Degrees:* certificates *Prof. Accred.:* EMT-Paramedic *CEO:* Dir. Louise A. Evans
(503) 297-5592

TARA LARA ACADEMY OF K-9 HAIR DESIGN
16307 S.E. McLoughlin Blvd., Portland 97267-5134 *Type:* Private *Accred.:* 1991 (ACCSCT) *Calendar:* Courses of varying lengths *Degrees:* certificates *CEO:* Dir. Arlene F. Steinle
(503) 653-7134

TREND COLLEGE
1050 Green Acres Rd., Eugene 97401-6501 *Type:* Private business *Accred.:* 1974/1990 (ACISC) *Calendar:* Courses of varying lengths *Degrees:* certificates, diplomas *CEO:* Dir. Richard Lyons
(503) 342-5377

TREND COLLEGE
1950 S.W. Sixth Ave., Portland 97201 *Type:* Private business *Accred.:* 1966/1989 (ACISC) *Calendar:* Qtr. plan *Degrees:* certificates, diplomas *CEO:* Dir. Gail Case
(503) 224-6410

TREND COLLEGE
210 S.E. Liberty St., Salem 97301 *Type:* Private business *Accred.:* 1970/1986 (ACISC) *Calendar:* Courses of varying lengths *Degrees:* certificates, diplomas *CEO:* Dir. Greg H. Otter
(503) 581-1476

BRANCH CAMPUS
400 Earhart St., Medford 97501 *Accred.:* 1981/1986 (ACISC) *CEO:* Acting Dir. Barbara Foster
(503) 779-5581

WEST COAST TRAINING
11919 N. Jensen Ave., Ste. 292, Portland 97217 *Type:* Private *Accred.:* 1986 (ACCSCT) *Calendar:* Courses of varying lengths *Degrees:* certificates *CEO:* Dir. William Myer
(503) 289-8661

BRANCH CAMPUS
2525 S.E. Stubb St., Milwaukie 97222-7323 *Accred.:* 1986 (ACCSCT) *CEO:* Dir. Russell L. Norton
(503) 659-5181

WESTERN BUSINESS COLLEGE
425 S.W. Washington St., Portland 97204 *Type:* Private business *Accred.:* 1969/1987 (ACISC) *Calendar:* Qtr. plan *Degrees:* certificates, diplomas *CEO:* Dir. F. William King
(503) 222-3225

BRANCH CAMPUS
6625 E. Mill Plain Blvd., Vancouver, WA 98661 *Accred.:* 1987 (ACISC) *CEO:* Dir. Randy Rogers
(206) 694-3225

WESTERN CULINARY INSTITUTE
1316 S.W. 13th Ave., Portland 97201-3355 *Type:* Private *Accred.:* 1991 (ACCSCT) *Calendar:* Courses of varying lengths *Degrees:* certificates *CEO:* Dir. Nick Fluge
(503) 223-2245

WESTERN MEDICAL COLLEGE OF ALLIED HEALTH CAREERS
3000 Market St., N.E., Ste. 541, Salem 97301 *Type:* Private *Accred.:* 1990 (ABHES) *Calendar:* Courses of varying lengths *Degrees:* certificates *CEO:* Dir. Marcella Arnold
(503) 363-4473

WESTERN TRUCK SCHOOL
10510 S.W. Industrial Way, Bldg. 1, Bay 1, Tualatin 97062-0826 *Type:* Private *Accred.:* 1991/1993 (ACCSCT) *Calendar:* Courses of varying lengths *Degrees:* certificates *CEO:* Dir. Art Hadduck
(503) 691-0113

PENNSYLVANIA

ACADEMY OF MEDICAL ARTS AND BUSINESS
279 Boas St., Harrisburg 17102-2944 *Type:*
Private *Accred.:* 1983/1988 (ACCSCT) *Calendar:* Courses of varying lengths *Degrees:*
diplomas *Prof. Accred.:* Medical Assisting
CEO: Dir./Pres. Gary Kay
(717) 233-2172

ALL-STATE CAREER SCHOOL
501 Seminole St., Lester 19029-1825 *Type:*
Private *Accred.:* 1988 (ACCSCT) *Calendar:*
Courses of varying lengths *Degrees:* certificates *CEO:* Pres. Joseph W. Marino
(215) 521-1818

BRANCH CAMPUS
201 S. Arlington Ave., Baltimore, MD
21223 *Accred.:* 1991 (ACCSCT) *CEO:*
Dir. Alex Teitelbaum
(410) 566-7111

ALLEGHENY BUSINESS INSTITUTE
3rd Fl., 339 Blvd. of the Allies, Pittsburgh
15222 *Type:* Private business *Accred.:* 1990
(ACISC) *Calendar:* Courses of varying
lengths *Degrees:* certificates, diplomas
CEO: Pres. James Rudolph
(412) 456-7100

ALLIED MEDICAL CAREERS
104 Woodward Hill Rd., Edwardsville
18704 *Type:* Private *Accred.:* 1990
(ABHES) *Calendar:* Courses of varying
lengths *Degrees:* certificates *CEO:* Pres.
Damon A. Young
(717) 288-8400

BRANCH CAMPUS
2901 Pittston Ave., Scranton 18505 *Accred.:* 1990 (ABHES) *CEO:* Pres. Damon
A. Young
(717) 342-8000

ANTONELLI MEDICAL AND PROFESSIONAL
INSTITUTE
1700 Industrial Hwy., Pottstown 19464-9250
Type: Private *Accred.:* 1989/1993 (ACCSCT) *Calendar:* Courses of varying lengths
Degrees: certificates, diplomas *CEO:* Dir. G.
Michael Orthaus
(215) 323-7270

AUTOMOTIVE TRAINING CENTER
114 Pickering Way, Exton 19341-1310
Type: Private *Accred.:* 1973/1993 (ACCSCT) *Calendar:* Courses of varying lengths
Degrees: certificates, diplomas *CEO:* Dir.
Steven C. Hiscox
(215) 363-6716

BARBER STYLING INSTITUTE
3447 Simpson Ferry Rd., Camp Hill 17011-
6485 *Type:* Private *Accred.:* 1983/1988
(ACCSCT) *Calendar:* Courses of varying
lengths *Degrees:* certificates *CEO:* Dir.
Gregory Mekulski
(717) 763-4787

BERKS TECHNICAL INSTITUTE
832 N. Park Rd., 4 Park Plaza, Wyomissing
19610-1341 *Type:* Private *Accred.:* 1991/
1993 (ACCSCT) *Calendar:* Courses of varying lengths *Degrees:* certificates *Prof. Accred.:* Medical Assisting (AMA) *CEO:* Pres.
Kenneth S. Snyder
(215) 372-1722

BIDWELL TRAINING CENTER
1815 Metropolitan St., Pittsburgh 15233
Type: Private *Accred.:* 1993 (ACCSCT) *Calendar:* Courses of varying lengths *Degrees:*
certificates *CEO:* Exec. Dir. William E.
Strickland
(412) 323-4000

BILL ALLEN'S POCONO INSTITUTE OF
TAXIDERMY
R.D. 2, Box 2038, Whitehaven 18661-9633
Type: Private *Accred.:* 1991 (ACCSCT) *Calendar:* Courses of varying lengths *Degrees:*
certificates *CEO:* Dir. William Allen
(717) 443-9166

THE CAREER INSTITUTE
1825 John F. Kennedy Blvd., Philadelphia
19103 *Type:* Private business *Accred.:* 1984/
1988 (ACISC) *Calendar:* Qtr. plan *Degrees:*
certificates, diplomas *CEO:* Dir. Eve M.
Corey
(215) 561-7600

BRANCH CAMPUS
711 Market St. Mall, Wilmington, DE 19801 *Accred.:* 1986 (ACISC) *CEO:* Dir. Sue Adams

(302) 575-1400

CAREER TRAINING ACADEMY
703 Fifth Ave., New Kensington 15068-6301 *Type:* Private *Accred.:* 1991 (ACCSCT) *Calendar:* Courses of varying lengths *Degrees:* certificates *Prof. Accred.:* Medical Assisting (AMA) *CEO:* C.E.O. John M. Reddy

(412) 337-1000

BRANCH CAMPUS
244 Center Rd., Monroeville 15146 *Accred.:* 1993 (ACCSCT) *CEO:* Dir. Maryagnes Luczak

(412) 372-3900

CHI INSTITUTE
520 Street Rd., Southampton 18966-3787 *Type:* Private *Accred.:* 1985/1990 (ACCSCT) *Calendar:* Courses of varying lengths *Degrees:* certificates *CEO:* Dir. Glenn B. Murray

(215) 357-5100

THE CLARISSA SCHOOL OF FASHION DESIGN
Warner Ctr., 332 Fifth Ave., Pittsburgh 15222-2411 *Type:* Private *Accred.:* 1976/1987 (ACCSCT) *Calendar:* Sem. plan *Degrees:* certificates, diplomas *CEO:* Dir. Penelope N. Smith

(412) 471-4414

COMPUTER LEARNING CENTER
3600 Market St., Philadelphia 19104-2684 *Type:* Private business *Accred.:* 1981/1991 (ACISC) *Calendar:* Courses of varying lengths *Degrees:* certificates, diplomas *CEO:* Dir. Joseph F. Reichard

(215) 222-6450

COMPUTER LEARNING NETWORK
1110 Fernwood Ave., Camp Hill 17011-6996 *Type:* Private *Accred.:* 1985/1990 (ACCSCT) *Calendar:* Courses of varying lengths *Degrees:* certificates *CEO:* Pres. Kenneth E. Whittington

(717) 761-1481

BRANCH CAMPUS
2900 Fairway Dr., Altoona 16602-4457 *Accred.:* 1992 (ACCSCT) *CEO:* Dir. Todd Fries

(814) 944-5643

THE CRAFT INSTITUTE
9 S. 12th St., Philadelphia 19107-3644 *Type:* Private *Accred.:* 1980/1993 (ACCSCT) *Calendar:* Courses of varying lengths *Degrees:* certificates *CEO:* Dir. Gail Zukerman

(215) 665-8546

DELAWARE COUNTY INSTITUTE OF TRAINING
615 Ave. of the States, Chester 19013-6022 *Type:* Private *Accred.:* 1984/1989 (ACCSCT) *Calendar:* Courses of varying lengths *Degrees:* certificates *CEO:* Dir. Howard K. Kauff

(215) 874-1888

DELAWARE VALLEY ACADEMY OF MEDICAL AND DENTAL ASSISTANTS
6539-43 Roosevelt Blvd., Philadelphia 19149-2998 *Type:* Private *Accred.:* 1986/1992 (ABHES) *Calendar:* Courses of varying lengths *Degrees:* certificates *CEO:* Dir. David M. Goldsmith

(215) 744-5300

ERIE INSTITUTE OF TECHNOLOGY
2221 Peninsula Dr., Erie 16506-2954 *Type:* Private *Accred.:* 1979/1989 (ACCSCT) *Calendar:* Courses of varying lengths *Degrees:* certificates *CEO:* Pres./Dir. Clinton L. Oviatt, Jr.

(814) 838-2711

FRANKLIN ACADEMY
324 N. Centre St., Pottsville 17901 *Type:* Private *Accred.:* 1992 (ACCSCT) *Calendar:* Courses of varying lengths *Degrees:* certificates *CEO:* Pres. Franklin K. Schoeneman

(717) 622-8370

GARFIELD BUSINESS INSTITUTE
709 Third Ave., New Brighton 15066 *Type:* Private business *Accred.:* 1988/1991 (ACISC) *Calendar:* Courses of varying lengths *Degrees:* certificates, diplomas *CEO:* Dir. Ed Latagliata

(412) 728-4050

GATEWAY TECHNICAL INSTITUTE
100 Seventh St., Pittsburgh 15222-3404
Type: Private *Accred.:* 1969/1993 (ACC-
SCT) *Calendar:* Tri. plan *Degrees:* diplomas
CEO: Dir. Wayne D. Smith
(412) 281-4111

GLEIM TECHNICAL INSTITUTE
200 S. Spring Garden St., Carlisle 17013
Type: Private *Accred.:* 1993 (ACCSCT) *Calendar:* Courses of varying lengths *Degrees:*
certificates *CEO:* Asst. Education Dir./Mgr.
Karen L. Gleim
(800) 922-8399

GREATER JOHNSTOWN AREA VOCATIONAL-
TECHNICAL SCHOOL
445 Schoolhouse Rd., Johnstown 15904-
2998 *Type:* Private *Calendar:* Courses of
varying lengths *Degrees:* certificates *Prof.
Accred.:* Respiratory Therapy Technology
CEO: Admin. Dir. Barry Dallara
(814) 266-6073

HIRAM G. ANDREWS CENTER
727 Goucher St., Johnstown 15905-3092
Type: Private *Accred.:* 1987 (ACCSCT) *Calendar:* Courses of varying lengths *Degrees:*
certificates, diplomas *CEO:* Dir. Joseph
Rizzo, Sr.
(814) 255-8200

INFORMATION COMPUTER SYSTEMS INSTITUTE
2201 Hangar Pl., Allentown 18103-9504
Type: Private *Accred.:* 1984/1989 (ACC-
SCT) *Calendar:* Courses of varying lengths
Degrees: certificates *CEO:* Owner/Pres.
William Barber
(215) 264-8029

JAMES MARTIN ADULT HEALTH OCCUPATIONS
Alvin A. Swenson Skills Ctr., 2600 Red
Lion Rd., Philadelphia 19114-1020 *Type:*
Public (city) *Calendar:* Courses of varying
lengths *Degrees:* certificates *Prof. Accred.:*
Medical Laboratory Technology, Respirato-
ry Therapy Technology *CEO:* Admin.
Richard L. Brown
(215) 961-2131

J.H. THOMPSON ACADEMIES
2908 State St., Erie 16508-1832 *Type:* Private *Accred.:* 1979/1989 (ACCSCT) *Calendar:* Courses of varying lengths *Degrees:*
diplomas *CEO:* Dir. Jack Thompson
(814) 456-6217

JOSEPH DONAHUE INTERNATIONAL SCHOOL OF
HAIRSTYLING
2485 Grant Ave., Philadelphia 19114-1004
Type: Private *Accred.:* 1984/1989 (ACC-
SCT) *Calendar:* Courses of varying lengths
Degrees: certificates *CEO:* Owner/Pres.
Nancy L. Johnson
(215) 969-1313

LEARNING AND EVALUATION CENTER
515 Market St., P.O. Box 616, Bloomsburg
17815 *Type:* Private home study *Accred.:*
1985/1989 (NHSC) *Calendar:* Courses of
varying lengths *Degrees:* certificates *CEO:*
Pres./Dir. I.L. McCloskey
(717) 784-5220

LIBERTY ACADEMY OF BUSINESS
Ste. 2000, 511 N. Broad St., Philadelphia
19123 *Type:* Private business *Accred.:* 1993
(ACISC) *Calendar:* Courses of varying
lengths *Degrees:* certificates, diplomas
CEO: C.E.O. Charlotte Matthews
(215) 925-8670

LIFETIME CAREER SCHOOLS
101 Harrison St., Archbald 18403 *Type:* Private home study *Accred.:* 1957/1990
(NHSC) *Calendar:* Courses of varying
lengths *Degrees:* certificates *CEO:* Pres.
Michael J. Zadarosni
(717) 876-6340

LINCOLN TECHNICAL INSTITUTE
5151 Tilghman St., Allentown 18104-3298
Type: Private *Accred.:* 1967/1988 (ACC-
SCT) *Calendar:* Courses of varying lengths
Degrees: certificates, diplomas *CEO:* Dir.
Robert G. Milot
(215) 398-5301

LINCOLN TECHNICAL INSTITUTE
9191 Torresdale Ave., Philadelphia 19136
Type: Private *Accred.:* 1969/1993 (ACC-
SCT) *Calendar:* Courses of varying lengths
Degrees: certificates, diplomas *CEO:* Dir.
Douglas M. Johnson
(215) 335-0800

MASTBAUM AREA VOCATIONAL-TECHNICAL
SCHOOL
3120 Frankford Ave., Philadelphia 19134
Type: Private *Calendar:* Courses of varying
lengths *Degrees:* certificates *Prof. Accred.:*

Dental Laboratory Technology *CEO:* Prin. Charles Clark

(215) 291-4703

NATIONAL EDUCATION CENTER ALLENTOWN CAMPUS
1501 Lehigh St., Allentown 18103 *Type:* Private business *Accred.:* 1968/1986 (ACISC) *Calendar:* Sem. plan *Degrees:* certificates, diplomas *CEO:* Dir. Virginia Carpenter

(215) 791-5100

NATIONAL EDUCATION CENTER—VALE TECHNICAL INSTITUTE CAMPUS
135 W. Market St., Blairsville 15717-1389 *Type:* Private *Accred.:* 1967/1993 (ACC-SCT) *Calendar:* Courses of varying lengths *Degrees:* diplomas *CEO:* Dir. Gary A. McGee

(412) 459-9500

NATIONAL EDUCATION CENTER—CLEVELAND CAMPUS
14445 Broadway Ave., Cleveland, OH 44125 *Accred.:* 1990 (ACCSCT) *CEO:* Exec. Dir. Bob Somers

(216) 475-7520

NAVAL DAMAGE CONTROL TRAINING CENTER
Naval Base, Philadelphia 19112 *Type:* Public (federal) *Accred.:* 1985/1990 (SACS-COEI) *Calendar:* Courses of varying lengths *Degrees:* certificates *CEO:* Commanding Ofcr. W.A. Smart, U.S.N.
FTE Enroll: 205   (215) 897-5677

NEW CASTLE SCHOOL OF TRADES
New Castle Youngstown Rd., Rte. 422, R.D. 1, Pulaski 16143-9721 *Type:* Private *Accred.:* 1973/1988 (ACCSCT) *Calendar:* Courses of varying lengths *Degrees:* certificates, diplomas *CEO:* Dir. Jason Whitehead

(412) 964-8811

NEW ENGLAND TRACTOR TRAILER TRAINING SCHOOL
3715 E. Thompson St., Philadelphia 19137-1483 *Type:* Private *Accred.:* 1991 (ACC-SCT) *Calendar:* Courses of varying lengths *Degrees:* certificates *CEO:* Dir. Diane M. Pelli

(215) 288-7800

NORTH HILLS SCHOOL OF HEALTH OCCUPATIONS
7805 McKnight Rd., Pittsburgh 15237 *Type:* Private *Accred.:* 1987 (ABHES) *Calendar:* Courses of varying lengths *Degrees:* certificates *CEO:* Exec. Dir. R. Gary Drent

(412) 367-8003

OAKBRIDGE ACADEMY OF ARTS
401 Ninth St., New Kensington 15068-6470 *Type:* Private *Accred.:* 1980/1990 (ACC-SCT) *Calendar:* Courses of varying lengths *Degrees:* certificates, diplomas *CEO:* Dir. William H. Breyak

(412) 335-5336

ORLEANS TECHNICAL INSTITUTE
1330 Rhawn St., Philadelphia 19111-2899 *Type:* Private *Accred.:* 1981/1986 (ACC-SCT) *Calendar:* Courses of varying lengths *Degrees:* certificates, diplomas *CEO:* Dir. Jayne Siniari

(215) 728-4700

THE COURT REPORTING INSTITUTE
1845 Walnut St., Ste. 700, Philadelphia 19103-4707 *Accred.:* 1988 (ACCSCT) *CEO:* Dir. Marlyn DeWitt

(215) 854-1823

PENN COMMERCIAL COLLEGE
82 S. Main St., Washington 15301 *Type:* Private business *Accred.:* 1960/1988 (ACISC) *Calendar:* Qtr. plan *Degrees:* certificates, diplomas *CEO:* Pres. Stanley S. Bazant, Sr.

(412) 222-5330

PENNSYLVANIA GUNSMITH SCHOOL
812 Ohio River Blvd., Pittsburgh 15202-2699 *Type:* Private *Accred.:* 1986 (ACC-SCT) *Calendar:* Courses of varying lengths *Degrees:* diplomas *CEO:* Dir. George Thacker

(412) 766-1812

PENNSYLVANIA INSTITUTE OF CULINARY ARTS
717 Liberty Ave., Pittsburgh 15222-3500 *Type:* Private *Accred.:* 1991 (ACCSCT) *Calendar:* Courses of varying lengths *Degrees:* certificates, diplomas *CEO:* Pres. Nicholas Hoban

(412) 566-2433

PENNSYLVANIA INSTITUTE OF TAXIDERMY
Rural Rte. 3, Box 188, Ebensburg 15931-8947 *Type:* Private *Accred.:* 1991 (ACC-

SCT) *Calendar:* Courses of varying lengths *Degrees:* certificates *CEO:* Pres. Dan A. Bantley

(814) 472-4510

PENNSYLVANIA SCHOOL OF ART AND DESIGN
204 N. Prince St., Lancaster 17603 *Type:* Private professional *Calendar:* Courses of varying lengths *Degrees:* diplomas *Prof. Accred.:* Art *CEO:* Pres. Mary C. Heil

(717) 396-7833

PHILADELPHIA WIRELESS TECHNICAL INSTITUTE
1533 Pine St., Philadelphia 19102-4693 *Type:* Private *Accred.:* 1985/1990 (ACC-SCT) *Calendar:* Courses of varying lengths *Degrees:* certificates *CEO:* Dir. Peter Honczar

(215) 546-0745

THE PJA SCHOOL
7900 W. Chester Pike, Upper Darby 19082-1926 *Type:* Private *Accred.:* 1985/1990 (ACCSCT) *Calendar:* Courses of varying lengths *Degrees:* diplomas *CEO:* Dir. David M. Hudiak

(215) 789-6700

PTC CAREER INSTITUTE
50 N. Second St., Center City, Philadelphia 19106 *Type:* Private *Accred.:* 1992 (ACC-SCT) *Calendar:* Courses of varying lengths *Degrees:* certificates *CEO:* Dir. Eugene Carboni

(215) 922-4400

PTC CAREER INSTITUTE
40 N. Second St., Philadelphia 19106-4504 *Type:* Private *Accred.:* 1978/1988 (ACC-SCT) *Calendar:* Courses of varying lengths *Degrees:* diplomas *CEO:* Dir. Eugene Carboni

(215) 922-4400

RALPH AMODEI INTERNATIONAL INSTITUTE OF HAIR DESIGN & TECHNOLOGY
4451 Frankford Ave., Philadelphia 19124-3636 *Type:* Private *Accred.:* 1986 (ACC-SCT) *Calendar:* Courses of varying lengths *Degrees:* certificates *CEO:* Pres. Ralph Amodei

(215) 289-4433

THE RESTAURANT SCHOOL
4207 Walnut St., Philadelphia 19104-3518 *Type:* Private *Accred.:* 1982/1987 (ACC-SCT) *Calendar:* Courses of varying lengths *Degrees:* diplomas *CEO:* Pres. Daniel Liberatoscioli

(215) 222-4200

RETS EDUCATION CENTER
2641 W. Chester Pike, Broomall 19008-1999 *Type:* Private *Accred.:* 1973/1988 (ACC-SCT) *Calendar:* Courses of varying lengths *Degrees:* certificates, diplomas *CEO:* Dir. Jane Chadwick

(215) 353-7630

ROSEDALE TECHNICAL INSTITUTE
4634 Browns Hill Rd., Pittsburgh 15217-2919 *Type:* Private *Accred.:* 1979/1989 (ACCSCT) *Calendar:* Qtr. plan *Degrees:* diplomas *CEO:* Exec. Vice Pres. David N. McCormick

(412) 521-6200

SETTLEMENT MUSIC SCHOOL
416 Queen St., Philadelphia 19147 *Type:* Private professional *Calendar:* Courses of varying lengths *Degrees:* certificates *Prof. Accred.:* Music *CEO:* Exec. Dir. Robert Capanna

(215) 336-0400

THE SHIRLEY ROCK SCHOOL OF THE PENNSYLVANIA BALLET
1101 S. Broad St., Philadelphia 19147 *Type:* Private *Calendar:* Courses of varying lengths *Degrees:* certificates *Prof. Accred.:* Dance (associate) *CEO:* Dir. Bojan Spassoff

(215) 551-7000

SWANSON'S DRIVING SCHOOLS INC.
9915 Frankstown Rd., Pittsburgh 15235-1646 *Type:* Private *Accred.:* 1992 (ACC-SCT) *Calendar:* Courses of varying lengths *Degrees:* certificates *CEO:* Vice Pres. Gene Swanson

(412) 241-6963

TRI-CITY BARBER SCHOOL
128 E. Main St., Norristown 19401-4917 *Type:* Private *Accred.:* 1987 (ACCSCT) *Calendar:* Courses of varying lengths *Degrees:* certificates *CEO:* Dir. Peggy Porche

(215) 279-4432

TRI-CITY BARBER SCHOOL
5901 N. Broad St., Philadelphia 19141-1801
Type: Private *Accred.:* 1986 (ACCSCT) *Calendar:* Courses of varying lengths *Degrees:* certificates *CEO:* Exec. Dir. Marc S. Jacobs
(215) 927-3232

WASHINGTON INSTITUTE OF TECHNOLOGY
82 S. Main St., Washington 15301-6810
Type: Private *Accred.:* 1974/1989 (ACCSCT) *Calendar:* Courses of varying lengths *Degrees:* certificates, diplomas *CEO:* Dir. Ron Davis
(412) 222-1942

WELDER TRAINING AND TESTING INSTITUTE
729 E. Highland St., Allentown 18103-1263
Type: Private *Accred.:* 1973/1988 (ACCSCT) *Calendar:* Courses of varying lengths *Degrees:* certificates *CEO:* Dir. Patrick F. Dorris
(215) 437-9720

WELDER TRAINING AND TESTING INSTITUTE
100 Pennsylvania Ave., Selinsgrove 17870-9339 *Type:* Private *Accred.:* 1985/1990 (ACCSCT) *Calendar:* Courses of varying lengths *Degrees:* certificates *CEO:* Exec. Dir. Ted S. Zenzinger
(800) 326-9306

WESTERN SCHOOL OF HEALTH AND BUSINESS CAREERS
411 Seventh Ave., 2nd Fl., Pittsburgh 15219-1905 *Type:* Private *Accred.:* 1986 (ACCSCT) *Calendar:* Courses of varying lengths *Degrees:* certificates *Prof. Accred.:* Histologic Technology, Medical Assisting *CEO:* Pres. Ross M. Perilman
(412) 281-2600

BRANCH CAMPUS
One Monroeville Ctr., Rte. 22 and 3824 Northern Pike, Monroeville 15146-2142 *Accred.:* 1986 (ACCSCT) *Prof. Accred.:* Medical Assisting *CEO:* Vice Pres. Karen Perilman
(412) 373-6400

THE WILLIAMSON FREE SCHOOL OF MECHANICAL TRADES
106 S. New Middletown Rd., Media 19063-5299 *Type:* Private *Accred.:* 1970/1993 (ACCSCT) *Calendar:* Courses of varying lengths *Degrees:* certificates, diplomas *CEO:* Pres. Barry G. Schuler
(215) 566-1776

WILMA BOYD CAREER SCHOOLS
One Chatham Ctr., Pittsburgh 15219 *Type:* Private business and home study *Accred.:* 1975/1990 (ACISC); 1979/1990 (NHSC) *Calendar:* Courses of varying lengths *Degrees:* certificates, diplomas *CEO:* Pres./Dir. Ruth A. Delach
(412) 456-1800

BRANCH CAMPUS
Concourse Tower II, 2090 Palm Beach Lakes Blvd., West Palm Beach, FL 33409 *Accred.:* 1990 (ACISC) *CEO:* Dir. Sam A. Gentile
(407) 684-1222

YORK TECHNICAL INSTITUTE
3351 Whiteford Rd., York 17402-9017
Type: Private *Accred.:* 1979/1989 (ACCSCT) *Calendar:* Courses of varying lengths *Degrees:* diplomas *CEO:* Dir. Harold L. Maley
(717) 757-1100

PUERTO RICO

ABBYNELL BEAUTY & TECHNICAL INSTITUTE
Box 7216, Caguas 00626-7216 *Type:* Private *Accred.:* 1989 (ACCSCT) *Calendar:* Courses of varying lengths *Degrees:* certificates, diplomas *CEO:* Pres. Magdalena Reyes Ortiz
(809) 743-3339

ACADEMIA LANIN
752 Andalucia St., Puerto Nuevo, Rio Piedras 00921 *Type:* Private *Accred.:* 1979/1989 (ACCSCT) *Calendar:* Courses of varying lengths *Degrees:* certificates *CEO:* Owner Lanin A. de Santana
(809) 782-5890

ACADEMIA SINGER DEALER AUTORIZADO INC.
101 Comercio St., Ponce 00731 *Type:* Private *Accred.:* 1991 (ACCSCT) *Calendar:* Courses of varying lengths *Degrees:* certificates *CEO:* Owner/Pres. Anabel Santiago Rivera
(809) 848-4949

ALLIED SCHOOLS OF PUERTO RICO
P.O. Box 98, Bayamon 00960-0098 *Type:* Private business *Accred.:* 1984/1990 (ACISC) *Calendar:* Courses of varying lengths *Degrees:* certificates, diplomas *CEO:* Dir. Gustavo Sanchez
(809) 780-1612

AMERICAN EDUCATIONAL COLLEGE
P.O. Box 62, Carretera No. 2, KM 11 HM 8, Edificio Federal, Bayamon 00960 *Type:* Private business *Accred.:* 1985/1991 (ACISC) *Calendar:* Courses of varying lengths *Degrees:* certificates, diplomas *CEO:* Pres. Joaquin E. Gonzalez Pinto
(809) 798-1199

ANTILLES SCHOOL OF TECHNICAL CAREERS
Calle Domenech No. 107, Hato Rey 00917 *Type:* Private *Accred.:* 1985/1992 (ABHES) *Calendar:* Courses of varying lengths *Degrees:* certificates, diplomas *Prof. Accred.:* Practical Nursing *CEO:* Pres. Martha Luz Bravo
(809) 764-7576

ARTS AND BUSINESS COLLEGE OF PUERTO RICO
P.O. Box 1269, Caguas 00726-1269 *Type:* Private *Accred.:* 1991 (ACCSCT) *Calendar:* Courses of varying lengths *Degrees:* certificates *CEO:* Chrmn. of the Bd. Humberto Garcia
(809) 744-5493

BAYAMON TECHNICAL & COMMERCIAL INC.
P.O. Box 6007, Sta. No. 1, Bayamon 00619 *Type:* Private business *Accred.:* 1984/1987 (ACISC) *Calendar:* Courses of varying lengths *Degrees:* certificates, diplomas *CEO:* Pres. Wilson Del Toro
(809) 787-8805

BENEDICT SCHOOL OF LANGUAGES AND COMMERCE
45 Munoz Rivera Ave., Hato Rey 00918 *Type:* Private business *Accred.:* 1982/1989 (ACISC) *Calendar:* Qtr. plan *Degrees:* certificates, diplomas *CEO:* Dir. Angel Lopez
(809) 754-1199

BRANCH CAMPUS
Carretera 719, Ave. Villa, Universitaria No. 15, Barranquitas 00794 *Accred.:* 1993 (ACISC) *CEO:* Dir. Alba Aponte
(809) 754-1199

BRANCH CAMPUS
112 St., Km. 6, Barrio Maro, Isabela 00662 *Accred.:* 1993 (ACISC) *CEO:* Dir. Anibal Gonzalez
(809) 754-1199

BRANCH CAMPUS
McKinley Ave., No. 101, Manati 00674 *Accred.:* 1993 (ACISC) *CEO:* Dir. Jose Torres Gonzalez
(809) 884-4441

CENTRO DE ESTUDIOS MULTIDISCIPLINARIOS
602 Barbosa Ave., 2nd Fl., Hato Rey 00917-4387 *Type:* Private *Accred.:* 1981/1986 (ACCSCT) *Degrees:* certificates *Prof. Accred.:* Practical Nursing *CEO:* Dir. Juan F. Pagani
(809) 765-4210

BRANCH CAMPUS
6 Dr. Vidal St., Humacao 00791 *Accred.:*
1981/1986 (ACCSCT) *CEO:* Dir. Felix
Rivera Resto
(809) 852-5530

COLEGIO MAYOR DE TECNOLOGIA
Calle Morse No. 151, Arroyo 00714 *Type:*
Private *Accred.:* 1988 (ACCSCT) *Calendar:*
Courses of varying lengths *Degrees:* certifi-
cates *CEO:* Pres. Mancio Vicente
(809) 839-5266

COLEGIO TECNICO DE ELECTRICIDAD
1251 Franklin D. Roosevelt Ave., Puerto
Nuevo 00920 *Type:* Private *Accred.:* 1992
(ACCSCT) *Calendar:* Courses of varying
lengths *Degrees:* certificates *CEO:* Vice
Pres. Jorge A. Melecio Rivera
(809) 782-5126

COLEGIO TECNOLOGICO Y COMERCIAL DE
PUERTO RICO
Calle Paz 165 Altos, Aguado 00602 *Type:*
Private business *Accred.:* 1990 (ACISC)
Calendar: Courses of varying lengths *De-
grees:* certificates, diplomas *CEO:* Dir.
Roberto Davila Martinez
(809) 868-2688

D'MART INSTITUTE
Jose de Diego No. 150 Altos, Box 2337,
Cayey 00737-2337 *Type:* Private *Accred.:*
1991 (ACCSCT) *Calendar:* Courses of varying lengths *Degrees:* certificates *CEO:* Pres./
Owner Marta L. Rivera Luna
(809) 738-5474

ESCUELA DE PERITOS ELECTRICISTAS DE ISABEL
P.O. Box 457, Ave. Aguadilla No. 242, Isabel 00662 *Type:* Private *Accred.:* 1993
(ACCSCT) *Calendar:* Courses of varying
lengths *Degrees:* certificates *CEO:* Dir.
Maria M. Santiago Maldonado
(809) 872-1747

FASHION DESIGN COLLEGE
Calle Degetau No. 5, Esq. Betances, Bayamon 00961-6208 *Type:* Private *Accred.:*
1988 (ACCSCT) *Calendar:* Courses of varying lengths *Degrees:* certificates *CEO:* Pres.
Arturo Auiles
(809) 785-2388

BRANCH CAMPUS
210 Arzuage St., Rio Piedras 00925 *Accred.:* 1989 (ACCSCT) *CEO:* Pres. Arturo
Auiles
(809) 765-0001

FASHION MERCHANDISING AND TECHNICAL
INSTITUTE
P.O. Box 2206, Bayamon 00621 *Type:* Private *Accred.:* 1988 (ACCSCT) *Calendar:*
Courses of varying lengths *Degrees:* certificates *CEO:* Pres. Ralph James
(809) 798-8870

INSTITUTE OF MULTIPLE TECHNOLOGY
P.O. Box 209, Mayaguez 00709 *Type:* Private business *Accred.:* 1985/1992 (ACISC)
Calendar: Courses of varying lengths *Degrees:* certificates, diplomas *CEO:* Pres.
Angel L. Negron
(809) 833-6305

BRANCH CAMPUS
Calle Antonio R. Barcelo 163, P.O. Box
707, Arecibo 00681-0209 *Accred.:* 1985/
1991 (ACISC) *CEO:* Dir. Benjamin
Pagdilla
(809) 878-6844

INSTITUTO CHAVIANO DE MAYAGUEZ
Calle Ramos Antonini, No. 116 Este,
Mayaguez 00608-5045 *Type:* Private *Accred.:* 1988 (ACCSCT) *Calendar:* Courses
of varying lengths *Degrees:* certificates
CEO: Vice Pres. Blanca Llantin
(809) 833-2474

INSTITUTO DE BANCA Y COMERCIO
996 Munoz Rivera Ave., Rio Piedras 00927
Type: Private business *Accred.:* 1978/1989
(ACISC) *Calendar:* Courses of varying
lengths *Degrees:* certificates, diplomas
CEO: Dir. Sairreio Diaz
(809) 765-8687

BRANCH CAMPUS
Box K, 164 Jose de Diego, Cayey 00634
Accred.: 1988/1989 (ACISC) *CEO:* Dir.
Josereul Jocman
(809) 738-5555

BRANCH CAMPUS
Munoz Rovera 205, Fajardo 00648 *Accred.:* 1978/1989 (ACISC) *CEO:* Dir.
Moises Rodriguez
(809) 860-6262

BRANCH CAMPUS
Box 6092, Edificio Iraola, St. No. 3 RR-1, Guayama 00654-9601 *Accred.:* 1988/1989 (ACISC) *CEO:* Chf. Admin. Edgardo Garcia Vasquez
(809) 864-3220

BRANCH CAMPUS
Carrera No. 2, KM 49.4, Manati 00701 *Accred.:* 1978/1989 (ACISC) *CEO:* Dir. Jaime Nez
(809) 854-6709

BRANCH CAMPUS
Calle Post No. 154 N., Mayaguez 00708 *Accred.:* 1986/1991 (ACISC) *CEO:* Vice Pres. Antonio Santos
(809) 833-4690

BRANCH CAMPUS
Edificio Torre de Oro, Ave. Las Americas, Ponce 00731 *Accred.:* 1983/1989 (ACISC) *CEO:* Dir. Jose Santiago
(809) 840-6119

INSTITUTO DE COSMETOLOGIA Y ESTETICA "LA REINE"
Ave. Colon No. 8A, Manati 00674 *Type:* Private *Accred.:* 1992 (ACCSCT) *Calendar:* Courses of varying lengths *Degrees:* certificates *CEO:* Owner Carmen Ocasio
(809) 854-1119

INSTITUTO DE EDUCACION UNIVERSIDAD
P.O. Box 1027, Sabana Seca 00947-1027 *Type:* Private *Accred.:* 1984/1989 (ACCSCT) *Calendar:* Courses of varying lengths *Degrees:* certificates *CEO:* Pres. Juan Jimenez
(809) 798-8606

BRANCH CAMPUS
Aptdo. 209, Carolina 00986 *Accred.:* 1989 (ACCSCT) *CEO:* Dir. Daisy Rodriguez Saea
(809) 757-5000

BRANCH CAMPUS
404 Ave. Barbosa, Hato Rey 00917-4302 *Accred.:* 1989 (ACCSCT) *CEO:* Dir. Gloria Lourdes Roman
(809) 767-2000

INSTITUTO DEL ARTE MODERNO
Ave. Monserrate FR-5, Villa Fontana, Carolina 00938-3912 *Type:* Private *Accred.:* 1986 (ACCSCT) *Calendar:* Courses of varying lengths *Degrees:* certificates *CEO:* Dir. Myriam Aponte
(809) 768-2532

INSTITUTO TECNICO DE LAS ARTES MANUALES
P.O. Box 2911, Marina Sta., Mayaguez 00681 *Type:* Private *Accred.:* 1993 (ACCSCT) *Calendar:* Courses of varying lengths *Degrees:* certificates *CEO:* Owner Kelmy Morales
(809) 851-1658

INSTITUTO VOCACIONAL CURELZA
P.O. Box 617, Corozal 00643 *Type:* Private *Accred.:* 1992 (ACCSCT) *Calendar:* Courses of varying lengths *Degrees:* certificates *CEO:* Owner Monserrate Rivera Rosado
(809) 859-1274

INSTITUTO VOCATIONAL Y COMERCIAL, EDCI
Calle 8, Equina 5 Urb., P.O. Box 9120, Caguas 00625 *Type:* Private business *Accred.:* 1990 (ACISC) *Calendar:* Courses of varying lengths *Degrees:* certificates, diplomas *CEO:* Pres. Jose Cartagena
(809) 743-4346

INTERAMERICAN BUSINESS COLLEGE
Box 202, Munoz Rivera No. 504 Altos, Hato Rey 00918 *Type:* Private business *Accred.:* 1983/1986 (ACISC) *Calendar:* Courses of varying lengths *Degrees:* certificates, diplomas *CEO:* Pres. Chris Burgos
(809) 753-1500

BRANCH CAMPUS
Calle Betances, Esq. Palmas, Arecibo 00612-1947 *Accred.:* 1986 (ACISC) *CEO:* Dir. Hector Vasquez
(809) 384-4481

BRANCH CAMPUS
Interior Rd. 923, BO.O, P.O. Box 823, Humacao 00661-0823 *Accred.:* 1987 (ACISC) *CEO:* Dir. Moses Gonzales
(809) 852-6444

INTERNATIONAL TECHNICAL COLLEGE
1302 Central Ave., Puerto Nuevo, Rio Piedras 00921 *Type:* Private *Accred.:* 1988 (ACCSCT) *Calendar:* Courses of varying

lengths *Degrees:* certificates *CEO:* Pres. Roberto Rios Rivera

(809) 792-5620

LICEO DE ARTE Y DISENOS
Calle Acosta No. 47, P.O. Box 1889, Caguas 00626-1889 *Type:* Private *Accred.:* 1991 (ACCSCT) *Calendar:* Courses of varying lengths *Degrees:* certificates *CEO:* Exec. Dir. Sylvia Rodriguez Aponte

(809) 743-7447

LICEO DE ARTE Y TECNOLOGIA
P.O. Box 2346, Hato Rey 00918-2346 *Type:* Private *Accred.:* 1978/1988 (ACCSCT) *Calendar:* Courses of varying lengths *Degrees:* certificates *CEO:* Dir. Carlos M. Valencia

(809) 754-9800

MBTI BUSINESS TRAINING INSTITUTE
1256 Ponce de Leon Ave., Santurce 00907 *Type:* Private business *Accred.:* 1974/1986 (ACISC) *Calendar:* Courses of varying lengths *Degrees:* certificates, diplomas *CEO:* Dir. John Barbosa

(809) 723-9402

MERLIX PROFESSIONAL & TECHNICAL INSTITUTE
Calle Betances No. 24, Box 6241, Sta. 1, Bayamon 00961-9998 *Type:* Private *Accred.:* 1988 (ACCSCT) *Calendar:* Courses of varying lengths *Degrees:* certificates *CEO:* Admin. Dir. Felix M. Vargas

(809) 786-7035

METRO COLLEGE, INC.
1126 Ponce de Leon Ave., Rio Piedras 00928 *Type:* Private business *Accred.:* 1989 (ACISC) *Calendar:* Courses of varying lengths *Degrees:* certificates, diplomas *CEO:* Pres. Luis E. Vazquez

(809) 754-7120

BRANCH CAMPUS
Mendez Vigo No. 20, Ponce 00731 *Accred.:* 1993 (ACISC) *CEO:* Dir. Raquel Reyes

(809) 754-7120

NATIONAL COMPUTER COLLEGE
P.O. Box 1009, Fajardo 00648 *Type:* Private business *Accred.:* 1986/1990 (ACISC) *Calendar:* Courses of varying lengths *Degrees:*

certificates, diplomas *CEO:* Pres. Antonio Caban

(809) 863-0593

PONCE COLLEGE OF TECHNOLOGY
Estrella St., No. 57, Box 1284, Ponce 00733-1284 *Type:* Private *Accred.:* 1980/1990 (ACCSCT) *Calendar:* Courses of varying lengths *Degrees:* certificates, diplomas *CEO:* Exec. Dir. William Hart

(809) 844-5325

PONCE PARAMEDICAL COLLEGE
L-15 Acacia St., Villa Flores Urbanization, Ponce 00731 *Type:* Private *Accred.:* 1988 (ACCSCT) *Calendar:* Courses of varying lengths *Degrees:* certificates *CEO:* Exec. Dir. Alberto Aristizabal

(809) 848-1589

PONCE TECHNICAL SCHOOL, INC.
16 Salud St., Ponce 00731 *Type:* Private *Accred.:* 1985/1992 (ABHES) *Calendar:* Courses of varying lengths *Degrees:* certificates, diplomas *Prof. Accred.:* Practical Nursing *CEO:* Pres. Fernando Torres

(809) 844-7940

PROFESSIONAL ELECTRICAL SCHOOL
Ramos Velez No. 3, P.O. Box 1797, Manati 00704 *Type:* Private *Accred.:* 1993 (ACCSCT) *Calendar:* Courses of varying lengths *Degrees:* certificates *CEO:* Dir. Paulino Delgado

(809) 854-4776

PROFESSIONAL TECHNICAL INSTITUTION
Betances Mail Sta., Ave. Betances No. 73, Ste. 491, Bayamon 00959-5200 *Type:* Private *Accred.:* 1993 (ACCSCT) *Calendar:* Courses of varying lengths *Degrees:* certificates *CEO:* Pres. Luis L. Montero

(809) 740-6810

PROFESSIONAL TRAINING ACADEMY OF ESTHETICS & BEAUTY COURSES
Cristina No. 74, P.O. Box 7716, Ponce 00732-7716 *Type:* Private *Accred.:* 1991 (ACCSCT) *Calendar:* Courses of varying lengths *Degrees:* certificates *CEO:* Pres. Carmen Molina

(809) 844-5960

BRANCH CAMPUS
Munoz Rivera No. 504, Hato Rey 00917 *Accred.:* 1991 (ACCSCT) *CEO:* Pres. Carmen Molina
(809) 766-2199

BRANCH CAMPUS
Mendez Vigo Corner to Pilar, Mayaguez 00680 *Accred.:* 1991 (ACCSCT) *CEO:* Pres. Carmen Molina
(809) 265-5270

PUERTO RICO BARBER COLLEGE
2018 Borinquen Ave., Box 14215, B.O. Obrero Sta., Santurce 00916-4215 *Type:* Private *Accred.:* 1988 (ACCSCT) *Calendar:* Courses of varying lengths *Degrees:* certificates *CEO:* Pres. Sergio Cardona
(809) 727-1961

BRANCH CAMPUS
E52 Garrido Morales St., Fajardo 00648 *Accred.:* 1988 (ACCSCT) *CEO:* Dir. Jose Rivera
(809) 863-2970

PUERTO RICO HOTEL SCHOOL
Box 4435, Old San Juan Sta., San Juan 00905 *Type:* Private business *Accred.:* 1993 (ACISC) *Calendar:* Courses of varying lengths *Degrees:* certificates *CEO:* Dir. Magal Gonzalez
(809) 791-6210

PUERTO RICO PROFESSIONAL COLLEGE
Calle Dr. Veve No. 51, Esq. Degetau, Baya-mon 00960 *Type:* Private *Accred.:* 1990 (ACCSCT) *Calendar:* Courses of varying lengths *Degrees:* certificates *CEO:* Pres. Ismael Mercado Hermandez
(809) 798-8200

PUERTO RICO TECHNICAL JUNIOR COLLEGE
Ave. Ponce de Leon No. 703, Hato Rey 00917 *Type:* Private *Accred.:* 1992 (ACC-SCT) *Calendar:* Courses of varying lengths *Degrees:* certificates *CEO:* Pres. Jose M. Muriente-Grana
(809) 751-0133

SAN JUAN CITY COLLEGE
501 Roberto H. Todd Ave., Call Box 9300, Santurce Sta., Santurce 00908-9998 *Type:* Private *Accred.:* 1984/1990 (ACCSCT) *Calendar:* Courses of varying lengths *Degrees:* certificates *CEO:* Pres. Americo Reyes Morales
(809) 725-5050

BRANCH CAMPUS
Call Box 4040, Arecibo 00613 *Accred.:* 1993 (ACCSCT) *CEO:* Dir. Americo Reyes Morales
(809) 724-5050

BRANCH CAMPUS
P.O. Box 1821, Juana Diaz 00665-1821 *Accred.:* 1990 (ACCSCT) *CEO:* Dir. Juan Rivera
(809) 837-5050

YORK COLLEGE
P.O. Box 5183, San Juan 00906-5183 *Type:* Private *Accred.:* 1988/1993 (ACCSCT) *Calendar:* Courses of varying lengths *Degrees:* certificates *CEO:* Pres./Dir. Victor Vega
(809) 722-2000

RHODE ISLAND

HALL INSTITUTE OF TECHNOLOGY
120 High St., Pawtucket 02860-2151 *Type:* Private *Accred.:* 1980/1993 (ACCSCT) *Calendar:* Courses of varying lengths *Degrees:* certificates *CEO:* Pres. Charles K. Rogers
(401) 722-2003

NASSON INSTITUTE
1080 Newport Ave., Pawtucket 02861 *Type:* Private business *Accred.:* 1980/1986 (ACISC) *Calendar:* Courses of varying lengths *Degrees:* certificates, diplomas *CEO:* Dir. Ella Cain
(401) 728-1570

BRANCH CAMPUS
1276 Bald Hill Rd., Warwick 02886 *Accred.:* 1993 (ACISC) *CEO:* Lead Instructor Betty Monahan
(401) 823-3773

BRANCH CAMPUS
191 Social St., Woonsocket 02895 *Accred.:* 1993 (ACISC) *CEO:* Lead Instructor Judy Shea
(401) 769-2066

NEW ENGLAND TECHNICAL COLLEGE
2500 Post Rd., Warwick 02886 *Type:* Private *Accred.:* 1991 (ACCSCT) *Calendar:* Courses of varying lengths *Degrees:* diplomas *CEO:* Pres. Richard I. Gouse
(401) 739-5000

NEW ENGLAND TRACTOR TRAILER TRAINING SCHOOL OF RHODE ISLAND
10 Dunnell La., Pawtucket 02860-5801 *Type:* Private *Accred.:* 1986/1993 (ACCSCT) *Calendar:* Courses of varying lengths *Degrees:* certificates *CEO:* Dir. Fred Hazard
(401) 725-1220

OCEAN STATE BUSINESS INSTITUTE
Mariner Sq., Boxes 1 and 2, 140 Point Judith Rd., Unit 3a, Narragansett 02882 *Type:* Private business *Accred.:* 1979/1991 (ACISC) *Calendar:* Courses of varying lengths *Degrees:* certificates, diplomas *CEO:* Dir. Assunta G. Pouliot
(401) 789-0287

RHODE ISLAND SCHOOL OF PHOTOGRAPHY
241 Webster Ave., Providence 02909-3891 *Type:* Private *Accred.:* 1982/1987 (ACCSCT) *Calendar:* Courses of varying lengths *Degrees:* diplomas *CEO:* Pres. Donald Folgo
(401) 943-7722

RHODE ISLAND TRADES SHOPS SCHOOL
361 W. Fountain St., Providence 02903-3513 *Type:* Private *Accred.:* 1971/1988 (ACCSCT) *Calendar:* Courses of varying lengths *Degrees:* diplomas *CEO:* Exec. Dir. John M. Anjos
(401) 331-3008

SAWYER SCHOOL
101 Main St., Pawtucket 02860 *Type:* Private business *Accred.:* 1973/1991 (ACISC) *Calendar:* Courses of varying lengths *Degrees:* certificates, diplomas *CEO:* Pres. John F. Crowley
(401) 272-8400

BRANCH CAMPUS
1109 Warwick Ave., Warwick 02888 *Accred.:* 1979/1989 (ACISC) *CEO:* Dir. Kristen Croce
(401) 781-2887

SCHOOL OF MEDICAL AND LEGAL SECRETARIAL SCIENCES
60 S. Angell St., Providence 02906-5208 *Type:* Private *Accred.:* 1981/1986 (ACCSCT) *Calendar:* Courses of varying lengths *Degrees:* certificates *CEO:* Pres. Norma M. Casale
(401) 331-1711

SOUTH CAROLINA

ALPHA BEAUTY SCHOOL
10 Liberty La., Greenville 29607 *Type:* Private *Accred.:* 1986/1991 (SACS-COEI) *Calendar:* Courses of varying lengths *Degrees:* certificates *CEO:* Dir. Kenneth W. Lochridge
FTE Enroll: 307   (803) 271-0020

BRANCH CAMPUS
Tunnel Rd., Innsbruck Mall, Asheville, NC 28805 *CEO:* Dir. Vera Hendricks
                (704) 253-2875

BRANCH CAMPUS
2619 S. Main St., Anderson 29624 *CEO:* Dir. Ethel Audrey
                (803) 224-8338

BRANCH CAMPUS
112 E. North and Second Sts., Seneca 29678 *CEO:* Dir. Deborah McCullough
                (803) 882-0936

BRANCH CAMPUS
653 N. Church St., Spartanburg 29301 *CEO:* Dir. Barbara Cash
                (803) 585-6666

BETTY STEVENS COSMETOLOGY INSTITUTE
301 Rainbow Dr., Florence 29501 *Type:* Private *Accred.:* 1985/1990 (SACS-COEI) *Calendar:* Courses of varying lengths *Degrees:* certificates *CEO:* Dir. Betty Humphries
FTE Enroll: 42   (803) 669-4452

CAMDEN SCHOOL OF HAIR DESIGN
2630 N. Broad St., Camden 29020 *Type:* Private *Accred.:* 1987 (SACS-COEI) *Calendar:* Courses of varying lengths *Degrees:* certificates *CEO:* Dir. Corliss Hinson
FTE Enroll: 94   (803) 425-1011

CHARLESTON COSMETOLOGY INSTITUTE
8484 Dorchester Rd., Charleston 29420 *Type:* Private *Accred.:* 1986/1991 (SACS-COEI) *Calendar:* Courses of varying lengths *Degrees:* certificates *CEO:* Dir. Jerry R. Poer, Jr.
FTE Enroll: 355   (803) 552-3670

CHARZANNE BEAUTY COLLEGE
1549 Hwy. 72, E., Greenwood 29649 *Type:* Private *Accred.:* 1986/1988 (SACS-COEI) *Calendar:* Courses of varying lengths *Degrees:* certificates *CEO:* Dir. Evangeline Levesque
FTE Enroll: 51   (803) 223-7321

CHRIS LOGAN CAREER COLLEGE
505 Seventh Ave., N., Myrtle Beach 29578 *Type:* Private *Accred.:* 1988 (SACS-COEI) *Calendar:* Courses of varying lengths *Degrees:* certificates *CEO:* Dir. Chris Logan
FTE Enroll: 2,041   (803) 448-6302

BRANCH CAMPUS
3420 Clemson Blvd., Anderson 29624 *CEO:* Dir. Chris Logan
                (803) 226-8438

BRANCH CAMPUS
1125 15-401 By-pass, Ste. A, Bennettsville 29512 *CEO:* Dir. Chris Logan
                (803) 479-4076

BRANCH CAMPUS
4830 Forest Dr., Columbia 29206 *CEO:* Dir. Chris Logan
                (803) 787-8621

BRANCH CAMPUS
1810-B Second Loop Rd., Florence 29501 *CEO:* Dir. Chris Logan
                (803) 665-4602

BRANCH CAMPUS
1235 S. Pleasantburg Dr., Ste. A, Greenville 29605 *CEO:* Dir. Chris Logan
                (803) 299-0000

BRANCH CAMPUS
Martintown Plaza, North Augusta 29841 *CEO:* Dir. Chris Logan
                (803) 278-1238

BRANCH CAMPUS
1930 N. Cherry Rd., Rock Hill 29730 *CEO:* Dir. Chris Logan
                (803) 328-1838

BRANCH CAMPUS
256 S. Pike Rd., Sumter 29150 *CEO:* Dir. Chris Logan
                (803) 773-8481

FARAH'S BEAUTY SCHOOL
520 Bush River Rd., Columbia 29210 *Type:*
Private *Accred.:* 1987 (SACS-COEI) *Calendar:* Courses of varying lengths *Degrees:*
certificates *CEO:* Dir. Rebecca Farah
FTE Enroll: 59   (803) 772-0101

FARAH'S BEAUTY SCHOOL
107 Central Ave., Goose Creek 29445 *Type:*
Private *Accred.:* 1985/1990 (SACS-COEI)
Calendar: Courses of varying lengths *Degrees:* certificates *CEO:* Dir. Albert D. Farah
FTE Enroll: 76   (803) 572-5705

MANGUM'S BARBER AND HAIRSTYLING COLLEGE
125 Hampton St., Rock Hill 29730-4509
Type: Private *Accred.:* 1985/1990 (ACC-SCT) *Calendar:* Courses of varying lengths
Degrees: diplomas *CEO:* Dir. Alice
Mangum
                                          (803) 328-0807

NAVY FLEET AND MINE WARFARE TRAINING
CENTER
Charleston Naval Base, Charleston 29408
Type: Public (federal) *Accred.:* 1988/1993
(SACS-COEI) *Calendar:* Courses of varying
lengths *Degrees:* certificates *CEO:* Commandant W.H. Sadler, U.S.N.
FTE Enroll: 201   (803) 743-4722

NIELSEN ELECTRONICS INSTITUTE
1600 Meeting St., Charleston 29405-9987
Type: Private *Accred.:* 1974/1989 (ACC-SCT) *Calendar:* Qtr. plan *Degrees:* certificates *CEO:* Pres./C.E.O. Robert R. Nielsen
                                          (803) 722-2344

NORTH AMERICAN INSTITUTE OF AVIATION
Conway-Horry County Airport, P.O. Box
680, Conway 29526-0680 *Type:* Private *Ac-*

cred.: 1981/1986 (ACCSCT) *Calendar:*
Courses of varying lengths *Degrees:* certificates *CEO:* Pres. Douglas W. Beckner
                                          (803) 397-9111

PETTIT SCHOOL OF RADIOLOGIC TECHNOLOGY
316 Calhoun St., Charleston 29401 *Type:*
Private *Calendar:* Courses of varying
lengths *Degrees:* certificates *Prof. Accred.:*
Radiography *CEO:* Dir. James Rogers
                                          (803) 724-2910

PROFESSIONAL HAIR DESIGN ACADEMY
1540 Wade Hampton Blvd., Greenville
29607-5063 *Type:* Private *Accred.:* 1987
(ACCSCT) *Calendar:* Courses of varying
lengths *Degrees:* diplomas *CEO:* Owner
Stewart A. Smith
                                          (803) 232-2676

ROYAL ACADEMY OF HAIR DESIGN
Clinton Plaza, Drawer 533, Clinton 29325
Type: Private *Accred.:* 1989 (SACS-COEI)
Calendar: Courses of varying lengths *Degrees:* diplomas *CEO:* Dir. David Alley
FTE Enroll: 73   (803) 833-6976

SOUTH CAROLINA CRIMINAL JUSTICE ACADEMY
5400 Broad River Rd., Columbia 29210
Type: Public (state) professional *Accred.:*
1991 (SACS-COEI) *Calendar:* Courses of
varying lengths *Degrees:* certificates, diplomas *CEO:* Dir. Walter J. Johnson, Jr.
FTE Enroll: 418   (803) 737-8400

SUMTER BEAUTY COLLEGE
921 Carolina Ave., Sumter 29150 *Type:* Private *Accred.:* 1988/1993 (SACS-COEI) *Calendar:* Courses of varying lengths *Degrees:*
certificates *CEO:* Dir. Faye Smith
FTE Enroll: 42   (803) 773-7311

SOUTH DAKOTA

STENOTYPE INSTITUTE OF SOUTH DAKOTA
705 West Ave. N., Sioux Falls 57104 *Type:*
Private business *Accred.:* 1975/1988
(ACISC) *Calendar:* Courses of varying
lengths *Degrees:* certificates, diplomas
CEO: Pres. Linda Clauson
(605) 336-1442

TENNESSEE

ARNOLD'S BEAUTY SCHOOL
1179 S. Second St., Milan 38358 *Type:* Private *Accred.:* 1983/1988 (SACS-COEI) *Calendar:* Courses of varying lengths *Degrees:* certificates *CEO:* Dir. Norma Arnold
FTE Enroll: 36   (901) 686-7351

ARTISTE SCHOOL OF COSMETOLOGY
129 Springbrook Dr., Johnson City 37601-1711 *Type:* Private *Accred.:* 1988 (ACC-SCT) *Calendar:* Courses of varying lengths *Degrees:* certificates *CEO:* Owner Phyllis Blair
           (615) 282-2279

BOBBIE'S SCHOOL OF BEAUTY ARTS
108 Decatur Pike, Athens 37371 *Type:* Private *Accred.:* 1992 (SACS-COEI) *Calendar:* Courses of varying lengths *Degrees:* certificates *CEO:* Dir. Bobbie Wallace
FTE Enroll: 47   (615) 744-7251

BRANELL INSTITUTE
6600 Bldg., 182 Eastgate Ctr., Chattanooga 37411 *Type:* Private business *Accred.:* 1979/1989 (ACISC); 1992 (SACS-COEI) *Calendar:* Courses of varying lengths *Degrees:* certificates, diplomas *CEO:* Dir. Darlene Johnston
FTE Enroll: 154   (615) 899-3060

BRANELL INSTITUTE
786 Two Mile Pkwy., Goodlettsville 37072 *Type:* Private business *Accred.:* 1986/1992 (ACISC); 1992/1993 (SACS-COEI) *Calendar:* Courses of varying lengths *Degrees:* certificates, diplomas *CEO:* Dir. Ron Hall
FTE Enroll: 221   (615) 851-1881

BRANELL INSTITUTE
5110 Park Ave., Memphis 38117 *Type:* Private business *Accred.:* 1987/1990 (ACISC); 1992 (SACS-COEI) *Calendar:* Courses of varying lengths *Degrees:* certificates, diplomas *CEO:* Dir. W.D. John Almond
FTE Enroll: 213   (901) 763-3400

BRANELL INSTITUTE
2424 Hillsboro Pike, No. 100, Nashville 37212 *Type:* Private business *Accred.:* 1986/1989 (ACISC); 1988 (SACS-COEI) *Calendar:* Courses of varying lengths *Degrees:*

certificates, diplomas *CEO:* Dir. Sherry Arnold
FTE Enroll: 214   (615) 297-1100

CHATTANOOGA BARBER COLLEGE
405 Market St., Chattanooga 37402-1204 *Type:* Private *Accred.:* 1987 (ACCSCT) *Calendar:* Courses of varying lengths *Degrees:* diplomas *CEO:* Owner Judy E. Griggs
           (615) 266-7013

CONCORDE CAREER INSTITUTE
5100 Poplar Ave., Ste. 132, Memphis 38137 *Type:* Private *Accred.:* 1980/1990 (SACS-COEI) *Calendar:* Courses of varying lengths *Degrees:* certificates *CEO:* Dir. Tommy Stewart
FTE Enroll: 462   (901) 761-9494

COURT REPORTING ACADEMY & SCHOOL OF PROFESSIONAL STUDIES
1101 Kermit Dr., Ste. 513, Nashville 37217 *Type:* Private *Accred.:* 1992 (SACS-COEI) *Calendar:* Courses of varying lengths *Degrees:* certificates *CEO:* Dir. Linda Bland
FTE Enroll: 36   (615) 366-0566

CUMBERLAND SCHOOL OF TECHNOLOGY
1065 E. Tenth St., Cookeville 38501 *Type:* Private 2-year *Accred.:* 1988/1993 (SACS-COEI) *Calendar:* Courses of varying lengths *Degrees:* diplomas *Prof. Accred.:* Medical Laboratory Technology, Medical Laboratory Technology (AMA) *CEO:* Pres. Laverne Floyd
FTE Enroll: 137   (615) 526-3660

BRANCH CAMPUS
4173 Government St., Baton Rouge, LA 70806 *CEO:* Dir. Laverne Floyd
           (504) 338-9085

DAVIDSON TECHNICAL COLLEGE
212 Pavilion Blvd., Nashville 37217 *Type:* Private *Accred.:* 1988 (SACS-COEI) *Calendar:* Courses of varying lengths *Degrees:* certificates *CEO:* Dir. Suzanne Davidson
FTE Enroll: 168   (615) 360-3300

BRANCH CAMPUS
525 E. Main St., Jackson 38301 *CEO:* Dir. Wanda Griffiths
           (901) 424-6795

DRAUGHONS COLLEGE
3200 Elvis Presley Blvd., Memphis 38116
Type: Private *Accred.:* 1960/1990 (ACISC)
Calendar: Qtr. plan *Degrees:* certificates,
diplomas *CEO:* Exec. Dir. Ann H. Gibson
(901) 332-7800

BRANCH CAMPUS
Ste. 101, 1430 W. Peachtree St., Atlanta,
GA 30309 *Accred.:* 1990 (ACISC) *CEO:*
Exec. Dir. Ann H. Gibson
(404) 892-0814

BRANCH CAMPUS
Ste. 111, 6202 S. Lewis Pl., Tulsa, OK
74136 *Accred.:* 1988 (ACISC) *CEO:* Dir.
Anita Bates
(918) 749-7700

ELECTRONIC COMPUTER PROGRAMMING COLLEGE
3805 Brainerd Rd., Chattanooga 37411-3798
Type: Private *Accred.:* 1982/1987 (ACC-
SCT) *Calendar:* Courses of varying lengths
Degrees: certificates *CEO:* Dir. Jo Ann
Pearson
(615) 624-0077

FORT SANDERS SCHOOL OF NURSING
1915 White Ave., Knoxville 37916 *Type:*
Private *Accred.:* 1993 (SACS-COEI) *Calendar:* Courses of varying lengths *Degrees:*
diplomas *Prof. Accred.:* Nursing (diplomas)
CEO: Dir. Margaret Heins
FTE Enroll: 86 (615) 541-1290

HEALTH CARE TRAINING INSTITUTE
1378 Union Ave., Memphis 38104 *Type:*
Private *Accred.:* 1988 (SACS-COEI) *Calendar:* Courses of varying lengths *Degrees:*
certificates *CEO:* Dir. Carl Gentry
FTE Enroll: 105 (901) 722-2288

INTERNATIONAL BARBER AND STYLE COLLEGE
619 S. Gallatin Rd., Madison 37115-4012
Type: Private *Accred.:* 1985/1990 (ACC-
SCT) *Calendar:* Courses of varying lengths
Degrees: certificates, diplomas *CEO:* Dir.
Janet C. Dunn
(615) 860-4247

INTERNATIONAL CAREER SCHOOL
7647 Bellfort St., Houston, TX 77061-
1707 *Accred.:* 1993 (ACCSCT) *CEO:* Dir.
Henry Perry
(713) 649-0067

NATIONAL SCHOOL OF HAIR DESIGN
3641 Brainerd Rd., Chattanooga 37411-
3604 *Accred.:* 1989 (ACCSCT) *CEO:* Dir.
Steve Barnett
(615) 624-6451

JETT COLLEGE OF COSMETOLOGY & BARBERING
3744 N. Watkins St., Memphis 38217 *Type:*
Private *Accred.:* 1983/1989 (SACS-COEI)
Calendar: Courses of varying lengths *De-
grees:* certificates *CEO:* Dir. Mary Leake
FTE Enroll: 68 (901) 358-5121

JETT COLLEGE OF COSMETOLOGY & BARBERING
3740 N. Watkins St., Memphis 38127 *Type:*
Private *Accred.:* 1989/1991 (SACS-COEI)
Calendar: Courses of varying lengths *De-
grees:* certificates *CEO:* Dir. Mary Lou
Holland
FTE Enroll: 116 (901) 357-0388

JETT COLLEGE OF COSMETOLOGY & BARBERING
1286 Southbrook Mall, Memphis 38116
Type: Private *Accred.:* 1989/1991 (SACS-
COEI) *Calendar:* Courses of varying lengths
Degrees: certificates *CEO:* Dir. Delores
Dunlap
FTE Enroll: 125 (901) 332-7330

JETT COLLEGE OF COSMETOLOGY & BARBERING
524 S. Cooper St., Memphis 38104 *Type:*
Private *Accred.:* 1989/1991 (SACS-COEI)
Calendar: Courses of varying lengths *De-
grees:* certificates *CEO:* Dir. Maggie Stewart
FTE Enroll: 47 (901) 276-1721

JETT COLLEGE OF COSMETOLOGY & BARBERING
5016 Navy Rd., Millington 38053 *Type:* Private *Accred.:* 1989/1991 (SACS-COEI) *Calendar:* Courses of varying lengths *Degrees:*
certificates *CEO:* Dir. Gerald Scott
FTE Enroll: 48 (901) 872-2208

KNOXVILLE INSTITUTE OF HAIR DESIGN
1221 N. Central St., Knoxville 37917-6366
Type: Private *Accred.:* 1979/1993 (ACC-
SCT) *Calendar:* Courses of varying lengths
Degrees: certificates *CEO:* Dir. Jack W.
Rogers
(615) 971-1529

KNOXVILLE JOB CORPS CENTER
621 Dale Ave., Knoxville 37921 *Type:* Private *Accred.:* 1990/1993 (SACS-COEI) *Cal-*

endar: Courses of varying lengths *Degrees:* certificates *CEO:* Dir. Rodney Chambers
FTE Enroll: 436   (615) 544-5600

MEDICAL CAREER COLLEGE
537 Main St., Nashville 37206 *Type:* Private *Accred.:* 1992 (SACS-COEI) *Calendar:* Qtr. plan *Degrees:* diplomas *CEO:* Pres. Nollie Long
FTE Enroll: 92   (615) 255-7531

MID-STATE BARBER STYLING COLLEGE INC.
510 Jefferson St., Nashville 37208-2626 *Type:* Private *Accred.:* 1991 (ACCSCT) *Calendar:* Courses of varying lengths *Degrees:* certificates *CEO:* Dir. James Oldham
                    (615) 242-9300

MIDSOUTH SCHOOL OF BEAUTY
3974 Elvis Presley Blvd., Memphis 38116 *Type:* Private *Accred.:* 1990 (SACS-COEI) *Calendar:* Courses of varying lengths *Degrees:* diplomas *CEO:* Dir. John Pitts
FTE Enroll: 156   (901) 332-6700

MILLER-HAWKINS BUSINESS COLLEGE
1399 Madison Ave., Memphis 38104 *Type:* Private business *Accred.:* 1965/1988 (ACISC) *Calendar:* Qtr. plan *Degrees:* certificates, diplomas *CEO:* Dir. Faith B. Barcroft
                    (901) 725-6614

MILLER-MOTTE BUSINESS COLLEGE
1820 Business Park Dr., Clarksville 37040 *Type:* Private *Accred.:* 1987/1992 (ACISC); 1990 (SACS-COEI) *Calendar:* Courses of varying lengths *Degrees:* certificates, diplomas *CEO:* Dir. Raymond M. Green
FTE Enroll: 161   (615) 553-0071

MISTER WAYNE'S SCHOOL OF UNISEX HAIR DESIGN
170 S. Willow Ave., Cookeville 38501 *Type:* Private *Accred.:* 1985/1990 (ACCSCT) *Calendar:* Courses of varying lengths *Degrees:* diplomas *CEO:* Owner Charles W. Fletcher
                    (615) 526-1478

NASHVILLE AUTO DIESEL COLLEGE
1524 Gallatin Rd., Nashville 37206-3298 *Type:* Private *Accred.:* 1967/1990 (ACCSCT) *Calendar:* Courses of varying lengths *Degrees:* diplomas *CEO:* Pres. Thomas Hooper
                    (615) 226-3990

NASHVILLE COLLEGE
402 Plaza Professional Bldg., Madison 37115-4696 *Type:* Private *Accred.:* 1990 (ACCSCT) *Calendar:* Courses of varying lengths *Degrees:* certificates *Prof. Accred.:* Medical Assisting *CEO:* Pres. Abdullah Malek
                    (615) 868-2963

NAVAL AIR TECHNICAL TRAINING CENTER
Naval Air Sta.—Memphis, Millington 38054 *Type:* Public (federal) *Accred.:* 1976/1991 (SACS-COEI) *Calendar:* Courses of varying lengths *Degrees:* certificates *CEO:* Commander J.W. Parker, Jr., U.S.N.
FTE Enroll: 3,998   (901) 872-5306

NORTH CENTRAL INSTITUTE
2469 Fort Campbell Blvd., Clarksville 37042 *Type:* Private *Accred.:* 1992 (SACS-COEI) *Calendar:* Courses of varying lengths *Degrees:* certificates, diplomas *CEO:* Dir. Larry Metcalf
FTE Enroll: 32   (615) 552-6200

NOSSI SCHOOL OF ART
907 Two Mile Pkwy., Goodlettsville 37072 *Type:* Private *Accred.:* 1988 (ACCSCT) *Calendar:* Courses of varying lengths *Degrees:* diplomas *CEO:* Exec. Dir. Nossi Vatandoost
                    (615) 851-1088

QUEEN CITY COLLEGE
1191 Fort Campbell Blvd., Clarksville 37042 *Type:* Private *Accred.:* 1987 (SACS-COEI) *Calendar:* Courses of varying lengths *Degrees:* certificates *CEO:* Dir. Greg Ross
FTE Enroll: 373   (615) 645-2361

BRANCH CAMPUS
800 Hwy. One, S., Greenville, MS 38701 *CEO:* Dir. Ralph Payne
                    (601) 334-9120

RICE COLLEGE
2485 Union Ave., Memphis 38112 *Type:* Private business *Accred.:* 1990 (SACS-COEI) *Calendar:* Courses of varying lengths *Degrees:* certificates, diplomas *CEO:* Pres. Richard K. Rice
FTE Enroll: 337   (901) 324-7423

BRANCH CAMPUS
5430 Norwood Ave., Jacksonville, FL 32208 *CEO:* Dir. Frank Kello
                    (904) 765-7300

BRANCH CAMPUS
2525 Robinson Rd., Jackson, MS 39219 *CEO:* Dir. John Pitts
(601) 355-8100

BRANCH CAMPUS
1515 Magnolia Ave., Knoxville 37917 *CEO:* Dir. James Babb
(615) 637-9899

SEMINARY EXTENSION INDEPENDENT STUDY INSTITUTE
901 Commerce St., Ste. 500, Nashville 37203-3697 *Type:* Private home study *Accred.:* 1972/1992 (NHSC) *Calendar:* Courses of varying lengths *Degrees:* certificates *CEO:* Dir. Doran C. McCarty, Ph.D.
(615) 242-2453

SOUTHEAST COLLEGE OF TECHNOLOGY
2731 Nonconnah Blvd., Memphis 38132-2199 *Type:* Private *Accred.:* 1989 (ACC-SCT) *Calendar:* Courses of varying lengths *Degrees:* certificates, diplomas *CEO:* Pres. David A. Podesta
(901) 345-1000

SOUTHEASTERN PARALEGAL INSTITUTE
Ste. 300, 2416 21st Ave., S., Nashville 37212 *Type:* Private *Accred.:* 1985/1990 (SACS-COEI) *Calendar:* Courses of varying lengths *Degrees:* certificates *CEO:* Dir. Bruce Mallard
FTE Enroll: 22   (615) 269-9900

STATE AREA VOCATIONAL-TECHNICAL SCHOOL—ATHENS
1634 Vo-Tech Dr., Athens 37371 *Type:* Public (state) technical *Accred.:* 1971/1992 (SACS-COEI) *Calendar:* Courses of varying lengths *Degrees:* certificates *CEO:* Dir. Margaret H. Mahery
FTE Enroll: 161   (615) 744-2814

STATE AREA VOCATIONAL-TECHNICAL SCHOOL—COVINGTON
1600 Hwy. 51 S., Covington 38019 *Type:* Public (state) technical *Accred.:* 1972/1992 (SACS-COEI) *Calendar:* Courses of varying lengths *Degrees:* certificates *CEO:* Dir. Joe D. Martin
FTE Enroll: 122   (901) 476-8634

STATE AREA VOCATIONAL-TECHNICAL SCHOOL—CROSSVILLE
715 N. Miller Ave., Crossville 38555 *Type:* Public (state) technical *Accred.:* 1971/1992

(SACS-COEI) *Calendar:* Courses of varying lengths *Degrees:* certificates *CEO:* Dir. James G. Purcell
FTE Enroll: 240   (615) 484-7502

STATE AREA VOCATIONAL-TECHNICAL SCHOOL—DICKSON
740 Hwy. 46, Dickson 37055 *Type:* Public (state) technical *Accred.:* 1974/1989 (SACS-COEI) *Calendar:* Courses of varying lengths *Degrees:* certificates *CEO:* Dir. Bobby Sullivan
FTE Enroll: 173   (615) 446-4710

STATE AREA VOCATIONAL-TECHNICAL SCHOOL—ELIZABETHTON
1500 Arney St., Elizabethton 37641 *Type:* Public (state) technical *Accred.:* 1973/1988 (SACS-COEI) *Calendar:* Courses of varying lengths *Degrees:* certificates *CEO:* Dir. Kelly C. Yates
FTE Enroll: 176   (615) 542-4174

STATE AREA VOCATIONAL-TECHNICAL SCHOOL—HARRIMAN
Hwy. 27, N., Harriman 37748 *Type:* Public (state) technical *Accred.:* 1973/1988 (SACS-COEI) *Calendar:* Courses of varying lengths *Degrees:* certificates *CEO:* Dir. Farrell W. Kennedy
FTE Enroll: 182   (615) 882-6703

STATE AREA VOCATIONAL-TECHNICAL SCHOOL—HARTSVILLE
716 McMurry Blvd., Hartsville 37074 *Type:* Public (state) technical *Accred.:* 1971/1992 (SACS-COEI) *Calendar:* Courses of varying lengths *Degrees:* certificates *CEO:* Dir. H. Dean Ward
FTE Enroll: 90   (615) 374-2147

STATE AREA VOCATIONAL-TECHNICAL SCHOOL—HOHENWALD
813 W. Main St., Hohenwald 38462 *Type:* Public (state) technical *Accred.:* 1972/1992 (SACS-COEI) *Calendar:* Courses of varying lengths *Degrees:* certificates *CEO:* Dir. Rick Brewer
FTE Enroll: 112   (615) 796-5351

STATE AREA VOCATIONAL-TECHNICAL SCHOOL—JACKSBORO
Rte. 1, Elkins Rd., Jacksboro 37757 *Type:* Public (state) technical *Accred.:* 1972/1992 (SACS-COEI) *Calendar:* Courses of varying

lengths *Degrees:* certificates *CEO:* Dir. Coy Gibson
FTE Enroll: 161   (615) 562-8648

STATE AREA VOCATIONAL-TECHNICAL SCHOOL—JACKSON
2468 Westover Rd., Jackson 38305 *Type:* Public (state) technical *Accred.:* 1972/1992 (SACS-COEI) *Calendar:* Courses of varying lengths *Degrees:* certificates *CEO:* Dir. Jo Evelyn Alred
FTE Enroll: 272   (901) 424-0691

STATE AREA VOCATIONAL-TECHNICAL SCHOOL—KNOXVILLE
1100 Liberty St., Knoxville 37919 *Type:* Public (state) technical *Accred.:* 1971/1992 (SACS-COEI) *Calendar:* Courses of varying lengths *Degrees:* certificates *Prof. Accred.:* Dental Assisting *CEO:* Dir. Phillip W. Johnston
FTE Enroll: 452   (615) 546-5567

STATE AREA VOCATIONAL-TECHNICAL SCHOOL—LIVINGSTON
Airport Rd., Livingston 38570 *Type:* Public (state) technical *Accred.:* 1971/1992 (SACS-COEI) *Calendar:* Courses of varying lengths *Degrees:* certificates *CEO:* Dir. Ralph E. Robbins
FTE Enroll: 269   (615) 823-5525

STATE AREA VOCATIONAL-TECHNICAL SCHOOL—MCKENZIE
905 Highland Dr., McKenzie 38201 *Type:* Public (state) technical *Accred.:* 1971/1992 (SACS-COEI) *Calendar:* Courses of varying lengths *Degrees:* certificates *CEO:* Dir. Kenneth D. Warren
FTE Enroll: 128   (901) 352-5364

STATE AREA VOCATIONAL-TECHNICAL SCHOOL—MCMINNVILLE
1507 Vo-Tech Dr., McMinnville 37110 *Type:* Public (state) technical *Accred.:* 1971/1992 (SACS-COEI) *Calendar:* Courses of varying lengths *Degrees:* certificates *CEO:* Dir. Charles Nunley
FTE Enroll: 171   (615) 473-5587

STATE AREA VOCATIONAL-TECHNICAL SCHOOL—MEMPHIS
550 Alabama Ave., Memphis 38105 *Type:* Public (state) technical *Accred.:* 1970/1990 (SACS-COEI) *Calendar:* Courses of varying lengths *Degrees:* certificates *Prof. Accred.:*

Dental Assisting, Medical Laboratory Technology (AMA), Respiratory Therapy Technology, Surgical Technology *CEO:* Dir. Joseph Cornelious
FTE Enroll: 524   (901) 527-8455

BRANCH CAMPUS
2752 Winchester Rd., Memphis 38116 *CEO:* Asst. Dir. Jay Clark
       (901) 345-1995

STATE AREA VOCATIONAL-TECHNICAL SCHOOL—MORRISTOWN
821 W. Louise Ave., Morristown 37813 *Type:* Public (state) technical *Accred.:* 1971/1993 (SACS-COEI) *Calendar:* Courses of varying lengths *Degrees:* certificates *CEO:* Dir. Lynn Elkins
FTE Enroll: 479   (615) 586-5771

BRANCH CAMPUS
316 E. Main St., Rogersville 37857 *CEO:* Asst. Dir. Dave Easterly
       (615) 272-2100

STATE AREA VOCATIONAL-TECHNICAL SCHOOL—MURFREESBORO
1303 Old Fort Pkwy., Murfreesboro 37129 *Type:* Public (state) technical *Accred.:* 1980/1990 (SACS-COEI) *Calendar:* Courses of varying lengths *Degrees:* certificates *CEO:* Dir. Wallace E. Burke
FTE Enroll: 157   (615) 898-8010

STATE AREA VOCATIONAL-TECHNICAL SCHOOL—NASHVILLE
100 White Bridge Rd., Nashville 37209 *Type:* Public (state) technical *Accred.:* 1972/1992 (SACS-COEI) *Calendar:* Courses of varying lengths *Degrees:* certificates *CEO:* Dir. Charles F. Malin
FTE Enroll: 436   (615) 741-1241

BRANCH CAMPUS
7204 Cockrill Bend Rd., Nashville 37209 *CEO:* Dir. Charles F. Malin
       (615) 350-6224

STATE AREA VOCATIONAL-TECHNICAL SCHOOL—NEWBERN
340 Washington St., Newbern 38059 *Type:* Public (state) technical *Accred.:* 1972/1992 (SACS-COEI) *Calendar:* Courses of varying lengths *Degrees:* certificates *CEO:* Dir. Wallace E. Sexton
FTE Enroll: 136   (901) 627-2511

STATE AREA VOCATIONAL-TECHNICAL
SCHOOL—ONEIDA
120 Eli La., Oneida 37841 *Type:* Public
(state) technical *Accred.:* 1973/1988 (SACS-
COEI) *Calendar:* Courses of varying lengths
Degrees: certificates *CEO:* Dir. Arvis Blakley
FTE Enroll: 133   (615) 569-8338

STATE AREA VOCATIONAL-TECHNICAL
SCHOOL—PARIS
312 S. Wilson St., Paris 38242 *Type:* Public
(state) technical *Accred.:* 1974/1992 (SACS-
COEI) *Calendar:* Courses of varying lengths
Degrees: certificates *CEO:* Dir. Jimmie R.
Pritchard
FTE Enroll: 187   (901) 642-7552

STATE AREA VOCATIONAL-TECHNICAL
SCHOOL—PULASKI
1233 E. College St., Pulaski 38478 *Type:*
Public (state) technical *Accred.:* 1973/1988
(SACS-COEI) *Calendar:* Courses of varying
lengths *Degrees:* certificates *CEO:* Dir.
Henry H. Sims
FTE Enroll: 156   (615) 363-1588

STATE AREA VOCATIONAL-TECHNICAL
SCHOOL—RIPLEY
S. Industrial Park, Ripley 38063 *Type:* Pub-
lic (state) technical *Accred.:* 1973/1993
(SACS-COEI) *Calendar:* Courses of varying
lengths *Degrees:* certificates *CEO:* Dir. Jerry
W. Little
FTE Enroll: 53   (901) 635-3368

STATE AREA VOCATIONAL-TECHNICAL
SCHOOL—SAVANNAH
Hwy. 64, W., Crump 38327 *Type:* Public
(state) technical *Accred.:* 1974/1992 (SACS-
COEI) *Calendar:* Courses of varying lengths
Degrees: certificates *CEO:* Dir. James King
FTE Enroll: 114   (901) 632-3393

STATE AREA VOCATIONAL-TECHNICAL
SCHOOL—SHELBYVILLE
1405 Madison St., Shelbyville 37160 *Type:*
Public (state) technical *Accred.:* 1972/1992

(SACS-COEI) *Calendar:* Courses of varying
lengths *Degrees:* certificates *CEO:* Dir.
Ronald Adcock
FTE Enroll: 222   (615) 685-5013

STATE AREA VOCATIONAL-TECHNICAL
SCHOOL—WHITEVILLE
330 Hwy. 100, Whiteville 30875 *Type:* Pub-
lic (state) technical *Accred.:* 1980/1990
(SACS-COEI) *Calendar:* Courses of varying
lengths *Degrees:* certificates *CEO:* Dir.
Russell Shelton
FTE Enroll: 75   (901) 254-8521

TENNESSEE INSTITUTE OF ELECTRONICS
3202 Tazewell Pike, Knoxville 37918-2530
Type: Private *Accred.:* 1967/1987 (ACC-
SCT) *Calendar:* Qtr. plan *Degrees:* certificates, diplomas *CEO:* Pres. Ronald R. Rackley
     (615) 688-9422

UNIVERSITY OF BEAUTY
1701-G S. Lee Plaza, Cleveland 37311 *Type:*
Private *Accred.:* 1988/1990 (SACS-COEI)
Calendar: Courses of varying lengths *De-
grees:* certificates *CEO:* Dir. Barry Babb
FTE Enroll: 75   (615) 472-1702

BRANCH CAMPUS
5798-A Brainerd Rd., Chattanooga 37411
CEO: Dir. M. Crocker
     (615) 899-0246

WEST TENNESSEE BUSINESS COLLEGE
P.O. Box 1668, 1186 Hwy. 45 By-Pass,
Jackson 38302-1668 *Type:* Private business
Accred.: 1953/1991 (ACISC) *Calendar:* Tri.
plan *Degrees:* certificates, diplomas *CEO:*
Exec. Dir. Vicki Burch
     (901) 668-7240

WILLIAM R. MOORE SCHOOL OF TECHNOLOGY
1200 Poplar Ave., Memphis 38104 *Type:*
Private *Accred.:* 1971/1991 (SACS-COEI)
Calendar: Courses of varying lengths *De-
grees:* certificates *CEO:* Dir. Gaylon S. Hall
FTE Enroll: 88   (901) 726-1977

TEXAS

ACTION CAREER TRAINING
Rte. 3, Box 41, Merkel 79536 *Type:* Private *Accred.:* 1989 (SACS-COEI) *Calendar:* Courses of varying lengths *Degrees:* certificates *CEO:* Dir. Don Balch
FTE Enroll: 156   (915) 676-3136

ADVANCED CAREER TRAINING
8800 N. Central Expy., Ste. 120, Dallas 75231-6416 *Type:* Private *Accred.:* 1989 (ACCSCT) *Calendar:* Courses of varying lengths *Degrees:* certificates *CEO:* Dir. Chris Padgett
                                     (214) 692-5400

AIMS ACADEMY
Ste. 305, 1106 N. Hwy. 360, Grand Prairie 75050 *Type:* Private technical *Accred.:* 1990 (SACS-COEI) *Calendar:* Courses of varying lengths *Degrees:* certificates, diplomas *CEO:* Dir. Kenneth J. Carden
FTE Enroll: 72   (214) 988-3202

BRANCH CAMPUS
10830 N. Central Expy., Dallas 75231 *CEO:* Exec. Dir. Kenneth J. Carden
                                     (214) 891-9672

ALLAN SHIVERS RADIATION THERAPY CENTER
2600 E. Martin Luther King, Jr. Blvd., Austin 78702 *Type:* Private *Calendar:* Courses of varying lengths *Degrees:* certificates *Prof. Accred.:* Radiation Therapy Technology *CEO:* Admin. E.B. Baker
                                     (512) 478-9681

ALLIED HEALTH CAREERS
5424 Hwy. 290, W., Ste. 105, Austin 78735-8828 *Type:* Private *Accred.:* 1991 (ACCSCT); 1991 (SACS-COEI) *Calendar:* Courses of varying lengths *Degrees:* certificates *CEO:* Dir. Sharon Maza
FTE Enroll: 66   (512) 892-5210

AMARILLO AFFILIATED SCHOOL OF MEDICAL TECHNOLOGY
P.O. Box 1110, Amarillo 79175 *Type:* Private *Calendar:* Courses of varying lengths *Degrees:* certificates *Prof. Accred.:* Medical Technology *CEO:* C.E.O. Kevin Gross
                                     (806) 354-1110

AMERICAN COMMERCIAL COLLEGE
402 Butternut St., Abilene 79602 *Type:* Private business *Accred.:* 1990 (ACISC) *Calendar:* Courses of varying lengths *Degrees:* certificates, diplomas *CEO:* Dir. Michael J. Otto
                                     (915) 672-8495

AMERICAN COMMERCIAL COLLEGE
2007 34th St., Lubbock 79411 *Type:* Private business *Accred.:* 1982/1987 (ACISC) *Calendar:* Courses of varying lengths *Degrees:* certificates, diplomas *CEO:* Dir. Brent Sheets
                                     (806) 747-4339

AMERICAN COMMERCIAL COLLEGE
2115 E. Eighth St., Odessa 79761 *Type:* Private business *Accred.:* 1970/1988 (ACISC) *Calendar:* Courses of varying lengths *Degrees:* certificates, diplomas *CEO:* Dir. Maurice Howell
                                     (915) 332-0768

AMERICAN COMMERCIAL COLLEGE
3177 Executive Dr., San Angelo 76904 *Type:* Private business *Accred.:* 1990 (ACISC) *Calendar:* Courses of varying lengths *Degrees:* certificates, diplomas *CEO:* Dir. B.A. Reed
                                     (915) 942-6797

AMERICAN INSTITUTE OF COMMERCE
Ste. 201, 5501 LBJ Fwy., Dallas 75240 *Type:* Private business *Accred.:* 1989 (ACISC) *Calendar:* Courses of varying lengths *Degrees:* certificates, diplomas *CEO:* Dir. Mary Witort
                                     (214) 458-1225

ARIT AIR ACADEMY
5125 Voyager Dr., Dallas 75376 *Type:* Private *Accred.:* 1992 (SACS-COEI) *Calendar:* Courses of varying lengths *Degrees:* certificates *CEO:* Dir. Cynthia Ndatah
FTE Enroll: 16   (214) 330-6060

ARLINGTON COURT REPORTING COLLEGE
1201 N. Watson Rd., Ste. 270, Arlington 76006-6120 *Type:* Private *Accred.:* 1988 (ACCSCT) *Calendar:* Courses of varying

lengths *Degrees:* certificates *CEO:* Dir. Ronda Vecchio

(817) 640-8852

COURT REPORTING INSTITUTE OF TENNESSEE
51 Century Blvd., Ste. 350, Nashville, TN 37214-3609 *Accred.:* 1989 (ACCSCT) *CEO:* Vice Pres. Tom Vecchio

(615) 885-9770

ARMY ACADEMY OF HEALTH SCIENCES
Fort Sam Houston, San Antonio 78234-6100 *Type:* Public (federal) professional *Accred.:* 1983/1988 (SACS-COEI) *Calendar:* Courses of varying lengths *Degrees:* certificates *Prof. Accred.:* Dental Laboratory Technology, Occupational Therapy Assisting, Physician Assisting, Radiography, Respiratory Therapy Technology *CEO:* Commandant William L. Moore, U.S.A.
FTE Enroll: 9,547   (512) 221-8542

ARMY MEDICAL EQUIPMENT AND OPTICIAN SCHOOL
Aurora, CO 80045-7040 *CEO:* Commander/Dean Donald E. Dunphy, U.S.A.

(303) 361-8898

SCHOOL OF AVIATION MEDICINE
Fort Rucker, AL 36362-5377 *CEO:* Commandant James Mitchell, U.S.A.

(205) 255-7393

ART INSTITUTE OF DALLAS
Two NorthPark E., 8080 Park La., Dallas 75231-9959 *Type:* Private *Accred.:* 1985/1990 (ACCSCT) *Calendar:* Qtr. plan *Degrees:* diplomas *CEO:* Pres. Thomas M. Hauser

(214) 692-8080

ART INSTITUTE OF HOUSTON
1900 Yorktown St., Houston 77056 *Type:* Private *Accred.:* 1979/1993 (ACCSCT) *Calendar:* Qtr. plan *Degrees:* diplomas *CEO:* Pres. Steve R. Gregg

(713) 623-2040

ATDS—PRAIRIE HILL
Farm Rd. 339, S. at Hwy. 84, Prairie Hill 76678 *Type:* Private *Accred.:* 1979/1991 (SACS-COEI) *Calendar:* Courses of varying lengths *Degrees:* certificates *CEO:* Dir. Jim Craddock
FTE Enroll: 21   (817) 344-2313

ATI—AMERICAN TRADES INSTITUTES
6627 Maple Ave., Dallas 75235-4623 *Type:* Private *Accred.:* 1975/1990 (ACCSCT) *Calendar:* Courses of varying lengths *Degrees:* certificates, diplomas *CEO:* Dir. Mike Thayer

(214) 352-2222

ATI—GRAPHIC ARTS INSTITUTE
11034 Shady Tr., Dallas 75229-5625 *Accred.:* 1989 (ACCSCT) *CEO:* Dir. Reza Nanbakhsh

(214) 353-9056

ATI CAREER TRAINING CENTER
2351 Northwest Hwy., Ste. 1301, Dallas 75220-4430 *Type:* Private *Accred.:* 1987 (ACCSCT) *Calendar:* Courses of varying lengths *Degrees:* certificates *CEO:* Dir. Gerald E. Parr

(214) 263-4284

ATI CAREER TRAINING CENTER
235 N.E. Loop 820, Ste. 110, Hurst 76053-7396 *Type:* Private *Accred.:* 1986/1993 (ACCSCT) *Calendar:* Courses of varying lengths *Degrees:* certificates *CEO:* Dir. Christine Bruce

(817) 284-1141

ATI—HEALTH EDUCATION CENTER
8150 Brookriver Dr., 5th Fl., Dallas 75247-4057 *Type:* Private *Accred.:* 1990 (ABHES); 1987/1993 (ACCSCT) *Calendar:* Courses of varying lengths *Degrees:* certificates *CEO:* Dir. Joseph P. Mehlmann

(214) 263-0512

ATI—HEALTH EDUCATION CENTER
1200 Summit Ave., Ste. 200, Fort Worth 76102-4403 *Type:* Private *Accred.:* 1990 (ABHES); 1989 (ACCSCT) *Calendar:* Courses of varying lengths *Degrees:* certificates *CEO:* Dir. Gail Crowe

(817) 429-1045

AVALON VOCATIONAL-TECHNICAL INSTITUTE
1407 Texas St., Fort Worth 76102 *Type:* Private *Accred.:* 1991 (SACS-COEI) *Calendar:* Courses of varying lengths *Degrees:* certificates *CEO:* Dir. Barbara Charles
FTE Enroll: 214   (817) 877-5511

AVALON VOCATIONAL-TECHNICAL INSTITUTE
4241 Tanglewood La., Odessa 79762 *Type:* Private *Accred.:* 1988/1992 (SACS-COEI)

Calendar: Courses of varying lengths *Degrees:* certificates *CEO:* Dir. Carole Paul
FTE Enroll: 391   (915) 367-2622

BRANCH CAMPUS
3301 Marshall St., Longview 76504 *CEO:* Dir. Bob Linthicum
(903) 295-2002

AVALON VOCATIONAL-TECHNICAL INSTITUTE
One Eureka Cir., Wichita Falls 76308 *Type:* Private *Accred.:* 1992 (SACS-COEI) *Calendar:* Courses of varying lengths *Degrees:* certificates *CEO:* Dir. Barbara Taylor
FTE Enroll: 398   (817) 692-6513

BELLAIRE BEAUTY COLLEGE
5014 Bellaire Blvd., Bellaire 77401 *Type:* Private *Accred.:* 1992 (SACS-COEI) *Calendar:* Courses of varying lengths *Degrees:* certificates *CEO:* Dir. Howard Conlon
FTE Enroll: 86   (713) 666-2318

BISH MATHIS INSTITUTE
2521 Judson Rd., Longview 75601 *Type:* Private business *Accred.:* 1971/1987 (ACISC) *Calendar:* Courses of varying lengths *Degrees:* certificates, diplomas *CEO:* Dir. Leslie Roberts
(903) 758-7300

BRADFORD SCHOOL OF BUSINESS
Ste. 300, 4669 Southwest Fwy., Houston 77027 *Type:* Private business *Accred.:* 1980/1986 (ACISC) *Calendar:* Courses of varying lengths *Degrees:* certificates, diplomas *CEO:* Dir. Kathy Hughston
(713) 629-8940

BRAZOS BUSINESS COLLEGE
1702 S. Texas Ave., Bryan 77802 *Type:* Private business *Accred.:* 1985/1991 (ACISC) *Calendar:* Courses of varying lengths *Degrees:* certificates, diplomas *CEO:* Dir. George Turner
(409) 822-6423

BRANCH CAMPUS
2017 N. Frazier St., Conroe 77301 *Accred.:* 1990 (ACISC) *CEO:* Dir. Craig Glensford
(409) 539-4006

BUSINESS SKILLS TRAINING CENTER
616 Fort Worth Dr., Ste. B, Denton 76201-7170 *Type:* Private *Accred.:* 1991 (ACCSCT) *Calendar:* Courses of varying lengths *Degrees:* certificates *CEO:* Pres. Jane M. Hadley
(817) 382-7922

CAPITOL CITY CAREERS
4630 Westgate Blvd., Austin 78749 *Type:* Private *Accred.:* 1989/1992 (SACS-COEI) *Calendar:* Courses of varying lengths *Degrees:* diplomas *CEO:* Dir. Sherie Sadlier
FTE Enroll: 156   (512) 892-4270

CAPITOL CITY TRADE & TECHNICAL SCHOOL
205 E. Riverside Dr., Austin 78704 *Type:* Private *Accred.:* 1979/1989 (SACS-COEI) *Calendar:* Courses of varying lengths *Degrees:* diplomas *CEO:* Dir. George W. Hollowell
FTE Enroll: 126   (512) 444-3257

CAREER ACADEMY
32 Oaklawn Village, Texarkana 75501 *Type:* Private *Accred.:* 1988/1991 (SACS-COEI) *Calendar:* Courses of varying lengths *Degrees:* certificates *CEO:* Dir. Monet Lasater
FTE Enroll: 84   (214) 832-1021

CAREER CENTERS OF TEXAS—EL PASO
8375 Burnham Rd., El Paso 79907 *Type:* Private *Accred.:* 1988/1989 (SACS-COEI) *Calendar:* Courses of varying lengths *Degrees:* certificates *Prof. Accred.:* Medical Assisting *CEO:* Dir. Rose Duenez
FTE Enroll: 279   (915) 595-1935

CAREER DEVELOPMENT CENTER
413 S. Chestnut St., Lufkin 75901 *Type:* Private *Accred.:* 1991 (SACS-COEI) *Calendar:* Courses of varying lengths *Degrees:* certificates *CEO:* Dir. Linda Amadon
FTE Enroll: 50   (409) 637-1740

CAREER POINT BUSINESS SCHOOL
485 Spencer La., San Antonio 78201 *Type:* Private business *Accred.:* 1984/1989 (ACISC) *Calendar:* Courses of varying lengths *Degrees:* certificates, diplomas *CEO:* Acting Dir. Larry Earle
(512) 732-3000

BRANCH CAMPUS
3138 S. Garnett Rd., Tulsa, OK 74146-1933 *Accred.:* 1987 (ACISC) *CEO:* Dir. Linda Burr
(918) 622-4100

CAREERS UNLIMITED
335 S. Bonner St., Tyler 75702 *Type:* Private *Accred.:* 1993 (ACCSCT) *Calendar:* Courses of varying lengths *Degrees:* certificates, diplomas *CEO:* Pres. Jim Craddock
(903) 593-4424

CENTER FOR ADVANCED LEGAL STUDIES
3015 Richmond Ave., Houston 77098 *Type:* Private *Accred.:* 1989/1990 (SACS-COEI) *Calendar:* Courses of varying lengths *Degrees:* certificates *CEO:* Dir. Doyle Happe
FTE Enroll: 146   (713) 529-2778

CENTRAL TEXAS COMMERCIAL COLLEGE
P.O. Box 1324, 315 N. Center St., Brownwood 76801 *Type:* Private business *Accred.:* 1971/1989 (ACISC) *Calendar:* Qtr. plan *Degrees:* certificates, diplomas *CEO:* Dir. Kathy Day
(915) 646-0521

BRANCH CAMPUS
Ste. 200, 9400 N. Central Expy., Dallas 75231 *Accred.:* 1987 (ACISC) *CEO:* Dir. Dianne Day
(214) 368-3680

CHENIER
6300 Richmond Ave., Ste. 300, Houston 77057 *Type:* Private *Accred.:* 1979/1989 (SACS-COEI) *Calendar:* Courses of varying lengths *Degrees:* certificates *CEO:* Dir. Timothy Connolly
FTE Enroll: 252   (713) 886-3102

CHENIER
845 Dal Sasso Dr., Orange 77630 *Type:* Private *Accred.:* 1991 (SACS-COEI) *Calendar:* Courses of varying lengths *Degrees:* certificates *CEO:* Dir. Melvin Broussard
FTE Enroll: 1,126   (409) 886-5260

CHENIER
2819 Loop 306, San Angelo 76904 *Type:* Private *Accred.:* 1990 (SACS-COEI) *Calendar:* Courses of varying lengths *Degrees:* certificates *CEO:* Dir. Thomas Tyler
FTE Enroll: 117   (915) 944-4404

CHENIER BUSINESS SCHOOL
4320 Calder Ave., Beaumont 77706 *Type:* Private *Accred.:* 1979/1990 (SACS-COEI) *Calendar:* Courses of varying lengths *Degrees:* certificates *CEO:* Dir. John Wagliardo
FTE Enroll: 264   (409) 899-3227

BRANCH CAMPUS
4375 Calder Ave., Beaumont 77706 *CEO:* Dir. John Wagliardo
(409) 899-3227

COMPUTER CAREER CENTER
8201 Lockheed Dr., Ste. 100, El Paso 79925 *Type:* Private *Accred.:* 1989 (SACS-COEI) *Calendar:* Courses of varying lengths *Degrees:* certificates *CEO:* Dir. Lee Chayes
FTE Enroll: 337   (915) 779-8031

BRANCH CAMPUS
4121 Wyoming Blvd., N.E., Albuquerque, NM 87111 *CEO:* Dir. Tom Colvin
(505) 271-8200

COURT REPORTING INSTITUTE OF DALLAS
Ste. 200, N., 8585 N. Stemmons Fwy., Dallas 75247 *Type:* Private business *Accred.:* 1986 (ACISC) *Calendar:* Courses of varying lengths *Degrees:* certificates, diplomas *CEO:* Dir. Carolyn S. Willard
(214) 350-9722

DALFORT AIRCRAFT TECH
7701 Lemmon Ave., Dallas 75209-3091 *Type:* Private *Accred.:* 1991 (ACCSCT) *Calendar:* Courses of varying lengths *Degrees:* certificates *CEO:* Exec. Dir. David Evans
(214) 358-7820

BRANCH CAMPUS
990 Toffie Terr., Atlanta, GA 30320 *Accred.:* 1993 (ACCSCT) *CEO:* Exec. Dir. David Evans
(404) 428-9056

DALLAS INSTITUTE OF FUNERAL SERVICES
3909 S. Buckner Blvd., Dallas 75227 *Type:* Private professional *Calendar:* Qtr. plan *Degrees:* diplomas *Prof. Accred.:* Funeral Service Education *CEO:* Pres. Robert P. Kite
FTE Enroll: 181   (214) 388-5466

DAVID L. CARRASCO JOB CORPS CENTER
11155 Gateway W., El Paso 79935 *Type:* Private *Accred.:* 1986 (SACS-COEI) *Calen-*

dar: Courses of varying lengths *Degrees:* certificates *CEO:* Dir. Mary Young
FTE Enroll: 451   (915) 594-0022

DELTA CAREER INSTITUTE
1310 Pennsylvania Ave., Beaumont 77701 *Type:* Private business *Accred.:* 1988 (ACISC); 1992 (SACS-COEI) *Calendar:* Qtr. plan *Degrees:* certificates, diplomas *CEO:* Dir. Willard R. Lively
FTE Enroll: 155   (409) 833-6161

DRAUGHON'S COLLEGE OF BUSINESS
2725 W. Seventh St., Fort Worth 76107 *Type:* Private *Accred.:* 1983/1988 (SACS-COEI) *Calendar:* Courses of varying lengths *Degrees:* certificates *CEO:* Dir. John L. Roberts
FTE Enroll: 16   (817) 335-2381

EURO HAIR SCHOOL
2301-A Morgan Ave., Corpus Christi 78405 *Type:* Private *Accred.:* 1993 (ACCSCT) *Calendar:* Courses of varying lengths *Degrees:* certificates *CEO:* Owner Stewart A. Smith
(512) 887-8494

EUROPEAN HEALTH & SCIENCES INSTITUTE
1201 Airway A-2, El Paso 79925 *Type:* Private *Accred.:* 1993 (ACCSCT) *Calendar:* Courses of varying lengths *Degrees:* certificates *CEO:* Owner Florencia M. Zelonis
(915) 772-4243

EXECUTIVE SECRETARIAL SCHOOL
4849 Greenville Ave., Ste. 200, Dallas 75206-4125 *Type:* Private *Accred.:* 1969/1990 (ACISC); 1977/1992 (SACS-COEI) *Calendar:* Tri. plan *Degrees:* certificates, diplomas *CEO:* Chrmn. of the Bd. Jan B. Friedheim
FTE Enroll: 520   (214) 369-9009

FOUR-C COLLEGE
P.O. Box 4, 205 N. 8th St., Waco 76703 *Type:* Private business *Accred.:* 1973/1991 (ACISC) *Calendar:* Courses of varying lengths *Degrees:* certificates, diplomas *CEO:* Dir. Camilla M. McKenzie
(817) 756-7201

GARY JOB CORPS CENTER
Hwy. 21, San Marcos 78667 *Type:* Public (federal) *Accred.:* 1985/1992 (SACS-COEI)

Calendar: Courses of varying lengths *Degrees:* certificates *CEO:* Dir. Albert Perkins
FTE Enroll: 2,054   (512) 396-6652

GULF COAST TRADES CENTER
FM 1375 W., New Waverly 77358 *Type:* Private *Accred.:* 1984/1989 (SACS-COEI) *Calendar:* Courses of varying lengths *Degrees:* certificates *CEO:* Dir. Thomas M. Buzbee
FTE Enroll: 209   (409) 344-6677

HALLMARK INSTITUTE OF TECHNOLOGY
1130 99th St., San Antonio 78214-9985 *Type:* Private *Accred.:* 1971/1988 (ACCSCT) *Calendar:* Courses of varying lengths *Degrees:* certificates *CEO:* Dir. Jeanne C. Martin
(512) 690-9000

HALLMARK INSTITUTE OF TECHNOLOGY
10401 IH 10 W., San Antonio 78230 *Type:* Private *Accred.:* 1987 (ACCSCT) *Calendar:* Courses of varying lengths *Degrees:* certificates *CEO:* Pres. Richard H. Fessler
(512) 924-8551

HOUSTON BALLET ACADEMY
1921 W. Bell St., P.O. Box 130487, Houston 77219-0487 *Type:* Private *Calendar:* Courses of varying lengths *Degrees:* certificates *Prof. Accred.:* Dance *CEO:* Admin. Kelli Walters Dunning
(713) 523-6300

HOUSTON TRAINING SCHOOL
709 Shotwell St., Houston 77020 *Type:* Private *Accred.:* 1979/1993 (SACS-COEI) *Calendar:* Courses of varying lengths *Degrees:* certificates *CEO:* Dir. Sherry Foster
FTE Enroll: 294   (713) 672-9607

BRANCH CAMPUS
Ste. 200, 6969 Gulf Fwy., Houston 77087 *CEO:* Dir. Jay Martinez
(713) 649-5050

INTERACTIVE LEARNING SYSTEMS
8585 N. Stemmons Fwy., Dallas 75247 *Type:* Private *Accred.:* 1989 (SACS-COEI) *Calendar:* Courses of varying lengths *Degrees:* certificates *CEO:* Dir. Malti Ayyr
FTE Enroll: 184   (214) 637-3377

BRANCH CAMPUS
10200 Richmond Ave., Houston 77042
CEO: Dir. Harry Mauz
(713) 782-5161

INTERNATIONAL AVIATION AND TRAVEL
ACADEMY
300 W. Arbrook Blvd., Arlington 76014-
3199 *Type:* Private *Accred.:* 1988/1992
(NHSC); 1979/1989 (SACS-COEI) *Calendar:* Courses of varying lengths *Degrees:*
certificates *CEO:* Pres. Kenneth D. Woods
FTE Enroll: 350   (800) 678-0700

BRANCH CAMPUS
5757 Alpha Rd., Ste. 101, Dallas 75240
CEO: Dir. Ben Sheldon
(214) 387-0553

INTERNATIONAL AVIATION AND TRAVEL
ACADEMY
9310 Max Conrad Dr., Spring 77379 *Type:*
Private *Accred.:* 1991 (SACS-COEI) *Calendar:* Courses of varying lengths *Degrees:*
certificates *CEO:* Dir. Dewayne Weeks
FTE Enroll: 315   (800) 627-4379

INTERNATIONAL BUSINESS COLLEGE
4121 Montana Ave., El Paso 79903 *Type:*
Private business *Accred.:* 1969/1987
(ACISC) *Calendar:* Courses of varying
lengths *Degrees:* certificates, diplomas
CEO: Dir. Robert C. Brown
(915) 566-8644

INTERNATIONAL BUSINESS COLLEGE
4630 50th St., Lubbock 79414 *Type:* Private
business *Accred.:* 1985/1987 (ACISC) *Calendar:* Courses of varying lengths *Degrees:*
certificates, diplomas *CEO:* Dir. Stephanie
Stone
(806) 797-1933

INTERNATIONAL BUSINESS SCHOOL
Ste. 138, 3801 I-35 N., Denton 76201 *Accred.:* 1993 (ACISC) *CEO:* Dir. Ray
Croff
(817) 380-0024

INTERNATIONAL BUSINESS SCHOOL
1002 N. Walnut St., Sherman 75090 *Accred.:* 1991 (ACISC) *CEO:* Dir. Robin
Counce
(806) 797-1933

IVERSON INSTITUTE OF COURT REPORTING
1200 Copeland Rd., Ste. 305, Arlington
76011 *Type:* Private *Accred.:* 1988 (SACS-COEI) *Calendar:* Courses of varying lengths
Degrees: certificates *CEO:* Dir. Audrey
Iverson
FTE Enroll: 84   (817) 274-6465

KEITH'S METRO HAIR ACADEMY
P.O. Box 7609, Amarillo 79114-7609 *Type:*
Private *Accred.:* 1988/1993 (ACCSCT) *Calendar:* Courses of varying lengths *Degrees:*
certificates *CEO:* Owner Frances Clark
(806) 355-7277

METRO BUSINESS ACADEMY
3225-B Commerce St., Amarillo 79114-
7609 *Accred.:* 1985 (ACCSCT) *CEO:* Dir.
Frances Clark
(806) 354-0580

LE HAIR DESIGN COLLEGE
217 Pleasant Grove Shopping Ctr., Dallas
75217-1700 *Type:* Private *Accred.:* 1991
(ACCSCT) *Calendar:* Courses of varying
lengths *Degrees:* diplomas *CEO:* Dir. Daniel
Ruidant
(214) 398-5905

LE HAIR DESIGN COLLEGE
505 Golden Triangle Shopping Ctr., Polk St.
at Marvin D. Love Fwy., Dallas 75224-4425
Type: Private *Accred.:* 1991 (ACCSCT) *Calendar:* Courses of varying lengths *Degrees:*
diplomas *CEO:* Dir. Lori Ruidant
(214) 375-0592

LE HAIR DESIGN COLLEGE
1125 E. Seminary Dr., Fort Worth 76115-
2829 *Type:* Private *Accred.:* 1986 (ACC-SCT) *Calendar:* Courses of varying lengths
Degrees: diplomas *CEO:* Dir. Thomas L.
Campo
(817) 926-7555

LE HAIR DESIGN COLLEGE
2410 W. Walnut St., Garland 75042-6623
Type: Private *Accred.:* 1991 (ACCSCT) *Calendar:* Courses of varying lengths *Degrees:*
diplomas *CEO:* Dir. Daniel Ruidant
(214) 272-8283

LE HAIR DESIGN COLLEGE
5201 E. Belknap, Haltom City 76117 *Type:*
Private *Accred.:* 1991 (ACCSCT) *Calendar:*

Courses of varying lengths *Degrees:* diplomas *CEO:* Dir. Thomas L. Campo
(817) 831-7261

LECHEF CULINARY ARTS SCHOOL
6020 Dillard Cir., Austin 78752 *Type:* Private *Accred.:* 1990 (SACS-COEI) *Calendar:* Courses of varying lengths *Degrees:* certificates *CEO:* Dir. Ronald Boston
FTE Enroll: 81   (512) 323-2511

LINCOLN TECHNICAL INSTITUTE
2501 E. Arkansas La., Grand Prairie 75051-9990 *Type:* Private *Accred.:* 1968/1988 (ACCSCT) *Calendar:* Courses of varying lengths *Degrees:* diplomas *CEO:* Dir. Paul R. McGuirk
(214) 660-5701

M & M WORD PROCESSING INSTITUTE
5050 Westheimer Rd., Ste. 300, Houston 77056 *Type:* Private *Accred.:* 1991 (ACCSCT) *Calendar:* Courses of varying lengths *Degrees:* certificates *CEO:* Owner Olgha Isid
(713) 961-0500

M. WEEKS WELDING LABORATORY TESTING & SCHOOL
4405 Hwy. 347, Nederland 77627 *Type:* Private *Accred.:* 1991 (SACS-COEI) *Calendar:* Courses of varying lengths *Degrees:* certificates, diplomas *CEO:* Pres. Morris Weeks
FTE Enroll: 7   (409) 727-7640

MASSEY BUSINESS COLLEGE
P.O. Box 630-444, Nacogdoches 75963 *Type:* Private business *Accred.:* 1966/1987 (ACISC) *Calendar:* Courses of varying lengths *Degrees:* certificates, diplomas *CEO:* Pres. Clarence E. Chandler
(409) 564-3788

MICROCOMPUTER TECHNOLOGY INSTITUTE
7277 Regency Square Blvd., Houston 77036-3163 *Type:* Private *Accred.:* 1983/1988 (ACCSCT) *Calendar:* Courses of varying lengths *Degrees:* certificates, diplomas *CEO:* Dir. Barbara Andrews
(713) 974-7181

BRANCH CAMPUS
17164 Blackhawk Blvd., Friendswood 77546-3446 *Accred.:* 1988 (ACCSCT) *CEO:* Dir. John Springhetti
(713) 996-8180

NATIONAL EDUCATION CENTER—BRYMAN CAMPUS
9724 Beechnut St., Ste. 300, Houston 77036-6564 *Type:* Private *Accred.:* 1973/1993 (ACCSCT) *Calendar:* Courses of varying lengths *Degrees:* diplomas *Prof. Accred.:* Medical Assisting *CEO:* Exec. Dir. Diana Mintner
(713) 776-3656

NATIONAL EDUCATION CENTER—BRYMAN CAMPUS
16416 Northchase Dr., Ste. 300, Houston 77060-2020 *Type:* Private *Accred.:* 1973/1988 (ACCSCT) *Calendar:* Courses of varying lengths *Degrees:* diplomas *CEO:* Dir. Ray White
(713) 447-6656

NATIONAL EDUCATION CENTER—NATIONAL INSTITUTE OF TECHNOLOGY CAMPUS
10945 Estates La., Dallas 75238-2378 *Type:* Private *Accred.:* 1969/1988 (ACCSCT) *Calendar:* Qtr. plan *Degrees:* diplomas *Prof. Accred.:* Medical Assisting (AMA) *CEO:* Dir. Paulette Gallerson
(214) 503-9373

NATIONAL EDUCATION CENTER—NATIONAL INSTITUTE OF TECHNOLOGY CAMPUS
3622 Fredericksburg Rd., San Antonio 78201-3841 *Type:* Private *Accred.:* 1985/1990 (ACCSCT) *Calendar:* Qtr. plan *Degrees:* diplomas *CEO:* Dir. Ed Howard
(210) 733-6000

THE NELL INSTITUTE
3rd Fl., 2101 IH 35 S., Austin 78741 *Type:* Private business *Accred.:* 1978/1987 (ACISC) *Calendar:* Courses of varying lengths *Degrees:* certificates, diplomas *CEO:* Dir. Jackie Ward
(512) 447-9415

OCCUPATIONAL SAFETY TRAINING INSTITUTE
8415 W. Bellfort St., Ste. 500, Houston 77031 *Type:* Private *Accred.:* 1991 (SACS-COEI) *Calendar:* Courses of varying lengths *Degrees:* certificates *CEO:* Dir. Eva Bonilla
FTE Enroll: 169   (713) 270-6882

THE OCEAN CORPORATION
10840 Rockley Rd., Houston 77099-3416 *Type:* Private *Accred.:* 1991 (ACCSCT) *Cal-*

endar: Courses of varying lengths *Degrees:* certificates *CEO:* Pres. Les Joiner
(713) 530-0202

THE OFFICE CAREERS CENTRE
7904-D N.E. Loop 820, Fort Worth 76180 *Type:* Private *Accred.:* 1988 (SACS-COEI) *Calendar:* Courses of varying lengths *Degrees:* certificates *CEO:* Dir. Susan Bauer
FTE Enroll: 19   (817) 284-8107

PCI HEALTH TRAINING CENTER
8101 John Carpenter Fwy., Dallas 75247-4720 *Type:* Private *Accred.:* 1991 (ACC-SCT) *Calendar:* Courses of varying lengths *Degrees:* certificates *CEO:* Dir. Bobby Prince
(214) 630-0568

PHILLIPS SCHOOL OF BUSINESS & TECHNOLOGY
119 W. Eighth St., Austin 78701 *Type:* Private business *Accred.:* 1967/1990 (ACISC) *Calendar:* Sem. plan *Degrees:* certificates, diplomas *CEO:* Dir. Gwinn Chunn
(512) 478-3446

POLYTECHNIC INSTITUTE
4625 North Fwy., Ste. 109, Houston 77022-2929 *Type:* Private *Accred.:* 1991 (ACC-SCT) *Calendar:* Courses of varying lengths *Degrees:* certificates *CEO:* Pres. Luis R. Cano
(713) 694-6027

PROFESSIONAL COURT REPORTING SCHOOL
1401 N. Central Expy., Richardson 75080 *Type:* Private *Accred.:* 1988 (ACCSCT) *Calendar:* Courses of varying lengths *Degrees:* certificates *CEO:* Pres. Ardith Spies
Enroll: 147   (214) 231-9502

R/S INSTITUTE
7122 Lawndale Ave., Houston 77023 *Type:* Private *Accred.:* 1984/1991 (SACS-COEI) *Calendar:* Courses of varying lengths *Degrees:* certificates *CEO:* Dir. Rhonda Morris
FTE Enroll: 20   (713) 923-6968

RHDC HAIR DESIGN COLLEGE
3209 N. Main St., Fort Worth 76106 *Type:* Private *Accred.:* 1993 (ACCSCT) *Calendar:* Courses of varying lengths *Degrees:* certificates *CEO:* Pres. Pat Collins
(817) 624-0871

RICE AVIATION, A DIVISION OF A&J ENTERPRISES
8880 Telephone Rd., Houston 77061 *Type:* Private *Accred.:* 1988/1991 (SACS-COEI) *Calendar:* Courses of varying lengths *Degrees:* certificates *CEO:* Dir. J. Michael Rice
FTE Enroll: 1,612   (713) 644-6616

BRANCH CAMPUS
3201 E. Broadway, Phoenix, AZ 85040 *CEO:* Dir. Jim Garvey
(602) 243-6611

BRANCH CAMPUS
8911 Aviation Blvd., Inglewood, CA 90301 *CEO:* Dir. James Tufo
(310) 337-4444

BRANCH CAMPUS
701 Wilson Point Rd., Baltimore, MD 21220 *CEO:* Dir. Richard Phillips
(410) 682-2226

BRANCH CAMPUS
7811 N. Shepherd Dr., Ste. 100, Houston 77088 *CEO:* Dir. Robert Taylor
(713) 591-2908

BRANCH CAMPUS
5202 W. Military Hwy., Hangar 7, Chesapeake, VA 23321 *CEO:* Dir. Margaret Perry
(804) 465-2813

SAN ANGELO HAIR ACADEMY
18 N. Chadbourne St., San Angelo 79603-0032 *Type:* Private *Accred.:* 1986 (ACC-SCT) *Calendar:* Courses of varying lengths *Degrees:* diplomas *CEO:* Dir. Frances Clark
(915) 653-2615

SAN ANTONIO COLLEGE OF MEDICAL & DENTAL ASSISTANTS
4205 San Pedro Ave., San Antonio 78212-1899 *Type:* Private *Accred.:* 1970/1985 (ACCSCT); 1984/1989 (SACS-COEI) *Calendar:* Courses of varying lengths *Degrees:* diplomas *Prof. Accred.:* Medical Assisting *CEO:* Pres. Comer M. Alden, Jr.
FTE Enroll: 635   (512) 733-0777

BRANCH CAMPUS
3900 N. 23rd St., McAllen 78501-6053 *Accred.:* 1990 (ACCSCT) *Prof. Accred.:*

Medical Assisting *CEO:* Dir. Bonita Mahannah

(210) 360-1499

BRANCH CAMPUS
5280 Medical Dr., Ste. 100, San Antonio 78229-9944 *Accred.:* 1990 (ACCSCT) *Prof. Accred.:* Surgical Technology *CEO:* Dir. Denise Cordova

(210) 692-3829

SAN ANTONIO TRADE SCHOOL
120 Playmoor St., San Antonio 78210 *Type:* Private *Accred.:* 1982/1992 (SACS-COEI) *Calendar:* Courses of varying lengths *Degrees:* certificates *CEO:* Dir. Charles Lee
FTE Enroll: 358   (512) 533-9126

BRANCH CAMPUS
117 W. Martin, Del Rio 78840 *CEO:* Dir. Arnold Manchaca

(512) 774-5646

SAN ANTONIO TRAINING DIVISION
9350 S. Presa, San Antonio 78223 *Type:* Private *Accred.:* 1984/1989 (SACS-COEI) *Calendar:* Courses of varying lengths *Degrees:* certificates *CEO:* Dir. James D. Partain
FTE Enroll: 261   (512) 633-1000

BRANCH CAMPUS
Hemisfair Park, Bldg. 277, San Antonio 78291 *CEO:* Dir. Patricia Turner

(512) 227-8217

SCHOOL OF AUTOMOTIVE MACHINISTS
1911 Antoine Dr., Houston 77055-1803 *Type:* Private *Accred.:* 1991 (ACCSCT); 1991 (SACS-COEI candidate) *Calendar:* Courses of varying lengths *Degrees:* certificates *CEO:* Dir. Linda Massingill
FTE Enroll: 67   (713) 683-3817

SEBRING CAREER SCHOOLS
842C W. 7th Ave., Corsicana 75110 *Type:* Private *Accred.:* 1992 (SACS-COEI) *Calendar:* Courses of varying lengths *Degrees:* certificates *CEO:* Dir. Joe Taylor
FTE Enroll: 253   (903) 874-7312

SEBRING CAREER SCHOOLS
2212 Ave. I, Huntsville 77340 *Type:* Private *Accred.:* 1985/1990 (SACS-COEI) *Calen-*

dar: Courses of varying lengths *Degrees:* certificates *CEO:* Dir. Reese Moore
FTE Enroll: 251   (409) 291-6299

BRANCH CAMPUS
6715 Bissonnet St., Houston 77074 *CEO:* Dir. Brooks Moore

(713) 772-6209

BRANCH CAMPUS
6672 Hwy. 6, S., Houston 77413 *CEO:* Dir. M. Turner

(713) 561-6352

SEGUIN BEAUTY SCHOOL
102 E. Court St., Seguin 78155 *Type:* Private *Accred.:* 1987/1992 (SACS-COEI) *Calendar:* Courses of varying lengths *Degrees:* certificates *CEO:* Dir. Joseph P. Evans
FTE Enroll: 47   (512) 372-0935

BRANCH CAMPUS
214 W. San Antonio St., New Braunfels 78130 *CEO:* Mgr. Maria Rosas

(512) 620-1301

SOUTH TEXAS VO-TECH INSTITUTE
2255 N. Coria St., Brownsville 78520 *Type:* Private *Accred.:* 1982/1992 (SACS-COEI) *Calendar:* Courses of varying lengths *Degrees:* certificates *CEO:* Dir. Maria Carrejo
FTE Enroll: 111   (512) 546-0353

SOUTH TEXAS VO-TECH INSTITUTE
2901 N. 23rd St., McAllen 78501 *Type:* Private *Accred.:* 1982/1992 (SACS-COEI) *Calendar:* Courses of varying lengths *Degrees:* certificates *CEO:* Dir. Adelina Garrett
FTE Enroll: 251   (512) 631-1107

SOUTH TEXAS VO-TECH INSTITUTE
2419 E. Haggar Ave., Weslaco 78596 *Type:* Private *Accred.:* 1982/1992 (SACS-COEI) *Calendar:* Courses of varying lengths *Degrees:* certificates *CEO:* Dir. Carlos Rodriguez, Jr.
FTE Enroll: 170   (512) 969-1564

SOUTHEASTERN PARALEGAL INSTITUTE
5440 Harvest Hill Rd., Ste. 200, Dallas 75230 *Type:* Private *Accred.:* 1989/1990 (SACS-COEI) *Calendar:* Courses of varying lengths *Degrees:* certificates *CEO:* Dir. Janice Bailey
FTE Enroll: 71   (214) 385-1446

SOUTHERN CAREERS INSTITUTE
2301 S. Congress Ave., Ste. 27, Austin 78704 *Type:* Private *Accred.:* 1991 (SACS-COEI) *Calendar:* Courses of varying lengths *Degrees:* certificates *CEO:* Dir. David Meck *FTE Enroll:* 57   (512) 326-1415

BRANCH CAMPUS
Bldg. C, 5333 Everhart Rd., Corpus Christi 78411 *CEO:* Dir. Charles David
(512) 702-2151

BRANCH CAMPUS
840 N. Cage, Pharr 78577 *CEO:* Dir. Chris Miteff
(512) 702-2151

SOUTHWEST INSTITUTE OF MERCHANDISING & DESIGN
9611 Acer Ave., El Paso 79925-6744 *Type:* Private *Accred.:* 1975/1990 (ACCSCT) *Calendar:* Courses of varying lengths *Degrees:* certificates *CEO:* Pres. Mary F. Simon
(915) 593-7328

SOUTHWEST SCHOOL OF ELECTRONICS
5424 Hwy. 290 W., Ste. 200, Austin 78735-8800 *Type:* Private *Accred.:* 1978/1988 (ACCSCT) *Calendar:* Courses of varying lengths *Degrees:* certificates, diplomas *CEO:* Dir. Joan Uribe
(512) 892-2640

SOUTHWEST SCHOOL OF MEDICAL ASSISTANTS
201 W. Sheridan, San Antonio 78204-1441 *Type:* Private *Accred.:* 1974/1988 (ACCSCT) *Calendar:* Courses of varying lengths *Degrees:* certificates *CEO:* Dir. Mark K. Kaleck
(512) 224-2296

SOUTHWEST SCHOOL OF HEALTH CAREERS
Plaza 24 Ctr., 2424 Williams Blvd., Kenner, LA 70062-4700 *Accred.:* 1988 (ACCSCT) *CEO:* Dir. Debra Hoffman
(504) 465-9677

S.W. SCHOOL OF BUSINESS & TECHNICAL CAREERS
100 Main St., Eagle Pass 78852 *Type:* Private *Accred.:* 1989/1991 (SACS-COEI) *Calendar:* Courses of varying lengths *Degrees:* certificates *CEO:* Dir. Guadalupe Limon *FTE Enroll:* 130   (512) 773-1373

S.W. SCHOOL OF BUSINESS & TECHNICAL CAREERS
602 W. Southcross Blvd., San Antonio 78221 *Type:* Private *Accred.:* 1982/1992 (SACS-COEI) *Calendar:* Courses of varying lengths *Degrees:* certificates *CEO:* Dir. Al Salazar
FTE Enroll: 287   (512) 921-0951

BRANCH CAMPUS
122 W. North St., Uvalde 78801 *CEO:* Dir. Paulette Hahn
(512) 278-4103

S.W. SCHOOL OF BUSINESS & TECHNICAL CAREERS
402 E. Travis St., San Antonio 78205 *Type:* Private *Accred.:* 1992 (SACS-COEI) *Calendar:* Courses of varying lengths *Degrees:* certificates *CEO:* Dir. Evangeline A. Vargas *FTE Enroll:* 55   (512) 225-7287

TEMPLE ACADEMY OF COSMETOLOGY
5 S. First St., Temple 76501 *Type:* Private *Accred.:* 1986/1991 (SACS-COEI) *Calendar:* Courses of varying lengths *Degrees:* certificates *CEO:* Dir. Lenda Tuck *FTE Enroll:* 59   (817) 778-2221

BRANCH CAMPUS
1408 W. Marshall Ave., Longview 75604 *CEO:* Dir. Shutona Vaughan
(903) 753-4717

TEXAS AERO TECH
6911 Lemmon Ave., Dallas 75209 *Type:* Private *Accred.:* 1979/1989 (SACS-COEI) *Calendar:* Courses of varying lengths *Degrees:* certificates *CEO:* Dir. Thomas A. Stose *FTE Enroll:* 594   (214) 358-7295

TEXAS BARBER COLLEGE
531 W. Jefferson Blvd., Dallas 75208 *Type:* Private *Accred.:* 1988 (SACS-COEI) *Calendar:* Courses of varying lengths *Degrees:* certificates *CEO:* Dir. Helen Spears *FTE Enroll:* 98   (214) 943-7255

BRANCH CAMPUS
2406 Gus Thomason Rd., Dallas 75228 *CEO:* Dir. Helen Spears
(214) 324-2851

BRANCH CAMPUS
525 W. Arapaho Rd., Richardson 75080
CEO: Dir. Helen Spears
(214) 644-4106

TEXAS DENTAL TECHNOLOGY SCHOOL
2414 Broadway, 2nd Fl., Houston 77102-3612 *Type:* Private *Accred.:* 1989 (ACC-SCT) *Calendar:* Courses of varying lengths *Degrees:* certificates *CEO:* Dir. Albert Marquez
(713) 645-1612

TEXAS SCHOOL OF BUSINESS
711 Airtex Blvd., Houston 77073 *Type:* Private business *Accred.:* 1985/1991 (ACISC) *Calendar:* Courses of varying lengths *Degrees:* certificates, diplomas *CEO:* Dir. Madeline Burillo
(713) 876-2888

TEXAS SCHOOL OF BUSINESS—SOUTHWEST
10250 Bissonnet St., Houston 77036 *Type:* Private business *Accred.:* 1989 (ACISC) *Calendar:* Courses of varying lengths *Degrees:* certificates, diplomas *CEO:* Dir. Jody Hawk
(713) 771-1177

TEXAS VOCATIONAL SCHOOL
Rte. 2, Box 254, Pharr 78577 *Type:* Private *Accred.:* 1982 (SACS-COEI) *Calendar:* Courses of varying lengths *Degrees:* certificates *CEO:* Dir. Gene Calhoun
FTE Enroll: 217   (512) 631-6181

TEXAS VOCATIONAL SCHOOL
1913 S. Flores St., San Antonio 78204-1934 *Type:* Private *Accred.:* 1982/1993 (SACS-COEI) *Calendar:* Courses of varying lengths *Degrees:* certificates *CEO:* Dir. Melvin Heitkamp
FTE Enroll: 246   (512) 225-3253

TEXAS VOCATIONAL SCHOOLS
1921 E. Red River, Victoria 77901 *Type:* Private *Accred.:* 1983/1993 (SACS-COEI) *Calendar:* Courses of varying lengths *Degrees:* certificates *CEO:* Dir. Angie S. Boone
FTE Enroll: 316   (512) 575-4768

BRANCH CAMPUS
201 E. Rio Grande, Victoria 77902 *CEO:* Dir. Angie S. Boone
(512) 575-4768

TYLER SCHOOL OF BUSINESS
621 E. Ferguson St., Tyler 75702 *Type:* Private business *Accred.:* 1986 (ACISC) *Calendar:* Courses of varying lengths *Degrees:* certificates, diplomas *CEO:* Pres. Marvin A. Gardner
(214) 592-2288

BRANCH CAMPUS
Rte. 14, Box 176, Hwy. 64E, Tyler 75701
Accred.: 1990 (ACISC) *CEO:* Dir. Wendell Gardner
(214) 566-1756

UNIVERSAL TECHNICAL INSTITUTE
721 Lockhaven Dr., Houston 77073-5598 *Type:* Private *Accred.:* 1986 (ACCSCT) *Calendar:* Courses of varying lengths *Degrees:* certificates *CEO:* Dir. Wendell Crabb
(713) 443-6262

USA HAIR ACADEMY
2525 N. Laurent St., Victoria 77901 *Type:* Private *Accred.:* 1990 (SACS-COEI) *Calendar:* Courses of varying lengths *Degrees:* certificates *CEO:* Pres. Paul Piwonka
FTE Enroll: 167   (512) 578-0035

VANGUARD INSTITUTE OF TECHNOLOGY
221 N. Eighth St., Edinburg 78539 *Type:* Private *Accred.:* 1990 (SACS-COEI) *Calendar:* Courses of varying lengths *Degrees:* certificates, diplomas *CEO:* Dir. Domingo Lopez, Jr.
FTE Enroll: 228   (210) 380-3264

BRANCH CAMPUS
603 Ed Carey Dr., Harlingen 78539 *CEO:* Dir. Domingo Lopez, Jr.
(210) 428-4999

WESTERN TECHNICAL INSTITUTE
1000 Texas Ave., El Paso 79901-1536 *Type:* Private *Accred.:* 1986 (ACCSCT) *Calendar:* Courses of varying lengths *Degrees:* diplomas *Prof. Accred.:* Medical Assisting (AMA) *CEO:* Dir. Allan Sharpe
(915) 532-3737

BRANCH CAMPUS
4710 Alabama St., El Paso 79930-2610
Accred.: 1990 (ACCSCT) *CEO:* Dir. James Bohanan
(915) 566-9621

UTAH

AMERICAN INSTITUTE OF MEDICAL-DENTAL
TECHNOLOGY
1675 N. Freedom Blvd., Bldg. 4, Provo
84604 *Type:* Private *Accred.:* 1984/1990
(ABHES) *Calendar:* Courses of varying
lengths *Degrees:* certificates *Prof. Accred.:*
Dental Assisting, Medical Assisting (AMA)
CEO: Admin. Keith T. Van Soest
(801) 377-2900

AMERICAN TECHNICAL CENTER
1144 W. 3300 S., Salt Lake City 84119-3330
Type: Private *Accred.:* 1976/1992 (ACC-
SCT) *Calendar:* Courses of varying lengths
Degrees: certificates *CEO:* Pres. John S.
Cowan
(801) 975-1000

THE BRYMAN SCHOOL
1144 W. 3300 S., Salt Lake City 84119-3330
Type: Private *Accred.:* 1973/1989 (ACC-
SCT) *Calendar:* Courses of varying lengths
Degrees: certificates *Prof. Accred.:* Dental
Assisting (prelim. provisional), Medical As-
sisting (AMA) *CEO:* Pres. John S. Cowan
(801) 975-7000

CERTIFIED CAREERS INSTITUTE
1455 W. 2200 S., No. 200, Salt Lake City
84119 *Type:* Private *Accred.:* 1988 (ACC-
SCT) *Calendar:* Courses of varying lengths
Degrees: diplomas *CEO:* C.E.O. Gene Curtis
(801) 973-7008

BRANCH CAMPUS
2661 Washington Blvd., Ste. 104, Ogden
84401-3697 *Accred.:* 1988 (ACCSCT)
CEO: Dir. John Cannon
(801) 621-4925

INTERMOUNTAIN COLLEGE OF COURT REPORTING
5980 S. 300 E., Murray 84107 *Type:* Private
business *Accred.:* 1981/1988 (ACISC) *Calendar:* Qtr. plan *Degrees:* certificates, diplomas *CEO:* Pres. Linda J. Smurthwaite
(801) 268-9271

MYOTHERAPY INSTITUTE OF UTAH
3350 S. 2300 E., Salt Lake City 84109 *Type:*
Private *Accred.:* 1992 (ACCSCT) *Calendar:*
Courses of varying lengths *Degrees:* certificates *CEO:* Owner Shirley Foster
(801) 484-7624

PROVO COLLEGE
1450 W. 820 N., Provo 84601 *Type:* Private
Accred.: 1988 (ACCSCT) *Calendar:* Courses of varying lengths *Degrees:* certificates
Prof. Accred.: Dental Assisting *CEO:* Pres.
Keith Poelman
(801) 375-1861

VERMONT

FANNY ALLEN MEMORIAL SCHOOL OF
PRACTICAL NURSING
  125 College Pkwy., Colchester 05446 *Type:*
  Private professional *Calendar:* Courses of
  varying lengths *Degrees:* certificates *Prof.*
  Accred.: Practical Nursing *CEO:* Dir. Phyllis
  Iorlano
                                  (802) 655-2540

NEW ENGLAND CULINARY INSTITUTE
  250 Main St., Montpelier 05602-9720 *Type:*
  Private *Accred.:* 1984/1989 (ACCSCT) *Cal-*
  endar: Courses of varying lengths *Degrees:*
  certificates *CEO:* Pres. Francis Voigt
                                  (802) 223-6324

NEW ENGLAND CULINARY INSTITUTE AT
ESSEX
  1700 Troy Ave., No. 1, Colchester 05446-
  3105 *Accred.:* 1989 (ACCSCT) *CEO:* Dir.
  John Turner
                                  (802) 655-0808

THOMPSON SCHOOL OF PRACTICAL NURSING
  30 Maple St., Brattleboro 05301 *Type:* Private professional *Calendar:* Courses of varying lengths *Degrees:* certificates *Prof. Ac-*
  cred.: Practical Nursing *CEO:* Interim Dir.
  Rosemary Tarbell
                                  (802) 254-5570

VIRGINIA

ALLIANCE TRACTOR TRAILER TRAINING
CENTERS II
100 Nye Rd., P.O. Box 804, Wytheville
24382-0804 *Type:* Private *Accred.:* 1988/
1993 (ACCSCT) *Calendar:* Courses of varying lengths *Degrees:* certificates *CEO:* Dir.
Mark Pressley
(703) 228-6101

ALLIANCE TRACTOR TRAILER TRAINING
CENTER V
P.O. Box 579, Benson, NC 27504-0579
Accred.: 1990 (ACCSCT) *CEO:* Dir.
Allan Rubio
(919) 892-8370

ANTHONY'S BARBER STYLING COLLEGE
1307 Jefferson Ave., Newport News 23607-
5617 *Type:* Private *Accred.:* 1989 (ACCSCT)
Calendar: Courses of varying lengths *Degrees:* certificates *CEO:* Dir. Irene Anthony
(804) 244-2311

APPRENTICE SCHOOL—NEWPORT NEWS
SHIPBUILDING
4101 Washington Ave., Newport News
23607 *Type:* Private *Accred.:* 1982/1992
(SACS-COEI) *Calendar:* Courses of varying
lengths *Degrees:* certificates *CEO:* Dir.
James H. Hughes
FTE Enroll: 684   (804) 380-2682

ARMED FORCES SCHOOL OF MUSIC
Bldg. 3602, Little Creek, Norfolk 23521
Type: Public (federal) *Accred.:* 1983/1988
(SACS-COEI) *Calendar:* Courses of varying
lengths *Degrees:* certificates *CEO:* Com-
manding Ofcr. Raymond A. Ascione, U.S.N.
FTE Enroll: 208   (804) 464-7501

THE ARMY INSTITUTE FOR PROFESSIONAL
DEVELOPMENT
U.S. Army Training Support Ctr., Fort Eustis
23604-5168 *Type:* Public (federal) home
study *Accred.:* 1978/1989 (NHSC) *Calendar:* Courses of varying lengths *Degrees:*
certificates *CEO:* Dir. Ned C. Motter
(804) 878-3305

ARMY QUARTERMASTER CENTER AND SCHOOL
Fort Lee 23801-5034 *Type:* Public (federal)
technical *Accred.:* 1975/1990 (SACS-COEI)
Calendar: Courses of varying lengths *De-
grees:* certificates *CEO:* Commanding Ofcr.
J. Cusick
FTE Enroll: 3,628   (804) 734-2555

ARMY TRANSPORTATION AND AVIATION
LOGISTICS SCHOOL
Bldg. 2731, Fort Eustis 23604-5450 *Type:*
Public (federal) technical *Accred.:* 1975/
1992 (SACS-COEI) *Calendar:* Courses of
varying lengths *Degrees:* certificates *CEO:*
Commandant Kenneth Wykle, U.S.A.
FTE Enroll: 2,173   (804) 878-4400

ATI CAREER INSTITUTE
7777 Leesburg Pike, No. 100, S., Falls
Church 22043 *Type:* Private *Accred.:* 1992
(SACS-COEI) *Calendar:* Courses of varying
lengths *Degrees:* certificates *CEO:* Pres.
Richard Shurtz
FTE Enroll: 164   (703) 821-8570

ATI—HOLLYWOOD
3024 Trinkle Ave., Roanoke 24012 *Type:*
Private *Accred.:* 1989/1992 (SACS-COEI)
Calendar: Courses of varying lengths *De-
grees:* certificates *CEO:* Pres. Todd Rothrock
FTE Enroll: 62   (703) 362-9338

BRANCH CAMPUS
1108 Brandon Ave., S.W., Roanoke
24015 *CEO:* Dir. Marie Mullens
(703) 343-0153

BRANCH CAMPUS
109 E. Main St., Salem 24153 *CEO:* Dir.
Priscilla Atkinson
(703) 389-1500

BARCLAY CAREER SCHOOL
645 Church St., Norfolk 23510-1712 *Type:*
Private *Accred.:* 1991 (ACCSCT) *Calendar:*
Courses of varying lengths *Degrees:* certificates *CEO:* Dir. Bob McNeeley
(804) 533-9500

THE BRAXTON SCHOOL
4917 Augusta Ave., Richmond 23230-3601
Type: Private business *Accred.:* 1988
(ACISC) *Calendar:* Courses of varying

lengths *Degrees:* certificates, diplomas
CEO: Dir. Emily Swelnis
(804) 353-4458

CAREER DEVELOPMENT CENTER
605 Thimble Shoals Blvd., Ste. 209, Newport News 23606 *Type:* Private *Accred.:*
1983/1993 (SACS-COEI) *Calendar:* Courses
of varying lengths *Degrees:* certificates
CEO: Dir. Patricia Ettus
FTE Enroll: 213   (804) 873-2423

CAREER TRAINING CENTER
4000 W. Broad St., Richmond 23230 *Type:*
Private *Accred.:* 1991 (SACS-COEI) *Calendar:* Courses of varying lengths *Degrees:*
certificates *CEO:* Dir. Joe Dillard
FTE Enroll: 244   (804) 342-1190

BRANCH CAMPUS
2600 Memorial Ave., No. 201, Lynchburg
24501 *CEO:* Dir. Donna Barrette
(804) 845-7949

BRANCH CAMPUS
3223 Brandon Ave., S.W., Roanoke
24018 *CEO:* Dir. Bob Bannock
(703) 981-0925

THE CATHOLIC HOME STUDY INSTITUTE
9 Loudoun St., S.E., Leesburg 22075 *Type:*
Private home study *Accred.:* 1986/1991
(NHSC) *Calendar:* Courses of varying
lengths *Degrees:* diplomas *CEO:* Exec. Dir.
Marianne E. Mount
(703) 777-8388

CENTRAL SCHOOL OF PRACTICAL NURSING
1330 N. Military Hwy., Norfolk 23502 *Type:*
Private professional *Calendar:* Courses of
varying lengths *Degrees:* certificates *Prof.
Accred.:* Practical Nursing *CEO:* Dir. Gloria
Rudibaugh
(804) 441-5625

COMPUTER DYNAMICS INSTITUTE
397 Little Neck Rd., Virginia Beach 23452
Type: Private *Accred.:* 1990 (SACS-COEI)
Calendar: Courses of varying lengths *De-
grees:* certificates *CEO:* Dir. Christine Carroll
FTE Enroll: 158   (804) 486-7300

COMPUTER LEARNING CENTER
6295 Edsall Rd., Ste. 210, Alexandria
22312-2617 *Type:* Private business *Accred.:*

1979/1991 (ACISC); 1984/1989 (SACS-
COEI) *Calendar:* Courses of varying lengths
Degrees: certificates, diplomas *CEO:* Dir.
Daniel J. Tokarski
FTE Enroll: 715   (703) 823-0300

DEFENSE MAPPING SCHOOL
21st St. and Belvoir Rd., Fort Belvoir 22060
Type: Public (federal) *Accred.:* 1975/1990
(SACS-COEI) *Calendar:* Courses of varying
lengths *Degrees:* certificates *CEO:* Commander James R. Nichols, U.S.A.
FTE Enroll: 202   (703) 805-2557

DOMINION BUSINESS SCHOOL
933 Reservoir St., Harrisonburg 22801 *Type:*
Private business *Accred.:* 1986/1990
(ACISC) *Calendar:* Courses of varying
lengths *Degrees:* certificates, diplomas
CEO: Dir. Dianne Phipps
(703) 433-6977

DOMINION BUSINESS SCHOOL
4142-1 Melrose Ave., N.W., No. 1, Roanoke
24017 *Type:* Private business *Accred.:* 1972/
1990 (ACISC) *Calendar:* Courses of varying
lengths *Degrees:* certificates, diplomas
CEO: Dir. Jon Coover
(703) 362-7738

DOMINION BUSINESS SCHOOL
825 Richmond Rd., Staunton 24401 *Type:*
Private business *Accred.:* 1986/1990
(ACISC) *Calendar:* Courses of varying
lengths *Degrees:* certificates, diplomas
CEO: Dir. Susan Race
(703) 886-3596

ECPI COMPUTER INSTITUTE
1030 Jefferson St., S.E., Roanoke 24016
Type: Private *Accred.:* 1986 (ACCSCT);
1992 (SACS-COEI) *Calendar:* Courses of
varying lengths *Degrees:* certificates *CEO:*
Dir. David Wesley Hansey
FTE Enroll: 112   (703) 343-5566

ECPI COMPUTER INSTITUTE
5555 Greenwich Rd., Ste. 300, Virginia
Beach 23462-6542 *Type:* Private *Accred.:*
1971/1991 (ACCSCT); 1984/1989 (SACS-
COEI) *Calendar:* Courses of varying lengths
Degrees: certificates *CEO:* Dir. Mark B.
Dreyfus
FTE Enroll: 1,105   (804) 671-7171

BRANCH CAMPUS
7015G Albert Pick Rd., Greensboro, NC 27409-9654 *Accred.:* 1986 (ACCSCT) *CEO:* Dir. Richard Wechner
(919) 665-1400

BRANCH CAMPUS
1919 Commerce Ave., No. 200, Hampton 23666-4246 *Accred.:* 1986 (ACCSCT) *CEO:* Vice Pres. Ronald J. Ballance
(804) 838-9191

ECPI OF CHARLOTTE
1121 Wood Ridge Center Dr., Ste. 150, Charlotte, NC 28217-1986 *Accred.:* 1986 (ACCSCT) *CEO:* Dir. H. Paul Shultz
(704) 357-0077

ECPI COMPUTER INSTITUTE OF RICHMOND
4303 W. Broad St., Richmond 23230-3305 *Type:* Private *Accred.:* 1986/1991 (ACCSCT); 1990/1991 (SACS-COEI) *Calendar:* Courses of varying lengths *Degrees:* certificates *CEO:* Dir. Bruce Misiaszek
FTE Enroll: 370 (804) 359-3535

ECPI COMPUTER INSTITUTE
4509 Creedmoor Rd., Raleigh, NC 27612 *Accred.:* 1986/1991 (ACCSCT) *CEO:* Dir. Steven Hitchner
(919) 571-0057

FLATWOODS CIVILIAN CONSERVATION CENTER
Rte. 1, Box 211, Coeburn 24230 *Type:* Private *Accred.:* 1989 (SACS-COEI) *Calendar:* Courses of varying lengths *Degrees:* certificates *CEO:* Dir. Al Lavergne
FTE Enroll: 225 (703) 395-3384

MICROCOMPUTER TECHNOLOGY CENTER
8303 Arlington Blvd., Ste. 210, Fairfax 22031 *Type:* Private home study *Accred.:* 1992 (NHSC) *Calendar:* Courses of varying lengths *Degrees:* certificates *CEO:* C.E.O. Marcellina Hawkes
(703) 573-1006

NATIONAL EDUCATION CENTER—KEE BUSINESS COLLEGE
803 Dilligence Dr., Newport News 23606 *Type:* Private business *Accred.:* 1955/1988 (ACISC) *Calendar:* Qtr. plan *Degrees:* certificates, diplomas *CEO:* Exec. Dir. Tom Wilson
(804) 873-1111

NATIONAL EDUCATION CENTER—KEE BUSINESS COLLEGE
861 Glenrock Rd., Norfolk 23502 *Type:* Private business *Accred.:* 1967/1988 (ACISC) *Calendar:* Qtr. plan *Degrees:* certificates, diplomas *Prof. Accred.:* Medical Assisting *CEO:* Exec. Dir. Joan L. Rhodes
(804) 461-2922

BRANCH CAMPUS
2106 County St., Portsmouth 23704 *Accred.:* 1988 (ACISC) *CEO:* Dir. Bettie Thomas
(804) 397-3800

BRANCH CAMPUS
6301 Midlothian Tpke., Richmond 23225 *Accred.:* 1988 (ACISC) *CEO:* Dir. Zoe S. Thompson
(804) 745-3300

NAVAL GUIDED MISSILES SCHOOL
Dam Neck, Virginia Beach 23461 *Type:* Public (federal) technical *Accred.:* 1983/1988 (SACS-COEI) *Calendar:* Courses of varying lengths *Degrees:* certificates *CEO:* Commandant T.L. Parry, Jr., U.S.N.
FTE Enroll: 273 (804) 433-6628

NAVY AND MARINE CORPS INTELLIGENCE TRAINING CENTER
Bldg. 420, Dam Neck, Virginia Beach 23461 *Type:* Public (federal) *Accred.:* 1987 (SACS-COEI) *Calendar:* Courses of varying lengths *Degrees:* certificates *CEO:* Commandant Frank Notz, U.S.N.
FTE Enroll: 263 (804) 433-8001

NORFOLK SKILLS CENTER
922 W. 21st St., Norfolk 23517 *Type:* Private *Accred.:* 1988/1992 (SACS-COEI) *Calendar:* Courses of varying lengths *Degrees:* certificates *CEO:* Dir. Raymond L. Murray
FTE Enroll: 165 (804) 441-2665

OMEGA TRAVEL SCHOOL
3102 Omega Office Park, Fairfax 22031 *Type:* Private *Accred.:* 1993 (ACCSCT) *Calendar:* Courses of varying lengths *Degrees:* certificates *CEO:* Pres./Owner Gloria Bohan
(703) 359-8830

PHILLIPS BUSINESS COLLEGE
P.O. Box 169, 1912 Memorial Ave., Lynchburg 24505 *Type:* Private business *Accred.:*

1953/1990 (ACISC) *Calendar:* Qtr. plan *Degrees:* certificates, diplomas *CEO:* Pres. Wynn F. Blanton

(804) 847-7701

POTOMAC ACADEMY OF HAIR DESIGN
9101 Center St., Manassas 22110-5405 *Type:* Private *Accred.:* 1991 (ACCSCT) *Calendar:* Courses of varying lengths *Degrees:* certificates *CEO:* Pres. Gail O. Donaway

(703) 361-7775

REPORTING ACADEMY OF VIRGINIA
Ste. 600, Pembroke One, Virginia Beach 23462 *Type:* Private business *Accred.:* 1986 (ACISC) *Calendar:* Qtr. plan *Degrees:* certificates, diplomas *CEO:* Pres. Jane F. Braithwaite

(804) 499-5447

BRANCH CAMPUS
Ste. 305, 1001 Boulders Pkwy., Richmond 23225 *Accred.:* 1988 (ACISC) *CEO:* Dir. Bonnie Rathjen

(804) 323-1020

BRANCH CAMPUS
5501 Backlick Rd., Springfield 22151 *Accred.:* 1990 (ACISC) *CEO:* Dir. Trudi F. Terry

(703) 658-0588

SOUTHSIDE TRAINING SKILLS CENTER
Hwy. 460, E., Crewe 23930 *Type:* Private *Accred.:* 1988/1991 (SACS-COEI) *Calendar:* Courses of varying lengths *Degrees:* certificates *CEO:* Dir. Gary Groneweg
FTE Enroll: 66   (804) 645-7471

TESST ELECTRONICS AND COMPUTER INSTITUTE
1400 Duke St., Alexandria 22314-3403 *Type:* Private *Accred.:* 1986/1993 (ACCSCT) *Calendar:* Courses of varying lengths *Degrees:* certificates *CEO:* Dir. Clete Mehringer

(703) 548-4800

TIDEWATER TECH
2697 Dean Dr., Ste. 100, Virginia Beach 23452 *Type:* Private *Accred.:* 1986 (ACCSCT) *Calendar:* Courses of varying lengths *Degrees:* certificates *CEO:* Dir. Carolyn Lake

(804) 340-2121

BRANCH CAMPUS
1417 N. Battlefield Blvd., Ste. 310, Chesapeake 23320 *Accred.:* 1993 (ACCSCT) *CEO:* Dir. Rob Richenbach

(804) 548-2828

BRANCH CAMPUS
616 Denbigh Blvd., Newport News 23402 *Accred.:* 1991 (ACCSCT) *CEO:* Dir. Maxine Stine

(804) 874-2121

BRANCH CAMPUS
1760 E. Little Creek Rd., Norfolk 23518-4202 *Accred.:* 1990 (ACCSCT) *CEO:* Dir. Yvonne Santos

(804) 588-2121

VIRGINIA HAIR ACADEMY
3312 Williamson Rd., N.W., Roanoke 24012-4049 *Type:* Private *Accred.:* 1981/1986 (ACCSCT) *Calendar:* Courses of varying lengths *Degrees:* certificates, diplomas *CEO:* Pres. Linwood Locklear

(703) 563-2015

VIRGINIA SCHOOL OF COSMETOLOGY
1516 Willow Lawn Dr., Richmond 23230 *Type:* Private *Accred.:* 1987/1992 (SACS-COEI) *Calendar:* Courses of varying lengths *Degrees:* certificates *CEO:* Dir. Francis Michael
FTE Enroll: 125   (804) 288-7923

WASHINGTON BUSINESS SCHOOL OF NORTHERN VIRGINIA
1980 Gallows Rd., Vienna 22182 *Type:* Private business *Accred.:* 1969/1990 (ACISC) *Calendar:* Qtr. plan *Degrees:* certificates, diplomas *CEO:* Dir. Katherine C. Embrey

(703) 556-8888

WASHINGTON COUNTY ADULT SKILL CENTER
848 Thompson Dr., Abingdon 24210 *Type:* Public (state) *Accred.:* 1990 (SACS-COEI) *Calendar:* Courses of varying lengths *Degrees:* certificates, diplomas *CEO:* Dir. Jerry Crabtree
FTE Enroll: 65   (703) 628-6641

WOODROW WILSON REHABILITATION CENTER
Fishersville 22939 *Type:* Private *Accred.:* 1983/1993 (SACS-COEI) *Calendar:* Courses of varying lengths *Degrees:* certificates *CEO:* Dir. Wendell Coleman
FTE Enroll: 400   (703) 332-7166

WASHINGTON

BATES TECHNICAL COLLEGE
1101 S. Yakima Ave., Tacoma 98405 *Type:* Public (district) *System:* Washington State Board for Community and Technical Colleges *Accred.:* 1988 (NASC) *Calendar:* Sem. plan *Degrees:* certificates *Prof. Accred.:* Dental Assisting, Dental Laboratory Technology *CEO:* Pres. William P. Mohler
Enroll: 8,834   (206) 596-1500

BELLINGHAM TECHNICAL COLLEGE
3028 Lindbergh Ave., Bellingham 98225 *Type:* Public (district) *System:* Washington State Board for Community and Technical Colleges *Calendar:* Courses of varying lengths *Degrees:* certificates *Prof. Accred.:* Dental Assisting, EMT-Paramedic *CEO:* Pres. Desmond McArdle
(206) 676-6490

CAPITOL BUSINESS COLLEGE
No. 13, 5005 Pacific Hwy. E., Fife 98424-2617 *Type:* Private business *Accred.:* 1993 (ACISC) *Calendar:* Courses of varying lengths *Degrees:* certificates, diplomas *CEO:* Dir. Deanna Jiles
(206) 357-9313

CAREER FLORAL DESIGN INSTITUTE
13200 Northup Way, Bellevue 98005-2004 *Type:* Private *Accred.:* 1992 (ACCSCT) *Calendar:* Courses of varying lengths *Degrees:* certificates *CEO:* Owner Katherine Salvog
(206) 746-8340

CLOVER PARK TECHNICAL COLLEGE
4500 Steilacoom Blvd., S.W., Tacoma 98498-4098 *Type:* Public (district) *System:* Washington State Board for Community and Technical Colleges *Calendar:* Courses of varying lengths *Degrees:* certificates *Prof. Accred.:* Dental Assisting, Medical Laboratory Technology (AMA) *CEO:* Admin. Alson E. Green, Jr.
(206) 589-5500

COMMERCIAL TRAINING SERVICES
24325 Pacific Hwy. S., Des Moines 98198-4026 *Type:* Private *Accred.:* 1973/1990 (ACCSCT) *Calendar:* Courses of varying lengths *Degrees:* certificates *CEO:* Dir. David F. Minear
(206) 824-3970

COURT REPORTING INSTITUTE
Ste. 2, 929 N. 130th St., Seattle 98133 *Type:* Private business *Accred.:* 1991 (ACISC) *Calendar:* Courses of varying lengths *Degrees:* certificates, diplomas *CEO:* Vice Pres. Ted Girgus
(206) 363-8300

CROWN ACADEMY
8739 S. Hosmer St., Tacoma 98444 *Type:* Private *Accred.:* 1979/1989 (ACCSCT) *Calendar:* Courses of varying lengths *Degrees:* diplomas *CEO:* Pres. John M. Wabel
(206) 531-3123

DIVERS INSTITUTE OF TECHNOLOGY
P.O. Box 70667, 4315 11th Ave., N.W., Seattle 98107-0667 *Type:* Private *Accred.:* 1973/1988 (ACCSCT) *Calendar:* Courses of varying lengths *Degrees:* certificates, diplomas *CEO:* Dir. John L. Ritter
(206) 783-5542

EMIL FRIES PIANO & TRAINING CENTER
2510 E. Evergreen Blvd., Vancouver 98661 *Type:* Private *Accred.:* 1993 (ACCSCT) *Calendar:* Courses of varying lengths *Degrees:* certificates *CEO:* Dir. Diane Dees
(206) 693-1511

ETON TECHNICAL INSTITUTE
3649 Frontage Rd., Port Orchard 98366 *Type:* Private business *Accred.:* 1979/1988 (ACISC) *Calendar:* Courses of varying lengths *Degrees:* certificates, diplomas *CEO:* Pres. Ron Heit
(206) 479-3866

BRANCH CAMPUS
209 E. Casino Rd., Everett 98208 *Accred.:* 1988 (ACISC) *CEO:* Dir. Teresa Ferguson
(206) 353-4888

BRANCH CAMPUS
31919 Sixth Ave. S., Federal Way 98063 *Accred.:* 1987/1988 (ACISC) *CEO:* Dir. Dennis Palmer
(206) 941-5800

FOX TRAVEL INSTITUTE
520 Pike St., Ste. 2800, Seattle 98101-4000
Type: Private *Accred.:* 1991 (ACCSCT) *Calendar:* Courses of varying lengths *Degrees:* certificates *CEO:* Vice Pres. Robert Veeder
(206) 224-7800

INTERNATIONAL AIR ACADEMY
2901 E. Mill Plain Blvd., Vancouver 98661-4899 *Type:* Private *Accred.:* 1983/1988 (ACCSCT) *Calendar:* Courses of varying lengths *Degrees:* certificates *CEO:* Pres. Arch Miller
(206) 695-2500

BRANCH CAMPUS
2980 Inland Empire Blvd., Ontario, CA 91764-4804 *Accred.:* 1991 (ACCSCT) *CEO:* Dir. Tracy Passariello
(714) 989-5222

LABORATORY OF PATHOLOGY OF SEATTLE
1229 Madison St., No. 500, P.O. Box 14950, Seattle 98114-0950 *Type:* Private *Calendar:* Courses of varying lengths *Degrees:* certificates *Prof. Accred.:* Medical Technology *CEO:* Dir. John D. Batjer, M.D.
(206) 386-2730

NATIONAL BROADCASTING SCHOOL
2615 Fourth Ave., No. 100, Seattle 98121-1233 *Type:* Private *Accred.:* 1987/1993 (ACCSCT) *Calendar:* Courses of varying lengths *Degrees:* diplomas *CEO:* Pres. Bill E. Brock
(206) 728-2346

NORTHWEST COLLEGE OF ART
16464 State Hwy. 305, Poulsbo 98370-0932 *Type:* Private *Accred.:* 1986 (ACCSCT) *Calendar:* Courses of varying lengths *Degrees:* certificates, diplomas *CEO:* Pres. Craig Freeman
(206) 779-9993

NORTHWEST SCHOOL OF WOODEN BOATBUILDING
251 Otto St., Port Townsend 98368 *Type:* Private *Accred.:* 1993 (ACCSCT) *Calendar:* Courses of varying lengths *Degrees:* certificates *CEO:* Dir. Andrew L. Patten
(206) 385-4948

PACIFIC NORTHWEST BALLET SCHOOL
4649 Sunnyside Ave. N., Seattle 98103 *Type:* Private *Calendar:* Courses of varying lengths *Degrees:* certificates *Prof. Accred.:* Dance *CEO:* Dir. Francia Russell
(206) 547-5910

PERRY TECHNICAL INSTITUTE
2011 W. Washington Ave., Yakima 98903-1296 *Type:* Private *Accred.:* 1969/1990 (ACCSCT) *Calendar:* Courses of varying lengths *Degrees:* certificates *CEO:* Dir. J. Tuman
(509) 453-0374

PHILLIPS JUNIOR COLLEGE OF SPOKANE
N. 1101 Fancher Rd., Spokane 99212-1204 *Type:* Private *Accred.:* 1991 (ACCSCT) *Calendar:* Courses of varying lengths *Degrees:* diplomas *CEO:* Dir. Carol Menck
(509) 535-7771

RESOURCE CENTER FOR THE HANDICAPPED
20150 45th Ave., N.E., Seattle 98155-1700 *Type:* Private *Accred.:* 1987/1993 (ACCSCT) *Calendar:* Courses of varying lengths *Degrees:* certificates *CEO:* Dir. of Opers. Cindi Strong
(206) 368-3327

TREND COLLEGE
Ste. 1201, 3311 W. Clearwater Ave., Kennewick 99336 *Type:* Private business *Accred.:* 1973/1989 (ACISC) *Calendar:* Courses of varying lengths *Degrees:* certificates, diplomas *CEO:* Dir. Jeffrey R. Brown
(509) 735-8515

TREND COLLEGE
1260 Commerce St., Longview 98632 *Type:* Private business *Accred.:* 1973/1990 (ACISC) *Calendar:* Courses of varying lengths *Degrees:* certificates, diplomas *CEO:* Dir. Robert Woodman
(206) 425-4790

TREND COLLEGE
N. 214 Wall St., Spokane 99201 *Type:* Private business *Accred.:* 1953/1986 (ACISC) *Calendar:* Courses of varying lengths *Degrees:* certificates, diplomas *Prof. Accred.:* Dental Assisting, Medical Assisting (AMA) *CEO:* Dir. Mark Lookabaugh
(509) 838-3521

BRANCH CAMPUS
230 Grant Rd., East Wenatchee 98801 *Accred.:* 1985/1991 (ACISC) *CEO:* Dir. Marcia Henkle
(509) 884-1587

TREND COLLEGE
112 Pierce Ave., Yakima 98902 *Type:* Private business *Accred.:* 1972/1989 (ACISC) *Calendar:* Courses of varying lengths *Degrees:* certificates, diplomas *CEO:* Dir. Judy Pilger
(509) 248-4806

TRIDENT TRAINING FACILITY
Silverdale 98315-5400 *Type:* Public (federal) *Accred.:* 1991 (NASC) *Calendar:* Courses of varying lengths *Degrees:* certificates *CEO:* Commanding Officer Jimmy Lee Ellis *Enroll:* 5,667
(206) 396-4068

VOCATIONAL TRAINING INSTITUTE
6400M N.E. Hwy. 99, Vancouver 98665 *Type:* Private *Accred.:* 1992 (ACCSCT) *Calendar:* Courses of varying lengths *Degrees:* certificates *CEO:* Pres. Charles Kroninger
(206) 695-5186

WEST VIRGINIA

B.M. SPURR SCHOOL OF PRACTICAL NURSING
800 Wheeling Ave., Glen Dale 26038 *Type:*
Public *Calendar:* Courses of varying lengths
Degrees: certificates *Prof. Accred.:* Practical
Nursing *CEO:* Dir. Dorothy McCulley
(304) 845-3211

BOONE COUNTY CAREER CENTER
Box 50 B, Danville 25053 *Type:* Private
Calendar: Courses of varying lengths *De-
grees:* certificates *Prof. Accred.:* Medical
Laboratory Technology *CEO:* Dir. Jimmy H.
Dolan
(304) 369-4585

CARVER CAREER AND TECHNICAL EDUCATION
CENTER
4799 Midland Dr., Charleston 25306 *Type:*
Private *Calendar:* Courses of varying
lengths *Degrees:* certificates *Prof. Accred.:*
Respiratory Therapy Technology *CEO:* Prin.
Norma Miller
(304) 348-1965

NATIONAL EDUCATION CENTER—CROSS LANES
NATIONAL INSTITUTE OF TECHNOLOGY CAMPUS
5514 Big Tyler Rd., Cross Lanes 25311-
9998 *Type:* Private *Accred.:* 1971/1986
(ACCSCT) *Calendar:* Courses of varying
lengths *Degrees:* diplomas *CEO:* Pres. Hans
Schmidt
(304) 776-6290

WHEELING COLLEGE OF HAIR DESIGN
1122 Main St., Wheeling 26003-2703 *Type:*
Private *Accred.:* 1978/1988 (ACCSCT) *Calendar:* Courses of varying lengths *Degrees:*
certificates *CEO:* Dir. of Opers. William
Devon
(304) 232-1957

WOOD COUNTY VOCATIONAL SCHOOL
1511 Blizzard Dr., Parkersburg 26101 *Type:*
Public *Calendar:* Courses of varying lengths
Degrees: certificates *Prof. Accred.:* Practical
Nursing *CEO:* Dir. William Gainer
(304) 420-9501

WISCONSIN

ACME INSTITUTE OF TECHNOLOGY
102 Revere Dr., Manitowoc 54220 *Type:* Private *Accred.:* 1967/1989 (ACCSCT) *Calendar:* Courses of varying lengths *Degrees:* diplomas *CEO:* Dir. Barbara A. Pitrowski
(414) 682-6144

ACME INSTITUTE OF TECHNOLOGY
819 S. 60th St., West Allis 53214-3365 *Type:* Private *Accred.:* 1967/1989 (ACCSCT) *Calendar:* Courses of varying lengths *Degrees:* diplomas *CEO:* Dir. Shirle A. Miick
(414) 257-1011

AURORA HEALTH CARE, INC.
3000 W. Montana Ave., P.O. Box 343910, Milwaukee 53234-3910 *Type:* Private *Calendar:* Courses of varying lengths *Degrees:* certificates *Prof. Accred.:* Medical Technology *CEO:* Pres. G. Edwin Howe
(414) 647-3000

DIESEL TRUCK DRIVER TRAINING SCHOOL
Hwy. 151 and Elder La., Rte. 2, Sun Prairie 53590-0047 *Type:* Private *Accred.:* 1973/1988 (ACCSCT) *Calendar:* Courses of varying lengths *Degrees:* certificates, diplomas *CEO:* Pres. Mark Klabacka
(608) 837-7800

FRANCISCAN SHARED LABORATORY, INC.
11020 W. Plank Ct., Ste. 100, Wauwatosa 53226 *Type:* Private *Calendar:* Courses of varying lengths *Degrees:* certificates *Prof. Accred.:* Medical Technology *CEO:* Pres. Earl C. Buck
(414) 476-3400

MARSHFIELD MEDICAL CENTER LABORATORY
1000 N. Oak Ave., Marshfield 54449 *Type:* Private *Calendar:* Courses of varying lengths *Degrees:* certificates *Prof. Accred.:* Cytotechnology *CEO:* Exec. Dir. Frederick J. Wenzel
(715) 387-5123

MBTI BUSINESS TRAINING INSTITUTE
820 N. Plankinton Ave., Milwaukee 53203 *Type:* Private business *Accred.:* 1969/1987 (ACISC) *Calendar:* Courses of varying lengths *Degrees:* certificates, diplomas *CEO:* Pres. Sandra C. Suzuki
(414) 272-2192

BRANCH CAMPUS
237 South St., Waukesha 53186 *Accred.:* 1993 (ACISC) *CEO:* Senior Vice Pres. Nancy J. Bush
(414) 527-3221

MIDWEST CENTER FOR THE STUDY OF ORIENTAL MEDICINE
6226 Bankers Rd., Stes. 5 and 6, Racine 53403 *Type:* Private professional *Calendar:* Qtr. plan *Degrees:* certificates *Prof. Accred.:* Acupuncture *CEO:* Pres. William Dunbar *FTE Enroll:* 57   (414) 554-2010

TRANS AMERICAN SCHOOL OF BROADCASTING
600 Williamson St., Madison 53703-3588 *Type:* Private *Accred.:* 1972/1987 (ACCSCT) *Calendar:* Sem. plan *Degrees:* diplomas *CEO:* Dir. Chris Hutchings
(608) 257-4600

WISCONSIN CONSERVATORY OF MUSIC, INC.
1584 N. Prospect Ave., Milwaukee 53202 *Type:* Independent *Calendar:* Courses of varying lengths *Degrees:* certificates, diplomas *Prof. Accred.:* Music *CEO:* Dir. Florence L. Ponzi
(414) 276-5760

WISCONSIN SCHOOL OF ELECTRONICS
1227 N. Sherman Ave., Madison 53704 *Type:* Private *Accred.:* 1970/1993 (ACCSCT) *Calendar:* Qtr. plan *Degrees:* certificates *CEO:* Dir. Donald G. Madelung
(608) 249-6611

WISCONSIN SCHOOL OF PROFESSIONAL PET GROOMING
34197 Wisconsin Ave., Okauchee 53069 *Type:* Private *Accred.:* 1992 (ACCSCT) *Calendar:* Courses of varying lengths *Degrees:* certificates *CEO:* Admin. Delores Lillge
(414) 569-9492

WYOMING

CHEYENNE AERO TECH
1204 Airport Pkwy., Cheyenne 82001-1552
Type: Private *Accred.:* 1983/1988 (ACC-SCT) *Calendar:* Courses of varying lengths
Degrees: certificates *CEO:* Exec. Dir.
Michael A. Smith

(800) 366-2376

WYOMING TECHNICAL INSTITUTE
4373 N. Third St., Laramie 82070 *Type:*
Private *Accred.:* 1969/1989 (ACCSCT)
Calendar: Courses of varying lengths
Degrees: diplomas *CEO:* Vice Pres. Jim
Mathis

(307) 742-3776

OUTSIDE THE UNITED STATES

BAHAMAS

BAHAMAS HOTEL TRAINING COLLEGE
College Ave., Oakes Field, Nassau *Type:*
Public technical *Accred.:* 1977/1990 (SACS-
COEI) *Calendar:* Courses of varying lengths
Degrees: certificates *CEO:* Dir. Kendal C.
Johnson
FTE Enroll: 63   (809) 323-8175

BRANCH CAMPUS
P.O. Box F-1679, Freeport *CEO:* Dir. Iva
Dahl-Brown
(809) 352-2896

CANADA

DAWSON COLLEGE
2120 Sherbrooke St. E., Montreal, Quebec
H2K 1C1 *Type:* Private *Calendar:* Sem. plan
Degrees: diplomas *Prof. Accred.:* Interior
Design *CEO:* Chrmn. Eugene Zamorski
(514) 931-8371

LAKELAND COLLEGE
Bag 5100, Vermillion, Alberta T0B 4M0
Type: Private *Calendar:* Sem. plan *Degrees:*
certificates, diplomas *Prof. Accred.:* Interior
Design *CEO:* Pres. D. Schmit
(403) 853-8400

MOUNT ROYAL COLLEGE
4825 Richard Rd., S.W., Calgary, Alberta
T3E 6K6 *Type:* Private *Calendar:* Sem. plan
Degrees: diplomas *Prof. Accred.:* Interior
Design *CEO:* Chrmn. Janice Smith
(403) 240-6100

QUEEN'S UNIVERSITY AT KINGSTON
Kingston, Ontario K7L 3N6 *Type:* Private
Calendar: Sem. plan *Prof. Accred.:* Clinical
Psychology, Medicine *CEO:* Chanc. Agnes
M. Benidickson
(613) 545-2000

FRANCE

INSTITUT HOTELIER CESAR RITZ
Le Bouveret CH-1897 *Type:* Private business *Accred.:* 1989 (ACISC) *Calendar:*
Courses of varying lengths *Degrees:* certificates, diplomas *CEO:* Dir. Martin Kisselef
[41] (25) 813-0150

SWISS HOSPITALITY INSTITUTE CESAR RITZ
101 Wykeham Rise Rd., Washington, CT
06793 *Accred.:* 1993 (ACISC) *CEO:* Dir.
Joseph D. Jaap
(203) 868-9555

ITALY

AMERICAN UNIVERSITY OF ROME
Via Collina 24, Rome 00187 *Type:* Private
Accred.: 1993 (ACISC) *Calendar:* Courses
of varying lengths *Degrees:* certificates,
diplomas *CEO:* Pres. Alessandro C. De
Bosis
[39] (6) 482-1819

SWITZERLAND

HOTEL INSTITUTE FOR MANAGEMENT
15 Ave. des Alpes, Montreux CH-1820
Type: Private business *Accred.:* 1990
(ACISC) *Calendar:* Courses of varying
lengths *Degrees:* certificates, diplomas
CEO: Dir. Edouard P.O. Dandrieux
[41] (21) 963-7404

HOTEL MANAGEMENT SCHOOL, "LES ROCHES"
Bluche Crans-Montana, Valais CH-3975
Type: Private *Accred.:* 1991 (NEASC-CTCI)
Calendar: Courses of varying lengths *De-
grees:* diplomas *CEO:* Dir. Peter Schlatter
FTE Enroll: 1,070   [41] (27) 41-1223

Major Changes

Alabama Christian School of Religion, AL, changed its name to Southern Christian University (summer 1992)

Asnuntuck Community College, CT, changed its name to Asnuntuck Community-Technical College (winter 1992)

Bastyr College, WA, changed its name to Bastyr University (winter 1993)

Belmont College, TN, changed its name to Belmont University (winter 1992)

Bishop Clarkson College, NE, changed its name to Clarkson College (winter 1992)

Brenau College, GA, changed its name to Brenau University (winter 1993)

Brewer State Junior College *and* Walker State Technical College, AL, merged to become Bevill State Community College (winter 1992)

Carver State Technical College *and* Southwest Technical College, AL, merged to become Bishop State Community College (winter 1992)

Catholic University of Puerto Rico, PR, changed its name to Pontifical Catholic University of Puerto Rico (winter 1992)

Chicago City-Wide College, IL, consolidated into Harold Washington College (winter 1992)

Chicago College of Osteopathic Medicine, IL, changed its name to Midwestern University (summer 1993)

Christ College Irvine, CA, changed its name to Concordia University (summer 1993)

Christopher Newport College, VA, changed its name to Christopher Newport University (spring 1992)

Clarke College, MS, closed (summer 1992)

College for Human Services, NY, changed its name to Audrey Cohen College (summer 1992)

Columbia Bible College and Seminary, SC, changed its name to Columbia International University (winter 1993)

Community College of Micronesia changed its name to College of Micronesia (summer 1993)

Dean Junior College, MA, changed its name to Dean College (summer 1993)

Delaware State College, DE, changed its name to Delaware State University (summer 1993)

Francis Marion College, SC, changed its name to Francis Marion University (spring 1992)

Gardner-Webb College, NC, changed its name to Gardner-Webb University (summer 1993)

Glassboro State College, NJ, changed its name to Rowan College of New Jersey (fall 1992)

Gordon Institute, MA, merged into Tufts University (winter 1992)

Goshen Biblical Seminary *and* Mennonite Biblical Seminary, IN, merged to become Associated Mennonite Biblical Seminary (summer 1993)

Great Lakes Bible College, MI, changed its name to Great Lakes Christian College (winter 1992)

Greater Hartford Community College *and* Hartford State Technical College, CT, merged to become Capital Community-Technical College (winter 1992)

Greater New Haven Technical College *and* South Central Community College, CT, merged to become Gateway Community-Technical College (winter 1992)

Griffin College, WA, closed (summer 1993)

Harcum Junior College, PA, changed its name to Harcum College (winter 1993)

Hartford College for Women, CT, merged into University of Hartford (winter 1992)

Hawaii Loa College, HI, merged into Hawaii Pacific University (winter 1992)

Hawkeye Institute of Technology, IA, changed its name to Hawkeye Community College (summer 1993)

High Point College, NC, changed its name to High Point University (winter 1992)

Hobson State Technical College *and* Patrick Henry State Junior College, AL, merged to become Alabama Southern Community College (winter 1992)

Housatonic Community College, CT, changed its name to Housatonic Community-Technical College (winter 1992)

Kansas College of Technology, KS, changed its name to Salina College of Technology and is a part of Kansas State University (summer 1992)

Lambuth College, TN, changed its name to Lambuth University (winter 1992)

Lander College, SC, changed its name to Lander University (winter 1992)

Manchester Community College, CT, changed its name to Manchester Community-Technical College (winter 1992)

Marylhurst College for Lifelong Learning, OR, changed its name to Marylhurst College (winter 1993)

Mattatuck Community College *and* Waterbury State Technical College, CT, merged to become Naugatuck Valley Community-Technical College (winter 1992)

Mesa Community College Chandler Extension, AZ, changed its name to Chandler-Gilbert Community College (winter 1992)

Miami Christian College, FL, changed its name to Trinity College at Miami and is a branch of Trinity College, IL (winter 1992)

Michael J. Owens Technical College, OH, changed its name to Owens Technical College (winter 1992)

Micronesian Occupational College changed its name to Palau Community College (summer 1993)

Middlesex Community College, CT, changed its name to Middlesex Community-Technical College (winter 1992)

Mitchell Vocational-Technical Institute, SD, changed its name to Mitchell Technical Institute (summer 1993)

Mobile College, AL, changed its name to University of Mobile (summer 1993)

Mohegan Community College *and* Thames Valley Technical College, CT, merged to become Three Rivers Community-Technical College (winter 1992)

Mount Aloysius Junior College, PA, changed its name to Mount Aloysius College (winter 1992)

Multnomah School of the Bible, OR, changed its name to Multnomah Bible College (fall 1993)

Nazareth College, MI, closed (summer 1992)

Northrop University, CA, closed (summer 1992)

Northwestern Connecticut Community College, CT, changed its name to Northwestern Connecticut Community-Technical College (winter 1992)

Norwalk Community College *and* Norwalk State Technical College, CT, merged to become Norwalk Community-Technical College (winter 1992)

Phillips College, KY, closed (summer 1992)

Pinebrook Junior College, PA, closed (summer 1992)

Portland School of Art, ME, changed its name to Maine College of Art (winter 1992)

Puerto Rico Junior College, PR, changed its name to Colegio Universitario del Este (spring 1992)

Quincy College, IL, changed its name to Quincy University (spring 1993)

Quinebaug Valley Community College, CT, changed its name to Quinebaug Valley Community-Technical College (winter 1992)

St. Bernard Parish Community College *and* Elaine P. Nunez Technical Institute, LA, merged to become Elaine P. Nunez Community College (winter 1992)

St. Joseph's College, CA, closed (fall 1993)

St. Mary of the Plains College, KS, closed (summer 1992)

Savannah Area Vocational Technical School, GA, changed its name to Savannah Technical Institute (summer 1992)

School for Lifelong Learning, NH, changed its name to College for Lifelong Learning (summer 1993)

South Carolina State College, SC, changed its name to South Carolina State University (spring 1992)

Southern Arkansas University—El Dorado, AR, changed its name to South Arkansas Community College (winter 1992)

Spring Garden College, PA, closed (summer 1992)

Summit Christian College, IN, became a branch of Taylor University (summer 1992)

Sumter Area Technical College, SC, changed its name to Central Carolina Technical College (fall 1992)

Laredo State University, TX, changed its name to Texas A&M International University (summer 1993)

Major Changes

Texas Southmost College, TX, entered into a legal partnership with The University of Texas at Brownsville (summer 1992)

Trinity College at Miami, FL, changed its name to Miami Christian College (fall 1993)

Tunxis Community College, CT, changed its name to Tunxis Community-Technical College (winter 1992)

University of Minnesota, Waseca, MN, closed (summer 1992)

University of South Carolina—Coastal Carolina, SC, changed its name to Coastal Carolina University (summer 1993)

Utah Valley Community College, UT, changed its name to Utah Valley State College (summer 1993)

Valley Forge Military Junior College, PA, changed its name to Valley Forge Military College (summer 1993)

Walsh College, OH, changed its name to Walsh University (winter 1993)

Washington County Vocational-Technical Institute, ME, changed its name to Washington County Technical College (summer 1993)

Watterson College, KY, closed (winter 1992)

West Texas State University, TX, changed its name to West Texas A&M University (summer 1993)

Western Dakota Vocational-Technical Institute, SD, changed its name to Western Dakota Technical Institute (summer 1993)

William Jennings Bryan College, TN, changed its name to Bryan College (summer 1993)

William Woods College, MO, changed its name to William Woods University (spring 1993)

Winthrop College, SC, changed its name to Winthrop University (summer 1992)

Wood Junior College, MS, changed its name to Wood College (winter 1993)

Candidates

Candidates for Accreditation

Candidate for Accreditation is a status of affiliation with a recognized accrediting commission which indicates that an institution has achieved initial recognition and is progressing toward, but does not assure, accreditation.

The Candidate for Accreditation classification is designed for postsecondary institutions which may or may not be fully operative. In either case the institution must provide evidence of sound planning, the resources to implement these plans, and appear to have the potential for attaining its goals within a reasonable time.

To be considered for Candidate for Accreditation status the applicant organization must be a postsecondary educational institution with the following characteristics:

1. Have a charter and/or formal authority from an appropriate governmental agency to award a certificate, diploma, or degree.
2. Have a governing board which includes representation reflecting the public interest.
3. Have employed a chief administrative officer.
4. Offer, or plan to offer, one or more educational programs of at least one academic year in length, or the equivalent at the postsecondary level, with clearly defined and published educational objectives, as well as a clear statement of the means for achieving them.
5. Include general education at the postsecondary level as a prerequisite to or an essential element in its principal educational programs.
6. Have admission policies compatible with its stated objectives.
7. Have developed a preliminary survey or evidence of basic planning for the development of the institution.
8. Have established an adequate financial base of funding commitments and have available a summary of its latest audited financial statement.

DEGREE GRANTING CANDIDATE INSTITUTIONS

ARKANSAS

OZARKA TECHNICAL COLLEGE
P.O. Box 10, Melbourne 72556 *Type:* Public technical *Accred.:* 1993 (NCA candidate) *Calendar:* Sem. plan *Degrees:* A, certificates, diplomas *CEO:* Pres. Douglas Rush
Enroll: 166   (501) 368-7371

PETIT JEAN TECHNICAL COLLEGE
Hwy. 9 N., P.O. Box 586, Morrilton 72110 *Type:* Public technical *Accred.:* 1993 (NCA candidate) *Calendar:* Sem. plan *Degrees:* A, certificates, diplomas *CEO:* Exec. Officer Nathan Crook
Enroll: 492   (501) 354-2465

CALIFORNIA

AMERICAN INSTITUTE OF ORIENTAL MEDICINE
4683 Mercury St., Ste. C, San Diego 92111 *Type:* Private professional *Calendar:* Tri. plan *Degrees:* M *Prof. Accred.:* Acupuncture (candidate) *CEO:* Pres. Penelope Wells
FTE Enroll: 39   (619) 467-9890

FIVE BRANCHES INSTITUTE COLLEGE OF TRADITIONAL CHINESE MEDICINE
200 7th Ave., Ste. 115, Santa Cruz 95062 *Type:* Private professional *Calendar:* Sem. plan *Degrees:* M *Prof. Accred.:* Acupuncture (candidate) *CEO:* Dean Ron Zaidman
FTE Enroll: 75   (408) 476-9424

INSTITUTE OF TRANSPERSONAL PSYCHOLOGY
250 Oak Grove, Menlo Park 94025 *Type:* Independent *Accred.:* 1992 (WASC-Sr. candidate) *Calendar:* Qtr. plan *Degrees:* M, D *CEO:* Pres. Ben A. Mancini
FTE Enroll: 320   (415) 326-1960

INTERNATIONAL SCHOOL OF THEOLOGY
Arrowhead Springs, San Bernardino 92414-0001 *Type:* Private (interdenominational) graduate only *Accred.:* 1991 (ATS candi-

date) *Calendar:* Sem. plan *Degrees:* M
CEO: Pres. Donald A. Weaver
FTE Enroll: 60   (909) 886-7876

PACIFICA GRADUATE INSTITUTE
249 Lambert Rd., Carpinteria 93013 Type:
Private professional Degrees: M, D Accred.:
1994 (WASC-Sr. candidate) CEO: Pres.
Stephen Alzenstrat

ROYAL UNIVERSITY OF AMERICA
1125 W. Sixth St., Los Angeles 90017 *Type:*
Private professional *Calendar:* Qtr. plan
Degrees: M *Prof. Accred.:* Acupuncture
(candidate) *CEO:* Pres. Dae Young Kim
FTE Enroll: 197   (213) 482-6646

SANTA BARBARA COLLEGE OF ORIENTAL
MEDICINE
1919 State St., Ste. 204, Santa Barbara
93101 *Type:* Private professional *Calendar:*
Tri. plan *Degrees:* M *Prof. Accred.:*
Acupuncture (candidate) *CEO:* Pres. JoAnn
Hickey
FTE Enroll: 40   (805) 682-9594

SOUTHERN CALIFORNIA INSTITUTE OF
ARCHITECTURE
5454 Beethoven St., Los Angeles 90066
Type: Independent professional *Accred.:*
1991 (WASC-Sr. candidate) *Calendar:* Sem.
plan *Degrees:* B, P, M *CEO:* Dir. Michael
Rotondi
FTE Enroll: 456   (310) 574-1123

COLORADO

COLLEGE FOR FINANCIAL PLANNING
4695 S. Monaco St., Denver 80237-3403
Type: Private professional *Accred.:* 1991/
1992 (NCA candidate) *Calendar:* Courses of
varying lengths *Degrees:* M, certificates
CEO: Pres. William L. Anthes
Enroll: 21,127   (303) 220-1200

CONNECTICUT

ST. VINCENT'S COLLEGE OF NURSING
2800 Main St., Bridgeport 06606 *Type:* Private professional *Accred.:* 1992 (NEASC-CTCI candidate) *Calendar:* Sem. plan
Degrees: A *CEO:* Pres. Anne T. Avallone
FTE Enroll: 146   (203) 576-5512

FLORIDA

FLORIDA NATIONAL COLLEGE
4206 W. 12th Ave., Hialeah 33012 *Type:*
Private *Accred.:* 1993 (SACS-CC candidate)
Calendar: Sem. plan *Degrees:* A *CEO:* Dir.
Jose Regueiro
FTE Enroll: 965   (305) 821-3333

INSTITUTO CENTROAMERICANO DE
ADMINISTRACION DE EMPRESAS
P.O. Box 025216-1358, Miami 33102-5216
Type: Private *Accred.:* 1992 (SACS-CC candidate) *Calendar:* Tri. plan *Degrees:* M
CEO: Rector Brizio Biondi-Morra
FTE Enroll: 687   (506) 041-2255

TRINITY COLLEGE OF FLORIDA
2430 Trinity Oaks Blvd., New Port Richey
34655 *Type:* Independent (nondenominational) *Accred.:* 1990 (AABC candidate) *Calendar:* Sem. plan *Degrees:* A, B, certificates,
diplomas *CEO:* Pres. Richard Williams
FTE Enroll: 55   (813) 376-6911

WORSLEY INSTITUTE OF CLASSICAL
ACUPUNCTURE
6175 N.W. 153rd St., Ste. 324, Miami Lakes
33014 *Type:* Private professional *Calendar:*
Tri. plan *Degrees:* M *Prof. Accred.:*
Acupuncture (candidate) *CEO:* Pres. J.R.
Worsley
FTE Enroll: 40   (305) 823-7270

GEORGIA

GEORGIA BAPTIST COLLEGE OF NURSING
300 Blvd. N.E., P.O. Box 411, Atlanta
30312 *Type:* Private (Protestant) *Accred.:*
1993 (SACS-CC candidate) *Calendar:* Qtr.
plan *Degrees:* B *CEO:* Pres. Susan S. Gunby
Enroll: 303   (404) 653-4512

ILLINOIS

HEARTLAND COMMUNITY COLLEGE
1226 Towanda Ave., Bloomington 61701
Type: Public (district) junior *System:* Illinois
Community College Board *Accred.:* 1992
(NCA candidate) *Calendar:* Sem. plan
Degrees: A, certificates *CEO:* Pres. Jonathan
M. Astroth
Enroll: 1,703   (309) 827-0500

INSTITUTE FOR CLINICAL SOCIAL WORK, INC.
30 N. Michigan Ave., Ste. 420, Chicago 60602 *Type:* Private professional; graduate only *Accred.:* 1988/1992 (NCA candidate) *Calendar:* Sem. plan *Degrees:* D *CEO:* Pres. Arnold M. Levin
Enroll: 34   (312) 726-8480

LAKEVIEW COLLEGE OF NURSING
812 N. Logan Ave., Danville 61832 *Type:* Private professional *Accred.:* 1989/1993 (NCA candidate) *Calendar:* Sem. plan *Degrees:* B *CEO:* Pres. Irene A. Steward
Enroll: 124   (217) 443-5238

ST. ANTHONY COLLEGE OF NURSING
5658 E. State St., Rockford 61108-2468 *Type:* Private professional *Accred.:* 1992 (NCA candidate) *Calendar:* Sem. plan *Degrees:* B *CEO:* Admin. Mary Linus
Enroll: 68   (815) 395-5091

ST. JOHN'S COLLEGE
421 N. Ninth St., Springfield 62702 *Type:* Private professional *Accred.:* 1993 (NCA candidate) *Calendar:* Sem. plan *Degrees:* B *CEO:* Chanc. Jane Schachtsiek
Enroll: 60   (217) 525-5628

KENTUCKY

KENTUCKY MOUNTAIN BIBLE COLLEGE
County Rd. 541, P.O. Box 10, Vancleve 41385 *Type:* Private (Kentucky Mountain Holiness Asscociation) *Accred.:* 1989 (AABC candidate) *Calendar:* Sem. plan *Degrees:* A, B *CEO:* Pres. Wilfred Fisher
FTE Enroll: 54   (606) 666-5000

MARYLAND

CARROLL COMMUNITY COLLEGE
1601 Washington Rd., Westminster 21157 *Type:* Public (local) two-year *System:* Maryland Higher Education Commission *Accred.:* 1993 (MSA candidate) *Calendar:* Sem. plan *Degrees:* A, certificates *CEO:* Pres. Joseph F. Shields
Enroll: 2,731   (410) 876-9635

MASSACHUSETTS

BOSTON ARCHITECTURAL CENTER
320 Newbury St., Boston 02115 *Type:* Private professional *Accred.:* 1991 (NEASC-

CIHE candidate) *Calendar:* Courses of varying lengths *Degrees:* B, certificates *CEO:* Pres. George B. Terrien
Enroll: 664   (617) 536-3170

MICHIGAN

BAY MILLS COMMUNITY COLLEGE
Rte. 1, Box 315A, Brimley 49715 *Type:* Public (district) junior *Accred.:* 1991/1993 (NCA candidate) *Calendar:* Sem. plan *Degrees:* A, certificates *CEO:* Pres. Martha McLeod
Enroll: 211   (906) 248-3354

JORDAN COLLEGE
360 W. Pine St., Cedar Springs 49319 *Type:* Private *Accred.:* 1988/1993 (NCA candidate) *Calendar:* Sem. plan *Degrees:* A, B *CEO:* Pres. Lexie K. Coxon
Enroll: 2,118   (616) 696-1180

SS. CYRIL & METHODIUS SEMINARY
Orchard Lake 48324 *Type:* Private (Roman Catholic) graduate only *Accred.:* 1991 (ATS candidate) *Calendar:* Sem. plan *Degrees:* M *CEO:* Rector Francis B. Koper
FTE Enroll: 39   (313) 683-0311

MINNESOTA

PILLSBURY BAPTIST BIBLE COLLEGE
315 S. Grove St., Owatonna 55060 *Type:* Private *Accred.:* 1990/1992 (NCA candidate) *Calendar:* Sem. plan *Degrees:* A, B, diplomas *CEO:* Pres. Alan L. Potter
Enroll: 336   (507) 451-2710

MISSOURI

BARNES COLLEGE
416 S. Kingshighway Blvd., St. Louis 63110 *Type:* Private *Accred.:* 1992 (NCA candidate) *Calendar:* Sem. plan *Degrees:* B *CEO:* Acting Chf. Admin. Ofcr. William Behrendt
Enroll: 358   (314) 362-5225

JEWISH HOSPITAL COLLEGE OF NURSING AND ALLIED HEALTH
306 S. Kingshighway Blvd., St. Louis 63110-1091 *Type:* Private professional *Accred.:* 1993 (NCA candidate) *Calendar:* Sem. plan *Degrees:* A, B, certificates, diplomas *CEO:* Pres./Dean Sharon L. Pontius
Enroll: 147   (314) 454-7055

ST. LUKE'S COLLEGE
4426 Wornall Rd., Kansas City 64111 *Type:*
Private liberal arts *Accred.:* 1992 (NCA candidate) *Calendar:* Sem. plan *Degrees:* B
CEO: Provost Patricia A. Teager
Enroll: 97   (816) 932-2233

SANFORD-BROWN COLLEGE
1655 Des Peres Rd., Ste. 150, St. Louis
63131 *Type:* Private *Accred.:* 1991 (NCA candidate) *Calendar:* Sem. plan *Degrees:* A, certificates *CEO:* Pres. Stephen M. Rothweiler
Enroll: 1,071   (800) 456-7222

MONTANA

DULL KNIFE MEMORIAL COLLEGE
P.O. Box 98, Lame Deer 59043 *Type:* Private (tribal) junior *Accred.:* 1990 (NASC candidate) *Calendar:* Sem. plan *Degrees:* A
CEO: Pres. Arthur L. McDonald
Enroll: 368   (406) 477-6215

NEW HAMPSHIRE

THE THOMAS MORE COLLEGE OF LIBERAL ARTS
6 Manchester St., Merrimack 03054-3805
Type: Private *Accred.:* 1990 (NEASC-CIHE candidate) *Calendar:* Sem. plan *Degrees:* B
CEO: Pres. Peter V. Sampo
Enroll: 63   (603) 880-8308

NEW JERSEY

RABBI JACOB JOSEPH SCHOOL
One Plainfield Ave., Edison 08817 *Type:*
Private professional *Accred.:* 1991 (AARTS candidate) *Calendar:* Sem. plan *Degrees:*
Talmudic (1st and Advanced) *CEO:* Pres. M.
Schick
Enroll: 47   (908) 985-6533

NEW MEXICO

SOUTHWESTERN COLLEGE
P.O. Box 4788, Santa Fe 87502 *Type:* Private *Accred.:* 1992 (NCA candidate) *Calendar:* Sem. plan *Degrees:* B, M *CEO:* Pres.
Robert Waterman
Enroll: 115   (505) 471-5756

NEW YORK

KOL YAAKOV TORAH CENTER
29 W. Maple Ave., P.O. Box 402, Monsey
10952 *Type:* Private professional *Accred.:*
1984/1990 (AARTS candidate) *Calendar:*
Sem. plan *Degrees:* Rabbinic (1st) *CEO:*
Pres. Leib Tropper
Enroll: 30   (914) 425-3863

MACHZIKEI HADATH RABBINICAL COLLEGE
5407 16th Ave., Brooklyn 11204 *Type:* Private professional *Accred.:* 1980/1989
(AARTS candidate) *Calendar:* Sem. plan
Degrees: Talmudic (1st and 2nd) *CEO:* Pres.
Avi Klein
Enroll: 120   (718) 331-6613

RABBINICAL COLLEGE OF OHR SHIMON YISROEL
215-217 Hewes St., Brooklyn 11211 *Type:*
Private professional *Accred.:* 1992 (AARTS candidate) *Calendar:* Sem. plan *Degrees:*
Talmudic (1st) *CEO:* Pres. Shulem Walter
Enroll: 45   (718) 387-5588

TALMUDICAL INSTITUTE OF UPSTATE NEW YORK
769 Park Ave., Rochester 14607 *Type:* Private professional *Accred.:* 1983/1988
(AARTS candidate) *Calendar:* Sem. plan
Degrees: Talmudic (1st and 2nd) *CEO:* Pres.
M. Davidowitz
Enroll: 29   (716) 473-2810

UNIFICATION THEOLOGICAL SEMINARY
10 Dock Rd., Barrytown 12507 *Type:* Private (Unification Church) *Accred.:* 1988
(MSA candidate) *Calendar:* Sem. plan
Degrees: P, M *CEO:* Pres. David S.C. Kim
Enroll: 146   (914) 758-6881

YESHIVA AND KOLEL BAIS MEDRASH ELYON
73 Main St., Monsey 10952 *Type:* Private
professional *Accred.:* 1989 (AARTS candidate) *Calendar:* Sem. plan *Degrees:* Talmudic (1st and 2nd) *CEO:* Pres. I. Falk
Enroll: 75   (914) 356-7064

YESHIVA AND KOLLEL HARBOTZAS TORAH
1049 E. 15th St., Brooklyn 11230 *Type:* Private professional *Accred.:* 1985/1991
(AARTS candidate) *Calendar:* Sem. plan
Degrees: Talmudic (1st and 2nd) *CEO:* Pres.
Y. Bittersfeld
Enroll: 48   (718) 692-0208

YESHIVA AND MESIVTA KOL TORAH
4823-B 48th St., Brooklyn 11224 *Type:* Private professional *Accred.:* 1989 (AARTS candidate) *Calendar:* Sem. plan *Degrees:* Talmudic (1st and 2nd) *CEO:* Pres. B. Klein
Enroll: 43   (718) 265-5840

YESHIVA GEDOLAH IMREI YOSEF D'SPINKA
1460 56th St., Brooklyn 11219 *Type:* Private professional *Accred.:* 1989 (AARTS candidate) *Calendar:* Sem. plan *Degrees:* Talmudic (1st) *CEO:* Pres. Mordechai Majerowitz
Enroll: 55   (718) 851-1600

OHIO

MERCY COLLEGE OF NORTHWEST OHIO
2238 Jefferson Ave., Toledo 43624-1197 *Type:* Private professional *Accred.:* 1993 (NCA candidate) *Calendar:* Sem. plan *Degrees:* A *CEO:* Pres. Patricia Ann Dahlke
Enroll: 93   (419) 259-1279

MOUNT CARMEL COLLEGE OF NURSING
127 S. Davis Ave., Columbus 43222 *Type:* Private professional *Accred.:* 1991 (NCA candidate) *Calendar:* Sem. plan *Degrees:* B *CEO:* Pres./Dean Ann E. Schiele
Enroll: 197   (614) 225-5800

OKLAHOMA

SPARTAN SCHOOL OF AERONAUTICS
Tulsa International Airport, 8820 E. Pine St., Tulsa 74115 *Type:* Private *Accred.:* 1991/1993 (NCA candidate) *Calendar:* Sem. plan *Degrees:* A, certificates *CEO:* Pres. Frank D. Iacobucci
Enroll: 3,013   (918) 836-6886

PENNSYLVANIA

REFORMED PRESBYTERIAN THEOLOGICAL SEMINARY
7418 Penn Ave., Pittsburgh 15208 *Type:* Private (Presbyterian) graduate only *Accred.:* 1991 (ATS candidate) *Calendar:* Sem. plan *Degrees:* M *CEO:* Pres. Bruce C. Stewart
FTE Enroll: 39   (412) 731-8690

PUERTO RICO

ESCUELA DE ARTES PLASTICAS DE PUERTO RICO INSTITUTO DE CULTURA PUERTORRIQUENA
Apartado 1112, San Juan 00902-1112 *Type:* Public (state) *Accred.:* 1988 (MSA candidate) *Calendar:* Sem. plan *Degrees:* B *CEO:* Chanc. Margarita Fernandez-Zavala
Enroll: 204   (809) 725-8120

SOUTH DAKOTA

CENTRAL INDIAN BIBLE COLLEGE
Riverfront Dr., P.O. Box 550, Mobridge 57601 *Type:* Private (Assemblies of God) *Accred.:* 1992 (AABC candidate) *Calendar:* Sem. plan *Degrees:* A, diplomas *CEO:* Pres. George Kallappa
FTE Enroll: 20   (605) 845-7801

TEXAS

AMBASSADOR COLLEGE
P.O. Box 111, Big Sandy 75755 *Type:* Private (Church of God) liberal arts *Accred.:* 1992 (SACS-CC candidate) *Calendar:* Sem. plan *Degrees:* A, B *CEO:* Pres. Donald L. Ward
FTE Enroll: 1,112   (903) 636-2000

THE COLLEGE OF ST. THOMAS MORE
3001 Lubbock Ave., Fort Worth 76109 *Type:* Private *Accred.:* 1992 (SACS-CC candidate) *Calendar:* Sem. plan *Degrees:* A *CEO:* Provost James A. Patrick
FTE Enroll: 16   (817) 923-8459

VIRGINIA

NOTRE DAME INSTITUTE
4420 Sano St., Alexandria 22312-1553 *Type:* Private graduate only *Accred.:* 1990 (SACS-CC candidate) *Calendar:* Sem. plan *Degrees:* M *CEO:* Pres. William P. Saunders
FTE Enroll: 74   (703) 658-4403

DEGREE GRANTING CANDIDATE INSTITUTIONS
OUTSIDE THE UNITED STATES
CANADA   COSTA RICA

CENTRAL PENTECOSTAL COLLEGE
1303 Jackson Ave., Saskatoon, Saskatche-
wan, S7H 2M9 *Type:* Private (Pentecostal
Assemblies of Canada) *Accred.:* 1992
(AABC candidate) *Calendar:* Sem. plan
Degrees: B *CEO:* Pres. Ronald Kadyschuk
FTE Enroll: 86   (306) 374-6655

HERITAGE BAPTIST COLLEGE
30 Grand Ave., London, Ontario, N6C 1K8
Type: Independent (Baptist) *Accred.:* 1991
(AABC candidate) *Calendar:* Sem. plan
Degrees: B, certificates *CEO:* Pres. Marvin
Brubacher
FTE Enroll: 105   (519) 434-6801

INSTITUTO CENTROAMERICANO DE
ADMINISTRACION DE EMPRESAS
Apartado Postal 960, 4050 Alajuela, La
Garita, Alajuela *Type:* Private graduate only
Accred.: 1992 (SACS-CC candidate) *Calen-
dar:* Sem. plan *Degrees:* M *CEO:* Pres.
Melvyn R. Copen
FTE Enroll: 428

NON-DEGREE GRANTING CANDIDATE INSTITUTIONS

ALABAMA

MITCHELL COSMETOLOGY COLLEGE
116 First St., S., Alabaster 35007 *Type:* Pri-
vate *Accred.:* 1991 (SACS-COEI candidate)
Calendar: Courses of varying lengths
Degrees: certificates *CEO:* Pres. Timothy
Mitchell
FTE Enroll: 80   (205) 663-7126

CALIFORNIA

NAVAL FLEET ANTI-SUBMARINE WARFARE
TRAINING CENTER—PACIFIC
San Diego 92147 *Type:* Public (federal)
technical *Accred.:* 1991 (SACS-COEI candi-
date) *Calendar:* Courses of varying lengths
Degrees: certificates *CEO:* Commandant
B.J. Binford, U.S.N.
FTE Enroll: 1,464   (619) 524-1665

CONNECTICUT

NAVAL SUBMARINE SCHOOL
Box 700, Bldg. 84, Code 01A, Groton
06340-5700 *Type:* Public (federal) *Accred.:*
1993 (NEASC-CTCI candidate) *Calendar:*

Courses of varying lengths *Degrees:* diplomas *CEO:* C.E.O. Warren A. Swanson
(203) 449-4369

FLORIDA

AMERICA DURAN SKIN CARE, MASSAGE AND
NAIL SCHOOL
3400 Coral Way, Ste. 105, Miami 33145
Type: Private *Accred.:* 1992 (SACS-COEI
candidate) *Calendar:* Courses of varying
lengths *Degrees:* certificates *CEO:* Pres.
America Duran
FTE Enroll: 5   (305) 642-4104

BRELY ACADEMY OF THE PERFORMING ARTS
9708 Coral Way, Miami 33165 *Type:* Private
Accred.: 1991 (SACS-COEI candidate) *Calendar:* Courses of varying lengths *Degrees:*
certificates *CEO:* Dir. Diana Gonzalez
FTE Enroll: 37   (305) 551-4673

C.C.G.I.
130 N.W. 79th St., Miami 33150 *Type:* Pri-
vate *Accred.:* 1991 (SACS-COEI candidate)
Calendar: Courses of varying lengths
Degrees: certificates, diplomas *CEO:* Dir.
Sharon Sapp
FTE Enroll: 35   (305) 758-3600

INSTITUTE OF SPECIALIZED TRAINING & MANAGEMENT
853 Semoran Blvd., Ste. 133, Casselberry 32707 *Type:* Private *Accred.:* 1992 (SACS-COEI candidate) *Calendar:* Courses of varying lengths *Degrees:* certificates *CEO:* Admin. Ofcr. Linda Hart
FTE Enroll: 3   (407) 831-8466

SARASOTA SCHOOL OF MASSAGE THERAPY
1970 Main St., Sarasota 34236 *Type:* Private *Accred.:* 1992 (SACS-COEI candidate) *Calendar:* Courses of varying lengths *Degrees:* certificates, diplomas *CEO:* Dir. Michael Rosen-Pyros
FTE Enroll: 50   (813) 957-0577

TAYLOR TECHNICAL INSTITUTE
3233 Hwy. 19, S., Perry 32347 *Type:* Private *Accred.:* 1992 (SACS-COEI candidate) *Calendar:* Courses of varying lengths *Degrees:* certificates *CEO:* Dir. Bryant J. Russell
FTE Enroll: 456   (904) 584-7603

GEORGIA

BEAUTY COLLEGE OF GEORGIA
6088 Beaufort Hwy., Doraville 30340 *Type:* Private *Accred.:* 1992 (SACS-COEI candidate) *Calendar:* Courses of varying lengths *Degrees:* certificates *CEO:* Pres. Thomas Carey
FTE Enroll: 99   (404) 449-1740

COBB BEAUTY COLLEGE
3096 Cherokee St., Kennesaw 30144 *Type:* Private *Accred.:* 1992 (SACS-COEI candidate) *Calendar:* Courses of varying lengths *Degrees:* certificates *CEO:* Dir. Gail Little
FTE Enroll: 46   (404) 424-6915

GEORGIA INSTITUTE OF COSMETOLOGY
3341 Lexington Rd., Athens 30605 *Type:* Private *Accred.:* 1992 (SACS-COEI candidate) *Calendar:* Courses of varying lengths *Degrees:* certificates *CEO:* Dir. Donna Vickers
FTE Enroll: 35   (706) 549-6400

HAWAII

ORIENTAL MEDICAL INSTITUTE OF HAWAII
181 S. Kukui St., Ste. 206, Honolulu 96813 *Type:* Private professional *Calendar:* Sem. plan *Degrees:* diplomas *Prof. Accred.:*
Acupuncture (candidate) *CEO:* Pres. Lucy Lee
FTE Enroll: 54   (808) 536-3611

LOUISIANA

THE ART OF BEAUTY COLLEGE
3026 Gentilly Blvd., New Orleans 70122 *Type:* Private *Accred.:* 1991 (SACS-COEI candidate) *Calendar:* Courses of varying lengths *Degrees:* certificates *CEO:* Dir. Elaine Joseph
FTE Enroll: 45

MANSFIELD TECHNICAL INSTITUTE
1001 Oxford Rd., Mansfield 71052 *Type:* Public (state) *Accred.:* 1989 (SACS-COEI candidate) *Calendar:* Courses of varying lengths *Degrees:* certificates, diplomas *CEO:* Dir. Ronald E. Wright
FTE Enroll: 105   (318) 872-2243

NEW YORK

NEW CENTER FOR WHOLISTIC HEALTH EDUCATION AND RESEARCH
6801 Jericho Tpke., Syosset 11791-4465 *Type:* Private professional *Calendar:* Tri. plan *Degrees:* certificates *Prof. Accred.:* Acupuncture (candidate) *CEO:* Pres. Steven Schenkman
FTE Enroll: 19   (516) 364-0808

NORTH CAROLINA

NORTH CAROLINA ACADEMY OF COSMETIC ARTS
131 Sixth Ave. E., Henderson 27536 *Type:* Private *Accred.:* 1993 (SACS-COEI candidate) *Calendar:* Courses of varying lengths *Degrees:* certificates *CEO:* Dir. Greg Johnson
(919) 876-9210

SCHOOL OF COMMUNICATION ARTS
3220 Spring Forest Rd., Raleigh 27604 *Type:* Private *Accred.:* 1993 (SACS-COEI candidate) *Calendar:* Courses of varying lengths *Degrees:* certificates *CEO:* Dir. Deborah Hooper
(919) 981-0972

TENNESSEE

BOBBIE'S SCHOOL OF BEAUTY ARTS
285 Second St., Cleveland 37311 *Type:* Private *Accred.:* 1992 (SACS-COEI candidate)

Calendar: Courses of varying lengths *Degrees:* certificates *CEO:* Dir. Bobbie Wallace
FTE Enroll: 24   (615) 476-3742

LaCARM SCHOOL OF COSMETOLOGY
1123-B Sparta St., McMinnville 37110
Type: Private *Accred.:* 1992 (SACS-COEI candidate) *Calendar:* Courses of varying lengths *Degrees:* certificates *CEO:* Dir. Margaret Herron
FTE Enroll: 22   (615) 473-2615

MEMPHIS AERO TECH
8582 Hwy. 51, N., Millington 38083 *Type:* Private *Accred.:* 1992 (SACS-COEI candidate) *Calendar:* Courses of varying lengths *Degrees:* certificates *CEO:* Dir. William Perkins
FTE Enroll: 75   (901) 872-7117

TEXAS

AMERICAN ACADEMY OF ACUPUNCTURE AND TRADITIONAL CHINESE MEDICINE
9100 Park West Dr., Houston 77063 *Type:* Private professional *Calendar:* Sem. plan *Degrees:* diplomas *Prof. Accred.:* Acupuncture (candidate) *CEO:* Pres. Shen Ping Liang
FTE Enroll: 14   (713) 780-9777

ICC TECHNICAL INSTITUTE
3333 Fannin St., Ste. 203, Houston 77004 *Type:* Private *Accred.:* 1991 (SACS-COEI candidate) *Calendar:* Courses of varying lengths *Degrees:* certificates *CEO:* Dir. Chi Do
FTE Enroll: 159

TEXAS COLLEGE OF COSMETOLOGY
918 Chadbourne St., San Angelo 76903
Type: Private *Accred.:* 1993 (SACS-COEI candidate) *Calendar:* Courses of varying lengths *Degrees:* certificates *CEO:* Dir. Tom Adams
                    (915) 659-2622

VIRGINIA

AEGIS TRAINING CENTER
Dahlgren 22448 *Type:* Public (federal) *Accred.:* 1991 (SACS-COEI candidate) *Calendar:* Courses of varying lengths *Degrees:* certificates *CEO:* Dir. Sheldon Margolis
FTE Enroll: 211   (703) 663-8531

APPLIED CAREER TRAINING INC.
1101 N. Wilson Blvd., Rosslyn 22209 *Type:* Private *Accred.:* 1992 (SACS-COEI candidate) *Calendar:* Courses of varying lengths *Degrees:* certificates *CEO:* Dir. Ginger McGlothlin
FTE Enroll: 21   (703) 527-6660

SUBMARINE TRAINING FACILITY
1915 C Ave., Norfolk 23504 *Type:* Public (federal) *Accred.:* 1993 (SACS-COEI candidate) *Calendar:* Courses of varying lengths *Degrees:* certificates *CEO:* Dir. John McCormack
                    (804) 936-0820

Public Systems of Higher Education

ALABAMA

The Alabama Commission on Higher Education
3465 Norman Bridge Rd., Montgomery 36105-2310
Exec. Dir. Henry J. Hector
(205) 281-1921

Alabama Agricultural and Mechanical University
P.O. Box 1357, Normal 35762
Pres. David B. Henson
(205) 851-5000

Alabama State University
915 S. Jackson St., Montgomery 36101-0271
Interim Pres. C.C. Baker
(205) 293-4100

Athens State College
300 N. Beaty St., Athens 35611
Pres. Jerry Bartlett
(205) 233-8100

Auburn University System
Auburn University 36849-5113
Pres. William V. Muse
(205) 844-4650

Auburn University
Auburn University 36849
Pres. William V. Muse
(205) 844-4000

Auburn University at Montgomery
7300 University Dr., Montgomery 36117-3596
Interim Chanc. Guin A. Nance
(205) 244-3000

Jacksonville State University
700 N. Pelham Rd., Jacksonville 36265-9982
Pres. Harold J. McGee
(205) 782-5781

Livingston University
205 N. Washington St., Livingston 35470
Pres. Donald C. Hines
(205) 652-9661

The Troy State University System
University Ave., Troy 36082
Chanc. Jack Hawkins, Jr.
(205) 670-3200

Troy State University
University Ave., Troy 36082
Chanc. Jack Hawkins, Jr.
(205) 670-3000

Troy State University at Dothan
P.O. Box 8368, 3601 U.S. Hwy. 231 N., Dothan 36304-0368
Pres. Thomas E. Harrison
(205) 983-6556

Troy State University in Montgomery
231 Montgomery St., P.O. Drawer 4419, Montgomery 36103-4419
Pres. Glenda S. McGaha
(205) 834-1400

The University of Alabama System
401 Queen City Ave., Tuscaloosa 35401-1551
Chanc. Philip E. Austin
(205) 348-5861

The University of Alabama
P.O. Box 870166, Tuscaloosa 35487-0166
Pres. E. Roger Sayers
(205) 348-6010

The University of Alabama at Birmingham
UAB Sta., Birmingham 35294
Pres. J. Claude Bennett
(205) 934-4011

The University of Alabama in Huntsville
Huntsville 35899
Pres. Frank A. Franz
(205) 895-6120

University of Montevallo
Sta. 6001, Montevallo 35115-6001
Pres. Robert M. McChesney
(205) 665-6000

University of North Alabama
Box 5121, Florence 35632-0001
Pres. Robert L. Potts
(205) 760-4100

University of South Alabama
307 University Blvd., Mobile 36688
Pres. Frederick P. Whiddon
(205) 460-6101

State of Alabama Department of Postsecondary Education
401 Adams Ave., Montgomery 36130
Chanc. Fred J. Gainous
(205) 242-2900

Alabama Southern Community College
P.O. Box 2000, Monroeville 36461
Pres. John A. Johnson
(205) 575-3156

Bishop State Community College
351 N. Broad St., Mobile 36603-5898
Pres. Yvonne Kennedy
(205) 690-6416

Central Alabama Community College
908 Cherokee Rd., P.O. Box 699,
Alexander City 35010
Pres. James H. Cornell
(205) 234-6346

Chattahoochee Valley State Community College
2602 College Dr., Phenix City 36869
Pres. Richard J. Frederinko
(205) 291-4900

Enterprise State Junior College
600 Plaza Dr., P.O. Box 1300, Enterprise 36331
Pres. Joseph D. Talmadge
(205) 347-2623

Gadsden State Community College
P.O. Box 227, Gadsden 35902-0227
Pres. Victor B. Ficker
(205) 549-8200

George C. Wallace State Community College
Dothan 36303
Pres. Larry Beaty
(205) 983-3521

George Corley Wallace State Community College
P.O. Drawer 1049, 3000 Range Line
Rd., Selma 36702-1049
Pres. Julius R. Brown
(205) 875-2634

James H. Faulkner State Community College
1900 Hwy. 31 S., Bay Minette 36507
Pres. Gary L. Branch
(205) 580-2100

Jefferson Davis State Junior College
P.O. Box 1119, Atmore 36504
Pres. Sandra K. McLeod
(205) 368-8118

Jefferson State Community College
2601 Carson Rd., Birmingham
35215-3098
Pres. Judy M. Merritt
(205) 853-1200

John C. Calhoun State Community College
P.O. Box 2216, Decatur 35609-2216
Pres. Richard G. Carpenter
(205) 306-2500

Lawson State Community College
3060 Wilson Rd., S.W., Birmingham
35221
Pres. Perry W. Ward
(205) 925-2515

Lurleen B. Wallace State Junior College
P.O. Box 1418, Andalusia 36420
Pres. Seth Hammett
(205) 222-6591

Northeast Alabama State Community College
P.O. Box 159, Hwy. 35, Rainsville
35986
Pres. Charles M. Pendley
(205) 228-6001

Northwest Alabama Community College
Rte. 3, Box 77, Phil Campbell 35581
Pres. Larry McCoy
(205) 993-5331

Shelton State Community College
202 Skyland Blvd., Tuscaloosa 35405
Pres. Thomas E. Umphrey
(205) 759-1541

Shoals Community College
P.O. Box 2545, George Wallace
Blvd., Muscle Shoals 35662
Pres. Larry McCoy
(205) 381-2813

Snead State Community College
P.O. Drawer D, 200 N. Walnut St.,
Boaz 35957
Pres. William H. Osborn
(205) 593-5120

Southern Union State Community College
Roberts St., Wadley 36276
Pres. Roy W. Johnson
(205) 395-2211

Wallace State Community College
801 Main St., Hanceville 35077
Pres. James C. Bailey
(205) 352-6403

ALASKA

University of Alaska System
Butrovich Bldg., Ste. 202, 910 Yukon Dr.,
Fairbanks 99775
Pres. Jerome Komisar
(907) 474-7311

Prince William Sound Community College
P.O. Box 97, Valdez 99686
Pres. Jo Ann C. McDowell
(907) 835-2421

University of Alaska Anchorage
3211 Providence Dr., Anchorage
99508
Chanc. Donald Behrend
(907) 786-1800

University of Alaska Fairbanks
320 Signers' Hall, Fairbanks 99775
Chanc. Joan K. Wadlow
(907) 474-7112

University of Alaska Southeast
11120 Glacier Hwy., Juneau 99801
Chanc. Marshall L. Lind
(907) 789-4509

ARIZONA

Arizona Board of Regents
2020 N. Central Ave., Ste. 230, Phoenix
85004
Exec. Dir. Frank H. Besnette
(602) 229-2500

Arizona State University
Tempe 85287
Pres. Lattie F. Coor
(602) 965-9011

Arizona State University West
4701 W. Thunderbird Rd., P.O. Box
37100, Phoenix 85069-7100
Provost Ben R. Forsyth
(602) 543-5500

Northern Arizona University
Box 4092, Flagstaff 86011-4092
Pres. Clara Lovett
(602) 523-9011

University of Arizona
Tucson 85721
Pres. Manuel T. Pacheco
(602) 621-2211

Arizona Community College Board
3225 N. Central Ave., Century Plaza, Ste.
1220, Phoenix 85012
Exec. Dir. Donald E. Puyear
(602) 255-4037

Arizona Western College
P.O. Box 929, Yuma 85366
Pres. James Carruthers
(602) 726-1000

Central Arizona College
8470 N. Overfield Rd., Coolidge
85228
Pres. John J. Klein
(602) 426-4444

Cochise College
Rte. 1, Box 100, Douglas 85607
Pres. Dan Rehurek
(602) 364-7943

Eastern Arizona College
600 Church St., Thatcher 85552
Pres. Gherald L. Hoopes, Jr.
(602) 428-8233

**Maricopa County Community College
District**
2411 W. 14th St., Tempe 85281-6941
Chanc. Paul A. Elsner
(602) 731-8000

*Chandler-Gilbert Community
College*
2626 E. Pecos Rd., Chandler
85225-2479
Chanc. Arnette S. Ward
(602) 732-7000

Gateway Community College
108 N. 40th St., Phoenix 85034
Pres. Phil D. Randolph
(602) 392-5000

Glendale Community College
6000 W. Olive Ave., Glendale
85302
Pres. John R. Waltrip
(602) 435-3000

Mesa Community College
1833 W. Southern Ave., Mesa
85202
Pres. Larry K. Christiansen
(602) 461-7000

Paradise Valley Community College
18401 N. 32nd St., Phoenix
85032
Pres. Raul Cardenas
(602) 493-2600

Phoenix College
1202 W. Thomas Rd., Phoenix
85013
Pres. Marie Pepicello
(602) 264-2462

Rio Salado Community College
640 N. First Ave., Phoenix
85003
Pres. Linda M. Thor
(602) 223-4000

Scottsdale Community College
9000 E. Chaparral Rd., Scottsdale 85250
Pres. Arthur W. DeCabooter
(602) 423-6000

South Mountain Community College
7050 S. 24th St., Phoenix 85040
Pres. John A. Cordova
(602) 243-8000

Mohave Community College
1971 Jagerson Ave., Kingman 86401
Pres. Charles W. Hall
(602) 757-4331

Northland Pioneer College
103 First Ave. at Hopi Dr., P.O. Box
610, Holbrook 86025
Pres. John H. Anderson
(602) 524-1993

Pima County Community College District
4907 E. Broadway Blvd., Tucson
85709-1010
Chanc. Johnas F. Hockaday
(602) 748-4999

Yavapai College
1100 E. Sheldon St., Prescott 86301
Pres. Doreen B. Dailey
(602) 445-7300

ARKANSAS

Arkansas Department of Higher Education
114 E. Capitol Ave., Little Rock 72201-3818
Dir. Diane S. Gilleland
(501) 324-9300

Arkansas State University System Office
P.O. Box 10, State University 72467
Pres. John N. Mangieri
(501) 972-3030

Arkansas State University
P.O. Box 10, State University 72467
Pres. John N. Mangieri
(501) 972-2100

Arkansas State University—Beebe Branch
Drawer H, Beebe 72012
Chanc. William H. Owen, Jr.
(501) 882-8254

Arkansas Tech University
Russellville 72801
Pres. Robert C. Brown
(501) 968-0389

Henderson State University
1100 Henderson St., Arkadelphia 71999-0001
Pres. Charles D. Dunn
(501) 246-5511

Southern Arkansas University
SAU Box 1402, Magnolia 71753
Pres. Steven G. Gamble
(501) 235-4001

University of Arkansas System Administration
Univ. Tower Bldg., Ste. 601, 1123 S. University Ave., Little Rock 72204
Pres. B. Alan Sugg
(501) 686-2500

University of Arkansas at Fayetteville
Fayetteville 72701
Chanc. Daniel E. Ferritor
(501) 575-2000

University of Arkansas at Little Rock
2801 S. University Ave., Little Rock 72204
Chanc. Charles E. Hathaway
(501) 569-3362

University of Arkansas at Monticello
Monticello 71655
Chanc. Fred J. Taylor
(501) 460-1020

University of Arkansas at Pine Bluff
Pine Bluff 71601
Chanc. Lawrence A. Davis, Jr
(501) 543-8000

University of Arkansas for Medical Sciences
4301 W. Markham St., Little Rock 72205
Chanc. Harry P. Ward
(501) 686-5000

University of Central Arkansas
Conway 73034
Pres. Winfred L. Thompson
(501) 450-3170

CALIFORNIA

California Community Colleges
1107 Ninth St., 6th Fl., Sacramento 95814
Chanc. David Mertes
(916) 322-4005

**Allan Hancock Joint Community
College District**
800 S. College Dr., Santa Maria 93454
Supt. Ann Foxworthy Stephenson
(805) 922-6966

Allan Hancock College
800 S. College Dr., Santa Maria
93454
Pres. Ann Foxworthy Stephenson
(805) 922-6966

**Antelope Valley Community College
District**
3041 W. Ave. K, Lancaster 93536-
5426
Supt. Allan W. Kurki
(805) 943-3241

Antelope Valley College
3041 W. Ave. K, Lancaster
93536
Pres. Allan W. Kurki
(805) 943-3241

Barstow Community College District
2700 Barstow Rd., Barstow 92311-
6699
Supt. Judith A. Strattan
(619) 252-2411

Barstow College
2700 Barstow Rd., Barstow
92311
Pres. Judith A. Strattan
(619) 252-2411

Butte Community College District
3536 Butte Campus Dr., Oroville
95965-8399
Supt. Betty M. Dean
(916) 895-2511

Butte College
3536 Butte Campus Dr.,
Oroville 95965
Pres. Betty M. Dean
(916) 895-2511

Cabrillo Community College District
6500 Soquel Dr., Aptos 95003
Supt. John D. Hurd
(408) 479-6100

Cabrillo College
6500 Soquel Dr., Aptos 95003
Pres. John D. Hurd
(408) 479-6100

Cerritos Community College District
11110 Alondra Blvd., Norwalk
90650-6298
Supt. Fred Gaskin
(310) 860-2451

Cerritos College
11110 Alondra Blvd., Norwalk
90650
Pres. Fred Gaskin
(310) 860-2451

**Chabot-Las Positas Community College
District**
5673 Gibraltar Dr., Ste. 100, Pleasan-
ton 94588
Chanc. Terry L. Dicianna
(510) 460-5334

Chabot College
25555 Hesperian Blvd., Hayward 94545
Pres. Raul Cardoza
(510) 786-6600

Las Positas College
3033 Collier Canyon Rd., Livermore 94550
Pres. Susan A. Cota
(510) 373-5800

Chaffey Community College District
5885 Haven Ave., Rancho Cucamonga 91737-3002
Supt. Jerry W. Young
(714) 987-1737

Chaffey College
5885 Haven Ave., Rancho
Cucamonga 91701
Pres. Jerry W. Young
(909) 941-2100

Citrus Community College District
1000 W. Foothill Blvd., Glendora
91741-1899
Supt. Louis E. Zellers
(818) 963-0323

Citrus College
1000 W. Foothill Blvd., Glendora 91741-1899
Pres. Louis E. Zellers
(818) 963-0323

Coast Community College District
1370 Adams Ave., Costa Mesa 92626
Chanc. William M. Vega
(714) 432-5813

Coastline Community College
11460 Warner Ave., Fountain Valley 92708
Acting Pres. Judith Valles
(714) 546-7600

Golden West College
15744 Golden West St., Huntington Beach 92647
Pres. Philip Westin
(714) 892-7711

Orange Coast College
2701 Fairview Rd., P.O. Box 5005, Costa Mesa 92628
Pres. David A. Grant
(714) 432-0202

Compton Community College District
1111 E. Artesia Blvd., Compton 90221
Pres./Supt. Byron R. Skinner
(310) 637-2660

Compton Community College
1111 E. Artesia Blvd., Compton 90221
Pres. Byron Skinner
(310) 637-2660

Contra Costa Community College District
500 Court St., Martinez 94553
Chanc. Robert D. Jensen
(510) 229-1000

Contra Costa College
2600 Mission Bell Dr., San Pablo 94806
Pres. D. Candy Rose
(510) 235-7800

Diablo Valley College
321 Golf Club Rd., Pleasant Hill
94523
Pres. Phyllis L. Peterson
(510) 685-1230

Los Medanos College
2700 E. Leland Rd., Pittsburg
94565
Pres. Stanley H. Chin
(510) 798-3500

Desert Community College District
43-500 Monterey Ave., Palm Desert
92260
Supt. David A. George
(619) 346-8041

College of the Desert
43-500 Monterey Ave., Palm Desert 92260
Pres. David A. George
(619) 346-8041

El Camino Community College District
16007 Crenshaw Blvd., Torrance
90506
Supt. Sam Schauerman
(310) 532-3670

El Camino College
16007 Crenshaw Blvd., Torrance 90506
Pres. Sam Schauerman
(310) 715-3111

Feather River Community College District
570 Golden Eagle Ave., P.O. Box 11110, Quincy 95971-6023
Supt./Pres. Donald J. Donato
(916) 283-0202

Feather River College
P.O. Box 11110, Quincy 95971
Pres. Donald J. Donato
(916) 283-0202

Foothill-DeAnza Community College District
12345 El Monte Rd., Los Altos Hills
94022-4599
Interim Chanc. Donald A. Perata
(415) 949-6100

De Anza College
21250 Stevens Creek Blvd.,
Cupertino 95014
Pres. Martha J. Kanter
(408) 864-5678

Foothill College
12345 El Monte Rd., Los Altos
Hills 94022
Pres. Thomas H. Clements
(415) 949-7200

Fremont-Newark Community College District
43600 Mission Blvd., P.O. Box 3909,
Fremont 94539-5884
Supt. Peter Blomerley
(510) 659-6000

Ohlone College
43600 Mission Blvd., Fremont
94539
Pres. Peter Blomerley
(510) 659-6000

Gavilan Joint Community College District
5055 Santa Teresa Blvd., Gilroy
95020
Supt. Glenn E. Mayle
(408) 847-1400

Gavilan College
5055 Santa Teresa Blvd., Gilroy
95020
Pres. Glenn E. Mayle
(408) 848-4712

Glendale Community College District
1500 N. Verdugo Rd., Glendale
91208
Supt. John A. Davitt
(818) 240-1000

Glendale Community College
1500 N. Verdugo Rd., Glendale
91208
Pres. John A. Davitt
(818) 240-1000

Grossmont-Cuyamaca Community College District
8800 Grossmont College Dr., El
Cajon 92020-1799
Chanc. Jeanne L. Atherton
(619) 697-9090

Cuyamaca College
2950 Jamacha Rd., El Cajon
92019-4304
Pres. Sherrill L. Amador
(619) 670-1980

Grossmont College
8800 Grossmont College Dr., El
Cajon 92020
Pres. Richard Sanchez
(619) 465-1700

Hartnell Community College District
156 Homestead Ave., Salinas 93901
Supt. James R. Hardt
(408) 755-6700

Hartnell College
156 Homestead Ave., Salinas
93901
Pres. James R. Hardt
(408) 755-6700

Imperial Community College District
P.O. Box 158, Imperial 92251-0158
Supt. John A. DePaoli, Jr.
(619) 352-8320

Imperial Valley College
P.O. Box 158, Imperial 92251
Pres. John A. DePaoli, Jr.
(619) 352-8320

Kern Community College District
2100 Chester Ave., Bakersfield
93301
Chanc. James C. Young
(805) 395-4100

Bakersfield College
1801 Panorama Dr., Bakersfield
93305
Pres. Richard L. Wright
(805) 395-4011

Cerro Coso Community College
3000 College Heights Blvd.,
Ridgecrest 93555
Pres. Raymond A. McCue
(619) 375-5001

Porterville College
100 E. College Ave., Porterville
93257
Interim Pres. John T. McCuen
(209) 781-3130

Lake Tahoe Community College District

One College Dr., South Lake Tahoe 96150
Supt. Guy F. Lease
(916) 541-4660

Lake Tahoe Community College
One College Dr., South Lake Tahoe 96150
Pres. Guy F. Lease
(916) 541-4660

Lassen Community College District

Hwy. 139, P.O. Box 3000, Susanville 96130
Supt. Larry J. Blake
(916) 257-6181

Lassen College
P.O. Box 3000, Susanville 96130
Pres. Larry J. Blake
(916) 257-6181

Long Beach Community College District

4901 E. Carson St., Long Beach 90808
Supt. Barbara A. Adams
(310) 420-4111

Long Beach City College
4901 E. Carson St., Long Beach 90808
Pres. Barbara A. Adams
(310) 420-4111

Los Angeles Community College District

770 Wilshore Blvd., Los Angeles 90017-3896
Interim Chanc. Neil Yoneji
(213) 891-2201

East Los Angeles College
1301 Brooklyn Ave., Monterey Park 91754
Acting Pres. Ernest Moreno
(213) 265-8650

Los Angeles City College
855 N. Vermont Ave., Los Angeles 90029
Pres. Jose Robledo
(213) 953-4000

Los Angeles Harbor College
1111 Figueroa Pl., Wilmington 90744
Pres. James Heinselman
(310) 522-8200

Los Angeles Mission College
13356 Eldridge Ave., Sylmar 91342-3244
Pres. Jack Fujimoto
(818) 364-7600

Los Angeles Pierce College
6201 Winnetka Ave., Woodland Hills 91371
Pres. Lowell J. Erickson
(818) 347-0551

Los Angeles Southwest College
1600 W. Imperial Hwy., Los Angeles 90047
Pres. Carolyn G. Williams
(213) 241-5273

Los Angeles Trade-Technical College
400 W. Washington Blvd., Los Angeles 90015
Pres. Thomas L. Stevens, Jr.
(213) 744-9500

Los Angeles Valley College
5800 Fulton Ave., Van Nuys 91401
Pres. Mary E. Lee
(818) 781-1200

West Los Angeles College
4800 Freshman Dr., Culver City 90230
Pres. Evelyn C. Wong
(310) 287-4200

Los Rios Community College District

1919 Spanos Ct., Sacramento 95825-3981
Pres. Queen F. Randall
(916) 568-3021

American River College
4700 College Oak Dr., Sacramento 95841
Interim Pres. Max McDonald
(916) 484-8011

Cosumnes River College
8401 Center Pkwy., Sacramento
95823
Pres. Marc E. Hall
(916) 688-7300

Sacramento City College
3835 Freeport Blvd., Sacramento 95822
Pres. Robert M. Harris
(916) 558-2100

Marin Community College District
Kentfield 94904
Supt. James E. Middleton
(415) 485-9500

College of Marin
835 College Ave., Kentfield
94904
Pres. James E. Middleton
(415) 457-8811

Mendocino-Lake Community College District
1000 Hensley Creek Rd., Ukiah
95482
Supt. Carl J. Ehmann
(707) 468-3073

Mendocino College
P.O. Box 3000, Ukiah 95482
Pres. Carl J. Ehmann
(707) 468-3100

Merced Community College District
3600 M St., Merced 95348-2898
Supt. E. Jan Moser
(209) 384-6000

Merced College
3600 M St., Merced 95340
Pres. E. Jan Moser
(209) 384-6000

MiraCosta Community College District
One Barnard Dr., Oceanside 92056
Supt. H. Deon Holt
(619) 757-2121

Mira Costa College
One Barnard Dr., Oceanside
92056
Pres. H. Deon Holt
(619) 757-2121

Monterey Peninsula Community College District
980 Fremont St., Monterey 93940
Supt. David W. Hopkins, Jr.
(408) 646-4000

Monterey Peninsula College
980 Fremont St., Monterey
93940
Pres. David W. Hopkins, Jr.
(408) 646-4000

Mount San Antonio Community College District
1100 N. Grand Ave., Walnut 91789
Supt. William H. Feddersen
(909) 594-5611

Mount San Antonio College
1100 N. Grand Ave., Walnut
91789
Pres. William H. Feddersen
(909) 594-5611

Mount San Jacinto Community College District
1499 N. State St., San Jacinto 92583
Supt. Roy B. Mason, II
(909) 654-8011

Mount San Jacinto College
1499 N. State St., San Jacinto
92583
Pres. Roy B. Mason, II
(909) 654-8011

Napa Valley Community College District
2277 Napa-Vallejo Hwy., Napa
94558
Supt. Diane E. Carey
(707) 253-3360

Napa Valley College
2277 Napa-Vallejo Hwy., Napa
94558
Pres. Diane E. Carey
(707) 253-3000

North Orange County Community College District
1000 N. Lemon St., Fullerton 92632-
1318
Chanc. Tom K. Harris, Jr.
(714) 871-4030

Cypress College
9200 Valley View St., Cypress 90630
Pres. Tom K. Harris, Jr.
(714) 826-2220

Fullerton College
321 E. Chapman Ave., Fullerton 92634
Pres. Philip W. Borst
(714) 992-7000

Palo Verde Community College District
811 W. Chanslor Way, Blythe 92225
Supt. Wilford J. Beumel
(619) 922-6168

Palo Verde College
811 W. Chanslorway, Blythe 92225
Pres. Wilford J. Beumel
(619) 922-6168

Palomar Community College District
1140 W. Mission Rd., San Marcos 92069-1487
Supt. George R. Boggs
(619) 744-5359

Palomar College
1140 W. Mission Rd., San Marcos 92069
Pres. George R. Boggs
(619) 744-1150

Pasadena Area Community College District
1570 E. Colorado Blvd., Pasadena 91106
Supt. Jack A. Scott
(818) 585-7201

Pasadena City College
1570 E. Colorado Blvd., Pasadena 91106
Pres. Jack A. Scott
(818) 585-7123

Peralta Community College District
333 E. Eighth St., Oakland 94606
Chanc. Robert J. Scannell
(510) 466-7200

College of Alameda
555 Atlantic Ave., Alameda 94501
Pres. Marie B. Smith
(510) 522-7221

Laney College
900 Fallon St., Oakland 94607
Pres. Odell Johnson
(510) 834-5740

Merritt College
12500 Campus Dr., Oakland 94619
Pres. Stan R. Arterberry
(510) 531-4911

Vista College
2020 Milvia St., Berkeley 94704
Pres. Barbara A. Beno
(510) 841-8431

Rancho Santiago Community College District
1530 W. 17th St., Santa Ana 92706
Supt. Vivian B. Blevins
(714) 564-6000

Rancho Santiago Community College
17th and Bristol Sts., Santa Ana 92706
Pres. Vivian B. Blevins
(714) 564-6053

Redwoods Community College District
7351 Tompkins Hill Rd., Eureka 95501
Supt. Cedric A. Sampson
(707) 445-6700

College of the Redwoods
7351 Tompkins Hill Rd., Eureka 95501
Pres. Cedric A. Sampson
(707) 445-6700

Rio Hondo Community College District
3600 Workman Mill Rd., Whittier 90608
Supt. Alex A. Sanchez
(310) 692-0921

Rio Hondo College
3600 Workman Mill Rd., Whittier 90608
Pres. Alex A. Sanchez
(310) 692-0921

Riverside Community College District
4800 Magnolia Ave., Riverside 92506-1299
Pres. Salvatore G. Rotella
(909) 684-3240

Riverside Community College
4800 Magnolia Ave., Riverside
92506-1299
Pres. Salvatore G. Rotella
(909) 684-3240

**Saddleback Community College
District**
28000 Marguerite Pkwy., Mission
Viejo 92692
Chanc. Robert A. Lombardi
(714) 582-4840

Irvine Valley College
5500 Irvine Center Dr., Irvine
92720
Pres. Anna L. McFarlin
(714) 559-9300

Saddleback College
28000 Marguerite Pkwy., Mission Viejo 92692
Pres. Ned Doffoney
(714) 582-4500

**San Bernardino Community College
District**
441 W. 8th St., San Bernardino
92401-1007
Chanc. Stuart M. Bundy
(714) 884-2533

Crafton Hills College
11711 Sand Canyon Rd.,
Yucaipa 92399
Pres. Luis S. Gomez
(714) 794-2161

San Bernardino Valley College
701 S. Mt. Vernon Ave., San
Bernardino 92410
Pres. Donald L. Singer
(714) 888-6511

San Diego Community College District
3375 Camino del Rio S., San Diego
92108
Chanc. Augustine P. Gallego
(619) 584-6957

San Diego City College
1313 Twelfth Ave., San Diego
92101
Pres. Jerome Hunter
(619) 230-2400

San Diego Mesa College
7250 Mesa College Dr., San
Diego 92111
Pres. Constance M. Carroll
(619) 627-2600

San Diego Miramar College
10440 Black Mountain Rd., San
Diego 92126
Pres. Louis C. Murillo
(619) 536-7800

**San Francisco Community College
District**
33 Gough St., San Francisco 94103
Chanc. Evan S. Dobelle
(415) 239-3000

City College of San Francisco
50 Phelan Ave., San Francisco
94112
Chanc. Evan S. Dobelle
(415) 239-3000

**San Joaquin Delta Community College
District**
5151 Pacific Ave., Stockton 95207-
6370
Supt. L.H. Horton, Jr.
(209) 474-5151

San Joaquin Delta College
5151 Pacific Ave., Stockton
95207
Pres. L.H. Horton, Jr.
(209) 474-5051

**San Jose-Evergreen Community
College District**
4750 San Felipe Rd., San Jose
95135-1599
Chanc. Ronald A. Kong
(408) 270-6402

Evergreen Valley College
3095 Yerba Buena Rd., San Jose
95135
Pres. Noelia Vela
(408) 274-7900

San Jose City College
2100 Moorpark Ave., San Jose
95128
Pres. Del M. Anderson
(408) 298-2181

San Luis Obispo Community College District
P.O. Box 8106, San Luis Obispo 93403-8106
Supt. Grace N. Mitchell
(805) 546-3100

Cuesta College
P.O. Box 8106, San Luis Obispo 93403
Pres. Grace N. Mitchell
(805) 546-3100

San Mateo County Community College District
3401 CSM Dr., San Mateo 94402-3699
Chanc./Supt. Lois A. Callahan
(415) 574-6550

Cañada College
4200 Farm Hill Blvd., Redwood City 94061
Pres. Miles Douglas Kechter
(415) 364-1212

College of San Mateo
1700 W. Hillsdale Blvd., San Mateo 94402
Pres. Peter J. Landsberger
(415) 574-6161

Skyline College
3300 College Dr., San Bruno 94066
Pres. Linda Graef Salter
(415) 355-7000

Santa Barbara Community College District
721 Cliff Dr., Santa Barbara 93109
Supt. Peter R. MacDougall
(805) 965-0581

Santa Barbara City College
721 Cliff Dr., Santa Barbara 93109
Pres. Peter R. MacDougall
(805) 965-0581

Santa Clarita Community College District
26455 N. Rockwell Canyon Rd., Santa Clarita 91355
Supt. Dianne G. Van Hook
(805) 259-7800

College of the Canyons
26455 N. Rockwell Canyon Rd., Santa Clarita 91355
Pres. Dianne G. Van Hook
(805) 259-7800

Santa Monica Community College District
1900 Pico Blvd., Santa Monica 90405
Supt. Richard L. Moore
(310) 450-5150

Santa Monica College
1900 Pico Blvd., Santa Monica 90405
Pres. Richard L. Moore
(310) 450-5150

Sequoias Community College District
915 S. Mooney Blvd., Visalia 93277
Interim Supt. David Erickson
(209) 730-3700

College of the Sequoias
915 S. Mooney Blvd., Visalia 93277
Interim Pres. David Erickson
(209) 730-3700

Shasta-Tehama-Trinity Joint Community College District
11555 Old Oregon Tr., Redding 96003
Supt. Douglas M. Treadway
(916) 225-4600

Shasta College
P.O. Box 496006, Redding 96049
Pres. Douglas M. Treadway
(916) 225-4600

Sierra Joint Community College District
5000 Rocklin Rd., Rocklin 95677
Supt. Kevin M. Ramirez
(916) 624-3333

Sierra College
5000 Rocklin Rd., Rocklin 95677
Pres. Kevin M. Ramirez
(916) 624-3333

Siskiyou Joint Community College District
800 College Ave., Weed 96094
Supt. Martha G. Romero
(916) 938-5200

College of the Siskiyous
800 College Ave., Weed 96094
Pres. Martha G. Romero
(916) 938-4461

Solano County Community College District
4000 Suisun Valley Rd., Suisun 94585
Supt. Virginia L. Holten
(707) 864-7112

Solano Community College
4000 Suisun Valley Rd., Suisun 94585
Pres. Virginia L. Holten
(707) 864-7000

Sonoma County Junior College District
1501 Mendocino Ave., Santa Rosa 95401
Supt. Robert F. Agrella
(707) 527-4431

Santa Rosa Junior College
1501 Mendocino Ave., Santa Rosa 95401
Pres. Robert F. Agrella
(707) 527-4431

Southwestern Community College District
900 Otay Lakes Rd., Chula Vista 91910-7299
Supt. Joseph M. Conte
(619) 421-6700

Southwestern College
900 Otay Lakes Rd., Chula Vista 91910
Pres. Joseph M. Conte
(619) 421-6700

State Center Community College District
1525 E. Weldon Ave., Fresno 93704
Chanc. Bill F. Stewart
(209) 244-5901

Fresno City College
1101 E. University Ave., Fresno 93741
Pres. Brice W. Harris
(209) 442-4600

Kings River Community College
995 N. Reed Ave., Reedley 93654
Pres. Richard J. Giese
(209) 638-3641

Ventura County Community College District
71 Day Rd., Ventura 93003
Chanc. Thomas G. Lakin
(805) 654-6412

Moorpark College
7075 Campus Rd., Moorpark 93021
Pres. James W. Walker
(805) 378-1400

Oxnard College
4000 S. Rose Ave., Oxnard 93033
Pres. Elise D. Schneider
(805) 986-5800

Ventura College
4667 Telegraph Rd., Ventura 93003
Pres. Jesus Carreon
(805) 642-3211

Victor Valley Community College District
18422 Bear Valley Rd., Victorville 92392
Supt. Edward O. Gould
(619) 245-4271

Victor Valley College
18422 Bear Valley Rd., Victorville 92392
Pres. Edward O. Gould
(619) 245-4271

West Hills Community College District
300 Cherry La., Coalinga 93210
Supt. Francis P. Gornick
(209) 935-0801

West Hills Community College
300 Cherry La., Coalinga 93210
Pres. Francis P. Gornick
(209) 935-0801

West Kern Community College District
29 Emmons Park Dr., Taft 93268
Supt. David Cothrun
(805) 763-4282

Taft College
29 Emmons Park Dr., Taft 93268
Pres. David Cothrun
(805) 763-4282

West Valley-Mission College District
14000 Fruitvale Ave., Saratoga 95070
Chanc. Rose Tseng
(408) 741-2011

Mission College
3000 Mission College Blvd.,
Santa Clara 95054
Pres. Floyd M. Hogue
(408) 988-2200

West Valley College
14000 Fruitvale Ave., Saratoga
95070
Pres. Leo E. Chavez
(408) 867-2200

Yosemite Community College District
P.O. Box 4065, Modesto 95352-4065
Chanc. Pamila J. Fisher
(209) 575-6508

Columbia College
P.O. Box 1849, Columbia 95310
Pres. Kenneth B. White
(209) 533-5100

Modesto Junior College
435 College Ave., Modesto
95350
Pres. Stanley L. Hodges
(209) 575-6067

Yuba Community College District
2088 N. Beale Rd., Marysville 95901
Supt. Patricia L. Wirth
(916) 741-6971

Yuba College
2088 N. Beale Rd., Marysville
95901
Pres. Patricia L. Wirth
(916) 741-6700

The California State University System
400 Golden Shore Dr., Long Beach
90802-4275
Chanc. Barry Munitz
(310) 985-2500

*California Polytechnic State University,
San Luis Obispo*
San Luis Obispo 93407
Pres. Warren J. Baker
(805) 756-1111

*California State Polytechnic University,
Pomona*
3801 W. Temple Ave., Pomona 91768
Pres. Bob H. Suzuki
(909) 869-7659

California State University, Bakersfield
9001 Stockdale Hwy., Bakersfield
93311-1099
Pres. Tomás A. Arciniega
(805) 664-2201

California State University, Chico
First and Normal Sts., Chico 95929-
0110
Pres. Manuel A. Esteban
(916) 898-6101

*California State University, Dominguez
Hills*
1000 E. Victoria St., Carson 90747
Pres. Robert C. Detweiler
(310) 516-3300

California State University, Fresno
5241 N. Maple Ave., Fresno 93740-
0054
Pres. John D. Welty
(209) 278-4240

California State University, Fullerton
800 N. State College Blvd., Fullerton
92634
Pres. Milton A. Gordon
(714) 773-2011

California State University, Hayward
25800 Carlos Bee Blvd., Hayward
94542
Pres. Norma S. Rees
(510) 881-3000

California State University, Long Beach
1250 Bellflower Blvd., Long Beach
90840
Interim Pres. Karl W.E. Anatol
(310) 985-4111

California State University, Los Angeles
5151 State University Dr., Los Angeles 90032
Pres. James M. Rosser
(213) 343-3030

California State University, Northridge
18111 Nordhoff St., Northridge 91330
Pres. Blenda J. Wilson
(818) 885-2121

California State University, Sacramento
6000 J St., Sacramento 95819-2694
Pres. Donald R. Gerth
(916) 278-6011

California State University, San Bernardino
5500 State University Pkwy., San Bernardino 92407-2397
Pres. Anthony H. Evans
(909) 880-5000

California State University, San Marcos
San Marcos 92069
Pres. Bill W. Stacy
(619) 471-4100

California State University, Stanislaus
801 W. Monte Vista Ave., Turlock 95382
Pres. Lee R. Kerschner
(209) 667-3082

Humboldt State University
Arcata 95521
Pres. Alistair W. McCrone
(707) 826-3011

San Diego State University
5300 Campanile Dr., San Diego 92182-0763
Pres. Thomas B. Day
(619) 594-5200

San Francisco State University
1600 Holloway Ave., San Francisco 94132
Pres. Robert A. Corrigan
(415) 338-1111

San Jose State University
One Washington Sq., San Jose 95192
Pres. J. Handel Evans
(408) 924-1000

Sonoma State University
1801 E. Cotati Ave., Rohnert Park 94928
Pres. Ruben Armiñana
(707) 664-2880

University of California Office of the President
300 Lakeside Dr., Oakland 94612-3550
Pres. Jack W. Peltason
(510) 987-0700

University of California, Berkeley
Berkeley 94720
Chanc. Chang-Lin Tien
(510) 642-6000

University of California, Davis
Davis 95616
Acting Chanc. Larry Vanderhoef
(916) 752-1011

University of California, Irvine
Irvine 92717
Chanc. Laurel L. Wilkening
(714) 856-5011

University of California, Los Angeles
405 Hilgard Ave., Los Angeles 90024
Chanc. Charles E. Young
(310) 825-4321

University of California, Riverside
Riverside 92521
Chanc. Raymond L. Orbach
(909) 787-1012

University of California, San Diego
La Jolla 92092
Chanc. Richard C. Atkinson
(619) 534-2230

University of California, San Francisco
513 Parnassus Ave., San Francisco 94143
Chanc. Joseph B. Martin
(415) 476-9000

University of California, Santa Barbara
Santa Barbara 93106
Chanc. Barbara S. Uehling
(805) 893-8000

University of California, Santa Cruz
1156 High St., Santa Cruz 95064
Chanc. Karl S. Pister
(408) 459-2058

COLORADO

Colorado Commission on Higher Education
1300 Broadway, 2nd Fl., Denver 80203
Acting Exec. Dir. Robert G. Moore
(303) 866-2723

**Colorado Community College and
Occupational Education System**
1391 N. Speer Blvd., Ste. 600,
Denver 80204-2554
Pres. Jerome F. Wartgow
(303) 620-4000

Arapahoe Community College
2500 W. College Dr., P.O. Box
9002, Littleton 80160-9002
Pres. James F. Weber
(303) 794-1550

Community College of Aurora
16000 E. Centretech Pkwy.,
Aurora 80011
Pres. Larry D. Carter
(303) 360-4700

Community College of Denver
P.O. Box 173363, Denver
80217-3363
Pres. Byron N. McClenney
(303) 556-2600

Front Range Community College
3645 W. 112th Ave., Westminster 80030
Pres. Thomas Gonzales
(303) 466-8811

Lamar Community College
2401 S. Main St., Lamar 81052
Pres. Marvin E. Lane
(719) 336-2248

Morgan Community College
17800 Rd. 20, Fort Morgan
80701
Pres. Richard Bond
(303) 867-3081

Otero Junior College
1802 Colorado Ave., La Junta
81050
Pres. Joe M. Treece
(719) 384-8721

Pikes Peak Community College
5675 S. Academy Blvd., Colorado Springs 80906
Pres. Marijane A. Paulsen
(719) 540-7551

Pueblo Community College
900 W. Orman Ave., Pueblo
81004
Pres. Joe D. May
(719) 549-3400

Red Rocks Community College
13300 W. Sixth Ave., Lakewood 80401
Pres. Dorothy Horrell
(303) 988-6160

Trinidad State Junior College
600 Prospect St., Trinidad
81082
Pres. Harold Deselms
(719) 621-8752

Colorado School of Mines
1500 Illinois St., Golden 80401
Pres. George S. Ansell
(303) 273-3000

Colorado State University
Fort Collins 80523
Pres. Albert C. Yates
(303) 491-1101

Fort Lewis College
Durango 81301
Pres. Joel M. Jones
(303) 247-7100

The State Colleges in Colorado
1580 Lincoln St., Ste. 750, Denver
80203
Pres. Glenn Burnham
(303) 874-2700

Adams State College
Alamosa 81102
Pres. William Fulkerson, Jr.
(719) 589-7341

Mesa State College
P.O. Box 2647, Grand Junction
81502
Pres. Raymond N. Kieft
(303) 248-1020

Metropolitan State College of Denver
P.O. Box 173362, Denver
80217-3362
Pres. Sheila Kaplan
(303) 556-3018

Western State College of Colorado
Gunnison 81231
Pres. Kaye Howe
(303) 943-2114

**University of Colorado Central
Administration**
Boulder 80309-0035
Pres. Judith E.N. Albino
(303) 492-6201

University of Colorado at Boulder
Boulder 80309
Chanc. James N. Corbridge, Jr.
(303) 492-1411

*University of Colorado at Colorado
Springs*
P.O. Box 7150, Colorado
Springs 80933-7150
Chanc. Linda Bunnell Jones
(719) 593-3000

University of Colorado at Denver
P.O. Box 173364, Denver
80217-3364
Chanc. John C. Buechner
(303) 556-2400

*University of Colorado Health
Sciences Center*
Denver 80262
Chanc. Vincent A. Fulginiti
(303) 399-1211

University of Northern Colorado
Greeley 80639
Pres. Herman D. Lujan
(303) 351-1890

University of Southern Colorado
2200 Bonforte Blvd., Pueblo 81001
Pres. Robert C. Shirley
(719) 549-2100

CONNECTICUT

State of Connecticut Department of Higher Education
61 Woodland St., Hartford 06105
Commissioner Andrew G. De Rocco
(203) 566-5766

Charter Oak State College
270 Farmington Ave., Ste. 171,
Farmington 06032-1934
Pres. Merle W. Harris
(203) 566-7230

Connecticut State University Central Office
P.O. Box 2008, New Britain 06050
Pres. Dallas K. Beal
(203) 827-7700

Central Connecticut State University
New Britain 06050
Pres. John W. Shumaker
(203) 827-7000

Eastern Connecticut State University
Willimantic 06226-2295
Pres. David G. Carter
(203) 456-2231

Southern Connecticut State University
New Haven 06515-0901
Pres. Michael J. Adanti
(203) 397-4000

Western Connecticut State University
Danbury 06810
Pres. James R. Roach
(203) 797-4347

State of Connecticut Board of Trustees of Community-Technical Colleges
61 Woodland St., Hartford 06105-2392
Exec. Dir. Andrew C. McKirdy
(203) 566-8760

Asnuntuck Community-Technical College
170 Elm St., Enfield 06082
Pres. Harvey S. Irlen
(203) 253-3000

Capital Community-Technical College
61 Woodland St., Hartford 06105
Pres. Conrad L. Mallett
(203) 520-7800

Gateway Community-Technical College
60 Sargent Dr., New Haven 06511
Pres. Antonio Perez
(203) 789-7071

Housatonic Community-Technical College
510 Barnum Ave., Bridgeport 06608
Pres. Vincent S. Darnowski
(203) 579-6400

Manchester Community-Technical College
60 Bidwell St., Manchester 06040
Pres. Jonathan M. Daube
(203) 647-6000

Middlesex Community-Technical College
100 Training Hill Rd., Middletown 06457
Pres. Leila G. Sullivan
(203) 344-3011

Naugatuck Valley Community-Technical College
750 Chase Pkwy., Waterbury 06708
Pres. Richard L. Sanders
(203) 575-8082

Northwestern Connecticut Community-Technical College
Park Pl. E., Winsted 06098
Pres. R. Eileen Baccus
(203) 738-6300

Norwalk Community-Technical College
188 Richards Ave., Norwalk 06854
Pres. William H. Schwab
(203) 857-7000

Quinebaug Valley Community-
Technical College
   724 Upper Maple St., Danielson
     06239
   Pres. Dianne E. Williams
   (203) 774-1130

Three Rivers Community-Technical
College
   P.O. Box 629, Mahan Dr., Nor-
     wich 06360
   Pres. Booker T. DeVaughn
   (203) 886-1931

Tunxis Community-Technical
College
   Rtes. 6 and 177, Farmington
     06032
   Pres. Cathryn L. Addy
   (203) 677-7701

The University of Connecticut
   Storrs 06269
   Pres. Harry J. Hartley
   (203) 486-2000

The University of Connecticut Health
Center
   263 Farmington Ave., Farmington
     06030-3800
   Vice Pres. Leslie S. Cutler
   (203) 679-2000

DELAWARE

Delaware Higher Education Commission
Carvel State Office Bldg., 820 N. French
St., Wilmington 19801
Exec. Dir. John F. Corrozi
(302) 571-3240

Delaware State University
1200 N. Dupont Hwy., Dover 19901
Pres. William B. DeLauder
(302) 739-4901

**Delaware Technical & Community
College Office of the President**
P.O. Box 897, Dover 19903
Pres. Thomas S. Kubala
(302) 739-4053

*Delaware Technical & Community
College Southern Campus*
P.O. Box 610, Georgetown
19947
Vice Pres./Campus Dir. Jack F.
Owens
(302) 856-5400

*Delaware Technical & Community
College Stanton/Wilmington
Campus*
400 Stanton Christiana Rd.,
Newark 19713
Vice Pres./Campus Dir. Orlando
J. George, Jr.
(302) 454-3917

*Delaware Technical & Community
College Terry Campus*
1832 N. Dupont Pkwy., Dover
19901
Acting Vice Pres./Campus Dir.
Wayne N. Dabson
(302) 739-5321

University of Delaware
Newark 19716
Pres. David P. Roselle
(302) 831-2000

FLORIDA

Florida State Board of Community Colleges
1314 Florida Educ. Ctr., 325 W. Gaines
St., Tallahassee 32399-0400
Exec. Dir. Clark Maxwell, Jr.
(904) 488-1721

Brevard Community College
1519 Clearlake Rd., Cocoa 32922
Pres. Maxwell C. King
(407) 632-1111

Broward Community College
225 E. Las Olas Blvd., Fort Lauderdale 33301
Pres. Willis N. Holcombe
(305) 761-7409

Central Florida Community College
P.O. Box 1388, Ocala 34478
Pres. William J. Campion
(904) 237-2111

Chipola Junior College
3094 Indian Cir., Marianna 32446-
2053
Pres. Jerry W. Kandzer
(904) 526-2761

Daytona Beach Community College
P.O. Box 2811, Daytona Beach
342120-2811
Pres. Philip R. Day, Jr.
(904) 255-8131

Edison Community College
8099 College Pkwy., S.W., P.O. Box
06210, Fort Myers 33906-6210
Pres. Kenneth P. Walker
(813) 489-9300

Florida Community College at Jacksonville
501 W. State St., Jacksonville 32202
Pres. Charles C. Spence
(904) 632-3000

Florida Keys Community College
5901 W. Junior College Rd., Key
West 33040
Pres. William A. Seeker
(305) 296-9081

Gulf Coast Community College
5230 W. U.S. Hwy. 98, Panama City
32401-1041
Pres. Robert L. McSpadden
(904) 769-1551

Hillsborough Community College
P.O. Box 31127, 39 Columbia Dr.,
Tampa 33631-3127
Pres. Andreas A. Paloumpis
(813) 253-7000

Indian River Community College
3209 Virginia Ave., Fort Pierce
34981-5599
Pres. Edwin R. Massey
(407) 462-4700

Lake City Community College
Rte. 3, Box 7, Lake City 32055
Pres. Muriel Kay Heimer
(904) 752-1822

Lake-Sumter Community College
9501 U.S. Hwy. 441, Leesburg
34788-8751
Pres. Robert W. Westrick
(904) 787-3747

Manatee Community College
5840 26th St. W., Bradenton 34207
Pres. Stephen J. Korcheck
(813) 755-1511

Miami-Dade Community College
300 N.E. Second Ave., Miami 33132
Pres. Robert H. McCabe
(305) 237-3221

North Florida Junior College
1000 Turner Davis Dr., Madison
32340
Pres. William H. McCoy
(904) 973-2288

Okaloosa-Walton Community College
100 College Blvd., Niceville 32578
Pres. James R. Richburg
(904) 678-5111

Palm Beach Community College
4200 Congress Ave., Lake Worth
33461-4796
Pres. Edward M. Eissey
(407) 439-8000

Pasco-Hernando Community College
36727 Blanton Rd., Dade City
33525-7599
Pres. Milton O. Jones
(904) 567-6701

Pensacola Junior College
1000 College Blvd., Pensacola 32504
Pres. Horace E. Hartsell
(904) 484-1000

Polk Community College
999 Ave. H, N.E., Winter Haven
33881-4299
Pres. Maryly VanLeer Peck
(813) 297-1000

St. Johns River Community College
5001 St. Johns Ave., Palatka 32177-
3897
Pres. Robert L. McLendon, Jr.
(904) 328-1571

St. Petersburg Junior College
P.O. Box 13489, St. Petersburg
33733-3489
Pres. Carl M. Kuttler, Jr.
(813) 341-3600

Santa Fe Community College
3000 N.W. 83rd St., Gainesville
32606
Pres. Lawrence W. Tyree
(904) 395-5000

Seminole Community College
100 Weldon Blvd., Sanford 32773-
6199
Pres. Earl S. Weldon
(407) 323-1450

South Florida Community College
600 W. College Dr., Avon Park 33825
Pres. Catherine P. Cornelius
(813) 453-6661

Tallahassee Community College
444 Appleyard Dr., Tallahassee
32304-2895
Pres. James H. Hinson, Jr.
(904) 488-9200

Valencia Community College
P.O. Box 3028, Orlando 32802-3028
Pres. Paul C. Gianini, Jr.
(407) 299-5000

State University System of Florida
325 W. Gaines St., Tallahassee 32399-1950
Chanc. Charles B. Reed
(904) 488-4234

*Florida Agricultural and Mechanical
University*
400 Lee Hall, Tallahassee 32307
Pres. Frederick S. Humphries
(904) 599-3000

Florida Atlantic University
500 N.W. 20th St., Boca Raton
33431-0991
Pres. Anthony J. Catanese
(407) 367-3000

Florida International University
University Park, Miami 33199
Pres. Modesto A. Maidique
(305) 348-2000

Florida State University
Tallahassee 32306
Pres. Talbot D'Alemberte
(904) 644-2525

University of Central Florida
4000 Central Florida Blvd., Orlando
32816
Pres. John C. Hitt
(407) 823-2000

University of Florida
226 Tigert Hall, Gainesville 32611
Pres. John V. Lombardi
(904) 392-3261

University of North Florida
4567 St. Johns Bluff Rd., S., Jacksonville 32224-2645
Pres. Adam W. Herbert, Jr.
(904) 646-2666

University of South Florida
4202 Fowler Ave., Tampa 33620-
6100
Pres. Betty Castor
(813) 974-2011

The University of West Florida
11000 University Pkwy., Pensacola
32514-5750
Pres. Morris L. Marx
(904) 474-2000

GEORGIA

Board of Regents of the University System of Georgia
244 Washington St., S.W., Atlanta 30334
Acting Chanc. Harry S. Downs
(404) 656-2202

Abraham Baldwin Agricultural College
P.O. Box 1, ABAC Sta., Tifton
31794-2601
Pres. Harold J. Loyd
(912) 386-3236

Albany State College
504 College Dr., Albany 31705-2794
Pres. Billy C. Black
(912) 430-4600

Armstrong State College
11935 Abercorn Ext., Savannah
31419-1997
Pres. Robert A. Burnett
(912) 927-5211

Atlanta Metropolitan College
1630 Stewart Ave., S.W., Atlanta
30310
Pres. Edwin A. Thompson
(404) 756-4441

Augusta College
2500 Walton Way, Augusta 30904-
2200
Pres. William A. Bloodworth
(706) 737-1400

Bainbridge College
Hwy. 84 E., Bainbridge 31717
Pres. Edward D. Mobley
(912) 248-2500

Brunswick College
Altama Ave. at Fourth St.,
Brunswick 31523
Pres. Dorothy L. Lord
(912) 264-7235

Clayton State College
P.O. Box 285, Morrow 30260
Pres. Richard Skinner
(404) 961-3400

Columbus College
4225 University Ave., Columbus
31907-5645
Pres. Frank D. Brown
(706) 568-2001

Dalton College
213 N. College Dr., Dalton 30720
Pres. Derrell C. Roberts
(706) 272-4436

Darton College
2400 Gillionville Rd., Albany 31707-
3098
Pres. Peter J. Sireno
(912) 430-6000

DeKalb College
3251 Panthersville Rd., Decatur 30034
Pres. Marvin M. Cole
(404) 244-5090

East Georgia College
237 Thigpen Dr., Swainsboro 30401
Pres. Jeremiah J. Ashcroft
(912) 237-7831

Floyd College
P.O. Box 1864, Rome 30162-1864
Pres. H. Lynn Cundiff
(706) 802-5000

Fort Valley State College
1005 State College Dr., Fort Valley
31030-3298
Pres. Oscar L. Prater
(912) 825-6315

Gainesville College
Mundy Mill Rd., P.O. Box 1358,
Gainesville 30503-1358
Pres. J. Foster Watkins
(404) 535-6239

Georgia College
C.P.O. Box 020, Milledgeville 31061
Pres. Edwin G. Speir, Jr.
(912) 453-5350

Georgia Institute of Technology
225 North Ave., N.W., Atlanta
30332-0325
Pres. John Patrick Crecine
(404) 894-2000

Georgia Southern University
Landrum Box 8033, Statesboro
30460-8033
Pres. Nicholas L. Henry
(912) 681-5611

Georgia Southwestern College
800 Wheatley St., Americus 31709-4693
Pres. William H. Capitan
(912) 928-1279

Georgia State University
University Plaza, Atlanta 30303-3083
Pres. Carl V. Patton
(404) 651-2000

Gordon College
419 College Dr., Barnesville 30204
Pres. Jerry M. Williamson
(404) 358-5016

Kennesaw State College
P.O. Box 444, Marietta 30061
Pres. Betty L. Siegel
(404) 423-6000

Macon College
100 College Station Dr., Macon 31297
Pres. S. Aaron Hyatt
(912) 471-2700

Medical College of Georgia
1120 15th St., Augusta 30912
Pres. Francis J. Tedesco
(706) 721-0211

Middle Georgia College
1100 Second St., S.E., Cochran 31014
Pres. Joe Ben Welch
(912) 934-6221

North Georgia College
College Ave., Dahlonega 30597
Pres. Delmas J. Allen
(706) 864-1400

Savannah State College
State College Branch, P.O. Box 20449, Savannah 31404
Pres. John T. Wolfe, Jr.
(912) 356-2187

South Georgia College
Douglas 31533-5098
Pres. Edward D. Jackson, Jr.
(912) 383-4220

Southern College of Technology
1100 S. Marietta Pkwy., Marietta 30060-2896
Pres. Stephen R. Cheshier
(404) 528-7230

The University of Georgia
Athens 30602-1661
Pres. Charles B. Knapp
(706) 542-3000

Valdosta State University
1500 N. Patterson St., Valdosta 31698
Pres. Hugh C. Bailey
(912) 333-5952

Waycross College
2001 Francis St., Waycross 31503
Pres. James M. Dye
(912) 285-6130

West Georgia College
Carrollton 30118-0001
Acting Pres. Bruce W. Lyon
(404) 836-6500

HAWAII

University of Hawaii Office of the President
2444 Dole St., Honolulu 96822
Pres. & Chanc. Kenneth P. Mortimer
(808) 956-8207

University of Hawaii at Hilo
200 W. Kawili St., Hilo 96720-4091
Chanc. Kenneth L. Perrin
(808) 933-3311

University of Hawaii at Manoa
2444 Dole St., Honolulu 96822
Chanc. Kenneth P. Mortimer
(808) 956-8111

University of Hawaii at West Oahu
96-043 Ala Ike, Pearl City 96782
Chanc. Kenneth L. Perrin
(808) 456-4718

**University of Hawaii Office of the
Chancellor for Community Colleges**
2327 Dole St., Honolulu 96822
Sr. V.P. & Chanc., Comm. Colleges
Joyce S. Tsunoda
(808) 956-7313

Hawaii Community College
523 W. Lanikaula St., Hilo
96720-4091
Provost Sandra Sakaguchi
(808) 933-3611

Honolulu Community College
874 Dillingham Blvd., Honolulu
96817
Provost Peter R. Kessinger
(808) 845-9225

Kapiolani Community College
4303 Diamond Head Rd., Honolulu 96816
Provost John E. Morton
(808) 734-9111

Kauai Community College
3-1901 Kaumualii Hwy., Lihue
96766
Provost David Iha
(808) 245-8311

Leeward Community College
96-045 Ala Ike, Pearl City
96782
Provost Barbara B. Polk
(808) 455-0011

Maui Community College
310 Kaahumanu Ave., Kahului
96732
Provost Clyde M. Sakamoto
(808) 244-9181

Windward Community College
45-720 Keaahala Rd., Kaneohe
96744
Provost Peter T. Dyer
(808) 235-0077

IDAHO

State Board of Education and Board of Regents of the University of Idaho
L.B. Jordan Bldg., Rm. 307, 650 W. State St., Boise 83720-3650
Exec. Dir. Rayburn Barton
(208) 334-2270

Boise State University
Boise 83725
Pres. Charles Ruch
(208) 385-1491

College of Southern Idaho
315 Falls Ave., P.O. Box 1238, Twin Falls 83303-1238
Pres. Gerald R. Meyerhoeffer
(208) 733-9554

Idaho State University
Pocatello 83209-0009
Pres. Richard L. Bowen
(208) 236-3340

Lewis-Clark State College
Lewiston 83501
Pres. Lee A. Vickers
(208) 799-2216

North Idaho College
Coeur d'Alene 83814
Pres. C. Robert Bennett
(208) 769-3300

University of Idaho
Moscow 83843
Pres. Elisabeth A. Zinser
(208) 885-6365

ILLINOIS

Illinois Board of Governors Universities
700 E. Adams St., Ste. 200, Springfield
62701
Chanc. Thomas D. Layzell
(217) 782-6392

Chicago State University
9501 S. King Dr., Chicago 60628
Pres. Dolores E. Cross
(312) 995-2000

Eastern Illinois University
600 Lincoln Ave., Charleston 61920
Pres. David L. Jorns
(217) 581-5000

Governors State University
University Park 60466
Pres. Paula Wolff
(708) 534-5000

Northeastern Illinois University
5500 N. St. Louis Ave., Chicago
60625
Pres. Gordon H. Lamb
(312) 794-4050

Western Illinois University
900 W. Adams St., Macomb 61455
Pres. Donald S. Spencer
(309) 295-1414

Illinois Community College Board
509 S. Sixth St., Rm. 400, Springfield
62701-1874
Exec. Dir. Cary Israel
(217) 785-0123

Belleville Area College
2500 Carlyle Rd., Belleville 62221
Pres. Joseph J. Cipfl
(618) 235-7000

Black Hawk College
6600 34th Ave., Moline 61265
Pres. Judith A. Redwine
(309) 796-1311

Carl Sandburg College
2232 S. Lake Storey Rd., Galesburg
61401
Pres. Donald G. Crist
(309) 344-2518

City Colleges of Chicago
226 W. Jackson Blvd., Chicago 60606
Chanc. Ronald J. Temple
(312) 641-0808

Harold Washington College
30 E. Lake St., Chicago 60601
Pres. Bernice J. Miller
(312) 781-9430

Harry S Truman College
1145 W. Wilson Ave., Chicago
60640
Pres. Wallace B. Appelson
(312) 878-1700

Kennedy-King College
6800 S. Wentworth Ave.,
Chicago 60621
Pres. Harold Pates
(312) 962-3200

Malcolm X College
1900 W. Van Buren St.,
Chicago 60612
Pres. Zerrie D. Campbell
(312) 850-7041

Olive-Harvey College
10001 S. Woodlawn Ave.,
Chicago 60628
Pres. Homer D. Franklin
(312) 291-6100

Richard J. Daley College
7500 S. Pulaski Rd., Chicago
60652
Interim Pres. Donald B. Smith
(312) 838-7500

Wilbur Wright College
4300 N. Narragansett Ave.,
Chicago 60634
Pres. Raymond F. Le Fevour
(312) 481-8182

College of DuPage
22nd St. and Lambert Rd., Glen
Ellyn 60137
Pres. Harold D. McAninch
(708) 858-2800

College of Lake County
19351 W. Washington St., Grayslake
60030
Pres. Daniel J. LaVista
(708) 223-6601

Danville Area Community College
2000 E. Main St., Danville 61832
Pres. Harry J. Braun
(217) 443-1811

Elgin Community College
1700 Spartan Dr., Elgin 60123
Pres. Paul R. Heath
(708) 697-1000

Highland Community College
2998 Pearl City Rd., Freeport 61032
Pres. Ruth Mercedes Smith
(815) 235-6121

Illinois Central College
One College Dr., East Peoria 61635
Pres. Thomas K. Thomas
(309) 694-5011

Illinois Eastern Community Colleges System
233 E. Chestnut St., Olney 62450-
2298
Chanc. Harry V. Smith, Jr.
(618) 393-2982

Frontier Community College
Frontier Dr., Fairfield 62837
Pres. Richard L. Mason
(618) 842-3711

Lincoln Trail College
Rte. 3, Robinson 62454
Pres. Donald E. Donnay
(618) 544-8657

Olney Central College
305 N. West St., Olney 62450
Pres. Judith Hansen
(618) 395-4351

Wabash Valley College
2200 College Dr., Mount
Carmel 62863
Pres. Harry K. Benson
(618) 262-8641

Illinois Valley Community College
2578 E. 350th Rd., Oglesby 61348
Pres. Alfred E. Wisgoski
(815) 224-2720

John A. Logan College
Carterville 62918
Pres. J. Ray Hancock
(618) 985-3741

John Wood Community College
150 S. 48th St., Quincy 62301
Pres. Robert C. Keys
(217) 224-6500

Joliet Junior College
1216 Houbolt Ave., Joliet 60436
Pres. Raymond A. Pietak
(815) 729-9020

Kankakee Community College
P.O. Box 888, Kankakee 60901
Pres. Lawrence D. Huffman
(815) 933-0345

Kaskaskia College
27210 College Rd., Centralia 62801
Pres. Raymond D. Woods
(618) 532-1981

Kishwaukee College
21193 Malta Rd., Malta 60150
Pres. Norman L. Jenkins
(815) 825-2086

Lake Land College
5001 Lake Land Blvd., Mattoon
61938
Pres. Robert K. Luther
(217) 235-3131

Lewis and Clark Community College
5800 Godfrey Rd., Godfrey 62035
Pres. Dale T. Chapman
(618) 466-3411

Lincoln Land Community College
Shepherd Rd., Springfield 62794
Pres. Norman L. Stephens, Jr.
(217) 786-2200

McHenry County College
8900 U.S. Hwy. 14, Crystal Lake
60012-2794
Pres. Robert C. Bartlett
(815) 455-3700

Moraine Valley Community College
10900 S. 88th Ave., Palos Hills
60465
Pres. Vernon O. Crawley
(708) 974-4300

Morton College
3801 S. Central Ave., Cicero 60650
Pres. Charles P. Ferro
(708) 656-8000

Oakton Community College
1600 E. Golf Rd., Des Plaines 60016
Pres. Thomas TenHoeve
(708) 635-1600

Parkland College
2400 W. Bradley Ave., Champaign
61821
Pres. Zelema M. Harris
(217) 351-2200

Prairie State College
202 S. Halsted St., Chicago Heights
60411
Pres. E. Timothy Lightfield
(708) 756-3110

Rend Lake College
Rural Rte. 1, Ina 62846
Pres. Mark S. Kern
(618) 437-5321

Richland Community College
One College Park, Decatur 62521
Pres. Charles R. Novak
(217) 875-7200

Rock Valley College
3301 N. Mulford Rd., Rockford 61114
Pres. Karl J. Jacobs
(815) 654-4250

Sauk Valley Community College
173 Illinois Rte. 2, Dixon 61021
Pres. Richard L. Behrendt
(815) 288-5511

Shawnee Community College
Rural Rte. 1, Box 53, Ullin 62992-
9725
Pres. Jack D. Hill
(618) 634-2242

South Suburban College of Cook County
15800 S. State St., South Holland
60473
Pres. Richard W. Fonte
(708) 596-2000

Southeastern Illinois College
3575 College Rd., Harrisburg 62946
Pres. Harry W. Abell
(618) 252-6376

Spoon River College
Rural Rte. 1, Canton 61520
Pres. Felix T. Haynes, Jr.
(309) 647-4645

State Community College of East St. Louis
601 James R. Thompson Blvd., East
St. Louis 62201
Interim Pres. Robert Randolph
(618) 583-2500

Triton College
2000 Fifth Ave., River Grove 60171
Pres. George T. Jorndt
(708) 456-0300

Waubonsee Community College
Illinois Rte. 47 at Harter Rd., Sugar
Grove 60554
Pres. John J. Swalec
(708) 466-4811

William Rainey Harper College
1200 W. Algonquin Rd., Palatine
60067-7398
Pres. Paul N. Thompson
(708) 397-3000

Regency Universities System Board of Regents
One W. Old State Capitol Plaza, Ste. 200,
Springfield 62701
Chanc. Roderick T. Groves
(217) 782-3770

Illinois State University
Normal 61790-1000
Pres. Thomas P. Wallace
(309) 438-2111

Northern Illinois University
De Kalb 60115
Pres. John E. LaTourette
(815) 753-9500

Sangamon State University
Springfield 62794-9243
Pres. Naomi B. Lynn
(217) 786-6600

Southern Illinois University System
Colyer Hall, Mail Code 6801, Carbondale
62901-6801
Chanc. James M. Brown
(618) 536-3331

*Southern Illinois University at
Carbondale*
Carbondale 62901
Pres. John C. Guyon
(618) 453-2121

*Southern Illinois University at
Edwardsville*
Edwardsville 62026
Pres. Nancy Belck
(618) 692-2000

University of Illinois Central Office
506 S. Wright St., Urbana 61801
Pres. Stanley O. Ikenberry
(217) 333-3070

University of Illinois at Chicago
P.O. Box 4348, Chicago 60680
Chanc. James J. Stukel
(312) 996-7000

*University of Illinois at Urbana-
Champaign*
601 E. John St., Champaign 61820
Chanc. Michael Aiken
(217) 333-6290

INDIANA

Indiana Commission for Higher Education
101 W. Ohio St., Ste. 550, Indianapolis
46204
Commissioner Clyde R. Ingle
(317) 232-1900

Ball State University
2000 University Ave., Muncie 47306
Pres. John E. Worthen
(317) 289-1241

Indiana State University
Terre Haute 47809
Pres. John W. Moore
(812) 237-6311

Indiana University System
Bryan Hall, Rm. 200, Bloomington
47405
Pres. Thomas Ehrlich
(812) 855-4613

Indiana University Bloomington
Bloomington 47405
Chanc. Kenneth R. Gros Louis
(812) 332-0211

Indiana University East
2325 N. Chester Blvd., Richmond 47374
Chanc. Charlie Nelms
(317) 966-8200

Indiana University Northwest
3400 Broadway, Gary 46408
Chanc. Hilda Richards
(219) 980-6500

Indiana University Southeast
4201 Grant Line Rd., New
Albany 47150
Chanc. Leon Rand
(812) 941-2000

Indiana University at Kokomo
P.O. Box 9003, Kokomo 46904-
9003
Chanc. Emita B. Hill
(317) 455-9200

Indiana University at South Bend
1700 Mishawaka Ave., P.O.
Box 7111, South Bend 46634
Chanc. H. Daniel Cohen
(219) 237-4111

*Indiana University-Purdue
University at Fort Wayne*
2101 Coliseum Blvd. E., Fort
Wayne 46805
Chanc. Joanne B. Lantz
(219) 481-6100

*Indiana University-Purdue
University at Indianapolis*
355 N. Lansing St., Indianapolis
46202
Chanc. Gerald L. Bepko
(317) 274-5555

Purdue University System
1031 Hovde Hall, Rm. 200, West
Lafayette 47907-1031
Pres. Steven C. Beering
(317) 494-9708

Purdue University
West Lafayette 47907
Pres. Steven C. Beering
(317) 494-4600

Purdue University Calumet
Hammond 46323
Chanc. James W. Yackel
(219) 989-2993

Purdue University North Central
1401 S. U.S. Hwy. 421, Westville 46391
Chanc. Dale W. Alspaugh
(219) 785-5200

University of Southern Indiana
8600 University Blvd., Evansville
47712
Pres. David L. Rice
(812) 464-8600

Vincennes University
1002 N. First St., Vincennes 47591
Pres. Phillip M. Summers
(812) 882-4208

**Indiana Vocational Technical College Office
of the President**
One W. 26th St., P.O. Box 1763, Indianapolis 46206
Pres. Gerald I. Lamkin
(317) 921-4861

Indiana Vocational Technical College—
Central Indiana Technical Institute
    One W. 26th St., P.O. Box 1763,
      Indianapolis 46206
    Vice Pres./Chanc. Meredith L. Carter
    (317) 921-4882

Indiana Vocational Technical College—
Columbus/Bloomington Technical
Institute
    4475 Central Ave., Columbus 47203
    Vice Pres./Chanc. Homer B. Smith
    (812) 372-9925

Indiana Vocational Technical College—
Eastcentral Technical Institute
    4301 S. Cowan Rd., P.O. Box 3100,
      Muncie 47307
    Exec. Dean Thomas Henry
    (317) 289-2291

Indiana Vocational Technical College—
Kokomo Technical Institute
    1815 E. Morgan St., Kokomo 46901
    Exec. Dean Shanon L. Christiansen
    (317) 459-0561

Indiana Vocational Technical College—
Lafayette Technical Institute
    3208 Ross Rd., P.O. Box 6299,
      Lafayette 47903
    Exec. Dean Elizabeth J. Doversberger
    (317) 477-9100

Indiana Vocational Technical College—
Northcentral Technical Institute
    1534 W. Sample St., South Bend
      46619
    Vice Pres./Chanc. Carl F. Lutz
    (219) 289-7001

Indiana Vocational Technical College—
Northeast Technical Institute
    3800 N. Anthony Blvd., Fort Wayne
      46805
    Vice Pres./Chanc. Jon L. Rupright
    (219) 482-9171

Indiana Vocational Technical College—
Northwest Technical Institute
    1440 E. 35th Ave., Gary 46409
    Vice Pres./Chanc. Darnell E. Cole
    (219) 981-1111

Indiana Vocational Technical College—
Southcentral Technical Institute
    8204 Hwy. 311 W., Sellersburg
      47172
    Exec. Dean Jonathan W. Thomas
    (812) 246-3301

Indiana Vocational Technical College—
Southeast Technical Institute
    590 Ivy Tech Dr., Madison 47250
    Vice Pres. Homer B. Smith
    (812) 265-2580

Indiana Vocational Technical College—
Southwest Technical Institute
    3501 First Ave., Evansville 47710
    Exec. Dean Daniel L. Schenk
    (812) 426-2865

Indiana Vocational Technical College—
Wabash Valley Technical Institute
    7999 U.S. Hwy. 41, Terre Haute
      47802
    Vice Pres./Chanc. Sam E. Borden
    (812) 299-1121

Indiana Vocational Technical College—
Whitewater Technical Institute
    2325 Chester Blvd., Richmond
      47374
    Exec. Dean Jim Steck
    (317) 966-2656

IOWA

Iowa Department of Education Division of Community Colleges
Grimes State Office Bldg., Des Moines 50319-0146
Acting Administrator Harriet Howell Custer, Ph.D.
(515) 281-8260

Des Moines Area Community College
2006 S. Ankeny Blvd., Ankeny 50021
Pres. Joseph A. Borgen, Ph.D.
(515) 964-6260

Eastern Iowa Community College District
306 W. River Dr., Davenport 52801
Chanc. John T. Blong
(319) 322-5015

Clinton Community College
1000 Lincoln Blvd., Clinton 52732
Pres. Desna L. Wallin
(319) 242-6841

Muscatine Community College
152 Colorado St., Muscatine 52761
Pres. Victor G. McAvoy
(319) 263-8250

Scott Community College
500 Belmont Rd., Bettendorf 52722
Pres. Lenny E. Stone
(319) 359-7531

Hawkeye Community College
1501 E. Orange Rd., Waterloo 50704
Pres. Phillip O. Barry
(319) 296-2320

Indian Hills Community College
525 Grandview Ave., Ottumwa 52501
Pres. Lyle Adrian Hellyer
(515) 683-5111

Iowa Central Community College
330 Ave. M, Fort Dodge 50501
Pres. Jack Bottenfield
(515) 576-7201

Iowa Lakes Community College
19 S. 7th St., Estherville 51334
Pres. Richard H. Blacker
(712) 362-2601

Iowa Valley Community College District
P.O. Box 536, Marshalltown 50158
Pres. Paul A. Tambrino
(515) 752-4643

Ellsworth Community College
1100 College Ave., Iowa Falls 50126
Dean Duane R. Lloyd
(515) 648-4611

Marshalltown Community College
3700 S. Center St., P.O. Box 430, Marshalltown 50158
Dean William M. Simpson
(515) 752-7106

Iowa Western Community College
2700 College Rd., Council Bluffs 51501
Pres. Carl L. Heinrich
(712) 325-3200

Kirkwood Community College
6301 Kirkwood Blvd., S.W., P.O. Box 2068, Cedar Rapids 52406-2068
Pres. Norman R. Nielsen
(319) 398-5501

North Iowa Area Community College
500 College Dr., Mason City 50401
Pres. David L. Buettner
(515) 423-1264

Northeast Iowa Community College
Box 400, Hwy. 150, Calmar 52132
Pres. Don Roby
(319) 562-3263

Northwest Iowa Community College
603 W. Park St., Sheldon 51201
Pres. Carl H. Rolf
(712) 324-5061

Southeastern Community College
Drawer F, West Burlington 52655
Pres. R. Gene Gardner
(319) 752-2731

Southwestern Community College
   1501 Townline St., Creston 50801
   Supt./Pres. Richard L. Byerly
   (515) 782-7081

Western Iowa Tech Community College
   4647 Stone Ave., P.O. Box 265,
      Sioux City 51102
   Pres. Robert E. Dunker
   (712) 274-6400

Iowa State Board of Regents
   Old Historical Bldg., Des Moines 50319
   Exec. Dir. R. Wayne Richey
   (515) 281-3934

Iowa State University
   Ames 50011
   Pres. Martin Charles Jischke
   (515) 294-2042

University of Iowa
   101 Jessup Hall, Iowa City 52242-
      1316
   Pres. Hunter R. Rawlings, III
   (319) 335-3500

University of Northern Iowa
   Cedar Falls 50614
   Pres. Constantine W. Curris
   (319) 273-2566

KANSAS

Kansas Board of Regents
700 S.W. Harrison St., Ste. 1410, Topeka
66603-3760
Exec. Dir. Stephen M. Jordan
(913) 296-3421

Emporia State University
1200 Commercial St., Emporia
66801
Pres. Robert E. Glennen, Jr.
(316) 343-1200

Fort Hays State University
600 Park St., Hays 67601
Pres. Edward H. Hammond
(913) 628-4000

Kansas State University
Manhattan 66506-0113
Pres. Jon Wefald
(913) 532-6011

Pittsburg State University
1701 S. Broadway, Pittsburg 66762
Pres. Donald W. Wilson
(316) 231-7000

University of Kansas
Lawrence 66045
Chanc. Gene A. Budig
(913) 864-2700

Wichita State University
1845 Fairmont St., Wichita 67260
Pres. Eugene M. Hughes
(316) 689-3001

Kansas State Board of Education
120 S.E. Tenth Ave., Topeka 66612-1182
Commissioner Lee Droegemueller
(913) 296-2635

Allen County Community College
1801 N. Cottonwood, Iola 66749
Pres. John A. Masterson
(316) 365-5116

Barton County Community College
Rural Rte. 3, Box 136Z, Great Bend
67530
Pres. Jimmie L. Downing
(316) 792-2701

Butler County Community College
901 S. Haverhill Rd., El Dorado
67042
Pres. Rodney V. Cox
(316) 312-2222

Cloud County Community College
2221 Campus Dr., P.O. Box 1002,
Concordia 66901-1002
Pres. James P. Ihrig
(913) 243-1435

Coffeyville Community College
11th and Willow Sts., Coffeyville
67337
Pres. Dan D. Kinney
(316) 251-7700

Colby Community College
1255 S. Range, Colby 67701
Pres. Mikel V. Ary
(913) 462-3984

Cowley County Community College
125 S. Second St., P.O. Box 1147,
Arkansas City 67005
Pres. Patrick J. McAtee
(316) 442-0430

Dodge City Community College
2501 N. 14th St., Dodge City 67801
Pres. Thomas E. Gamble
(316) 225-1321

Fort Scott Community College
2108 S. Horton St., Fort Scott 66701
Pres. Laura Meeks
(316) 223-2700

Garden City Community College
801 Campus Dr., Garden City 67846
Pres. James H. Tangeman
(316) 276-7611

Highland Community College
Box 68, Highland 66035
Pres. Eric M. Priest
(913) 442-3236

Hutchinson Community College
1300 N. Plum St., Hutchinson 67501
Pres. Edward E. Berger
(316) 665-3500

Independence Community College
    College Ave. and Brookside Dr.,
        Independence 67301
    Pres. Don Schoening
    (316) 331-4100

Johnson County Community College
    12345 College Blvd. at Quivira Rd.,
        Overland Park 66210
    Pres. Charles J. Carlsen
    (913) 469-8500

Kansas City Kansas Community College
    7250 State Ave., Kansas City 66112
    Pres. Thomas R. Burke
    (913) 334-1100

Labette Community College
    200 S. 14th St., Parsons 67357
    Pres. Joe Birmingham
    (316) 421-6700

Neosho County Community College
    1000 S. Allen, Chanute 66720
    Pres. Theodore W. Wischropp
    (316) 431-2820

Pratt Community College
    Hwy. 61, Pratt 67124
    Pres. William A. Wojciechowski
    (316) 672-5641

Seward County Community College
    1801 N. Kansas St., Box 1137, Liberal 67901
    Pres. Donald E. Guild
    (316) 624-1951

KENTUCKY

Kentucky Council on Higher Education
1050 U.S. 127 S., Ste. 101, W. Frankfort
Office Complex, Frankfort 40601-4395
Exec. Dir. Gary S. Cox
(502) 564-3553

Eastern Kentucky University
Richmond 40475-3101
Pres. H. Hanly Funderburk, Jr.
(606) 622-1000

Kentucky State University
E. Main St., Frankfort 40601
Pres. Mary L. Smith
(502) 227-6000

Morehead State University
University Blvd., Morehead 40351
Pres. Ronald G. Eaglin
(606) 783-2221

Murray State University
One Murray St., Murray 42071-3305
Pres. Ronald J. Kurth
(502) 762-3011

Northern Kentucky University
Nunn Dr., Highland Heights 41099
Pres. Leon E. Boothe
(606) 572-5100

University of Kentucky
206 Administration Bldg., Lexington
40506-0032
Pres. Charles T. Wethington, Jr.
(606) 257-9000

**University of Kentucky Community
College System**
Breckinridge Hall, Lexington 40506-
0056
Chanc. Ben W. Carr, Jr.
(606) 257-8607

Ashland Community College
1400 College Dr., Ashland
41101-3683
Pres. Charles R. Dassance
(606) 329-2999

Elizabethtown Community College
600 College Street Rd., Elizabethtown 42701
Pres. Charles E. Stebbins
(502) 769-2371

Hazard Community College
One Community College Dr.,
Hazard 41701
Pres. G. Edward Hughes
(606) 436-5721

Henderson Community College
2660 S. Green St., Henderson
42420
Pres. Patrick R. Lake
(502) 827-1867

Hopkinsville Community College
P.O. Box 2100, Hopkinsville
42241-2100
Pres. A. James Kerley
(502) 886-3921

Jefferson Community College
109 E. Broadway, Louisville
40202
Pres. Ronald J. Horvath
(502) 584-0181

Lexington Community College
Oswald Bldg., Cooper Dr., Lexington 40506-0235
Acting Pres. Anthony Newberry
(606) 257-4872

Madisonville Community College
2000 College Dr., Madisonville
42431
Pres. Arthur D. Stumpf
(502) 821-2250

Maysville Community College
1755 U.S. 68, Maysville 41056
Pres. James C. Shires
(606) 759-7141

Owensboro Community College
4800 New Hartford Rd., Owensboro 42303
Pres. John M. McGuire
(502) 686-4400

Paducah Community College
P.O. Box 7380, Paducah 42002-
7380
Pres. Leonard F. O'Hara
(502) 554-9200

Prestonsburg Community College
One Bert T. Combs Dr., Prestonsburg 41653
Pres. Deborah Lee Floyd
(606) 886-3863

Somerset Community College
808 Monticello Rd., Somerset 42501
Pres. Rollin J. Watson
(606) 679-8501

Southeast Community College
700 College Rd., Cumberland 40823-1099
Pres. W. Bruce Ayers
(606) 589-2145

University of Louisville
2301 S. Third St., Louisville 40292-0001
Pres. Donald C. Swain
(502) 588-5555

Western Kentucky University
1526 Big Red Way, Bowling Green 42101
Pres. Thomas C. Meredith
(502) 745-0111

Kentucky Tech North Central Region
150 Vo-Tech Rd., Lexington 40510-1001
Regional Exec. Dir. W. Michael Wright
(606) 252-3418

Kentucky Tech—Boone County Area Vocational Education Center
3320 Cougar Path, Hebron 41048
Coord. Stephanie Rottman
(606) 689-7855

Kentucky Tech—Carroll County Area Vocational Education Center
1704 Highland Ave., Carrollton 41008
Coord. Donald W. Garner
(502) 732-4479

Kentucky Tech—Central Kentucky State Vocational-Technical School
105 Vo-Tech Rd., Lexington 40510
Prin. Ron Baugh
(606) 255-8500

Kentucky Tech—Clark County Area Vocational Education Center
650 Boone Ave., Winchester 40391
Coord. William Lockhart
(606) 744-1250

Kentucky Tech—Danville School of Health Occupations
448 S. Third St., Danville 40422
Coord. Sandra Houston
(606) 236-2053

Kentucky Tech—Garrard County Area Vocational Education Center
306 W. Maple Ave., Lancaster 40444
Coord. James Spurlin
(606) 792-2144

Kentucky Tech—Harrison County Area Vocational Education Center
551 Webster Ave., Cynthiana 41031
Coord. James Plummer
(606) 234-5286

Kentucky Tech—Harrodsburg Area Vocational Education Center
661 Tapt Rd., P.O. Box 628, Harrodsburg 40330
Coord. L. Hughes Jones
(606) 734-9329

Kentucky Tech—Madison County Area Vocational Education Center
P.O. Box 809, 703 N. Second St., Richmond 40476-0809
Coord. Evelyn Watson
(606) 623-4061

Kentucky Tech—McCormick Area Vocational Education Center
50 Orchard La., Alexandria 41001
Coord. Kenneth McCormick
(606) 635-4101

Kentucky Tech—Northern Campbell County Vocational-Technical School
Campbell Dr., Highland Heights 41076
Coord. Earl Wittenrock
(606) 441-2010

Kentucky Tech—Northern Kentucky Health Occupations Center
790 Thomas More Pkwy., Edgewood 41017
Coord. Wade Halsey
(606) 341-5200

Kentucky Tech—Northern Kentucky State
Vocational-Technical School
　1025 Amsterdam Rd., Covington
　41018
　Prin. Edward Burton
　(606) 431-2700

Kentucky Tech—Patton Area Vocational
Education Center
　3234 Turkeyfoot Rd., Fort Mitchell
　41017
　Coord. Eugene Penn
　(606) 341-2266

Kentucky Tech Northeast Region
　4818 Roberts Dr., Ashland 41102-9046
　Regional Exec. Dir. Howard W. Moore
　(606) 928-6427

Kentucky Tech—Ashland State
Vocational-Technical School
　4818 Roberts Dr., Ashland 41102
　Prin. Marsha Burks
　(606) 928-6427

Kentucky Tech—Belfry Area Vocational
Education Center
　P.O. Box 280, Belfry 41514
　Prin. Brad W. May
　(606) 353-4951

Kentucky Tech—Garth Area Vocational
Education Center
　HC 79, Box 205, Martin 41649
　Prin. Ronald Turner
　(606) 285-3088

Kentucky Tech—Greenup County Area
Vocational Education Center
　P.O. Box 7, South Shore 41175
　Coord. Helen Spears
　(606) 932-3107

Kentucky Tech—Martin County Area
Vocational Education Center
　HC 68, Box 2177, Inez 41224
　Coord. Robert L. Allen
　(606) 298-3879

Kentucky Tech—Mason County Area
Vocational Education Center
　646 Kent Station Rd., Maysville
　41056
　Coord. Glenn Collins
　(606) 759-7101

Kentucky Tech—Mayo State Vocational-
Technical School
　513 Third St., Paintsville 41240
　Prin. Gary Coleman
　(606) 789-5321

Kentucky Tech—Millard Area Vocational
Education Center
　430 Millard Hwy., Pikeville 41501
　Prin. William Justice
　(606) 437-6059

Kentucky Tech—Montgomery County
Area Vocational Education Center
　682 Woodford Dr., Mount Sterling
　40353
　Coord. Norma Willoughby
　(606) 498-1103

Kentucky Tech—Morgan County Area
Vocational Education Center
　P.O. Box 249, West Liberty 41472
　Coord. Willis Lyon
　(606) 743-4321

Kentucky Tech—Phelps Area Vocational
Education Center
　HC 67, No. 1002, Phelps 41553
　Prin. Curtis Akers
　(606) 456-8136

Kentucky Tech—Rowan State Vocational-
Technical School
　100 Vo-Tech Dr., 32 N., Morehead
　40351
　Prin. Jamie Brown
　(606) 783-1538

Kentucky Tech—Russell Area Vocational
Education Center
　705 Red Devil La., Russell 41169
　Coord. Michael Chapman
　(606) 836-1256

Kentucky Tech Northwest Region
　505 University Dr., Elizabethtown 42701
　Regional Exec. Dir. Roye S. Wilson
　(502) 769-2326

Kentucky Tech—Breckinridge County
Area Vocational Education Center
　P.O. Box 68, Harnet 40144
　Coord. Wayne A. Spencer
　(502) 756-2138

Kentucky Tech—Bullitt County Area Vocational Education Center
395 High School Dr., Sheperdsville 40165
Coord. Robert Hazelrigg
(502) 543-7018

Kentucky Tech—Elizabethtown State Vocational-Technical School
505 University Dr., Elizabethtown 42701
Prin. Neil Ramer
(502) 765-2104

Kentucky Tech—Jefferson State Vocational-Technical Center
727 W. Chestnut St., Louisville 40202
Prin. Sandra Parks
(502) 588-4223

Kentucky Tech—Marion County Area Vocational Education Center
Rte. 3, Box 100, Lebanon 40033
Coord. John Coyle
(502) 692-3155

Kentucky Tech—Meade County Area Vocational Education Center
Old State Rd., Brandenburg 40108
Coord. William Whalen
(502) 422-3955

Kentucky Tech—Nelson County Area Vocational Education Center
1060 Bloomfield Rd., Bardstown 40004
Coord. John T. Kromer
(502) 348-9096

Kentucky Tech—Oldham County Area Vocational Education Center
P.O. Box 127, Hwy. 393, Buckner 40065
Prin. Jeanette Stratton
(502) 222-0131

Kentucky Tech—Shelby County Area Vocational Education Center
Rte. 7, Box 331, Shelbyville 40065
Coord. Ruth Bunch
(502) 633-6554

Kentucky Tech Southeast Region
101 Vo-Tech Dr., Hazard 41701
Regional Exec. Dir. Finley Begley
(606) 439-2500

Kentucky Tech—Bell County Area Vocational Education Center
Box 199-A, Rte. 7, Pineville 40977
Coord. Ron Mason
(606) 337-3094

Kentucky Tech—Breathitt County Area Vocational Education Center
P.O. Box 786, Jackson 41339
Coord. Fred Deaton
(606) 666-5153

Kentucky Tech—Clay County Area Vocational Education Center
Rte. 2, Box 256, Manchester 40962
Coord. Charles McWhorter
(606) 598-2194

Kentucky Tech—Corbin Area Vocational Education Center
1909 S. Snyder Ave., Corbin 40701
Coord. Ronnie Partin
(606) 528-5338

Kentucky Tech—Cumberland Valley Health Occupations Center
U.S. 25E S., P.O. Box 187, Pineville 40977
Coord. Mildred Winkler
(606) 337-3106

Kentucky Tech—Harlan State Vocational-Technical School
21 Ballpark Rd., Harlan 40831
Prin. Harve J. Couch
(606) 573-1506

Kentucky Tech—Hazard State Vocational-Technical School
101 Vo-Tech Dr., Hazard 41701
Prin. Connie W. Johnson
(606) 436-3101

Kentucky Tech—Knott County Area Vocational Education Center
HCR 60, Box 1100, Hindman 41822
Coord. Sonny Smith
(606) 785-5350

Kentucky Tech—Knox County Area Vocational Education Center
210 Wall St., Barbourville 40906
Coord. Charles Frasier
(606) 546-5320

Kentucky Tech—Laurel County State
Vocational-Technical School
　1711 S. Main St., London 40741
　Prin. Ronnie Partin
　(606) 864-7311

Kentucky Tech—Lee County Area
Vocational Education Center
　P.O. Box B, Beattyville 41311
　Coord. Fred Kincaid
　(606) 464-2475

Kentucky Tech—Leslie County Area
Vocational Education Center
　P.O. Box 902, Hyden 41749
　Coord. Betty Huff
　(606) 672-2859

Kentucky Tech—Letcher County Area
Vocational Education Center
　610 Circle Dr., Whitesburg 41858
　Coord. James G. Estep
　(606) 633-5053

Kentucky Tech—Rockcastle County Area
Vocational Education Center
　P.O. Box 275, Mount Vernon 40456
　Coord. Donna Hopkins
　(606) 256-4346

Kentucky Tech Southern Region
1845 Loop Dr., Bowling Green 42101-3601
Regional Exec. Dir. Ann W. Cline
(502) 843-5467

Kentucky Tech—Barren County Area
Vocational Education Center
　491 Trojan Tr., Glasgow 42141
　Coord. Max Doty
　(502) 651-2196

Kentucky Tech—Bowling Green State
Vocational-Technical School
　1845 Loop Dr., Bowling Green 42102
　Prin. Donald R. Williams
　(502) 843-5461

Kentucky Tech—Casey County Area
Vocational Education Center
　Rte. 4, Box 49, Liberty 42539
　Coord. J.D. Shugars
　(606) 787-6241

Kentucky Tech—Clinton County Area
Vocational Education Center
　Rte. 3, Box 8, Albany 42602
　Coord. Preston Sparks
　(606) 387-6448

Kentucky Tech—Glasgow Health
Occupations School
　1215 N. Race St., Glasgow 42141
　Coord. Rebecca Forrest
　(502) 651-5673

Kentucky Tech—Green County Area
Vocational Education Center
　P.O. Box H, Greensburg 42743
　Coord. Jerry O. Rogers
　(502) 932-4263

Kentucky Tech—Kentucky Advanced
Technology Center
　1845 Loop Dr., Bowling Green 42102
　Coord. Jack Thomas
　(502) 843-5807

Kentucky Tech—Monroe County Area
Vocational Education Center
　4th and Emmerton Sts., Tomp-
　　kinsville 42167
　Coord. Bill Polland
　(502) 487-8261

Kentucky Tech—Russell County Area
Vocational Education Center
　P.O. Box 599, Russell Springs 42642
　Prin. Chester Taylor
　(502) 866-6175

Kentucky Tech—Russellville Area
Vocational Education Center
　1103 W. 9th St., Russellville 42276
　Coord. Maurice Grayson
　(502) 726-8433

Kentucky Tech—Somerset State
Vocational-Technical School
　714 Airport Rd., Somerset 42501
　Prin. Carol Ann Van Hook
　(606) 679-4303

Kentucky Tech—Wayne County Area
Vocational Education Center
　Rte. 4, Box 1B, Monticello 42633
　Coord. Sharon Tiller
　(606) 348-8424

Kentucky Tech West Region
100 School Ave., Madisonville 42431
Regional Exec. Dir. Bill M. Hatley
(502) 825-6546

Kentucky Tech—Caldwell County Area
Vocational Education Center
　P.O. Box 350, Princeton 42445
　Coord. Arthur Dunn
　(502) 365-5563

Kentucky Tech—Christian County Area
Vocational Education Center
  109 Hamond Plaza, Ste. 2, Fort
    Campbell Blvd., Hopkinsville
    42240
  Coord. Ann Claxton
  (502) 887-2524

Kentucky Tech—Daviess County
Vocational-Technical School
  P.O. Box 1677, Owensboro 42303-
    1677
  Prin. Ray Gillaspie
  (502) 686-3321

Kentucky Tech—Fulton County Area
Vocational Education Center
  Rte. 4, Hickman 42050
  Coord. Larry Lynch
  (502) 236-2517

Kentucky Tech—Henderson County Area
Vocational Education Center
  2440 Zion Rd., Henderson 42420
  Prin. Dennis Harrell
  (502) 827-3810

Kentucky Tech—Madisonville Health
Occupations School
  701 N. Laffoon, Madisonville 42431
  Coord. Mary Stanley
  (502) 825-6552

Kentucky Tech—Madisonville State
Vocational-Technical School
  150 School Ave., Madisonville 42431
  Prin. James Pfeffer, Jr.
  (502) 825-6544

Kentucky Tech—Mayfield Area
Vocational Education Center
  710 Doughtit Rd., Mayfield 42066
  Coord. Jim Lawson
  (502) 247-4710

Kentucky Tech—Muhlenberg County Area
Vocational Education Center
  R.R. Box 67, Greenville 42345
  Coord. Andrew Swansey
  (502) 338-1271

Kentucky Tech—Murray Area Vocational
Education Center
  18th and Sycamore Sts., Murray
    42071
  Prin. Lynn Tackett
  (502) 753-1870

Kentucky Tech—Ohio County Area
Vocational Education Center
  P.O. Box 1406, U.S. 231 S., Hartford
    42347
  Coord. Ray Price
  (502) 274-9612

Kentucky Tech—Owensboro Vocational-
Technical School
  1501 Frederica St., Owensboro 42301
  Prin. Beverly Bosley
  (502) 686-3255

Kentucky Tech—Paducah Area
Vocational Education Center
  2400 Adams St., Paducah 42001
  Prin. Robert Rouff
  (502) 443-6592

Kentucky Tech—Webster County Area
Vocational Education Center
  P.O. Box 188, Dixon 42409
  Coord. Claude Hicks
  (502) 639-5035

Kentucky Tech—West Kentucky State
Vocational-Technical School
  Hwy. 60, W., Paducah 42002
  Prin. Lee Hicklin
  (502) 554-4991

LOUISIANA

State of Louisiana Board of Trustees for State Colleges and Universities
State Office Bldg., 3rd Fl., 150 Third St.,
Baton Rouge 70801
Pres. James A. Caillier
(504) 342-6950

Delgado Community College
501 City Park Ave., New Orleans
70119-4399
Pres. Ione H. Elioff
(504) 483-4114

Elaine P. Nunez Community College
3700 LaFontaine St., Chalmette 70043
Pres. Carol F. Hopson
(504) 278-7440

Grambling State University
P.O. Drawer 607, Grambling 71245
Pres. Harold W. Lundy
(318) 274-2000

Louisiana State University System
3810 W. Lakeshore Dr., Baton
Rouge 70808
Pres. Allen A. Copping
(504) 388-2111

*Louisiana State University Medical
Center*
433 Bolivar St., New Orleans
70112-2223
Chanc. Perry G. Rigby
(504) 568-4808

*Louisiana State University and
Agricultural and Mechanical
College*
Baton Rouge 70803
Chanc. William E. Davis
(504) 388-3202

*Louisiana State University at
Alexandria*
8100 Hwy. 71 S., Alexandria
71302-9121
Acting Chanc. Fred Beckerdite
(318) 445-3672

Louisiana State University at Eunice
P.O. Box 1129, Eunice 70535
Chanc. Michael Smith
(318) 457-7311

*Louisiana State University in
Shreveport*
One University Pl., Shreveport
71115-2399
Chanc. John R. Darling
(318) 797-5000

University of New Orleans
Lakefront, New Orleans 70148
Chanc. Gregory M. St. L.
O'Brien
(504) 286-6000

Louisiana Tech University
P.O. Box 3168, Tech Sta., Ruston
71272
Pres. Daniel D. Reneau
(318) 257-0211

McNeese State University
4100 Ryan St., Lake Charles 70609
Pres. Robert D. Hebert
(318) 475-5000

Nicholls State University
Louisiana Hwy. 1, Thibodaux 70310
Pres. Donald J. Ayo
(504) 446-8111

Northeast Louisiana University
700 University Ave., Monroe 71209
Pres. Lawson L. Swearingen, Jr.
(318) 342-1000

Northwestern State University
College Ave., Natchitoches 71497
Pres. Robert A. Alost
(318) 357-6491

Southeastern Louisiana University
P.O. Box 784, University Sta., Hammond 70402
Pres. G. Warren Smith
(504) 549-2000

**Southern University and Agricultural
and Mechanical College System**
Baton Rouge 70813
Pres. Dolores R. Spikes
(504) 771-4680

Southern University and Agricultural and Mechanical College at Baton Rouge
Southern Branch Post Office, Baton Rouge 70813
Chanc. Marvin L. Yates
(504) 771-4500

Southern University at New Orleans
6400 Press Dr., New Orleans 70126
Chanc. Robert B. Gex
(504) 286-5000

Southern University/Shreveport Bossier Campus
3050 Martin Luther King, Jr. Dr., Shreveport 71107
Chanc. Jerome G. Greene, Jr.
(318) 674-3300

University of Southwestern Louisiana
E. University Ave., Lafayette 70503
Pres. Ray P. Authement
(318) 231-6000

MAINE

University of Maine System
107 Maine Ave., Bangor 04401-1805
Chanc. J. Michael Orenduff
(207) 947-0336

University of Maine
Orono 04469-0102
Pres. Frederick E. Hutchinson
(207) 581-1512

University of Maine at Augusta
Augusta 04330
Pres. George P. Connick
(207) 621-3403

University of Maine at Farmington
86 Main St., Farmington 04938
Acting Pres. Sue A. Huseman
(207) 778-7000

University of Maine at Fort Kent
Pleasant St., Fort Kent 04743
Pres. Richard G. Dumont
(207) 834-3162

University of Maine at Machias
Machias 04654
Pres. Paul E. Nordstrom
(207) 255-3313

University of Maine at Presque Isle
181 Main St., Presque Isle 04769
Pres. W. Michael Easton
(207) 764-0311

University of Southern Maine
96 Falmouth St., Portland 04103
Pres. Richard L. Pattenaude
(207) 780-4141

MARYLAND

Maryland Higher Education Commission
The Jeffrey Bldg., 16 Francis St., Annapolis 21401-1781
Secretary of Education Shaila R. Aery
(410) 974-2971

Allegany Community College
Willowbrook Rd., Cumberland 21502
Pres. Donald L. Alexander
(301) 724-7700

Anne Arundel Community College
101 College Pkwy., Arnold 21012
Pres. Thomas E. Florestano
(410) 647-7100

Baltimore City Community College
2901 Liberty Heights Ave., Baltimore 21215
Pres. James D. Tschechtelin
(410) 333-5555

Catonsville Community College
800 S. Rolling Rd., Catonsville 21228
Pres. Frederick J. Walsh
(410) 455-6050

Cecil Community College
1000 North East Rd., North East 21901-1999
Pres. Robert L. Gell
(410) 287-6060

Charles County Community College
Mitchell Rd., P.O. Box 910, La Plata 20646
Pres. John M. Sine
(301) 934-2251

Chesapeake College
P.O. Box 8, Wye Mills 21679-0008
Pres. John R. Kotula
(410) 822-5400

Dundalk Community College
7200 Sollers Point Rd., Dundalk 21222-4692
Pres. Martha A. Smith
(410) 282-6700

Essex Community College
7201 Rossville Blvd., Baltimore 21237
Pres. Donald J. Slowinski
(410) 682-6000

Frederick Community College
7932 Oppossumtown Pike, Frederick 21702
Pres. Lee John Betts
(301) 846-2400

Garrett Community College
P.O. Box 151, Mosser Rd., McHenry 21541
Pres. Stephen J. Herman
(301) 387-6666

Hagerstown Junior College
11400 Robinwood Dr., Hagerstown 21742-6590
Pres. Norman P. Shea
(301) 790-2800

Harford Community College
401 Thomas Run Rd., Bel Air 21015
Pres. Richard J. Pappas
(410) 836-4000

Howard Community College
10901 Little Patuxent Pkwy., Columbia 21044
Pres. Dwight A. Burrill
(410) 992-4800

Montgomery College Central Administration
900 Hungerford Dr., Rockville 20850
Pres. Robert E. Parilla
(301) 279-5000

Montgomery College—Germantown Campus
20200 Observation Dr., Germantown 20874
Provost Noreen A. Lyne
(301) 353-7700

Montgomery College—Rockville Campus
51 Mannakee St., Rockville 20850
Provost Antoinette P. Hastings
(301) 279-5000

Montgomery College—Takoma Park Campus
Takoma Ave. and Fenton St., Takoma Park 20912
Provost O. Robert Brown
(301) 650-1300

Morgan State University
Hillen Rd. and Cold Spring La., Baltimore 21239
Pres. Earl S. Richardson
(410) 319-3333

Prince George's Community College
301 Largo Rd., Largo 20772-2199
Pres. Robert I. Bickford
(301) 336-6000

St. Mary's College of Maryland
St. Mary's City 20686
Pres. Edward T. Lewis
(301) 862-0200

University of Maryland System
3330 Metzerott Rd., Adelphi 20783-1690
Chanc. Donald N. Langenberg
(301) 445-1901

Bowie State University
14000 Jericho Park Rd., Bowie 20715
Pres. Nathaniel Pollard, Jr.
(301) 464-3000

Coppin State College
2500 W. North Ave., Baltimore 21216-3698
Pres. Calvin W. Burnett
(410) 383-5585

Frostburg State University
Frostburg 21532-1099
Pres. Catherine R. Gira
(301) 689-4000

Salisbury State University
Salisbury 21801
Pres. Thomas E. Bellavance
(410) 543-6000

Towson State University
Towson 21204-7097
Pres. Hoke L. Smith
(410) 830-2000

University of Baltimore
1420 N. Charles St., Baltimore 21201
Pres. H. Mebane Turner
(410) 625-3000

University of Maryland Baltimore County
5401 Wilkens Ave., Baltimore 21228
Pres. Freeman A. Hrabowski, III
(410) 455-1000

University of Maryland College Park
College Park 20742
Pres. William E. Kirwan
(301) 405-1000

University of Maryland Eastern Shore
Princess Anne 21853
Pres. William P. Hytche
(410) 651-6101

University of Maryland University College
University Blvd. at Adelphi Rd., College Park 20742-1600
Pres. T. Benjamin Massey
(301) 985-7000

University of Maryland at Baltimore
520 W. Lombard St., Baltimore 21201
Interim Pres. John W. Ryan
(410) 706-3100

Wor-Wic Community College
1409 Wesley Dr., Salisbury 21801
Pres. Arnold H. Maner
(410) 749-8181

MASSACHUSETTS

The Commonwealth of Massachusetts
Higher Education Coordinating Council
McCormack Bldg., Rm. 1401, One Ash-
burton Pl., Boston 02108-1696
Chanc. Stanley Z. Koplik
(617) 727-7785

Berkshire Community College
West St., Pittsfield 01201
Pres. Barbara Viniar
(413) 499-4660

Bridgewater State College
Bridgewater 02325
Pres. Adrian Tinsley
(508) 697-1200

Bristol Community College
777 Elsbree St., Fall River 02720-
7395
Pres. Eileen T. Farley
(508) 678-2811

Bunker Hill Community College
Rutherford Ave., Boston 02129
Pres. C. Scully Stikes
(617) 241-8600 x400

Cape Cod Community College
Rte. 132, West Barnstable 02668
Pres. Richard A. Kraus
(508) 362-2131

Fitchburg State College
160 Pearl St., Fitchburg 01420
Pres. Vincent J. Mara
(508) 345-2151

Framingham State College
100 State St., Framingham 01701-
9101
Pres. Paul F. Weller
(508) 626-4575

Greenfield Community College
One College Dr., Greenfield 01301
Pres. Katherine H. Sloan
(413) 774-3131

Holyoke Community College
303 Homestead Ave., Holyoke 01040
Pres. David M. Bartley
(413) 538-7000

Massachusetts Bay Community College
50 Oakland St., Wellesley Hills
02181-5399
Pres. Roger A. Van Winkle
(617) 237-1100

Massachusetts College of Art
621 Huntington Ave., Boston 02115
Pres. William F. O'Neil
(617) 232-1555

Massachusetts Maritime Academy
Academy Dr., Buzzards Bay 02532
Interim Pres. Christine M. Griffin
(617) 759-5761

Massasoit Community College
One Massasoit Blvd., Brockton 02402
Pres. Gerard F. Burke
(508) 588-9100

Middlesex Community College
Springs Rd., Bedford 01730
Pres. Carole A. Cowan
(617) 275-8910

Mount Wachusett Community College
444 Green St., Gardner 01440
Pres. Daniel M. Asquino
(508) 632-6600

North Adams State College
North Adams 01247
Pres. Thomas D. Aceto
(413) 664-4511

North Shore Community College
1 Ferncroft Rd., Danvers 01923-4093
Pres. George Traicoff
(508) 762-4000

Northern Essex Community College
100 Elliott Way, Haverhill 01830-
2399
Pres. John R. Dimitry
(508) 374-3900

Quinsigamond Community College
670 W. Boylston St., Worcester
01606
Pres. Clifford S. Peterson
(508) 853-2300

Roxbury Community College
1234 Columbus Ave., Roxbury
Crossing 02120-3400
Pres. Grace Carolyn Brown
(617) 427-0060

Salem State College
352 Lafayette St., Salem 01970-4589
Pres. Nancy D. Harrington
(508) 741-6000

Springfield Technical Community College
One Armory Sq., Springfield 01105
Pres. Andrew M. Scibelli
(413) 781-7822

University of Massachusetts President's Office
18 Tremont St., Ste. 800, Boston
02108
Pres. Michael K. Hooker
(617) 287-7000

University of Massachusetts Boston
100 Morrisey Blvd., Boston
02125-3393
Chanc. Sherry H. Penney
(617) 287-6800

University of Massachusetts Dartmouth
North Dartmouth 02747
Chanc. Peter Cressy
(508) 999-8004

University of Massachusetts Lowell
One University Ave., Lowell
01854
Chanc. William T. Hogan
(508) 934-4000

University of Massachusetts Medical Center at Worcester
55 Lake Ave., N., Worcester
01605
Chanc. Aaron Lazare
(508) 856-6630

University of Massachusetts at Amherst
Amherst 01003
Chanc. David K. Scott
(413) 545-3171

Westfield State College
Western Ave., Westfield 01086
Pres. Ronald L. Applbaum
(413) 568-3311

Worcester State College
486 Chandler St., Worcester 01602-2597
Pres. Kalyan K. Ghosh
(508) 793-8000

MICHIGAN

Michigan Department of Education
Community Coll. Services Unit, P.O. Box 30008, Lansing 48909
Dir. Ronald L. Root
(517) 373-3900

Alpena Community College
666 Johnson St., Alpena 49707
Pres. Donald L. Newport
(517) 356-9021

Bay de Noc Community College
2001 N. Lincoln Rd., Escanaba 49829
Pres. Dwight E. Link
(906) 786-5802

Central Michigan University
Mount Pleasant 48859
Pres. Leonard E. Plachta
(517) 774-4000

Charles Stewart Mott Community College
1401 E. Court St., Flint 48503
Pres. Allen D. Arnold
(313) 762-0200

Delta College
University Center 48710
Pres. Peter D. Boyse
(517) 686-9000

Eastern Michigan University
Ypsilanti 48197
Pres. William E. Shelton
(313) 487-1849

Ferris State University
Big Rapids 49307
Pres. Helen Popovich
(616) 592-2100

Glen Oaks Community College
62249 Shimmel Rd., Centreville 49032
Pres. Philip G. Ward
(616) 467-9945

Gogebic Community College
E-4946 Jackson Rd., Ironwood 49938
Pres. James R. Grote
(906) 932-4231

Grand Rapids Community College
143 Bostwick St., N.E., Grand Rapids 49503
Pres. Richard W. Calkins
(616) 771-4000

Grand Valley State University
One Campus Dr., Allendale 49401
Pres. Arend D. Lubbers
(616) 895-6611

Henry Ford Community College
5101 Evergreen Rd., Dearborn 48128
Pres. Andrew A. Mazzara
(313) 271-2750

Highland Park Community College
Glendale Ave. at Third St., Highland Park 48203
Pres. Thomas Lloyd
(313) 252-0475

Jackson Community College
2111 Emmons Rd., Jackson 49201
Pres. E. Lee Howser
(517) 787-0800

Kalamazoo Valley Community College
6767 W. O Ave., Kalamazoo 49009
Pres. Marilyn J. Schlack
(616) 372-5200

Kellogg Community College
450 North Ave., Battle Creek 49017-3397
Pres. Paul R. Ohm
(616) 965-3931

Kirtland Community College
10775 N. St. Helen Rd., Roscommon 48653
Pres. Dorothy N. Franke
(517) 275-5121

Lake Michigan College
2755 E. Napier St., Benton Harbor 49022
Interim Pres. Greg Korock
(616) 927-3571

Lake Superior State University
1000 College Dr., Sault Ste. Marie 49783
Pres. Robert D. Arbuckle
(906) 632-6841

Lansing Community College
521 N. Washington Sq., Box 40010,
Lansing 48901-7210
Pres. Abel B. Sykes, Jr.
(517) 483-1851

Macomb Community College
14500 E. Twelve Mile Rd., Warren
48093
Pres. Albert L. Lorenzo
(313) 445-7000

Michigan State University
East Lansing 48824
Pres. M. Peter McPherson
(517) 355-1855

Michigan Technological University
1400 Townsend Dr., Houghton 49931
Pres. Curtis J. Tompkins
(906) 487-1885

Mid Michigan Community College
1375 S. Clare Ave., Harrison 48625
Pres. Charles J. Corrigan, Ph.D.
(517) 386-6622

Monroe County Community College
1555 S. Raisinville Rd., Monroe
48161
Pres. Gerald D. Welch
(313) 242-7300

Montcalm Community College
2800 College Dr., S.W., Sidney
48885
Pres. Donald C. Burns
(517) 328-2111

Muskegon Community College
221 S. Quarterline Rd., Muskegon
49442
Pres. James L. Stevenson
(616) 773-0643

North Central Michigan College
1515 Howard St., Petoskey 49770
Pres. Robert B. Graham
(616) 348-6600

Northern Michigan University
Marquette 49855
Pres. William E. Vandament
(906) 227-2242

Northwestern Michigan College
1701 E. Front St., Traverse City
49684
Pres. Timothy G. Quinn
(616) 922-0650

Oakland Community College
2480 Opdyke Rd., Bloomfield Hills
48304-2266
Chanc. Patsy J. Fulton
(313) 540-1500

Oakland University
Rochester 48309
Pres. Sandra Packard
(313) 370-2100

Saginaw Valley State University
7400 Bay Rd., University Center
48710
Pres. Eric R. Gilbertson
(517) 790-4000

Schoolcraft College
18600 Haggerty Rd., Livonia 48152
Pres. Richard W. McDowell
(313) 462-4400

Southwestern Michigan College
58900 Cherry Grove Rd., Dowagiac
49047-9793
Pres. David C. Briegel
(616) 782-5113

St. Clair County Community College
323 Erie St., P.O. Box 5015, Port
Huron 48061-5015
Pres. R. Ernest Dear
(313) 984-3881

Washtenaw Community College
4800 E. Huron River Dr., P.O. Box
D-1, Ann Arbor 48106
Pres. Gunder A. Myran
(313) 973-3300

Wayne County Community College
801 W. Fort St., Detroit 48226-3010
Pres. Rafael L. Cortada
(313) 496-2510

Wayne State University
Detroit 48202
Pres. David W. Adamany
(313) 577-2424

West Shore Community College
  3000 N. Stiles Rd., P.O. Box 277,
    Scottville 49454
  Pres. William M. Anderson
  (616) 845-6211

Western Michigan University
  Kalamazoo 49008
  Pres. Diether H. Haenicke
  (616) 387-1000

The University of Michigan System
  Ann Arbor 48109
  Pres. James J. Duderstadt
  (313) 764-1817

University of Michigan
  Ann Arbor 48109
  Pres. James J. Duderstadt
  (313) 764-1817

University of Michigan—Dearborn
  4901 Evergreen Rd., Dearborn 48128
  Chanc. James C. Renick
  (313) 593-5000

University of Michigan—Flint
  Flint 48502
  Chanc. James Renick
  (313) 762-3000

MINNESOTA

Minnesota Community College System
203 Capitol Square Bldg., 550 Cedar St.,
St. Paul 55101
Chanc. Geraldine A. Evans
(612) 296-3990

Anoka-Ramsey Community College
11200 Mississippi Blvd., Coon
Rapids 55433
Pres. Patrick M. Johns
(612) 422-3435

Arrowhead Community College Region
1855 E. Hwy. 169, Grand Rapids
55744
Pres. Greg Braxton-Brown
(218) 327-4380

Hibbing Community College
1515 E. 25th St., Hibbing 55746
Pres. Anthony J. Kuznik
(218) 262-6700

Itasca Community College
1851 E. Hwy. 169, Grand
Rapids 55744
Pres. Lawrence Dukes
(218) 327-4461

Mesabi Community College
905 W. Chestnut St., Virginia
55792
Pres. Richard N. Kohlhase
(800) 657-3860

Rainy River Community College
Hwy. 11-71 and 15th St., International Falls 56649
Pres. Allen Rasmussen
(218) 285-7722

Vermilion Community College
1900 E. Camp St., Ely 55731
Pres. Jon Harris
(218) 365-7200

Austin Community College
1600 8th Ave., N.W., Austin 55912
Pres. Vicky R. Smith
(507) 433-0508

Brainerd Community College
501 W. College Dr., Brainerd 56401
Pres. Sally Jane Ihne
(218) 828-2525

Fergus Falls Community College
1414 College Way, Fergus Falls 56537
Pres. Daniel F. True
(218) 739-7500

Inver Hills Community College
8445 College Tr., Inver Grove
Heights 55076
Pres. Steven R. Wallace
(612) 450-8500

Lakewood Community College
3401 Century Ave., White Bear Lake
55110
Pres. James Meznek
(612) 779-3200

Minneapolis Community College
1501 Hennepin Ave., Minneapolis
55403
Pres. Jacquelyn M. Belcher
(612) 341-7000

Normandale Community College
9700 France Ave. S., Bloomington
55431
Pres. Thomas J. Horak
(612) 832-6000

North Hennepin Community College
7411 85th Ave. N., Brooklyn Park
55445
Pres. Frederick W. Capshaw
(612) 424-0820

Northland Community College
Hwy. 1 E., Thief River Falls 56701
Provost James Haviland
(218) 681-2181

Rochester Community College
851 30th Ave., S.E., Rochester
55904-4999
Pres. Karen E. Nagle
(507) 285-7210

Willmar Community College
P.O. Box 797, Willmar 56201
Pres. Harold G. Conradi
(612) 231-5102

Worthington Community College
1450 Collegeway, Worthington 56187
Pres. Conrad W. Burchill
(507) 372-2107

Minnesota State University System
230 Park Office Bldg., 555 Park St., St. Paul 55103
Chanc. Terrence J. MacTaggart
(612) 296-2844

Bemidji State University
1500 Birchmont Dr., N.E., Bemidji 56601-2699
Interim Pres. Linda L. Baer
(218) 755-2000

Mankato State University
Mankato 56002-8400
Pres. Richard R. Rush
(507) 389-1111

Metropolitan State University
700 E. 7th St., St. Paul 55106-5000
Pres. Susan A. Cole
(612) 772-7777

Moorhead State University
1104 7th Ave. S., Moorhead 56563
Pres. Roland Dille
(218) 236-2011

Southwest State University
1501 State St., Marshall 56258
Pres. Oliver J. Ford, III
(507) 537-6272

St. Cloud State University
740 Fourth Ave. S., St. Cloud 56301-4498
Pres. Robert Bess
(612) 255-0121

Winona State University
Winona 55987
Pres. Darrell W. Krueger
(507) 457-5003

University of Minnesota System
100 Church St., S.E., Minneapolis 55455-0110
Pres. Nils Hasselmo
(612) 625-5000

University of Minnesota—Crookston
Hwys. 2 and 75 N., Crookston 56716
Chanc. Donald G. Sargeant
(218) 281-6510

University of Minnesota—Duluth
Duluth 55812
Chanc. Lawrence A. Ianni
(218) 726-8000

University of Minnesota—Morris
600 E. Fourth St., Morris 56267
Chanc. David C. Johnson
(612) 589-2211

University of Minnesota—Twin Cities
100 Church St., S.E., Minneapolis 55455
Pres. Nils Hasselmo
(612) 625-5000

MISSISSIPPI

Mississippi Board of Trustees of State Institutions of Higher Learning
3825 Ridgewood Rd., Jackson 39211
Commissioner W. Ray Cleere
(601) 982-6611

Alcorn State University
P.O. Box 359, Lorman 39096-9402
Pres. Walter Washington
(601) 877-6100

Delta State University
Hwy. 8 W., Cleveland 38733
Pres. F. Kent Wyatt
(601) 846-3000

Jackson State University
1400 J.R. Lynch St., Jackson 39217
Pres. James E. Lyons
(601) 968-2121

Mississippi State University
Mississippi State 39762
Pres. Donald W. Zacharias
(601) 325-2323

Mississippi University for Women
P.O. Box W-1600, Columbus 39701
Pres. Clyda S. Rent
(601) 329-4750

Mississippi Valley State University
1400 Hwy. 82 W., Itta Bena 38941
Pres. William W. Sutton
(601) 254-9041

University of Mississippi
University 38677
Chanc. R. Gerald Turner
(601) 232-7211

University of Mississippi Medical Center
2500 N. State St., Jackson 39216-4505
Vice Chanc. Norman Crooks Nelson, M.D.
(601) 984-1000

The University of Southern Mississippi
Southern Sta., Box 5001, Hattiesburg 39406-5001
Pres. Aubrey K. Lucas
(601) 266-4111

Mississippi State Board for Community and Junior Colleges
3825 Ridgewood Rd., Jackson 39211
Exec. Dir. Olon E. Ray
(601) 982-6518

Coahoma Community College
3240 Friars Point Rd., Clarksdale 38614
Pres. Vivian M. Presley
(601) 627-2571

Copiah-Lincoln Community College
P.O. Box 457, Wesson 39191
Pres. Billy B. Thames
(601) 643-5101

East Central Community College
P.O. Box 129, Decatur 39327-0129
Pres. Eddie M. Smith
(601) 635-2111

East Mississippi Community College
P.O. Box 158, Scooba 39358
Pres. Thomas L. Davis
(601) 476-8442

Hinds Community College
Raymond 39154
Pres. V. Clyde Muse
(601) 857-5261

Holmes Community College
P.O. Box 369, Goodman 39079
Pres. Starkey A. Morgan
(601) 472-2312

Itawamba Community College
602 W. Hill St., Fulton 38843-1099
Pres. David Cole
(601) 862-3101

Jones County Junior College
900 Court St., Ellisville 39437
Pres. T. Terrel Tisdale
(601) 477-4000

Meridian Community College
910 Hwy. 19 N., Meridian 39307
Pres. William F. Scaggs
(601) 483-8241

Mississippi Delta Community College
P.O. Box 668, Moorhead 38761
Pres. Bobby S. Garvin
(601) 246-5631

*Mississippi Gulf Coast Community
    College*
    P.O. Box 67, Perkinston 39573
    Pres. Barry L. Mellinger
    (601) 928-5211

Northeast Mississippi Community College
    Cunningham Blvd., Booneville
        38829
    Pres. Joe M. Childers
    (601) 728-7751

Northwest Mississippi Community College
    510 N. Panola, Senatobia 38668
    Pres. David M. Haraway
    (601) 562-3200

Pearl River Community College
    101 Hwy. 11 N., Poplarville 39470-
        2298
    Pres. Ted J. Alexander
    (601) 795-6801

Southwest Mississippi Community College
    Summit 39666
    Pres. Horace C. Holmes
    (601) 276-2000

MISSOURI

Missouri Coordinating Board for Higher Education
3515 Amazonas, Jefferson City 65109
Commissioner Charles J. McClain
(314) 751-2361

Central Missouri State University
Warrensburg 64093
Pres. Ed M. Elliott
(816) 543-4111

Crowder College
601 Laclede, Neosho 64850
Pres. Kent Farnsworth
(417) 451-3223

East Central College
P.O. Box 529, Union 63084
Pres. Dale L. Gibson
(314) 583-5193

Harris-Stowe State College
3026 Laclede Ave., St. Louis 63103
Pres. Henry Givens, Jr.
(314) 340-3366

Heart of the Ozarks Technical Community College
1417 N. Jefferson Ave., Springfield 65802
Pres. Norman K. Myers
(417) 895-7000

Jefferson College
1000 Viking Dr., Hillsboro 63050
Interim Pres. Ronald J. Fundis
(314) 789-3951

Lincoln University
820 Chestnut St., Jefferson City 65102-0029
Pres. Wendell G. Rayburn, Sr.
(314) 681-5000

The Metropolitan Community College District
3200 Broadway, Kansas City 64111-2429
Chanc. Wayne E. Giles
(816) 759-1011

Longview Community College
500 Longview Rd., Lee's Summit 64081
Pres. Aldo W. Leker
(816) 672-2000

Maple Woods Community College
2601 N.E. Barry Rd., Kansas City 64156
Pres. Stephen R. Brainard
(816) 437-3000

Penn Valley Community College
3201 S.W. Trafficway, Kansas City 64111
Pres. E. Paul Williams
(816) 759-4000

Mineral Area College
P.O. Box 1000, Hwy. 67 and 32, Park Hills 63601
Pres. Dixie A. Kohn
(314) 431-4593

Missouri Southern State College
3950 Newman Rd., Joplin 64801
Pres. Julio S. Leon
(417) 625-9300

Missouri Western State College
4525 Downs Dr., St. Joseph 64507
Pres. Janet G. Murphy
(816) 271-4200

Moberly Area Community College
College and Rollins Sts., Moberly 65270
Pres. Andrew Komar, Jr.
(816) 263-4110

North Central Missouri College
1301 Main St., Trenton 64683
Pres. James E. Selby
(816) 359-3948

Northeast Missouri State University
Kirksville 63501
Pres. Russell G. Warren
(816) 785-4000

Northwest Missouri State University
800 University Dr., Maryville 64468-6001
Pres. Dean L. Hubbard
(816) 562-1110

Southeast Missouri State University
One University Plaza, Cape Girardeau 63701
Pres. Kala M. Stroup
(314) 651-2000

Southwest Missouri State University
901 S. National Ave., Springfield 65804
Pres. John H. Keiser
(417) 836-5000

St. Charles County Community College
4601 Mid Rivers Mall Dr., P.O. Box 76975, St. Peters 63376
Pres. Donald D. Shook
(314) 922-8000

St. Louis Community College Center
300 S. Broadway, St. Louis 63102-1708
Chanc. Gwendolyn W. Stephenson
(314) 539-5150

> *St. Louis Community College at Florissant Valley*
> 3400 Pershall Rd., St. Louis 63135
> Pres. Michael T. Murphy
> (314) 595-4200

> *St. Louis Community College at Forest Park*
> 5600 Oakland Ave., St. Louis 63110
> Pres. Henry D. Shannon
> (314) 644-9100

> *St. Louis Community College at Meramec*
> 11333 Big Bend Blvd., Kirkwood 63122
> Pres. Richard A. Black
> (314) 984-7500

State Fair Community College
3201 W. 16th St., Sedalia 65301
Pres. Marvin R. Fielding
(816) 530-5800

Three Rivers Community College
2080 Three Rivers Blvd., Poplar Bluff 63901
Pres. Stephen M. Poort
(314) 840-9600

University of Missouri System
321 University Hall, Columbia 65211
Pres. George A. Russell
(314) 882-2011

> *University of Missouri—Columbia*
> Columbia 65211
> Chanc. Charles A. Kiesler
> (314) 882-2121

> *University of Missouri—Kansas City*
> 5100 Rockhill Rd., Kansas City 64110
> Chanc. Eleanor B. Schwartz
> (816) 235-1000

> *University of Missouri—Rolla*
> Rolla 65401
> Chanc. John T. Park
> (314) 341-4114

> *University of Missouri—St. Louis*
> 8001 Natural Bridge Rd., St. Louis 63121
> Chanc. Blanche M. Touhill
> (314) 553-5000

MONTANA

Montana Community College System
2500 Broadway, Helena 59620-3101
Coord. David L. Toppen, Ph.D.
(406) 444-6570

Dawson Community College
Glendive 59330
Pres. Donald H. Kettner
(406) 365-3396

Flathead Valley Community College
777 Grandview Dr., Kalispell 59901
Pres. Howard L. Fryett
(406) 756-3822

Miles Community College
Miles City 59301
Pres. Judson H. Flower
(406) 232-3031

Montana University System
2500 Broadway, Helena 59620
Commissioner Jeff Baker
(406) 444-6570

Billings Vocational-Technical Center
3803 Central Ave., Billings 59102
Dir. George E. Bell
(406) 656-4445

Butte Vocational-Technical Center
Basin Creek Rd., Butte 59701
Dir. Jane G. Baker
(406) 494-2894

Eastern Montana College
Billings 59101
Pres. Bruce H. Carpenter
(406) 657-2011

Great Falls Vocational-Technical Center
2100 16th Ave., S., Great Falls
59405
Dir. Willard R. Weaver
(406) 771-1240

Helena Vocational-Technical Center
115 N. Roberts St., Helena 59620
Dir. Alex Capdeville
(406) 444-6800

Missoula Vocational-Technical Center
909 South Ave., W., Missoula 59801
Dir. Dennis N. Lerum
(406) 542-6811

Montana College of Mineral Science and Technology
Butte 59701
Pres. Lindsay D. Norman, Jr.
(406) 496-4101

Montana State University
Bozeman 59717
Pres. Michael Malone
(406) 994-0211

Northern Montana College
P.O. Box 7751, Havre 59501
Pres. William Daehling
(406) 265-3221

The University of Montana
Missoula 59812
Pres. George M. Dennison
(406) 243-0211

Western Montana College
710 S. Atlantic St., Dillon 59725-3511
Pres. Sheila Sterns
(406) 683-7151

NEBRASKA

Nebraska Coordinating Commission for Postsecondary Education
140 N. 8th St., Ste. 300, P.O. Box 95005, Lincoln 68509-5005
Exec. Dir. Bruce G. Stahl
(402) 471-2847

Central Community College
P.O. Box 4903, Grand Island 68802-4903
Pres. Joseph W. Preusser
(308) 384-5220

Chadron State College
10th and Main Sts., Chadron 69337
Pres. Samuel H. Rankin, Jr.
(308) 432-4451

Metropolitan Community College
P.O. Box 3777, Omaha 68103
Pres. J. Richard Gilliland
(402) 449-8400

Mid-Plains Community College Area
416 N. Jeffers, North Platte 69101
Chanc. William G. Hasemeyer
(308) 534-9265

McCook Community College
1205 E. Third St., McCook 69001
Pres. Robert G. Smallfoot
(800) 658-4348

Mid-Plains Community College
Rte. 4, Box 1, North Platte 69101
Pres. Kenneth L. Aten
(308) 532-8740

Northeast Community College
801 E. Benjamin Ave., P.O. Box 469, Norfolk 68702-0469
Pres. Robert P. Cox
(402) 371-2020

Peru State College
Peru 68421
Pres. Robert L. Burns
(402) 872-2239

Southeast Community College
8800 O St., Lincoln 68520
Interim Chanc. Jack Huck
(402) 437-2500

University of Nebraska
3835 Holdrege St., Lincoln 68583
Pres. L. Dennis Smith
(402) 472-2111

University of Nebraska Medical Center
600 S. 42nd St., Omaha 68198-6605
Chanc. Carol A. Aschenbrener
(402) 559-4000

University of Nebraska at Kearney
905 W. 25th St., Kearney 68849
Chanc. Gladys Styles Johnston, Ph.D.
(308) 236-8441

University of Nebraska at Omaha
60th and Dodge Sts., Omaha 68182
Chanc. Delbert D. Weber
(402) 554-2800

University of Nebraska—Lincoln
Lincoln 68583
Chanc. Graham B. Spanier
(402) 472-7211

Wayne State College
200 E. 10th St., Wayne 68787
Pres. Donald J. Mash
(402) 375-7200

Western Nebraska Community College
1601 E. 27th St., Scottsbluff 69361
Pres. John N. Harms
(308) 635-3606

NEVADA

University and Community College System of Nevada
2601 Enterprise Rd., Reno 89512
Interim Chanc. John Richardson
(702) 784-4901

Community College of Southern Nevada
3200 E. Cheyenne Ave., North Las
Vegas 89030
Pres. Paul E. Meacham
(702) 643-6060

Northern Nevada Community College
901 Elm St., Elko 89801
Pres. Ronald Remington
(702) 738-8493

Truckee Meadows Community College
7000 Dandini Blvd., Reno 89512
Pres. John W. Gwaltney
(702) 673-7000

University of Nevada, Las Vegas
4505 Maryland Pkwy., Las Vegas
89154
Pres. Robert C. Maxson
(702) 739-3201

University of Nevada, Reno
Reno 89557
Pres. Joseph N. Crowley
(702) 784-4805

Western Nevada Community College
2201 W. Nye La., Carson City 89703
Pres. Anthony D. Calabro
(702) 887-3000

NEW HAMPSHIRE

University System of New Hampshire
Dunlap Ctr., 25 Concord Rd., Durham
03824-3563
Chanc. William J. Farrell
(603) 868-1800

College for Lifelong Learning
Durham 03824-3547
Dean Victor B. Montana
(603) 862-1692

Keene State College
229 Main St., Keene 03431
Interim Pres. Richard E. Cunningham
(603) 352-1909

Plymouth State College
Plymouth 03264
Pres. Donald P. Wharton
(603) 535-5000

University of New Hampshire
Durham 03824
Pres. Dale F. Nitzschke
(603) 862-1234

NEW JERSEY

State of New Jersey Department of Higher Education
20 W. State St., CN 542, Trenton 08625
Chanc. Edward D. Goldberg, Ph.D.
(609) 292-4310

Office of Community Colleges
20 W. State St., CN 542, Trenton 08625
Dir. Michael B. Villano
(609) 984-2680

Atlantic Community College
5100 Black Horse Pike, Mays Landing 08330-2699
Interim Pres. John T. May
(609) 625-1111

Bergen Community College
400 Paramus Rd., Paramus 07652
Pres. Jose Lopez-Isa
(201) 447-7100

Brookdale Community College
Newman Springs Rd., Lincroft 07738
Pres. Peter F. Burnham
(908) 842-1900

Burlington County College
County Rte. 530, Pemberton 08068-1599
Pres. Robert C. Messina, Jr.
(609) 894-9311

Camden County College
P.O. Box 200, Blackwood 08012
Pres. Phyllis Della Vecchia
(609) 227-7200

County College of Morris
Rte. 10 and Center Grove Rd., Randolph 07869
Pres. Edward J. Yaw
(201) 328-5000

Cumberland County College
College Dr., P.O. Box 517, Vineland 08360
Pres. Roland J. Chapdelaine
(609) 691-8600

Essex County College
303 University Ave., Newark 07102
Pres. A. Zachary Yamba
(201) 877-3000

Gloucester County College
Tanyard Rd., Deptford Twp., R.R. 4, P.O. Box 203, Sewell 08080
Pres. Richard H. Jones
(609) 468-5000

Hudson County Community College
901 Bergen Ave., Jersey City 07306
Pres. Glen Gabert
(201) 656-2020

Mercer County Community College
1200 Old Trenton Rd., Box B, Trenton 08690-0182
Pres. Thomas D. Sepe
(609) 586-4800

Middlesex County College
155 Mill Rd., P.O. Box 3050, Edison 08818
Pres. Flora Mancuso-Edwards
(908) 548-6000

Ocean County College
College Dr., CN 2001, Toms River 08753-2001
Pres. Milton Shaw
(908) 255-4000

Passaic County Community College
One College Blvd., Paterson 07505-1179
Pres. Elliott Collins
(201) 684-6800

Raritan Valley Community College
P.O. Box 3300, Hwy. 28 and Lamington Rd., Somerville 08876
Pres. S. Charles Irace
(908) 526-1200

Salem Community College
460 Hollywood Ave., Carneys Point 08069
Pres. Linda C. Jolly
(609) 299-2100

Sussex County Community College
College Hill, Newton 07860
Pres. William A. Connor
(201) 579-5400

Union County College
1033 Springfield Ave., Cranford
07016
Pres. Thomas H. Brown, Ph.D.
(908) 709-7000

Warren County Community College
Box 55A, Rte. 57 W., Washington 07882
Pres. Vincent De Sanctis
(908) 689-1090

Office of Senior Institutions
20 W. State St., CN 542, Trenton
08625
Dir. Sarah Kleinman
(609) 292-7170

Jersey City State College
2039 Kennedy Blvd., Jersey
City 07305
Pres. Carlos Hernandez
(201) 200-2000

Kean College of New Jersey
1000 Morris Ave., Union 07083
Pres. Elsa Gomez
(908) 527-2000

Montclair State College
Valley Rd. and Normal Ave.,
Upper Montclair 07043-1624
Pres. Irvin D. Reid
(201) 893-4000

New Jersey Institute of Technology
Univ. Heights, Newark 07102-
9938
Pres. Saul K. Fenster
(201) 596-3000

Ramapo College of New Jersey
505 Ramapo Valley Rd., Mahwah 07430-1680
Pres. Robert A. Scott
(201) 529-7500

Rowan College of New Jersey
201 Mullica Hill Rd., Glassboro
08028-1701
Pres. Herman D. James
(609) 863-5000

**Rutgers, The State University of
New Jersey Central Office**
Old Queens Bldg., New
Brunswick 08903
Pres. Francis L. Lawrence
(908) 932-7495

*Rutgers, The State University of
New Jersey Camden Campus*
311 N. Fifth St., Camden
08102
Provost Walter K. Gordon
(609) 757-1766

*Rutgers, The State University of
New Jersey New Brunswick
Campus*
Old Queens Bldg., New
Brunswick 08903
Provost Joseph A. Potenza
(908) 932-1766

*Rutgers, The State University of
New Jersey Newark Campus*
15 Washington St., Newark
07102
Provost Norman Samuels
(201) 648-1766

Stockton State College
Jimmy Leeds Rd., Pomona 08240
Pres. Vera King Farris
(609) 652-1776

Thomas A. Edison State College
101 W. State St., Trenton
08608-1176
Pres. George A. Pruitt
(609) 984-1100

Trenton State College
Hillwood Lakes, CN 4700,
Trenton 08650-4700
Pres. Harold W. Eickhoff
(609) 771-1855

*University of Medicine and Dentistry
of New Jersey*
30 Bergen St., Newark 07107-
3000
Pres. Stanley S. Bergen, Jr.
(201) 982-4300

*William Paterson College of New
Jersey*
300 Pompton Rd., Wayne 07470
Pres. Arnold S. Speert
(201) 595-2000

NEW MEXICO

New Mexico Commission on Higher Education
1068 Cerrillos Rd., Santa Fe 87501-4295
Exec. Dir. Bruce D. Hamlett
(505) 827-7383

Albuquerque Technical Vocational Institute
525 Buena Vista Dr., S.E., Albuquerque 87106
Pres. Ted F. Martinez
(505) 224-3000

Clovis Community College
417 Schepps Blvd., Clovis 88101
Pres. Jay Gurley
(505) 769-2811

Eastern New Mexico University
Portales 88130
Pres. Everett L. Frost
(505) 562-2121

Luna Vocational Technical Institute
P.O. Drawer K, Las Vegas 87701
Pres. Samuel F. Vigil
(505) 454-2500

New Mexico Highlands University
National Ave., Las Vegas 87701
Pres. Gilbert Sanchez
(505) 454-3229

New Mexico Institute of Mining and Technology
Socorro 87801
Pres. Daniel H. Lopez
(505) 835-5011

New Mexico Junior College
5317 Lovington Hwy., Hobbs 88240
Pres. Charles D. Hays, Jr.
(505) 392-4510

New Mexico Military Institute
100 W. College Blvd., Roswell 88201
Supt. Winfield W. Scott, Jr.
(505) 624-8000

New Mexico State University System
Las Cruces 88003-8001
Pres. James E. Halligan
(505) 646-2035

Dona Ana Branch Community College
Box 30001, Las Cruces 88003
Provost Donaciano Gonzalez
(505) 527-7510

New Mexico State University
Box 30001, Las Cruces 88003
Pres. James E. Halligan
(505) 885-8831

New Mexico State University at Alamogordo
P.O. Box 477, Alamogordo 88311-0477
Provost Charles R. Reidlinger
(505) 439-3600

New Mexico State University at Carlsbad
1500 University Dr., Carlsbad 88220
Provost Douglas E. Burgham
(505) 885-8831

Northern New Mexico Community College
1002 N. Onate St., Espanola 87532
Pres. Connie A. Valdez
(505) 747-2100

San Juan College
4601 College Blvd., Farmington 87402
Pres. James C. Henderson
(505) 326-3311

Santa Fe Community College
P.O. Box 4187, Santa Fe 87502-4187
Pres. Leonardo de La Garza
(505) 471-8200

The University of New Mexico
Albuquerque 87131
Pres. Richard E. Peck
(505) 277-0111

Western New Mexico University
P.O. Box 680, 1000 W. College Ave., Silver City 88062
Pres. John E. Counts
(505) 538-6238

NEW YORK

The City University of New York Office of the Chancellor
535 E. 80th St., New York 10021
Chanc. W. Ann Reynolds
(212) 794-5555

Bernard M. Baruch College
17 Lexington Ave., New York 10010
Pres. Matthew Goldstein
(212) 447-3000

Borough of Manhattan Community College
199 Chambers St., New York 10007
Acting Pres. Stephen Curtis
(212) 346-8000

Bronx Community College
W. 181st St. and University Ave., Bronx 10453
Acting President Leo A. Corbie
(718) 220-6920

Brooklyn College
2900 Bedford Ave., Brooklyn 11210-2889
Pres. Vernon E. Lattin
(718) 951-5000

City College
Convent Ave. at 138th St., New York 10031
Pres. Yolanda T. Moses
(212) 650-7000

College of Staten Island
130 Stuyvesant Pl., Staten Island 10301
Interim Pres. Felix Cardegna
(718) 982-2000

Graduate School and University Center
33 W. 42nd St., New York 10036
Pres. Frances Degen Horowitz
(212) 642-1600

Herbert H. Lehman College
Bedford Park Blvd. W., Bronx 10468
Pres. Ricardo R. Fernandez
(718) 960-8000

Hostos Community College
475 Grand Concourse, Bronx 10451
Pres. Isaura Santiago
(718) 518-4444

Hunter College
695 Park Ave., New York 10021
Acting Pres. Blanche D. Blank
(212) 772-4000

John Jay College of Criminal Justice
899 10th Ave., New York 10019
Pres. Gerald W. Lynch
(212) 237-8000

Kingsborough Community College
2001 Oriental Blvd., Manhattan Beach, Brooklyn 11235
Pres. Leon M. Goldstein
(718) 368-5000

La Guardia Community College
31-10 Thomson Ave., Long Island City 11101
Pres. Raymond C. Bowen
(718) 482-7000

Medgar Evers College
1650 Bedford Ave., Brooklyn 11225
Pres. Edison O. Jackson
(718) 270-4900

New York City Technical College
300 Jay St., Brooklyn 11201
Pres. Charles W. Meredith
(718) 260-5000

Queens College
65-30 Kissena Blvd., Flushing 11367
Pres. Shirley Strum Kenny
(718) 997-5000

Queensborough Community College
222-05 56th Ave., Bayside 11364-1497
Pres. Kurt R. Schmeller
(718) 631-6262

York College
94-20 Guy R. Brewer Blvd., Jamaica 11451
Pres. Josephine D. Davis
(718) 262-2000

State University of New York System Office
State University Plaza, Albany 12246
Interim Chanc. Joseph C. Burke
(518) 443-5355

State University College at Brockport
Brockport 14420
Pres. John E. Van de Wetering
(716) 395-2211

State University College at Buffalo
1300 Elmwood Ave., Buffalo 14222
Pres. F.C. Richardson
(716) 878-4000

State University College at Cortland
P.O. Box 2000, Cortland 13045
Pres. James M. Clark
(607) 753-2201

State University College at Fredonia
Fredonia 14063
Pres. Donald A. MacPhee
(716) 673-3111

State University College at Geneseo
Geneseo 14454
Pres. Carol C. Harter
(716) 245-5211

State University College at New Paltz
New Paltz 12561
Pres. Alice Chandler
(914) 257-2121

State University College at Old Westbury
P.O. Box 210, Old Westbury 11568
Pres. L. Eudora Pettigrew
(516) 876-3000

State University College at Oneonta
Oneonta 13820-4015
Pres. Alan B. Donovan
(607) 436-3500

State University College at Oswego
Oswego 13126
Pres. Stephen L. Weber
(315) 341-2500

State University College at Plattsburgh
Plattsburgh 12901
Interim Pres. Walter Vom Saal
(518) 564-2000

State University College at Potsdam
Pierrepont Ave., Potsdam 13676
Pres. William C. Merwin
(315) 267-2000

State University College at Purchase
735 Anderson Hill Rd., Purchase
10577-1400
Pres. Bill Lacy
(914) 251-6000

*State University of New York College of
Agriculture and Technology at
Cobleskill*
Cobleskill 12043
Pres. Kenneth E. Wing
(518) 234-5011

*State University of New York College of
Agriculture and Technology at
Morrisville*
Morrisville 13408
Pres. Frederick Woodward
(315) 684-6000

*State University of New York College of
Environmental Science and Forestry at
Syracuse*
Syracuse 13210
Pres. Ross S. Whaley
(315) 470-6500

*State University of New York College of
Optometry at New York City*
100 E. 24th St., New York 10010
Pres. Alden N. Haffner
(212) 420-4900

*State University of New York College of
Technology at Alfred*
Huntington Bldg., Alfred 14802
Pres. William D. Rezak
(607) 587-4111

*State University of New York College of
Technology at Canton*
Cornell Dr., Canton 13617
Pres. Joseph L. Kennedy
(315) 386-7011

*State University of New York College of
Technology at Delhi*
Delhi 13753
Pres. Mary Ellen Duncan
(607) 746-4111

State University of New York College of Technology at Farmingdale
Melville Rd., Farmingdale 11735
Pres. Frank A. Cipriani
(516) 420-2000

State University of New York Empire State College
One Union Ave., Saratoga Springs 12866
Pres. James W. Hall
(518) 587-2100

State University of New York Health Science Center at Brooklyn
450 Clarkson Ave., Brooklyn 11203
Interim Pres. Richard H. Schwarz
(718) 270-1000

State University of New York Health Science Center at Syracuse
750 E. Adams St., Syracuse 13210
Pres. Gregory L. Eastwood
(315) 464-5540

State University of New York Institute of Technology at Utica/Rome
P.O. Box 3050, Utica 13504-3050
Pres. Peter J. Cayan
(315) 792-7100

State University of New York Maritime College
Fort Schuyler, Throggs Neck 10465
Pres. Floyd H. Miller, U.S.N. (Ret.)
(212) 409-7200

State University of New York Office of Community Colleges
State University Plaza, Rm. T-705, Albany 12246
Dep. to the Chanc. Ernest A. Martinez
(518) 443-5134

Adirondack Community College
Queensbury 12804
Pres. Roger C. Andersen
(518) 793-4491

Broome Community College
Upper Front St., P.O. Box 1017, Binghamton 13902
Pres. Donald A. Dellow
(607) 778-5000

Cayuga County Community College
Franklin St., Auburn 13021
Pres. Lawrence H. Poole
(315) 255-1743

Clinton Community College
Rural Rte. 3, Box 8A, Plattsburgh 12901-9573
Pres. Jay L. Fennell
(518) 562-4200

Columbia-Greene Community College
P.O. Box 1000, Hudson 12534
Pres. Terry A. Cline
(518) 828-4181

Corning Community College
Spencer Hill, Corning 14830
Pres. Donald H. Hangen
(607) 962-9011

Dutchess Community College
53 Pendell Rd., Poughkeepsie 12601-1595
Pres. D. David Conklin
(914) 471-4500

Erie Community College Central Office
121 Ellicott St., Buffalo 14203
Pres. Louis M. Ricci
(716) 851-1200

Erie Community College City Campus
121 Ellicott St., Buffalo 14203
Acting Vice Pres. Thomas Adkins
(716) 851-1001

Erie Community College North (Amherst) Campus
6205 Main St., Williamsville 14221-7095
Interim Vice Pres. Dennis DiGiacomo
(716) 634-0800

Erie Community College South Campus
S-4041 Southwestern Blvd., Orchard Park 14127-2199
Vice Pres. Kenneth Gubala
(716) 851-1003

Fashion Institute of Technology
Seventh Ave. at 27th St., New
York 10001-5992
Pres. Allan F. Hershfield
(212) 760-7660

Finger Lakes Community College
4355 Lake Shore Dr.,
Canandaigua 14424
Pres. Daniel T. Hayes
(716) 394-3500

*Fulton-Montgomery Community
College*
Rte. 67, Johnstown 12095
Pres. Jacqueline D. Taylor
(518) 762-4651

Genesee Community College
One College Rd., Batavia 14020
Pres. Stuart Steiner
(716) 343-0055

*Herkimer County Community
College*
Reservoir Rd., Herkimer 13350
Pres. Ronald F. Williams
(315) 866-0300

Hudson Valley Community College
80 Vandenburgh Ave., Troy
12180
Pres. Joseph J. Bulmer
(518) 283-1100

Jamestown Community College
525 Falconer St., Jamestown
14701
Pres. Timothy G. Davies
(716) 665-5220

Jefferson Community College
Outer Coffeen St., Watertown
13601
Pres. John W. Deans
(315) 786-2200

Mohawk Valley Community College
1101 Sherman Dr., Utica 13501
Pres. Michael I. Schafer
(315) 792-5400

Monroe Community College
1000 E. Henrietta Rd.,
Rochester 14623
Pres. Peter A. Spina
(716) 292-2000

Nassau Community College
One Education Dr., Garden City
11530
Pres. Sean A. Fanelli
(516) 222-7205

Niagara County Community College
3111 Saunders Settlement Rd.,
Sanborn 14132
Pres. Gerald L. Miller
(716) 731-3271

North Country Community College
20 Winona Ave., P.O. Box 89,
Saranac Lake 12983
Pres. Gail Rogers Rice
(518) 891-2915

Onondaga Community College
Rte. 173, Syracuse 13215
Pres. Bruce H. Leslie
(315) 469-7741

Orange County Community College
115 South St., Middletown
10940
Pres. William F. Messner
(914) 343-1121

Rockland Community College
145 College Rd., Suffern 10901
Pres. Neal A. Raisman
(914) 574-4000

*Schenectady County Community
College*
78 Washington Ave., Schenectady 12305
Pres. Gabriel J. Basil
(518) 346-6211

**Suffolk County Community
College Central Administration**
533 College Rd., Selden 11784
Pres. John F. Cooper
(516) 451-4110

*Suffolk County Community
College Ammerman Campus*
533 College Rd., Selden
11784
Exec. Dean William C.
Hudson
(516) 451-4110

Suffolk County Community College Eastern Campus
Speonk-Riverhead Rd., Riverhead 11901
Exec. Dean Steven T. Kenny
(516) 548-2500

Suffolk County Community College Western Campus
Crooked Hill Rd., Brentwood 11717
Provost Salvatore La Lima
(516) 434-6750

Sullivan County Community College
College Rd., Loch Sheldrake 12759
Pres. Jeffrey B. Willens
(914) 434-5750

Tompkins Cortland Community College
P.O. Box 139, 170 North St., Dryden 13053
Pres. Eduardo J. Marti
(607) 844-8211

Ulster County Community College
Stone Ridge 12484
Pres. Robert T. Brown
(914) 687-5000

Westchester Community College
75 Grasslands Rd., Valhalla 10595
Pres. Joseph N. Hankin
(914) 285-6600

State University of New York at Albany
1400 Washington Ave., Albany 12222
Pres. H. Patrick Swygert
(518) 442-3300

State University of New York at Binghamton
P.O. Box 6000, Binghamton 13902-6000
Pres. Lois B. DeFleur
(607) 777-2000

State University of New York at Buffalo
Buffalo 14260
Pres. William R. Greiner
(716) 645-2000

State University of New York at Stony Brook
Nicolls Rd., Stony Brook 11794-0701
Pres. John H. Marburger, III
(516) 632-6000

NORTH CAROLINA

North Carolina Department of Community Colleges
200 W. Jones St., Raleigh 27603-1337
Pres. Robert W. Scott
(919) 733-7051

Alamance Community College
P.O. Box 8000, Graham 27253-8000
Pres. W. Ronald McCarter
(919) 578-2002

Anson Community College
P.O. Box 126, Polkton 28135
Pres. Donald P. Altieri
(704) 272-7635

Asheville-Buncombe Technical
*   Community College*
340 Victoria Rd., Asheville 28801
Pres. K. Ray Bailey
(704) 254-1921

Beaufort County Community College
P.O. Box 1069, Washington 27889
Pres. U. Ronald Champion
(919) 946-6194

Bladen Community College
P.O. Box 266, Dublin 28332-0266
Pres. Lynn G. King
(910) 862-2164

Blue Ridge Community College
College Dr., Flat Rock 28731-9624
Pres. David W. Sink, Jr.
(704) 692-3572

Brunswick Community College
P.O. Box 30, Supply 28462-0030
Pres. W. Michael Reaves
(910) 754-6900

Caldwell Community College and
*   Technical Institute*
P.O. Box 600, Lenoir 28645
Pres. Eric B. McKeithan
(704) 726-2200

Cape Fear Community College
411 N. Front St., Wilmington 28401-
3993
Interim Pres. Raymond A. Stone
(910) 251-5100

Carteret Community College
3505 Arendell St., Morehead City
28557
Pres. Donald W. Bryant
(919) 247-6000

Catawba Valley Community College
2550 Hwy. 70 SE, Hickory 28602-
9699
Pres. Cuyler A. Dunbar
(704) 327-7000

Central Carolina Community College
1105 Kelly Dr., Sanford 27330
Pres. Marvin R. Joyner
(919) 775-5401

Central Piedmont Community College
P.O. Box 35009, Charlotte 28235
Pres. Paul Anthony Zeiss
(704) 342-6633

Cleveland Community College
137 S. Post Rd., Shelby 28150
Pres. L. Steve Thornburg
(704) 484-4000

Coastal Carolina Community College
444 Western Blvd., Jacksonville
28546-6877
Pres. Ronald K. Lingle
(910) 455-1221

College of the Albemarle
P.O. Box 2327, Elizabeth City
27906-2327
Pres. Larry R. Donnithorne
(919) 335-0821

Craven Community College
800 College Ct., New Bern 28562
Pres. Lewis S. Redd
(919) 638-4131

Davidson County Community College
P.O. Box 1287, Lexington 27293-
1287
Pres. J. Bryan Brooks
(704) 249-8186

Durham Technical Community College
1637 Lawson St., Durham 27703
Pres. Phail Wynn, Jr.
(919) 598-9222

Edgecombe Community College
2009 W. Wilson St., Tarboro 27886
Interim Pres. Hartwell H. Fuller
(919) 823-5166

Fayetteville Technical Community College
P.O. Box 35236, 2201 Hull Rd.,
Fayetteville 28303-0236
Pres. Robert Craig Allen
(910) 678-8400

Forsyth Technical Community College
2100 Silas Creek Pkwy., Winston-
Salem 27103-5197
Pres. Bob H. Greene
(919) 723-0371

Gaston College
201 Hwy. 321 S., Dallas 28034-1499
Interim Pres. Paul Berrier
(704) 922-6200

Guilford Technical Community College
P.O. Box 309, Jamestown 27282
Pres. Donald W. Cameron
(910) 334-4822

Halifax Community College
P.O. Drawer 809, Weldon 27890
Pres. Elton L. Newbern, Jr.
(919) 536-2551

Haywood Community College
Freedlander Dr., Clyde 28721
Pres. Dan W. Moore
(704) 627-2821

Isothermal Community College
P.O. Box 804, Spindale 28160
Pres. Willard L. Lewis, III
(704) 286-3636

James Sprunt Community College
P.O. Box 398, Kenansville 28349
Pres. Donald L. Reichard
(910) 296-2400

Johnston Community College
P.O. Box 2350, Smithfield 27577
Pres. John L. Tart
(919) 934-3051

Lenoir Community College
P.O. Box 188, Kinston 28502-0188
Pres. Lonnie H. Blizzard
(919) 527-6223

Martin Community College
Kehukee Park Rd., Williamston
27892-9988
Pres. Martin H. Nadelman
(919) 792-1521

Mayland Community College
P.O. Box 547, Spruce Pine 28777
Interim Pres. Kenneth A. Bohan
(704) 765-7351

McDowell Technical Community College
Rte. 1, Box 170, Marion 28752
Pres. Robert M. Boggs
(704) 652-6021

Mitchell Community College
500 W. Broad St., Statesville 28677
Pres. Douglas O. Eason
(704) 878-3200

Montgomery Community College
P.O. Box 787, Troy 27371
Pres. Theodore H. Gasper, Jr.
(910) 572-3691

Nash Community College
P.O. Box 7488, Rocky Mount 27804-
0488
Pres. J. Reid Parrott, Jr.
(919) 443-4011

Pamlico Community College
P.O. Box 185, Hwy. 306 S., Grantsboro 28529
Pres. E. Douglas Kearney, Jr.
(919) 249-1851

Piedmont Community College
P.O. Box 1197, Roxboro 27573
Pres. H. James Owen
(910) 599-1181

Pitt Community College
P.O. Drawer 7007, Greenville 27835-
7007
Pres. Charles E. Russell
(919) 355-4200

Randolph Community College
P.O. Box 1009, Asheboro 27204-1009
Pres. Larry K. Linker
(910) 629-1471

Richmond Community College
P.O. Box 1189, Hamlet 28345
Pres. Joseph W. Grimsley
(919) 582-7000

Roanoke-Chowan Community College
Rte. 2, Box 46-A, Ahoskie 27910
Pres. Harold E. Mitchell
(910) 332-5921

Robeson Community College
P.O. Box 1420, Lumberton 28359
Pres. Frederick G. Williams, Jr.
(910) 738-7101

Rockingham Community College
P.O. Box 38, Wentworth 27375-0038
Pres. N. Jerry Owens, Jr.
(910) 342-4261

Rowan-Cabarrus Community College
P.O. Box 1595, Salisbury 28144-
1595
Pres. Richard L. Brownell
(704) 637-0760

Sampson Community College
P.O. Drawer 318, Clinton 28328
Pres. Clifton W. Paderick
(910) 592-8081

Sandhills Community College
2200 Airport Rd., Pinehurst 28374
Pres. John R. Dempsey
(919) 692-6185

Southeastern Community College
P.O. Box 151, Whiteville 28472
Pres. Stephen C. Scott
(910) 642-7141

Southwestern Community College
275 Webster Rd., Sylva 28779
Pres. Barry W. Russell
(704) 586-4091

Stanly Community College
141 College Dr., Albemarle 28001
Pres. Jan J. Crawford
(704) 982-0121

Surry Community College
P.O. Box 304, Dobson 27017
Pres. Swanson Richards
(919) 386-8121

Tri-County Community College
2300 Hwy. 64 E., Murphy 28906
Pres. W. Harry Jarrett
(704) 837-6810

Vance-Granville Community College
P.O. Box 917, Poplar Creek Rd.,
Henderson 27536
Pres. Benjamin F. Currin
(919) 492-2061

Wake Technical Community College
9101 Fayetteville Rd., Raleigh
27603-5696
Pres. Bruce I. Howell
(919) 662-3240

Wayne Community College
Caller Box 8002, Goldsboro 27533-
8002
Pres. Edward H. Wilson
(919) 735-5151

Western Piedmont Community College
1001 Burkemont Ave., Morganton
28655-9978
Pres. James A. Richardson
(704) 438-6000

Wilkes Community College
P.O. Box 120, Collegiate Dr.,
Wilkesboro 28697-0120
Pres. James R. Randolph
(919) 651-8600

Wilson Technical Community College
902 Herring Ave., P.O. Box 4305,
Wilson 27893
Pres. Frank L. Eagles
(919) 291-1195

The University of North Carolina General Administration
P.O. Box 2688, Chapel Hill 27515-2688
Pres. C.D. Spangler, Jr.
(919) 962-1000

Appalachian State University
Boone 28608
Chanc. Francis T. Borkowski
(704) 262-2000

East Carolina University
Fifth St., Greenville 27858-4353
Chanc. Richard R. Eakin
(919) 757-6131

Elizabeth City State University
ECSU Box 790, Elizabeth City
27909
Chanc. Jimmy R. Jenkins
(919) 335-3230

Fayetteville State University
1200 Murchison Rd., Newbold Sta.,
Fayetteville 28301-4298
Chanc. Lloyd V. Hackley
(910) 486-1111

*North Carolina Agricultural and
Technical State University*
1601 E. Market St., Greensboro 27411
Chanc. Edward B. Fort
(910) 334-7500

North Carolina Central University
1801 Fayetteville St., Durham 27707
Chanc. Julius L. Chambers
(919) 560-6100

North Carolina School of the Arts
200 Waughtown St., P.O. Box 12189,
Winston-Salem 27117-2189
Chanc. Alexander C. Ewing
(919) 770-3399

North Carolina State University
P.O. Box 7001, Raleigh 27695-7001
Chanc. Larry K. Monteith
(919) 515-2011

Pembroke State University
One University Dr., Pembroke 28372
Chanc. Joseph B. Oxendine
(910) 521-6000

*The University of North Carolina at
Asheville*
One University Heights, Asheville
28804
Interim Chanc. Larry Wilson
(704) 251-6600

*The University of North Carolina at
Chapel Hill*
CB #9100, 103 South Bldg., Chapel
Hill 27599-9100
Chanc. Paul Hardin
(919) 962-2211

*The University of North Carolina at
Charlotte*
University City Blvd., Charlotte
28223
Chanc. James H. Woodward, Jr.
(704) 547-2000

*The University of North Carolina at
Greensboro*
1000 Spring Garden St., Greensboro
27412
Chanc. William E. Moran
(910) 334-5000

*The University of North Carolina at
Wilmington*
601 S. College Rd., Wilmington
28403-3297
Chanc. James R. Leutze
(910) 395-3000

Western Carolina University
Cullowhee 28723
Chanc. Myron L. Coulter
(704) 227-7211

Winston-Salem State University
601 Martin Luther King, Jr. Dr.,
Winston-Salem 27110
Chanc. Cleon F. Thompson, Jr.
(910) 750-2000

NORTH DAKOTA

North Dakota University System
State Capitol, 600 E. Boulevard Ave., Bismarck 58505-0230
Chanc. (Vacant)
(701) 224-2960

Bismarck State College
1500 Edwards Ave., Bismarck 58501
Pres. Kermit Lidstrom
(701) 224-5400

Dickinson State University
291 Campus Dr., Dickinson 58601
Pres. Albert A. Watrel
(701) 227-2507

Mayville State University
330 Third St., N.E., Mayville 58257
Pres. Ellen E. Chaffee, Ph.D.
(701) 786-2301

Minot State University
Minot 58701
Pres. H. Erik Shaar
(701) 857-3300

North Dakota State College of Science
800 N. Sixth St., Wahpeton 58076
Pres. Jerry C. Olson
(701) 671-2221

North Dakota State University
Fargo 58105
Pres. Jim L. Ozbun
(701) 237-8011

North Dakota State University—Bottineau
First St. and Simrall Blvd., Bottineau 58318
Dean J.W. Smith
(701) 228-2277

University of North Dakota
Box 8232, University Sta., Grand Forks 58202-8232
Pres. Kendall L. Baker
(701) 777-2011

University of North Dakota—Lake Region
N. College Dr., Devils Lake 58301
Exec. Dean Sharon L. Etemad
(701) 662-1600

University of North Dakota—Williston
P.O. Box 1326, Williston 58801
Exec. Dean Garvin L. Stevens
(701) 774-4200

Valley City State University
College St., Valley City 58072
Pres. Ellen E. Chaffee
(701) 845-7100

OHIO

Ohio Board of Regents
30 E. Broad St., 36th Fl., Columbus
43266-0417
Chanc. Elaine H. Hairston
(614) 466-6000

Belmont Technical College
120 Fox-Shannon Pl., St. Clairsville
43950
Pres. Wesley R. Channell
(614) 695-9500

Bowling Green State University
Bowling Green 43403
Pres. Paul J. Olscamp
(419) 372-2531

Central Ohio Technical College
1179 University Dr., Newark 43055-
1767
Pres. Julius S. Greenstein
(614) 366-1351

Central State University
1400 Brush Row Rd., Wilberforce
45384
Pres. Arthur E. Thomas
(513) 376-6011

Cincinnati Technical College
3520 Central Pkwy., Cincinnati
45223
Pres. James P. Long
(513) 569-1500

Clark State Community College
570 E. Leffels La., P.O. Box 570,
Springfield 45505
Pres. Albert A. Salerno
(513) 325-0691

Clermont College
4200 Clermont College Dr., Batavia
45103
Dean Roger J. Barry
(513) 732-5200

Cleveland State University
Euclid Ave. at E. 24th St., Cleveland
44115
Pres. Claire A. Van Ummersen
(216) 687-2000

Columbus State Community College
550 E. Spring St., P.O. Box 1609,
Columbus 43216-1609
Pres. Harold M. Nestor
(614) 227-2400

Cuyahoga Community College
700 Carnegie Ave., Cleveland 44115
Pres. Jerry Sue Owens
(216) 987-6000

Edison State Community College
1973 Edison Dr., Piqua 45356
Pres. Kenneth A. Yowell
(513) 778-8600

Hocking Technical College
3301 Hocking Pkwy., Nelsonville
45764
Pres. John J. Light
(614) 753-3591

Jefferson Technical College
4000 Sunset Blvd., Steubenville
43952
Pres. Edward L. Florak
(614) 264-5591

Kent State University
P.O. Box 5190, Kent 44242
Pres. Carol A. Cartwright
(216) 672-3000

Lakeland Community College
7700 Clocktower Dr., Mentor 44060
Pres. Ralph R. Doty
(216) 953-7118

Lima Technical College
4240 Campus Dr., Lima 45804
Pres. James J. Countryman
(419) 221-1112

Lorain County Community College
1005 N. Abbe Rd., Elyria 44035
Pres. Roy A. Church
(216) 365-4191

Marion Technical College
1467 Mt. Vernon Ave., Marion
43302-5694
Pres. John Richard Bryson
(614) 389-4636

Medical College of Ohio
  Caller Service No. 10008, Toledo
    43699
  Pres. Roger C. Bone
  (419) 381-4267

Miami University
  Oxford 45056
  Pres. Paul G. Risser
  (513) 529-1809

Muskingum Area Technical College
  1555 Newark Rd., Zanesville 43701
  Pres. Lynn H. Willett
  (614) 454-2501

North Central Technical College
  P.O. Box 698, Mansfield 44901-0698
  Pres. Byron E. Kee
  (419) 755-4800

Northeastern Ohio Universities College of
  Medicine
  4209 State Rte. 44, P.O. Box 95,
    Rootstown 44272-0095
  Pres. Robert S. Blacklow, M.D.
  (216) 325-2511

Northwest Technical College
  22-600 State Rte. 34, Archbold 43502
  Pres. Larry G. McDougle
  (419) 267-5511

The Ohio State University
  190 N. Oval Dr., Columbus 43210
  Pres. E. Gordon Gee
  (614) 292-6446

Ohio University
  Athens 45701
  Pres. Charles J. Ping
  (614) 593-1000

Owens Technical College
  P.O. Box 10000, 30335 Oregon Rd.,
    Toledo 43699
  Pres. Daniel H. Brown
  (419) 666-0580

Raymond Walters College
  9555 Plainfield Rd., Cincinnati 45236
  Acting Dean Roger J. Barry
  (513) 745-5600

Shawnee State University
  940 Second St., Portsmouth 45662
  Pres. Clive C. Veri
  (614) 355-3205

Sinclair Community College
  444 W. Third St., Dayton 45402
  Pres. David H. Ponitz
  (513) 226-2500

Southern State Community College
  200 Hobart Dr., Hillsboro 45133
  Pres. George R. McCormick
  (513) 393-3431

Stark Technical College
  6200 Frank Ave., N.W., Canton
    44720
  Pres. John J. McGrath, Jr.
  (216) 494-6170

Terra Technical College
  2830 Napoleon Rd., Fremont 43420
  Pres. Charlotte J. Lee
  (419) 334-8400

The University of Akron
  Akron 44325
  Pres. Peggy Gordon Elliott
  (216) 972-7111

University of Cincinnati
  2624 Clifton Ave., Cincinnati 45221
  Pres. Joseph A. Steger
  (513) 556-6000

University of Toledo
  2801 W. Bancroft St., Toledo 43606
  Pres. Frank E. Horton
  (419) 537-2696

Washington State Community College
  710 Colegate Dr., Marietta 45750
  Pres. Carson K. Miller
  (614) 374-8716

Wayne College
  1901 Smucker Rd., Orrville 44667
  Dean Tyrone M. Turning
  (216) 683-2010

Wright State University
  3640 Colonel Glenn Hwy., Dayton
    45435
  Pres. Harley E. Flack
  (513) 873-3333

Youngstown State University
  410 Wick Ave., Youngstown 44555
  Pres. Leslie H. Cochran
  (216) 742-3000

OKLAHOMA

Oklahoma State Regents for Higher Education
500 Education Bldg., State Capitol Complex, Oklahoma City 73105-4503
Chanc. Hans Brisch
(405) 524-9120

Cameron University
2800 Gore Blvd., Lawton 73505
Pres. Don Davis
(405) 581-2200

Carl Albert State College
1507 S. McKenna, Poteau 74953-5208
Pres. Joe E. White
(918) 647-8660

Connors State College
Rte. 1, Box 1000, Warner 74469
Pres. Carl O. Westbrook
(918) 463-2931

East Central University
Ada 74820
Pres. Bill S. Cole
(405) 332-8000

Eastern Oklahoma State College
1301 W. Main St., Wilburton 74578
Pres. Bill H. Hill
(918) 465-2361

Langston University
P.O. Box 907, Langston 73050-0907
Pres. Ernest L. Holloway
(405) 466-3201

Murray State College
1100 S. Murray, Tishomingo 73460
Pres. Clyde R. Kindell
(405) 371-2371

Northeastern Oklahoma A&M College
200 I St. N.E., Miami 74354
Pres. Jerry D. Carroll
(918) 542-8441

Northeastern State University
Tahlequah 74464
Pres. W. Roger Webb
(918) 456-5511

Northern Oklahoma College
P.O. Box 310, Tonkawa 74653-0310
Pres. Joe M. Kinzer, Jr.
(405) 628-6200

Northwestern Oklahoma State University
709 Oklahoma Blvd., Alva 73717
Pres. Joe J. Struckle
(405) 327-1700

Oklahoma City Community College
7777 S. May Ave., Oklahoma City 73159
Pres. Bob D. Gaines
(405) 682-1611

Oklahoma Panhandle State University
Box 430, Goodwell 73939
Pres. Ron Meek
(405) 349-2611

Oklahoma State University Office of the President
Stillwater 74078
Interim Pres. Ray M. Bowen
(405) 744-5000

Oklahoma State University
Stillwater 74078
Interim Pres. Ray M. Bowen
(405) 744-5000

Oklahoma State University College of Osteopathic Medicine
1111 W. 17th St., Tulsa 74107
Provost/Dean Thomas Wesley Allen
(918) 582-1972

Oklahoma State University— Oklahoma City
900 N. Portland Ave., Oklahoma City 73107
Provost James E. Hooper
(405) 947-4421

Oklahoma State University— Okmulgee
1801 E. Fourth St., Okmulgee 74447
Provost Robert Klabenes
(918) 756-6211

Redlands Community College
P.O. Box 370, El Reno 73036-0370
Pres. Larry F. Devane
(405) 262-2552

Rogers State College
Will Rogers and College Hill, Claremore 74017
Pres. Richard H. Mosier
(918) 341-7510

Rose State College
6420 S.E. 15th St., Midwest City
73110
Pres. Larry Nutter
(405) 733-7311

Seminole Junior College
P.O. Box 351, Seminole 74868-0351
Pres. James J. Cook
(405) 382-9950

Southeastern Oklahoma State University
Sta. A, Durant 74701
Pres. Larry Williams
(405) 924-0121

Southwestern Oklahoma State University
100 Campus Dr., Weatherford 73096
Pres. Joe Anna Hibler
(405) 772-6611

Tulsa Junior College
6111 E. Skelly Dr., Tulsa 74135
Pres. Dean P. Van Trease
(918) 631-7000

University of Central Oklahoma
100 N. University Dr., Edmond
73060
Pres. George Nigh
(405) 341-2980

University of Oklahoma President's Office
660 Parrington Oval, Rm. 110, Norman 73019
Pres. Richard L. Van Horn
(405) 325-3916

University of Oklahoma
660 Parrington Oval, Norman
73019
Pres. Richard L. Van Horn
(405) 325-0311

University of Oklahoma Health Sciences Center
P.O. Box 26901, Oklahoma City
73126-0901
Provost Jay H. Stein
(405) 271-4000

University of Science and Arts of Oklahoma
P.O. Box 82345, Chickasha 73018
Pres. Roy Troutt
(405) 224-3140

Western Oklahoma State College
2801 N. Main St., Altus 73521
Pres. Stephen R. Hensley
(405) 477-2000

OREGON

Oregon Office of Community College Services
255 Capitol St., N.E., Salem 97310-0203
Commissioner Roger J. Bassett
(503) 378-8648

Blue Mountain Community College
P.O. Box 100, Pendleton 97801
Pres. Ronald L. Daniels
(503) 276-1260

Central Oregon Community College
Bend 97701-5998
Pres. Robert Barber
(503) 385-6112

Chemeketa Community College
P.O. Box 14007, Salem 97309
Pres. Gerard J. Berger
(503) 399-5000

Clackamas Community College
19600 S. Molalla Ave., Oregon City 97045
Pres. John S. Keyser
(503) 657-6958

Clatsop Community College
1653 Jerome Ave., Astoria 97103
Pres. John W. Wubben
(503) 325-0910

Lane Community College
4000 E. 30th Ave., Eugene 97405
Pres. Jerry Moskus
(503) 747-4501

Linn-Benton Community College
Albany 97321
Pres. Jon Carnahan
(503) 967-6100

Mount Hood Community College
26000 S.E. Stark St., Gresham 97030
Pres. Paul E. Kreider
(503) 667-6422

Portland Community College
P.O. Box 19000, Portland 97219-0990
Pres. Daniel F. Moriarty
(503) 244-6111

Rogue Community College
3345 Redwood Hwy., Grants Pass 97527
Pres. Harvey Bennett
(503) 479-5541

Southwestern Oregon Community College
1988 Newmark, Coos Bay 97420
Pres. Stephen Kridelbaugh
(503) 888-2525

Treasure Valley Community College
Ontario 97914
Pres. Berton Glandon
(503) 889-6493

Umpqua Community College
Roseburg 97470
Pres. James M. Kraby
(503) 440-4600

Oregon State System of Higher Education
P.O. Box 3175, Eugene 97403-0175
Chanc. Thomas A. Bartlett
(503) 346-5700

Eastern Oregon State College
La Grande 97850
Pres. David E. Gilbert
(503) 962-3512

Oregon Health Sciences University
3181 S.W. Sam Jackson Park Rd., Portland 97201
Pres. Peter O. Kohler, M.D.
(503) 494-8252

Oregon Institute of Technology
Klamath Falls 97601-8801
Pres. Lawrence J. Wolf
(503) 885-1103

Oregon State University
Corvallis 97331
Pres. John V. Byrne
(503) 737-2565

Portland State University
P.O. Box 751, Portland 97207
Pres. Judith A. Ramaley
(503) 725-4419

Southern Oregon State College
Ashland 97520
Pres. Joseph W. Cox
(503) 552-6111

University of Oregon
Eugene 97403-1226
Pres. Myles Brand
(503) 346-3036

Western Oregon State College
Monmouth 97361
Pres. Richard S. Meyers
(503) 838-8215

PENNSYLVANIA

Community College of Allegheny County College Office
800 Allegheny Ave., Pittsburgh 15233
Pres. John M. Kingsmore
(412) 237-3040

Community College of Allegheny County Allegheny Campus
808 Ridge Ave., Pittsburgh 15212
Exec. Dean/Vice Pres. J. David Griffin
(412) 237-2525

Community College of Allegheny County Boyce Campus
595 Beatty Rd., Monroeville 15146
Exec. Dean/Vice Pres. Carl A. DiSibio
(412) 371-8651

Community College of Allegheny County North Campus
8701 Perry Hwy., Pittsburgh 15237
Exec. Dean/Vice Pres. Fred F. Bartok
(412) 366-7000

Community College of Allegheny County South Campus
1750 Clairton Rd., Rte. 885, West Mifflin 15122
Exec. Dean/Vice Pres. Thomas A. Juravich
(412) 469-1100

Pennsylvania State System of Higher Education
Box 809, 301 Market St., Harrisburg 17108
Chanc. James H. McCormick
(717) 783-8887

Bloomsburg University of Pennsylvania
Bloomsburg 17815
Interim Pres. Curtis R. English
(717) 389-4000

California University of Pennsylvania
250 University Ave., California 15419-1934
Pres. Angelo Armenti, Jr.
(412) 938-4000

Cheyney University of Pennsylvania
Cheyney and Creek Rds., Cheyney 19319
Pres. H. Douglas Covington
(215) 399-2000

Clarion University of Pennsylvania
Clarion 16214
Pres. Diane L. Reinhard
(814) 226-2000

East Stroudsburg University of Pennsylvania
200 Prospect St., East Stroudsburg 18301
Pres. James E. Gilbert
(717) 424-3545

Edinboro University of Pennsylvania
Edinboro 16444
Pres. Foster F. Diebold
(814) 732-2000

Indiana University of Pennsylvania
Indiana 15705
Pres. Lawrence K. Pettit
(412) 357-2100

Kutztown University of Pennsylvania
Kutztown 19530
Pres. David E. McFarland
(215) 683-4000

Lock Haven University of Pennsylvania
Lock Haven 17745
Pres. Craig D. Willis
(717) 893-2011

Mansfield University of Pennsylvania
Academy St., Mansfield 16933
Pres. Rodney C. Kelchner
(717) 662-4000

Millersville University of Pennsylvania
P.O. Box 1002, Millersville 17551-1002
Pres. Joseph A. Caputo
(717) 872-3011

Shippensburg University of Pennsylvania
Shippensburg 17257
Pres. Anthony F. Ceddia
(717) 532-9121

Slippery Rock University of Pennsylvania
Slippery Rock 16057
Pres. Robert N. Aebersold
(412) 738-0512

West Chester University of Pennsylvania
S. High St., West Chester 19383
Pres. Madeleine Wing Adler
(215) 436-1000

PUERTO RICO

**Inter American University of Puerto Rico
Central Administration**
G.P.O. Box 3255, San Juan 00936
Pres. Jose R. Gonzalez
(809) 766-1912

*Inter American University of Puerto Rico
Aguadilla Campus*
Call Box 20000, Aguadilla 00605
Chanc. Hilda M. Bacó
(809) 891-0925

*Inter American University of Puerto Rico
Arecibo Campus*
Call Box UI, Arecibo 00613
Chanc. Zaida Vega-Lugo
(809) 878-5475

*Inter American University of Puerto Rico
Barranquitas Campus*
P.O. Box 517, Barranquitas 00794
Chanc. Vidal Rivera-Garcia
(809) 857-4040

*Inter American University of Puerto Rico
Bayamon Campus*
RD 174, Minillas Industrial Park,
Bayamon 00959
Chanc. Felix Torres-Leon
(809) 780-4040

*Inter American University of Puerto Rico
Fajardo Campus*
P.O. Box 1029, Fajardo 00738
Chanc. Yolanda Robles-Garcia
(809) 863-2390

*Inter American University of Puerto Rico
Guayama Campus*
Call Box 10004, Guayama 00785
Chanc. Samuel F. Febres-Santiago
(809) 864-2222

*Inter American University of Puerto Rico
Metropolitan Campus*
P.O. Box 1293, Hato Rey 00919-
1293
Chanc. Manuel J. Fernos
(809) 250-1912

*Inter American University of Puerto Rico
Ponce Campus*
Mercedita 00715
Chanc. Marilina L. Wayland
(809) 840-9090

*Inter American University of Puerto Rico
San German Campus*
Harris Dr., Call Box 5100, San Ger-
man 00683
Chanc. Agnes Mojica
(809) 264-1912

*Inter American University of Puerto Rico
School of Law*
P.O. Box 8897, Fernandez Juncos
Sta., Santurce 00910
Dean Carlos E. Ramos-Gonzalez
(809) 727-1930

*Inter American University of Puerto Rico
School of Optometry*
118 Eleanor Roosevelt St., Hato Rey
00919
Dean Arthur J. Afanador
(809) 754-6690

**University of Puerto Rico Central
Administration**
P.O. Box 364984, San Juan 00936-4984
Interim Pres. Salvador E. Alemañy
(809) 765-5610

Cayey University College
Antonio R. Barcelo Ave., Cayey
00633
Chanc. Margarita Benitez
(809) 738-2161

Humacao University College
CUH Sta., Rd. 908, Bo. Tejas,
Humacao 00661
Chanc. Felix A. Castrodad Ortiz
(809) 850-0000

*University of Puerto Rico Mayaguez
Campus*
P.O. Box 5000, Mayaguez 00681
Chanc. Alejandro Ruiz-Acevedo
(809) 832-4040

*University of Puerto Rico Medical
Sciences Campus*
   Box 365067, San Juan 00936-5067
   Interim Rector Uveles Garcia
   (809) 758-2525

**University of Puerto Rico Regional
Colleges Administration**
   P.O. Box 21876, U.P.R. Sta., San
   Juan 00931
   Interim Pres. Salvador E. Alemañy
   (809) 758-3454

Aguadilla Regional College
   P.O. Box 160, Ramey 00604
   Dean/Dir. Miguel A. Gonzalez
   (809) 890-2681

*Arecibo Technological University
College*
   Box 4010, Arecibo 00613
   Dir. de Cano Ireneo Martin
   Duque
   (809) 878-2830

*Bayamon Technological University
College*
   Bayamon 00959-1919
   Dean/Dir. Aida Canals de Bird
   (809) 786-2885

Carolina Regional College
   P.O. Box 4800, Carolina 00984-
   4800
   Dean/Dir. Marta Arroyo
   (809) 257-0000

La Montaña Regional College
   Call Box 2500, Utuado 00641
   Dean/Dir. Ramon A. Toro
   (809) 894-2828

*Ponce Technological University
College*
   Box 7186, Ponce 00732
   Dean/Dir. Pedro E. Laboy-
   Zengotita
   (809) 844-8181

*University of Puerto Rico Rio Piedras
Campus*
   P.O. Box 23300, San Juan 00931-
   3300
   Rector Efrain Gonzales Tejera
   (809) 764-0000

RHODE ISLAND

State of Rhode Island Office of Higher Education
301 Promenade St., Providence 02908-5089
Commissioner Americo W. Petrocelli, Ph.D.
(401) 277-6560

Community College of Rhode Island
400 East Ave., Warwick 02886-1805
Pres. Edward J. Liston
(401) 825-1000

Rhode Island College
Providence 02908
Pres. John Nazarian
(401) 456-8000

University of Rhode Island
Kingston 02881-0806
Pres. Robert L. Carothers
(401) 792-1000

SOUTH CAROLINA

South Carolina Commission on Higher Education
1333 Main St., Ste. 200, Columbia 29201
Commissioner Fred R. Sheheen
(803) 253-6260

The Citadel
Citadel Sta., 171 Moultrie St.,
Charleston 29409
Pres. Claudius E. Watts, III
(803) 792-5000

Clemson University
201 Sikes Hall, Clemson 29634
Pres. A. Max Lennon
(803) 656-3311

Coastal Carolina University
P.O. Box 1954, Myrtle Beach 29577
Pres. Ronald R. Ingle
(803) 347-3161

College of Charleston
66 George St., Charleston 29424
Pres. Alexander M. Sanders, Jr.
(803) 953-5507

Francis Marion University
P.O. Box 100547, Florence 29501-
0547
Pres. Thomas C. Stanton
(803) 661-1362

Lander University
320 Stanley Ave., Greenwood
29649-2099
Pres. William C. Moran
(803) 229-8300

Medical University of South Carolina
171 Ashley Ave., Charleston 29425
Pres. James B. Edwards
(803) 792-2211

South Carolina State University
300 College Ave. N.E., Orangeburg
29117
Pres. Barbara Hatton
(803) 536-7000

University of South Carolina Central Office
Columbia 29208
Pres. John M. Palms
(803) 777-2001

University of South Carolina—Aiken
171 University Pkwy., Aiken
29801
Chanc. Robert E. Alexander
(803) 648-6851

*University of South Carolina—
Beaufort*
801 Carteret St., Beaufort 29902
Dean Chris Plyler
(803) 521-4100

*University of South Carolina—
Columbia*
Columbia 29208
Pres. John M. Palms
(803) 777-7000

*University of South Carolina—
Lancaster*
P.O. Box 889, Lancaster 29721
Dean John R. Arnold
(803) 285-7471

*University of South Carolina—
Salkehatchie*
P.O. Box 617, Allendale 29810
Dean Carl A. Clayton
(803) 584-3446

*University of South Carolina—
Spartanburg*
800 University Way, Spartanburg 29303
Interim Chanc. William J.
Whitener
(803) 599-2000

*University of South Carolina—
Sumter*
200 Miller Rd., Sumter 29150
Dean C. Leslie Carpenter
(803) 775-6341

University of South Carolina—Union
P.O. Drawer 729, Union 29379
Dean James W. Edwards
(803) 429-8728

Winthrop University
701 Oakland Ave., Rock Hill 29733
Pres. Anthony J. DiGiorgio
(803) 323-2211

**South Carolina State Board for Technical
and Comprehensive Education**
111 Executive Center Dr., Columbia
29210
Exec. Dir. James R. Morris, Jr.
(803) 737-9320

Aiken Technical College
P.O. Box 696, Aiken 29802-0696
Interim Pres. Don B. Campbell
(803) 593-9231

Central Carolina Technical College
506 N. Guignard Dr., Sumter 29150-
2499
Pres. Herbert C. Robbins
(803) 778-1961

Chesterfield-Marlboro Technical College
1201 Chesterfield Hwy., No. 9 W.,
P.O. Drawer 1007, Cheraw 29520-
1007
Pres. Ronald W. Hampton
(803) 537-5286

Denmark Technical College
P.O. Box 327, Denmark 29042
Pres. Joann R.G. Boyd
(803) 793-3301

Florence-Darlington Technical College
P.O. Box 100548, Florence 29501-
0548
Pres. Charles W. Gould
(803) 661-8324

Greenville Technical College
P.O. Box 5616, Greenville 29606
Pres. Thomas E. Barton, Jr.
(803) 250-8000

Horry-Georgetown Technical College
P.O. Box 1966, Conway 29526
Pres. D. Kent Sharples
(803) 347-3286

Midlands Technical College
P.O. Box 2408, Columbia 29202
Pres. James L. Hudgins
(803) 738-1400

Orangeburg-Calhoun Technical College
3250 St. Matthews Rd., Orangeburg
29115
Pres. M. Rudolph Groomes
(803) 536-1500

Piedmont Technical College
P.O. Drawer 1467, Greenwood
29648
Pres. Lex D. Walters
(803) 941-8324

Spartanburg Technical College
P.O. Drawer 4386, Spartanburg
29305-4386
Pres. Jack A. Powers
(803) 591-3600

Technical College of the Lowcountry
100 S. Ribaut Rd., P.O. Box 1288,
Beaufort 29901
Pres. Anne S. McNutt
(803) 525-8324

Tri-County Technical College
Hwy. 76, P.O. Box 587, Pendleton
29670
Pres. Don C. Garrison
(803) 646-8361

Trident Technical College
P.O. Box 10367, Charleston 29423-
8067
Pres. Mary Dellamura Thornley
(803) 572-6111

Williamsburg Technical College
601 Lane Rd., Kingstree 29556-4197
Interim Pres. James M. Donnelly
(803) 354-7423

York Technical College
452 S. Anderson Rd., Rock Hill 29730
Pres. Dennis F. Merrell
(803) 327-8000

SOUTH DAKOTA

South Dakota Board of Regents
207 E. Capitol Ave., Pierre 57501-3159
Exec. Dir. Howell W. Todd
(605) 773-3455

Black Hills State University
1200 University Ave., Spearfish
57799-9500
Pres. Clifford M. Trump
(605) 642-6011

Dakota State University
820 N. Washington St., Madison
57042
Pres. Jerald A. Tunheim
(605) 256-5111

Northern State University
1200 S. Jay St., Aberdeen 57401
Pres. John Hutchinson
(605) 622-2521

*South Dakota School of Mines and
Technology*
501 E. St. Joseph St., Rapid City
57701
Pres. Richard J. Gowen
(605) 394-2411

South Dakota State University
Box 2201, University Sta., Brookings
57007
Pres. Robert T. Wagner
(605) 688-4121

The University of South Dakota
414 E. Clark St., Vermillion 57069-
2390
Pres. Betty Turner Asher
(605) 677-5011

TENNESSEE

Tennessee Board of Regents
1415 Murfreesboro Rd., Ste. 350,
Nashville 37217-2833
Chanc. Charles E. Smith
(615) 366-4403

Austin Peay State University
601 College St., Clarksville 37044
Pres. Oscar C. Page
(615) 648-7011

*Chattanooga State Technical Community
College*
4501 Amnicola Hwy., Chattanooga
37406
Pres. James L. Catanzaro
(615) 697-4000

Cleveland State Community College
P.O. Box 3570, Cleveland 37320-
3570
Pres. Owen F. Cargol
(615) 472-7141

Columbia State Community College
P.O. Box 1315, Hwy. 412 W.,
Columbia 38402-1315
Pres. L. Paul Sands
(615) 540-2722

Dyersburg State Community College
P.O. Box 648, Dyersburg 38025-
0648
Pres. Karen A. Bowyer
(901) 286-3200

East Tennessee State University
P.O. Box 70734, Johnson City
37614-0734
Pres. Roy S. Nicks
(615) 929-4112

Jackson State Community College
2046 North Pkwy., Jackson 38301-
3797
Pres. Walter L. Nelms
(901) 424-3520

Memphis State University
Memphis 38152
Pres. V. Lane Rawlins
(901) 678-2000

Middle Tennessee State University
Murfreesboro 37132
Pres. James E. Walker
(615) 898-2300

Motlow State Community College
P.O. Box 88100, Tullahoma 37388-
8100
Pres. A. Frank Glass
(615) 455-8511

Nashville State Technical Institute
120 White Bridge Rd., Nashville
37209-4515
Pres. George H. Van Allen
(615) 353-3333

*Northeast State Technical Community
College*
P.O. Box 246, 2425 Hwy. 75,
Blountville 37617-0246
Pres. R. Wade Powers
(615) 323-3191

*Pellissippi State Technical Community
College*
10915 Hardin Valley Rd., P.O. Box
22990, Knoxville 37933-0990
Pres. Allen G. Edwards
(615) 694-6400

Roane State Community College
Rte. 8, Box 69, Patton La., Harriman
37748
Pres. Sherry L. Hoppe
(615) 354-3000

Shelby State Community College
P.O. Box 40568, Memphis 38174-
0568
Pres. Lawrence M. Cox
(901) 544-5000

State Technical Institute at Memphis
5983 Macon Cove, Memphis 38134-
7693
Pres. Charles M. Temple
(901) 377-4100

Tennessee State University
3500 John Merritt Blvd., Nashville
37209-1561
Pres. James A. Hefner
(615) 320-3131

Tennessee Technological University
N. Dixie Ave., Cookeville 38505
Pres. Angelo A. Volpe
(615) 372-3101

Volunteer State Community College
1360 Nashville Pike, Gallatin 37066
Pres. Hal R. Ramer
(615) 452-8600

Walters State Community College
500 S. Davy Crockett Pkwy., Morristown 37813-6899
Pres. Jack E. Campbell
(615) 587-2600

The University of Tennessee System
Knoxville 37996
Pres. Joseph E. Johnson
(615) 974-2241

*The University of Tennessee at
Chattanooga*
615 McCallie Ave., Chattanooga
37403-2598
Chanc. Frederick W. Obear
(615) 744-4111

The University of Tennessee at Martin
University St., Martin 38238
Chanc. Margaret N. Perry
(901) 587-7000

The University of Tennessee, Knoxville
527 Andy Holt Tower, Knoxville
37996-0150
Pres. Joseph E. Johnson
(615) 974-1000

The University of Tennessee, Memphis
800 Madison Ave., Memphis 38163
Chanc. William R. Rice
(901) 448-5500

TEXAS

Texas Higher Education Coordinating Board
P.O. Box 12788, Capitol Sta., Austin 78711
Commissioner Kenneth H. Ashworth
(512) 483-6100

Alamo Community College District
811 W. Houston St., San Antonio 78207-3033
Chanc. Robert W. Ramsay
(210) 220-1520

Palo Alto College
1400 W. Villaret Blvd., San Antonio 78224-2499
Pres. Joel E. Vela
(512) 921-5000

St. Philip's College
1801 Martin Luther King Dr., San Antonio 78203
Pres. Hamice R. James
(210) 531-3200

San Antonio College
1300 San Pedro Ave., San Antonio 78212-4299
Pres. Ruth Burgos-Sasscer
(210) 733-2000

Alvin Community College
3110 Mustang Rd., Alvin 77511-4898
Pres. A. Rodney Allbright
(713) 331-6111

Amarillo College
P.O. Box 447, Amarillo 79178
Pres. Luther Bud Joyner
(806) 371-5000

Angelina College
P.O. Box 1768, Lufkin 75902
Pres. Larry M. Phillips
(409) 639-1301

Austin Community College
5930 Middle Fiskville Rd., Austin 78752-4390
Pres. William E. Segura
(512) 483-7000

Bee County College
3800 Charco Rd., Beeville 78102
Pres. Norman E. Wallace
(512) 358-3130

Blinn College
902 College Ave., Brenham 77833
Pres. Walter C. Schwartz
(409) 830-4000

Brazosport College
500 College Dr., Lake Jackson 77566
Pres. John R. Grable
(409) 266-3000

Central Texas College
P.O. Box 1800, Killeen 76540-9990
Chanc. James R. Anderson
(817) 526-7161

Cisco Junior College
Rte. 3, Box 3, Cisco 76437
Pres. Roger C. Schustereit
(817) 442-2567

Clarendon College
P.O. Box 968, Clarendon 79226
Pres. Jerry D. Stockton
(806) 874-3571

College of the Mainland
1200 Amburn Rd., Texas City 77591
Pres. Larry L. Stanley
(409) 938-1211

Collin County Community College
2200 W. University Dr., P.O. Box 8001, McKinney 75070
Pres. John H. Anthony
(214) 548-6790

Cooke County College
1525 W. California St., Gainesville 76240-4699
Pres. Ronnie Glassock
(817) 668-7731

Dallas County Community College District
701 Elm St., Dallas 75202-3299
Chanc. J. William Wenrich
(214) 746-2125

Brookhaven College
3939 Valley View La., Farmers
Branch 75244-4997
Pres. Walter G. Bumphus
(214) 620-4700

Cedar Valley College
3030 N. Dallas Ave., Lancaster
75134
Pres. Carol J. Spencer
(214) 372-8201

Eastfield College
3737 Motley Dr., Mesquite
75150-2099
Pres. Roberto Aguero
(214) 324-7001

El Centro College
Main and Lamar Sts., Dallas
75202-3604
Pres. Wright L. Lassiter, Jr.
(214) 746-2010

Mountain View College
4849 W. Illinois Ave., Dallas
75211-6599
Pres. Monique Amerman
(214) 333-8700

North Lake College
5001 N. MacArthur Blvd.,
Irving 75038-3899
Pres. James F. Horton
(214) 659-5230

Richland College
12800 Abrams Rd., Dallas
75243-2199
Pres. Stephen K. Mittelstet
(214) 238-6209

Del Mar College
101 Baldwin Blvd., Corpus Christi
78404-3897
Pres. Buddy R. Venters
(512) 886-1200

East Texas State University
ETSU Sta., Commerce 75429-3011
Pres. Jerry D. Morris
(903) 886-5012

East Texas State University at Texarkana
P.O. Box 5518, Texarkana 75505-
0518
Pres. John F. Moss
(903) 838-6514

El Paso Community College
P.O. Box 20500, El Paso 79998
Interim Pres. Adriana Barrera
(915) 594-2000

Frank Phillips College
P.O. Box 5118, Borger 79008-5118
Pres. Vance W. Gipson
(806) 274-5311

Galveston College
4015 Ave. Q, Galveston 77550
Pres. Marc A. Nigliazzo
(409) 763-6551

Grayson County College
6101 Grayson Dr., Denison 75020
Pres. James M. Williams, Jr.
(903) 465-6030

Hill College
P.O. Box 619, 112 Lamar Dr., Hillsboro 76645
Pres. William R. Auvenshine
(817) 582-2555

Houston Community College
P.O. Box 7819, Houston 77270-7849
Chanc. Charles A. Green
(713) 869-5021

Howard County Junior College District
1001 Birdwell La., Big Spring 79720
Pres. Cheryl T. Sparks
(915) 264-5000

Howard College
1001 Birdwell La., Big Spring
79720
Pres. Cheryl T. Sparks
(915) 264-5000

Kilgore College
1100 Broadway, Kilgore 75662-3299
Pres. J. Frank Thornton
(903) 984-8531

Lamar University System
P.O. Box 11900, Beaumont 77710
Interim Chanc. James A. Norton
(409) 880-2304

Lamar University at Beaumont
4400 M.L. King, Jr. Pkwy.
Blvd, Beaumont 77705
Pres. Rex L. Cottle
(409) 880-7011

Lamar University at Orange
410 W. Front St., Orange 77630
Pres. Steve Maradian
(409) 883-7750

Lamar University at Port Arthur
P.O. Box 310, Port Arthur
77641-0310
Pres. W. Sam Monroe
(409) 983-4921

Laredo Community College
W. End Washington St., Laredo
78040-4395
Pres. Roger L. Worsley
(210) 722-0521

Lee College
511 S. Whiting St., Baytown 77520-
0818
Pres. Jackson N. Sasser
(713) 427-5611

McLennan Community College
1400 College Dr., Waco 76708
Pres. Dennis F. Michaelis
(817) 756-6551

Midland College
3600 N. Garfield St., Midland 79705
Pres. David E. Daniel
(915) 685-4500

Midwestern State University
3400 Taft Blvd., Wichita Falls
76308-2099
Pres. Louis J. Rodriguez
(817) 689-4000

Navarro College
3200 W. Seventh Ave., Corsicana
75110
Pres. Gerald E. Burson
(903) 874-6501

North Harris Montgomery County College
250 N. Sam Houston Pkwy., E.,
Houston 77060
Pres. John E. Pickelman
(713) 591-3500

Northeast Texas Community College
P.O. Drawer 1307, Mount Pleasant
75456-1307
Pres. Michael C. Bruner
(903) 572-1911

Odessa College
201 W. University Blvd., Odessa
79764
Pres. Philip T. Speegle
(915) 335-6400

Panola College
1109 W. Panola St., Carthage 75633
Pres. William Edmonson
(903) 693-2000

Paris Junior College
2400 Clarksville St., Paris 75460
Pres. Bobby R. Walters
(903) 785-7661

Ranger Junior College
College Cir., Ranger 76470-3298
Pres. Joe Mills
(817) 647-3234

San Jacinto College
4624 Fairmont Pkwy., Pasadena 77504
Chanc. Thomas S. Sewell
(713) 998-6100

South Plains College
1401 College Ave., Levelland 79336
Pres. Gary McDaniel
(806) 894-9611

Southwest Texas Junior College
2401 Garner Field Rd., Uvalde
78801-6297
Pres. Billy Word
(210) 278-4401

Stephen F. Austin State University
P.O. Box 6078, SFA Sta., Nacogdoches 75962
Pres. Daniel D. Angel
(409) 568-2011

Tarrant County Junior College
1500 Houston St., Fort Worth 76102-
6599
Chanc. C.A. Roberson
(817) 336-7851

Temple Junior College
2600 S. First St., Temple 76504-7435
Pres. Marvin R. Felder
(817) 773-9961

Texarkana College
2500 N. Robinson Rd., Texarkana
75599
Pres. Carl M. Nelson
(903) 838-4541

The Texas A&M University System
State Headquarters Bldg., 301 Tar-
row, 7th Fl., College Station
77843-1122
Chanc. William H. Mobley
(409) 845-4331

Prairie View A&M University
P.O. Box 519, Prairie View
77446
Pres. Julius W. Becton, Jr.
(409) 857-3311

Tarleton State University
1297 W. Washington St., Tarleton Sta., Stephenville 76402
Pres. Dennis P. McCabe
(817) 968-9100

Texas A&M International University
One W. End Washington St.,
Laredo 78041
Pres. Leo Sayavedra
(210) 722-8001

Texas A&M University
College Station 77843
Interim Pres. E. Dean Gage
(409) 845-2217

Texas A&M University at Galveston
P.O. Box 1675, Galveston
77553
Pres. David J. Schmidly
(409) 740-4400

*Texas A&M University—Corpus
Christi*
6300 Ocean Dr., Corpus Christi
78412
Pres. Robert R. Furgason
(512) 991-6810

Texas A&M University—Kingsville
Campus Box 101, Kingsville
78363
Pres. Manuel L. Ibanez
(512) 595-2111

West Texas A&M University
2501 Fourth Ave., P.O. Box
999, W.T. Sta., Canyon
79016
Pres. Barry B. Thompson
(806) 656-2000

Texas Southern University
3100 Cleburne St., Houston 77004
Pres. Joann A. Horton
(713) 527-7011

Texas Southmost College
80 Fort Brown St., Brownsville 78520
Exec. Dir. Michael Putegnat
(210) 544-8200

Texas State Technical College System
3801 Campus Dr., Waco 76705
Chanc. Cecil L. Groves
(817) 867-4891

*Texas State Technical College—
Amarillo*
P.O. Box 11197, Amarillo 79111
Pres. Ronald L. DeSpain
(806) 335-2316

*Texas State Technical College—
Harlingen*
2424 Boxwood, Harlingen
78550-3697
Pres. J. Gilbert Leal
(210) 425-0600

*Texas State Technical College—
Sweetwater*
300 College Dr., Sweetwater
79556
Pres. Clay G. Johnson
(915) 235-7300

*Texas State Technical College—
Waco*
3801 Campus Dr., Waco 76705
Pres. Don E. Goodwin
(817) 867-4800

The Texas State University System
333 Guadalupe St., Tower III, Ste.
810, Austin 78701-3942
Chanc. Lamar Urbanovsky
(512) 463-1808

Angelo State University
2601 West Ave. N., San Angelo
76909
Pres. Lloyd D. Vincent
(915) 942-2073

Sam Houston State University
Huntsville 77341
Pres. Martin J. Anisman
(409) 294-1111

Southwest Texas State University
601 University Dr., San Marcos
78666-4616
Pres. Jerome H. Supple
(512) 245-2111

Sul Ross State University
Hwy. 90, Alpine 79832
Pres. R. Victor Morgan
(915) 837-8011

Texas Tech University
Lubbock 79409
Pres. Robert W. Lawless
(806) 742-2011

*Texas Tech University Health Sciences
Center*
3601 Fourth St., Lubbock 79430
Pres. Robert W. Lawless, Ph.D.
(806) 743-2975

Texas Woman's University
P.O. Box 23925, Denton 76204
Interim Pres. Patricia A. Sullivan
(817) 898-2000

Trinity Valley Community College
500 S. Prairieville, Athens 75751
Pres. Ronald C. Baugh
(903) 675-6200

Tyler Junior College
P.O. Box 9020, Tyler 75711
Pres. Raymond M. Hawkins
(903) 510-2200

University of Houston System
1600 Smith St., Ste. 3400, Houston
77002
Chanc. Alexander F. Schilt
(713) 754-7406

University of Houston—Clear Lake
2700 Bay Area Blvd., Houston
77058
Pres. Glenn A. Goerke
(713) 283-7600

University of Houston—Downtown
One Main St., Houston 77002
Pres. Max Castillo
(713) 221-8000

*University of Houston—University
Park*
4800 Calhoun Blvd., Houston
77204-2162
Pres. James H. Pickering
(713) 743-1000

University of Houston—Victoria
2506 E. Red River, Victoria
77901-4450
Pres. Lesta Van Der Wert
Turchen
(512) 576-3151

University of North Texas
P.O. Box 13737, Denton 76203
Chanc. Alfred F. Hurley
(817) 565-2000

*University of North Texas Health Science
Center at Fort Worth*
3500 Camp Bowie Blvd., Fort Worth
76107-2970
Pres. David M. Richards, D.O.
(817) 735-2000

The University of Texas System
601 Colorado St., Austin 78701
Chanc. William H. Cunningham
(512) 499-4201

*The University of Texas Health
Science Center at Houston*
P.O. Box 20036, Houston 77225
Pres. M. David Low
(713) 792-4975

*The University of Texas Health
Science Center at San Antonio*
7703 Floyd Curl Dr., San
Antonio 78284-7834
Pres. John P. Howe, III
(210) 567-7000

*The University of Texas Medical
Branch at Galveston*
300 University Blvd., Galveston
77550-0133
Pres. Thomas N. James
(409) 772-1687

*The University of Texas
Southwestern Medical Center at
Dallas*
5323 Harry Hines Blvd., Dallas
75235-9002
Pres. C. Kern Wildenthal
(214) 688-3111

The University of Texas at Arlington
UTA Box 19125, Arlington
76019
Pres. Ryan C. Amacher
(817) 273-2011

The University of Texas at Austin
P.O. Box T, Austin 78713-7389
Pres. Robert M. Berdahl
(512) 471-3434

The University of Texas at Brownsville
80 Fort Brown, Brownsville
78520
Pres. Juliet V. Garcia
(210) 544-8200

The University of Texas at Dallas
P.O. Box 830688, Richardson
75083-0688
Pres. Robert H. Rutford
(214) 690-2111

The University of Texas at El Paso
500 W. University Ave., El Paso
79968
Pres. Diana S. Natalicio
(915) 747-5000

The University of Texas at San Antonio
6900 N. Loop 1604 W., San
Antonio 78249-0617
Pres. Samuel A. Kirkpatrick
(210) 691-4100

The University of Texas at Tyler
3900 University Blvd., Tyler
75799
Pres. George F. Hamm
(903) 566-7000

The University of Texas of the Permian Basin
4901 E. University Blvd.,
Odessa 79762
Pres. Charles A. Sorber
(915) 367-2011

The University of Texas—Pan American
1201 W. University Dr., Edinburg 78539-2999
Pres. Miguel A. Nevarez
(210) 381-2011

Vernon Regional Junior College
4400 College Dr., Vernon 76384-
4092
Pres. R. Wade Kirk
(817) 552-6291

The Victoria College
2200 E. Red River St., Victoria
77901-4494
Pres. Jimmy L. Goodson
(512) 573-3291

Weatherford College
308 E. Park Ave., Weatherford 76086
Pres. James Boyd
(817) 594-5471

Western Texas College
6200 S. College Ave., Snyder 79549
Pres. Harry L. Krenek
(915) 573-8511

Wharton County Junior College
911 Boling Hwy., Wharton 77488
Pres. Elbert C. Hutchins
(409) 532-4560

UTAH

Utah System of Higher Education
355 West N. Temple, 3 Triad Ctr., Ste.
550, Salt Lake City 84180-1205
Commissioner Cecelia H. Foxley
(801) 321-7103

College of Eastern Utah
Price 84501
Pres. Michael A. Petersen
(801) 637-2120

Dixie College
St. George 84770
Pres. Robert C. Huddleston
(801) 673-4811

Salt Lake Community College
P.O. Box 30808, Salt Lake City
84130
Pres. Frank W. Budd
(801) 967-4111

Snow College
Ephraim 84627
Pres. Gerald J. Day
(801) 283-4021

Southern Utah University
Cedar City 84720
Pres. Gerald R. Sherratt
(801) 586-7710

University of Utah
Salt Lake City 84112
Pres. Arthur K. Smith
(801) 581-7200

Utah State University
Logan 84322-1400
Pres. George H. Emert
(801) 750-1000

Utah Valley State College
800 W. 1200 S., Orem 84058
Pres. Kerry D. Romesburg
(801) 226-5000

Weber State University
3750 Harrison Blvd., Ogden 84408-
1004
Pres. Paul H. Thompson
(801) 626-6140

VERMONT

Vermont State Colleges
P.O. Box 359, Waterbury 05676-0359
Chanc. Charles I. Bunting
(802) 241-2520

Castleton State College
Castleton 05735
Interim Pres. Joseph T. Mack
(802) 468-5611

Community College of Vermont
Waterbury 05676
Pres. Michael Holland
(802) 241-3535

Johnson State College
Johnson 05656
Pres. Robert T. Hahn
(802) 635-2356

Lyndon State College
Vail Hill, Lyndonville 05851
Pres. Margaret R. Williams
(802) 626-9371

Vermont Technical College
Randolph Center 05061
Pres. Robert G. Clarke
(802) 728-3391

VIRGINIA

Commonwealth of Virginia Council of Higher Education
James Monroe Bldg., 101 N. 14th St.,
Richmond 23219
Dir. Gordon K. Davies
(804) 225-2600

Christopher Newport University
50 Shoe La., Newport News 23606-2998
Pres. Anthony R. Santoro
(804) 594-7000

George Mason University
4400 University Dr., Fairfax 22030-4444
Pres. George W. Johnson
(703) 993-1000

James Madison University
Harrisonburg 22807
Pres. Ronald E. Carrier
(703) 568-6211

Longwood College
201 High St., Farmville 23909
Pres. William F. Dorrill
(804) 395-2000

Mary Washington College
1301 College Ave., Fredericksburg 22401
Pres. William M. Anderson, Jr.
(703) 899-4100

Norfolk State University
2401 Corprew Ave., Norfolk 23504
Pres. Harrison B. Wilson
(804) 683-8600

Old Dominion University
5215 Hampton Blvd., Norfolk 23529
Pres. James V. Koch
(804) 683-3000

Radford University
Radford 24142
Pres. Donald N. Dedmon
(703) 831-5000

University of Virginia Central Office
Charlottesville 22906-9011
Pres. John T. Casteen, III
(804) 924-3337

Clinch Valley College of the University of Virginia
College Ave., Wise 24293
Chanc. L. Jay Lemons
(703) 328-0100

University of Virginia
P.O. Box 9011, Charlottesville 22906
Pres. John T. Casteen, III
(804) 924-3337

Virginia Commonwealth University
910 W. Franklin St., Richmond 23284-2512
Pres. Eugene P. Trani
(804) 367-0100

Virginia Community College System
James Monroe Bldg., 101 N. 14th St.,
Richmond 23219
Chanc. Arnold R. Oliver
(804) 225-2117

Blue Ridge Community College
P.O. Box 80, Weyers Cave 24486
Pres. James R. Perkins
(703) 234-9261

Central Virginia Community College
3506 Wards Rd., Lynchburg 24502-2498
Pres. Belle S. Wheelan
(804) 386-4500

Dabney S. Lancaster Community College
P.O. Box 1000, Clifton Forge 24422-1000
Pres. John F. Backels
(703) 862-4246

Danville Community College
1008 S. Main St., Danville 24541
Pres. B. Carlyle Ramsey
(804) 797-2222

Eastern Shore Community College
29300 Lankford Hwy., Melfa 23410
Pres. John C. Fiege
(804) 787-5900

Germanna Community College
P.O. Box 339, Locust Grove
22508
Pres. Francis S. Turnage
(703) 423-1333

*J. Sargeant Reynolds Community
College*
P.O. Box 85622, Richmond
23285-5622
Pres. S.A. Burnette
(804) 371-3200

John Tyler Community College
13101 Jefferson Davis Hwy.,
Chester 23831-5399
Pres. Marshall W. Smith
(804) 796-4000

Lord Fairfax Community College
P.O. Box 47, Middletown 22645
Pres. Marilyn C. Beck
(703) 869-1120

*Mountain Empire Community
College*
P.O. Drawer 700, Big Stone
Gap 24219
Pres. Robert H. Sandel
(703) 523-2400

New River Community College
P.O. Drawer 1127, Dublin
24084
Pres. Edwin L. Barnes
(703) 674-3600

*Northern Virginia Community
College*
4001 Wakefield Chapel Rd.,
Annandale 22003-3723
Pres. Richard J. Ernst
(703) 323-3000

Patrick Henry Community College
P.O. Drawer 5311, Martinsville
24115-5311
Pres. Max F. Wingett
(703) 638-8777

Paul D. Camp Community College
100 N. College Rd., P.O. Box
737, Franklin 23851
Pres. Jerome J. Friga
(804) 562-2171

*Piedmont Virginia Community
College*
Rte. 6, Box 1, Charlottesville
22902
Pres. Deborah M. DiCroce
(804) 977-3900

Rappahannock Community College
P.O. Box 287, Glenns 23149
Pres. John H. Upton
(804) 758-6700

*Southside Virginia Community
College*
Rte. 1, Box 60, Alberta 23821
Pres. John J. Cavan
(804) 949-7111

*Southwest Virginia Community
College*
P.O. Box SVCC, Richlands
24641
Pres. Charles R. King
(703) 964-2555

Thomas Nelson Community College
P.O. Box 9407, Hampton 23670
Pres. Robert G. Templin, Jr.
(804) 825-2700

Tidewater Community College
7000 College Dr., Portsmouth
23703
Pres. Larry L. Whitworth
(804) 484-2121

*Virginia Highlands Community
College*
P.O. Box 828, State Rte. 372 off
Rte. 140, Abingdon 24210
Pres. N. DeWitt Moore, Jr.
(703) 628-6094

Virginia Western Community College
3095 Colonial Ave., S.W., P.O.
Box 14045, Roanoke 24038
Pres. Charles L. Downs
(703) 857-7311

Wytheville Community College
1000 E. Main St., Wytheville
24382
Pres. William F. Snyder
(703) 228-5541

Virginia Military Institute
  Lexington 24450
  Supt. John W. Knapp
  (703) 464-7000

Virginia Polytechnic Institute and State
  University
  210 Burruss Hall, Blacksburg 24061-
    0131
  Pres. Paul E. Torgersen
  (703) 231-6000

Virginia State University
  P.O. Box 9001, One Hayden Dr.,
    Petersburg 23806
  Pres. Eddie N. Moore, Jr.
  (804) 524-5000

WASHINGTON

Washington Higher Education Coordinating Board
917 Lakeridge Way, P.O. Box 43430, Olympia 98504-3430
Executive Dir. Elson S. Floyd
(206) 753-3241

Central Washington University
208 Bouillon, Ellensburg 98926
Pres. Ivory V. Nelson
(509) 963-1111

Eastern Washington University
Cheney 99004
Pres. Marshall E. Drummond
(509) 359-6200

Evergreen State College
Olympia 98505
Pres. Jane L. Jervis
(206) 866-6000

University of Washington
Seattle 98195
Pres. William P. Gerberding
(206) 543-2100

Washington State University
Pullman 99164-1046
Pres. Samuel H. Smith
(509) 335-3564

Western Washington University
Bellingham 98225
Pres. Karen W. Morse
(206) 650-3000

Washington State Board for Community and Technical Colleges
319 Seventh Ave., P.O. Box 42495, Olympia 98504-2495
Exec. Dir. Earl Hale
(206) 753-7412

Bates Technical College
1101 S. Yakima Ave., Tacoma 98405
Pres. William P. Mohler
(206) 596-1500

Bellevue Community College
3000 Landerholm Cir., S.E., Bellevue 98007-6484
Pres. B. Jean Floten
(206) 641-0111

Bellingham Technical College
3028 Lindbergh Ave., Bellingham 98225
Pres. Desmond McArdle
(206) 676-6490

Big Bend Community College
7662 Chanute St., Moses Lake 98837-3299
Pres. Gregory G. Fitch
(509) 762-5351

Centralia College
600 W. Locust St., Centralia 98531
Pres. Henry P. Kirk
(206) 736-9391

Clark College
1800 E. McLoughlin Blvd., Vancouver 98663
Pres. Earl P. Johnson
(206) 694-6521

Clover Park Technical College
4500 Steilacoom Blvd., S.W., Tacoma 98498-4098
Admin. Alson E. Green, Jr.
(206) 589-5500

Columbia Basin College
2600 N. 20th Ave., Pasco 99302
Pres. Marvin Weiss
(509) 547-0511

Community Colleges of Spokane
N2000 Greene St., Spokane 99207-5499
C.E.O. Terrance R. Brown
(509) 533-7401

Spokane Community College
N. 1810 Greene St., Spokane 99207
Pres. Donald R. Kolb
(509) 533-7000

Spokane Falls Community College
W. 3410 Fort George Wright Dr., Spokane 99204
Pres. Vern Jerome Loland
(509) 459-3500

Edmonds Community College
20000 68th Ave. W., Lynnwood
98036
Pres. Thomas C. Nielsen
(206) 771-1500

Everett Community College
801 Wetmore Ave., Everett 98201-
1327
Pres. Susan Carroll
(206) 259-7151

Grays Harbor College
Aberdeen 98520
Pres. Jewell C. Manspeaker
(206) 532-9020

Green River Community College
12401 S.E. 320th St., Auburn 98002
Pres. Richard A. Rutkowski
(206) 833-9111

Highline Community College
P.O. Box 98000, Des Moines 98198-
9800
Pres. Edward M. Command
(206) 878-3710

Lake Washington Technical College
11605 132nd Ave., N.E., Kirkland
98034
Pres. Donald W. Fowler
(206) 828-5600

Lower Columbia College
P.O. Box 3010, Longview 98632-
0310
President Vernon R. Pickett
(206) 577-2300

Olympic College
1600 Chester Ave., Bremerton 98310
Pres. Wallace A. Simpson
(206) 478-4544

Peninsula College
1502 E. Lauridsen Blvd., Port Angeles 98362
Pres. Joyce Helens
(206) 452-9277

Pierce College
9401 Farwest Dr., S.W., Tacoma
98498
Pres. George A. Delaney
(206) 964-6500

Renton Technical College
3000 Fourth St., N.E., Renton 98056
Pres. Robert C. Roberts
(206) 235-2352

Seattle Community College District
1500 Harvard St., Seattle 98122
Chanc. Charles A. Kane
(206) 587-3872

North Seattle Community College
9600 College Way N., Seattle
98103
Pres. Peter Ku
(206) 527-3600

Seattle Central Community College
1701 Broadway, Seattle 98122
Pres. Charles H. Mitchell
(206) 587-3800

South Seattle Community College
6000 16th Ave., S.W., Seattle
98106
Pres. Jerry M. Brockey
(206) 764-5300

Shoreline Community College
16101 Greenwood Ave. N., Seattle
98133
Pres. Ronald E. Bell
(206) 546-4101

Skagit Valley College
2405 College Way, Mount Vernon
98273
Pres. James M. Ford
(206) 428-1261

South Puget Sound Community College
2011 Mottman Rd., S.W., Olympia
98502
Pres. Kenneth J. Minnaert
(206) 754-7711

Tacoma Community College
5900 S. 12th St., Tacoma 98465
Pres. Raymond J. Needham
(206) 566-5000

Walla Walla Community College
500 Tausick Way, Walla Walla
99362
Pres. Steven L. Van Ausdle
(509) 522-2500

Wenatchee Valley College
    1300 Fifth St., Wenatchee 98801
    Interim Pres. Woody Ahn
    (509) 662-1651

Whatcom Community College
    237 W. Kellogg Rd., Bellingham
        98226
    Pres. Harold G. Heiner
    (206) 676-2170

Yakima Valley Community College
    P.O. Box 1647, Yakima 98907
    Pres. V. Phillip Tullar
    (509) 575-2350

WEST VIRGINIA

State College System of West Virginia
1018 Kanawha Blvd., E., Charleston
25301
Interim Chanc. James W. Rowley
(304) 558-0699

Bluefield State College
219 Rock St., Bluefield 24701
Pres. Robert E. Moore
(304) 327-4030

Concord College
Athens 24712
Pres. Jerry L. Beasley
(304) 384-3115

Fairmont State College
Locust Ave., Fairmont 26554
Pres. Robert J. Dillman
(304) 367-4151

Glenville State College
200 High St., Glenville 26351
Pres. William K. Simmons
(304) 462-7361

Shepherd College
Shepherdstown 25443
Pres. Michael P. Riccards
(304) 876-2511

*Southern West Virginia Community
College*
P.O. Box 2900, Dempsey Branch
Rd., Logan 25601-2900
Pres. Harry J. Boyer
(304) 792-4300

West Liberty State College
West Liberty 26074
Pres. Clyde D. Campbell
(304) 336-5000

West Virginia Institute of Technology
Montgomery 25136
Pres. John P. Carrier
(304) 442-3071

*West Virginia Northern Community
College*
College Sq., Wheeling 26003
Pres. Ronald M. Hutkin
(304) 233-5900

West Virginia State College
Institute 25112
Pres. Hazo W. Carter, Jr.
(304) 766-3000

University System of West Virginia
1018 Kanawha Blvd., E., Ste. 700,
Charleston 25301
Chanc. Charles W. Manning
(304) 558-0267

Marshall University
Huntington 25755
Pres. J. Wade Gilley
(304) 696-2300

*Potomac State College of West Virginia
University*
Fort Ave., Keyser 26726
Pres. Joseph M. Gratto
(304) 788-3011

West Virginia Graduate College
P.O. Box 1003, Institute 25112
Pres. Dennis P. Prisk
(304) 766-2000

*West Virginia School of Osteopathic
Medicine*
400 N. Lee St., Lewisburg 24901
Pres. Olen E. Jones, Jr., PhD
(304) 645-6270

West Virginia University
Box 6201, Morgantown 26506-6201
Pres. Neil S. Bucklew
(304) 293-0111

West Virginia University at Parkersburg
Rte. 5, Box 167-A, Parkersburg
26101
Pres. Eldon L. Miller
(304) 424-8000

WISCONSIN

The University of Wisconsin System
1220 Linden Dr., Madison 53706
Pres. Katharine C. Lyall
(608) 262-2321

University of Wisconsin Centers
150 E. Gilman St., P.O. Box 8680,
Madison 53708-8680
Chanc. Lee E. Grugel
(608) 262-1783

University of Wisconsin—Eau Claire
P.O. Box 4004, Eau Claire 54702
Chanc. Larry G. Schnack
(715) 836-2637

University of Wisconsin—Green Bay
2420 Nicolet Dr., Green Bay 54311
Chanc. Mark Perkins
(414) 465-2000

University of Wisconsin—La Crosse
1725 State St., La Crosse 54601
Chanc. Judith L. Kuipers, Ph.D.
(608) 785-8000

University of Wisconsin—Madison
500 Lincoln Dr., Madison 53706
Chanc. David Ward
(608) 262-1234

University of Wisconsin—Milwaukee
P.O. Box 413, Milwaukee 53201
Chanc. John H. Schroeder
(414) 229-4331

University of Wisconsin—Oshkosh
800 Algoma Blvd., Oshkosh 54901
Chanc. John E. Kerrigan
(414) 424-1234

University of Wisconsin—Parkside
Box 2000, Kenosha 53141-2000
Interim Chanc. John C. Stockwell
(414) 595-2345

University of Wisconsin—Platteville
One University Plaza, Platteville
53818-3099
Chanc. Robert G. Culbertson
(608) 342-1234

University of Wisconsin—River Falls
River Falls 54022
Chanc. Gary A. Thibodeau
(715) 425-3201

University of Wisconsin—Stevens Point
2100 Main St., Stevens Point 54481
Chanc. Keith R. Sanders
(715) 346-0123

University of Wisconsin—Stout
Menomonie 54751-0790
Chanc. Charles W. Sorensen
(715) 232-2441

University of Wisconsin—Superior
1800 Grand Ave., Superior 54880
Chanc. Betty J. Youngblood
(715) 394-8101

University of Wisconsin—Whitewater
800 W. Main St., Whitewater 53190
Chanc. H. Gaylon Greenhill
(414) 472-1918

WYOMING

Wyoming Community College Commission
122 W. 25th St. at West, Cheyenne 82002
Exec. Dir. James Meznek
(307) 777-7763

Casper College
125 College Dr., Casper 82601
Pres. Leroy Strausner
(307) 268-2110

Central Wyoming College
2660 Peck Ave., Riverton 82501
Pres. Jo Anne McFarland
(307) 856-9291

Eastern Wyoming College
3200 W. C St., Torrington 82240
Pres. Roy B. Mason
(307) 532-7111

Laramie County Community College
1400 E. College Dr., Cheyenne
82007
Pres. Charles H. Bohlen
(307) 778-1102

Northwest College
231 W. Sixth St., Powell 82435
Pres. John P. Hanna
(307) 754-6111

Sheridan College
P.O. Box 1500, Sheridan 82801
Pres. Stephen J. Maier
(307) 674-6446

Western Wyoming College
P.O. Box 428, Rock Springs 82901
Pres. Tex Boggs
(307) 382-1600

OUTSIDE THE UNITED STATES

College of Micronesia
P.O. Drawer F, Kolonia, Pohnpei,
Micronesia FSM 96941
Chanc. Singeru Sigeo
(691) 320-2462

College of Micronesia
P.O. Box 159, Kolonia, Pohnpei,
FSM 96941
Pres. Paul Gallen
(691) 320-2480

College of the Marshall Islands
P.O. Box 1258, Majuro, RMI 96960
Pres. Dorothy Nook
(692) 625-3394

Palau Community College
P.O. Box 9, Koror, RP 96940
Pres. Francis M. Matsutaro
(680) 488-2471

Appendices

A. The Accrediting Process

Accreditation is a system for recognizing educational institutions and professional programs affiliated with those institutions for a level of performance, integrity, and quality which entitles them to the confidence of the educational community and the public they serve. In the United States, this recognition is extended primarily through nongovernmental, voluntary institutional or professional associations. These groups establish criteria for accreditation, arrange site visits, evaluate those institutions and professional programs which desire accredited status, and publicly designate those which meet their criteria.

In most other countries, the establishment and maintenance of educational standards are the responsibilities of a central government bureau. In the United States, however, public authority in education is constitutionally reserved to the states. The system of voluntary nongovernmental evaluation, called accreditation, has evolved to promote both regional and national approaches to the determination of educational quality. While accreditation is basically a private, voluntary process, accrediting decisions are used as a consideration in many formal actions—by governmental funding agencies, scholarship commissions, foundations, employers, counselors, and potential students. Accrediting bodies have, therefore, come to be viewed as quasi-public entities with certain responsibilities to the many groups which interact with the educational community.

In America, accreditation at the postsecondary level performs a number of important functions, including the encouragement of efforts toward maximum educational effectiveness. The accrediting process requires institutions and programs to examine their goals, activities, and achievements; to consider the expert criticism and suggestions of a visiting team; and to determine internal procedures for action on recommendations from the accrediting body. Since accreditation status is reviewed on a periodic basis, recognized institutions and professional programs are encouraged to maintain continuous self-study and improvement mechanisms.

Types of Accreditation

Institutional accreditation is granted by the regional and national accrediting commissions of schools and colleges, which collectively serve most of the institutions chartered or licensed in the United States and its possessions. These commissions and associations accredit total operating units only.

Specialized accreditation of professional or occupational schools and programs is granted by national professional organizations in such fields as business, dentistry, engineering, and law. Each of these groups has its distinctive definitions of eligibility, criteria for accreditation, and operating procedures, but all have undertaken accreditation activities primarily to provide quality assurances concerning educational preparation of members of the profession or occupation. Many of the specialized accrediting bodies will consider requests for accreditation reviews only from programs affiliated with institutions holding comprehensive accreditation. Some specialized agencies, however, accredit professional programs at institutions not otherwise accredited. These are generally independent institutions which offer only the particular specified discipline or course of study in question.

Procedures in Accreditation

The accrediting process is continuously evolving. The trend has been qualitative criteria, from the early days of simple checklists to an increasing interest and emphasis on measuring the outcomes of educational experiences.

The process begins with the institutional or programmatic self-study, a comprehensive effort to measure progress according to previously accepted objectives. The self-study considers the interests of a broad cross-section of constituencies—students, faculty, administrators, alumni, trustees, and, in some circumstances, the local community.

The resulting report is reviewed by the appropriate commission and serves as the basis for evaluation by a site-visit team from the accrediting group. The site-visit team normally consists of professional educators (faculty and administrators), specialists selected according to the nature of the institution, and members representing specific interests. The visiting team assesses the institution or program in light of the self-study and adds judgments based on its own expertise and its external perspective. The team prepares an evaluation report, which is reviewed by the institution or program for factual accuracy.

The original self-study, the team report, and any response the institution or program may wish to make are forwarded to the accreditation commission. The review body uses these materials as the basis for action regarding the accreditation status of the institution or program. Negative actions may be appealed according to established procedures of the accrediting body.

Although accreditation is generally granted for a specific term (e.g., five or ten years), accrediting bodies reserve the right to review member institutions or programs at any time for cause. They also reserve the right to review any substantive change, such as an expansion from undergraduate to graduate offerings. Such changes may require prior approval and/or review upon implementation. In this way, accrediting bodies hold their member institutions and programs continually responsible to their educational peers, to the constituents they serve, and to the public.

Accreditation's Purposes
Throughout the evolution of its procedures, postsecondary accreditation's aims have been and are to:
- foster excellence in postsecondary education through the development of uniform national criteria and guidelines for assessing educational effectiveness;
- encourage improvement through continuous self-study and review;
- assure the educational community, the general public, and other agencies or organizations that an institution or program has clearly defined and appropriate objectives, maintains conditions under which their achievement can reasonably be expected, is in fact accomplishing them substantially, and can be expected to continue to do so;
- provide counsel and assistance to established and developing institutions and programs; and
- endeavor to protect institutions against encroachments which might jeopardize their educational effectiveness or academic freedom.

Postsecondary education in the United States derives its strength and excellence from the unique and diverse character of its many individual institutions. Such qualities are best sustained and extended by the freedom of these institutions to determine their own objectives and to experiment in the ways and means of education within the framework of their respective authority and responsibilities.

Public as well as educational needs must be served simultaneously in determining and fostering standards of quality and integrity in the institutions and such specialized programs as they offer. Accreditation, through nongovernmental institutional and specialized agencies, provides a major means for meeting those needs.

Role of the Commission on Recognition of Postsecondary Accreditation
The Commission on Recognition of Postsecondary Accreditation (CORPA) is a voluntary, nongovernmental organization that works to foster and facilitate the role of accrediting bodies in promoting and insuring the quality and diversity of American postsecondary education. The accrediting bodies, while established and supported by their membership, are intended to serve the broader interests of society as well. To promote these ends, CORPA recognizes, coordinates, and periodically reviews the work of its recognized accrediting bodies, and the appropriateness of existing or proposed accrediting bodies and their activities, through its granting of recognition and performance of other related functions.

B. Accrediting Groups Recognized by CORPA

CORPA periodically evaluates the accrediting activities of institutional and professional associations. Upon determining that those activities meet or exceed CORPA provisions, the accrediting organizations are publicly recognized through this listing. Groups that are regional in nature are identified with their geographical areas; all others are national in their activities.

NATIONAL INSTITUTIONAL ACCREDITING BODIES

ACCREDITING BUREAU OF HEALTH EDUCATION
SCHOOLS
Jeanne Russell, *Administrator*
Oak Manor Offices
29089 U.S. 20 West
Elkhart, IN 46514
(219) 293-0124, Fax: (219) 295-8564

ACCREDITING COMMISSION FOR CAREER
SCHOOLS/COLLEGES OF TECHNOLOGY
Thomas A. Kube, *Executive Director*
750 First Street, N.E.
Suite 905
Washington, DC 20002-4242
(202) 336-6850, Fax: (202) 842-2585

ACCREDITING COUNCIL FOR INDEPENDENT
COLLEGES AND SCHOOLS
Stephen D. Parker, *Executive Director*
750 First Street, N.E.
Suite 900
Washington, DC 20002-4242
(202) 336-6700, Fax: (202) 337-0566

AMERICAN ASSOCIATION OF BIBLE COLLEGES
Randall E. Bell, *Executive Director*
Commission on Accrediting
P.O. Box 1523
Fayetteville, AR 72702
(501) 521-8164, Fax: (501) 521-9202

ASSOCIATION OF ADVANCED RABBINICAL AND
TALMUDIC SCHOOLS
Dr. Bernard Fryshman, *Executive Vice
President*
Accreditation Commission
175 Fifth Avenue
Suite 711
New York, NY 10010
(212) 477-0950, Fax: (212) 533-5335

THE ASSOCIATION OF THEOLOGICAL SCHOOLS IN
THE UNITED STATES AND CANADA
James L. Waits, *Executive Director*
Commission on Accrediting
10 Summit Park Drive
Pittsburgh, PA 15275-1103
(412) 788-6505, Fax: (412) 788-6510

NATIONAL HOME STUDY COUNCIL
Michael P. Lambert, *Executive Secretary*
Accrediting Commission
1601 18th Street, N.W.
Washington, DC 20009
(202) 234-5100, Fax: (202) 332-1386

REGIONAL INSTITUTIONAL ACCREDITING BODIES

MIDDLE STATES ASSOCIATION OF COLLEGES AND SCHOOLS
Delaware, District of Columbia, Maryland, New Jersey, New York, Pennsylvania, Puerto Rico, Virgin Islands
Howard L. Simmons, *Executive Director*
The Commission on Higher Education
3624 Market Street
Philadelphia, PA 19104
(215) 662-5606, Fax: (215) 662-5950

NEW ENGLAND ASSOCIATION OF SCHOOLS AND COLLEGES, INC.
Connecticut, Maine, Massachusetts, New Hampshire, Rhode Island, Vermont
209 Burlington Road
Bedford, MA 01730-1433
(617) 271-0022, Fax: (617) 271-0950
Charles M. Cook, *Director*
Commission on Institutions of Higher Education
Richard E. Mandeville, *Director*
Commission on Technical and Career Institutions

NORTH CENTRAL ASSOCIATION OF COLLEGES AND SCHOOLS
Arizona, Arkansas, Colorado, Illinois, Indiana, Iowa, Kansas, Michigan, Minnesota, Missouri, Nebraska, New Mexico, North Dakota, Ohio, Oklahoma, South Dakota, West Virginia, Wisconsin, Wyoming
Dr. Patricia A. Thrash, *Executive Director*
Commission on Institutions of Higher Education
30 N. LaSalle Street, Suite 2400
Chicago, IL 60602
(312) 263-0456, Fax: (312) 263-7462

THE NORTHWEST ASSOCIATION OF SCHOOLS AND COLLEGES
Alaska, Idaho, Montana, Nevada, Oregon, Utah, Washington
Joseph A. Malik, *Executive Director*
Commission on Colleges
3700-B University Way, N.E.
Seattle, WA 98105
(206) 543-0195

SOUTHERN ASSOCIATION OF COLLEGES AND SCHOOLS
Alabama, Florida, Georgia, Kentucky, Louisiana, Mississippi, North Carolina, South Carolina, Tennessee, Texas, Virginia
1866 Southern Lane
Decatur, GA 30033-4097
(404) 679-4500, Fax: (404) 679-4558
James T. Rogers, *Executive Director*
Commission on Colleges
Harry L. Bowman, *Executive Director*
Commission on Occupational Education Institutions
(404) 679-4500, Fax: (404) 679-4556

WESTERN ASSOCIATION OF SCHOOLS AND COLLEGES
California, Guam, Hawaii
Stephen S. Weiner, *Executive Director*
Accrediting Commission for Senior Colleges and Universities
P.O. Box 9990
Mills College
Oakland, CA 94613
(510) 632-5000, Fax: (510) 632-8361

John C. Petersen, *Executive Director*
Accrediting Commission for Community and Junior Colleges
3060 Valencia Avenue
Aptos, CA 95003
(408) 688-7575, Fax: (408) 688-1841

SPECIALIZED ACCREDITING BODIES

ACCREDITATION BOARD FOR ENGINEERING AND
TECHNOLOGY, INC.
Professional engineering programs at the baccalaureate and master's levels preparing for
entry into the engineering profession; baccalaureate and two-year programs (including those
leading to the associate degree) in engineering
technology; programs in industrial hygiene at
the master's level; programs in occupational
health and safety at the baccalaureate and master's level; and programs in surveying or surveying and mapping at the baccalaureate level.
Engineering Accreditation Commission
Technology Accreditation Commission
George D. Peterson, *Executive Director*
345 East 47th Street
New York, NY 10017-2397
(212) 705-7685, Fax: (212) 838-8062

ACCREDITING COMMISSION ON EDUCATION FOR
HEALTH SERVICES ADMINISTRATION
Graduate programs at the master's degree level
or the equivalent in health services administra-
tion, health planning, and health policy analysis.
Sherril B. Gelmon, DrPH, *Executive Director*
1911 North Fort Myer Drive
Suite 503
Arlington, VA 22209
(703) 524-0511, Fax: (703) 525-4791

ACCREDITING COUNCIL ON EDUCATION IN
JOURNALISM AND MASS COMMUNICATIONS
Units within institutions, a major part of the
unit's activities being to offer professional pro-
grams preparing students at the bachelor's and
master's levels for careers in journalism and
mass communications.
Susanne Shaw, *Executive Director*
Stauffer-Flint Hall
University of Kansas
Lawrence, KS 66045
(913) 864-3973, Fax: (913) 864-4755

AMERICAN ASSEMBLY OF COLLEGIATE SCHOOLS
OF BUSINESS
Baccalaureate and master's degree programs in
business administration and management and
baccalaureate and master's degree programs in
accounting.
Accreditation Council
Milton Blood, *Managing Director*
600 Emerson Road
Suite 300
St. Louis, MO 63141-6762
(314) 872-8481, Fax: (314) 872-8495

AMERICAN ASSOCIATION FOR MARRIAGE AND
FAMILY THERAPY
Graduate programs at the master's, doctoral
and post-graduate levels for careers in marriage
and family therapy.
Commission on Accreditation for
Marriage and Family Therapy
Education
Denise Heaman Calvert, *Executive Director*
1100 17th Street, N.W.
10th Floor
Washington, DC 20036-4601
(202) 452-0109

AMERICAN BAR ASSOCIATION/ASSOCIATION OF
AMERICAN LAW SCHOOLS
Programs leading to the first professional
degree and advanced degrees in law.
Council of the Section of Legal Education
and Admissions to the Bar
James P. White, *Consultant on Legal*
Education
American Bar Association
550 West North Street
Indianapolis, IN 46202
(317) 264-8340, Fax: (317) 264-8355

Programs leading to the first professional
degree.
Carl C. Monk, *Executive Vice President*
Association of American Law Schools
1201 Connecticut Avenue, N.W.
Suite 800
Washington, DC 20036
(202) 296-8851, Fax: (202) 296-8869

AMERICAN BOARD OF FUNERAL SERVICE
EDUCATION, INC.
Institutions and programs offering diplomas,
associate and baccalaureate degrees in funeral
service education and mortuary science education.
Committee on Accreditation
Gordon S. Bigelow, *Executive Director*
14 Crestwood Road
Cumberland, ME 04021
(207) 829-5715, Fax: (207) 829-4443

AMERICAN COUNCIL FOR CONSTRUCTION
EDUCATION
Associate degree programs in construction, and
baccalaureate programs in construction, construction science, construction management,
and construction technology.
Daniel E. Dupree, *Executive Vice President*
901 Hudson Lane
Monroe, LA 71201
(318) 328-2413, Fax: (318) 323-2413

AMERICAN COUNSELING ASSOCIATION
Master's degree programs designed to prepare individuals for community counseling, mental health counseling, marriage and family counseling/therapy, school counseling, and student affairs practice in higher education; and doctoral level programs in counselor education and supervision.
Council for Accreditation of Counseling and Related Educational Programs
Dr. Carol L. Bobby, *Executive Director*
5999 Stevenson Avenue
Alexandria, VA 22304
(703) 823-9800, Fax: (703) 823-0252

AMERICAN DENTAL ASSOCIATION
First professional degree programs in dental education; degree, certificate, and diploma programs in allied dental education (dental assisting, dental hygiene, and dental laboratory technology); and advanced degrees and certificate programs in dental education (dental public health, endodontics, oral pathology; oral and maxillofacial surgery, orthodontics, pediatric dentistry, periodontics, prosthodontics, general practice residency and general dentistry).
Commission on Dental Accreditation
Cynthia Davenport, *Program Manager*
211 East Chicago Avenue
Chicago, IL 60611
(312) 440-2719, Fax: (312) 440-2915

AMERICAN DIETETIC ASSOCIATION
Coordinated bachelor's degree programs, post-baccalaureate dietetic internship programs, and coordinated master's degree programs in dietetics.
Council on Education
Beverly Mitchell, *Administrator*
216 West Jackson Boulevard
Suite 800
Chicago, IL 60606-6995
(312) 899-0400, Fax: (312) 899-1758

AMERICAN HOME ECONOMICS ASSOCIATION
Baccalaureate programs in home economics.
Office of Accreditation
Katherine Hall, *Director of Accreditation*
1555 King Street
Alexandria, VA 22314
(703) 706-4600, Fax: (703) 706-HOME

AMERICAN LIBRARY ASSOCIATION
First professional degree programs at the master's level in librarianship.
Committee on Accreditation
Prudence Dalrymple, *Accreditation Officer*
50 East Huron Street
Chicago, IL 60611-2795
(312) 280-2432, Fax: (312) 280-2433

AMERICAN MEDICAL ASSOCIATION
CORPA recognizes the Committee on Allied Health Education and Accreditation (CAHEA) as an umbrella agency for 20 review committees representing professional organizations collaborating in the accreditation of programs in the following areas of allied health. All questions concerning accreditation of these programs should be directed to CAHEA at the address given. The review committees are:
- Accreditation Review Committee for the *Anesthesiologist Assistant*;
- Committee on *Athletic Trainer* Education;
- Committee on Accreditation (AABB), *Specialist in Blood Bank Technology Schools*;
- Joint Review Committee on Education in *Cardiovascular Technology*;
- *Cytotechnology* Programs Review Committee;
- Joint Review Committee on Education in *Diagnostic Medical Sonography*;
- Joint Review Committee on Education in *Electroneurodiagnostic Technology*;
- Joint Review Committee on Educational Programs for the *EMT-Paramedic*;
- National Accrediting Agency for Clinical Laboratory Science, *Histologic Technician/Technologist, Medical Laboratory Technician (associate degree), Medical Laboratory Technician (certificate), Medical Technologist*;
- Curriculum Review Board (AAMA), *Medical Assistant*;
- Accreditation Review Committee for the *Medical Illustrator*;
- Council on Education (AMRA), *Medical Record Technician, Medical Record Administrator*;
- Joint Review Committee on Educational Programs in *Nuclear Medicine Technology*;
- Accreditation Committee (AOTA), *Occupational Therapy, Occupational Therapy Assistant*;
- Joint Review Committee on Education Programs for the *Ophthalmic Medical Technician/Technologist*;
- Joint Review Committee for *Perfusion Education*;
- Accreditation Review Committee on Education for the *Physician Assistant, Surgeon's Assistant*;
- Joint Review Committee on Education in Radiologic Technology, *Radiologic Technology, Radiation Therapy Technologist, Radiographer*;

·Joint Review Committee for Respiratory Therapy Education, *Respiratory Therapist, Respiratory Therapy Technician*;
·Accreditation Review Committee on Educational Programs for the *Surgical Technologist*.
Committee on Allied Health Education and Accreditation
Division of Allied Health Education and Accreditation
L.M. Detmer, *Director*
515 North State Street
Chicago, IL 60610
(312) 464-4660, Fax: (312) 464-5830

AMERICAN MEDICAL ASSOCIATION/ASSOCIATION OF AMERICAN MEDICAL COLLEGES
Programs leading to the professional degree in medicine (Doctor of Medicine) and to post-baccalaureate programs in the basic medical sciences.

Liaison Committee on Medical Education
(in odd-numbered years beginning July 1st)
Harry S. Jonas, M.D., *Secretary*
American Medical Association
515 North State Street
Chicago, IL 60610
(312) 464-4933, Fax: (312) 464-5830

(in even-numbered years beginning July 1st)
Donald G. Kassebaum, M.D., *Secretary*
Association of American Medical Colleges
2450 N Street, N.W.
Washington, DC 20037-1126
(202) 828-0596, Fax: (202) 785-5027

AMERICAN OPTOMETRIC ASSOCIATION
Optometric technician associate degree programs, professional optometric doctoral degree programs, and optometric post-doctoral residency programs.
Council on Optometric Education
Joyce Urbek, *Manager*
243 North Lindbergh Boulevard
St. Louis, MO 63141
(314) 991-4100, Fax: (314) 991-4101

AMERICAN OSTEOPATHIC ASSOCIATION
Programs leading to the Doctor of Osteopathy degree.
Bureau of Professional Education
Department of Education
W. Douglas Ward, Ph.D., *Director*
142 East Ontario Street
Chicago, IL 60611-2864
(312) 280-5840, Fax: (312) 280-5893

AMERICAN PHYSICAL THERAPY ASSOCIATION
Physical therapist assistant programs at the associate degree level and physical therapist programs at the baccalaureate, post-baccalaureate certificate, and master's degree levels.
Commission on Accreditation in Physical Therapy Education
Virginia M. Nieland, *Director*
1111 North Fairfax Street
Alexandria, VA 22314
(703) 706-3245, Fax: (703) 684-7343

AMERICAN PODIATRIC MEDICAL ASSOCIATION
Programs leading to the degree of Doctor of Podiatric Medicine.
Council on Podiatric Medical Education
Jay Levrio, *Director*
9312 Old Georgetown Road
Bethesda, MD 20814-1621
(301) 571-9200, Fax: (301) 530-2752

AMERICAN PSYCHOLOGICAL ASSOCIATION
Doctoral programs in professional specialties of psychology and pre-doctoral internship training programs in professional psychology.
Committee on Accreditation
Paul D. Nelson, *Director, Office of Accreditation*
750 First Street, N.E.
Washington, DC 20002-4242
(202) 336-5979, Fax: (202) 336-5978

AMERICAN SOCIETY OF LANDSCAPE ARCHITECTS
First professional programs at the bachelor's or master's level in landscape architecture.
Landscape Architecture Accreditation Board
Ronald C. Leighton, *Accreditation Manager*
4401 Connecticut Avenue, N.W., 5th Floor
Washington, DC 20008-2302
(202) 686-2752, Fax: (202) 686-1001

AMERICAN SPEECH-LANGUAGE-HEARING ASSOCIATION
Master's degree programs in speech-language pathology and/or audiology.
Educational Standards Board
Sharon Goldsmith, *Director*
10801 Rockville Pike
Rockville, MD 20852
(301) 897-5700, Fax: (301) 571-0457

AMERICAN VETERINARY MEDICAL ASSOCIATION
First professional degree programs in veterinary medicine.
Council on Education
Edward R. Ames, *Director*
1931 North Meacham Road
Schaumburg, IL 60173-4360
(708) 925-8070, Fax: (708) 925-1329

COMPUTING SCIENCES ACCREDITATION BOARD
Baccalaureate degree programs designated as computer science programs which prepare students for entry into the computer science profession.
Computer Science Accreditation Commission
Patrick M. LaMalva, *Executive Director*
Two Landmark Square
Suite 209
Stamford, CT 06901
(203) 975-1117, Fax: (203) 975-1222

COUNCIL ON ACCREDITATION OF NURSE ANESTHESIA EDUCATIONAL PROGRAMS
Generic nurse anesthesia educational programs.
Betty J. Horton, CRNA, MA, *Director of Accreditation*
216 Higgins Road
Park Ridge, IL 60068-5790
(708) 692-7050, Fax: (708) 692-6968

THE COUNCIL ON CHIROPRACTIC EDUCATION
Institutions offering the doctor of chiropractic degree.
Commission on Accreditation
Ralph G. Miller, *Executive Vice President*
4401 Westown Parkway, Suite 120
West Des Moines, IA 50265
(515) 226-9001, Fax: (515) 226-9031

THE COUNCIL ON EDUCATION FOR PUBLIC HEALTH
Graduate schools of public health and graduate programs outside schools of public health in community health education and community health/preventive medicine.
Patricia P. Evans, *Executive Director*
1015 15th Street, N.W.
Suite 403
Washington, DC 20005
(202) 789-1050, Fax: (202) 289-8274

COUNCIL ON REHABILITATION EDUCATION
Master's degree programs in rehabilitation counselor education.
Commission on Standards and Accreditation
Emer D. Broadbent, *Executive Director*
P.O. Box 1680
1207 South Oak Street
Champaign, IL 61824-1680
(217) 333-6688, Fax: (217) 244-6784

COUNCIL ON SOCIAL WORK EDUCATION
Baccalaureate and master's degree programs in social work education.
Commission on Accreditation
Nancy Randolph, *Director*
1600 Duke Street
Alexandria, VA 22314-3421
(703) 683-8080, Fax: (703) 683-8099

FOUNDATION FOR INTERIOR DESIGN EDUCATION RESEARCH
Programs from the junior college through the graduate level in interior design.
Kayem Dunn, *Executive Director*
60 Monroe Center, N.W.
Grand Rapids, MI 49503
(616) 458-0400

NATIONAL ACCREDITATION COMMISSION FOR SCHOOLS AND COLLEGES OF ACUPUNCTURE AND ORIENTAL MEDICINE
First professional master's degree programs and professional master's level certificate or diploma programs in acupuncture that are based upon the theory of Oriental medicine with a concentration in herbology, that are at least three academic years in length, and that follow at least two years of college level general education.
Penelope Ward, *Executive Director*
1424 16th Street, N.W.
Suite 501
Washington, DC 20036
(202) 265-3370

NATIONAL ASSOCIATION OF SCHOOLS OF ART AND DESIGN
Institutions and units within institutions which offer associate, baccalaureate, and/or graduate degree programs in art, design, and art/design related disciplines; also nondegree-granting institutions having programs in these areas.
Commission on Accreditation
Samuel Hope, *Executive Director*
11250 Roger Bacon Drive
Suite 21
Reston, VA 22090
(703) 437-0700, Fax: (703) 437-6312

NATIONAL ASSOCIATION OF SCHOOLS OF DANCE
Institutions and units within institutions which offer associate, baccalaureate, and/or graduate degree programs in dance and dance-related disciplines; and nondegree-granting institutions having programs in these areas.
Commission on Accreditation
Samuel Hope, *Director*
11250 Roger Bacon Drive
Suite 21
Reston, VA 22090
(703) 437-0700, Fax: (703) 437-6312

NATIONAL ASSOCIATION OF SCHOOLS OF MUSIC
Institutions and units within institutions which
offer associate, baccalaureate, and/or degree
programs in music and/or music-related disciplines, and nondegree-granting institutions having programs in these areas.
Commission on Accreditation
Samuel Hope, *Executive Director*
11250 Roger Bacon Drive
Suite 21
Reston, VA 22090
(703) 437-0700, Fax: (703) 437-6312

NATIONAL ASSOCIATION OF SCHOOLS OF PUBLIC
AFFAIRS AND ADMINISTRATION
Master's degree programs in public affairs and
administration.
**Commission on Peer Review and
Accreditation**
Alfred M. Zuck, *Executive Director*
1120 G Street, N.W.
Suite 730
Washington, DC 20005
(202) 628-8965, Fax: (202) 626-4978

NATIONAL ASSOCIATION OF SCHOOLS OF
THEATRE
Institutions and units within institutions which
offer associate, baccalaureate and/or graduate
degree programs in theatre and theatre-related
disciplines; and nondegree-granting institutions
having programs in these areas.
Commission on Accreditation
Samuel Hope, *Executive Director*
11250 Roger Bacon Drive
Suite 21
Reston, VA 22090
(703) 437-0700, Fax: (703) 437-6312

NATIONAL COUNCIL FOR ACCREDITATION OF
TEACHER EDUCATION
Units within institutions offering professional
education programs at the basic and advanced
levels.
Arthur E. Wise, *President*
2010 Massachusetts Avenue, N.W.
Suite 200
Washington, DC 20036
(202) 466-7496, Fax: (202) 296-6620

NATIONAL LEAGUE FOR NURSING
Practical nurse, diploma, associate, baccalaure-
ate, and higher degree programs.
Division of Education and Accreditation
Patricia Moccia, Ph.D., *Executive Vice
President*
350 Hudson Street
New York, NY 10014
(718) 989-9393, Fax: (718) 989-3710

NATIONAL RECREATION AND PARK ASSOCIATION
Programs in recreation, park resources, and
leisure services at the baccalaureate level.
Council on Accreditation
Michelle Park, *Professional Services
Director*
3101 Park Center Drive
Alexandria, VA 22302
(703) 820-4940, Fax: (703) 671-6772

PLANNING ACCREDITATION BOARD
Programs in planning at the baccalaureate and
master's level.
Planning Accreditation Board
Beatrice Clupper, *Director*
Iowa State University
Research Park
2501 North Loop Drive
Suite 800
Ames, IA 50010
(515) 296-7030, Fax: (515) 296-9910

SOCIETY OF AMERICAN FORESTERS
First professional degree programs, baccalaure-
ate or graduate, in forestry education.
Committee on Accreditation
P. Gregory Smith, *Director, Science and
Education*
5400 Grosvenor Lane
Bethesda, MD 20814-2198
(301) 897-9720, Fax: (301) 897-3690

C. Joint Statement on Transfer and Award of Academic Credit

The following set of guidelines originally was developed by three national associations in higher education whose member institutions are directly involved in the transfer and award of academic credit. In 1990, a fourth national association joined the original three by officially approving the statement. It is one in a series of policy guidelines developed through the American Council on Education to respond to issues in higher education by means of voluntary self-regulation. Each statement is developed through a process of wide review among representatives of different types of institutions and professional responsibilities in higher education. They are intended to summarize general principles of good practice that can be adapted to the specific circumstances of each college and university.

Transfer of credit is a concept that now involves transfer between dissimilar institutions and curricula and recognition of extra-institutional learning, as well as transfer between institutions and curricula of similar characteristics. As their personal circumstances and educational objectives change, students seek to have their learning, wherever and however attained, recognized by educational institutions where they enroll for further study. It is important for reasons of social equity and educational effectiveness, as well as the wide use of resources, for all institutions to develop reasonable and definitive policies and procedures for acceptance of transfer credit. Such policies and procedures should provide maximum consideration for the individual student who has changed institutions or objectives. It is the receiving institution's responsibility to provide reasonable and definitive policies and procedures for determining a student's knowledge in required subject areas. All institutions have a responsibility to furnish transcripts and other documents necessary for a receiving institution to judge the quality and quantity of the work. Institutions also have a responsibility to advise the students that the work *reflected* on the transcript *may or may not* be accepted by a receiving institution.

Inter-Institutional Transfer of Credit

Transfer of credit from one institution to another involves at least three considerations:

(1) the educational quality of the institution from which the student transfers;
(2) the comparability of the nature, content, and level of credit earned to that offered by the receiving institution; and
(3) the appropriateness and applicability of the credit earned to the programs offered by the receiving institution, in light of the student's educational goals.

Accredited Institutions

Accreditation speaks primarily to the first of these considerations, serving as the basic indicator that an institution meets certain minimum standards. Users of accreditation are urged to give careful attention to the accreditation conferred by accrediting bodies recognized by the Commission on Recognition of Postsecondary Accreditation (CORPA). CORPA has a formal process of recognition which requires that any accrediting body so recognized must meet the same standards. Under these standards, CORPA has recognized a number of accrediting bodies, including:

(1) regional accrediting commissions (which historically accredited the more traditional colleges and universities, but which now accredit proprietary, vocational-technical, and single-purpose institutions as well);
(2) national accrediting bodies that accredit various kinds of specialized institutions; and
(3) certain professional organizations that accredit free-standing professional schools, in addition to programs within multi-purpose institutions. (CORPA annually publishes a list of recognized accrediting bodies, and the American Council on Education publishes for CORPA a directory of institutions accredited by these organizations.)

Although accrediting agencies vary in the ways they are organized and in their statements of scope and mission, all accrediting bodies that meet CORPA's provisions for recognition function to assure that the institutions or programs they accredit have met generally accepted minimum standards for accreditation.

Accreditation affords reason for confidence in an institution's or a program's purposes, in the appropriateness of its resources and plans for carrying out these purposes, and in its effectiveness in accomplishing its goals, insofar as these things can be judged. Accreditation speaks to the probability, but does not guarantee, that students have met acceptable standards of educational accomplishment.

Comparability and Applicability

Comparability of the nature, content, and level of transfer credit and the appropriateness and applicability of the credit earned to programs offered by the receiving institution are as important in the evaluation process as the accreditation status of the institution at which the transfer credit was awarded. Since accreditation does not address these questions, this information must be obtained from catalogues and other materials and from direct contact between knowledgeable and experienced faculty and staff at both the receiving and sending institutions. When such considerations as comparability and appropriateness of credit are satisfied, however, the receiving institution should have reasonable confidence that students from accredited institutions are qualified to undertake the receiving institution's educational program.

Admissions and Degree Purposes

At some institutions there may be differences between the acceptance of credit for admission purposes and applicability of credit for degree purposes. A receiving institution may accept previous work, place a credit value on it, and enter it on the transcript. However, that previous work, because of its nature and not its inherent quality, may be determined to have no applicability to a specific degree to be pursued by the student.

Institutions have a responsibility to make this distinction and its implications clear to students before they decide to enroll. This should be a matter of full disclosure, with the best interests of the student in mind. Institutions also should make every reasonable effort to reduce the gap between credits accepted and credits applied toward an educational credential.

Unaccredited Institutions

Institutions of postsecondary education that are not accredited by CORPA-recognized accrediting bodies may lack that status for reasons unrelated to questions of quality. Such institutions, however, cannot provide a reliable, third-party assurance that they meet or exceed minimum standards. That being the case, students transferring from such institutions may encounter special problems in gaining acceptance and transferring credits to accredited institutions. Institutions admitting students from unaccredited institutions should take steps to validate credits previously earned.

Foreign Institutions

In most cases, foreign institutions are chartered and authorized by their national governments, usually through a ministry of education. Although this provides for a standardization within a country, it does not produce useful information about comparability from one country to another. No other nation has a system comparable to voluntary accreditation. At the operational level, three organizations—the National Council on the Evaluation of Foreign Student Credentials (CEC), the National Association for Foreign Student Affairs (NAFSA), and the National Liaison Committee on Foreign Student Admissions (NLC)—often can assist institutions by distributing general or specific guidelines on admission and placement of foreign students. Equivalency or placement recommendations are to be evaluated in terms of the programs and policies of the individual receiving institution.

Validation of Extra-Institutional and Experiential Learning for Transfer Purposes

Transfer-of-credit policies should encompass educational accomplishment attained in extra-institutional settings as well as at accredited postsecondary institutions. In deciding on the award of credit for extra-institutional learning, institutions will find the service of the American Council on Education's Center for Adult Learning and Educational Credentials helpful. One of the Center's functions is to operate and foster programs to determine credit equivalencies for various modes of extra-institutional learning. The Center maintains evaluation programs for formally structured courses offered by the military and civilian noncollegiate sponsors such as businesses, corporations, government agencies, and labor unions. Evaluation services are also available for examination programs, for occupations with validated job proficiency evaluation systems, and for correspondence courses offered by schools accredited by the National Home Study Council. The results are published in a *Guide* series. Another resource is the General Educational Development (GED) Testing Program, which provides a means for assessing high school equivalency.

For learning that has not been validated through the ACE formal credit recommendation process or through credit-by-examination programs, institutions are urged to explore the Council for Adult and Experiential Learning (CAEL) procedures and processes. Pertinent CAEL publications designed for this purpose are available from CAEL National Headquarters, 223 West Jackson Boulevard, Suite 510, Chicago, IL 60606.

Uses of this Statement

This statement has been endorsed by the four national associations most concerned with practices in the area of transfer and awarding of credit—the American Association of Collegiate Registrars and Admissions Officers, the American Council on Education/Commission on Educational Credit and Credentials, the Council on Postsecondary Accreditation (now functioning as the Commission on Recognition of Postsecondary Accreditation), and the American Association of Community and Junior Colleges.

Institutions are encouraged to use this statement as a basis for discussions in developing or reviewing institutional policies with regard to transfer. If the statement reflects an institution's policies, that institution might want to use this publication to inform faculty, staff, and students.

It is recommended that accrediting bodies reflect the essential precepts of this statement in their criteria.

Approved by the COPA Board
October 10, 1978; Reaffirmed April 25, 1990

Approved by the American Council on Education/Commission on Educational Credit
December 5, 1978; Reaffirmed by the Commission on Educational Credit and Credentials
September 26, 1990

Approved by the Executive Committee, American Association of Collegiate Registrars and Admission Officers
November 21, 1978; Reaffirmed February 1989

Approved by the Board of Directors, American Association of Community and Junior Colleges
April 1990

Institutional Index

A

Aaker's Business Coll. 486
Abbeville Beauty Acad. 436
Abbie Business Inst. 445
Abbynell Beauty & Technical Inst. 501
ABC Technical & Trade Schs. 371
Abilene Christian Univ. 309
Abilene Intercollegiate Sch. of Nursing 309
Abraham Baldwin Agricultural Coll. 72, 580
ABS Training Ctr. 376
ACA Coll. of Design 487
Acad. Education Ctr. 457
Acad. for Career Education 475
Acad. Lanin 501
Acad. of Art Coll. 21
Acad. of Artistic Hair Design 483
Acad. of Business Coll. 12
Acad. of Chinese Culture and Health Sciences 21
Acad. of Court Reporting 241
Acad. of Creative Hair Design 399
Acad. of Floral Design 391
Acad. of Hair Design 422 (IN); 487 (OH)
Acad. of Healing Arts, Massage & Facial Skin Care 399
Acad. of Health Careers 452
Acad. of Medical Arts and Business 495
Acad. of Medical Careers 468
Acad. of Professional Development 470
Acad. of the New Church 265
Acad. Pacific Business and Travel Coll. 376
Acad. Singer Dealer Autorizado Inc. 501
Acadia Divinity Coll. 357
Acadian Technical Inst. 436
Acme Inst. of Technology 537
Action Career Training 516
Adams State Coll. 48, 573
Adelphi Univ. 201
Adirondack Community Coll. 201, 625
Adler Inst. of Minnesota (see: Alfred Adler Inst. of Minnesota)
Adler Sch. of Professional Psychology 85
Adolphus Coll. (see: Gustavus Adolphus Coll.)
Adrian Coll. 151
Adult and Experiental Learning Sch. (see: Sch. for Adult and Experiential Learning)
Advance Inst. 483
Advanced Career Training 516

Advanced Hair Tech 424
Advanced International Studies Sch. (see: Sch. of Advanced International Studies)
Advanced Legal Studies Ctr. (see: Ctr. for Advanced Legal Studies)
Advanced Software Analysis 475
Advertising Art Sch. (see: Sch. of Advertising Art)
Advertising Arts Coll. 376
AEGIS Training Ctr. 551
Aero Mechanics Sch. 462
Aeronautics Coll. (see: Coll. of Aeronautics)
Agnes Scott Coll. 72
Aguadilla Regional Coll. 285, 641
Aiken Technical Coll. 292, 644
Ailey American Dance Ctr. (see: Alvin Ailey American Dance Ctr.)
AIMS Acad. 516
Aims Community Coll. 48
Air Force Acad. (see: U.S. Air Force Acad.)
Air Force Community Coll. (see: Community Coll. of the Air Force)
Air Force Inst. of Technology 241
Air-Tech Inc. 444
Airman Proficiency Ctr. 493
Akron Barber Coll. 487
Akron Machining Inst. Inc. 487
Akron Medical-Dental Inst. 487
Akron Sch. of Practical Nursing 487
Al Collins Graphic Design Sch. 371
Al-Med Acad. 462
Alabama Agricultural and Mechanical Univ. 3, 555
Alabama Aviation and Technical Coll. 3
Alabama Christian Sch. of Religion (see: Southern Christian Univ.)
Alabama Commission on Higher Education 555
Alabama Dept. of Postsecondary Education (see: State of Alabama Dept. of Postsecondary Education)
Alabama Reference Laboratories, Inc. 367
Alabama Southern Community Coll. 3, 540, 556
Alabama State Coll. of Barber Styling 367
Alabama State Univ. 3, 555
Alamance Community Coll. 227, 628

Alameda Coll. (see: Coll. of Alameda)
Alamo Community Coll. District 648
Alaska Bible Coll. 10
Alaska Jr. Coll. 10
Alaska Pacific Univ. 10
Alaskan Native Culture and Arts Development Inst. (see: Inst. of American Indian and Alaskan Native Culture and Arts Development)
Albany Coll. of Pharmacy of Union Univ. 201
Albany Law Sch. 201
Albany Medical Coll. of Union Univ. 201
Albany State Coll. 72, 580
Albany State Univ. (see: State Univ. of New York at Albany)
Albany Technical Inst. 410
Albemarle Coll. (see: Coll. of the Albemarle)
Albert I. Prince Regional Vocational-Technical Sch. 394
Albert State Coll. (see: Carl Albert State Coll.)
Albertson Coll. 83
Albertus Magnus Coll. 54
Albion Coll. 151
Albright Coll. 265
Albuquerque Barber Coll. 474
Albuquerque Technical Vocational Inst. 198, 622
Alcorn State Univ. 168, 612
Alderson-Broaddus Coll. 345
Alexandria Regional Technical Inst. 436
Alexandria Technical Coll. 160
Alfred Adler Inst. of Minnesota 160
Alfred Coll. of Technology (see: State Univ. of New York Coll. of Technology at Alfred)
Alfred Univ. 201
Alice Lloyd Coll. 121
All-State Career Sch. 495
Allan Hancock Coll. 21, 562
Allan Hancock Joint Community Coll. District 562
Allan Shivers Radiation Therapy Ctr. 516
Allegany Community Coll. 134, 603
Allegheny Business Inst. 495
Allegheny Coll. 265
Allegheny County Community Coll. Allegheny Campus (see: Community Coll. of Allegheny County Allegheny Campus)

Antelope Valley Coll. 21, 562
Antelope Valley Community Coll. District 562
Anthony's Barber Styling Coll. 529
Antilles Sch. of Technical Careers 501
Antioch Coll. 241
Antioch New England Graduate Sch. 241
Antioch Seattle 241
Antioch Southern California—Los Angeles 241
Antioch Southern California—Santa Barbara 241
Antioch Univ. 241
Antonelli Inst. 265
Antonelli Inst. of Art and Photography 241
Antonelli Medical and Professional Inst. 495
Apex Technical Sch. 475
Apollo Coll. of Medical-Dental Careers 493
Apollo Coll.—Phoenix, Inc. 371
Apollo Coll.—Tri-City, Inc. 371
Apollo Coll.—Tucson, Inc. 371
Apollo Coll.—Westridge, Inc. 371
Appalachian Bible Coll. 345
Appalachian State Univ. 227, 630
Applied Career Training Inc. 551
Apprentice Sch.—Newport News Shipbuilding 529
Aquinas Coll. 151, 301 (see also: St. Thomas Aquinas Coll.; see also: Thomas Aquinas Coll.)
Aquinas Coll. at Milton 140
Aquinas Coll. at Newton 140
Aquinas Inst. of Theology 172
Arapahoe Community Coll. 48, 573
Arecibo Technological Univ. Coll. 285, 641
Aristotle Coll. of Medical and Dental Technology 422
Aristotle Inst. of Medical and Dental Technology 487
Arit Air Acad. 516
Arizona Automotive Inst. (see: National Education Ctr.—Arizona Automotive Inst.)
Arizona Board of Regents 559
Arizona Coll. of the Bible 12
Arizona Community Coll. Board 559
Arizona Inst. of Business and Technology 12
Arizona State Univ. 12, 559
Arizona State Univ. West 12, 559
Arizona Western Coll. 12, 559
Arkansas Baptist Coll. 17

Arkansas Coll. 17
Arkansas Coll. of Barbering and Hair Design 375
Arkansas Coll. of Technology (see: National Education Ctr.—Arkansas Coll. of Technology)
Arkansas Dept. of Higher Education 561
Arkansas State Univ. 17, 561
Arkansas State Univ.—Beebe Branch 17, 561
Arkansas State Univ. System Ofc. 561
Arkansas Tech Univ. 17, 561
Arkansas Valley Technical Inst. 375
Arlington Baptist Coll. 309
Arlington Court Reporting Coll. 516
Armed Forces Sch. of Music 529
Armstrong State Coll. 72, 580
Armstrong Univ. 21
Armstrong Univ. of Beauty 410
Army Acad. of Health Sciences 517
Army Command and General Staff Coll. (see: U.S. Army Command and General Staff Coll.)
Army Inst. for Professional Development 529
Army Intelligence Ctr. (see: U.S. Army Intelligence Ctr. and Fort Huachuca)
Army Medical Equipment and Optician Sch. 517
Army Ordnance Ctr. and Sch. 445
Army Ordnance Missile and Munitions Ctr. and Sch. 367
Army Quartermaster Ctr. and Sch. 529
Army Signal Ctr. and Sch. 410
Army Soldier Support Inst. (see: U.S. Army Soldier Support Inst.)
Army Transportation and Aviation Logistics Sch. 529
Arnold's Beauty Coll. 483
Arnold's Beauty Sch. 510
Arrowhead Community Coll. Region 610
Art Acad. of Cincinnati 241
Art Advertising Acad. 487
Art Ctr. 371
Art Ctr. Coll. of Design 21
Art Inst. of Atlanta 72
Art Inst. of Boston 140
Art Inst. of Chicago Sch. (see: Sch. of the Art Inst. of Chicago)
Art Inst. of Dallas 517
Art Inst. of Fort Lauderdale 62

Art Inst. of Houston 517
Art Inst. of Philadelphia 265
Art Inst. of Pittsburgh 265
Art Inst. of Seattle 339
Art Inst. of Southern California 22
Art Instruction Schs. 457
Art of Beauty Coll. 550
Arte Moderno Inst. (see: Inst. del Arte Moderno)
Arthur D. Little Management Education Inst., Inc. 140
Artiste Sch. of Cosmetology 510
Artistic Beauty Coll. 410
Artistic Hair Design Acad. (see: Acad. of Artistic Hair Design)
Arts and Business Coll. of Puerto Rico 501
Arundel Inst. of Technology 445
Asbury Coll. 121
Asbury Park Learning Ctr. 191
Asbury Theological Seminary 121
Ascension Coll. 436
Ascension Technical Inst. 436
Asher Sch. of Business 410
Asheville-Buncombe Technical Community Coll. 227, 628
Ashland Community Coll. 121, 594
Ashland State Vocational-Technical Sch. (see: Kentucky Tech—Ashland State Vocational-Technical Sch.)
Ashland Univ. 242
Asnuntuck Community-Technical Coll. 54, 540, 575
Assemblies of God Theological Seminary 172
Associated Arts Coll. (see: Coll. of Associated Arts)
Associated Mennonite Biblical Seminary 101, 540
Associated Technical Coll. 376-377
Associated Technical Inst. 448
Assumption Coll. 140
Assumption Coll. for Sisters 191
ATDS—Prairie Hill 517
Athenaeum of Ohio 242
Athens Area Technical Inst. 72
Athens State Coll. 3, 555
ATI—American Trades Insts. 517
ATI Career Inst. 529
ATI Career Training Ctr. 399 (FL); 517 (TX)
ATI Career Training Ctr. Electronic Campus 399
ATI—Graphic Arts Inst. 517
ATI—Health Education Ctr. 399 (FL); 517 (TX)
ATI—Hollywood 529
Atlanta Area Technical Sch. 410

Atlanta Art Inst. (see: Art Inst. of
Atlanta)
Atlanta Christian Coll. 72
Atlanta Coll. of Art 72
Atlanta Job Corps Ctr. 410
Atlanta Metropolitan Coll. 72, 580
Atlanta Sch. of Massage 410
Atlantic Coll. 285 (see also: Coll.
of the Atlantic)
Atlantic Community Coll. 191,
620
Atlantic Sch. of Theology 357
Atlantic Union Coll. 140
Atlantic Vocational-Technical Ctr.
399
Auburn Univ. 3, 555
Auburn Univ. at Montgomery 3,
555
Auburn Univ. System 555
Audio Research Inst. (see: Inst. of
Audio Research)
Audrey Cohen Coll. 201, 540
Augsburg Coll. 160
Augusta Coll. 73, 580
Augusta Technical Inst. 73
Augustana Coll. 85 (IL); 298 (SD)
Aurora Community Coll. (see:
Community Coll. of Aurora)
Aurora Health Care, Inc. 537
Aurora Univ. 85
Austin Coll. 309
Austin Community Coll. 160, 610
(MN); 309, 648 (TX)
Austin Peay State Univ. 301, 646
Austin Presbyterian Theological
Seminary 309
Austin State Univ. (see: Stephen F.
Austin State Univ.)
Automation Acad. 398
Automotive Machinists Sch. (see:
Sch. of Automotive Machinists)
Automotive Technical Inst. 419
Automotive Training Ctr. 495
Automotive Transmission Sch. 399
Autry Area Vocational-Technical
Ctr. (see: O.T. Autry Area
Vocational-Technical Ctr.)
Avalon Vocational-Technical Inst.
517-518
Avante Sch. of Cosmetology 457
Avanti Hair Tech 399
Averett Coll. 331
Aviation Career Acad. 470
Avila Coll. 172
Avoyelles Technical Inst. 436
Ayers Inst. 436
Ayers State Technical Coll. (see:
Harry M. Ayers State Technical
Coll.)
AzTech Coll. 371
Azusa Pacific Univ. 22

B

Babson Coll. 140
Bacone Coll. 256
Bahamas Hotel Training Coll. 539
Bailey Fashion Coll. (see: Mable
Bailey Fashion Coll.)
Bainbridge Coll. 73, 580
Baker Aviation Sch. (see: George
T. Baker Aviation Sch.)
Baker Coll. of Flint 151
Baker Coll. of Muskegon 151
Baker Coll. of Owosso 151
Baker Univ. 116
Bakersfield Coll. 22, 564
Baldwin Agricultural Coll. (see:
Abraham Baldwin Agricultural
Coll.)
Baldwin Coll. (see: Mary Baldwin
Coll.)
Baldwin-Wallace Coll. 242
Ball State Univ. 101, 588
Ballard County Area Vocational
Ctr. 426
Baltimore City Community Coll.
134, 603
Baltimore Hebrew Univ. 134
Baltimore International Culinary
Coll. 134
Bancroft Sch. of Massage Therapy
448
Bangor Theological Seminary 131
Bank Street Coll. of Education 201
Baptist Bible Coll. 172
Baptist Bible Coll. and Seminary
265
Baptist Missionary Association
Theological Seminary 310
Baran Inst. of Technology 394
Barat Coll. 85
Barber-Scotia Coll. 227
Barber Styling Inst. 495
Barclay Career Sch. 529
Barclay Coll. 116
Bard Coll. 201
Barna Inst. 399
Barnard Coll. 201
Barnes Business Coll. 391
Barnes Coll. 546
Barren County Area Vocational
Education Ctr. (see: Kentucky
Tech—Barren County Area
Vocational Education Ctr.)
Barrett & Company Sch. of Hair
Design 426
Barry Univ. 62
Barstow Coll. 22, 562
Barstow Community Coll. District
562
Bartlesville Wesleyan Coll. 256
Barton Coll. 227

Barton County Community Coll.
116, 592
Baruch Coll. (see: Bernard M.
Baruch Coll.)
Basic Inst. of Technology 172
Bassist Coll. 261
Bastrop Technical Inst. 436
Bastyr Coll. 339
Bates Coll. 131
Bates Technical Coll. 533, 659
Batesville Job Corps Ctr. 460
Baton Rouge Commercial Coll.
(see: Commercial Coll. of Baton
Rouge)
Baton Rouge Regional Technical
Inst. 436
Baton Rouge Sch. of Computers
436
Bauder Coll. 73
Bauder Fashion Coll.—Arlington
310
Bay Area Legal Acad. 62
Bay Area Vocational-Technical
Sch. 400
Bay de Noc Community Coll. 151,
607
Bay Mills Community Coll. 546
Bay Path Coll. 140
Bay State Coll. 140
Bay State Sch. of Appliances 448
Bayamon Central Univ. 285
Bayamon Technical &
Commercial Inc. 501
Bayamon Technological Univ.
Coll. 285, 641
Baylor Coll. of Dentistry 310
Baylor Coll. of Medicine 310
Baylor Univ. 310
Bayshore Learning Ctr. 191
Beacon Career Inst. 400
Beal Coll. 131
Beaufort County Community Coll.
227, 628
Beauty Coll. of Georgia 550
Beauty Schs. of America 400
Beaver Coll. 265
Beaver County Community Coll.
(see: Community Coll. of
Beaver County)
Becker Coll. 141
Bee County Coll. 310, 648
Bel-Rea Inst. of Animal
Technology 48
Belfry Area Vocational Education
Ctr. (see: Kentucky Tech—
Belfry Area Vocational
Education Ctr.)
Belhaven Coll. 168

Bradford Sch. of Business 518
Bradley Acad. for the Visual Arts 266
Bradley Univ. 86
Brainerd Community Coll. 160, 610
Brainerd/Staples Regional Technical Coll. 457
Branch Campus 480
Brandeis Univ. 141
Branell Inst. 400 (FL); 411 (GA); 510 (TN)
Branford Hall Career Inst. 394
Braxton Sch. 529
Brazos Business Coll. 518
Brazosport Coll. 310, 648
Breathitt County Area Vocational Education Ctr. (see: Kentucky Tech—Breathitt County Area Vocational Education Ctr.)
Breckinridge County Area Vocational Education Ctr. (see: Kentucky Tech—Breckinridge County Area Vocational Education Ctr.)
Brely Acad. of the Performing Arts 549
Brenau Univ. 73
Brescia Coll. 121
Brevard Coll. 228
Brevard Community Coll. 62, 578
Brewer State Jr. Coll. (see: Bevill State Community Coll.)
Brewster Technical Ctr. (see: Henry W. Brewster Technical Ctr.)
Brewton-Parker Coll. 73
Briar Cliff Coll. 110
Briarcliff Coll. 62
Briarcliffe Sch., Inc. 202
Briarwood Coll. 54
Brick Computer Science Inst. 470
Bridgeport Engineering Inst. 54
Bridgewater Coll. 331
Bridgewater State Coll. 141, 605
Briercrest Bible Coll. 357
Brigham Young Univ. 326
Brigham Young Univ.—Hawaii Campus 81
Bristol Community Coll. 142, 605
Bristol Univ. 301
Broadcast Professionals Complete Sch. of Radio Broadcasting 493
Broadcasting Inst. of Maryland 445
Brockport Coll. (see: State Univ. Coll. at Brockport)
Brock's Hair Design Coll. 460
Bronx Community Coll. 202, 623
Brookdale Community Coll. 191, 620

Brookhaven Coll. 310, 649
Brooklyn Coll. 202, 623
Brooklyn Health Science Ctr. (see: State Univ. of New York Health Science Ctr. at Brooklyn)
Brooklyn Law Sch. 202
Brooks Coll. 22
Brooks Inst. of Photography 22
Brookstone Coll. of Business 483
Broome Community Coll. 203, 625
Broward Community Coll. 62, 578
Brown Coll. (see: Morris Brown Coll.)
Brown Coll. of Court Reporting & Medical Transcription 411
Brown Inst. (see: National Education Ctr.—Brown Inst. Campus)
Brown Mackie Coll. 116
Brown Univ. 290 (see also: John Brown Univ.)
Brown's Business Coll. 419
Brunswick Coll. 73, 580
Brunswick Community Coll. 228, 628
Bryan Coll. 301, 542
Bryan Coll. of Court Reporting 377
Bryan Inst. 424 (KS); 462 (MO); 491 (OK)
Bryan Travel Coll. 424 (KS); 462 (MO)
Bryant & Stratton Business Inst. 203 (NY); 242 (OH)
Bryant Coll. 290
Bryman Sch. 372 (AZ); 527 (UT)
Bryn Mawr Coll. 266
Bucknell Univ. 266
Bucks County Community Coll. 266
Buena Vista Coll. 110
Buffalo Coll. (see: State Univ. Coll. at Buffalo)
Buffalo State Univ. (see: State Univ. of New York at Buffalo)
Bullitt County Area Vocational Education Ctr. (see: Kentucky Tech—Bullitt County Area Vocational Education Ctr.)
Bunker Hill Community Coll. 142, 605
Burdett Sch. 448
Burke Acad. of Cosmetic Art 483
Burlington Coll. 328
Burlington County Coll. 192, 620
Business and Industry Training Ctr. (see: Ctr. for Training in Business and Industry)

Business and Medical Technology Inst. (see: Inst. of Business and Medical Technology)
Business & Technology Inst. 400 (see also: Inst. for Business & Technology)
Business Careers Inst. 281
Business Informatics Ctr. 475
Business Skills Training Ctr. 518
Business Training Inst. 400 (FL); 470 (NJ)
Butera Sch. of Art 448
Butler Business Sch. 394
Butler County Community Coll. 116, 592 (KS); 266 (PA)
Butler Univ. 101
Butte Coll. 22, 562
Butte Community Coll. District 562
Butte Vocational-Technical Ctr. 181, 616

C

Cabot Coll. 377
Cabrillo Coll. 22, 562
Cabrillo Community Coll. District 562
Cabrini Coll. 266
CAD Inst. 372
Cain's Barber Coll. 419
Caldwell Coll. 192
Caldwell Community Coll. and Technical Inst. 228, 628
Caldwell County Area Vocational Education Ctr. (see: Kentucky Tech—Caldwell County Area Vocational Education Ctr.)
Calhoun State Community Coll. (see: John C. Calhoun State Community Coll.)
California Acad. of Merchandising, Art & Design 377
California Baptist Coll. 22
California Career Schs. 377
California Coll. for Health Sciences 22
California Coll. of Arts and Crafts 22
California Coll. of Podiatric Medicine 23
California Community Colls. 562
California Culinary Acad. 377
California Family Study Ctr. 23
California Inst. of Integral Studies 23
California Inst. of Locksmithing 377
California Inst. of Technology 23

California Inst. of the Arts 23
California Lutheran Univ. 23
California Maritime Acad. 23
California Nannie Coll. 377
California Paramedical & Technical Coll. 377
California Polytechnic State Univ., San Luis Obispo 23, 571
California Sch. of Court Reporting 377
California Sch. of Professional Psychology, Berkeley/Alameda 23
California Sch. of Professional Psychology, Fresno 23
California Sch. of Professional Psychology, Los Angeles 23
California Sch. of Professional Psychology, San Diego 24
California State Polytechnic Univ., Pomona 24, 571
California State Univ., Bakersfield 24, 571
California State Univ., Chico 24, 571
California State Univ., Dominguez Hills 24, 571
California State Univ., Fresno 24, 571
California State Univ., Fullerton 24, 571
California State Univ., Hayward 24, 571
California State Univ., Long Beach 24, 571
California State Univ., Los Angeles 25, 572
California State Univ., Northridge 25, 572
California State Univ., Sacramento 25, 572
California State Univ., San Bernardino 25, 572
California State Univ., San Marcos 25, 572
California State Univ., Stanislaus 25, 572
California State Univ. System 571
California Univ. of Pennsylvania 266, 639
California Western Sch. of Law 25
Calumet Coll. of St. Joseph 101
Calvary Bible Coll. 172
Calvin Coll. 151
Calvin Theological Seminary 151
Cambria-Rowe Business Coll. 266
Cambridge Coll. 142
Cambridge Sch. of Culinary Arts 448
Camden County Coll. 192, 620
Camden Sch. of Hair Design 507

Camelot Career Coll. 436
Cameron Coll. 437
Cameron Univ. 256, 635
Camp Community Coll. (see: Paul D. Camp Community Coll.)
Campbell Univ. 228
Campbellsville Coll. 121
Cañada Coll. 25, 569
Canadian Bible Coll. and Theological Seminary 357
Canisius Coll. 203
Cannon's International Business Coll. 81
Canton Coll. of Technology (see: State Univ. of New York Coll. of Technology at Canton)
Canyons Coll. (see: Coll. of the Canyons)
Cape Cod Community Coll. 142, 605
Cape Fear Community Coll. 228, 628
Cape Girardeau Area Vocational-Technical Sch. 462
Capital Area Vocational Ctr. 419
Capital City Jr. Coll. 17
Capital Community-Technical Coll. 54, 540, 575
Capital Univ. 242
Capitol Business Coll. 533
Capitol City Careers 518
Capitol City Trade & Technical Sch. 518
Capitol Coll. 134
Capps Coll. 367
Capri Cosmetology Coll. 423
Cardinal Stritch Coll. 349
Career Acad. 518
Career Ctr. 400
Career Ctrs. of Texas—El Paso 518
Career City Coll. 62
Career Coll. of Northern Nevada 468
Career Development Ctr. 518 (TX); 530 (VA)
Career Development Inst. 367
Career Education Acad. (see: Acad. for Career Education)
Career Floral Design Inst. 533
Career Inst. 475 (NY); 495 (PA)
Career Management Inst. 377
Career Point Business Sch. 518
Career Training Acad. 496
Career Training Ctr. 530
Career Training Inst. 400
Career Training Specialists 437
Career West Acad. 378
CareerCom Jr. Coll. of Business 121
Careers Unlimited 519

Carey Coll. (see: William Carey Coll.)
Caribbean Ctr. for Advanced Studies 285
Caribbean Univ. 285
Carl Albert State Coll. 256, 635
Carl D. Perkins Job Corps Ctr. 426
Carl Sandburg Coll. 86, 584
Carleton Coll. 161
Carlow Coll. 267
Carnegie Inst. 452
Carnegie Mellon Univ. 267
Carolina Beauty Coll. 483
Carolina Regional Coll. 285, 641
Carrasco Job Corps Ctr. (see: David L. Carrasco Job Corps Ctr.)
Carroll Coll. 181 (MT); 349 (WI)
Carroll Community Coll. 546
Carroll County Area Vocational Education Ctr. (see: Kentucky Tech—Carroll County Area Vocational Education Ctr.)
Carroll Technical Inst. 411
Carroll Univ. (see: John Carroll Univ.)
Carson-Newman Coll. 301
Carteret Community Coll. 228, 628
Carthage Coll. 349
CARTI Sch. of Radiation Therapy Technology 375
Carver Career and Technical Education Ctr. 536
Carver State Technical Coll. (see: Bishop State Community Coll.)
Casco Bay Coll. 131
Case Western Reserve Univ. 242
Casey County Area Vocational Education Ctr. (see: Kentucky Tech—Casey County Area Vocational Education Ctr.)
Cashier Training Inst. 475
Casper Coll. 356, 664
Castle Coll. 188
Castleton State Coll. 328, 655
Catawba Coll. 228
Catawba Valley Community Coll. 228, 628
Catherine Booth Bible Coll. 357
Catherine Coll. 378 (CA); 419 (IL)
Catherine E. Hinds Inst. of Esthetics 448
Catholic Home Study Inst. 530
Catholic Theological Union 86
Catholic Univ. of America 60
Catholic Univ. of Puerto Rico (see: Pontifical Catholic Univ. of Puerto Rico)
Catonsville Community Coll. 134, 603

Denham Springs Beauty Coll. 438
Denison Univ. 245
Denmark Technical Coll. 293, 644
Dental Technology Inst. 379
Denver Acad. of Court Reporting 392
Denver Automotive and Diesel Coll. 392
Denver Business Coll. 49
Denver Community Coll. (see: Community Coll. of Denver)
Denver Conservative Baptist Seminary 49
Denver Inst. of Technology 49
Denver Paralegal Inst. 392
Denver Technical Coll. 49
Denver Technical Coll. at Colorado Springs 50
DePaul Univ. 87
DePauw Univ. 102
Deree Coll. 362
Derma Clinic Acad. 411
Des Moines Area Community Coll. 110, 590
Desert Coll. (see: Coll. of the Desert)
Desert Community Coll. District 563
Desert Inst. of the Healing Arts 372
Design Inst. of San Diego 29
Detroit Business Inst. 452
Detroit Business Inst.—Downriver 452
Detroit Coll. of Business 153
Detroit Coll. of Law 153
Detroit Inst. of Ophthalmology 452
DeVry Inst. of Technology, Atlanta 74
DeVry Inst. of Technology, Chicago 87
DeVry Inst. of Technology, City of Industry 29
DeVry Inst. of Technology, Columbus 245
DeVry Inst. of Technology, Dallas 312
DeVry Inst. of Technology, DuPage 87
DeVry Inst. of Technology, Kansas City 173
DeVry Inst. of Technology, Phoenix 13
DeVry Insts. 87
DeVry Technical Inst. 192
Diablo Valley Coll. 29, 563
Diamond Council of America 462
Diana Ramsay's Specialty Beauty Sch. 401

Dick Hill International Flight Sch. 462
Dickinson Coll. 269
Dickinson Sch. of Law 269
Dickinson State Univ. 239, 632
Dickinson-Warren Business Coll. 379
Diesel Driving Acad. 438
Diesel Inst. of America 445
Diesel Truck Driver Training Sch. 493 (OR); 537 (WI)
Dillard Univ. 127
District of Columbia Sch. of Law 60
Divers Acad. of the Eastern Seaboard 471
Divers Inst. of Technology 533
Divine Word Coll. 110
Dixie Coll. 326, 654
D'Mart Inst. 502
Doane Coll. 183
Dr. Martin Luther Coll. 161
Dr. Welbes Coll. of Massage Therapy 467
Dr. William M. Scholl Coll. of Podiatric Medicine 87
Dodge City Community Coll. 117, 592
Domestic Health Care Inst. 438
Dominican Coll. of Blauvelt 206
Dominican Coll. of San Rafael 29
Dominican House of Studies 60
Dominican Sch. of Philosophy and Theology 29
Dominion Business Sch. 530
Don Bosco Technical Inst. 29
Dona Ana Branch Community Coll. 198, 622
Donahue International Sch. of Hairstyling (see: Joseph Donahue International Sch. of Hairstyling)
Donnelly Coll. 117
Dordt Coll. 111
Dorsey Business Sch. 452
Douglas MacArthur State Technical Coll. 4
Douglas Sch. of Business 269
Dover Business Coll. 471
Dowling Coll. 206
D-Q Univ. 29
Drake Business Sch. 476
Drake Coll. of Business 471
Drake State Technical Coll. (see: J.F. Drake State Technical Coll.)
Drake Univ. 111
Draughons Coll. 511
Draughon's Coll. of Business 520
Draughons Jr. Coll. 4 (AL); 302 (TN)

Drew Univ. 192
Drew Univ. of Medicine and Science (see: Charles R. Drew Univ. of Medicine and Science)
Drexel Univ. 269
Drury Coll. 173
du Cret Sch. of the Arts 471
DuBois Business Coll. 269
Duff's Business Inst. 269
Duke Univ. 229
Dull Knife Memorial Coll. 547
Duluth Business Univ. 457
Duluth Technical Coll. 161
Dundalk Community Coll. 135, 603
Dunwoody Industrial Inst. 457
DuPage Coll. (see: Coll. of DuPage)
Duquesne Univ. 269
Duran Skin Care, Massage and Nail Sch. (see: America Duran Skin Care, Massage and Nail Sch.)
Durango Air Service 392
Durham Technical Community Coll. 229, 628
Dutchess Community Coll. 206, 625
Dyersburg State Community Coll. 302, 646
Dyke Coll. 245
D'Youville Coll. 206

E

Earle C. Clements Job Corps Ctr. 426
Earlham Coll. 102
East Arkansas Community Coll. 17
East Carolina Univ. 229, 630
East Central Coll. 173, 614
East Central Community Coll. 168, 612
East Central Univ. 256, 635
East Coast Aero Technical Sch. 448
East Coast Bible Coll. 230
East Georgia Coll. 74, 580
East Grand Forks Technical Coll. 161
East Los Angeles Coll. 29, 565
East Los Angeles Occupational Ctr. 379
East Mississippi Community Coll. 168, 612
East St. Louis Community Coll. (see: State Community Coll. of East St. Louis)

Erie Community Coll. City Campus 206, 625
Erie Community Coll. North (Amherst) Campus 206, 625
Erie Community Coll. South Campus 206, 625
Erie Inst. of Technology 496
Erskine Coll. 293
Erwin Technical Ctr. (see: David G. Erwin Technical Ctr.)
Escuela de Artes Plasticas de Puerto Rico Inst. de Cultura Puertorriquena 548
Escuela de Peritos Electricistas de Isabel 502
ESI Career Ctr. 488
Essex Agricultural and Technical Inst. 143
Essex Community Coll. 135, 603
Essex County Coll. 192, 620
Estelle Harman Actors Workshop 380
ETI Technical Coll. 245
ETI Technical Coll. of Niles 245
Eton Technical Inst. 533
Eugene Bible Coll. 261
Eureka Coll. 88
Euro Hair Design Inst. 401
Euro Hair Sch. 520
Euro-Skill Therapeutic Training Ctr. 401
European Health & Sciences Inst. 520
European Inst. for International Communication 142
Evangel Coll. 173
Evangelical Sch. of Theology 270
Evangelical Seminary of Puerto Rico 286
Evangeline Technical Inst. 438
Everett Community Coll. 340, 660
Evergreen State Coll. 340, 659
Evergreen Valley Coll. 30, 568
Evers Coll. (see: Medgar Evers Coll.)
Executive Secretarial Sch. 520
Executive Travel Inst. 411
Extension Course Inst. of the U.S. Air Force 367

F

FAA Ctr. for Management Development 401
Fairfax Community Coll. (see: Lord Fairfax Community Coll.)
Fairfield Univ. 55
Fairleigh Dickinson Univ. 193
Fairmont State Coll. 345, 662

Faith Baptist Bible Coll. and Theological Seminary 111
Fanny Allen Memorial Sch. of Practical Nursing 528
Farah's Beauty Sch. 508
Farmingdale Coll. of Technology (see: State Univ. of New York Coll. of Technology at Farmingdale)
Fashion Careers of California 380
Fashion Design Coll. 502
Fashion Inst. of Design and Merchandising 30
Fashion Inst. of Technology 206, 626
Fashion Merchandising and Technical Inst. 502
Faulkner State Jr. Coll. (see: James H. Faulkner State Community Coll.)
Faulkner Univ. 4
Fayetteville Beauty Coll. 484
Fayetteville State Univ. 230, 631
Fayetteville Technical Community Coll. 230, 629
Feather River Coll. 30, 563
Feather River Community Coll. District 563
Federal Correctional Inst. 401
FEGS Trades and Business Sch. 476
Felician Coll. 193
Fell's Sch. of Business (see: Cheryl Fell's Sch. of Business)
Fergus Falls Community Coll. 162, 610
Ferris State Univ. 153, 607
Ferrum Coll. 332
Field Medical Service Sch. 446
Fielding Inst. 30
Financial Planning Coll. (see: Coll. for Financial Planning)
FinEd, Sch. of Financial Education 438
Finger Lakes Community Coll. 207, 626
Firelands Coll. 242
Fisher Coll. 143 (see also: St. John Fisher Coll.)
Fisk Univ. 303
Fitchburg State Coll. 143, 605
Five Branches Inst. Coll. of Traditional Chinese Medicine 544
Five Towns Coll. 207
Flagler Career Inst. 63
Flagler Coll. 63
Flathead Valley Community Coll. 181, 616
Flatwoods Civilian Conservation Ctr. 531

Fleet Business Sch. 445
FlightSafety International 401
Flint Hills Technical Sch. 424
Flint Inst. of Barbering 453
Flint River Technical Inst. 411
Floral Design Acad. (see: Acad. of Floral Design)
Florence-Darlington Technical Coll. 293, 644
Florida Agricultural and Mechanical Univ. 63, 579
Florida Atlantic Univ. 63, 579
Florida Baptist Theological Coll. 64
Florida Bible Coll. 64
Florida Career Inst. 64
Florida Christian Coll. 64
Florida Coll. 64
Florida Community Coll. at Jacksonville 64, 578
Florida Computer & Business Sch. 64
Florida Inst. of Massage Therapy & Esthetics 402
Florida Inst. of Technology 64
Florida Inst. of Ultrasound, Inc. 402
Florida International Univ. 64, 579
Florida Keys Community Coll. 64, 578
Florida Memorial Coll. 64
Florida National Coll. 545
Florida Parishes Technical Inst. 439
Florida Sch. of Business 402
Florida Southern Coll. 65
Florida State Board of Community Colls. 578
Florida State Univ. 65, 579
Florida State Univ. System (see: State Univ. System of Florida)
Florida Technical Coll. 65, 402
Florissant Upholstery Sch. 462
Floyd Coll. 75, 580
Folk Art Inst. of the Museum of American Folk Art 477
Folkes Technical Inst. 439
Fontbonne Coll. 174
Foothill Coll. 30, 564
Foothill-DeAnza Community Coll. District 563
Ford Community Coll. (see: Henry Ford Community Coll.)
Fordham Univ. 207
Forest Inst. of Professional Psychology 174
Forrest Jr. Coll. 293
Forsyth Sch. for Dental Hygienists 449
Forsyth Technical Community Coll. 230, 629

H

Harlan State Vocational-Technical Sch. (see: Kentucky Tech—Harlan State Vocational-Technical Sch.)

Harman Actors Workshop (see: Estelle Harman Actors Workshop)

Harold Washington Coll. 88, 540, 584

Harper Coll. (see: William Rainey Harper Coll.)

Harrington Inst. of Interior Design 88

Harris Sch. of Business 471

Harris-Stowe State Coll. 174, 614

Harris Technical Inst. (see: T.H. Harris Technical Inst.)

Harrisburg Area Community Coll. 271

Harrisburg-Capital Coll. (see: Pennsylvania State Univ. at Harrisburg-Capital Coll.)

Harrison Career Sch. (see: Hannah Harrison Career Sch.)

Harrison County Area Vocational Education Ctr. (see: Kentucky Tech—Harrison County Area Vocational Education Ctr.)

Harrodsburg Area Vocational Education Ctr. (see: Kentucky Tech—Harrodsburg Area Vocational Education Ctr.)

Harry M. Ayers State Technical Coll. 5

Harry S Truman Coll. 88, 584

Hart Sch. of Practical Nursing (see: Isabella G. Hart Sch. of Practical Nursing)

Hartford Ballet Sch. (see: Sch. of the Hartford Ballet)

Hartford Camerata Conservatory 395

Hartford Coll. for Women (see: Univ. of Hartford)

Hartford Graduate Ctr. 55

Hartford Secretarial Sch. 395

Hartford Seminary 55

Hartford State Technical Coll. (see: Capital Community-Technical Coll.)

Hartnell Coll. 31, 564

Hartnell Community Coll. District 564

Hartwick Coll. 207

Harvard Univ. 143

Harvey Mudd Coll. 31

Haskell Indian Jr. Coll. 117

Hastings Coll. 184

Hastings Coll. of the Law (see: Univ. of California, Hastings Coll. of the Law)

Hattiesburg Radiology Group 460

Haverford Coll. 271

Haverstraw Learning Ctr. 217

Hawaii Business Coll. 417

Hawaii Community Coll. 81, 582

Hawaii Inst. of Hair Design 417

Hawaii Loa Coll. (see: Hawaii Pacific Univ.)

Hawaii Loa Coll. Campus 81

Hawaii Pacific Univ. 81, 540

Hawkeye Community Coll. 111, 540, 590

Hawkeye Inst. of Technology (see: Hawkeye Community Coll.)

Haywood Community Coll. 231, 629

Hazard Community Coll. 122, 594

Hazard State Vocational-Technical Sch. (see: Kentucky Tech—Hazard State Vocational-Technical Sch.)

Heald Business Coll.—Concord 31

Heald Business Coll.—Fresno 31

Heald Business Coll.—Hayward 32

Heald Business Coll.—Oakland 32

Heald Business Coll.—Sacramento 32

Heald Business Coll.—Salinas 32

Heald Business Coll.—San Francisco 32

Heald Business Coll.—San Jose 32

Heald Business Coll.—Santa Rosa 32

Heald Business Coll.—Stockton 32

Heald Inst. of Technology—Hayward 32

Heald Inst. of Technology—Martinez 32

Heald Inst. of Technology—Sacramento 32

Heald Inst. of Technology—San Francisco 32

Heald Inst. of Technology—San Jose 32

Health Care Training Inst. 511

Health-Related Professions Sch. (see: Sch. of Health-Related Professions)

Health Science Ctr. at Brooklyn (see: State Univ. of New York Health Science Ctr. at Brooklyn)

Health Science Ctr. at Syracuse (see: State Univ. of New York Health Science Ctr. at Syracuse)

Heart of Georgia Technical Inst. 412

Heart of the Ozarks Technical Community Coll. 174, 614

Heartland Community Coll. 545

Heartland Sch. of Business 420

Hebrew Coll. 144

Hebrew Union Coll.—Jewish Inst. of Religion 32 (CA); 207 (NY); 246 (OH)

Heidelberg Coll. 246

Helena Vocational-Technical Ctr. 181, 616

Helene Fuld Sch. of Nursing 207

Hellenic Coll./Holy Cross Greek Orthodox Sch. of Theology 144

Hemphill Schs. 381

Henderson Community Coll. 122, 594

Henderson County Area Vocational Education Ctr. (see: Kentucky Tech—Henderson County Area Vocational Education Ctr.)

Henderson State Univ. 18, 561

Hendrix Coll. 18

Hennepin Technical Coll. 457

Henry Community Coll. (see: Patrick Henry Community Coll.)

Henry Ford Community Coll. 154, 607

Henry W. Brewster Technical Ctr. 402

Herbert H. Lehman Coll. 207, 623

Heritage Baptist Coll. 549

Heritage Coll. 340

Heritage Coll. of Health Careers 392

Herkimer County Community Coll. 208, 626

Hershey Medical Ctr. 277

Herzing Inst. 368

Hesser Coll. 188

Hesston Coll. 117

Hi-Tech Sch. of Miami 402

Hialeah Technical Ctr. 402

Hibbing Community Coll. 162, 610

Hickey Sch. 174

Hickox Sch. 449

High Point Coll. (see: High Point Univ.)

High Point Univ. 231, 540

High-Tech Inst. 372

Highland Community Coll. 88, 585 (IL); 118, 592 (KS)

Highland Park Community Coll. 154, 607

Highline Community Coll. 340, 660

Hilbert Coll. 208

Hill Coll. 313, 649

International Coll. of Broadcasting 246

International Coll. of Business & Technology 288

International Correspondence Schs. 272

International Dealers Sch. 381 (CA); 468 (NV)

International Fine Arts Coll. 66

International Hair Inst. 463

International Inst. of Chinese Medicine 198

International Sch. 474

International Sch. of Skin & Nailcare 412

International Sch. of Theology 544

International Technical Coll. 503

International Training Sch. (see: Sch. for International Training)

Interstate Business Coll. 486

Inver Hills Community Coll. 162, 610

Iona Coll. 208

Iowa Central Community Coll. 111, 590

Iowa Dept. of Education Div. of Community Colls. 590

Iowa Lakes Community Coll. 112, 590

Iowa Sch. of Barbering and Hairstyling 423

Iowa State Board of Regents 591

Iowa State Univ. 112, 591

Iowa Valley Community Coll. District 590

Iowa Wesleyan Coll. 112

Iowa Western Community Coll. 112, 590

Irvine Coll. of Business 381

Irvine Valley Coll. 33, 568

Isabella G. Hart Sch. of Practical Nursing 477

Island Drafting & Technical Inst. 477

Isothermal Community Coll. 231, 629

Itasca Community Coll. 162, 610

Itawamba Community Coll. 168, 612

Ithaca Coll. 209

ITI Technical Coll. 439

ITT Technical Inst. 13 (AZ); 33 (CA); 50 (CO); 66 (FL); 83 (ID); 106 (IN); 453 (MI); 174 (MO); 246 (OH); 261 (OR); 303 (TN); 314 (TX); 326 (UT); 340 (WA); 350 (WI)

Iverson Inst. of Court Reporting 521

J

J. Sargeant Reynolds Community Coll. 333, 657

Jackson Acad. of Beauty 460

Jackson Business Inst. 453

Jackson Community Coll. 154, 607

Jackson Hair Design Coll. 460

Jackson State Community Coll. 303, 646

Jackson State Univ. 169, 612

Jacksonville Coll. 314

Jacksonville Community Coll. (see: Florida Community Coll. at Jacksonville)

Jacksonville State Univ. 5, 555

Jacksonville Univ. 66

James H. Faulkner State Community Coll. 5, 556

James L. Walker Vocational-Technical Ctr. 403

James Madison Univ. 333, 656

James Martin Adult Health Occupations 497

James Sprunt Community Coll. 231, 629

Jamestown Business Coll. 209

Jamestown Coll. 239

Jamestown Community Coll. 209, 626

Jarvis Christian Coll. 314

Jay Coll. of Criminal Justice (see: John Jay Coll. of Criminal Justice)

Jefferson Coll. 439 (LA); 174, 614 (MO)

Jefferson Community Coll. 122, 594 (KY); 209, 626 (NY)

Jefferson Davis State Jr. Coll. 5, 556

Jefferson Davis Technical Inst. 439

Jefferson State Community Coll. 5, 556

Jefferson State Vocational-Technical Ctr. (see: Kentucky Tech—Jefferson State Vocational-Technical Ctr.)

Jefferson Technical Coll. 246, 633

Jefferson Technical Inst. 439

Jefferson Univ. (see: Thomas Jefferson Univ.)

Jersey City State Coll. 193, 621

Jesuit Sch. of Theology at Berkeley 33

Jett Coll. of Cosmetology & Barbering 511

Jewell Coll. (see: William Jewell Coll.)

Jewish Hospital Coll. of Nursing and Allied Health 546

Jewish Inst. of Religion (see: Hebrew Union Coll.—Jewish Inst. of Religion)

Jewish Theological Seminary of America 209

J.F. Drake State Technical Coll. 5

J.F. Ingram State Technical Coll. 6

J.H. Thompson Acads. 497

J.M. Frazier Vocational-Technical Sch. 436

Jocelyn Daspit Beauty Coll. 439

Joe Kubert Sch. of Cartoon and Graphic Art 472

Joffrey Ballet Sch. (see: American Ballet Ctr./Joffrey Balley Sch.)

John A. Gupton Coll. 303

John A. Logan Coll. 89, 585

John B. Stetson Univ. 66

John Brown Univ. 18

John C. Calhoun State Community Coll. 6, 556

John Carroll Univ. 246

John F. Kennedy Univ. 34

John Jay Coll. of Criminal Justice 209, 623

John M. Patterson State Technical Coll. 6

John Marshall Law Sch. 89

John Pope Eden Area Vocational Education Ctr. 368

John Tracy Clinic 382

John Tyler Community Coll. 333, 657

John Wesley Coll. 231

John Wood Community Coll. 89, 585

Johns Hopkins Univ. 136

Johnson & Wales Univ. 290

Johnson Bible Coll. 303

Johnson C. Smith Univ. 231

Johnson Civilian Conservation Ctr. (see: Lyndon B. Johnson Civilian Conservation Ctr.)

Johnson County Community Coll. 118, 593

Johnson Medical Sch. (see: Robert Wood Johnson Medical Sch.)

Johnson State Coll. 328, 655

Johnson Technical Inst. 272

Johnston Community Coll. 231, 629

Johnston Sch. of Practical Nursing 445

Joint Board of Theological Colls. 358

Joliet Jr. Coll. 89, 585

Jones Coll. 66

Jones County Jr. Coll. 169, 612

Jordan Coll. 546

Joseph Donahue International Sch. of Hairstyling 497

Lenoir Community Coll. 231, 629
Lenoir-Rhyne Coll. 232
Leonard's Barber Coll. 463
Lesley Coll. 144
Leslie County Area Vocational Education Ctr. (see: Kentucky Tech—Leslie County Area Vocational Education Ctr.)
Letcher County Area Vocational Education Ctr. (see: Kentucky Tech—Letcher County Area Vocational Education Ctr.)
LeTourneau Univ. 315
Levine Sch. of Music 398
Lewis A. Wilson Technical Ctr. 477
Lewis and Clark Coll. 262
Lewis and Clark Community Coll. 91, 585
Lewis-Clark State Coll. 83, 583
Lewis Coll. of Business 155
Lewis Univ. 91
Lexington Community Coll. 123, 594
Lexington Electronics Inst. 122
Lexington Inst. of Hospitality Careers 91
Lexington Theological Seminary 123
Liberty Acad. of Business 497
Liberty Univ. 333
Liceo de Arte y Disenos 504
Liceo de Arte y Tecnologia 504
L.I.F.E. Bible Coll. 34
Life Chiropractic Coll.-West 34
Life Coll. 76
Life Laboratories 449
Lifelong Learning Coll. (see: Coll. for Lifelong Learning)
Lifetime Career Schs. 497
Lima Technical Coll. 247, 633
Limestone Coll. 294
Lincoln Christian Coll. and Seminary 91
Lincoln Coll. 91
Lincoln Land Community Coll. 91, 585
Lincoln Memorial Univ. 304
Lincoln Sch. of Commerce 184
Lincoln Technical Inst. 420 (IL); 422 (IN); 445 (MD); 472 (NJ); 497 (PA); 522 (TX)
Lincoln Trail Coll. 91, 585
Lincoln Univ. 34 (CA); 175, 614 (MO); 273 (PA)
Lindenwood Coll. 175
Lindsey Hopkins Technical Education Ctr. 403
Lindsey Wilson Coll. 123
Linfield Coll. 262

Linn-Benton Community Coll. 262, 637
Lipscomb Univ. (see: David Lipscomb Univ.)
Little Big Horn Coll. 181
Little Hoop Community Coll. 239
Little Management Education Inst. (see: Arthur D. Little Management Education Inst., Inc.)
Lively Area Vocational-Technical Ctr. 403
Livingston Univ. 6, 555
Livingstone Coll. 232
Lloyd Coll. (see: Alice Lloyd Coll.)
Lock Haven Univ. of Pennsylvania 273, 639
Locklin Vocational-Technical Ctr. (see: Radford M. Locklin Vocational-Technical Ctr.)
Logan Career Coll. (see: Chris Logan Career Coll.)
Logan Coll. (see: John A. Logan Coll.)
Logan Coll. of Chiropractic 175
Loma Linda Univ. 34
Lon Morris Coll. 315
Long Beach City Coll. 35, 565
Long Beach Community Coll. District 565
Long Branch Learning Ctr. 191
Long Island Business Inst. 478
Long Island Univ. 210
Long Medical Inst. 372
Long Technical Inst. (see: Huey P. Long Technical Inst.)
Longview Community Coll. 175, 614
Longwood Coll. 333, 656
Longy Sch. of Music, Inc. 449
Lorain County Community Coll. 247, 633
Loras Coll. 112
Lord Fairfax Community Coll. 333, 657
Los Angeles City Coll. 35, 565
Los Angeles Coll. of Chiropractic 35
Los Angeles Community Coll. District 565
Los Angeles Harbor Coll. 35, 565
Los Angeles Mission Coll. 35, 565
Los Angeles ORT Technical Inst. 382
Los Angeles Pierce Coll. 35, 565
Los Angeles Southwest Coll. 35, 565
Los Angeles Trade-Technical Coll. 35, 565
Los Angeles Valley Coll. 35, 565

Los Medanos Coll. 35, 563
Los Rios Community Coll. District 565
Louisburg Coll. 232
Louise Salinger Acad. of Fashion 35
Louisiana Art Inst. 440
Louisiana Board of Trustees for State Colls. and Univs. (see: State of Louisiana Board of Trustees for State Colls. and Univs.)
Louisiana Coll. 128
Louisiana Hair Design Coll. 440
Louisiana Inst. of Technology 440
Louisiana State Univ. and Agricultural and Mechanical Coll. 128, 600
Louisiana State Univ. at Alexandria 128, 600
Louisiana State Univ. at Eunice 128, 600
Louisiana State Univ. in Shreveport 128, 600
Louisiana State Univ. Medical Ctr. 128, 600
Louisiana State Univ. System 600
Louisiana Tech Univ. 128, 600
Louisiana Training Ctr. 440
Louisville Presbyterian Theological Seminary 123
Louisville Technical Inst. 123
Lourdes Coll. 247
Lowcountry Technical Coll. (see: Technical Coll. of the Lowcountry)
Lower Columbia Coll. 340, 660
Lowthian Coll. 162
Loyola Coll. in Maryland 136
Loyola Marymount Univ. 35
Loyola Univ. 128
Loyola Univ. of Chicago 92
Lubbock Christian Univ. 315
Lujac Business Coll. 474
Luna Vocational Technical Inst. 198, 622
Lurleen B. Wallace State Jr. Coll. 6, 556
Luther Coll. 112 (see also: Dr. Martin Luther Coll.)
Luther Northwestern Theological Seminary 162
Lutheran Bible Inst. of Seattle 341
Lutheran Coll. of Health Professions 106
Lutheran Sch. of Theology at Chicago 92
Lutheran Theological Seminary 358
Lutheran Theological Seminary at Gettysburg 273

Accredited Institutions of Postsecondary Education | 1993-94

Missoula Vocational-Technical Ctr. 182, 616

Missouri Baptist Coll. 175

Missouri Coordinating Board for Higher Education 614

Missouri Sch. for Doctors' Assistants 463

Missouri Sch. of Barbering and Hairstyling 463

Missouri Southern State Coll. 175, 614

Missouri Technical Sch. 463

Missouri Valley Coll. 175

Missouri Western State Coll. 175, 614

Mr. David's Sch. of Hair Design 484

Mister Wayne's Sch. of Unisex Hair Design 512

Mitchell Coll. 55

Mitchell Coll. of Law (see: William Mitchell Coll. of Law)

Mitchell Community Coll. 232, 629

Mitchell Cosmetology Coll. 549

Mitchell Technical Inst. 298, 541

Mitchell Vocational-Technical Inst. (see: Mitchell Technical Inst.)

Moberly Area Community Coll. 176, 614

Mobile Coll. (see: Univ. of Mobile)

Modern Schs. of America, Inc. 372

Modern Technology Sch. of X-Ray 382-383

Modern Welding Sch. 478

Modesto Jr. Coll. 36, 571

Mohave Community Coll. 14, 560

Mohawk Valley Community Coll. 212, 626

Mohegan Community Coll. (see: Three Rivers Community-Technical Coll.)

Moler Barber Coll. 383 (CA); 493 (OR)

Moler Barber Coll. of Hairstyling 486

Moler Barber Sch. of Hairstyling 458

Moler Hairstyling Coll. 420

Molloy Coll. 212

Monmouth Coll. 93 (IL); 194 (NJ)

Monroe Coll. 212

Monroe Community Coll. 212, 626

Monroe County Area Vocational Education Ctr. (see: Kentucky Tech—Monroe County Area Vocational Education Ctr.)

Monroe County Community Coll. 156, 608

Monroeville Sch. of Business 281

Montana Coll. of Mineral Science and Technology 182, 616

Montana Community Coll. System 616

Montana State Univ. 182, 616

Montana Univ. System 616

Montay Coll. 93

Montcalm Community Coll. 156, 608

Montclair State Coll. 194, 621

Monterey Inst. of International Studies 36

Monterey Peninsula Coll. 36, 566

Monterey Peninsula Community Coll. District 566

Montgomery Coll. Central Administration 603

Montgomery Coll.—Germantown Campus 137, 603

Montgomery Coll.—Rockville Campus 137, 603

Montgomery Coll.—Takoma Park Campus 137, 603

Montgomery Community Coll. 232, 629

Montgomery County Area Vocational Education Ctr. (see: Kentucky Tech—Montgomery County Area Vocational Education Ctr.)

Montgomery County Community Coll. 275

Montreat-Anderson Coll. 232

Montserrat Coll. of Art 145

Moody Bible Inst. 93

Moore Career Coll. 460

Moore Coll. of Art and Design 275

Moore Sch. of Technology (see: William R. Moore Sch. of Technology)

Moore Studio of the Theatre (see: Sonia Moore Studio of the Theatre)

Moorhead State Univ. 163, 611

Moorpark Coll. 37, 570

Moraine Park Technical Coll. 351

Moraine Valley Community Coll. 93, 585

Moravian Coll. 275

More Coll. (see: Thomas More Coll.)

More Coll. of Liberal Arts (see: Thomas More Coll. of Liberal Arts)

Morehead State Univ. 124, 594

Morehouse Coll. 77

Morehouse Sch. of Medicine 77

Morgan Community Coll. 50, 573

Morgan County Area Vocational Education Ctr. (see: Kentucky Tech—Morgan County Area Vocational Education Ctr.)

Morgan State Univ. 137, 604

Morgan Vocational-Technical Inst. (see: Robert Morgan Vocational-Technical Ctr.)

Morningside Coll. 113

Morris Brown Coll. 77

Morris Coll. 295 (see also: Lon Morris Coll.; see also: Robert Morris Coll.)

Morris County Coll. (see: County Coll. of Morris)

Morrison Coll.—Reno 187

Morrison Inst. of Technology 93

Morrisville Agriculture and Technology Coll. (see: State Univ. of New York Coll. of Agriculture and Technology at Morrisville)

Morse Sch. of Business 395

Morton Coll. 93, 586

Motech Education Ctr. 454

Motlow State Community Coll. 305, 646

Motorcycle/Marine Mechanics Inst. 372

Mott Community Coll. (see: Charles Stewart Mott Community Coll.)

Moultrie Area Technical Inst. 413

Mount Aloysius Coll. 275, 541

Mount Aloysius Jr. Coll. (see: Mount Aloysius Coll.)

Mount Angel Seminary 262

Mount Carmel Coll. of Nursing 548

Mount Holyoke Coll. 145

Mount Hood Community Coll. 262, 637

Mount Ida Coll. 145

Mount Marty Coll. 298

Mount Mary Coll. 351

Mount Mercy Coll. 113

Mount Olive Coll. 233

Mount Royal Coll. 539

Mount St. Clare Coll. 113

Mount St. Joseph Coll. (see: Coll. of Mount St. Joseph)

Mount St. Mary Coll. 212

Mount St. Mary's Coll. 37

Mount St. Mary's Coll. and Seminary 137

Mount St. Vincent Coll. (see: Coll. of Mount St. Vincent)

Mount San Antonio Coll. 37, 566

Mount San Antonio Community Coll. District 566

Mount San Jacinto Coll. 37, 566

Naval Damage Control Training Ctr. 498
Naval Dental Sch.—Maxillofacial 446
Naval Diving and Salvage Training Ctr. 405
Naval Fleet Anti-Submarine Warfare Training Ctr.—Pacific 549
Naval Guided Missiles Sch. 531
Naval Health Sciences Education and Training Command 446
Naval Hospital Corps Sch. 446
Naval Postgraduate Sch. 37
Naval Sch. of Dental Assisting 446
Naval Sch. of Health Science 446
Naval Service Sch. Command 384 (CA); 405 (FL)
Naval Submarine Sch. 549
Naval Technical Training Ctr. 384 (CA); 405 (FL); 461 (MS)
Naval Transportation Management Sch. 385
Naval Undersea Medical Inst. 446
Naval War Coll. 290
Navarro Coll. 316, 650
Navy and Marine Corps Intelligence Training Ctr. 531
Navy Fleet and Mine Warfare Training Ctr. 508
Navy Supply Corps Sch. 414
Nazarene Bible Coll. 51
Nazarene Indian Bible Coll. 51
Nazarene Theological Seminary 176
Nazareth Coll. of Rochester 213
Nebraska Christian Coll. 184
Nebraska Coll. of Business 184
Nebraska Coll. of Technical Agriculture 184
Nebraska Coordinating Commission for Postsecondary Education 617
Nebraska Custom Diesel Driver Training 467
Nebraska Indian Community Coll. 184
Nebraska Methodist Coll. of Nursing and Allied Health 184
Nebraska Wesleyan Univ. 184
NEI Coll. of Technology 458
Nell Inst. 522
Nelson Community Coll. (see: Thomas Nelson Community Coll.)
Nelson County Area Vocational Education Ctr. (see: Kentucky Tech—Nelson County Area Vocational Education Ctr.)
Neosho County Community Coll. 119, 593

Ner Israel Rabbinical Coll. 137
Ner Israel Yeshiva Coll. of Toronto 358
Nettleton Jr. Coll. 298
Neumann Coll. 275
Nevada Univ. and Community Coll. System (see: Univ. and Community Coll. System of Nevada)
New Brunswick Theological Seminary 194
New Castle Sch. of Trades 498
New Ctr. for Wholistic Health Education and Research 550
New Church Acad. (see: Acad. of the New Church)
New Coll. of California 37
New England Banking Inst. 146
New England Coll. 188
New England Coll. of Optometry 146
New England Conservatory of Music 146
New England Culinary Inst. 528
New England Culinary Inst. at Essex 528
New England Hair Acad. 449
New England Inst. of Technology 290
New England Inst. of Technology at Palm Beach 405
New England Sch. of Accounting 449
New England Sch. of Acupuncture 449
New England Sch. of Art and Design 449
New England Sch. of Broadcasting 444
New England Sch. of Law 146
New England Sch. of Photography 449
New England Technical Coll. 506
New England Technical Inst. of Connecticut 395
New England Tractor Trailer Training Sch. 446 (MD); 498 (PA)
New England Tractor Trailer Training Sch. of Connecticut 395
New England Tractor Trailer Training Sch. of Massachusetts 449
New England Tractor Trailer Training Sch. of Rhode Island 506
New Hampshire Coll. 188
New Hampshire Technical Coll. at Berlin 188

New Hampshire Technical Coll. at Claremont 188
New Hampshire Technical Coll. at Laconia 189
New Hampshire Technical Coll. at Manchester 189
New Hampshire Technical Coll. at Nashua 189
New Hampshire Technical Coll. at Stratham 189
New Hampshire Technical Inst. 189
New Hampshire Univ. System (see: Univ. System of New Hampshire)
New Image Careers 434
New Jersey Dental Sch. 197
New Jersey Dept. of Higher Education (see: State of New Jersey Dept. of Higher Education)
New Jersey Inst. of Technology 194, 621
New Jersey Medical Sch. 197
New Jersey Sch. of Osteopathic Medicine 197
New Kensington Commercial Sch. 275
New Mexico Commission on Higher Education 622
New Mexico Highlands Univ. 198, 622
New Mexico Inst. of Mining and Technology 198, 622
New Mexico Jr. Coll. 199, 622
New Mexico Military Inst. 199, 622
New Mexico State Univ. 199, 622
New Mexico State Univ. at Alamogordo 199, 622
New Mexico State Univ. at Carlsbad 199, 622
New Mexico State Univ. at Grants 199
New Mexico State Univ. System 622
New Orleans Baptist Theological Seminary 129
New Orleans Regional Technical Inst. 440
New Paltz Coll. (see: State Univ. Coll. at New Paltz)
New River Community Coll. 334, 657
New Rochelle Coll. (see: Coll. of New Rochelle)
New Sch. for Social Research 213
New Sch. of Contemporary Radio 478
New Tyler Barber Coll. Inc. 375
New World Coll. of Business 368

Northeastern State Univ. 257, 635
Northeastern Univ. 146
Northern Arizona Coll. of Health Careers 373
Northern Arizona Inst. of Technology 373
Northern Arizona Univ. 14, 559
Northern Baptist Theological Seminary 94
Northern Campbell County Vocational-Technical Sch. (see: Kentucky Tech—Northern Campbell County Vocational-Technical Sch.)
Northern Essex Community Coll. 146, 605
Northern Hospital of Surry County Sch. of Medical Technology 485
Northern Illinois Univ. 94, 586
Northern Kentucky Health Occupations Ctr. (see: Kentucky Tech—Northern Kentucky Health Occupations Ctr.)
Northern Kentucky State Vocational-Technical Sch. (see: Kentucky Tech—Northern Kentucky State Vocational-Technical Sch.)
Northern Kentucky Univ. 124, 594
Northern Maine Technical Coll. 132
Northern Marianas Coll. 362
Northern Michigan Univ. 156, 608
Northern Montana Coll. 182, 616
Northern Nevada Career Coll. (see: Career Coll. of Northern Nevada)
Northern Nevada Community Coll. 187, 618
Northern New Mexico Community Coll. 199, 622
Northern Oklahoma Coll. 257, 635
Northern State Univ. 299, 645
Northern Virginia Community Coll. 335, 657
Northland Coll. 352
Northland Community Coll. 164, 610
Northland Pioneer Coll. 14, 560
Northwest Alabama Community Coll. 6, 556
NorthWest Arkansas Community Coll. 18
Northwest Baptist Theological Coll. 358
Northwest Christian Coll. 262
Northwest Coll. 313 (TX); 356, 664 (WY)
Northwest Coll. of Art 534

Northwest Coll. of Medical & Dental Assistants 385
Northwest Coll. of the Assemblies of God 341
Northwest Indian Coll. 341
Northwest Inst. of Acupuncture and Oriental Medicine 341
Northwest Iowa Community Coll. 113, 590
Northwest Louisiana Technical Inst. 441
Northwest Mississippi Community Coll. 170, 613
Northwest Missouri Community Coll. 176
Northwest Missouri State Univ. 176, 614
Northwest Nazarene Coll. 83
Northwest Sch. of Wooden Boatbuilding 534
Northwest Technical Coll. 249, 634
Northwest Technical Coll.—Moorhead 164
Northwest Technical Inst. (see: Indiana Vocational Technical Coll.—Northwest Technical Inst.)
Northwest Technical Inst. 164
Northwestern Business Coll. 94
Northwestern Coll. 113 (IA); 164 (MN); 249 (OH); 352 (WI)
Northwestern Coll. of Chiropractic 164
Northwestern Connecticut Community-Technical Coll. 56, 541, 575
Northwestern Michigan Coll. 156, 608
Northwestern Oklahoma State Univ. 257, 635
Northwestern State Univ. 129, 600
Northwestern Univ. 94
Northwood Univ. 156
Norwalk Community-Technical Coll. 56, 541, 575
Norwalk State Technical Coll. (see: Norwalk Community-Technical Coll.)
Norwich Univ. 328
Nossi Sch. of Art 512
Notre Dame Coll. 189 (NH); 249 (OH); (see also: Coll. of Notre Dame)
Notre Dame Coll. of Maryland (see: Coll. of Notre Dame of Maryland)
Notre Dame Inst. 548
Notre Dame Seminary Graduate Sch. of Theology 129

Nova Inst. of Health Technology 385
Nova Southeastern Univ. 67
NRI Schs. 398
Nu-Tek Acad. of Beauty 434
Nunez Community Coll. (see: Elaine P. Nunez Community Coll.)
Nyack Coll. 214
Nyack Learning Ctr. 217

O

Oak Hills Bible Coll. 164
Oakbridge Acad. of Arts 498
Oakdale Technical Inst. 441
Oakland City Coll. 107
Oakland Coll. of Court Reporting 385
Oakland Community Coll. 157, 608
Oakland Univ. 157, 608
Oakton Community Coll. 94, 586
Oakwood Coll. 6
Oberlin Coll. 249
Oblate Coll. 61
Oblate Sch. of Theology 316
Occidental Coll. 37
Occupational Education Ctr.—Central 414
Occupational Education Ctr.—North 414
Occupational Education Ctr.—South 414
Occupational Safety Training Inst. 522
Ocean Corporation 522
Ocean County Coll. 194, 620
Ocean State Business Inst. 506
Oceaneering Coll. (see: Coll. of Oceaneering)
Ochsner Sch. of Allied Health Sciences 441
Oconaluftee Job Corps Civilian Conservation Ctr. 485
Odessa Coll. 316, 650
Office Careers Ctr. 523
Office Technology Coll. (see: Coll. of Office Technology)
Ogeechee Technical Inst. 414
Oglala Lakota Coll. 299
Oglethorpe Univ. 77
Ohio Auto-Diesel Technical Inst. 489
Ohio Board of Regents 633
Ohio Coll. of Podiatric Medicine 249

Ohio County Area Vocational Education Ctr. (see: Kentucky Tech—Ohio County Area Vocational Education Ctr.)
Ohio Dominican Coll. 249
Ohio Inst. of Photography and Technology 489
Ohio Northern Univ. 249
Ohio State Coll. of Barber Styling 489
Ohio State Univ. 249, 634
Ohio Univ. 250, 634
Ohio Valley Business Coll. 250
Ohio Valley Coll. 346
Ohio Wesleyan Univ. 250
Ohlone Coll. 38, 564
Ohr HaMeir Theological Seminary 214
Ohr Somayach-Tanenbaum Educational Ctr. 214
Okaloosa-Walton Community Coll. 67, 578
Okefenokee Technical Inst. 414
Oklahoma Baptist Univ. 257
Oklahoma Christian Univ. of Science and Arts 257
Oklahoma City Community Coll. 257, 635
Oklahoma City Univ. 257
Oklahoma Farrier's Coll. 491
Oklahoma Horseshoeing Sch. 492
Oklahoma Jr. Coll. 257
Oklahoma Panhandle State Univ. 257, 635
Oklahoma State Horseshoeing Sch. 492
Oklahoma State Regents for Higher Education 635
Oklahoma State Univ. 257, 635
Oklahoma State Univ. Coll. of Osteopathic Medicine 258, 635
Oklahoma State Univ. Ofc. of the President 635
Oklahoma State Univ.—Oklahoma City 258, 635
Oklahoma State Univ.—Okmulgee 258, 635
Old Dominion Univ. 335, 656
Old Westbury Coll. (see: State Univ. Coll. at Old Westbury)
Oldham County Area Vocational Education Ctr. (see: Kentucky Tech—Oldham County Area Vocational Education Ctr.)
Olean Business Inst. 214
Olive-Harvey Coll. 94, 584
Olivet Coll. 157
Olivet Nazarene Univ. 94
Olney Central Coll. 94, 585
Olympic Coll. 341, 660
Omaha Coll. of Business 467

Omaha Coll. of Health Careers 467
Omaha Opportunities Industrialization Ctr. 467
Omar Rivas Acad. of Barber Arts and Science 421
Omega Inst. 472
Omega Travel Sch. 531
Omni Technical Sch. 405
O'More Coll. of Design 305
Oneonta Coll. (see: State Univ. Coll. at Oneonta)
Onondaga Community Coll. 214, 626
Ontario Bible Coll. and Theological Seminary 358
Opelika State Technical Coll. 6
Oral Roberts Univ. 258
Orange Coast Coll. 38, 563
Orange County Business Coll. 386
Orange County Community Coll. 215, 626
Orangeburg-Calhoun Technical Coll. 295, 644
Oregon Coll. of Oriental Medicine 262
Oregon Denturist Coll. 493
Oregon Graduate Inst. of Science and Technology 262
Oregon Health Sciences Univ. 262, 637
Oregon Inst. of Technology 262, 637
Oregon Ofc. of Community Coll. Services 637
Oregon Polytechnic Inst. 263
Oregon Sch. of Arts and Crafts 493
Oregon State System of Higher Education 637
Oregon State Univ. 263, 637
Oriental Medical Inst. of Hawaii 550
Orlando Coll. 67
Orlando Vocational-Technical Ctr. 405
Orleans Technical Inst. 498
Oscar B. Hunter Memorial Laboratory 447
Osteopathic Medicine Coll. (see: Coll. of Osteopathic Medicine of the Pacific)
Oswego Coll. (see: State Univ. Coll. at Oswego)
O.T. Autry Area Vocational-Technical Ctr. 492
Otero Jr. Coll. 51, 573
Otis Coll. of Art and Design 38
Ottawa Univ. 119
Otterbein Coll. 250
Ouachita Baptist Univ. 18
Our Lady of Holy Cross Coll. 129

Our Lady of the Elms Coll. (see: Coll. of Our Lady of the Elms)
Our Lady of the Lake Coll. of Nursing and Allied Health 441
Our Lady of the Lake Univ. 316
Owens Technical Coll. 251, 541, 634
Owensboro Community Coll. 124, 594
Owensboro Jr. Coll. of Business 124
Owensboro Vocational-Technical Sch. (see: Kentucky Tech— Owensboro Vocational-Technical Sch.)
Oxnard Coll. 38, 570
Ozark Christian Coll. 176
Ozarka Technical Coll. 544
Ozarks Coll. (see: Coll. of the Ozarks)

P

Pace Business Sch. 479
Pace Inst. 276
Pace Univ. 215
Pacific Christian Coll. 38
Pacific Coast Coll. 386
Pacific Coll. of Oriental Medicine 38
Pacific Gateway Coll. 386
Pacific Graduate Sch. of Psychology 38
Pacific Lutheran Theological Seminary 38
Pacific Lutheran Univ. 341
Pacific Northwest Ballet Sch. 534
Pacific Northwest Coll. of Art 263
Pacific Oaks Coll. 38
Pacific Sch. of Religion 38
Pacific Travel Sch. 386
Pacific Union Coll. 38
Pacific Univ. 263
Pacifica Grad. Inst. 545
Paducah Area Vocational Education Ctr. (see: Kentucky Tech—Paducah Area Vocational Education Ctr.)
Paducah Community Coll. 124, 594
Paier Coll. of Art 56
Paine Coll. 77
Palau Community Coll. 362, 541, 665
Palm Beach Atlantic Coll. 67
Palm Beach Beauty & Barber Sch. 405
Palm Beach Community Coll. 67, 578
Palmer Business Inst. 276

Accredited Institutions of Postsecondary Education | 1993-94

St. Francis Coll. 108 (IN); 217 (NY); 279 (PA); (see also: Coll. of St. Francis)
St. Francis De Sales Coll. (see: Allentown Coll. of St. Francis De Sales)
St. Francis Medical Ctr. Coll. of Nursing 96
St. Francis Sch. of Practical Nursing 479
St. Francis Seminary 352
St. Gregory's Coll. 258
St. Hyacinth Coll. and Seminary 147
St. John Fisher Coll. 217
St. John Vianney Coll. Seminary 68
St. John's Coll. 546 (IL); 137 (MD); 199 (NM)
St. Johns River Community Coll. 68, 579
St. John's Sch. of Business 450
St. John's Seminary 40 (CA); 147 (MA)
St. John's Seminary Coll. 40
St. John's Univ. 165 (MN); 217 (NY)
St. Joseph Coll. 56 (see also: Coll. of St. Joseph)
St. Joseph Coll. of Nursing 96
St. Joseph Seminary Coll. 129
St. Joseph's Coll. 108 (IN); 132 (ME); 217 (NY)
St. Joseph's Seminary 218
St. Joseph's Univ. 279
St. Lawrence Univ. 218
St. Leo Coll. 68
St. Louis Christian Coll. 177
St. Louis Coll. of Health Careers 464
St. Louis Coll. of Pharmacy 177
St. Louis Community Coll. at Florissant Valley 177, 615
St. Louis Community Coll. at Forest Park 177, 615
St. Louis Community Coll. at Meramec 177, 615
St. Louis Community Coll. Ctr. 615
St. Louis Conservatory and Schs. for the Arts 464
St. Louis Tech 464
St. Louis Univ. 177
St. Luke's Coll. 547
St. Martin's Coll. 342
St. Mary Coll. 119 (see also: Coll. of St. Mary)
St. Mary of the Lake Univ. (see: Univ. of St. Mary of the Lake Mundelein Seminary)
St. Mary-of-the-Woods Coll. 108

St. Mary Seminary 251
St. Mary's Coll. 108 (IN); 157 (MI); 235 (NC)
St. Mary's Coll. of California 40
St. Mary's Coll. of Maryland 137, 604
St. Mary's Coll. of Minnesota 165
St. Mary's Seminary and Univ. 137
St. Mary's Univ. 317
St. Meinrad Coll. 108
St. Meinrad Sch. of Theology 108
St. Michael's Coll. 329 (see also: Univ. of St. Michael's Coll.)
St. Norbert Coll. 352
St. Olaf Coll. 165
St. Patrick's Seminary 40
St. Paul Sch. of Theology 177
St. Paul Technical Coll. 165
St. Paul's Coll. 336
St. Peter's Coll. 195
St. Peter's Seminary 359
St. Petersburg Jr. Coll. 69, 579
St. Philip's Coll. 317, 648
St. Rose Coll. (see: Coll. of St. Rose)
St. Scholastica Coll. (see: Coll. of St. Scholastica)
St. Thomas Aquinas Coll. 218
St. Thomas More Coll. (see: Coll. of St. Thomas More)
St. Thomas Theological Seminary 52
St. Thomas Univ. 69
St. Vincent Coll. and Seminary 280
St. Vincent's Coll. of Nursing 545
St. Vladimir's Orthodox Theological Seminary 218
St. Xavier Univ. 96
Ste. Genevieve Beauty Coll. 464
Salem Coll. 235
Salem Community Coll. 196, 620
Salem State Coll. 147, 606
Salem-Teikyo Univ. 346
Salina Coll. of Technology 118, 540
Salinger Acad. of Fashion (see: Louise Salinger Acad. of Fashion)
Salisbury Business Coll. 485
Salisbury State Univ. 137, 604
Salish Kootenai Coll. 182
Salt Lake Community Coll. 326, 654
Salter Sch. 450
Salter Technical Inst. (see: Lamar Salter Technical Inst.)
Salvation Army Sch. for Officers' Training 40
Salve Regina Univ. 291

Sam Houston State Univ. 317, 651
Samford Univ. 7
Sampson Community Coll. 235, 630
Samra Univ. of Oriental Medicine 40
Samuel Merritt Coll. 41
SamVerly Coll. 415
San Angelo Hair Acad. 523
San Antonio Coll. 318, 648
San Antonio Coll. of Medical & Dental Assistants 523
San Antonio Trade Sch. 524
San Antonio Training Div. 524
San Bernardino Community Coll. District 568
San Bernardino Valley Coll. 41, 568
San Diego City Coll. 41, 568
San Diego Community Coll. District 568
San Diego Mesa Coll. 41, 568
San Diego Miramar Coll. 41, 568
San Diego State Univ. 41, 572
San Francisco Art Inst. 41
San Francisco Ballet Sch. 386
San Francisco Barber Coll. 387
San Francisco City Coll. (see: City Coll. of San Francisco)
San Francisco Coll. of Mortuary Science 41
San Francisco Community Coll. District 568
San Francisco Conservatory of Music 41
San Francisco State Univ. 41, 572
San Francisco Theological Seminary 42
San Jacinto Coll. 318, 650
San Joaquin Coll. of Law 42
San Joaquin Delta Coll. 42, 568
San Joaquin Delta Community Coll. District 568
San Joaquin Valley Coll. 387
San Joaquin Valley Coll. of Aeronautics 387
San Jose Christian Coll. 42
San Jose City Coll. 42, 568
San Jose-Evergreen Community Coll. District 568
San Jose State Univ. 42, 572
San Juan City Coll. 505
San Juan Coll. 199, 622
San Juan Technological Coll. (see: Technological Coll. of the Municipality of San Juan)
San Luis Obispo Community Coll. District 569
San Mateo Coll. (see: Coll. of San Mateo)

Stuart Sch. of Diamond Setting
(see: Charles Stuart Sch. of
Diamond Setting)
Submarine Training Facility 551
Suburban Technical Sch. 480
Sue Bennett Coll. 125
Suffolk County Community Coll.
Ammerman Campus 222, 626
Suffolk County Community Coll.
Central Administration 626
Suffolk County Community Coll.
Eastern Campus 222, 627
Suffolk County Community Coll.
Western Campus 222, 627
Suffolk Univ. 148
Sul Ross State Univ. 319, 652
Sullivan Coll. 125
Sullivan County Community Coll.
222, 627
Sullivan Educational Ctrs. 464
Sullivan Technical Inst. 442
Summit Christian Coll. 541
Sumter Area Technical Coll. (see:
Central Carolina Technical
Coll.)
Sumter Beauty Coll. 508
Suncoast Ctr. for Natural
Health/Suncoast Sch. 407
Sunstate Acad. of Hair Design 407
Suomi Coll. 158
Superior Career Inst. 480
Surry Community Coll. 236, 630
Susquehanna Univ. 280
Sussex County Community Coll.
196, 621
SUTECH Sch. of Vocational-
Technical Training 388
Suwanee-Hamilton Area
Vocational-Technical and Adult
Education Ctr. 408
S.W. Sch. of Business & Technical
Careers 525
Swainsboro Technical Inst. 415
Swanson's Driving Schs. Inc. 499
Swarthmore Coll. 280
Swedish Inst. 481
Sweet Briar Coll. 336
Swiss Hospitality Inst. Cesar Ritz
539
Syracuse Environmental Science
and Forestry Coll. (see: State
Univ. of New York Coll. of
Environmental Science and
Forestry at Syracuse)
Syracuse Health Science Ctr. (see:
State Univ. of New York Health
Science Ctr. at Syracuse)
Syracuse Univ. 223
SYRIT Computer Sch. Systems
481

Systems Programming
Development Inst. 388

T

Tabor Coll. 119
Tacoma Community Coll. 342,
660
TAD Technical Inst. 450 (MA);
464 (MO)
Taft Coll. 44, 571
Tai Hsuan Foundation Coll. of
Acupuncture and Herbal
Medicine 82
Talladega Coll. 8
Tallahassee Community Coll. 70,
579
Tallapoosa-Alexander City Area
Vocational Ctr. 368
Tallulah Technical Inst. 442
Talmudic Coll. of Florida 70
Talmudical Acad. of New Jersey
196
Talmudical Inst. of Upstate New
York 547
Talmudical Seminary Oholei
Torah 223
Talmudical Yeshiva of
Philadelphia 280
Tampa Coll. 70
Tampa Technical Inst. (see:
National Education Ctr.—
Tampa Technical Inst.)
Tara Lara Acad. of K-9 Hair
Design 494
Tarleton State Univ. 319, 651
Tarrant County Jr. Coll. 319, 650
Taylor Business Inst. 98 (IL); 223
(NY)
Taylor Technical Inst. 550
Taylor Univ. 108
TDDS 490
Teachers Coll. of Columbia Univ.
223
Teche Area Technical Inst. 442
Technical Career Inst. 408 (FL);
223 (NY)
Technical Careers Inst. 396
Technical Coll. of the Lowcountry
295, 644
Technical Health Careers Sch. 388
Technical Inst. of Camden County
473
Technical Trades Inst. 392-393
Techno-Dent Training Ctr. 481
Technological Coll. of the
Municipality of San Juan 289
Technology Education Ctr. 490
Teikyo Marycrest Univ. 114
Teikyo Post Univ. 56

Teikyo Westmar Univ. 114
Telshe Yeshiva-Chicago 98
Temple Acad. of Cosmetology 525
Temple Jr. Coll. 319, 650
Temple Univ. 280
Tennessee Board of Regents 646
Tennessee Inst. of Electronics 515
Tennessee State Univ. 306, 646
Tennessee Technological Univ.
306, 647
Tennessee Temple Univ. 306
Tennessee Wesleyan Coll. 306
Terra Technical Coll. 253, 634
TESST Electronics and Computer
Inst. 447 (MD); 532 (VA)
Teterboro Sch. of Aeronautics 473
Texarkana Coll. 319, 650
Texas A&M International Univ.
319, 541, 651
Texas A&M Univ. 320, 651
Texas A&M Univ. at Galveston
320, 651
Texas A&M Univ.—Corpus
Christi 320, 651
Texas A&M Univ.—Kingsville
320, 651
Texas A&M Univ. System 651
Texas Aero Tech 525
Texas Barber Coll. 525
Texas Chiropractic Coll. 320
Texas Christian Univ. 320
Texas Coll. 320
Texas Coll. of Cosmetology 551
Texas Dental Technology Sch. 526
Texas Higher Education
Coordinating Board 648
Texas Lutheran Coll. 320
Texas Sch. of Business 526
Texas Sch. of Business—
Southwest 526
Texas Southern Univ. 320, 651
Texas Southmost Coll. 320, 651
Texas State Technical Coll.—
Amarillo 321, 651
Texas State Technical Coll.—
Harlingen 321, 651
Texas State Technical Coll.—
Sweetwater 321, 651
Texas State Technical Coll.
System 651
Texas State Technical Coll.—
Waco 321, 651
Texas State Univ. System 651
Texas Tech Univ. 321, 652
Texas Tech Univ. Health Sciences
Ctr. 321, 652
Texas Vocational Sch. 526
Texas Vocational Schs. 526
Texas Wesleyan Univ. 321
Texas Woman's Univ. 321, 652

Textile Technology Inst. (see: Inst. of Textile Technology)
T.H. Harris Technical Inst. 442
T.H. Pickens Technical Ctr. 393
Thaddeus Stevens State Sch. of Technology 281
Thames Valley Technical Coll. (see: Three Rivers Community-Technical Coll.)
Theological Colls. Joint Board (see: Joint Board of Theological Colls.)
Thibodaux Area Technical Inst. 442
Thiel Coll. 281
Thomas A. Edison State Coll. 196, 621
Thomas Aquinas Coll. 44
Thomas Coll. 78 (GA); 132 (ME)
Thomas Jefferson Univ. 281
Thomas M. Cooley Law Sch. 158
Thomas More Coll. 125
Thomas More Coll. of Liberal Arts 547
Thomas Nelson Community Coll. 337, 657
Thomas Technical Inst. 415
Thompson Acads. (see: J.H. Thompson Acads.)
Thompson Sch. of Practical Nursing 528
Three Rivers Community Coll. 178, 615
Three Rivers Community-Technical Coll. 56, 541, 576
Tidewater Community Coll. 337, 657
Tidewater Tech 532
Tiffin Univ. 253
Titan Helicopter Acad. 473
Toccoa Falls Coll. 78
Tom P. Haney Vocational-Technical Ctr. 408
Tomball Coll. 316
Tompkins Cortland Community Coll. 223, 627
Topeka Sch. of Medical Technology 119
Topeka Technical Coll. 424
Torah Temimah Talmudical Seminary 223
Toronto Sch. of Theology 359
Total Technical Inst. 490
Tougaloo Coll. 171
Touro Coll. 223
Towson State Univ. 138, 604
Tracy Clinic (see: John Tracy Clinic)
Traditional Acupuncture Inst. 138
Trans American Sch. of Broadcasting 537

Trans World Travel Acad. 464
Transpersonal Psychology Inst. (see: Inst. of Transpersonal Psychology)
Transylvania Univ. 125
Travel Acad. 370
Travel and Trade Career Inst. 388
Travel Career Inst. 486
Travel Education Ctr. 450
Travel Inst. 481
Travel Inst. of the Pacific 417
Travel Sch. of America 450
Travel Training Ctr. 456
Travel Univ. International 389
Traviss Vocational-Technical Ctr. 408
Treasure Valley Community Coll. 264, 637
Trend Coll. 494 (OR); 534-535 (WA)
Trenholm State Technical Coll. 8
Trenton State Coll. 196, 621
Trevecca Nazarene Coll. 306
Tri-City Barber Sch. 499-500
Tri-College Univ. 240
Tri-County Community Coll. 236, 630
Tri-County Technical Coll. 296, 644
Tri-State Beauty Acad. 435
Tri-State Business Inst. 281
Tri-State Inst. of Traditional Chinese Acupuncture 481
Tri-State Univ. 108
Triangle Tech 281
Trident Technical Coll. 296, 644
Trident Training Facility 415 (GA); 535 (WA)
Trinidad State Jr. Coll. 52, 573
Trinity Bible Coll. 240
Trinity Christian Coll. 98
Trinity Coll. 57 (CT); 61 (DC); 98 (IL); 359 (Canada)
Trinity Coll. at Miami 541
Trinity Coll. of Florida 545
Trinity Coll. of Vermont 329
Trinity Episcopal Sch. for Ministry 281
Trinity Evangelical Divinity Sch. 98
Trinity Lutheran Seminary 253
Trinity Univ. 321
Trinity Valley Community Coll. 322, 652
Triton Coll. 98, 586
Trocaire Coll. 223
Troy State Univ. 8, 555
Troy State Univ. at Dothan 8, 555
Troy State Univ. in Montgomery 8, 555
Troy State Univ. System 555

Truck Driving Acad. 389
Truck Marketing Inst. 389
Truckee Meadows Community Coll. 187, 618
Truett McConnell Coll. 78
Truman Coll. (see: Harry S Truman Coll.)
Trumbull Business Coll. 253
Tucson Coll. 373
Tufts Univ. 148, 540
Tulane Univ. 130
Tulsa Barber Styling Coll. 492
Tulsa Jr. Coll. 259, 636
Tulsa Technology Ctr. 492
Tulsa Welding Sch. 492
Tunxis Community-Technical Coll. 57, 541, 576
Turabo Univ. (see: Univ. del Turabo)
Turner Job Corps Ctr. 415
Turtle Mountain Community Coll. 240
Turtle Mountain Sch. of Paramedical Technique 486
Tusculum Coll. 306
Tuskegee Univ. 8
Tuttle Vocational-Technical Ctr. (see: Francis Tuttle Vocational-Technical Ctr.)
Twin City Sch. of Pet Grooming Inc. 459
Tyler Community Coll. (see: John Tyler Community Coll.)
Tyler Jr. Coll. 322, 652
Tyler Sch. of Business 526
Tyler Sch. of Secretarial Sciences 421
Tyndale Coll. (see: William Tyndale Coll.)

U

UCC Vocational Ctr. 389
Ulster County Community Coll. 223, 627
Ultrasound Diagnostic Sch. 481
Umpqua Community Coll. 264, 637
Unification Theological Seminary 547
Uniformed Services Univ. of the Health Sciences 138
Union Coll. 125 (KY); 185 (NE); 224 (NY)
Union County Coll. 196, 621
Union Inst. 253
Union Theological Seminary 224
Union Theological Seminary in Virginia 337
Union Univ. 306

Accredited Institutions of Postsecondary Education | 1993-94

Institutional Index

Univ. of Nebraska Medical Ctr. 185, 617
Univ. of Nevada, Las Vegas 187, 618
Univ. of Nevada, Reno 187, 618
Univ. of New England 133
Univ. of New Hampshire 189, 619
Univ. of New Hampshire at Manchester 189
Univ. of New Haven 57
Univ. of New Mexico 200, 622
Univ. of New Orleans 130, 600
Univ. of North Alabama 9, 556
Univ. of North Carolina at Asheville 236, 631
Univ. of North Carolina at Chapel Hill 236, 631
Univ. of North Carolina at Charlotte 236, 631
Univ. of North Carolina at Greensboro 236, 631
Univ. of North Carolina at Wilmington 236, 631
Univ. of North Carolina General Administration 630
Univ. of North Dakota 240, 632
Univ. of North Dakota—Lake Region 240, 632
Univ. of North Dakota—Williston 240, 632
Univ. of North Florida 71, 579
Univ. of North Texas 322, 652
Univ. of North Texas Health Science Ctr. at Fort Worth 323, 652
Univ. of Northern Colorado 53, 574
Univ. of Northern Iowa 114, 591
Univ. of Notre Dame 109
Univ. of Oklahoma 259, 636
Univ. of Oklahoma Health Sciences Ctr. 259, 636
Univ. of Oklahoma President's Ofc. 636
Univ. of Oregon 264, 638
Univ. of Osteopathic Medicine and Health Sciences 114
Univ. of Ottawa 360
Univ. of Pennsylvania 282
Univ. of Phoenix 16
Univ. of Pittsburgh 282
Univ. of Portland 264
Univ. of Prince Edward Island 360
Univ. of Puerto Rico Central Administration 640
Univ. of Puerto Rico Mayaguez Campus 289, 640
Univ. of Puerto Rico Medical Sciences Campus 289, 641
Univ. of Puerto Rico Regional Colls. Administration 641

Univ. of Puerto Rico Rio Piedras Campus 289, 641
Univ. of Puget Sound 343
Univ. of Redlands 45
Univ. of Rhode Island 291, 642
Univ. of Richmond 337
Univ. of Rio Grande 254
Univ. of Rochester 224
Univ. of St. Mary of the Lake Mundelein Seminary 99
Univ. of St. Michael's Coll. 360
Univ. of St. Thomas 166 (MN); 323 (TX)
Univ. of San Diego 46
Univ. of San Francisco 46
Univ. of Sarasota 71
Univ. of Saskatchewan 360
Univ. of Science and Arts of Oklahoma 260, 636
Univ. of Scranton 282
Univ. of South Alabama 9, 556
Univ. of South Carolina—Aiken 296, 643
Univ. of South Carolina—Beaufort 296, 643
Univ. of South Carolina Central Ofc. 643
Univ. of South Carolina—Coastal Carolina (see: Coastal Carolina Univ.)
Univ. of South Carolina—Columbia 296, 643
Univ. of South Carolina—Lancaster 296, 643
Univ. of South Carolina—Salkehatchie 296, 643
Univ. of South Carolina—Spartanburg 296, 643
Univ. of South Carolina—Sumter 296, 643
Univ. of South Carolina—Union 297, 643
Univ. of South Dakota 299, 645
Univ. of South Florida 71, 579
Univ. of Southern California 46
Univ. of Southern Colorado 53, 574
Univ. of Southern Indiana 109, 588
Univ. of Southern Maine 133, 602
Univ. of Southern Mississippi 171, 612
Univ. of Southwestern Louisiana 130, 601
Univ. of Tampa 71
Univ. of Tennessee at Chattanooga 307, 647
Univ. of Tennessee at Martin 307, 647
Univ. of Tennessee, Knoxville 307, 647

Univ. of Tennessee, Memphis 307, 647
Univ. of Tennessee System 647
Univ. of Texas at Arlington 323, 653
Univ. of Texas at Austin 323, 653
Univ. of Texas at Brownsville 323, 653
Univ. of Texas at Dallas 323, 653
Univ. of Texas at El Paso 323, 653
Univ. of Texas at San Antonio 323, 653
Univ. of Texas at Tyler 323, 653
Univ. of Texas Health Science Ctr. at Houston 324, 652
Univ. of Texas Health Science Ctr. at San Antonio 324, 652
Univ. of Texas Medical Branch at Galveston 324, 652
Univ. of Texas of the Permian Basin 324, 653
Univ. of Texas—Pan American 324, 653
Univ. of Texas Southwestern Medical Ctr. at Dallas 324, 652
Univ. of Texas System 652
Univ. of the Arts 282
Univ. of the District of Columbia 61
Univ. of the Ozarks 20
Univ. of the Pacific 46
Univ. of the Sacred Heart 289
Univ. of the South 307
Univ. of the Virgin Islands 330
Univ. of Toledo 254, 634
Univ. of Toronto 360
Univ. of Tulsa 260
Univ. of Utah 326, 654
Univ. of Vermont 329
Univ. of Virginia 337, 656
Univ. of Virginia Central Ofc. 656
Univ. of Washington 343, 659
Univ. of Waterloo 360
Univ. of West Florida 71, 579
Univ. of West Los Angeles 46
Univ. of Western Ontario 360
Univ. of Windsor 360
Univ. of Wisconsin Ctr.—Baraboo-Sauk County 352
Univ. of Wisconsin Ctr.—Barron County 352
Univ. of Wisconsin Ctr.—Fond du Lac 352
Univ. of Wisconsin Ctr.—Fox Valley 352
Univ. of Wisconsin Ctr.—Manitowoc County 353
Univ. of Wisconsin Ctr.—Marathon County 353
Univ. of Wisconsin Ctr.—Marinette County 353

Accredited Institutions of Postsecondary Education | 1993-94

Walker Vocational-Technical Ctr.
(see: James L. Walker
Vocational-Technical Ctr.)
Walla Walla Coll. 343
Walla Walla Community Coll.
343, 660
Wallace State Community Coll. 9,
557 (see also: George C.
Wallace State Community
Coll.; see also: George Corley
Wallace State Community
Coll.)
Wallace State Jr. Coll. (see:
Lurleen B. Wallace State Jr.
Coll.)
Walsh Coll. (see: Walsh Univ.)
Walsh Coll. of Accountancy and
Business Administration 158
Walsh Univ. 254, 542
Walters Coll. (see: Raymond
Walters Coll.)
Walters State Community Coll.
308, 647
Ward Stone Coll. 71
Warner Pacific Coll. 264
Warner Southern Coll. 71
Warren County Community Coll.
197, 621
Warren Wilson Coll. 237
Wartburg Coll. 115
Wartburg Theological Seminary
115
Washburn Univ. of Topeka 120
Washington and Jefferson Coll.
283
Washington and Lee Univ. 338
Washington Bible Coll. 139
Washington Business Sch. of
Northern Virginia 532
Washington Coll. 139 (see also:
Harold Washington Coll.; see
also: Mary Washington Coll.)
Washington Conservatory of
Music, Inc. 398
Washington County Adult Skill
Ctr. 532
Washington County Technical
Coll. 133, 542
Washington County Vocational-
Technical Inst. (see:
Washington County Technical
Coll.)
Washington Higher Education
Coordinating Board 659
Washington-Holmes Area
Vocational-Technical Ctr. 408
Washington Inst. of Technology
500
Washington State Board for
Community and Technical
Colls. 659

Washington State Community
Coll. 254, 634
Washington State Univ. 343, 659
Washington Theological Union
139
Washington Univ. 179 (see also:
George Washington Univ.)
Washtenaw Community Coll. 159,
608
Waterbury State Technical Coll.
(see: Naugatuck Valley
Community-Technical Coll.)
Waterloo Lutheran Seminary 361
Waters Coll. (see: Edward Waters
Coll.)
Watterson Coll. 389 (CA); 465
(MO)
Watterson Coll. Pacific 389
Waubonsee Community Coll. 99,
586
Waukesha County Technical Coll.
355
Waycross Coll. 79, 581
Wayland Baptist Univ. 325
Wayne Coll. 254, 634
Wayne Community Coll. 237, 630
Wayne County Area Vocational
Education Ctr. (see: Kentucky
Tech—Wayne County Area
Vocational Education Ctr.)
Wayne County Community Coll.
159, 608
Wayne State Coll. 186, 617
Wayne State Univ. 159, 608
Wayne's Sch. of Unisex Hair
Design (see: Mister Wayne's
Sch. of Unisex Hair Design)
Waynesburg Coll. 283
Weatherford Coll. 325, 653
Webb Inst. of Naval Architecture
225
Webber Coll. 71
Weber State Univ. 327, 654
Webster Coll. 346 (see also:
Daniel Webster Coll.)
Webster County Area Vocational
Education Ctr. (see: Kentucky
Tech—Webster County Area
Vocational Education Ctr.)
Webster Univ. 179
Weeks Welding Laboratory
Testing & Sch. (see: M. Weeks
Welding Laboratory Testing &
Sch.)
Welbes Coll. of Massage Therapy
(see: Dr. Welbes Coll. of
Massage Therapy)
Welder Training and Testing Inst.
500
Wellesley Coll. 149
Wells Coll. 225

Wenatchee Valley Coll. 343, 661
Wentworth Inst. of Technology
149
Wentworth Military Acad. and Jr.
Coll. 179
Wentworth Technical Sch. 451
Wesley Biblical Seminary 171
Wesley Coll. 59 (DE); 171 (MS);
(see also: John Wesley Coll.)
Wesley Theological Seminary 61
Wesleyan Coll. 79
Wesleyan Univ. 57
West Chester Univ. of
Pennsylvania 283, 639
West Coast Talmudic Seminary
(see: Yeshiva Ohr Elchonon-
Chabad/West Coast Talmudic
Seminary)
West Coast Training 494
West Coast Univ. 46
West Georgia Coll. 79, 581
West Georgia Technical Inst. 415
West Hills Community Coll. 46,
571
West Hills Community Coll.
District 570
West Jefferson Technical Inst. 442
West Kentucky State Vocational-
Technical Sch. (see: Kentucky
Tech—West Kentucky State
Vocational-Technical Sch.)
West Kern Community Coll.
District 571
West Liberty State Coll. 346, 662
West Los Angeles Coll. 47, 565
West Shore Community Coll. 159,
609
West Side Inst. of Technology 490
West Suburban Coll. of Nursing 99
West Technical Education Ctr. 408
West Tennessee Business Coll.
515
West Texas A&M Univ. 325, 542,
651
West Texas State Univ. (see: West
Texas A&M Univ.)
West Valley Coll. 47, 571
West Valley-Mission Coll. District
571
West Virginia Business Coll. 346
West Virginia Career Coll. 347
West Virginia Coll. (see: Coll. of
West Virginia)
West Virginia Graduate Coll. 347,
662
West Virginia Inst. of Technology
347, 662
West Virginia Northern
Community Coll. 347, 662
West Virginia Sch. of Osteopathic
Medicine 347, 662

West Virginia State Coll. 347, 662
West Virginia State Coll. System (see: State Coll. System of West Virginia)
West Virginia Univ. 347, 662
West Virginia Univ. at Parkersburg 348, 662
West Virginia Univ. System (see: Univ. System of West Virginia)
West Virginia Wesleyan Coll. 348
Westark Community Coll. 20
Westbrook Coll. 133
Westchester Business Inst. 225
Westchester Community Coll. 225, 627
Westchester Conservatory of Music 482
Westech Coll. 389
Western Baptist Coll. 264
Western Business Coll. 494
Western Career Coll. 389
Western Carolina Univ. 237, 631
Western Connecticut State Univ. 58, 575
Western Conservative Baptist Seminary 264
Western Culinary Inst. 494
Western Dakota Technical Inst. 300, 542
Western Dakota Vocational-Technical Inst. (see: Western Dakota Technical Inst.)
Western Evangelical Seminary 264
Western Illinois Univ. 99, 584
Western International Univ. 16
Western Iowa Tech Community Coll. 115, 591
Western Kentucky Univ. 126, 595
Western Maryland Coll. 139
Western Medical Coll. of Allied Health Careers 494
Western Michigan Univ. 159, 609
Western Montana Coll. 182, 616
Western Nebraska Community Coll. 186, 617
Western Nevada Community Coll. 187, 618
Western New England Coll. 149
Western New Mexico Univ. 200, 622
Western Oklahoma State Coll. 260, 636
Western Oregon State Coll. 264, 638
Western Pentecostal Bible Coll. 361
Western Piedmont Community Coll. 237, 630
Western Sch. of Health and Business Careers 500

Western State Coll. of Colorado 53, 574
Western State Univ. Coll. of Law of Orange County 47
Western State Univ. Coll. of Law of San Diego 47
Western States Chiropractic Coll. 264
Western Technical Inst. 526
Western Texas Coll. 325, 653
Western Theological Seminary 159
Western Truck Sch. 389-390 (CA); 494 (OR)
Western Washington Univ. 343, 659
Western Wisconsin Technical Coll. 355
Western Wyoming Coll. 356, 664
Westfield State Coll. 149, 606
Westlake Inst. of Technology 390
Westlawn Sch. of Marine Technology 396
Westminster Choir Coll. 195
Westminster Coll. 179 (MO); 283 (PA)
Westminster Coll. of Salt Lake City 327
Westminster Theological Seminary 283
Westminster Theological Seminary in California 47
Westmont Coll. 47
Westmoreland County Community Coll. 283
Weston Sch. of Theology 149
Westside Technical Inst. 443
Westside Vocational-Technical Ctr. 408
Wharton County Jr. Coll. 325, 653
Whatcom Community Coll. 344, 661
Wheaton Coll. 99 (IL); 149 (MA)
Wheeling Coll. of Hair Design 536
Wheeling Jesuit Coll. 348
Wheelock Coll. 149
Whelan Sch. of Practical Nursing (see: Marion S. Whelan Sch. of Practical Nursing)
White Pines Coll. 190
Whitewater Technical Inst. (see: Indiana Vocational Technical Coll.—Whitewater Technical Inst.)
Whitman Coll. 344
Whitney Regional Vocational-Technical Sch. (see: Eli Whitney Regional Vocational-Technical Sch.)
Whittier Coll. 47
Whitworth Coll. 344

Wichita Area Vocational-Technical Sch. 424
Wichita Business Coll. 425
Wichita State Univ. 120, 592
Wichita Technical Inst. 425
Widener Univ. 283
Widener Univ. at Harrisburg 283
Wilberforce Univ. 254
Wilbur Wright Coll. 99, 584
Wilcox Coll. of Nursing 58
Wiley Coll. 325
Wilkes Community Coll. 237, 630
Wilkes Univ. 283
Willamette Univ. 264
William and Mary Coll. (see: Coll. of William and Mary)
William Carey Coll. 171
William Jennings Bryan Coll. (see: Bryan Coll.)
William Jewell Coll. 179
William M. Scholl Coll. of Podiatric Medicine (see: Dr. William M. Scholl Coll. of Podiatric Medicine)
William Marsh Rice Univ. 325
William Mitchell Coll. of Law 166
William Paterson Coll. of New Jersey 197, 621
William Penn Coll. 115
William R. Moore Sch. of Technology 515
William Rainey Harper Coll. 100, 586
William T. McFatter Vocational-Technical Ctr. 408
William Tyndale Coll. 159
William Woods Coll. (see: William Woods Univ.)
William Woods Univ. 180, 542
Williams Baptist Coll. 20
Williams Coll. 149
Williams Univ. (see: Roger Williams Univ.)
Williamsburg Technical Coll. 297, 644
Williamson Free Sch. of Mechanical Trades 500
Williamsport Sch. of Commerce 283
Willmar Community Coll. 166, 610
Wilma Boyd Career Schs. 500
Wilmington Coll. 59 (DE); 255 (OH)
Wilson Coll. 283 (see also: Lindsey Wilson Coll.; see also: Warren Wilson Coll.)
Wilson Rehabilitation Ctr. (see: Woodrow Wilson Rehabilitation Ctr.)